Brain Perspectives

There are three basic planes, or orientations, that are typically used to view internal areas of a brain: coronal, horizontal, and sagittal. The following descriptions offer useful analogies that may help you in becoming familiar with these orientations.

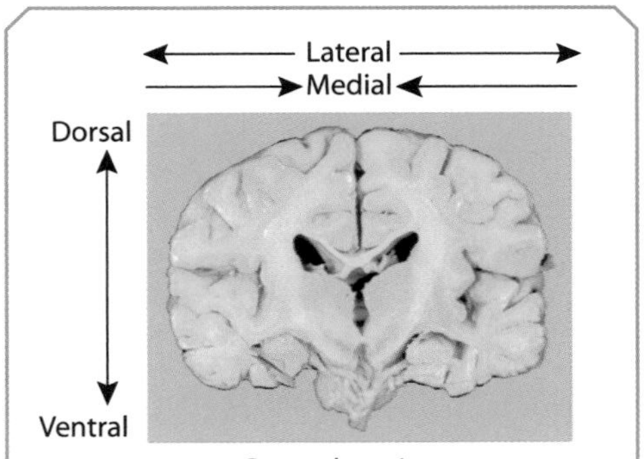

Coronal section

Coronal. Think of an ordinary loaf of sliced bread for sandwiches, with the end slices at the "front" and "back" of the loaf. Now imagine a brain, sliced similarly top to bottom from the front (anterior surface) to the back (posterior surface). When viewing a coronal brain section you will be able to visualize the brain's two distinct hemispheres. A coronal section generally has greater width than height. In a series of coronal sections you can visualize dorsal and ventral movements, as well as medial and lateral movements; you cannot visualize anterior and posterior movements.

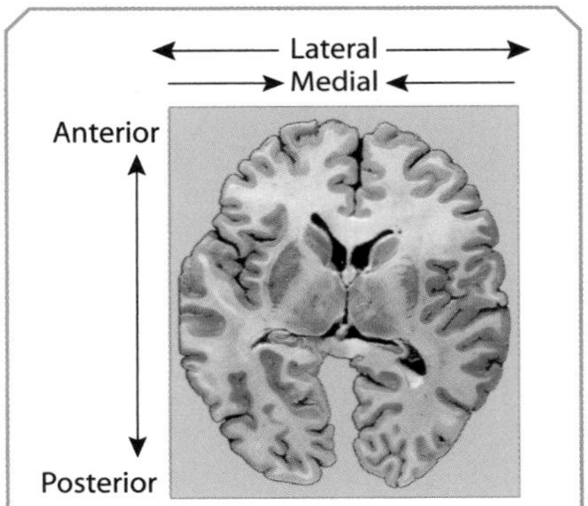

Horizontal section

Horizontal. Think of a hamburger bun as it sits on your plate. A brain can be sliced similarly, the cuts going side to side separate the top (dorsal surface) from the bottom (ventral surface). When viewing a horizontal brain section you should, as in viewing a coronal section, also clearly see two hemispheres. But unlike coronal sections, images of horizontal sections typically have greater height than width; the front of the brain is almost always shown facing up or down, not left or right, when depicting this perspective. In a series of horizontal sections you can visualize anterior and posterior movements as well as medial and lateral movements; you cannot visualize dorsal and ventral movements.

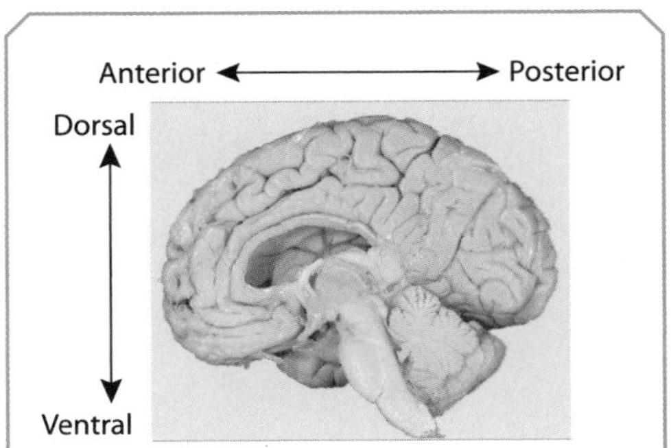

Sagittal section

Sagittal. Think of a hotdog bun as it approaches your mouth, open end up. In this position, the slice through the bun goes top to bottom, parallel to the sides. Similarly, sagittal sections of the brain are taken from one side (lateral surface) to the other. Sagittal sections are distinct from coronal and horizontal sections in that they do not show two hemispheres. In a series of sagittal sections you can visualize anterior and posterior movements as well as dorsal and ventral movements; you cannot visualize medial and lateral movements.

Primer by Terence J. Bazzett, State University of New York at Geneseo

Continued on the back

Biological Psychology

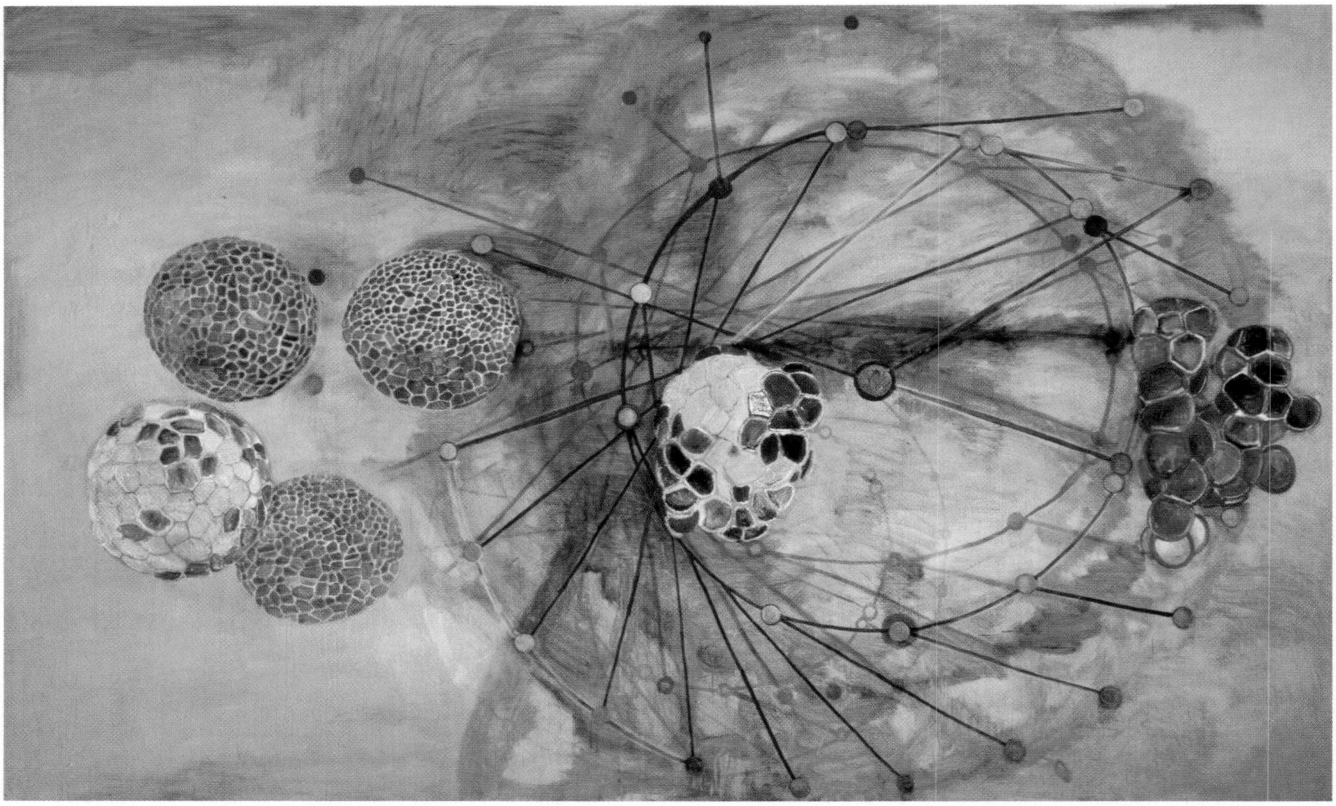

Eureka, 1988-91, Oil on linen, 96 x 156 inches

Terry Winters (b. 1949, Brooklyn, NY) has exhibited widely in the United States and abroad since the early 1980's. The first one-person exhibition of his paintings was held in 1982 at the Sonnabend Gallery in New York. Winters' work is included in many public collections, including the Tate Gallery, London; the Reina Sofia, Madrid; and, in New York, the Whitney Museum of American Art, Metropolitan Museum of Art, and the Museum of Modern Art. Winters is interested in the organizing structures and systems beneath the seeming randomness of nature's complexity. His paintings are metaphors for social structures, means of communication, and modes of living. They also represent psychological states and human relationships.

Biological Psychology

STEPHEN B. KLEIN • B. MICHAEL THORNE
Mississippi State University Mississippi State University

Worth Publishers

Publisher: Catherine Woods
Acquisitions Editor: Charles Linsmeier
Development Editor: Linda Strange
Associate Managing Editor: Tracey Kuehn
Project Editor: Kerry O'Shaughnessy
Editorial Assistant: Justin Kruger
Marketing Manager: Amy Shefferd
Production Manager: Sarah Segal
Art Director and Cover Design: Babs Reingold
Interior Design: Lissi Sigillo
Illustrations: Mike Demaray (Dragonfly), Matthew Holt, Northeastern Graphic
Photo Editors: Patricia Marx, Christina Micek
Composition: Northeastern Graphic
Printing and Binding: R. R. Donnelley & Sons

We gratefully acknowledge the following artists and agencies for providing the illustrations on the chapter opening pages: p. 0: ©Kevin Ghiglione/i2iart.com; p. 32: Ferruccio Sardella; p. 72: ©Phil/i2iart.com; p. 108: Ferruccio Sardella; p. 146: Fred Tomaselli/Airborne Event, 2003/mixed media, acrylic paint, resin on wood, 84 x 60 x 1 1/2 inches/Image courtesy of James Cohan Gallery, New York; p. 190: Joyce Hesselberth; p. 226: Sandra Speidel/Corbis; p. 266: Leigh Wells; p. 306: Philippe Lardy/www.lardy.com; p. 340: Karine Daisay/www.marlenaagency.com; p. 384: Karine Daisay/www.marlenaagency.com; p. 420: Sean Qualls; p. 460: Leigh Wells; p. 502: Leigh Wells; p. 544: Jim Dandy/Images.com

ISBN-13: 978-0-7167-9922-1
ISBN-10: 0-7167-9922-7
Library of Congress Control Number: 2006930552

Printed in the United States of America

First printing, 2006

Worth Publishers
41 Madison Avenue
New York, NY 10010
www.worthpublishers.com

To my brother Michael, who has shown me the meaning of courage.

Steve

To Wanda, my wife and best friend, and to my children, Dean and Erin.

Mike

About the Authors

Stephen B. Klein has been professor and head of the Department of Psychology at Mississippi State University since 1990. He has written numerous articles on the biological basis of learning and memory and is the author of six textbooks, including *Learning: Principles and Applications* (McGraw-Hill, adopted by several hundred universities and translated into Spanish). He also coedited the two-volume text *Contemporary Learning Theories* (1989) and *Handbook of Contemporary Learning Theories* (2001), both published by Lawrence Erlbaum.

B. Michael Thorne is Professor Emeritus in the Psychology Department at Mississippi State University, serving as Graduate Coordinator for the last decade of his career. He has published numerous articles on biological psychology, the history of psychology, and the teaching of psychology, and is the senior author of *Statistics for the Behavioral Sciences* (McGraw-Hill) and *Connections in the History and Systems of Psychology* (Houghton Mifflin).

Contributing Editors

Michelle Butler
Associate Professor
Department of Behavioral Sciences and Leadership
United States Air Force Academy

Patricia Wallace
Compliance Coordinator
Division of Research and Graduate Studies
Northern Illinois University

Brief Contents

Contents

Preface

Rationale and Goals

Biological Psychology is intended to provide a general introduction to and overview of the structure and processes of the nervous system and their role in determining behavior. Our goal has been to write a biological psychology textbook that is both comprehensive and understandable to a person with little or no background in the biological sciences.

We decided to write such a textbook after teaching biological psychology to a variety of students over a period of many years. In developing our courses, one of the biggest challenges we faced was deciding on an appropriate textbook. Although the market offers many excellent, extremely detailed biological psychology texts, our students invariably had difficulty in comprehending the mass of complex material the books contained and particularly in relating the material to their world. We concluded from our experience that a biological psychology textbook appropriate for our students, who we believe are representative of the vast majority of students at public (and many private) universities, needs to be pedagogically engaging and approachable as well as academically sound.

We firmly believe that every student majoring in psychology needs to have a comprehensive course in the fundamentals of biological psychology. Such a course is also of relevance to students in the biological sciences in general, in premedicine and prenursing programs in particular, as well as in such diverse areas as educational psychology and veterinary medicine.

But a need for a basic course in biological psychology is not confined to the academic setting. In today's world, all you have to do is turn on your television, log onto the Internet, or buy a news magazine to be inundated with increasingly technical information about such fundamentally neurological disorders as Alzheimer's disease, Parkinson's disease, depression and bipolar disorder, and schizophrenia. The explosion of information about the brain and its functions has created a need for a comprehensive yet easily understandable textbook of biological psychology. Our text was designed with that need in mind.

Content and Organization

We have often found that beginning students are "turned off" by their initial contact with biological psychology because they find the terminology incomprehensible and the material irrelevant. Thus, we set out to write a textbook that would demonstrate the relationship between biological psychology and everyday behaviors in a readable, understandable way for students with little or no neuroscience background. Our plan for accomplishing this goal included a straightforward, engaging writing style, the incorporation of numerous pedagogical features (described in detail in the next section), and the judicious use of appropriate, interesting examples and research studies.

We wrote this book primarily for the unprepared student. This student has perhaps not taken a science course since wading through some required courses in high school. We have done our best to make the book readable, striving to present even the most complex material clearly and concisely. Our informal writing style, along with the inclusion of relevant examples, should help students make connections between biological psychology and their everyday lives.

Among the examples we have included are hypothetical case histories as well as actual situations reported in the popular press. From our experience, we know that students can grasp complex concepts more readily if relevant applications are provided. For example, in Chapter 13 we discuss in detail the split-brain research of Roger Sperry and his colleagues. Sperry took advantage of a surgical procedure designed to treat intractable epileptic seizures—cutting the major connections between the hemispheres of the brain—to learn profound truths about the human brain and its control over such vitally important human functions as language. In Chapter 14, we use the case history of H. M., a man with brain damage that significantly affected his memory, to illustrate how a person's memory depends on the effective functioning of specific neural systems. H. M.'s story also dramatically reveals how the quality of a person's life and the lives of those around him or her can be profoundly affected by a neurological disorder.

We have included research studies that best clarify the concepts being discussed as well as illustrate how neuroscientists gather information and solve problems. We have chosen both classic experiments and recent major-impact studies to demonstrate to the reader that some ideas are enduring whereas others are quite new.

Art Program

The illustrations in this textbook were created specifically for it. The entire art program was developed to assure its dynamism, accuracy, and clarity.

It is our experience, however, that many students have difficulty understanding anatomical and biological art no matter how clear it is. For that reason we have included a Primer for Anatomical and Biological Art. Created by Terry Bazzett at SUNY–Geneseo, this art primer is designed to provide an introduction and serve as a reference for students learning the importance and necessity of understanding biological art in this course.

Engaging, High Interest Topics

To help spur students' enthusiasm and involvement in the course, *Biological Psychology* features in each chapter high-interest topics woven throughout the narrative as well as displayed in chapter boxes and *Scientific American* Spotlights. Fascinating topics and research relevant to students' lives and to the significance of contemporary study in biological psychology are included in the following:

Cutting Edge Research

Each chapter in *Biological Psychology* includes relevant and important research from recent years. To illustrate the nature of biological psychology as a living field as well as to reflect on the progress of the field in recent years, we highlight the following topics.

- Imaging techniques (PET, fMRI) that give pictures of the brain at work (pp. 17–19)
- Prefrontal cortex serving an executive function for the brain (pp. 66–67)
- Fetal tissue implantation as a treatment for degenerative neurological disorders (pp. 101–103)
- Electrical synapses as a means of communication within the cerebral cortex (p. 139)

- Dopamine and addictive behaviors such as smoking and gambling (pp. 178–181)
- Parietal lobe and the binding of features (i.e., shape, color, movement, distance) of visual events (pp. 220–222)
- Cochlear implants as a treatment for deafness (p. 238)
- Mirror neurons and the imitation of observed behaviors (pp. 281–282)
- Light therapy as a treatment for seasonal affective disorder (p. 312)
- Rimonabant, a THC antagonist, as a treatment for obesity (pp. 353–354)
- Pheromones and the synchrony of the menstrual cycle (pp. 400-401)
- Testosterone and serotonin's role in anger, rage, and aggressive behavior (pp. 437–438)
- The right hemisphere's role in language (pp. 473–474)
- Synaptic changes and learning (pp. 519–522)
- Stress, hypothalamic-pituitary-adrenal axis and depression (pp. 561–562)

Scientific American Spotlight

Unique to this text, each chapter of *Biological Psychology* features a *Scientific American* Spotlight, an intriguing and illuminating selection from the pages of America's leading scientific magazine. The *Scientific American* Spotlights include the following topics:

- Single Neuron Speaks p. 17
- Glia Control Synapses p. 43
- Baby to Brain p. 102
- The "Magic" of Lithium p. 126
- Beating Abuse p. 168
- Seeing Is Believing p. 216
- Quieting Phantom Limbs p. 250
- Probing Cerebellar Function p. 294
- From Bulimia to Jet Lag p. 315
- The Diet That Fits p. 361
- Olfaction: What's Smell Got to Do With It? p. 412
- Don't Stress p. 448
- Same Brain for Speech or Sign p. 475
- Senile Words p. 534
- Fever In, Schizophrenia Out p. 577

Chapter Boxes

Most chapters feature high-interest boxes that provide an in-depth examination of various key concepts discussed in the chapter text. These boxes include the following wide-ranging topics:

Box 2.2 The Tragedy of a Prefrontal Lobotomy p. 66

Box 3.1 Huntington's disease p. 78

Box 4.1 Multiple Sclerosis p. 120

Box 4.2 Drug Treatment for Depression p. 132

Box 4.3 Multiple Sclerosis: New Treatments p. 141

Box 6.1 Testing for Visual Field Deficits p. 200

Box 7.1 Cochlear Implants and the Plasticity of the Auditory Cortex p. 238

Box 8.1 Myasthenia Gravis p. 273

Box 8.2 Apraxia p. 286

Box 8.3 Amyotrophic Lateral Sclerosis p. 288

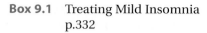

Pedagogy and Student Learning Aids

Students first encounter the material in the chapter through the **chapter-opening vignettes.** These fictional stories provide a backdrop for the students as they immerse themselves in the concepts and content of the chapter. Grounded in this storyline, students are able to make a case for the relevance of biological psychology.

A **running glossary** provides definitions of key terms throughout the textbook, a proven method for engaging students in the vocabulary. Key terms are then revisited in the end-of-chapter pedagogy. **Checkpoints** appear at the end of each major section to give students an opportunity to reflect on the significance of the reading. The Checkpoints are matched with **Review** sections that appear frequently throughout each chapter.

The **Chapter Review** serves as a built-in **study guide,** averting the need to purchase a separate study aid. With correct answers and feedback available on the companion website, each chapter review consists of the following:

- Key Terms
- Suggested Readings
- Critical Thinking Questions
- Fill-in-the-Blank Questions
- Multiple-Choice Questions

The Chapter Review provides an opportunity for students to review and master the material in the chapter after their reading. Built to support the reading of the text, not to replace it, the questions provide further insight and extend comprehension of the major concepts and terms in the chapter.

Supplements

For Students

Foundations of Behavioral Neuroscience CD-ROM, created by Uri Hasson, New York University, and Yehuda Shavit, Hebrew University of Jerusalem, and produced by the Open University of Israel and CADRE Design. This innovative CD has five modules: Neural Communication, Central Nervous System, Vision, Movement, and Research Methods. The CD-ROM features rotating three-dimensional models of the human brain and eye; more than 25 video clips; animations of key physiological mechanisms; interactive examples of neuroimaging technologies, including MRI and CT; and a number of pedagogical features, including a clickable glossary, a search engine, and multiple-choice questions.

Each module on the CD-ROM is enhanced by a "Test Yourself" component. Written by Paul Currie, Barnard College, these additional assessment questions and drag-and-drop activities offer students an opportunity to test their understanding of the material presented in each module. Customized for *Biological Psychology,* the CD also includes quizzes and flashcards for every chapter of the text. *(CD-ROM is available packaged with the textbook upon request.)*

***Biological Psychology* Companion Website** by Joe Morrissey and Laura Cook, State University of New York at Binghamton, and Meredith Woitach, University of Rochester. Available at www.worthpublishers.com/klein. The companion website is an online educational setting for students providing a virtual study guide 24 hours a day, 7 days a week. The resources are free and do not require any special access codes or passwords. Tools on the site include chapter outlines and summaries, learning objectives, annotated web links, interactive flashcards, research exercises, selections from *PsychSim 5.0* by Thomas Ludwig, Hope College, and online quizzes with immediate feedback and instructor notification. It also includes answers to the questions in the chapter reviews.

For the instructor, the site offers online testing (with access to a quiz gradebook for viewing student results), a syllabus posting service, PowerPoint presentation files, electronic versions of the artwork (also included in Worth Publishers' Image and Lecture Gallery) and photos in the book, and links to additional tools, including Course Management Systems course cartridges.

Lecture Notebook and Study Guide by Billy L. Smith and Chrystal McChristian, University of Central Arkansas. Unique to *Biological Psychology,* and featuring selections of key figures, tables, and photos from the textbook (including labels), the Lecture Notebook allows students to concentrate on the lecture while taking notes in spaces provided next to each art piece or table. Annotated with the page numbers on which the art originates, the Lecture Notebook is a great tool for students to use during the lecture and out of the classroom.

The Study Guide features chapter summaries and space for students to quiz themselves on the textbook's key terminology. It also includes a selection of unlabeled art for students to use in assessing their understanding of biological figures.

Clinical Neuroscience Reader from *Scientific American.* Upon request, this reader is free when packaged with the textbook. Created to emphasize the importance of biological psychology, this new reader from *Scientific American* focuses on such neurological disorders and traumas as schizophrenia, ADHD, and traumatic brain injury (TBI), as well as on advances in treatments, including the use of light therapy to treat seasonal affective disorder (SAD) and insights into new technologies.

***Scientific American* Explores the Hidden Mind: A Collector's Edition.** Upon request, this reader is free when packaged with the textbook. In the past decade, we have learned more about the brain and how it creates the mind than we learned in the entire previous century. In a special collector's edition, *Scientific American* provides a must-have compilation of updated feature articles that explore and reveal the mysterious inner workings of our minds and brains.

Improving the Mind and Brain: A *Scientific American* Special Issue. Upon request, this reader is free when packaged with the textbook. This single-topic issue of *Scientific American* magazine features the latest findings from the most distinguished researchers in the field.

iClicker Radio Frequency Classroom Response System. Offered by Worth Publishers in partnership with iClicker and available for fall 2006 classes, iClicker is Worth's new polling system, created by educators for educators. This radio frequency system is the hassle-free way to make your class time more interactive. The system allows you to pause to ask questions and instantly record responses, as well as take attendance, direct students through lectures, and gauge students' understanding of the material.

For Instructors

Instructor's Resource Manual and Test Bank by Charles C. Swart, Trinity College, and Robert Mowrer, Angelo State University (with additional material by Michelle Butler, United States Air Force Academy). The Instructor's Resource Manual features chapter-by-chapter learning objectives and topic overviews, detailed lecture outlines, thorough chapter summaries, chapter key terms, in-class demonstrations and activities, springboard topics for discussion and debate, ideas for research and term paper projects, homework assignments, extra-credit projects, exercises that highlight the *Scientific American* Spotlights, suggestions for additional reading materials (from journals and periodicals), and a guide to video and Internet resources, including the new Worth Publishers: Neuroscience Video Collection.

The Test Bank includes more than 1,600 multiple-choice, true/false, fill-in, and essay questions—a wide variety of applied, conceptual, and factual questions, which have been thoroughly reviewed and edited for accuracy. Each item is keyed to the topic and page in the text on which the answer can be found. In addition, each chapter features diagram exercises tied to the major illustrations in the text.

Diploma Computerized Test Bank. Available on a dual-platform CD-ROM. Instructors are guided step-by-step through the process of creating a test; they can add an unlimited number of questions, edit, scramble, or reorder items, and format a test. The accompanying gradebook enables them to record students' scores throughout the course, and it includes the capacity to sort student records, view detailed analyses of test items, curve tests, generate reports, and add weights to grades. The CD-ROM is the access point for Diploma Online Testing, allowing instructors to create and administer secure exams over a network and over the Internet, as well as containing Blackboard- and WebCT-formatted versions of each item in the Test Bank.

Online Testing Powered by Diploma. Available at www.brownstone.net. With Diploma, instructors can create and administer secure exams over a network and over the Internet, with questions that incorporate multimedia and interactive exercises. The program also allows them to restrict tests to specific computers or time blocks and includes a suite of grade-book and result-analysis features. For more information on Diploma, please visit the www.brownstone.net website.

Online Quizzing, Powered by Questionmark. Access via the companion website at www.worthpublishers.com/klein. Instructors can easily and securely quiz students online using prewritten multiple-choice questions for each chapter. Students receive instant feedback and can take the quizzes multiple times. Using the online quiz gradebook, instructors can view results by quiz, student, or question, or they can get weekly results via e-mail.

Presentation

Chapter Art and Outline PowerPoint Slides. Available at www.worthpublishers.com/klein or on the Instructor's Resource CD-ROM. These PowerPoint slides can be used directly or customized to fit instructor needs. There are two customizable slide sets for each chapter of the book—one featuring chapter text, the other featuring all chapter figures, tables, and photographs.

Enhanced Lecture PowerPoint Slides by Billy L. Smith and Chrystal McChristian, University of Central Arkansas. Available at www.worthpublishers.com/klein or on the Instructor's Resource CD-ROM. These customized slides focus on key terms and themes, reflect the main points in significant detail, and feature tables, figures, and photos from the *Biological Psychology* text.

Digital Photo Library. Available at www.worthpublishers.com/klein or on the Instructor's Resource CD-ROM. This collection gives you access to all the photographs in *Biological Psychology.*

Image and Lecture Gallery. Available at www.worthpublishers.com/ilg. The Image and Lecture Gallery is a convenient way to access electronic versions of lecture materials. Instructors can browse, search, and download illustrations from every Worth title, as well as prebuilt PowerPoint presentations that contain all chapter art or chapter section headings in text form. Users can also create personal folders on a personalized home page for easy organization of the materials.

Overhead Transparencies. This set of over 100 full-color transparencies consists of key photos, figures, and tables from the text and is available for use in classroom presentations.

Video

Worth Publishers: Neuroscience Video Collection, edited by Ronald J. Comer, Princeton University. Available on VHS, DVD, and CD-ROM (in MPEG format). This all-new video collection consists of dozens of video segments, each 1 to 10 minutes in length. Clinical documentaries, television news reports, and archival footage are only a few of the exciting sources for each video. Each segment has been created to provide illustrations that help bring the lecture to life, engaging students and enabling them to apply neuroscience theory to the real world. The collection offers powerful and memorable demonstrations such as the links between the brain and behavior, neuroanatomical animations, cutting-edge neuroscience research, brain assessment in action, important historical events, interviews, and a wide sampling of brain phenomena and brain dysfunction. A special cluster of segments reveals the range of research methods used to study the brain. The accompanying Faculty Guide (also included in the Instructor's Resource Manual) offers a description of each segment so that instructors can make informed decisions about how best to use the videos to enhance their lectures.

The Brain and Behavior Video Segments. Available on VHS. This special collection includes targeted selections from the revised edition of the highly praised *Scientific American* Frontiers series. Hosted by Alan Alda, these video clips provide instructors with an excellent tool for showing how neuroscience research is actually conducted. The 10-to-12-minute modules focus on the work of Steve Sumi, Renee Baillargeon, Car Rosengren, Laura Pettito, Steven Pinker, Barbara Rothbaum, Bob Stickgold, Irene Pepperberg, Marc Hauser, Linda Bartoshuk, and Michael Gazzaniga.

***The Mind* Video Teaching Modules, Second Edition,** edited by Frank J. Vattano, Colorado State University, with the consultation of Charles Brewer, Furman University, and David Myers in association with WNET. Available on VHS and DVD. The 35 brief, engaging video clips dramatically enhance and illustrate lecture topics. This completely revised collection of short clips contains updated segments on language processing, infant cognitive development, heredity factors in alcoholism, and living without memory (featuring a dramatic new interview with Clive Wearing). The accompanying Faculty Guide offers descriptions for each module as well as suggestions on how they might be incorporated into class presentations.

***The Brain* Video Teaching Modules, Second Edition,** edited by Frank J. Vattano and Thomas L. Bennet, Colorado State University, and Michelle Butler, United States Air Force Academy. Available on VHS and DVD. A great source of classroom discussion ideas, this collection of 32 short clips provides vivid examples of brain development, function, disorders, and research. The Second Edition contains 10 new and 13 revised modules using added material, new audio, and new graphics. Individual segments range from 3 to 15 minutes long, providing flexibility in highlighting specific topics. The accompanying Faculty Guide offers descriptions of each module as well as suggestions as to how the modules might be incorporated into class presentations.

Course Management

Enhanced Course Management Solutions: Superior Content, All in One Place. Available at www.bfwpub.com/lms for WebCT, Blackboard, Desire2Learn, and Angel. As a service for adopters, Worth Publishers is launching an enhanced turnkey course for *Biological Psychology.* The enhanced course includes a suite of robust teaching and learning materials in one location, organized so that instructors can quickly customize the content for individual needs, eliminating hours of work. For instructors, the *Biological Psychology* enhanced cartridge includes the complete Test Bank and all PowerPoint slides. For students, the course offers interactive flashcards, quizzes, chapter outlines, annotated web links, and research exercises.

Acknowledgments

This project was the product of tireless work on the part of many dedicated people. We would like to take a moment to recognize the contributions of our supplements team:

Charles C. Swart, Trinity College, for his efforts in compiling a thorough Instructor's Resource Manual that will help instructors bring the material alive during lectures.

Michelle Butler, United States Air Force Academy, for her contributions to the Instructor's Resource Manual. Michelle also provided a chapter-by-chapter commentary on our coverage and accuracy. Her thoughts and insights have immensely helped the final product.

Robert R. Mowrer, Angelo State University, for compiling a Test Bank that matches our textbook in both tone and content.

Billy L. Smith and **Chrystal McChristian,** University of Central Arkansas, for creating the Lecture Notebook and Study Guide, a supplement unique to our textbook that stresses the importance of an accurately developed art program.

Joe Morrissey and **Laura Cook,** State University of New York at Binghamton, for their contributions to a sound and complete Companion Website for our textbook.

Meredith Woitach, University of Rochester, for her contributions to the Companion Website.

We are eternally grateful to those colleagues who provided invaluable feedback during the development of this book. Their comments and criticisms were vital in making the book what it is today. To all of you, we thank you for your time, energy, and commitment to improving the study of psychology.

Chalon Anderson,
Central Oklahoma University

Mike Babcock,
Montana State University

Ronald Baenninger,
Temple University

Christopher Bloom,
University of Southern Indiana

Jay Coleman,
University of South Carolina

Catherine DeSoto,
University of Northern Iowa

Marcia Finkelstein,
University of South Florida

Lauren Fowler,
Weber State University

Paul Greenberg,
University of California, San Diego

David Holtzman,
SUNY Brockport

Anna Marsland,
University of Pittsburgh

Laurence Nolan,
Wagner College

Claire Novosad,
Southern Connecticut State University

Heywood Petry,
University of Louisville

Joseph Porter,
Virginia Commonwealth University

Amira Rezec,
Saddleback College

John Ruys,
Evergreen Valley College

Lawrence Ryan,
Oregon State University

Jennifer Sage,
University of California, San Diego

Douglas Shore,
University of Windsor

Douglas Smith,
Southern Illinois University

Linda Walsh,
University of Northern Iowa

Beth Wee,
Tulane University

Scott Wersinger,
University at Buffalo, SUNY

The extraordinary people at Worth Publishers have once again lived up to their reputation for producing college textbooks that are second to none. From the outset, their exhaustive commitment to excellence never ceased to amaze us. We are grateful for each of their individual contributions, without which we might never have completed this project. We would especially like to acknowledge the contributions of our developmental editor, Linda Strange, whose commitment to excellence in writing and knowledge of science in general were most appreciated. Charles Linsmeier ably guided the development of the text to its final form, and we are grateful for his assistance and encouragement. We would also like to acknowledge the efforts of Kerry O'Shaughnessy, whose unending patience and dedication to seeing us achieve our goals with the illustrations went well beyond the call of duty. Worth's production group, including Sarah Segal, Tracey Kuehn, and Justin Kruger, as well as Art Director Babs Reingold, produced a textbook that we can all be proud of. Danny Pucci, along with Stacey Alexander and Eve Conte, guided the supplements program with competence and attention to detail, producing the best package for instructors and students using our book. Amy Shefferd led the charge in placing our book in your hands with her able efforts as marketing manager. And last, we would like to thank Laura Pople and Kim Smith for bringing our book to Worth Publishers. Their confidence in our project allowed this journey to take place.

We wish to thank Rita Christopher and Brenda Lambert for their secretarial assistance. Their help allowed the project to progress smoothly. In addition, our families have been quite supportive of our work on this textbook, and we are grateful for their help and understanding.

To the Student

We have always enjoyed teaching biological psychology and have tried to convey this enjoyment, as well as the conversational style of our lectures, in our writing. As you would imagine, over the many years since we received our final degrees and began teaching, there have been incredible advances both in neuroscience and in our understanding of the influence of biology on behavior. We hope that you will become as excited by the material covered in this textbook as we are about conveying it to you. We also hope that you will be motivated enough by our enthusiasm and what you learn from us to decide to learn more about biological psychology from sources beyond this book.

As you have undoubtedly learned in other courses, one of the best sources for additional information about biological psychology or any other field is the Internet. A number of fascinating sites are listed and described at www.worthpublishers.com/klein.

We would very much like to know what you think of our textbook. To help us, as well as future readers of the book, please send your thoughts to either of us at the Department of Psychology, Post Office Box 6161, Mississippi State, MS 39762. You can also send us e-mail at either sbk1@ra.msstate.edu or bmt2@ra.msstate.edu. We look forward to hearing from you.

Stephen B. Klein
B. Michael Thorne
Mississippi State University

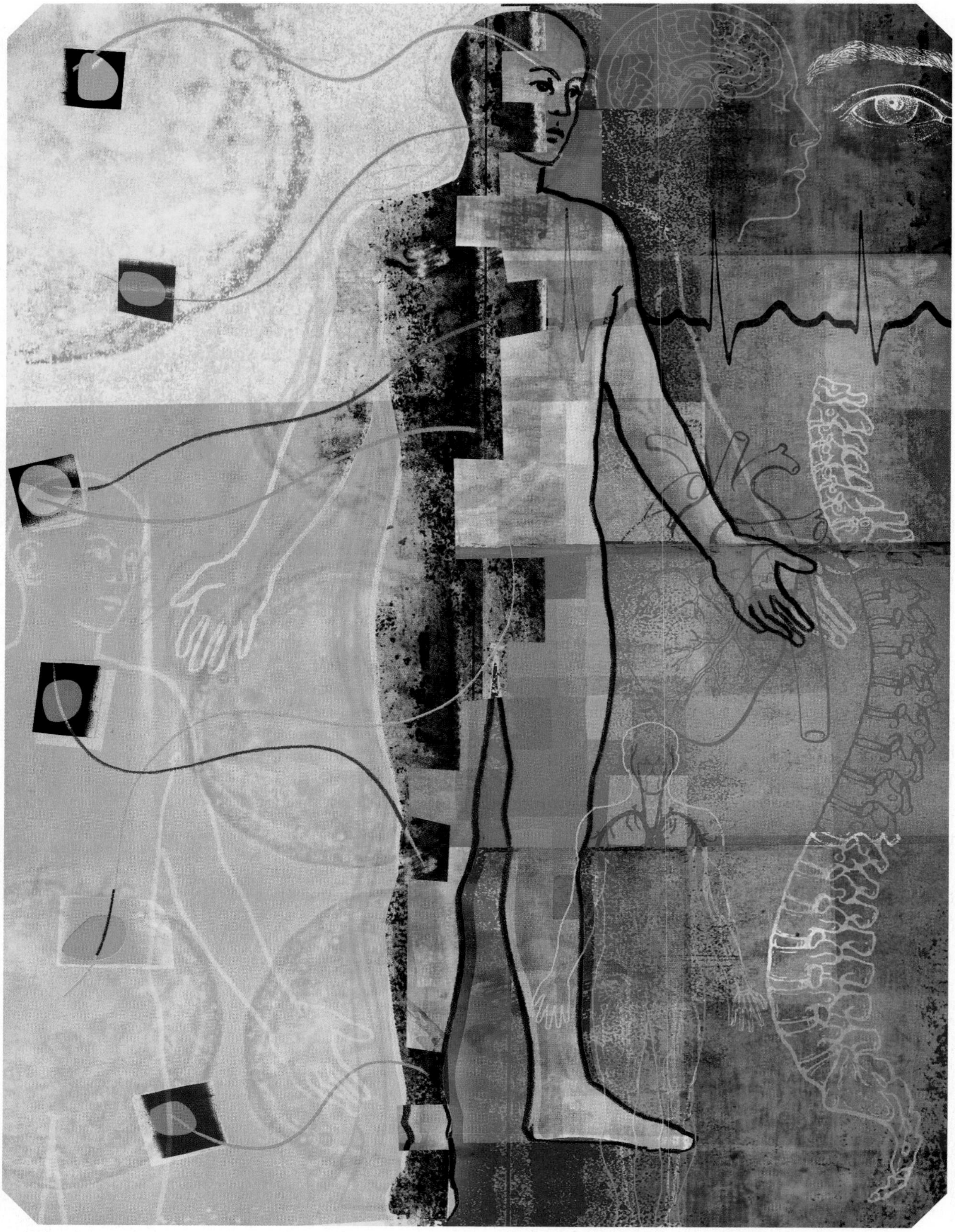

An Introduction to Biological Psychology

1

A New Focus

Because of her mother's periodic struggles with depression, Laura began her college career determined to major in psychology, perhaps to become, eventually, a clinical psychologist. "After all," her mother had told her more than once, "maybe you could learn how to help me." Laura would just smile, but secretly she hoped for just such an outcome.

Nothing in Laura's first 2 years in college caused her to question her decision to be a psychology major; she enjoyed all her courses, even such "tough" ones as learning, experimental, and cognitive psychology. Her vague desire to become a clinical psychologist was strengthened by her abnormal psychology course, but at the same time, some doubts arose about this plan as she learned about treatment methods. Although the instructor told the class that many people with depression could be helped by psychotherapy, he also stressed the importance of antidepressant drugs. And from her mother's experience, Laura knew that both the family physician and the psychiatrist had emphasized the use of prescription medicines.

In her junior year, Laura enrolled in a course that she hoped would help her understand the root of her mother's problem—that is, the biological basis of depression. Taking a quick look through the textbook for the biological psychology course, she found information about some of the drugs her mother had tried over the years: how they affect chemicals in the brain, where in the brain they operate, and so forth. These topics interested her greatly. Although she hadn't formalized anything consciously, Laura was beginning to lean more toward being a biological psychologist than a clinician.

Keep an open mind as you read through this text. Like Laura, maybe you will find that biological psychology contains the answers to many of the questions that have occurred to you in your other psychology courses.

BEFORE YOU BEGIN

- ➤ **What is biological psychology?**
- ➤ **Why should Laura (or you) take a course in biological psychology?**
- ➤ **Who are some of the major figures in the history of biological psychology?**
- ➤ **What are the major solutions to the mind/body problem? To which of the solutions do you subscribe?**
- ➤ **What is meant by localization and nonlocalization of function?**
- ➤ **What are the major research techniques used by biological psychologists?**

> ➤ **What are the various fields of biological psychology from which Laura has to choose?**
> ➤ **What safeguards help protect animals used in research and prevent humans from being harmed while they participate in research?**
>
> **In this chapter, you will find the answers to these questions and many others.**

What Biological Psychology Is and Why We Study It

Laura is thinking of going home this weekend to see how her mother is doing. In the past, Laura's departure for a new semester has precipitated a depressive reaction in her mom and, although her mother sounded all right on the phone, Laura wants to go home and see for herself. Laura's preparation for the trip involves deciding to go, thinking about the condition of her car (Need gas? Check the oil? Water? Air in the tires?), and planning what to take (dirty laundry, perhaps a textbook or two). Deciding, thinking, and planning are all behaviors, or activities of the brain/mind.

Biological psychology is the study of the influences of biological systems, especially the nervous system, on behavior. In the context of biological psychology, **behavior** is anything that an organism does that involves action and response to stimulation. Laura's decision to go home for the weekend and her planning for the trip are behaviors, as are her mother's insomnia and frequent crying sessions. Further, the behavior that biological psychologists are interested in can include not just the entire organism but parts of an organism. In Chapter 6, for example, we will discuss the research of Nobel Prize winners David Hubel and Torsten Wiesel, who studied the behavior of individual neurons (nerve cells) in response to visual stimulation.

We know from experience that some students have reservations about their first biological psychology course. One reason for this reservation is that biological psychology employs the language of biology, a vocabulary with which most psychology majors are not familiar. Terminology, often involving Latin-based words, can be intimidating to the uninitiated. Thus, we are devoting a few paragraphs to why we think such a course is so important to your undergraduate experience in psychology.

In most introductory psychology textbooks, you will find psychology defined as the scientific study of behavior, or perhaps as the scientific study of behavior and the mind. What is the organ of mind and the source of all behavior? Is it the liver? The kidneys? The heart? Most of us believe, of course, that the brain is the organ of mind and the author of all behavior, although as we discuss the historical origins of biological psychology, you will find that this belief has not been universal.

If the brain is the organ of mind and the source of all behavior, and if the definition of psychology is the study of behavior and the mind, then it stands to reason that biological psychology is fundamental to everything else in psychology. For this reason alone, students of psychology should take a biological psychology course.

Consider the material in what most undergraduate students find the most interesting psychology course—abnormal psychology. Abnormal psychology deals with "mental disorders" such as schizophrenia, obsessive-compulsive disorder, phobias, and, of course, depression. When Laura was working on a high school science paper, she asked her mother to list her main symptoms. Her mother responded with the following: insomnia, lack of appetite and energy, obsessive thoughts, and anxiety. It should not surprise you to learn that all these symptoms originate (like everything else we are and do) in the brain. And this is why Laura is enthusiastic about her biological psychology textbook: It contains the information she needs for a deeper understanding of her mother's problems.

You have probably taken a course in learning and memory or remember the topic from your introductory course. What is the organ of learning? Where are

biological psychology The study of the influence of biological systems on behavior.

behavior Anything that an organism does that involves action and response to stimulation.

memories stored? The answer to both questions is in the central nervous system—the brain and spinal cord. Does your school offer a course in human sexual behavior? If so, it is certainly one of the most popular courses on campus. When long-time advice columnist Ann Landers wrote that sex is all in your mind, she was correct. You cannot fully comprehend the human sexual response without knowing something about the nervous system's control of it. We could go on like this, mentioning most of the undergraduate psychology courses you are likely to encounter, but you get the idea: Biological psychology is basic to everything else in psychology.

We would like to begin by discussing where we have been—the historical origins of biological psychology—as a prelude to looking at where we are now—the subject of the rest of the book.

monism The idea that there is only one underlying reality, either body or mind.

dualism The idea that both body and mind exist.

Checkpoint

Beginning with the definition of psychology, explain to another student majoring in psychology why taking a course in biological psychology is important.

Historical Origins of Biological Psychology

So far, as you may have inferred, we have been treating the brain and mind as synonymous. (By mind, we generally mean consciousness—what we are consciously aware of—which includes thought, reason, emotion, and memory.) Throughout the history of psychology, however, scientists have been concerned with the so-called mind/body problem. Do both body and mind exist, or is there only body or only mind? The whole issue often has had religious connotations, and in some languages the words for mind and soul are the same (for example, in French, *l'âme*). If you believe in an immortal soul and a mortal body, then you probably subscribe to some version of René Descartes' mind/body solution: the existence of both body and mind (dualism), with a material body and an immaterial mind/soul.

Monism Versus Dualism

Briefly, the major solutions to the mind/body problem fall into two categories: monism and dualism. **Monism** posits one underlying reality—either body or mind. The "body" solution is called *materialism,* the idea that the underlying reality is physical. Critics of this solution say that the materialists have lost their minds. This materialist position has an ancient origin, with the Greek philosopher Democritus (ca. 460–370 B.C.E.), but the contemporary belief that all thought and action are ultimately reducible to electrochemical activity is a materialist view. The "mind" solution, by contrast, contends that reality ultimately exists in the mind; all that can be proved to exist is mind, not body. This type of monism is often called *immaterialism,* and the modern version is usually attributed to British philosopher George Berkeley (1685–1753).

Dualism, the idea that both body and mind exist, takes two major forms: interactionism and parallelism. As already indicated, René Descartes (1596–1650) was the chief architect of the *interactionism* version of dualism, contending that the interaction of the material body and the immaterial mind takes place in the brain, and particularly in the movements of a small brain structure called the pineal gland (Figure 1.1). One reason Descartes chose the pineal gland was that he knew it was an unpaired structure in the brain and thus one of the leading candidates for the place where our dual sensory messages are transformed into unitary object perceptions. Descartes had rejected another unpaired structure, the pituitary, because it is below the brain and "already had an assigned function about which there seemed to be little disagreement. From ancient times, people thought it acted as a drain or pump for removing waste (phlegm) from the brain" (Finger, 2000, p. 78).

The other major dualism position, called *parallelism* or psychophysical parallelism, holds the view that both mind and body exist, but the two do not interact. Rather, they only *appear* to interact because,

Figure 1.1

A drawing of the human brain by René Descartes Descartes theorized that the pineal gland (labeled H in the drawing) is where the mind and the body interact.

How do we know that the pineal gland is not where body and mind interact?

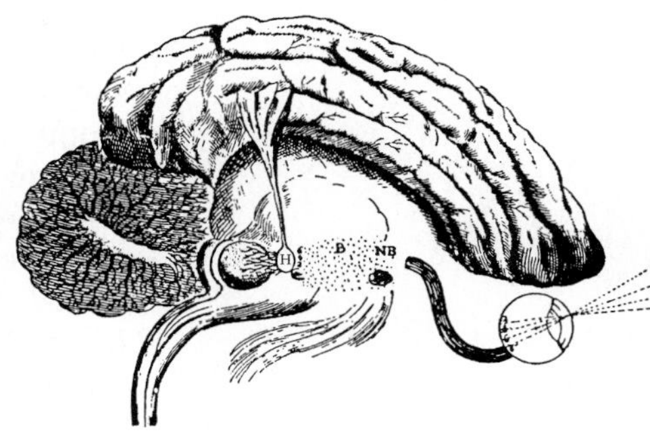

THE GRANGER COLLECTION, NEW YORK

René Descartes (1596–1650).

as Gottfried Wilhelm Leibniz (1646–1716) contended, they are like two perfectly constructed clocks set in motion simultaneously.

Of the many other mind/body solutions, one of the most interesting is *epiphenomenalism.* This philosophical position holds that the activities of the brain produce mind as a sort of accidental by-product and that the activities of the mind are irrelevant to the workings of the brain. The analogy often used to illustrate epiphenomenalism is the noise made by a lawnmower: The noise produced is an epiphenomenon and is totally unnecessary for cutting the grass, just as the mind is unnecessary for the functioning of the brain. Epiphenomenalism is attributed to the famous British philosopher Thomas Hobbes (1588–1679).

The Location of the Mind

In addition to the philosophical musings on the mind/body problem, until relatively modern times there has been no definitive answer to the question of the physical location of the mind. Aristotle (384–322 B.C.E.), one of the most important early philosophers, taught that the mind resides in the heart. He reasoned that the origin of blood must be the site where life or the soul originates; the brain merely serves to cool the blood. The Egyptians also believed that the heart is the source of life; when they embalmed a person, the heart was preserved and the brain discarded.

Most of the early Greeks, however, believed that the brain, not the heart, is the locus of the mind. Hippocrates (460–377 B.C.E.), the famous Greek physician, speculated some 50 years earlier than Aristotle that the brain gives rise to human actions. Even Plato (427–347 B.C.E.), Aristotle's teacher, believed that the mind resides in the brain. Because the sphere is a perfect geometric shape, Plato reasoned, the mind must be located in the spherical head (or the summit) of the human body.

Living some 600 years after Hippocrates, Galen (ca. A.D. 130–200) was greatly influenced by both Hippocrates and Aristotle, although he accepted the Hippocratic belief in the brain as the organ of the mind. Galen's views were particularly important because they were accepted by the early Christian Church and became dogma until the beginnings of what we call the Renaissance, in about the 14th century.

Following Galen, the Church proposed that nutrients absorbed from the intestines are converted by the liver into natural spirits. Upon reaching the heart, natural spirits become vital spirits, which are carried to a network of blood vessels at the base of the brain and there converted to animal spirits. Animal spirits are stored in the three fluid-filled chambers, or ventricles, in the brain. The ventricles were seen, incorrectly, as chambers located one behind the other: the first ventricle analyzing sensory input, the second ventricle responsible for reason and thought, and the third storing memories.

This view of the brain was challenged by Leonardo da Vinci (1452–1519), whose dissections led him to conclude in the early 1500s that sensory nerves, which, according to the view of the Church, should end in the first ventricle, actually end near the second ventricle. Although this conclusion too was inaccurate, the finding cast doubt on the Church's model.

In his resolve to doubt everything, Descartes broke completely with the conception of the Church. His hydraulic model of the nervous system envisioned nerves as a group of hollow tubes containing delicate threads that connect sensory receptors to the brain. Other hollow tubes lead to the muscles, which are empty bladders. Stimulation of a sensory organ tightens the threads to the brain, opening a "pore." Animal spirits, released from the brain when the "pore" opens, flow through the hollow tubes, fill the bladders, and produce movement. Descartes' conception of the nervous system was based on the operation of the animated statues, or automata, seen in the gardens of St. Germain at the palace of Louis XIV; the limbs of these statues moved when a visitor to the gardens stepped on a plate connected to the hydraulic system of the statues.

Using a preparation consisting of a leg muscle and attached motor nerve of a frog, Luigi Galvani (1737–1798) provided convincing evidence against Descartes' theory. If the hydraulic model was valid, removal of the motor nerve and leg muscle from the body of the frog would prevent the animal spirits from flowing from brain to muscle; stimulation of the motor nerve after removal from the body (and disconnection from the brain) should no longer produce a muscle twitch. However, Galvani observed that an electrical stimulus applied to the motor nerve did cause the leg muscle to twitch, strongly suggesting that electricity is an essential element in the functioning of the nervous system. This was confirmed when an instrument to measure electric current—appropriately called a galvanometer—was first applied to nerve tissue.

reflex An involuntary response to a stimulus, caused by a direct connection between a sensory receptor and a muscle.

The Reflex

Although Descartes' notion of how the nervous system works was quickly disproved, another aspect of his theory was more successful—specifically, the idea that external events could cause muscle movements. For example, Descartes (1662/1972) believed that when someone's foot gets too close to a fire, the heat stimulates sensory spots on the skin and results in movement of the foot away from the fire (Figure 1.2). Descartes envisioned the external environmental stimulation being reflected by the muscles, and thus coined the term **reflex.** His general concept of a reflex has been accepted by modern scientists, although the mechanism is radically different from the one Descartes proposed (Chapter 2).

Robert Whytt (1714–1766) did not accept Descartes' idea that muscle movements are simply reflections of external stimulation. He observed that reflex movements occur too rapidly to be dependent on mental processes. Instead, Whytt proposed that reflexes are controlled by the spinal cord. He found that movement of a leg of a frog could be produced by the electrical stimulation of a small segment of the spinal cord (Whytt, 1768).

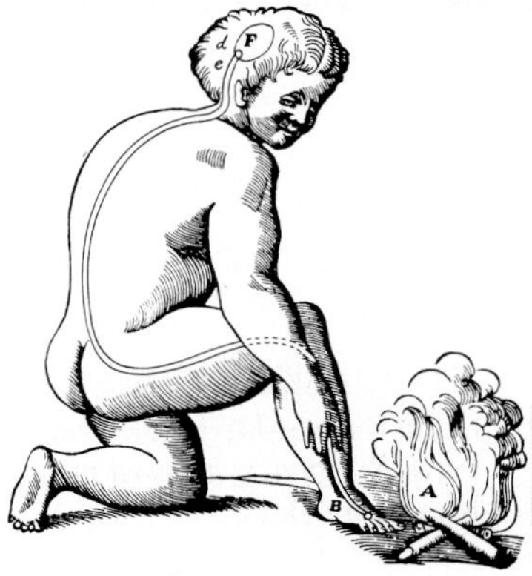

Figure 1.2

Descartes' view of reflex action The detection of heat (A) on the skin (B) tightens nerve threads that open "pores" (F) in the brain, causing the release of animal spirits into the hollow tube that travels to the muscles. The animal spirits fill a bladder in the muscle, causing the muscle to expand and produce movement that pulls the foot away from the fire.

➾ **What is the origin of the term *reflex*?**

The classic research of English physiologist Charles Bell (1774–1842) provided new insights into the sensory and motor systems. (*Sensory* refers to the detection of environmental events either inside or outside the body, and *motor* refers to actions.) In 1811, Bell reported his research on spinal nerves, the fibers that enter and exit the spinal cord and carry sensory and motor information. Spinal nerves divide into two roots: a dorsal ("toward the back") root and a ventral ("toward the belly") root. Working on rabbits, Bell observed that touching the ventral root with a probe produced muscle contractions, whereas similarly probing the dorsal root did not produce movement. He thus concluded that sensory and motor nerves are separate, with sensory information probably entering the spinal cord through the dorsal root and motor information leaving through the ventral root. Bell published 100 copies of a pamphlet describing his research and gave them to his friends.

Eleven years after Bell distributed his pamphlets, French physiologist François Magendie (1783–1855) published his studies of spinal nerves, in which he used 6-week-old puppies as subjects. (Not surprisingly, antivivisectionists—people who oppose research on live animals—find Magendie's research particularly offensive.) If you have ever tried to clip your dog's nails, you know that a dog's paws are very sensitive. If you pinch a dog's leg or prick it with a pin, the dog normally jerks the leg away. Magendie found that after cutting the dorsal root of the nerves of a limb, pinching or pricking produced no movement, but the dog could still move the limb voluntarily. Magendie concluded that the limb was anesthetized but not paralyzed. When the ventral root was cut, however, the puppy yelped when the limb was pinched but did not move it away, indicating that the limb was paralyzed but not anesthetized. Magendie concluded from these observations that the dorsal root carries sensory information, and the ventral root carries motor messages (Figure 1.3). This finding is today known as

Figure 1.3

A cross-sectional view of part of the spinal cord The sensory nerves enter the spinal cord through the dorsal root of the spinal nerves, and the motor nerves exit through the ventral root.

➾ **What is the significance of the Bell-Magendie law for psychology? For the concept of localization of function?**

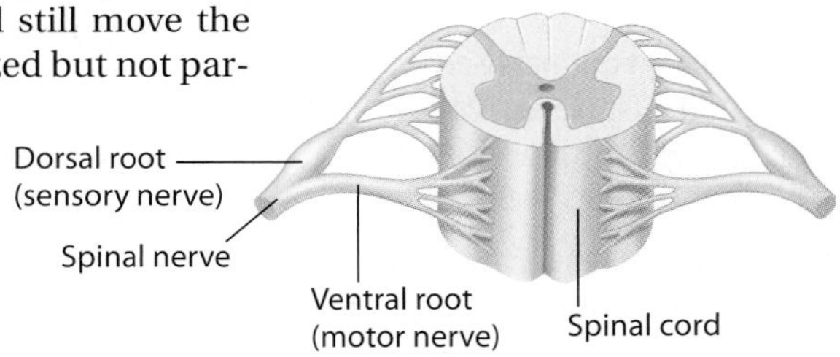

Charles Bell (1774–1842)

the **Bell-Magendie law,** recognizing the initial importance of Bell's research and the more thorough and convincing evidence of Magendie.

Johannes Müller (1801–1858) went a step further, suggesting that each sensory nerve carries specific information about the quality and location of sensory events. For example, touching a flame with your right index finger activates pain receptors on that finger. The pain receptors send a message through the sensory nerve that pain is being detected at the tip of the index finger of your right hand. According to Müller, if these same pain receptors were activated by electrical stimulation, the signal sent would be the same—that is, that pain is being experienced in the tip of your right index finger. So, stimulation of this particular sensory nerve anywhere along its path to the brain would send the same message. Likewise, activation of the optic nerve would produce visual sensations, and activation of the auditory nerve would lead to auditory sensations. The idea that the event detected by the brain depends on which nerve carries the message is known as Müller's **doctrine of specific nerve energies** (Müller, 1838).

You can demonstrate the doctrine of specific nerve energies by gently pressing the right side of your right eyeball. The pressure on your eye activates the optic nerve and causes you to experience a visual sensation called a **pressure phosphene.** The brain detects stimulation of the optic nerve as a visual sensation even though the nerve is being activated by pressure from your finger. We will have more to say about the doctrine of specific nerve energies when we discuss vision in Chapter 6.

➤Checkpoint

Using the Bell-Magendie law, explain what happens when someone tickles your foot or taps you on the shoulder to get your attention. Using the doctrine of specific nerve energies, explain how you know in which direction to turn.

REVIEW

- Biological psychology is the study of the influence of biological systems, especially the nervous system, on behavior.
- The major perspectives on the mind/body problem are monism (there is only one underlying reality—body/materialism or mind/immaterialism) and dualism (both body and mind exist).
- Aristotle believed the heart was the locus of the mind, although some 50 years earlier Plato and Hippocrates had taught that the mind was in the brain.
- Greatly influenced by Hippocrates, Galen considered the ventricles of the brain particularly important for mental activities, and this view was accepted by the Christian Church until the beginnings of the Renaissance.
- Descartes described the nervous system as a group of hollow tubes connecting the sensory organs to the brain and the brain to the muscles. Galvani's research disproved Descartes' hydraulic model by showing that a muscle of a frog twitched in response to electrical stimulation even when the muscle and attached motor nerve had been removed from the body.
- Descartes coined the term *reflex,* suggesting that muscle movements reflect external stimulation. Whytt proposed that reflex movements are controlled by the spinal cord, and he showed that the stimulation of small segments of the cord elicited motor responses.
- The Bell-Magendie law states that the dorsal roots of spinal nerves carry in sensory information, and the ventral roots take out motor impulses to the muscles.
- In Müller's doctrine of specific nerve energies, the particular message detected by the brain depends on which nerve carries the message.

Localization of Function

Although the issue is much older, the idea that specific functions are located in particular places in the nervous system was a major theme running through 19th and 20th century studies of the brain. The Bell-Magendie law supports this local-

Bell-Magendie law The principle that the dorsal root of a spinal nerve carries sensory information to the spinal cord and the ventral root conveys commands to the muscles.

doctrine of specific nerve energies The theory that the message detected by the nervous system is determined by which nerve carries the message.

pressure phosphene A visual sensation caused by pressure on the optic nerve.

izationist view, as does Müller's doctrine of specific nerve energies. Further support came from other areas of research ranging from phrenology to Darwin's theory of evolution and studies of brain-damaged human subjects.

phrenology Gall's "science of the mind," which assumed that mental functions are localized in certain brain areas and that the moral and intellectual character of a person can be determined by studying the bumps and indentations on the skull.

cerebrum The uppermost portion of the brain.

Phrenology

German physician and anatomist Franz Joseph Gall (1758–1828), founder of the pseudoscience of **phrenology** (meaning "science of the mind"), examined the brains of many different animal species and of humans of different ages and capacities. He concluded that mental functioning, or the strength of mental functioning, was related to the size and integrity of the brain. He argued further that mental character could be divided into a limited number of moral and intellectual faculties, located in specific brain areas. Gall believed that an individual who demonstrated an above-average faculty had a corresponding brain area that was larger than normal, whereas a person with a below-average faculty had a correspondingly reduced brain area. He also argued that an enlarged brain area produced a bump on the skull above that area, whereas a diminished brain area produced an indentation. The examination of these bumps and indentations, called *cranioscopy,* thus revealed the strength of the mental faculties of an individual. According to Gall, humans have 27 highly specific faculties, including acquisitiveness, amativeness, benevolence, firmness, mirthfulness, secretiveness, and veneration, that reside in different areas of the brain (Figure 1.4).

Gall's phrenology was quite popular in the 19th century, but never accepted by most of the scientific community. One of the most tireless critics of phrenology was Marie-Jean-Pierre Flourens (1794–1867). Using ablation (the removal of tissue, a method discussed later in the chapter), Flourens (1824/1965) removed parts of the brain from animals of several species in order to demonstrate that the functions claimed by the phrenologists for specific brain areas did not reside in those areas. For example, to examine the mental functions of the **cerebrum** (the uppermost portion of the brain), Flourens removed this area, nursed the animal back to health, then noted any changes in its behavior. He found that a pigeon without a cerebrum, kept alive by force feeding, showed neither voluntary movements nor responses to light or sound. Flourens concluded that the cerebrum controlled voluntary movements, perception, and the will—not the functions claimed by phrenologists.

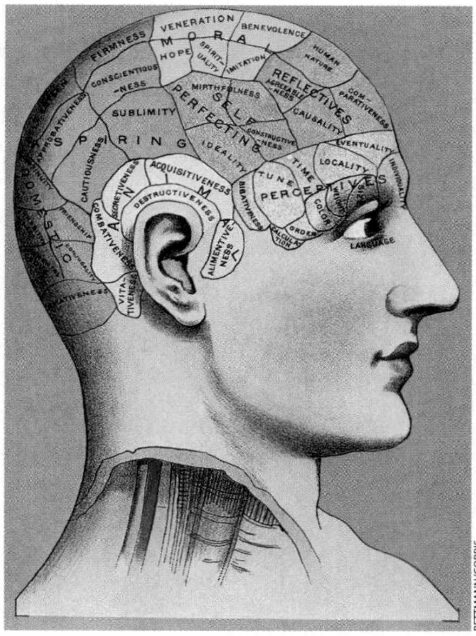

BETTMANN/CORBIS

Figure 1.4

A phrenology map Gall suggested that faculties are located in specific areas of the cortex and that personality can be revealed by measuring the bumps and indentations on a person's head.

➡ **What research demolished the validity of phrenology in the scientific community?**

Despite finding specific functions for the areas of the nervous system he examined, Flourens was most struck by the common action of the nervous system acting as a whole—an illustration of nonlocalization of function. In comparing the contributions of Gall and Flourens, "it is possible to think of Gall as the visionary who had the right idea [localization of function] but the wrong method, and of Flourens as a laboratory scientist with the better method but the wrong theory [nonlocalization of function]" (Finger, 1994, p. 36).

Implicit in Flourens's work was the idea that we can generalize from animals to humans. Otherwise, his research, no matter how carefully conducted, would not have been relevant as an argument against the teachings of phrenology. The work of a contemporary of Flourens in England soon provided the scientific basis to make explicit what had been implicit in much earlier research.

Darwin, Wallace, and Evolution

In 1859, Charles Darwin (1809–1882) published a book that contains, according to Daniel Dennett (1995, p. 21), "the single best idea anyone has ever had": the idea of evolution by natural selection. The development of Darwin from a rather indifferent student at Cambridge to the most famous naturalist in England has been the subject of many books and continues to fascinate nearly a century and a half after the publication of his best-known work, *On the Origin of Species by Means of*

Natural Selection, or the Preservation of Favoured Races in the Struggle for Life, generally known as *The Origin of Species.*

The most formative aspect of Darwin's early adult life was his nearly 5-year voyage on the HMS *Beagle* as an unpaid naturalist. As a result of his discoveries on the voyage and his reading and study, Darwin became convinced that species of animals could change as a result of their struggle for survival; individuals with beneficial variations relative to their environment would be more likely to survive, breed, and pass on these beneficial characteristics to their offspring. With no knowledge of genetics, Darwin deduced the core ideas of organic evolution. We will have more to say about genetics and the evolution of the nervous system in Chapter 3.

Charles Darwin (1809–1882).

Darwin did not rush to publish his ideas, however, and more than 2 decades passed between his return from the voyage and publication of *The Origin of Species.* In fact, Darwin was working on a monumental treatise to present all his evidence for evolution when, in 1858, he received a letter and essay from a young naturalist, Alfred Russel Wallace (1823–1913), that outlined a theory of evolution remarkably like Darwin's.

Darwin's inclination was to allow Wallace to have the priority of discovery, but his friends argued against this. Darwin, prostrated with grief over the death of one of his children, turned the matter over to his friends, and the result was that Wallace's paper was presented at the next meeting of the Linnean Society along with some of Darwin's work that established him as the discoverer of evolution by natural selection (Rachels, 1986).

The 1858 presentation at the Linnean Society had little effect on the scientific community or society at large, and Darwin quickly produced a brief summary of his evidence for evolution, which was published the following year as *The Origin of Species.* Although Darwin did not explicitly discuss the place of humankind in evolution in the book, the implication was there, and we can confidently state that the publication of *The Origin of Species* in 1859 forever changed our view of the animal kingdom and the place of humans in it. People who accepted the arguments presented in the book—and virtually all of the scientific community did—could no longer argue for a Cartesian dualism in the animal kingdom, with humans as rational beings possessing both mind and body and nonhuman animals as automatons without a mind (or soul). The implicit assumption that research on animals would generate knowledge relevant for humans now became explicit, and the person usually credited with founding the field of comparative psychology, George John Romanes (1848–1894), was a protégé of Darwin.

Darwin's explicit linking of humans with the rest of the animal kingdom came in *The Descent of Man* (1874). In this work, we can see why Darwin thought the study of animal physiology, including neurophysiology, would generalize to humans:

> It is notorious that man is constructed on the same general type or model as other mammals. All the bones in his skeleton can be compared with corresponding bones in a monkey, bat, or seal. So it is with his muscles, nerves, blood-vessels, and internal viscera. The brain . . . follows the same law, as shown by Huxley and other anatomists. Bischoff, who is a hostile witness, admits that every chief fissure and fold in the brain of man has its analogy in that of the orang[utan]. (Darwin, 1874, p. 6)

Darwin's idea of a basic continuity in the animal kingdom has implications far beyond the study of animals closely related to humans (i.e., the great apes) as a way of learning about matters of relevance to humans. The idea has encouraged scientists to search for the biological origins of a variety of behaviors and systems in species far removed (in an evolutionary sense) from humans. For example, if we assume that the neurological correlates of learning and memory share a common set of features throughout the animal kingdom, then it becomes relevant to study these phenomena in such primitive creatures as *Aplysia,* a sea slug, which is a useful research animal because of its relative simplicity and small number of neurons. Similarly, if we accept that the same mechanisms of neuronal transmission are

Broca's area An area in the frontal lobe of the left hemisphere of the brain that contributes to speech production.

used in all animals with neurons, then it becomes worthwhile to study neuronal transmission in the giant axon of the squid. As you will see, a significant amount of the information we have gained about the nervous system and its operations in the last century rests on Darwin's fundamental concept.

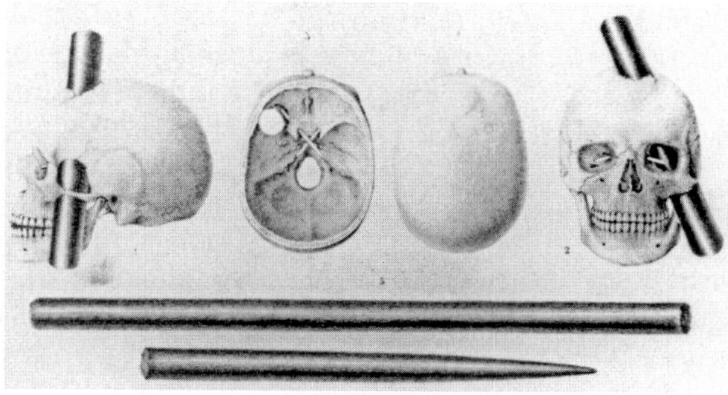

Figure 1.5

The case of Phineas P. Gage This photograph illustrates the size of the tamping rod and Gage's skull. Gage's personality changed dramatically after his accident.

➡ **What is the significance of the case of Phineas P. Gage?**

The Case of Phineas P. Gage

On September 13, 1848, while railroad construction supervisor Phineas P. Gage was tamping explosive powder into a hole, a premature explosion sent the tamping rod through Gage's left cheek and out the top of his head (Figure 1.5). Amazingly, Gage survived his accidental lobotomy, but "his friends and acquaintances said he was 'no longer Gage'" (Harlow, 1868, p. 340). Using modern brain imaging techniques, Hanna Damasio and her colleagues have studied Gage's skull (Damasio & others, 1994). They have confirmed the location of the prefrontal (front part of the brain) damage that produces defects in the ability to make rational decisions and the processing of emotional information—both problems Gage exhibited after his accident.

Localization of Language Areas

Although the 19th-century work of Flourens appeared to show evidence for nonlocalization of function, most brain research has supported localization. This support has been particularly evident in the examination of people with brain damage affecting their language abilities. The first discovery in this area involved French physician Pierre-Paul Broca (1824–1880), who successfully identified a language area in the frontal lobe. In 1861, Broca treated and reported on a man named Leborgne who had been transferred to his surgical ward because of gangrene in his paralyzed right leg. Leborgne appeared to understand what was said to him, but, despite having intact vocal cords, could only say *"tan, tan,"* or, when extremely frustrated because of his inability to communicate, would say the curse words *"Sacré nom de Dieu."*

When Leborgne died 6 days after admission to Broca's ward, Broca performed an autopsy. He found a large tumor in the third convolution of the frontal lobe on the left side of the brain. Shortly after the autopsy, Broca reported his findings to the Société d'Anthropologie (Anthropological Society). Broca continued to accumulate evidence from other patients, providing additional documentation for a language area in the left frontal lobe. Damage to this brain area, today called **Broca's area** (Figure 1.6), often produces *nonfluent aphasia.* (*Aphasia* refers to a deficit in language.) A person with nonfluent aphasia has great difficulty speaking but has relatively good (although not perfect) language comprehension.

German neurologist Carl Wernicke (1848–1905) identified a second language area (Wernicke, 1874). Some of Wernicke's patients could verbalize clearly but were

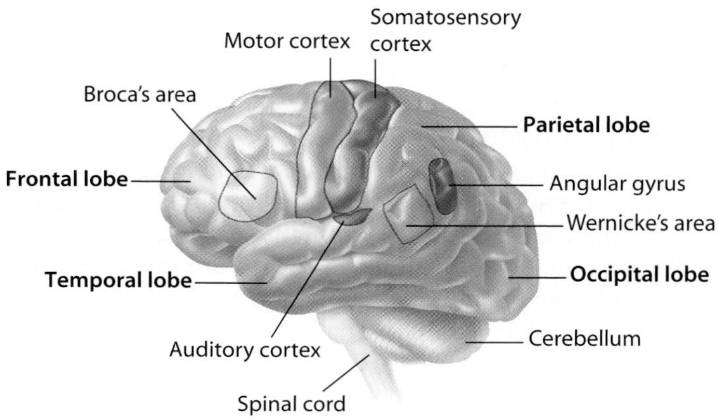

Figure 1.6

The four lobes of the cerebral cortex Broca's and Wernicke's areas are shown, as well as the areas of the cerebral cortex that control skin senses (somatosensory cortex) and movement (motor cortex).

➡ **What would probably happen following damage to either Broca's area or Wernicke's area?**

Wernicke's area An area in the temporal lobe of the left hemisphere of the brain that contributes to understanding language and producing intelligible speech.

engram A memory trace, or the physical location of specific memories.

mass action Lashley's finding that the greater the brain area destroyed, the more severe the impact on learning.

equipotentiality The idea that any part of a functional area can carry out the function of that area.

unable to speak intelligibly to others or to understand their speech. Wernicke found that this type of language deficit was associated with damage to the upper portion of the left temporal lobe. Damage to this area, now called **Wernicke's area** (Figure 1.6), typically produces *fluent aphasia.* A person with fluent aphasia can speak easily, but his or her speech is meaningless, and the person also has poor language comprehension. In Chapter 13, we will look more closely at neural structures, which include Broca's area and Wernicke's area, that are involved in language comprehension and production.

Sensory and Motor Localization

Additional 19th-century work provided evidence for the localization of motor functions and sensory perception. In 1870, German scientists Gustav Fritsch (1838–1927) and Eduard Hitzig (1838–1907) demonstrated that direct electrical stimulation of the frontal cortex of a dog produced muscle actions on the opposite side of the body. Fritsch and Hitzig also showed that increasing the stimulation intensity increased the number of muscle groups activated, and moving the electrical stimulation to different areas of the cortex produced different movements. We will have more to say about the brain's control of movement in Chapter 8.

Scottish neurologist David Ferrier (1843–1928) and German physiologist Hermann Munk (1839–1912) used electrical stimulation, as well as ablation, in monkey subjects to identify areas in the brain that control specific sensory systems. Their work showed that vision is controlled by occipital lobe areas, audition (hearing) by areas in the temporal lobe, and the skin senses (e.g., touch, temperature) by portions of the parietal lobe (Figure 1.6). We discuss vision in Chapter 6 and audition and the skin senses in Chapter 7.

Mass Action and Equipotentiality

Our discussion to this point has focused on the localization of function within specific neural structures. Karl Lashley's research, however, appeared to support a nonlocalizationist point of view. Although he considered himself a psychologist, Karl Spencer Lashley (1890–1958) earned a master's degree in bacteriology at Pittsburgh and a doctorate in genetics at Johns Hopkins University, where he developed an interest in behavior while studying under the noted psychologist John Watson. Lashley also worked with Shepard Ivory Franz (1874–1933), who was the first investigator to combine the animal training methods of a psychologist with the ablation technique of a physiologist. Franz argued that the return of partial functioning after brain damage contradicted strict localization of function. Lashley's research, published in *Brain Mechanisms and Intelligence* in 1929, involved testing brain-damaged rats on several different learning tasks.

In his search for the **engram,** a memory trace or the physical location of specific memories, Lashley developed the concepts for which he is most remembered: mass action and equipotentiality. Lashley found that the amount of damage to cortical tissue (the outer covering of the brain) rather than the exact location of the damage influenced rats' impairment on complex learning tasks such as negotiating a maze. This was his **mass action** concept—the greater the area destroyed, the more severe the impact on learning. Note that mass action was intended to apply only to the learning of complex tasks involving many different cues and motor responses—and correspondingly many different cortical areas.

Karl Spencer Lashley (1890–1958).

By **equipotentiality,** Lashley meant that any part of a functional area could carry out the function of that area—that is, the functions were not strictly localized in some cortical "units" but were distributed within the particular brain area. Lashley proposed that equipotentiality occurs only in cortical *association areas*—areas that are neither primarily sensory nor primarily motor—and only for relatively complex functions. He considered equipotentiality responsible for the mass action effect: All neurons in a particular area are involved in a complex learning task because each neuron in the area has an equivalent function. Equipotentiality explains why partial functioning is retained following brain damage, provided some part of the functional unit is intact. Lashley's view also explains the recovery of functioning that often follows damage.

By appearing to show the brain as a relatively homogeneous structure governed by the principle of equipotentiality, Lashley's publication of *Brain Mechanisms and Intelligence* (1929/1963) discouraged interest in neurophysiological explanations for behavioral events (Hebb, 1959). For 2 decades after the publication of Lashley's book, experimental psychology concentrated on the behavioral aspects of learning. This was the heyday of such neobehaviorists (behaviorists who followed John Watson, the founder of behaviorism) as Edward Tolman and Clark Hull and their comprehensive, nonneurological theories of learning.

Interest in neurological explanations for behavior was reawakened by the work of one of Lashley's students, Donald Olding Hebb (1904–1985). In *The Organization of Behavior,* Hebb (1949) developed several hypothetical mechanisms that he used to account for a wide range of behavior, including learning and memory. We will discuss the importance of Hebb's theorizing in Chapter 14.

Checkpoint

What is phrenology? What was its lasting contribution to biological psychology? Who was the most ardent opponent of phrenology? What did his research show definitively about animals? What is the relevance of Darwin's theory of evolution for biological psychology?

REVIEW

- Gall, the founder of phrenology, suggested that mental functioning could be divided into moral and intellectual faculties localized in different areas in the brain.
- Flourens was the chief opponent of phrenology. He developed the ablation method to study the brain in experimental animals, concluding that some abilities associated with mind were abolished following removal of the cerebrum. Flourens appeared to find evidence for nonlocalization of function, which was opposed to the extreme localizationist teachings of phrenology.
- Darwin's idea of organic evolution, expressed in *The Origin of Species* and *The Descent of Man,* made explicit the place of humans in the animal kingdom and made the study of animals and animal systems relevant for learning about basic neurophysiological mechanisms that also apply to humans.
- Gage's accident and his subsequent changed behavior definitively established the brain as the organ of mind in humans.
- Broca successfully identified a language area involved in speech production in the left frontal lobe (Broca's area). Wernicke later identified a second language area (Wernicke's area) in the left temporal lobe.
- Fritsch and Hitzig electrically stimulated the frontal cortex of a dog and observed limb movement on the opposite side of the body, providing support for the localization of motor behavior.
- Ferrier and Munk reported that vision is controlled by areas in the occipital lobe, audition by the temporal lobe, and the skin senses by the parietal lobe, supporting the localization of sensory perception.
- Lashley suggested that functioning is not localized for complex learning tasks governed by the association areas of the cortex. He proposed two concepts: mass action (the amount of neural tissue destroyed is more important than the locus of the tissue) and equipotentiality (all neurons within a functional area contribute equally to the function).
- Lashley's nonlocalizationist viewpoint suppressed interest in the search for neural explanations for behavior, which was rescued by one of Lashley's students, D. O. Hebb, with publication of *The Organization of Behavior.*

The Neuron

By the end of the 19th century, researchers had amassed a great deal of evidence to support the localization of specific functions in specific areas of the brain. The evidence had come from the development of two experimental techniques: ablation of specific nervous system structures and electrical stimulation of these structures.

nerve net theory The idea that the nervous system consists of a network of connected nerves.

neuronal theory The idea that the nervous system is made up of individual nerve cells.

neuron A nerve cell.

synapse The point of functional contact between a neuron and its target.

The last great neurological discovery of the 19th century was the identification of the structural unit in the brain that is responsible for these functions. Many scientists had assumed that the nervous system consists of a network of connected nerves, and Flourens's nonlocalizationist position was consistent with such a **nerve net theory.** Today, however, we accept **neuronal theory,** which is the idea that the nervous system is made up of individual nerve cells, called **neurons.** The development of a third technique to investigate the nervous system—the staining of cells—enabled researchers to accept the neuron as a discrete structure, contiguous but not continuous with its neighbors.

Italian histologist and physician Camillo Golgi (1843–1926) developed the stain, called in his honor the *Golgi stain,* that led to the acceptance of neuronal theory. (*Histology* is the study of the cellular structure of tissues.) Using methods introduced earlier for hardening and staining tissues, Golgi developed a staining technique that colors only a few cells in a slice of brain tissue; these cells are stained entirely black, whereas the other cells are not affected. Using the Golgi stain, Spanish histologist and neurologist Santiago Ramón y Cajal (1852–1934) found that nervous tissue consisted of individual cells. For their discoveries, Golgi and Cajal shared the Nobel Prize in Physiology or Medicine in 1906. At the award ceremony, "the speech given by Golgi was largely devoted to resurrecting the defunct nerve net theory" (Finger, 2000, p. 215), and Golgi was quite critical of the theory of the man with whom he shared the prize. Cajal, by contrast, praised Golgi for developing the stain that Cajal had used to demolish the nerve net idea.

The Synapse

The acceptance of neuronal theory following Cajal's work raised the question of how information was transmitted across the spaces between individual neurons. The research of English physician and physiologist Charles Scott Sherrington (1857–1952) helped answer this question.

Sherrington called the point of functional contact between neurons the **synapse,** which means "binding together." His understanding of synaptic transmission came from his studies of spinal reflexes in dogs. The basic spinal reflex consists of at least three neurons: a sensory neuron, a motor neuron, and a third neuron (an interneuron) that connects the sensory and motor neurons. Sherrington measured the time required for an electric current to travel along a neuron, and then compared it with the time required for a spinal reflex. He found that the spinal reflex (with its three synapses) takes longer, suggesting that transmission across the synapse is not as fast as transmission along the neuron. Sherrington also observed other properties of the spinal reflex, such as an addition or summation of influences at the synapse. For his work, he shared the 1932 Nobel Prize in Physiology or Medicine.

Although the prevailing view in the early part of the 20th century was that synaptic transmission was an electrical process, German pharmacologist and physician Otto Loewi (1873–1961) believed that because stimulation of certain nerves decreases rather than increases the functioning of an organ, transmission across synapses must take place by some other means. Loewi thought that nerves might contain chemicals that are released into the synapse and act to stimulate the target neuron, but for many years he could think of no way to prove chemical transmission. Finally, the answer came to him.

To test his idea, Loewi removed the hearts of two frogs (Loewi, 1960). He left the nerves of one heart attached but removed the nerves of the other. Both hearts were placed in containers with Ringer's solution—physiological saline containing chemicals that preserve tissue functioning; this treatment allowed the hearts to continue beating. Loewi electrically stimulated the vagus nerve of the first heart (the donor heart), which caused its beating to slow down. When some of the Ringer's solution from around the donor heart reached the second (recipient) heart, the beating of this heart slowed as if it, too, had had its vagus nerve stimulated (Figure 1.7). Loewi reasoned that stimulation of the vagus nerve of the donor heart had produced a chemical that acted on the heart to slow its beating, and this chemical was released into the Ringer's solution; when the chemical reached the recipient heart, its rate decreased as well. To confirm these observations, Loewi stimulated the accelerator nerve of the donor heart, which increased its heart rate, then transferred some of the surrounding Ringer's solution to the recipient heart, which increased its rate of beating as well.

Loewi called the chemical that decreased heart rate ***vagusstoff,*** "stuff from the vagus nerve." He soon discovered that *vagusstoff* was really acetylcholine, one of the major neurotransmitters (Chapter 4). He later found that the chemical released by the accelerator nerve was epinephrine (also known as adrenalin or adrenaline). Otto Loewi shared the Nobel Prize in Physiology or Medicine in 1936 for his discovery that communication between neurons is a chemical process.

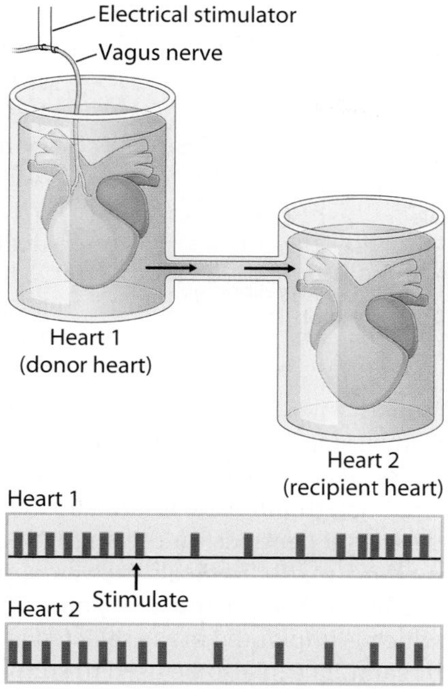

Figure 1.7
Loewi's experiment Using isolated frog hearts, Otto Loewi showed that stimulating the vagus nerve of one heart (the donor) lowered its heart rate because of the release of a chemical that, when added to a second heart (the recipient), lowered its rate as well.

➜ What was the significance of Loewi's experiment?

➤Checkpoint

Imagine you are an 18th century biologist. Describe the nervous system without mentioning the neuron, the synapse, or chemical communication across the synapse. How did Loewi demonstrate that communication between neurons was a chemical process?

REVIEW

- Cajal used Golgi's cell-staining technique to show that nervous tissue consists of individual cells, the neurons.
- Sherrington called the point of functional contact between neurons the synapse. His research showed that the transmission of impulses across the synapse is not as fast as electrical transmission along the neuron.
- Loewi demonstrated that communication across the synapse is a chemical process. He later identified the chemical released into the synapse between the vagus nerve and the heart as acetylcholine.

Techniques for Studying Brain Function

In our historical overview, we have mentioned several major research techniques used by neuroscientists, without going into detail about any specific method. Here, we take a closer look at several of the tools used to unlock the mysteries of the nervous system. Additional methods for studying the nervous system will be introduced throughout the text.

The Ablation of Neural Tissue

Flourens developed the **ablation** method as a way to identify the behavioral function of a particular neural area. Sometimes called *lesioning,* ablation is the experimental destruction of neurons in a selected area. The method is typically performed on nonhuman subjects, for obvious ethical reasons, although ablation has been used in humans clinically to treat neurological disorders. For example, destruction of the neural locus of epilepsy—the area of the brain in which the seizure begins—has been an effective treatment in certain cases (Penfield & Jasper, 1954).

vagusstoff Loewi's term for the chemical that acts to decrease the heart rate.

ablation The experimental destruction of neurons or the surgical removal of a part of the brain.

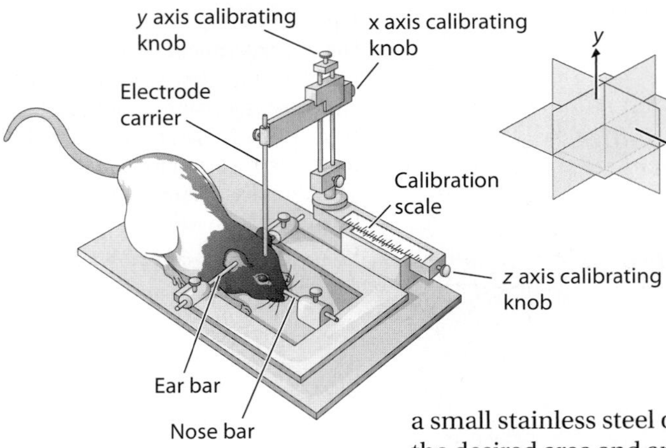

Figure 1.8

A stereotaxic instrument in use in an ablation The animal's head is immobilized while an electric current is passed through the uninsulated tip of an electrode to destroy a specific site in the brain of the animal. The stereotaxic instrument can also be used in stimulation experiments.

➔ **What information about the brain can be obtained with the use of a stereotaxic apparatus to produce brain lesions?**

In the ablation method, an animal is first anesthetized and then placed in a special surgical instrument, called a **stereotaxic apparatus** (Figure 1.8), which enables the researcher to place a lesion with precision. The stereotaxic apparatus was introduced early in the 20th century by Victor Horsley and Robert Clarke for making subcortical lesions, or lesions below the cortex.

There are many methods for producing a brain lesion. In one, bone is removed to expose the brain, the outer cover of the brain (dura mater) is cut away, and the underlying cortical tissue is removed by cutting or suction. In a second method, a small stainless steel or platinum wire, insulated except for the tip, is inserted into the desired area and an electric current is passed through the wire. The current carries enough intensity to destroy the targeted neurons; the amount of brain tissue destroyed depends on the strength of the current and how long it lasts. In a third method, toxic chemicals such as kainic acid are injected to destroy specific areas of the brain. The chemical is administered through a small tube called a cannula, which is implanted in the selected area of the brain. The implantation of electrodes or cannula can also be used to stimulate portions of the brain rather than destroying them; we discuss the stimulation method later.

A *stereotaxic atlas* is used to locate the area to be lesioned. A stereotaxic atlas is analogous to a geographic atlas of the United States, which has outline maps of each state, along with grid coordinates that permit the user to locate a given city or physical feature (e.g., mountain, river). Similarly, the stereotaxic atlas has pictures of sections through the brain, along with grid coordinates that allow the experimenter to locate a particular structure inside the brain. Using a skull feature such as the bregma—the junction of the sagittal and coronal sutures, the joint between flat bones of the skull—as a guide, the atlas indicates where and how deep the electrode or cannula should be placed. By observing the behavioral changes that occur after the animal has recovered from the surgery, a biological psychologist can hypothesize the influence of a particular area of the brain on behavior.

At the end of an experiment, the researcher examines the cell structure of the brain of the animal to determine whether the ablation was performed on the correct area. After the animal is euthanized, its brain is extracted and frozen or otherwise hardened and then cut into thin slices with a device called a *microtome.* Staining may be used on the tissue slices to identify the structures that have been damaged either directly or indirectly by the lesion. By using particular stains, researchers may be able to identify both the ablated area of the brain and the structures anatomically connected to it.

By themselves, ablation techniques cannot establish the function of a particular neural area. Consider the following example: After a particular area of the brain of a rat is destroyed, the animal no longer becomes aggressive when frustrated. Does this mean the destroyed area motivates aggressive behavior? Reduced aggression after lesioning could be the result of a lessening of aggressive emotional states, but other interpretations are possible. For example, the destroyed area may have controlled the ability of the animal to engage in aggressive behavior—a motor ability—rather than the experience of an aggressive emotional state. Another possibility is that the animal may no longer recognize the signals that normally elicit aggressive behavior. To summarize, although ablation can provide some evidence of the function of a specific neural area, in order to understand functioning more fully, we need information from other techniques as well.

The same can also be said for data from human neurological patients. These are patients, such as those studied by Broca and Wernicke, with brain damage caused by such things as injury, tumor, or stroke. Human clinical cases provide correlational data that may eventually lead to useful deductions about functional localiza-

stereotaxic apparatus A surgical instrument that allows a neuroscientist to create a lesion in a specific region of the brain.

computerized axial tomography (CT) A technique that produces a static image of the brain by shooting a narrow beam of x-rays from all angles to produce a cross-sectional image, referred to as a CT scan or CAT scan.

magnetic resonance imaging (MRI) A technique that produces a static image of the brain by passing a strong magnetic field through the brain, followed by a radio wave, then measuring the radiation emitted from hydrogen atoms.

tion in the human brain, but much additional research with different techniques is usually needed before we can draw definitive conclusions.

One additional reason for the difficulty with functional localization is the incredible complexity we find in the nervous system and its control of behavior. One way to illustrate this complexity is to consider the interconnections among neurons. Each neuron may have as many as 1,000 or more synapses on it from other neurons. When you consider that there are perhaps 10 billion neurons, the number of synapses is truly mind-boggling and rivals our current national debt.

However, it turns out that each neuron is likely to be in communication with only a few of its neighbors, not with the untold billions of other neurons. Thus, neurons are typically part of local circuits of neurons, and these circuits make up behavioral systems. The brain, then, can be considered a "supersystem of systems" (Damasio, 1994), with areas of specialization, such as for sensation and perception, emotion, or learning and memory. Each area of specialization may have within it systems, which are made up of local circuits of neurons. Localizing a function within this complex framework is difficult, to say the least, and requires the efforts of a variety of experts, using many different techniques.

Figure 1.9
Computerized axial tomography (CT) This CT scan reveals an area of stroke damage (arrow) in the left hemisphere.

Describe the value of a CT scan for identifying damage to the brain. What are the limitations of this technology?

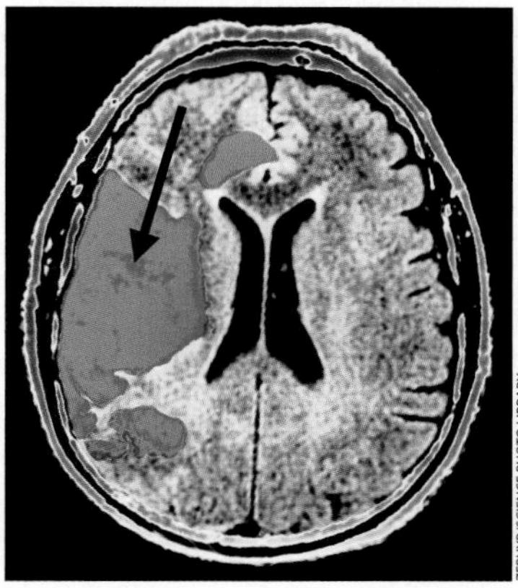

ZEPHYR/SCIENCE PHOTO LIBRARY

Static Images of the Nervous System: CT and MRI

With recent technological advances, neuroscientists can observe the nervous systems of living subjects relatively noninvasively. Computerized axial tomography and magnetic resonance imaging are two such techniques.

Damage to specific brain areas as a result of tumors, strokes, or accidents is common and can lead to significant behavioral impairments. One way to identify the area of damage is to use **computerized axial tomography (CT),** which employs x-ray imaging. The subject lies with his or her head inside the CT scanner, which slowly rotates over 180 degrees (a half-circle) while passing a narrow beam of x-rays through the head. When the rotation is completed, the computer constructs a cross-sectional image from the pictures (Figure 1.9), which the technician observes on the monitor. Once the area of damage is identified, appropriate treatment(s) can be prescribed.

Magnetic resonance imaging (MRI) uses radio waves to obtain a picture of the brain. A strong magnetic field is first passed through the patient's head, which causes the nuclei of some molecules in the brain to spin with a particular orientation. When a radio wave is then passed through the brain, these spinning nuclei emit radio waves. The MRI scanner measures the radiation emitted from rotating hydrogen atoms. Because the hydrogen atoms are present in different concentrations in different parts of the brain, the MRI scanner can use this information to provide an extremely clear three-dimensional view of the brain (Figure 1.10). Several Nobel Prizes have been awarded for discoveries involving MRI, including the 2003 Nobel Prize in Physiology or Medicine shared by Paul Lauterbur (University of Illinois, Urbana) and Peter Mansfield (University of Nottingham, England).

Figure 1.10
Magnetic resonance imaging (MRI) This MRI image on the monitor shows a sagittal section through the head.

What is the advantage of MRI over CT?

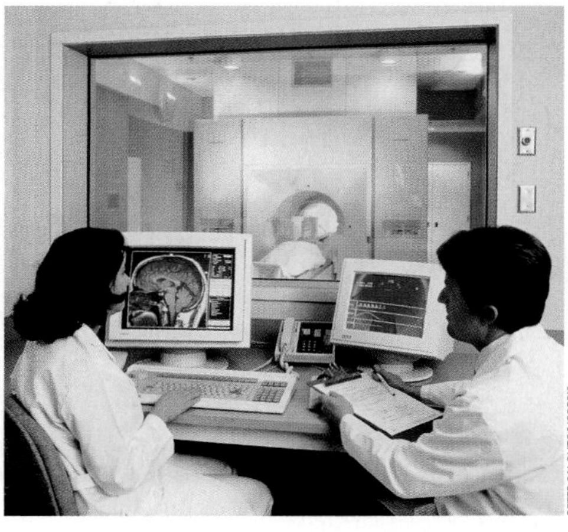

PETER SALOUTOS/CORBIS

Although much useful information is provided by CT and MRI, both techniques have some limitations. Both methods yield static images and cannot visualize the brain at work, and any behavioral changes produced by brain damage can result from a variety of causes. The specific functioning of particular brain areas cannot be determined solely from these methods.

Another limitation is the initial cost of the equipment, and you may wonder about the cost effectiveness of these expensive imaging techniques. The small amount of research that has been done in this area presents a mixed picture. For example, McMahon and colleagues (2000) examined the cost effectiveness of two different neuroimaging methods for the diagnosis of Alzheimer's disease. The researchers concluded that adding neuroimaging to the usual diagnostic procedures was not cost effective for diagnosing Alzheimer's disease, given the current ineffectiveness of treatment methods for the disease.

macroelectrode An electrode designed to record from many neurons at once.

electroencephalogram (EEG) A graphical record of the electrical activity of the cerebral cortex.

evoked potential A neural response to sensory stimulation introduced by an experimenter.

microelectrode An electrode designed to record the activity of one or a few neurons.

positron emission tomography (PET) A technique that measures the metabolic activity of a specific structure in the nervous system in order to determine neural functioning.

In a study comparing the use of CT and MRI in the diagnostic evaluation of patients with suspected multiple sclerosis, Mushlin and colleagues (1997) concluded that CT imaging was cost effective, whereas MRI was not, at least in patients with equivocal neurological signs and symptoms. With an increasing likelihood of disease, however, MRI cost effectiveness improved, and it was particularly useful for patients with a low probability of multiple sclerosis who needed reassurance that they did not have the disease.

In 2001, the International Panel on MS Diagnosis established revised diagnostic criteria for MS that included MRI for the first time (McDonald & others, 2001). A follow-up review concluded that the McDonald criteria are either as good as or better than the previously used criteria (Polman & others, 2005).

Wardlaw and coworkers (2004) assessed the cost effectiveness of CT scanning after acute stroke and found that the procedure was quite sensitive and worthwhile if used soon after the stroke. In addition, CT scanning was specific for determining hemorrhagic stroke, or bleeding from a ruptured blood vessel in the brain. This ability to detect hemorrhagic stroke is particularly helpful, because the use of aspirin therapy, desirable in ischemic stroke (blood vessel blockage), can exacerbate hemorrhagic stroke.

Recording Nervous System Activity

Biological psychologists have developed several methods for recording activity in the nervous system, especially the brain, to better ascertain function. One of these methods measures electrical activity, a second infers neural activity from metabolic functioning, and a third infers the level of neural activity from cerebral blood flow.

Electrical Recording

One method for studying the function of an area of the nervous system involves amplifying and recording the natural electrical activity of that area during the performance of a particular behavior. The changes in electrical potential can be recorded in two ways: In the first, **macroelectrodes** (electrodes designed to record from many neurons at once) are placed on the scalp, and the cortical activity is recorded (Figure 1.11). An electroencephalograph measures electrical potentials in the cerebral cortex and provides a record of this activity, called an **electroencephalogram (EEG).** The cortical EEG can be used, for example, to determine objectively whether an animal (or human) is asleep. In addition to recording these naturally occurring electrical signals, researchers are often interested in recording the neural response to sensory stimulation that the experimenter introduces. The resulting **evoked potentials** may be used to determine the particular brain areas that respond to specific sensory messages, to identify the types of sensory stimulation different people respond to, or for many other purposes (Figure 1.11).

In the second, more invasive method (typically used on nonhuman subjects), a tiny stainless steel or platinum wire called a **microelectrode,** which can record the

Figure 1.11

An electroencephalograph

(a) Recording electrodes are attached to the surface of the subject's scalp. The EEG records the level of activity in different areas of the brain, displayed as line tracings called brain waves. **(b)** These EEG tracings illustrate evoked potentials, generated by a stimulus (flash of light) presented to the subject. Tracings are shown for four separate responses.

➡ **What is one use of a cortical EEG? What is the significance of an evoked potential?**

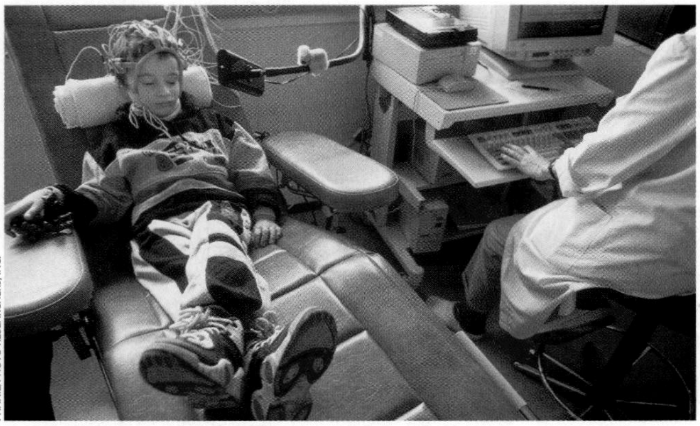

(a)

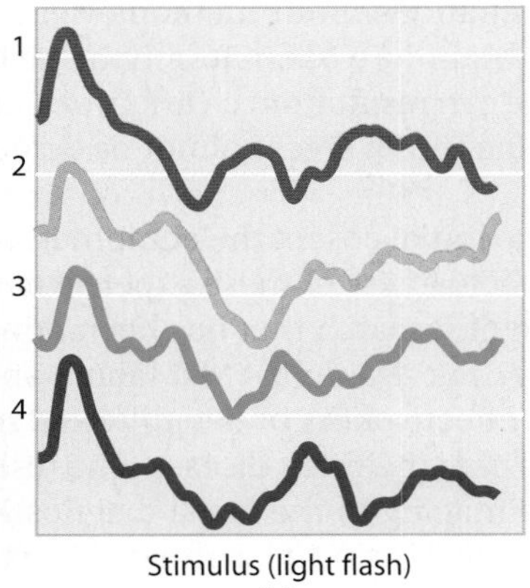

(b)

activity of one or several neurons, is inserted into the brain. An electrical socket, attached to the electrode, is then cemented to the animal's skull with dental plastic. After surgery, the psychologist can literally "plug" the animal into the recording system and detect the electrical activity of the neurons while the animal is engaged in various behaviors (Figure 1.12). An *oscillograph,* or polygraph, amplifies the electrical activity and creates a record of the changes in electrical potential. The *Scientific American* Spotlight, "Single Neuron Speaks," provides an illustration of a discovery (a given neuron, but not its neighbors, responds to a particular stimulus) made through the use of single-cell recording with a microelectrode.

How can the information provided by electrical recording be used? Suppose we notice that neurons in a particular area show increased activity just before a rat engages in aggressive behavior, but when the aggressive behavior ends, the neural activity decreases to the level observed before the behavior began. This information suggests that this brain area motivates aggressive activity. Or does it? Although the evidence shows that the electrical activity in the area is related to aggression, we cannot conclude that the activity actually *caused* the aggressive behavior. There is a relevant statistical principle here: Correlation does not necessarily mean causation. Just because the electrical activity and aggression occurred together, we cannot automatically assume that the activity caused the aggression.

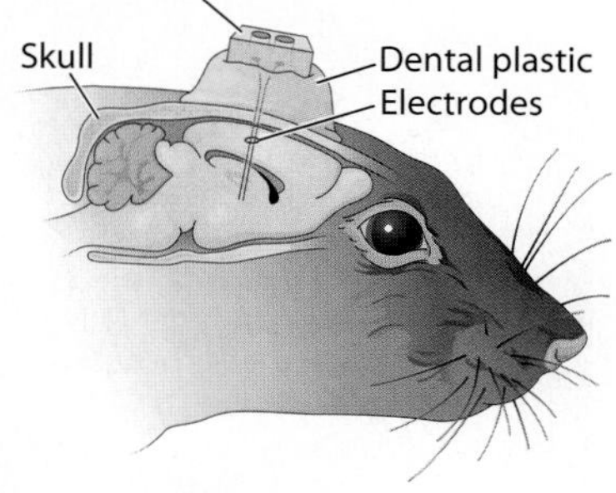

Figure 1.12
The permanent implantation of a microelectrode in an animal's brain
Implantation of the electrode is performed using a stereotaxic instrument (see Figure 1.8). After surgery, the animal can be plugged into a recording system that detects electrical activity in the brain.

➜ Why is the implantation technique more useful than the use of surface electrodes in some cases?

Positron Emission Tomography

Rather than directly measuring electrical activity, the technique of **positron emission tomography (PET)** infers neural activity by measuring metabolic activity in the nervous system, especially the brain. Neurons use glucose as an energy source for metabolism. Because little glucose is stored in the neurons, increased

Scientific American Spotlight

Single Neuron Speaks

Nicole Gabarini

A lone neuron in one of the brain's key memory centers may be able to distinguish a specific person or place, negating a long-standing tenet that a group of neurons is needed to encode any memory. The single-neuron hypothesis comes from a recent study of epilepsy patients. A team led by researchers at the California Institute of Technology and the University of California at Los Angeles implanted small electrodes in the epileptics' brains to monitor seizure activity. The patients volunteered to watch a rapid slide show of random images, including photographs of famous landmarks, politicians and celebrities. The researchers found that single cells responded to single images, by sorting neural activity based on the cells' unique timing and response characteristics. One patient had a neuron that responded to a photograph of actress Halle Berry but not to images of other actresses. The same neuron fired when the patient was shown line drawings of the actress or her name typed on a screen but not other drawings or names. A single neuron in another patient responded to photographs and words denoting the Sydney Opera House but not other landmarks. The experiments advance work the group started two years ago that prompted media discussion of a Bill Clinton gene. Although the single-concept neuron theory dates back to the 1960s, it had been dismissed by scientists. Itzhak Fried, one of the current investigators, suggests that one-to-one correlations may be key to efficient memory storage. It is possible, however, that neurons not monitored during the procedure were responding to the people or places presented. Conversely, some neurons fired when two different images were presented. Co-investigator Rodrigo Quian Quiroga suggests this might occur if we "associate one particular person with one particular object and we want to store this association in long-term memory."

From: *Scientific American Mind,* vol. 16(3), p. 10.

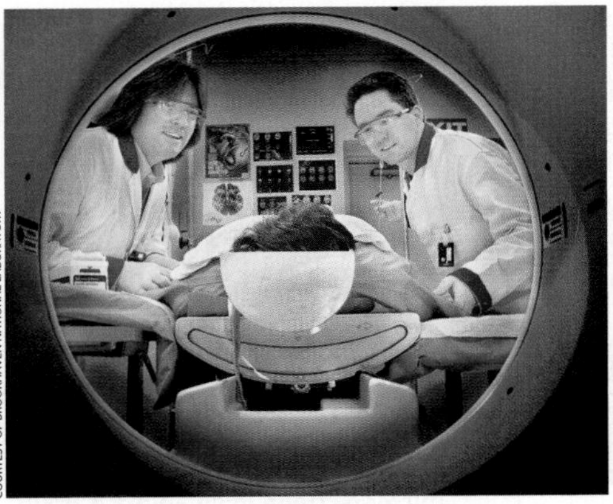

COURTESY OF BROOKHAVEN NATIONAL LABORATORY

(a)

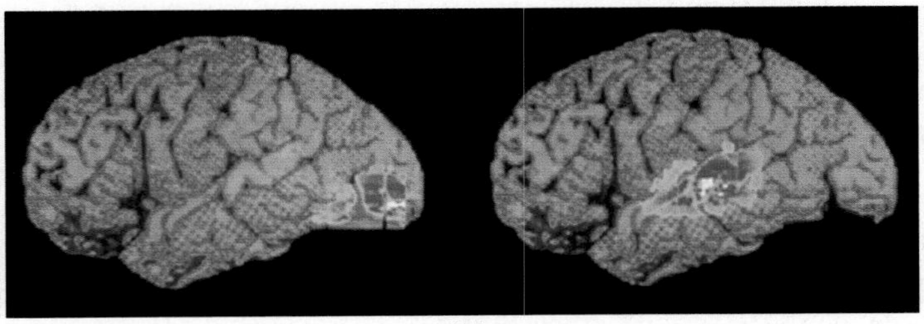

WELLCOME DEPT OF COGNITIVE NEUROLOGY/ SCIENCE PHOTO LIBRARY

(b)

Figure 1.13

PET scans (a) The subject is prepared for a scan. **(b)** These PET scans were taken while the subject was seeing words (left) and hearing words (right). The colors indicate the level of activity in specific areas of the cortex. Green areas indicate average cortical activity; yellow and red, higher-than-average activity; and blue, lower-than-average activity.

➡ **How does a PET scan differ from a CT scan and MRI? What are the advantages of a PET scan?**

neural activity causes increased absorption of glucose from the bloodstream. One way to measure glucose use is to inject a radioactively tagged chemical, such as 2-deoxyglucose (2-DG), into the bloodstream. Brain cells absorb 2-DG (along with glucose) but cannot metabolize it. The PET scanner measures the stream of positrons (positively charged particles with the same mass and same numerical charge as electrons) emitted from the nuclei of the radioactive carbon atoms of 2-DG. A computer combines the signals into a record of neural activity. This record of radioactive 2-DG absorption into the neurons can tell us which neural areas are most engaged during a particular activity. This is information about the structures that are part of the system that mediates the activity we are studying. We would still need to determine the role that each structure plays in the system.

How can information provided by the PET scanner be used? Suppose Laura's mother undergoes a PET scan while in a depressed state and experiencing ruminative (obsessive) thoughts. The PET scan will reveal the areas of the brain that are most active during the obsessive thoughts and will show a depression of activity in areas that should be active. Later PET scans, after Laura's mother has begun to respond to therapy, would probably reveal a more normal pattern of neural activity.

PET scans reveal that during such activities as seeing and hearing words, certain areas of the brain are more active than others (Figure 1.13). This technology also can be modified to provide a measure of cerebral blood flow. In this procedure, called *regional cerebral blood flow (rCBF),* a person is injected with or inhales a radioactive form of xenon gas. Because xenon accumulates in brain areas in which blood flow is high, its presence highlights the most active brain areas.

Positron emission technology has proved especially valuable to **cognitive neuroscience,** the study of the relationship between the nervous system and mental processes. We present the results of such investigations in many places throughout the text.

Functional Magnetic Resonance Imaging

Like PET technology, MRI technology can be modified to measure cerebral blood flow. This modified MRI procedure, called **functional MRI (fMRI),** uses high-powered, rapidly oscillating magnetic fields and powerful computation to measure the cerebral blood flow and thereby assess neural activity in the brain. An increase in the activity of a region of the brain requires more energy, which is supplied by the oxygen and glucose in blood. The image of neural activity is obtained by setting the fMRI equipment to detect the energy released from hemoglobin, the oxygen-carrying protein of vertebrate red blood cells. Neural areas with more energy release are assumed to be more active. One advantage of fMRI over PET scans is that functional MRI scans have greater resolution, so they present more detailed information. Functional MRI has been used to study neural activity in different types of memory, in emotions and depressed moods (Mandzia &

cognitive neuroscience The study of the relationship between the nervous system and mental processes.

functional MRI (fMRI) A technique that uses high-powered, rapidly oscillating magnetic fields and powerful computation to measure cerebral blood flow in the brain and obtain an image of the neural activity in a specific brain area.

Black, 2001), in human epilepsy (Kuzniecky, 1997), and in other clinical disorders (Hennig & others, 2003). Although the cost of fMRI may seem prohibitive, in a cost analysis comparing a traditional method for determining language lateralization (locating the brain hemisphere that controls most language functions by injecting a fast-acting anesthetic into one hemisphere or the other) with fMRI, Medina and colleagues (2004) found that the cost of the traditional method was nearly four times that of fMRI.

autoradiography The injection of radioactive chemicals into the bloodstream and subsequent analysis of neural tissue to determine where a specific chemical is found in the nervous system.

microdialysis A technique for identifying the neurotransmitter in a specific area of the nervous system by measuring the chemical constituents of fluid from neural tissue.

Measuring Chemical Activity: Autoradiography and Microdialysis

Some neuroscientists are interested in identifying the neurotransmitters that are active in a specific part of the brain, whereas others would like to determine the neural structure(s) affected by a particular drug. Autoradiography and microdialysis are two ways to measure the chemical activity in the nervous system.

Autoradiography can reveal the area of the nervous system in which a particular chemical is located. In this method, a neuroscientist first injects a radioactive chemical into the bloodstream of an animal and waits for the chemical to reach the nervous system. The animal is then euthanized, and the target neural tissue is extracted and sliced into thin sections. Each tissue slice is placed against a piece of x-ray film to record the radioactivity emitted. This autoradiograph shows which neural areas absorbed the radioactive chemical, reflecting the chemical activity in these areas (Figure 1.14).

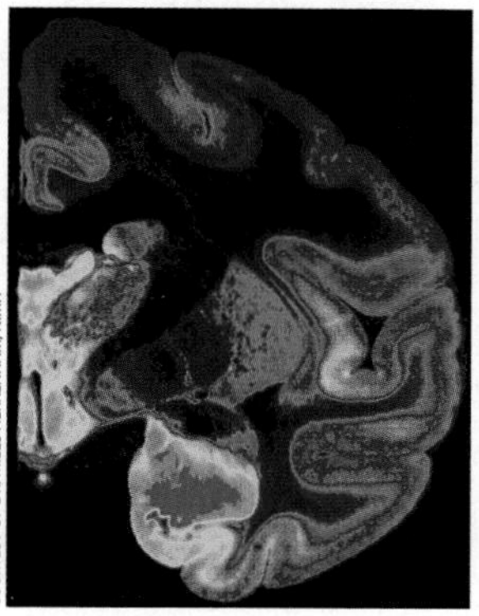

COURTESY OF DR. MILES HERKENHAM, NIMH

Figure 1.14

Autoradiograph This picture is color coded to show opiate receptor binding in the brain of a monkey at the level of the hypothalamus and amygdala. Lighter colors (red, orange, yellow) indicate a high density of receptors; darker colors (green, blue, violet) signify lower-density binding.

How is an autoradiograph made?

In **microdialysis,** chemical analysis can be made on a living animal. A fine tube is passed through the neural tissue, placing a short, semipermeable section of the tube in a specific area of the nervous system. Neurochemicals in that area then diffuse into the tube. An automated *chromatograph,* an instrument that separates and measures the chemical constituents of blood and other liquids, detects which neurotransmitters are present in the neural area under study (Figure 1.15).

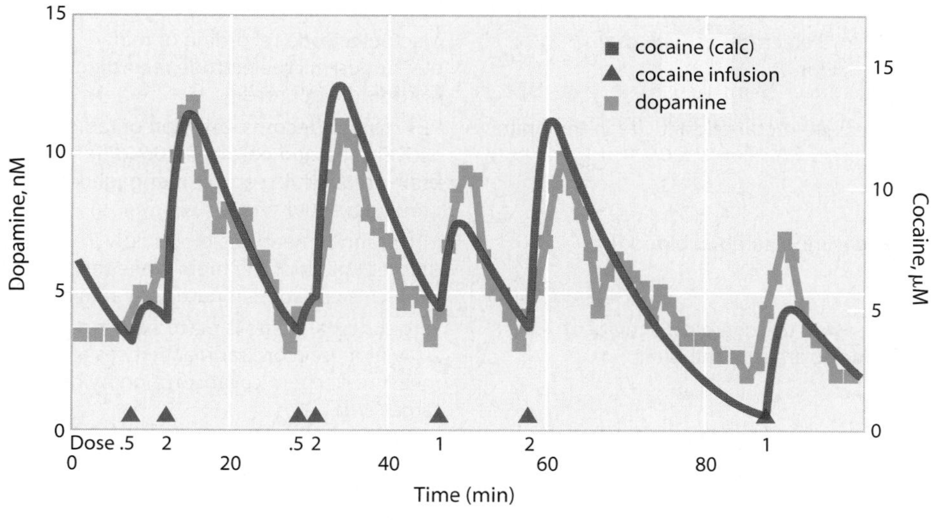

Figure 1.15

Microdialysis and gas chromatography In this experiment, a rat was equipped to self-administer cocaine and the researcher used chromatography to measure the dopamine level and estimate cocaine levels in a region of the brain called the nucleus accumbens. The graph shows dopamine level (green) in the nucleus accumbens as a function of cocaine (red) level. The solid triangles indicate the time of cocaine self-administration; the numbers below each triangle indicate the amount of cocaine received (in milligrams).

How is the dopamine extracted from the brain?

Direct Stimulation of the Nervous System

Rather than destroying a particular area of the nervous system or recording its natural activity, an experimenter can assess the function of the area by stimulating its neurons. As already noted, the stimulation can be produced either by

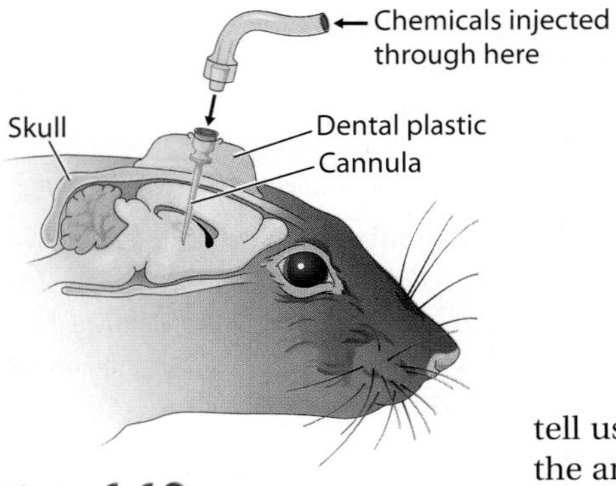

Figure 1.16

The permanent implantation of a cannula into the brain of an animal After surgery, chemicals can be injected into the brain through the cannula.

➡ **What information can be obtained by chemically stimulating a specific brain structure? What are some limitations of this technique?**

passing a weak electric current through a small wire, or by administering a chemical through a cannula (Figure 1.16). The behavior produced by direct stimulation provides yet another source of information about the role of that neural area in behavior. Chemical stimulation can also be used to identify which neurotransmitter acts in a particular brain area.

As in the other research methods, the results of stimulation must be viewed cautiously. Suppose we stimulate a particular brain area, and the animal then becomes aggressive. This would indicate that the stimulated area is somehow involved in aggressive behavior, but it does not tell us that activity in this area directly *causes* aggression. Perhaps stimulation of the area inhibits another brain structure that had been preventing aggression, so the stimulation may be releasing the neural inhibition of aggression rather than directly eliciting aggressive behavior. Or perhaps the stimulation produces a painful sensation, and the animal's aggression is a response to the pain rather than a direct elicitation of aggression.

Why do we need so many different methods to study brain functioning? (Table 1.1 summarizes methodologies.) The answer lies in the complexity of the information-processing tasks performed by the nervous system. The results of different techniques must be considered together in order to get a complete picture. Suppose that damage to a particular area of the brain causes no change in a behavior of interest. We might conclude that this area plays no role in the behavior. However, electrically stimulating the area may activate the behavior by releasing it from inhibition. Or perhaps a PET scan will indicate that one area of the brain is active when a specific behavior occurs, but stimulation of that area alone does not

Table 1.1
Methods for Studying Brain Function

Method	Purpose	How It Is Done
Ablation, lesion	Destroy neurons in specific area	Cutting or suction, electric current, toxic chemicals
Computerized axial tomography (CT)	Produce static image of nervous system	X-ray imaging with CT scanner
Magnetic resonance imaging (MRI)	Produce static image of nervous system	Radio waves measured with MRI scanner
Electrical recording	Record electrical activity during behavior	Macroelectrode recording of many electrodes; microelectrode recording from single neurons
Positron emission tomography (PET)	Measure metabolic activity in the brain	PET scanner records emission of radioactively charged particles from different brain areas while subject is engaged in particular activity
Functional magnetic resonance imaging (fMRI)	Measuring cerebral blood flow	MRI scanner measures blood flow in different parts of the brain while the subject is engaged in particular activity
Autoradiography	Measure the chemical activity of specific areas of the brain	Target neural tissue is placed against x-ray film to record radioactivity as a measure of chemical absorption by the target area
Microdialysis	Detect presence of specific neurotransmitters in an area of the brain	Neurochemicals diffuse into a fine tube implanted into a brain area and are assessed with an automated chromatograph
Electrical stimulation	Elicit behavior through direct stimulation of brain area	Weak electric current passed through small wire
Chemical stimulation	Elicit behavior through direct stimulation of brain area	Chemical administered to brain through tube called a cannula

elicit the behavior—because other areas must also be activated for the behavior to occur. Recall our earlier note about the complexity of the brain and its systems and circuits; only by using a combination of techniques can we identify the function of a specific area of the nervous system.

neuroscience The study of the nervous system.

Checkpoint

What information about the brain can be provided by ablation experiments? What information is ablation not able to provide? Describe the techniques you would use to determine which parts of your brain are active as you read this sentence.

REVIEW

- Many different methods are used to study brain functioning.
- Ablation (lesioning) is the destruction of specific neurons in the nervous system.
- Computerized axial tomography (CT) produces a static, cross-sectional image by passing a narrow beam of x-rays from all angles through the brain.
- Magnetic resonance imaging (MRI) produces a static image by passing a strong magnetic field through the brain, followed by a radio wave, and then measuring the radiation emitted from spinning hydrogen atoms.
- The electroencephalogram (EEG) is a graphic record of the electrical activity of areas of the brain.
- Positron emission tomography (PET) measures the metabolic activity of nervous system structures in order to assess functional localization.
- Functional MRI (fMRI) uses high-powered, rapidly oscillating magnetic fields to measure cerebral blood flow in the brain in order to obtain an image of the brain's neural activity.
- In autoradiography, radioactive chemicals are injected into the bloodstream, and subsequent analysis of neural tissue reveals where a specific chemical is located.
- Microdialysis and chromatography can identify the neurotransmitter in a specific area of the nervous system by measuring the chemical constituents of that area.
- Direct stimulation of the brain in order to determine the function of a particular area is performed by administering chemicals or an electric current to the area.
- Evaluation of the results of various methods must be considered together to give an accurate picture of the function of a particular area of the nervous system.

Current Approaches to Biological Psychology

You have now been introduced to the history and some of the techniques of biological psychology. What opportunities are available for students interested in this field? Perhaps, like Laura in the opening vignette, you are trying to decide what career to pursue. Biological psychology offers a multitude of choices.

Biological psychology is part of a larger discipline—**neuroscience,** the study of the nervous system. Among other things, a neuroscientist can study the anatomy of the nervous system, investigate the chemical basis of neural activity, or study the development of the nervous system. Table 1.2 lists specializations within neuroscience. Among them is behavioral neuroscience, which, as you can see, is a major part of biological psychology.

Biological psychology, because of its interdisciplinary nature, relies heavily on knowledge from the other neuroscience disciplines. For example, the drug alprazolam (trade name Xanax) can be used therapeutically to reduce anxiety levels.

Table 1.2
Specializations Within Neuroscience

Specialization	Area of Investigation
Behavioral neuroscience	Impact of the nervous system on behavior
Cognitive neuroscience	Relationship between the nervous system and mental processes
Developmental neurobiology	Development of the nervous system
Neuroanatomy	Structure of the nervous system
Neurochemistry	Chemical basis of neural activity
Neuroendocrinology	Influence of hormones on the nervous system and of the nervous system on endocrine (hormone) function
Neuropathology	Disorders of the nervous system
Neuropharmacology	Effects of drugs on the nervous system
Neuropsychology	Behavioral consequences of disorders of the nervous system

Our understanding of its effect on behavior has come from such disciplines as neurochemistry (How does the drug influence the chemical balance in the nervous system?) and neuroanatomy (Which nervous system structures are affected by the drug?). Throughout this text, you will find information about the physiology (function) and anatomy (structure) of the nervous system, information that adds to our understanding of how the nervous system controls behavior.

Now that you know how biological psychology fits in the big picture of neuroscience, we will narrow our focus to five different areas of study within biological psychology that sound similar but are, in fact, quite different: physiological psychology, psychophysiology, psychopharmacology, neuropsychology, and comparative psychology (Figure 1.17).

Physiological psychology is the investigation of the relationship between the nervous system and behavior by experimentally altering specific nervous system functions and then observing the effects on behavior. For example, a physiological psychologist might electrically stimulate a specific structure in the brain of a female rat and then observe any changes in the rat's maternal care of her offspring. Research in physiological psychology is conducted under tightly controlled conditions primarily with nonhuman subjects (Figure 1.17a), because most such in-

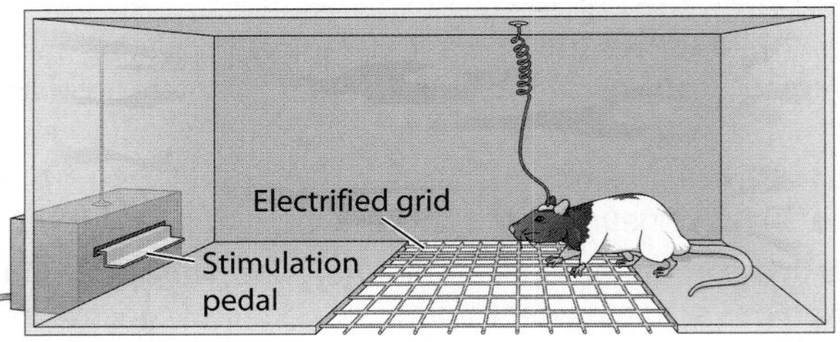

(a)

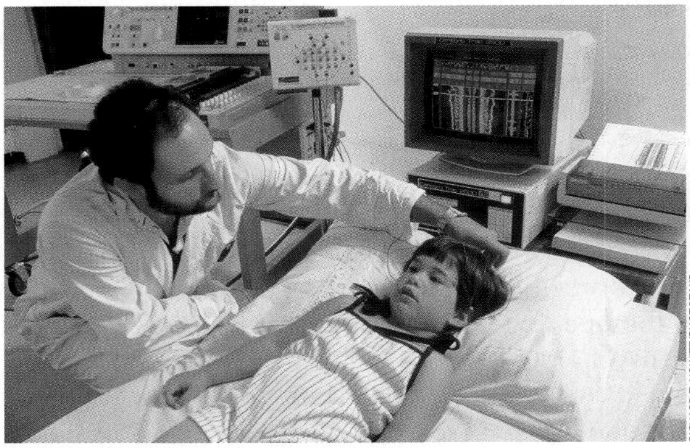

RICHARD T. NOWITZ/PHOTOTAKE

(b)

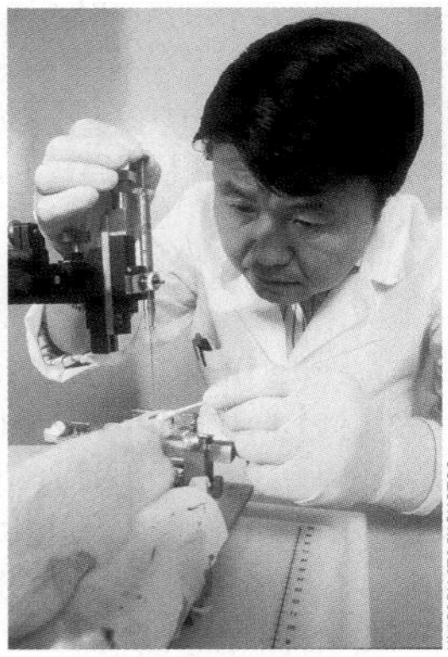

UNICORN STOCK PHOTOS

(c)

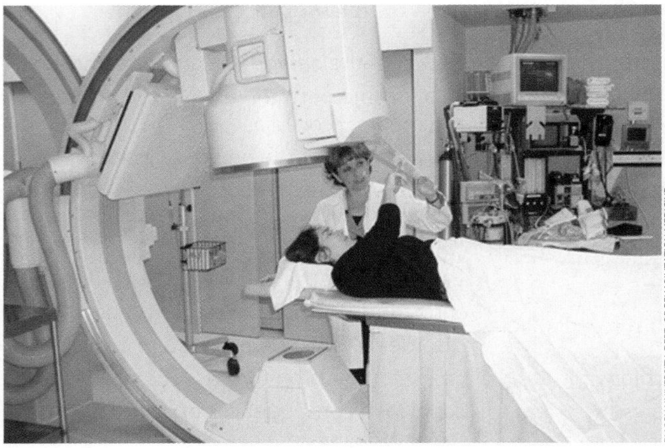

EMORY UNIVERSITY, DEPT. OF REHABILITATION MEDICINE

(d)

KARL AMMANN/CORBIS

(e)

Figure 1.17

Research methods in biological psychology **(a)** In this physiological psychology experiment, a rat with an electrode in its "reward area" crosses an electrified floor to press a lever that delivers stimulation to its brain. **(b)** By watching the monitor, which displays tracings of heart rate, brain wave activity, and other physiological changes, the psychophysiologist observes any changes in nervous system activity. **(c)** In psychopharmacology research, a drug is injected into an animal to assess its effect on the animal's behavior. **(d)** This patient is part of a neuropsychology research study of cognitive (language) functioning after traumatic brain injury. **(e)** A comparative psychology researcher observes the social interactions of primates in a seminatural environment.

➜ **How do physiological psychology and psychophysiology research differ? What are some limitations of psychopharmacology research? Of neuropsychology research? Name two fields of research closely related to comparative psychology.**

vestigations would be unethical to conduct with human subjects (we will have more to say about the ethics of animal research later in this chapter). Strict laboratory control should provide scientifically valid results, but the application of the results to our understanding of human behavior can be somewhat limited. As we indicate below, the knowledge gained from physiological psychology research can be combined with findings from other areas of biological psychology to better understand the relationship between the nervous system and behavior.

Psychophysiology is the study of the relationship between physiology and behavior through analysis of the physiological responses of human subjects engaged in various activities (Figure 1.17b). The psychophysiologist measures changes in brain activity, heart rate, and other bodily functions and tries to relate the measurements to observed behavioral changes. These correlations are used to establish potential physiology-behavior relationships. (Recall the statistical principle we mentioned earlier: Correlation between two things does not equal causation; that is, just because two measurements are correlated, it does not mean that one causes the other.) For example, if heart rate increases as stress levels increase (as revealed in an electrocardiogram), the psychophysiologist hypothesizes a relationship between heart rate and stress level. This hypothesis is later confirmed or refuted by additional tests.

Clinically, psychophysiological techniques have been used to assess seizure activity and to evaluate and diagnose sleep disorders. More recently, psychophysiology research has focused on enhancing our understanding of the physiology of psychological processes such as emotion, learning, and memory. Unlike most research in physiological psychology, psychophysiological studies use human subjects and measure nervous system functioning with noninvasive techniques. Psychophysiology research in the past was conducted primarily with normal, healthy subjects, but recent studies are measuring physiological responses in clinical populations (groups of individuals with particular psychological disorders). For example, individuals with anxiety disorders show greater physiological reactions to stressors than do healthy subjects (Sarason & Sarason, 2004). But does this greater physiological responsiveness contribute to the anxiety disorder or result from it? Remember that research in psychophysiology is correlational; only controlled experimentation can establish causal relationships. Significant insight into the relationship between the nervous system and behavior can come from combining the highly controlled research of physiological psychology and the correlational studies of psychophysiology.

Psychopharmacology is the investigation of the effects of drugs on behavior, focusing mostly on **psychoactive drugs,** which are drugs that affect mental functioning (Figure 1.17c). For example, a psychopharmacologist might administer cocaine directly into a specific structure in the brain of a rat and then observe whether the rat's memory of the place in a maze where a reward was previously located is enhanced or impaired as a result. Psychopharmacological research attempts to determine not only the relationship between a drug and behavior but also the neural mechanism by which the drug influences behavior. Thus, the psychopharmacologist in a cocaine study would also want to know which neural circuits in the brain of a rat are affected by the drug. Although most psychopharmacological research uses nonhuman animals as subjects, the therapeutic value of a drug can be established only by examining its effect in humans. We will look closely at the effects of drugs on behavior in Chapter 5.

We define **neuropsychology** as the study of the behavioral effects of brain damage in humans, although it can have a broader definition. For example, Lashley used the term to refer to what today we would call behavioral neuroscience. Research in neuropsychology uses subjects with brain damage that results from such sources as disease, accident, or neurosurgery. The goal of research in neuropsychology is to understand better the structure and function of the nervous system and how alterations to the nervous system can lead to behavioral impairment (Figure 1.17d). For example, a head trauma caused by an automobile accident may

physiological psychology The study of the relationship between the nervous system and behavior by experimentally altering specific nervous system structures and observing the effects on behavior.

psychophysiology The study of the relationship between behavior and physiology through the analysis of the physiological responses of human subjects engaged in various activities.

psychopharmacology The study of the effects of psychoactive drugs on behavior.

psychoactive drug A drug that influences mental functioning.

neuropsychology The study of the behavioral effects of brain damage in humans.

comparative psychology The comparative study of the behavior of different species of animals, generally in a laboratory setting.

ethology The study of the behavior of animals, usually in their natural environments.

behavior genetics The study of how inheritance affects the behavior of a species.

leave a person with relatively intact language comprehension but an inability to speak. (Which area of the brain would be more likely to have received damage—Broca's area or Wernicke's area?) Studying brain-damaged patients helps us understand how the brain produces and comprehends speech, and how damage to a particular neural area can lead to language deficits.

Neuropsychological research does have limitations, however. As you may already have noted, unlike physiological psychology research with animals, in which a specific area of the brain can be damaged and the results studied, the damage from disease or accident cannot be controlled—for example, a bullet to the brain rarely causes damage to a specific, limited area, and the damage varies from subject to subject (depending on the trajectory of the bullet). Hence, the research is by nature very individualized. However, combining the results of research studies in physiological psychology and neuropsychology can help clarify the role of a specific nervous system structure in behavior.

Comparative psychology, as the name implies, is the study of the behavior of different animal species, focusing on the influence of genetics and evolution on behavior. For example, a comparative psychologist's research might examine the differences in aggressive behavior in two monkey species. Observed behavioral differences, along with knowledge of anatomical and physiological differences, can reveal important information about the biological basis of aggression. (Recall that Darwin's theory of evolution made possible the field of comparative psychology, which began with the work of George Romanes, Darwin's friend and protégé.)

Research in comparative psychology is generally conducted under controlled, seminatural settings (settings modeled after the natural environment), often in the laboratory. For example, a setting that resembles the natural environment of a primate might be used to study its social behaviors (Figure 1.17e). In a related field, **ethology,** the behavior of animals is generally observed in their natural environments, although some ethologists have studied behavior in laboratory settings. In another related field, **behavior genetics,** selective breeding is used to determine how genetic inheritance affects the behavior of a species. The observational research of comparative psychology and ethology, like the correlational studies of psychophysiology, can only suggest possible relationships between genetics and behavior. However, when considered with the controlled laboratory research of the behavior geneticist, the findings of comparative psychologists can establish the impact of biology on behavior.

➤Checkpoint

How is biological psychology related to neuroscience? What are the five major areas of specialization within biological psychology? How do they differ?

REVIEW

- ➤ Biological psychology, the study of the influences of biological systems on behavior, can be considered part of a larger discipline, neuroscience, which is the scientific study of the nervous system.
- ➤ Physiological psychology is the study of the neural control of behavior through invasive experimentation mainly on nonhuman subjects.
- ➤ Psychophysiology is the study of the physiology of human psychological processes through noninvasive tests.
- ➤ Psychopharmacology is the study of the effects of drugs on behavior.
- ➤ Neuropsychology is the study of the behavioral effects of brain damage.
- ➤ Comparative psychology is the study, often in laboratory settings, of the influence of genetics and evolution on behavior through behavioral comparisons of different animal species.
- ➤ Ethology is the study of the behavior of species, generally in their natural environments.
- ➤ Behavior genetics involves the selective breeding of animals to determine the effects of inherited biological characteristics on behavior.

The Ethics of Conducting Research

Before proceeding further with the study of biological psychology and the research on which this science is based, we need to consider the ethics involved in applying research methods to human and animal subjects. Although many people feel uneasy about nervous system research on living organisms, such studies are a necessary part of the scientific search for answers to the question of why we behave as we do. Keep in mind that far more animals are sacrificed for food, hunting, and furs than for research and education (Nichols & Russell, 1990).

Conducting Research on Human Subjects

When a biological psychologist plans a study using human subjects (Figure 1.18), an ethics committee at the research institution decides whether that research is permissible under guidelines issued by the United States Department of Health and Human Services (DHHS) (Title 45 Code of Federal Regulations, Part 46, Protection of Human Subjects). Title 45 CFR Part 46 was based on the ethical principles of The Belmont Report, which established guidelines for protecting human subjects in research. These guidelines specify the benefits and risks of conducting human research, as well as the procedures that are used in the review of proposals to conduct human research by the local Institutional Review Board (IRB). The Office of Human Research Protection of the DHHS oversees IRBs to ensure that the welfare of human subjects is protected. The American Psychological Association (1992) also provides guidelines for psychological research using human subjects. In essence, all of these guidelines require a researcher to demonstrate that the planned study maximizes potential gain in knowledge and minimizes potential risks to its participants.

All subjects must participate *of their own free will.* No person should be forced into research participation. Students at many universities are required to take part in psychological experiments as a course requirement in introductory psychology; this course requirement is permissible only if an alternative activity is available to students. At other universities, students can volunteer to participate, but choosing not to volunteer cannot be counted against the student.

The biological psychologist enters into a written agreement with each human subject, explaining the general purpose of the study and the potential risks of participating. The anonymity and confidentiality of the behavior of the subject in the study must be guaranteed and maintained, if the identity of the subject can be tied to his or her data. As part of this agreement, the participant must be told that he or she will receive tangible rewards (e.g., money), personal help (e.g., counseling), and/or information about the study (e.g., its results). This agreement is considered a contract between the researcher and subject. After the study is completed, information about the results may be made available to the participant. The subject must sign this agreement to indicate informed consent but is free to withdraw from the study at any time.

Figure 1.18

Research on a human subject This woman is participating in a study on sleep (see Chapter 9).

➔ **If your roommate persuaded you to participate in a sleep study for her psychology class, could you get out of it?**

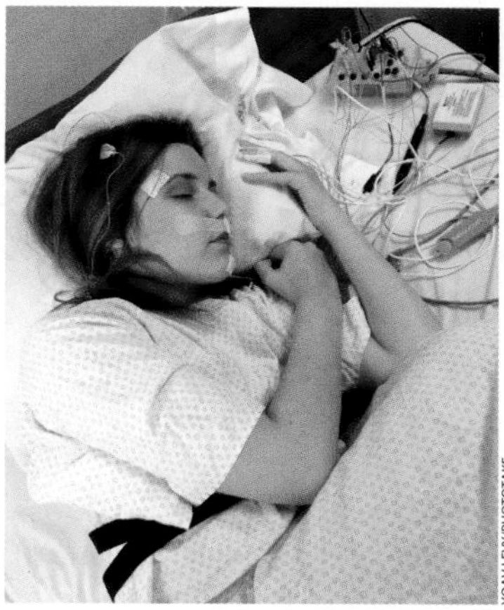

YOAV LEVY/PHOTOTAKE

Conducting Research on Nonhuman Subjects

Many of the studies described in this text have used such subjects as mice, rats, birds, cats, dogs, and monkeys or apes (Figure 1.19). Some of this research involves treatments that are stressful and/or painful. Many people have expressed serious concerns about the use of nonhuman animals in research, particularly when it involves pain or suffering (Bowd & Shapiro, 1993; Plous, 1996). The animal rights movement contends that animals have the right to be protected from use in research or for other purposes, such as for food and clothing.

In 1996, Plous published the results of a survey of the members of the American Psychological Association concerning attitudes toward

Figure 1.19

Research on a nonhuman subject Strict guidelines determine what research can be done with these young primates and how the animals are cared for.

➔ **What are some reasons for conducting research on animal rather than human subjects?**

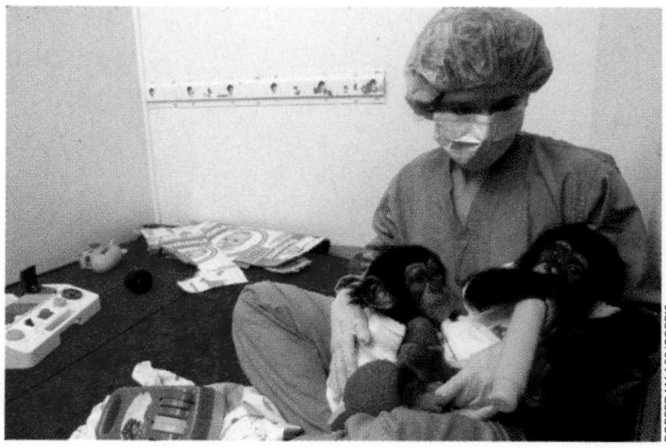

ROBERT MAASS/CORBIS

the use of animals in psychological research and teaching. He found that the majority of his respondents supported the use of animals in studies involving observation or confinement but were not in favor of experiments resulting in pain or death. Further, despite majority support for the use of animals in teaching, most respondents opposed a requirement for laboratory work with animals as a part of the psychology curriculum. In a response to Plous's article, Vonk (1997) argued that the treatment animals receive in research is a form of discrimination analogous to racism and sexism. As humans, we have been able to justify our treatment of nonhuman animals by viewing them as completely different and therefore beyond the protection we afford to our own species. Vonk notes a problem here: If animals are so different from us, would not research on animals be pointless? Yet if we perceive that animals are enough like us that research on them allows us to learn more about the human condition, how could we justify doing things to them that we would not do to our own species?

For those in the animal rights movement, the consequences of nonhuman animal research—the pain and suffering—make such research unacceptable. But nonhuman animal research continues, suggesting that the scientists who do the research believe it is important enough to outweigh any reservations they might have. Perhaps the main reason for continuing to use nonhuman animals in research is the consequence of *not* doing the studies. Biomedical disorders inflict a great deal of pain and suffering on both humans and nonhuman animals, and it is abundantly clear that research conducted on animals has led to major advances in the alleviation and treatment of such disorders (Carroll & Overmier, 2001).

As a result of research on nonhuman animals, biological psychologists have a better understanding of the causes of and treatments for such problems as alcoholism (Spanagel, 2003), anxiety disorders (Uys & others, 2003; Zinbarg & Mineka, 2001), learned helplessness and depression (LoLordo, 2001), drug abuse (Grabowski, 2001), Parkinson's disease (Schwarzschild & others, 2003), and Alzheimer's disease (Gotz & others, 2004; Woodruff-Pak, 2001). Research on nonhuman animals has also led to procedures that can maximize recovery after spinal cord injury (Grau & Joynes, 2001). Some examples of human benefits from animal research that are not directly relevant to biological psychology include organ transplantation techniques, gene therapy, chemotherapy for cancer patients, advances in the treatment of heart disease, and corneal and bone marrow transplantation.

Still, there are examples of biomedical research findings using nonhuman animals that proved not to be applicable to humans. For example, the differences between the effects of cyclosporine on tissue rejection in nonhuman animals and in humans are so great that the approval of this immunosuppressant drug for human transplant recipients was delayed. And research on nonhuman animals suggested that the use of corticosteroids would benefit human patients with toxic shock; in reality, the use of these steroids increased the death rate among toxic shock patients (Greek & Greek, 2000). However, according to Carskadon (2000, p. 744), "The examples cited by Drs Greek and Greek are a tiny drop compared with the ocean of positive benefits derived from biomedical research with nonhumans."

Obviously, significant advances have been made through biomedical research on nonhuman animals, but we might ask at this point if there are experimental reasons favoring such research over similar work on humans. In other words, is there any rationale for using animals in preference to humans, other than the obvious ethical issues? One reason why biological psychologists use animals is the problem in humans of documenting the causes of behavior. The wide variations in human behavior make it difficult to get a representative sample of people to use for investigation of any particular question. Because the behavior of nonhuman animals is generally less variable, causal relationships are easier to demonstrate. In other words, the greater simplicity and lower variability in nonhuman animals increase the likelihood of useful results in experimentation.

Another reason for using nonhuman animals is that it would be unethical to conduct some types of research on humans. For example, suppose a biological psychologist suspects that a particular brain structure is responsible for memory storage. The psychologist may have arrived at this idea by studying case histories of individuals with memory disorders who have a tumor in this brain area. However, the fact that these people have memory disorders does not mean that the area damaged by the tumor is responsible for memory storage. The only way to begin to demonstrate causality is to damage this area of the brain experimentally and then observe whether memory storage problems result. Obviously, we cannot do this type of research on humans.

Using nonhuman animals as subjects circumvents this difficulty, although it introduces again the issue of whether it is ethical to subject nonhuman animals to this type of treatment. As noted earlier, many people think the use of nonhuman animals in such research is unacceptable. However, much attitude research has shown that most respondents do approve of psychological and biopsychological research on nonhuman animals (e.g., Navarro & others, 2001). And, again, animal models of disease have led to significant advances in the understanding and treatment of human diseases.

Some research on nonhuman animals also has had significant benefits for animals (Baldwin, 1993). For example, such research has led to improvements in the environment of captive primates (Novak & Petto, 1991), to vaccines against such diseases as rabies and feline leukemia, and to advances in many practices in veterinary medicine. Additional benefits to animals of nonhuman animal research include cataract surgery for blindness, organ transplantation techniques, drug therapies to treat illnesses such as diabetes and heart failure, the use of in vitro fertilization methods to help preserve endangered species, treatment for parasites, experimental radiation techniques and immunotherapy for cancer, and the use of ultrasound, MRI, and CT scans in removing brain tumors and correcting birth defects in animals.

Virtually no researcher wants to expose nonhuman animals to unnecessary pain and suffering. A number of federal laws, most notably the Animal Welfare Act, protect nonhuman animals and ensure their proper care. Currently, animal research is conducted only when approved by a committee, such as an Institutional Animal Care and Use Committee (IACUC), which acts to ensure that animals are used humanely and in strict accordance with local, state, and federal regulations. Several federal agencies, including the United States Department of Agriculture and some Public Health Service agencies such as the National Institutes of Health and the Centers for Disease Control and Prevention, oversee the IACUCs. Such oversight helps prevent any deviation from federal animal welfare regulations by imposing severe penalties for any violations. The American Psychological Association also provides guidelines for research on animal subjects, specifying how such research is to be conducted and how research animals are to be cared for.

Checkpoint

Would you volunteer to participate in a biological psychology study? Explain why or why not. Why do psychologists use animals in their research? What mechanisms are in place to ensure the proper care and use of research animals?

REVIEW

- Ethical principles established by the American Psychological Association govern what kind of research is permissible using humans as subjects.
- A researcher must demonstrate to an ethics committee that a planned human study both maximizes the potential gain in psychological knowledge and minimizes the costs and potential risks to its human subjects.
- Causal relationships can be demonstrated more readily in animals, using certain experimental designs that cannot be used ethically for humans.
- Animal research must be approved by a committee such as an IACUC, which ensures that animals are used in accordance with local, state, and federal regulations.

Chapter Review

Key Terms

ablation (p. 13)
autoradiography (p. 19)
behavior (p. 2)
behavior genetics (p. 24)
Bell-Magendie law (p. 6)
biological psychology (p. 2)
Broca's area (p. 9)
cerebrum (p. 7)
cognitive neuroscience (p. 18)
comparative psychology (p. 24)
computerized axial tomography (CT) (p. 15)
doctrine of specific nerve energies (p. 6)
dualism (p. 3)
electroencephalogram (EEG) (p. 16)
engram (p. 10)
equipotentiality (p. 10)
ethology (p. 24)
evoked potential (p. 16)
functional MRI (fMRI) (p. 18)
macroelectrode (p. 16)
magnetic resonance imaging (MRI) (p. 15)
mass action (p. 10)
microdialysis (p. 19)
microelectrode (p. 16)
monism (p. 3)
nerve net theory (p. 12)
neuron (p. 12)
neuronal theory (p. 12)
neuropsychology (p. 23)
neuroscience (p. 21)
phrenology (p. 7)
physiological psychology (p. 22)
positron emission tomography (PET) (p. 17)
pressure phosphene (p. 6)
psychoactive drug (p. 23)
psychopharmacology (p. 23)
psychophysiology (p. 23)
reflex (p. 5)
stereotaxic apparatus (p. 14)
synapse (p. 12)
vagusstoff (p. 13)
Wernicke's area (p. 10)

Suggested Readings

Carroll, M. E., & Overmier, J. B. (Eds.) (2001). *Animal research and human health: Advancing human welfare through behavioral science.* Washington, DC: American Psychological Association.

Finger, S. (2000). *Minds behind the brains: A history of the pioneers and their discoveries.* New York: Oxford University Press.

Thorne, B. M., & Henley, T. B. (2005). *Connections in the history and systems of psychology* (3rd ed.). Boston: Houghton Mifflin.

Critical Thinking Questions

1. Laura and her boyfriend are studying for a test in her dorm room. Taking a break from reading *Biological Psychology,* Laura observes her boyfriend concentrating on his accounting textbook. His breathing is deep and even (she checked), his eyes are open, he is resting his head in his left hand and rubbing his forehead with his right, and he is sighing occasionally as he turns a page. Which of these activities is behavior, according to the definition in this chapter?
2. What is your view of the mind/body problem? Do you believe in both a mind and a body, with the body material and the mind immaterial? Or do you subscribe to one of the monism positions or to epiphenomenalism?
3. Imagine that you are interested in which areas of the brain are most involved when you read aloud. Using what you have learned about the research methods of biopsychologists, design an experiment to investigate your interest.
4. Michael is opposed to the use of animals in biological psychology research. What might be some of his objections? What are some reasons for using nonhuman animals in research? Is there room for compromise in this debate?

Fill-in-the-Blank Questions

1. The study of the influence of biological systems on behavior is called ______; ______ is anything and everything an organism does.
2. The debate over the nature and relationship of the mind to the body is called the ______ problem.
3. The idea that both the body and the mind exist is called ______, whereas ______ is the notion that there is only one underlying reality, either body or mind.
4. ______ is the idea that both body and mind exist, but the two do not interact.
5. The idea that the body produces mind as an accidental by-product is called ______.
6. Aristotle held that the mind is located in the ______.
7. ______ coined the term *reflex*.
8. The notion that the dorsal roots of spinal nerves carry in sensory information and the ventral roots carry out motor impulses is called the ______ law.
9. The ______ is the idea that the event detected by the brain depends on which nerve carries the message.
10. The pseudoscience that taught that the bumps and the indentations on the skull are a reflection of underlying mental faculties is called ______.
11. Flourens used the ______ technique in animals to show that mental processes are controlled by the brain.
12. Darwin published *The Origin of Species* after receiving an essay from ______ that described a theory of evolution remarkably like Darwin's.
13. Darwin explicitly linked humans with the rest of the animal kingdom in his book ______.
14. Definitive proof that the brain is the organ of the mind in humans came from the results of ______'s accident.
15. Damage to ______'s area produces a nonfluent aphasia, whereas damage to ______'s area produces a fluent aphasia.
16. German scientists ______ and ______ were the first to demonstrate successfully that electrical stimulation of the brain can produce muscle actions.
17. According to Lashley's concept of ______, the greater the amount of damage to a cortical area, the more severe the impact on complex learning.
18. According to the ______ theory, the nervous system consists of a network of connected nerves.
19. Cajal used the Golgi stain to provide evidence for the ______ theory.
20. The point of functional contact between neurons is called a(n) ______.
21. ______ received a Nobel Prize for demonstrating that synaptic transmission from the vagus nerve to the heart is chemical.
22. Using the ______ method, neurons in a given area are destroyed.
23. In ______, radio waves are used to obtain a static picture of the brain.
24. A(n) ______ is used to study the activity of a single neuron in the nervous system.
25. ______ infers neural activity by measuring metabolic activity in the nervous system, especially the brain.
26. In ______, MRI technology is modified to measure cerebral blood flow.
27. Chemical analysis of the brain can be made in a living animal through a technique called ______.
28. ______ is the study of the effects of drugs on behavior.
29. ______ is the study of the behavioral effects of brain damage on humans.
30. In ______, selective breeding is used to determine how genetic inheritance affects the behavior of a species.

Multiple-Choice Questions

1. Descartes' solution to the mind/body problem is called
   a. parallelism.
   b. epiphenomenalism.
   c. interactionism.
   d. double aspectism.
2. The earliest proponent of materialism was the Greek philosopher
   a. Aristotle.
   b. Socrates.
   c. Plato.
   d. Democritus.
3. The mind/body solution in which the mind is merely an accidental by-product of the brain's activities is called
   a. interactionism.
   b. epiphenomenalism.
   c. parallelism.
   d. immaterialism.
4. Galen's views about the mind emphasized which area of the brain?
   a. the ventricles
   b. the pineal gland
   c. the cortex
   d. the basal ganglia
5. ______ observation that an electrical stimulus applied to a frog's motor nerve caused its leg muscle to twitch strongly suggested that electricity was an essential element in the functioning of the nervous system.
   a. Descartes'
   b. Galen's
   c. Leonardo da Vinci's
   d. Galvani's

6. The term *reflex* was coined by
a. Galvani.
b. Golgi.
c. Whytt.
d. Descartes.

7. The Bell-Magendie law asserts that sensory nerves enter the spinal cord through the ______ root and motor nerves leave the spinal cord through the ______ root.
a. anterior, posterior
b. posterior, anterior
c. dorsal, ventral
d. ventral, dorsal

8. According to the doctrine of specific nerve energies, stimulation of the optic nerve would produce a(n) ______ sensation.
a. tactile
b. auditory
c. olfactory
d. visual

9. Gall's phrenology suggested that individuals' intellectual faculties are determined by
a. the strength of their character.
b. their ancestry.
c. the size of their brain.
d. the size of specific locations in their brain.

10. In his attacks on phrenology, Flourens developed the ______ method for studying the brain.
a. electrical stimulation
b. ablation
c. staining
d. anatomical

11. Darwin went public with his theory of evolution after receiving a letter and essay from Wallace that described
a. a theory of evolution.
b. the voyage of the *Beagle.*
c. a theory of genetics.
d. comparative psychology.

12. Darwin explicitly put humans into the animal kingdom in his book
a. *Man in the Animal Kingdom.*
b. *The Origin of Species.*
c. *The Expression of Emotions in Man and Animals.*
d. *The Descent of Man.*

13. The event that definitively showed that the brain ______ was an accident involving a tamping rod and Phineas P. Gage.
a. has two language areas
b. is the organ of mind
c. has four lobes
d. consists of neurons

14. Juan has recently suffered brain damage in an automobile accident. His primary symptom is an inability to understand speech/language. Some brain-damaged people with this type of aphasia have damage to
a. Broca's area.
b. Wernicke's area.
c. the occipital lobe.
d. the parietal lobe.

15. Damage to ______ area often produces a fluent aphasia, in which the person speaks fluently but nonsensically.
a. Broca's
b. Wernicke's
c. Hitzig's
d. Ferrier's

16. In 1870, ______ and ______ used electrical stimulation to show that stimulation produced movement.
a. Ferrier, Munk
b. Lashley, Franz
c. Fritsch, Hitzig
d. Darwin, Wallace

17. By ______, Lashley meant that any part of a functional area of the nervous system could carry out the function of that area.
a. equipotentiality
b. mass action
c. engram
d. psychophysiology

18. ______ used the Golgi stain to produce evidence that led to acceptance of the neuronal theory.
a. Gerlach
b. Cajal
c. Sherrington
d. Golgi

19. Following a stroke, Miriam can no longer identify objects by feeling them. She has probably suffered damage to the ______ lobe.
a. parietal
b. temporal
c. frontal
d. occipital

20. In an experiment with a pair of frog hearts, Loewi showed that
a. synaptic transmission is chemical.
b. synaptic transmission is electrical.
c. the beating of a heart does not involve synaptic transmission.
d. *vagusstoff* is adrenalin.

21. A stereotaxic atlas is used to
a. locate the region of the brain to be lesioned.
b. obtain cross-sectional images of the brain.
c. create thin slices of brain tissue for examination.
d. pass electric current through the brain.

22. ______ are often used to determine the particular brain areas that respond to specific sensory messages.
a. EEGs
b. Evoked potentials
c. Microelectrodes
d. Oscillographs

23. Ashley wants to determine the most active area of the brain when a person reads a book. To do this, she will probably use
a. EEG.
b. MRI.
c. CT.
d. PET.

24. Following a gunshot wound to the head, Philip has great difficulty producing meaningful speech, although he seems to have reasonably good language comprehension. To determine the area of his brain that is damaged, his physician will probably order a(n)
a. cortical EEG.
b. MRI.
c. autoradiograph.
d. PET scan.

25. ______ is a technique for determining the area of the nervous system in which a particular chemical is found.
a. MRI
b. CT scan
c. EEG
d. Autoradiography

26. Allison administers methadone directly into the brain of a rat to study how methadone works in the treatment of heroin addiction. Allison specializes in
   a. neuropsychology.
   b. psychopharmacology.
   c. comparative psychology.
   d. psychophysiology.

27. Sarah assesses the behavioral changes in persons following a stroke. Sarah specializes in
   a. neuropsychology.
   b. psychopharmacology.
   c. comparative psychology.
   d. psychophysiology.

28. In ______, selective breeding is used to determine how inheritance affects behavior.
   a. artificial selection
   b. natural selection
   c. developmental neurobiology
   d. behavior genetics

Answers can be found on the companion website at www.worthpublishers.com/klein.

Think!

2

Exploring the Nervous System

One Too Many

Sugar Ray Martin had been a contender in his day, but that day was long past. The reporter watched as the aging welterweight—whose current weight would better suit the heavyweight class—shuffled slowly into the cafeteria to meet her. His expression never changing, Sugar Ray pulled out a chair opposite the reporter and slowly lowered himself onto the seat. His hands, resting on the table, showed their usual tremor.

"How's it going, Sugar Ray?" the reporter asked.

"Been better," was the soft reply.

"Last time we met, you were starting to tell me about your shot at the championship," the reporter said. "What happened that night?"

Sugar Ray's gaze shifted from the reporter to the far corner of the room. The reporter could almost see the ex-fighter's mental wheels turning as he returned in his memory to the night of the fight, billed as the fight of the decade. Instead it became Sugar Ray's greatest disaster and his last big fight.

"I was greased lightning back then," Sugar Ray said. "Man, I was so fast that by the time you saw my first punch, I had already sent a half dozen more your way. Problem was that the champ—Buster Guidry—was just as fast and had a helluva punch to boot. He caught me with a uppercut in the third round, and I don't remember much after that. Just stayed on my feet and kept swinging. Shoulda gone down, looking back on it now."

The reporter had watched film of the fight. Guidry hit Sugar Ray with everything but the ring posts, yet somehow the challenger's iron will had kept him upright. The decision, when it came, was merely a formality, as Guidry had won every round after the second.

"When did you start having trouble moving?" the reporter asked.

"It was a few years after that fight," Sugar Ray said. "I noticed I was starting to freeze up and getting slower and slower doing anything. And the shaking, that started a little earlier than the freezing up. Sometimes I wish I had a time machine to take me back to that night. If I had just slipped that uppercut . . . ."

If Sugar Ray had only slipped the uppercut, he might have avoided that savage beating. The repeated head shots, on top of a long boxing career that continued for another year after the fight with Guidry, had led to Parkinson's-like symptoms (e.g., tremors, muscle rigidity, slowed movement). If he'd slipped that uppercut, he might even have become champion.

BEFORE YOU BEGIN

- What part or parts of Sugar Ray's brain probably were damaged during his boxing career?
- How did his brain injury affect how his body functions?
- How do the two major divisions of the nervous system work together to perform the nervous system's primary functions, and what are these primary functions?
- What types of cells make up the structures in the nervous system? What are their functions?
- What are the major structures of the brain? What are their primary functions?

In this chapter, you will find the answers to these questions and many others.

The Importance of the Nervous System

As we go about our daily lives, we encounter an enormous amount of information—some pleasant, some not so pleasant. For example, Sugar Ray enjoys talking to the reporter. He walks into the cafeteria expecting to meet her, and he spots her sitting alone at a table. Detecting this information allows him to keep his appointment. Or, let us suppose that Sugar Ray is still driving his car occasionally, even though his doctor tells him he should not be doing so. And suppose he'd planned a short trip today, but it is 5 degrees below zero and his car battery is weak. Aware that his car may not start in the extreme cold, he may choose to stay inside and thereby avoid the frustration of trying and failing to start the car.

In each of the examples, Sugar Ray must first *detect* the relevant information from among the many stimuli present in the environment (e.g., the reporter in the cafeteria, the low outside temperature). Having detected the relevant stimuli, he must *recognize* their significance. For example, he may remember past good times he has spent talking to the reporter, or he may understand that his weak car battery may not start his car today.

2: Recognition: It's close to dinner time, nothing to eat
3: Decision: Order pizza
1: Detection: Looks at watch/clock
4: Execution: Find number for pizza parlor, dial number, order pizza

Figure 2.1
The four-stage response to stimuli
These responses are made possible by the nervous system.

➡ Given the same events in stages 1 and 2, what would be some alternative responses in stages 3 and 4?

He must next *decide* how to respond to the significant event. In some instances, the decision is relatively straightforward: Once he remembers past positive encounters with the reporter, the decision to sit and talk with her is made easily. Other decisions are more difficult: Although his weak car battery might fail, it *might* work, and he does enjoy getting out for a while. Finally, Sugar Ray needs to *execute* the appropriate behaviors after completing the decision process. In the first example, execution involves shuffling to the table and sitting down across from the reporter. In the second example, it involves going outside and trying to start the car or sitting on the couch in his room to watch *Seinfeld* reruns, depending on the result of the previous step.

Thus, there are four functional stages in reacting to environmental events: detection, recognition, decision, and execution (Figure 2.1). The ability to perform these four functions is governed by the nervous system. To understand how the nervous system accomplishes this, we must first understand its structure. We describe here the nervous system as a whole and each of its components, focusing on how the nervous system carries out the four basic functions.

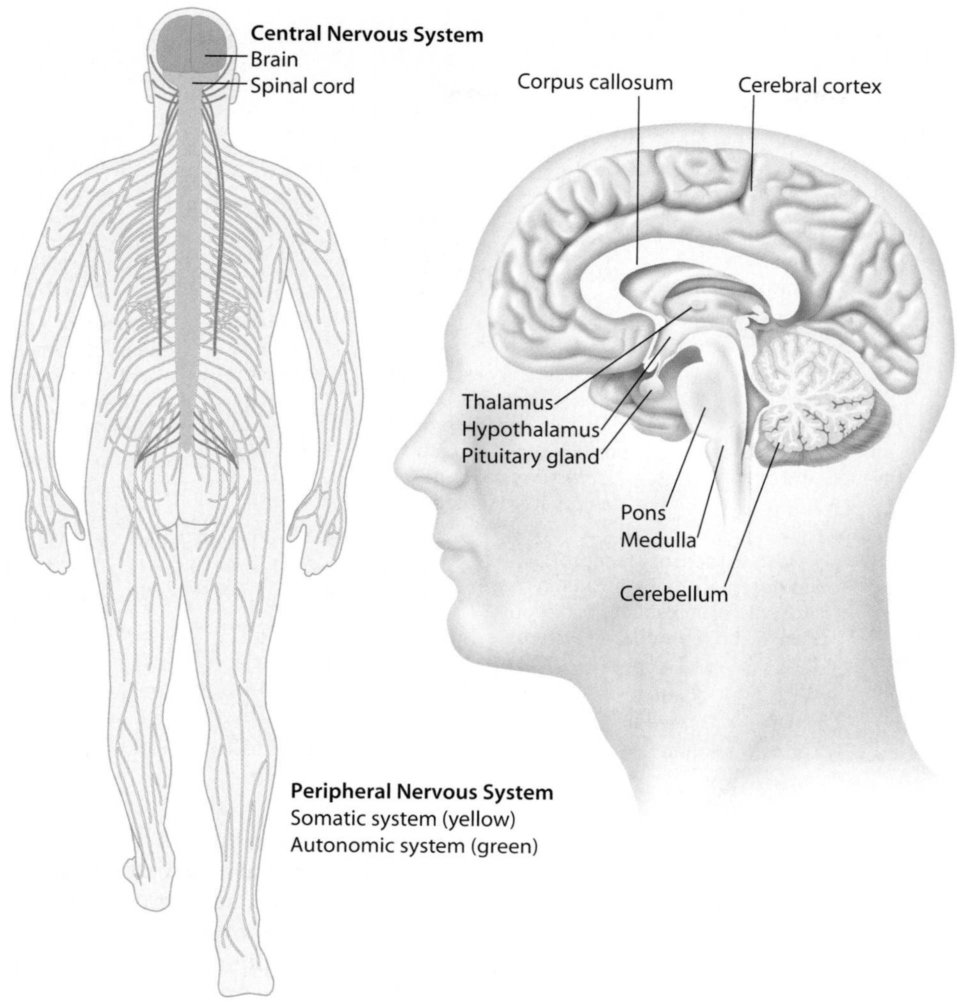

Figure 2.2

The human nervous system The standing figure illustrates the major divisions of the nervous system. More details of parts of the central nervous system (discussed later in the chapter) are shown in the enlargement on the right.

→ **In the four-stage response to stimuli, which stages are functions of the CNS? Of the PNS?**

The Organization of the Nervous System

The vertebrate nervous system is classified into two divisions: the peripheral nervous system and the central nervous system (Figure 2.2). The **peripheral nervous system (PNS)** detects environmental information both inside and outside the body. The PNS then transmits this information to the central nervous system for recognition, analysis, and decision; it then transmits the decision to the muscles, glands, and organs for execution. Sensory receptors located in the PNS detect environmental events (stimuli), and sensory nerves carry the information detected by the sensory receptors to the central nervous system. (Note that there is one major exception: The sensory receptors for vision are part of the central nervous system, not the peripheral nervous system.) For example, the sensory receptors in Sugar Ray's PNS enable him to detect the extremely low temperature when he goes outside, and they send that information via his sensory nerves to his central nervous system. The PNS also consists of motor nerves that convey orders to the muscles. Sugar Ray's motor nerves send messages to his skeletal muscles to propel him back to the warmth of his home.

Like the nervous system as a whole, the PNS has two divisions: the somatic nervous system and the autonomic nervous system (Figure 2.3). The **somatic nervous system** consists of both the sensory receptors that detect environmental (external and internal) stimuli and the nerves that activate the skeletal muscles. The **autonomic nervous system** includes the nerves that regulate the functioning

peripheral nervous system (PNS) The division of the nervous system that detects environmental information, transmits that information to the CNS, and executes CNS decisions.

somatic nervous system The division of the PNS containing sensory receptors that detect environmental stimuli and motor nerves that activate skeletal muscles.

autonomic nervous system The division of the PNS containing the nerves that regulate the functioning of internal organs.

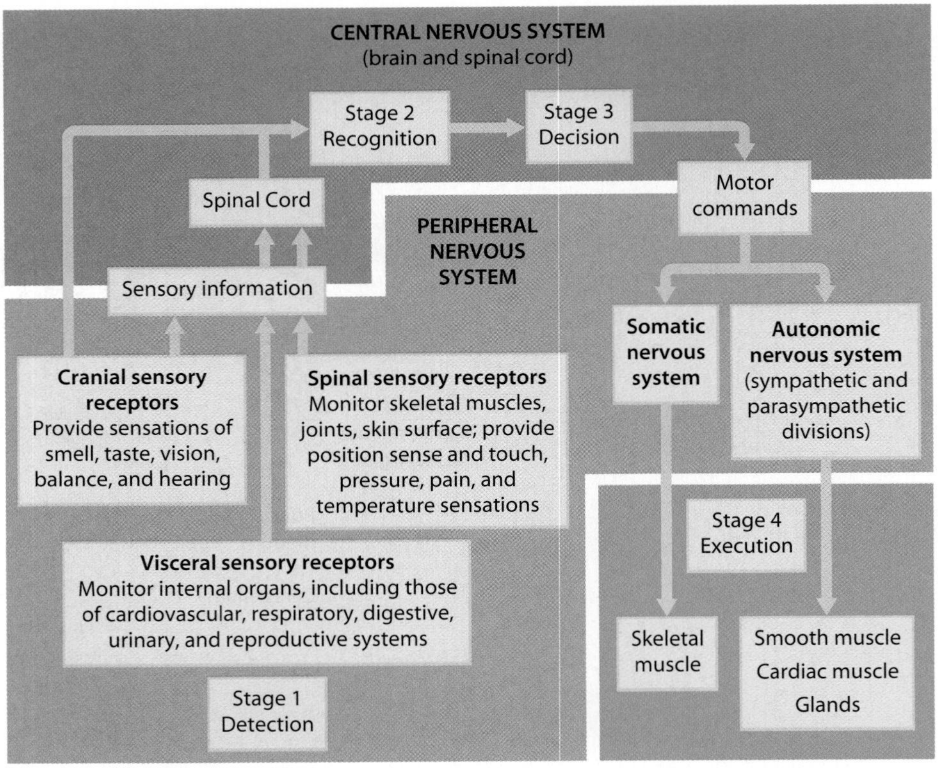

Figure 2.3

The organization and functions of the nervous system Responses to stimuli occur in four functional stages. Sensory receptors detect stimuli (stage 1). The central nervous system recognizes the stimuli and analyzes them for meaning (stage 2) and decides on an appropriate response (stage 3). A muscle response is then executed (stage 4). Note: You will find it useful to consult this overview of the nervous system as you read through the chapter.

➡ **You just refused an invitation to a party tonight because you have to catch up on some reading. In your response to this situation, what occurred in stage 2? Stage 3? Stage 4?**

of our internal organs. Sugar Ray's somatic nervous system detects the reporter's presence in the cafeteria and conveys the orders to his muscles so that he can approach and sit down at the table. His autonomic nervous system increases his heart rate and respiration rate in response to seeing the reporter.

If detection and execution are controlled by the peripheral nervous system, recognition and decision must be the responsibility of the **central nervous system (CNS).** The central nervous system also has two parts: the spinal cord and the brain (see Figure 2.3). The **spinal cord,** the part of the CNS located within the vertebral column (also called the spinal column), plays a limited role in analysis and decision; it either responds directly to a sensory stimulus via a spinal reflex, or it carries a sensory message to the brain or a motor command from the brain to the muscles. The **brain,** the portion of the CNS located within the skull, is responsible for analyzing sensory information and deciding the appropriate behavioral responses to the sensory input. Sugar Ray's brain enables him to recognize that the reporter is present and to decide that he should sit down across from her; his spinal cord serves as a conduit for sensory messages from his spinal nerves to his brain and from his brain to his motor nerves.

Before we begin our tour of the nervous system, we need to introduce *anatomical directions.* Just as we use geographic directions (north, northeast, south, etc.) to locate places as we travel, anatomists use a system for locating structures in the body (Figure 2.4). Structures toward the front end of an organism are referred to as **anterior,** structures toward the rear as **posterior.** For example, the nose of a dog is anterior to the rest of its body, and its tail is posterior. Note that all the terms for anatomical directions are used in a relative sense: A dog's ears are posterior to its nose but anterior to its tail.

Ventral means toward the belly, and **dorsal** means toward the back. To help you remember this, think of the dorsal fin of a shark, which is on the top of its body (its back) as it swims along. In referring to the human brain, dorsal means the top of the brain—above versus below (ventral).

central nervous system (CNS) The division of the nervous system that recognizes and analyzes the significance of sensory information, decides how to respond to that information, and sends the message to execute that response to the PNS.

spinal cord The division of the CNS located within the vertebrate spinal column, which receives sensory messages from the body below the head and sends motor commands to the PNS. Most sensory messages are sent to the brain and most motor commands originate in the brain.

brain The division of the CNS within the vertebrate skull, which interprets sensory messages and determines the appropriate behavioral response.

anterior Toward the front end.

posterior Toward the rear end.

ventral Toward the belly.

dorsal Toward the back.

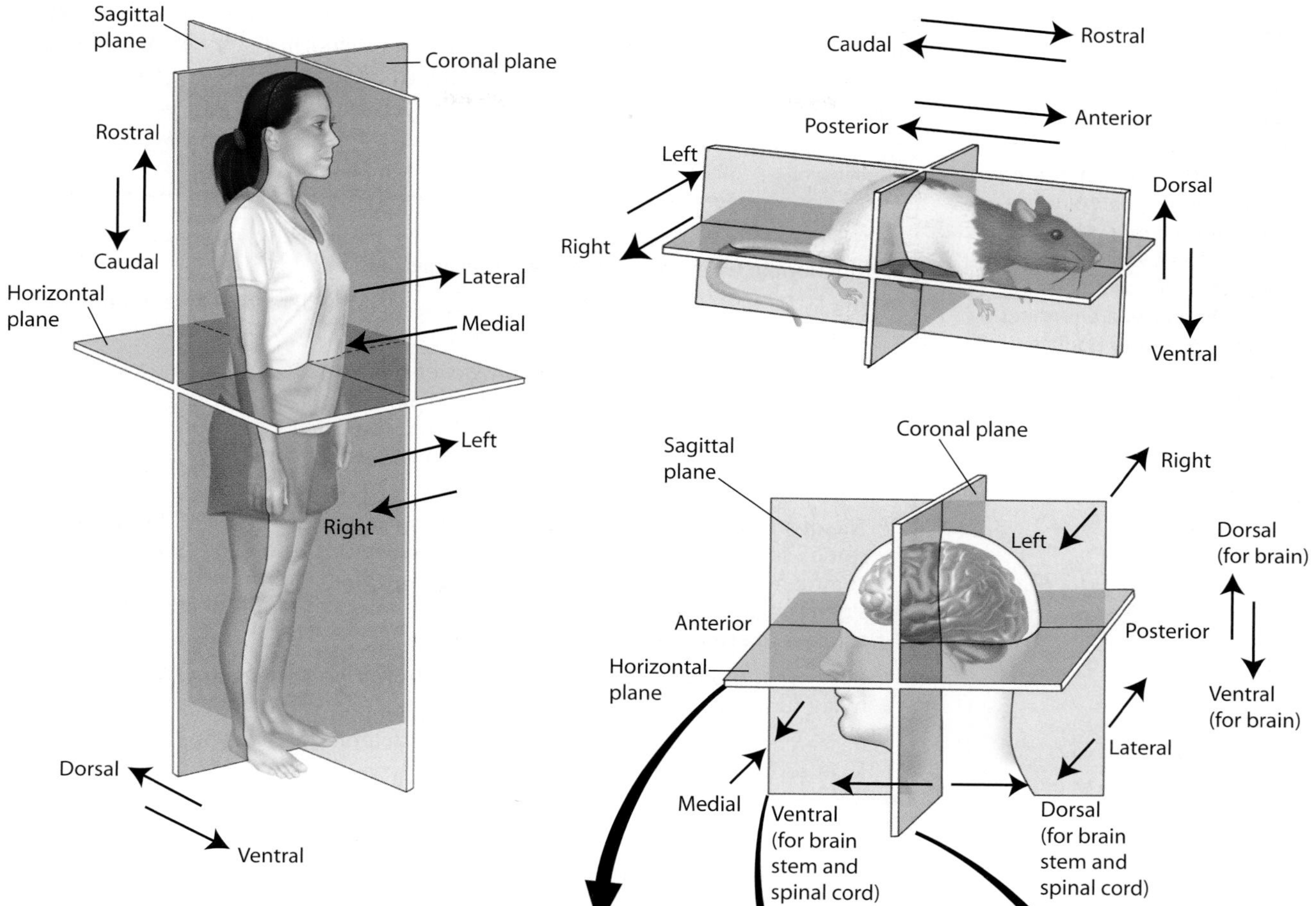

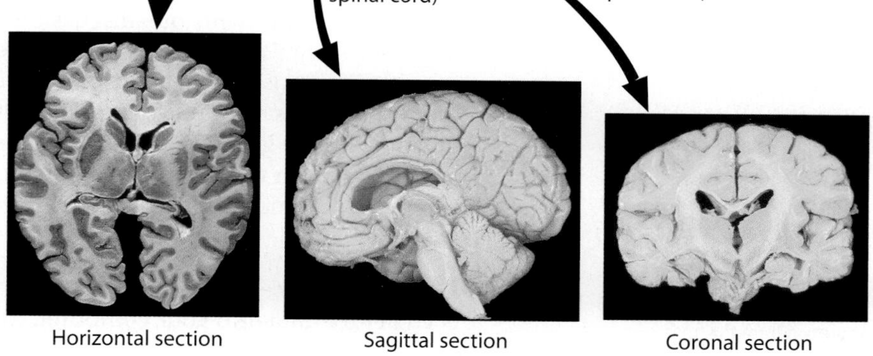

Figure 2.4

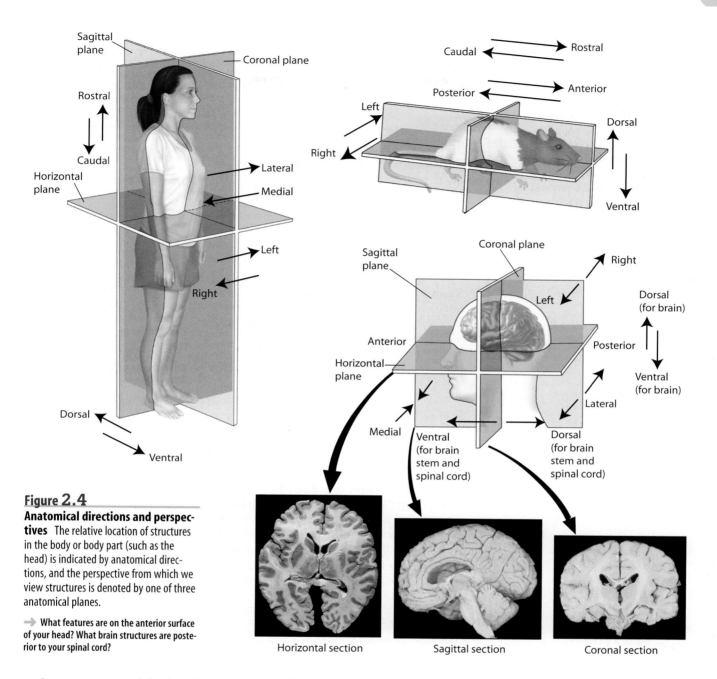

Anatomical directions and perspectives The relative location of structures in the body or body part (such as the head) is indicated by anatomical directions, and the perspective from which we view structures is denoted by one of three anatomical planes.

→ **What features are on the anterior surface of your head? What brain structures are posterior to your spinal cord?**

Structures toward the head end of an organism are **rostral;** structures toward the tail end are **caudal.** In terms of the brain, rostral and caudal are used synonymously with anterior and posterior, respectively.

The term **medial** means toward the midline, and **lateral** means away from the midline. For example, a cat's ears are lateral and its tongue is medial relative to the midline of its face. Your right nostril is medial relative to your right cheek, and your right eye is medial relative to your right ear.

Superior means above a structure, and **inferior** means below a structure. For example, in humans, the brain is superior to the spinal cord, which in turn is inferior to the brain.

Structures—and their internal arrangements—can be viewed from several perspectives, reflecting the planes of three-dimensional space (Figure 2.4). A plane that cuts the structure at right angles to the spine produces a **horizontal section,** a section as it would be seen from above in a human; a **sagittal section** is produced

rostral Toward the head.

caudal Toward the tail.

medial Toward the midline.

lateral Away from the midline.

superior Above a structure.

inferior Below a structure.

horizontal section A section of a structure as viewed from above.

sagittal section A section of a structure produced by a plane that cuts the structure into left and right parts.

by a plane that divides the structure into left and right parts; and a **coronal section** (also known as a *frontal section* or a *cross section*) results from a plane that cuts the structure vertically between front and back.

➤Checkpoint

Illustrate the four functions of the nervous system by using an example of an activity you perform every day, such as crossing the street or getting dressed. Which part of your nervous system is primarily in control when you are reading? When you are digesting food? When you are running? What part of your body is caudal to your chest? What would a sagittal view of your head show?

REVIEW

- ➤ The nervous system regulates the body's internal state and integrates the body's functioning with events in the external environment.
- ➤ The four major functions of the nervous system are detection, recognition, decision, and execution.
- ➤ The peripheral nervous system consists of the somatic and autonomic nervous systems. The somatic nervous system contains the sensory receptors that detect external stimuli and the nerves that execute the activity of the skeletal muscles. The autonomic nervous system includes the nerves that regulate the functioning of the internal organs.
- ➤ The central nervous system consists of the spinal cord and brain. The spinal cord carries sensory messages to the brain from regions below the head and motor commands from the brain to the muscles. The brain interprets, or recognizes, the significance of sensory information and determines the appropriate behavioral responses to sensory input.
- ➤ All the components of the nervous system must work together to perform its major functions.
- ➤ Researchers and physicians use a system of anatomical directions to describe the location of the parts of the body.

Cells of the Nervous System

Before proceeding with our discussion of how the various components of the nervous system work together to produce behavior, we need to look at the activities of the nervous system at the cellular level. We introduced the neuron briefly in Chapter 1. In this chapter, you will become much better acquainted with the neuron and with the glial cell, a second type of neural cell. Neurons communicate information within the nervous system and between the nervous system and other systems in the body. Glial cells perform various support functions for neurons.

Neurons

As you enter data into your computer, the computer chip, the computer's central element, processes the information, breaks it into its simplest form, and relays messages to different parts of the computer. Collections of neurons perform analogous functions in the nervous system.

Neurons are the cells that perform the information-processing and communication functions of the nervous system. Neurons can communicate with other neurons, with blood vessels, with muscles, or with glands. The human nervous system contains about 100 billion neurons.

Like other cells, each neuron contains a nucleus, cytoplasm, and a cell membrane. The **nucleus,** like that of all cells, contains chromosomes and genes, which consist of **deoxyribonucleic acid (DNA),** the genetic blueprint for the entire organism (Chapter 3). DNA controls the production of **ribonucleic acid (RNA),** which governs the manufacture of proteins, which in turn regulate cell functioning. (As you will see, the term *nucleus* can also refer to a collection of neuronal cell bodies.) The **cytoplasm** is the jellylike semiliquid substance inside the cell and the various structures it contains, including *mitochondria,* which extract energy from foods, and *ribosomes,* which synthesize new proteins. The **cell membrane** surrounds the cytoplasm and controls the flow of substances into and out of the neu-

coronal section A section of a structure as viewed from the front.

nucleus (of cell) The part of a cell containing chromosomes, genes, and DNA.

deoxyribonucleic acid (DNA) An organism's genetic material; controls the production of RNA.

ribonucleic acid (RNA) A substance that controls the manufacture of proteins, which regulate cell functioning.

cytoplasm The jellylike semiliquid substance inside a cell and the intracellular structures it contains; all cell contents other than the nucleus and cell membrane.

cell membrane The structure that surrounds a cell and controls the flow of substances into and out of the cell.

ron, allowing some substances to enter and keeping others out. We describe the cell membrane in more detail in Chapter 4.

Neurons have several unique structures that enable them to perform their information-processing and communication functions (Figure 2.5). **Dendrites** are thin, widely branching projections from the **cell body, or soma.** (*Soma* is Greek for "body"; *dendron* is Greek for "tree," a good term to describe the branching of dendrites.) The dendritic spines (small buds) on the surface of the dendrites contain specialized junctions, called receptor sites, that receive information from other neurons. Neural messages also can be received by receptor sites on the cell body.

Information received by the dendrites and the cell body is transmitted away from the cell body by a single long, relatively thick fiber called an **axon** (from the Greek word *axis;* this fiber resembles an axis projecting from one pole of the neuron). The axon is joined to the cell body at the **axon hillock**, which is where the nerve impulse begins (Chapter 4). Generally, each neuron has a single axon, but the axon may have many branches at its end, known as **telodendria** (singular: telodendron, meaning "tree at end").

Groups of neurons, or neuron parts, cluster together in four functional groups: nerves, tracts, ganglia, and nuclei. A **nerve** is a collection of axons outside the central nervous system—meaning within the peripheral nervous system. One major exception to this definition is the optic nerve; because the retina is really an outgrowth of the brain, the optic nerve is actually part of the CNS and is incorrectly named. A **tract** is a collection of axons within the CNS (or outside the PNS). Thus what we call the optic nerve should really be the optic tract. A **ganglion** (plural, ganglia) is a collection of neuronal cell bodies outside the CNS, and a **nucleus** (plural, nuclei; not to be confused with the DNA-containing structure inside the cell) is a collection of neuronal cell bodies within the CNS. Keeping these definitions in mind, you will recognize that when we discuss the red *nucleus,* for example, we are talking about a group of cell bodies within the CNS. If we refer to the auditory *nerve,* you will recognize that we are talking about a collection of axons outside the CNS. Similarly, the spiral *ganglion* must be a collection of cell bodies outside the CNS, and the olfactory *tract* is a collection of axons within the CNS.

Located at the end of the axon or telodendron is a swelling called the **presynaptic terminal.** Like many important terms in neuroscience, *presynaptic terminal* has

dendrite A thin, widely branching projection from the cell body of a neuron that receives neural impulses.

cell body (soma) The body of a neuron from which the dendrites and axon project.

axon A long, relatively thick fiber that transmits neural impulses away from the neural cell body.

axon hillock The area between the cell body and axon of a neuron where neural impulses are generated.

telodendron A branch at the end of an axon.

nerve A collection of axons outside the CNS, within the PNS.

tract A collection of axons within the CNS, outside the PNS.

ganglion A collection of neuronal cell bodies outside the CNS.

nucleus (of CNS) A collection of neuronal cell bodies within the CNS.

presynaptic terminal A swelling at the end of an axon.

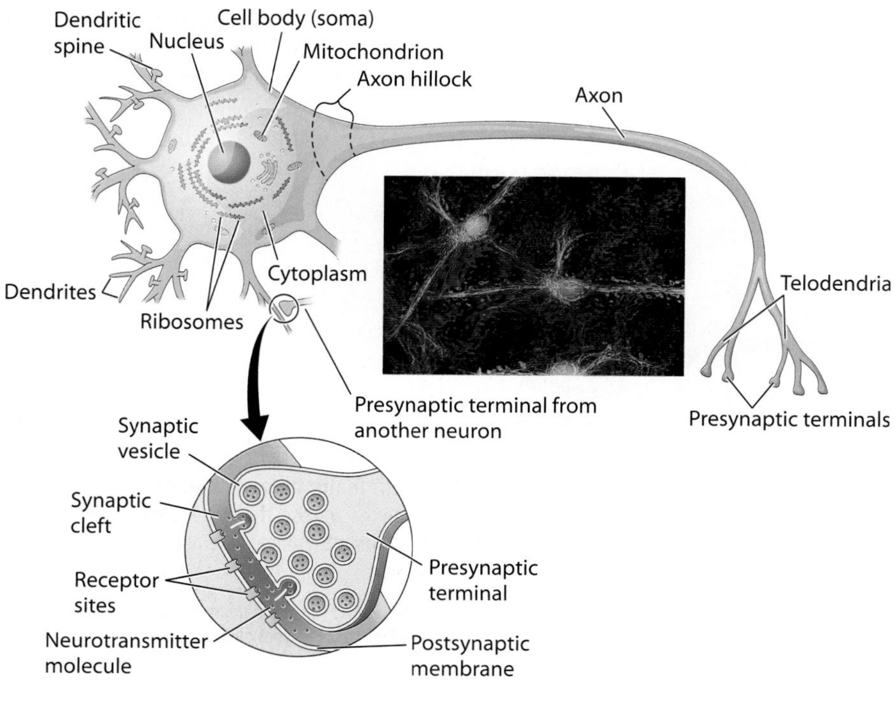

Figure 2.5

A typical neuron and synapse

Shown here are the principal structures related to the neural transmission of information. At the synapse, neurotransmitter molecules, stored in synaptic vesicles, are released at the presynaptic membrane. They diffuse across the synaptic cleft and affect the receptors of the next neuron in the information pathway.

Which part(s) of a neuron receive information from other neurons? Which part(s) transmit information to other neurons? Which structures constitute the synapse?

synaptic vesicle A sac within the presynaptic terminal that contains neurotransmitters.

neurotransmitter A chemical stored in the synaptic vesicles that is released into the synaptic cleft and transmits messages to other neurons, blood vessels, or muscles.

synaptic cleft The space between the presynaptic and postsynaptic membranes.

axodendritic synapse A synapse between the axon of one neuron and the dendrite of another neuron.

axosomatic synapse A synapse between the axon of one neuron and the cell body of another neuron.

dendrodendritic synapse A synapse between the dendrite of one neuron and the dendrite of another neuron.

axoaxonic synapse A synapse between the axon of one neuron and the axon of another neuron.

presynaptic membrane The outer surface of the presynaptic terminal, the site of release of neurotransmitters into the synaptic cleft.

postsynaptic membrane The outer surface of a target cell that receives messages from the presynaptic membrane.

synapse The point of functional contact between a neuron and its target.

neuromuscular junction The point of contact between a neuron and a muscle.

sensory neuron A specialized neuron that detects information from inside the body or from the outside world.

motor neuron A specialized neuron that carries messages from the CNS to muscles.

interneuron A neuron that connects a sensory and a motor neuron or communicates with other neurons.

many synonyms, including terminal bouton, terminal button, and end foot. A presynaptic terminal contains sacs, called **synaptic vesicles,** that contain chemical substances called **neurotransmitters.** Neurotransmitters transmit information between neurons or from neurons to blood vessels, muscles, or glands. The small space that separates the presynaptic terminal from the dendrites, cell body, or axon of a neighboring neuron or from its target blood vessel, gland, or muscle is the **synaptic cleft.** The axon of one neuron usually synapses with, or meets, the dendrites or cell body of the next neuron, resulting in an **axodendritic synapse** or **axosomatic synapse,** respectively, but there are other possibilities (Figure 2.6). In some cases, the dendrites of one neuron synapse with the dendrites of another neuron to produce a **dendrodendritic synapse.** In other cases, the axon of one neuron synapses with the axon of another neuron at an **axoaxonic synapse.** We will have more to say about these various connections between neurons in Chapter 4.

When a message reaches the end of an axon, the synaptic vesicles move to the outer surface, or **presynaptic membrane,** of the presynaptic terminal and release a neurotransmitter into the synaptic cleft. The neurotransmitter then diffuses across the synaptic cleft to the **postsynaptic membrane** of the target (see Figure 2.5). Thus, the function of the axon is to relay information to a target: another neuron, a muscle, a gland, or a blood vessel. We examine communication between neurons in Chapter 4 and between neurons and muscles in Chapter 8.

Together, the presynaptic terminal, synaptic cleft, and postsynaptic membrane make up the **synapse,** the point of functional contact between a neuron and its target. Another name for the synapse between a neuron and a muscle is the **neuromuscular junction.**

Although neurons come in a bewildering variety of forms, we can classify them by *structure* into three main types: unipolar, bipolar, and multipolar. As the name implies, a *unipolar neuron* has just one projection from the cell body, which then divides into two branches. The branch that extends toward the periphery (outside) of the organism is a single dendritic tree, and the branch that extends toward the brain is the axon (Figure 2.7a). A *bipolar neuron* has one dendritic tree and one axon at opposite ends of the cell body (Figure 2.7b); as in the unipolar neuron, the dendrites extend toward the periphery, the axon toward the brain. A *multipolar neuron* has many dendritic trees extending from the cell body and one long axon (Figure 2.7c).

Neurons are of three *functional* types: sensory neurons, motor neurons, and interneurons. **Sensory neurons** detect information from the external or internal environment and transmit the information to the central nervous system. Some sensory neurons are unipolar; bipolar neurons are often found between a sensory

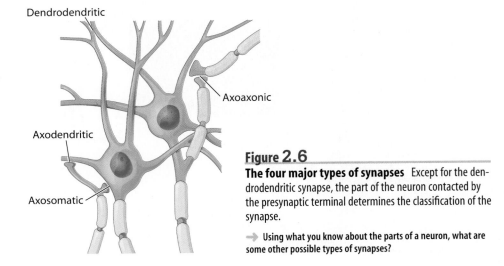

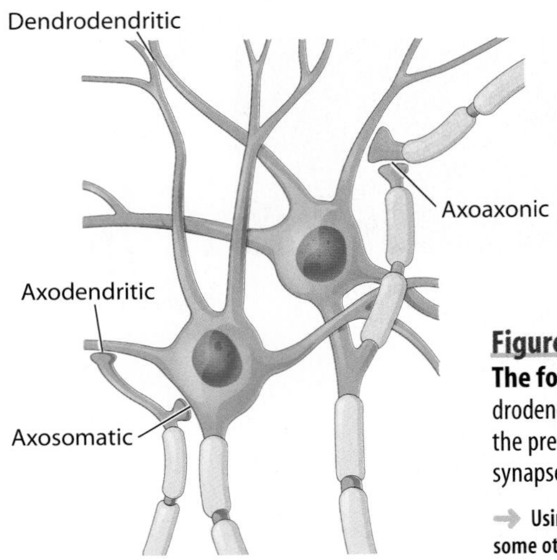

Figure 2.6

The four major types of synapses Except for the dendrodendritic synapse, the part of the neuron contacted by the presynaptic terminal determines the classification of the synapse.

➜ **Using what you know about the parts of a neuron, what are some other possible types of synapses?**

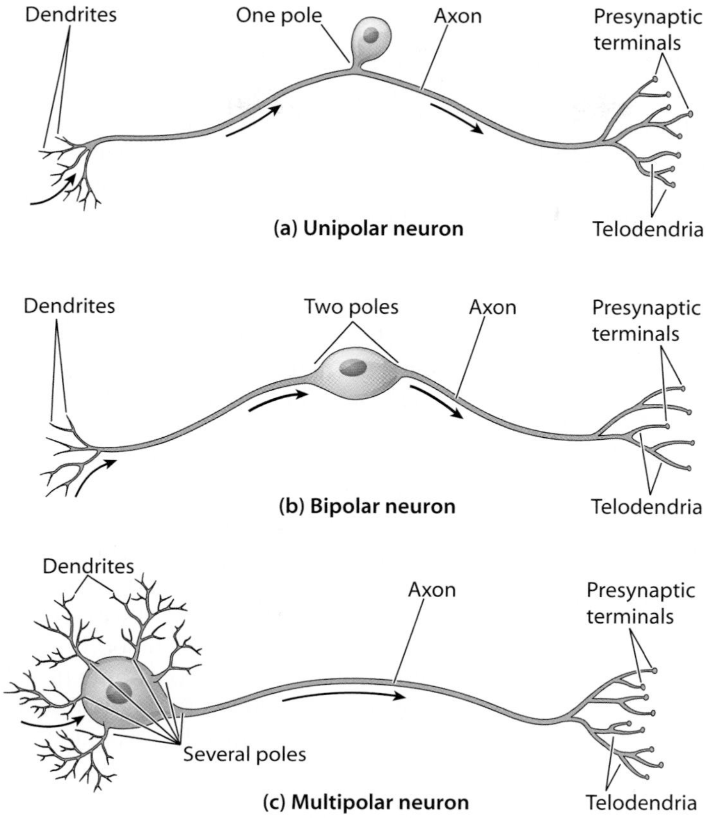

Figure 2.7
Three types of neurons The types are classified by the number of projections extending from the cell body: (a) one projection, unipolar; (b) two projections, bipolar; (c) more than two projections, multipolar.

→ **Why are motor neurons and interneurons typically multipolar? Why are sensory neurons typically unipolar or bipolar?**

neuron and the rest of the nervous system. You will see this pattern in both the visual system and the auditory system. **Motor neurons** carry information from the CNS to the muscles to control their functioning. **Interneurons** connect sensory and motor neurons or communicate with other interneurons. Interneurons and motor neurons are typically multipolar and can assume dramatically different shapes (Figure 2.8).

Checkpoint

Name the structures that are unique to neurons. What are the functions of these structures? What parts of neurons are also found in other cells? What are the three main structural types of neurons? Describe the three functional types of neurons.

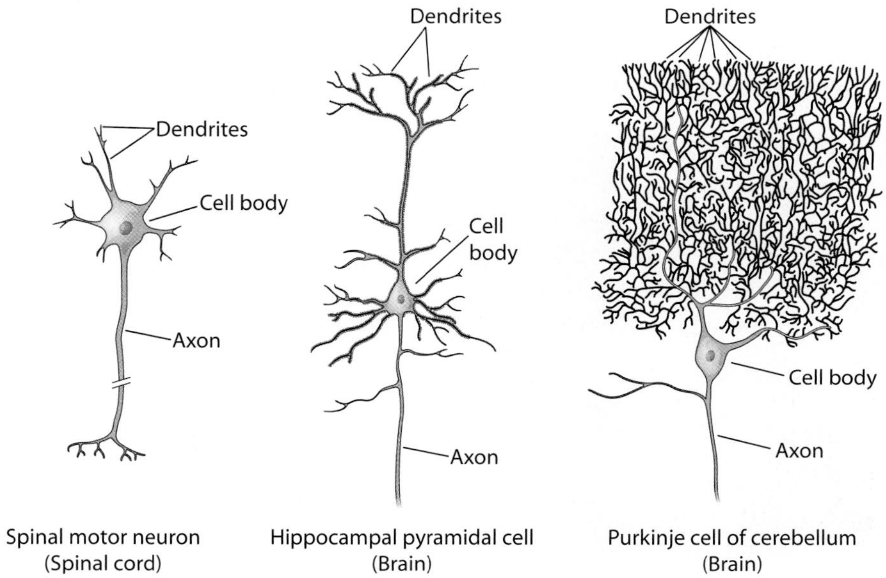

Figure 2.8
Three examples of multipolar neurons The number of dendritic projections on a multipolar neuron varies from a few in a spinal motor neuron to many in a Purkinje cell of the cerebellum, a cell type involved in skilled movements. Hippocampal pyramidal cells, so named for their pyramid-shaped cell bodies, are involved in memory formation.

→ **Which end of the spinal motor neuron extends toward the brain?**

Glial Cells

The **glial cell** (or *neuroglial cell*), the second type of cell found in the nervous system, generally plays a supporting role. (*Glia* is from the Greek word meaning "glue"; it was once thought that glial cells were like glue holding neurons together. Neuroglial thus means "nerve glue.") Glial cells are about one-tenth the size of a neuron but are approximately 10 times as numerous, which means the two cell types occupy approximately the same volume in the nervous system.

Figure 2.9

Types of glial cells Glial cells of the CNS include astrocytes, microglial cells, and oligodendrocytes. The inset shows Schwann cells.

➔ **What is the function of each type of glial cell?**

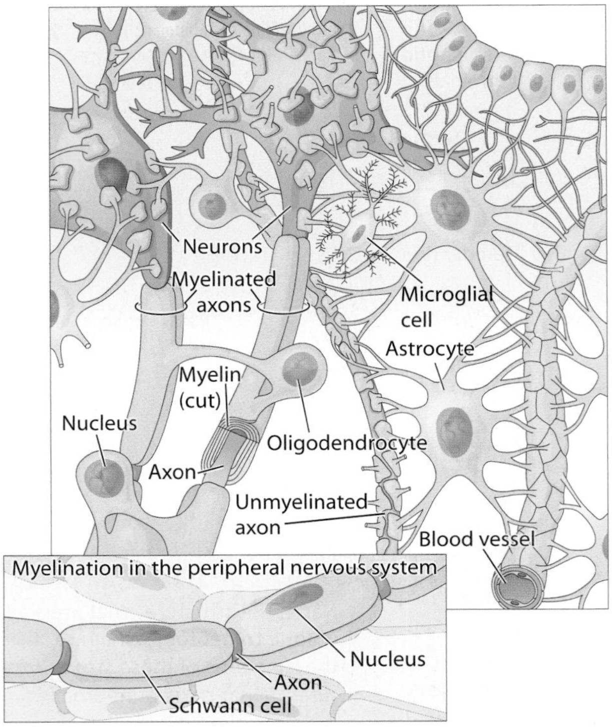

As you can see in Figure 2.9, glial cells come in a variety of types. The largest of the glial cells is the **astrocyte** (from the Greek *astron,* "star," and *cyte,* "cell"). Astrocytes provide physical support for neurons by protecting them and holding them in place; they also isolate neurons from each other to prevent the accidental transmission of neural messages. Astrocytes transport nutrients into the neuron, remove waste products from it, regulate blood flow in the CNS, and guide neuronal development in the embryo and fetus. Astrocytes also cover the blood vessels that form the blood-brain barrier (Chapter 4), which is a neural structure that prevents most compounds from entering the brain from the blood. Although astrocytes are involved in the development and maintenance of the blood-brain barrier (Abbott, 2002), they probably do not contribute to its barrier function (Ballabh & others, 2004). Traditionally, it has been thought that astrocytes perform only those support functions just stated, but extensive evidence suggests that they also integrate neuronal messages and release neurotransmitters that affect the sensitivity of synapses (Alvarez-Maubecin & others, 2000; Hansson & Ronnback, 2003; Haydon, 2001).

Some astrocytes and a second type of glial cell, a **microglial cell,** remove the debris of neurons that have died. (As their name implies, microglia are much smaller than astrocytes.) Astrocytes and microglia travel through the nervous system, locate dead or dying neurons, and digest the debris. They leave behind a network of astrocytes to form scar tissue, walling off the cleaned-up area. (In Chapter 3 we discuss how neural tissue can recover from damage. In Chapter 3 we also discuss radial glial cells, which are specialized to aid in the migration of new neurons to their appropriate destinations.)

Two additional types of glial cells produce a complex, fatty substance called **myelin** that surrounds and insulates certain axons to speed the transmission of neural messages. We discuss the transmission of messages in myelinated axons in Chapter 4. **Oligodendrocytes** (or *oligodendroglia*) protect and insulate the axons of certain neurons in the CNS, and **Schwann cells** perform the same function in the PNS. The two types of glial cells differ in their ability to support axonal regeneration after injury, however. Schwann cells facili-

A woman with multiple sclerosis (MS), a disease caused by the death of cells that form the myelin sheath in the nervous system. The symptoms suffered by a person with MS depend on which part of the nervous system is damaged. We have more to say about MS in Chapter 4.

glial cell A nervous system cell that has a support function.

astrocyte A star-shaped glial cell that provides physical support for a neuron, transports nutrients into and waste products out of the neuron, regulates blood flow, and guides neural development.

microglial cell A type of glial cell that removes the debris of dead neurons.

myelin A fatlike substance that surrounds and insulates the axons of certain neurons.

oligodendrocyte A type of glial cell that myelinates certain neurons in the CNS.

Schwann cell A type of glial cell that myelinates certain neurons in the PNS.

tate such regeneration (Chapter 3), whereas oligodendrocytes may actively inhibit it through growth inhibitory proteins (Kocsis & others, 2002). Because oligodendrocytes are destroyed in a demyelinating disease such as multiple sclerosis (Chapter 4), the lack of axonal regeneration results in little functional recovery. Extensive research is underway to try to enhance the remyelination potential in the CNS (Kocsis & others).

The *Scientific American* Spotlight, "Glia Control Synapses," highlights the role played by glial cells in determining both the location and number of synapses a neuron forms.

Checkpoint

What are the different types of glial cells? What are their functions? What types of glial cells myelinate neurons?

Scientific American Spotlight

GLIA CONTROL SYNAPSES

R. Douglas Fields

For years, scientists assumed that only neurons specify the connections they make to other neurons. But evidence shows that glia can strongly influence how many synapses a neuron forms and where it forms them.

Ben A. Barres and his colleagues at Stanford University found that when they grew neurons from a rat's retina in a lab culture devoid of glial cells known as astrocytes, the neurons created very few synapses. When the researchers added astrocytes or culture medium that had been in contact with astrocytes, synapses formed abundantly. Barres could see the synapses and count them through a microscope as well as detect them by recording electrical activity (a sign that signals were flowing through synapses) with a microelectrode. He then detected in the medium two chemicals that are released by astrocytes to stimulate synapse formation—a fatty complex called apoE/cholesterol and the protein thrombospondin.

Meanwhile, Jeff W. Lichtman's group at Washington University recorded muscle synapses in mice over several days or weeks as they formed and as they were removed during development (the time when unneeded synapses get pruned) or after injury. When the images were spliced into a time-lapse movie, it appeared that both synapse formation and elimination were influenced by nonneuronal cells, seen as ghostlike forces acting on the axon terminal.

Most recently, Le Tian, Wesley Thompson, and their associates at the University of Texas at Austin experimented with a mouse that had been engineered so that its Schwann glia cells fluoresced. This trait allowed Thompson's team to collaborate with Lichtman's group and watch glial cells operate at the junction where neurons meet muscle—a feat previously not possible. After a muscle axon is injured or cut, it withdraws, but a cluster of neurotransmitter receptors remains on the recipient side of a synapse. Investigators knew that an axon can regenerate and find its way back to the abandoned receptors by following the Schwann cells that remain.

But what happens if the axon cannot find its way? Tracking the fluorescence, Thompson's group saw that Schwann cells at intact synapses somehow sensed that a neighboring synapse was in trouble. Mysteriously, the Schwann cells sprouted branches that extended to the damaged synapse, forming a bridge along which the axon could grow a new projection to the receptors (as shown in the accompanying photographs).

This work clearly shows that glia help to determine where synaptic connections form. Researchers are now trying to exploit this power to treat spinal cord injuries by transplanting Schwann cells into damaged spinal regions in lab animals.

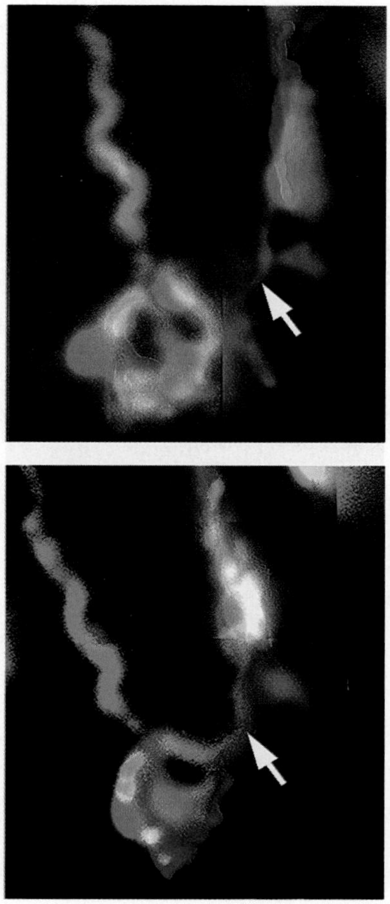

Glia can guide the formation of synapses. Neurobiologist Le Tian severed a muscle nerve synapse in a mouse whose cells had been engineered to fluoresce. Two days later (*top*) Schwann glia cells (*dark red*) had formed a bridge across the divide (*arrow*). In another two days (*bottom*), an axon (*green*) had regrown along the bridge to create a synapse.

From: *Scientific American*, vol. 290(4), p. 61.

REVIEW

- ➤ The nervous system is composed of neurons and glial cells.
- ➤ Neurons transmit neural messages from cell to cell over long distances.
- ➤ Sensory neurons detect information outside and inside the body and transmit it to the central nervous system. Motor neurons transmit messages from the CNS to the muscles and glands. Interneurons connect sensory and motor neurons.
- ➤ Glial cells have several functions. Astrocytes support and protect neurons, integrate neuronal inputs, and affect synaptic responsiveness. Microglia and astrocytes remove the debris of dead neurons. Oligodendrocytes and Schwann cells produce myelin, a protective substance that surrounds the axons of certain neurons and speeds the transmission of messages.

◆ The Peripheral Nervous System

You will recall that the four functions of the nervous system are detection, recognition, decision, and execution. As we indicated earlier, the peripheral nervous system detects information about external events and internal states, and executes the decisions made by the central nervous system in response to that input.

The sensory receptors in our sense organs detect a variety of environmental events. For example, the receptor cells in our eyes detect light, and the receptors in our ears react to sound. Other specialized receptors respond to events within the body, such as the proprioceptive receptors that detect the stretch and tension of a muscle. (These receptors let you know how much force to exert when you lift your backpack full of books.) In executing CNS decisions, the PNS conveys signals from the CNS to peripheral organs and muscles. For example, for most of his boxing

Figure 2.10

Spinal nerves and dermatomes

Each of the 31 pairs of spinal nerves serves a specific area of the body (left). The different colored areas designate the corresponding dermatomes (right), regions of the body surface innervated by the different pairs.

➡ **Why are there so many spinal nerves? What is the effect of damage to sensory or motor nerves?**

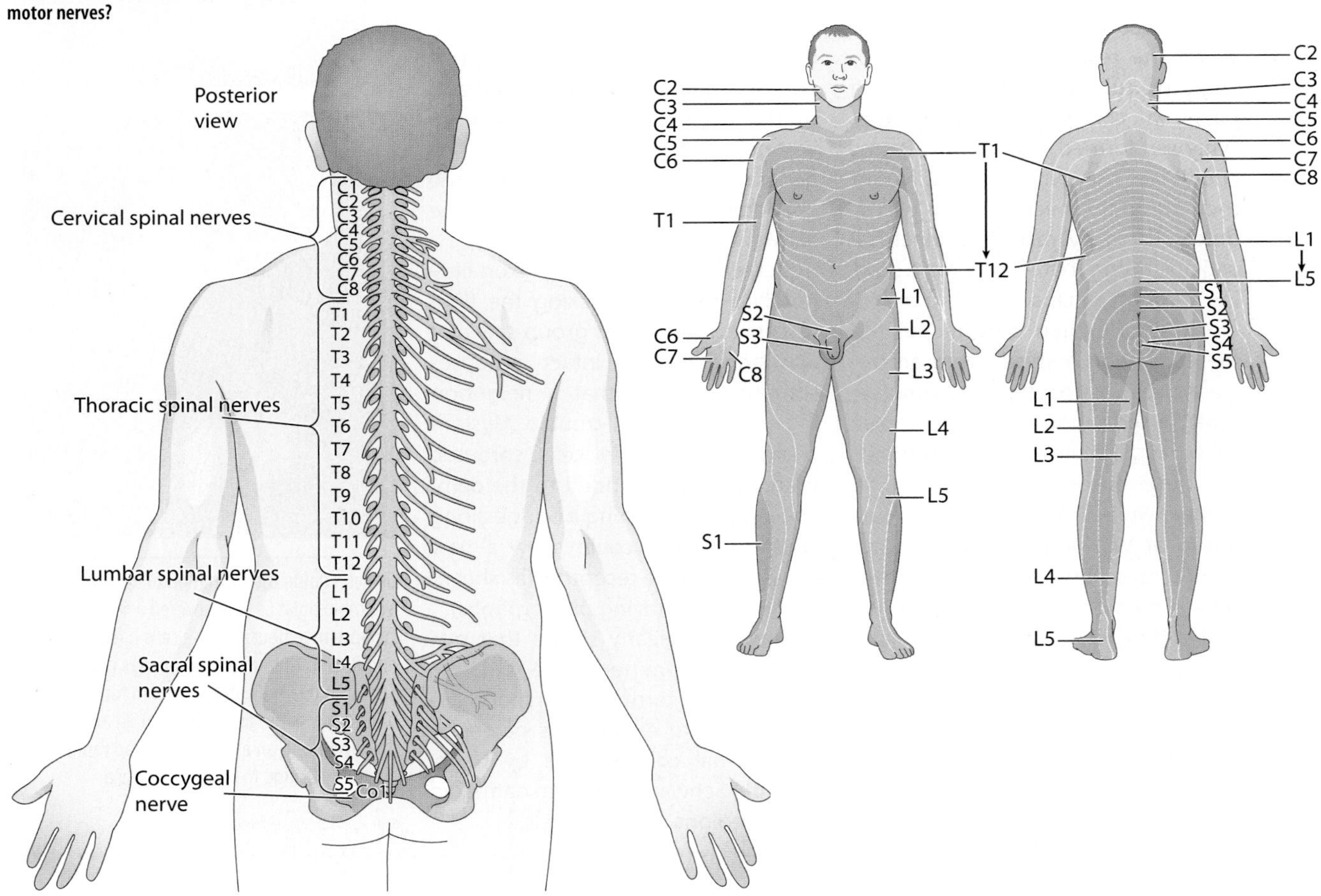

career, Sugar Ray's CNS sent a message to his PNS that caused him to duck when his opponent threw a punch. Unfortunately, in his fight with Guidry, he may have "ducked" into the uppercut. The PNS also activated the skeletal muscles that allowed Sugar Ray—for most of his career—to block punches.

The Somatic Nervous System

It is the neurons of the somatic nervous system, one of the two subsystems of the PNS (see Figure 2.3), that enable us to interact with our physical environment. **Afferent neurons** bring messages from the sensory receptors *to* the central nervous system (unless the receptors are already part of the CNS), and **efferent neurons** take messages *from* the CNS to the skeletal muscles. *Afferent* means coming toward, and *efferent* means going away from.

The somatic nervous system has two main types of nerves. **Spinal nerves** send messages to and from the brain through the spinal cord, and **cranial nerves** (so-named because they are inside the cranium, or skull) directly link the sensory receptors of the head to the brain and the brain to certain muscles. Both spinal and cranial nerves have afferent sensory input nerves and efferent motor output nerves.

We have 31 pairs of spinal nerves and 12 pairs of cranial nerves. Figure 2.10 shows the spinal nerves and the area of the body that each pair serves. The different colored areas on the body show the **dermatomes,** areas of skin innervated by the spinal nerves from a particular segment of the spinal cord. Table 2.1 shows the sensory and motor information conveyed by the cranial nerves. All but four cranial nerves have a single function, either sensory or motor.

The Autonomic Nervous System

The autonomic nervous system contains efferent neurons that control glandular activity and internal organ functioning. The system has two divisions: the sympathetic division and the parasympathetic division (Figure 2.11). The actions of the two divisions are typically antagonistic (act in opposition to each other).

The **sympathetic nervous system** is activated by conditions that promote arousal, particularly in situations involving emotional reactions to stressors (Berry

afferent neuron A neuron that transmits messages from sensory receptors to the CNS, unless the receptors are already part of the CNS.

efferent neuron A neuron that transmits messages from the CNS to skeletal muscles.

spinal nerve A group of axons that transmits messages to and from the brain through the spinal cord.

cranial nerve A group of axons that directly links sensory receptors to the brain, and the brain to certain muscles.

dermatome A segment of skin innervated by a spinal nerve from a particular segment of the spinal cord.

sympathetic nervous system A division of the autonomic nervous system that is activated by challenging, stimulating, or dangerous situations.

Table 2.1
The 12 Pairs of Cranial Nerves

Number	Name	Type	Function
I	Olfactory	Sensory	Smell
II	Optic	Sensory	Vision
III	Oculomotor	Motor	Eye movement
IV	Trochlear	Motor	Eye movement
V	Trigeminal	Motor	Chewing movements
		Sensory	Sensitivity of face
VI	Abducens	Motor	Eye movement
VII	Facial	Motor	Muscles of facial expression
		Sensory	Taste from anterior two-thirds of tongue
VIII	Auditory	Sensory	Hearing, balance
IX	Glossopharyngeal	Motor	Movement of pharynx, salivary secretion
		Sensory	Taste from posterior one-third of tongue
X	Vagus	Sensory, motor	Sensitivity and movement of heart, lungs, gastrointestinal tract, larynx
XI	Spinal accessory	Motor	Movement of neck muscles and viscera, swallowing
XII	Hypoglossal	Motor	Tongue movement

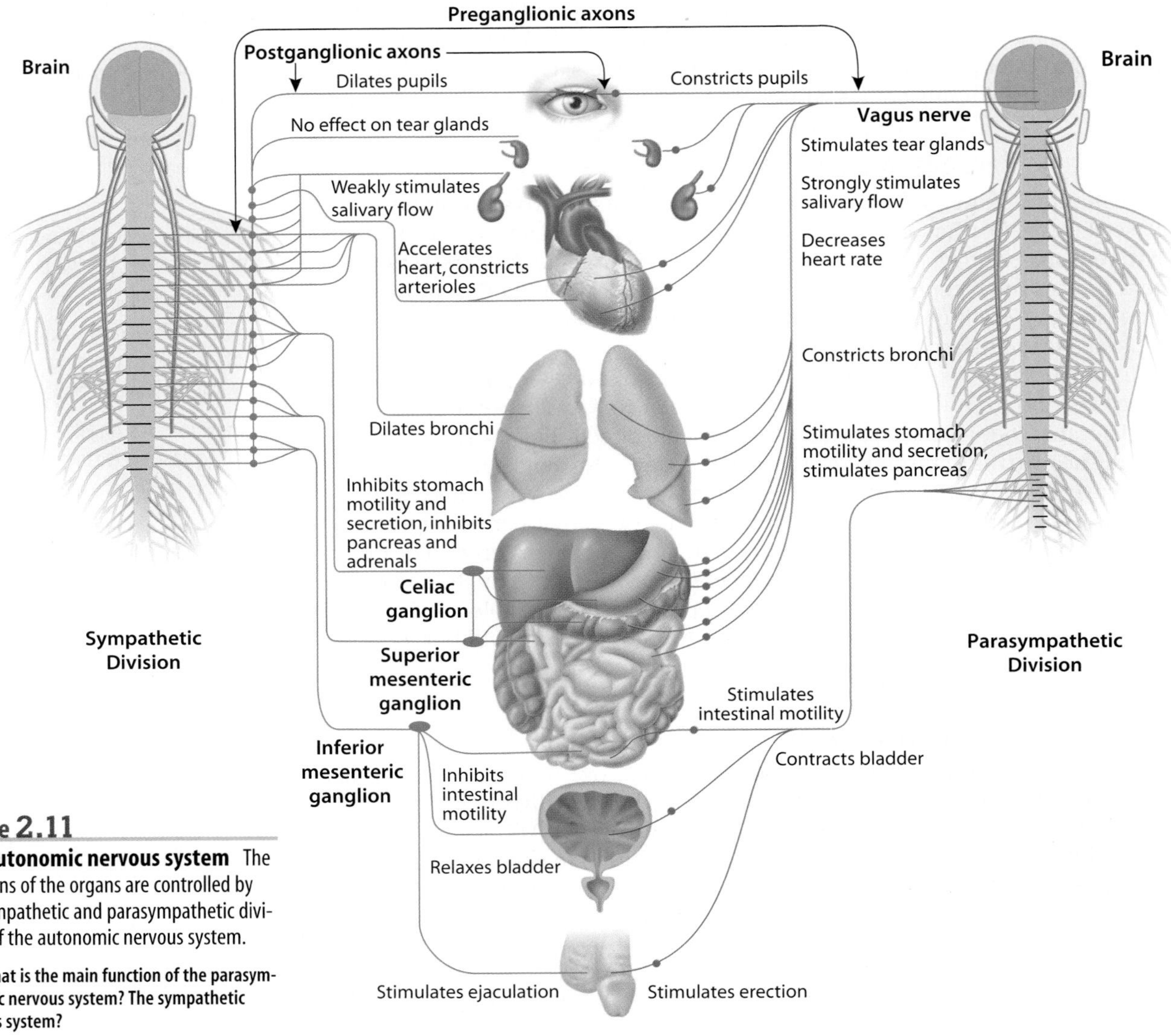

Figure 2.11

The autonomic nervous system The functions of the organs are controlled by the sympathetic and parasympathetic divisions of the autonomic nervous system.

➔ **What is the main function of the parasympathetic nervous system? The sympathetic nervous system?**

& Pennebaker, 1993; Oshima & others, 2001). Thus, stimulation of the sympathetic nervous system prepares the organism to respond to challenging or dangerous conditions, which is why the well-known Harvard physiologist Walter B. Cannon called it the fight-or-flight system (see the drawing of the boxer on the next page). For example, think of the last time you had to speak in public. Chances are good that you were aware of your racing heart, your sweaty palms and armpits, and your dry mouth. Although you were not aware of it, your pupils probably dilated, and your digestive activities stopped. These were all responses caused by sympathetic nervous system stimulation. We can be sure, too, that Sugar Ray's sympathetic system was active before a fight. The sympathetic nervous system also is likely to be stimulated by such positive events as attending an exciting concert, going skiing or snowboarding, or learning you have won a lottery.

parasympathetic nervous system A division of the autonomic nervous system that is activated by conditions of recovery or the termination of stress.

In contrast, the **parasympathetic nervous system** is activated by conditions of recovery, or the termination of stressors, and it allows the organism to replenish energy-depleted stores. For example, after you finished speaking and took your seat, your parasympathetic system became dominant, your heart rate slowed, your blood pressure dropped, and your digestive system resumed working on your lunch. The activation of the parasympathetic nervous system after sympathetic nervous system activation ends, a process called *parasympathetic rebound,* helps to ensure that we are ready to respond to our next challenge. At its extreme,

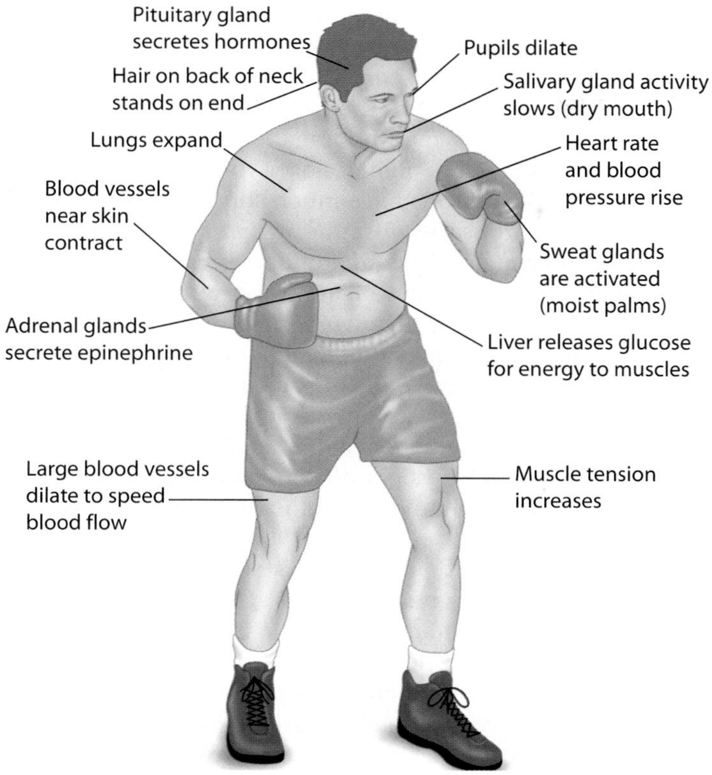
Pituitary gland secretes hormones
Hair on back of neck stands on end
Lungs expand
Blood vessels near skin contract
Adrenal glands secrete epinephrine
Large blood vessels dilate to speed blood flow
Pupils dilate
Salivary gland activity slows (dry mouth)
Heart rate and blood pressure rise
Sweat glands are activated (moist palms)
Liver releases glucose for energy to muscles
Muscle tension increases

A young man demonstrating the "fight or flight" reaction.

parasympathetic rebound can kill an organism by causing its heart rate to slow too much (Richter, 1957). This phenomenon, also known as "voodoo death" or stress-induced sudden death, has been documented (Cannon, 1957; Sternberg, 2002), although its cause may stem more from excessive sympathetic stimulation than from parasympathetic rebound (Brown & Fee, 2002).

Although the sympathetic and parasympathetic actions are typically antagonistic, there is some cooperative functioning between the two systems. An example is the sexual response. Suppose a man sees an attractive woman. This sight might stimulate his sympathetic nervous system, leading to an increase in heart rate and blood pressure. At the same time, the parasympathetic nervous system might be activated, causing the arteries of the penis to dilate (enlarge), which increases blood flow to the genital area. This causes the erectile tissue to become engorged with blood and produces penile erection. (There is a similar parasympathetic engorgement in the clitoris in women.) Continued sympathetic nervous system arousal may lead to ejaculation.

Have you noticed that the effects of exposure to a stressful event, such as running in a 5K race, occur more quickly than the effects of a pleasant event, like listening to soothing music? When you line up for the start of the race, your heart rate almost immediately quickens, your breathing becomes more rapid, and your mouth almost instantly becomes dry. By contrast, it seems to take much longer for the opposite physiological effects to occur when you listen to soothing music. One reason for the difference lies in structural differences between the sympathetic and parasympathetic nervous systems. Both contain ganglia—which, you will recall, are groupings of neuronal cell bodies with a common function in the PNS—but the ganglia occur in different positions in the two systems. (The following discussion can be confusing because of the similarity and length of the terms. To make it easier, keep the word roots in mind: *Preganglionic* means before the ganglion, and *postganglionic* means after the ganglion.)

The axons of the preganglionic *sympathetic* neurons that leave the spinal cord are short, synapsing with the postganglionic sympathetic neurons in the sympathetic ganglia (see the red spheres in Figure 2.11). The axons of the postganglionic sympathetic neurons are long, synapsing directly with the target organ (e.g., the heart). By contrast, the axons of the preganglionic *parasympathetic* neurons are long, and they synapse with postganglionic parasympathetic neurons at the parasympathetic ganglia close to the target organ (the blue spheres in Figure 2.11). Being closer to the target organ, the postganglionic parasympathetic neurons have much shorter axons than do the postganglionic sympathetic neurons. Because the *sympathetic* ganglia are so far from a target organ, one preganglionic sympathetic neuron can activate up to 20 or 30 postganglionic neurons, which can, in turn, stimulate several different target organs. By contrast, because the *parasympathetic* ganglia are so much closer to the target organ, the activation of a preganglionic parasympathetic neuron produces a more specific effect, activating only a few postganglionic parasympathetic neurons, which in turn activate only a single target organ. This makes sense if you think about it—the body needs to respond much more quickly to sympathetic stimulation, such as the sight of a growling dog approaching, so it is an advantage that the preganglionic sympathetic neurons can activate more organs in a shorter time.

The parasympathetic nervous system, then, tends to act more slowly and more discretely—one or a few organs stimulated at a time rather than many organs stimulated simultaneously, which occurs in sympathetic activation. The "all-or-none" sympathetic activation is enhanced by its stimulation of the adrenal gland (part of the endocrine system of glands that secrete substances inside the body) and the subsequent release of epinephrine or norepinephrine. These neurochemicals enter the bloodstream and from there can activate many organs simultaneously. We have more to say about the actions of epinephrine and norepinephrine—as well as about the many endocrine hormones that affect nervous system functioning—in Chapter 4.

➤ Checkpoint

Explain the difference between afferent and efferent nerves. What are the different functions of the somatic and autonomic nervous systems? Give an example of the antagonistic effects of the sympathetic and parasympathetic nervous systems.

REVIEW

- The somatic and autonomic nervous systems are the two divisions of the peripheral nervous system.
- The somatic nervous system consists of the spinal and cranial nerves, receives input from sensory receptors located throughout the body, and activates the skeletal muscles.
- The autonomic nervous system, which consists of the sympathetic and parasympathetic systems, activates the glands and organs that control the functions of the body.
- The sympathetic nervous system, activated by arousing or stimulating conditions, prepares the body to cope with challenge or danger.
- The parasympathetic nervous system is most active during conditions of rest. It mainly functions to conserve and replenish energy stores.

◆ The Protective Features of the Central Nervous System

You drop your pencil, which rolls under the desk, and you crouch under the desk to search for it. At this point, a friend knocks on your door. Without thinking, you rear up and strike the top of your head sharply against the bottom of the desk drawer. Although the blow is very painful, in all likelihood its most serious consequences will be a headache and maybe a bump on the head. The explanation for the lack of a long-term effect lies in three protective features of the CNS: (1) the skull and vertebral column, or backbone; (2) the meninges; and (3) the ventricular system. (We discuss a fourth feature—the blood-brain barrier—in Chapter 4.) Of course, these features cannot protect against extreme damage such as Sugar Ray had experienced by the end of his career. (Box 2.1 describes various forms of brain damage and their consequences.)

skull The outer bony covering that protects the brain.

vertebral column The outer bony covering that protects the spinal cord; also called the spinal column, spine, or backbone.

meninges The three layers of tissue between the skull and brain and between the vertebral column and spinal cord.

dura mater The thick, tough, and flexible outermost layer of the meninges.

The Skull and Vertebral Column

The brain is protected from injury by a set of bones that comprise the **skull;** the spinal cord by the bones of the **vertebral column** (also called the *spinal column, spine,* or *backbone*). The vertebral column is composed of 24 individual vertebrae, as well as the fused vertebrae of the sacral and coccygeal regions (Figure 2.12). The hard, bony composition of the vertebral column and the skull provides important protection for the soft tissue of the central nervous system.

The Meninges

Between the skull and the brain, and between the spinal cord and the vertebral column, are three layers of tissue called the **meninges** (singular: meninx; from the Greek word for "membrane") (see Figure 2.12). The outermost layer is the **dura mater** (Latin for "hard mother"), which is thick, tough, and flexible. The

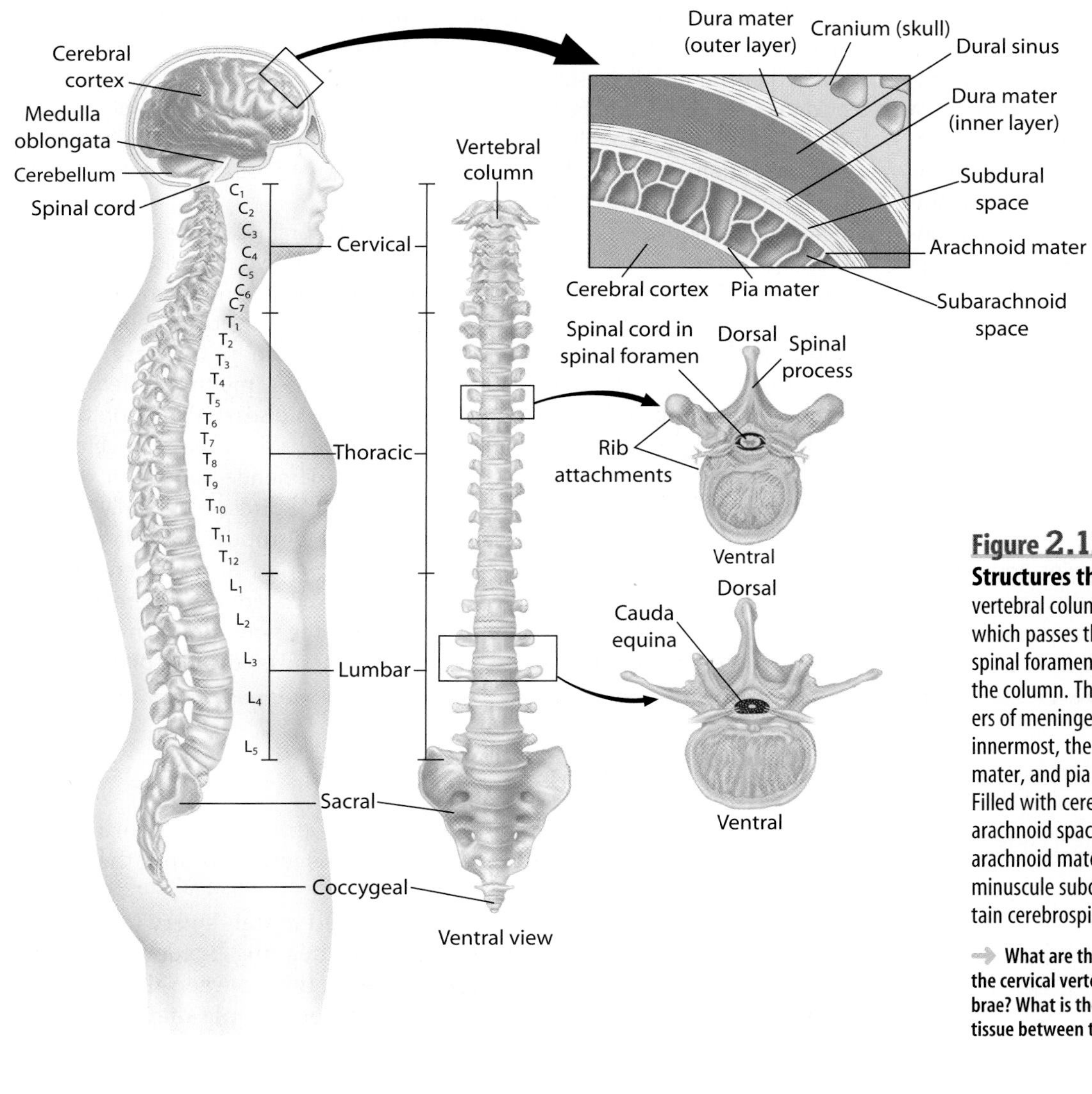

Figure 2.12

Structures that protect the CNS The vertebral column protects the spinal cord, which passes through the canal and the spinal foramen, in the upper two-thirds of the column. The bony skull and three layers of meninges (from outermost to innermost, the dura mater, arachnoid mater, and pia mater) protect the brain. Filled with cerebrospinal fluid, the subarachnoid space lies between the arachnoid mater and the pia mater. The minuscule subdural space may also contain cerebrospinal fluid.

→ What are the consequences of damage to the cervical vertebrae? To the lumbar vertebrae? What is the role of the many layers of tissue between the brain and the skull?

Box 2.1

Brain Damage

Sugar Ray Martin's motor impairments, described in the opening vignette, are almost certainly a result of brain damage caused by repeated blows to his head. Here we examine several major causes of brain damage. Later in the chapter we discuss the specific areas of the brain that were probably injured during Sugar Ray's boxing career.

Trauma is a major source of brain damage (Davis, 2000; Fawcett & others, 2002). Trauma can occur from injuries sustained during such sports as boxing and football and from gunshot wounds or automobile or motorcycle accidents. There are two classes of trauma: penetrating head injury and closed head injury. Brain damage caused by boxing is an example of a closed head injury, and all boxers experience it; Muhammad Ali is a well-known example. A gunshot wound (such as that suffered by President John F. Kennedy and by his brother Robert F. Kennedy) is an example of a penetrating head injury; another example is Phineas P. Gage's accident with the tamping rod (see Figure 1.5).

Other causes of brain damage include **congenital disorders** (disorders present at birth), vascular disorders, infections, tumors, and degenerative diseases (Davis, 2000; Fawcett & others, 2002). Congenital disorders include conditions such as cerebral palsy, which involves defects in motor behavior and coordination, and Down syndrome, a type of mental retardation accompanied by particular physical characteristics.

Strokes, or *cerebral vascular accidents (CVAs),* are a major category of vascular disorders (Figure 2.13a). A CVA can result from obstruction of a blood vessel by a clot or from bleeding in the brain caused by the rupture of a blood vessel. Other vascular disorders include *transient ischemic attacks (TIAs),* which are temporary disruptions of the blood supply that produce specific neurological problems such as blurring of vision or speech difficulty, and *pseudobulbar palsy,* a permanent muscular paralysis in the head and neck area.

Brain damage can result from a variety of infections, such as encephalitis, meningitis, abscesses, and syphilis. *Syphilis* is a sexually transmitted disease caused by a microorganism that may attack the nervous system.

Brain damage can also result from the blocking of CSF flow from the brain. This blocking produces a condition known as **hydrocephalus** (Figure 2.13b), which literally means "water head" (although the fluid is CSF, not water). In adults, this condition is life-threatening unless the pressure is relieved. In young children, whose skull bones have not yet fused completely, hydrocephalus can cause the skull bones to spread, resulting in an overgrown head and mental retardation from brain damage if the pressure is not alleviated.

A **tumor,** or abnormal proliferation of cells, is another cause of brain damage (Figure 2.13c). Within the brain, a tumor may develop from excessive glial cell duplication. As the tumor grows, it puts increasing pressure on neural tissue, which adversely affects neuronal functioning. Tumors are generally classified by grade, which is an indication of the severity of the tumor or the degree of abnormality of cancer cells compared with normal cells. Malignant grades 3 and 4 *astrocytomas* (proliferations of astrocytes) are the most common primary brain tumors in adults. (A primary tumor is the first tumor to develop; secondary tumors result from metastasis—the spread of the disease to other regions of the body.) These tumors mainly occur in the frontal and temporal lobes of the cerebral cortex and grow quite rapidly, causing death in about a year. Grades 1 and 2 astrocytomas and oligodendrogliomas develop more slowly than grades 3 and 4 astrocytomas, and patients have an average survival time of 5 to 6 years. Arising from the arachnoid cells of the meninges, meningiomas are benign tumors with a favorable prognosis, as they usually do not invade the brain.

Finally, brain damage can be caused by degenerative neurological diseases, progressive deterioration of function caused by the death of neurons. Examples are Parkinson's disease, Huntington's disease, multiple sclerosis, and Alzheimer's disease. Parkinson's disease is primarily a disorder of movement, although dementia can occur, whereas Alzheimer's disease primarily involves cognitive disruption. Huntington's disease begins as a movement disorder and is associated with severe dementia, whereas the symptoms of multiple sclerosis depend on the part of the nervous

congenital disorder A disorder that is present at birth.

hydrocephalus A blockage of CSF flow from the brain.

tumor An abnormal proliferation of cells.

arachnoid mater A thin weblike sheet of tissue that is the middle layer of meninges.

dura actually consists of two layers of tissue, closely united except for the open areas (venous sinuses or dural sinuses) where blood is returned from the brain to the heart.

The middle layer of the meninges is the **arachnoid mater,** a very thin weblike sheet of tissue (*arachnoid* is from the Greek word meaning "spider track"). The **subarachnoid space,** filled with cerebrospinal fluid, lies between the arachnoid mater and the pia mater, which is the innermost layer. The **pia mater** ("pious or

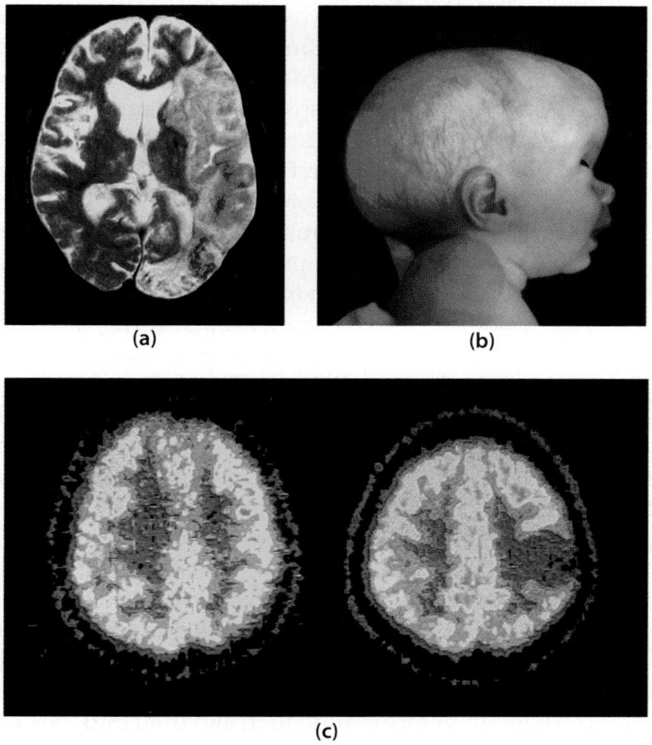

Figure 2.13

Some types of brain damage (a) Stroke; MRI scan shows a brain with massive stroke damage. Tissue damage is shown in brown in the left hemisphere (shown on the right of the figure). (b) Hydrocephalus; when left untreated, the build-up of CSF caused by blockage of the cerebral aqueduct or constriction of the subarachnoid space results in distortion of the brain and enlargement of the skull, as shown in this child. (c) A tumor, shown in an MRI scan next to a normal brain (on the left).

➔ **What might be done to prevent the development of hydrocephalus?**

system damaged, with sensory, motor, cognitive, and emotional changes possible. We discuss Parkinson's disease and Huntington's disease briefly later in this chapter and again, in more detail, in Chapter 8; multiple sclerosis is discussed in Chapter 4, and Alzheimer's disease in Chapter 14.

Some types of brain damage can be detected by a *spinal tap,* which involves removing and testing a small amount of cerebrospinal fluid from the subarachnoid space. For example, a CNS infection elevates the white blood cell count and the protein content in the CSF. Chemicals in the CSF can provide information about such brain disorders as encephalitis, an inflammation of the brain, and meningitis, an inflammation of the meninges of the brain or the spinal cord.

Analysis of CSF can also provide information about behavior pathology. For example, a low level of 5-HIAA (5-hydroxyindoleacetic acid)—a product of the metabolism (i.e., a metabolite) of the neurotransmitter serotonin—is a marker for suicidal tendency among people with depression and thus is a useful warning sign for a clinical psychologist or psychiatrist (Spreux-Varoquaux & others, 2001; Westrin & Nimeus, 2003).

An understanding of the causes and consequences of brain damage can tell us much about how the brain functions, as well as contribute to the development of effective methods of preventing or treating neurological disorders. In this book, we discuss the known causes and treatments for several neurological disorders. Unfortunately, for some disorders, such as Alzheimer's disease, the cause is unknown and effective treatment is not yet available. Research on this disorder and many others is continuing, and sometime in the near future we hope to have treatments for these devastating diseases.

gentle mother"), a thin membrane with a rich blood supply, adheres closely to the surface of the brain.

Meningitis is the infection or inflammation of the meninges and can be caused either by a bacterium, a virus, or a fungus. Symptoms generally include an excruciating headache, stiff neck, fever, and extreme sensitivity to light. The disorder can be fatal, although cure is virtually certain with prompt diagnosis and treatment with modern antibiotics.

subarachnoid space The space between the arachnoid mater and pia mater that is filled with cerebrospinal fluid.

pia mater A thin membrane that adheres closely to the surface of the brain and is the innermost layer of the meninges.

The Ventricular System

Figure 2.14
The ventricular system (a) Sagittal view; (b) coronal view.

→ **What are the functions of the cerebrospinal fluid?**

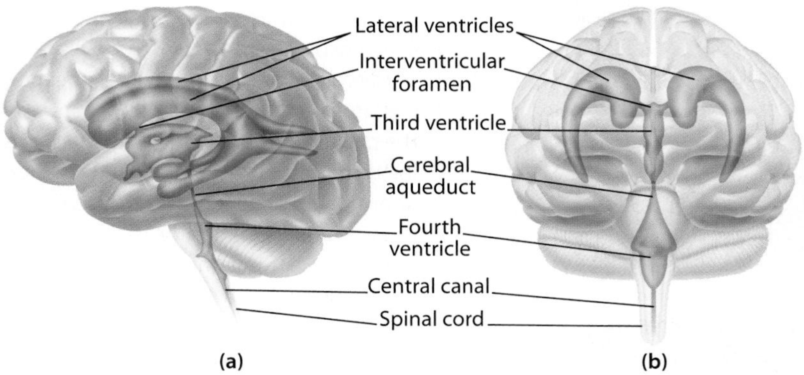

The **ventricular system** is a series of hollow interconnected chambers in the brain and spinal cord. The **ventricles** in the brain consist of two lateral ventricles, the third ventricle, and the fourth ventricle. (The lateral ventricles would have been the first and second ventricles, but the early anatomists could not decide which was first and which was second.) The **central canal** is the chamber passing through the spinal cord (Figure 2.14).

Like the subarachnoid space, the chambers of the ventricular system contain **cerebrospinal fluid (CSF),** a clear fluid that resembles blood plasma. CSF cushions and protects the brain and spinal cord from injury, provides buoyancy to support the brain against gravity, and contains nutrients needed by the central nervous system. As an illustration of the importance of the buoyancy provided by the CSF, in the days before CT scans and MRIs, one way to visualize the living brain was to remove the CSF, fill the ventricles with air, and then take X-ray pictures (pneumoencephalography). After this procedure, the patient was advised to remain perfectly still while the CSF replenished itself, as any head movement resulted in an excruciating headache. CSF is constantly manufactured by cells covering the **choroid plexus,** a rich network of blood vessels inside each ventricle. The absorption of CSF into the bloodstream prevents its excess accumulation.

Cerebrospinal fluid from the two lateral ventricles passes into the third ventricle through the interventricular foramen (an opening between the ventricles), into the fourth ventricle through the cerebral aqueduct, and then into the central canal of the spinal cord.

➤Checkpoint

Explain how the skull, the meninges, and the ventricular system protect your brain when you hit your head.

REVIEW

- ➤ The central nervous system is protected by the skull and vertebral column, the meninges, and the ventricular system.
- ➤ The meninges are three layers of tissue—the dura mater, arachnoid mater, and pia mater—that separate the CNS structures from the skull and vertebrae. The subarachnoid space, between the arachnoid mater and pia mater, contains protective cerebrospinal fluid.
- ➤ The ventricular system is a series of interconnected hollow spaces in the brain and spinal column including four ventricles in the brain and the central canal of the spinal cord. The ventricular system is filled with CSF, which cushions and protects the brain and spinal cord.

ventricular system A series of interconnected hollow chambers in the brain and spinal cord that contain cerebrospinal fluid.

ventricle One of four chambers of the ventricular system in the brain.

central canal The chamber of the ventricular system that runs through the spinal cord.

cerebrospinal fluid (CSF) The clear fluid contained in the ventricular system and arachnoid space that supports and protects the CNS and provides it with nutrients.

choroid plexus A rich network of blood vessels in the ventricles that manufactures CSF.

◆ The Central Nervous System: The Spinal Cord

We turn now to the functional components of the central nervous system. As we have indicated, the peripheral nervous system consists of the sensory (afferent) nerves and the motor (efferent) nerves of the somatic nervous system and the motor nerves of the autonomic nervous system. The somatic system detects environmental events and internal states and activates the muscles that produce movement in the external environment, and the autonomic system controls the functioning of internal organs. Many afferent nerves enter the CNS through the spinal cord, and the corresponding efferent nerves exit through the spinal cord. In the case of spinal reflexes, a response to environmental input is controlled solely by the spinal cord, but in other situations, the spinal cord is merely a conduit for information to and from the brain. In this section we examine the spinal cord to discover how it influences our actions.

Structure and Function

The spinal cord is a long, cylindrical structure that runs through the vertebral column. Its main function is to carry sensory input to and motor output from the brain. Thirty-one pairs of spinal nerves enter and exit the spinal cord: 8 pairs of cervical nerves, 12 pairs of thoracic nerves, 5 pairs of lumbar nerves, 5 pairs of sacral nerves, and 1 pair of coccygeal nerves (see Figure 2.10). For each spinal nerve pair, incoming sensory input from the PNS enters through the dorsal (back) side of the cord, and the outgoing motor neurons exit through the ventral (belly) side (recall the Bell-Magendie law from Chapter 1).

Figure 2.15 shows a cross-sectional view of a segment of the spinal cord. The sensory nerves that enter through the dorsal root are axons of sensory neurons, and the motor nerves that exit through the ventral root are axons of motor neurons. Each spinal nerve pair receives sensory input from and sends motor output to a specific part of the body, although there is some overlap in the nerves controlling certain areas, such as those controlling respiration. Because respiration is controlled by several spinal nerves (cervical nerves C3 through C5), respiration may be affected by damage to one cervical nerve, but it can continue because of the ongoing activity of the other two cervical nerves.

Viewing the spinal cord in cross section, we see **gray matter,** consisting of neuronal cell bodies, and **white matter,** consisting of groups of nerve fibers. The axons of these nerves appear white because they are myelinated, and myelin consists of lipids, which are white. *Myelination* increases the speed of transmission of neural information (in Chapter 4 we discuss why myelinated neurons transmit messages faster than unmyelinated neurons).

Figure 2.15

Section of the spinal cord Afferent sensory neurons enter through the dorsal root, and efferent motor neurons exit through the ventral root.

What are the main functions of the spinal cord?

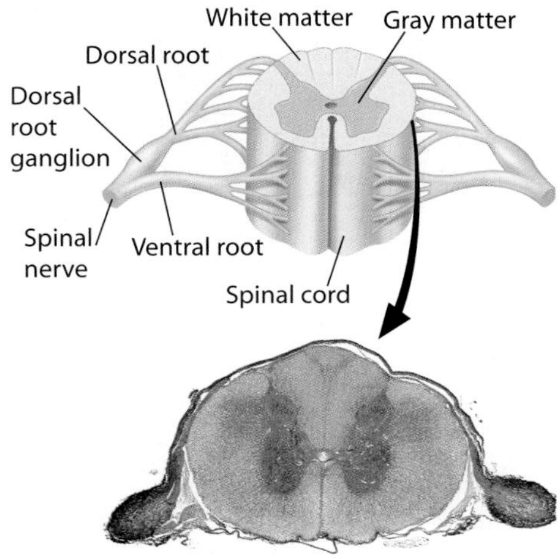

Spinal Reflexes

Remember Descartes' model of the reflex (see Figure 1.2)? Although our brain controls most of our behavior, some activities occur without the brain's intervention. In **spinal reflexes,** afferent sensory input enters the spinal cord and quickly activates the appropriate efferent motor neuron.

Spinal reflexes are important because they allow rapid reactions to environmental events, when even minimal analysis of information would introduce an injury-producing delay. Think about the last time you accidentally touched a hot burner on a stove, and you will understand the importance of the spinal *withdrawal reflex*. Further responses, or adjustments to the initial response, can occur later, after the information that triggered the reflex has traveled on to the brain and has been processed by higher neuronal structures. Spinal reflexes also play an important role in posture and postural adjustments.

Another type of spinal reflex is the *patellar reflex* (also known as the knee-jerk reflex). To visualize the patellar reflex, imagine being in your doctor's office for a physical exam. The doctor strikes you below the kneecap with a rubber mallet and, without your conscious effort, your leg extends, or moves away from the body (Figure 2.16). The receptors in the extensor muscle of the leg react to the sudden stretching that occurs when the tendon below your kneecap is struck by the mallet. The sensory message is carried to the spinal cord by sensory neurons that synapse with the motor neurons that control the same leg extensor muscle. Sudden stretching of this muscle, caused by the blow from the hammer, causes your leg to extend. The patellar reflex plays an important role in maintaining posture and allowing you to stay upright. It also can reveal some motor disorders. For example, a hyperactive

gray matter The cell bodies of neurons.

white matter Myelinated axons of neurons.

spinal reflex A reflex in which afferent sensory input enters the spinal cord and then directly innervates an efferent motor neuron.

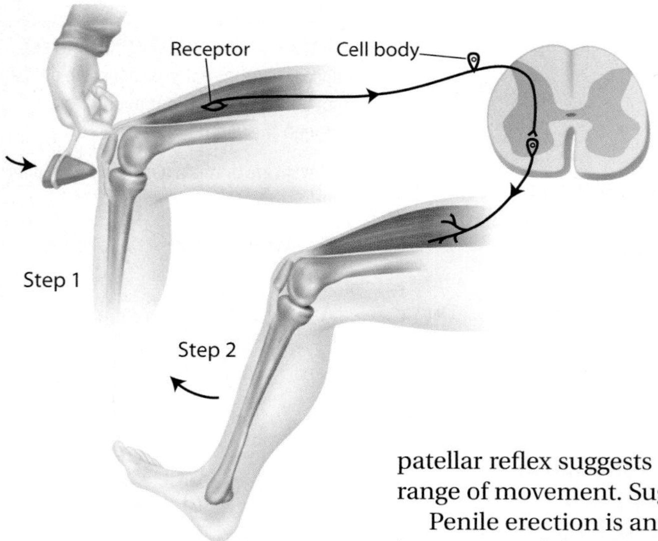

Figure 2.16

The patellar or knee-jerk reflex When the doctor strikes your knee (step 1), a sensory neuron is activated and carries the message to the spinal cord. Here, the sensory nerve synapses with a motor neuron. Activation of the motor neuron carries the message to a muscle in your thigh. Contraction of this muscle causes your leg to extend (step 2).

➜ **What can a doctor learn by testing your patellar reflex?**

patellar reflex suggests *spasticity,* a motor disorder characterized by a slow, limited range of movement. Sugar Ray, by contrast, has no patellar reflex.

Penile erection is another spinal reflex. Because the erection reflex involves the lower part of the spinal cord, stimulation by a touch to the genitals can elicit an erection in men with injuries to the upper part of the cord, but not in men with certain lower spinal cord injuries.

➤Checkpoint

What is the difference between white matter and gray matter in the spinal cord? Describe a spinal reflex. What benefit is provided by the spinal reflex short-circuiting the brain?

REVIEW

- Thirty-one pairs of spinal nerves carry sensory information to and motor information away from the spinal cord. The spinal cord relays the sensory information to the brain and the motor information from the brain to the muscles.
- The spinal cord is composed of gray matter, or neuronal cell bodies, and white matter, or axons, which appear white because they are myelinated.
- Spinal reflexes allow sensory input to affect motor neurons directly, without processing by the brain. The withdrawal reflex, the patellar (knee-jerk) reflex, and penile erection are examples of spinal reflexes.

The Central Nervous System: The Brain

We can think of the brain as having three main functions: recognizing detected sensory events, analyzing the information and deciding how to respond, and executing the appropriate response. Take a moment to review the four-stage model of the behavioral functions of the nervous system that we introduced at the beginning of the chapter (see Figures 2.1, 2.3). Detecting events (stage 1) is the function of the peripheral nervous system (or the CNS in the case of vision). This sensory information travels to specific parts of the brain for recognition (stage 2).

The significance of an event depends not only on the recognition of its physical characteristics but also on the ability to recall relevant past experiences and to detect the emotional and motivational states accompanying the experience of the present event. For example, suppose a friend asks you to go with him to a new movie playing at the local theater. The question is detected by your ears and transmitted to your brain. Your brain recognizes the question's meaning, enables you to remember previous trips to the movie theater and previous outings with this friend, and considers these memories along with information about whether you feel like going today (your emotional and motivational states).

This analysis yields a decision (stage 3) to go or not go to the movie. After the brain decides how to respond to a specific sensory input, it then executes the decision (stage 4) by controlling the muscles that produce the desired motor response (in this case, saying either yes or no).

Table 2.2
The Major Structures of the Human Brain and Their Primary Functions

Structure	Function
Hindbrain	
Myelencephalon	
Medulla oblongata	Controls vital functions; relays sensory information to thalamus
Metencephalon	
Cerebellum	Coordinates complex motor responses
Pons	Relays sensory information to cerebellum and thalamus
Raphé system	Controls sleep-wake cycle
Midbrain	
Mesencephalon	
Tectum	
Inferior colliculi	Relay auditory information, auditory localization
Superior colliculi	Mediate visual reflexes, visual localization, gross pattern discrimination
Tegmentum	
Red nucleus	Controls basic body and limb movements
Reticular formation	Controls arousal and consciousness
Substantia nigra	Integrates voluntary movements
Forebrain	
Diencephalon	
Epithalamus	
Habenula	Functions in olfaction
Pineal gland	Coordinates seasonal rhythms
Thalamus	
Lateral geniculate nucleus	Relays visual information to cerebral cortex
Medial geniculate nucleus	Relays auditory information to cerebral cortex
Ventrolateral nucleus	Relays information from cerebellum to motor cortex
Hypothalamus	Detects need states; controls pituitary hormone production and release
Pituitary gland	Controls other glands (anterior lobe); releases oxytocin and vasopressin (posterior lobe)
Telencephalon	
Limbic system	
Amygdala	Controls anger and fear
Cingulate gyrus	Elicits positive and negative emotional responses
Hippocampus	Participates in memory storage and retrieval
Basal ganglia	Integrate voluntary movement; maintain posture and muscle tone
Caudate nucleus, Putamen }	Corpus striatum
Globus pallidus	
Cerebral cortex	
Occipital lobes	Control vision
Parietal lobes	Control skin senses, spatial functions
Temporal lobes	Control audition, language in left hemisphere, visual functions
Frontal lobes	Control motor functions, planning, speech in left hemisphere

But this is by no means all that the brain does. Activities such as dreaming and remembering can occur without sensory input and may or may not lead to a motor response. Think about it (thinking is another brain function): The brain is a complex, fascinating organ that has inspired entire disciplines and a multitude of books—including this one.

Now that we have covered in a very general way the major brain functions, we will discuss brain structure and how the various components of this organ work together. The three main divisions of the brain are the hindbrain, the midbrain, and the forebrain (Table 2.2).

The Hindbrain

Located just above the spinal cord is the **hindbrain** (Figure 2.17), which has two major divisions: the myelencephalon and the metencephalon. The **myelencephalon** (from the Greek *myelos,* "marrow," and *enkephalos,* "in the head") contains the **medulla oblongata** ("oblong marrow"), located rostral to the spinal cord. The medulla controls basic functions essential to life, such as respiration and heart rate. It also stimulates reflexive responses (via cranial nerves) such as coughing, sneezing, vomiting, and salivating. Sensory information from some of the cranial nerves is received in the medulla oblongata and then relayed to higher structures, such as the thalamus. For example, audition first enters the brain at this level. Sensory information from the spinal cord is also relayed through the medulla, and motor output passes through this area on its way to the spinal cord. The failure of activity in such essential autonomic nuclei as those that control breathing and heartbeat is fatal. Presidential candidate and former attorney general Robert F. Kennedy died from damage to the medulla caused by a gunshot wound to the side of the head.

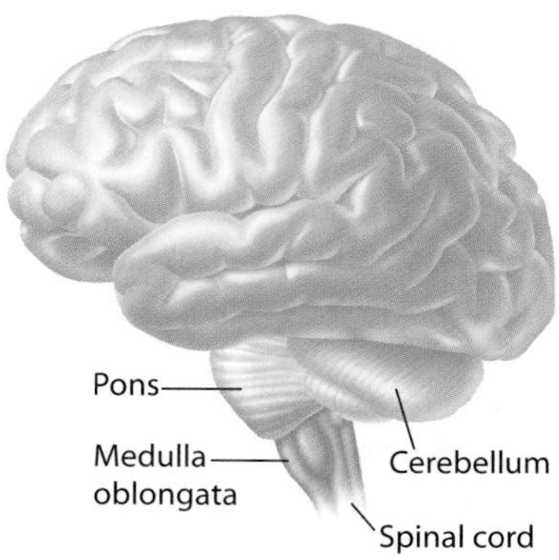

Figure 2.17
The hindbrain Key structures in the hindbrain are the medulla oblongata (shown in red), pons (purple), and cerebellum (green).

➔ **Describe the hindbrain's location in relation to the spinal cord and midbrain, using the anatomical directions you learned earlier in the chapter. What might be the effect on a person of damage to the medulla?**

The **reticular formation** (sometimes called the *reticular activating system* or *RAS*) is a diffuse, interconnected network of neurons that begins in the medulla, extends through the midbrain, and continues into higher brain structures. It maintains consciousness and plays an important role in arousal (Jones, 2003; Steriade, 1996). The role of the reticular formation is addressed more fully in Chapter 9.

The next region of the hindbrain is the **metencephalon** (*meta* is Greek for "between"). The two major structures of the metencephalon are the pons and the cerebellum. The **pons** (Latin for "bridge"; so named because many fibers cross from one side of the brain to the other at this point) is superior (anterior) to the medulla; many neural messages pass through this structure on their way from the sensory receptors via cranial nerves and the spinal cord, and from the areas of the cerebral cortex controlling movement to the cerebellum. Additional neural messages travel through the pons to relay information on arousal, sleep, and dreaming to higher brain structures, such as the thalamus.

The **cerebellum** (Latin for "little brain") is involved in the development and coordination of movement. This structure provides information about body and limb position. It receives information from other brain structures about intended movement and from sense organs about actual motor responses. The cerebellum, then, compares actual and intended movements and makes adjustments to correct movement errors. According to one interpretation of its function, the cerebellum develops representations of moving systems, including our body, its parts, and objects outside the body (Paulin, 1997). Through cerebellar influence, awkward movements become fluid, skilled actions, and it should not surprise you to learn that alcohol intoxication affects cerebellar functioning. By the same token, people with cerebellar damage may appear to be intoxicated. We will have much more to say about the important roles of the cerebellum in movement (Chapter 8) and in certain types of motor learning, such as eyeblink conditioning (Chapter 14).

The **raphé system** is a group of nuclei located along the midline of the hindbrain between the medulla and the midbrain. The raphé system plays a crucial role in the sleep-wake cycle (Gao & others, 2002), which we discuss in Chapter 9.

hindbrain The division of the brain just above the spinal cord that contains the medulla oblongata, the pons, the cerebellum, and the raphé system.

myelencephalon One of two divisions of the hindbrain; contains the medulla oblongata.

medulla oblongata A hindbrain structure located just rostral to the spinal cord; controls essential functions such as respiration and heart rate.

reticular formation A network of neurons that controls arousal and consciousness.

metencephalon One of two divisions of the hindbrain; contains the cerebellum and the pons.

pons A hindbrain structure located superior to the medulla; relays sensory information to the cerebellum and thalamus.

cerebellum A hindbrain structure located posterior to the medulla; develops and coordinates complex movement.

raphé system A group of nuclei located along the midline of the hindbrain between the medulla and midbrain; controls the sleep-wake cycle.

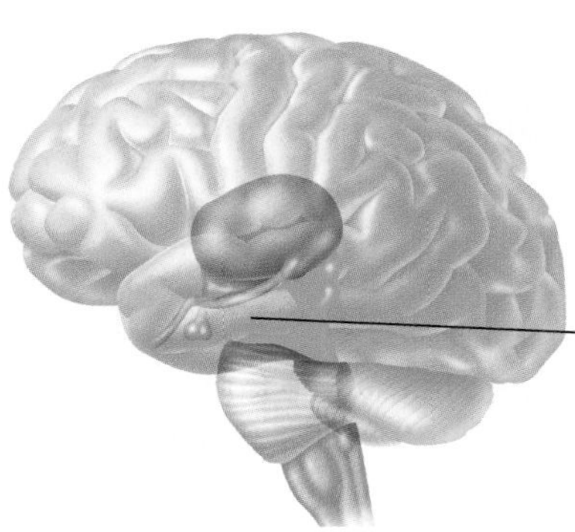

Figure 2.18
The midbrain The midbrain (shown in yellow) lies between the hindbrain and the forebrain.

→ **Name the major structures of the midbrain's tectum and tegmentum.**

midbrain A division of the CNS that contains the tectum and the tegmentum.

tectum A midbrain structure that controls simple reflexes and orients eye and ear movements.

superior colliculus A structure in the tectum that relays visual information.

inferior colliculus A structure in the tectum that relays auditory information.

tegmentum A division of the midbrain that contains the substantia nigra, the red nucleus, and the reticular formation.

substantia nigra A structure in the tegmentum that is involved in the integration of voluntary movements.

red nucleus A structure in the tegmentum that controls basic body and limb movements.

brain stem A group of structures consisting of the hindbrain (minus the cerebellum) and the midbrain.

The Midbrain

Located above (or anterior to) the pons, the **midbrain** (or *mesencephalon,* from the Greek *mesos,* "middle") has two parts: the tectum and the tegmentum (Table 2.2 and Figure 2.18). The **tectum** (Latin for "roof") contains neurons that relay visual and auditory information and control simple reflexes such as blinking. Visual information is relayed through the **superior colliculus** ("little hills"), and auditory information is relayed through the **inferior colliculus.** The tectum also controls eye and ear movements that orient an animal to external stimuli and is generally concerned with detecting where something is.

The **tegmentum** ("floor covering") contains three main structures: the substantia nigra and the red nucleus, which are components of the motor system, and the reticular formation. The **substantia nigra** is involved in the integration of voluntary movements. Damage to this area is almost certainly responsible for Sugar Ray's parkinsonian (Parkinson's-like, but with a different origin) symptoms. The **red nucleus** is involved in controlling basic body movements, such as postural adjustments.

As a unit, the hindbrain (minus the cerebellum) and the midbrain are often referred to as the **brain stem,** because these structures contain all the connections between the spinal cord and the cerebral cortex (Figure 2.19). The structures also form the "stem" from which the two hemispheres of the forebrain branch.

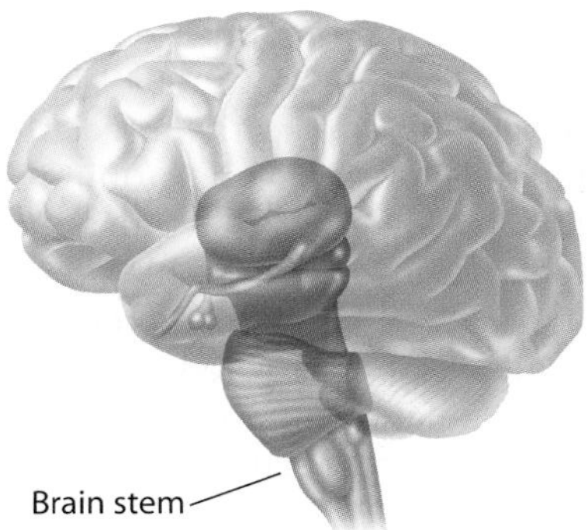

Figure 2.19
The brain stem The brain stem (shown in blue) consists of the hindbrain (minus the cerebellum) and the midbrain.

→ **Why is this portion of the brain called the brain stem?**

REVIEW

- The three major divisions of the brain are the hindbrain, the midbrain, and the forebrain.
- The hindbrain contains the medulla oblongata, the pons, the cerebellum, and the raphé system.
- The medulla oblongata controls breathing and heart rate and stimulates basic reflexive responses. Audition and some other sensory information enter the brain at this level, and the reticular formation begins here. The reticular formation, which connects with higher brain structures, maintains consciousness and produces arousal.
- The pons brings information to the cerebellum and relays messages to higher brain structures. The cerebellum develops and coordinates complex movements. The raphé system influences the sleep-wake cycle.
- The midbrain contains the tectum and tegmentum. The tectum, which includes the superior and inferior colliculi, receives and relays visual and auditory information and controls simple reflexes.

Checkpoint

Explain this statement: "A person would probably survive considerable damage to the cerebral cortex but could not survive extensive damage to the medulla oblongata." Describe how the cerebellum coordinates activity with the sensory receptors and with other brain structures. Why is this coordination important? What structures are included in the brain stem? Why do scientists group these structures together?

forebrain The division of the brain containing the telencephalon and the diencephalon.

diencephalon The division of the forebrain containing the epithalamus, thalamus, hypothalamus, and the pituitary gland.

epithalamus An area of the diencephalon above the thalamus; contains the pineal gland and the habenula.

habenula A structure of the epithalamus with olfactory functions.

pineal gland A structure of the epithalamus that controls seasonal rhythms in behavior through its release of melatonin.

melatonin A hormone secreted by the pineal gland in response to daylight and darkness.

thalamus A forebrain structure that relays information from sensory receptors to the cerebral cortex.

medial geniculate nucleus (MGN) A structure in the thalamus that relays auditory information to the cortex.

➤ The tegmentum contains the substantia nigra, the red nucleus, and the reticular formation. The substantia nigra is involved in integrating voluntary motor movements, and damage to this region results in parkinsonian symptoms. The red nucleus controls basic body and limb movements.

The Forebrain

The **forebrain,** located rostral to and surrounding the midbrain, has two divisions: the diencephalon and the telencephalon. Table 2.2 lists the major structures of the forebrain.

The Diencephalon

The **diencephalon** (from the Greek *dia,* "between") contains the epithalamus, the thalamus, the hypothalamus, and the pituitary gland, also known as the hypophysis (Figure 2.20).

The Epithalamus The **epithalamus** (*epi* means "upon" or "over"), lying over the thalamus, the largest structure of the diencephalon, contains the habenula and the pineal gland. The **habenula** has olfactory functions. The **pineal gland,** which Descartes suggested was the point where mind and body interact (Chapter 1), in fact plays a role in seasonal changes in behavior.

The pineal gland manufactures and secretes the hormone **melatonin,** which is covered in more depth in Chapter 9 in our discussion of sleep. In all mammalian species, melatonin production is stimulated by darkness and inhibited by light. Because the amount of lightness and darkness depends on the seasons, the pineal gland, through melatonin secretion, controls seasonal rhythms in behavior (Luboshitzky & Lavie, 1999; Pevet, 2000, 2003; Reiter, 1993). For example, in seasonally breeding mammals, changes in day length provide a signal for reproductive readiness (Goldman, 1999). This signal is mediated by melatonin production and release. In animals that breed in springtime, as the days get longer after the winter, the duration of melatonin release decreases as the nights get shorter. Because melatonin tends to have an antigonadal (against the gonads) effect, lower levels of melatonin mean that the animal becomes increasingly ready to breed as spring approaches. Although some research has suggested that changes in melatonin production are related to puberty and menopause onset in humans, the functional relationship between melatonin and the human reproductive system has not been demonstrated conclusively (Reiter, 1998).

The Thalamus The **thalamus** (from the Greek for "inner chamber") is the main relay station for most sensory messages—visual, auditory, somatosensory, gustatory (Figure 2.21; see also Figure 2.20). This structure receives information from sensory receptors in the PNS (the CNS in the case of vision) and transmits this information to the appropriate cortical structures for analysis. The nuclei in the thalamus that receive information from a specific sensory receptor (e.g., the eye) connect to the sensory areas of the cerebral cortex that recognize that particular sensory message (e.g., the visual message).

Figure 2.20

The diencephalon The epithalamus (not shown), thalamus, hypothalamus, and pituitary gland make up the diencephalon.

➜ What are the two structures of the epithalamus and what are their functions?

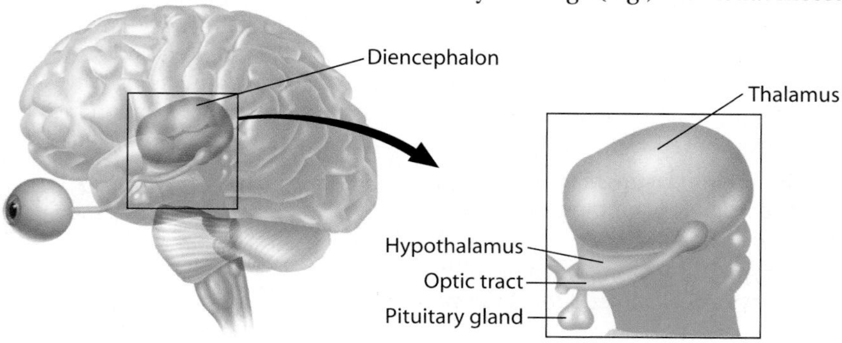

Consider the following example: In his fight with Buster Guidry, Sugar Ray heard the bell signaling the end of the second round (he did not hear any other bells that night). The sensory receptors in his auditory system detected the ringing, and this message was sent through the hindbrain and midbrain structures to the **medial geniculate nucleus (MGN)** of the thalamus (see Figure 2.21). The MGN then transmitted the neural record of the bell ring to the area of Sugar Ray's cortex that recognized the meaning of the sound and motivated him to stop fighting and return to his corner. If the stimulation were visual instead of auditory (e.g., a light flash signaling the end of the round), the sensory receptors in the visual system would send the message to the **lateral geniculate nucleus (LGN)** instead of to the MGN. The LGN would then relay the information to a different cortical area than for audition. As you will see shortly, each sensory modality is understood by a different brain structure.

Although some thalamic neurons send sensory messages to the appropriate higher cortical structures, others connect to cortical areas not related to the reception of sensory information, including to areas mediating motor functions (Herrero & others, 2002). For example, the **ventrolateral nucleus** receives information from the cerebellum and relays this information to the motor cortex, so that the brain can determine whether its decision, or intended movement, corresponds to the actual movement executed. This information allows the cortex to make adjustments to ensure that the message from the motor cortex is executed smoothly by the motor neurons of the PNS. Suppose the motor cortex executes a message for you to reach for your pen on the top of your desk, but your hand starts heading away from the pen. Your cerebellum recognizes the movement is off target and sends a message to your motor cortex via the thalamus, so that you change the course of your movement as needed. The thalamus is also an important area for processing certain pain sensations (Schnitzler & Ploner, 2000) and organizing the sleep-wake cycle (Moore, 1997; Novak & others, 2000).

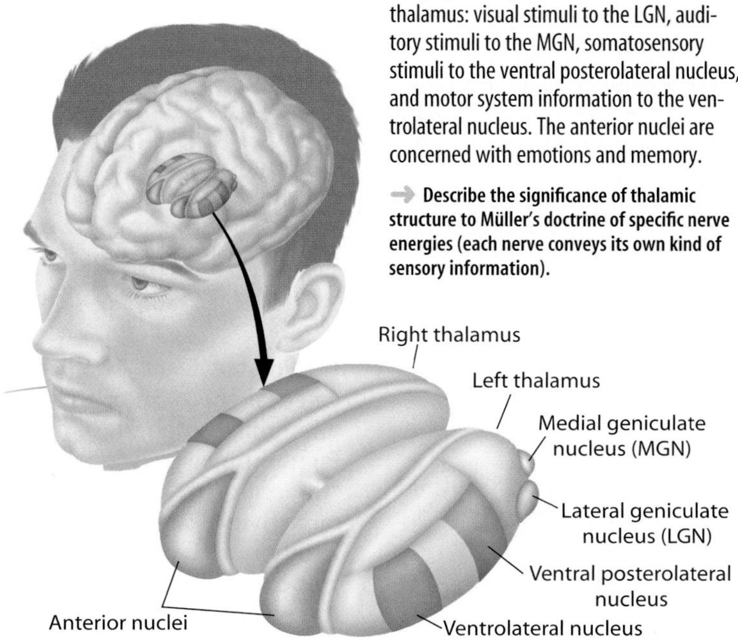

Figure 2.21

The thalamus Neural messages carrying sensory information travel to the thalamus: visual stimuli to the LGN, auditory stimuli to the MGN, somatosensory stimuli to the ventral posterolateral nucleus, and motor system information to the ventrolateral nucleus. The anterior nuclei are concerned with emotions and memory.

→ **Describe the significance of thalamic structure to Müller's doctrine of specific nerve energies (each nerve conveys its own kind of sensory information).**

lateral geniculate nucleus (LGN) A structure in the thalamus that relays visual information to the cortex.

ventrolateral nucleus A structure in the thalamus that receives information from the cerebellum and relays this information to the motor cortex so the brain can determine whether its intended movement corresponds to the actual movement executed.

hypothalamus A forebrain structure that detects need states and controls pituitary hormone production and release.

The Hypothalamus The **hypothalamus,** a small structure below the thalamus, is about the size of two peanuts and takes up less than 1% of the brain (Hoffman & Swaab, 1994). Despite its diminutive size, the hypothalamus has sensors that can detect internal conditions throughout the body (e.g., levels of glucose, testosterone, or estrogen) that are used as stimuli for such basic motives as hunger, thirst, and sex (e.g., Yamanaka & others, 2003). These internal need states stimulate specific hypothalamic neurons, thereby leading to the motivation to respond in specific ways (Figure 2.22).

Imagine you are walking by a bakery. You smell bread baking, and the aroma makes you hungry; you go inside and buy a fresh, warm loaf. Just outside the

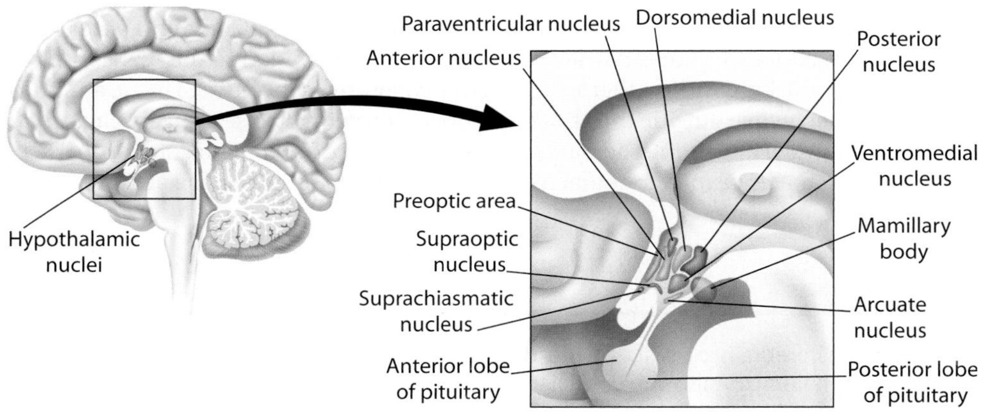

Figure 2.22

The hypothalamus The hypothalamus has many types of nuclei, as shown here. The nuclei are concerned with such motives as hunger, thirst, and sex. The hypothalamus is also intimately associated with the two lobes of the pituitary gland.

→ **What is the significance of the connection between the hypothalamus and the pituitary gland?**

pituitary gland A gland located just ventral to the hypothalamus; divided into two lobes: the anterior pituitary gland and the posterior pituitary gland; also called the hypophysis.

anterior pituitary gland The part of the pituitary gland that manufactures and secretes releasing hormones; also called the adenohypophysis.

posterior pituitary gland The part of the pituitary gland, considered an extension of the hypothalamus, that produces and releases oxytocin and antidiuretic hormone; also called the neurohypophysis.

somatotropin A growth-promoting hormone released by the anterior pituitary; also called growth hormone.

thyroid-stimulating hormone (TSH) An anterior pituitary hormone that regulates the thyroid gland.

adrenocorticotropic hormone (ACTH) An anterior pituitary hormone that stimulates the production and release of hormones by the adrenal cortex.

gonadotropin An anterior pituitary hormone that regulates the activities of the gonads.

oxytocin A posterior pituitary hormone that stimulates uterine contractions and milk secretion in females and causes prostate gland contractions in males.

antidiuretic hormone (ADH) A posterior pituitary hormone that helps conserve bodily fluids by concentrating urine; also called vasopressin.

bakery, you sit on a bench and tear off a piece of the loaf and consume it on the spot. Why did you feel hungry when you smelled the bread? Generally, smelling food stimulates the lateral hypothalamus, which produces sensations of hunger and motivates eating (Klein, 2002). You will learn more about the important influence of the hypothalamus on hunger and eating (Chapter 10) and on sexual behavior (Chapter 11).

Because of its intimate association with and control of the autonomic nervous system, the hypothalamus has been called the "head ganglion of the autonomic nervous system." It is also involved in motivated behaviors such as copulating, fighting, fleeing, and eating and drinking. The hypothalamus has an additional important function: It controls the production and release of pituitary hormones from the pituitary gland, located just ventral to it. Finally, through one of its nuclei, the suprachiasmatic nucleus, the hypothalamus is involved in the control of biological rhythms.

The Pituitary Gland The **pituitary gland** (the Latin *pituita* means "phlegm") is located at the base of the brain, above the nose. Its location suggests why early anatomists might have thought the function of the pituitary gland was to manufacture phlegm, or mucus. The pituitary is also called the *hypophysis* (Greek for "undergrowth"). In terms of one of its functions—the regulation of other glandular activity—the pituitary is often called the "master gland of the body." This designation actually refers only to the anterior part of the pituitary. The pituitary gland has two major parts: the **anterior pituitary gland** (or *adenohypophysis*) and the **posterior pituitary gland** (or *neurohypophysis*) (Figure 2.22). The hypothalamus influences the anterior pituitary gland through a system of blood vessels called the *hypophyseal portal system*. Hormones known as releasing hormones are produced in the hypothalamus and released into the portal system to travel to the anterior pituitary. There, they stimulate the production and release of several anterior pituitary hormones, which include somatotropin, thyrotropin, adrenocorticotropin, and the gonadotropins.

Somatotropin, also called *growth hormone,* is a general growth-promoting hormone; its presence at certain stages of development is necessary for normal growth. Too much can produce a distorted growth condition called acromegaly; too little results in dwarfism. **Thyroid-stimulating hormone (TSH)** regulates the action of the thyroid gland, which is concerned with the body's metabolism. **Adrenocorticotropic hormone (ACTH)** is produced in times of stress to stimulate the production and release of hormones by the outer part of the adrenal gland (the adrenal cortex). The **gonadotropins** regulate the activities of the gonads—the testes of the male and the ovaries of the female.

Unlike the anterior pituitary, the posterior pituitary does not manufacture the substances it secretes. The two chemicals it releases—**oxytocin** and **antidiuretic hormone (ADH)**—are made in two hypothalamic nuclei: the paraventricular nuclei and the supraoptic nuclei, respectively (Figure 2.22). Oxytocin stimulates uterine contractions during labor and milk secretion by the mammary glands (in males, oxytocin is responsible for prostate gland contractions) (Chapter 4). ADH (also called *vasopressin*) helps conserve bodily fluids by stimulating the reabsorption of water by the kidneys. In other words, ADH concentrates the urine. The next time you have been active outside on a hot day, notice the color of your urine; because of the action of ADH, it should be darker than usual. A lack of ADH results in a disorder called *diabetes insipidus,* characterized by colorless (insipid) urine and great thirst.

➤Checkpoint

Explain the role of the thalamus in transmitting visual signals. Why would obesity researchers be interested in studying the functions of the hypothalamus? Why is the anterior pituitary called the "master gland of the body"?

REVIEW

- The forebrain consists of the diencephalon and the telencephalon. The diencephalon contains the epithalamus, the thalamus, the hypothalamus, and the pituitary gland.

- The epithalamus consists of the habenula, which has olfactory functions, and the pineal gland, which manufactures and releases melatonin in response to light. The pineal gland regulates reproductive readiness in seasonally breeding mammals.
- The thalamus receives sensory messages and relays them to the proper part of the cerebral cortex for processing. It also works with the cerebellum to coordinate and evaluate movement.
- The hypothalamus detects need states, such as hunger and thirst. It also controls the production and release of pituitary hormones.
- The pituitary gland, or hypophysis, has two major parts: the anterior lobe and the posterior lobe. The anterior lobe releases hormones that regulate the functioning of the glands of the body, whereas the posterior lobe releases oxytocin (uterine and prostate gland contractions) and antidiuretic hormone (concentrates urine).

telencephalon The division of the forebrain that consists of the cerebral cortex, limbic system, and basal ganglia.

limbic system A group of forebrain structures, surrounding the brain stem, that processes emotional expression and the storage and retrieval of memories.

amygdala A limbic system structure at the base of the temporal lobe that processes the emotions of anger and fear.

cingulate gyrus A limbic system structure involved in positive and negative emotional response.

The Telencephalon

The **telencephalon,** or "end brain," is the other main division of the forebrain. It consists of the limbic system, the basal ganglia, and the cerebral cortex.

The Limbic System Sportscasters often speak of "the thrill of victory and the agony of defeat." The emotional impact of these two experiences is related to activity in the **limbic system,** which is the evolutionarily older part of the telencephalon. Other emotions, such as anger, frustration, and fear, are also governed by limbic system structures. We have more to say about the limbic system's role in emotions in Chapter 12.

The limbic system is not a single brain structure but a group of structures surrounding the brain stem (the Latin *limbus* means "edge" or "border"). Some important limbic system structures are the amygdala, the cingulate gyrus, and the hippocampus (Figure 2.23).

The **amygdala,** located at the base of the temporal lobe, plays a central role in our experience of the emotions of anger and fear (Hariri & others, 2000; Skuse & others, 2003). Destruction of the amygdala can produce either heightened defensiveness or extreme passivity, depending on the particular region destroyed. This observation suggests that certain parts of the amygdala trigger anger or fear, whereas others inhibit these emotions.

The **cingulate gyrus** has a significant role in the control of emotional behavior (Hadland & others, 2003; Phan & others, 2004) and in the subjective experience of the unpleasantness of pain (Rainville, 2002). It receives input from many structures, including the decision-making centers of the cerebral cortex, the limbic system structures that elicit specific emotions, and the neural systems controlling movement. Activity in the cingulate gyrus produces either positive or negative emotional responses and plays an important role in attention.

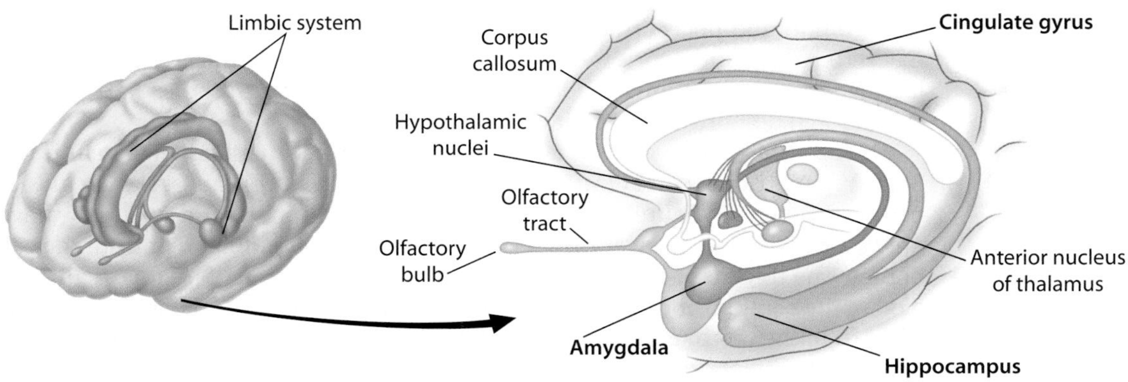

Figure 2.23
The limbic system The amygdala, the cingulate gyrus, and the hippocampus are clustered around the brain stem.

How does the limbic system contribute to the thrill of victory and the agony of defeat?

DAVID YOUNG-WOLFF/GETTY IMAGES

Alzheimer's disease is often harder on the caregiver than on the person with the disease. We discuss Alzheimer's disease at greater length in Chapter 14.

The **hippocampus** (Latin for "seahorse") plays an essential role in memory processes (Manns & others, 2003; Teng & others, 2000). Hippocampal damage is linked to an inability to store and later recall previously acquired information. As you might expect, this area of the brain is particularly affected in Alzheimer's disease. The role of the hippocampus in memory storage and retrieval is discussed in detail in Chapter 14.

The Basal Ganglia The **basal ganglia** consist of three large nuclei: the caudate nucleus, the putamen, and the globus pallidus (Figure 2.24). Together, the caudate nucleus and the putamen are sometimes referred to as the *corpus striatum* ("striped body") because of the appearance of this brain area in a sagittal section. The basal ganglia play a crucial role in initiating voluntary movements and maintaining posture and muscle tone (Takakusaki & others, 2004) and in learning or choosing appropriate motor or behavioral programs (Groenewegen, 2003).

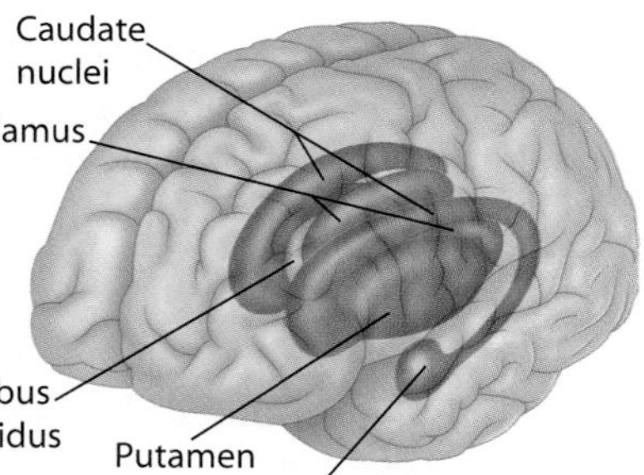

Figure 2.24
The basal ganglia The three large nuclei—the caudate nucleus, putamen, and globus pallidus—have widespread connections to the cerebral cortex and midbrain.

➡ **How are the basal ganglia involved in Parkinson's disease and Huntington's disease?**

The basal ganglia receive input from the substantia nigra and the cerebral cortex and send messages back to both the midbrain and the cortex. Degeneration of the dopamine-producing (dopamine is a neurotransmitter) neurons that link the substantia nigra to the basal ganglia leads to Parkinson's disease. This disorder is characterized by rigidity, tremors at rest, and difficulty integrating movement. Damage to this fiber tract system, as from repeated blows to the head, produces Parkinson's-like symptoms; Sugar Ray has parkinsonian symptoms rather than Parkinson's disease. Degeneration of neurons in the caudate nucleus and putamen leads to Huntington's disease, a hereditary disorder characterized by uncontrollable, jerky limb movements and severe dementia. The movements appear to be fragments of normally purposeful actions.

Checkpoint

What would be the effects of a lack of input from the substantia nigra to the basal ganglia? Describe the results of damage to the connections between the basal ganglia and the substantia nigra of the tegmentum.

The Cerebral Cortex Much of what we would see if the top of your skull were removed is the **cerebral cortex** (cortex means "rind" or "outer covering"), the outer layer of the brain that is responsible for higher mental processes (Figure 2.25). The cerebral cortex is sometimes divided into sensory areas, motor areas, and so-called association areas: certain areas responsible for the perception of sensory events (sensory detection areas), others controlling motor movements (motor execution areas), and the remainder enabling us to think, reason, and communicate (recognition and decision areas). This final functional division was once designated the association cortex, because it was assumed to be the site of the stimulus-response associations made during learning. Among others, Karl Lashley (1929/1963) demonstrated the fallacy of this notion.

The cerebral cortex contains layers of cell bodies that run parallel to its surface. Some regions of the cortex (referred to as the neocortex) contain six layers, designated I through VI (Figure 2.26), others contain fewer than six, and still others have only a single layer. The layers are separated by fibers extending to or from the cell bodies. The thickness of each layer is related to the function of that particular region of the cerebral cortex. For example, the thickness of cortical layers V and VI is greatest in the motor cortex, because that is where the large cells that control voluntary movement originate. By contrast, cortical layer IV is thickest in the primary sensory areas for vision, audition, taste, and the somatosenses, where the axons

hippocampus A limbic system structure that processes or contributes to memory storage and retrieval.

basal ganglia A collective forebrain structure that integrates voluntary movement; consists of three nuclei: the caudate nucleus, the putamen, and the globus pallidus.

cerebral cortex The outer layer of the forebrain that processes sensory information, controls thinking and decision making, stores and retrieves memories, and initiates motor responses.

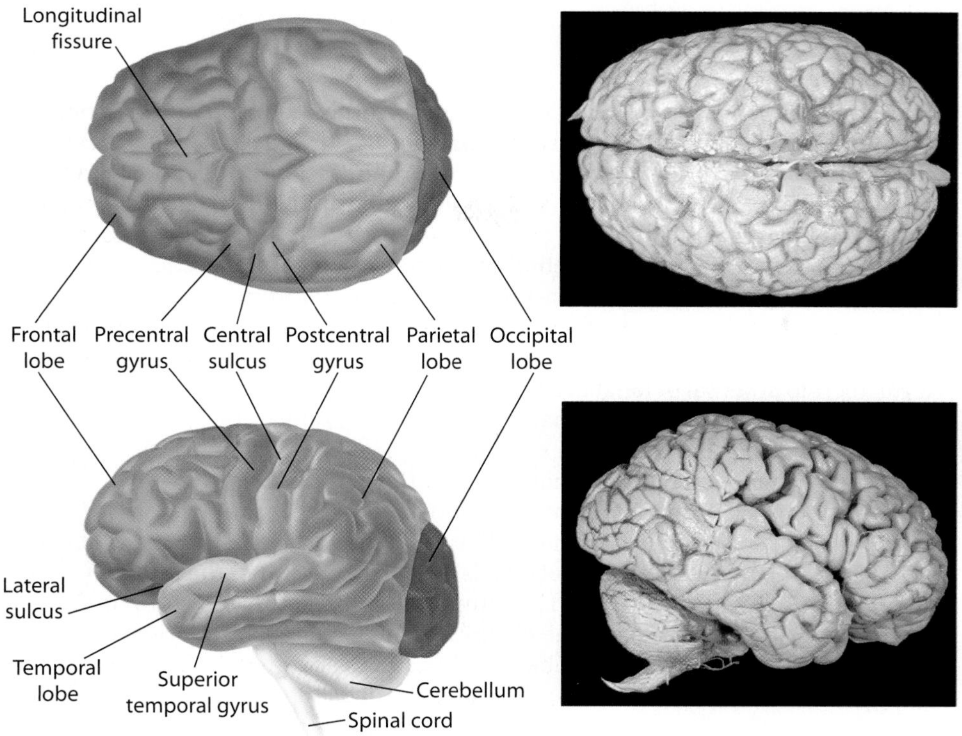

Figure 2.25

The cerebral cortex, dorsal and lateral views The two cerebral hemispheres are separated by the longitudinal fissure and connected by the cerebral commissures, the largest of which is the corpus callosum (not shown). The central sulcus separates the frontal and parietal lobes; the lateral sulcus separates the temporal and frontal lobes. The precentral gyrus is also known as the motor cortex, and the postcentral gyrus as the somatosensory cortex.

➡ **What is meant by lateralization of function?**

from sensory nuclei in the thalamus terminate. Because layer IV is where sensory information is received, it is absent in the motor cortex. We have more to say about the structure of the sensory systems in Chapters 6 and 7, and about the motor system in Chapter 8.

The cortex consists of the right and the left hemispheres, separated by the **longitudinal fissure** (Figure 2.25). The two hemispheres are connected by axons

longitudinal fissure A deep groove that separates the right and left hemispheres.

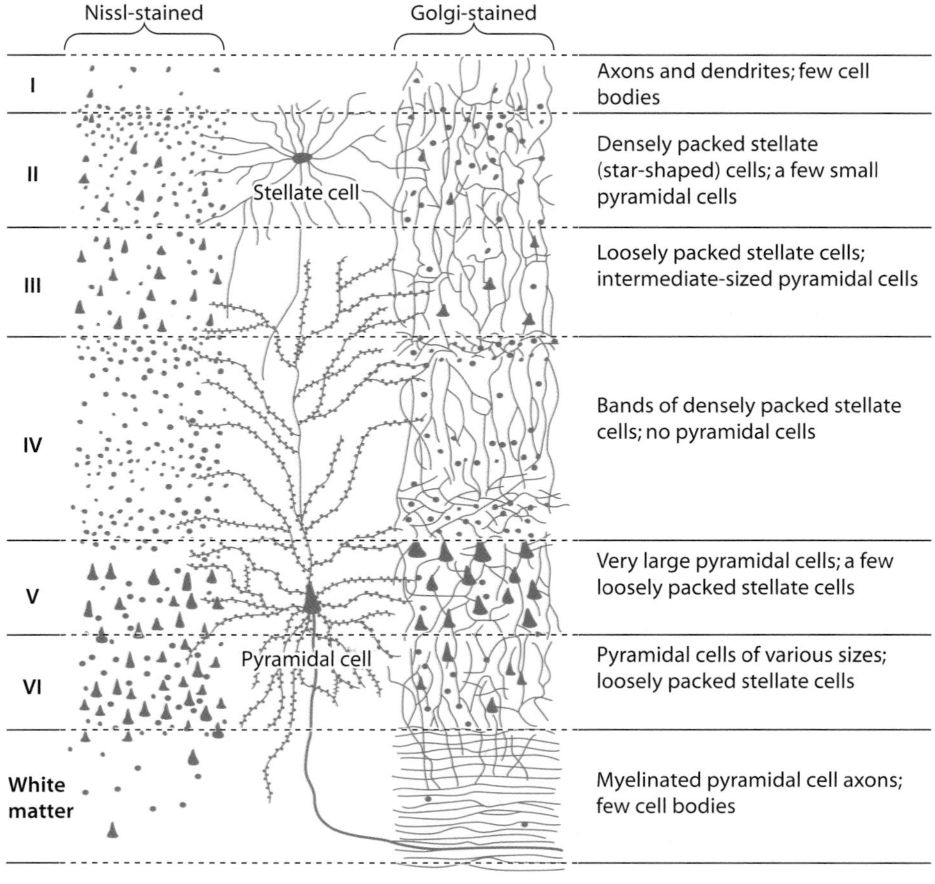

Figure 2.26

The six layers of the neocortex Shown here are the different types of cells that constitute the neocortex, the cerebral cortex that has all six cell layers. The Nissl stain colors cell bodies; the Golgi stain selectively colors a few neurons in each slice of brain tissue.

➡ **What is white matter? What makes it white?**

cerebral commissure A fiber tract that connects the two hemispheres of the brain.

corpus callosum The largest of the cerebral commissures.

contralateral control The process by which one side of the brain controls movements on the opposite side of the body.

lateralization of function The differentiation of the functions of the two hemispheres of the brain.

lateral sulcus A deep groove that separates the temporal from the frontal and parietal lobes of the cerebral cortex.

central sulcus A deep groove that separates the anterior and posterior halves of the cerebral cortex.

occipital lobe The lobe located in the most posterior part of the cerebral cortex; responsible for the analysis of visual stimuli.

primary visual cortex An area in the occipital lobe that receives visual information from the thalamus.

parietal lobe The lobe of the cerebral cortex located between the central sulcus and the occipital lobe; responsible for the analysis of somatosensory stimuli.

somatosensory cortex An area in the anterior part of the parietal lobe that receives information about touch, pain, pressure, temperature, and body position from the thalamus.

sensory neglect A condition resulting from parietal lobe damage (usually on the right side) in which a person shows clumsiness or neglect of the side of the body opposite the damage.

that cross over and synapse with neurons in the other hemisphere. The connecting axons are grouped into **cerebral commissures,** the largest of which is the **corpus callosum.** Note the *convolutions* in the hemispheres; the purpose of this feature is to increase the brain's surface area (and number of cortical neurons) without increasing its volume.

The left hemisphere of the cerebral cortex controls motor responses on the right side of the body, and the right hemisphere controls motor movement on the left side of the body—an arrangement known as **contralateral control** (Chapter 8). There is a great deal of evidence indicating that, for most people, the left hemisphere plays a greater role in verbal or language functions and the right hemisphere has a greater influence on nonverbal, visual-spatial functions (Gazzaniga, 1995). We have much more to say about **lateralization of function** (the idea that the two hemispheres have somewhat different functional specializations) in Chapter 13.

Each hemisphere is divided into four lobes—occipital, parietal, temporal, and frontal (Figure 2.25)—which are named for the bones of the skull under which they lie. As its name implies, the frontal lobe is the most anterior of the four lobes, with the parietal lobe posterior to it. The temporal lobe is lateral, or more to the side (where your temples are), and the occipital lobe is the most posterior of the four lobes. Except for the occipital lobe, the lobes are separated from each other by grooves, or *sulci* (singular: sulcus). The **lateral sulcus** separates the temporal lobe from the frontal and parietal lobes, and the **central sulcus** divides the frontal and parietal lobes. You may also encounter the term *fissure,* which is sometimes used to denote a particularly deep groove. In some cases, the same groove has names using each of the terms; for example, the lateral sulcus is also known as the fissure of Sylvius (or Sylvian fissure), and the central sulcus is also called the fissure of Rolando. Let us briefly examine the structure and function of each lobe.

The role of the **occipital lobe** is the easiest to characterize: Its primary function is the analysis of visual information. Information from the visual sensory receptors arrives at the **primary visual cortex** via pathways from the LGN in the thalamus. Destruction of the primary visual cortex produces absolute cortical blindness (Stoerig & Cowey, 1997), in which a person is able to see light but is unable to recognize visual patterns (such as the shape of an object) in the part of the visual scene that sends information to the damaged area of the occipital lobe. For example, damage to the left occipital lobe would produce cortical blindness in the right visual field. We discuss the role of the occipital lobe in vision in Chapter 6.

The **parietal lobe** is located between the central sulcus and the occipital lobe, dorsal to the temporal lobe (Figure 2.25). The anterior portion of the parietal lobe is called the **somatosensory cortex,** because sensory information about touch, pain, pressure, temperature, and body position is analyzed in this area. The posterior portion of the parietal lobe receives visual information from the occipital lobe and is involved in spatial perception. The neurons of the somatosensory cortex are organized in such a way that the body is represented in an orderly, but upside-down fashion; that is, information from the toes is transmitted to the "top" of the parietal lobe (which is actually down in the longitudinal fissure), and sensory information from the mouth travels to the bottom of the lobe.

As you can see from Figure 2.27, sensory information from the face and hands is overrepresented in the human somatosensory cortex, reflecting the relative significance of information coming from these areas of the body. In humans, facial stimulation provides significant information; we can feel happy or sad depending on feedback provided by our facial muscles, which are differentially reactive to environmental circumstances. In other species, other parts of the body are overrepresented. In bats, for example, which use their feet to hang from trees, a relatively greater area of the parietal lobes is devoted to the representation of their feet (Calford & others, 1985).

Individuals with parietal lobe damage, particularly on the right side of the brain, often show clumsiness or neglect on the side of their body opposite the damage, a condition known as **sensory neglect,** or *visuospatial neglect* (Halligan & Marshall, 2001). They also have difficulty identifying objects by touch, and they cannot draw

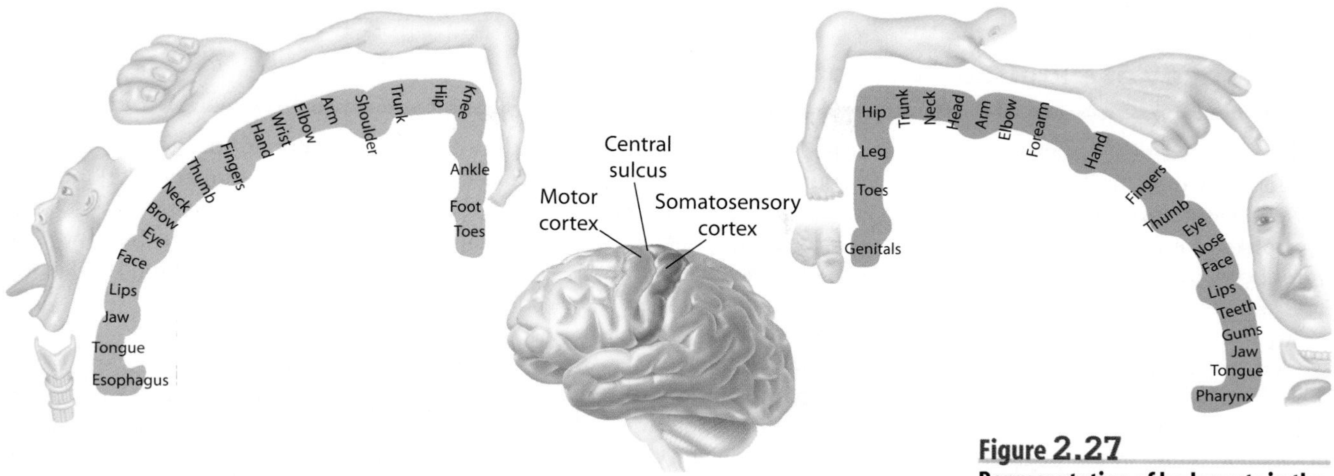

Figure 2.27
Representation of body parts in the somatosensory cortex and motor cortex These "maps" show the areas of the somatosensory cortex that receive sensory information from various parts of the body and the areas of the motor cortex that send messages to various muscles. Notice the unequal representation of the face, hands, and feet in both the motor cortex and somatosensory cortex.

➜ **Why is the face overrepresented in both the motor cortex and the somatosensory cortex?**

or follow maps or describe how to get from one place to another. As just one illustration of this problem: An individual will eat half the food on a plate and then complain about not having enough to eat, even though half the food is still there. If the plate is rotated so that the uneaten portion of the meal is now on the nonneglected side, the person will eat half of what is left, neglecting the remainder.

Separated from the frontal and parietal lobes by the lateral sulcus, the **temporal lobe** contains the **primary auditory cortex** as well as a visual area and language centers (Figure 2.25). Information from the auditory receptors (in the ears) arrives at the auditory cortex by way of the MGN in the thalamus. Destruction of the primary auditory cortex in both hemispheres leads to cortical deafness, an inability to recognize sounds (such as the sound of a baby's cry; Brookshire, 1997). Auditory messages are sent from the primary auditory cortex to an adjacent part of the left temporal lobe for analysis. If the stimulus is verbal, it is interpreted in a system of structures that includes Wernicke's area (see Figure 1.7), and damage to this area may lead to profound language comprehension difficulties. We have more to say about the temporal lobe and language comprehension in Chapter 13.

Visual object recognition is also a temporal lobe function, as is the processing of information about balance and equilibrium transmitted from the vestibular organs of the inner ear. The temporal lobe may also be involved in our emotional reaction to events. Klüver and Bucy (1939) found that destruction of the temporal lobe, which included the amygdala underneath the temporal cortex, caused male monkeys to exhibit dramatic behavioral changes, including a lack of understanding of the meaning of previously familiar visual stimuli, compulsive orality, and bizarre sexual behavior (e.g., attempts to mate with other species). Comparable changes have been observed in human males who have sustained temporal lobe damage (Terzian & Ore, 1955) and may even occur after mild head injury and unilateral temporal lobe damage (Salim & others, 2002). More about the role of the temporal lobe and the amygdala in the control of aggressive behavior appears in Chapter 12 and of sexual behavior in Chapter 11.

Located anterior to the parietal lobe and dorsal to the temporal lobe is the **frontal lobe,** the largest of the four lobes (Figure 2.25). The area of the frontal lobe just anterior to the central sulcus is called the **motor cortex.** As its name suggests, the motor cortex is involved in the control of voluntary body movements, and, like the somatosensory cortex, the motor cortex is organized upside down (Figure 2.27). Also as in the somatosensory cortex, the facial muscles are overrepresented in the motor cortex. This allows the production of the precise movements characteristic of different facial expressions, as well as the intricate oral motor movements needed for speech.

The frontal lobe in the left hemisphere also contains Broca's area (see Figure 1.7). This area is implicated in the programming and sequencing of motor movements for speech production. Damage to Broca's area often leads to difficulty with speech production (see Chapters 1 and 13).

temporal lobe The lobe of the cerebral cortex that is ventral to the lateral sulcus; responsible for the analysis of auditory stimuli, language, and some visual information.

primary auditory cortex An area in the temporal lobe that receives auditory information from the thalamus.

frontal lobe The lobe in the most anterior part of the cerebral cortex; responsible for executive functioning and the control of movement.

motor cortex An area in the frontal lobe involved in the control of voluntary body movements.

Box 2.2
The Tragedy of a Prefrontal Lobotomy

In the 1940s and 1950s, about 40,000 people in the United States underwent a surgical procedure called a **prefrontal lobotomy** (Shutts, 1982). Introduced by Portuguese neurologist Egas Moniz (1874–1955) in the late 1930s, the prefrontal lobotomy was intended to make psychotic patients more manageable at a time before the introduction of the first effective antipsychotic drugs. In the operation, the surgeon severed the neural connections of the prefrontal cortex, the anterior part of the frontal lobe (Figure 2.28). American neurosurgeon Walter Freeman, shown performing an operation in the figure, was one of the leading popularizers of the technique. Along with James Watts, Freeman performed more than 1,000 such operations by 1950 (Thorne & Henley, 1997). One justification for the operation was evidence indicating that prefrontal damage in chimpanzees made them tamer without influencing sensory or motor functions (Fulton & Jacobsen, 1935). However, the early research that provided this evidence did not measure prefrontal lobe functions accurately, and many prefrontal lobotomies performed on humans were unsuccessful in producing the intended effect, caused unintended side effects, or both.

Subsequent research has shown that the prefrontal cortex plays a central role in thinking, memory, emotional expression, and social inhibition. Individuals with prefrontal damage often show apathy, lack of motivation to plan and initiate behavior, memory deficits, distractibility, lack of facial expressions, and blunted emotionality. Further, prefrontal damage sometimes causes a person to lose social inhibitions and thus to act in a callous and rude fashion. Not all of the symptoms are present in all people with prefrontal damage, and the severity of symptoms varies among individuals. Although the prefrontal lobotomy is rarely performed today, other forms of psychosurgery (surgery designed to treat a psychiatric condition) are still employed, and Pedrosa-Sanchez and Sola (2003) envision a promising future for psychiatric neurosurgery.

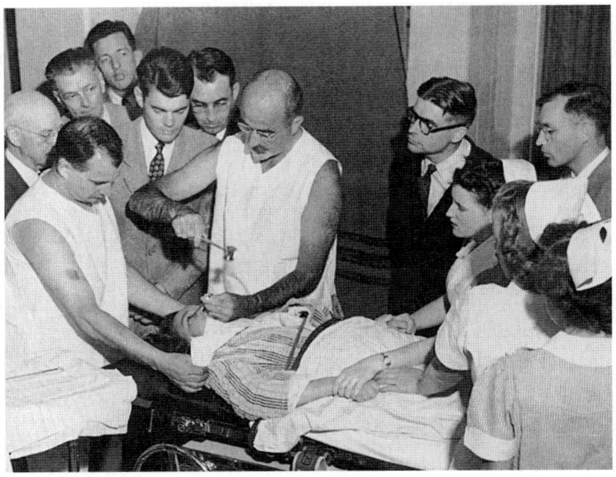

Figure 2.28
The prefrontal lobotomy The surgeon, Walter Freeman, is performing what he sometimes called "icepick" surgery. He is preparing to drive a special surgical knife, a leucotome, through the back of the patient's eyesocket into her brain. The operation was also called a transorbital (through the eyesocket) leucotomy.

→ **What effect would you expect the operation to have on the patient's behavior?**

The **prefrontal cortex,** the part of the frontal lobe anterior to the motor cortex, controls complex intellectual functions such as the planning and sequencing of behavior (Elliott, 2003). Damage to this area of the brain is associated with a diminished ability to plan future actions effectively (Colvin & others, 2001). Phineas P. Gage had damage from the tamping rod that effectively separated the prefrontal area from the rest of his brain (see Figure 1.5). After his accident, he was never again able to make plans or carry them out, which is typical of people with prefrontal damage. (See Box 2.2 for the consequences of the use of prefrontal damage as a surgical treatment for "unmanageable" psychiatric patients.)

Using fMRI imaging of human subjects performing a variety of cognitive tasks, Jonathan Cohen and his associates have found evidence that the prefrontal cortex has a central role in the cognitive control of behavior (e.g., MacDonald & others, 2000; Miller & Cohen, 2001). These findings suggest that the prefrontal cortex coordinates thought and action in accordance with internal goals by accessing memories from the hippocampus; by regulating a balance between focused attention, or "concentration," and a state of distributed awareness, or "alertness"; and by producing specific patterns of neural activity, or "thoughts," that motivate specific "actions." Cohen and his colleagues believe that, once behavior is initiated,

prefrontal lobotomy A surgical procedure that severs the connections of the prefrontal cortex to the rest of the brain.

prefrontal cortex An area in the anterior part of the frontal lobe that controls complex intellectual functions.

the anterior cingulate cortex (part of the limbic system) monitors performance and signals when behavioral adjustments are needed.

The prefrontal cortex is also involved in attentional and emotional processes (Yamasaki & others, 2002). These disparate functions are contained in separate prefrontal networks in the human brain, with further integration in the anterior cingulate cortex. As further evidence of the interaction of the prefrontal cortex and the anterior cingulate cortex, Eisenberger and others (2003), using fMRI, found that part of the prefrontal cortex regulates the emotional distress people feel from social exclusion through its effect on the anterior cingulate cortex.

In studies of people with schizophrenia, Cohen and his colleagues have observed lowered activity levels in the prefrontal cortex and have suggested that such *hypofrontality* is responsible for the cognitive impairments associated with schizophrenia (Cohen & others, 1999; Perlstein & others, 2003). In Chapter 15, we further examine evidence for the role of a dysfunctional prefrontal cortex in schizophrenia.

Checkpoint

When you pick up a pencil with your right hand, which side of your cerebral cortex is controlling this behavior? Why is sensory information from the face overrepresented in the human somatosensory cortex? In the human motor cortex? Distinguish between the types of language difficulties often produced by damage to either Wernicke's area or Broca's area.

REVIEW

- The telencephalon, or end brain, consists of the limbic system, the basal ganglia, and the cerebral cortex.
- The limbic system is a group of interconnected structures that control basic emotions, such as anger and fear, and the storage and retrieval of memories.
- The basal ganglia are a set of three nuclei (caudate nucleus, putamen, and globus pallidus) involved in integrating voluntary movements and in maintaining posture and muscle tone.
- The cerebral cortex consists of two hemispheres, each of which is composed of four lobes. Each hemisphere controls motor functions on the opposite side of the body.
- The primary function of the occipital lobe is to analyze visual information.
- The somatosensory cortex, located in the parietal lobe, analyzes sensory information about touch, pain, pressure, temperature, and body position.
- The temporal lobe contains the primary auditory cortex, which receives auditory information from the ears via the thalamus. The temporal lobe also is involved in visual object recognition, balance, and emotional response. Wernicke's area, involved in the interpretation of language, is located in the left temporal lobe.
- The frontal lobe contains the motor cortex, which is involved in the control of voluntary body movement. Broca's area, involved in the programming and sequencing of speech production, is located in the left frontal lobe.
- The prefrontal cortex plays a role in attentional and emotional processes and in the planning and sequencing of behavior.

Chapter Review

Key Terms

adrenocorticotropic hormone (ACTH) (p. 60)
afferent neuron (p. 45)
amygdala (p. 61)
anterior (p. 36)
anterior pituitary gland (p. 60)
antidiuretic hormone (ADH) (p. 60)
arachnoid mater (p. 50)
astrocyte (p. 42)
autonomic nervous system (p. 35)
axoaxonic synapse (p. 40)
axodendritic synapse (p. 40)
axon (p. 39)
axon hillock (p. 39)
axosomatic synapse (p. 40)
basal ganglia (p. 62)
brain (p. 36)
brain stem (p. 57)

caudal (p. 37)
cell body (soma) (p. 39)
cell membrane (p. 38)
central canal (p. 52)
central nervous system (CNS) (p. 36)
central sulcus (p. 64)
cerebellum (p. 56)
cerebral commissure (p. 64)
cerebral cortex (p. 62)
cerebrospinal fluid (CSF) (p. 52)
choroid plexus (p. 52)
cingulate gyrus (p. 61)
congenital disorder (p. 50)
contralateral control (p. 64)
coronal section (p. 38)
corpus callosum (p. 64)
cranial nerve (p. 45)
cytoplasm (p. 38)
dendrite (p. 39)
dendrodendritic synapse (p. 40)
dermatome (p. 45)
deoxyribonucleic acid (DNA) (p. 38)
diencephalon (p. 58)
dorsal (p. 36)
dura mater (p. 49)
efferent neuron (p. 45)
epithalamus (p. 58)
forebrain (p. 58)
frontal lobe (p. 65)
ganglion (p. 39)
glial cell (p. 42)
gonadotropin (p. 60)
gray matter (p. 53)
habenula (p. 58)
hindbrain (p. 56)
hippocampus (p. 62)
horizontal section (p. 37)
hydrocephalus (p. 50)
hypothalamus (p. 59)
inferior (p. 37)
inferior colliculus (p. 57)
interneuron (p. 40)
lateral (p. 37)
lateral geniculate nucleus (LGN) (p. 59)
lateralization of function (p. 64)
lateral sulcus (p. 64)
limbic system (p. 61)
longitudinal fissure (p. 63)
medial (p. 37)
medial geniculate nucleus (MGN) (p. 58)
medulla oblongata (p. 56)
melatonin (p. 58)
meninges (p. 49)
metencephalon (p. 56)
microglial cell (p. 42)
midbrain (p. 57)
motor cortex (p. 65)
motor neuron (p. 40)
myelencephalon (p. 56)
myelin (p. 42)
nerve (p. 39)
neuromuscular junction (p. 40)
neurotransmitter (p. 40)
nucleus (of cell) (p. 38)
nucleus (of CNS) (p. 39)
occipital lobe (p. 64)
oligodendrocyte (p. 42)
oxytocin (p. 60)
parasympathetic nervous system (p. 46)
parietal lobe (p. 64)
peripheral nervous system (PNS) (p. 35)
pia mater (p. 51)
pineal gland (p. 58)
pituitary gland (p. 60)
pons (p. 56)
posterior (p. 36)
posterior pituitary gland (p. 60)
postsynaptic membrane (p. 40)
prefrontal cortex (p. 66)
prefrontal lobotomy (p. 66)
presynaptic membrane (p. 40)
presynaptic terminal (p. 39)
primary auditory cortex (p. 65)
primary visual cortex (p. 64)
raphé system (p. 56)
red nucleus (p. 57)
reticular formation (p. 56)
ribonucleic acid (RNA) (p. 38)
rostral (p. 37)
sagittal section (p. 37)
Schwann cell (p. 42)
sensory neglect (p. 64)
sensory neuron (p. 40)
skull (p. 49)
soma (p. 39)
somatic nervous system (p. 35)
somatosensory cortex (p. 64)
somatotropin (p. 60)
spinal cord (p. 36)
spinal nerve (p. 45)
spinal reflex (p. 53)
subarachnoid space (p. 51)
substantia nigra (p. 57)
superior (p. 37)
superior colliculus (p. 57)
sympathetic nervous system (p. 45)
synapse (p. 40)
synaptic cleft (p. 40)
synaptic vesicle (p. 40)
tectum (p. 57)
tegmentum (p. 57)
telencephalon (p. 61)
telodendron (p. 39)
temporal lobe (p. 65)
thalamus (p. 58)
thyroid-stimulating hormone (TSH) (p. 60)
tract (p. 39)
tumor (p. 50)
ventral (p. 36)
ventricle (p. 52)
ventricular system (p. 52)
ventrolateral nucleus (p. 59)
vertebral column (p. 49)
white matter (p. 53)

Suggested Readings

Afifi, A. K., & Bergman, R. A. (1998). *Functional neuroanatomy.* New York: McGraw-Hill.

Diamond, M. C., Scheibel, A. B., & Elson, L. M. (1985). *The human brain coloring book.* New York: Barnes & Noble Books.

Haines, D. E. (1991). *Neuroanatomy: An atlas of structures, sections and systems* (3rd ed.). Baltimore: Urban and Schwarzenberg.

Heimer, L. (1995). *The human brain and spinal cord* (2nd ed.). New York: Springer-Verlag.

Martin, J. H. (1989). *Neuroanatomy: Text and atlas.* New York: Elsevier.

Critical Thinking Questions

1. Describe the organizational structure of the nervous system. Indicate the key differences between the functions of the PNS and the CNS. How does the differentiation allow the nervous system to carry out its varied functions?
2. Using what you have learned about the functions of the various areas of the brain, including Broca's area and Wernicke's area, explain why there is lateralization of function in the human brain. Would lateralization of function differ in right-handed and left-handed people?
3. As we discussed in Chapter 1, biological psychologists use various methods to study how the nervous system influences behavior. Suppose you are interested in identifying the neural structures responsible for depression. Describe the various methods you could use to reveal the involvement of the nervous system in depression.

Fill-in-the-Blank Questions

1. The part of the nervous system that analyzes the significance of events and decides how to respond is the ______.
2. The part of the nervous system that contains both the sensory receptors that detect environmental stimulation and the nerves that activate skeletal muscles is the ______.
3. Anatomical structures toward the tail end of an organism are described as ______, which means toward the tail.
4. A(n) ______ plane of section through an organism shows structures as they would be seen from above.
5. The ______ is the jellylike substance inside the cell and the various structures involved in cell functioning it contains.
6. The axon is joined to the cell body at the ______.
7. A(n) ______ is a collection of neuronal cell bodies outside the CNS.
8. The synapse between the axon of one neuron and the axon of another neuron is called a(n) ______ synapse.
9. The location where messages are transmitted between two neurons is a(n) ______.
10. The synapse between a neuron and a muscle is called a(n) ______ junction.
11. ______ are neurons that send messages from sensory receptors to the CNS.
12. Generally speaking, ______ cells play a supporting role in the nervous system.
13. Conditions that promote arousal activate the ______ nervous system.
14. "Voodoo death" is caused by excessive activation of the ______ nervous system.
15. The layers of tissue that protect the brain and spinal cord are called the ______.
16. The interconnected hollow chambers within the brain are the ______.
17. When CSF flow from the brain is blocked, a condition known as ______ develops.
18. In a(n) ______, an afferent sensory neuron enters the spinal cord and synapses directly with an efferent neuron.
19. The brain structure that controls breathing and heart rate is the ______.
20. The hindbrain (minus the cerebellum) and the midbrain are referred to as the ______.
21. In the tegmentum of the midbrain, the ______ is involved in the integration of voluntary movements.
22. The ______ is a glandular structure in the epithalamus that is involved in seasonal rhythms in behavior.
23. The part of the forebrain involved in hunger and sex is the ______.
24. One of the main functions of the structure in the diencephalon called the ______ is to relay sensory information to the cerebral cortex.
25. The ______ is sometimes called the master gland of the body.
26. Too little ______ causes diabetes insipidus.
27. The limbic structure that plays an important role in memory processes is called the ______, because early anatomists thought it looked like a seahorse.
28. The ______ is a vertical groove that separates the anterior and posterior halves of the cerebral cortex.
29. The largest of the cerebral commissures is the ______.
30. The analysis of visual information is the primary function of the ______.
31. The primary auditory cortex is located in the ______ lobe.

Multiple-Choice Questions

1. The four main functions of the nervous system are
   a. seeing, hearing, tasting, and movement.
   b. balance, movement, language, and memory.
   c. detection, recognition, decision, and execution.
   d. storage, processing, integration, and motor control.
2. The two main divisions of the nervous system are the
   a. central nervous system and peripheral nervous system.
   b. sympathetic nervous system and parasympathetic nervous system.
   c. autonomic nervous system and somatic nervous system.
   d. brain and spinal cord.
3. ______ means toward the belly, and ______ means toward the back.
   a. rostral, caudal
   b. ventral, dorsal
   c. medial, lateral
   d. anterior, posterior
4. The ______ plane presents structures as viewed from the front.
   a. horizontal
   b. sagittal
   c. coronal
   d. commuter
5. The point at which the axon leaves the cell body is called the
   a. telodendron.
   b. axosomatic synapse.
   c. axon hillock.
   d. dendrite.
6. A collection of axons outside the central nervous system is called a
   a. ganglion.
   b. tract.
   c. nucleus.
   d. nerve.
7. The sacs containing neurotransmitter substance are called
   a. synaptic vesicles.
   b. synaptic clefts.
   c. presynaptic terminals.
   d. ganglia.
8. Sensory neurons carry information from the
   a. central nervous system to the muscles.
   b. motor neurons to other sensory neurons.
   c. outside world to the central nervous system.
   d. central nervous system to the peripheral nervous system.
9. A major function of astrocytes is to
   a. provide physical support for neurons.
   b. form the lining of fluid-filled spaces.
   c. produce myelin.
   d. connect motor and sensory neurons.
10. ______ form the myelin sheath in the PNS.
    a. Schwann cells
    b. Oligodendrocytes
    c. Microglial cells
    d. Astrocytes
11. The cranial nerves directly connect the
    a. spinal cord and brain.
    b. sympathetic and parasympathetic nervous systems.
    c. sensory receptors in the head and brain.
    d. brain and skeletal muscles.
12. A car nearly hit Theresa as she crossed the street. After the incident, Theresa sat on a bench to recover. As she sat, her heart rate decreased and her breathing slowed. Which nervous system was primarily responsible for her recovery?
    a. central nervous system
    b. somatic nervous system
    c. parasympathetic nervous system
    d. sympathetic nervous system
13. The innermost layer of the meninges is called the
    a. arachnoid mater.
    b. pia mater.
    c. dura mater.
    d. subarachnoid space.
14. Which of the following is *not* a function of cerebrospinal fluid?
    a. provides nutrients to the brain
    b. carries messages to the brain
    c. cushions and protects the brain
    d. provides buoyancy and support to the brain
15. The gray matter in the spinal cord consists of
    a. cerebrospinal fluid.
    b. myelinated axon sheaths.
    c. dendrites.
    d. neuronal cell bodies.
16. The hindbrain structure that controls functions essential to life is the
    a. cerebellum.
    b. pons.
    c. medulla oblongata.
    d. raphé system.

17. Which hindbrain structure coordinates motor movement?
   a. medulla oblongata
   b. pons
   c. cerebellum
   d. reticular formation
18. Which midbrain structure controls simple reflexes such as blinking?
   a. tectum
   b. substantia nigra
   c. red nucleus
   d. tegmentum
19. Carlos has rigidity, difficulty initiating movement, and tremors at rest. He probably would be diagnosed as having
   a. multiple sclerosis.
   b. Huntington's disease.
   c. Alzheimer's disease.
   d. Parkinson's disease.
20. One important function of the thalamus is to
   a. detect hunger and thirst.
   b. relay sensory messages.
   c. control release of pituitary hormones.
   d. control emotions.
21. Which of the following thalamic nuclei sends visual messages to the cerebral cortex?
   a. LGN
   b. MGN
   c. ventrolateral nucleus
   d. ventromedial nucleus
22. The structure in the diencephalon that controls such basic motivations as fighting, fleeing, feeding, and sexual behavior is the
   a. thalamus.
   b. habenula.
   c. hypothalamus.
   d. pineal gland.
23. Too much ______ can cause acromegaly.
   a. gonadotropin
   b. ADH
   c. somatotropin
   d. ACTH
24. Huntington's disease results from damage to the
   a. cerebral commissures.
   b. basal ganglia.
   c. hippocampus.
   d. cerebral cortex.
25. The two hemispheres of the cerebral cortex are connected at the
   a. basal ganglia.
   b. central fissure.
   c. cerebral commissures.
   d. somatosensory cortex.
26. For most people, the left hemisphere has more control than the right hemisphere over
   a. sensory perception.
   b. language functions.
   c. motor functions.
   d. memory.
27. The primary visual cortex is located in the
   a. occipital lobe.
   b. parietal lobe.
   c. temporal lobe.
   d. frontal lobe.
28. After a car accident and head injury, Jennifer has clumsiness on the side of her body opposite the brain damage, has difficulty identifying objects by touch, and cannot describe how to get from one place to another. She probably has damage to her ______ lobe.
   a. frontal
   b. parietal
   c. temporal
   d. occipital
29. Primary functions of the temporal lobe relate to
   a. seeing and speaking.
   b. hearing, object recognition by sight, and balance.
   c. movement, following maps or charts, and sight.
   d. smell and taste.
30. While riding his bicycle without a helmet, Armando hit a large rock and flew over the handle bars, hitting his head on a tree. After this injury, Armando finds it impossible to make plans for the future and carry them through. Armando probably has damage to his ______ lobes.
   a. frontal
   b. parietal
   c. occipital
   d. temporal

Answers can be found on the companion web site at www.worthpublishers.com/klein.

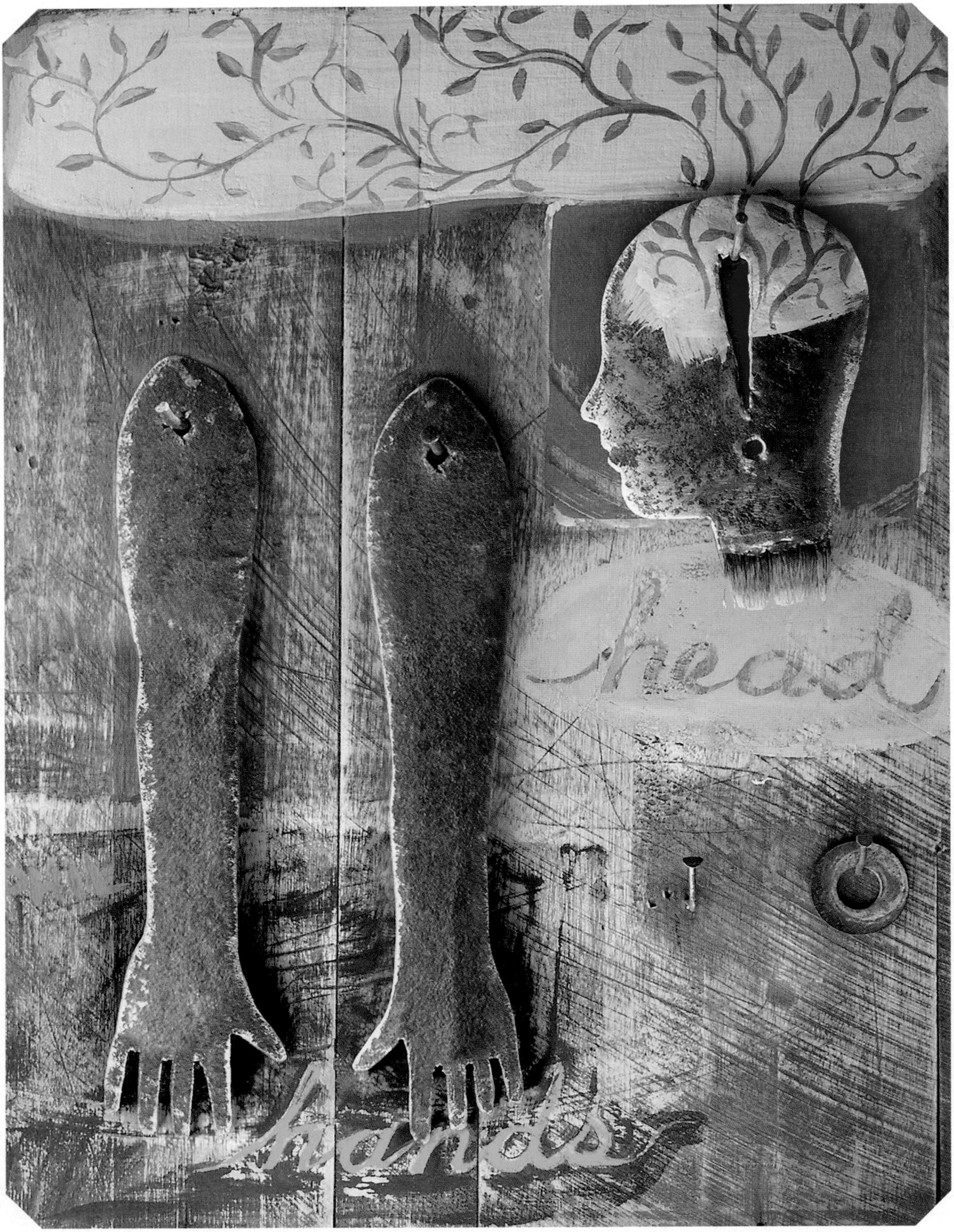
head
hands

3

The Development and Plasticity of the Nervous System

The Long Needle

"I shouldn't have looked," Anne told herself, obsessing over the needle that was going to be inserted into her uterus. Her obstetrician, Dr. Threadgill, had told her the procedure wasn't especially painful, but she had seen the needle, and having been a psychology major in college, she knew how much expectations could affect a person's perception of pain.

"This should be interesting, honey," Nathan said, patting her hand.

Easy for you to say, Anne thought, fighting panic as the preparations for her amniocentesis neared completion. She clutched Nathan's hand more tightly and closed her eyes as the doctor readied the needle.

"You'll feel just a little prick, Anne," the physician said, and Anne felt Nathan squeeze her hand to comfort her. Just that momentary distraction broke the cycle of anxiety, and the slender needle slipped easily through her taut belly and into the amniotic sac enclosing their son.

"Is that what I think it is?" Anne had asked a few days earlier as the technician performed an ultrasound.

"It sure is," the young man said, while he, Nathan, and Anne stared at the flickering image on the monitor. "You're going to have a little boy."

But was their baby developing normally? That was the question that had prompted Dr. Threadgill some weeks ago to recommend either chorionic villus sampling (CVS) or amniocentesis for Anne. Anne remembered enough from her psychology classes to know the reason for the extensive testing in her case. She was 40, and the risk of birth defects or Down syndrome is greater for women over 35. In addition, the obstetrician had told Anne and Nathan about improved survivability of infants if certain problems were diagnosed and treated before birth. Dr. Threadgill had carefully discussed with them the risks and benefits of both amniocentesis and CVS, and Anne had opted for "amnio," as Dr. Threadgill called it, and she had signed the informed consent form the doctor provided.

So here she was in her 16th week of pregnancy, lying on a hospital table, with Nathan clutching her hand and looking slightly green around the gills, waiting for the physician to finish withdrawing the small sample of amniotic fluid that would be tested for genetic defects and metabolic abnormalities. Anne just wished the results weren't going to take so long—Dr. Threadgill had told them to expect a wait of 3 to 4 weeks. At least the result of the triple screen test—a standard prenatal blood test assessing alpha-fetoprotein, human chorionic gonadotropic hormone, and estradiol levels—had been completely normal. That gave Anne hope that the amniocentesis results would be equally benign.

genetics The study of heredity or inheritance.

gene A unit of heredity; a region of DNA that directs the making of a protein.

chromosome The structure in a cell that contains genes.

deoxyribonucleic acid (DNA) A large, double-stranded molecule consisting of the nitrogen-containing bases adenine, guanine, cytosine, and thymine, which are attached to the sugar deoxyribose; the hereditary material.

ribonucleic acid (RNA) A single-stranded molecule consisting of four nitrogenous bases: adenine, guanine, cytosine, and uracil; directs the synthesis of proteins.

After all her fears at the sight of the needle, the amnio had been a piece of cake, Anne decided. She just hoped Nathan would be okay: He had muttered something about feeling sick and had hurried out of the room before the doctor finished withdrawing the needle. Anne thought for perhaps the hundredth time since she learned she was pregnant that it was a good thing men didn't have babies. Nathan obviously didn't have the stomach for it.

BEFORE YOU BEGIN

- What happens during the development of the human nervous system?
- How do neurons develop and form the millions of connections that enable us to live and behave?
- What causes birth defects?
- When does the development of the nervous system end?
- Can the nervous system recover from injury?

In this chapter, you will find the answer to these questions and many others.

◆ A Look at the Basics of Genetics

Some weeks before Anne's sophisticated medical testing, she and Nathan had met with a genetic counselor at the hospital. The counselor had questioned them about their family histories, which, they were relieved to discover, did not suggest any genetic defects on either side. As Anne remembered from her reading in college, genetics underlies the development of a fetus—of its nervous system and all its other characteristics. So, as a prelude to our discussion of how the nervous system develops, we briefly examine the basics of genetics and, in the next section, how the nervous system itself evolved. **Genetics,** the science of heredity, teaches us about the molecular building blocks that form the cells that in turn form the systems that control behavior.

We all inherit characteristics, or *traits,* from our parents. For example, Anne may be said to have her mother's eyes, her father's hair, and her grandmother's nose. But visible characteristics are not all we inherit. The characteristics of every cell in our body are determined by the combination of our parents' genes in the fertilized egg from which we developed. These **genes,** or units of heredity, are located on **chromosomes,** structures contained within the nucleus of each cell (except our red blood cells, which lack a nucleus). A gene is a portion of **deoxyribonucleic acid (DNA),** a large, double-stranded molecule consisting of the nitrogen-containing bases adenine, guanine, cytosine, and thymine, which are attached to a sugar called deoxyribose. (Bases are substances that form salts when they interact with acids.) Hydrogen bonds between pairs of bases hold together the two strands that constitute the DNA molecule, with an adenine pairing with a thymine and a cytosine pairing with a guanine (Figure 3.1). DNA is the principal active compound of each chromosome, and the DNA in our cells determines such inherited physical characteristics as

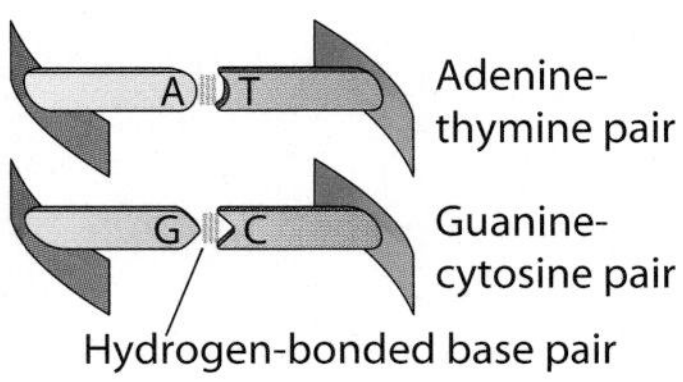

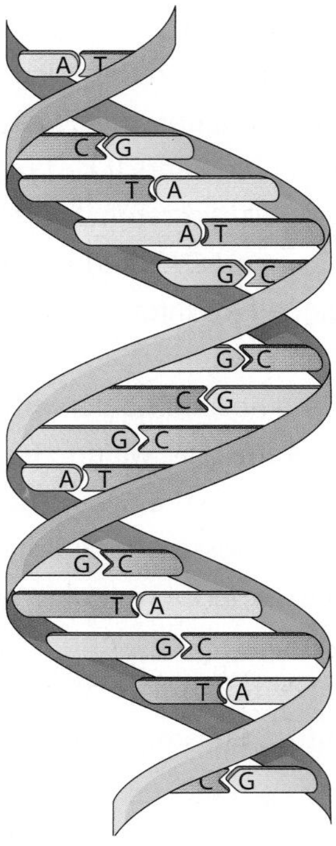

Figure 3.1

Portion of a DNA molecule DNA consists of paired strands of complementary bases linked by hydrogen bonding—adenine with thymine and guanine with cytosine.

→ **How is the DNA molecule related to physical and behavioral characteristics?**

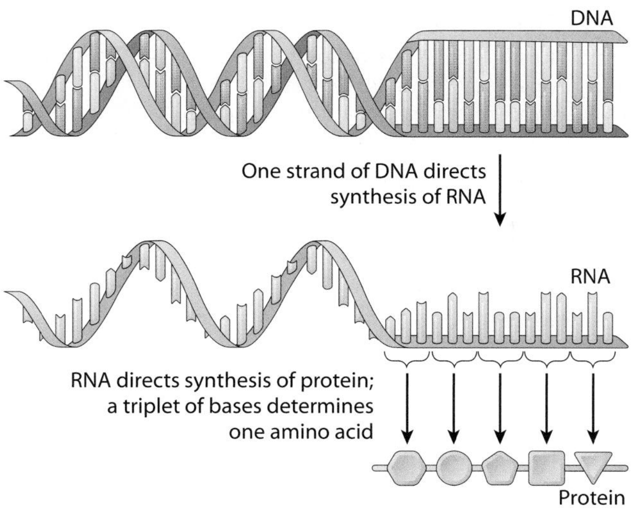

Figure 3.2
The relationships between DNA, RNA, and proteins DNA directs the production of RNA, which in turn directs the production of proteins.

➡ How is a particular RNA molecule related to a specific protein?

hair color, eye color, and blood type and is involved in such behavioral characteristics as emotional disposition and intelligence.

Because DNA molecules provide the information to build proteins, DNA is involved in every aspect of the body's structure and function. It controls the production of our enzyme proteins and our structural proteins and thus affects all aspects of our cellular metabolism and physical characteristics. DNA exerts its control through **ribonucleic acid (RNA),** which is a single-stranded molecule. Like DNA, RNA consists of four nitrogenous bases; three—adenine, guanine, and cytosine—are the same as in DNA; the fourth base in RNA is uracil. DNA directs RNA synthesis, and RNA, in turn, directs protein synthesis.

A protein consists of a string of amino acids, with different proteins having different amino acid sequences. Each amino acid in the protein is determined (through RNA as an intermediary) by a sequence of three bases in the DNA molecule. This *triplet* of bases governs the specific amino acid inserted into a protein during its synthesis. For example, the DNA triplet thymine-guanine-thymine (TGT) leads to the insertion of the amino acid cysteine in a protein molecule. Thus, the *genetic code* is really a triplet code, because the sequence of bases in the DNA triplet governs protein synthesis and, ultimately, the inherited physical and behavioral characteristics of the individual. The relationships between DNA, RNA, and protein synthesis are shown in Figure 3.2.

All cells in a human body (except sperm and egg cells)—that is, all *somatic cells*—contain 46 chromosomes, or 23 pairs of chromosomes (Figure 3.3). One chromosome of each pair is inherited from the father and the other from the mother. These somatic cells are said to be *diploid,* meaning they have two complete sets of chromosomes, a set being one of each of the 23 chromosomes. The reason

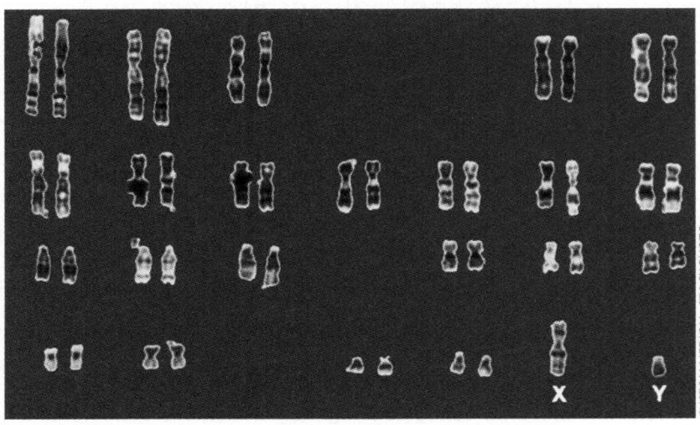

CUSTOM MEDICAL STOCK PHOTO

Figure 3.3
Human male chromosomes This enlarged photograph shows the 46 chromosomes (23 pairs) of a human male.

➡ Which chromosome pair would differ in a human female?

Figure 3.4

Crossing over During meiosis, the paired members of replicated chromosomes sometimes exchange pieces of genetic material (DNA).

➡ **What effect would crossing over have on the genetic makeup of siblings?**

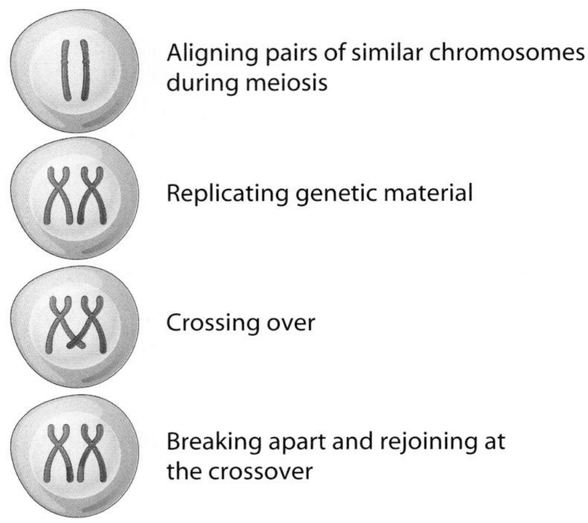

that each of our somatic cells contains only one chromosome of each pair from our father and one from our mother is that the sperm and the egg, the sex cells, or *gametes,* have exactly half the number of chromosomes found in somatic cells (23, or 23 half-pairs)—they are *haploid* cells. Once the sperm and the egg fuse at fertilization, the resulting cell has 46 chromosomes (23 full pairs).

Gametes are formed in a complex process called **meiosis:** two consecutive cell divisions that are preceded by a single round of replication of the DNA, so that a single diploid cell (one with 46 chromosomes, each of which has replicated to form two "daughter" chromosomes) is converted into four haploid cells (with 23 chromosomes each). During meiosis, some exchange of genetic material occurs through a process called **crossing over** (Figure 3.4). Crossing over allows genetic material to be transferred from one chromosome of a pair to the other, thereby mixing the original genes inherited from the two parents. This exchange increases the genetic variation among offspring, which is responsible for differences among individuals. Genetic variation is also responsible for the differences among species.

If chromosomes occur in pairs, then the genes on the chromosomes must also occur in pairs. Actually, this is true for all except the sex chromosomes, which determine gender. You may remember the manipulation of Xs and Ys from your high school biology course: Boys do not have a true pair of sex chromosomes (they have a mixed pair, XY), whereas girls have a true pair (XX). For now, let us consider the 44 human chromosomes that are paired in both males and females. (Sexual development and the sex hormones are topics covered in Chapter 11.)

The location of a gene on a chromosome is called its **locus.** At any given locus, a gene can have alternative forms, which are called **alleles.** The expression of one allele may dominate expression of the other allele (in genetics, when a gene is *expressed* it means it codes for a protein that produces the characteristic, or trait, associated with that gene). The dominant trait (controlled by a **dominant allele**) will appear in the offspring regardless of the trait carried by the other allele. A trait controlled by a **recessive allele** is expressed only when both alleles are recessive.

To illustrate the action of dominant and recessive alleles consider the characteristic of freckles, which is determined by a single gene (Figure 3.5). Because the absence of freckles is dominant to having freckles, if a child inherits a nonfreckles allele (designated *F*) from either parent, the child will not have freckles. (Remember, a child receives one chromosome of each pair of chromosomes, and each chromosome carries one of two possible alleles.) A child has freckles only when two freckles alleles (designated *f*) are inherited—that is, when the pair of alleles is **homozygous** for freckles (*homo* means "same")—*ff.* Of course, an allele pair homozygous for a lack of freckles (*FF*) is also possible.

A child can have freckles even if both parents do not have freckles, as long as each parent carries one recessive freckles allele—that is, the parent's allele pairs are

meiosis The process by which gametes, sperm and egg cells with half the number of chromosomes found in other cells, are formed.

crossing over The exchange of genetic material between chromosomes of a chromosome pair during meiosis.

locus The location of a gene on a chromosome.

allele An alternative form of a gene.

dominant allele The form of a gene that determines the expression of a physical characteristic, when either or both members of a pair of alleles are in that form.

recessive allele The form of a gene that can determine the expression of a specific physical characteristic only when both members of a pair of alleles are in that form.

homozygous Describing an allele pair with identical alleles.

heterozygous Describing an allele pair in which the two alleles are different.

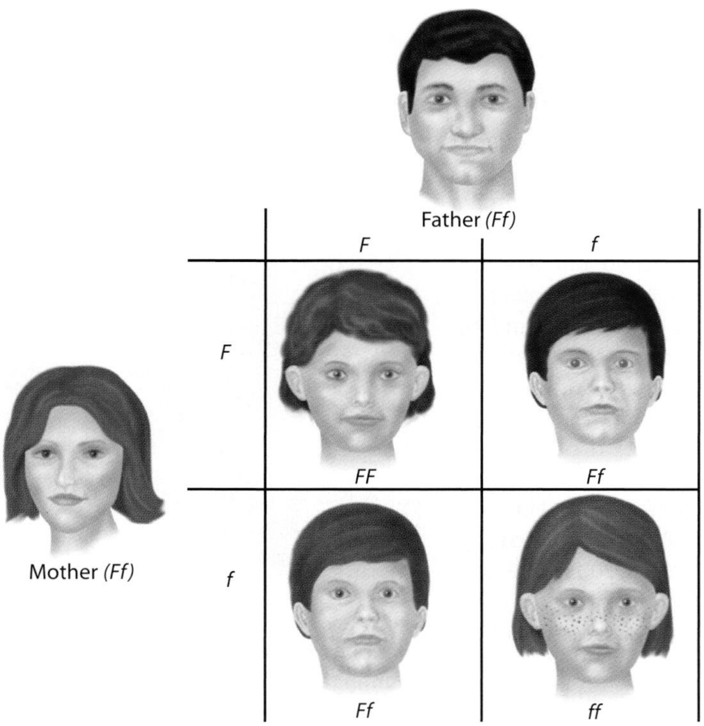

Figure 3.5

The inheritance of freckles In this illustration, each parent carries one allele for nonfreckles (*F*) and one allele for freckles (*f*). On average, three-fourths of the offspring of this couple will not have freckles and one-fourth will have freckles; put differently, each child has a 1 in 4 chance of having freckles. This box is called a Punnett square. The *F* and *f* along the top and sides of the box represent the alleles for this trait in the parents' gametes.

➜ If the father were homozygous for nonfreckles (FF), could any of the children have freckles?

heterozygous (*hetero* means "different")—*Ff.* Figure 3.5 shows how two parents without freckles can have a freckled child. However, two parents with freckles cannot have a child without freckles, as they do not have the dominant nonfreckles allele (if they did, they would not have freckles). Similarly, if one of the parents in the pictured example were homozygous for nonfreckles, none of the children could have freckles, as they would all have at least one dominant allele (*F*). Other characteristics determined by a single dominant allele include free ear lobes (ear lobes that are not attached to the head) and curly hair. Another example of a human condition controlled by a single dominant allele is the neurological disorder Huntington's disease (Box 3.1).

➤Checkpoint

You have free ear lobes, and your spouse has attached ear lobes. Your father has attached ear lobes, and your mother has free ear lobes. What are the chances that your children will have attached ear lobes? (Hint: Use Punnett squares like the one shown in Figure 3.5, starting with your parents' generation.) Why are the ear lobes of your spouse's parents unimportant for answering this question?

REVIEW

- ➤ Genetics is the study of genes, the units of heredity. Genes are located on chromosomes in the nucleus of each cell of the human body.
- ➤ A gene is a portion of DNA, a double-stranded molecule that makes RNA, which directs protein synthesis. Through proteins, genes determine the inherited physical and behavioral characteristics, or traits, of the individual.
- ➤ Humans have 23 pairs of chromosomes, 46 chromosomes in all.
- ➤ An allele is said to be dominant if the characteristic it produces (such as nonfreckles, allele *F*) is expressed regardless of the characteristic produced by the other allele of the pair (freckles, allele *f*).
- ➤ An allele is said to be recessive if its characteristic (such as freckles) is expressed only when two copies of the allele are present (*ff*).
- ➤ A pair of alleles is homozygous if both alleles produce the same characteristic (e.g., *FF* or *ff*), and heterozygous if the alleles produce different characteristics (e.g., *Ff*).
- ➤ Huntington's disease is a neurological disorder caused by a single dominant allele.

Box 3.1
Huntington's Disease

Described by George Huntington (1850–1916) in 1872, Huntington's disease is an invariably fatal neurological disorder with a known genetic basis (Wexler & others, 2004). (Nancy Wexler [Figure 3.6], one of the discoverers of the location of the Huntington's gene, has been motivated in her search for information about Huntington's by family history—her mother died from the disease.) **Huntington's disease** is characterized by psychiatric symptoms, severe dementia, and a slow deterioration of muscle control (Ho & others, 2001; MacDonald & others, 2003). The first symptom is often a facial twitch, with tremors developing in other body parts as the disease progresses. The resulting abnormal movements are sometimes called choreiform movements, and an alternative name for the disease is *Huntington's chorea* (chorea means a type of dance). Voluntary movements, such as walking and speaking, become slow and clumsy, and eventually impossible. These physical symptoms are accompanied by such behavioral symptoms as loss of energy and initiative, impaired judgment, and emotional blunting, along with affective (emotional) symptoms such as apathy, depression, anxiety, and irritability (Craufurd & others, 2001; Thompson & others, 2002). Patients with early Huntington's disease also become progressively more impaired in such cognitive abilities as attention and immediate memory, with less impairment in general cognition and semantic (language-related) memory (Ho & others, 2003).

Although the onset of the symptoms of Huntington's disease can occur at any time from childhood to old age, the symptoms usually begin in midlife—between the ages of about 30 and 40. As there is no treatment for Huntington's disease at the present time, mental and physical functioning continue to deteriorate over a period of 10 to 15 years, until the person dies.

The gene responsible for Huntington's is located on human chromosome 4 (MacDonald & others, 2003). The non-Huntington form of this gene contains a sequence of three bases (cytosine, adenine, guanine—CAG) that is normally repeated 11 to 24 times but can be repeated up to 34 times. However, if the sequence is repeated more than 37 times, the dominant allele will produce Huntington's disease. Further, the more base repetitions, the earlier the disease begins (Antonini & others, 1998; Langbehn & others, 2004; Mahant & others, 2003): A person with 40 or so CAG repeats will probably begin to exhibit symptoms after age 40, whereas someone with more than 50 repeats will generally become symptomatic before age 30.

Although the number of CAG repeats is associated with when symptoms first appear, it is not a perfect correlation, and individuals with the same number of repeats may differ markedly in age at onset of symptoms (Holzmann & others, 2001; Wexler & others, 2004). In a study of 370 individuals, Rosenblatt and colleagues (2001) found that the CAG number alone accounted for about two-thirds of the variation in age of onset and suggested that additional modifiers of age of onset might include other genes not presently identified.

The CAG triplet codes for the amino acid glutamine, which is closely related

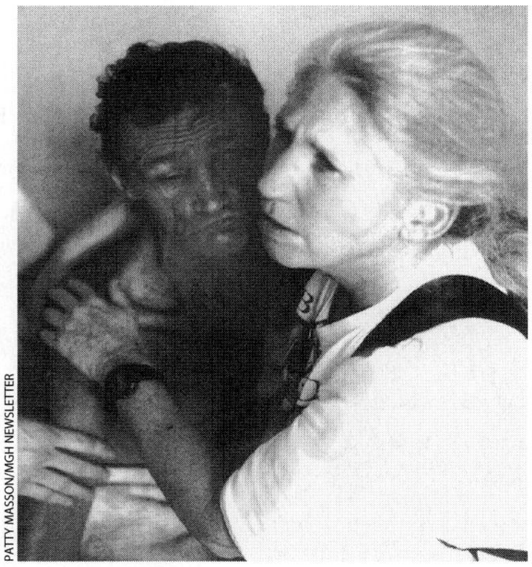

Figure 3.6
Nancy Wexler and Venezuelan man with Huntington's disease In looking for the gene for Huntington's disease, Wexler studied a group of people in Lake Maracaibo, Venezuela, many of whom have the disorder. All of these individuals are descended from a single woman, who died from the disease.

→ **Why has Wexler been so devoted to the search for the Huntington's disease gene?**

◆ The Evolution of the Nervous System

Huntington's disease A progressive neurological disorder characterized by psychiatric symptoms, dementia, and a slow deterioration of muscle control; caused by a single dominant gene.

evolution The process by which succeeding generations of organisms change in physical appearance, function, and behavior through a process of natural selection.

As we noted earlier, variations in genetic makeup are responsible for both individual differences within a species and differences among species. Have you ever asked yourself why we have a nervous system? Some species survive perfectly well without one and have done so for hundreds of millions of years. Primitive forerunners of animals such as single-celled protozoa or primitive multicellular organisms such as sponges do not have specialized nerve cells or an organized nervous system to respond to environmental stimulation (Figure 3.7). So how did we come to possess a complex system that enables us to laugh, cry, throw a ball, enjoy a great meal, and appreciate a painting? We can find the answer by studying the evolution of the nervous system.

to the excitatory neurotransmitter glutamate (which we discuss in Chapter 4). The gene on chromosome 4 codes for a protein of unknown function, called *huntingtin* (Ho & others, 2001; Rosser & Dunnett, 2003). Both the buildup of a mutant form of huntingtin and excitotoxicity caused by an excess of glutamate may be involved in the selective death of cells in the corpus striatum (part of the basal ganglia) and neocortex (Sawa & others, 2003). Using a mouse model of Huntington's, Behrens and colleagues (2002) found an age-dependent reduction in glutamate transport function, with a corresponding increase in extracellular glutamate levels.

Additional mechanisms that have been proposed to account for Huntington's neuropathology include impaired energy metabolism, abnormal protein interactions, and *apoptosis,* or genetically programmed cellular suicide (Hickey & Chesselet, 2003). In fact, a defect in a key regulator of apoptosis has been implicated in the excessive cell death seen in several neurological disorders, including Huntington's disease (Ethell & Buhler, 2003). (We have more to say about the brain damage and motor disorders associated with Huntington's disease in Chapter 8.)

The identification of the gene causing Huntington's disease, and the abnormal sequence of bases associated with it, has enabled professionals to predict whether a person will get the disease and, if so, when. Unfortunately, genetic testing for Huntington's is a mixed blessing, at best. For example, if a person at risk because of a family history of the disease chooses to be tested and finds he or she does not have the gene, then this should provide a tremendous sense of relief. Learning of a positive test result could also be considered beneficial, as the individual can do such things as start to prepare for the inevitable, develop support systems, or decide to live life to the fullest, taking maximum advantage of the time left (Drellishak, 1996).

Some might argue, however, that testing is of dubious value. At this point, there is nothing a person can do about the disease other than prepare for it. In addition, approximately 5% of persons tested do not receive definitive results, which means that testing has not removed their doubts. Also, because of the variability in age at onset of symptoms, even with the same number of CAG repeats (Holzmann & others, 2001; Wexler & others, 2004), a person testing positive still does not know for sure when the symptoms will begin. Either result—learning that you have the gene or that you do not have it—can be emotionally traumatic. For example, a person who tests negative for the gene may experience guilt at being spared when relatives are not (Greicius, 1996).

A positive test result, if it becomes known to the person's insurance company or a potential employer, can result in discrimination for life, health, or disability insurance or in employment. In addition, if an insurance company can prove a person knew about his or her diagnosis and lied about it on application forms, then the company can terminate the coverage. Testing can also be quite expensive, particularly if the person pays out-of-pocket for the test in order to keep the insurance company from knowing about it. According to Drellishak (1996), the total cost of testing, including psychiatric and genetic counseling sessions, can be nearly $1,000. Greicius (1996) cited costs ranging from $600 to $1,500.

One of the most unfortunate aspects of Huntington's disease is that its symptoms usually do not develop until after the child-bearing years. This, of course, can be an argument in favor of genetic testing for a person who is at risk. If he or she has inherited the gene, then the decision may be made not to have children, because there is a 50:50 chance that the offspring of a gene carrier will inherit the disease. This assumes the potential parent has only one copy of the gene associated with Huntington's disease. To be homozygous for this gene, a person would have to have inherited a copy from both parents, which is quite rare. When it does occur, the age of symptom onset is not affected, but the disease progresses more rapidly (Squitieri & others, 2003). Fortunately, unlike Huntington's disease, most human characteristics are governed by several genes.

Evolution is the process by which succeeding generations of organisms change in physical appearance, function, and behavior, according to Darwin's theory of evolution—the origin of species by natural selection (Chapter 1). These changes begin with an increase or decrease in the frequency with which specific genes are represented in the population of a species over successive generations, and the changes occur as species adapt to changing environmental conditions. We can trace the evolutionary development of the nervous system by looking at present-day animals, from the most primitive to the most advanced, highly complex species.

Figure 3.7

Two primitive organisms (a) The protozoan *Paramecium caudatum.* (b) A sponge.

→ **Do protozoans and sponges have a nervous system?**

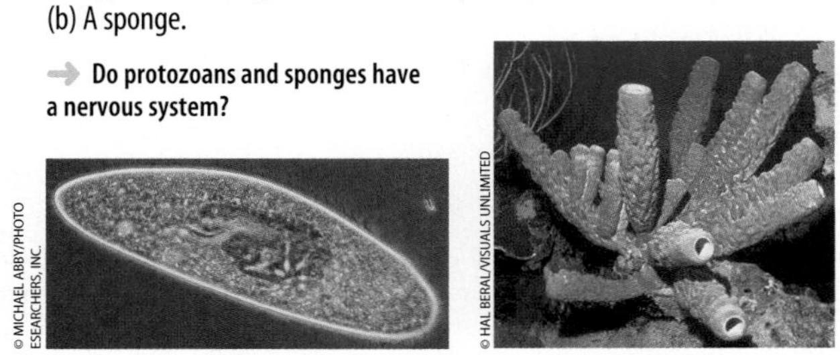

(a) (b)

invertebrate An animal without a backbone.

ganglion A group of neurons with a specialized function.

The Emergence of the Nervous System in Invertebrates

Most of the animals on Earth are **invertebrates,** or animals without a backbone. Most invertebrates have much simpler nervous systems than vertebrates but are nevertheless highly successful at adapting to a large number of situations. Insects, for example, outnumber humans a billion to one. Many invertebrates have elaborate sensory systems that make them extremely sensitive to environmental events such as tactile or light stimuli. We describe here some of the variations in nervous system complexity among invertebrate species.

The jellyfish has specialized neurons that respond to touch, light, and chemicals in the environment, but has no true nervous system (Figure 3.8a). By reacting to these stimuli, the jellyfish can capture food and avoid danger. The nerve cells of the jellyfish are interconnected in a *nerve net,* with individual nerve cells having either a sensory or a motor function.

In more complex organisms such as the flatworm (or planarian, Figure 3.8b), neurons are grouped into clusters called **ganglia**. (Recall from Chapter 2 that a ganglion is a collection of neurons outside the central nervous system.) Two ganglia in the head region, the cerebral ganglia, and pairs of ganglia along the sides of the body are connected by bridges of nerve fibers called *nerve cords* to form a true nervous system. Each ganglion receives information from one side of the body and controls the functioning on that side. This specialization of function makes the ladder-like flatworm nervous system more complex than related structures in the jellyfish. The nerve cords also allow information received on one side of the animal to be relayed to neurons on the other side.

Somewhat more advanced is the "brain" of the roundworm (Figure 3.8c), actually a simple ring of nerves around the pharynx, the *circumpharyngeal nerve ring.* This nerve ring controls action throughout the roundworm's nervous system and

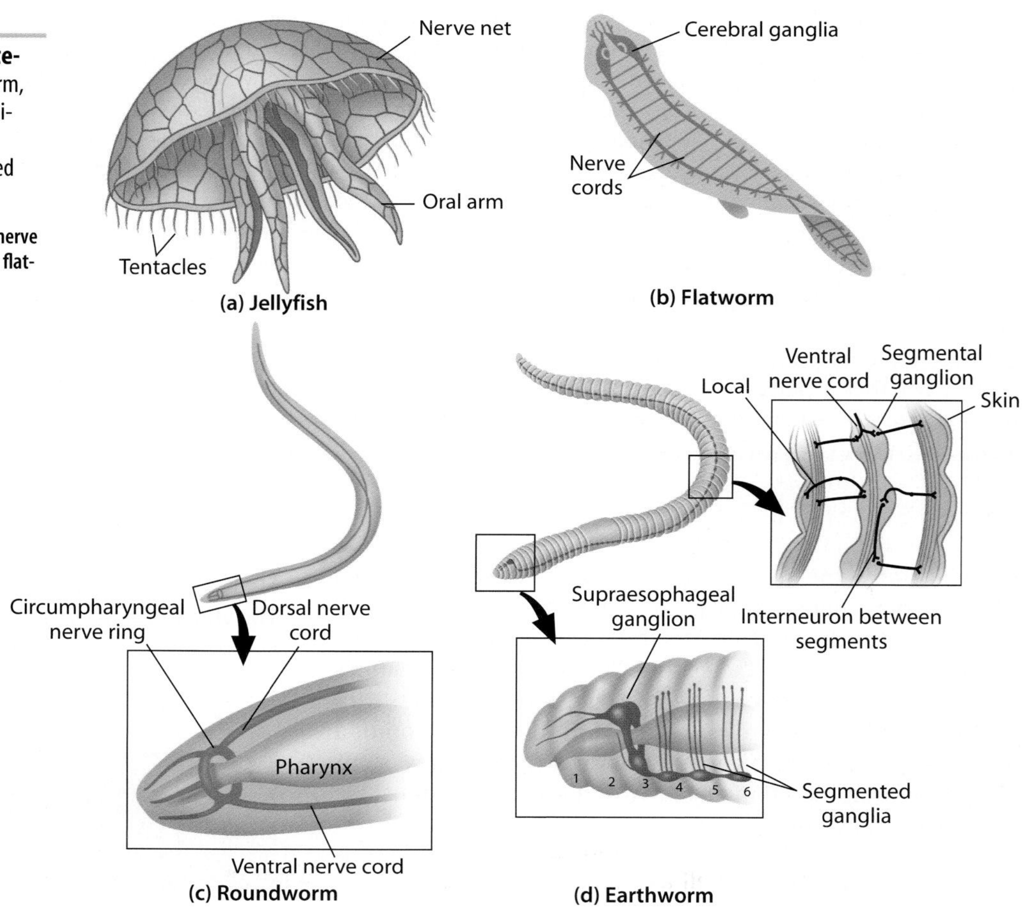

Figure 3.8
Nervous systems of some invertebrate species The jellyfish, flatworm, and roundworm are unsegmented animals. Segmentation, as seen in the earthworm, produces a more advanced nervous system.

➡ **What is the difference between the nerve net of the jellyfish and the ganglia of the flatworm?**

can be considered a primitive brain. The evolutionary process of concentrating neurons in the head region is called **cephalization,** or *encephalization.* As we move from primitive invertebrates to more complex invertebrates and then to the vertebrates, cephalization increases, with greater fusion of neurons and larger, more complex brains.

The nervous systems of the flatworm and roundworm are unsegmented; that is, their nervous system acts as a single system. By contrast, the nervous system of the earthworm is segmented, and each segment can act independently from the others. The belly of an earthworm contains a series of segmental ganglia, consisting of joined neurons (Figure 3.8d). Sensory neurons convey information from the outside world to the ganglion in only one segment, and motor neurons control the responses of that segment; interneurons connect the sensory and motor neurons. The segments communicate with each other by means of other interneurons that connect adjacent local segments. The fusion of neurons that is first evident in flatworms increases in the earthworm. Some local segments are fused in the earthworm's abdomen and thorax, and greater fusion of the neurons is observed in the **supraesophageal ganglion,** a primitive brain located above the esophagus.

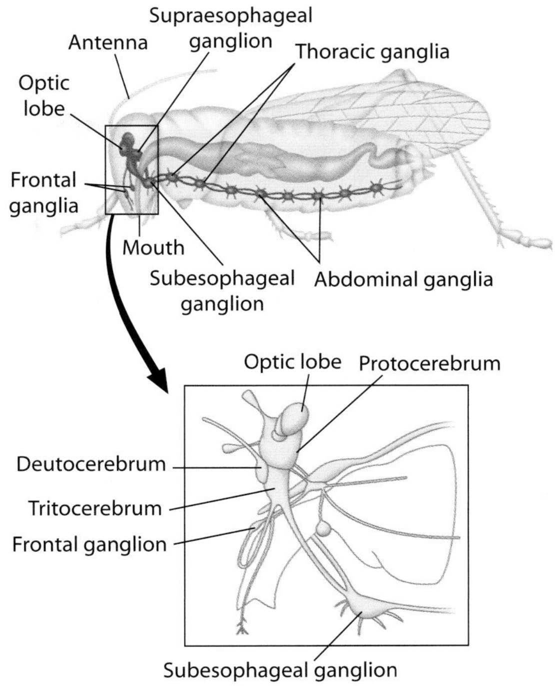

Figure 3.9

The nervous system of an insect
Many neurons are combined to form a large supraesophageal ganglion (brain) and paired ganglia in each body segment below the brain, with nerve fibers connecting each ganglion to the brain.

→ **Why is the insect considered a more advanced invertebrate than the earthworm?**

As you know from being outside on a warm summer evening, there are many different insect species. Insects have no rivals in the animal kingdom in terms of variety of color, structure, and habitat. Yet, despite this diversity, the central nervous system of all insects is quite similar (Edwards & Palka, 1971), consisting of a relatively larger supraesophageal ganglion than is seen in the earthworm and paired ganglia in each body segment behind the brain (Figure 3.9).

The insect brain is divided into three vesicles: the protocerebrum, the deutocerebrum, and the tritocerebrum. The *protocerebrum* has a right lobe and a left lobe, each connected to a large optic lobe. Neurons in the optic lobe receive input from both the compound eye and the brain.

The division of the protocerebrum into different parts suggests that function is localized in different areas of the insect brain. Also, the difference in the relative size of the parts of the protocerebrum among insects appears to be related to behavioral variations (Edwards & Palka, 1971). For example, one part of the protocerebrum is larger in social insects, such as bees, than in solitary insects, such as most wasps and mud daubers.

The Vertebrate Nervous System

The nervous systems of vertebrates are much more complex than those of invertebrates. A **vertebrate** has a protective covering over its spinal cord and brain—the vertebral column and bony skull—one of the major differences between the nervous systems of invertebrates and vertebrates. The cell bodies (somas) of vertebrate neurons tend to be located inside the bony coverings and the axons on the outside; in invertebrates, the axons are in the inner core of ganglia and cell bodies in an outer ring.

The spinal cord and brain of vertebrates are located on the back, or dorsal surface, of the body, whereas the nerve cord of invertebrates is usually on the ventral surface. In invertebrates, motor responses on each side of the body are controlled *ipsilaterally*—by the same side of the brain. In vertebrates, motor responses are controlled *contralaterally*—by the opposite side of the brain; in other words, instructions from the left side of the brain control actions on the right side of the body, and vice versa.

In the vertebrate brain, sensory information from one side of the body is transmitted contralaterally as well as ipsilaterally; in the invertebrate brain, sensory

cephalization The evolutionary process of concentrating neurons in the head region; the fusion of many ganglion pairs to form an increasingly larger and more complex brain.

supraesophageal ganglion A primitive brain above the esophagus, formed by the fusion of several ganglion pairs in certain invertebrates.

vertebrate An animal with a protective covering over its spinal cord and brain.

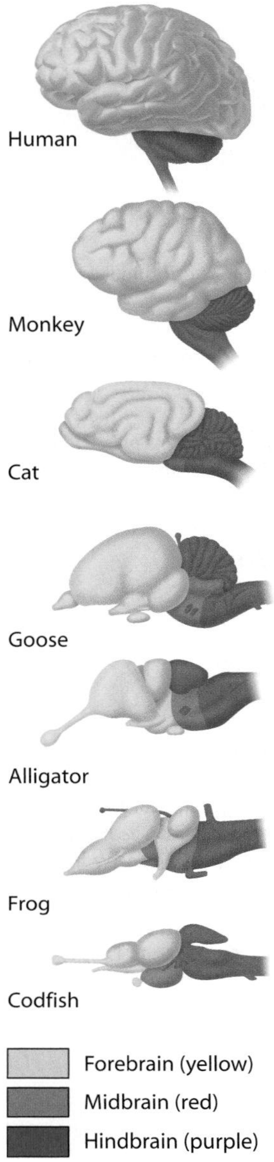

Figure 3.10
The brains of several vertebrate species The size of the forebrain relative to the hindbrain and midbrain increases in the more advanced vertebrates. The midbrain and part of the hindbrain are surrounded by the forebrain in humans.

➡ **Why can an alligator not use the phrase "You silly goose!"?**

Table 3.1
Comparison of Vertebrate and Invertebrate Nervous Systems

Vertebrate	Invertebrate
Protective covering over CNS	No protective covering over CNS
Cell bodies inside bony coverings; axons outside	Axons in inner core of ganglia; cell bodies in outer ring
CNS located on dorsal surface	Nerve cord usually on ventral surface
Motor responses controlled contralaterally	Motor responses controlled ipsilaterally
Sensory information contralateral and ipsilateral	Sensory information exclusively ipsilateral
Myelinated axons for rapid transmission of neural messages	Few giant axons for rapid transmission of neural messages
Larger number of neurons	Smaller number of neurons

transmission is exclusively ipsilateral. Invertebrates have a few giant axons that transmit neural messages rapidly; in mammalian vertebrates (as we discuss in Chapter 2), many axons are myelinated, which enables them to conduct impulses even more quickly. Table 3.1 summarizes the differences between the vertebrate and invertebrate nervous systems.

The vertebrate brain has a much larger number of neurons than the invertebrate brain. As noted earlier, the more extensive grouping or incorporation of neurons into a brain (cephalization) represents a major step in nervous system evolution. Much of the evolution of the vertebrate nervous system is evident within the brain. There are three distinct major divisions of the vertebrate brain: the hindbrain, the midbrain, and the forebrain (Chapter 2). These three regions are evident in the codfish (Figure 3.10). Note the large midbrain and hindbrain relative to the small forebrain. In a more advanced vertebrate such as the frog, the size of the forebrain relative to the other two regions is greatly increased. Development of the forebrain continues to increase in the more evolutionarily advanced vertebrate species. In humans, for example, the midbrain and much of the hindbrain are surrounded by the much larger forebrain.

The size of the forebrain is not the only difference among vertebrate nervous systems. The cerebral cortex, the part of the forebrain associated with human consciousness and intellectual functioning, is present in reptiles as a three-layered structure. Interestingly, part of the cerebral cortex in reptiles is analogous to the hippocampus in mammals, which also is a three-layered structure. The mammalian cerebral cortex, by contrast, generally has six layers of cells. The percentage of brain volume occupied by the cerebral cortex increases in mammals, accounting for more than half the volume in more advanced species.

In mammalian species, the cerebral cortex is deeply folded, or convoluted, which gives it greater surface area and a correspondingly larger number of neurons (Figure 3.11). In fact, two-thirds of the cortical surface in humans is hidden in the grooves. The total surface area of the human cerebral cortex is approximately 2.5 square feet of flat surface (Martini, 2003).

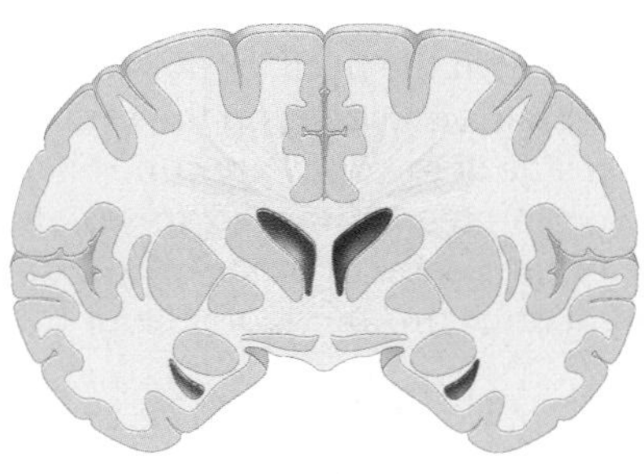

Figure 3.11
A cross section of the human brain This view reveals the extensive folding of the cerebral cortex.

➡ **What is the significance of the convolutions of the cortical surface?**

As the brain evolved, there were changes in function as well as in structure. For example, most visual processing occurs in the midbrain in fish, amphibians, reptiles, and birds, and in the cerebral cortex in mammals. The midbrain in mammals mainly controls certain reflexes and relays neural impulses to higher brain structures.

As you may already have guessed, as the forebrain becomes larger, the size of its

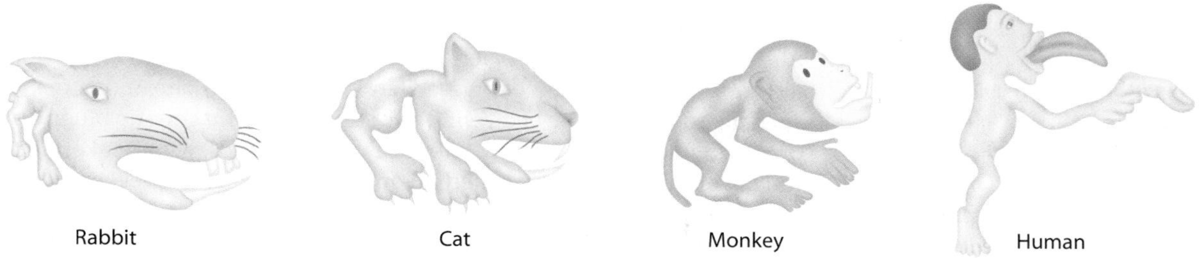

Figure 3.12
Proportional amount of cortex devoted to different body parts in some mammals The proportional size of cortical representation of different body parts, illustrated by these distorted images, depends on the species.

➡ **Other than the fingers and tongue, what body areas would you expect to find overrepresented in the human cortex?**

neurons and the number of synaptic connections between them increase. For example, the *pyramidal neurons* of the motor cortex play a significant role in the initiation of fine motor responses (Chapter 8); the size and number of dendrites and the size and number of axons of pyramidal neurons increase in more advanced mammalian species.

One difference between primates (including humans) and other mammals is that larger sensory and motor areas of the primate cerebral cortex are devoted to the hands (Figure 3.12) and certain other functionally important parts of the body (see Figure 2.27). This evolutionary adaptation is related to a greater ability to manipulate the environment. Humans also have large cortical areas devoted to speech recognition and production, which is associated with the significant role of language in our lives (Chapter 13). Moreover, larger areas of the cerebral cortex are devoted to nonsensory and nonmotor processes, allowing for greater analysis of information and for more varied behavioral responses to environmental stimuli. For example, our prefrontal cortex is involved in the planning and coordination of activities rather than in the recognition of environmental events or the initiation of motor responses.

Checkpoint

What is the advantage of encasing the cell bodies of neurons in a bony skull and vertebral column? Compare and contrast the nervous systems of a butterfly and a rabbit.

REVIEW

- Specialized nerve cells are present in simple invertebrates such as the jellyfish. Neurons are grouped into clusters in more complex invertebrates such as the flatworm. The primitive brain, or supraesophageal ganglion, of the earthworm is the first appearance of a segmented nervous system. Localization of function within the primitive brain is evident in insects.
- The vertebrate central nervous system is encased in a bony skull and vertebral column. The spinal cord and brain are on the dorsal or back surface rather than the ventral surface as in invertebrates.
- In mammalian species, many axons are covered by myelin, which increases the speed of neural impulses.
- In vertebrates, the brain has distinct forebrain, midbrain, and hindbrain regions; and in the more advanced vertebrates, the forebrain becomes larger relative to the other two regions.
- The sensory functions controlled by the midbrain in fish, amphibians, reptiles, and birds are taken over by the cerebral cortex in mammals.
- Nonsensory and nonmotor functions such as planning and coordination of activities are controlled by the cerebral cortex in humans and other primates.

The Structural Development of the Human Nervous System

Of most interest to biological psychologists, of course, is the human nervous system. Remarkable changes will occur during the development of Anne and Nathan's baby—from the time of **conception,** the moment of **fertilization** of an egg by a sperm, to his birth and beyond.

conception The moment of fertilization of an egg by a sperm.

fertilization The fusion of an egg nucleus and sperm nucleus.

zygote A single cell formed when the sperm fertilizes the egg.

embryo The human developmental stage for the first 8 weeks after conception.

fetus The human developmental stage beginning at 8 weeks and continuing for the remainder of the pregnancy.

endoderm The innermost layer of the embryo, which will form linings of the intestines, lungs, and liver.

mesoderm The middle layer of the embryo, which will form the connective tissue, muscle, and blood and blood vessel linings.

ectoderm The outermost layer of the embryo, which will become the nervous system, the skin, and parts of the eyes and ears.

differentiation The creation of different cell types.

neural plate The thickened ectodermal layer of the embryo.

neural fold The lateral edge of the neural plate.

The Human Embryo

After a sperm successfully penetrates the wall of the egg, the two nuclei fuse and a **zygote** is formed. The single-celled zygote has 46 chromosomes (23 from the sperm and 23 from the egg), which contain the entire genetic blueprint for embryonic and fetal development. After the zygote divides, which takes about 12 hours, the developing human is called an **embryo** for its first 8 weeks and a **fetus** for the remainder of the pregnancy. The cells of the embryo continue dividing, and after 3 days the result is a mass of homogeneous cells that looks like a cluster of grapes.

Figure 3.13
The cell layers of a 2-week-old embryo The three embryonic cell layers—endoderm, mesoderm, and ectoderm—will give rise to the body's linings, connective tissues, and nervous system, respectively.

➡ **Which layer will give rise to the spinal cord?**

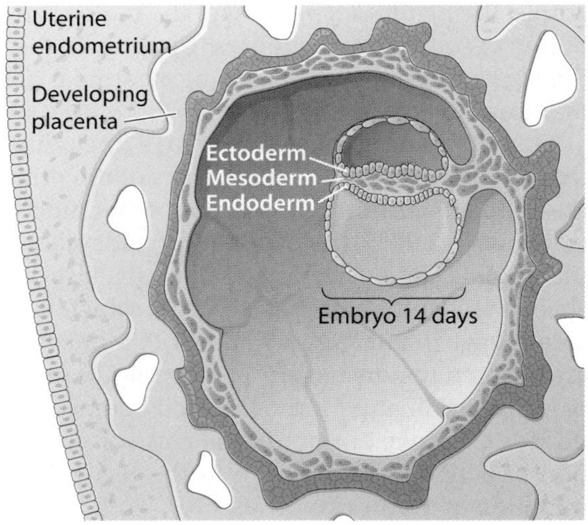

Within 2 weeks after conception, the embryo has divided into three distinct layers of cells (Figure 3.13). The **endoderm,** the innermost layer, will form many of the body's linings, including the linings of the intestines, lungs, and liver. The middle layer, the **mesoderm,** will form the connective tissues, such as muscle, bone and cartilage, and the blood and blood vessel linings. The layer of most interest to us is the **ectoderm,** the outermost layer, which will become the nervous system, as well as the epidermis (skin) and parts of the eyes and ears. **Differentiation,** the creation of different cell types, continues throughout embryonic and fetal development in the amazing process that produces a human being from a single fertilized egg cell. Our focus here is on the differentiation of the nervous system into the structures that enable us to walk, talk, and otherwise behave.

The Formation of the Nervous System

As cell division proceeds, the three embryonic layers thicken into three flat oval plates. The thickened ectodermal layer is called the **neural plate** (Figure 3.14). The lateral edges of the neural plate, the **neural folds,** push up to form a space called

Figure 3.14
Formation of the neural tube and central nervous system in the human embryo The neural groove begins to form in the neural plate at 20 days. At 21 days, the neural folds begin to fuse, forming the neural tube. At 23 days, the neural tube is completely formed, and the brain begins to emerge. The notochord is a rodlike supporting structure found in the lowest vertebrates and in the embryos of higher vertebrates.

➡ **What happens if the neural folds do not meet?**

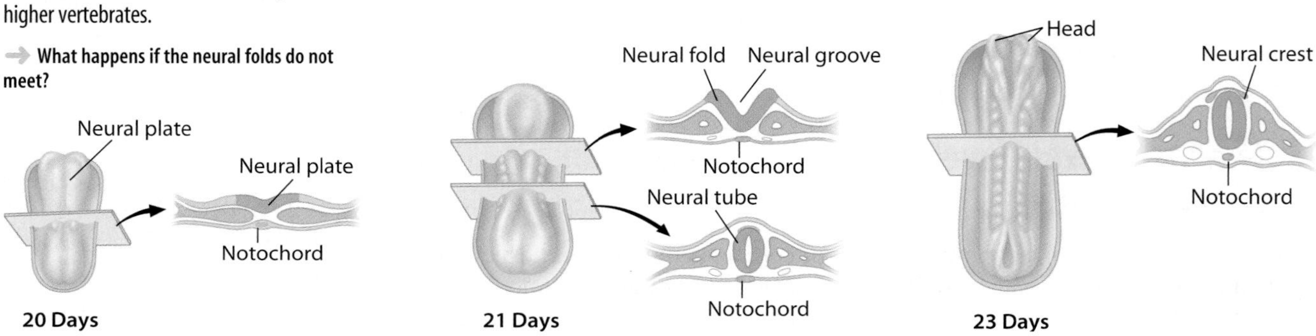

the **neural groove.** The groove begins to develop by day 20, and the neural folds continue to move toward each other for the next 3 days. If development proceeds normally, by day 23 the neural folds meet along the length of the embryo, and the neural groove becomes the **neural tube.** The brain and spinal cord then develop from the walls of the enclosed neural tube.

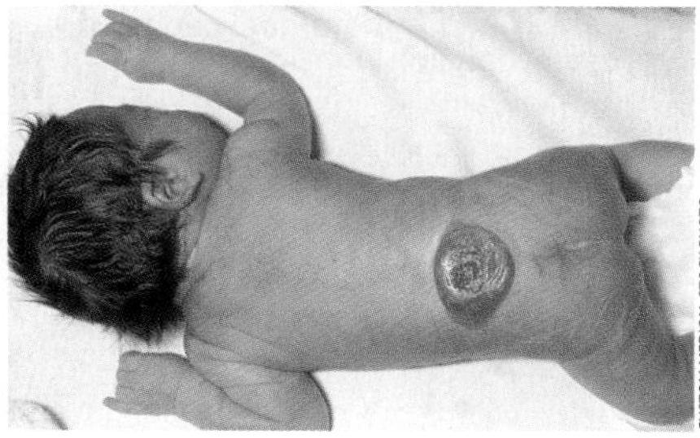

CUSTOM MEDICAL STOCK PHOTO

Figure 3.15

Neural tube defect Spina bifida is a common neural tube defect.

➔ **What recommendation would you give to a woman who is pregnant or wants to become pregnant to decrease the likelihood that she will have a baby with a neural tube defect?**

In some embryos, however, the neural folds fail to close, producing what is called a *neural tube defect (NTD)*. Spina bifida and anencephaly are two common NTDs. **Spina bifida** results when some part of the neural folds that gives rise to the spinal cord fails to close (Figure 3.15). A small opening may lead to minor problems, which can in some cases be corrected surgically. A large opening, especially one high in the spinal cord, can produce profound impairments, such as paralysis, limb deformities, and mental retardation. Some fetuses with spina bifida do not survive, but this disorder does occur in 1 of every 1,000 live births worldwide. Yet 50% to 75% of spina bifida cases could be prevented simply by adding supplemental folic acid, a common B vitamin, to the diet of women of childbearing age. In the United States, all breads and enriched cereal grains have been fortified with folic acid since January 1, 1998 (Folic Acid Information, 2001), and by 2001 the occurrence of spina bifida had undergone a 19% reduction (Folic Acid, 2001).

Anencephaly (literally, "no brain") is a defect that results when the brain or a major part of it fails to develop. Fetuses with this NTD are usually stillborn, and infants born with anencephaly die shortly after birth.

Anne's obstetrician recommended that she undergo amniocentesis in the 16th or 17th week of pregnancy because, in addition to detecting the genetic defects that chorionic villus sampling (CVS) can reveal (such as Down syndrome), amniocentesis can also detect neural tube defects such as spina bifida and anencephaly. The danger of miscarriage is also less with amniocentesis than with chorionic villus sampling, because CVS is done earlier in the pregnancy (between the 10th and 12th weeks), when the fetus is less well established.

When development proceeds normally, the neural tube cavity becomes the ventricular system, and the cells that line the neural tube walls produce the neurons and glial cells of the CNS. These cells also produce a specialized group of migratory cells, which form the **neural crest** (see Figure 3.14). Shortly after forming, neural crest cells leave the dorsal region of the neural tube, migrating away from it to form several types of tissue, including the sensory and autonomic neurons of the peripheral nervous system.

The Developing Brain

From its beginning at a relatively late stage of embryogenesis, the structural development of the nervous system proceeds rapidly (Jessell & Sanes, 2000). The rostral (toward the head) part of the neural tube becomes the brain, and the caudal (tailward) part becomes the spinal cord. The brain initially differentiates into three vesicles: the forebrain, or **prosencephalon;** the midbrain, or **mesencephalon;** and the hindbrain, or **rhombencephalon** (Figure 3.16).

At about the 4th week of embryonic development, the forebrain and the hindbrain divide again (see Figure 3.16). The forebrain subdivides into the **telencephalon,** which includes the cerebral cortex, the basal ganglia, and the limbic system, and the **diencephalon,** which includes the epithalamus, the thalamus, and the hypothalamus. The midbrain does not divide. The hindbrain divides into the **metencephalon,** which includes the pons and the cerebellum, and the **myelencephalon,** which includes the medulla oblongata. By the 11th week of embryonic

neural groove The space formed between the edges of the neural folds.

neural tube The closed space that is formed when the neural folds meet and close the neural groove.

spina bifida A neural tube defect that results when some part of the neural folds fails to close.

anencephaly A neural tube defect that results when the brain or a major part of it fails to develop.

neural crest A specialized group of cells that migrate away from the neural tube to form several types of tissue, including the sensory and autonomic neurons of the PNS.

prosencephalon Another name for the forebrain, which divides into the telencephalon and the diencephalon.

mesencephalon Another name for the midbrain.

rhombencephalon Another name for the hindbrain.

telencephalon The division of the forebrain that becomes the cerebral cortex, the basal ganglia, and the limbic system.

diencephalon The division of the forebrain that becomes the epithalamus, the thalamus, and the hypothalamus.

metencephalon The division of the hindbrain that becomes the pons and the cerebellum.

myelencephalon The division of the hindbrain that becomes the medulla.

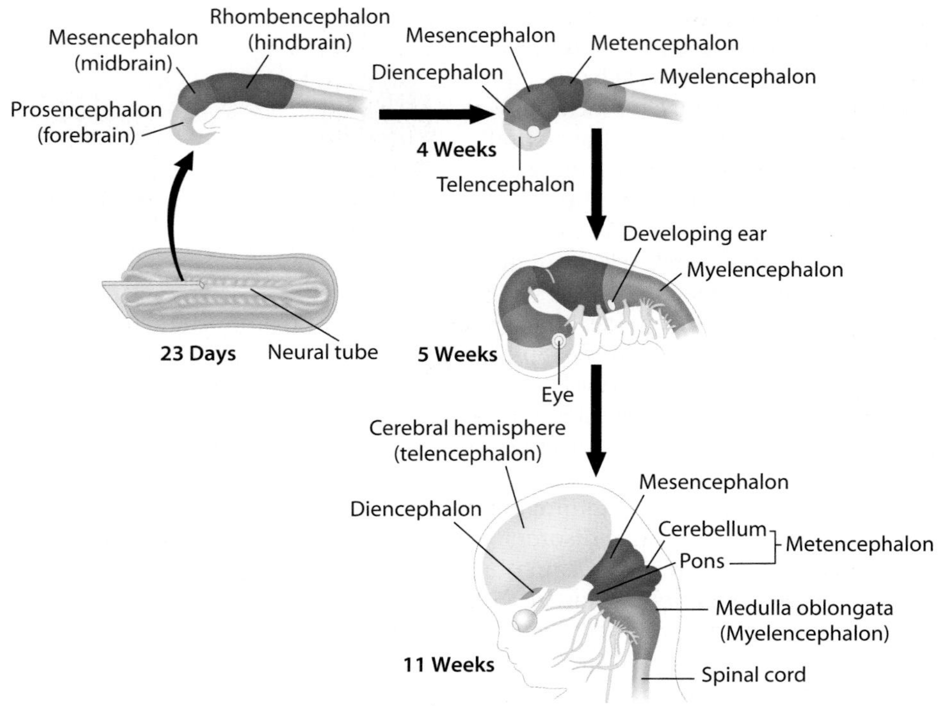

Figure 3.16
Development of the neural tube into the spinal cord and brain of the human embryo By day 23, the brain has differentiated into three separate structures: the forebrain, the midbrain, and the hindbrain. Development is shown at 4, 5, and 11 weeks; the major divisions of the brain are apparent at 11 weeks.

➔ Which of the three structures shown at 23 days will develop into the cerebral cortex? Which structures form from the telencephalon? The mesencephalon?

development, many of the key brain structures have developed and are clearly visible. Figure 3.17 provides a flow chart illustrating the differentiation of the brain.

➤Checkpoint
What causes spina bifida? What are the three initial divisions of the brain? Which mature (adult) brain structures develop from these divisions?

The Developing Spinal Cord

As we indicated in Chapter 2, the mature spinal cord has a dorsal root, with neurons that bring sensory input from the body and a ventral root, with neurons that control motor responses (see Figure 2.15 to review these spinal cord structures). This organization emerges during embryonic development and is complete when a baby is born. Two major zones of cells appear in the developing spinal cord (Figure 3.18). The **alar plate,** the dorsal portion of the neural tube, gives rise to the sensory neurons and the interneurons of the spinal cord's dorsal horn. The **basal plate,** the ventral portion of the spinal cord, gives rise to the motor neurons and

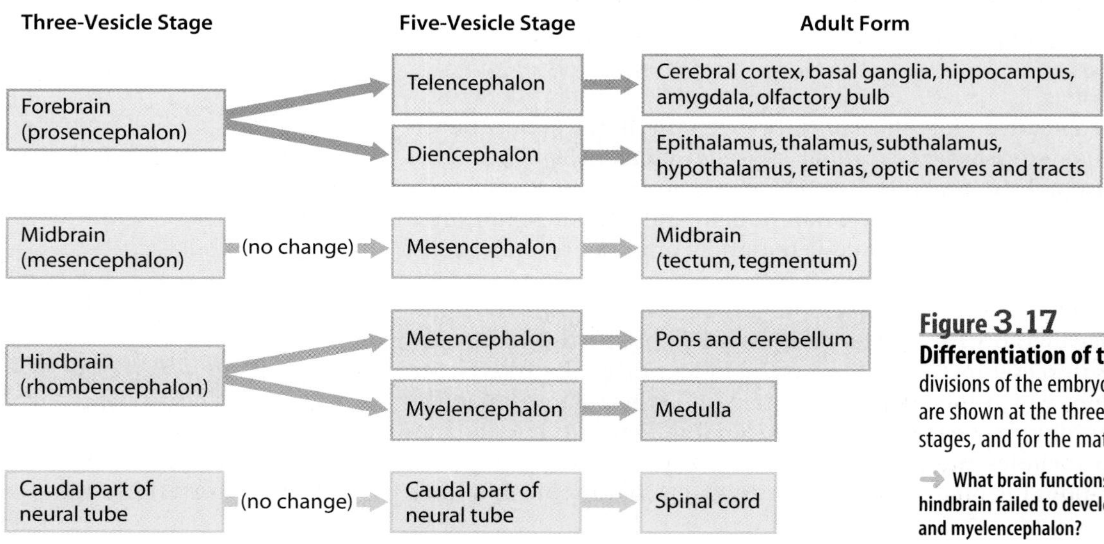

Figure 3.17
Differentiation of the brain The main subdivisions of the embryonic central nervous system are shown at the three-vesicle and five-vesicle stages, and for the mature adult.

➔ What brain functions would be impaired if the hindbrain failed to develop into the metencephalon and myelencephalon?

the interneurons of the ventral root. The sympathetic and parasympathetic nervous systems also derive from the basal plate.

The spinal cord of the 3-month-old fetus runs the length of the vertebral column. As the fetus develops, however, the vertebral column lengthens more than the spinal cord. This results in a spinal cord that extends only to the level of the third lumbar vertebra in the newborn and only to the first lumbar vertebra in the adult. Thus, the spinal nerves that extend to and from the lumbar and sacral vertebral segments are quite long, which is why they form a structure called the *cauda equina*, or horse's tail. Think about it: Nerves have to run from the middle of your back all the way down to your toes. Although the spinal nerves are covered with the protective meninges, with additional protection provided by the cerebrospinal fluid, because of their length these nerves are still subject to damage. As we get older, many of us develop sciatica, or pain in the lower back and leg from irritation of the long sciatic nerve that runs down the back of the thigh.

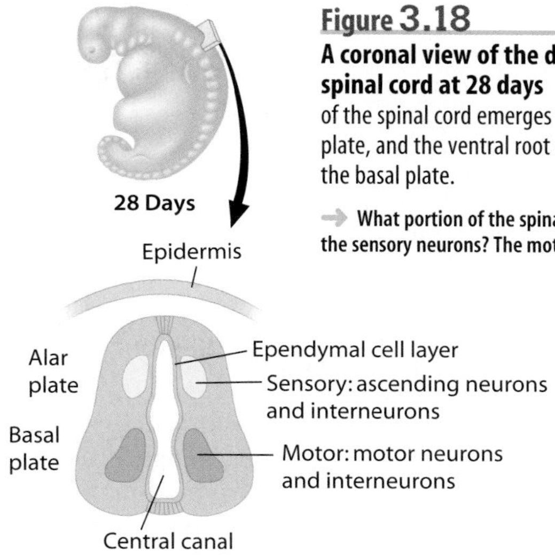

Figure 3.18

A coronal view of the developing spinal cord at 28 days The dorsal root of the spinal cord emerges from the alar plate, and the ventral root emerges from the basal plate.

➔ What portion of the spinal cord contains the sensory neurons? The motor neurons?

The Developing Ventricular System

As noted earlier, the ventricular system develops in the cavity inside the neural tube. The ventricles contain the CSF, which will cushion and nourish the central nervous system. The brain's four ventricles (the two lateral ventricles, third ventricle, and fourth ventricle) and the central canal of the spinal cord all develop during the embryonic stage.

Checkpoint

What would happen if the dorsal horn of the spinal cord did not develop properly from the alar plate? Or the ventral horn from the basal plate? What are the four components of the ventricular system? What is the function of this system?

REVIEW

- During embryonic development, the nervous system emerges from the ectodermal layer to form the neural plate and then the neural tube. The ventricular system forms in the cavity of the neural tube.
- The inner cells of the neural tube give rise to the central nervous system and to neural crest cells.
- The brain initially differentiates into three vesicles: the forebrain, the midbrain, and the hindbrain. The hindbrain develops into the metencephalon, which becomes the pons and cerebellum, and the myelencephalon, which becomes the medulla.
- The forebrain develops into the telencephalon, which becomes the cerebral cortex, the basal ganglia, and the limbic system, and the diencephalon, which becomes the epithalamus, the thalamus, and the hypothalamus.
- The dorsal horn of the spinal cord develops from the alar plate and receives sensory input from the peripheral nervous system. The ventral horn of the spinal cord develops from the basal plate and controls motor responses.
- The ventricular system consists of four ventricles—the two lateral ventricles, the third ventricle, and the fourth ventricle—and the central canal.

The Cellular Development of the Nervous System

Our discussion to this point has focused on the development of the gross structures of the nervous system. These structures, as you know, are composed of millions of neurons and supporting cells. How are these individual neurons formed and how do they make the billions of connections that will enable Anne and Nathan's baby to smile for the first time, take his first steps, and speak his first words?

alar plate A zone of cells in the dorsal portion of the neural tube that develops into the sensory neurons and the interneurons of the dorsal horn of the spinal cord.

basal plate A zone of cells in the ventral portion of the neural tube that develops into motor neurons and interneurons of the ventral horn of the spinal cord and the sympathetic and parasympathetic nervous systems.

The Formation of Neurons and Glial Cells

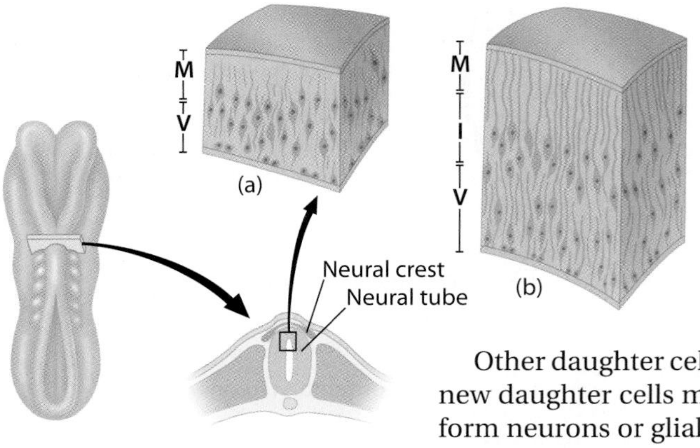

Figure 3.19
The proliferation of neurons and glial cells on the inner surface of the neural tube (a) At an early stage of embryonic development (23 days), only the inner ventricular layer (V) and outer marginal layer (M) are present. (b) A few days later, as the embryo develops, the intermediate layer (I) emerges as the neural tube thickens. Daughter cells migrate from the ventricular to the intermediate and marginal layers. Some daughter cells become neurons and glial cells, and others return to the ventricular layer, where they divide again; these new cells then return to the intermediate and marginal layers.

➡ **From which of the three layers of cells do neurons and glial cells develop?**

With its extensive capacity for thought, memory, action, and simple reflexes, the nervous system begins as a single layer of ectodermal cells along the inner surface of the neural tube (see Figure 3.13). These cells divide and eventually form a closely packed layer of cells called the **ventricular layer** (unrelated to the ventricular system). Further division of these ventricular layer cells produces daughter cells, which migrate initially to the outer surface or *marginal layer* and later to the *intermediate layer* of the neural tube. Some daughter cells are destined to become neurons or glial cells (Figure 3.19).

Other daughter cells return to the ventricular layer and divide further, and these new daughter cells migrate to the marginal or intermediate layer, where they will form neurons or glial cells or return again to the ventricular layer. The intermediate layer thickens over time, and when it becomes well-established, two new layers are formed. Some daughter cells migrate to a layer between the intermediate and marginal layers, the **cortical plate.** The cortical plate eventually develops into the neurons and glial cells of the cerebral cortex.

Daughter cells also form the **subventricular layer** between the intermediate and ventricular layer. These cells become either glial cells or interneurons. Daughter cells that remain in the ventricular layer after the migration develop into *ependymal cells,* which form the lining of the brain's fluid-filled cavities—the ventricles—and the central canal of the spinal cord (see Figure 3.18).

Division of the daughter cells continues throughout embryonic and fetal development. The formation of new neurons, called **neurogenesis,** continues until birth in most mammalian species (Jacobson, 1991). In humans, few neurons are formed after birth, although there are exceptions. Specifically, cerebellar cells continue to form for several months after birth, olfactory receptor neurons are replaced throughout our lives, and hippocampal neurons and some cortical neurons continue to form. Research by Elizabeth Gould and her associates (e.g., Gould, Tanapat, & others, 1999; Shors & others, 2002) suggests that the birth of hippocampal cells is important for learning and memory (Chapter 14). Gould and her coworkers have also proposed that the birth of new neurons in the cortex of the prefrontal, inferior temporal, and posterior parietal lobes is important for cognitive function (Gould, Reeves, & others, 1999). This neurogenesis in cognitive areas endows the brain with sufficient plasticity, known as **neuroplasticity,** to adapt to changing environmental conditions. We return to this subject in later chapters, especially in Chapter 14 in the context of learning and memory.

Some daughter cells become neurons as they migrate from the inner to the outer surface of the developing nervous system. Their migration is not random but is guided by specialized **radial glial cells** (Figure 3.20). These cells radiate outward from the inner to the outer surface of the developing nervous system, like the spokes of a bicycle wheel. A newly formed neuron, with short extensions at its "head" and "tail" ends, creeps along the radial glial cell as if it were shinnying up a rope. Radial glial cells act like guide wires, enabling the new neurons to migrate to the appropriate locations. Once the initial neurons have migrated, their axons can serve as guides for further neuronal migration, so later-migrating cells can use either radial glial cells or the axons of previously migrated neurons as their guides (Hatten, 1990; Rakic, 2003).

What might be the effect of abnormalities in the neuronal migration process? Increasing evidence has accumulated in the last 2 decades for the idea that schizophrenia is a neurodevelopmental disorder (Beauregard & Bachevalier, 1996; Harrison, 1999). At least one neurodevelopmental hypothesis suggests that the disorder begins with an abnormal migration of neurons into the hippocampus (Kovelman & Scheibel, 1984). As evidence for this hypothesis, abnormal distri-

ventricular layer The innermost layer of the developing nervous system; its cells become daughter cells, some of which become neurons or glial cells.

cortical plate A layer of daughter cells between the intermediate and marginal layers that develop into the neurons and glial cells of the cerebral cortex.

subventricular layer A layer of daughter cells between the intermediate and marginal layers that become either glial cells or interneurons.

neurogenesis The formation of new neurons.

neuroplasticity The ability of some areas of the brain to form new neurons.

radial glial cell A glial cell that guides the migration of daughter cells during the embryonic development of the nervous system.

butions of neurotrophins that guide cell migration have been found in post-mortem brain tissue from schizophrenic patients (Durany & others, 2001). The researchers found a significant increase of brain-derived neurotrophic factor (a chemical that directs cell migration) in cortical areas and a significant decrease in the hippocampus relative to control subjects. Further, Akbarian and colleagues (1996) found an abnormal distribution of neurons left over from neural development in the frontal lobes of schizophrenics, suggesting a problem with either neuronal migration or with the pattern of programmed cellular death. Either problem could produce defective circuits in the brains of schizophrenics. We discuss schizophrenia in greater detail in Chapter 15.

In addition to the structural help provided by radial glial cells and by other neurons, neurons are aided by **glycoprotein** molecules—compounds in which a protein is combined with a carbohydrate group (Sanes & Jessell, 2000b). Neural cell adhesion molecules and cadherins (two types of glycoprotein molecules) are found on the surfaces of neurons and radial glial cells (Karagogeos, 2003; Tepass & others, 2000). These molecules allow neurons to bind to other neurons or to radial glial cells by providing sticky neuron-to-glial-cell or neuron-to-neuron handholds to help the migrating neuron shinny up the "rope."

Similarly, integrins (another type of glycoprotein) on the surface of the neuron bind with integrins in the extracellular matrix. If these molecules fail to guide neuronal migration properly, the result can be either a reduced number or a disorganized arrangement of neurons. In either case, neurological disorders are likely to result from glycoprotein failure. For example, mice deficient in neural cell adhesion molecules have been found to display such behavioral deficits as reduced exploratory behavior, impaired spatial learning, and increased aggressive behavior (Stork & others, 1997).

Rakic and Caviness (1995) have described the effects of a failure of normal cell migration in a genetic mutant mice strain. In the normal mouse, neurons accumulate in the cortex from the inside out. By contrast, in the genetic mutant mouse, the first generation of cortical neurons lies near the surface and the last generation lies deepest, resulting in an inverted cortex. Unusual reeling movements are just one consequence of this abnormal cell migration in the mutant mouse.

Until recently, scientists who wanted to study mutant animals had to depend on either spontaneous mutations, which are rare, or animals that had been treated in a way known to produce mutations, such as exposure to radiation. Now, however, researchers use either *knockout* mice, animals in which a gene of interest has been deleted, or knocked out, or *transgenic* mice, animals in which a gene has been transplanted into its genome (the animal's complete set of genes). In later chapters, we discuss research using either knockout mice or transgenic mice in order to create mutations of interest.

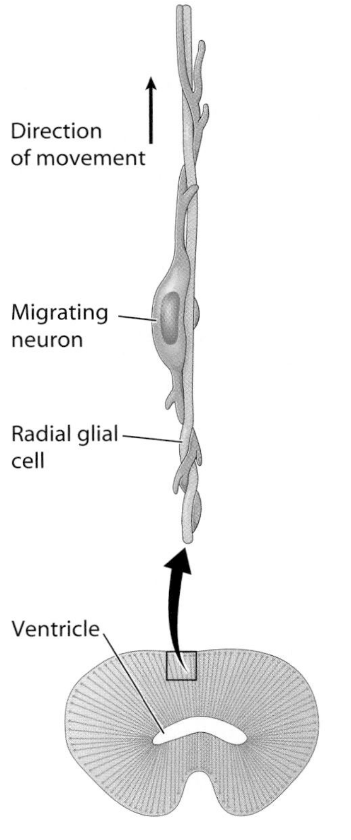

Figure 3.20
The migration of a neuron along a radial glial cell The radial glial cells extend outward like the spokes of a bicycle wheel. The neuron creeps along a radial glial cell to its predetermined location in the emerging nervous system.

→ **What chemical substance helps the neuron move along the radial glial cell?**

Checkpoint

What is neurogenesis? Describe the migration of daughter cells among the cell layers of the neural tube. How do radial glial cells and glycoproteins differ in guiding neuronal migration?

Neural Cell Differentiation

The cells that migrate from the inner ventricular layer to the outer marginal layer of the developing nervous system look more like most other cell types. Neurons do not assume their distinctive appearance until they reach their intended location (see Figure 2.4 for a typical neuron structure). As we noted in Chapter 2, not all neurons look alike. Spinal motor neurons are large, multipolar cells, whereas sensory neurons can be either unipolar or bipolar (see Figure 2.6). Neurons achieve their differentiation in one of two ways: cell-autonomous differentiation or induction.

Cell-autonomous differentiation occurs when neurons develop without outside influence, by genetic programming that directs them to develop in a particular way. The Purkinje cell illustrates cell-autonomous differentiation (Figure 3.21). *Purkinje cells* are found in the cerebellum, which, as you will recall from Chapter 2, is involved in developing and coordinating skilled movements. A Purkinje cell will develop into

glycoprotein A class of compounds in which a protein is combined with a carbohydrate group.

cell-autonomous differentiation A process by which neurons develop without outside influence.

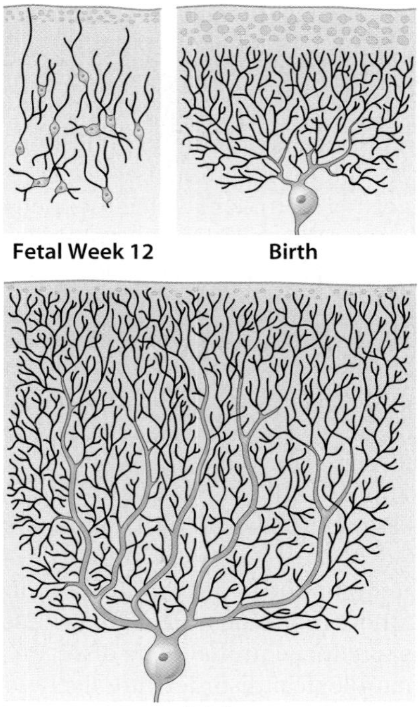

Figure 3.21
Purkinje cells at different developmental ages Shown here are Purkinje cells of the cerebellum at week 12, at birth, and in the adult. A Purkinje cell develops extensive dendritic trees; this development is determined solely by the cell's genetic makeup and, unlike some other types of neural cell development, is not influenced by other cells.

➔ **How would the nervous system be affected if Purkinje cells did not develop extensive dendritic trees?**

its final distinctive form even when it is extracted from its natural environment and grown in culture (Gianola & others, 2003; Marino & others, 2003), and thus it must contain the genetic instructions sufficient for developing its distinctive dendritic branching without any influence from other cells. (The role of Purkinje cells in movement is discussed in Chapter 8.)

In **induction,** neurons rely on other cells to determine their final form. The other cells release chemicals to effect the change. One example is the differentiation of the spinal motor neuron. The notochord, which lies just beneath the developing nervous system (see Figure 3.14)**,** influences some (but not all) of the cells in the spinal cord to become motor neurons (Roelink & others, 1994). Some researchers have found that the extracellular protein vitronectin is the chemical that directs certain neurons to become spinal motor neurons (Pons & Marti, 2000).

Glial Cell Development

Glial cells develop in the ventricular layer from the same daughter cells that produce neurons, but we do not know what determines whether a daughter cell differentiates into a neuron or into a glial cell. Glial cell production from immature cells in the ventricular layer starts in the embryonic period and continues into the postnatal period. In fact, the most intense glial cell production occurs after birth.

Myelination, the wrapping of the nerve axon with a protective myelin sheath, is an important glial cell function (see Figure 2.8), beginning in the cranial and spinal nerves at about 24 weeks. In the CNS, myelination starts in the fiber tracts within the spinal cord, spreads to the hindbrain, then to the midbrain, and finally to the forebrain. The cortical sensory areas are myelinated before the motor areas, which is why sensory functions mature ahead of motor functions. Anne and Nathan's son will have a well-developed sense of smell, taste, and hearing before he learns to walk.

➤Checkpoint

Compare and contrast the two types of neural cell differentiation. Suggest why the most intense period of glial cell production occurs after birth.

REVIEW

- ➤ The nervous system begins as a single layer of cells along the inner surface of the neural tube that divides into a closely packed ventricular layer.
- ➤ Daughter cells migrate from the ventricular layer to predetermined locations in the marginal or intermediate layers of the neural tube to become either neurons or glial cells.
- ➤ Radial glial cells and previously formed neurons guide the migration of neurons, as newly formed neurons creep along their surfaces.
- ➤ Neural cell differentiation occurs either by cell-autonomous differentiation or by induction.
- ➤ Glial cells emerge from the immature cells of the ventricular layer during both the prenatal and postnatal periods to myelinate neurons of the peripheral nervous system, the spinal cord, and the brain.

induction A process in which neurons rely on the influence of other cells to determine their final form.

The Formation of Neural Connections

Once a neuron has migrated to its destination and has achieved its characteristic form through induction or cell-autonomous differentiation, it is ready to establish the connections that will allow it to function as an effective part of the nervous system. These connections are established by the growth of axons toward their **target cells,** which can be other neurons, muscles, glands, blood vessels, or organs, such as the liver. The axon emerges from the **growth cone,** the swollen end of the developing neuron. Spinelike extensions called **filopodia** ("thread feet") extend from the growth cone (Figure 3.22), stretching and retracting as though searching for something. Once they find it, they appear to adhere to the extracellular environment and pull the growth cone in a particular direction, elongating the developing axon without moving the cell body.

In addition to being the person responsible for the acceptance of neuronal theory (Chapter 1), Ramón y Cajal proposed in 1911 that chemicals guide the direction of axonal growth, in a process called **chemotropism** (from the Greek *tropos,* meaning "turn"). The target cell releases **neurotrophins,** chemicals that attract the filopodia and guide the axon to its appropriate location (Crone & Lee, 2002; Dickson, 2002). Several well-known neurotrophins include nerve growth factor (NGF), brain-derived neurotrophic factor (BDNF), neurotrophin 3 (NT3), and neurotrophin 4 (NT4). Filopodia are believed to use the concentration gradient of the chemical released by the target cell to guide their movement. That is, they are thought to move toward the area with the highest concentration of the chemical, much like a fox hunts a rabbit by the strength of its scent. Figure 3.23 illustrates the movement of the filopodia and growth cone toward the target cell.

Working together, Rita Levi-Montalcini and Stanley Cohen discovered the first neurotrophin, NGF, which is produced by target cells in the sympathetic nervous system (Cohen, 1959; Levi-Montalcini & Hamburger, 1951). When they injected newborn mice with NGF antibodies, total degeneration of sympathetic ganglia occurred. (An *antibody* is a protein produced by blood cells that binds to a specific antigen and helps to destroy it.) For discovering NGF and demonstrating its necessity for the development of the sympathetic nervous system, Levi-Montalcini and Cohen shared the 1986 Nobel Prize in Physiology or Medicine.

Different neurotrophins are involved in the development of different parts of the nervous system. NGF is necessary for the development of sympathetic nerves in the PNS, and BDNF is involved in the development of visual pathways (Caleo & others, 2000). In addition, chemical signals may attract the growth cone of some cells but repel that of others, thus ensuring that only the appropriate axon moves toward a particular target cell (Cook & others, 1998).

The path an axon takes to reach its target cell may be long, and there may be abrupt directional changes along the way. The map that guides the axon in making these changes is composed of cells appropriately called **guidepost cells** (Johansen & Johansen, 1997). When the filopodia reach a guidepost cell, the growth cone adheres to it, and the guidepost cell then redirects axonal growth toward the target cell (Figure 3.24).

When an axon reaches its target cell, a synaptic connection forms between the two. As the synapse is formed, the neurotransmitter that will be used for communication between the two neurons is also established through chemicals released

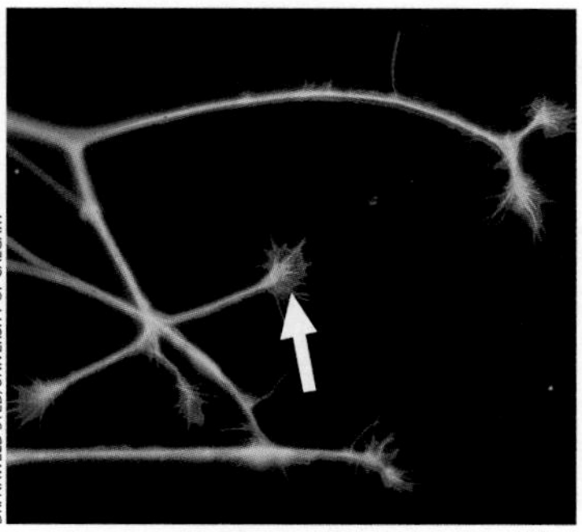

DR. NAWEED SYED/UNIVERSITY OF CALGARY

Figure 3.22

The growth cone This photomicrograph shows growth cones of a developing neuron, each with its many filopodia. (The arrow points to one growth cone.)

→ **What is the function of the filopodia in the development of the neuron?**

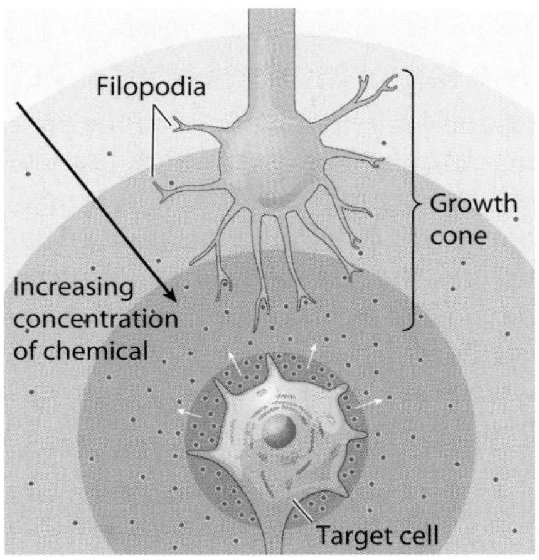

Figure 3.23

The movement of filopodia and the growth cone As the filopodia move, they pull the growth cone toward target neurons that are releasing a particular chemical (represented by the red dots). This allows the axon to establish new neural connections.

→ **How do the filopodia pull the growth cone to its destination?**

target cell A cell with which a neuron establishes synaptic connections.

growth cone The swollen end of the developing neuron from which an axon emerges.

filopodia Spinelike extensions from the growth cone that pull the axon to the target cell.

chemotropism The process by which a target cell releases chemicals that attract filopodia and guide the axon to its appropriate location in the nervous system.

neurotrophin A chemical released by a target cell that attracts the filopodia of a developing neuron.

guidepost cell A cell that redirects the growth of the axon toward the target cell.

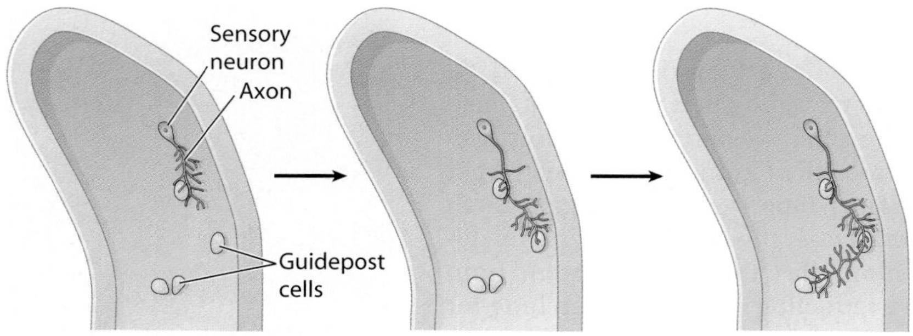

Figure 3.24
Migration of the axon of a sensory neuron The axon of a sensory neuron grows toward its predetermined location in the nervous system. Guidepost cells direct the axon on its long and circuitous route.

➡ **What happens when the filopodia reach a guidepost cell?**

by the target cell (Perrone-Capano & Di Porzio, 2000). Schotzinger and colleagues (1994) have provided compelling evidence that the target determines the neurotransmitter released from the presynaptic neuron.

Norepinephrine is the neurotransmitter found in most sympathetic neurons of the autonomic nervous system (noradrenergic neurons; see Chapter 4). The sympathetic neurons that innervate sweat glands in the footpads of rats are an exception: They are cholinergic, using acetylcholine as the neurotransmitter. Newly differentiated sympathetic neurons destined for the sweat glands initially have the same properties as other sympathetic neurons, but as the axon of a sympathetic neuron approaches the sweat gland, the neuron adopts acetylcholine as its neurotransmitter. Schotzinger and colleagues (1994) found that if the sweat glands of the rat footpad were replaced with a parotid gland, which is naturally innervated by noradrenergic sympathetic neurons, cholinergic synapses did not develop. Noradrenergic synapses did develop, however, revealing that the target (the parotid gland, in this case) determines the transmitter released by the neurons growing toward it.

The Importance of Neural Activity

Not all final neural connections are established during neural development. During axon growth, many side branches emerge. Some of these branches are lost; others become more elaborate and eventually form synaptic connections with the appropriate neural areas. Carla Shatz and her associates have shown that adult neural connections emerge during development by a process Shatz calls *axonal remodeling* (Kanold & others, 2003; Katz & Shatz, 1996; Lein & others, 2000). According to Katz and Shatz, axons grow to many different "addresses," some of which are correct and some of which are not. Axons at the correct addresses remain, and those at the incorrect addresses are eliminated.

A brief look at the development of the visual system will illustrate the complexity of axonal remodeling. The axons of the ganglion cells of the retina migrate to specific sites in the thalamus, where they synapse with particular neurons in the lateral geniculate nucleus (Figure 3.25). The axons of these LGN neurons in turn migrate to specific sites in the occipital lobe of the cerebral cortex, where they synapse with specific neurons. The axons of ganglion neurons do not migrate to just any neuron in the LGN; instead, the axons of adjacent ganglion neurons synapse with the dendrites of adjacent LGN neurons, which then synapse with adjacent neurons in the cerebral cortex. Thus, neurons in the visual system not only develop to specific target sites but do so in alignment with adjacent cells.

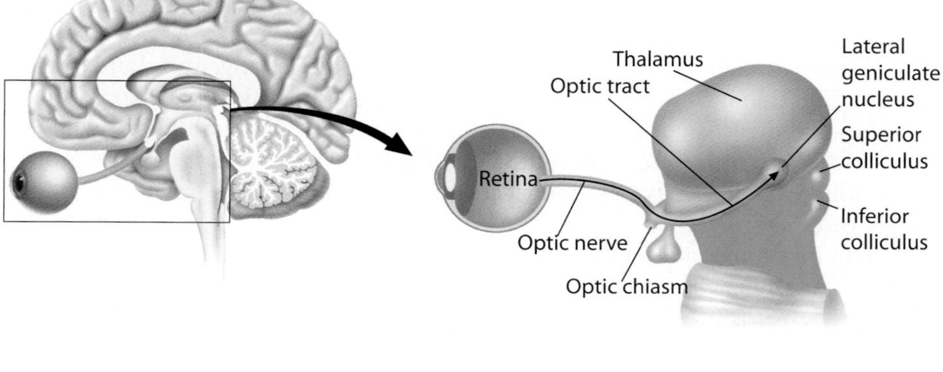

Figure 3.25
Development of the visual pathway from the retina to the LGN The neural circuit between the retina and primary visual cortex is set up when the growth cones of ganglion cell bodies grow toward their target cells, the neurons in the LGN.

➡ **What is the significance of the cell migration process?**

As we discuss in Chapter 6, this alignment ensures that neural activity in the visual system is not random but temporally and spatially defined. That is, an object in our visual field activates specific receptors in our eyes, which in turn send their information to specific cells feeding into specific portions of the LGN and from there to particular parts of the occipital lobe. This continuing specificity through the visual "pipeline" enables us to perceive the characteristics of our visual environment accurately—to know precisely where and what an object is, for example.

Katz and Shatz (1996) have suggested that neurons that fire together in temporal and spatial sequences get wired together, which is why adjacent ganglion neurons synapse with adjacent LGN neurons. As described earlier, axonal growth is controlled by chemicals that attract the growth cone to the target neuron, or repel it. However, a specific neurotrophin is not sufficient for neural development; neurons must also respond, or conduct a neural impulse, in order for axonal growth to progress to the target neuron. Without neural activity, the neuron will connect to both correct and incorrect addresses. As Shatz (1992) found, administering a drug (tetrodotoxin) that blocks neural impulses traveling from ganglion neurons to LGN neurons produced more extensive rather than more restricted neural connections. Apparently, neural activity is necessary for ensuring that the correct wiring takes place (Shatz, 1996).

Maffei and Galli-Resta (1990) reported spontaneous discharges of neural activity from fetal ganglion cells, and this spontaneous neural activity occurred in the darkness of the developing eye. Further, they found that such activity occurred in predictable and rhythmic bursts. The activities of these ganglion cells were highly correlated; that is, simultaneous activity was much more likely in neighboring cells than in ganglion neurons distant from one another. Apparently, patterns of neural activity in the developing fetus lead to nervous system wiring that enables environmental events to produce similar patterns of neural activity. In addition, such neural activity patterns have been shown to occur during a brief critical period early in development (McLaughlin & others, 2003).

Shatz and her colleagues have shown that this spontaneous neural activity and the activity-dependent changes in synaptic connectivity are governed by a type of antigen called class 1 major histocompatibility complex antigen (Huh & others, 2000). Mice deficient in this antigen fail to develop normal adult patterns of synaptic activity.

We have seen that almost all neuron formation and growth occurs during prenatal development. At birth, Anne's baby's brain will weigh approximately 350 g, and it will increase in size to approximately 800 g by his first birthday. By adulthood, the young man's brain will weigh approximately 1,350 g. This increase in brain weight comes mainly from the increasing size of existing neurons rather than the formation of new neurons. Thus, the brain becomes bigger because of increases in the size of neurons, the number of axons and dendrites, and the number of synaptic connections between axons and dendrites (Shatz, 1992).

New synaptic connections continue to form after birth. These new connections permit the increasingly sophisticated analysis of information and the varied behavioral responses to the environment that develop during infancy and childhood. For example, at birth Anne's baby will be able to see things at a distance of approximately 75 cm, just far enough to see his mother's face when she is cradling or nursing him. By 6 months he will be able to see things at approximately 7.5 m, and as an adult he will be able to read a road sign from at least 100 m. In Chapter 14, we examine the formation of the new synaptic connections that develop from postnatal experience—learning.

Neural Cell Death

Although you are unlikely to think of cell death as having any place in a discussion of normal neural development, neural cell death is a natural developmental process. In fact, in some regions of the CNS, most neurons die during development,

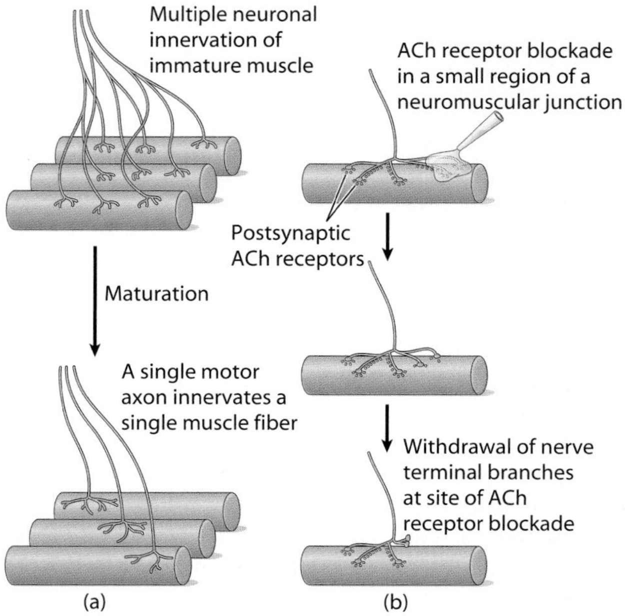

Figure 3.26

Pruning of synaptic connections with maturation (a) Before birth, each muscle fiber is innervated by several motor axons; after birth, only one terminal remains, and it enlarges. (b) Local postsynaptic inactivity (in this case, produced by blockade of acetylcholine [ACh] receptors) causes withdrawal of nerve terminal branches.

➡ **Does the decline in multiple innervation of a muscle fiber weaken the reaction of the muscle fiber?**

and overall, the extent of cell death is quite large (Oppenheim, 1991). In a study of genetically programmed cell death (apoptosis), Rakic and Zecevic (2000) found that embryonic cell death is probably unrelated to the establishment of neuronal circuitry, whereas fetal apoptosis does appear to be related to such circuitry.

One theory about neural cell death is that neurons compete for connections to target cells; neurons that establish adequate connections survive, and the remainder die. A second theory is that neurons that receive a certain amount of the chemical released by the target cells survive, and neurons that receive less than this amount die.

Some synaptic connections are lost during development through a process analogous to the pruning of a tree or a bush. For example, Redfern (1970) recorded the synaptic responses from skeletal muscle fibers in newborn rats and observed a declining number of synaptic inputs to a single muscle fiber over the first weeks after birth. This reduction is caused by the withdrawal of some presynaptic terminals from the muscle fiber, not a decrease in motor neurons. Because of this withdrawal, over the course of development, the number of muscles activated by a motor neuron declines. But the strength of the muscle fiber reaction does not decline. Instead, the one remaining presynaptic terminal is joined by additional presynaptic terminals and postsynaptic receptor sites, which allows the single motor neuron to produce a stronger synaptic input to the muscle fiber, thereby substituting for innervation from several different motor neurons.

Synaptic elimination also occurs in the CNS (Goda & Davis, 2003). For example, over the course of development, the number of one type of fiber that innervates a Purkinje cell in the cerebellum declines from several to a single fiber that synapses with the cell in the mature cerebellum (Hashimoto & Kano, 2003). Figure 3.26 illustrates synaptic elimination in motor axons.

Human brain growth slows by late childhood or young adulthood and begins to reverse at about age 40. The weight of the brain decreases because of a reduction in the size of brain cells as well as an increase in rate of neuronal death. This normal change in the number and size of brain cells does not significantly affect a person's intellect. However, diseases such as Alzheimer's cause a substantial death of brain cells and are thus quite different from the normal aging process.

➤Checkpoint

Describe the physical and chemical means used by filopodia to reach a target cell. Why do some neurons die during development? Why are some synaptic connections lost during development?

REVIEW

- Axons grow toward target cells to establish neural connections. Filopodia extend from the growth cones of the axons and pull the growing axons toward their target cell.
- Neurotrophins, chemicals released by target cells, attract the filopodia. Different neurotrophins guide the development of different parts of the nervous system.
- Guidepost cells direct axons along a sometimes long and circuitous route to their target cells.
- Neurotrophins released by a target cell also influence the type of neurotransmitter released by the axon.
- Neural development occurs in response to neural activity; axon remodeling involves a selective strengthening of appropriate synaptic connections and an elimination of inappropriate ones by neural cell death.

Failures of Neural Development

As you learned in Chapter 2, the nervous system is designed to detect information, recognize its relevance, decide on a response, and execute that response. Normal development produces a system that can perform all four tasks. Developmental defects (such as spina bifida and anencephaly) can lead to failures in any or all of the major functions. In some cases, the failures are preventable, but in other cases they are not.

Genetic defects also can result in impaired neural development (Mochida & Walsh, 2001; Nissenkorn & others, 2001). In broad terms, an altered gene leads to altered cellular proteins and thus altered cellular functions. The result may be a change in the behavior controlled by the neurons. For example, earlier in the chapter we mentioned that amniocentesis could detect **Down syndrome.** This condition is characterized by altered facial features, decreased mental functioning, and abnormalities in several internal organs. Down syndrome is caused by a defect that produces three copies of chromosome 21 instead of the usual two (the syndrome is also called trisomy 21; Figure 3.27). Down syndrome is much more likely to occur in babies born to women over age 35, and recent evidence suggests advanced paternal age may also be a factor (Fisch & others, 2003).

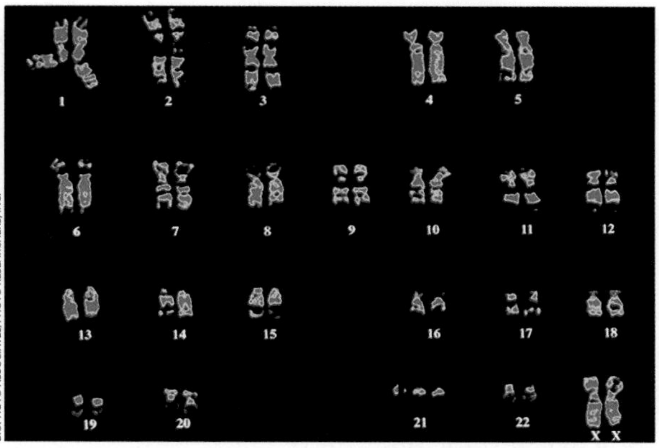

BIOPHOTO ASSOCIATES/PHOTO RESEARCHERS, INC.

HATTIE YOUNG/SCIENCE PHOTO LIBRARY

Figure 3.27
Down syndrome An extra copy of chromosome 21 results in Down syndrome, with its characteristic altered facial features.

➜ **What are some other characteristics of this disorder?**

Phenylketonuria (PKU) is caused by the absence of an enzyme needed to break down phenylalanine, an amino acid present in many foods. If the disease is untreated, phenylalanine accumulates in the body and prevents the normal myelination of neurons, resulting in severe mental retardation. PKU is caused by a recessive allele carried by approximately 1 in 50 people, and it occurs in about 1 in 13,500 to 1 in 19,000 live births in the United States (Phenylketonuria, 2000). Fortunately, PKU is easy to detect through early screening of phenylalanine levels, and Anne's baby will be tested for it before he leaves the hospital. If he is found to have the disorder, a diet low in phenylalanine for the early years, especially the first two, will prevent the nervous system impairment and mental retardation typically associated with PKU. Continued dietary restriction has been associated with a better long-term outcome than an unrestricted diet (Koch & others, 2002; Poustie & Rutherford, 2000), and some groups recommend that the restrictive diet be maintained throughout life (Cleary & Walter, 2001; Merrick & others, 2003). Such dietary restriction is particularly important for women with PKU who become pregnant. In one study, more than 90% of infants born to mothers with PKU who did not maintain an optimal low blood level of phenylalanine during pregnancy had some degree of mental retardation (Levy, 1987). Now you know why diet soda cans and bottles carry the warning: "Phenylketonurics: contains phenylalanine." (A phenylketonuric is a person who has PKU.)

Fragile X syndrome is the leading inherited cause of mental retardation (Oostra & Willemsen, 2002). People with this disorder have abnormal facial features—a long, narrow face; large, prominent ears; and a prominent forehead and jaw (Figure 3.28)—and mild to severe mental retardation (Baumgardner & others, 1994). Hyperactivity and attention deficits are also associated with the disorder. As the name implies, fragile X syndrome is caused by a mutant gene at one site on the large arm of the X chromosome that can cause the X chromosome to break. Normally, the gene is responsible for producing a protein called FMR-1, but the

Down syndrome A genetic disorder caused by an extra copy of chromosome 21; characterized by altered facial features, decreased mental functioning, and abnormalities in several internal organs.

phenylketonuria (PKU) A genetic disorder involving the absence of an enzyme needed to break down phenylalanine; the resulting buildup of phenylalanine can lead to mental retardation.

fragile X syndrome A disorder caused by a fragile gene at one site on the large arm of the X chromosome that can cause the chromosome to break; characterized by an abnormal facial appearance and mental retardation.

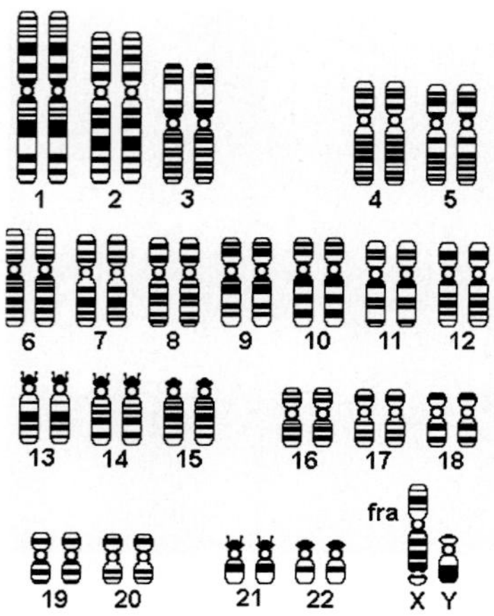

Figure 3.28
Fragile X chromosome disorder An abnormal X chromosome results in the high forehead, large ears, and slightly crossed eyes that are characteristic of people with this disorder.

➡ **What are some other characteristics of this disorder?**

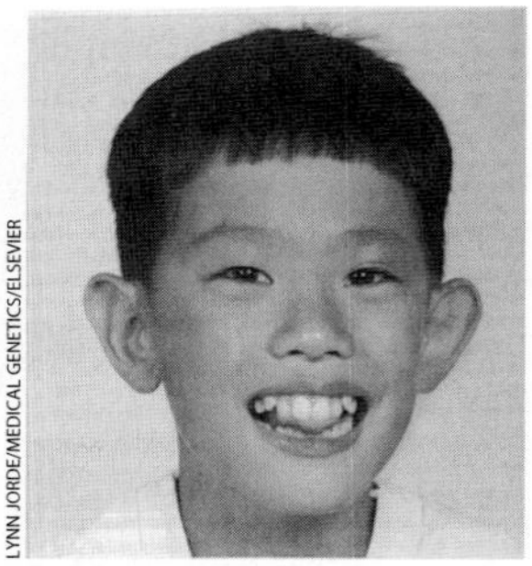
LYNN JORDE/MEDICAL GENETICS/ELSEVIER

fragile gene produces drastically reduced levels of FMR-1 (Paulson & Fischbeck, 1996). The consequences of reduced FMR-1 protein are widespread, because this protein is widely distributed in fetal tissue, especially in differentiating and migrating neurons (Dykens & others, 1994).

A variety of external factors also can affect the developing nervous system. Here we look at two such factors that demonstrate how sensitive the developing nervous system is to disruption: malnutrition and alcohol consumption.

You may have heard or seen public health announcements urging women to seek medical care during pregnancy. One reason for this advice is to ensure that pregnant women receive nutritionally sound dietary information. Failure to provide sufficient nutrients to the developing fetal brain can have a variety of negative consequences. For example, malnutrition has extremely detrimental effects on the developing brain (Gordon, 1997; Rao & Georgieff, 2000) and is associated with lowered performance on tests of mental capacity (Sanchez-Lastres & others, 2003); it can also cause problems such as decreased birth weight and increased infant mortality (Darnton-Hill & Coyne, 1998). The damaging effects of malnutrition can sometimes be reversed with early and prolonged intervention (Gunston & others, 1992; Meeks & others, 1995). For example, using CT scans, Akinyinka and colleagues (1995) found that cerebral shrinkage and ventricular dilation following protein malnutrition could be reversed by 2 months of nutritional rehabilitation.

Malnutrition and stunted child development are particularly common in some less developed countries (Figure 3.29). For example, a recent investigation of the problem in Sierra Leone, a western African nation, concluded that 46% of child deaths in the country are the result of malnutrition (Aguayo & others, 2003). Further, without appropriate policy changes, an estimated 74,000 children will die from malnutrition over the next 5 years, and if the current levels of iodine deficiency are not reversed, an estimated 252,000 children could be born with various degrees of mental retardation.

Figure 3.29
Malnutrition This child shows the physical effects of extreme malnutrition.

➡ **Can malnutrition's effects be reversed? If so, how?**

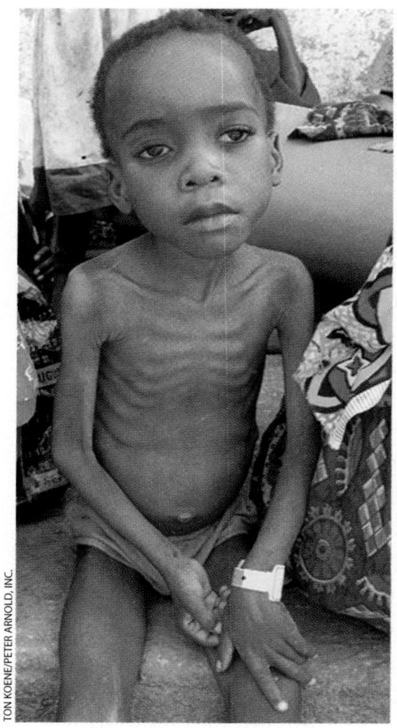
TON KOENE/PETER ARNOLD, INC.

Malnutrition can be prevented by the nutritional counseling included in prenatal medical care. Even if an expectant mother thinks she is eating properly, a deficiency in a single nutrient can cause irreversible damage to the developing fetus. Earlier we noted that a diet deficient in folic acid can cause neural tube defects such as spina bifida and anencephaly in the first few weeks of development, possibly before the woman even realizes she is pregnant. For this reason, in the United States, folic acid has been added to food staples such as bread, just as Vitamin D is added to milk.

A mother's consumption of even moderate amounts of alcohol during pregnancy sometimes causes significant physical and behavioral problems in her child (Meschke & others, 2003; Sood & others, 2001), which can be recognized within the first year of life (Van Der Leeden & others, 2001). Individuals born with **fetal alcohol syndrome (FAS)** have low birth weight and diminished height, distinctive facial features (sunken nasal bridge, altered shape of nose and eyelids; Figure 3.30), and cognitive/behavioral problems (men-

fetal alcohol syndrome (FAS) A disorder caused by alcohol consumption by the mother during pregnancy; characterized by low birth weight and diminished height, distinctive facial features, mental retardation, and behavioral problems (hyperactivity and irritability).

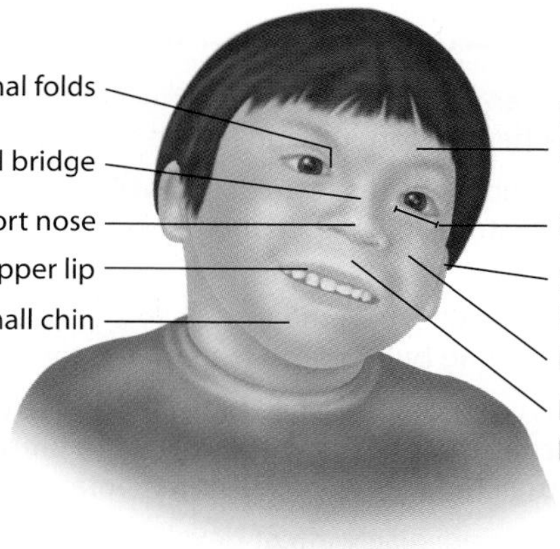

Figure 3.30
Fetal alcohol syndrome Individuals with FAS typically have the facial features identified at the left.

→ **What are some other characteristics of this disorder?**

tal retardation, hyperactivity, and irritability). Behavioral disturbances such as hyperactivity and relatively poor performance on a learning task were seen in adolescent monkeys whose mothers had ingested moderate amounts of alcohol during pregnancy (Schneider & others, 2001, 2004). Further, Wass and colleagues (2001) found that maternal alcohol consumption during pregnancy was associated with a reduction in the size of the frontal cortex in human fetuses; such reduction might account for the behavioral problems observed in other studies. Because a threshold for alcohol consumption that causes FAS has not been established, pregnant women are generally advised to avoid consuming alcohol.

Although FAS is known throughout the world, the incidence is apparently much greater in the United States than in European and other countries (Abel, 1995), which Abel (1998) has dubbed the "American Paradox." The difference in rates does not seem to be related to alcohol consumption. In both the United States and other countries, low socioeconomic status appears to be the major factor associated with FAS (Abel, 1995; Viljoen & others, 2002).

Table 3.2 summarizes these defects resulting from abnormal neural development.

Checkpoint

Give two examples of genetic failures of neural development. Why is what a pregnant woman eats and drinks important to the development of the fetal nervous system?

Table 3.2
Failures of Neural Development

Type of Defect	Characterized by
Developmental defect	
Spina bifida	Paralysis below the level of the defect
Anencephaly	Failure in all major functions
Genetic defect	
Down syndrome	Altered facial features, decreased mental functioning, organ abnormalities
Phenylketonuria	If untreated, accumulation of phenylalanine and severe mental retardation
Fragile X syndrome	Abnormal facial features, mild to severe mental retardation
Defect from external factors	
Malnutrition	Decreased birth weight and increased mortality, low performance on tests of mental capacity
Fetal alcohol syndrome	Low birth weight, diminished height, distinctive facial features, hyperactivity and irritability, mental retardation

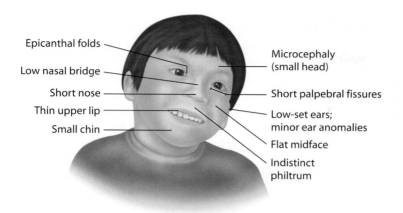

REVIEW

- Neural development can be impaired by defective genes, causing such disorders as Down syndrome, phenylketonuria, and fragile X syndrome.
- Down syndrome, in which there are three copies of chromosome 21, is characterized by altered facial features, decreased mental functioning, and abnormalities in several internal organs.
- Phenylketonuria (PKU) results from the lack of an enzyme needed to break down phenylalanine; the resulting buildup can lead to mental retardation.
- Fragile X syndrome is caused by a fragile gene at one site on the large arm of the X chromosome, which can cause the chromosome to break; people with this disorder have an abnormal facial appearance and mental retardation.
- External factors that can adversely affect development include malnutrition during pregnancy, which can lead to low birth weight, increased risk of infant mortality, and neural tube defects; and alcohol consumption during pregnancy, which can lead to fetal alcohol syndrome.

Neuroplasticity

We have discussed several ways in which the developing nervous system can be damaged, and in Chapters 1 and 2 we cited a number of instances of damage to the nervous system after development is complete (e.g., penetrating head injury such as that suffered by Phineas Gage, and closed head injury as described in the opening vignette of Chapter 2). Here we revisit what can happen if the nervous system is damaged after development is completed. Consider, for example, the case of actor Christopher Reeve, who in 1995 fell from his horse in a riding accident, broke his neck, and was paralyzed from the neck down. What happened to Reeve's damaged neurons and how much function had he recovered by the time of his death in 2004?

ARNALDO MAGNANI/GETTY

Christopher Reeve with his wife, Dana, and daughter, Alexandra (far left), in April 2000.

Neural Degeneration

The nervous system can suffer damage in many ways, including blunt trauma from a blow (or many blows, in the case of Sugar Ray Martin), invasive trauma from a projectile such as a bullet or a tamping rod, and the death of neurons as a result of tumors, infections, drugs and other toxic substances, exposure to radiation, and degenerative conditions such as Parkinson's disease. (Some of the causes of brain damage are discussed in Chapter 2.)

If damage to a neuron involves the cell body, the neuron will die, because the cell body is the neuron's metabolic heart. Damage to the axon, however, leads to degenerative changes that may or may not kill the neuron. When an axon is damaged, the part between the injury and the presynaptic terminals, the distal part of the axon, breaks down through a process called **anterograde degeneration** (Figure 3.31). Anterograde degeneration is triggered by the separation of the distal part of the axon from the cell body and its metabolic activities. Degeneration back toward the cell body may also occur, through a process called **retrograde degeneration.** In some cases, the axonal cut leads to degenerative changes in the cell body, whereas in others, regenerative changes (discussed below) occur (Goldberg & Barres, 2000). In the former case, the cell body breaks down through the process of **chromatolysis.** It is easy to remember the difference between anterograde and retrograde degeneration if you recall that the transmission of neural messages is a one-way process from the cell body, down the axon, and to the synapse (Chapter 2): Anterograde degeneration is forward (toward the synapse) from the damage, and retrograde degeneration is backward (toward the cell body).

anterograde degeneration The breakdown of an axon from the site of damage to the presynaptic terminals.

retrograde degeneration The progressive breakdown of an axon between the site of the break and the cell body.

chromatolysis The breakdown of a neuronal cell body following damage to the axon.

A degenerating neuron may in turn damage neurons with which it has synaptic connections. The result may be slight changes in connecting neurons, or the changes may be severe enough to cause affected neurons to degenerate through **transneuronal degeneration.** This can occur in neurons receiving synaptic input from the degenerating neuron (*anterograde transneuronal degeneration*) and in neurons that synapse onto the degenerating neuron (*retrograde transneuronal degeneration*).

Transneuronal degeneration can lead to widespread nervous system damage (Johnson & Cowey, 2000; Kodama & others, 2003). For example, suppose the axons of some retinal ganglion cells that are part of the optic nerve are severed. The degeneration of these cells will lead to anterograde degeneration of neurons in the LGN. From there, the degeneration may spread to the connecting neurons in the occipital lobe, to adjacent cortical neurons, and then back to the LGN and retinal ganglion layer. From the initially severed ganglion cell axons, the end result is a severely damaged visual system, with a consequent loss of the ability to process visual information. A more detailed discussion of the visual system and the effects of damage to it is presented in Chapter 6.

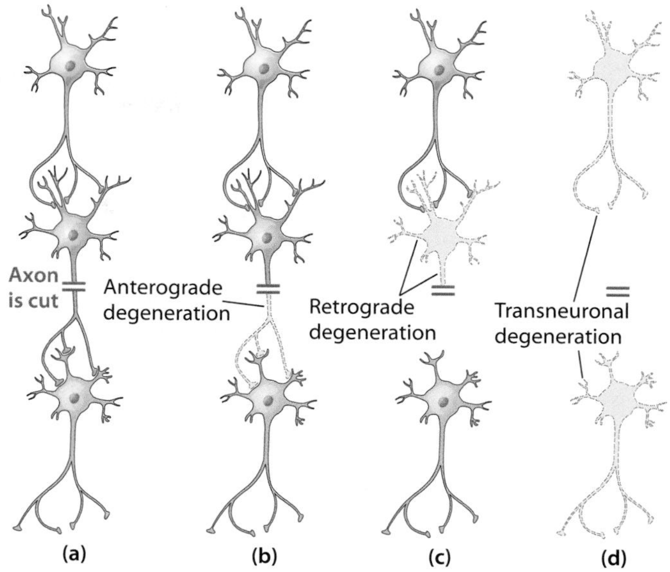

Figure 3.31
Degeneration of a neuron or neurons following damage to an axon
After (a) axotomy (the severing of an axon), (b) the portion of the axon beyond the cut degenerates (anterograde degeneration), (c) the remainder of the cut neuron may degenerate (retrograde degeneration), and (d) other neurons in that neural pathway may degenerate—those before the cut neuron (retrograde transneuronal degeneration) and those after (anterograde transneuronal degeneration).

→ Describe how anterograde, retrograde, and transneuronal degeneration might severely affect a neural system's ability to function.

The Regeneration of Damaged Neurons

Whether or not regeneration occurs depends on the location of the damage to the nervous system and the age at which the damage occurs (Prang & others, 2001). If the damaged axon is in the peripheral nervous system, the neuron can regrow and reestablish its connections to other neurons. However, such **neural regeneration** generally does not occur for damaged axons in the CNS of an adult (Figure 3.31); exceptions include regeneration in the olfactory system (Miwa & others, 2002) and the regeneration of some retinal cells (Campbell & others, 2003; Taylor & Bampton, 2004) (Table 3.3).

Although regeneration usually does not occur in the mature nervous system, it does take place in embryonic and neonatal nervous systems (Prang & others, 2001). Apparently the difference between mature and younger systems lies in the loss of specific proteins that promote axon growth in the younger systems (Goldberg & Barres, 2000). For example, in the retina, Bcl-2 is a protein that controls the ability of neurons to grow axons. In a review of studies, Merry and Korsmeyer (1997) concluded that the loss of Bcl-2 occurs at the same time that retinal ganglion cells lose their ability to regenerate. Researchers have also found that retinal ganglion cells

Table 3.3
The potential for neural regeneration

Regeneration	Lack of Regeneration
PNS, immature CNS	Mature CNS (exceptions: olfactory system, some retinal cells)
Damaged CNS neurons transplanted into PNS	Damaged PNS neurons transplanted into CNS
Aided by glycoproteins (laminin, fibronectin) that promote cone growth	Caused by loss of axon growth-promoting proteins
Myelin-forming Schwann cells in PNS do not synthesize growth-inhibiting glycoproteins	Myelin-forming oligodendrocytes in CNS synthesize axon growth-inhibiting glycoproteins

transneuronal degeneration Damage to neurons with which a degenerating neuron has synaptic connections.

neural regeneration The regrowth of a neuron and the reestablishment of its connections to other neurons.

are more likely to regenerate in transgenic mice (mice that have received foreign genes) that express Bcl-2 into adulthood than in other mice (Chen & others, 1997).

Factors external to the damaged neuron account for at least some of the difference in regeneration potential in the CNS and the PNS of mature animals. We know this because damaged CNS neurons will regenerate if they are transplanted into the PNS, but damaged PNS neurons transplanted into the CNS do not regenerate (Bray & others, 1987). Thus, whether regeneration occurs depends on something intrinsic to the PNS other than the neurons themselves.

Sanes and Jessell (2000a) have identified a variety of factors that may explain regeneration in the PNS but not in the CNS. For example, two glycoproteins that promote cone growth—laminin and fibronectin—are present in the mature mammalian PNS but not in the mature CNS. These glycoproteins facilitate the regeneration of damaged axons in the PNS; their absence from the CNS makes regeneration unlikely. In addition, the oligodendrocytes that form the myelin sheath in the CNS synthesize a glycoprotein that inhibits axonal growth, but this is not true of the myelin-forming Schwann cells of the PNS.

Enhancing Regeneration

Earlier in this chapter we noted that chemical signals can repel as well as attract axon growth toward a target cell during nervous system development. Several researchers have investigated the possibility that suppression of growth-inhibiting chemicals in adult rats following CNS damage might facilitate regeneration in the damaged neurons. Some of these studies looked at regeneration of corticospinal motor axons (axons of neurons connecting the cerebral cortex with the spinal cord) following spinal cord lesions in adult rats exposed to antibodies that neutralize axon growth-inhibitory proteins (GrandPre & Strittmatter, 2002; Raineteau & others, 2002). Such antibody exposure led to significant long-distance regeneration of the axons of corticospinal motor neurons.

Additional studies have examined the recovery of motor functions in similarly treated rats and have reported the recovery of some, but not all, motor functions (Bregman & others, 1995; Kunkel-Bagden & others, 1993). For example, although the length of a rat's stride is shortened by such spinal cord damage, animals treated with the antibodies displayed a normal stride length. Other motor functions remained impaired despite antibody administration, however. For example, the same researchers found that contact placement—lifting a limb and placing it on a surface for support following light skin contact such as a pin prick—in spinal cord–damaged animals was not improved by antibody administration. Contact placement is a more precise sensory-motor response than stride length, which may explain the different results. Research continues on axon growth with inhibitory protein antibodies as a way to regenerate axons in the CNS. The usefulness of this approach for people with spinal cord damage appears promising, but much more research is needed.

Figure 3.32

Collateral sprouting (a) Undamaged neurons. (b) Degeneration of one neuron following damage to the axon leads to collateral sprouting of another neuron. The new axon terminals synapse with the receptor sites formerly occupied by the degenerating neuron.

➔ **What is the purpose of collateral sprouting?**

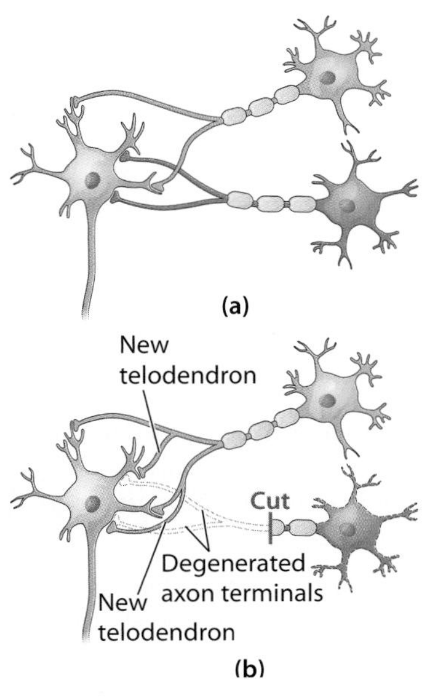

Collateral Sprouting

Although mature CNS neurons cannot regenerate after damage, research shows that nearby neurons can compensate for the loss of neural connections through **collateral sprouting.** When a neuron degenerates, neighboring neurons sometimes sprout new axonal endings to connect to the vacated receptor sites (Figure 3.32). Goldstein and colleagues (1997) observed collateral sprouting in the lumbar region of the spinal cord in adult rats following an incomplete midthoracic injury. It is also possible that such sprouting can reinstate normal functioning, as Kolb (1995) has reported. After hippocampal damage in rats, collateral sprouts developed between the hippocampus and the cerebral cortex at the same time that the animals recovered behaviors that had been lost following the damage. Such a recovery process in humans is known to extend over a period of years (Raineteau & Schwab, 2001)

More recent studies have suggested several options for enhancing collateral sprouting after brain damage. For example, Mearow (1998) reported that electrical stimulation of the intact nerve accelerated the collateral sprouting of thoracic dorsal cutaneous nerves in adult rats. In other studies, repeated electroconvulsive shock promoted the sprouting of serotonergic (serotonin-producing) neurons in adult rats following hippocampal lesioning (Madhav & others, 2000), which might account for some of the therapeutic effect of electroconvulsive shock in depressed patients. Future research will determine whether these techniques can promote collateral sprouting as a means of restoring lost functions after nerve damage in humans.

collateral sprouting A process by which neighboring neurons of a degenerating neuron sprout new axonal endings to connect to the receptor sites left vacant by the degenerated neuron.

The Transplantation of Neural Tissue

The transplantation of fetal tissue into a damaged area of the CNS is another field of active research that holds promise for restoring lost functions after neuronal damage. *Fetal tissue implantation* may be the ideal treatment, because undifferentiated cells at this early stage of neural development have the flexibility needed to reestablish critical neural circuits. However, many people believe that the use of fetal tissue is unethical for this or any other purpose. For them, taking the tissue from aborted fetuses is tantamount to condoning murder, because they view the fetus at any stage as fully human. Despite the potential benefits of fetal tissue implantation, investigations of these procedures at the present time are controversial.

Damage to dopaminergic (dopamine-producing) neurons that connect the substantia nigra to the basal ganglia leads to Parkinson's disease, which is characterized by rigidity and difficulty integrating voluntary motor responses (Chapter 2). In animal studies, fetal tissue (cells from the substantia nigra of the fetal donors) has been transplanted into the brains of adult rats with substantia nigra lesions (Baker & others, 2002; Kirik & others, 2001). Such transplants have restored some movement, although the recovery is not complete. Kirik and colleagues found that recovery depended on the extent of the damage to the nigrostriatal system (the system of connections between the substantia nigra and the corpus striatum of the basal ganglia), with graft-induced functional recovery seen only in animals with greater than 70% denervation of the striatum. Fetal tissue implants have also improved motor function in several humans with Parkinson's-like symptoms that were induced by MPTP, a neurotoxic contaminant in synthetic heroin (Lindvall, 1998; Widner & others, 1992). Nonhuman primates with MPTP-induced Parkinson's-like symptoms have also shown some behavioral recovery following transplantation of fetal dopamine neurons (Elsworth & others, 1996; Starr & others, 1999).

Improved movement has also been reported following fetal tissue implants in humans with Parkinson's disease (Freed & others, 2001; Lindvall & Hagell, 2001). In the most responsive patients, transplantation of fetal tissue has permitted them to discontinue L-dopa drug treatment and resume an independent lifestyle. (We have more to say about the use of L-dopa in treating Parkinson's disease in Chapter 8.) In most cases, however, there is only partial recovery of motor abilities. Further, Freed and colleagues found such recovery only in younger patients (60 and younger). One small group of younger patients developed excessive movement and muscle spasms rather than a lack of movement, implying an overgrowth of transplanted fibers and a corresponding excess of dopamine. The authors suggested that the simplest solution to this problem would be to transplant less fetal tissue in future operations.

In studies examining the brains of rats receiving fetal tissue implants after dopamine-depleting treatments, the fetal dopaminergic neurons reinnervated the striatum, suggesting the repair of brain microcircuitry (Stromberg & others, 2001). Other studies suggest that fetal tissue implantation into the caudate-putamen area (part of the basal ganglia) caused dopaminergic neurons to grow from the graft site and establish synaptic connections to neurons in the area (Deacon & others, 1997; Kordower & others, 1996). These animal studies suggest that the motor function improvement observed in Parkinson's patients following fetal tissue implants results from new dopaminergic synapses in the basal ganglia.

You most likely have heard about the potential use of stem cells in treating neurological disorders. Stem cells are cells from which other cells are derived.

Scientific American Spotlight

Baby to Brain

Therapy Clues From Fetal Cells That Enter Mom's Brain

Charles Q. Choi

Mothers could literally always have their kids on their minds. Researchers find that in mice, cells from fetuses can migrate into a mother's brain and apparently develop into nervous system cells.

The discovery comes from Gavin S. Dawe of the National University of Singapore and Zhi-Cheng Xiao of Singapore General Hospital, along with their colleagues from China and Japan. They were looking to design therapies for stroke or diseases such as Alzheimer's. Scientists have known for years that fetal cells can enter a mother's blood; in humans, they may remain there at least 27 years after birth. Like stem cells, they can become many other kinds of cells and in theory might help repair damaged organs.

The neurobiologists bred normal female mice with males genetically modified to uniformly express a green fluorescent protein. They found green fetal cells in the mothers' brains. "In some regions of some mothers' brains, there are as many as one in 1,000 to sometimes even 10 in 1,000 cells of fetal origin," Xiao reports.

The fetal cells transformed into what seem like neurons, astrocytes (which help to feed neurons), oligodendrocytes (which insulate neurons), and macrophages (which ingest germs and damaged cells). Moreover, after the scientists chemically injured the mouse brains, nearly six times as many fetal cells made their way to damaged areas than elsewhere, suggesting the cells could be responding to molecular distress signals released by the brain.

Just how the fetal cells make it through the capillaries separating the brain from the blood system is not known—the cells of the vessels are densely packed, preventing most compounds from crossing the barrier. The researchers speculate that biomolecules such as proteins or sugars adorning fetal cell surfaces interact with the blood-brain barrier and allow the cells to wriggle past. The team feels confident that fetal cells can also pass to the brains of males and nonpregnant females, given little evidence of major differences between their blood-brain barriers and those of pregnant females, Dawe says. The scientists hope next to show that the fetal cells become functional neurons.

The finding, published online August 10, 2005, by *Stem Cells,* gives fresh hope in treating brain disorders. Because of the blood-brain barrier, transplant therapies for the brain normally evoke thoughts of drilling into the skull. Identifying the molecules typical of fetal cells that enter the brain and become nervous system cells could help find similar cells from sources other than fetuses, such as umbilical cord blood. Such research could lead to noninvasive cell transplants for the brain requiring only intravenous injections. Any cells used for therapies would be matched to patients as closely as possible to avoid triggering immune disease. It remains uncertain whether injected cells meant for the brain could end up grafting somewhere else, "but we don't know yet if that happening would even be a problem," Dawe says.

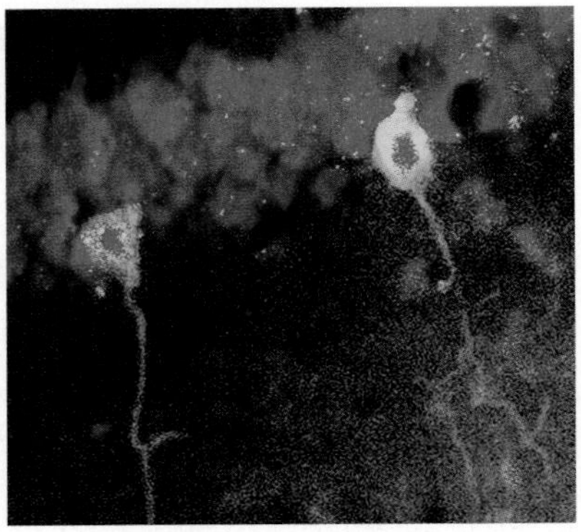

Fetal cells (*green*) can make their way to a mother's brain. Neuronal nuclei are stained red.

The investigators are also now looking to see if the passage of fetal cells to the brain occurs in humans as readily as it does in mice. They plan on looking at postmortem brain tissue from mothers of boys. Signs of a Y chromosome would confirm the effect in humans. It would also, Xiao points out, raise the issue of "whether there are any behavioral or psychological implications."

From: *Scientific American,* vol. 293(5), pp. 22, 24.

Embryonic stem cells, obtained from the early stages of embryonic development, have the capability to develop into any type of cell. As larger amounts of fetal tissue are needed for therapeutic transplants in Parkinson's disease patients, embryonic stem cells that could develop into dopaminergic neurons are being considered as an alternative for the treatment of this and other neurodegenerative disorders. Unfortunately, initial attempts to use embryonic stem cells have not been promising, and the generated neurons have not survived well after transplantation in animals (Lindvall, 2003). Future research will determine whether the use of embryonic stem cells represents a viable alternative to fetal tissue implantation (Langston, 2005). At present, both approaches—using embryonic stem cells or fetal tissue from specific brain areas—seem equally controversial.

Box 3.2
Rehabilitation

By undergoing **rehabilitation,** some individuals with nerve damage can develop compensatory behaviors that substitute for lost functions. For example, speech-language pathologists use several treatment approaches to help patients regain language abilities following a stroke or other brain injury. We will be discussing various rehabilitation approaches throughout the text.

Rehabilitation may also have been the key to Christopher Reeve's recovery of function. According to traditional dogma, most recovery from spinal cord injury occurs in the first 6 months and is essentially complete within the first 2 years following the injury. But Reeve continued to recover sensations and slight movements in the affected regions of his body more than 9 years after his fall. Such recovery may have been the result of the consistent exercise regimen Reeve followed. He did not recover bladder or bowel control, but his ability to move certain joints and to feel touch over much of his body dramatically improved his outlook on life. Toward the end of his life, Reeve was even able to go long periods of time without using a ventilator to aid his breathing. "It does appear that with the proper rehabilitative approach, many individuals with a spinal cord injury can relearn how to walk even many years after an injury" (Christopher Reeve, 2002, p. 7). That was Reeve's goal, and unfortunately his life ended before he was able to see if it was possible.

Less controversial would be the use of adult stem cells, which are found in small numbers in most parts of the body. Their function is to maintain the tissues in which they are located. Recent evidence suggests, however, that some adult stem cells may be able to differentiate into multiple types of cells including neurons, glia, and liver cells (Ulloa-Montoya & others, 2005). If they prove to be as potentially useful as embryonic stem cells, adult stem cells will avoid the ethical problem many see in sacrificing human embryos for their stem cells or in sacrificing fetuses to harvest neural tissue for implantation.

The *Scientific American* Spotlight, "Baby to Brain: Therapy Clues From Fetal Cells That Enter Mom's Brain," shows that undifferentiated fetal cells can pass through the blood-brain barrier and enter the brain of the mother, at least in mice. In the brain, the fetal cells appear to become nervous system cells, such as neurons, astrocytes, and oligodendrocytes. A similar phenomenon in humans might lead to a new approach to central nervous system repair.

Apart from these possible medical interventions, some individuals benefit from rehabilitation, as described in Box 3.2.

Checkpoint

What is the difference in response to neuron damage in the central and peripheral nervous systems? Why might the implantation of fetal tissue help in the treatment of nervous system damage?

REVIEW

- Damage to the cell body of a neuron leads to the breakdown or degeneration of the entire neuron.
- Axonal damage causes degeneration toward the presynaptic terminal, called anterograde degeneration, and degeneration of the axon toward the cell body, called retrograde degeneration. Chromatolysis is the breakdown of the neuronal cell body.
- Transneuronal degeneration causes the death of neurons that have synaptic connections with the damaged neuron; this damage can be widespread.
- An axon in the PNS can regenerate after damage, because of the presence of laminin and fibronectin, glycoproteins that promote cone growth. A lack of laminin and fibronectin, and the presence of inhibitory glycoproteins synthesized by oligodendrocytes, prevent CNS neurons from regenerating.
- Several research areas hold promise for treating damaged CNS neurons in adult humans, including the promotion of collateral sprouting, the administration of antibodies to axon growth-inhibitory proteins, and the implantation of fetal tissue.
- Rehabilitation can sometimes compensate for lost function.

rehabilitation The process of developing compensatory behaviors that substitute for lost functions.

Chapter Review

Key Terms

Suggested Readings

Brown, M. C., Hopkins, W. G., & Keynes, R. J. (1991). *Essentials of neural development.* Cambridge University Press: Cambridge.

Cook, G., Tannahill, D., & Keynes, R. (1998). Axon guidance to and from choice points. *Current Opinion in Neurobiology, 8,* 64–72.

Goldberg, J. L., & Barres, B. A. (2000). The relationship between neuronal survival and regeneration. *Annual Review of Neuroscience, 23,* 579–612.

Ho, L. W., Carmichael, J., Swartz, J., Wittenbach, A., Rankin, J., & Rubinsztein, D. C. (2001). The molecular biology of Huntington's disease. *Psychological Medicine, 31,* 3–14.

Shatz, C. J. (1992). The developing brain. *Scientific American, 267,* 61–67.

Tatagiba, M., Brosamle, C., & Schwab, M. E. (1997). Regeneration of injured axons in the adult mammalian central nervous system. *Neurosurgery, 40,* 541–546.

Wexler, N. S., Rose, E. A., & Housman, D. E. (1991). Molecular approaches to hereditary diseases of the nervous system: Huntington's disease as a paradigm. *Annual Review of Neuroscience, 14,* 503–529.

Critical Thinking Questions

1. Miscarriage (spontaneous abortion) is a relatively common occurrence. Using your knowledge of the processes responsible for the developing nervous system, suggest several reasons an embryo or fetus might not survive.
2. The development of new neurons ceases shortly after birth, with a few minor exceptions. Why is it that the nervous system does not continue to generate new neurons throughout the life cycle?
3. Many individuals become paralyzed as a result of accidents. Describe what might be done to enable people with spinal cord damage to regain the use of their limbs. Your answer should make use of your understanding of nerve migration and the formation of synaptic connections.

Fill-in-the Blank Questions

1. ______ is the science of heredity and ______ are the units of heredity.
2. An allele is ______ if its expression always occurs, no matter what characteristic is carried by the other gene with which it is paired.
3. A pair of alleles is ______ if both members of the pair control the same characteristic; an allele pair is ______ if each member of the pair controls different characteristics.
4. ______ are animals without backbones; ______ are animals with backbones.
5. The evolutionary process of concentrating neurons around the head region is called ______ or ______.
6. The ______ of the roundworm can be considered a primitive brain.
7. The spinal cord and brain of vertebrates are located on the ______ surface of the body.
8. The developing human is called a(n) ______ for its first 8 weeks and a(n) ______ for the remainder of the pregnancy.
9. The three distinct layers of cells formed by the embryo within 2 weeks of conception are the ______, the ______, and the ______.
10. A(n) ______ defect such as ______ or ______ occurs when some portion of the neural folds fails to close to form the neural tube.
11. During development, the forebrain divides into the ______ and the ______.
12. The ______ subdivision of the forebrain develops into the cerebral cortex, the basal ganglia, and the ______ system.
13. The ______ subdivision of the forebrain develops into the epithalamus, thalamus, and ______.
14. During development, the hindbrain divides into the ______ (which includes the ______ and cerebellum) and the ______ (which includes the ______).
15. The layer of cells between the intermediate and marginal layers that gives rise to the neurons and glial cells of the cerebral cortex is called the ______.
16. The formation of new neurons is called ______.
17. ______ cells guide the migration of daughter cells from the inner to the outer surface of the developing nervous system.
18. The two types of neural cell differentiation are ______ and ______.
19. The axon emerges from the ______, which is the swollen end of the developing neuron.
20. ______ is the guidance of axon growth by chemical signals.
21. ______ are chemicals released by the target cells that attract filopodia and guide the axon to its appropriate location.
22. ______ cells are involved in abrupt directional changes by an axon on the way to its target.
23. ______, or trisomy 21, is a genetic disorder caused by an extra copy of chromosome 21.
24. ______ is a genetic disorder caused by an abnormality in a gene on the X chromosome that causes the X chromosome to break.
25. ______ is the disorder caused by the lack of an enzyme needed to break down phenylalanine.
26. The consumption of alcohol during pregnancy can cause ______ syndrome.
27. The breakdown of an axon back toward the cell body of the neuron is called ______.
28. The cell body breaks down through a process called ______.
29. Damage to neighboring neurons by a degenerating neuron is called ______ degeneration.
30. The growth of new axons by neurons adjacent to degenerating neurons is called ______.
31. ______ may allow individuals with nerve damage to develop compensatory behaviors that substitute for lost functions.

Multiple-Choice Questions

1. _____ are located on _____ contained in the nucleus of every cell (except red blood cells) of the human body.
   a. Chromosomes, genes
   b. Genes, mitochondria
   c. Genes, chromosomes
   d. Chromosomes, ganglia
2. Gametes are formed through a process called
   a. crossing over.
   b. homozygosity.
   c. mitosis.
   d. meiosis.
3. If an allele is _____, the characteristic determined by the allele will be present regardless of the characteristic carried by the other member of the pair of alleles.
   a. recessive
   b. sex-linked
   c. paternal
   d. dominant
4. If both parents carry one allele for curly hair (*C*) and one allele for noncurly hair (*c*), what percentage of their children would you expect to have curly hair?
   a. 25%
   b. 50%
   c. 75%
   d. 100%
5. Which neurological disease is caused by a gene mutation on chromosome 4 and has symptoms that generally do not appear until the person is between the ages of 30 and 40?
   a. Parkinson's disease
   b. Lou Gehrig's disease
   c. Huntington's disease
   d. multiple sclerosis
6. Most of the animals on Earth are
   a. invertebrates.
   b. vertebrates.
   c. protovertebrates.
   d. polyvertebrates.
7. The evolutionary process that concentrates neurons around the head region is called
   a. gangliation.
   b. nucleation.
   c. cephalization.
   d. concentration.
8. The brain of an insect is divided into the
   a. protocerebrum, deuterocerebrum, and cerebellum.
   b. protocerebrum, diencephalon, and tritocerebrum.
   c. protocerebrum, deuterocerebrum, and tritocerebrum.
   d. protocerebrum, cerebellum, and pituitary gland.
9. The mammalian cerebral cortex has _____ layers of cells.
   a. 3
   b. 5
   c. 10
   d. 6
10. The purpose of the folding that occurs in the mammalian cerebral cortex is to
    a. increase the surface area without increasing the volume.
    b. increase the volume without increasing the surface area.
    c. increase the flexibility of the axons.
    d. increase the size of subcortical areas without increasing the size of the cortex.
11. For its first 8 weeks, the developing human is called a(n)
    a. fetus.
    b. embryo.
    c. infant.
    d. child.
12. The embryonic cell layer that forms the various parts of the nervous system is the
    a. endoderm.
    b. mesoderm.
    c. ectoderm.
    d. marginal layer.
13. The brain initially differentiates into the
    a. forebrain, midbrain, and hindbrain.
    b. forebrain, medulla, and hypothalamus.
    c. pons, medulla, and cerebellum.
    d. thalamus, hypothalamus, and cerebral cortex.
14. _____ is a neural tube defect caused by the failure of the neural folds to close.
    a. Spina bifida
    b. Hydrocephalus
    c. Microcephaly
    d. Cauda equina
15. The addition of _____ to the diet of pregnant women dramatically decreases the incidence of neural tube defects.
    a. acetic acid
    b. folic acid
    c. Vitamin A
    d. Vitamin E
16. The ventral portion of the spinal cord, the motor neurons, and the interneurons of the ventral root of the spinal cord develop from the
    a. alar plate.
    b. rhombencephalon.
    c. basal plate.
    d. cauda equina.
17. The four _____ of the _____ system protect and provide nutrients to the brain.
    a. divisions, peripheral nervous
    b. ventricles, ventricular
    c. ganglia, peripheral
    d. cell layers, limbic
18. The formation of new neurons is called
    a. chemotropism.
    b. chromatolysis.
    c. regeneration.
    d. neurogenesis.
19. Newly formed neurons are guided toward their destinations by glycoproteins such as
    a. neural cell adhesion molecules, cadherins, and integrins.
    b. adherins, radial glial cells, and daughter cells.
    c. Purkinje cells, glial cells, and cadherins.
    d. neural cell adhesion molecules, daughter cells, and glial cells.
20. The layer of cells between the intermediate and marginal layers that develops into the neurons and glial cells of the cerebral cortex is called the
    a. alar plate.
    b. basal plate.
    c. neural plate.
    d. cortical plate.
21. The _____ extend from the _____ to guide the developing axon toward its proper destination.
    a. growth cones, axon
    b. filopodia, growth cone
    c. growth cones, synapse
    d. filopodia, axon

22. The growth cone may be redirected toward its destination by
a. daughter cells.
b. glial cells.
c. target cells.
d. guidepost cells.

23. One important function of ______ cells is ______, the wrapping of the nerve axon with myelin.
a. daughter, chemotropism
b. glial, neurogenesis
c. daughter, myelination
d. glial, myelination

24. The particular neurotransmitter that will be used at a developing synapse is determined by the
a. filopodia.
b. growth cone.
c. target cell.
d. cell body.

25. Because he has three copies of chromosome 21 rather than two, André has altered facial features, impaired mental functioning, and abnormalities in several internal organs. His genetic disorder is called
a. FAS.
b. Down syndrome.
c. fragile X syndrome.
d. PKU

26. A person with a long, narrow face; large, prominent ears; a prominent forehead and jaw; and mild to severe mental retardation is likely to have
a. Down syndrome.
b. phenylketonuria.
c. fetal alcohol syndrome.
d. fragile X syndrome.

27. Sheritha is short, has distinctive facial features, and has cognitive/behavioral problems such as mental retardation, hyperactivity, and irritability. After her mother is questioned about certain habits during pregnancy, Sheritha is diagnosed as having
a. Down syndrome.
b. PKU.
c. FAS.
d. fragile X syndrome.

28. The neuron degenerates toward the synapse in ______ degeneration and toward the cell body in ______ degeneration.
a. retrograde, anterograde
b. anterograde, retrograde
c. transneuronal, anterograde
d. retrograde, transneuronal

29. Regeneration occurs in the ______ system but not in the ______ system.
a. central nervous, peripheral nervous
b. limbic, digestive
c. peripheral nervous, central nervous
d. vertebral, cranial

30. Experimental approaches to recovery of function after nervous system damage include
a. collateral sprouting and fetal tissue implantation.
b. rehabilitation and neurogenesis.
c. induction and chemotropism.
d. regeneration and collateral sprouting.

Answers can be found on the companion website at www.worthpublishers.com/klein.

Communication Within the Nervous System

4

Why Me?

Multiple sclerosis! Was that really what she'd heard? Dr. Stewart, the neurologist, continued talking soothingly, but Michelle heard little of what he was saying. All she could think about was how innocuous her symptoms had been—most of them, anyway—and how young she was. And most of all she was thinking, Why me? What have I done to deserve this?

Perhaps sensing her shock at the news, Dr. Stewart paused in his discussion of what she might expect to experience from her disease. "Do you have any particular questions at this time, Michelle?"

"Why me?" she wanted to blurt out, but she knew the doctor wouldn't have an answer, so she asked, "Is there any treatment?" Aware of the quaver in her voice, she hoped she'd be able to leave the doctor's office without dissolving into tears.

"There certainly is, Michelle. I'll start you on a form of beta interferon that you'll receive as a once-a-week injection." Dr. Stewart carefully told Michelle about the different forms of MS, explaining that it was likely she had the relapsing-remitting variety, as this is by far the most common form.

"We know that beta interferon can reduce the exacerbations, or flare-ups, of the disorder. But notice I said *reduce* the attacks; unfortunately, we don't yet have anything to eliminate them entirely. But if you do experience an exacerbation, I'll give you a corticosteroid medication to reduce the inflammation in your nerve tissue."

Michelle thought about her earlier episodes. In retrospect, she now realized her first attack had been around Christmas, about 6 months earlier. She had awakened one morning with an odd tingling in her left hand that gradually spread to include the whole left side of her body. Over several days, the unusual sensations fluctuated and gradually disappeared, and Michelle had chalked the whole thing up to holiday stress.

Her next episode began on her 25th birthday. Her boyfriend, Jerry, and some of her friends from work had taken her to a Polynesian restaurant, where she'd consumed several tall drinks with little parasols in them. At some point, she had become aware of numbness in her left hand and her left leg and on the left side of her face; she'd attributed this to the rum in the drinks. The numbness in this second attack had lasted longer than expected given her rationalization for it, but she quickly forgot the whole thing when the symptoms disappeared after about a week.

Her latest attack finally convinced her she needed to find out what was wrong. She'd had a touch of the virus that was making the rounds in her office but seemed to be getting over it when, out of the blue, she woke up with weakness on the right side of her face and blindness in her right eye. This was very alarming. When she called to make an appointment to see her family physician, she realized she was slurring her words. After examining her, the physician referred her to Dr. Stewart.

And now she understood what it all meant. What she didn't know and the doctor couldn't yet tell her was what kind of MS she had. Was it the rapidly progressive kind, or was it the kind a character in her favorite TV show had? Before he left office, President Bartlett of *The West Wing* seemed to have done quite well with his disease, but of course, he had a physician for a wife. And he never seemed to ask the question she couldn't get out of her mind: Why me?

As you will see, the symptoms of multiple sclerosis well illustrate what can happen when communication in the nervous system malfunctions. Such communication involves many different structures and processes, which we explore in this chapter.

BEFORE YOU BEGIN

- **How does the nervous system process information?**
- **How do neurons communicate with each other?**
- **What is myelin, and why is it so important? What happens when the immune system destroys the myelin sheath?**
- **Why do drugs influence the function of the nervous system?**

In this chapter, you will find the answers to these questions and many others.

◆ The Exchange of Information

Neurons receive information from other neurons and from the external and internal environments. Our focus in this chapter is on the process responsible for information exchange between neurons. This information exchange, occurring at the synapse, usually involves transmission from the axon of one neuron to the dendrite of another—*axodendritic;* or from axon to cell body—*axosomatic.* In some cases, transmission is *axoaxonic,* from axon to axon; or *dendrodendritic,* from dendrite to dendrite. We begin by discussing *axonal transmission,* the process by which information travels along the length of the axon. Then we will examine *synaptic transmission* and several major neurotransmitters.

channel protein A protein embedded in the cell membrane that provides a channel through which substances can pass from one side of the membrane to the other.

receptor protein A protein in the cell membrane that recognizes and binds a specific neurotransmitter.

pump protein A protein in the cell membrane that exchanges one type of ion on one side of the membrane for another ion on the other side of the membrane.

resting membrane potential The difference in polarity between the inside and the outside of the cell membrane when the neuron is at rest.

ion A charged particle, such as a sodium (Na^+), potassium (K^+), or chloride (Cl^-) ion.

diffusion The tendency of molecules to move from areas of higher concentration to areas of lower concentration.

To paraphrase Shakespeare, "To fire or not to fire, that is the question." And the end result of information exchange between neurons is essentially a yes or no response. For example, suppose you have a pebble in your shoe. A neuron in your brain "asks" the question, Is there something in my shoe? If the answer is yes, the more likely one in this case, the neuron conveys this answer, as a neural impulse, to other neurons by releasing neurotransmitters that travel across the synapse and bind to receptor sites on the postsynaptic membrane. You feel the pebble and, most likely, remove it from your shoe. If the answer is no, then no neural impulse is conveyed. For example, neurons in your touch detection system might not respond to the pebble stimulus if you have recently consumed several glasses of wine (we discuss the effects of alcohol on sensory detection in Chapter 5). The way sensory receptors, such as touch receptors, detect environmental stimuli differs from the way neurons detect information from other neurons. We have more to say about the detection of sensory information by sensory receptors in Chapters 6 and 7.

We begin our discussion with an examination of what makes the neuron uniquely suited for receiving and transmitting information.

The Resting Membrane Potential

The cell membrane (Figure 4.1) is a marvelous structure, consisting of a lipid bilayer (a double layer of fat molecules) embedded with several different kinds of protein molecules. **Channel proteins** provide channels for the passage of substances from one side of the membrane to the other, **receptor proteins** recognize and bind to neurotransmitters or other chemicals, and **pump proteins** exchange one type of substance for another. Like all cell membranes, the cell membrane of a neuron allows some substances to enter the cell while keeping other substances out. However, the neuronal cell membrane has a special quality (shared only with muscle cell membranes): *polarity*—the membrane is electrically charged, or polarized. Think of this membrane charge as being similar to the positive and negative poles on a battery. When the neuron is at rest—not receiving information from other neurons—the fluid inside the cell (intracellular fluid) is more negatively charged than the fluid outside the cell (extracellular fluid), so the extracellular fluid is like the positive pole of the battery and the intracellular fluid is like its negative pole. This difference in polarity is called the **resting membrane potential.**

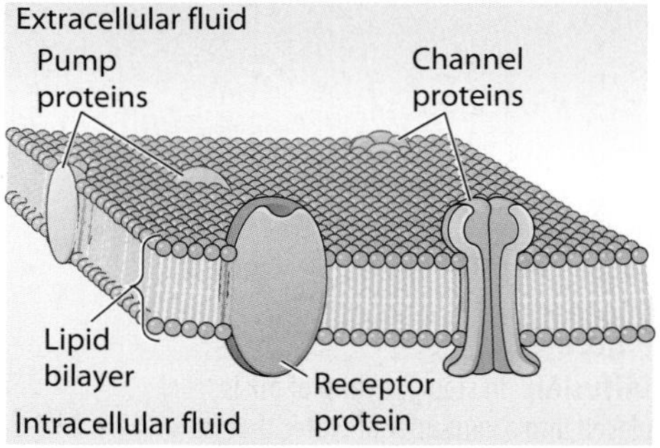

Figure 4.1

The cell membrane The cell membrane is a double layer of lipid molecules with embedded proteins. Ions move in and out of the cell through channel proteins or pump proteins. Receptor proteins bind neurotransmitters or other substances.

What is the general function of the protein molecules embedded in the neuronal cell membrane?

The charge across the cell membrane is much smaller than that of a battery. The typical polarization of the cell membrane is 70 mV (mV is a millivolt, one thousandth of a volt), compared with 9,000 mV in a 9-volt battery. Using the intracellular fluid as the reference point, the typical resting membrane potential is −70 mV, meaning that the inside of the cell is 70 mV more negatively charged than the extracellular fluid (Figure 4.2).

This difference in charge across the cell membrane is caused by a greater concentration of positive ions outside the cell than inside the cell. **Ions** are charged particles such as sodium (Na^+), potassium (K^+), and chloride (Cl^-); the plus and minus signs indicate whether the particular ions are positively or negatively charged.

When the neuron is at rest, Na^+, K^+, and Cl^- ions enter and exit the neuron through channels (or gates) in channel proteins embedded in the cell membrane (see Figure 4.1). However, there are different concentrations of the various ions on either side of the cell membrane, with more Na^+ and Cl^- ions outside and more K^+ and negatively charged protein molecules inside. Protein molecules are large and cannot leave the cell, whereas the other three ions (Na^+, K^+, Cl^-) enter and leave through ion channels—although the cell membrane is much more permeable to K^+ and Cl^- ions than to Na^+ ions. Two passive forces, diffusion and electrostatic pressure, and one active process, the sodium-potassium pump, affect ion movement across the cell membrane and thus the different concentration of ions.

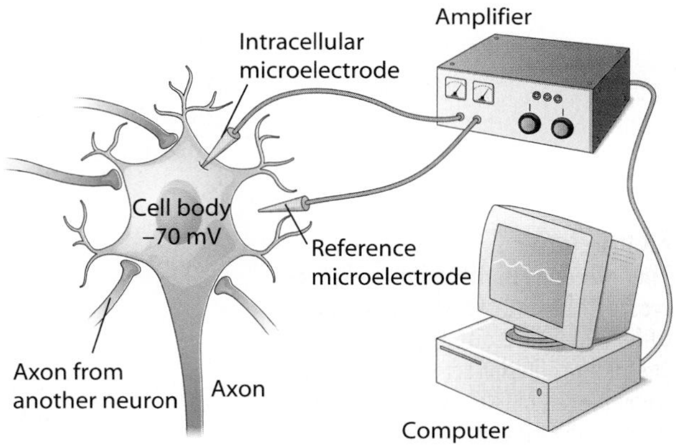

Figure 4.2

Recording the resting membrane potential of a neuron The resting potential can be recorded by inserting into the cell a very small electrode (a microelectrode—a micropipette filled with a liquid that conducts electricity) connected to an amplifier that is connected to a computer. Recordings show that the inside of the cell is 70 mV more negatively charged than the outside of the cell.

What ion differences exist across the resting neuronal cell membrane?

Diffusion and Electrostatic Pressure

Diffusion is the tendency of molecules to move from areas of higher concentration to areas of lower concentration. Technically speaking, the difference in concentration between areas produces a *concentration gradient,* and the concentration gradient causes the diffusion. If it is the only force at work, diffusion eventually produces an even distribution of molecules. You can see the result of diffusion for yourself by placing a drop of ink into a glass of water. Initially concentrated at the point of entry into the water, the ink particles quickly spread out, moving to areas of lower concentration, and the end result is that the water soon takes on an even, darker hue throughout (Figure 4.3). The same thing—equal dispersion throughout—would happen if we placed positive and negative ions into a glass of water divided in half by a completely permeable membrane. If we placed

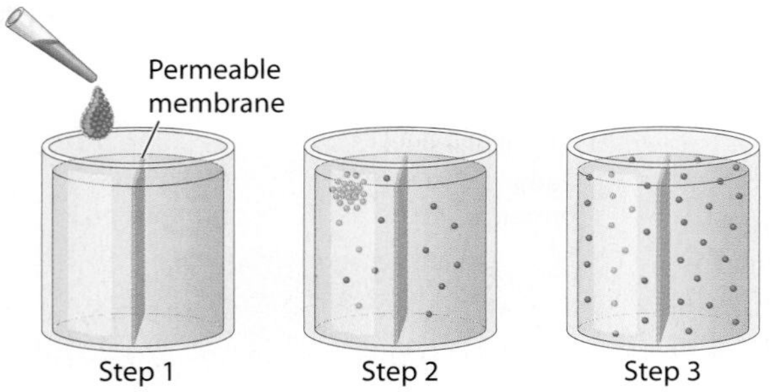

Figure 4.3

Diffusion In step 1, a drop of ink is placed into a container of water that is divided by a permeable membrane. As diffusion occurs (step 2), the dye molecules in the ink move from the area of higher concentration (the drop at the upper left) to the area of lower concentration (the surrounding water). Eventually diffusion results in an even distribution of molecules on both sides of the membrane (step 3).

➡ What forces other than diffusion affect the movement of ions across the cell membrane?

all the ions on one side of the membrane, they would diffuse across the membrane and end up equally concentrated on both sides.

For cell membranes, however, ionic movement is also affected by electrical charge. You probably remember from chemistry that unlike charges attract and like charges repel. If you place two bar magnets end to end, they will attach to one another if the unlike poles are placed together or push away from one another if the same-sign poles are placed together. **Electrostatic pressure** refers to the attraction of opposite-polarity molecules and the repulsion of same-polarity molecules. Electrostatic pressure tends to even out the number of ions on either side of the cell membrane, based on electrical charge rather than on concentration. Thus, if electrostatic pressure were the only force at work and the membrane were completely permeable to all ions, even negatively charged protein molecules, the resulting membrane potential would be 0 mV, not −70 mV.

Of course, neither diffusion nor electrostatic pressure acts alone, and the cell membrane is *selectively* permeable (impermeable to protein molecules, relatively permeable to K^+ and Cl^- ions, and relatively impermeable to Na^+ ions). At this point, let us look at each ion in turn and see where it tends to move in terms of diffusion and electrostatic pressure.

Because there are more Cl^- ions outside the cell than inside, they would tend to diffuse into the cell. However, the force of diffusion is counteracted by the electrostatic pressure created by the greater negative charge inside the cell; that is, the repulsion of like charges tends to prevent Cl^- ions from entering the cell. As shown in Figure 4.4, the opposing forces of diffusion and electrostatic pressure keep the Cl^- ion concentration higher outside the cell. Similarly, diffusion and electrostatic pressure act to keep most K^+ ions inside the cell. Although diffusion would tend to move K^+ ions out of the cell, the higher positive charge outside the cell (the electrostatic pressure) tends to keep the K^+ ions where they are—inside the cell.

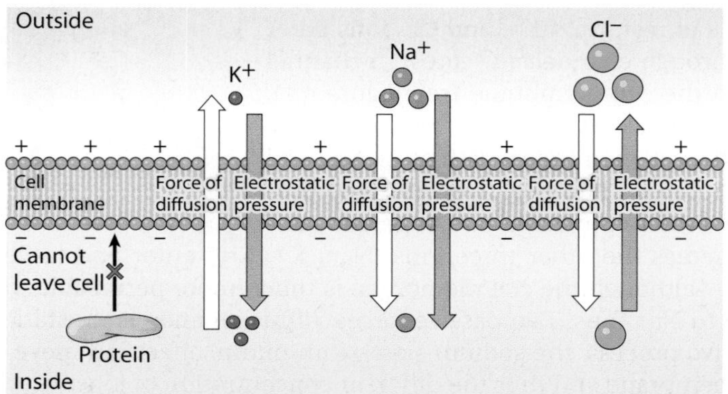

Figure 4.4

The influence of diffusion and electrostatic pressure on the movement of ions into and out of the neuron The force of diffusion acts to move K^+ ions out of the cell and Na^+ and Cl^- ions into the cell, whereas electrostatic pressure acts to move Cl^- ions out of the cell and K^+ and Na^+ ions into the cell.

➡ Given the forces acting on Na^+ ions shown here, how does the cell prevent the free flow of Na^+ ions into the cell?

For K^+ and Cl^- ions, then, the two passive forces counteract each other, and the ions tend to stay where they are. For Na^+ ions, however, both diffusion (a higher concentration outside) and electrostatic pressure (a more negative charge inside) would tend to move Na^+ ions into the cell. But they remain outside during the resting state for two reasons: The Na^+ channels of the cell membrane are typically closed, and the sodium-potassium pump acts to expel any Na^+ ions that do manage to leak into the cell and to replace them with K^+ ions.

electrostatic pressure The attraction of opposite-polarity (+/−) particles and the repulsion of same-polarity (+/+ or −/−) particles.

sodium-potassium pump A protein in the cell membrane that expels three Na^+ ions for every two K^+ ions it brings into the cell.

The Sodium-Potassium Pump

In contrast to diffusion and electrostatic pressure, the **sodium-potassium pump** (Figure 4.5) is an active process that expels three Na^+ ions for every two K^+ ions it carries into the cell. The difference in the rate of Na^+ ion expulsion and the rate of

K^+ ion entry helps maintain the polarization of the resting cell membrane; that is, the larger number of Na^+ ions on the outside than K^+ ions on the inside causes the extracellular fluid to be more positively charged than the intracellular fluid.

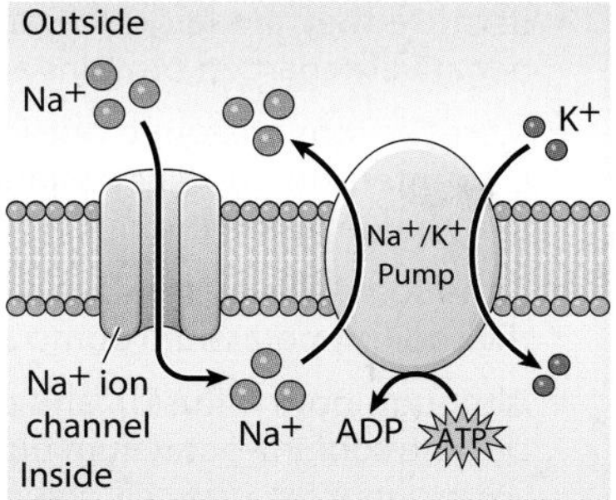

Figure 4.5

The sodium-potassium pump The sodium-potassium pump actively expels three Na^+ ions from the cell for every two K^+ ions that it allows in. The pump requires a lot of energy, which is provided by the conversion of ATP to ADP.

→ How does the sodium-potassium pump help establish the resting membrane of a cell?

The large amount of energy required to operate the sodium-potassium pump is provided by adenosine triphosphate (ATP). ATP is a high-energy compound consisting of adenosine and three phosphate groups, which is produced by the mitochondria (see Figure 2.4). The sodium-potassium pump converts ATP to ADP (adenosine diphosphate) by removing a phosphate group, and this releases the energy needed to operate the pump.

Once the resting potential is established by the sodium-potassium pump, diffusion and electrostatic pressure keep most Cl^- ions out of the cell and most K^+ ions in the cell. Any K^+ ions that escape are retrieved by the sodium-potassium pump. As discussed above, both diffusion and electrostatic pressure tend to drive Na^+ ions into the cell, but the continued activity of the sodium-potassium pump expels any Na^+ ions that leak through the cell membrane; thus the membrane's resting potential is maintained. A summary of the neuron at rest is illustrated in Figure 4.6.

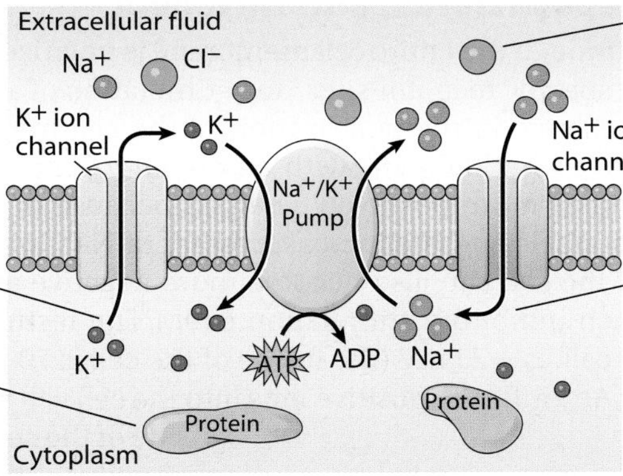

A. K+ ion concentration is higher inside the cell so diffusion tends to push K+ out. But the inside of the cell is more negative than the outside, so electrostatic pressure tends to pull K+ in. Because the force of diffusion is slightly greater than the electrostatic pressure, some K+ leaves the cell and is returned by the sodium-potassium pump.
C. Negatively charged protein molecules cannot leave the cell; they create a negative charge inside the cell.
Extracellular fluid
Na+
Cl−
K+ ion channel
K+
Na+/K+ Pump
Na+ ion channel
K+
ATP
ADP
Na+
Protein
Protein
Cytoplasm
B. Cl− ion concentration is higher outside the cell, so diffusion tends to pull Cl− in. But because the inside of the cell is more negative than the outside, electrostatic pressure tends to push Cl− out.
D. Na+ ion concentration is higher outside the cell, and the inside of the cell is more negative than the outside, so both diffusion and electrostatic pressure tend to pull Na+ in. But the sodium-potassium pump actively transports Na+ out.

Figure 4.6

The neuron at rest Overall, diffusion, electrostatic pressure, and the activity of the sodium-potassium pump result in a resting membrane potential of −70 mV.

→ What happens to the levels of Na^+, K^+, and Cl^- ions when the neuron is transmitting a message?

Although we use the word "rest" to describe a certain state of the neuron, this is really something of a misnomer. In fact, "resting potential" is more descriptive, as it implies that during the resting state the neuron has the potential, or power, to act. The sodium-potassium pump has created this potential by placing ions in positions they would not be if allowed to move passively. In the so-called resting state, the neuron is really analogous to a cocked mouse trap or pistol; it has the potential for explosive action. The actions of the sodium-potassium pump and the selectively permeable cell membrane set the stage for the action potential, which we discuss next.

Checkpoint

Describe how diffusion, electrostatic pressure, and the sodium-potassium pump act on sodium and potassium ions. What is the purpose of the sodium-potassium pump?

REVIEW

- Cell membranes are lipid bilayers with embedded channel proteins, receptor proteins, and pump proteins.
- The cell membrane of neurons is electrically charged. When the cell is at rest, the inside of the cell is negatively charged relative to the outside; the difference in charge is the resting membrane potential.

action potential The changes that occur within the neuron in response to a stimulus; also called the spike potential or firing of the neuron.

depolarization A reduction in electrical charge across the neuronal cell membrane.

threshold The level of cell membrane depolarization required for an action potential to occur.

- Because they are large molecules and cannot pass through the cell membrane, negatively charged proteins are retained inside the cell.
- More Cl^- ions are found outside than inside the cell because the force of diffusion is counteracted by electrostatic pressure: Cl^- ions are repelled by the more negative charge inside the cell.
- Although diffusion tends to push K^+ ions out of the cell, electrostatic pressure and the sodium-potassium pump act together to maintain high inside levels of K^+ ions.
- Although both diffusion and electrostatic pressure tend to pull Na^+ ions into the cell, the sodium-potassium pump expels three Na^+ ions for every two K^+ ions that are brought into the cell; this establishes and helps maintain the membrane's resting potential.

The Action Potential

What happens to the resting neuron when it receives information? A series of events occurs, which are collectively referred to as the **action potential,** the *spike potential,* or sometimes the *firing* of the neuron. The sequential events are depolarization to the threshold level, reversal of the membrane polarity, repolarization to the resting potential, and the refractory period. Note that the *action potential* refers just to the axon; the dendrites and cell body use another type of potential—the graded potential—to transfer the information they receive, as you will see.

Depolarization and Threshold

Although the entire cell membrane is polarized, neural messages are detected only at specific receptor sites, and stimulation of a neuron by another neuron produces a change in the polarization of the cell membrane at that point. Here we consider what happens with an *excitatory stimulus,* when the inside of the cell becomes more positively charged because of the temporary opening of Na^+ ion channels and the increased entry of Na^+ ions into the cell. (Note that the inside of the cell can also become more negative as a result of stimulation. We discuss such inhibitory stimulation later.) The resting membrane potential, you will recall, is −70 mV (the inside of the cell is 70 mV more negative than the outside). Any influx of positive ions into the cell will reduce the negative charge (make the inside of the cell less negative, or more positive) and thus reduce the charge across the membrane; this process is called **depolarization.**

Whether or not an axon generates an action potential upon receiving a message depends on the amount of depolarization produced—that is, whether it reaches a crucial level called the threshold. The **threshold** is the level of depolarization required for the neuron to pass on the message it has received. For example, consider again the pebble in your shoe. If the stimulus is sufficient to cause touch receptors to reach the threshold level, the message that you have a pebble in your shoe will continue on its way to your brain and your awareness. However, the touch neuron will not transmit any information if the membrane potential depolarization does not reach the threshold. In such a case, you will not notice the pebble.

If enough sodium enters the neuron and the threshold is reached (about −55 mV, as shown in Figure 4.7), the cell membrane undergoes a more

Figure 4.7
Changes in the membrane potential during the action (spike) potential
When depolarization reaches the threshold, Na^+ ion channels open, allowing more Na^+ ions to enter the cell and changing the polarity so that the inside becomes positively charged relative to the outside. Soon after the threshold is reached, K^+ ion channels open and K^+ ions begin to leave the cell. Next, Na^+ ion channels close, and the continuing exit of K^+ ions causes the membrane to become more negatively charged inside than outside again. For a brief time, the cell is slightly more polarized than normal. It quickly returns to the resting potential.

➔ **How is the original ion distribution restored after depolarization?**

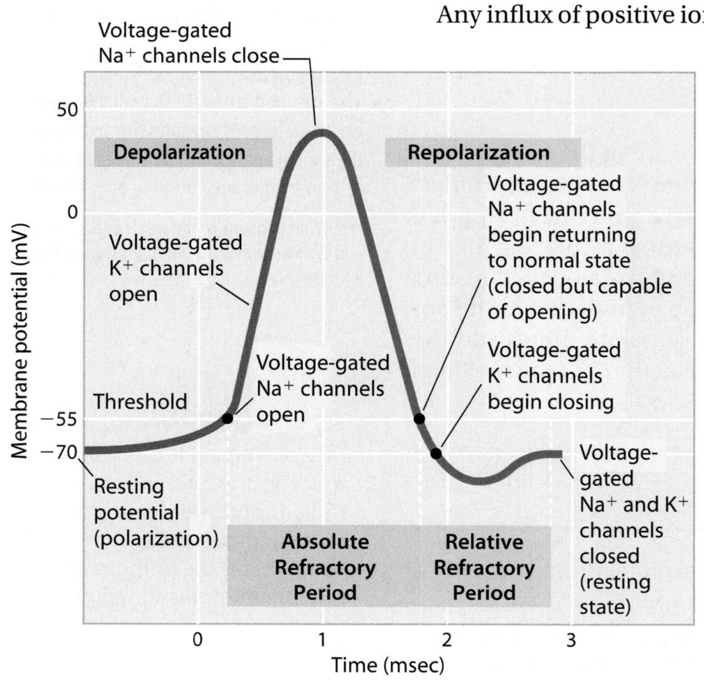

radical change in polarization. Many Na^+ ion channels now open and Na^+ ions pour in, causing the inside of the cell to become positive relative to the outside (about +50 mV; Figure 4.7). The Na^+ ion channels open because of their sensitivity to changes in membrane potential: The ion channels are said to be voltage-gated. **Voltage-gated ion channels** are opened or closed by changes in membrane potential.

voltage-gated ion channel An ion channel sensitive to changes in the cell membrane potential.

absolute refractory period The time during which the neuron is insensitive to further stimulation.

relative refractory period The time following the absolute refractory period during which a neuron can be activated but only by a more intense stimulus than normal.

hyperpolarized Having an electrical charge across the cell membrane that is more negative than normal.

repolarization The process of recovery of the resting membrane potential.

Repolarization and the Refractory Period

Next, the K^+ ion channels open and K^+ ions leave the cell. (The K^+ ion channels are less sensitive to changes in membrane potential than are Na^+ ion channels and therefore open later.) The K^+ ions leave because they are repelled by what is now a higher level of Na^+ ions in the cell. Shortly after the K^+ ion channels open, Na^+ ion channels close, and Na^+ ions stop entering the cell. The continuing exit of K^+ ions causes the inside of the cell to again become more negatively charged than the outside. Look carefully at Figure 4.7. Notice that sodium entry causes the line representing membrane potential to shoot up and that potassium exit brings it back down sharply; this is why the action potential is sometimes called the spike potential.

For a brief period of time during the generation of the action potential, the neuron is completely resistant to further stimulation. This period is called the **absolute refractory period,** during which the neuron cannot generate another action potential (or fire) no matter how intense the stimulus. The absolute refractory period is followed by another brief period, the **relative refractory period,** during which the neuron can generate another action potential only in response to a more intense stimulus than normal. In the graph in Figure 4.7, the relative refractory period corresponds to the portion where the membrane potential actually becomes slightly more negative (on the inside) than normal during the recovery process. During this period of greater negativity (e.g., −80 mV instead of −70 mV), the cell membrane is said to be **hyperpolarized.**

Although the distribution of Na^+ and K^+ ions changes as the result of depolarization and the action potential, the distribution quickly returns to normal through a process called **repolarization.** As soon as the resting membrane potential is restored, the sodium-potassium pump acts to maintain the ion concentration differences until it is changed by a depolarizing (or hyperpolarizing) stimulus.

Checkpoint

Describe what happens during an action potential, using the terms resting membrane potential, depolarization, threshold, repolarization, Na^+ ions, K^+ ions, and sodium-potassium pump.

REVIEW

- Stimulation of a neuron by another neuron causes depolarization of the cell membrane, a reduction in the electrical charge across the membrane.
- The process that includes depolarization of the membrane to its threshold, reversal of the membrane polarity, repolarization and restoration of the resting membrane potential, and the refractory period is called an action potential. This leads to the transmission of a neural impulse along the axon.
- Depolarization is caused by the temporary opening of Na^+ ion channels and the increased flow of Na^+ ions into the cell.
- If the depolarization reaches a particular threshold value, further depolarization occurs in which many Na^+ ion channels open and Na^+ ions flow rapidly into the cell, causing the inside of the cell to become momentarily positive relative to the outside.
- K^+ ion channels open and Na^+ channels close, leading to repolarization, because the increased exit of K^+ ions from the cell causes the inside of the cell to again become more negatively charged than the outside. During the action potential, the

all-or-none law A principle stating that the strength of an action potential is independent of the intensity of the stimulus that elicits it.

rate law A principle stating that the greater the stimulus intensity, the faster the rate of neural firing (up to the maximum rate possible for the neuron).

neuron cannot generate another impulse no matter how intense the stimulus—this is the absolute refractory period.

- The absolute refractory period is followed by the relative refractory period, during which the neuron can generate another impulse only in response to a more intense stimulus than normal.
- The distribution of ions across the cell membrane quickly returns to normal, and the sodium-potassium pump maintains the resting potential until it is again changed by a depolarizing or hyperpolarizing stimulus.

The Intensity of a Stimulus

Information about the intensity of a stimulus is not provided by a single action potential, because once the threshold is reached, the strength of the action potential is independent of the intensity of the stimulus. This lack of relationship between stimulus intensity and the action potential is known as the **all-or-none law:** If the stimulus causes enough Na^+ ions to enter the cell membrane so that the threshold is reached, then the action potential is generated from one end of the axon to the other. If too little sodium enters the cell to push the membrane potential to the threshold, then the neuron does not "fire" and the message dies out. Thus, there is no "weak" or "strong" action potential; it either occurs or does not occur—in other words, it is an all-or-none process.

Information about stimulus intensity can be important, as you undoubtedly realize. Suppose you order a glass of iced tea with lunch. You take a sip and find that it is unsweetened tea, which you do not like. You add one packet of sugar and take another sip. This time you perceive the tea as slightly sweet, but still not sweet enough, so you add another packet of sugar. Another sip tells you the tea is just right, sweet enough but not too sweet. How can you tell the difference in the two stimuli (tea with one packet of sugar vs. tea with two packets), which obviously differ in intensity? The nervous system has two mechanisms for assessing stimulus intensity. One is the rate of firing of a neuron, as measured by the number of action potentials per unit of time (Figure 4.8). An intense stimulus causes a neuron to fire more often than a weak stimulus. Thus, the tea with two packets of sugar generates a greater number of action potentials in the affected neurons than does the tea sweetened with only one packet. The **rate law,** which states that the greater the stimulus intensity, the faster the rate of neural firing (up to the maximum rate possible for the neuron), describes this relationship between the rate of firing and the intensity of a stimulus.

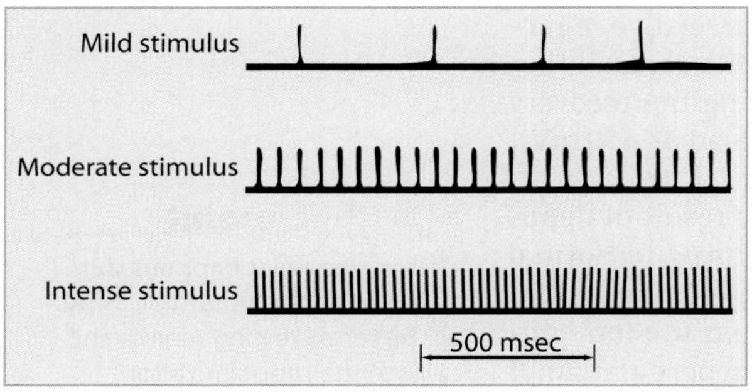

Figure 4.8

Illustration of the rate law The firing rate of a neuron is shown as a function of stimulus intensity. Each vertical line represents an action potential. Note that stimulus intensity is coded by the rate of firing, not by the size (height) of the action potential.

➡ **Why is the action potential (the spike) not higher for more intense stimuli?**

To understand how the rate law works, you must recall that the relative refractory period is a time during which the neuron can generate another action potential, but only to a more intense stimulus than normal. In our example, the iced tea with the second packet of sugar causes the stimulated neurons to fire during their relative refractory period, thus producing a greater number of action potentials per unit of time than the tea with only one packet, which is not an intense enough stimulus to cause firing during the period of hyperpolarization.

The other mechanism by which the nervous system assesses the intensity of a stimulus is by the number of neurons firing in a given area—a more intense stimulus causes more neurons to fire in an area than a less intense stimulus. Using our tea-sweetening example, adding the second packet of sugar causes more neurons in the area of the stimulus to generate action potentials, whereas the tea with only one packet of sugar causes fewer neurons to fire. Because the second packet causes more neurons to fire, the tea tastes sweeter than it did after you added only one packet of sugar.

One more point deserves mentioning. We may have given the impression that neurons exist in one of two states: either at rest or firing. This is indeed true for neurons in the peripheral nervous system, but it is not true for central nervous system neurons. As you will see, CNS neurons are typically active all the time, with information detected by changes in a neuron's firing rate.

The length of the absolute refractory period determines the maximum firing rate. A neuron with a short absolute refractory period can fire more rapidly than a neuron with a long absolute refractory period. Some input may increase the firing rate, whereas other input may decrease it in a specific neuron. One of the challenges of the CNS is to recognize the meaning of a specific change in the firing rate.

Now you know about each of the events that constitute the action potential: depolarization to threshold, reversal of the membrane polarity, repolarization to the resting potential, and the refractory period. At this point, however, we have discussed only what happens at the beginning of the action potential, at the point where the axon leaves the cell body of the neuron—at the **axon hillock.** We next consider the transmission of the neural impulse along the axon.

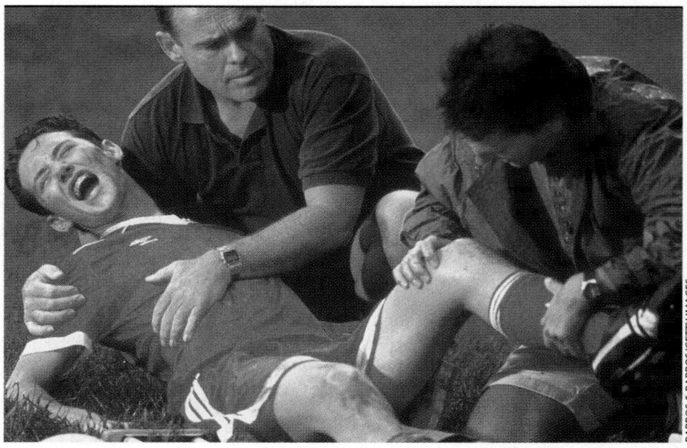

BARROS & BARROS/GETTY IMAGES

The intensity of pain experienced following an injury depends on the number of pain messages per second and the number of neurons firing in the injured area of the body.

Checkpoint

How does the brain tell whether one stimulus is more intense than another? What difference does it make to your brain whether a neuron's absolute refractory stage is short or long?

REVIEW

- Because of the all-or-none response, the size and speed of the nerve impulse are independent of the intensity of the stimulus.
- Perceived stimulus intensity is related to a neuron's firing rate and the number of neurons firing in a given area: the greater the stimulus intensity, the higher the firing rate and the greater the number of neurons firing in a given area.

The Neural Impulse

An action potential has been generated at the axon hillock. What happens next? Here we describe the propagation of the action potential along the axon—that is, the **neural impulse.** We first look at propagation in an unmyelinated axon, then propagation in a myelinated axon.

Propagation of the Impulse

As we indicated in Chapter 2, a neuron receives most of its messages from other neurons or from sensory receptors through synapses on its dendrites and cell body. These messages do not ordinarily produce action potentials, which, as we have noted, begin at the axon hillock, where the threshold for activation is lower. Here, all the various inputs the cell receives from many synapses are summed (a neuron may receive 1,000 or more synapses from other neurons). If the threshold is reached, an action potential is generated.

The axon is a continuous structure, of course, but it will help you to understand impulse propagation if you think of the axon as segmented, with action potentials repeated from one segment to the next along the length of the axon (Figure 4.9). At the same time that the ion channels in the first segment close to Na^+ ions, the Na^+ ions that entered this first segment are attracted to a region where there are fewer Na^+ ions and a more negative charge—the inside of the next segment of the axon. When these ions reach the next segment, the resulting depolarization brings this second segment of the axon to the threshold level,

axon hillock The part of the neuron where the axon and the action potential begin.

neural impulse The propagation of an action potential along an axon.

more sodium channels open, more Na^+ ions enter, and these Na^+ ions are attracted to the next segment—and thus the action potential continues along the length of the axon. Before the threshold is reached in a given segment, there is a change in membrane potential because of the Na^+ ions that have entered the segment. We can call this depolarization that has not reached threshold a *graded depolarization* (see Figure 4.9).

An action potential is propagated (spread) in one direction only, from the axon hillock to the presynaptic terminals. The reason for this one-way travel is the absolute refractory period. An action potential cannot return to the previous segment, because at that moment, that part of the axon is absolutely refractory to further stimulation.

The speed of impulse transmission is not the same for all neurons and is independent of stimulus intensity—another aspect of the all-or-none law. In fact, the speed with which information travels from point A to point B in the nervous system depends on three factors: thickness of the axon, the presence or absence of myelination, and the number of synapses. Larger neurons transmit messages faster than smaller neurons; myelinated axons transmit faster than unmyelinated axons; and the greater the number of synapses, the slower the message travels.

As you have seen, when an action potential occurs, Na^+ ions flow along the inside of the cell membrane, depolarizing the segment of the membrane that lies just ahead. The thicker the axon, the faster the local membrane depolarization will occur. And the faster the segments are depolarized, the faster the neural impulse will travel along the axon.

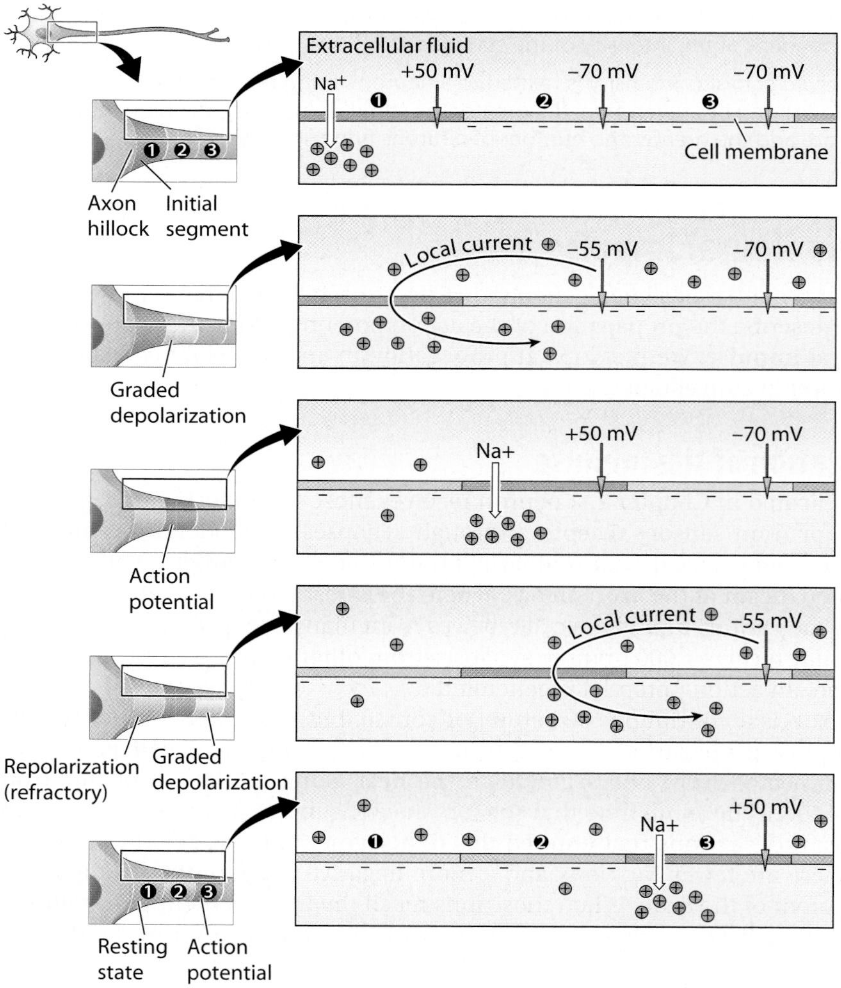

Figure 4.9

Propagation of the action potential along an unmyelinated axon Na^+ ion entry into one "segment" of the axon causes a polarity change in that segment (an action potential). The polarity of the first segment returns to normal as K^+ ions leave the cell. The movement of Na^+ ions into the next portion of the axon causes the polarity of that part to change, with the inside becoming positively charged. These changes in polarity (the action potential) continue along the axon until reaching the presynaptic terminals.

➜ What attracts the Na^+ ions to flow from one portion of the axon to the next?

Consider the following analogy to illustrate why axon thickness affects rate of transmission. Water flows more quickly through a wide-bore hose than through a narrow-bore one, in part because there is less resistance to the flow of water in the thicker hose. Similarly, Na^+ ions flow faster along the membrane of a thick axon than a thin axon.

myelin sheath The segments of myelin covering certain axons; myelinated axons transmit a neural impulse faster than unmyelinated axons.

node of Ranvier The space between myelinated segments of a myelinated axon.

saltatory conduction The propagation of an action potential from node to node in myelinated axons.

Saltatory Conduction

The axons of many neurons are covered with myelin, a complex mixture of fat and protein produced by certain types of glial cells (oligodendrocytes in the CNS, Schwann cells in the PNS) (Chapter 2). Although the axon is a continuous structure, myelin is wrapped around the axon in segments. The myelinated segments, collectively called the **myelin sheath,** are separated by small spaces, known as **nodes of Ranvier** (Figure 4.10), where the cell membrane is exposed to the extracellular fluid. These nodes are the only places along the axon with ion channels and thus the only places where extracellular and intracellular fluid can be exchanged. Given that an action potential is generated by the movement of ions into and out of the cell through the ion channels, only the nodes can respond to a depolarizing stimulus such as the flow of Na^+ ions. In this way, the action potential is propagated from node to node. This "jumping" movement from node to node is called **saltatory conduction** (from the Latin *saltare,* "to jump"). Note that the action potential only seems to jump. It is really traveling passively between the nodes and being recreated at the nodes.

Saltatory conduction dramatically increases the speed of information transmission. By way of analogy, picture yourself walking a dog. You are probably

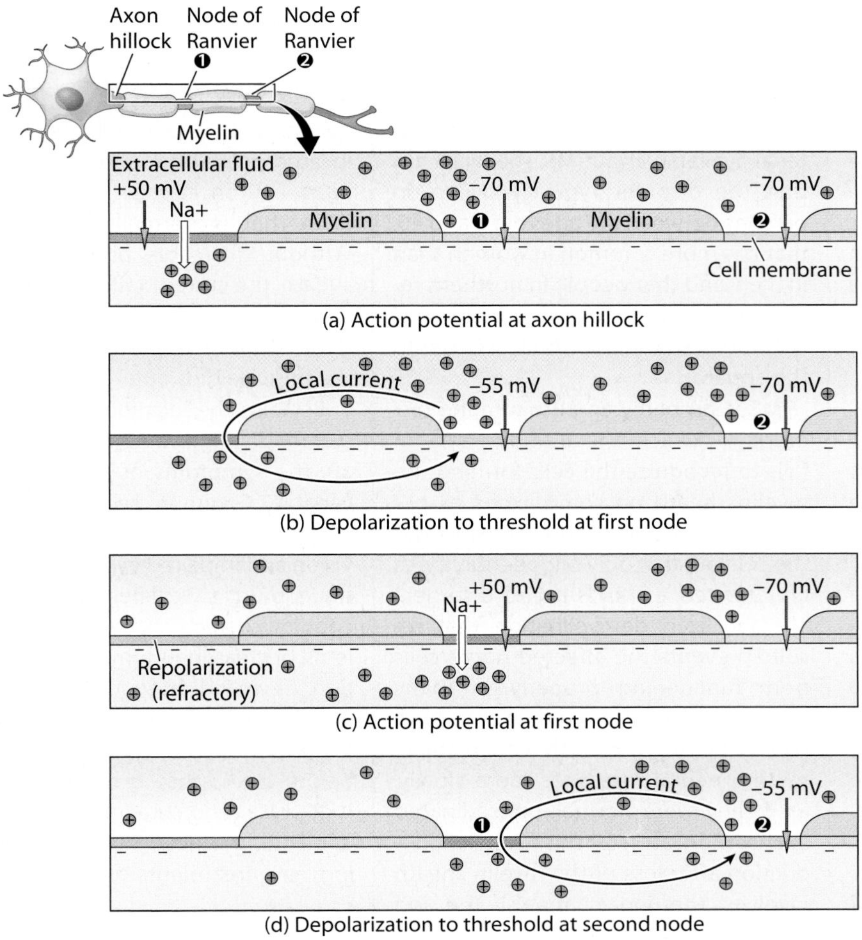

Figure 4.10

Propagation of the action potential along a myelinated axon The action potential that develops at the axon hillock is propagated as the depolarizing Na^+ ions move along the axon between nodes of Ranvier.

Why is transmission faster along a myelinated axon than along an unmyelinated axon?

multiple sclerosis (MS) A progressive neurological disorder caused by the degeneration of the myelin sheath in the central nervous system.

taking normal steps, but if the dog slips the leash to go after a cat, you will run, taking longer strides in an effort to catch the dog. The speed with which you travel depends not only on how fast you move your legs but also on the length of your stride—how much ground you cover with each step. An action potential has to "walk" down an unmyelinated axon from segment to segment, whereas it can "run" (or "jump") along a myelinated axon from node to node.

The reason for the "running" versus "walking" is that the myelin sheath acts like a cable conducting an electric current. These cable properties allow the current to flow through myelinated regions of the axon from one node of Ranvier to the next. Although the depolarizing current diminishes along the length of a myelin segment, it is still sufficient to generate another action potential at the next node. Because Na^+ ions only have to enter the axon at each node, the action potential is propagated more swiftly along a myelinated axon than along an unmyelinated one, in which Na^+ ions must flow into the cell many times along the length of the axon.

The difference in the rate of transmission in myelinated and unmyelinated axons is striking. For example, in mammals, a myelinated axon with a diameter of 1.5 mm can conduct information at speeds up to 100 m/sec. By contrast, an unmyelinated neuron of the same size can conduct action potentials at a rate of only about 1 m/sec. In Box 4.1, we explain why a myelinated axon typically cannot conduct a nerve impulse when it loses its myelin sheath.

Myelination provides another benefit as well. The sodium-potassium pump uses a considerable amount of energy to expel Na^+ ions that enter the neuron dur-

Box 4.1
Multiple Sclerosis

In the chapter-opening vignette, Michelle receives a diagnosis of **multiple sclerosis (MS),** a progressive neurological disorder whose symptoms are caused by the degeneration of the myelin sheath at places in the nervous system (Bjartmar & others, 2003; Bruck & Stadelmann, 2003). As Michelle learned from the neurologist, there are several types of MS. The *relapsing-remitting* variety, in which occasional flare-ups are followed by periods of remission of symptoms, is by far the most common. The other forms are *benign,* in which the symptoms are mild to moderate and do not worsen or lead to permanent disability; *primary progressive,* in which deterioration occurs without remission; *secondary progressive,* in which people with the relapsing-remitting variety (in about half of all cases) enter a stage of progressive deterioration; and *progressive relapsing,* which is primary progressive with sudden episodes of new symptoms or a worsening of older symptoms. If Michelle reads any of the abundant material available about MS, she will learn that the disorder typically occurs in persons between the ages of 20 and 40, that it is more common in women than in men, and that people in northern regions of the world are more likely to be afflicted than people who live closer to the equator.

MS is probably an autoimmune disorder, in which the immune system fails to recognize the cells forming the myelin sheath on some axons as belonging to the "self" and thus destroys them. (Note that only oligodendrocytes are affected, as MS is a CNS disorder.) The localized demyelination that results prevents the affected nerve cells from functioning properly. In many cases, the demyelinated axons completely fail to work, rather than transmitting neural messages more slowly, as if they were normal, unmyelinated axons. The reason for this failure of conduction after loss of the myelin sheath involves the ion channels: The ion channels of the demyelinated axon are located only at the nodes, so the damaged neuron cannot function like an axon that is normally unmyelinated. Without the cable properties of the sheath, the current fails to travel to the next node with enough strength to generate a new action potential, and the impulse dies out.

Because the location of the nervous system damage varies among individuals, the symptoms of MS patients are variable. Common symptoms include numbness in one or both limbs, double vision and impaired eye movements, fatigue, muscle weakness, dizziness, and cognitive defects such as memory problems, decreased judgment, and inattention. As we indicated, MS usually begins in young adulthood, but symptoms may be present for months or even years before the disease is diagnosed. There is at present no cure for this potentially debilitating illness, but some promising new treatments are available (see Box 4.3).

ing an action potential. Because Na^+ ions enter myelinated axons only at the nodes of Ranvier, rather than along the entire axon as with unmyelinated axons, far less energy is expended to pump out the excess Na^+ ions.

Checkpoint

Compare the propagation of the action potential along an unmyelinated axon and along a myelinated axon. Other than myelination, in what ways can the nervous system increase the speed with which a message gets from one place to another?

REVIEW

- In an unmyelinated axon, an action potential is propagated through a continuous process of Na^+ entry and K^+ exit, until it reaches the presynaptic terminals.
- The axons of some neurons are covered by a myelin sheath, a segmented fatty covering produced by glial cells. Ion channels occur only at the spaces between myelinated segments, called nodes of Ranvier.
- Propagation along a myelinated axon, which involves the jumping of the action potential from one node of Ranvier to the next, is called saltatory conduction and is much faster than transmission in unmyelinated axons.

Synaptic Transmission

Although each neuron has only one axon, it may have many branches at the end, called telodendria. The swelling at the end of each telodendron, the *presynaptic terminal,* contains synaptic vesicles filled with *neurotransmitter,* which provides one means of communication among neurons throughout the nervous system. Let us look at what happens when a neural impulse arrives at the synapse.

Neurotransmitter Release

When an action potential reaches the presynaptic terminal (Figure 4.11a), calcium ion channels open and Ca^{2+} ions enter the cell (Figure 4.11b). Calcium entry causes the synaptic vesicles to move to the release sites on the presynaptic membrane, where they release neurotransmitter molecules into the synaptic cleft (see Figure 4.11b). Many action potentials fail to release any neurotransmitter molecules (Goda & Sudhof, 1997). Moreover, the same amount of neurotransmitter is not released each time, although neurotransmitter molecules are released in a fixed amount, called a quantum. Thus, the neuron may release few, many, or even no neurotransmitter molecules in response to an action potential. We discuss the factors affecting how much neurotransmitter is released later in the chapter.

Diffusion carries the neurotransmitter molecules across the synaptic cleft, and they encounter and attach to specific receptor sites on the postsynaptic membrane. Binding to the receptors causes the opening of ion channels (Figure 4.11c). Earlier we described ion channels that are sensitive to changes in membrane potential and are thus said to be voltage-gated. Other ion channels are sensitive to specific

Figure 4.11
Overview of synaptic transmission
(a) The action potential reaches the presynaptic terminal, (b) neurotransmitter molecules are released, and (c) they bind to receptors on the postsynaptic membrane. The neurotransmitter causes depolarization (excitation) in this illustration but can also hyperpolarize (inhibit) the postsynaptic membrane.

What event triggers movement of the synaptic vesicles to the presynaptic membrane? What triggers release of a neurotransmitter?

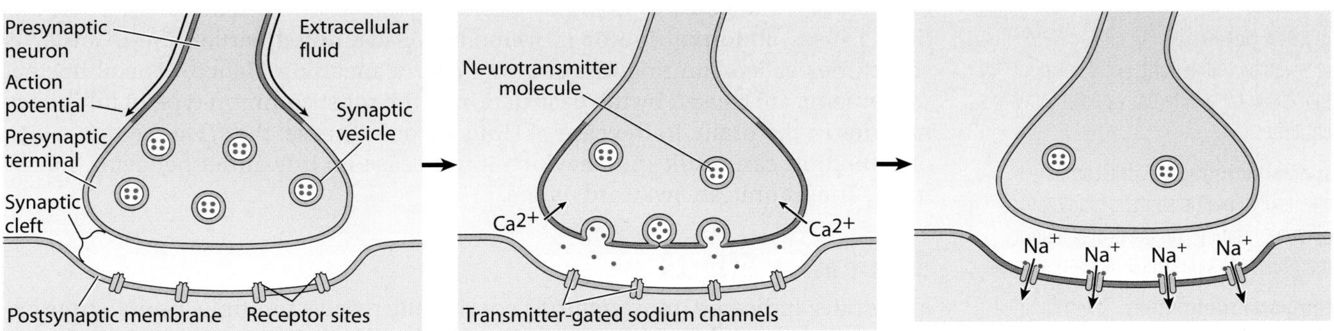

(a) Arrival of action potential at presynaptic terminal

(b) Entry of Ca^{2+} ions into presynaptic terminal and release of neurotransmitter molecules into synaptic cleft

(c) Binding of neurotransmitter to receptors and depolarization of postsynaptic membrane

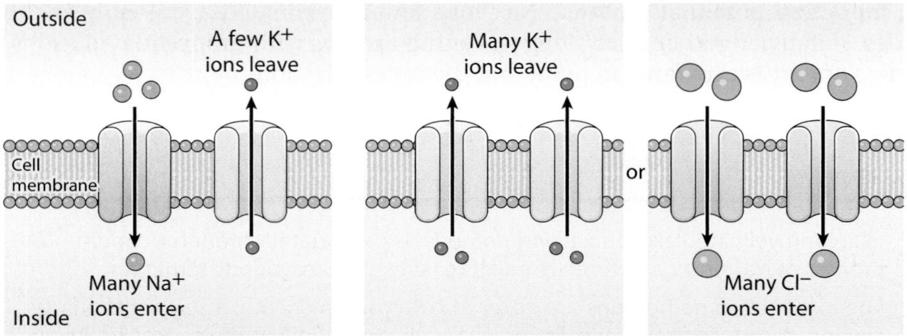

(a) EPSP (depolarization) (b) IPSP (hyperpolarization)

Figure 4.12

Ionic changes caused by neurotransmitters interacting with the postsynaptic membrane Interacting with receptors on the postsynaptic membrane, a neurotransmitter causes either depolarization or hyperpolarization. (a) Entry of more Na^+ ions into the cell causes depolarization (excitatory postsynaptic potential, or EPSP). (b) Entry of more Cl^- ions or exit of more K^+ ions causes hyperpolarization (inhibitory postsynaptic potential, or IPSP).

➜ **How does depolarization cause increased Na^+ ion entry into the neuron?**

neurotransmitter molecules and are called **transmitter-gated ion channels.** Opening of the transmitter-gated ion channels in the postsynaptic membrane produces either depolarization or hyperpolarization, depending on which channels open.

The neurotransmitter can have either an excitatory or an inhibitory influence on the postsynaptic membrane. An excitatory influence produces depolarization at the postsynaptic membrane by increasing the number of Na^+ ion channels that open, allowing more Na^+ ions to enter the cell. This depolarization is called an **excitatory postsynaptic potential,** or **EPSP** (Figure 4.12a).

Neurotransmitters that have an inhibitory effect on the postsynaptic membrane either cause K^+ ions to leave the cell or cause Cl^- ions to enter. Both potassium exit and chloride entry hyperpolarize the cell membrane—that is, increase the difference in charge across the membrane. This hyperpolarization is called an **inhibitory postsynaptic potential,** or **IPSP** (Figure 4.12b); the affected neuron is now less likely to generate an action potential in response to stimulation. The reason for this is that the IPSP moves the membrane potential *farther* from the threshold value than it was during the resting state.

The IPSP is just one mechanism by which the nervous system decreases its activity. Later in the chapter we discuss presynaptic inhibition and autoreceptors as two additional inhibitory mechanisms. At this point, you may be wondering about the purpose of all these inhibitory mechanisms; you might expect the nervous system to have only excitatory processes—sending messages to get something done. One reason for the inhibitory processes is that neurons are highly interconnected. Once activity is initiated in a neuronal circuit, without some way to dampen the activity, there would be nothing to stop the firing; neurons would excite neurons, which would excite other neurons, which would re-excite the original neurons, and so on. Seizure activity, in which groups of neurons recruit other groups until all are out of control, is seen as a failure of the inhibitory mechanisms.

Do not confuse neural inhibition with behavioral inhibition. Neural inhibition can even produce behavior if the inhibited system normally suppresses activity. In Chapter 3, we talked about Huntington's disease, an inherited disorder that initially causes abnormal motor movements. As we noted earlier, the disorder is sometimes called Huntington's chorea—*chorea* meaning "dance." The abnormal movements are caused by the destruction of the most common type of inhibitory neurons in the brain. In the case of Huntington's disease, then, we see that a lack of inhibition can result in behavior—in this case an unwanted behavior, movements that mimic an awkward dance.

transmitter-gated ion channel An ion channel sensitive to a specific neurotransmitter.

excitatory postsynaptic potential (EPSP) The depolarization produced by neurotransmitter molecules acting on receptors on the postsynaptic membrane.

inhibitory postsynaptic potential (IPSP) The hyperpolarization produced by neurotransmitter molecules acting on receptors on the postsynaptic membrane.

graded potential An EPSP or IPSP received by the dendrites and cell body that can have a different value at different times.

spatial summation The combined effects of neurotransmitters binding to different locations on the postsynaptic membrane at a particular moment in time.

temporal summation The combined effects of neurotransmitter binding over time.

Summation Effects

As we have indicated, most neurons continually receive multiple inputs, some excitatory, some inhibitory (Figure 4.13). The net effect of excitation and inhibition determines whether or not the neuron is activated and will fire.

Unlike action potentials, which are all-or-none events, the EPSPs and IPSPs received by the dendrites and cell bodies are **graded potentials,** with different values at different times. Each EPSP causes a depolarization and each IPSP causes a hyperpolarization of the postsynaptic membrane. The various EPSPs received by the postsynaptic membrane can be added together to produce a combined level of depolarization, and the various IPSPs received by the postsynaptic membrane can be added together to produce a combined level of hyperpolarization.

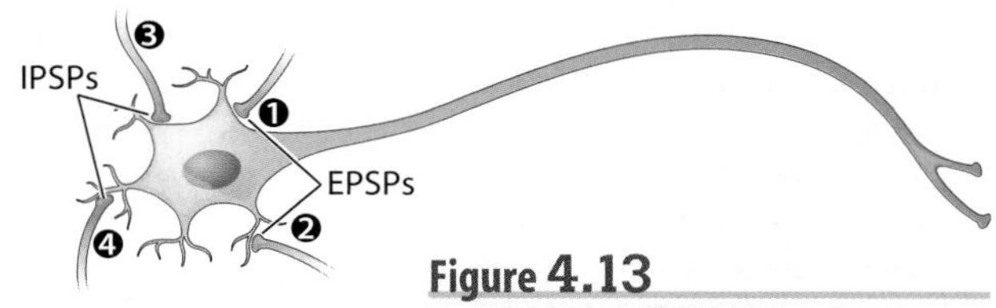

Figure 4.13
Excitatory and inhibitory synapses to a postsynaptic membrane An action potential is generated only if the combined EPSPs at synapses 1 and 2 minus the combined IPSPs at synapses 3 and 4 reach the threshold.

Use this figure to explain the principle of spatial summation.

This process of adding positive and negative influences on the cell membrane is called summation. **Spatial summation** (Figure 4.14a) refers to the combined effects of neurotransmitters arriving at and binding to different locations on the postsynaptic membrane at a particular moment in time—that is, the combined influence of EPSPs and IPSPs across an area or space on the postsynaptic membrane. If the summation of excitatory and inhibitory influences causes sufficient depolarization, the neuron will fire; if the depolarization is not sufficient, the cell will not fire. The nervous system assesses stimulus intensity by the number of neurons firing in a given area and the rate of firing of individual neurons. The more neurons firing in a given area, the greater the spatial summation and the more likely it is that a neuron acted upon by other neurons will generate an action potential.

The neurotransmitter's influence on the postsynaptic membrane—either an EPSP or an IPSP—is short-lived, and the affected cell membrane quickly returns to its resting state. However, summation can also occur across time, if the action potentials in the presynaptic neuron occur sufficiently close together. **Temporal summation** (Figure 4.14b) refers to the combined effects of depolarizing or hyperpolarizing stimuli over time. For example, a neuron may receive several depolarizing stimuli in succession. If the postsynaptic membrane is still depolarized from the first stimulus when the neuron is activated again, the combined level of depolarization from both stimuli is greater than that from a single stimulus. If temporal summation causes the postsynaptic membrane to reach the threshold level, an action potential is generated and the neuron fires. As you may have guessed by now, temporal summation is the other mechanism the nervous system has for assessing stimulus intensity. That is, if the presynaptic neuron is being activated by an intense stimulus, then it will be generating action potentials during its relative refractory period and its rate of firing will be greater than normal. This faster rate of firing increases temporal summation on the postsynaptic membrane and increases the likelihood that the postsynaptic neuron will generate an action potential.

Of course, temporal and spatial summation rarely operate in isolation from each other. An intense stimulus will cause *both* a high rate of firing and more neurons to fire in a given area, and the result is both temporal summation and spatial summa-

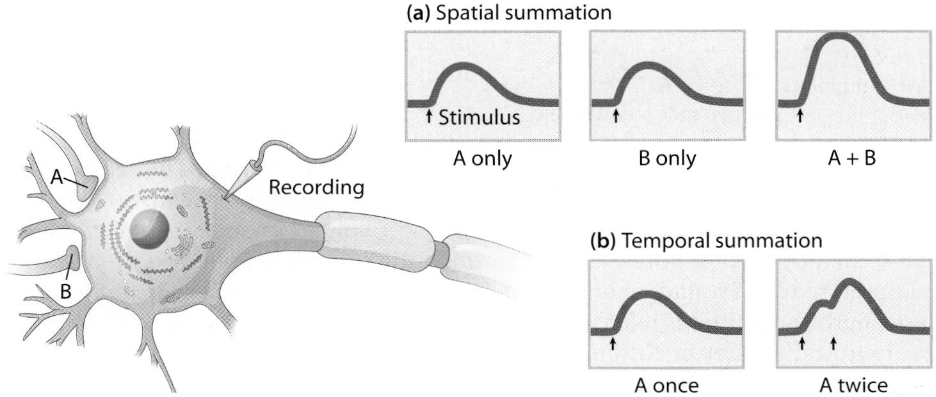

Figure 4.14
Spatial summation and temporal summation (a) Spatial summation occurs when multiple stimuli (here, A + B) exert their effects at the same time on different receptor sites on the postsynaptic membrane. (b) Temporal summation occurs when stimuli (A twice) are close enough in time that their effects are additive.

Why do the stimuli have to be close together for temporal summation to occur?

➤Checkpoint

What is the difference between EPSPs and IPSPs? A postsynaptic membrane receives EPSPs that, when combined, produce 40 mV of change in the postsynaptic membrane potential and IPSPs that, when combined, produce 25 mV of change. Will the postsynaptic neuron fire? (Assume a resting potential of −70 mV and a threshold of −55 mV.)

tion on the postsynaptic neurons. Note that both types of summation may involve IPSPs as well as EPSPs, with the result that they may combine to make it *less* likely that a given neuron will generate an action potential.

REVIEW

- Once the action potential reaches the presynaptic terminals, Ca^{2+} ions move into the cell, causing the synaptic vesicles to move to the presynaptic membrane and release their neurotransmitter into the synaptic cleft.
- The neurotransmitter diffuses across the synaptic cleft, binds to receptor sites on the postsynaptic membrane, and depolarizes or hyperpolarizes the membrane.
- Depolarization (excitation) of the postsynaptic membrane, called an excitatory postsynaptic potential (EPSP), shifts the postsynaptic neuron's membrane potential closer to the threshold, which may ultimately cause the cell to fire.
- Hyperpolarization (inhibition) of the postsynaptic membrane, called an inhibitory postsynaptic potential (IPSP), can prevent the neuron from firing by shifting the potential farther from the threshold. Hyperpolarization results from more K^+ ions leaving the cell or more Cl^- ions entering.
- The various EPSPs occurring at the postsynaptic membrane are summed to produce a combined level of depolarization. The various IPSPs are summed to produce a combined level of hyperpolarization. If the combined EPSPs and IPSPs produce a voltage change that reaches the threshold level, the postsynaptic neuron will fire.
- Spatial summation is the combined influence of EPSPs and IPSPs occurring on different parts of the postsynaptic membrane at a particular moment in time. Temporal summation is the combined effects of EPSPs and IPSPs over time.

Presynaptic Effects

When a neuron fires, neurotransmitter release from the presynaptic terminals is not automatic, and the amount of neurotransmitter released can be influenced by several processes. One such process is **presynaptic inhibition,** a decrease in the amount of neurotransmitter released despite the occurrence of an action potential in the presynaptic neuron. Presynaptic inhibition is caused by the release of a neurotransmitter from another neuron and is an example of the influence of an axoaxonic synapse (Wu & Saggau, 1997) (Figure 4.15). The binding of a neurotransmitter from the influencing neuron to receptors on the presynaptic neuron causes some *depolarization* of the presynaptic membrane (an EPSP, in other words). This decreased polarity (say, −60 mV rather than −70 mV) means that fewer Ca^{2+} ion channels open, fewer Ca^{2+} ions enter, and therefore less neurotransmitter is released. The reason that fewer Ca^{2+} ion channels open is that they are voltage gated, and because of the partial depolarization at the axoaxonic synapse, less voltage change than normal occurs when the action potential goes through the slightly depolarized membrane. With this reduced voltage change, fewer voltage-gated Ca^{2+} ion channels open and less neurotransmitter is released. The opposite effect can also occur: If the release of neurotransmitter at the axoaxonic synapse causes hyperpolarization rather than depolarization, the result is a greater amount of neurotransmitter release, or **presynaptic facilitation** (see Figure 4.15). We discuss these axoaxonic processes

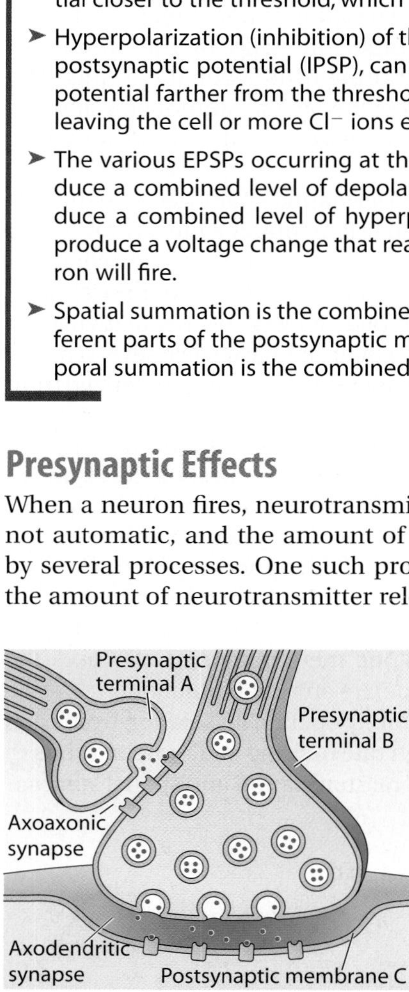

Figure 4.15
An axoaxonic synapse and presynaptic inhibition and facilitation
If activity at presynaptic terminal A slightly depolarizes presynaptic terminal B, then B will release less neurotransmitter onto postsynaptic membrane C (presynaptic inhibition). If activity at presynaptic terminal A slightly hyperpolarizes B, then B will release more neurotransmitter onto postsynaptic membrane C (presynaptic facilitation).

➜ **What is the purpose of presynaptic inhibition? Presynaptic facilitation?**

presynaptic inhibition A decrease in the release of neurotransmitter from the presynaptic membrane (despite the occurrence of an action potential) caused by the action of another neuron.

further in our treatment of learning and memory in Chapter 14.

A neuron can also be inhibited by its own neurotransmitter (Figure 4.16). In some cases, a neurotransmitter not only affects the postsynaptic membrane but also binds to receptors on the presynaptic membrane. Stimulation of these presynaptic receptors, or **autoreceptors,** decreases the amount of neurotransmitter released by the presynaptic neuron. This process allows the neuron to regulate its own neurotransmitter release.

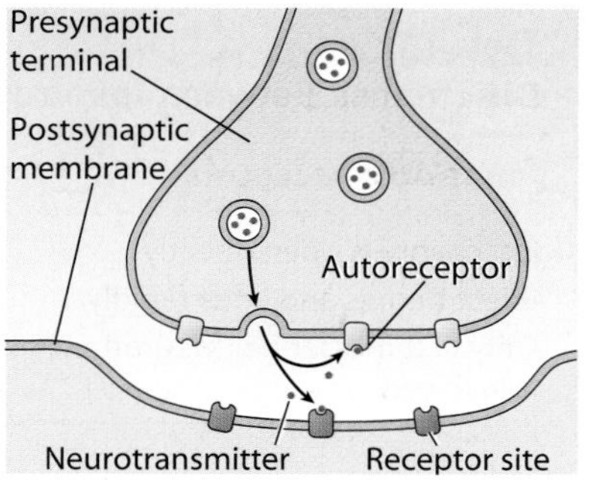

Figure 4.16

Autoreceptors Released neurotransmitter can act on an autoreceptor to decrease subsequent neurotransmitter release.

What is the role of autoreceptors on the presynaptic membrane?

Postsynaptic Receptors

The neurotransmitter effects on the postsynaptic membrane that we have discussed so far, in which a neurotransmitter produces a rapid opening of ion channels through the membrane, involve **ionotropic receptors.** One example of an ionotropic effect occurs at the neuromuscular junction, where acetylcholine (ACh) is the neurotransmitter. Binding of ACh molecules to the ionotropic receptors on the postsynaptic membrane (a muscle cell membrane) causes a rapid opening of Na^+ ion channels to produce an EPSP. Ionotropic effects begin and end rapidly.

This is but one of the possible postsynaptic actions, however. A neurotransmitter can also produce ion channel changes indirectly, by acting on a **metabotropic receptor** (Figure 4.17). In a metabotropic effect, binding of the neurotransmitter to the metabotropic receptor activates another protein attached to the inside of the cell membrane—a *G protein.* The G protein initiates chemical changes within the cell that ultimately produce a chemical called a **second messenger** (the first messenger is the neurotransmitter itself). The second messenger then causes ion channels to open in the postsynaptic membrane. *Cyclic adenosine monophosphate (cyclic AMP)* is one such second messenger. Cyclic AMP is produced from adenosine triphosphate (ATP), which as we noted earlier is a prime source of energy for cellular metabolism. Cyclic AMP is involved in the sedative effects of alcohol and in alcohol consumption (Misra & Pandey, 2003; Wand & others, 2001). It also appears to have an important role in the formation of long-term memories (Bauman & others, 2004; Jackson & Ramaswami, 2003), which we discuss in Chapter 14. In addition to opening ion channels, second messengers can influence gene expression (Baker & Kelly, 2004).

Because ionic changes at metabotropic receptors occur only after the chemical changes required to produce the second messenger, metabotropic effects take

presynaptic facilitation The enhanced release of neurotransmitter from the presynaptic membrane caused by the action of another neuron.

autoreceptor A presynaptic receptor whose stimulation decreases the amount of neurotransmitter released by that presynaptic neuron.

ionotropic receptor A receptor whose ion channels are rapidly opened by the direct action of a neurotransmitter.

metabotropic receptor A receptor whose ion channels are opened indirectly by a second messenger.

second messenger A chemical that causes changes inside the cell in response to a neurotransmitter that lead to ion channel changes.

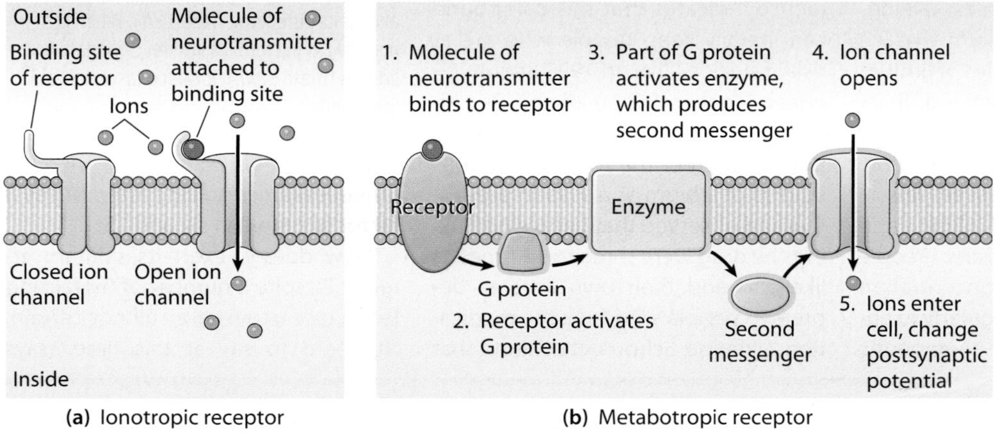

Figure 4.17

Ionotropic and metabotropic receptors (a) When a neurotransmitter molecule binds to an ionotropic receptor, an ion channel opens directly. (b) When a neurotransmitter binds to a metabotropic receptor, the ion channel opens after a series of steps.

What are the major differences between metabotropic and ionotropic receptors?

enzymatic degradation Breakdown and thus deactivation of neurotransmitter molecules by an enzyme.

neurotransmitter reuptake The return of neurotransmitter to the presynaptic neuron.

Table 4.1
Differences Between Ionotropic and Metabotropic Receptors

Ionotropic Receptors	Metabotropic Receptors
Ion channels open directly	Ion channels open indirectly
Effect begins and ends rapidly	Effect begins and ends relatively slowly
Only first messenger (neurotransmitter) is involved	Both neurotransmitter and a second messenger (another chemical) are involved

longer to develop than ionotropic effects; they also last longer. Most of the receptors for ACh in the brain are metabotropic receptors. Table 4.1 summarizes the differences between ionotropic and metabotropic receptors.

Termination of Neurotransmitter Effects

The influence of the neurotransmitter on the postsynaptic membrane is quite brief. In the case of acetylcholine, once it has bound to the receptors on the postsynaptic membrane, it is deactivated by an enzyme, acetylcholinesterase, in the synapse—that is, by **enzymatic degradation.** With other neurotransmitters, the transmitter substance is returned to the presynaptic membrane through **neurotransmitter reuptake.** A pumplike mechanism in the presynaptic membrane conveys released neurotransmitter molecules to the reuptake site and then into the cytoplasm, where they are again stored in synaptic vesicles (Figure 4.18). Both en-

Scientific American Spotlight

The "Magic" of Lithium

Carol Ezzell

"Only crazy people take lithium!" my mother shouted during one of our many arguments over her not receiving the best treatment for her manic-depression. She accused me and my stepfather of wanting to medicate her so she would "just shut up." To be honest, she was partially right: it is very trying to be around someone in the grip of a mania, which often brings on incessant, stream-of-consciousness talking.

Many people find lithium—which generally comes in capsules of lithium carbonate or lithium citrate—difficult to take. It can cause hand tremors, constant thirst, frequent urination, weight gain, lethargy, reduced muscle coordination, blurred thinking, and short-term memory deficits. People on it must also have its concentration in their blood assessed regularly to ensure that it is within the therapeutic range: the drug is usually ineffective below 0.6 millimole per liter of blood serum and can cause life-threatening toxic reactions if the level becomes higher than two millimoles per liter.

Lithium is used routinely to even out the extreme mood swings of patients with manic-depressive illness, or bipolar disorder. Increasingly, however, it is also offered to people with depression. But a growing body of evidence indicates that this compound can literally keep people who are at risk of suicide alive. In 1998 lithium pioneer Mogens Schou of the Psychiatric Hospital in Risskov, Denmark, pulled together the results of various studies of lithium as a suicide preventive and observed that people not taking the drug were three to 17 times as likely to end their own lives as depressed people who took the medication. Likewise, Schou determined that lithium reduced suicide attempts by a factor of between six and 15.

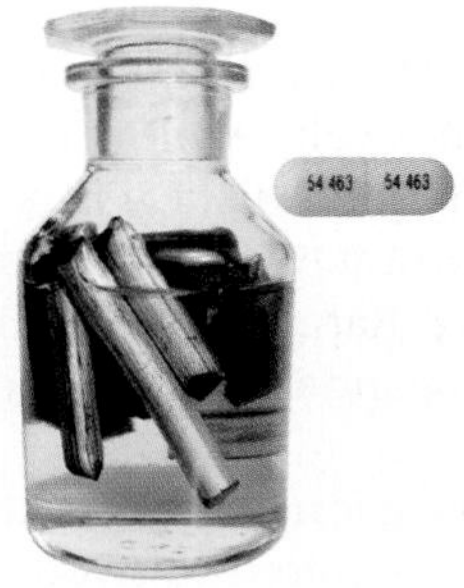

Lithum is the lightest of the solid elements and, in its pure form, floats (*left*). When compounded in pill form as lithium carbonate or lithium citrate (*right*), it can be taken to stabilize moods.

How does it exert its salutary effects? Despite a number of tantalizing leads, researchers are still not certain. "It's hard to say at this time," says

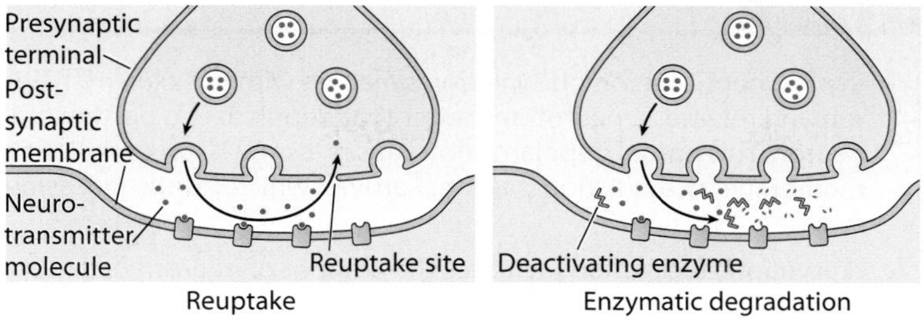

Figure 4.18

Termination of neural transmission In reuptake, the molecules of neurotransmitter are taken back into the presynaptic membrane after they have had their effect on the postsynaptic receptors. In enzymatic degradation, the molecules of neurotransmitter are inactivated by being broken into pieces.

What is the advantage of neurotransmitter reuptake over enzymatic degradation?

zymatic degradation and reuptake occur within a fraction of a second after the neurotransmitter acts on the postsynaptic membrane. In addition, although the major mechanisms of neurotransmitter inactivation are enzymatic degradation and reuptake, the action of all neurotransmitters is affected by *diffusion,* in which neurotransmitter molecules simply drift away from the synapse.

The rapid reuptake or degradation of neurotransmitter, and thus the rapid termination of its effect, allows neurons to transmit many messages each second. The production of an almost continuous flow of impulses is what allows the nervous system to process the enormous amount of information necessary for survival.

The *Scientific American* Spotlight, "The 'Magic' of Lithium," discusses the importance of lithium, in pill form, in the treatment of manic-depressive illness (bipolar disorder) and in preventing suicide. Although researchers are not certain exactly how lithium performs its "magic," the author outlines some of the possible modes of action, which involve the processes and structures discussed in this chapter.

Checkpoint

What is the advantage of presynaptic inhibition? What are the major differences between ionotropic receptors and metabotropic receptors? Nerve poisons such as pesticides block acetylcholinesterase activity. Describe their impact on the nervous system, using what you have learned about enzymatic degradation.

"Lithium . . . is the lightest of the solid elements, and it is perhaps not surprising that it should in consequence possess certain modest magical qualities."—G. P. Hartigan, psychiatrist

Ghanshyam N. Pandey of the University of Illinois. "There are so many modes of action." Lithium is thought to affect tiny ports called ion channels on the surfaces of nerve cells, or neurons. As they open and close, ion channels admit or bar charged atoms that determine the electrical potential within the cells, thereby dictating their activity and ability to communicate with other neurons. Scientists posit that the drug stabilizes the excitability of the neurons by influencing the ion channels or by skewing the chain reaction of biochemical events that occur within an excited cell.

A drug only works, though, if someone takes it properly. In the May 2002 issue of the *Journal of Clinical Psychiatry,* Jan Scott and Marie Pope of the University of Glasgow reported that half of a group of 98 patients who were taking a mood-stabilizing drug such as lithium failed to stick with their drug regimen. Yet, the researchers noted, just 1 percent of scientific publications on the subject of mood stabilizers looked at why patients did not take their lithium as prescribed.

J. John Mann of the New York State Psychiatric Institute says that a major factor in noncompliance is the human desire not to want to think of oneself as ill. "There's a natural reluctance to take any medicine long-term," Mann explains. "When a person is depressed, they have a problem imagining ever getting better. When they're well, they can't imagine getting sick again."

The side effects of lithium also play a role. Kay Redfield Jamison, a psychiatrist at Johns Hopkins University who studies manic-depression and suicide—and who is a manic-depressive herself—has found that the most common reasons patients stop taking the drug are cognitive side effects, weight gain and impaired coordination. In her moving memoir, *An Unquiet Mind,* she recounts her own struggle to come to terms with the fact that she will probably be coping with lithium's side effects for the rest of her life. Perhaps if my mother had lived to read it, she would have been heartened by Jamison's example and motivated to begin lithium therapy.

From: *Scientific American,* vol. 288(2), p. 49.

glutamate An amino acid neurotransmitter, the most common excitatory neurotransmitter in the CNS.

gamma-aminobutyric acid (GABA) An amino acid neurotransmitter, the most common inhibitory neurotransmitter in the brain.

GABAergic Describing a synapse or synaptic transmission with GABA as the neurotransmitter.

glutamatergic Describing a synapse or synaptic transmission with glutamate as the neurotransmitter.

REVIEW

- In presynaptic inhibition, a neuron synapses with the axon of the presynaptic neuron and releases a neurotransmitter that depolarizes a portion of the presynaptic neuron. This partial depolarization causes less Ca^{2+} ion entry into the presynaptic membrane as the action potential arrives, which results in less neurotransmitter release.
- Presynaptic facilitation increases the amount of neurotransmitter released by hyperpolarizing a portion of the presynaptic membrane.
- Neurotransmitter molecules can bind to autoreceptors on the presynaptic membrane, decreasing the amount of neurotransmitter released.
- Binding of a neurotransmitter to ionotropic receptors directly affects ion channels. Binding to metabotropic receptors produces metabolic changes in the cell that lead to ion channel changes. This occurs through production of a second messenger such as cyclic AMP.
- Neurotransmitter molecules in the synaptic cleft are deactivated by enzymatic degradation and by reuptake into the presynaptic neuron.

◆ Agents of Synaptic Transmission

Now that you have learned the basics of synaptic transmission, it is time to examine the actions of several specific neurotransmitters. Dozens of different neurotransmitters are found in the nervous system, and scientists have devised different schemes for categorizing them. Here we will divide them into *small-molecule neurotransmitters* and *large-molecule neurotransmitters.* The small-molecule category includes amino acids, monoamines, soluble gases, and acetylcholine—a neurotransmitter that is in a class by itself. The peptides or neuropeptides are large-molecule neurotransmitters. Table 4.2 outlines the neurotransmitter classification system we are using.

Why are there so many different neurotransmitters? In many parts of the nervous system, especially the brain, neurons with different behavioral functions are in close physical proximity. Thus, one explanation for different neurotransmitters for different functions is that they are needed to prevent unwanted or inadvertent communication between neurons. For example, the neurons controlling eating and sexual behavior are located in the same general area of the brain, but because the chemical transmitters controlling each behavior are different, we can engage in each behavior separately. Another possibility is that the different neurotransmitter systems evolved separately and just happen to occupy the same space (or nearly the same space).

Table 4.2
Classification of Neurotransmitters, With Some Examples

Small-molecule neurotransmitters
Amino acids
Glutamate
Gamma-amino butyric acid (GABA)
Aspartate
Glycine
Monoamines
Catecholamines
Epinephrine (adrenalin)
Norepinephrine (noradrenalin)
Dopamine
Indoleamines
Serotonin
Melatonin
Soluble gases
Nitric oxide
Carbon monoxide
Acetylcholine
Large-molecule neurotransmitters
Endogenous opioids
Substance P
Oxytocin
Antidiuretic hormone (ADH)
Cholecystokinin (CCK)

Small-Molecule Neurotransmitters

As stated earlier, this category of neurotransmitters includes such diverse substances as amino acids, monoamines, soluble gases, and acetylcholine. We begin with amino acids, a group that contains possibly the first neurotransmitters.

The Amino Acids

Some neurons use amino acids—compounds with an amino group (NH_2) and a carboxyl group (COOH)—as neurotransmitters. The four amino acid neurotransmitters we will consider are glutamate, aspartate, glycine, and gamma-aminobutyric acid (GABA). Both GABA and glutamate are present in primitive species, suggesting they were the first neurotransmitters to evolve. Glutamate and aspartate are excitatory neurotransmitters; GABA and glycine are inhibitory neurotransmitters. (An important note here: For simplicity, we say that certain neurotransmitters are excitatory or inhibitory or both. Actually, whether an IPSP or an EPSP is produced at a particular synapse depends on the ion channels controlled by the receptor proteins on the postsynaptic membrane. If Na^+ ion channels open and Na^+ ions enter the postsynaptic neuron, an EPSP is produced; exit of K^+ ions or entry of Cl^- ions causes an IPSP. Thus, it would be more accurate to say that at synapses where glutamate or aspartate are the neurotransmitters, ionic movement results in EPSPs, whereas at synapses employing GABA or glycine, ionic movement produces IPSPs. So, although we refer to a particular neurotransmitter as excitatory or inhibitory, keep in mind that it is not the neurotransmitter itself that has this property; rather, the action of the postsynaptic receptor on particular ion channels is what determines whether an EPSP or an IPSP is produced.)

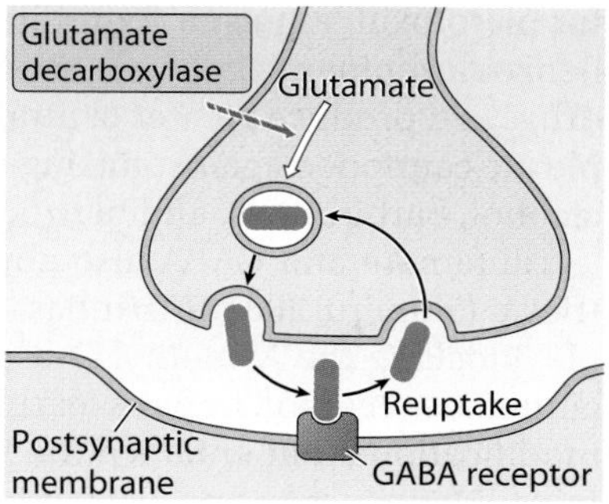

Figure 4.19
A GABAergic synapse Gamma-aminobutyric acid (GABA) is synthesized from the amino acid glutamate by the enzyme glutamate decarboxylase and stored in synaptic vesicles. When released into the synaptic cleft, GABA diffuses across the cleft and binds to receptors on the postsynaptic membrane. A few milliseconds after binding, GABA is inactivated by reuptake into the presynaptic neuron.

→ How does GABAergic transmission differ from serotonergic transmission?

Glutamate is the most common excitatory neurotransmitter in the central nervous system, and **gamma-aminobutyric acid (GABA)** is the most common inhibitory neurotransmitter in the brain. GABA is produced from glutamate by the enzyme glutamate decarboxylase. Synapses that use GABA are called **GABAergic,** and the activity of GABA on the postsynaptic membrane is terminated by reuptake (Figure 4.19), as is the case for all the amino acid neurotransmitters. Synapses that use glutamate are called **glutamatergic.** GABA and glutamate activate both ionotropic and metabotropic receptors, GABA to produce IPSPs and glutamate to produce EPSPs.

The primary role of the inhibitory action of GABA is to keep the brain from becoming excessively aroused. There are at least five types of GABA receptors (Enz, 2001), of which $GABA_A$ (Figure 4.20) and $GABA_B$ are the most studied. $GABA_A$ receptors are believed to produce IPSPs by causing Cl^- ions to enter the postsynaptic neuron; $GABA_B$ receptors produce IPSPs by opening K^+ ion channels to allow K^+ ions to leave the postsynaptic neuron. Hyperpolarization of the postsynaptic membrane results in both cases.

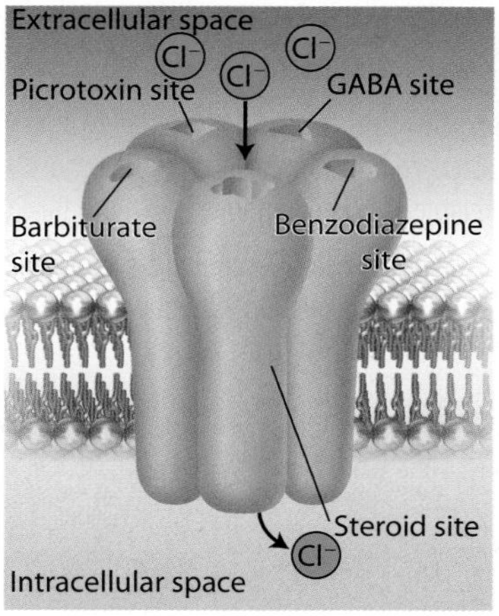

Figure 4.20
$GABA_A$ receptor Receptor protein, showing the major binding sites.

→ Why is the combination of alcohol and Xanax potentially deadly?

GABA deficiencies have been linked to a number of disorders. For example, because GABA is the primary inhibitory neurotransmitter in the brain, any problem with its function increases the likelihood of seizures (Chang & others, 2003; Pearl & others, 2004). Epilepsy is the most common disorder in which modification of GABA is the goal of treatment (Wong & others, 2003). In addition, a decrease in GABAergic neurons appears to be responsible for Huntington's disease (Kendall & others, 2000). Glutamate may also be involved, producing a toxic effect through excessive activity that kills selected neurons primarily in the corpus striatum but also in the neocortex (Alberch & others, 2002; Mattson, 2003). We discuss the genetic basis of Huntington's disease in Chapter 3 and examine its neural basis in Chapter 8.

Extreme anxiety, characterized by intense physiological arousal and strong feelings of apprehension, guilt, and a sense of impending doom, has also been linked to below-normal GABA levels (Chang & others, 2003). People are likely to be anxious when GABA levels decline, and drugs that increase GABA activity, such as diazepam (Valium) and alcohol, decrease anxiety levels (Nutt & Malizia, 2001).

Diazepam and alcohol produce their GABA effects by attaching to the same binding site on the $GABA_A$ receptor, which has at least five different binding sites. As you would expect, the primary site is for GABA itself, but secondary sites are available for the benzodiazepines (diazepam and alprazolam [Xanax] are in this class of "minor" tranquilizers) and alcohol; for the barbiturates (e.g., phenobarbital); for various steroids, including some that cause general anesthesia; and

monoamine One of a class of neurotransmitters that contain an amino group (NH_2); includes epinephrine, norepinephrine, dopamine, and serotonin.

catecholamine One of a subclass of monoamine neurotransmitters that includes epinephrine, norepinephrine, and dopamine.

indoleamine One of a subclass of monoamine neurotransmitters that includes serotonin and melatonin.

norepinephrine A neurotransmitter synthesized from the amino acid tyrosine; sometimes called noradrenalin (noradrenaline).

epinephrine A neurotransmitter closely related to norepinephrine; also called adrenalin (adrenaline).

noradrenergic (adrenergic) Describing a synapse or synaptic transmission with norepinephrine as the neurotransmitter.

monoamine oxidase (MAO) An enzyme that deactivates norepinephrine, dopamine, and serotonin.

dopamine A neurotransmitter synthesized from the amino acid tyrosine; closely related to norepinephrine.

dopaminergic Describing a synapse or synaptic transmission with dopamine as the neurotransmitter.

for picrotoxin, a poison found in an East Indian shrub. Because alcohol and the benzodiazepines occupy the same GABA-binding sites, the combination of these drugs can produce greater central inhibition than either alone, which is why people are cautioned against mixing the two. We have more to say about the effects of alcohol, barbiturates, and benzodiazepines in Chapter 5.

Glutamate and GABA also appear to be involved in memory storage and retrieval (Shapiro, 2001; Zarrindast & others, 2002). According to Shapiro, for example, blocking the *N*-methyl D-aspartate (NMDA) receptor, which is a subtype of glutamate receptor, impairs learning in tasks requiring the hippocampus, whereas modifications that enhance the function of these receptors improve learning in mice. Zarrindast and colleagues found that drugs that activate GABA receptors impaired retention, whereas antagonists improved it. The influence of glutamate and GABA on memory are further examined in Chapter 14.

The Monoamines

The **monoamines,** which are amine compounds with a single amino group (NH_2), are divided into two subclasses—the catecholamines and the indoleamines. Epinephrine, norepinephrine, and dopamine are **catecholamines;** serotonin and melatonin are **indoleamines.**

Norepinephrine, sometimes called *noradrenalin* (or *noradrenaline*), is synthesized from the amino acid tyrosine. You may be more familiar with norepinephrine's close relative, **epinephrine** or *adrenalin* (*adrenaline*). We are discussing norepinephrine here because, of the two, it is much more important in the CNS. Note that the terms *adrenalin* and *epinephrine* have similar meanings in different languages. *Adrenalin* comes from the Latin *ad,* "at," and *ren,* "kidney"; epinephrine comes from the Greek *epi,* "upon" and *nephron,* "kidney." Both epinephrine and norepinephrine are made in the adrenal gland, which is located at the top of the kidneys in mammals, as well as in the nervous system.

Synaptic transmission involving norepinephrine is referred to as **noradrenergic,** or just **adrenergic,** because the receptors also respond to epinephrine (Figure 4.21). There are four major types of adrenergic receptors, which are found in the brain and elsewhere. Stimulation of the different receptor types can produce either excitatory or inhibitory effects at the synapse, but the behavioral effects of norepinephrine release tend to be excitatory. Noradrenergic transmission stops with the reuptake of norepinephrine by the presynaptic membrane. Excess norepinephrine in the cytoplasm of the cell (not stored in synaptic vesicles) may be broken down by the enzyme **monoamine oxidase (MAO),** which also inactivates some norepinephrine in the synaptic cleft, along with the enzyme catechol-*O*-methyltransferase (COMT).

Norepinephrine is widely distributed throughout the nervous system and is involved in a number of important behavioral functions. For example, in the PNS, norepinephrine is the neurotransmitter of the sympathetic nervous system. In the brain, norepinephrine appears to have a prominent role in regulating attention, concentration, arousal, and sleep, and it has been implicated in the pathophysiology of depression (Fava, 2003). We have more to say about its role in depression in Chapter 15.

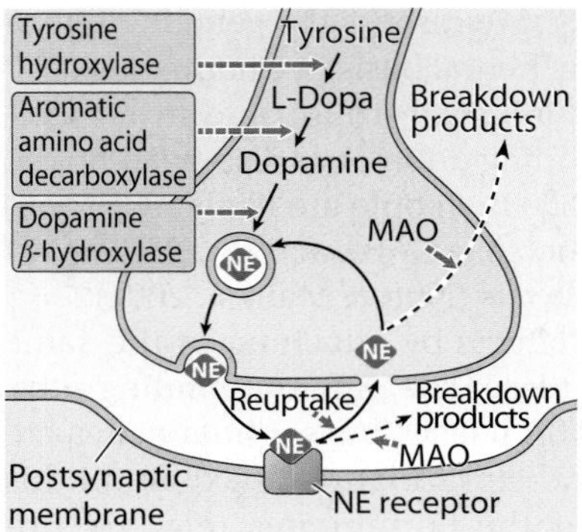

Figure 4.21
A noradrenergic synapse Norepinephrine (NE) is synthesized from the amino acid tyrosine by a series of enzyme reactions. Termination of norepinephrine activity occurs through reuptake by the presynaptic membrane or deactivation by the enzyme monoamine oxidase (MAO).

➡ How does noradrenergic transmission differ from cholinergic transmission?

Like norepinephrine, **dopamine** is synthesized from the amino acid tyrosine. In fact, norepinephrine and dopamine are close chemical relatives; norepinephrine is produced when the enzyme dopamine *β*-hydroxylase attaches a hydroxyl group to dopamine. Synaptic transmission involving dopamine is referred to as **dopaminergic**

(Figure 4.22). There appear to be at least five types of dopamine receptors (Baldessarini & Tarazi, 1996). Of these five, the D_1 and D_2 receptors have been most studied. D_1 receptors are found only on the postsynaptic membrane, whereas D_2 receptors are found on both presynaptic and postsynaptic membranes. Like norepinephrine, dopamine activity is mainly terminated by reuptake. Also like norepinephrine, some dopamine is inactivated by MAO and COMT.

Dopamine is the neurotransmitter at synapses between the substantia nigra and the basal ganglia, which act to integrate voluntary movements (Chapter 2), and the degeneration of dopaminergic neurons in the substantia nigra has been implicated in Parkinson's disease (Fernandez-Espejo, 2004). Parkinson's disease is characterized by severe tremors, muscular rigidity, and decreased control of voluntary movements.

Defective dopaminergic transmission is also involved in schizophrenia, a severe mental illness marked by irrational thought, hallucinations, poor contact with reality, and deterioration of adaptive behavior. Some investigators have proposed that schizophrenia is caused by an excess of activity at dopaminergic synapses. Supporting this hypothesis is the finding that drugs that block dopaminergic transmission are often effective in reducing some of the major symptoms of schizophrenia (Pani, 2002). Movement disorders such as Parkinson's disease and tardive dyskinesia (involuntary, repetitive, stereotyped movements) are among the possible side effects of the antipsychotic drugs used to treat schizophrenia. Later in the book we discuss the role of dopamine in Parkinson's disease (Chapter 8) and schizophrenia (Chapter 15). Dopaminergic transmission has also been implicated in a variety of addictions, including addiction to heroin, nicotine, alcohol, and marijuana (Gianoulakis, 2004) (discussed further in Chapter 5).

Serotonin, also known as *5-hydroxytryptamine (5-HT),* is another monoamine neurotransmitter; it is an indoleamine rather than a catecholamine. Widely distributed throughout the CNS, serotonin is synthesized from the amino acid tryptophan. Synaptic transmission involving serotonin is called **serotonergic** (Figure 4.23). There appear to be at least seven classes of serotonin receptors, with one class alone (5-HT_1) having five receptor subtypes (Lanfumey & Hamon, 2004). Some serotonin receptors are found on both presynaptic and postsynaptic membranes; the 5-HT_2 receptor occurs only on the postsynaptic membrane (Struder & Weicker, 2001). Like the other monoamines, postsynaptic action of serotonin is primarily terminated by reuptake.

Serotonergic neurons play an important role in a variety of behaviors, including the regulation of sleep (Huwig-Poppe & others, 1999). A depletion of serotonin decreases sleep duration (Voderholzer & others, 1998), whereas the ingestion of a metabolite of the amino acid tryptophan, which can be converted to serotonin, seems to help some people go to sleep (Birdsall, 1998). This may be why drinking a glass of milk, which contains tryptophan, can be an aid to falling asleep. Melatonin, the hormone secreted by the pineal gland (Chapter 2), is closely related to serotonin and has long been assumed to play a role in sleep (Cardinali & others, 2002). We have more to say about the role of serotonin in sleep in Chapter 9.

A strong fear reaction is primarily mediated by the release of norepinephrine. This is a still from *I Was a Teenage Werewolf.*

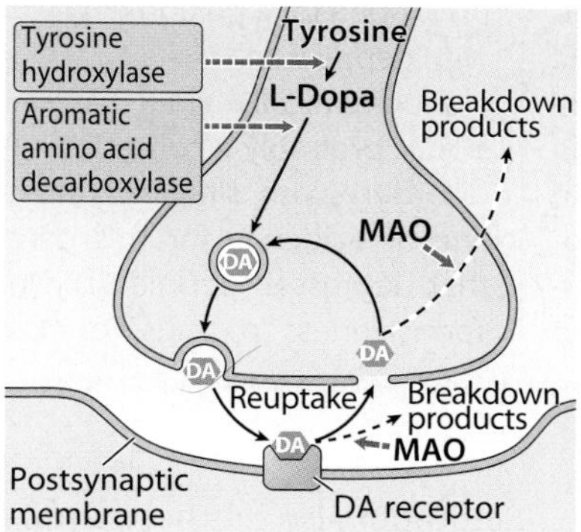

Figure 4.22

A dopaminergic synapse Dopamine (DA) is synthesized from the amino acid tyrosine in two steps. Dopamine activity is terminated by reuptake by the presynaptic membrane or deactivation by the enzyme monoamine oxidase (MAO).

How does dopaminergic transmission differ from noradrenergic transmission?

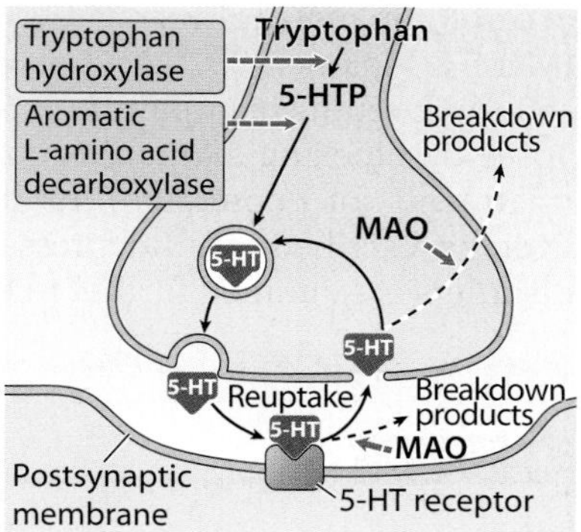

Figure 4.23

A serotonergic synapse Serotonin (5-hydroxytryptamine, 5-HT) is synthesized from the amino acid tryptophan in two steps. 5-HT activity is terminated by reuptake by the presynaptic membrane or deactivation by the enzyme MAO.

How does serotonergic transmission differ from dopaminergic transmission?

serotonin A neurotransmitter synthesized from the amino acid tryptophan; also known as 5-HT.

serotonergic Describing a synapse or synaptic transmission with serotonin as the neurotransmitter.

Box 4.2
Drug Treatment for Depression

The neuropathology of clinical depression is discussed at length in Chapter 15, but here we look briefly at how the different drug therapies affect synaptic transmission. One theory of depression holds that it is caused by reduced activity at monoaminergic synapses, particularly the synapses that use serotonin or norepinephrine. One piece of evidence supporting this theory is that drugs that elevate monoamine levels decrease depressive symptoms (Bymaster & others, 2003).

Two classes of drugs have been used for many years to provide clinical relief for depressed individuals. Discovered more than 40 years ago, the **tricyclic compounds** increase norepinephrine and serotonin levels without affecting dopamine levels, by interfering with neurotransmitter reuptake. The **monoamine oxidase inhibitors (MAOIs)** increase monoamine levels by preventing monoamine oxidase from degrading any excess monoamine neurotransmitter in the cytoplasm of the presynaptic neuron; as a result, more neurotransmitter is available for release.

Introduced more recently, the **selective serotonin reuptake inhibitors (SSRIs;** also sometimes called *serotonin-specific reuptake inhibitors)* target serotonin almost exclusively, increasing its availability by inhibiting its reuptake. Because of their selectivity, the SSRIs tend to have fewer side effects than either of the other classes of drugs (Baldwin, 2001; Donoghue, 2000). For this reason, they are likely to be the first drugs prescribed for a person newly diagnosed with depression.

Biochemically, what we call depression is probably a collection of different disorders with similar symptoms. One line of evidence for this conclusion is that depressed people vary in their responsiveness to drugs. For example, the tricyclics may be more effective than the SSRIs for treating persons with severe depression (Anderson, 2000), and the MAOIs are helpful for some depressed individuals who fail to respond to other antidepressant treatments (Shelton, 1999; Thase & others, 1995). One problem with the MAOIs is that they also inhibit MAO *outside* the brain, so a person taking such a drug is unable to break down a substance, tyramine, found in many foods. Without rather severe dietary restrictions, the MAOIs can cause a severe blood pressure increase that has proved fatal in some cases.

The reason for the varying responses to the different drug treatments is not yet clear, but a number of brain structures and specific systems are probably involved in depression. The success of any drug treatment thus depends on whether the drug alters the specific neurotransmitters and receptors involved in a particular individual's depression.

Serotonin also has been implicated in depression, and individuals with severe depression as indicated by high-lethality suicide attempts have decreased levels of serotonin metabolites relative to depressed patients with low-lethality attempts (Mann & Malone, 1997). A whole class of drugs has been developed—the selective serotonin reuptake inhibitors or SSRIs—that increase activity at serotonergic synapses by blocking serotonin reuptake (Box 4.2 discusses these and other drug treatments for depression). Its representatives, such as fluoxetine (Prozac), are widely prescribed as antidepressants (Julien, 2005). The role of serotonin in mood disorders is examined further in Chapter 15.

Checkpoint

Distinguish between amino acid and monoamine neurotransmitters. Give several examples of each. What would happen if GABA release were suddenly inhibited? Glutamate release?

REVIEW

- The neurotransmitters can be classified as small-molecule and large-molecule neurotransmitters. The small-molecule neurotransmitters include amino acids, monoamines, soluble gases, and acetylcholine.
- Amino acids used as neurotransmitters include glutamate and aspartate, which are both excitatory, and gamma-aminobutyric acid (GABA) and glycine, which are both inhibitory. Glutamate and GABA are the most common excitatory and inhibitory neurotransmitters, respectively, and may have been the first neurotransmitters to have evolved.
- Deficiencies of GABA have been linked to Huntington's disease and to excessive anxiety.
- The $GABA_A$ receptor has binding sites for GABA, the benzodiazepines and alcohol, the barbiturates, certain steroids, and picrotoxin.

- The monoamines are divided into the catecholamines (epinephrine, dopamine, and norepinephrine) and the indoleamines (serotonin and melatonin).
- Norepinephrine is involved in arousal and mood, with lowered levels implicated in depression.
- Dopamine is involved in the integration of voluntary behavior, with the degeneration of dopamine neurons in the substantia nigra associated with Parkinson's disease; excess activity at dopaminergic synapses is considered a possible cause of schizophrenia.
- Serotonin is involved in sleep regulation, and serotonin depletion has been associated with decreased sleep and depression.

The Soluble Gases

The neurotransmitters we have discussed to this point are packaged in synaptic vesicles and released from terminal buttons to diffuse across the synapse and make contact with receptor proteins on the postsynaptic membrane of another neuron. The **soluble gases,** recently discovered small-molecule neurotransmitters, break all the "rules." They are manufactured in all parts of a neuron, are released as soon as they are made, and do not affect postsynaptic receptors. Instead, they diffuse through cell membranes and activate a second messenger before being quickly inactivated.

The soluble gas neurotransmitters so far identified are nitric oxide and carbon monoxide (Hartsfield, 2002; Morse & others, 2002). Of the two, **nitric oxide (NO)** has received more research attention and has been found to be involved in such disparate functions as penile erection (Andersson, 2003), dilation of blood vessels in metabolically active brain regions (Gulbenkian & others, 2001), and, perhaps most importantly, learning (Susswein & others, 2004)—a function we discuss further in Chapter 14.

Acetylcholine

Found in both the CNS and the PNS, acetylcholine is one of the most widespread neurotransmitters. **Acetylcholine (ACh)** is synthesized from acetyl CoA and choline by the enzyme choline acetyltransferase. Synaptic transmission involving ACh is said to be **cholinergic** (Figure 4.24).

There are two types of cholinergic receptors, named for the substances other than ACh that have also been found to stimulate them. *Nicotinic receptors* are activated by nicotine, which is the main addictive component in cigarettes, and *muscarinic receptors* are stimulated by muscarine, a poison found in mushrooms. Studies of cholinergic receptors have identified four subtypes of nicotinic receptors and five subtypes of muscarinic receptors (McCormick, 1989). Virtually all cholinergic receptors in the CNS are muscarinic. The cholinergic receptors at the neuromuscular junctions, as well as those at autonomic ganglia, are nicotinic.

After producing either an EPSP or an IPSP, molecules of ACh are quickly deactivated by the enzyme **acetylcholinesterase (AChE),** which is present in the synaptic cleft. AChE splits ACh into acetate and choline, neither of which is effective by itself. Most of the choline is taken up by the presynaptic membrane and stored in the presynaptic terminal, where it can be used to synthesize new ACh.

Acetylcholine has a variety of important behavioral functions. As you will recall from Chapter 1, Otto Loewi discovered *vagusstoff,* which decreased heart rate, and this turned out to be ACh. Thus, one of the main functions of ACh is as a

tricyclic compound A type of drug that increases brain levels of norepinephrine and serotonin by interfering with neurotransmitter reuptake.

monoamine oxidase inhibitor (MAOI) A type of drug that increases monoamine levels by preventing MAO from degrading excess monoamine neurotransmitters.

selective serotonin reuptake inhibitor (SSRI) A type of drug that increases the availability of serotonin by inhibiting its reuptake.

soluble gas A class of neurotransmitters that includes nitric oxide and carbon monoxide.

nitric oxide (NO) A soluble gas neurotransmitter involved in such disparate functions as penile erection and learning.

acetylcholine (ACh) A neurotransmitter synthesized from acetyl CoA and choline by the enzyme choline acetyltransferase.

cholinergic Describing a synapse or synaptic transmission with ACh as the neurotransmitter.

acetylcholinesterase (AChE) An enzyme present in the synaptic cleft that quickly deactivates ACh after it is released.

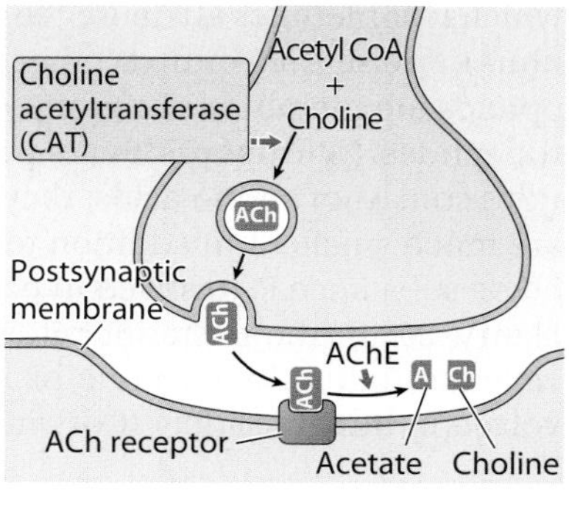

Figure 4.24

A cholinergic synapse Acetylcholine (ACh) is synthesized from acetyl CoA and choline by the enzyme choline acetyltransferase (CAT). ACh is deactivated by acetylcholinesterase (AChE), which splits ACh into choline and acetate.

How is the process ending cholinergic transmission different from that of other neurotransmitters?

neurotransmitter in the parasympathetic nervous system. Acetylcholine is also the neurotransmitter at the neuromuscular junction, transmitting messages from motor nerves to skeletal muscles. Its role in movement and movement disorders, such as myasthenia gravis, is discussed in Chapter 8. A forebrain structure called the nucleus basalis of Meynert contains cells that manufacture ACh and distribute it widely to the cerebral cortex. The finding of a depletion of ACh in the brains of Alzheimer's patients led to a popular theory of cholinergic involvement in the disease (Mesulam, 1998) and treatments for the disorder involving acetylcholinesterase inhibitors (Zhang & others, 2004). Talesa (2001) and Rees and Brimijoin (2003) have suggested that acetylcholinesterase itself may be involved in the neurological development of Alzheimer's disease. Further research has revealed a neural depletion of other neurotransmitters as well (Heneka & others, 2002; Porter & others, 2003; Seidl & others, 2001). We have more to say about neurotransmission and Alzheimer's disease in Chapter 14.

Chemical warfare agents, such as nerve gases, often work by disrupting the action of AChE. One example is sarin, which is a clear, odorless, and tasteless liquid. Exposure to sarin either in liquid or gaseous form can cause loss of consciousness, convulsions, paralysis, and respiratory failure that leads to death. At least two of the anticholinesterase effects of sarin can prove lethal: The first is that knocking out the action of AChE magnifies the effect of ACh on the heart, which is to slow it down. The second effect, and this is what is likely to kill a victim of sarin poisoning, is that blocking the action of AChE disrupts breathing. Through the action of ACh on the breathing muscles of the chest, abdomen, and diaphragm, the sarin victim is able to inhale, but without AChE to break down the ACh, the breathing muscles are unable to relax and the victim is therefore unable to exhale. In other words, voluntary breathing ceases.

Checkpoint

How do the soluble gases differ in function from the other neurotransmitters? Name as many of the functions of acetylcholine as you can. What would you expect to happen if ACh activity were blocked at the neuromuscular junctions?

Large-Molecule Neurotransmitters

Jerry, Michelle's boyfriend, is a committed runner who jogs at least 6 miles on most days. Jerry has run in several 10K races in the past 2 years and generally finishes among the top five in his age group. Because he lives in Ohio, there are times, particularly in the winter, when Jerry is tempted to stay inside his warm apartment rather than venture out into the cold. But if the streets are cleared of snow, Jerry runs. He is sure Michelle thinks he is crazy to run in bad weather, but he is compelled to do it.

After a few minutes of stretching, Jerry starts running slowly, and then he picks up his pace about a mile into his run. After a couple of miles, he starts to feel pretty good, and after about 5 miles, he enters what he likes to think of as a state of nirvana. Jerry has a hard time describing the feeling to Michelle, but it is one of great exhilaration—an unbearable lightness of being, he thinks, recalling the title of one of his favorite movies. His whole body tingles, and he feels as though he is floating rather than running. And, if only for a while, he forgets his worries about Michelle's illness.

Jerry's state of exhilaration illustrates a phenomenon called "runner's high," which is sometimes attributed to a release of endogenous opioids following strenuous exercise (Heitkamp & others, 1993; Rahkila & others, 1988). The endogenous opioids are members of a group of large-molecule neurotransmitters called neuropeptides. **Neuropeptides** are peptides that function as neurotransmitters. (Peptides consist of amino acids; they have the same type of structure as proteins but are much smaller.) In addition to the endogenous opioids, the neuropeptides include substance P, involved in pain perception (Paukert & others, 2001; Pitcher & Henry, 2004); the posterior pituitary substances oxytocin and vasopressin (also called antidiuretic hormone or ADH); and cholecystokinin (CCK), which is involved in hunger satiety (Corwin & others, 1991; Smith & Gibbs, 1975; Halford &

neuropeptide A peptide that functions as a neurotransmitter.

others, 2004). CCK and neuropeptide Y (NPY), which is also involved in hunger, are discussed further in Chapter 10. Most of these peptides also act as neuromodulators, which we discuss later in the chapter.

Of the neuropeptides, probably the most investigated are members of the family of **endogenous opioids** (*endogenous* means "coming from within," and *opioid* means "opium-like"). Three major classes of endogenous opioids are currently recognized—enkephalins, dynorphins, and endorphins—each of which is derived from a different precursor. Together, the endogenous opioids are sometimes called *endorphins,* short for endogenous morphine-like substance. The use of this term can be confusing, however, as it also refers to one of the three classes of endogenous opioids, as we indicated. We will use the term "endogenous opioids" throughout this discussion.

As you probably realize, opiates, such as heroin and morphine, have a powerful effect on people, producing such sensations as analgesia (a decreased perception of pain) and a strong sense of emotional well-being (Chapter 5). Interest in the effects of opiate drugs led to the 1973 discovery of opiate receptors in the brain, by scientists working in three different laboratories: Candace Pert and Solomon Snyder at Johns Hopkins University School of Medicine, Eric Simon of the New York University School of Medicine, and Lars Terenius of Uppsala University in Sweden. Obviously, these receptors did not evolve on the off-chance that someone would ingest opium; humans must have a naturally occurring neurochemical that binds to opiate receptors, and discovery of the receptors initiated an intense search for such a chemical or chemicals.

PHILIP GREENSPUN

For some runners, racing in a marathon can produce "runner's high."

In 1975, John Hughes, working in the laboratory of Hans Kosterlitz at the University of Aberdeen in Scotland, announced that he had found two endogenous opioids, which he called *enkephalins,* meaning "in the head" (Hughes & others, 1975). Soon, other endogenous opioids were discovered, and in 1976 Abram Goldstein suggested that opiate drugs affect behavior by mimicking the naturally occurring opiates and activating the same neurons. In fact, Goldstein found that when opium was ingested, it concentrated in specific neural areas associated with the perception of pain and with emotions. Like the opiate drugs, the endogenous opioids are involved in euphoria (Singh & others, 1999) and analgesia (Hall & Sykes, 2004; Przewlocki & Przewlocka, 2001), and both functions probably contribute to Jerry's runner's high. That is, endogenous opioid release blocks any pain Jerry might experience from running and also produces a feeling of euphoria, which he interprets as runner's high. We have more to say about the opioids in Chapter 5.

Neuromodulators

Unlike neurotransmitters, which are used for isolated communication between neurons in close proximity to each other, **neuromodulators** are chemical transmitters that affect groups of cells, modifying their sensitivity to neurotransmitter release or altering the amount of neurotransmitter released. As noted below, the endogenous opioids and other neuropeptides can function as neuromodulators as well as neurotransmitters.

Instead of influencing a single neuron, neuromodulators diffuse throughout a region, affecting all the neurons in the area, including the one that released the neuromodulator. Because of this regional effect, neuromodulators function somewhat like hormones, which we discuss later. However, hormones act even more broadly and at greater distances from where they were released. Thus, although the endogenous opioids and other neuromodulators share some qualities with both neurotransmitters and hormones, neuromodulators are a distinct type of chemical transmitter; their function is to modify cells' responsiveness to neurotransmitters. For example, one effect of caffeine is to block the action of the neuromodulator adenosine. Adenosine acts to decrease the release of

endogenous opioid One of a class of neurotransmitters that have opiate-like characteristics.

neuromodulator A type of chemical that modifies the sensitivity of groups of cells to neurotransmitters or the amount of neurotransmitter released.

many neurotransmitters, including glutamate, GABA, norepinephrine, serotonin, and acetylcholine. When caffeine blocks adenosine receptors, more neurotransmitter is released. The general effect of adenosine in the brain is to decrease neural activity; caffeine, by blocking adenosine receptors, increases such activity and thus arousal (e.g., Carter & others, 1995). Some of the functions in which neuromodulators may be involved include pain sensitivity, attention, and fearfulness.

➤Checkpoint

What triggered the search that led to the discovery of the endogenous opioids? What is "runner's high"? How does caffeine act on the brain to increase arousal?

REVIEW

- ➤ Carbon monoxide (CO) and nitric oxide (NO) are soluble gases that function as small-molecule neurotransmitters. They are manufactured in all parts of neurons, are released as soon as they are made, and diffuse through cell membranes and activate a second messenger before being quickly inactivated.
- ➤ Acetylcholine (ACh) is a widespread small-molecule neurotransmitter in the CNS and PNS. It is the neurotransmitter of the parasympathetic nervous system and neuromuscular junctions. Lowered levels of ACh and other neurotransmitters are associated with Alzheimer's disease.
- ➤ The large-molecule neurotransmitters are the neuropeptides, which include substance P, oxytocin, and vasopressin (antidiuretic hormone, ADH), cholecystokinin, and the endogenous opioids. The main effects of the endogenous opioids are analgesia and euphoria.
- ➤ Neuromodulators are chemicals that modify the sensitivity of neurons to neurotransmitter or that affect the release of neurotransmitter.

◆ Hormones and the Endocrine System

So far we have discussed the action of neurotransmitters, which transmit impulses from one neuron to the next, and neuromodulators, which modify the effects of neurotransmitters. But for many purposes, communication must be more widespread. For such situations, the glands of the **endocrine system** release chemical transmitters called **hormones** into the bloodstream, which carries the transmitters to distant target areas.

The endocrine glands are located throughout the body (Figure 4.25). Hormones are a slower means of communication than neurotransmitters, but they transmit information more widely. For example, testosterone is produced by the testes but can have effects as far away as the brain.

Like neurotransmitters, hormones stimulate the membranes of specific target cells. Table 4.3 lists the major endocrine glands and some of the hormones they release. For example, stimulation of the adrenal gland releases epinephrine and norepinephrine into the bloodstream, and stimulation of specific neurons by epinephrine and norepinephrine produces intense internal arousal. Note that norepinephrine is listed in Table 4.3 as a hormone released from the adrenal medulla, although we discussed it earlier as a major neurotransmitter. Norepinephrine is considered a neurotransmitter when it is communicating from neuron to neuron and a hormone when it is distributed by the bloodstream. Therefore, *distribution* differentiates neurotransmitters from hormones.

Hormones carry messages to neurons, muscles, and organs, and can also stimulate the development of these targets; for example, testosterone controls the maturation of the male repro-

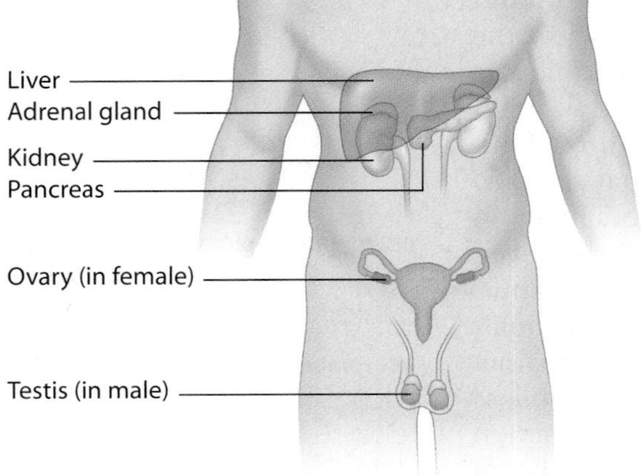

Figure 4.25
The location of major endocrine glands These glands have an important influence on biological processes and behavior. Table 4.3 shows the hormones released by each gland. Although the liver and kidneys are shown in the drawing, they are not endocrine glands.

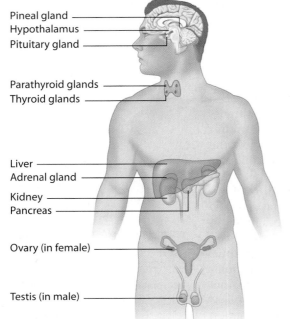

➡ **How do hormones travel from the gland in which they are produced to the target organs?**

Table 4.3

Major Endocrine Glands, the Hormones They Secrete, and Their Principal Functions

Gland	Hormone	Function
Adrenal gland		
Cortex	Aldosterone	Retention of sodium and excretion of potassium by kidneys
	Androstenedione	Growth of pubic and underarm hair, sex drive (women)
	Cortisol	Metabolism; response to stress
Medulla	Epinephrine, norepinephrine	Metabolism; response to stress
Hypothalamus*	Releasing hormones	Control of anterior pituitary hormone secretion
Pancreas	Insulin, glucagon	Regulation of glucose use and storage as glycogen
Pineal	Melatonin	Regulation of circadian rhythms
Pituitary gland		
Anterior	Adrenocorticotropic hormone (ACTH)	Control of adrenal cortex
	Gonadotropic hormones: follicle-stimulating hormone (FSH) and luteinizing hormone (LH)	Control of testes and ovaries
	Somatotropin or growth hormone (STH or GH)	Growth; control of metabolism
	Prolactin (PRL)	Milk production
	Thyroid-stimulating hormone (TSH)	Control of thyroid gland
Posterior	Antidiuretic hormone (ADH)**	Retention of water by kidneys
	Oxytocin	Release of milk, contraction of uterus, contraction of prostate gland
Ovaries	Estrogen	Maturation of female reproductive system; secondary sex characteristics
	Progesterone	Maintenance of uterine lining; facilitation of pregnancy
	Inhibin	Control of FSH release
Testes	Androgens	Maturation of male reproductive system; sperm production; secondary sex characteristics; sex drive (men)
	Inhibin	Control of FSH release
Thyroid gland	Thyroxine, triiodothyronine	Energy metabolism; growth and development
	Calcitonin	Helps regulate the level of calcium in the blood
Parathyroids	Parathyroid hormone	Helps regulate the level of calcium in the blood

*The hypothalamus, although it is part of the brain, secrets hormones; thus, it can be considered an endocrine gland.

**These hormones are produced by the hypothalamus but are transported to and released from the posterior pituitary gland.

ductive system. As we will see throughout the text, hormones have important influences on our behavior.

Many hormones are controlled by the brain through feedback loops, which can be either positive or negative. In a **positive feedback loop,** the release of a hormone promotes the further release of that hormone. For example, consider what happens during childbirth; once it begins, it must be completed quickly. Triggered by the distortion of the uterus by the growing fetus, oxytocin secretion initiates labor. Stretch receptors on the uterine wall detect contractions and activate the hypothalamus to continue oxytocin release from the posterior lobe of the pituitary (Figure 4.26). A positive feedback loop increases the level of oxytocin release and the strength of uterine contractions until the baby is delivered.

In some cases, hormonal release inhibits its subsequent release in a **negative feedback loop.** For example, estrogen release is controlled by negative feedback

endocrine system The system of glands that releases hormones into the bloodstream, where they are carried to distant target areas.

hormone A chemical produced by the endocrine glands that is circulated widely throughout the body via the bloodstream.

positive feedback loop The release of a substance that acts to promote its further release.

negative feedback loop The release of a substance that acts to inhibit its subsequent release.

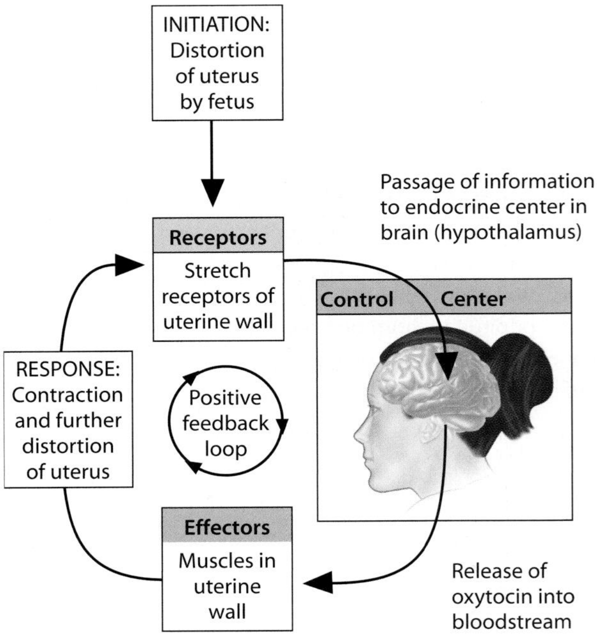

Figure 4.26

The positive feedback loop involved in labor and childbirth Distortion of the uterus by the growing fetus causes release of oxytocin, which initiates uterine contractions. These contractions in turn stimulate further oxytocin release and stronger uterine contractions.

Why is the positive feedback loop important in childbirth?

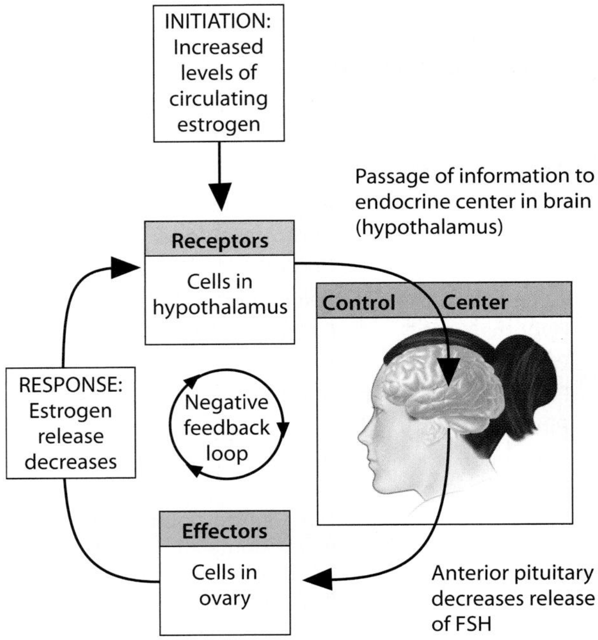

Figure 4.27

The negative feedback loop involved in regulating estrogen levels Increased estrogen levels activate processes that lead to reduced estrogen levels, which then activate processes that elevate estrogen levels.

Does the negative feedback loop maintain a consistent level of estrogen?

(Figure 4.27). Stimulation of part of the hypothalamus in sexually mature females causes the anterior pituitary to release follice-stimulating hormone (FSH), one effect of which is to cause the ovary to secrete estrogen. When the bloodstream carries estrogen to the hypothalamus, one of its actions is to inhibit FSH release, which causes estrogen levels to fall. The lowered estrogen level then removes this inhibition, and FSH production resumes.

Pheromones are chemicals released into the air rather than into the bloodstream. Their detection can have a powerful effect on the behavior of members of the same species. When a female dog is in heat, it is difficult to keep male dogs away. This attraction is produced by pheromones released by female dogs when they are sexually receptive (Goodwin, Gooding, & Regnier, 1979).

Checkpoint

Why do male dogs in a neighborhood without a leash law sometimes congregate around the house of a family with a female dog? Compare the effects of neuromodulators and hormones. How do they differ and what are their similarities of action?

REVIEW

- The endocrine glands release hormones into the bloodstream, and the hormones affect distant target organs. Hormones provide a slower means of communication than neurotransmitters but allow more widespread information transmission.
- In positive feedback, hormonal release promotes further release of that hormone; in negative feedback, a hormone inhibits its further release.
- Pheromones are chemicals released into the air that affect the behavior of other members of the same species.

pheromone A chemical released into the air, rather than into the bloodstream, that affects other members of a species.

Electrical Synaptic Transmission

Our discussion has focused on axonal transmission, but some neurons in the mammalian nervous system are anaxonic, meaning they do not have axons. **Anaxonic neurons** are components of complex interneuronal circuits in which neural impulses can move in either direction rather than by the one-way axonal transmission described thus far. These circuits occur primarily in brain areas that control complex activities such as learning and memory (Chapter 14). Because there are no axons, communication occurs from the dendrites of one neuron to the dendrites of another neuron, hence the name **dendrodendritic transmission.**

Unlike neurons with axons, which produce action potentials and communicate by chemical transmission, neurons with only dendrites and a cell body produce small localized depolarizations and hyperpolarizations on the dendrites of adjacent neurons (Hormuzdi & others, 2004; Rozental & others, 2000). This communication occurs across **electrical synapses,** where ions move across a **gap junction** between dendrites (Figure 4.28). Electrical synapses also are found in cardiac and smooth muscle, as well as in many invertebrates.

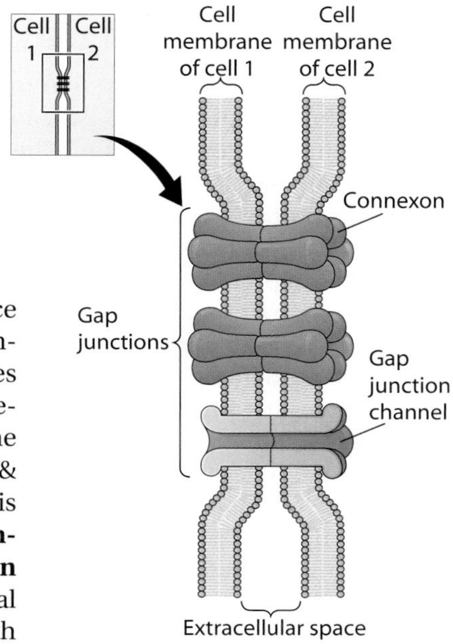

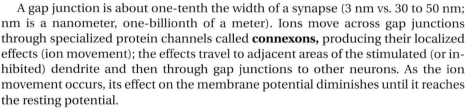

Figure 4.28
Gap junctions Ions travel through the connexons of a gap junction from the dendrites of one neuron to the dendrites of another neuron.

What is the advantage of neurons without axons?

A gap junction is about one-tenth the width of a synapse (3 nm vs. 30 to 50 nm; nm is a nanometer, one-billionth of a meter). Ions move across gap junctions through specialized protein channels called **connexons,** producing their localized effects (ion movement); the effects travel to adjacent areas of the stimulated (or inhibited) dendrite and then through gap junctions to other neurons. As the ion movement occurs, its effect on the membrane potential diminishes until it reaches the resting potential.

As you will recall, an action potential is an all-or-none event, and stimulus intensity is determined by the rate of neuronal firing and by the number of neurons firing in a given area. In dendrodendritic transmission, however, there are no action potentials, and the level of depolarization or hyperpolarization varies directly with stimulus intensity in these graded potentials. In other words, a more intense stimulus causes greater depolarization or hyperpolarization of the cell membrane of the dendrite.

At least in the goldfish, electrical synapses and nearby chemical synapses are highly interrelated, with chemical synapses affecting the conductance of their electrical neighbors (Smith & Pereda, 2003). Pereda and colleagues (1998) have noted striking similarities between the regulation of gap junctions and mechanisms proposed for certain communications at mammalian synapses employing glutamate.

anaxonic neuron A neuron without an axon.

dendrodendritic transmission Communication between anaxonic neurons from the dendrites of one neuron to the dendrites of another neuron.

electrical synapse The junction between the dendrites of two neurons where localized depolarization or hyperpolarization is produced.

gap junction The narrow space between the dendrites of two neurons; another name for an electrical synapse.

connexon A specialized protein channel through which ions move across gap junctions.

Checkpoint

How does the transmission of a neural impulse differ across electrical and chemical synapses? What might be the advantage of dendrodendritic transmission?

REVIEW

- Anaxonic neurons, which do not have axons, transmit impulses between dendrites (dendrodendritic transmission).
- Anaxonic neurons are components of complex interneuronal circuits in neural areas that control activities such as learning and memory.

➤ Communication between the dendrites of two neurons occurs across an electrical synapse. Ions move across gap junctions through protein channels called connexons. The ionic movement produces either depolarization or hyperpolarization of the postsynaptic membrane.

The Blood-Brain Barrier

The ability of the nervous system to process and respond effectively to environmental stimuli depends on a delicate chemical balance between the fluid outside and the fluid inside the neuron. This critical balance is maintained in part by the **blood-brain barrier,** a collective structure that prevents the free flow of substances from the bloodstream into the brain. Note that the blood-brain barrier helps protect the brain, just as do the skull, meninges, and ventricular system discussed in Chapter 2.

Of course, many substances entering our body are essential to our survival. And the brain needs oxygen and glucose to fuel metabolic processes, but it is unable to store even moderate amounts of either substance. Fortunately, the circulatory system provides the brain with these essential resources. Other substances entering the bloodstream, such as alcohol, can disrupt the functioning of the brain and therefore are potentially harmful.

Because of the critical nature of the brain's nutritional needs, several major arteries supply it with blood. These large arteries branch into many smaller arteries and then into fine channels called capillaries, which deliver nutrients to the neurons. The endothelial cells that form the walls of the capillaries form a protective lining. In most capillaries, gaps between the endothelial cells allow relatively large molecules to pass from the bloodstream into nearby cells. In the brain, however, the endothelial cells are closely joined by tight junctions, thereby preventing the free flow of substances from the blood into the neurons (Figure 4.29). In addition to this layer of tightly joined endothelial cells, access to the brain is limited by astrocytes, glial cells surrounding the capillaries. For example, astrocytes keep certain blood-borne toxic substances from entering neurons.

Figure 4.29

The blood-brain barrier The tight joining of the endothelial cells of the capillaries surrounding the brain limits the movement of large molecules. Some substances enter the brain by passing freely through the capillary walls. Other substances enter the brain by attaching to the lipids in the capillary walls or by being actively transported out of the bloodstream. Note that the glial feet are not shown on the left side of the blood vessel in order to show the passage of substances through the blood vessel wall into the brain tissue.

➜ **How does nicotine cross the blood-brain barrier?**

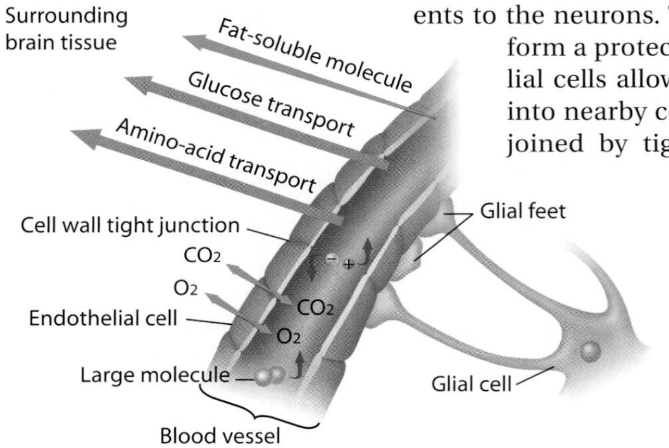

The blood-brain barrier is far from perfect, however. Small uncharged molecules, such as oxygen and carbon dioxide, pass readily through the endothelial layer. In addition, any lipid- or fat-soluble substance can pass from the bloodstream into the brain. (Recall that cell membranes are composed of a lipid bilayer.) For example, heroin and nicotine can enter the brain by attaching to the lipids in the capillary walls.

In addition to excluding harmful substances, the blood-brain barrier also keeps out most sources of nutrition. Thus, active, energy-expending systems transport the needed materials (for example, glucose, amino acids, vitamins) from the blood through the blood-brain barrier into the brain.

The blood-brain barrier is not uniformly effective throughout the brain. For example, the barrier is relatively weak in the area postrema, a region of the medulla oblongata that controls vomiting. The greater permeability in this area increases the chances that an ingested poison will be discharged from the body: Toxic substances can leave the bloodstream in the area postrema, stimulating its neurons to produce vomiting. However, the same toxic substances cannot cross the barrier in other areas of the brain, protecting it from their dangerous effects.

The blood-brain barrier also prevents many substances from leaving brain cells and entering the bloodstream. Although most waste products are removed

blood-brain barrier A barrier between the blood and the brain that prevents the free flow of substances between the two.

experimental allergic encephalomyelitis A neurological disorder resembling MS produced by injecting myelin proteins into the bloodstreams of laboratory animals.

Box 4.3

Multiple Sclerosis: New Treatments

As noted in Box 4.1, the symptoms of MS are caused by the progressive degeneration of the myelin sheath covering the axons of some neurons in the central nervous system; this degeneration leads primarily to sensory and motor impairment. In some cases, the immune system attacks myelin as if it were a foreign substance. One theory for the attack is that damage to the blood-brain barrier allows myelin proteins to enter the bloodstream. Because under normal circumstances the immune system does not encounter these proteins, it does not recognize them and thus reacts to them as it would to any foreign substance: It forms antibodies to myelin proteins.

Based on the idea that at least some cases of MS are maladaptive autoimmune responses, MS is frequently treated with corticosteroids, such as methylprednisone, which suppress the immune system (National Multiple Sclerosis Society, 2003). Clinical trials are underway to determine the effectiveness of immune system suppressant drugs such as interferon beta-1b (Betaseron) and interferon beta-1a (Avonex). (*Interferons* are peptides released by virus-infected cells, which make other cells more resistant to the virus.) The monoclonal antibody drug natalizumab (Antegren) is another experimental treatment. (*Monoclonal antibodies* are genetically engineered antibodies.) The hope is that these new treatments will reduce the severity and duration of acute attacks experienced by MS patients.

Although natalizumab does not appear to reduce the effects of an acute exacerbation of MS, long-term treatment with the drug significantly reduces the likelihood of further exacerbations (Sheremata & others, 2005). Unfortunately, its use has been suspended recently because of safety concerns, as three patients taking it have died from progressive multifocal leukoencephalopathy (PML). PML is a rare disease of the CNS that is caused by a virus typically acquired in childhood. The virus usually remains dormant in people with normal immune function.

Evidence supporting the idea that MS is an autoimmune disorder triggered by brain proteins that have escaped the blood-brain barrier comes from studies of a neurological disorder with symptoms that resemble multiple sclerosis. **Experimental allergic encephalomyelitis** (**EAE**) is produced when myelin proteins are injected into the bloodstreams of laboratory animals, and it has been extensively investigated as an animal model of MS (Ucelli & others, 2003). This suggests that the immune system can be triggered to attack and destroy myelin in reaction to myelin protein in the bloodstream. If this model is correct, then Michelle and other people with MS should have myelin protein in their blood; in fact, myelin protein has been found in the blood of some MS patients. In studies employing the animal model, Brok and colleagues (2002) and Laman and colleagues (2002) have used monoclonal antibodies to block the inflammatory agent that would normally damage the myelin sheath. Such treatment prevents the development of clinical symptoms in animals and suggests a promising approach to treating MS.

from the neuron by active transport systems, large molecules, such as proteins, remain within the neuron. When these proteins are lost through various disease processes, the result can be damage to the brain. In fact, Michelle's multiple sclerosis may have developed because of a failure of her blood-brain barrier (see Box 4.3).

Checkpoint

Name three substances that can cross the blood-brain barrier, and describe how they gain entry to the brain. What might happen if myelin could cross the blood-brain barrier and enter the bloodstream?

REVIEW

- The tight junctions between the endothelial cells that form the walls of the brain capillaries contribute to the blood-brain barrier, which restricts the movement of substances from the bloodstream into the brain.
- Astrocytes also control the movement of substances into the brain.
- Uncharged small molecules and lipid-soluble substances can pass from the bloodstream into the brain.
- Multiple sclerosis may be caused by damage to the blood-brain barrier.

Chapter Review

Key Terms

absolute refractory period (p. 115)
acetylcholine (ACh) (p. 133)
acetylcholinesterase (AChE) (p. 133)
action potential (p. 114)
adrenergic (p. 130)
all-or-none law (p. 116)
anaxonic neuron (p. 139)
autoreceptor (p. 125)
axon hillock (p. 117)
blood-brain barrier (p. 140)
catecholamines (p. 130)
channel protein (p. 111)
cholinergic (p. 133)
connexon (p. 139)
dendrodendritic transmission (p. 139)
depolarization (p. 114)
diffusion (p. 111)
dopamine (p. 130)
dopaminergic (p. 130)
electrical synapse (p. 139)
electrostatic pressure (p. 112)
endocrine system (p. 136)
endogenous opioid (p. 135)
enzymatic degradation (p. 126)
epinephrine (p. 130)
excitatory postsynaptic potential (EPSP) (p. 122)
experimental allergic encephalomyelitis (EAE) (p. 141)
GABAergic (p. 129)
gamma-aminobutyric acid (GABA) (p. 129)
gap junction (p. 139)
glutamate (p. 129)
glutamatergic (p. 129)
graded potential (p. 123)
hormone (p. 136)
hyperpolarized (p. 115)
indoleamine (p. 130)
inhibitory postsynaptic potential (IPSP) (p. 122)
ion (p. 111)
ionotropic receptor (p. 125)
metabotropic receptor (p. 125)
monoamine (p. 130)
monoamine oxidase (MAO) (p. 130)
monoamine oxidase inhibitor (MAOI) (p. 132)
multiple sclerosis (MS) (p. 120)
myelin sheath (p. 119)
negative feedback loop (p. 137)
neural impulse (p. 117)
neuromodulator (p. 135)
neuropeptide (p. 134)
neurotransmitter reuptake (p. 126)
nitric oxide (p. 133)
node of Ranvier (p. 119)
noradrenergic (p. 130)
norepinephrine (p. 130)
pheromone (p. 138)
positive feedback loop (p. 137)
presynaptic facilitation (p. 125)
presynaptic inhibition (p. 124)
pump protein (p. 111)
rate law (p. 116)
receptor protein (p. 111)
relative refractory period (p. 115)
repolarization (p. 115)
resting membrane potential (p. 111)
saltatory conduction (p. 119)
second messenger (p. 125)
selective serotonin reuptake inhibitor (SSRI) (p. 132)
serotonergic (p. 131)
serotonin (p. 131)
sodium-potassium pump (p. 112)
soluble gas (p. 133)
spatial summation (p. 123)
temporal summation (p. 123)
threshold (p. 114)
transmitter-gated ion channel (p. 122)
tricyclic compound (p. 132)
voltage-gated ion channel (p. 115)

Suggested Readings

Cooper, J. R., Bloom, F. E., & Roth, R. H. (1996). *The biochemical basis of neuropharmacology* (7th ed.). New York: Oxford University Press.

Kandel, E. R., Schwartz, J. H., & Jessell, T. M. (2000). *Principles of neural science* (4th ed.). New York: McGraw-Hill.

Levitan, I. B., & Kaczmarck, C. K. (1996). *The neuron* (2nd ed.). New York: Oxford University Press.

Nicolls, J. G., Martin, A. R., Wallace, B. G., & Kuffer, S. W. (1993). *From neuron to brain* (3rd ed.). Sutherland, MA: Sinauer.

Critical Thinking Questions

1. Neuron A is a taste neuron that detects whether a food is bitter. Using what you know about the functioning of neurons, explain how neuron A "decides" whether a food is bitter. Use the terms synapse, postsynaptic membrane, threshold, summation, and action potentials.
2. June asked her friend Michelle how she was feeling. Michelle did not hear June's question the first time, but she heard it when June asked a second time. Suggest several reasons why Michelle was able to hear the question the second time, but not the first. Use what you have learned about temporal and spatial summation.

3. Describe a possible treatment for multiple sclerosis, using what you have learned about the destruction of myelin and the leakage of myelin proteins through the blood-brain barrier. Would it be best to target the immune system? The blood-brain barrier?

Fill-in-the-Blank Questions

1. Transmission from the axon of one neuron to the axon of another neuron occurs across a(n) ______ synapse.
2. ______ proteins provide openings through the neuronal cell membrane through which particles can pass.
3. The difference in polarity between the outside and inside of the neuronal cell membrane at rest is called the ______.
4. ______ is the tendency of molecules to move from areas of higher concentration to areas of lower concentration; ______ refers to the attraction of opposite-polarity molecules.
5. The ______ promotes an active process that trades Na^+ ions for K^+ ions.
6. A reduction in the charge across the neuronal cell membrane is called ______.
7. ______ are pathways through the cell membrane that are opened or closed by changes in membrane potential.
8. A period when the neuron cannot generate another action potential no matter how intense the stimulus is called the ______; this period is followed by the ______.
9. According to the ______, the size and speed of the nerve impulse are independent of the intensity of the stimulus.
10. The rate law states that the ______ the stimulus intensity, the ______ the rate of neural firing.
11. The action potential moves down the ______ from the axon hillock to the presynaptic terminal.
12. The action potential moves along myelinated axons by ______ conduction, in which the impulse "jumps" from node to node.
13. The depolarization of the postsynaptic membrane is called a(n) ______, and the hyperpolarization of the postsynaptic membrane is called a(n) ______.
14. ______ results from the combined influence of neurotransmitters released at different locations on the postsynaptic membrane.
15. The decreased release of neurotransmitter despite the occurrence of an action potential is called ______; the release of a greater-than-normal amount of neurotransmitter caused by hyperpolarization of the presynaptic membrane is called ______.
16. A ______ receptor is a postsynaptic receptor that almost immediately opens an ion channel in the membrane. A ______ receptor ultimately produces a second messenger to open ion channels.
17. ______ is the mechanism for terminating the postsynaptic effects of acetylcholine, whereas the effects of other neurotransmitters are terminated mainly by ______.
18. ______ is the most common inhibitory neurotransmitter in the brain; ______ is the most common excitatory neurotransmitter.
19. The monoamines are divided into two subclasses: the ______ and the ______.
20. Excess norepinephrine in the presynaptic terminal is broken down by the enzyme ______.
21. Excess activity at dopaminergic synapses is thought to be responsible for ______, whereas too little dopamine in the brain is associated with ______.
22. Along with norepinephrine, the neurotransmitter ______ has been implicated in depression.
23. The ______ increase levels of monoamine neurotransmitters by preventing monoamine oxidase from degrading excess monoamine in the synaptic terminals.
24. The ______ are antidepressants that target serotonin almost exclusively, increasing serotonin levels in the brain by preventing its reuptake.
25. The ______ are small-molecule neurotransmitters that are released as soon as they are produced, diffuse through cell membranes, and activate a second messenger before being inactivated.
26. Most of the receptors for ACh in the brain are ______ receptors, so called because they also respond to ______, a poison found in mushrooms.
27. Probably the most investigated of the neuropeptides are the ______, whose main functions are ______ and ______.
28. At electrical synapses, ions move across a(n) ______ between dendrites.
29. The ______ is the structure that prevents the free flow of substances from the bloodstream into the brain.
30. ______ develops when myelin proteins are injected into the bloodstreams of laboratory animals; it has been used as an animal model of ______.
31. In a(n) ______ feedback loop, the release of a hormone promotes its further release; in a(n) ______ feedback loop, the release of a hormone inhibits its further release.
32. ______ are chemical transmitters that affect the sensitivity of groups of cells to other neurotransmitters.

Multiple-Choice Questions

1. Of the protein molecules embedded in the cell membrane of a neuron, the ones that recognize and bind to neurotransmitters are the ______ proteins.
   a. channel
   b. receptor
   c. pump
   d. structural

2. The neuronal cell membrane differs from the membranes of other cells, because it
   a. is composed of a lipid bilayer.
   b. contains protein channels.
   c. allows nothing to pass into or out of the cell.
   d. is polarized.

3. The three forces that affect the movement of ions across the cell membrane are
   a. diffusion, electrolysis, and the chloride pump.
   b. diffusion, electrostatic pressure, and the sodium-potassium pump.
   c. diversion, electrostatic pressure, and the sump pump.
   d. diversion, ion charges, and the sodium-potassium pump.

4. Sodium and potassium are ______ charged; chloride is ______ charged.
   a. not, negatively
   b. positively, not
   c. positively, negatively
   d. negatively, positively

5. The sodium-potassium pump expels ______ sodium ions from the cell for every ______ potassium ions it brings into the cell.
   a. three, two
   b. two, three
   c. one, two
   d. two, one

6. For an action potential to occur, the membrane must be depolarized to the ______ potential.
   a. action
   b. resting membrane
   c. threshold
   d. excitatory postsynaptic

7. The period when the neuron can generate another action potential only if the stimulus is greater than normal is called the ______ period.
   a. absolute refractory
   b. relative refractory
   c. marginally refractory
   d. strongly refractory

8. The ______ law states that the size and speed of the nerve impulse are independent of the stimulus intensity.
   a. Bell-Magendie
   b. specific nerve energies
   c. all-or-none
   d. Young-Helmholtz

9. The greater the stimulus intensity, the faster the rate of neural firing up to the maximum possible for the neuron. This is a statement of the
   a. all-or-none law.
   b. rate law.
   c. Bell-Magendie law.
   d. law of specific nerve energies.

10. The propagation of an action potential from node to node along a myelinated axon is called
    a. saltatory conduction.
    b. an inhibitory postsynaptic potential.
    c. nodes of Ranvier.
    d. an excitatory postsynaptic potential.

11. ______ is a progressive neurological disorder whose symptoms are caused by the degeneration of the myelin sheath at places in the central nervous system.
    a. ALS
    b. Tay-Sachs disease
    c. MS
    d. Parkinson's disease

12. Neurotransmitters are released from synaptic vesicles into the ______, where they attach to receptor sites on the ______.
    a. inhibitory neuron, presynaptic membrane
    b. presynaptic membrane, axon
    c. synaptic cleft, postsynaptic membrane
    d. synaptic cleft, inhibitory neuron

13. Depolarization of the postsynaptic membrane produces an ______, whereas hyperpolarization produces an ______
    a. IPSP, EPSP.
    b. EPSP, IPSP.
    c. action potential, inhibitory potential.
    d. autoimmune response, autoimmune inhibition.

14. The first time Lawanda told her roommate she was going to the library, Shawna, engrossed in her favorite TV show, did not hear her. Shawna did hear Lawanda when she repeated her statement, however. Shawna's failure to hear Lawanda the first time but not the second time could be the result of
    a. spatial summation.
    b. temporary deafness.
    c. temporal summation.
    d. the volume of the TV.

15. The EPSPs and IPSPs received by the dendrites and the cell body are
    a. action potentials.
    b. spatial potentials.
    c. temporal potentials.
    d. graded potentials.

16. An autoreceptor is sensitive to the neurotransmitter released by
    a. its own neuron.
    b. a neighboring neuron.
    c. an inhibitory neuron.
    d. an automatic neuron.

17. A postsynaptic effect that directly results in a rapid opening of ion channels involves a(n) ______ receptor.
    a. ionotropic
    b. metabotropic
    c. neuromodulatory
    d. electrostatic

18. A neurotransmitter is broken down in the synaptic cleft by ______. A neurotransmitter returns to the presynaptic neuron by ______.
a. reuptake, autoreception
b. enzymatic degradation, autoreception
c. enzymatic degradation, reuptake
d. reuptake, presynaptic inhibition

19. ______ is the most common excitatory neurotransmitter.
a. GABA
b. Acetylcholine
c. Glutamate
d. Glycine

20. Drugs that increase GABA activity tend to ______ anxiety.
a. increase
b. decrease
c. have no effect on
d. sometimes increase and sometimes decrease

21. Excess norepinephrine in the presynaptic terminal may be broken down by the enzyme
a. choline acetyltransferase.
b. monoamine oxidase.
c. cholinesterase.
d. 5-hydroxytryptophan.

22. The neurotransmitter implicated in Parkinson's disease, schizophrenia, and various addictions is
a. serotonin.
b. norepinephrine.
c. dopamine.
d. epinephrine.

23. Whenever Doug has difficulty falling asleep, he finds that a glass of warm milk often does the trick. The reason that milk probably helps him fall asleep is that it contains tryptophan, which is converted in the brain to
a. GABA.
b. norepinephrine.
c. dopamine.
d. serotonin.

24. ______ is the soluble gas that has been most extensively investigated as a neurotransmitter.
a. NO
b. CO
c. CO_2
d. O_2

25. Almost all of the cholinergic receptors in the brain are
a. muscarinic.
b. nicotinic.
c. picrotinic.
d. in the cerebellum.

26. The major effects of the endogenous opioids are
a. euphoria and analgesia.
b. hunger and thirst.
c. hunger satiety and pain perception.
d. hallucinations and delusions.

27. Ions move across gap junctions through specialized protein channels called
a. ion-gated channels.
b. transmitter-gated channels.
c. connexons.
d. reflexons.

28. The blood-brain barrier is relatively weak in a region of the medulla oblongata that controls vomiting; this is the
a. pineal gland.
b. area postrema.
c. pars nervosa.
d. infundibular stalk.

29. The glands of the ______ system produce hormones that are circulated by the bloodstream to targets throughout the body.
a. circulatory
b. nervous
c. digestive
d. endocrine

30. Jaime is extremely anxious about an upcoming examination in biological psychology. His anxiety may be the result of low levels of
a. GABA.
b. ACh.
c. serotonin.
d. norepinephrine.

31. Chemical transmitters whose function is to modify responsiveness to neurotransmitters are called
a. neuromodulators.
b. hormones.
c. connexons.
d. pheromones.

Answers can be found on the companion website at www.worthpublishers.com/klein.

5

The Effects of Psychoactive Drugs

It's Not All It's Cracked Up to Be

When she got to the bottom of the stairs, Evelyn made the mistake of glancing in the mirror.

"When did I start looking so unhealthy?" she muttered, repelled yet fascinated by her image. When had she become so pale and thin?

"Hell, I'm only . . . ." But she couldn't remember when she had last celebrated a birthday. Man, that's pathetic when you can't even remember your own age, she thought. All she knew was that she was still in her twenties.

But what she saw in the mirror was even more pathetic. Her skin was sallow, with a slightly yellow tinge. Was she jaundiced? Her hair was tangled and dirty looking. When did she stop taking proper care of herself? How had her life gone so wrong?

It had all started innocently enough. Evelyn had smoked a little pot in high school with her friends, and of course, she'd had beer and wine and occasionally some harder stuff—not that she'd ever been all that interested in alcohol. No, alcohol had never been the problem, and the pot was just something fun at the time. She could take it or leave it.

College was a blast. Evelyn had joined a sorority, made decent grades, met a guy, and graduated in 4 years. Her marriage to Bill had lasted—how long, 2 years? She couldn't remember. Actually, she couldn't remember much of her life after she met "Big C."

They were introduced one night at a party she and Bill had gone to. She'd noticed some people congregated around a coffee table in the living room. Several of the women were giggling, and the guys were talking too loudly.

"Let's check it out, Bill," she said, pulling him with her. And that was the first time she saw Big C: lines of white powder on the glass tabletop, a guy leaning over with a rolled-up dollar bill, using it like a straw to sniff in a line. The guy sat back, rubbing his nose, with a grin a mile wide. Evelyn felt Bill moving away.

"What's the matter, honey?" she asked. "Don't you want to try it?"

Bill didn't want to try it, and he left the party. She stayed and had a great time. It was amazing how energized the powder made her feel and how aroused she was when one of the guys (she couldn't remember his name) invited her into a bedroom.

"So long ago," she told herself, wistfully, still captivated by the stranger staring back at her from the mirror. After a few more episodes like that first party, Bill had packed his things and moved out.

Soon after, Evelyn lost her job at the bank where she had worked after finishing college. Her savings carried her and her habit for a while, but she found it increasingly difficult to come up with the money she needed for cocaine. She began to sell the jewelry she'd inherited from her grandmother, and when that was gone, she sold the furniture she and Bill had bought together. Evelyn found all this a little sad at first, but her cravings soon overcame any reservations.

She slipped into prostitution for a while, but her ability to "turn a trick" quickly vanished as her appearance deteriorated. Now she was shoplifting. She would put on her most presentable outfit, take a bus to a different part of town, and just blend in with all the people mall-walking. She would duck into a store every now and then, slip something she could sell under her jacket, and glide out. It was so easy; she just looked for the store with the most bored-looking teenaged clerk, and that was the one she would target.

Crack was Evelyn's new friend now, as she could no longer afford the powdered stuff. But she found "Little C" almost as much fun. Sometimes, though, usually in these in-between periods, Evelyn wished she had gone home that night with Bill.

BEFORE YOU BEGIN

- **What caused Evelyn to become addicted to cocaine?**
- **Physiologically speaking, what is addiction?**
- **What is a psychoactive drug? What are the different classes of psychoactive drugs?**
- **How does a person become addicted to a drug? What happens inside the body when addiction occurs?**
- **How do different kinds of psychoactive drugs affect the brain? What effects do drugs have on synaptic functioning?**
- **How do drugs affect mood and behavior?**

In this chapter, you will find the answers to these questions and many others.

The Definition of a Drug

Defined broadly, a drug is any substance we can take into our body that has the power to change us either functionally or structurally. Although we often equate drugs with drug abuse, if you think about it for a moment, you will realize that we use drugs in a variety of positive ways. For example, we are using drugs to prevent illness when we receive a vaccination against diphtheria, polio, and tetanus. Antibiotics and antiviral agents are often prescribed to treat infections, and antidepressants and antipsychotics can allay symptoms of major mental disorders.

Our focus in this chapter is on one particular category of drugs—the **psychoactive drugs,** which we defined in Chapter 1 as drugs that affect mental functioning. Psychoactive drugs can be used appropriately to treat adverse mental conditions, or they can be abused when taken for nonmedical purposes, as Evelyn is doing with cocaine.

Cocaine in its various forms is just one example of a psychoactive drug. Psychoactive drugs vary widely in their effects on the body and the brain. For example, morphine's pain-inhibiting effects contrast sharply with the arousing effects of amphetamines. We examine here the biological and psychological influences of psychoactive drugs, and the biological basis of addiction, to find out why drugs like cocaine are so habit-forming that people are willing to risk their lives for the next high—or low, in the case of sedating, relaxing drugs like alcohol.

psychoactive drug A drug that affects mental functioning.

The Basic Principles of Psychopharmacology

Let us begin with some basic principles of **psychopharmacology,** the study of the effects of drugs on behavior. The study of the ways in which a drug affects the living organism, its effects on the organs of the body, is called **pharmacodynamics.** In order to affect the brain and behavior, a psychoactive drug must reach its target in the brain, and the study of how a drug moves through the body, which includes the processes of absorption, metabolism, distribution to tissues, and elimination, is called **pharmacokinetics.** Often, the molecules of the drug must surmount many hurdles to get to where they are going—such hurdles as the skin, the linings of the stomach and the intestines, and the blood-brain barrier (Chapter 4); in addition, from the moment a drug enters the body, enzymes begin to break it down. One important factor in determining whether or how soon a substance will reach its neural target is how it is taken in—its route of administration.

psychopharmacology The study of the effects of drugs on behavior.

pharmacodynamics The study of the effects of a drug on the living organism, on the organs of the body.

pharmacokinetics The study of how a drug moves through the body, including absorption, metabolism, distribution to tissues, and elimination.

oral ingestion The administration of a drug through the mouth.

intramuscular (IM) injection An injection of a drug into a muscle.

intraperitoneal (IP) injection An injection of a drug through the abdominal wall into the peritoneal cavity, or space surrounding major organs.

intravenous (IV) injection An injection of a drug into a vein.

subcutaneous (SC) injection An injection of a drug under the skin.

intracerebral injection An injection of a drug directly into the brain.

Routes of Administration

From your own experience, you can probably think of at least two of the main routes of drug administration: oral ingestion (by mouth) and injection. If you smoke, or if you have ever breathed second-hand smoke, then you are familiar with the inhalation route. Another route of drug administration is absorption through the mucous membranes, the route Evelyn used when she was first introduced to cocaine. She "snorted" it into her nasal passages, where it was quickly absorbed.

Oral Ingestion

We typically take medicines orally. However, the **oral ingestion** route is less likely to be used in laboratory animals, because they tend to reject anything that is distasteful to them. Taken orally, drugs dissolve in the fluids of the mouth, esophagus, or stomach and are carried to the intestines, where some drugs are absorbed into the bloodstream. Other drugs are destroyed by the digestive juices, and yet others are simply not absorbed from the digestive system. Insulin, for example, cannot be taken orally, because it is broken down by enzymes in the digestive tract.

Injection

Most of us are familiar with **intramuscular (IM) injection,** or injection into a muscle. Such injections are usually into the shoulder, the upper arm, or the thigh, or perhaps the buttocks, and the injected drug is absorbed into the capillaries supplying the muscle. Small laboratory animals are often given **intraperitoneal (IP) injections,** in which the substance is injected through the abdominal wall directly into the peritoneal cavity, the space surrounding major organs such as the stomach, liver, and intestines. The drug enters the bloodstream faster than by IM injection. One of the most rapid routes to the brain, however, is by **intravenous (IV) injection.** If Evelyn were interested in heroin, this is undoubtedly the way she would self-administer the drug. For someone addicted to a drug, the extremely rapid action of a drug administered by IV injection is both a blessing (a faster high) and a curse, as it allows little time to do anything to counteract the effects of an overdose or a bad reaction. In **subcutaneous (SC) injections,** drugs are injected under the skin. This route can be used for substances that need to be absorbed slowly into the body, such as long-acting contraceptive drugs.

Shooting heroin, an illustration of the injection route of drug administration.

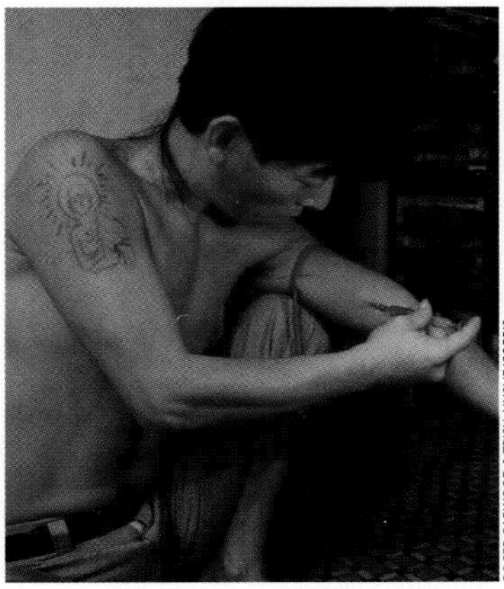

Finally, drugs can be injected directly into the brain or into its ventricles. For example, to measure the effect of a particular chemical on a thalamic nucleus, a researcher would administer an **intracerebral injection** of a tiny amount of the chemical into a laboratory animal. Substances are sometimes injected into the cerebral ventricles in order to produce widespread distribution in the brain while bypassing the blood-brain barrier. Such **intraventricular injections** are sometimes used in humans to treat brain infections directly with antibiotics.

Inhalation

Popular psychoactive drugs such as nicotine, freebase cocaine (cocaine base separated from regular cocaine [cocaine hydrochloride] through the use of ammonia and ether), and marijuana are typically self-administered through the lungs by **inhalation.** Inhaled drugs produce their actions quickly, and this route is also often used to administer general anesthesia before surgery.

Figure 5.1
The blood plasma concentration of cocaine after different methods of administration

➔ If you did not want to inject it, which route would give you the highest concentration of cocaine?

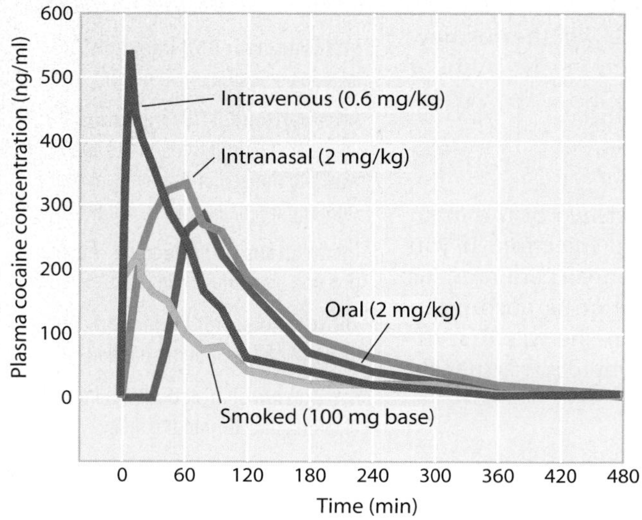

Absorption Through the Skin or Mucous Membranes

Some drugs can be absorbed through the skin, and this can be useful for people who are trying to quit smoking; a nicotine patch delivers nicotine via the skin rather than through inhalation. A fentanyl (Sublimaze) patch delivers a short-acting, but potent, analgesic to surgical patients. Fentanyl in lollipop form became available in 1998 to treat surgical pain in children; the drug is absorbed through the mucous membranes of the mouth as the child sucks on the lollipop. As noted above, absorption through mucous membranes is also the route employed by users of powdered cocaine.

Figure 5.1 illustrates how the different routes of administration affect how quickly and how much of a substance actually reaches its CNS target, by showing what happens when cocaine is either injected intravenously, smoked (inhaled), ingested orally, or sniffed and absorbed through the mucous membranes of the nasal passages. Despite some variation in the amount of cocaine administered by each route, the graph gives a sense of the relative effectiveness of the different routes of administration.

Checkpoint

Name all the routes by which you have ingested drugs. Have you ever received a particular drug by more than one route? If so, did one way have a quicker effect than another?

The Distribution of Drugs in the Body

Once a drug is introduced into the body, where does it go and what obstacles does it encounter before reaching its target? In some cases, drugs can diffuse across cell membranes and thus produce effects throughout the body. Alcohol is one such example. In other cases, in order to have a psychoactive effect, a drug must cross the blood-brain barrier, which is an obstacle for water-soluble substances but not for fat-soluble ones. For example, heroin is more fat-soluble than morphine; therefore, heroin reaches its sites of action in the brain more quickly than morphine. As a result, drug abusers much prefer heroin to morphine because of its quicker and more intense "rush."

The Elimination of Drugs From the Body

The speed with which the body eliminates a drug is a factor in how long the effect of the drug will last. The effect of a drug is usually expressed as its **half-life,** the amount of time required for the body to eliminate half of the drug. The longer the half-life, the longer the drug continues to have a physiological effect. Most drugs are broken down, or metabolized, by the liver into their component molecules, or **metabolites,** which generally have little or none of the effect of the parent compound. For some drugs, however, a metabolite has a longer-lasting effect than the parent compound. For example, trimipramine, one of the tricyclic antidepressants, has a half-life of 8 to 10 hours, whereas its active metabolite, protriptyline, has a half-life more than 5 to 10 times longer. This type of action can be beneficial if the drug has the intended effect (i.e., if it adequately functions as an antidepressant) but not if it produces undesirable side effects.

The Long-Term Effects of Drug Use

Some of the long-term effects of taking a drug are substance abuse, substance dependence, tolerance, and withdrawal symptoms. **Substance abuse** refers to a pattern of drug use that results in such negative effects as legal and financial difficulties associated with the drug use, difficulties in a marriage or other intimate relationship, or decreases in work or school abilities. Continuing abuse can lead to **substance dependence** (or *addiction*), defined as the compulsive use of a substance and the existence of at least three of seven symptoms over a 12-month period, according to the American Psychiatric Association (1994). Examples of the symptoms are developing **tolerance,** a decrease in the effects of a drug resulting from repeated use; experiencing **withdrawal symptoms,** physical problems upon stopping use of the drug; investing a considerable amount of time in the effort to obtain and use the drug; and continuing to use the drug despite the problems likely to be caused or worsened by doing so. Substance dependence can be either physical or psychological (or both), although we hasten to remind you that the psychological is ultimately physiological, the result of activity in neurons in the brain. *Physical dependence* involves changes in the body that produce intense physical symptoms when the drug taking is stopped. *Psychological dependence* is illustrated by a craving for the way the drug makes the individual feel, for the pleasure and/or relief from discomfort that come from taking the drug.

In the minds of many people, addiction is nothing more than physical dependence on the abused substance; that is, addicted users continue their compulsive activities in order to prevent the withdrawal symptoms that follow attempts to curtail use. If this were true, however, then addiction could be cured by forcing individuals to undergo withdrawal until the drug was completely out of their system. Unfortunately, this does not work for most people; they can be "dried out" and drug-free for months but then resume their drug habit.

As you probably realize, we are discussing psychoactive drugs, also called *psychotropic* or *mind-altering drugs,* because they exert their influence through their actions on the nervous system, particularly the brain and spinal cord, although they affect other biological systems as well. In order to affect the brain and behavior, psychoactive drugs must be able to penetrate the blood-brain barrier (Chapter 4). They have their effect—producing pleasant feelings or relieving unpleasant ones—by modifying synaptic transmission in critical nervous system structures; the resulting affective, or emotional, reactions alone can often lead to substance dependence.

Note that the long-term use of a drug in a physically distinctive environment, with intense reinforcement, at least initially, is critical for *learning* to crave that drug (psychological dependence). There is extensive evidence for the involvement of such learning in the craving for the drug experience that produces relapse. For example, a PET study of cocaine abusers who were shown drug-related stimuli showed increased activity in several areas of the brain implicated in different types of memory (Grant & others, 1996). Metabolic increases occurred, for example, in the dorsolateral prefrontal cortex, the amygdala, and the cerebellum and were correlated with self-reports of craving for cocaine. In another PET study, autobiographical memories were used to induce drug craving in crack cocaine-dependent subjects (Kilts & others, 2001). The craving was associated with activation that included the amygdala, the anterior cingulate gyrus, and the nucleus accumbens, which, as we discuss below, is vitally involved in reinforcement. The researchers concluded that these areas are part of a network of structures involved in stimulus-reward association (amygdala), incentive

intraventricular injection An injection of a drug into the cerebral ventricles in order to achieve widespread distribution in the brain and bypass the blood-brain barrier.

inhalation The administration of a drug through the lungs.

half-life The amount of time it takes the body to eliminate half of a drug.

metabolite A component molecule of a drug, produced by enzymatic breakdown, that typically has little or none of the effect of the parent compound.

substance abuse A pattern of drug use that results in negative effects.

substance dependence The compulsive use of a substance; also known as addiction.

tolerance A decrease in the effects of a drug as a result of repeated use.

withdrawal symptom A physical or psychological problem that results from stopping the use of a drug.

agonist A drug that mimics or enhances the activity of a neurotransmitter.

antagonist A drug that blocks the activity of a neurotransmitter.

motivation (nucleus accumbens), and anticipation (anterior cingulate cortex). According to Franken (2003), conditioning involving this same network creates an "attentional bias," which draws the subject's attention toward drug-related stimuli and ultimately leads to further craving and relapse. A review of factors related to relapse following withdrawal stressed the importance of the conditioning of drug craving to contextual stimuli in both alcohol and cocaine addiction (Weiss & others, 2001).

The Mechanisms of Drug Action

As we noted in Chapter 4, drugs can either facilitate or inhibit the transmission of neural impulses (see Box 4.2: Drug Treatment for Depression, p. 132). Drugs that mimic or enhance the activities of a neurotransmitter are called **agonists** (from the Greek for "contest"). You can think of agonists as competing with neurotransmitters to produce similar effects; nicotine, for example, competes successfully with acetylcholine at neuromuscular junctions. Drugs that block or inhibit the postsynaptic effects of a neurotransmitter are called **antagonists.** Antagonists compete with neurotransmitters to produce opposite effects; botulinum toxin, for example, competes with acetylcholine at neuromuscular junctions in an antagonistic way to produce paralysis.

Agonist Drugs

A drug can act as an agonist in several different ways, as shown in Figure 5.2, mechanisms 1 through 6. In one mechanism (1), the drug attaches to a receptor and produces the same effect on the postsynaptic membrane as the normal neurotransmitter, either an excitatory postsynaptic potential (EPSP) or an inhibitory postsynaptic potential (IPSP). For example, heroin activates receptors for the endorphins to produce its analgesic and/or euphoric effects (recall the runner's high that Jerry experienced, in Chapter 4). A drug can also bind to a receptor and increase the action of the neurotransmitter on the postsynaptic membrane, rather than directly affecting the receptor. For example, the sedating effect of alcohol is produced by enhancing the influence of GABA on a binding site on the $GABA_A$ receptor. Drugs that bind to a postsynaptic receptor to produce their agonist effect are called *direct agonists.*

Agonist drugs can affect synaptic transmission less directly, and these are called, appropriately enough, *indirect agonists.* A drug can block either enzymatic degradation or reuptake of the neurotransmitter (2), prolonging the effects of the neurotransmitter on the postsynaptic membrane. Evelyn's nemesis, cocaine, blocks norepinephrine and dopamine reuptake, allowing the neurotransmitters to produce the enhanced alertness and pleasure that characterize a cocaine high. As another example, the drug physostigmine blocks the degrading action of acetyl-

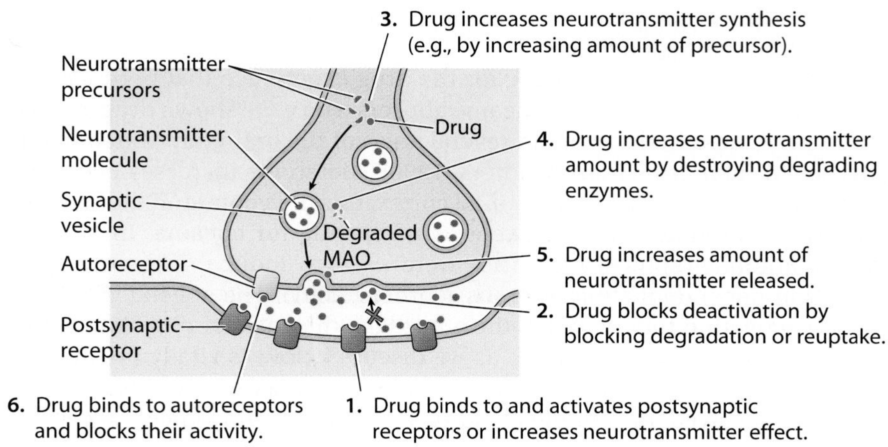

Figure 5.2

The actions of agonist drugs Drugs can enhance synaptic transmission in one or more of the six ways shown here. Mechanism 1 refers to a direct agonist drug, mechanisms 2 through 6 to indirect agonists.

➡ **Which of these mechanisms produces the analgesic effects of heroin?**

cholinesterase, which enhances the effect of ACh at neuromuscular junctions; this drug can be used to treat the extreme fatigue of myasthenia gravis (Chapter 8).

In another indirect mechanism, a drug can increase the amount of neurotransmitter stored in the synaptic vesicles. This occurs in one of two ways: Either neurotransmitter synthesis is increased (3), or the action of the degrading enzyme inside the presynaptic terminal is inhibited (4). The drug L-dopa illustrates the first of these mechanisms. By increasing the synthesis of dopamine, L-dopa can, at least for a time, decrease the motor rigidity and tremor of Parkinson's disease. The class of antidepressants called monoamine oxidase inhibitors (MAOIs) illustrate the second mechanism. They block the action of MAO in the cytoplasm of the presynaptic terminal, so more of the monoamine (e.g., norepinephrine, serotonin) is available for packaging into synaptic vesicles and subsequent release.

Some agonist drugs can enhance neurotransmitter release from the presynaptic membrane (5) or prevent decreased neurotransmitter release by binding to and suppressing the neuron's autoreceptors, which decrease neurotransmitter release, as we indicated in Chapter 4 (6). One example of the first of these effects is the increased arousal produced by the drug nicotine. Nicotine increases the release of dopamine and glutamate by stimulating cholinergic receptors on the presynaptic membrane of dopaminergic and glutamatergic neurons. An example of the second mechanism is the arousing effect of amphetamine. Amphetamine binds to the norepinephrine and dopamine autoreceptors on the presynaptic membrane, thus delaying the signal to decrease the release of these neurotransmitters. The effect is to increase the number of neurotransmitter molecules that can bind to the postsynaptic membrane receptors.

A specific drug may use only one of the six mechanisms described above, or it may combine two or more. For example, the arousing effect of nicotine is caused by both the direct activation of postsynaptic cholinergic receptors (mechanism 1) and the increased release of dopamine and glutamate by stimulation of cholinergic receptors on the presynaptic membrane of dopaminergic and glutamatergic neurons (mechanism 5).

false transmitter A drug that prevents a neurotransmitter from binding to a receptor by attaching to the receptor on the postsynaptic membrane.

Checkpoint

Describe two different mechanisms of agonist drug action, and include examples of each.

Antagonist Drugs

Drugs can also antagonize or impair synaptic transmission, via several mechanisms, many of which are similar to those of agonist drugs (Figure 5.3, mechanisms 1 through 5). For example, a drug can attach to the postsynaptic membrane and yet not exert the effect of the neurotransmitter (1). This prevents the neurotransmitter from binding to the receptors and thereby blocks its postsynaptic action. A drug that impairs synaptic transmission in this way is called a **false transmitter** or a *receptor blocker.* Synaptic transmission remains blocked as long as the drug occupies the receptor sites. One example of false transmitters is the major antipsychotic drugs that reduce schizophrenic symptoms such as hallucinations and delusions by binding to dopaminergic receptors and reducing dopaminergic activity at these sites. The nerve poison curare is another false transmitter; by blocking cholinergic

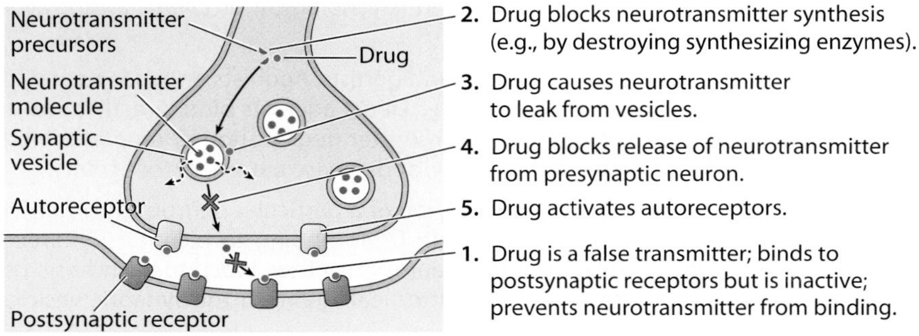
Neurotransmitter precursors
Drug
Neurotransmitter molecule
Synaptic vesicle
Autoreceptor
Postsynaptic receptor
2. Drug blocks neurotransmitter synthesis (e.g., by destroying synthesizing enzymes).
3. Drug causes neurotransmitter to leak from vesicles.
4. Drug blocks release of neurotransmitter from presynaptic neuron.
5. Drug activates autoreceptors.
1. Drug is a false transmitter; binds to postsynaptic receptors but is inactive; prevents neurotransmitter from binding.

Figure 5.3

The actions of antagonist drugs

Drugs can reduce synaptic transmission in one or more of the five ways shown here. Mechanism 1 refers to a direct antagonist drug, mechanisms 2 through 5 to indirect antagonists.

➜ By which of these mechanisms do antipsychotics alleviate the symptoms of schizophrenia?

receptors at neuromuscular junctions, curare produces paralysis and death. As we saw with agonist drugs, antagonist drugs that produce their effect directly, by binding to postsynaptic receptors, are called *direct antagonists.*

Drugs do not have to bind to receptors in order to have an antagonistic action, and those that have an indirect effect are called *indirect antagonists.* A drug may decrease the level of available neurotransmitter by causing either a decrease in neurotransmitter synthesis (2) or a loss of the neurotransmitter from the synaptic vesicles so that it is destroyed by enzymes in the cell (3). The drug AMPT (alpha-methyl-*p*-tyrosine) is an example of the first type. AMPT inactivates an enzyme involved in the synthesis of dopamine and norepinephrine, which means that it functions as a catecholamine antagonist. It has been used in laboratory animals but is not used in human treatment. Reserpine illustrates the second type of effect. Once used in treating hypertension (high blood pressure), reserpine acts by making the monoamine-containing synaptic vesicles leaky; as a result, neurotransmitter molecules diffuse out and are broken down presynaptically by MAO. Use of reserpine has been discontinued, however, because a sizable minority of people taking it became depressed.

A drug also can inhibit neurotransmitter release from the presynaptic membrane (4) or decrease neurotransmitter release by activating the autoreceptors of the neuron (5). Botulinum toxin illustrates the first type of effect. It blocks the presynaptic release of ACh at neuromuscular junctions, producing paralysis. An illustration of the second mechanism is the stimulating effect of caffeine, which comes from its ability to inhibit the release of the neurotransmitter adenosine by activating autoreceptors. As we discuss later in this chapter, adenosine is an inhibitory neurotransmitter for glutamate receptors. As with the agonist drugs, a specific antagonist drug may impair synaptic transmission by one or more of these five mechanisms.

To repeat, whether they act as agonists or antagonists, psychoactive drugs affect behavior by altering synaptic function. For example, you drink alcohol and this changes synaptic activity in the CNS. As a result, your behavior changes.

➤Checkpoint

Explain how a drug can have an antagonistic effect without binding to a receptor. Give an example. Do the same for a drug with an agonistic effect.

REVIEW

- Psychoactive drugs are substances that affect mental functioning.
- Drugs can be taken into the body orally, by injection, by inhalation, or by absorption through the skin or mucous membranes.
- Once a drug enters the body, it encounters obstacles on its way to its targets, including the blood-brain barrier and enzymes that break down the drug into inactive metabolites.
- The long-term effects of drug use include substance abuse, substance dependence, tolerance, and withdrawal symptoms.
- Substance abuse is a pattern of drug use that results in a variety of negative consequences; substance dependence, or addiction, is the compulsive use of a substance.
- Tolerance is a decrease in the effects of a drug that results from repeated use. Withdrawal symptoms are physical and psychological problems arising when a person tries to stop taking a drug.
- Drugs can function as agonists or as antagonists. Agonists enhance neural transmission of a particular neurotransmitter. Direct agonists bind directly to receptor sites; indirect agonists block neurotransmitter degradation or reuptake, increase neurotransmitter synthesis and release, or decrease autoreceptor activity.
- Antagonists decrease neural transmission of a particular neurotransmitter. Direct antagonists block the neurotransmitter from binding to receptors; indirect antagonists inhibit the release of the neurotransmitter, block the synthesis of the neurotransmitter, cause neurotransmitter leakage from the synaptic vesicles, or activate autoreceptors.

Classification of Psychoactive Drugs

One difficulty with classifying the vast number of psychoactive drugs is that many of them have multiple effects on the brain and on behavior. In addition, drugs with quite different effects on the brain may produce similar behavioral outcomes. For our discussion of the psychoactive drugs of abuse, the following classification is most useful: *opioids, depressants, psychostimulants, psychedelic drugs, and marijuana* (Table 5.1). Drugs used to treat mental illness are also psychoactive drugs, and we discuss these elsewhere: *antipsychotic drugs* in Chapter 15; *antidepressant drugs* in Chapter 4 and, further, in Chapter 15.

Table 5.1
The Psychoactive Drugs and Their Physical and Psychological Effects

Category	Typical Effects	Tolerance/Dependence
Opioids		
Codeine, heroin, morphine, meperidine, opium	Analgesia, euphoria, drowsiness, a rush of pleasure, psychological functions mostly spared	Tolerance, physical and psychological dependence, severe withdrawal symptoms
Depressants		
Alcohol	**Low doses:** decreased alertness, feelings of relaxation	Tolerance, physical and psychological dependence, severe withdrawal symptoms
	Moderate doses: mild sedation, impairment of sensory-motor functions	
	High doses: severe motor disturbances, unconsciousness, coma, death	
Barbiturate and nonbarbiturate sedative-hypnotic drugs Pentobarbital (Nembutal), methaqualone (Quaalude)	Calming effect, muscle relaxation; reduced tension, anxiety, and irritability; sleep-inducing, anesthetic, anticonvulsant effects	Tolerance, psychological and physical dependence, withdrawal symptoms
Benzodiazepines and nonbenzodiazepine anxiolytics Diazepam (Valium), zolpidem (Ambien)	Reduced nervousness, anxiety, or fear	Tolerance, low physical and high psychological dependence, withdrawal symptoms
Psychostimulants		
Amphetamine, cocaine	Increased alertness, euphoria, sense of well-being; sleeplessness; appetite suppression	Tolerance, psychological and physical dependence, withdrawal symptoms
Caffeine, nicotine	Increased alertness, sleeplessness, more rapid reaction times, increased metabolism	Tolerance, physical and psychological dependence, withdrawal symptoms
Psychedelic Drugs		
Peyote	Visual hallucinations	None known
Psilocybin, psilocin	Illusions, hallucinations, distortions in time perception, loss of contact with reality	None known
LSD	Illusions, hallucinations, distortions in time perception, loss of contact with reality	None known
PCP	Illusions, hallucinations, distortions in time perception, loss of contact with reality	Psychological dependence
MDMA (Ecstasy)	Euphoric mood state, mild hallucinations	Tolerance, withdrawal symptoms
Marijuana		
Marijuana, hashish, THC	Euphoria, relaxed inhibitions, increased vividness of experiences, increased appetite, mild hallucinations, possible disorientation, impaired motor coordination, decreased reaction time, distortions in time perception	Psychological dependence

Figure 5.4
Opium poppies Grown in Southwest Asia, the opium poppy plant is the source of the opioid drugs codeine and morphine. Shown here are the unripe seed pods, with the red flowers visible in the background.

→ **What are the effects of the opiate drugs?**

◆ Opioids

If you have ever undergone surgery, the doctor may have prescribed meperidine (Demerol) for relief of pain, or *analgesia*, for the first few days of your recovery. Meperidine belongs to a class of drugs called **opioids,** or *opiates,* which are drugs derived from the opium poppy plant or that have an action comparable to drugs from the opium poppy (Figure 5.4).

Analgesia is not the only defining effect of opioid drugs, however. To qualify as an opioid, a drug also must act on the CNS to produce stupor or a sleep-inducing effect. As you may know, Demerol not only eliminates pain, it also makes you drowsy and induces a feeling of well-being or euphoria, which is yet another effect of opioids. Opioids are also effective cough suppressants and antidiarrheal medications. Opioids are classified by their origins, as natural, semisynthetic, or synthetic.

Opioids of Natural Origin

Sometimes called "the mother drug," **opium** is extracted directly from the opium poppy, a lovely red flower (Figure 5.4). When the unripe seedpod is slit, a milky fluid oozes out. After drying, the brownish gum becomes crude or raw opium. Although crude opium is sometimes eaten, inhaling the vapors of smoked opium is the typical method for experiencing its various effects.

Opium contains several *alkaloid* compounds, which are nitrogen compounds that contain an organic base. The main alkaloid compound is **morphine,** which, depending on the plant, makes up 4% to 21% of the seedpod. An extremely potent analgesic, morphine has a bitter taste; it is usually administered intravenously. Morphine also induces powerful feelings of well-being. It is administered to patients with severe pain, such as that caused by terminal cancer.

Codeine is another alkaloid found in opium. Less potent than morphine, codeine is often combined with aspirin and cough suppressants as a prescription analgesic and cough medicine. Tylenol 3, which combines codeine with acetaminophen, can be obtained only by prescription because of the potential for abuse.

Semisynthetic Opioids

Some opiates are combinations of natural opiates and other chemicals. Heroin is the most common semisynthetic opioid, and 90% of opiate abuse involves this drug (Carroll, 2000). **Heroin** is made by reacting acetic anhydride with morphine, creating a compound with the chemical name *diacetylmorphine.* The drug was introduced as a cough suppressant in 1898. *Heroin* is from the German word meaning "long" or "powerful," and, like morphine, it has a bitter taste. When injected, heroin induces an intense euphoric response that lasts from 3 to 6 hours.

Synthetic Opioids

Drugs with opiate properties can also be manufactured in the laboratory. Meperidine (Demerol) was the first synthetic opioid. It can eliminate even intense pain. Propoxyphene (Darvon) is a synthetic opioid with weaker action than meperidine. An estimated 30 million prescriptions for Darvon are written in the United States each year (Carroll, 2000). Two other widely prescribed synthetic opioids are oxycodone (Percodan, OxyContin) and hydromorphone (Dilaudid). Percodan is the short-acting form of oxycodone and is primarily prescribed for acute pain. OxyContin is the long-acting form of oxycodone and is prescribed for chronic pain, such as from terminal cancer or a severe back injury. Both Percodan and OxyContin are widely abused. In the case of OxyContin, the pills are crushed and the resulting powder is either snorted like cocaine or dissolved in water and injected. Because of the widespread abuse, efforts are underway to add an opioid antagonist

opioid A drug derived from the opium poppy, or a drug that has an action comparable to that of drugs derived from the opium poppy.

opium A natural opiate drug obtained directly from the opium poppy.

morphine An extremely potent natural opioid that is the main alkaloid compound found in opium.

codeine An alkaloid found in opium that is less potent than morphine.

heroin A powerful semisynthetic opioid made by reacting acetic anhydride with morphine.

to the drug, so that its injection would trigger withdrawal (Julien, 2005). Celebrities with publicized addictions to OxyContin include conservative talk show host Rush Limbaugh and singer/actress Courtney Love.

The Mechanisms of Opioid Action

In Chapter 4, we described the brain neuromodulators called *endorphins,* which produce the opiate-like effects of analgesia and euphoria. Endorphins suppress the pain induced by injury and enable us to cope with such damage. Opioid drugs are endorphin agonists that work by binding to opioid receptors and activating the same neurons in the brain that are stimulated by the endogenous opioids (see Figure 5.2, mechanism 1). The opioids have their effects on at least three different receptors—mu, delta, and kappa—which are differentially distributed in the nervous system. Of the three receptor types, mu receptors are most involved in mediating the analgesic effects of the opioids (Barry & Zuo, 2005); kappa agonists produce modest analgesia, and delta receptors are believed to modulate the actions of the mu receptors (Julien, 2005). Table 5.2 summarizes the effects of opioid drugs (and the other psychoactive drugs discussed below) on synaptic transmission.

Individual opioid drugs can be classified according to their effects on the opioid receptors: *pure agonists, partial agonists, mixed agonist-antagonists,* and *pure*

Table 5.2
Some Psychoactive Drugs and Their Effects on Synaptic Transmission

Category	Main Effect(s)	Effect on Synaptic Transmission
Opioids		
Heroin, morphine	Stimulate endorphin receptors	Direct agonist
Depressants		
Alcohol	Binds to endorphin and $GABA_A$ receptors	Direct agonist
Barbiturate and nonbarbiturate sedative-hypnotic drugs	Binds to $GABA_A$ receptors	Direct agonist
Thiopental (Pentothal)		
Phenobarbital (Luminal)		
Benzodiazepines and nonbenzodiazepine anxiolytics	Binds to $GABA_A$ receptors	Direct agonist
Alprazolam (Xanax)		
Chlordiazepoxide (Librium)		
Diazepam (Valium)		
Meprobamate (Miltown)		
Psychostimulants		
Amphetamine	Stimulates dopamine and norepinephrine release and blocks reuptake of both	Indirect agonist
Cocaine	Blocks dopamine and norepinephrine reuptake	Indirect agonist
Caffeine	Blocks adenosine release	Indirect antagonist
Nicotine	Stimulates ACh receptors and increases dopamine, ACh, and glutamate release	Direct and indirect agonist
Psychedelic Drugs		
LSD	Stimulates 5-HT receptors	Direct agonist
PCP	Inhibits NMDA receptors	Direct antagonist
MDMA	Stimulates D_2 and serotonin receptors	Direct agonist
Marijuana		
Marijuana	Binds to THC receptors	Direct agonist

depressant A type of psychoactive drug that acts on the CNS to slow down mental and physical functioning.

sedative-hypnotic drug A drug that has a calming (sedative) effect at low doses and a sleep-inducing effect at higher doses.

alcohol Ethyl alcohol (ethanol); a powerful depressant that strongly influences consciousness and the ability to respond effectively to the environment.

antagonists. Morphine is an example of a pure agonist, producing its effect on the mu receptors, as is the case with all of the strong opioids. Other examples include codeine, heroin, and methadone.

Partial agonists bind to opioid receptors without producing as great an effect as pure agonists, which makes them useful in treating opioid dependence. Thus, *buprenorphine* (in Suboxone; Suboxone's other ingredient is naloxone, a pure opioid antagonist) has an analgesic effect, but it is less than the effect produced by a pure agonist such as methadone. Gerra and colleagues (2004) found that methadone and buprenorphine were equally effective in treating opioid dependence. Further, buprenorphine is the first drug approved for office-based treatment of opioid dependency; methadone, by contrast, can be prescribed only by a specially licensed physician through a federally licensed methadone clinic (Julien, 2005).

Mixed agonist-antagonist opioids produce an agonistic effect at one receptor and an antagonistic effect at another. Pentazocine (Talwin), which activates the kappa receptor and binds to the mu receptor without activating it, is an example of a mixed agonist-antagonist opioid.

The Long-Term Effects of Opioid Use

Like all drugs, if abused, opioid drugs can be dangerous. Of course, the danger of opioid abuse arises not only from the physiological effects of the drug but also from the fact that such opioid use is often illegal and has social consequences. The medical use of opioid drugs for pain relief can be both beneficial and essential for someone suffering from intractable pain, but long-term use for the euphoria these drugs produce can be addictive. When opioids are taken frequently, tolerance soon develops, especially to the powerful opiates. Withdrawal symptoms include chills, diarrhea, nausea, and sweating, with tremors and intense cramps occurring during extremely intense withdrawal. These symptoms may persist. For example, heroin withdrawal symptoms may last for 2 to 3 days.

Physical dependence on opioids results from the suppression of endorphin production that occurs with repeated use. The psychological dependence or intense craving results in part from the conditioning of the drug abuser to the cues associated with drug use. Such cues (e.g., darkened room, drug paraphernalia) have been strongly associated in the past with intense pleasure, and the association is difficult to extinguish. Although most people are aware of the negative effects of heroin and other opioid abuse on people's lives, it is worth noting that, every year, tobacco use and alcohol abuse kill far more people than opioid abuse. Table 5.1 summarizes the major long-term effects of opioid use.

Checkpoint

What distinguishes opioids from other painkillers and other classes of psychoactive drugs? Why are opioids so addictive? Explain their effects on the nervous system.

REVIEW

- Opioids—including opium, codeine, heroin, and morphine—are strongly addictive psychoactive drugs that reduce pain and induce sleep and feelings of well-being.
- Opioids act as endorphin agonists that directly stimulate at least three types of opioid receptors—mu, delta, and kappa—with the mu receptors being most involved in the analgesic effect.
- The long-term use of opioids can lead to tolerance, withdrawal, and psychological and physical dependence.

Depressants

You have a major examination coming up that you are extremely nervous about, because of its importance for your grade in the course. As the test date approaches, your anxiety intensifies, preventing you from concentrating. You visit a doctor, who prescribes diazepam (Valium). Shortly after taking the medication, you no longer feel as anxious and are able to study.

For many years, diazepam was the most frequently prescribed psychoactive drug (Ray & Ksir, 2006). It belongs to a class of drugs called **depressants,** or **sedative-hypnotic drugs,** which act on the CNS to slow down mental and physical functioning. At low doses, depressants reduce anxiety, tension, or irritability; at higher doses, they produce drowsiness and sleep.

The major types of depressants are alcohol, barbiturate and nonbarbiturate drugs, and the benzodiazepines and nonbenzodiazepine sedative-hypnotics. Alcohol includes wine, beer, and distilled spirits (the so-called hard liquors, such as vodka or bourbon). (Note that opioids have some effects similar to those of alcohol and other sedative-hypnotics, but they also produce analgesia.)

Alcohol

Alcohol is so widely consumed in many societies that most people do not consider it a drug, thinking of it instead as a social beverage. However, despite its widespread acceptance, **alcohol** is a powerful sedative-hypnotic that has a significant influence on consciousness and on the ability to respond effectively to the environment. The consumption of even a small amount reduces effectiveness at school or at work. Alcohol abuse, in addition to the damage it does to the CNS and other parts of the body, dramatically increases the probability of having a motor vehicle accident (Figure 5.5).

Figure 5.5
The risks of drinking and driving This graph shows the detrimental effect of drinking on driving: the higher the alcohol level, the higher the probability of an accident.

➜ **What is the relative probability of an accident at a blood alcohol level of 0.10%? Based on this graph, at what level do you think the legal limit should be set?**

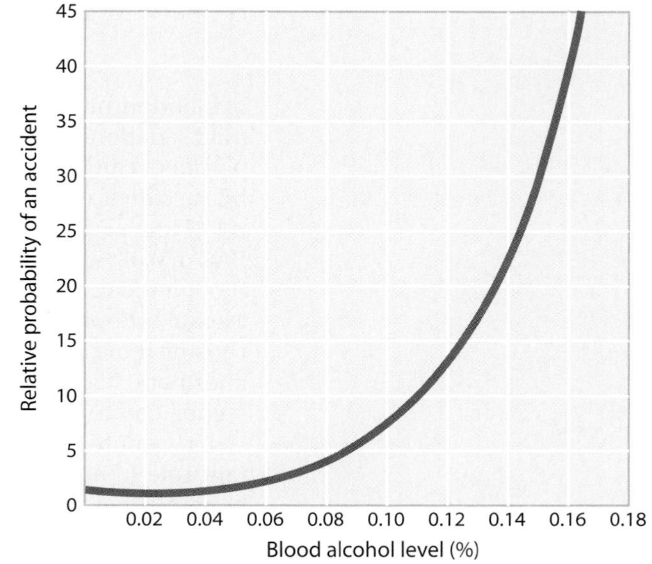

Types of Alcohol

The alcohol used for social drinking is *ethyl alcohol,* or *ethanol,* a clear, colorless fluid with a mild, aromatic odor and pungent taste. Ethyl alcohol is produced by fermenting certain grains and fruits. Fermentation occurs when yeast cells convert the sugar in the grain or fruit to carbon dioxide and alcohol. Wine is made by fermenting grapes or other fruits and has an alcohol content of 10% to 14%. Beer is made in two stages: First, the starch in cereal grains is converted to sugar by a process called *brewing;* next, the sugar is fermented. Beer has an alcohol content of 3.6% to 6.0%. Distilled spirits are produced by heating fermented cereal grains or fruits. Ethyl alcohol boils at a lower temperature than the other fermentation products and can be collected by cooling and condensing the vapors to produce a distilled spirit with an alcohol concentration typically between 40% and 50%.

Alcohol Intoxication

As with all drugs, the effects of alcohol depend on dose level. Although distilled spirits have a higher concentration of alcohol than beer, people typically drink more beer at a sitting than they do liquor. In fact, a 1.25-ounce shot of 80-proof whiskey, a 5-ounce glass of wine, and a typical 12-ounce can of beer contain about the same amount of alcohol (Figure 5.6).

The behavioral effects caused by alcohol vary from person to person. Although a couple of beers will typically make someone either tipsy or drowsy, some chain beer drinkers can consume vast quantities of alcohol daily without showing any outward signs of intoxication.

Because of the variation in the ethyl alcohol concentration of drinks and in the behavioral changes it produces, *blood alcohol content (BAC)* provides an objective measure for examining alcohol's effects (Table 5.3). Low blood alcohol levels (0.05%, or 0.05 milligrams of alcohol per 100 milliliters

Figure 5.6
Equivalent alcohol in different forms A 1.25-ounce shot of 80 proof whiskey, a 5-ounce glass of wine, and a 12-ounce can of beer all contain the same amount of alcohol.

➜ **Why do people perceive "hard" liquor to be more intoxicating than wine or beer?**

Table 5.3
Blood Alcohol Concentration (BAC) and Behavioral Effects

BAC (%)	Behavioral Effects
0.05	Lowered alertness, increased relaxation
0.10	Mild sedation; impaired sensory-motor functions causing increased reaction time
0.15	Greatly increased reaction time
0.20	Marked suppression of sensory-motor abilities
0.25	Severe motor disturbances, such as staggering; greatly impaired perception
0.30	Semistupor
0.35	Level for surgical anesthesia; possibly death
0.40	Death (usually caused by respiratory failure)

Adapted from Ray, O. S., & Ksir, C. (2006). *Drugs, society, and human behavior* (11th ed.). New York: McGraw-Hill.

of blood) produce relaxation and lowered alertness. Modest levels (0.10%) lead to mild sedation and some sensory-motor impairment. Even this relatively mild impairment can be quite dangerous, however, as the likelihood of having an automobile accident with a BAC of 0.10% is six to seven times greater than when the BAC is 0 (Figure 5.5), primarily because of a decreased reaction time. Someone with a BAC of 0.08% is considered legally intoxicated in all states of the United States, although the last state to enforce this, Minnesota, did not do so until August 2005. Mental and physical functions decline further with greater blood alcohol levels, causing more substantial impairments. At a BAC of 0.35 percent, alcohol acts as an anesthetic, causing unconsciousness. Higher blood alcohol levels may produce stupor, coma, or death from respiratory failure.

As we noted in Chapter 2, the reticular formation of the brain plays an important role in arousal, and alcohol depresses reticular formation activity: A small amount of alcohol-induced depression leads to relaxation and feelings of well-being. With greater depression of the reticular formation, cortical activity is lowered to a point at which mental and physical functioning is impaired. High levels of neural suppression can cause sleep, coma, or even death, generally from respiratory depression.

The Mechanisms of Action of Alcohol

Alcohol exerts its major effects on four nervous system activities: the movement of Na^+ ions across cell membranes, the binding of GABA to its receptors, the responsiveness of NMDA receptors to glutamate, and activity at opiate receptors. Alcohol inhibits the movement of Na^+ ions across the cell membrane, and the higher the dose, the greater the general reduction in CNS functioning. Decreased nervous system functioning leads to the diminished judgment and impaired sensory-motor coordination characteristic of intoxication.

Alcohol influences the $GABA_A$ receptor, which controls Cl^- ion movement into the neuron, producing IPSPs (Chapter 4). Alcohol attaches to the $GABA_A$ receptor but does not directly influence its activity; instead, alcohol enables the neurotransmitter to bind more tightly to its receptors, increasing its effect on the postsynaptic membrane (Sudzak & others, 1986). The enhanced influence of GABA produces relaxation and decreases anxiety (i.e., alcohol has an *anxiolytic effect* through its influence on the GABA receptors).

Alcohol also affects the NMDA-subtype of receptor for glutamate, the brain's most common excitatory neurotransmitter (Davis & Wu, 2001; Heinz & others, 2003). In the short term, alcohol disrupts glutamatergic transmission by inhibiting the NMDA receptor (Tsai & others, 1998). Continued ingestion of alcohol causes an up-regulation (increase) in the number of NMDA receptors. With an abrupt cessation of drinking, the excess of NMDA receptors contributes to a hyperexcitable state (withdrawal) that produces seizures, delirium tremens (confusion, hallucinations), and neuronal death (Tsai & Coyle, 1998).

Alcohol consumption is also pleasurable. According to Gianoulakis (2001), some of these reinforcing properties are caused by the agonistic action of alcohol on opiate receptors, which increases their stimulation by endorphins (Figure 5.2, mechanism 1).

The Long-Term Effects of Alcohol Use

As indicated above, tolerance, withdrawal, and physical and psychological dependence characterize addiction, and all of these effects can be consequences of repeated alcohol consumption. For example, repeated consumption leads to tolerance, which allows a person to consume larger and larger amounts of alcohol. Long-term alcohol consumption can lead both to physical dependence, revealed in withdrawal symptoms ranging from restlessness to tremors, insomnia, anxiety, mental confusion, and hallucinations, and to psychological dependence, indicated by intense craving.

Alcoholism, or *alcohol dependence,* is a major public health problem in the United States. Approximately 10% of adult drinkers abuse alcohol, or deliberately use alcohol at a level that produces physical, mental, emotional, and/or social impairment (Carroll, 2000). We have more to say about the genetic basis for alcoholism and other addictions later in the chapter. Table 5.1 summarizes the major long-term effects of alcohol use.

Women who consume alcohol during pregnancy have an increased risk of giving birth to a child with *fetal alcohol syndrome* (FAS) or with milder developmental problems (*fetal alcohol effects,* FAE). Despite an extensive literature on the effects of alcohol during pregnancy (e.g., Cook, 2004; O'Leary, 2004), the "safe" amount of alcohol consumption during pregnancy is unknown, as are the physiological mechanisms that make alcohol toxic for the developing fetus (Eustace & others, 2003). We discussed FAS at greater length in Chapter 3.

Barbiturate and Nonbarbiturate Sedative-Hypnotic Drugs

Derivatives of barbituric acid, the **barbiturates** are powerful sedative-hypnotic drugs. They can be classified as ultrashort-acting, short-intermediate-acting, and long-acting, depending on time of onset and duration of effect. For the ultrashort-acting barbiturates, such as thiopental (Pentothal) and thiamylal (Surital), the effect takes place within a minute and lasts up to 3 hours. These types of barbiturates are frequently used as *anesthetics* during surgery. Short-intermediate-acting barbiturates begin their effect after about 15 to 40 minutes and act for up to 6 hours; these include pentobarbital (Nembutal) and secobarbital (Seconal), which are widely used as sedatives. Finally, the long-acting barbiturates, such as phenobarbital (Luminal), begin to have an effect after 1 hour and can be effective for as long as 16 hours. Because of the length of time they are effective, these drugs are used as *anticonvulsants* in treating epilepsy.

Nonbarbiturate sedative-hypnotic drugs are sedative-hypnotic drugs that are not derived from barbituric acid but have the same mode of action as the barbiturates. They are frequently used to treat insomnia. First synthesized in 1862, chloral hydrate, with street names such as "Mickey Finn" and "knockout drops," produces sleep lasting for up to 5 hours shortly after being taken. If you have seen any of the old film noir detective movies, you have probably witnessed the effect of chloral hydrate on one or more of the characters. Methaqualone (Quaalude) is another nonbarbiturate sedative-hypnotic drug. Once prescribed for insomnia, this drug is now considered to have a high potential for abuse and is no longer prescribed.

alcoholism A dependence on alcohol.

barbiturate A type of sedative-hypnotic drug that is a derivative of barbituric acid.

nonbarbiturate sedative-hypnotic drug A type of sedative-hypnotic drug that is not derived from barbituric acid but has the same mode of action as barbiturates.

anxiolytic A sedative-hypnotic drug often used to reduce nervousness, anxiety, or fear.

benzodiazepine A widely prescribed subclass of antianxiety drugs.

Benzodiazepines and Nonbenzodiazepine Anxiolytics

Anxiolytics, or antianxiety drugs, are often used to reduce nervousness, fear, or anxiety. Meprobamate (Miltown), the first antianxiety drug, was introduced in the mid-1950s. Meprobamate produces rapid anxiety relief and was once widely used. In 1960, chlordiazepoxide (Librium) was marketed as an antianxiety drug, followed by diazepam (Valium) 3 years later; these two drugs belong to a subclass called the **benzodiazepines,** which continue to be widely prescribed tranquilizers. In fact, diazepam was the most frequently used anxiolytic drug for almost 20 years (Ray & Ksir, 2006). There is an amusing scene in the 1979 movie *Starting Over* in which a character has an anxiety attack in a furniture store. His brother, a psychiatrist, quickly diagnoses the problem and asks the assembled onlookers if anyone has a Valium. He is pelted by dozens of capsules from the crowd. Alprazolam (Xanax) has now replaced diazepam as the most frequently used benzodiazepine. Faster acting and more powerful, alprazolam also, unfortunately, has more potential for abuse.

Nonbenzodiazepine anxiolytics include drugs that, like the benzodiazepines, target the $GABA_A$ receptor. Examples include zolpidem (Ambien) and zaleplon (Sonata). Zolpidem was marketed in the early 1990s as a sedative drug to treat insomnia. Because it acts on the same receptor as the benzodiazepines, zolpidem has quite similar effects, although its sedative actions outweigh any anxiolytic action. Zaleplon has an extremely short-acting effect and induces sleep quickly, which makes it particularly useful as a sleep aid. A person can take zaleplon to fall asleep, without having to worry about negative effects on functioning the next day. Research comparing the residual effects of zolpidem and zaleplon on driving ability the day after use has shown that zolpidem produces significant impairment, particularly in a 20 mg dose, when the drug is taken during the middle of the night (i.e., 4 hours before testing) (Verster & others, 2002). If taken at bedtime, the drug did not produce a significant effect (Verster & others, 2004). Zaleplon did not significantly affect driving ability at the doses tested, following either bedtime or middle-of-the-night administration.

Another group of nonbenzodiazepine anxiolytics targets serotonin rather than GABA receptors. One well-known example of this group is buspirone (BuSpar), which was approved for clinical use in 1986. Buspirone has a number of characteristics that make it particularly useful in treating anxiety, with or without depression: It produces its anxiolytic effect without sedation; memory loss, mental confusion, and psychomotor impairment are minimal; unlike the benzodiazepines, it does not potentiate the depressant effects of alcohol; it has little addiction potential; and it also has an antidepressant effect. It is ineffective as a sleep aid, because it has a gradual onset of action (Julien, 2005).

The Mechanisms of Sedative-Hypnotic Action

All of the sedative-hypnotic drugs produce some general depression of CNS activity, and any other effects are specific to a particular drug. As noted earlier, alcohol attaches to $GABA_A$ receptors and enhances the binding of GABA to other binding sites on the receptor. Other sedative-hypnotic drugs appear to affect GABA receptors similarly.

Barbiturate and Nonbarbiturate Sedative-Hypnotics. Barbiturate and nonbarbiturate sedative-hypnotic drugs bind to a different $GABA_A$ binding site than alcohol. However, like alcohol, they increase the action of GABA on the postsynaptic membrane (Majewska & others, 1986). At low doses, the result is a calming effect; higher doses lead to drowsiness and sleep.

Anxiolytic Drugs. Specific sites on the $GABA_A$ receptor (different from the barbiturate/nonbarbiturate sites but probably the same as the alcohol binding site) are sensitive to the antianxiety drugs. Like alcohol and the barbiturates, anxiolytic drugs are indirect agonists of GABA, attaching to $GABA_A$ receptors without directly activating GABA neurons. Instead, they enhance the action of GABA, leading to decreased anxiety. Although antianxiety drugs also produce CNS depression, they are safer than the barbiturates because they are less toxic and less sleep-inducing.

People sometimes mix alcohol and drugs such as the benzodiazepines and barbiturates. Because alcohol, benzodiazepines, and barbiturates act on the same GABA neurons, combining alcohol with either of the other two sedative-hypnotics increases the risk of overdose. In fact, the chance of dying as a result of taking both alcohol and barbiturates is greater than the likelihood of dying from taking twice as much of either drug separately (Goode, 1998).

The Long-Term Effects of Sedative-Hypnotic Drugs Other Than Alcohol

The calming effect of sedative-hypnotic drugs is pleasurable and may even lead to mild euphoria, which can lead to repeated use. Tolerance quickly develops, and withdrawal symptoms can be severe (Julien, 2005). Thus, the use of sedative-hypnotics can easily become habit-forming, both because of the way the drugs make people feel and because of the unpleasantness of withdrawal. As tolerance develops, even greater doses are required to maintain the same level of sedative effect, increasing the risk of overdose. This type of overdose is apparently what killed the singer and actress Judy Garland (you may be familiar with her as a child actress in the 1939 classic, *The Wizard of Oz*) at the age of 47. She had used Seconal for years to fight insomnia, and her autopsy revealed a Seconal level high enough to kill most people instantly.

Because of the rapid development of tolerance, the severity of withdrawal symptoms, and the conditioning associated with their use, sedative-hypnotic drugs have a high potential for addiction, and their repeated use produces both physical and psychological dependence. During withdrawal, the individual feels extremely tense, anxious, and irritable, and may suffer from prolonged insomnia. There is also a danger of convulsions and seizures, which can be fatal. The major long-term effects of sedative-hypnotic drug use are summarized in Table 5.1.

Note that the symptoms of withdrawal tend to be the opposite of the effects of drug use. Thus, withdrawal can be seen as the compensatory reaction of the body and brain to the absence of the drug.

Checkpoint

Can a person become as drunk from drinking beer as from drinking whiskey? Explain your answer. Why is it particularly dangerous to mix alcohol and other sedative-hypnotic drugs?

REVIEW

- Depressants slow down mental and physical functions. At low doses, depressants produce relaxation and decreased anxiety. At higher doses, they produce drowsiness and sleep.
- Alcohol, barbiturates and nonbarbiturates, and anxiolytic (antianxiety) drugs function as GABA agonists. Alcohol also reduces Na^+ ion movement across the cell membrane, affects the responsiveness of NMDA receptors to glutamate, and has an agonistic effect on opiate receptors.
- Long-term sedative-hypnotic use can lead to tolerance, withdrawal, and physical and psychological dependence.

Psychostimulants

Before her cocaine addiction, Evelyn usually awakened in the morning feeling tired. Staggering into the kitchen, she would pour herself a cup of coffee, drain it, and then pour another. After finishing the second cup, she generally felt sufficiently alive to start her day. Coffee has this effect because it contains caffeine, which belongs to a class of drugs called stimulants. A **psychostimulant** produces alertness by enhancing the functioning of the sympathetic nervous system and the reticular

psychostimulant A drug that produces alertness by enhancing the functioning of the sympathetic nervous system and the reticular formation.

amphetamine A collective term for psychostimulant drugs typically used to treat attention deficit hyperactivity disorder and sleep disorders.

cocaine A psychostimulant extracted from the leaves of the coca plant that increases alertness, decreases fatigue, and produces a pleasurable emotional state.

caffeine A psychostimulant found in various plants that increases alertness and decreases fatigue.

nicotine A psychostimulant found in the leaves of the tobacco plant that increases alertness and decreases fatigue.

formation. The caffeine in Evelyn's two cups of coffee produced sufficient alertness to enable her to begin her day. Caffeine is one of the four types of psychostimulants; the others are amphetamine, cocaine, and nicotine (Julien, 2005).

Amphetamines

The term **amphetamine** encompasses three closely related drugs: amphetamine or levoamphetamine (Benzedrine), dextroamphetamine (Dexedrine), and methamphetamine or "speed," the most commonly abused amphetamine. Amphetamines are usually taken orally, but crystalline amphetamine can be smoked or, after dilution, injected intravenously. Amphetamines are currently prescribed primarily to treat attention deficit hyperactivity disorder (ADHD) and sleep disorders, such as narcolepsy. After taking amphetamine, an individual experiences greater energy, a decreased need to sleep, reduced appetite, and positive affect (mood). Paradoxically, when used in the treatment of childhood ADHD, amphetamine has a calming effect.

Cocaine

Extracted from the leaves of the coca plant, **cocaine** is an alkaloid compound obtained as white, odorless crystals or crystalline powder. Although its medical use is now rare, in the latter part of the 19th century, cocaine was used to treat a number of ailments in both children and adults (Figure 5.7), and Sigmund Freud was initially enthusiastic about its medical potential (Thorne & Henley, 2005). Applied to the mucous membranes of the nose, throat, larynx, or lower respiratory passages, cocaine acts as a local anesthetic. Cocaine also stops bleeding during surgery on the nose, because of its ability to constrict the blood vessels. Like amphetamine, cocaine produces increased alertness, greater energy, a decreased need for sleep, and an extremely pleasurable emotional state.

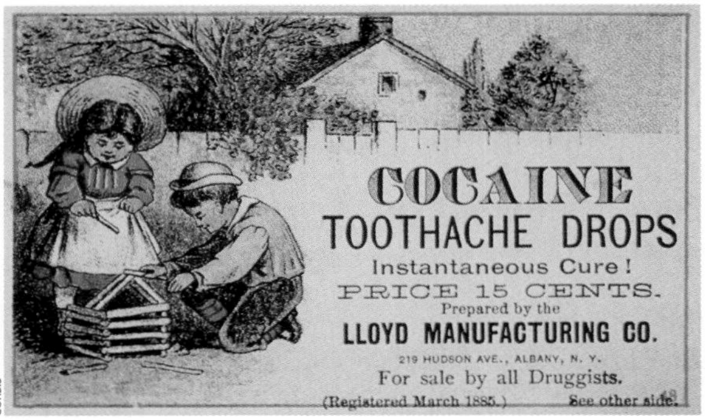

CORBIS

Figure 5.7

Cocaine and toothache Cocaine was not always considered a dangerous drug. This ad, from 1885, promotes the benefit of cocaine as a cure for toothache.

➡ **What are the effects of cocaine?**

Until recently, snorting, or sniffing through the nose, was the most common way to self-administer cocaine. It can also be taken orally by chewing coca leaves or can be converted to a smokable form, called a freebase, by mixing it with a strong alkali compound and ether. The freebase is then smoked in a pipe. Because of the combustibility of ether, freebasing is particularly dangerous. The late comedian Richard Pryor once set his clothes and himself on fire while freebasing cocaine. He sustained third-degree burns over most of the upper half of his body.

Cocaine use seems to be particularly popular with celebrities and often leads to legal difficulties. For example, rock singer Courtney Love's name is frequently in the news for arrests involving illicit drugs. In the past decade, Robert Downey, Jr., who received an Oscar nomination for his lead role in the 1992 movie *Chaplin* and an Emmy for work on the television show *Ally McBeal,* has been in and out of jail and rehabilitation facilities for his cocaine and heroin addictions. After photographs and videotapes were published in late 2005 of British supermodel Kate Moss using cocaine, she spent time in a rehabilitation facility, apparently determined to put her drug use behind her.

Introduced in 1985, crack cocaine has become a popular way of using cocaine, as the effects are similar to those produced by freebasing. *Crack* is made by mixing cocaine hydrochloride with ammonia or baking soda and water; the resulting crystals are smoked in a pipe. Crack is a potent form of cocaine and can quickly lead to addiction.

Caffeine

Caffeine is a bitter-tasting, odorless compound found in various plants. In the United States, the majority of caffeine is consumed in coffee (Figure 5.8), an extract from the fruit of the *Coffee arabica* plant and related species. It is estimated that the

Figure 5.8

A cup of coffee The energizing effects of caffeine are clearly depicted in this Garfield cartoon.

→ **In what circumstances do you use stimulants like caffeine and nicotine?**

average American drinks about 1,000 cups of coffee annually (Carroll, 2000). Caffeine is also found in cola drinks as well as in cocoa, chocolate, and tea (Table 5.4). Although mostly consumed in drinks or foods, caffeine also can be taken in pill form, usually as appetite-suppressant nonprescription diet pills. The effects of caffeine are similar to, but milder than, those of amphetamines and cocaine. Unless a person has little or no experience with it, coffee use leads to clearer thought processing, reduced drowsiness, more rapid reaction times, enhanced intellectual functioning, and an overall positive feeling.

Table 5.4

The Caffeine Content of Some Frequently Used Products

Product	Amount	Caffeine (mg)
Brewed coffee	8 fl. oz.	135
Instant coffee	8 fl. oz.	95
Decaffeinated coffee	8 fl. oz.	5
Tea, leaf or bag	8 fl. oz.	50
Cola beverages	12 fl. oz.	23–58
Hershey bar (dark chocolate)	1.5 oz.	31
Hershey bar (milk chocolate)	1.5 oz.	10
NoDoz, regular strength	1 tablet	100
NoDoz, maximum strength	1 tablet	200
Anacin	2 tablets	64

Source: Center for Science in the Public Interest (CSPI), Caffeine Content of Foods and Drugs Chart (July 31, 1997), found online at http://www.cspinet.org/new/cafchart.html

Nicotine

Found in the leaves of the tobacco plant, **nicotine** is most commonly ingested by smoking cigarettes, cigars, or pipes. It also can be ingested orally as chewing tobacco or by chewing nicotine gum. The newest method of taking nicotine is absorption through the skin via a nicotine patch; the patch and nicotine gum are used by people who are trying to stop the other, more dangerous, methods of nicotine consumption—primarily, smoking.

Increased alertness and reduced fatigue are the two primary effects of nicotine use. It is perhaps surprising to nonsmokers that smoking a cigarette has the same energizing effect as drinking a cup of coffee. Nicotine also increases metabolism, with the result that people typically gain weight when they stop smoking. However, such weight gain is usually trivial and is more than offset by the health benefits gained from smoking cessation (Perkins & others, 1997).

The Mechanisms of Psychostimulant Action

All psychostimulants produce arousal, but by different mechanisms. For example, amphetamine increases norepinephrine and dopamine release from the presynaptic membrane (Figure 5.2, mechanism 5) and blocks the reuptake of both neurotransmitters (Figure 5.2, mechanism 2). Cocaine increases norepinephrine and dopamine availability, but only by blocking neurotransmitter reuptake (Unterwald, 2001). The agonistic actions of amphetamine and cocaine increase the noradrenergic and dopaminergic activity in neural areas that control arousal and pleasure.

The stimulating effect of caffeine results from increased activity in neurons that use glutamate as the neurotransmitter. Glutamate release is increased following caffeine consumption, but not directly (Figure 5.9). Caffeine blocks the release of the inhibitory neurotransmitter adenosine, which normally inhibits glutamate release. By preventing adenosine release, caffeine indirectly increases glutamate activity (Quarta & others, 2004). Evidence also indicates that caffeine has an agonistic action on dopaminergic neurons in the prefrontal cortex (Nehlig, 1999).

Rick Bender, former baseball player and poster boy for the potential effects of long-term use of smokeless tobacco.

RICK BENDER

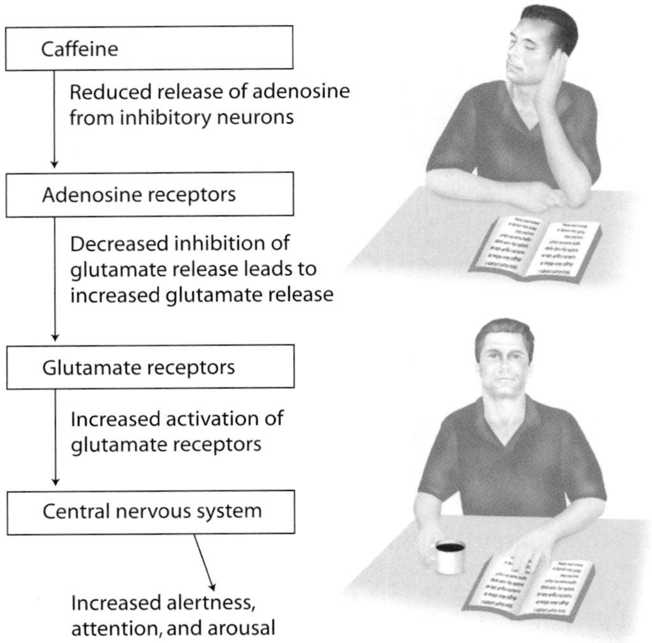

Figure 5.9

How caffeine produces alertness, attention, and arousal Caffeine blocks adenosine release, which normally inhibits glutamate release. As a result, caffeine produces CNS arousal.

➔ **How are the physiological effects of caffeine different from the effects of amphetamine and cocaine?**

The arousing effects of nicotine result from its activation of cholinergic receptors (the nicotinic receptors) in both the PNS and the CNS. In the PNS, such activation increases blood pressure and heart rate and stimulates epinephrine release from the adrenal glands. In the CNS, nicotinic receptors are widespread and stimulation seems to enhance the release of dopamine, acetylcholine, and glutamate. Increased dopamine levels probably account for the reinforcing, psychostimulant, antidepressant, and addictive actions of nicotine (Julien, 2005). Table 5.2 summarizes the major effects of the stimulants on synaptic transmission.

The Dangers of Psychostimulant Abuse

Psychostimulants are widely used, powerful drugs that are often abused. The dangers of cocaine use have become particularly evident in recent years, especially since the death of the University of Maryland's star basketball player Len Bias in 1986. Just 2 days after he was drafted by the Boston Celtics, Bias died from a cocaine overdose. His death was widely publicized, and attitudes toward the use of cocaine changed drastically, with the result that cocaine use is down nearly 80% from the level in Bias's time (Pasierb & Harrison, 2002). Still, cocaine use continues in some circles, and people continue to succumb to its dangers. On October 10, 2004, the sports world was shocked to learn of the death of former baseball star Ken Caminiti from a sudden heart attack at the age of 41. Unfortunately, Caminiti had two strikes against him, as he was a former user of anabolic steroids and a user of cocaine in the months and weeks before his death (Mundell, 2004). Both substances have deleterious effects on the cardiovascular system. Cocaine increases both heart rate and blood pressure, sometimes to fatal levels, as in the case of Len Bias.

The dangers of amphetamine and nicotine are now widely recognized. Among these psychostimulants, most are readily available, with or without prescription. For example, amphetamines are still prescribed for short-term weight control (Ray & Ksir, 2006), and nicotine is easily obtained in many different forms. The age restrictions for the sale and use of cigarettes and related sources of nicotine in the United States and some other countries do not appear to work, as most tobacco users develop their habits as teenagers or preteens.

The Controlled Substances Act of 1970 designated cocaine as a Schedule II drug, which means it is illegal to sell cocaine without a U.S. Drug Enforcement Administration (DEA) license, and it is illegal to buy or possess cocaine without a license or prescription. Because it has some limited use in medicine as an anesthetic, physicians can administer cocaine legally in surgery. The Controlled Substances Act established five schedules of controlled substances. Schedule I contains drugs considered to have the highest potential for abuse, with no accepted medical use; examples include ecstasy, heroin, LSD, and marijuana. Schedule II drugs have a high potential for abuse, but they also have an accepted medical use; examples are amphetamines, cocaine, codeine, morphine, and opium. Schedules III to V drugs also have medical uses and are considered to have decreasing potential for abuse (in the order III $>$ IV $>$ V). Schedule III drugs include anabolic steroids, barbiturates, and testosterone; Schedule IV includes the benzodiazepines, such as Xanax, Librium, and Valium; Schedule V drugs include codeine preparations such as the cough medicine Robitussin and opium preparations such as the antidiarrheal medicine Parepectolin.

Tolerance develops rapidly to all psychostimulants, and tolerance to nicotine is at least part of the reason why some individuals smoke 2 or 3 (or more) packs of cigarettes each day. Similarly, some people drink 8 to 10 cups of coffee daily because their caffeine tolerance is so high.

Symptoms of withdrawal from psychostimulants range from mild to severe. Mild withdrawal is experienced as a lack of alertness and feelings of lethargy; intense withdrawal symptoms include sleeping for up to 48 hours, followed by depression lasting for several days or weeks (Wilford, 1981). The process of withdrawal from a psychostimulant drug can be so severe that it is known as "crashing," and the intense depression resulting from withdrawal may present a suicide risk. Withdrawal symptoms indicate that a physical dependence, which can occur with all the psychostimulant drugs, has developed (Julien, 2005).

Psychological dependence is common with the repeated use of psychostimulants. Cravings in individuals can occur even after the drug has not been used for a long time. People who have not smoked for years may still have the desire to smoke, especially when around others who are smoking or when in situations in which they smoked in the past. This, of course, reflects the importance of conditioning for psychological dependence.

Stimulant-induced psychosis is another serious consequence of psychostimulant abuse, particularly the abuse of amphetamines and cocaine. Frequent or excessive use of either amphetamines or cocaine can lead to paranoia, or feelings of persecution, as well as to delusions and hallucinations. Stimulant-induced psychosis can even lead to violent behavior. Table 5.1 summarizes the effects of psychostimulant drug use.

The long-term abuse of cocaine or methamphetamine leads to demonstrable cognitive impairment and brain damage, which continues long after the person stops taking the drug. For example, crack-cocaine abusers exhibited abnormal EEG measures at 5 to 10 days after their last use of cocaine, and these abnormalities persisted following 6 months of abstinence (Alper & others, 1998). Brain imaging revealed reduced integrity of the anterior corpus callosum in cocaine-dependent subjects, which was related to impaired function of the prefrontal cortex and increased impulsivity in the subjects (Moeller & others, 2005). In a study comparing the cognitive function of 20 abstinent crack users, 37 abstinent crack- and alcohol-dependent subjects, and 29 healthy controls, both substance-dependent groups were significantly impaired on a wide range of tests relative to the control subjects (Di Sclafani & others, 2002). Further, both substance-dependent groups were still significantly impaired after 6 months of abstinence.

As we indicated in Chapter 4, the neurotransmitter dopamine is apparently involved in all of the addictions; therefore, it should come as no surprise that changes in dopaminergic activity are found in cocaine- and methamphetamine-addicted subjects. For example, reductions in dopamine D_2 receptors are consistently found in cocaine abusers, and these reductions are associated with lowered metabolism in the orbitofrontal cortex and compulsive behavior (Volkow & others, 2001a). Using PET scans, Volkow and colleagues (2001c) found a similar reduction in D_2 receptors in methamphetamine abusers, and this reduction was still apparent in abusers who had been detoxified for 11 months or more. The changes in dopamine function are associated with motor and cognitive impairments. Former methamphetamine abusers have been studied after even longer periods of abstinence, and there is some evidence for improvement both in the number of D_2 receptors and in some of the motor and cognitive tests (Volkow & others, 2001b). However, a study of brain glucose metabolism in methamphetamine abusers after 12 to 17 months of abstinence revealed that the metabolic recovery was greater in the thalamus than in the striatum, with the residual deficit particularly evident in the caudate nucleus and nucleus accumbens (G. J. Wang & others, 2004). The researchers suggested that decreased nucleus accumbens activity might explain the persistent lack of motivation and lack of pleasure seen in detoxified methamphetamine abusers.

The *Scientific American* Spotlight, "Beating Abuse: Glutamate May Hold a Key to Drug Addiction," suggests that the neurotransmitter glutamate, as well as

Scientific American Spotlight

Beating Abuse

Glutamate May Hold a Key to Drug Addiction Tabitha Powledge

Addiction has long been thought to be a form of learning. In the past few years, molecular biologists have amassed chemical evidence to prove it, in the process generating new ideas for combating drug use.

Some of the most striking recent studies have examined the affinity between cocaine and glutamate, one of several chemical neurotransmitters that govern communication between nerve cells and are involved particularly with memory. For example, Stanislav R. Vorel and his colleagues at the Albert Einstein College of Medicine discovered that electrically stimulating the hippocampus, a brain structure central to memory and rich in glutamate, causes dependence relapse in rats formerly addicted to cocaine. Other researchers found that glutamate activates brain cells devoted to dopamine, a neurotransmitter associated with feelings of reward and pleasure. Indeed, the dopamine reward circuit in the brain has been regarded as the addiction pathway, commandeered not just by cocaine but by all addictive drugs. The fact that glutamate modifies dopamine action demonstrates a direct connection between brain reward circuits and those for learning and memory.

The reward and memory systems may harbor the secrets to addiction, but they also serve as a barrier to developing treatments. Altering either of these fundamental brain circuits without subverting some essential function is tricky business. "That's why there was excitement about the possibility that the glutamate system might be involved. But at this point, we're not there," says Francis J. White, a pharmacologist at Finch University of Health Sciences/The Chicago Medical School.

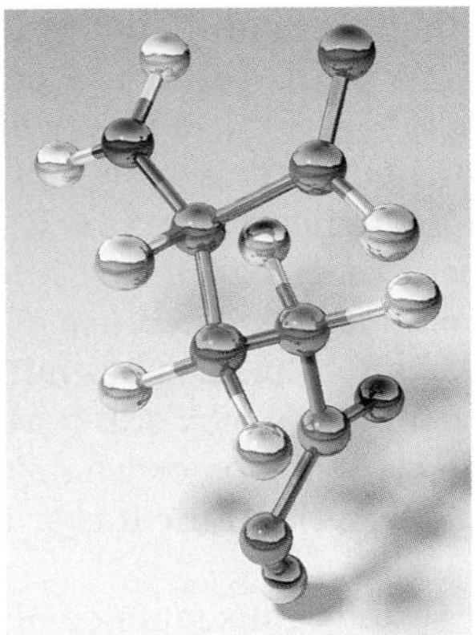

Glutamate is a brain-signaling molecule involved in addiction.

A discovery published in September 2001 may nudge that process along. Researchers studying mice identified a particular glutamate receptor, known as mGluR5, that is crucial for cocaine dependence. Mice that lack the receptor do not become dependent no matter how much cocaine they are given. The mGluR5 findings are significant in part because the receptor's action appears to be selective. The mutant mouse takes food and water just like other mice, which suggests that lack of the receptor does not affect "natural" rewards, only interest in cocaine.

Eliot Gardner, a senior research investigator at the National Institute on Drug Abuse, identifies two major hurdles to basing addiction treatments on glutamate. The first is figuring out which glutamate receptors are involved. (Even if mGluR5 is related to human cocaine dependence, it is not the only receptor significant in addiction.) The second problem is glutamate's ubiquity. "It's found all over the brain in lots of circuits subserving lots of behavior and mental processes that one would not want to manipulate," Gardner says. Researchers will need to find precise delivery systems that will target only specific brain circuits, leaving alone the dozens, or perhaps hundreds, of other circuits that use glutamate as a neurotransmitter.

Intriguingly, the glutamate studies could strengthen that old nonpharmaceutical standby: behavioral therapy. One of the most promising treatments "is to have people unlearn aspects of addiction and relearn new things to do in life," says renowned molecular biologist and addiction specialist Eric J. Nestler of the University of Texas Southwestern Medical Center. "An argument can be made that Alcoholics Anonymous provides that type of alternative focus."

Or pharmacotherapies could be combined with "talking cures" to yield fewer relapses. "If we could develop medications that could address the underlying biology, the powerful biological forces that drive addiction, then we can make a person more amenable to other treatments," such as behavior therapy, Nestler says. "You really need both."

From: *Scientific American*, Vol. 286(1), p. 20.

dopamine, may play a part in the addictions. The fact that glutamate modifies dopaminergic action is important because glutamate is critical for learning and memory, and addiction has long been considered to be the result of learning. It is hoped that this insight about glutamate and addiction will lead to the "unlearning" of addiction.

Little research seems to have been done on the prenatal effects of exposure to amphetamines on the developing fetus. However, based on animal research and the few human studies reported, amphetamines and methamphetamines increase the risk of adverse fetal effects when they are abused during pregnancy (Plessinger, 1998). Physical effects such as cleft palate, cardiac abnormalities, and reduced growth (low birth weight) have been observed.

Cocaine easily diffuses across the placenta and is thus readily available to the developing fetus. At midgestation the fetus may experience high concentrations of cocaine in the amniotic fluid, which prolongs the exposure during critical periods of neurodevelopment (Woods, 1998). Binge use of cocaine can have decidedly adverse effects on pregnancy, including an increase in placental detachment, low birth weight and small head circumference, precipitous initiation of labor, or stillbirth (Burkett & others, 1994). In animal research, prenatal exposure to cocaine has been associated with cognitive deficits. For example, as adults, rats prenatally exposed to cocaine based on a drug-administration model designed to mimic the pharmacokinetics of human use performed more poorly on a short-term memory task than control rats (that received saline) (Morrow & others, 2002). Using a rabbit model, Harvey and colleagues (Harvey, 2004; Harvey & others, 2001) found that prenatally exposed animals exhibit cognitive deficits involving the ability to focus attention, with morphological abnormalities in the anterior cingulate cortex. Consistent with the animal research, impaired attention and decreased adaptability to stress have been seen in humans prenatally exposed to cocaine (Harvey & others; Walker & others, 1999).

Research on the effects of prenatal exposure to tobacco/nicotine is both extensive and relatively consistent. Prenatal tobacco exposure is causally related to growth retardation that results in low birth weight, with an inverse relationship between maternal smoking rates and infant's weight at birth (Cornelius, 2003; Cornelius & Day, 2000; Ernst & others, 2001). In animal research, low birth weight, increased locomotor activity, and cognitive impairments have been found consistently after prenatal tobacco exposure (Ernst & others). Cognitive impairments have also been found in human studies, including deficits in language, reading, and vocabulary, and on tests of memory and reasoning (Cornelius & Day; Morrow & others, 2004). Prenatal tobacco exposure has also been associated with an increased incidence of behavior problems and school failure (Weitzman & others, 2002), ADHD (Linnet & others, 2003), and delinquency and criminality in adolescence and adulthood (Cornelius & Day).

Checkpoint

Describe the effects of psychostimulants on the brain and the body. Linda has to drink at least four cups of coffee before she can start work in the morning. Explain the effect of caffeine on her brain.

REVIEW

- Psychostimulant drugs—amphetamines, cocaine, nicotine, and caffeine—produce increased alertness, reduced appetite, and increased energy.
- Amphetamine and cocaine are noradrenergic and dopaminergic agonists. Caffeine is an adenosine antagonist. Nicotine is a cholinergic, dopaminergic, and glutamatergic agonist.
- People who use psychostimulants quickly develop tolerance; withdrawal symptoms can range from mild to severe, and physical and psychological dependence sometimes result from long-term use.
- The long-term use of methamphetamine or cocaine damages the brain and produces cognitive impairment.

Psychedelic Drugs

I lost all count of time. . . . everything appeared deformed as in a faulty mirror. Space and time became more and more disorganized and I was overcome by a fear that I was going out of my mind. The worst part of it being that I was clearly aware of my condition. . . . Occasionally, I felt as if I were out of my body. I thought I had died. My ego seemed suspended somewhere in space, from where I saw my dead body lying on the sofa. . . . acoustic percep-

> tions, such as the noise of water gushing from a tap or the spoken word, were transformed into optical illusions. . . . (Quoted in Julien, 2005, p. 605)

This is a 1938 description of Swiss chemist Albert Hofmann's experience with a drug called lysergic acid diethylamide, or LSD, which belongs to a class of drugs known as psychedelic drugs. Sometimes called *hallucinogens,* **psychedelic drugs** profoundly alter a person's state of consciousness, including sensory experiences (Julien, 2005). For example, the person may perceive vivid but unreal images, referred to as illusions, or "pseudohallucinations."

Psychedelic-induced perceptual changes include an increased sensory awareness; heightened clarity of a sensory experience; the perception of routine elements of the environment as novel, beautiful, or harmonious; and a decreased capacity to distinguish between the self and the environment. Emotional changes include a reduced control over reactions to environmental circumstances and the assigning of profound meaning to even the slightest sensation.

Each experience with a psychedelic drug is different, even for the same person. In one experience, an individual may perceive that objects are moving in slow motion. At another time, using the same drug, the individual may perceive the same objects as moving blindingly fast.

Figure 5.10

Plant sources of psychedelic drugs
(a) A peyote cactus, the source of peyote and mescaline. This cactus is native to southern Texas and the northern and central parts of the Mexican plateau region. **(b)** A psilocybin mushroom, source of the psychoactive drug psilocybin.

➜ **What are the effects of smoking peyote? Of ingesting psilocybin?**

COURTESY OF JOHN AT HTTP://WWW.PEYOTES1.COM

(a)

WILLOW S. HEMPHILL

(b)

Peyote

Several interesting psychedelic drugs are obtained from plants. For example, native peoples of the southwestern United States and northern Mexico have for thousands of years experienced powerful psychedelic experiences, primarily visual hallucinations, after ingesting part of the peyote cactus during their religious rituals. The psychoactive ingredient in **peyote,** the drug obtained from the cactus, is **mescaline.** The mescal buttons, the tips of the fleshy cactus, are removed and dried (Figure 5.10a). Because the buttons taste bitter, native peoples of Mexico smoke the ground-up peyote or drink it in tea. The psychedelic experience lasts 6 to 10 hours. In pure form, mescaline is an extremely powerful psychedelic with effects resembling those produced by LSD (see below).

Psilocybin and Psilocin

Other psychedelic drugs are obtained from fungi. *Psilocybin* and *psilocin* are present in at least 15 species of mushrooms. Mushrooms with psilocybin and psilocin are found throughout the world (Figure 5.10b), and the mushroom *Psilocybe mexicana* is an integral part of the religious ceremonies of native peoples of Central America. These two psychedelic drugs produce effects similar to, but weaker than, those of LSD; their duration of action is much shorter (2 to 4 hours compared with 10 to 12 hours).

Timothy Leary (right) , Harvard professor, who advocated the use of psychoactive drugs.

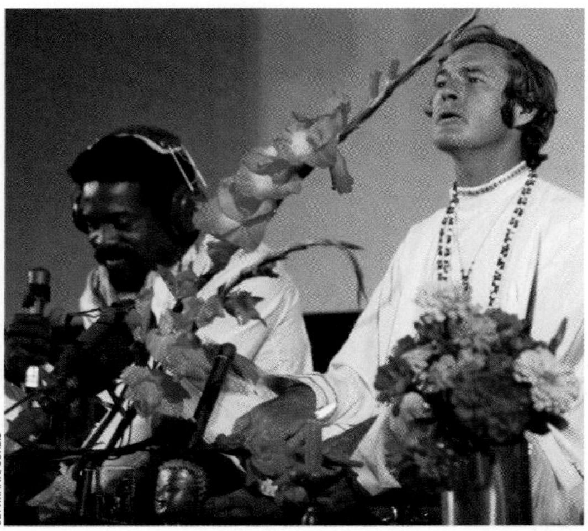

BETTMANN/CORBIS

LSD

In addition to the plant- and fungus-derived psychedelics, some psychedelic drugs have been created in the laboratory. The drug effects Albert Hofmann described were caused by **lysergic acid diethylamide (LSD),** or *acid,* the classic example of a synthetic psychedelic drug. Figure 5.11 provides a vivid example of the hallucinogenic effect of LSD.

When it was first synthesized, LSD was welcomed as a research tool for studying serious mental disorders, because its effects seemed to mimic psychoses. The value of the LSD experience was widely touted by psychologists Timothy Leary and Richard Alpert of Harvard University during the early 1960s. Despite Leary and Alpert's dismissal from the university in 1963 for drug use and for advocating drug use, LSD has remained a widely used psychoactive drug. LSD is consumed orally in tablets or tiny squares of gelatin.

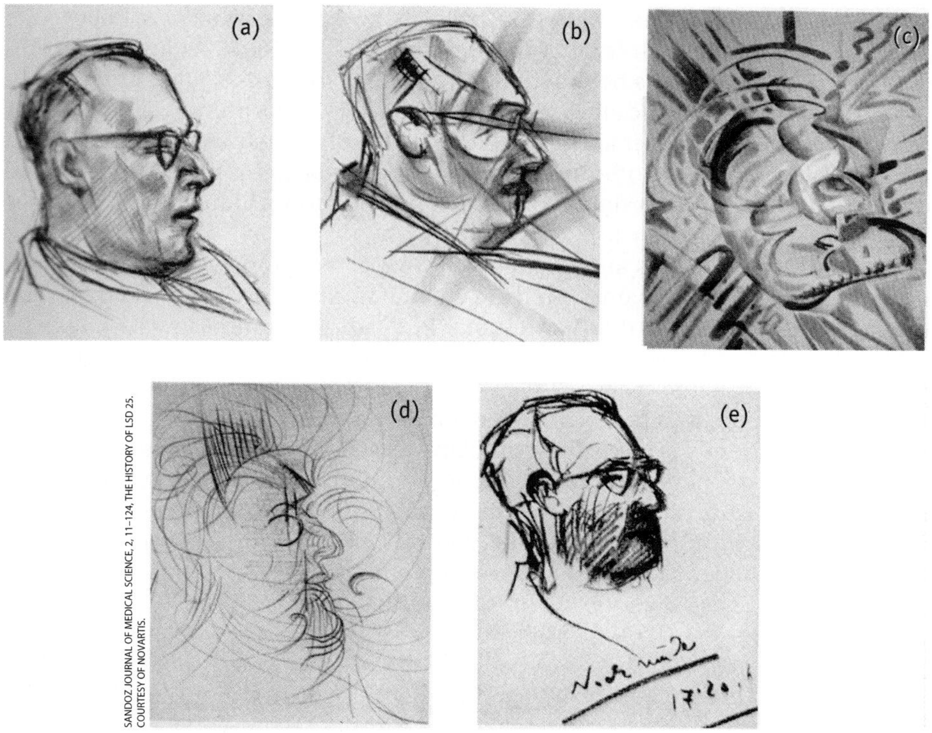

Figure 5.11
Drawings done by an artist under the influence of LSD The artist chose to sketch the person who administered the dose of LSD. **(a)** Using charcoal to make his sketch, the artist shows no effect from the drug 20 minutes after the first dose. **(b)** Some perceptual alterations are evident 85 minutes after the first dose and 20 minutes after a second dose. **(c)** Using tempera for his sketch, the artist shows the most intense effects of LSD 2 hours and 45 minutes after the first dose. **(d)** Using a crayon to make his drawing, the subject reports that the drug's effects are beginning to wear off 5 hours and 45 minutes after the first dose. **(e)** Eight hours after the first dose, the artist produces a final drawing with little enthusiasm. "I want to go home now," he says.

➜ **From these drawings, what are your impressions of the changes in perception produced by LSD?**

PCP

Phencyclidine (PCP) is another synthetic psychedelic drug. PCP was first introduced as a surgical anesthetic in the 1950s. Sometimes referred to as "angel dust," PCP is a white powder that can be injected, smoked, inhaled, or sniffed. It may produce auditory or visual hallucinations and an altered perception of time and distance. There is considerable research interest in PCP effects as a model of schizophrenia (Balla & others, 2003; Murray, 2002).

MDMA

Commonly known as *ecstasy,* **MDMA** (3,4-methylenedioxymethamphetamine) is another popular synthetic psychoactive drug. MDMA was first described in a patent filed in 1912 by E. Merck Pharmaceuticals in Germany; the patent listed its use as an intermediate in the production of therapeutic substances (Pentney, 2001). Psychotherapists began using MDMA as an adjunct to treatment in the 1970s, because of its ability to produce a state of consciousness that facilitates communication. Meanwhile, ecstasy use was gradually growing in popularity as a recreational drug that was "fun" and "good to dance to."

In the mid-1980s, the DEA classified MDMA as a Schedule I controlled substance (Pentney, 2001). Despite this status, ecstasy use has increased over the years. In fact, according to a survey displayed on the National Institute on Drug Abuse website (www.nida.nih.gov/Infofax/ecstasy.html), the number of high school seniors in the United States who had used ecstasy increased from 5.8% in 1998 to 8.0% in 1999. Ecstasy is often used at "raves," where participants dance to loud, rhythmic music for hours on end; it is one of the so-called club drugs (Smith & others, 2002).

The Mechanisms of Action of Psychedelic Drugs

The hallucinogenic effect of LSD is thought to be caused either by an agonistic action on one type of serotonergic neuron or by an antagonistic action on another type of serotonergic neuron. There are few definitive answers, but because of their

psychedelic drug A drug that profoundly alters a person's state of consciousness.

peyote A psychedelic drug obtained from the peyote cactus plant.

mescaline The psychoactive ingredient in peyote.

lysergic acid diethylamide (LSD) A powerful synthetic psychedelic drug, also known as acid.

phencyclidine (PCP) A powerful synthetic psychedelic drug, also known as angel dust.

MDMA The abbreviation for 3,4-methylenedioxymethamphetamine, a synthetic psychoactive drug, known as ecstasy, that induces a state of consciousness that facilitates communication.

structural similarity to serotonin, LSD, psilocin, and psilocybin all are believed to exert their effects through serotonergic neurons (Julien, 2005). As just one example of this, psilocybin has been found to induce a psychosis-like disorder in humans through its agonistic effect on serotonin (5-HT_{2A}) receptors (Vollenweider & others, 1998). Vollenweider and colleagues (1999) subsequently found that the effect of psilocybin on serotonin receptors was related to an increase in striatal dopamine release, supporting a hypothesis of a serotonin/dopamine imbalance in schizophrenia (Chapter 15).

Phencyclidine (PCP) is an antagonist of NMDA receptors, which are involved in the regulation of dopamine release in the striatum (Chapter 4). Balla and colleagues (2001) found that continuous PCP administration in rats caused a schizophrenia-like hyperreactivity of striatal dopamine release to amphetamine stimulation, suggesting that NMDA dysfunction might be responsible for the excessive dopaminergic activity characteristic of schizophrenia.

MDMA apparently produces its stimulant-like euphoric mood state through its stimulation of dopamine D_2 receptors. In addition, the MDMA-produced mild hallucinogenic state may result from its stimulation of a particular group of serotonin receptors (Liechti & Vollenweider, 2001; Oesterheld & others, 2004). Table 5.2 lists some psychedelic drugs and their major effects on synaptic transmission.

The Dangers of Psychedelic Drugs

Perhaps the biggest danger of psychedelic drug use is unpredictability. Individuals who take hallucinogenic drugs can experience panic reactions, or "bad trips," characterized by extreme distress and, in some cases, feelings of persecution.

Another danger is the occurrence of *flashbacks*, or hallucinations experienced long after the original "trip" has ended (Halpern & Pope, 2003). The flashback may be a recurrence of the original hallucinogenic experience, or it may be a totally new hallucinogenic experience. It can occur spontaneously or can be triggered by an environmental stressor. The physical danger of a flashback is obvious, as it could occur at any time, perhaps when the person is driving or performing some other activity that requires concentration. Such unexpected events can be quite frightening, leaving the drug user unsure of what has happened and fearful of additional episodes. LSD-induced flashbacks have been alleviated in some patients with clonidine, an antihypertensive drug (Lerner & others, 2000).

Tolerance is observed with most other psychedelic drugs, with no evidence of withdrawal after the drug usage stops (Carroll, 2000). However, more serious permanent damage is seen in PCP users; long-term use can lead to psychological dependence and neurological problems, including memory deficits (Ellison, 1995). PCP may also have a neurotoxic effect on the developing fetus when ingested during pregnancy (Olney, 2002).

Repeated MDMA use often produces tolerance, which leads to dosage escalation, and lethargy and depression are common following the stimulating effects of the drug (Parrott, 2001). Toxic reactions to MDMA are also possible; symptoms include accelerated heart rate, sweating, and hyperthermia (Teter & Guthrie, 2001). Hyperthermia can be particularly life-threatening, as it involves activation of the sympathetic nervous system and the release of norepinephrine, which has the dual effect of causing heat generation and loss of heat dissipation through sympathetic nervous system-mediated constriction of blood vessels (Mills & others, 2004). Using an animal model of human drug use of MDMA (social interaction, warm temperature), Brown and Kiyatkin (2004) found that the drug produced highly elevated brain temperatures; under certain conditions, most tested animals died. This suggests that under typical "party" conditions, MDMA is a particularly dangerous drug. In the most severe cases, death results from causes such as hyperthermia, cerebral edema, or acute renal failure (Doyon, 2001; Parrott).

Parrott (2001) has reported that regular MDMA users who become abstinent often exhibit reduced levels of serotonin and its metabolites and precursors, with such functional consequences as sleep difficulties, loss of sexual interest, and deficits in learning and memory. The problems are worse in heavy users, possibly reflecting a loss of serotonergic neurons in higher brain areas (Reneman, 2003). Short-term use of MDMA can result in subtle changes in brain function, and long-term use might produce major deficits (Jacobsen & others, 2004). Table 5.1 summarizes the typical effects of psychedelic drugs.

Marijuana

Marijuana is obtained from a mixture of the crushed leaves, flowers, stems, and seeds of the hemp plant, *Cannabis sativa* (Figure 5.12). The resinous secretions of *Cannabis sativa* can be dried into a solid form known as *hashish.* The psychoactive ingredient in both hashish and marijuana is *delta-9-tetrahydrocannabinol,* or **THC.** Marijuana, hashish, and THC are sometimes referred to as cannabis; the psychoactive substances found in marijuana are called *cannabinoids.* At low doses, both marijuana and hashish have a weak sedative effect. At higher doses, they often produce experiences that have been compared to those of the psychedelics. Panic, depressive reactions, and mild paranoia can occur and are probably the result of altered perceptions (Julien, 2005).

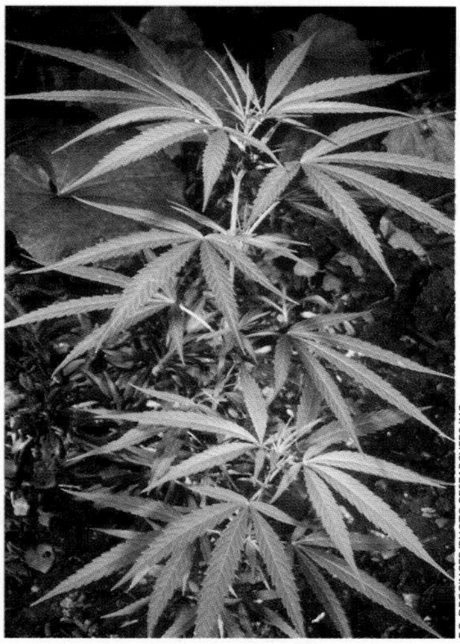

E.R. DEGGINGER/PHOTO RESEARCHERS INC.

Figure 5.12
Marijuana plant The psychoactive ingredient of marijuana is delta-9-tetrahydrocannibinol (THC).

What are the effects of smoking marijuana?

Although the DEA considers marijuana a drug without medical usefulness, its active ingredient, THC, has been used medically to treat nausea and stimulate appetite (Carlini, 2004; Gorter, 1999). The drug dronabinol, which contains THC, has helped cancer patients gain weight by reducing their nausea from chemotherapy (Walsh & others, 2003) and has stimulated appetite in AIDS patients (Nemechek & others, 2000). Dronabinol also has been used to reduce muscle spasms and pain in people with multiple sclerosis (Pertwee, 2002), but, in the case of pain, it may not be superior to existing treatments (Smith, 2002). Killestein and colleagues (2004) concluded that convincing evidence of the efficacy of the cannabinoids in treating multiple sclerosis is not available. The cannabinoids can effectively lower intraocular pressure and may be useful in the treatment of glaucoma (Tomida & others, 2004).

The primary psychedelic effect of both hashish and marijuana is perceptual. After taking either drug, a person's experiences seem more vivid. For example, food tastes better or worse; one young man, a former student in our department, commented that he had not realized foods had different tastes until he ate a meal after smoking marijuana. Odors seem more intense, and visual and auditory sensations seem more powerful. Another widely reported effect is a change in time perception: Time seems to move at a crawl. Hallucinations sometimes occur, and thought processes are occasionally fragmented. Balance is impaired without necessarily affecting braking reaction time, so driving after smoking marijuana or hashish may not be as dangerous as driving while intoxicated (Liguori & others, 2002). However, some research has pointed to impairments of such parameters as perceptual motor speed and accuracy after marijuana ingestion, which suggests that the drug may have a negative effect on driving ability (Kurzthaler & others, 1999).

marijuana A drug obtained from a mixture of crushed leaves, flowers, stems, and seeds of the hemp plant, *Cannabis sativa.*

THC The abbreviation and commonly used name for delta-9-tetrahydrocannabinol, the psychoactive ingredient in marijuana.

The Mechanism of Action of Marijuana

Just as the discovery of opiate receptors preceded the discovery of endogenous opioids, so neural receptors for THC (the active ingredient in marijuana) were found a couple of years before the discovery of a naturally occurring, THC-like substance,

anandamide A naturally occurring THC-like substance.

which was called **anandamide** (Axelrod & Felder, 1998). Because the THC receptor was discovered first, the family of chemicals that includes anandamide is called, in somewhat backward fashion, the endogenous cannabinoids. (As mentioned earlier, *Cannabis* is the genus name for the marijuana plant; *ananda* is Sanskrit for "bliss.")

Studies have suggested that marijuana binds to cannabinoid receptors in the basal ganglia, cerebellum, hippocampus, and cerebral cortex. The effects of THC on cannabinoid receptors in the basal ganglia and cerebellum might account for the influence of marijuana on movement and postural controls; its effects on the cerebral cortex might explain such psychoactive effects of marijuana as the characteristic "high" and changes in sensory perception; and hippocampal involvement might be related to marijuana-induced memory problems (Iversen, 2003).

If cannabinoid agonists produce the psychological effects of marijuana by activating cannabinoid receptors, then cannabinoid *antagonists* might be useful in helping people who would like to stop using marijuana. Because marijuana enhances food intake, another potential use of a cannabinoid antagonist might be as an aid to weight loss. The cannabinoid antagonist rimonabant is currently in clinical trials as a treatment for obesity (Bays, 2004) and as an aid to smoking cessation (Fernandez & Allison, 2004; Le Foll & Goldberg, 2005). We discuss this in greater detail in Chapter 10. A cannabinoid antagonist may also be useful in reducing cocaine-seeking behavior induced by cocaine-associated conditioned stimuli (Le Foll & Goldberg).

The Dangers of Marijuana Use

Tolerance develops with the repeated use of marijuana and hashish. Withdrawal symptoms include restlessness, irritability, insomnia, and nausea. Because marijuana is smoked, users are vulnerable to the same types of cancers and other respiratory problems as cigarette smokers. Also, marijuana users experience a craving for the drug, indicating psychological dependence.

In comparison to other drugs that we have considered, prenatal exposure to marijuana appears to have less of an effect on the development of offspring. For example, in a review of the effects of fetal alcohol and other drugs, Chiriboga (2003) concluded that marijuana exposure is not consistently associated with the outcome of pregnancy. Another review reported that both prenatal alcohol and marijuana were associated with growth deficits, with exposure to any marijuana during the second trimester of pregnancy related to short stature in children (Cornelius & others, 2002).

In a series of studies in Canada involving adolescents prenatally exposed to marijuana or cigarettes, marijuana exposure was negatively associated with tasks requiring visual memory, visual integration and analysis, and sustained attention (Fried, 2002; Fried & others, 2003). Similarly, prenatal cigarette exposure was associated with lowered intelligence and poor impulse control. As part of the same longitudinal study, young adults with prenatal marijuana exposure performed a task that required response inhibition while undergoing fMRI (Smith & others, 2004). According to the fMRI, increased marijuana exposure was associated with a significant change in activity in the prefrontal cortex and in the right premotor cortex during response inhibition. This suggests that prenatal marijuana exposure leads to changes in neural activity during response inhibition that last at least into young adulthood. Other neural changes seen following prenatal marijuana exposure include abnormal amygdala dopamine D_2 gene expression in the human fetus (X. Wang & others, 2004) and a decrease in hippocampal glutamate release in rats, which led to a passive avoidance task memory impairment (Mereu & others, 2003).

Emotional changes have also been observed in children prenatally exposed to marijuana. For example, prenatal exposure during the first and third trimesters of pregnancy was related to significantly elevated levels of depressive symptoms (Gray & others, 2005).

Checkpoint

Describe the effects of psychedelic drugs on the brain and the body. Evan has unknowingly taken LSD. Explain the effects he might experience. How long might these effects last?

REVIEW

- Psychedelic drugs, or hallucinogens, which include peyote, LSD, PCP, and MDMA, induce substantial changes in the way a person thinks, feels, and perceives.
- LSD, mescaline, psilocin, and psilocybin probably exert their effects through their influence on serotonergic neurons.
- PCP is an antagonist of NMDA receptors, which are involved in the regulation of dopamine release in the striatum. Psychological dependence and permanent neurological damage can result from the extended use of PCP.
- MDMA stimulates dopamine D_2 receptors to produce its euphoric mood state and serotonergic receptors to cause a mild hallucinogenic state. Continued use of MDMA can lead to tolerance, dosage escalation, and functional deficits that might signal brain damage.
- THC, the active ingredient in marijuana, binds to cannabinoid receptors in the basal ganglia, cerebellum, cerebral cortex, and hippocampus, affecting motor functions, sensory perceptions, and memory. Marijuana use can result in tolerance and psychological dependence.

Addiction: The Biology of Reinforcement

When it happened, all Sam felt was pressure, as if he were being pushed by a giant, invisible hand. Next, he was aware of lying on his back, but now he felt nothing, heard nothing, saw nothing. Was this death? Had he "crossed over," as his buddies were always talking about? But then came the pain, first in his shoulder and later in his legs, and Sam knew he was still alive. Unless he was in hell.

The pain was all-consuming, so intense it took his breath away, but Sam realized in the midst of his agony that he could see again. A medic loomed over him, filling a syringe with a clear liquid. Sam mouthed, or perhaps said—he still couldn't hear anything—"Hurry." The medic bent over, something pricked his thigh, and Sam's world went black.

He came to in a hospital—far from Iraq, he hoped. Aware of voices from his left, he knew he'd regained his hearing. Instead of the fiery pain he'd experienced earlier, he now felt only a dull ache from his lower body; nothing from his shoulder. Was that good or bad? He cleared his throat, and a nurse materialized. Sam thought she looked like an angel, and he wondered again if he had "crossed over."

"Can I get you anything?" she asked. "The button by your left hand"—Sam moved his hand and felt it—"delivers pain medication on demand, Samuel."

"Sam," he whispered. "And what's the medication?"

"Morphine," the nurse said. For many weeks, this was the sweetest word he heard.

A self-administered morphine pump provides pain relief after surgery.

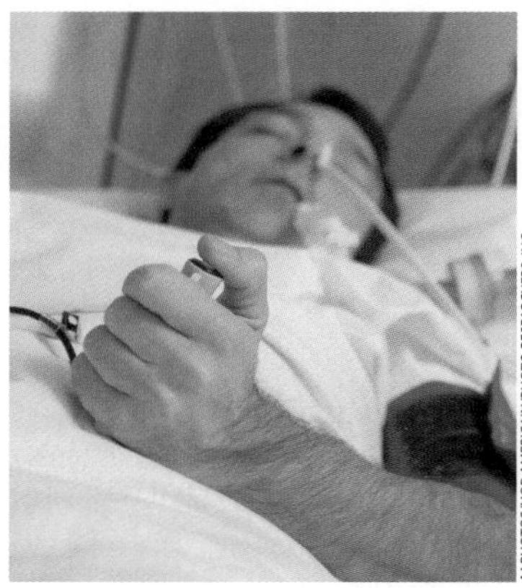

AJ PHOTOS/HOP AMERICAIN/PHOTO RESEARCHERS, INC.

Like other opiates, morphine has dual effects: It functions as an analgesic to eliminate pain, and it produces pleasurable feelings. Because a person who feels these effects is likely to try to experience them again, the drug is considered a powerful reinforcer. A *reinforcer* is a substance, an event, or an activity that increases the frequency of the behavior preceding it (Klein, 2002). (Note that nothing in this definition indicates that a reinforcer has to be pleasurable. In the next section, we define reward or reinforcement biologically as the stimulation of particular areas of the brain. Such stimulation may or may not be associated with a feeling of pleasure.) In this case, the effects of morphine act as a reinforcer of subsequent attempts to obtain the drug. In this section, we discuss the biology of reinforcement, focusing on the CNS structures that enable us to experience pleasure, as well as the influence of reinforcers on our actions. You will learn why drugs such as cocaine, nicotine, and heroin are so reinforcing and how drug use can lead to addiction.

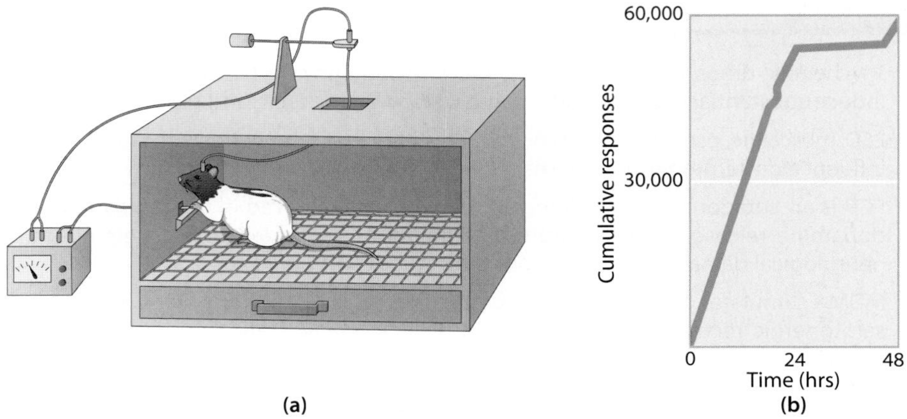

Figure 5.13
Learning to stimulate the reward area **(a)** A rat presses a bar for electrical stimulation of the brain (ESB). **(b)** Sample cumulative response curve; note the high rate of responding (more than 2,000 bar presses per hour) for more than 24 hours, followed by a period of sleep.

➔ In the graph, can the curve ever turn downward? What does the flat part of the curve indicate?

Discovering the Reward Areas of the Brain

Like many other important findings, the discovery of the neurophysiological basis for reward or reinforcement began with a scientific accident. In 1953, a young psychologist named James Olds, trained as a social psychologist at Harvard, arrived at Quebec's McGill University, hoping to work with Donald Hebb, a student of the renowned psychologist Karl Lashley. Hebb introduced Olds to Peter Milner, a doctoral student in physiological psychology. Milner later wrote, "When I discovered the extent of [Olds's] knowledge of physiological psychology I was not very [optimistic] that he would achieve a successful metamorphosis [from social psychologist to physiological psychologist]" (Milner, 1989, p. 62).

In fact, Olds's inexperience in rat brain surgery led to a gross error in electrode implantation in his first experimental animal. Olds's mistake produced a rat that, in the learning apparatus, sought out and remained in places where it received stimulation. In other words, stimulation of the septal area (part of the limbic system; the structure in which Olds had accidentally implanted the electrode) appeared to be highly reinforcing. To confirm Olds's observations, Olds and Milner (1954) implanted electrodes into many different areas of the rat brain and made the brain stimulation of the animal dependent on its pressing a bar in a Skinner box (Figure 5.13). They found that rats quickly learned to press the bar to receive brain stimulation. Subsequent studies demonstrated that many species, including dogs (Wauquier & Sadowski, 1978), primates (Aou & others, 1988), and humans (Ervin & others, 1969), find electrical stimulation of particular brain areas reinforcing.

➤Checkpoint

Based on what you learned about the hypothalamus in Chapter 2, why would you expect stimulation of the hypothalamus to be reinforcing?

The Influence of the Medial Forebrain Bundle

In the 1960s, researchers suggested that a pathway of nerve fibers, the **medial forebrain bundle (MFB),** which interconnects areas in the limbic system with brain stem structures, is the physical location of the reinforcement mechanism (Margules & Stein, 1967; Stein & Wise, 1973). The MFB fiber system appeared to be a sort of "reinforcement center." The researchers based this suggestion on the finding that stimulation of the MFB has four characteristics: It is highly reinforcing, it motivates behavior, its functioning is stimulated by reinforcers, and its reinforcing effects are enhanced by deprivation. We discuss each of these characteristics in turn.

medial forebrain bundle (MFB)
A pathway of nerve fibers that interconnects structures in the limbic system with brain stem areas; considered part of the reinforcement system of the brain.

The Reinforcing Influence of MFB Stimulation

Back in the United States, Sam has recovered from his wounds and is enjoying some leisure time. He places a dollar in a video poker machine and pulls the lever. The hand he "draws" consists of four aces and a jack—he has won $200. He pumps his right fist and cries, "Yessss!" One explanation for Sam's joy at having won is stimulation of his MFB fiber system.

In early studies of the reinforcing properties of MFB stimulation, researchers found that rats would press a bar at high rates for brain stimulation, and in one study, animals literally starved to death when given the choice of bar pressing either for MFB stimulation or for food (Routtenberg & Lindy, 1965). Such apparently reinforcing properties of MFB fiber system stimulation were also found in humans. For example, Ervin and colleagues (1969) reported that MFB stimulation in cancer patients not only eliminated pain but also produced euphoria. Sem-Jacobson (1968) found that patients suffering intense depression, fear, or physical pain experienced brain stimulation as pleasurable; subjects who felt well before electrical stimulation of the brain (ESB) experienced only mild pleasure.

stimulus-bound behavior Behavior motivated by brain stimulation in the presence of appropriate environmental stimuli.

The Motivational Influence of MFB Stimulation

At the bank, Sam cashes the $50 birthday check he has received from an aunt, receiving two $20 bills and one $10 bill. In all likelihood, he experiences a little pleasure from feeling the bills in his palm. Sam might save the money for next week's grocery bill, or he might take it to the casino today and play video poker. What do you think Sam will do? Of course, he goes to the casino. Spending the money right away demonstrates that reinforcers often have both pleasurable and motivating properties. The pleasurable property is the feeling Sam experiences when he receives the reinforcer (money); his desire to perform another behavior (spend it) demonstrates the motivating property.

On a more personal level, you may find it very reinforcing to receive a good grade on a test in your biological psychology class. The way you feel when you see the letter or number on your test paper illustrates the pleasurable properties of the event. Your desire to study hard for the next exam shows the motivational properties of the good grade.

Valenstein and colleagues (1969) demonstrated that the specific response motivated by brain stimulation depends on the prevailing environmental conditions: Brain stimulation motivates eating when food is available and drinking when water is available. This phenomenon is called **stimulus-bound behavior.**

Obviously, we do not have electrodes implanted in our MFB fiber system; the neurons there must be activated by naturally occurring processes. We now know that reinforcement and deprivation naturally stimulate the MFB fiber system and increase our search for reinforcement.

The Influence of Reinforcers on the MFB Fiber System

Sam finds sexual activity with his wife more pleasurable after watching an erotic film. We can speculate that the movie activates his MFB fiber system, which then increases the reinforcing quality of sex. A number of studies have demonstrated that a reinforcing activity, or a stimulus associated with a reinforcing activity, enhances the functioning of the structures connected by the MFB fiber system (e.g., septal area, lateral hypothalamus).

For example, one study found that rats pressed a bar to receive ESB significantly more often when water was present than when it was absent (Mendelson, 1967). Similarly, other studies found that the presence of food increased attempts to obtain brain stimulation (Coons & Cruce, 1968) and that a peppermint odor or a few drops of sugar in the mouth had the same effect (Hoebel, 1969). These results suggest that the presence of reinforcement enhances MFB functioning, which leads to increased responses to reinforcers. Reinforcers may then become more pleasurable because of the higher level of MFB activity. Thus, watching an erotic film may activate Sam's MFB, which motivates him to engage in sexual activity, which he finds pleasurable because it further stimulates his MFB fiber system.

The Influence of Deprivation on the MFB Fiber System

Sam goes to the ballpark on a hot day and drinks several beers. The next time he goes to the ballpark, it is cold, and he drinks only one beer. The effect of deprivation on MFB functioning may explain the difference in Sam's behavior.

Deprivation can be defined as a restriction in access to a reinforcer. Drinking something cold is satisfying on a hot day but has less incentive value on a cold day. This illustrates one characteristic of deprivation: A physiological need increases the incentive value of reinforcers (Klein, 2002). Thirst on a hot day enhances the reinforcement value of ice water or a cold beer. Increased activity in the reinforcement system of the brain is one probable mechanism for this enhancement. In support of this mechanism, Brady (1961) showed that the rate of self-stimulation by a rat directly depended on its hunger level; greater hunger led to a higher rate of bar pressing. Similarly, Olds (1962) found that water deprivation enhanced the value of brain stimulation.

In summary (Figure 5.14), MFB fiber system activity is reinforcing. Environmental reinforcers such as food and drink, and internal needs such as hunger, thirst, and the desire for sex, apparently activate the MFB fiber system and associated structures, and stimulating this system motivates the behavior necessary to obtain reinforcers. Psychoactive drugs, such as cocaine, nicotine, and heroin, act on the same brain reinforcement system, with the craving for a drug acting in the same manner as hunger or thirst.

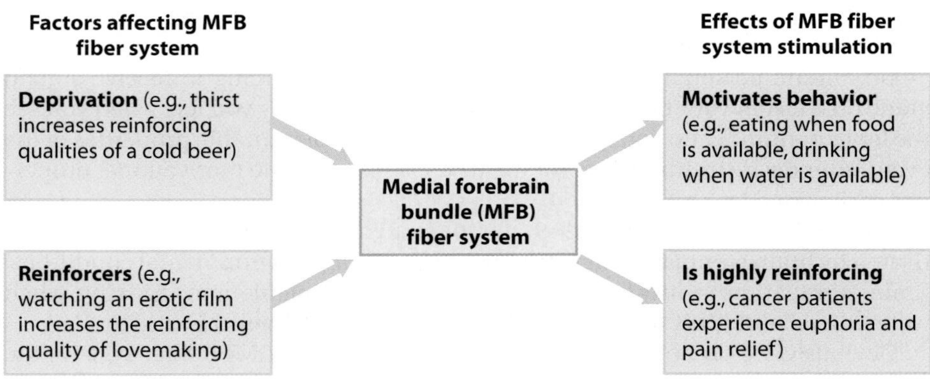
Factors affecting MFB fiber system
Effects of MFB fiber system stimulation
Deprivation (e.g., thirst increases reinforcing qualities of a cold beer)
Reinforcers (e.g., watching an erotic film increases the reinforcing quality of lovemaking)
Medial forebrain bundle (MFB) fiber system
Motivates behavior (e.g., eating when food is available, drinking when water is available)
Is highly reinforcing (e.g., cancer patients experience euphoria and pain relief)

Figure 5.14
The medial forebrain bundle (MFB) fiber system and reinforcement
Deprivation and reinforcement act on the MFB fiber system, motivating behavior; stimulation is highly reinforcing.

→ *What other reinforcers act on the MFB fiber system?*

Checkpoint

Explain how scientists discovered the effect of the medial forebrain bundle fiber system on reinforcement. How might acquiring money act on the MFB fiber system? Would a person's need for money or the amount of money acquired affect the influence of the MFB on the motivating qualities of the money?

The Mesolimbic Reinforcement System

As we have indicated, the neurotransmitter dopamine is involved in all addictions, which implies that it is also involved in reinforcement. Indeed, dopaminergic pathways are important components of the reinforcement system of the brain. Dopaminergic neurons originate in two midbrain areas: the substantia nigra and the ventral tegmental area. Cells of the substantia nigra form the *nigrostriatal pathway,* which projects, as its name implies, to the striatum. This pathway is primarily involved in movement and action, as we see in Chapter 8. Cells from the ventral tegmental area form the **mesolimbic reinforcement system (MRS)**; Figure 5.15), which courses through the MFB to end in various limbic structures, such as the amygdala, septal area, and, in particular, the *nucleus accumbens* (DeSousa & Vaccarino, 2001). There are also projections to the frontal cortex.

Dopaminergic Control of Reinforcement

Dopamine plays a key role in regulating the behavioral effects of reinforcement (Schultz, 2002; Wise, 2002). The neurotransmitter governs the activity of the neurons that connect the ventral tegmental area to the nucleus accumbens, septum, and frontal cortex (Figure 5.15). Several lines of evidence indicate that dopamine plays an important role in the effect of reinforcement on behavior.

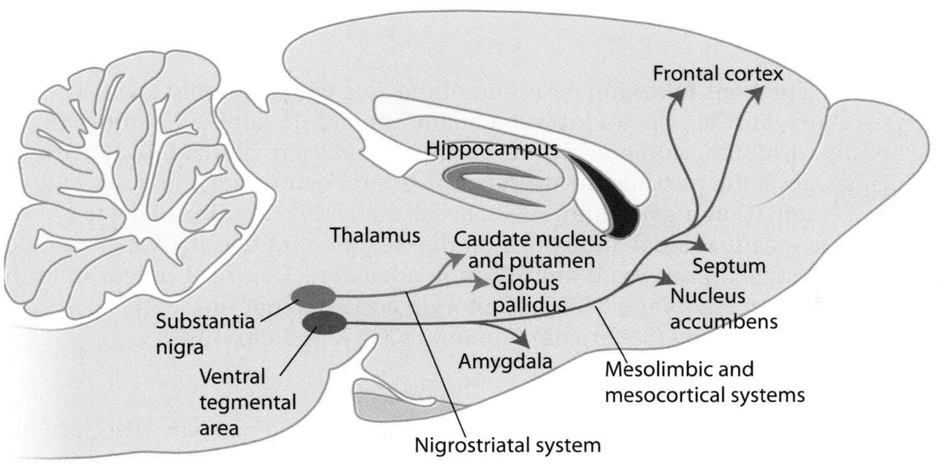

Figure 5.15

Structures of the mesolimbic reinforcement system in the rat brain (sagittal plane) The mesolimbic pathway (red) begins in the ventral tegmental area and travels through the medial forebrain bundle fiber system to the amygdala, nucleus accumbens, septum, and frontal cortex. The nigrostriatal pathway (blue) begins in the substantia nigra and projects to the striatum (caudate nucleus, putamen, and globus pallidus).

→ **How are these structures involved in the experience of pleasure produced by cocaine and heroin?**

One indication of dopaminergic influence is the effect of the dopamine agonists amphetamine and cocaine, which have powerful reinforcing properties (Figure 5.16). Evelyn, in our opening vignette, is highly motivated to obtain cocaine. The reinforcing property of cocaine, and of amphetamines, results in part from their ability to activate the dopaminergic mesolimbic pathway. Many researchers have shown that animals quickly learn a behavior that enables them to self-administer amphetamine (e.g., Bush & others, 1999) and cocaine (e.g., Norman & others, 1999). They also learn to perform at a high rate any behavior that triggers cocaine or amphetamine injection into the nucleus accumbens (Carr & White, 1986). Further, studies have revealed elevated dopamine levels in the nucleus accumbens after the administration of amphetamine or cocaine (Carboni & others, 2000; Zhang & others, 2001).

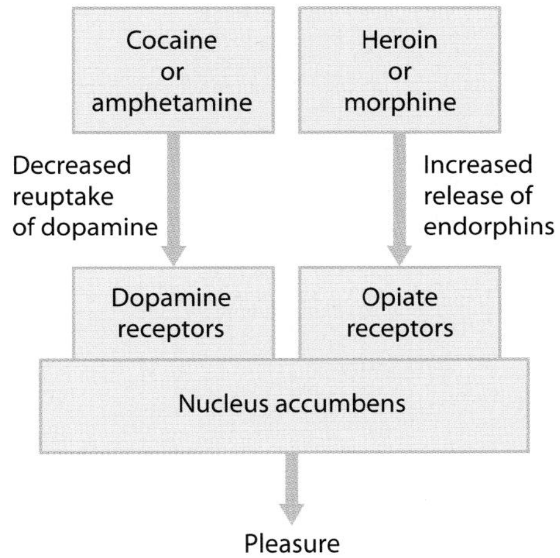

Figure 5.16

The separate mechanism by which cocaine and heroin activate the nucleus accumbens Activity in the nucleus accumbens produces extreme pleasure.

→ **Why do cocaine and heroin activate the nucleus accumbens by different mechanisms?**

Reinforcers other than cocaine and amphetamine trigger dopamine release, providing further support for dopaminergic involvement in the neural control of reinforcement. For example, electrical stimulation of the lateral hypothalamus (You & others, 2001), the MFB (Gardner, 2002), and the ventral tegmental area (Fiorino & others, 1993; Gardner) causes dopamine release in the nucleus accumbens. When animals perform a behavior for stimulation of the MFB or ventral tegmental area, dopamine is also released. Natural reinforcers, such as food and water, also cause the release of dopamine in the nucleus accumbens, probably because of the reinforcing properties of drinking or eating in water- or food-deprived animals (Bassareo & Di Chiara, 1999). In addition, stimuli associated through conditioning with a natural reinforcer increase dopamine levels in the nucleus accumbens (Datla & others, 2002). Researchers have found increased dopamine levels in the nucleus accumbens following the administration of alcohol (Melendez & others, 2002), cannabis (Mechoulam & Parker, 2003), and nicotine (Fadda & others, 2003).

Studies on animals with impaired functioning of dopaminergic neurons in the mesolimbic pathway further support the dopaminergic control of reinforcement. For example, destruction of dopaminergic neurons in this pathway weakens the reinforcing properties of both electrical stimulation and dopamine agonists such as amphetamine and cocaine (Gerrits & Van Ree, 1996). In addition, drugs that block dopamine receptors cause animals to reduce or stop behaviors they have been using to obtain cocaine or amphetamine (Fletcher, 1998) or alcohol (Files & others, 1998).

Although we have focused here on the involvement of dopamine in reward, evidence implicates other neurotransmitters as well (Bardo, 1998). For example, treatment with serotonin agonists may facilitate reward-related behavior (Sasaki-Adams & Kelley, 2001), and the infusion of serotonin into the ventral tegmental area enhances the release of dopamine in the nucleus accumbens (Van Bockstaele & others, 1994). Other studies have found an increase in dopamine release in the

mesolimbic reinforcement system (MRS) The brain reinforcement system traveling from the ventral tegmental area through the MFB to end in limbic structures, particularly the nucleus accumbens.

nucleus accumbens following perfusion of the area with serotonin agonists (Yan & Yan, 2001). Further, dopaminergic metabolism and dopamine neurons are affected by serotonin, norepinephrine, GABA, opioid, and cannabinoid neurons, which suggests the possible involvement of several neurotransmitter systems in reinforcement (Comings & Blum, 2000). Recall our earlier mention of the use of rimonabant, a cannabinoid antagonist, in the treatment of obesity (which can be seen as an addiction to food) and nicotine addiction. The involvement of both nicotinic ACh receptors and GABA receptors in dopaminergic reward mechanisms has also been reported (Soderpalm & others, 2000; Xi & Stein, 1998).

Opiate Activation of the Mesolimbic Pathway

The opiate drugs also appear to stimulate the mesolimbic pathway (Vaccarino & others, 1989). Animals can learn to self-administer the opiates heroin or morphine just as they learn to self-administer amphetamine and cocaine (Li & others, 2003; Mierzejewski & others, 2003), although the opiates appear less reinforcing than the stimulants. Animals also will press a bar to receive injections of morphine into the ventral tegmental area (Devine & Wise, 1994) or injections of an endogenous opiate into the nucleus accumbens (Goeders & others, 1984). Injection of opiate antagonists causes rats to stop bar pressing for stimulation of the nucleus accumbens (Trujillo & others, 1989).

Studies suggest that opiate drugs activate opiate receptors rather than dopamine receptors (see Figure 5.16). For example, drugs that antagonize dopamine receptors reduce self-administration of amphetamine or cocaine but do not affect self-stimulation by opiate drugs (Ettenberg & others, 1982). Also, the destruction of dopaminergic neurons in the nucleus accumbens decreased cocaine intake without influencing heroin self-administration (Gerrits & Van Ree, 1996). An opposite pattern is found when opiate receptors are blocked. Walker and colleagues (2000) have reported that opiate antagonists cause animals to stop self-administering heroin.

Koob (1992) suggested that the mesolimbic pathway contains two separate types of receptors, and that dopaminergic agonists activate dopamine receptors and opiates stimulate opiate receptors, with the same result: dopamine release in the nucleus accumbens—and pleasure (see Figure 5.16). In support of this idea, Gianoulakis (2004) has reported that stimulation of opioid receptors in either the ventral tegmental area or the nucleus accumbens increases the release of dopamine in the nucleus accumbens.

Individual Differences in the Functioning of the Mesolimbic Reinforcement System

Some people find gambling highly reinforcing; others can take it or leave it. Although these differences could be the result of different reinforcement experiences (people who like gambling have been reinforced for it, and people who dislike gambling have not), variations in the functioning of the mesolimbic reinforcement system also could be involved. Individual differences in responding to other reinforcers, both drug and nondrug, also could reflect differences in the functioning of the reinforcement system of the brain.

DeSousa and Vaccarino (2001) have suggested that the motivational and reinforcing effects of reinforcers are positively correlated with activity level in the mesolimbic reinforcement system. One way to assess this idea is to examine the activity of this system in animals that respond differently to various reinforcers. For example, some rats consume high levels of sucrose (high sucrose feeders, or HSFs), whereas others consume low levels (low sucrose feeders, or LSFs). Sills and colleagues (1998) found greater dopamine release in the nucleus accumbens of HSFs that were given access to sucrose than in LSFs given the same access. One interpretation is that HSFs find sucrose more reinforcing than do LSFs (and thus consume more sucrose), because the mesolimbic reinforcement system is more responsive to sucrose in HSFs.

If this is a valid interpretation, then HSFs should also be more responsive than LSFs to other reinforcers. Consistent with this interpretation, self-administration of amphetamine, which as we have noted is a powerful reinforcer that causes the release of dopamine in the nucleus accumbens, is indeed significantly higher in HSFs than in LSFs (DeSousa & others, 2000).

Animals also differ in their responsiveness to novel environments: Low responders (LRs) show much less locomotor response in a novel environment than do high responders (HRs). Not surprisingly, HRs self-administer amphetamine more than do LRs (Cain & others, 2004; Klebaur & others, 2001). Further, dopamine release in response to cocaine is significantly higher in HRs than in LRs (Hooks & others, 1992).

Let us return to the gambling example. Our discussion suggests that reinforcement (winning) releases more dopamine in the nucleus accumbens of people attracted to gambling than in those who are not attracted. And the greater release of dopamine is one reason some people gamble and others do not—and why some people smoke and others do not, and perhaps why gamblers seem so likely to smoke. The same biological mechanism—greater release of dopamine in the nucleus accumbens—might also be applied to people who frequently engage in dangerous behavior, who seek the thrill that they get from thwarting death or serious injury. In such individuals, the risky activity perhaps triggers the release of large amounts of dopamine in their nucleus accumbens.

Genes and Addiction

Genetic differences appear to be one important cause of the variability in response to reinforcers, which may explain why some people exhibit a greater potential for substance dependence (addiction) than others. According to one hypothesis, a defect in the dopaminergic system, caused by a variant of the D_2 receptor gene, causes people who have this variation to abuse certain substances in order to obtain greater stimulation of their dopaminergic reward system (Noble, 2000, 2003). The abused substances include alcohol, cocaine, nicotine, the opiates, and food. Comings and Blum (2000) cited an even greater number of addictive and impulsive disorders that might be caused by a genetic lack of dopamine D_2 receptors, including marijuana use, pathological gambling, sex addiction, chronic violence, and antisocial behavior.

As we pointed out earlier, several different neurotransmitter systems can modify dopamine metabolism and dopaminergic neurons. Comings and Blum (2000) have proposed a reward deficiency syndrome that could involve defects in various genes responsible for neurotransmitters such as serotonin, norepinephrine, and GABA, all of which can affect dopamine transmission. Individuals with reward deficiency syndrome would be at risk for abusing "unnatural rewards" such as alcohol, cocaine, heroin, and gambling.

A defect in the gene for one of the opioid receptors, the mu opioid receptor, also has been implicated in alcohol addiction (Rommelspacher & others, 2001) and in heroin addiction (Szeto & others, 2001). Rommelspacher and colleagues have suggested that the pattern of physiological results seen in alcohol-dependent subjects with the variant gene indicates a reduced activity in dopaminergic neurons along with a compensating increase in dopamine receptor activity. Dopamine involvement occurs because the dopaminergic reward system is sensitive to both alcohol and opioids. The researchers concluded that genetic differences in the sensitivity of the opioid system to alcohol may underlie the development of alcohol substance abuse.

Although the dopaminergic reward system may be responsible for initiating drug self-administration, Volkow and Fowler (2000) have suggested that a dysfunction of the orbitofrontal cortex (the part of the frontal lobes that lies above the eyes) may have a role in continued craving, even after tolerance to the abused substance develops. Because the orbitofrontal cortex is involved in drive and compulsive repetitive behaviors, its abnormal activation by drug use might explain the compulsive drug-seeking behaviors of the addict. In support of this idea, neuroimaging studies have revealed hypoactivity in the orbitofrontal cortex of addicts during drug withdrawal, and hyperactivity when subjects are tested shortly after their last drug use or during drug-induced craving. Based on this model, Volkow and Fowler suggest that drugs that interfere with the activation of the orbitofrontal cortex might be beneficial in treating drug addiction. Examples of such drugs include gamma vinyl GABA (GVG) for treating cocaine or nicotine addiction (Dewey & others, 1998, 1999) and phentermine, either alone or in combination with fenfluramine, for treating cocaine abuse (Glowa & others, 1997). The combination of fenfluramine and phentermine, called fen-phen, was at one time prescribed for treating obesity. However, some people developed heart-valve disease while taking fen-phen, and the drug was taken off the market. We have more to say about these drugs in Chapter 10.

Here we have highlighted the possible influence of genes on addictive behavior, but it is important to keep in mind that behavior is always a complex interaction of genetic potential and individual experiences. Previous experience with reinforcement undoubtedly plays a key role in how a person responds to subsequent reinforcement. An early experience that results in a large amount of reinforcement might predispose a person with little genetic potential for addiction to become addicted.

Checkpoint

Describe the two dopaminergic pathways that originate in different midbrain structures. What is the role of dopamine in amphetamine and cocaine addiction? In opiate addiction? In nicotine addiction?

REVIEW

- Early self-stimulation research on laboratory animals suggested the importance of the medial forebrain bundle (MFB) fiber system in reinforcement. Environmental reinforcers and internal need states activate the MFB and associated brain areas.
- The mesolimbic reinforcement system mediates the influence of reward on behavior. Dopamine controls the activity of neurons in the mesolimbic reinforcement system and thus plays a major role in the behavioral effects of reinforcement.
- The pleasurable effects of amphetamine and cocaine may result from the activation of dopaminergic receptors in the mesolimbic pathway, and the pleasurable effects of opiate agonists such as heroin and morphine may result from the stimulation of opiate receptors in the same pathway.
- Opiate agonists and dopamine agonists activate different receptors in the mesolimbic pathway, with the same end result: activation of the nucleus accumbens.
- Evidence indicates a genetic component to addiction, involving dysfunction in the dopaminergic reward system.

Use of Opiate Agonists to Treat Heroin Addiction

As we have described in this chapter, heroin is an endorphin agonist, binding to opiate receptors and mimicking the effects of naturally occurring endorphins; it produces feelings of pleasure by activating the mesolimbic pathway; and repeated heroin use leads to physical and psychological dependence.

Until recently, the assumption was that heroin addicts could not overcome their dependence on the drug. Now, however, heroin addiction can in many cases be treated with a combination of intense psychological counseling and the administration of methadone (Julien, 2005). Methadone is an endorphin agonist that, like heroin, binds to opiate receptors (Figure 5.17). In fact, **methadone** is an opioid drug with effects similar to those of heroin. Unlike heroin, which is broken down in the digestive tract, methadone can be taken in pill form. In this form, the effects of methadone develop gradually over several hours rather than producing

methadone An opioid drug with pleasurable effects similar to those of heroin, used to treat heroin addiction.

the "rush" associated with the IV injection of heroin and other opiates. Methadone alleviates the craving for heroin and prevents the withdrawal symptoms that otherwise would result from abstinence.

The methadone user thus substitutes a less powerful opioid for heroin. Methadone maintenance treatment aims to rehabilitate the heroin-dependent person by reducing illicit drug use, the incidence of diseases associated with intravenous drug use, and crime (Julien, 2005). Providing the appropriate daily methadone dose is crucial to the success of methadone maintenance programs. Doses that are too low may result in withdrawal, craving, and relapse into heroin use; therefore, drug prescribers must be able to adjust the recommended dosage to fit the needs of the addicted individual. To illustrate, in one study of patients in a methadone-maintenance program who continued to use heroin, increasing the dose of methadone above the 50 mg used at the beginning of the study proved effective in reducing heroin use (Preston & others, 2000).

Early studies of methadone programs suggested that heroin addicts stopped taking heroin and eventually gave up methadone. Criminal activity also diminished. However, later research suggests that these early evaluations were unreasonably optimistic and that the majority of patients relapsed to heroin use (Amato & others, 2003). Persuading heroin users to seek treatment has proved difficult. Also, individuals who receive methadone treatment often switch from heroin to other drugs, such as alcohol, barbiturates, cocaine, or amphetamines. And methadone itself has become an illicit street drug, with the same harmful consequences as heroin use.

Alternatives to methadone treatment have been developed. For example, *LAAM (levo-alpha acetylmethadol)* is a methadone relative approved in 1993 for the management of opioid dependence in heroin addicts (Julien, 2005). LAAM's longer lasting effect (72 hours vs. 24 hours) means that the individual takes an oral dose only two or three times a week rather than daily. In a meta-analysis of studies comparing the efficacy of LAAM relative to methadone, LAAM seemed to be more effective at reducing heroin use (Clark & others, 2002). Unfortunately, more individuals in the LAAM group stopped taking their medication, although many switched to methadone.

Buprenorphine (Buprenex) is another alternative for heroin abusers. Unlike methadone and LAAM, buprenorphine is a partial opioid agonist rather than a full agonist. It binds tightly to opioid mu receptors but produces less of a stimulating effect than the full agonists, which means there is a ceiling on both its euphoric properties and its depression of respiration. As we indicated earlier, buprenorphine can be prescribed by physicians who are not specially licensed. In addition, it is effective in maintenance therapy for heroin dependence, although not more effective than methadone (Gerra & others, 2004; Mattick & others, 2004).

Despite drawbacks for each of the drugs approved for opioid replacement therapy, the opioid maintenance model seems to offer greater public health benefits than opioid detoxification treatment (Krantz & Mehler, 2004). This approach is widely accepted in Europe and is now being applied in the United States.

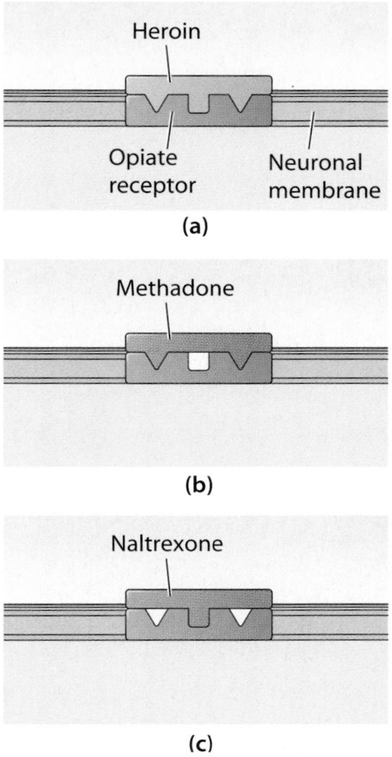

Figure 5.17
The effects of heroin, methadone, and naltrexone on opiate receptors (a) Heroin attaches to opiate receptors. **(b)** Methadone also binds to opiate receptors, but not as closely, and **(c)** naltrexone attaches to opiate receptors even less strongly.

How does naltrexone prevent heroin from producing pleasuarble effects?

Use of an Opiate Antagonist to Treat Heroin and Alcohol Addiction

One difficulty with methadone maintenance therapy is that methadone is an addictive drug, albeit one with less intense effects than those of heroin. An alternative to opioid agonist treatment may be the use of the opiate antagonist **naltrexone** (see Figure 5.17), which binds to the same opiate receptors as heroin and methadone and blocks the action of heroin and other opiates. Without the rush and high of heroin, drug craving might decline, along with the destructive behaviors associated with drug use. In fact, Gerra and colleagues (1995) found that naltrexone does reduce the cravings for heroin and other opiates.

naltrexone An opiate antagonist that binds to opiate receptors and blocks the action of heroin and other opiates.

Unfortunately, there are major drawbacks in using naltrexone to treat heroin dependence. For one thing, naltrexone treatment reduces tolerance to heroin, which means that the heroin dose used before taking naltrexone may be an overdose after taking naltrexone. In fact, an Australian study found a significantly elevated risk of nonfatal heroin overdose after naltrexone treatment (Ritter, 2002). Ritter suggested that clinicians should warn patients of the reduction in tolerance when prescribing naltrexone and noted that agonist treatments have much less risk of overdose.

Another drawback is that the individual must take naltrexone daily. Patient compliance is often poor, and only individuals highly motivated to quit are likely to continue to take naltrexone. One possible answer to the compliance problem is to use an intramuscular injection of naltrexone in a suspension (forming a "depot") that releases the drug gradually, over a period of weeks or months. Clinical trials have found that treatment with a depot opioid antagonist is safe and more effective than oral administration, with improved patient retention in the programs and better compliance (Carreno & others, 2003; Comer & others, 2002).

Recently, an approach to maintenance therapy using a combination of an opioid agonist and antagonist has been approved. Suboxone, the combination of buprenorphine (agonist) and naloxone (antagonist), has been studied in a short-term opioid detoxification program (Amass & others, 2004). In the study, medication compliance was high, and 68% of the subjects completed the detoxification. In an Australian study, a selected group of patients on buprenorphine maintenance was switched to Suboxone and allowed to take the combination medication without supervision (Bell & others, 2004). Suboxone was well tolerated, and 15 of the 17 recruited subjects remained in the trial for a full 6 months. This suggests that in a carefully selected group of former opioid abusers, Suboxone might be effective for maintenance therapy under minimal supervision.

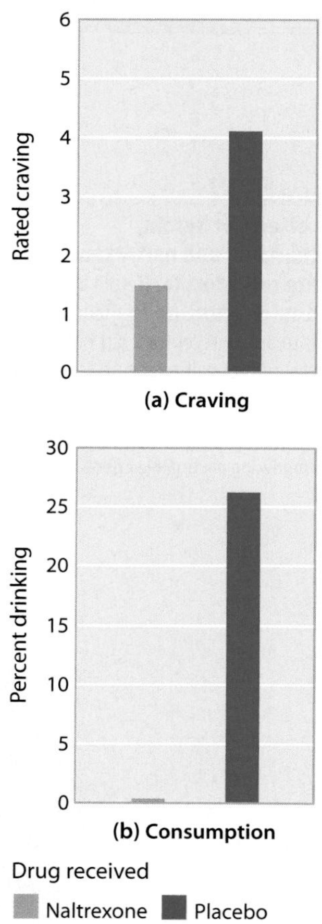

Figure 5.18

The effects of naltrexone on alcohol craving and consumption The administration of naltrexone to individuals with a history of alcohol abuse reduced craving for alcohol and stopped its consumption.

→ **How does naltrexone reduce the craving for alcohol?**

Naltrexone, which decreases the craving for alcohol in alcoholics (Mann, 2004; Rohsenow, 2004), has also been used for treating alcohol abuse. For example, Volpicelli and colleagues (1992) gave two groups of alcohol abusers either naltrexone or a placebo for 12 weeks. Naltrexone led to weaker cravings for alcohol than did the placebo (Figure 5.18). Further, the level of alcohol consumption was significantly lower in the naltrexone treatment group.

Pettinati and colleagues (2000) observed that naltrexone was an effective treatment for the alcohol abusers who adhered to the prescribed treatment, whereas for noncompliant individuals, relapse rates were comparable to those for placebo-treated subjects (43% vs. 40%, respectively). In another study, patients with either high levels of craving for alcohol or those with a strong family history of problems with alcohol were more likely than other alcoholics to benefit from naltrexone treatment (Monterosso & others, 2001). In addition, O'Brien and colleagues (1996) reported that naltrexone provided a useful pharmacological adjunct to a psychosocial intervention program, particularly if the patients attended all the sessions. Finally, Berg and coworkers (1996) concluded that naltrexone offers significant therapeutic benefits at relatively low risk.

As we indicated above, compliance with treatment can be improved by using long-lasting intramuscular depots of the drug. This approach has also been used with alcohol-dependent subjects (Garbutt & others, 2005). A high dose of long-acting naltrexone (380 mg) produced a 25% decrease in heavy drinking days relative to a placebo, and a low dose (190 mg) resulted in a 17% decrease. These results suggest that long-acting naltrexone may be beneficial in treating alcohol dependence.

A review of animal studies of opiate and alcohol addiction revealed that opiate antagonists reduce alcohol intake in rats without affecting the intake of other biological reinforcers such as food or water (Ulm & others, 1995; Bienkowski & others, 1999). Another study found that the administration of an opiate antagonist into the nucleus accumbens of rats decreased ethanol intake (Heyser & others,

1999), which suggests that the beneficial effects of opiate antagonists in humans lie in their ability to block opiate receptors in the nucleus accumbens.

As we have noted, alcohol, like the opiates, is an opiate agonist that increases the stimulation of opiate receptors. The desirable effects of alcohol stem at least in part from this action on opiate receptors in the reinforcement system of the brain. By blocking the effect of alcohol on this system, naltrexone reduces the craving for and consumption of alcohol.

In general, dopaminergic and opiate antagonists suppress drug self-administration rates and brain-stimulation rates in laboratory animals. In some cases, however, such response rates have actually risen rather than fallen after exposure to dopaminergic and opiate antagonists (Corrigall & Coen, 1991; Maldonado & others, 1993). For example, Maldonado and colleagues found that following injection of a dopaminergic antagonist into the nucleus accumbens of rats, the self-administration of cocaine increased significantly. These researchers suggested that the dopaminergic antagonist reduced cocaine's reinforcer value, and therefore the rats increased self-administration to compensate for this lower value.

Finally, alcohol, like the other dependence-producing drugs, stimulates the dopaminergic reward system. And several other neurotransmitter systems can affect dopamine release in the nucleus accumbens, including some of the nicotinic receptors of the brain. In fact, the dopamine-activating properties of alcohol are enhanced by subchronic nicotine treatment (i.e., by smoking), which suggests a neurological explanation for the frequently observed co-abuse of alcohol and nicotine (Soderpalm & others, 2000). In addition, this association suggests that selectively blocking these particular nicotinic ACh receptors could lead to a new pharmacological treatment for alcoholism and, not coincidentally, to a new treatment for nicotine addiction.

Checkpoint

How is an opioid agonist used to treat heroin addiction? How is an opioid antagonist used to treat heroin addiction? Alcohol addiction?

REVIEW

- The opiate antagonist naltrexone may be a useful alternative to methadone treatment for heroin addiction, particularly if used as depot injections.
- Suboxone, a combination opioid agonist and antagonist, may be useful for treating carefully selected detoxified opioid addicts.
- Because naltrexone decreases the craving for alcohol and nicotine in alcoholics, it may also be beneficial in the treatment of these addictions.

CHAPTER REVIEW

Key Terms

agonist (p. 152)
alcohol (p. 159)
alcoholism (p. 161)
amphetamine (p. 164)
anandamide (p. 174)
antagonist (p. 152)
anxiolytic (p. 162)
barbiturate (p. 161)
benzodiazepine (p. 162)
caffeine (p. 164)
cocaine (p. 164)
codeine (p. 156)
depressant (p. 159)
false transmitter (p. 153)
half-life (p. 150)
heroin (p. 156)
inhalation (p. 150)
intracerebral injection (p. 149)
intramuscular (IM) injection (p. 149)
intraperitoneal (IP) injection (p. 149)
intravenous (IV) injection (p. 149)

intraventricular injection (p. 150)
lysergic acid diethylamide (LSD) (p. 170)
marijuana (p. 173)
MDMA (p. 171)
medial forebrain bundle (MFB) (p. 176)
mescaline (p. 170)
mesolimbic reinforcement system (MRS) (p. 178)
metabolite (p. 150)
methadone (p. 182)
morphine (p. 156)
naltrexone (p. 183)
nicotine (p. 165)
nonbarbiturate sedative-hypnotic drug (p. 161)
opioid (p. 156)
opium (p. 156)
oral ingestion (p. 149)
peyote (p. 170)
pharmacodynamics (p. 149)
pharmacokinetics (p. 149)
phencyclidine (PCP) (p. 171)
psychedelic drug (p. 170)
psychoactive drug (p. 148)
psychopharmacology (p. 149)
psychostimulant (p. 163)
sedative-hypnotic drug (p. 159)
stimulus-bound behavior (p. 177)
subcutaneous (SC) injection (p. 149)
substance abuse (p. 151)
substance dependence (p. 151)
THC (p. 173)
tolerance (p. 151)
withdrawal symptom (p. 151)

Suggested Readings

Carroll, C. R. (2000). *Drugs in modern society* (5th ed.). New York: McGraw-Hill.

Goode, E. (1998). *Drugs in American society* (5th ed.). New York: McGraw-Hill.

Julien, R. M. (2005). *A primer of drug action* (10th ed.). New York: Worth.

Olds, J., & Milner, P. M. (1954). Positive reinforcement produced by electrical stimulation of septal area and other regions of rat brain. *Journal of Comparative and Physiological Psychology, 47,* 419–427.

Ray, O., & Ksir, C. (2006). *Drugs, society, and human behavior* (11th ed.). New York: McGraw-Hill.

Vaccarino, F. J., Schiff, B., & Glickman, S. E. (1989). Biological view of reinforcement. In S. B. Klein & R. R. Mowrer (Eds.), *Contemporary learning theories: Instrumental conditioning theory and the impact of biological constraints on learning* (pp. 111–142). Hillsdale, NJ: Erlbaum.

Wise, R. A. (1996). Addictive drugs and brain stimulation reward. *Annual Review of Neuroscience, 19,* 319–340.

Critical Thinking Questions

1. Neal enjoys a few beers after work. He claims that it calms him after a hard day at the office. Is Neal correct about the calming effect of alcohol? Describe the physiological actions of alcohol. Could Neal substitute another drug for alcohol? Suggest several alternatives, and explain the basis of your suggestions.
2. Evelyn finds using cocaine extremely pleasurable. Describe the neural system involved in Evelyn's experience of pleasure from cocaine, and explain why cocaine is such a powerful reinforcer.
3. Why is heroin such a powerful reinforcer? Are the brain structures that produce the reinforcing effects of heroin the same as or different from those mediating the effects of cocaine? Give a possible explanation for the common or differing effects of these two drugs, based on what you have learned about their mechanisms of action and their mechanisms of reinforcement.

Fill-in-the-Blank Questions

1. Drugs that affect mental functioning are called ______.
2. ______ is the study of the effects of drugs on behavior.
3. ______ injections deliver drugs under the skin for slow absorption.
4. The time required for the body to eliminate half of a drug is the drug's ______.
5. Another name for substance dependence is ______.
6. A person who has developed ______ will require increasingly higher amounts of a drug to feel the same effect.
7. Drugs that mimic or enhance the way a neurotransmitter acts are called ______; drugs that block the activity of a neurotransmitter are called ______.
8. A(n) ______ is a drug that impairs synaptic transmission by binding to receptors and preventing the neurotransmitter from having its effect.
9. ______ is the main alkaloid compound obtained from the poppy plant.
10. ______ is a semisynthetic opioid made from reacting acetic anhydride with morphine.

11. Drugs that act on the CNS to slow down mental and physical functioning are called ______.
12. Another name for alcohol dependence is ______.
13. The sedative-hypnotic drugs derived from barbituric acid are called ______; long-acting drugs of this type are used as ______ in treating epilepsy.
14. Antianxiety drugs, also called ______, are used to reduce nervousness, anxiety, or fear.
15. Valium, Librium, and Xanax are trade names for drugs of the subclass called the ______.
16. ______ are drugs typically used to treat attention deficit hyperactivity disorder.
17. ______ is made by mixing cocaine hydrochloride with ammonia or baking soda and water.
18. ______ is a type of psychostimulant drug that is most commonly consumed in coffee in the United States.
19. The stimulating effect of caffeine results from increased activity in neurons that use ______ as the neurotransmitter.
20. Sometimes called hallucinogens, ______ drugs profoundly alter a person's state of consciousness, including sensory experiences.
21. ______ is a drug obtained from cactus tips that is used in Native American religious ceremonies.
22. Also called "acid," ______ is the classic example of a synthetic psychedelic drug.
23. First introduced as a surgical anesthetic in the 1950s, ______ is sometimes referred to as "angel dust."
24. ______ is a drug often used at large parties called "raves."
25. MDMA's euphoria-producing effect probably results from its stimulation of ______ receptors, whereas its mild hallucinogenic properties may result from its stimulation of ______ receptors.
26. ______ is a naturally occurring substance that binds to the brain's THC receptors.
27. Discovery of the reward areas in the brain is attributed to ______, a young social psychologist.
28. In a phenomenon called ______, brain stimulation motivates eating when food is available and drinking when water is available.
29. The ______ is the brain reinforcement system that includes the MFB fiber system.
30. ______ is the neurotransmitter that plays a key role in regulating the behavioral effects of reinforcement.
31. ______ is an opioid drug that resembles heroin and can be taken in pill form; it is used in treatment programs aimed at eliminating heroin addiction.
32. One alternative to methadone treatment may be the use of opiate antagonists, such as ______.

Multiple-Choice Questions

1. The study of the effects of drugs on behavior is
   a. psychoactivity.
   b. psychopharmacology.
   c. psychoneurology.
   d. psychophysiology.
2. Heroin reaches its sites of action in the brain sooner than morphine because heroin is
   a. more fat soluble.
   b. more water soluble.
   c. more likely to be ingested by inhalation.
   d. more likely to be administered orally.
3. Andy generally has several bottles of beer when he gets home, to unwind from work, and he usually kills the rest of a 12-pack before falling asleep on the sofa watching TV. The large quantity of beer Andy can consume before getting sleepy is caused by
   a. tolerance.
   b. abuse.
   c. withdrawal syndrome.
   d. addiction.
4. A drug that enhances the release of a neurotransmitter is referred to as a(n)
   a. antagonist.
   b. agonist.
   c. synapse.
   d. hallucinogen.
5. One way in which a drug can have an antagonistic effect is by
   a. increasing neurotransmitter release.
   b. blocking neurotransmitter degradation.
   c. producing the same effect on the postsynaptic membrane as the neurotransmitter.
   d. preventing the neurotransmitter from binding to the receptors.
6. Physostigmine, a cholinergic agonist, has its effect by ______ at the neuromuscular junction.
   a. mimicking the effect of ACh
   b. blocking ACh reuptake
   c. increasing ACh synthesis
   d. blocking the action of acetylcholinesterase
7. A drug that impairs synaptic transmission by binding to receptors and preventing the neurotransmitter from binding to them is called a
   a. false transmitter.
   b. fake antagonist.
   c. binding blocker.
   d. reuptake inhibitor.
8. ______ is a drug that decreases action at monoaminergic synapses by making the synaptic vesicles leaky.
   a. AMPT
   b. Reserpine
   c. Caffeine
   d. Botulinum toxin

9. Madelyn's doctor prescribed a long-acting pain medication when she was suffering from a ruptured vertebral disk. Madelyn no longer has the back pain, but she has continued taking her pain medication, which she now gets any way she can, even if it means forging her doctor's signature on a blank prescription form. Madelyn is probably addicted to
   a. Percodan c. OxyContin.
   b. Darvon. d. alprazolam.

10. Physical dependence on opioids such as heroin results from the suppression of
   a. endorphin production. c. anandamide production.
   b. appetite. d. pleasure.

11. At low doses, depressants act to
   a. produce drowsiness. c. reduce tension.
   b. relieve pain. d. create hallucinations.

12. _____ is made by fermenting grapes or other fruits and has an alcohol content of 10% to 14%.
   a. Beer c. Whiskey
   b. Wine d. Scotch

13. What blood alcohol level constitutes legal intoxication in all U.S. states?
   a. 0.01% c. 0.05%
   b. 0.03% d. 0.08%

14. Part of the effect of alcohol on functioning results from its influence on _____ receptors.
   a. $GABA_A$ c. THC
   b. $GABA_B$ d. BAC

15. The effect of high doses of sedative-hypnotic drugs is to
   a. reduce pain. c. relieve tension.
   b. induce sleep. d. suppress appetite.

16. Alcohol, antianxiety drugs, and barbiturates work by attaching to receptors on _____ neurons.
   a. dopaminergic c. GABAergic
   b. cholinergic d. serotonergic

17. _____ barbiturates are frequently used as anesthetics during surgery.
   a. Ultrashort-acting c. Long-acting
   b. Short-intermediate-acting d. Medium-short-acting

18. Because of Sean's anxiety about an upcoming job interview, his physician prescribed _____ for his situational anxiety.
   a. Prozac c. Darvon
   b. Xanax d. chloral hydrate

19. _____ drugs produce alertness by enhancing the function of the sympathetic nervous system and the reticular formation.
   a. Psychedelic c. Psychostimulant
   b. Analgesic d. Antianxiety

20. _____ is the most commonly abused amphetamine.
   a. Levoamphetamine c. Morphoamphetamine
   b. Dextroamphetamine d. Methamphetamine

21. Sigmund Freud was initially enthusiastic about the medical use of
   a. cocaine. c. amphetamine.
   b. demerol. d. caffeine.

22. The two primary effects of nicotine use are
   a. relaxation and mild euphoria.
   b. decreased metabolism and weight loss.
   c. increased alertness and reduced fatigue.
   d. increased metabolism and fatigue.

23. Amphetamine acts by increasing the release of
   a. glutamate and GABA. c. norepinephrine and dopamine.
   b. acetylcholine and serotonin. d. GABA and glycine.

24. Intense withdrawal symptoms on stopping the use of psychostimulants include
   a. wakefulness and appetite suppression.
   b. prolonged sleeping and depression.
   c. hallucinations and delusions.
   d. increased alertness and loss of appetite.

25. Psychedelic drugs are sometimes called _____, because they profoundly alter a person's state of consciousness, including sensory experiences.
   a. antipsychotics c. hallucinogens
   b. psychotics d. antidepressants

26. Native peoples of the Southwest have traditionally used the cactus-derived _____ to produce psychedelic experiences.
   a. peyote c. hashish
   b. LSD d. psilocin

27. Which of the following drugs once was of interest to psychotherapists because it facilitates communication?
   a. MDMA c. anandamide
   b. PCP d. THC

28. Anandamide is the natural chemical for receptors that also respond to
   a. PCP. c. THC.
   b. LSD. d. psilocybin.

29. Brain stimulation motivates eating when food is present and drinking when water is present, in a phenomenon called
   a. MFB stimulation.
   b. stimulus-response learning.
   c. stimulus-driven responding.
   d. stimulus-bound behavior.

30. Which of the following neurotransmitters appears to play a key role in the behavioral effects of reinforcement?
   a. GABA c. glycine
   b. acetylcholine d. dopamine

31. Research suggests that the reason some people are more attracted to gambling than others is that the reinforcement they receive causes
   a. a greater sense of relaxation.
   b. the release of more dopamine in their nucleus accumbens.
   c. the release of more sex hormone in their hypothalamus.
   d. an enhancement of the muscarinic effect of nicotine on their brains.

32. ______ is an opioid drug that, taken in pill form, is used to treat heroin addiction.
   a. Codeine
   b. Morphine
   c. Methadone
   d. Methamphetamine

Answers can be found on the companion website at www.worthpublishers.com/klein.

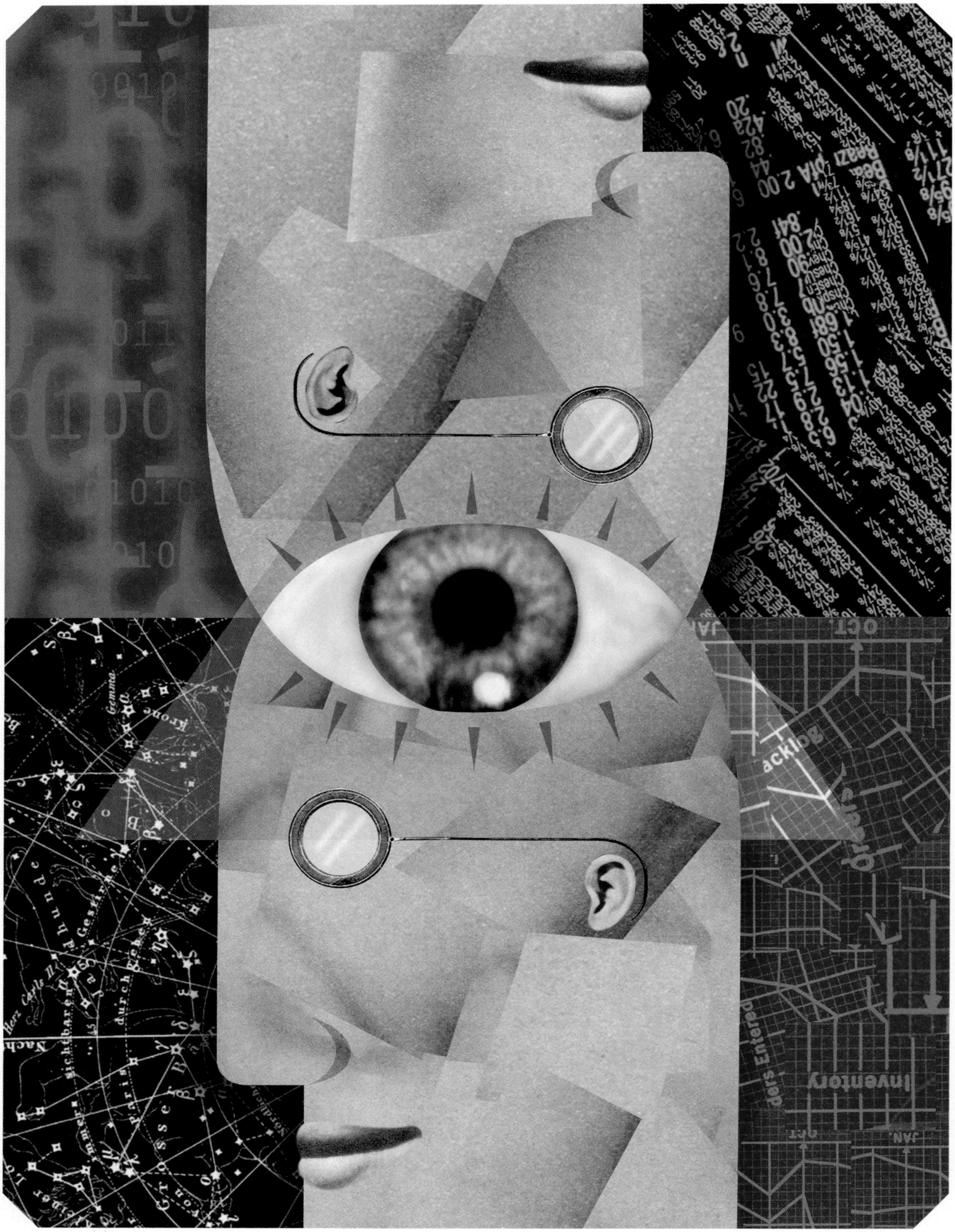

Vision

6

Out of Sight

Alan stared into the eyepiece, willing himself to see something. The same thing had just happened with his other eye—surely too much time was going by between flashes. Was he missing something he should have seen? But there, just on the edge of his vision, was that a tiny flash? He pressed the button. Long seconds crawled by before he saw another flash and pressed the button. He felt perspiration on his forehead. The test was too hard. Or maybe—and this was what worried him most—there really was something wrong with his eyesight. He saw another flash and pressed the button again. Finally, the visual field test was over, and Alan was back in the office, waiting to see Dr. Bradley, the ophthalmologist.

While he waited, he had time to worry. Could he be losing his sight? What would he do? Reading, watching movies, painting—these were his life. But he was letting his fears run away with him. Surely there was nothing really wrong.

At last Dr. Bradley came in. "I don't think I did all that well on the test," Alan said, his voice shaky.

"No, you didn't, Alan," the doctor said. "You've lost almost 20% of your peripheral vision."

"How can that be?" Alan asked, his heart thumping. "I'm not aware of any change."

"The mind's a wonderful thing, Alan," Dr. Bradley said. "It fills in the gaps in our vision. No one's aware of having a blind spot, a hole in their vision, but everyone does. Not only that, but we know of people who've lost a whole side of their visual field—half of what they see in front of them—without realizing it."

"Is there anything we can do, Dr. Bradley?"

"There isn't any treatment, " the doctor began, "but it's extremely unlikely you'll lose your central vision. And that means you'll be able to continue doing all the things you've been doing."

Alan began to feel calmer. He wanted to know why this had happened, why he'd lost some of his peripheral vision, but Dr. Bradley had said the magic words: It was extremely unlikely he would lose his central vision.

"You have something called optic nerve head drusen," she said, printing the last word for him on a prescription pad, "pronounced 'drew-sin,' which I noticed when I checked your retina. It's an inherited disorder. There are small, hard particles in the front part of your optic nerve. You've always had them, and they haven't caused any problems you're aware of. Most people with this condition don't have symptoms, and the drusen are usually detected during a routine eye exam."

"Any dietary changes I can make? Medication? Laser surgery?" The doctor shook her head. "Just come back every 6 months or so, and we'll do the visual field test again to check that the condition hasn't gotten any worse. Although drusen are almost always benign, in a very small percentage of cases, they do enlarge and then they begin to affect your sight."

Alan felt his heartbeat quicken and was sure his blood pressure had gone up, too. He knew he'd have some anxious moments in the next 6 months until he took the test again.

BEFORE YOU BEGIN

- **How does Alan's visual system recognize the words in the books he reads?**
- **What is the structure of the optic nerve, and how would drusen destroy Alan's peripheral vision?**
- **What path does a visual stimulus take through the visual system?**
- **What is light, and how is it converted into a neural signal?**
- **What processes enable Alan to read? To see his dog in the backyard at night?**
- **How do we perceive our world in three dimensions?**
- **What is the neurological basis of color vision?**

In this chapter, you will find the answers to these questions and many others.

Detecting Environmental Events: Transduction and Coding

Alan's fear about losing his vision reflects the importance of the visual sense. Try to imagine what it would be like to lose your sight—how would it affect your life at home, at school and work, and in your social and leisure activities? You could never see another sunrise or drive down the open highway, and you would have to learn to read with your fingers. Suppose Alan liked to visit Lake Tahoe, a resort area between California and Nevada, with a breathtaking view of the crystal clear lake surrounded by snow-capped mountains. If Alan's central vision were impaired, he would still be able to feel the cool breeze and smell the wildflowers, but he would be unable to see the mountains reflected in the lake or the eagle in flight above it. In this chapter, we discuss how the visual system enables us to perceive these beautiful aspects of our environment, as well as those that are more mundane or definitely not beautiful. Vision is just one of the senses, of course, and before examining it in detail, we need to consider some of the general principles of sensory detection.

Is the sky blue? Is the song loud? Is the ball smooth? Is the orange sweet? The function of our senses is to answer these and many other questions about environmental events. A **sense** is what we use to detect and react to stimuli, the mechanism that transforms environmental stimulation into information that the nervous system can use to form a picture of the world around us. The senses enable the nervous system to connect us with the outside world. We use our senses to detect significant events in our physical environment and then decide whether (and how) to respond to them.

The types of information detected by sensory receptors differ, but all of the receptors perform three basic functions: absorption, transduction, and coding. Sensory receptors first absorb physical energy from the environment. The particular kind of physical energy is different for each type of sensory receptor—the visual receptors absorb light energy from which they detect colors (and many other things as well), and the auditory receptors (discussed in Chapter 7) absorb energy from moving air molecules beating against the eardrum, which enables them to detect sounds.

After a sensory receptor absorbs the energy from an environmental stimulus, it must then convert that energy into a neural impulse. This process of **transduction**

sense The mechanism we use to detect and react to stimuli, so as to transform environmental stimulation into information the nervous system can use.

transduction The conversion of physical energy into a neural impulse.

differs for different sensory systems. Some sensory receptors follow the all-or-none law; that is, the receptor will fire and a neural impulse will be generated only if the level of depolarization is sufficient to reach a threshold value. For other sensory receptors, the level of response is determined by stimulus intensity—the greater the intensity, the higher the level of receptor response. In this chapter, we focus on how light is transduced into a neural message in the visual system; Chapter 7 describes the processes for several other sensory systems: the auditory sense (hearing), the vestibular sense (balance), the somatosenses (touch, temperature, pain), the gustatory sense (taste), and the olfactory sense (smell).

The sensory receptors generate a specific pattern of neural activity through a process called coding. **Coding** enables the nervous system to construct a representation of the physical world; that is, the coded message contains information about stimuli in the physical environment.

In Chapter 1, we briefly discussed Müller's doctrine of specific nerve energies, which states that the particular event detected by the brain depends on which nerve carries the message. One reason that the brain recognizes the meanings of different neural impulses is that different messages are carried by different neurons. For example, a particular set of neurons carries information to the brain about blue things, and a different set transmits messages about things that are loud. Sensory receptors transmit specific information about the environment through different neural connections to different parts of the cerebral cortex for analysis and decision making.

We can also detect differences in stimuli within a particular sensory system. For example, our visual system can detect that a car is either maroon or white. The gustatory system can detect that a food is sweet or bitter. The differences between maroon and white and between sweet and bitter are detected through two different types of coding.

In **labeled-line coding,** different receptors within a sensory system react to different stimulation. This type of coding occurs in the gustatory system, where separate taste receptors detect sweet and bitter. If a food is bitter, certain taste receptors are activated and transmit an action potential to the cerebral cortex, which recognizes that the food is bitter because of the activity in the set of cortical neurons activated only by bitter foods. We do not, however, have different sensory receptors for every color. Instead, the cerebral cortex recognizes a particular *pattern* of responses from a number of visual receptors to determine whether a color is maroon or white. The process that allows us to distinguish colors is referred to as **across-fiber pattern coding.**

These examples might suggest that labeled-line coding is the mechanism used by the gustatory system and across-fiber pattern coding is that used by the visual system, but the process of coding sensory information is of course more complex than this. The gustatory system uses across-fiber pattern coding when two flavors are combined; the taste of bittersweet candy, for example, is produced by across-fiber coding. Labeled-line coding is used in the visual system when a primary color, such as blue, activates a single type of visual sensory receptor. The visual sensory system, and how it receives and interprets the physical energy of light, is the main topic of this chapter.

coding A process involving a specific pattern of neural activity that contains information about stimuli in the environment.

labeled-line coding The type of coding in which information about a stimulus is determined by the particular receptor reacting to the stimulus.

across-fiber pattern coding The type of coding in which information about a stimulus is determined by the pattern of neural impulses.

Checkpoint

What type of physical energy is absorbed by the sensory receptors of the visual system to enable Alan to read a book? What type of coding is used in the visual perception of a bouquet of red roses? (Do not forget the green leaves and stems.)

REVIEW

- A sense is the mechanism the nervous system uses for detecting a specific set of stimuli.
- The three basic functions of all sensory receptors are absorption, transduction, and coding: absorbing physical energy from the environment; converting the energy into a neural stimulus; and generating a specific pattern of neural activity that enables the nervous system to construct a representation of the physical world.

> ➤ In labeled-line coding, different receptors within a sensory system react to different stimuli. In across-fiber pattern coding, a particular pattern of neural activity is produced by each kind of stimulus.

Components of the Visual System

The physical energy to which visual receptors respond is light, a form of electromagnetic radiation. Visible light—light detected by our visual system—is just a small part of the electromagnetic spectrum; other parts include television and radio broadcast bands, infrared rays, ultraviolet rays, radar, x-rays, and gamma radiation. We will return to the physical characteristics of light later in the chapter. First, to understand how the visual system detects light, we must look at the structure of the eye.

Figure 6.1
A cross-sectional view of the human eye This illustration shows the projection of the image of a pen onto the retina at the back of the eye.

➡ **At what point is the image turned right side up?**

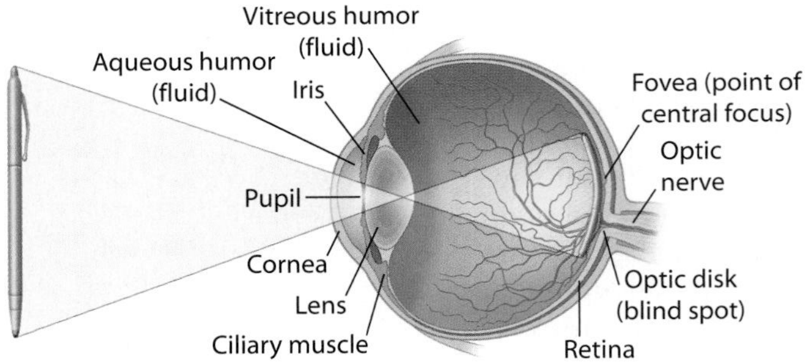

The Eye

If we are to see an object, a stimulus must be detected by the receptor cells located at the back of our eyes. These receptor cells, called **photoreceptors,** transmit information about the detected stimulus to other cells that transmit the information to the primary visual cortex, in the occipital lobe of the brain.

Figure 6.1 presents a cross-sectional view of an eye and the path of light. Light passes through the **cornea,** the transparent outer layer of the eyeball, and then through the **aqueous humor,** a clear fluid similar to blood plasma, in the anterior chamber (aqueous means "watery"). Behind the aqueous fluid is the **iris,** which consists of bands of muscles covered by colored tissue (blue, green, brown). Light passes through an opening in the iris called the **pupil.** In bright light the muscles of the iris cause the pupil to constrict (decrease in size), limiting the amount of light allowed into the eye. The pupil dilates (becomes larger) when the light is dim, allowing more light to enter the eye.

Because the muscles of the iris are innervated by the autonomic nervous system, pupil size also is related to emotions and interest. For example, great excitement, interest, and fear all stimulate the sympathetic nervous system, which causes the pupils to dilate. Remember this the next time you are in a car showroom. If you really like a particular model of car, chances are good that your pupils will dilate. If this happens and your salesperson is aware that dilated pupils signal great interest, your haggling over price might be much less effective. But before you rush out to purchase a pair of dark glasses, it should be noted that it is often difficult to detect changes in pupil size, particularly if the person has dark eyes.

After passing through the pupil, light reaches the **lens,** which consists of a series of transparent, onion-like layers of tissue. The shape of the lens, which changes to focus images on the retina, is controlled by the contraction of the **ciliary muscles** pulling on attached ligaments. The lens becomes more convex (rounded) to focus on nearby objects and less convex (flattened) to focus on distant objects. The change of the shape of the lens to maintain the focus of an image on the retina is called **accommodation** (Figure 6.2). After passing through the lens and a clear, jelly-like fluid called the **vitreous humor** (vitreous means "glassy"), light reaches the **retina,** the interior lining at the back of the eye. The process of accommodation by changing the shape of the lens is counterintuitive, if you compare it to how a film camera accomplishes the same feat. The camera moves the lens either closer to or farther from the light-sensitive film in order to adjust the focus.

The image focused on the retina, the **retinal image,** is not exactly like the stimulus that gave rise to the image. First, the focused image is upside down (Figure 6.1). Second, the image is reversed; that is, the right side of the image is focused on the left part of the retina, and the left side of the image on the right part of the

photoreceptor The receptor cell located at the back of the eye that transduces light into a neural impulse.

cornea The transparent outer layer of the eyeball.

aqueous humor A clear fluid that fills the anterior chamber of the eye.

iris Bands of muscles covered by the colored tissue of the eye.

pupil The opening in the iris through which light passes.

lens A structure made of a series of transparent, onionlike layers of tissue that changes shape to focus images on the retina.

ciliary muscle One of several muscles that control the shape of the lens of the eye.

accommodation The change of the shape of the lens to maintain the focus of an image on the retina.

vitreous humor A clear, jelly-like fluid between the lens and the retina.

retina The interior lining at the back of the eye that contains the photoreceptors.

retinal image The image focused on the retina; it is upside down and reversed relative to the stimulus that created it.

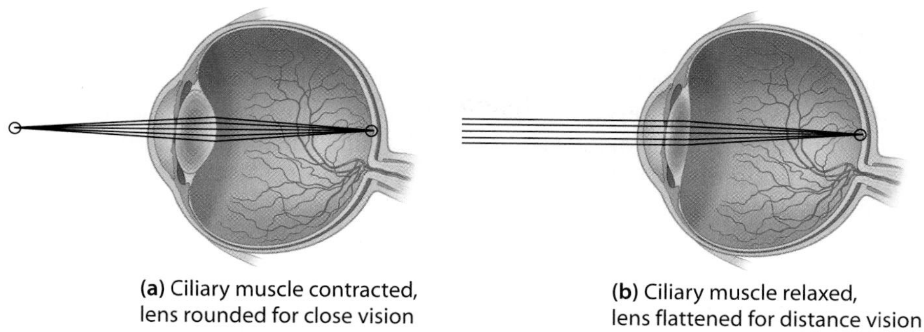

(a) Ciliary muscle contracted, lens rounded for close vision
(b) Ciliary muscle relaxed, lens flattened for distance vision

Figure 6.2
Accommodation The lens becomes (a) more convex (rounded) when focusing on a close object and (b) less convex (flattened) when focusing on a distant object.

→ **What is the path of the light after it passes through the lens?**

retina. This upside-down, backward image is encoded by the nervous system as neural activity and this information is sent to the cerebral cortex, where it is transformed and assimilated into the right-side-up image we normally have of the world.

The reason the retinal image is upside down and backward is that light rays travel in a straight line, as illustrated in Figure 6.1. As a result, the rays from the top of the object (the pen) wind up at the bottom on the retina and those at the bottom go to the top. The same is true for rays coming from the left and right sides of the object, which explains why the retinal image is reversed as well as being upside down.

Checkpoint
Describe the path of light through the eye from the cornea to the retina. Explain why you should consider wearing light-reflecting sunglasses the next time you are shopping for a new car.

The Retina

The recognition of a visual stimulus begins in the retina, the light-sensitive portion of the eye. The retina is composed of several layers of cells, of which three are particularly important for vision: the photoreceptors (of two types, as you will see), the **bipolar cells** and the **ganglion cells** (Figure 6.3). The photoreceptors are actually specialized sensory cells with neuron-like properties. One end of the photoreceptor absorbs photons ("particles") of light, and the other end relays this information about light absorption to bipolar cells through the release of neurotransmitter. We have more to say about how light rays are changed (transduced) into nervous system "information" later in the chapter. The focused light passes through the ganglion cells and bipolar cells before reaching the photoreceptors. Note that there are two additional layers of cells in the retina: horizontal cells and amacrine cells. The horizontal cells interconnect the photoreceptor cells, and the amacrine cells interconnect the ganglion cells. We discuss the functions of these cells later in the chapter.

bipolar cell A cell between a photoreceptor and a ganglion cell in the retina.

ganglion cell A cell in the third layer of cells in the retina.

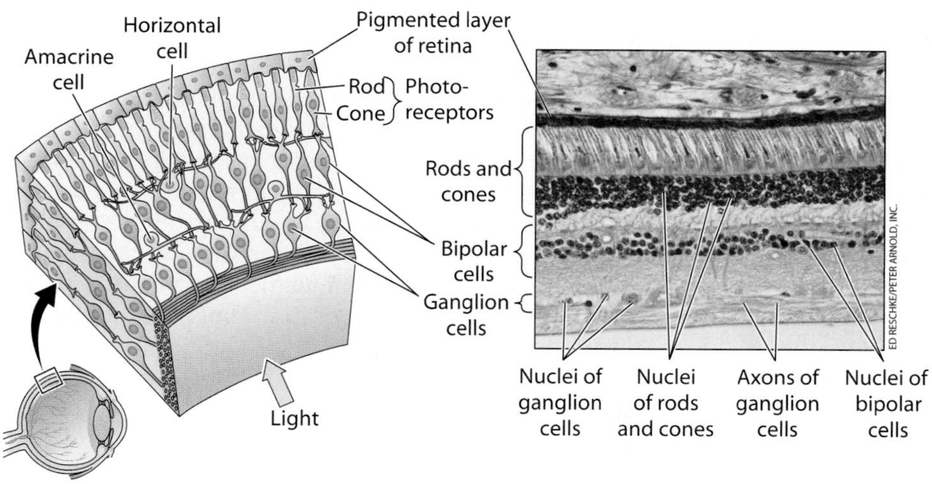

Figure 6.3
Cellular organization of the retina
Light passes through ganglion and bipolar cells before reaching the photoreceptors (rods and cones) at the back of the eye.

→ **Why are the photoreceptors at the back of the eye rather than at the front?**

rod A type of photoreceptor concentrated in the periphery of the retina; operates in low light.

cone A type of photoreceptor relatively concentrated in the center of the retina; detects fine details and colors in bright light.

fovea The central region of the retina, where cones are most concentrated.

duplex theory A theory of vision proposed by Max Schultze that summarizes the differences between rods and cones.

Given that the photoreceptors are the cells that transduce light stimulation into neural activity, it may seem odd that they are the cell layer farthest from the light. The explanation lies in the energy requirements of the photoreceptor cells. Because they use a lot of energy, the photoreceptors lie close to the blood vessels supplying the nutrients. The blood vessels, which unlike the bipolar and ganglion cells are not transparent, are at the back of the eye; therefore, this is where the photoreceptors are located.

The two types of photoreceptors are **rods** and **cones** (see Figure 6.3). The human retina contains approximately 120 million rods and 6 million cones. The cones are most concentrated in the central region of the retina, called the **fovea** (see Figure 6.1), and the rods are most concentrated at the periphery.

As no doubt you have noticed, you can see details of an object more clearly in the daytime than at night; that is, visual acuity is greater in daylight (or under high illumination levels at night). The reason for this day-night difference is that cones, which can detect small details and colors, operate more effectively in bright light. Rods are more sensitive to light than cones and can detect visual stimuli even in dim lighting conditions, but they are less able to detect small details and colors.

Another visual phenomenon you may have noticed is that you can see things better at night if you do not look straight at them but look at them out of the corner of your eye. The reason for this, again, is that the cones do not function well in the dark, and if you look straight at something, you are primarily stimulating the cones, which are concentrated in the central portion of the retina. Therefore, in order to see an object at night, you need to look slightly away from it, so that you are primarily stimulating the rods in the periphery.

What gives the cones better acuity and the rods more light sensitivity? The answer lies in the relative number of photoreceptors that send their input to a particular ganglion cell, a mechanism called *convergence* (Figure 6.4). Only a few cones send their input to a particular ganglion cell, allowing the brain to detect the input from each cone better. The greater number of rods connected (by way of bipolar cells) to ganglion cells reduces the detected detail of objects, but dramatically increases the sensitivity to light of the ganglion cells.

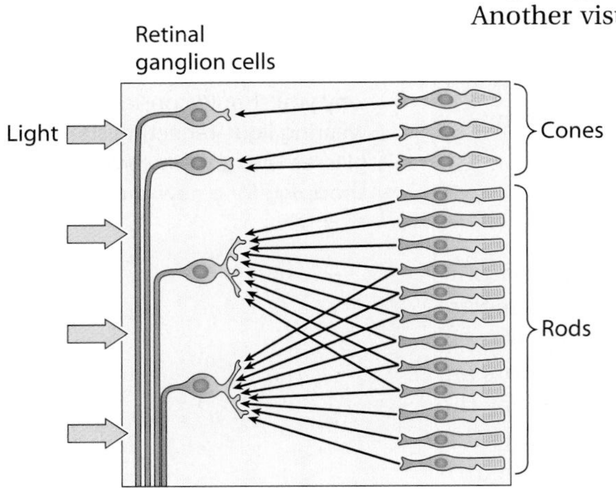

Figure 6.4

The convergence of cones and rods onto ganglion cells Notice that fewer cones than rods converge onto a ganglion cell; this leads to greater visual acuity mediated by cones than by rods. (For simplicity, the bipolar, horizontal, and amacrine cells have been omitted.)

➡ **Are rods and cones part of the peripheral nervous system or the central nervous system?**

The differences between rods and cones that we have discussed to this point are sometimes summarized in the **duplex theory** of vision (or the *duplicity theory*). The central idea of the duplex theory was proposed in the 1860s by Max Schultze, a German anatomist. Schultze theorized that we have two visual systems, one that functions under low light and depends on the rods and another that operates in bright light and depends on the cones. The basic differences in the rods and the cones—duplex theory—are summarized in Table 6.1.

Because of evolutionary adaptations, not all animals have the same arrangement of rods and cones in the fovea as humans do. For example, some predatory bird species (e.g., falcons, hawks, eagles) have two foveas in each eye, the deep fovea and the shallow fovea (Tucker, 2000). The deep fovea has a wider range of vision and higher acuity than the shallow fovea and is typically used when the object of interest is relatively far away. Tucker found, for example, that these birds look sideways at an object more than 80% of the time when the object is 40 m or more away. When the object is within 8 m, the birds tend to look straight at it, thus stimulating the shallow fovea, with its narrow field of view about the central axis of the bird.

Bipolar and ganglion cells are much more than conduits for conveying neural messages about light stimuli between the photoreceptors and the primary visual cortex. Although most of the analysis of light stimuli takes place in the cortex, the initial processing begins in the retina. For example, detection of the edges of an

Table 6.1
The Duplex Theory: Differences Between Rods and Cones

Rods	Cones
Located mostly in the periphery of the retina	Located mostly in the center of the retina
Relatively sensitive to light	Relatively insensitive to light
Operate under low light levels (at night)	Operate under high light levels (during the day)
Achromatic (colorless) vision	Chromatic (color) vision
Low visual acuity	High visual acuity
120 million in each retina (in humans)	6 million in each retina (in humans)
High convergence of information	Low convergence of information

optic disk The point at the back of the eye where axons from ganglion cells converge.

blind spot An area of the retina lacking photoreceptors, where no visual processsing occurs.

object, distinguishing it from its background, occurs in the retina. The sharpening of edges that occurs in the retina involves the horizontal cells and the amacrine cells. Because the retina is actually an extension of the brain, its sensory receptors have much greater complexity than those of other sensory systems. You will learn more about the important role of bipolar and ganglion cells, as well as horizontal and amacrine cells, in analyzing light stimuli throughout this chapter.

Checkpoint
Why are rods better adapted to night vision? Why are cones better able to detect small details?

REVIEW

- The form of energy detected by the visual system is light, electromagnetic radiation reflected by stimuli in the environment.
- Light passes through the transparent cornea, the clear aqueous humor, and the pupil before reaching the lens, which focuses the image of an object on the retina. The image on the retina is upside down and reversed.
- The retina contains several layers of cells, the most important for detecting the visual signal being the photoreceptors (rods and cones), the bipolar cells, and the ganglion cells.
- Light passes through the ganglion and bipolar layers before reaching the photoreceptors, which then transduce the light into neural impulses.
- Cones are most concentrated in the central part of the retina; rods are most concentrated at the periphery of the retina.
- Cones detect colors and the details of daytime vision; rods detect stimuli even under dim lighting conditions. The contrasting characteristics of rods and cones comprise the duplex theory of vision.

Pathways to the Primary Visual Cortex

The photoreceptors transduce light into a neural message that is passed to the bipolar cells with which they synapse, then from the bipolar cells to the ganglion cells. The axons of the ganglion cells come together at the **optic disk,** the blind spot at the back of the eye, where arteries enter and veins exit the eye. The **blind spot** is approximately 16 mm to the side of the fovea (see Figure 6.1). An object focused only on this area of the eye would not be visible. However, because objects are focused on large parts of the retina and our eyes continually move, we are not aware of our blind spot. Our visual system fills in the gap created by the blind spot, as Dr. Bradley told Alan. You can use Figure 6.5 to demonstrate your blind spot to yourself.

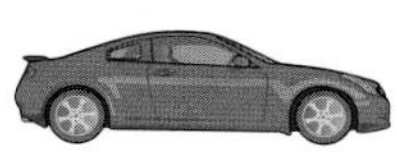

Figure 6.5
The blind spot To demonstrate the existence of the blind spot, close your right eye and focus on the black circle with your left eye. Start with the page a few inches from your face. Slowly move the book away from you. The image of the car will disappear when it is focused on your blind spot.

Why do we have a blind spot?

Although ganglion cells vary in distance from the optic disk, the neural messages about a particular visual stimulus coming from all the ganglion cells are conveyed to higher neural structures at the same time. This *synchrony of input* allows us to see an entire visual stimulus as a complete whole, rather than as separate stimuli. Synchrony of input is possible because of differential propagation rates of neural impulses along ganglion cell axons: The farther a ganglion cell is from the optic disk, the faster its axon propagates action potentials (Stanford, 1987).

After leaving the optic disk, the axons of the ganglion cells form the **optic nerve,** one from each eye. Remember that the retina, which includes the ganglion cells, is really part of the CNS. Therefore, the optic nerve is incorrectly named (a nerve is a collection of axons within the PNS); it should be the optic tract.

The two optic nerves, or second cranial nerves (see Table 2.1), meet at the **optic chiasm.** In some vertebrates, for example amphibians and reptiles, all the fibers of each optic nerve cross over to the opposite side of the brain at the optic chiasm. In most mammals, some fibers of the optic nerve cross over to the opposite side of the brain, and others project to the same side. In humans and other primates, about 50% of the optic nerve fibers cross at the optic chiasm. The optic nerve fibers that originate in the nasal half (closest to the nose) of each retina cross over to the contralateral (opposite) side of the brain, whereas those that originate in the lateral half of each retina stay on the ipsilateral (same) side of the brain. This arrangement means that input from the right visual field is transmitted to the left hemisphere, and information from the left visual field to the right hemisphere. (Because of brain damage, a person may be unable to see a portion of the visual field. Box 6.1 describes some visual field deficits and how they are diagnosed.)

The **optic tracts** are the continuation of the optic nerve fibers beyond the optic chiasm. Approximately 80% of these fibers project to the **lateral geniculate nucleus (LGN)** of the thalamus (Figure 6.6). Each LGN has six layers, and adjacent LGN areas are activated by adjacent areas of the retina. This organization allows the form of the visual stimulus to remain intact as it is processed by the visual system—so that we can see the pen in Figure 6.1, for example, instead of a mishmash of colors and lines.

The top four layers of cells in the LGN are the parvocellular layers, and the bottom two layers are the magnocellular layers. The **parvocellular layers** are composed of neurons with small cell bodies that receive projections from a type of ganglion cell called an **X ganglion cell.** X ganglion cells originate mostly from the fovea, the central portion of the retina, which suggests they receive input mostly from cones. The **magnocellular layers** are composed of neurons with large cell bodies that receive input from a **Y ganglion cell.** As you may have guessed, the Y ganglion cells originate mostly from the periphery of the retina, which suggests their input comes mostly from rods.

Figure 6.6
Pathways to the primary visual cortex Because of the fiber crossing that occurs in the optic chiasm, input from the right visual field (blue) goes initially to the left hemisphere, and input from the left visual field (red) to the right hemisphere.

➡ **Where does the first synapse occur in the visual portion of the CNS beyond the retina?**

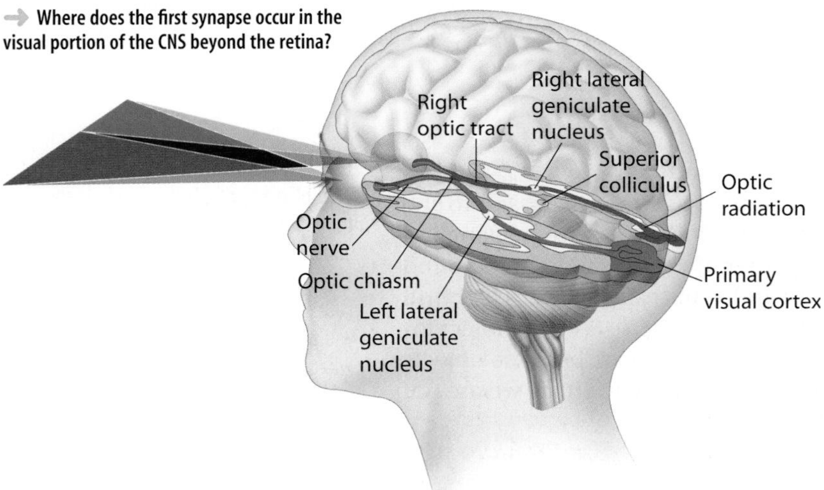

The nerve fibers that reach the LGN are the axons of the retinal ganglion cells. Thus, the first synapse in the visual analysis of information outside the retina is located in the thalamus. Like the LGN, the primary visual cortex is organized spatially like a map of the retina, so in a sense, the image of the pen remains intact from the beginning to the end of its journey through the visual system.

In our discussion of the duplex theory of vision, we noted that there is less convergence of cones, which are more concentrated in the central part of the retina (the fovea), than of rods, which are more concentrated in the periphery. Because of this, about 25% of the primary visual cortex receives input from the fovea, even though the fovea occupies a disproportionately small percentage of the retina. The greater foveal representation is one reason why details of objects seen in the daylight are so much clearer than details seen at night.

Recall that 80% of the optic tract fibers go to the LGN (the dorsal LGN). Most of the remaining 20% project to a structure in the tectum of the midbrain called the *superior colliculus* (see Figure 6.6). The superior colliculus projects to parts of the parietal and temporal lobes and is responsible for attention to visual stimuli and coordination of eye movements. Other projections of the optic tract go to several targets: the ventral LGN, which sends messages to other subcortical areas; the accessory optic nuclei of the midbrain, which influence certain eye movements; the suprachiasmatic nucleus of the hypothalamus, which regulates circadian rhythms through its influence on the pineal gland (as described in Chapter 9); and the pretectal area of the midbrain, which influences pupil size.

Additional subcortical areas receiving visual information include the amygdala and the hippocampus. For example, Shi and Davis (2001) studied visual pathways to the amygdala, which is critical in fear conditioning, as we discuss in Chapter 14. The researchers found that lesions of both the LGN and the lateral posterior nucleus of the thalamus after fear conditioning in rats completely blocked the startle reaction of the animals to a visual conditioned stimulus. Damage to either structure by itself had no effect on the conditioned startle reaction, however. Shi and Davis concluded that during fear conditioning, visual information reaches the amygdala either by way of pathways through cortical regions or directly from the thalamus.

Using fMRI in nine healthy men, Critchley and colleagues (2000) found that the processing of facial expressions (pictures of men and women exhibiting either happy, angry, or neutral expressions) increased activity in temporal lobe areas, the hippocampus, the amygdalohippocampal junction, and the pulvinar nucleus in the thalamus. Explicit processing of the expressions (subjects were asked to identify the emotions expressed) activated different neural areas than implicit processing (subjects were asked to identify the gender of the person expressing the emotion). Temporal lobe areas were activated in explicit (conscious) processing, the amygdala in implicit (unconscious) processing.

The Structure of the Primary Visual Cortex

Like the LGN, the **primary visual cortex,** also called striate cortex, has six layers. The input from the parvocellular layers and the magnocellular layers of the LGN is projected to layer IV of the primary visual cortex through the *optic radiations* (see Figure 6.6). Margaret Wong-Riley (1979) discovered that the parvocellular pathways of the primary visual cortex contain clusters of neurons, which she named **blobs.** (The sections of cortex between the blobs are called interblobs.) These blob-shaped clusters can be distinguished from other neurons in the primary visual cortex by a staining reaction with the enzyme cytochrome oxidase. The blobs are sensitive to specific colors (Dow, 2002; Landisman & Ts'o, 2002; Shostak & others, 2002). Other neurons in the parvocellular pathways are sensitive to stationary objects and detect stimulus boundaries, and neurons in the magnocellular pathways are responsive to moving objects, detecting movement as well as stimulus orientation and retinal disparity—the slight differences in visual scenes seen by each eye.

According to Livingstone and Hubel (1988), the magnocellular layers are more primitive (in an evolutionary sense) and are found in all mammalian species. The existence in these pathways of neurons selectively sensitive to a specific stimulus moving in a particular direction is consistent with the view that these neurons provide the basic visual information needed to move around in the environment, to

optic nerve A nerve formed by the axons of ganglion cells after leaving the optic disk.

optic chiasm The place where the two optic nerves meet and some or all of the optic nerve fibers cross to the opposite side of the brain.

optic tract The continuation of the optic nerve fibers beyond the optic chiasm.

lateral geniculate nucleus (LGN) A group of neurons in the thalamus that receive neural impulses from the ganglion cells of the retina.

parvocellular layer One of the top four layers of the LGN, consisting of neurons with small cell bodies.

X ganglion cell A type of ganglion cell that originates mostly from the central part of the retina.

magnocellular layer One of the bottom two layers of the LGN, consisting of neurons with large cell bodies.

Y ganglion cell A type of ganglion cell that originates mostly from the peripheral part of the retina.

primary visual cortex The area of the cerebral cortex that detects features of the visual environment; also called striate cortex.

blob A cluster of neurons in the primary visual cortex that are sensitive to specific colors.

Box 6.1

Testing for Visual Field Deficits

Following a stroke, Alan's mother, Margaret, has had difficulty naming objects placed in what should be full view. A therapist is testing Margaret for a number of possible causes. One of the most likely is *aphasia,* a language impairment, especially if the stroke damaged the left frontal lobe (Broca's area). In this case, Margaret could see the object but would be unable to produce the word for it. Another possibility is *amnesia,* or memory loss, for the names of objects learned before the stroke. Again, she would be able to see the object, but in this case, she would be unable to remember what it is or what it is called. A third possibility is a **visual field deficit,** an inability to see objects placed in a particular part of the visual field, caused by damage either to a portion of an occipital lobe or to the pathways leading to it (Brookshire, 1997). Here, Margaret would simply be unable to see the object. Other possibilities include visual agnosia (an inability to recognize or interpret objects) and contralateral neglect (lack of response to part of the body or space on the side opposite to the location of the lesion).

If the damage is posterior to the optic chiasm, the visual field deficit will be contralateral to the damage (remember the crossing over of nerve fibers at the optic chiasm). If upper nerve fibers are damaged, the deficit will be in the opposite lower quadrant (Figure 6.7a); if lower nerve fibers are damaged, the deficit will be in the opposite upper quadrant (Figure 6.7b). Damage to both upper and lower nerve fibers will result in a condition called *homonymous hemianopsia.* The term *hemianopsia* indicates that half the visual field is affected; *homonymous* means the same part of the visual field is affected in each eye (Figure 6.7c).

To rule out aphasia and amnesia, the therapist places objects in different quadrants of space and asks Margaret to point to them. She consistently fails to detect objects only when they are placed in the upper right quadrant. To confirm this, the therapist then places objects only in unimpaired portions of Margaret's visual field. Because she can name objects in the entire left visual field and in the lower right visual field, the therapist concludes that Margaret does not suffer from either aphasia or amnesia but instead from a visual field deficit of the upper right quadrant. The therapist can help Margaret compensate for this deficit by training her to move her head to detect objects with the intact portions of her visual field. Most patients quickly learn to compensate in this way.

Visual field deficits also can be caused by damage to the occipital lobe, from strokes, tumors, or injury. One interesting phenomenon observed in people with occipital lobe damage is known as **blindsight**—the ability to respond to objects in a missing visual field without being consciously aware of seeing anything.

Lawrence Weiskrantz first used the word *blindsight* to describe observations he and his colleagues made on a patient referred to in the literature as D. B. (Weiskrantz & others, 1974). D. B. had a tumor removed from his right occipital lobe, which left him apparently blind in his left visual field; that is, when visual stimuli were presented in his left visual field, D. B. said he did not see them. However, when D. B. was required to guess where the stimulus he could not see might be, he "guessed" the location with great accuracy. In addition, when asked to guess whether the stimulus was a horizontal or vertical line, or an X versus an O, he again showed remarkable accuracy, protesting all the while that he could not see anything.

One explanation for blindsight is that the ability to respond to stimuli in the missing area of the visual field is a func-

---

locate prey, and to avoid predators. Livingstone and Hubel further suggested that the parvocellular layers evolved more recently, allowing the detection of finer details and colors.

➤Checkpoint

Describe the pathway from the photoreceptors in a human eye to the primary visual cortex that results in a visual perception. Why does visual information go to the amygdala and the hippocampus?

REVIEW

- ➤ The photoreceptors synapse with bipolar cells, which synapse with ganglion cells.
- ➤ Ganglion cells converge at the optic disk to form the optic nerve.
- ➤ In humans and most other primates, the optic nerve fibers originating in the nasal half of each retina cross over to the contralateral side of the brain at the optic chiasm, and fibers originating in the lateral half remain on the ipsilateral side.
- ➤ The optic nerve, or second cranial nerve, is a continuation of ganglion cell axons, as is the optic tract, the extension of the optic nerve beyond the optic chiasm.

tion of activity in the visual pathway that bypasses the LGN and goes directly to the superior colliculus and pretectal area. As we have noted, these areas are responsible for attention to visual stimuli and the coordination of eye movements and other visual reflexes. Presumably, the noncortical areas detect the visual stimuli in the "missing" visual field and signal this detection by allowing the person to "guess" (or, in some cases, point to) whatever was presented.

Blindsight is controversial. At least one researcher believes that in people who exhibit blindsight, the cortical damage is incomplete and the ability to detect objects comes from this spared cortical tissue rather than from the stimulation of subcortical regions such as the superior colliculus (Fendrich & others, 2001; Gazzaniga & others, 1994). This explanation could indeed account for some of the blindsight cases, but research with monkeys argues convincingly for the reality of the phenomenon. Monkeys with demonstrably complete visual cortical ablations display the same blindsight ability observed in humans (Cowey & Stoerig, 2004; Stoerig & Cowey, 1997; Weiskrantz, 2004), with, also like humans, apparently no awareness of having seen anything (Cowey & Stoerig, 1997).

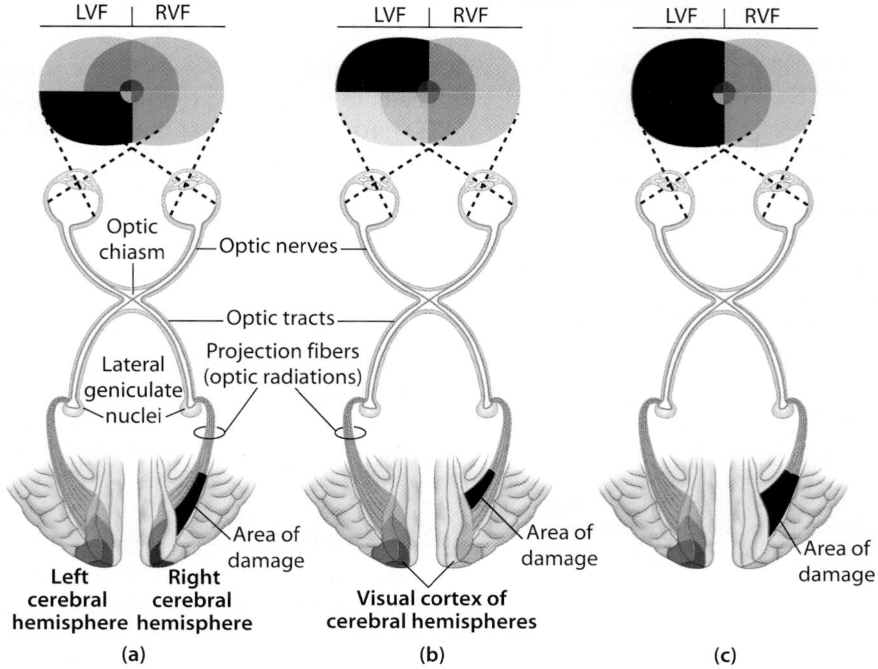

Figure 6.7

Visual field deficits Damage to optic tract fibers posterior to the optic chiasm causes contralateral visual field deficits. The colors (red, green, blue, yellow) in the visual fields and in the brains are included to indicate where the information in a particular part of the visual field is projected in the brain. (a) Damage to nerve fibers connecting to the upper right visual hemisphere causes a visual field deficit in the lower left quadrant (black area). (b) Damage to fibers connecting to the lower right visual hemisphere causes a visual field deficit in the upper left quadrant. (c) Damage to fibers connecting to both upper and lower portions of the right hemisphere causes homonymous hemianopsia, a deficit in the left half of the visual field of each eye. (LVF and RVF indicate left and right visual field, respectively.)

What deficit would result if nerve fibers connecting the lower right visual field to the left hemisphere were damaged?

- Most fibers of the optic tract project to the LGN, where they synapse with neurons projecting to the primary visual cortex (striate cortex).
- The remaining optic tract fibers extend to other subcortical structures, including the superior colliculus, the ventral LGN, the accessory optic nuclei, the suprachiasmatic nucleus, and the pretectal area. Other subcortical structures receiving visual information include the amygdala and the hippocampus.
- The X ganglion cells originate mostly from the central part of the retina and project to the top four layers, the parvocellular layers, of the LGN.
- The Y ganglion cells originate mostly from the peripheral part of the retina and project to the bottom two layers, the magnocellular layers, of the LGN.

Pathways to the Secondary Visual Cortex

The primary visual cortex detects features of the visual environment (the lines and colors that make up the pen in Figure 6.1), and the **secondary visual cortex** combines the visual features into a recognizable visual perception (the pen). The

visual field deficit An inability to see objects in a specific part of the visual field, caused by damage to a region of the occipital lobe or the pathways leading to it.

blindsight The ability of a person to respond to objects in a missing visual field without being conscious of seeing anything.

secondary visual cortex The area of the cerebral cortex that combines visual features into a recognizable visual perception; also called prestriate cortex.

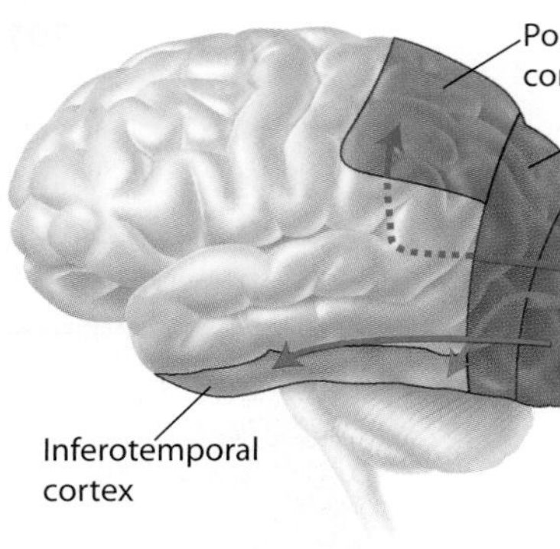

Figure 6.8

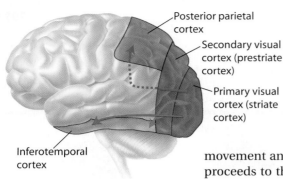

Visual pathways beyond the primary visual cortex The green arrow represents the visual pathway that detects shapes; the red arrow, the visual pathway that detects color; and the blue arrow, the visual pathway that detects movement and depth. Because of their buried location in the superior temporal gyrus, areas MT and MST are not shown here (the blue line is dashed where it passes through areas MT and MST).

➔ **What are the three pathways that relay information to the secondary visual cortex?**

visual pathway that detects the shape of objects begins in the primary visual cortex, travels to the prestriate cortex, and ends at the inferotemporal cortex (green arrow in Figure 6.8). The pathway that detects color begins in the striate cortex, travels to the prestriate cortex, and ends at the posterior inferotemporal cortex (red arrow in Figure 6.8). The pathway that detects movement and depth begins in the striate cortex, travels to the prestriate cortex, proceeds to the middle temporal (MT) cortex and the medial superior temporal (MST) cortex, and ends at the posterior parietal cortex (blue arrow in Figure 6.8). We address how these visual pathways enable us to detect the shape, color, distance, and movement of objects later in the chapter.

◆ Transducing Light Into Neural Messages

So far we have seen how electromagnetic radiation—light—travels through the eye to the photoreceptors (rods and cones), which transduce or change it into neural messages, and how messages are carried through the optic nerve to the cerebral cortex. Here we consider the characteristics of light and how the photoreceptor cells transform it into the messages conveyed to the visual cortex.

The Characteristics of Light

The light we see, which is the light reflected off objects or radiated from a source, varies along three physical dimensions: wavelength, intensity, and purity. Wavelength is measured in nanometers (1 nm is a billionth of a meter), and humans can see wavelengths in the range of 380 to 760 nm (Figure 6.9). Wavelength is related to the perceived characteristic known as **hue** or color, so that when our visual system detects a particular wavelength, we generally perceive that wavelength as a specific color. Light of a short wavelength (e.g., 420 nm) is usually perceived as blue, light of a medium wavelength (e.g., 530 nm) as green, light of a medium-to-long wavelength (e.g., 580 nm) as yellow, and light of a long wavelength (e.g., 660 nm) as red. These wavelengths are associated with what we consider the primary colors.

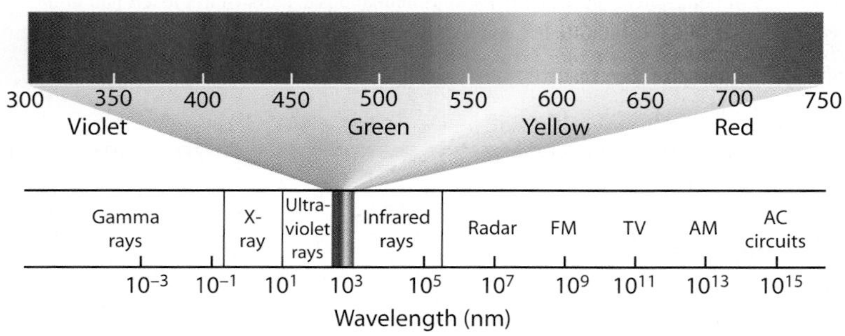

Figure 6.9

The electromagnetic spectrum The human visual system can detect only a small portion of the electromagnetic spectrum as different colors. For help in remembering the basic colors of the visual spectrum, think of the name ROY G BIV, as a mnemonic device standing for red orange yellow green blue indigo violet—in this case, in the order of decreasing wavelength.

➔ **If a light stimulus contains all wavelengths, what color is it perceived to be?**

As is evident in Figure 6.9, humans can detect only a small part of the electromagnetic spectrum. Many insects can detect ultraviolet rays, which are shorter wavelengths than we can see, and many fish and reptiles are sensitive to infrared rays, which are longer wavelengths than we can detect.

Light also varies in intensity, which is related to the perceived characteristic of **brightness.** Some stimuli, such as aluminum foil, reflect a great deal of light and are perceived as bright, whereas other stimuli, such as coal, reflect little light and are perceived as dark.

The third dimension of light is its purity, which refers to the number of wavelengths it contains. A light consisting of only one wavelength is called monochromatic (meaning "one color") and is the purest light possible. In fact, truly monochromatic light is difficult to produce, and when we refer to a light as monochromatic, what we really mean is a light that contains wavelengths within a very narrow range. Purity is related to the perceived characteristic of **saturation,** which refers to the amount of color a stimulus contains. A stimulus perceived as completely saturated would be one with only color, with an absence of white. The more white in a light, the less saturated it seems. Light from the sun contains nearly equal amounts of all the wavelengths that we can detect, and we perceive it as white, or completely pure.

The Detection of Visual Stimuli

George Wald was the first to describe how photoreceptors transduce light into neural signals, and for this he shared the Nobel Prize in Physiology or Medicine in 1967 with Ragnar Granit and Haldan Keffer Hartline, both of whom also studied the visual system. (We discuss some of Hartline's work later.) Wald found that a photoreceptor consists of an outer segment connected to an inner segment by hair-like extensions called *cilia* (Figure 6.10a). The inner segment contains the cell nucleus, and the outer segment is made up of several hundred thin membranes that form discs, called **lamellae.**

The lamellae contain molecules called **photopigments,** chemicals that absorb light. The photopigments have two molecular components: a protein **opsin** and a lipid **retinal** (Figure 6.10b). All rods contain a single type of opsin called **rod opsin.** There are three forms of opsin in cones, corresponding to the three different types of cones; cones are involved in color recognition, discussed later in the chapter. Retinal is synthesized from vitamin A, commonly found in vegetables (carrots are a good source). **Rhodopsin,** made of rod opsin and retinal, is the photopigment in rods. As many as 10 million photopigment molecules are found in each photoreceptor cell.

Rhodopsin has a rosy or pink color before it is exposed to light (the Greek *rhodon* means "rose"). When exposed to light, it breaks down into rod opsin and *trans*-retinal and has a pale yellow color. In darkness, and with the help of vitamin A and several enzymes, rod opsin and *cis*-retinal (produced from *trans*-retinal by the enzyme retinal isomerase) recombine into rhodopsin, and the rosy color returns (Figure 6.11). Light bleaches the rhodopsin in an extremely rapid chemical reaction (Chen & others, 2001; Schoenlein & others, 1991).

The splitting of rhodopsin into rod opsin and retinal by a light stimulus is the key to the detection of light. Photoreceptor cells continuously release neurotransmitter molecules that inhibit the bipolar cells they innervate (see Figure 6.3). Thus, a photoreceptor that is not being stimulated by light inhibits (hyperpolarizes) its

hue The color a particular wavelength of light is perceived to be.

brightness The intensity of a light stimulus.

saturation The purity of a light stimulus.

lamella In the eye, a thin membranous disc in the outer segment of a photoreceptor.

photopigment A chemical molecule in the lamellae of the eye that absorbs light.

opsin The protein component of a photopigment.

retinal The lipid component of a photopigment, synthesized from vitamin A.

rod opsin The form of opsin found in rods.

rhodopsin The photopigment in rods; consists of rod opsin and retinal.

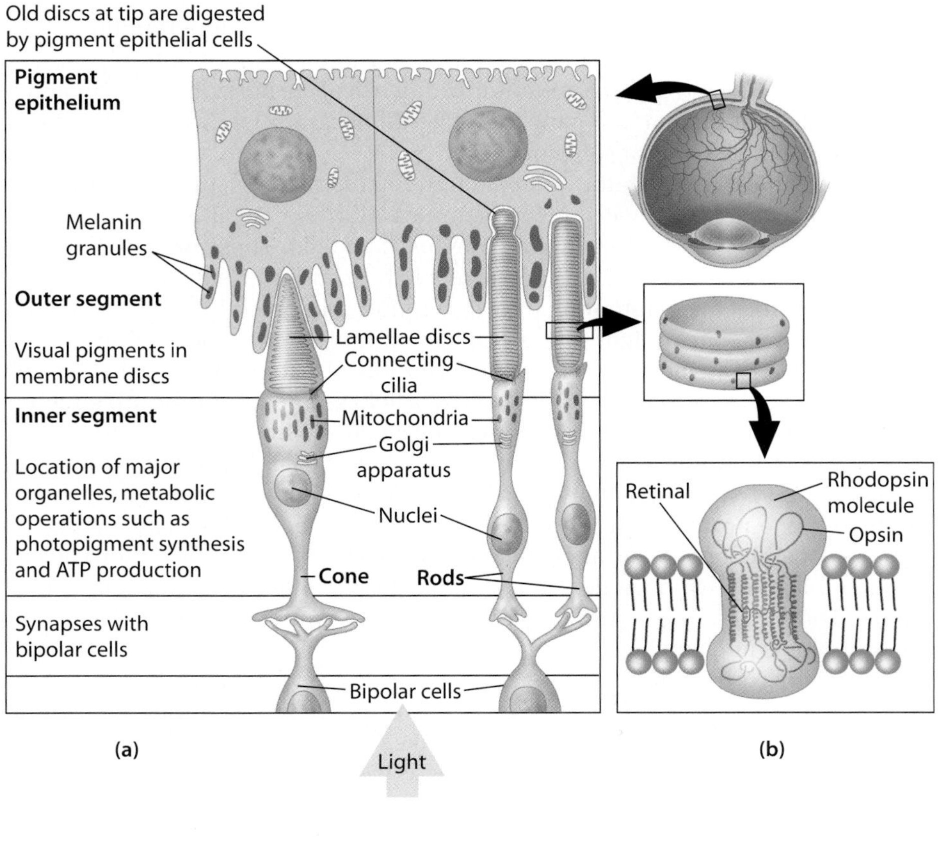

Figure 6.10
Photoreceptors Structural components of photoreceptor cells: rods and cones.

→ **Where in the eye are the rods and cones located?**

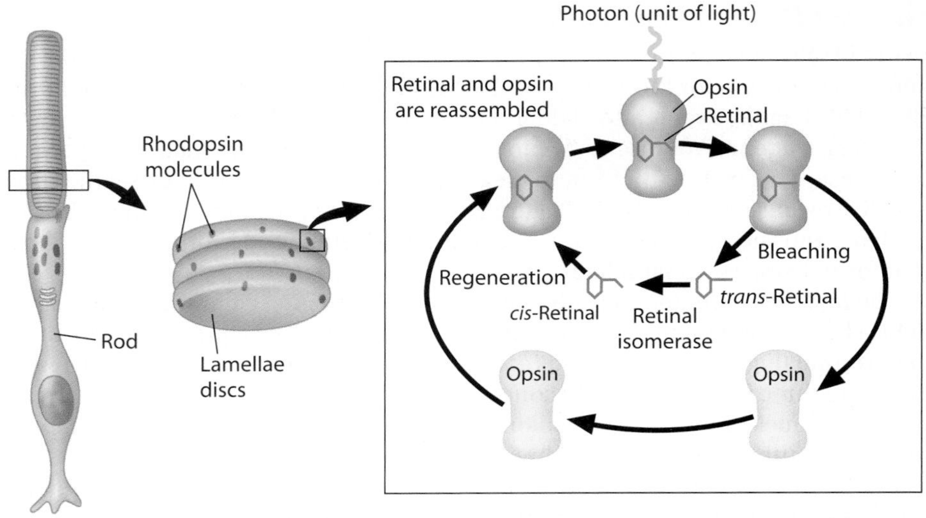

Figure 6.11

The bleaching and regeneration of visual pigments in rods Light breaks down rhodopsin into its components, rod opsin and retinal; when light is removed, rod opsin and retinal recombine into rhodopsin.

➡ **How does the splitting of rhodopsin stimulate a rod cell?**

bipolar cell. When light splits rhodopsin, chemical reactions cause Na^+ ion channels in the photoreceptor membrane to close (Alberts & others, 1994), thereby increasing the polarity of the membrane (Schnapf & Baylor, 1987). In turn, hyperpolarization of the photoreceptor membrane decreases neurotransmitter release (Yau, 1991), thus reducing bipolar cell inhibition. As a result, the bipolar cell membrane becomes depolarized. Bipolar cells have a graded depolarization: The greater the depolarization, the more neurotransmitter molecules they release into the synaptic cleft between the bipolar and ganglion cells. Bipolar cells have an excitatory influence on the ganglion cells, whose axons, as we have seen, make up the optic nerves (Doly, 1994).

As mentioned earlier, the retina contains two additional types of cells that lie in layers parallel to its surface: **horizontal cells** and **amacrine cells.** As shown in Figure 6.3, the photoreceptors synapse with horizontal cells as well as with bipolar cells. In turn, horizontal cells synapse with and have an inhibitory influence on bipolar cells. Similarly, amacrine cells synapse with and inhibit both bipolar and ganglion cells. The effect of this inhibitory influence of the horizontal and amacrine cells on adjacent bipolar and ganglion cells will become clear as we describe the action of the three types of ganglion cells.

As the earliest investigator of single optic nerve fibers (remember, these are axons of ganglion cells) with microelectrodes, Hartline (1938) found that some ganglion cells respond when a light stimulus is applied. These **on ganglion cells** are excited by bipolar cells in response to a light stimulus. Ganglion cells excited when a light stimulus is removed, the **off ganglion cells,** are inhibited by amacrine cells in the presence of light. When the light stimulus ends, the inhibition is removed, and the ganglion cells are excited. Hartline also found some ganglion cells that respond to both the start and the end of a light stimulus—the **on-off ganglion cells.** On-off cells are excited by a bipolar cell when a light stimulus is present and released from inhibition by an amacrine cell when the light stimulus is removed.

In summary, some ganglion cells respond to the presence of a light stimulus, some to the removal of a light stimulus, and some to both. If the same visual receptors are stimulated continuously by the same visual image, the pattern of ganglion cell activity we have described should result in the disappearance of the image. That is, the three types of ganglion cells are responding to change, and if the stimulus is unchanging, they should stop responding. This is indeed what happens. So why do we continue to detect visual events in our environment? The explanation is that the same photoreceptors are not exposed continuously to the same visual stimuli. Our eyes constantly make rapid, jerky **saccadic movements,** shifting abruptly from one point to another as we scan the physical environment

horizontal cell A type of retinal neuron that receives neural messages from photoreceptors; synapses with and has an inhibitory influence on bipolar cells.

amacrine cell A type of retinal neuron that receives neural messages from bipolar cells; synapses with and inhibits both bipolar and ganglion cells.

on ganglion cell A type of ganglion cell excited by bipolar cells in response to a light stimulus.

off ganglion cell A type of ganglion cell excited when a light stimulus is removed.

on-off ganglion cell A type of ganglion cell excited by both the presence and removal of a light stimulus.

saccadic movement The rapid, jerky movement of the eye from one point to another as the physical environment is scanned.

(*saccade* is from French meaning a twitch or spasmodic jerk). During this scanning process, eye movements start and stop and then start again. The occurrence and speed of a saccade cannot be consciously controlled. Saccadic eye movements slow down when we attempt to follow a moving object, in a smoother type of eye movement called **pursuit movement.** When the object stops and our eyes focus on it, the saccadic movements begin again, scanning the object to maintain the stimulation of the visual system.

Checkpoint

Describe the three physical characteristics of light and the perceived characteristics to which they are related. Why is it important to be able to recognize when a light goes off as well as when it comes on?

REVIEW

- Information from the primary visual cortex travels by three pathways to the secondary visual cortex for analysis.
- The pathway involved in shape recognition projects to the prestriate cortex and then to the inferotemporal cortex.
- The pathway providing information about color projects to the prestriate cortex and then to the posterior inferotemporal cortex.
- The pathway involved in the detection of depth and movement projects to the prestriate cortex, then to the middle temporal cortex and the medial superior temporal cortex, and finally to the posterior parietal cortex.
- Light varies in wavelength (related to what we perceive as hue), intensity (related to brightness), and purity (related to saturation).
- Photoreceptors (rods and cones) transduce light into neural impulses.
- Photoreceptors contain photopigments, which consist of the protein opsin and the lipid retinal. Light breaks down the photopigment into two separate molecules. When light is removed, the opsin and retinal recombine with the help of vitamin A and enzymes.
- Photoreceptors continually release neurotransmitter molecules that inhibit bipolar cells.
- When light splits the photopigment, Na^+ ion channels close, the photoreceptor membrane becomes hyperpolarized, and less neurotransmitter is released; this leads to depolarization of the bipolar cells.
- Bipolar cells have an excitatory influence on ganglion cells, whereas horizontal cells and amacrine cells have an inhibitory influence.
- On ganglion cells respond when a light is turned on, because of the excitatory influence of bipolar cells. Off ganglion cells respond when a light is turned off, because of the removal of the inhibitory influence of amacrine cells. On-off ganglion cells respond when a light stimulus begins and ends.

Object Recognition

Alan is no longer as worried about his visual problem as he was in the ophthalmologist's office. Sitting on his patio reading a magazine, he detects movement on the bird feeder hanging from a tree. He looks at the feeder and sees that a male cardinal has come to visit. The cardinal is just one of a multitude of objects in Alan's environment. His visual system, even with drusen, enables him to recognize objects and to distinguish between them: He can tell it is a cardinal and not another type of bird or a squirrel. Alan also sees colors, such as the bright red of the cardinal's feathers, and the movement of the bird as it hops about on the feeder. And he perceives the cardinal in three dimensions. Form, depth, movement, and color are properties of objects recognized through discrete functions of our visual system. We focus in this section on the recognition of the form of an object.

Alan now looks down at his magazine and sees a picture of a sailboat, which he can recognize as a sailboat and not a cruise ship. His ability to make this distinction

pursuit movement The smooth movement of the eyes following a moving object.

lateral inhibition A decrease in activity of one neuron caused by the stimulation of its neighbors.

receptive field The part of the retina that, when stimulated, causes a change in the activity of the cell.

center-on, surround-off ganglion cell A type of ganglion cell stimulated when the center of the receptive field is illuminated.

center-off, surround-on ganglion cell A type of ganglion cell stimulated when the surround is illuminated.

is aided by *lateral inhibition,* which enables him to sense the edges of an object—to distinguish the sails of the sailboat from the smokestacks of a cruise ship. But object recognition also requires other, highly complex mechanisms—as you will see.

Lateral Inhibition

The white sails of the sailboat are surrounded by a dark blue sky. From our previous discussion, you would expect the whiteness of the sails to stimulate Alan's photoreceptors more than the dark blue of the sky does. Although this differential photoreceptor activity would allow him to recognize that he was viewing an object, the object would appear merely as a light blur against a dark background; that is, the object would appear out of focus and might not be recognizable. To see where the sailboat ends and the sky begins, Alan must be able to sense both the brightness differences between an object and its background and the edges of the object (e.g., where the sails end and the sky begins).

When light reaches the retina, photoreceptors are hyperpolarized, causing a decreased release of neurotransmitter molecules. This decrease not only activates the bipolar cells by reducing their inhibition but also excites the interconnecting horizontal cells. Horizontal cell activation decreases the activity in bipolar cells adjacent to those activated. The reduced activity of the bipolar cells just outside a light stimulus (and the increased activity just inside the light stimulus) is caused by **lateral inhibition,** a decrease in the activity of one neuron resulting from the stimulation of its neighbors. Lateral inhibition enables us to sense edges by enhancing the contrast between an object and its background. Thus, the white sails are clearly focused against the blue sky because of the greater inhibition of bipolar cells connected to the photoreceptors on the "sail" side than on the "sky" side of the stimulus.

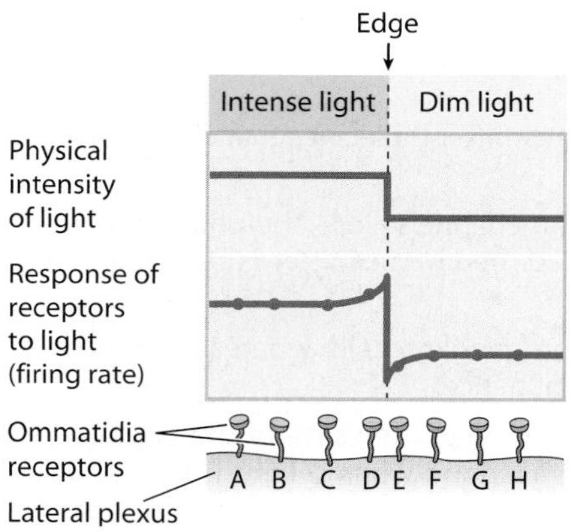

Figure 6.12

Lateral inhibition and the perception of edges This graph shows the firing rate of ommatidia receptors A to H in a horseshoe crab, when adjacent intense and dim lights are projected onto the retina. The increased firing rate of receptor D and decreased firing rate of receptor E create an edge between the intense and dim lights.

➡ **The lateral plexus of the horseshoe crab is analogous to what vertebrate structure?**

Figure 6.12 illustrates how lateral inhibition enhances contrast and creates the perception of edges. These results were obtained in a horseshoe crab, the subject of a classic study by Hartline (1949). The eye of the horseshoe crab consists of many little eyes, called *ommatidia* (singular: ommatidium), each of which has a lens and a receptor cell. The ommatidia synapse with a single large neuron called the eccentric cell. They also relay information to each other via a connection called the *lateral plexus,* which is analogous to the horizontal and amacrine cells of vertebrates. Activation of the lateral plexus by an ommatidium decreases the activity of ommatidia adjacent to the one that stimulated the lateral plexus.

Suppose that an intense light appears against a dimly lit background. In Figure 6.12, the activity of ommatidia receptors A, B, and C (those exposed to intense light) is decreased by inhibition from adjacent receptors via the lateral plexus. Because receptor D is next to receptors exposed to a dimly lit background as well as to receptors exposed to the intense light, it is inhibited less than receptors A, B, and C. In addition, ommatidia receptors F, G, and H are acted on only by receptors exposed to the dimly lit background. By contrast, receptor E is inhibited by receptor D as well as by receptors F, G, and H. The lateral inhibition of receptor E by receptor D results in a smaller response of receptor E than of receptors F, G, and H. This greater activation of receptor D and greater inhibition of receptor E enhances the contrast between the intense light and dimly lit background, thereby producing the perception of the edge between the two different light stimuli. Lateral inhibition sharpens our perception of edges.

Checkpoint

Describe how lateral inhibition works to sharpen the perception of edges. What structure in the horseshoe crab interconnects the ommatidia and accounts for lateral inhibition?

Receptive Fields

Lateral inhibition is only part of the object-recognition process. The recognition of objects also involves receptive fields. In a classic study using microelectrode recordings of single cells, Kuffler (1953) found that a particular ganglion cell in the optic nerve of a cat responded to a small light stimulus only when the stimulus was presented to a limited, circular area of the retina. He called this limited area the receptive field of the ganglion cell whose activity he was recording. A **receptive field** of a cell in the visual system is a region of the retina that, when stimulated, causes a change in the activity of that cell. Stated another way, the receptive field of a cell is what the cell "sees," what sort of pattern it responds to. A broader definition, one that applies to all sensory system cells, is that a receptive field of a cell is a region on the *receptor* that, when stimulated, causes a change in the activity of that cell. Figure 6.13 illustrates how the receptive field of a ganglion cell is determined.

Earlier we talked about Hartline's finding of on, off, and on-off ganglion cells. Kuffler's work indicates that there are actually two receptive fields for each type of on or off ganglion cell (Figure 6.14). Suppose the environment contains a dark object against a light background. Kuffler found that some ganglion cells respond when the *center* of the receptive field is dark and the periphery, or the *surround,* is light, whereas other cells respond when the center is light and the surround is dark. Ganglion cells stimulated when the center of the receptive field is illuminated are called **center-on, surround-off ganglion cells;** cells activated when the surround is illuminated are called **center-off, surround-on ganglion cells.** The general name for this type of receptive field is *center-surround;* that is, there is a central area, which responds to a light being on or off, and a surround, which at any time gives a response opposite to that of the center.

Microelectrode research has revealed additional information about the center-surround receptive fields of ganglion cells. For example, the size of the receptive field depends on the part of the retina from which the ganglion cell originates. X ganglion cells, which are innervated mainly by cones in the central part of the retina, have relatively small receptive fields, whereas Y ganglion cells generally have larger receptive fields, consistent with their innervation mostly by rods in the periphery. In addition, X ganglion cells tend to respond to color, with red center-on, green surround-off and vice versa, and blue center-on, yellow surround-off and vice versa. This response to color by the X ganglion cells is also consistent with their

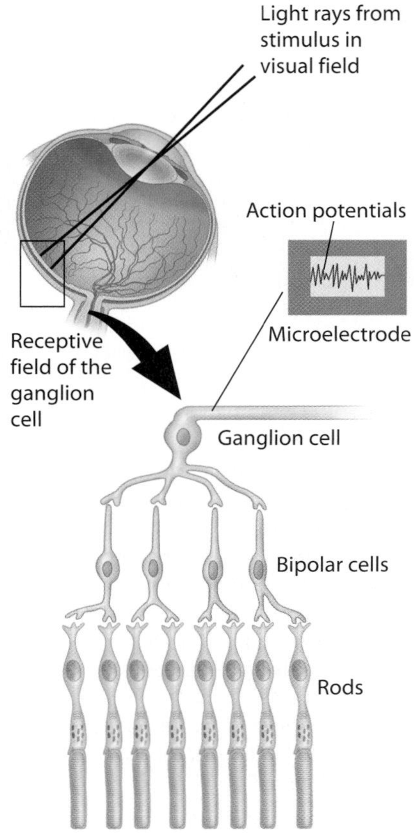

Figure 6.13
The receptive field of a ganglion cell in the periphery of the retina Light rays from part of the visual field hit a particular region on the retina and cause a change in the firing rate of a particular ganglion cell. The stimulated region on the retina is the receptive field of the cell.

Are the receptive fields of all ganglion cells the same size? Explain your answer.

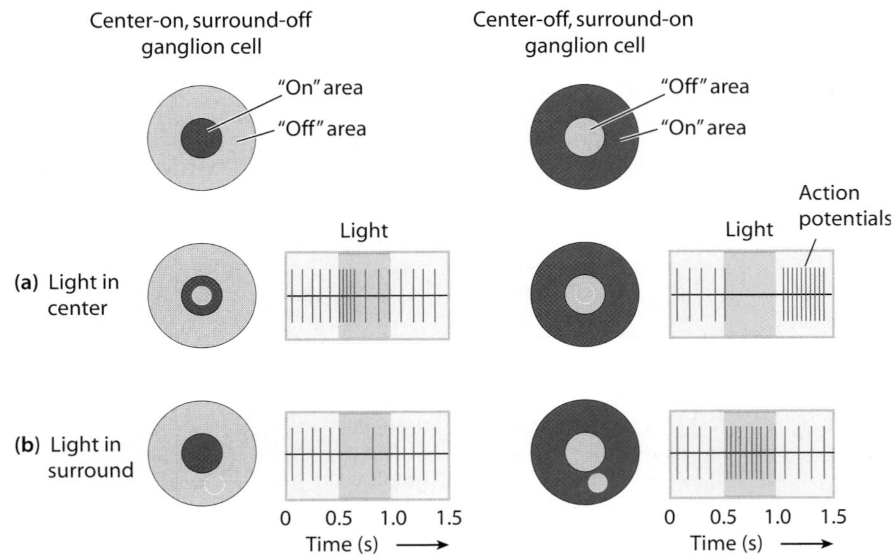

Figure 6.14
The receptive fields of center-on, surround-off and center-off, surround-on ganglion cells (a) A spot of light in the center of the field increases activity in a center-on, surround-off cell and decreases activity in a center-off, surround-on cell. (b) A spot of light in the surround of the field decreases activity in a center-on, surround-off cell and increases activity in a center-off, surround-on cell.

How many receptive fields does each ganglion cell have?

simple cell A neuron in the striate cortex that responds to lines (edges) in a specific part of the visual field having a specific orientation.

innervation by cones. Finally, the receptive fields of ganglion cells tend to be larger than the receptive fields of bipolar cells, which is consistent with the observation that several bipolar cells, all of which have center-surround receptive fields, contribute their information to a single ganglion cell. In other words, the receptive field of the ganglion cell is larger, because it is the combination of the receptive fields of several bipolar cells.

Using microelectrodes, David Hubel and Torsten Wiesel, cowinners of the Nobel Prize for Physiology or Medicine in 1981, recorded the activity of single cells at different levels of the primate visual system in response to stimulation of the eyes with different types of visual stimuli. They found that the center-surround type of receptive field continues in the LGN:

> To sum up, the retinal ganglion cells and the cells of the lateral geniculate—the cells supplying the input to the visual cortex—are cells with concentric, center-surround receptive fields. They are primarily concerned . . . with making a comparison between the light level in one area of the visual scene and the average illumination of the immediate surround. (Hubel & Wiesel, 1979, p. 154)

In the visual cortex, Hubel and Wiesel (1979) found two major differences with what had been found at lower levels of the visual system. First, most cells in the visual cortex beyond layer IV (the layer to which LGN cells project) respond to binocular input—stimulation from both eyes—rather than monocular input, as is found as far as the LGN. Second, the receptive fields of the cortical cells no longer seem to be the center-surround variety found as far as layer IV. Instead, the cells in the visual cortex seem to respond best to lines and edges.

Hubel and Wiesel identified several different types of cells in the visual cortex. So-called **simple cells,** found only in the primary visual cortex, respond to lines (edges) that have a specific orientation and occur in a specific part of the visual field. If the orientation or the location of a line is changed, the particular simple cell either fails to respond or has a drastically reduced response. As shown in Fig-

Figure 6.15

The receptive field of a simple cell of the primary visual cortex (a) The responses of a simple cell, with a vertical orientation, to a light stimulus in different locations and orientations relative to the receptive field of the cell. (b) Examples of receptive fields of simple cells in the primary visual cortex. (c) Model to explain the receptive field of a simple cell in the cortex, which receives input from several cells in the LGN with center-surround receptive fields.

➡ **What are some of the other cell types that Hubel and Wiesel found in the visual cortex?**

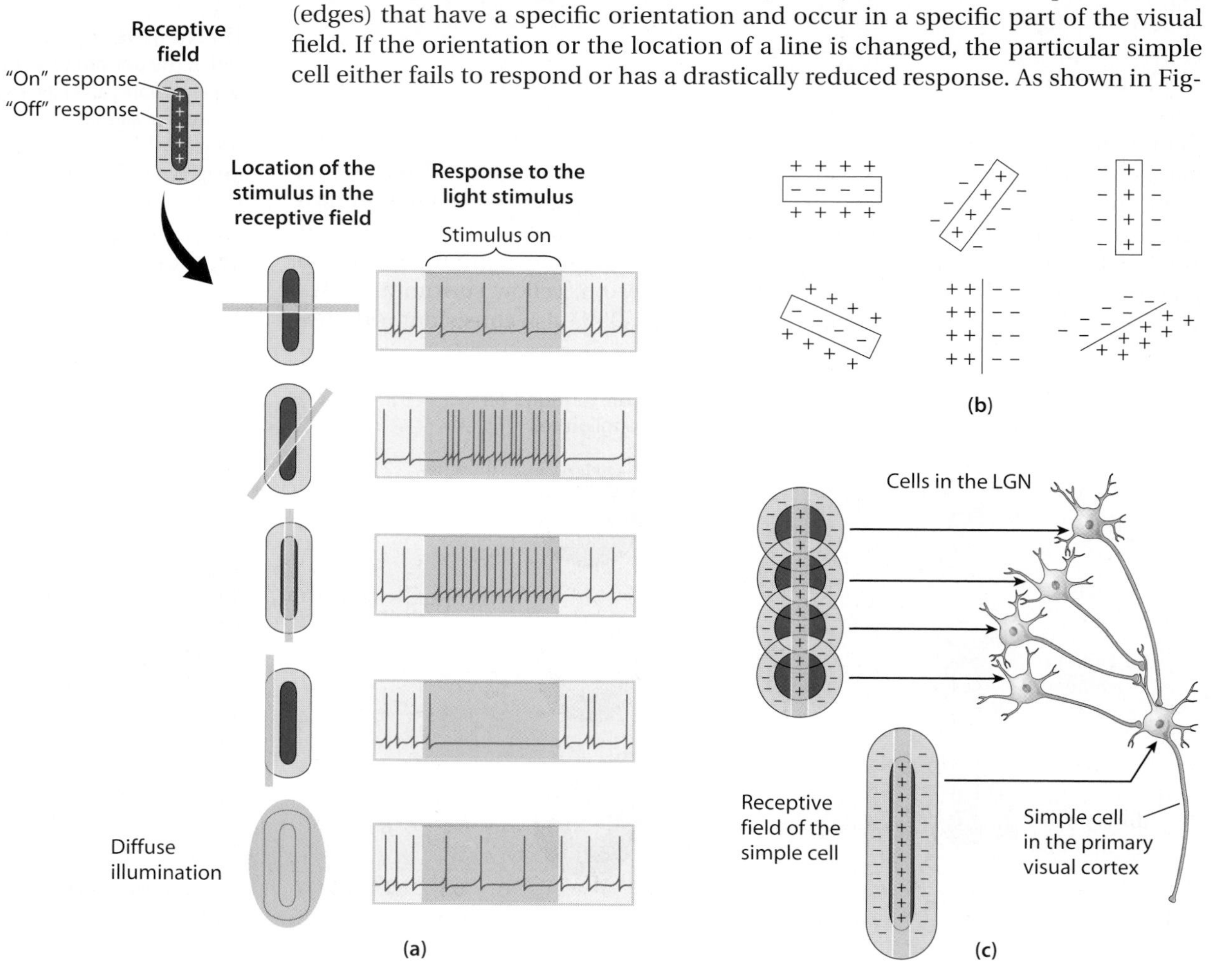

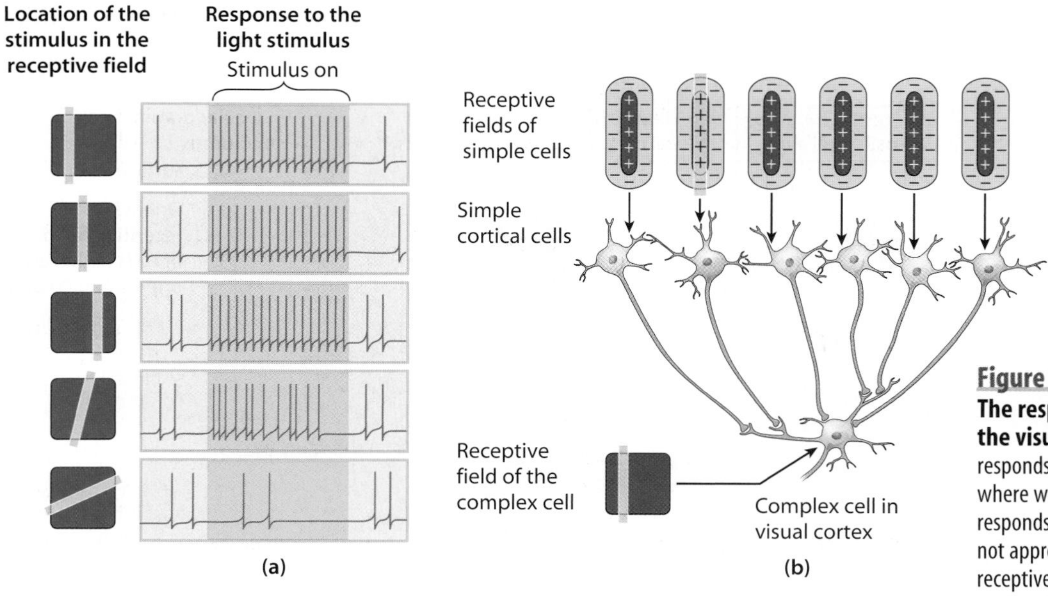

Figure 6.16

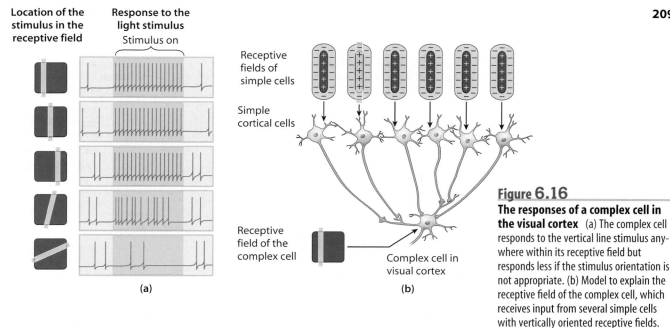

The responses of a complex cell in the visual cortex (a) The complex cell responds to the vertical line stimulus anywhere within its receptive field but responds less if the stimulus orientation is not appropriate. (b) Model to explain the receptive field of the complex cell, which receives input from several simple cells with vertically oriented receptive fields.

→ **List the differences between simple cells and complex cells.**

ure 6.15a, only a specific line will activate the simple cell, which in this case responds best to a vertical light stimulus covering its center "on" region. Diffuse light covering the entire receptive field results in little response. Figure 6.15b shows several other possible receptive fields of simple cells. As you can see from the model in Figure 6.15c, the simple cell may be responding to the input it receives from several LGN cells with center-surround, circularly symmetrical fields. Again, these cells respond to binocular input—that is, to a line with a specific orientation that is stimulating the same part of the retina of each eye.

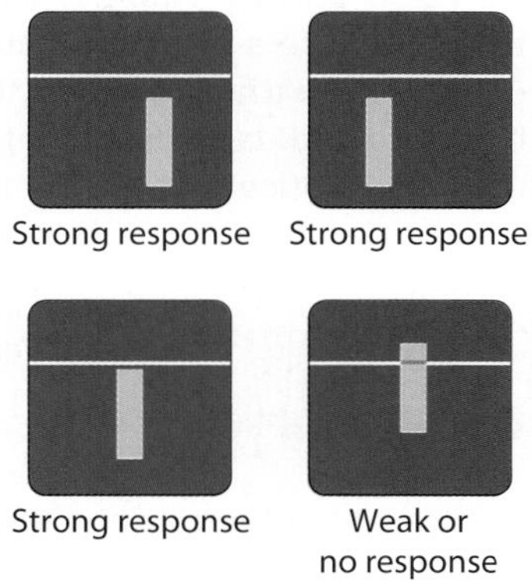

Figure 6.17

The responses of a hypercomplex (end-stopped) cell in the visual cortex The cell responds strongly to a bar of light with a particular orientation (vertical, in this case) anywhere within the receptive field, as long as the bar does not extend beyond a certain point. If this boundary is crossed, the cell produces little or no response.

→ **What is the difference between complex cells and hypercomplex cells?**

Like simple cells, the more numerous **complex cells** found in striate and prestriate cortex are sensitive to a line stimulus oriented in a particular direction. Unlike in simple cells, the line can be anywhere within a rather large receptive field (Figure 6.16a). Because the receptive fields of complex cells are larger than those of simple cells, the stimulus can appear in several different locations and still activate the complex cell. Some complex cells also respond when the line moves in a specific direction, whereas others react to line movement in any direction. Complex cells appear to be responding to input from several simple cells, all with the same receptive-field orientation but differing slightly in where the fields are located (Figure 6.16b).

Like complex cells, **hypercomplex cells** respond to visual stimuli of a particular orientation (line-tilt) within a relatively large receptive field. The difference is that hypercomplex cells do not respond if the line stimulus extends beyond a specific point, and hypercomplex cells are sometimes called *end-stopped* because of this feature (Figure 6.17). As you can see in Figure 6.17, a line extending beyond the boundaries of the receptive field elicits little or no firing.

Hubel and Wiesel (1977) also found that the visual cortex has a columnar organization. Cells within a given column may exhibit the same degree of dominance of either the right or the left eye—for example, in one column, the input from the left eye may account for most of the activity of the cells, and all the cells in the column have the same amount of left-eye dominance. Columns with this feature are called **ocular dominance columns.** In addition, all the cells within a column respond to the same orientation of a line stimulus (line-tilt). If one responds to a vertical line, then all the orientation-specific cells in the **orientation column** respond maximally to a vertical line. Ocular dominance columns, orientation columns, and blobs (mentioned earlier) are contained in a *hypercolumn* in which several types of

complex cell A neuron in striate or prestriate cortex that is sensitive to a line stimulus oriented in a particular direction and occurring anywhere in the receptive field.

hypercomplex cell A neuron that responds to visual stimuli of a particular orientation and a specific length in a relatively large receptive field.

ocular dominance column A column of cells in the visual cortex all having the same amount of dominance of input from either the left or the right eye.

orientation column A column of cells in the visual cortex all responding to the same orientation of a line stimulus (line-tilt).

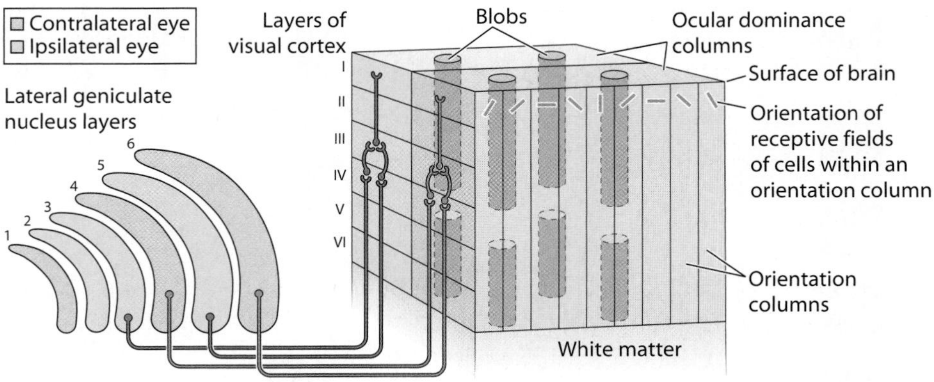

Figure 6.18
A hypercolumn A hypercolumn includes a set (one from each eye) of ocular dominance columns, blobs, and orientation columns.

➡ **What happens in a hypercolumn?**

visual information are combined into a picture of a particular region of the visual field (Figure 6.18).

On the basis of their work, Hubel and Wiesel concluded that our visual system analyzes the visual scene by breaking it down into lines and edges, moving lines and edges, moving lines of a specific length, and so on. The cells of the primary visual cortex appear to be **feature detectors,** responding to specific features of the visual scene.

Figure 6.19
Spatial-frequency analysis A visual scene can be represented by plotting changes in lightness and darkness along "slices" of the scene.

➡ **How is a visual scene analyzed according to spatial-frequency theory?**

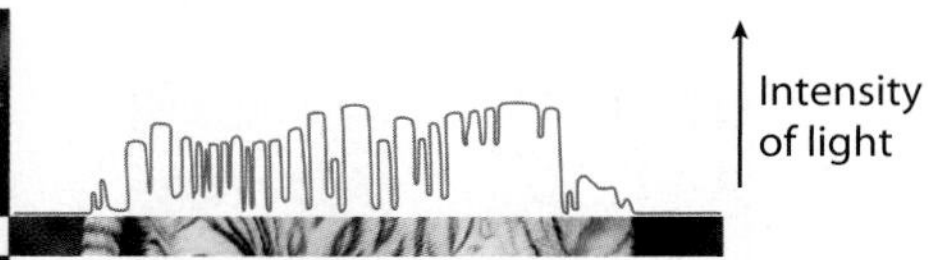

But do these cells respond best to lines and edges, or do they respond better to some other characteristic of the visual scene? If they respond better to some other feature, what might it be? Based on earlier work by Campbell and Robson (1968), De Valois and De Valois (1988) suggested that the cortical cells may actually be responding to a different feature of the visual scene—its spatial frequencies. According to **spatial-frequency theory,** any visual scene can be broken into areas of lightness and darkness (Figure 6.19), as represented in a **sine-wave grating** (Figure 6.20). Notice that the intensity of light varies in the sine-wave grating, becoming alternately lighter and darker. The complex pattern of light and dark consists of many simple sine waves, which can vary in frequency (cycles per second), amplitude (height of the wave), and angle. A complex mathematical procedure called Fourier analysis can break down any complex curve into its constituent sine waves (Figure 6.21). Sine-wave gratings are identified by their spatial frequency, or variation in brightness measured in cycles per degree of visual angle.

De Valois and De Valois (1988) suggested that the cells in the visual cortex are actually responding to specific spatial frequencies rather than to lines or edges. In support of the spatial-frequency theory, they found that neurons of the type that Hubel and Wiesel studied give a greater response to specific sine-wave gratings than to lines or edges. Further, different neurons in the primary visual cortex respond to different sine-wave patterns. As yet, it is not clear whether neurons in the primary visual cortex respond to both straight lines and sine-wave gratings, or

Figure 6.20
A sine-wave grating The increasing and decreasing brightness of light within the circle is depicted as a sine wave. (From De Valois & De Valois, 1988.)

➡ **In what three ways can sine waves differ from one another?**

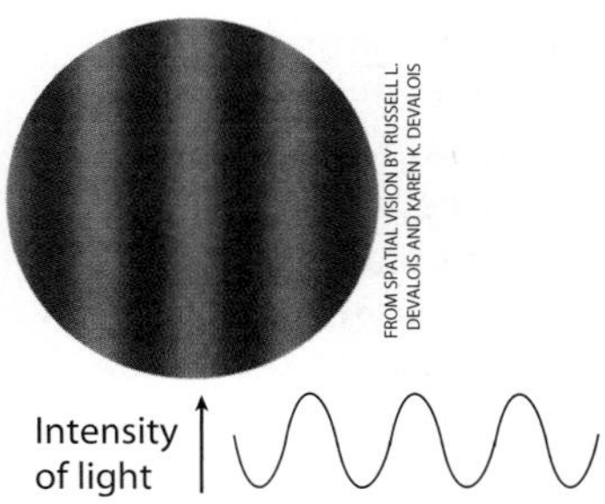

Figure 6.21
Analyzing a complex curve into its component sine waves
Fourier analysis shows that the complex curve at the top is composed of the three sine waves shown below.

➡ **How many different neurons would be needed to respond to the complex pattern at the top of this figure?**

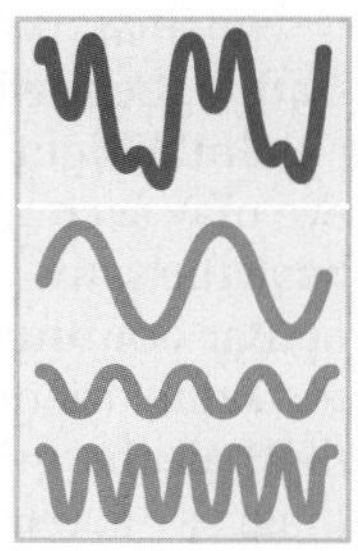

just to sine-wave gratings, or to something else entirely. Researchers are attempting to answer this question, as well as the question of how the visual system reconstructs the basic elements to which it responds into the perception of a specific object (e.g., Hegde & Van Essen, 2000; Petkov & Kruizinga, 1997).

feature detector A cell in the visual cortex that appears to respond to a specific feature of the visual scene.

spatial-frequency theory The theory that cells in the visual cortex are responding to spatial frequencies of lightness and darkness in a visual scene.

sine-wave grating The alternating lighter and darker intensities in a light stimulus.

The Influence of Experience on the Development of the Visual System

Thus far, our discussion of receptive fields of neurons in the visual system has assumed normal development. In the 1960s, Hubel and Wiesel began to study the visual system of cats after varying amounts of visual deprivation (Hubel, 1967). For example, when the experimenters sewed shut the right eye of newborn kittens and opened it 3 months later, virtually no cells in the visual cortex of the animals responded to the closed eye; most cells responded to the left eye only (Wiesel & Hubel, 1963). Not surprisingly, the kittens behaved as though they were blind in their right eye.

In their studies on newborn kittens, Hubel and Wiesel (1963) found that all the specific cell types they had observed in the visual cortex of adult cats were present in the newborns, which suggests that the connections are innately determined—an observation verified by Crair and colleagues (1998). However, if these connections are not used soon after birth, they become nonfunctional. Further research indicated that the critical period for such use in cats is between the 4th and 6th weeks of life, as monocular deprivation ending before the 4th week had little effect, but deprivation for 6 weeks or more produced the kind of deficit seen in kittens monocularly deprived (by sewing shut one eye) for 3 months. Hubel and Wiesel also found that deprivation beginning at 3 months of age had no effect on the cat's visual system. The corresponding critical period for the visual system of monkeys appears to be much longer than for cats, beginning soon after birth and extending through the first year of life or longer (Hubel, 1967). In humans, the period of plasticity of the visual system may last to the age of 4 or 5 years or even beyond.

In an effort to study the human clinical implications of their research, Hubel and Wiesel (1965) cut the eye muscles of kittens to create *strabismus,* a condition occurring in humans in which one eye cannot focus with the other because of an imbalance of the eye muscles (sometimes called *crossed-eye* or *wall-eye*). After 3 months, the experimenters were surprised to find that the kittens had normal vision in both eyes. However, when Hubel and Wiesel recorded activity in the visual cortical cells of the animals, they found that most cells (79%) were monocularly driven, which occurs in only about 20% of cortical cells in a cat with normal vision.

Strabismus is the main cause of *amblyopia,* or lazy eye, in which one eye (the "lazy" one) does not develop properly because the other eye dominates vision. Research into the neurological basis for amblyopia essentially began with Hubel and Wiesel's early work on kittens (Barrett & others, 2004). The treatment for amblyopia generally requires forcing the patient to use the "lazy" eye by wearing a patch over the stronger eye. Goodyear and colleagues (2002) used fMRI to show greater ocular dominance of the strong eye in adults with early-onset amblyopia, but not in adults with later-onset amblyopia. The researchers suggested that the shift in ocular dominance occurs only if amblyopia develops within the critical period for development of the visual system.

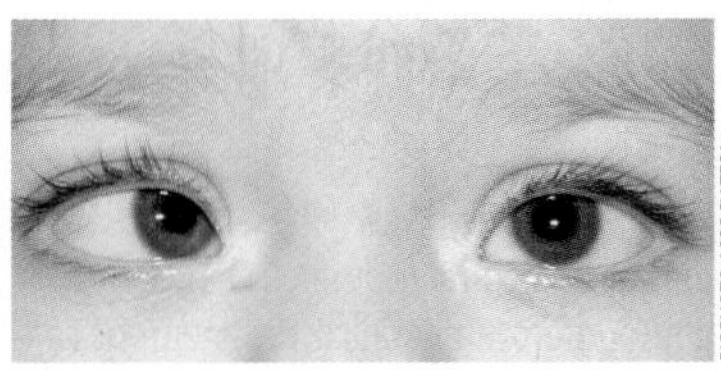
BIOPHOTO ASSOCIATES/PHOTO RESEARCHERS, INC.

Strabismus is the main cause of amblyopia (lazy eye).

Although most research into development of the visual system has focused on the effects of visual deprivation, Cancedda and coworkers (2004) took the opposite approach, by examining visual development following environmental enrichment. The researchers raised mice in an environment that provided complex sensory-motor stimulation, and observed earlier eye opening and precocious development of visual acuity as well as electrophysiological and molecular changes indicative of accelerated development.

Checkpoint

From their microelectrode work, how would Hubel and Wiesel characterize the receptive fields of neurons in the primary visual cortex and beyond? Do De Valois and De Valois agree with Hubel and Wiesel? If not, how do they differ?

visual agnosia A perceptual problem involving the inability to name an object when it is presented visually but not when it is presented in another sensory modality.

fusiform face area The region of the inferotemporal cortex most responsible for recognition of faces.

prosopagnosia An impaired ability to recognize familiar faces visually.

The Role of the Secondary Visual Cortex

As we noted earlier, three pathways relay information from the primary visual cortex to the secondary visual cortex. Of these, the pathway extending through the prestriate cortex to the inferotemporal cortex appears to be involved in object recognition.

Remember Margaret's visual field deficit? She is unable to detect objects in the upper right quadrant of her visual field because of damage to some of the visual pathway. Her visual field deficit is a *sensory* problem, in which the path from the sensory organ to the cerebral cortex is damaged. If a person is unable to name objects that he or she can see—a *perceptual* problem—the pathway from the sensory organ to the cerebral cortex is intact, but there is damage within the cerebral cortex. In one such perceptual problem, **visual agnosia,** a person is unable to name an object presented visually but can identify it when it is presented in another sensory mode (e.g., the person cannot identify a cube visually but can identify it by touch). Visual agnosia usually results from bilateral damage to the inferotemporal cortex (Goodale & others, 1994; Ridley & others, 2001). The person with visual agnosia is not blind and can respond to some, especially visually familiar, objects in the environment. The person sees individual features of an object but cannot assemble them into a meaningful whole—a percept.

Vision researchers have long sought what they sometimes call "grandmother detectors," cortical neurons that respond to something as specific and as highly familiar as an image of your grandmother (or any other familiar image or object). Although grandmother detectors per se have not yet been found, the brain does contain neurons that respond differentially to familiar and unfamiliar faces. For example, Rossion and colleagues (2001) measured brain activity using PET as individuals viewed faces they had been shown earlier and completely novel faces. Large relative increases in activation occurred in several parts of the occipitotemporal pathway when subjects saw unfamiliar faces, but no increase in activation occurred with familiar faces. By their activation in response to novel faces and their failure to respond to familiar faces, these neurons seem to be differentiating faces on the basis of new information provided. Obviously, the unfamiliar faces provide more new information than the ones seen before.

An analysis of functional brain-imaging studies suggests that facial recognition is particularly a function of a region of the inferotemporal cortex called the fusiform gyrus, or the **fusiform face area** (Joseph, 2001). Further, the fusiform face area appears to be specifically activated by faces rather than by nonface objects such as cars, as seen by car experts, or lepidoptera (butterflies and moths), as seen by lepidoptera experts (Grill-Spector & others, 2004; Rhodes & others, 2004).

Keiji Tanaka's research (2000) suggests how we learn to recognize specific faces. For example, Kobatake and Tanaka (1994) trained monkeys to discriminate between 28 moderately complex shapes by presenting pairs of stimuli and reinforcing an animal for responding to one stimulus but not the other (Figure 6.22). After a year of discrimination training, 39% of the neurons in the anterior part of the inferotemporal cortex of the monkey responded to some of these shapes. By contrast, only 9% of these neurons in monkeys that had not received discrimination training responded to any of the shapes. The research results indicate that experience enables neurons in the inferotemporal cortex to recognize complex light stimuli, such as the face of a particular person. Damage to these neurons should produce a failure to recognize familiar faces, and indeed it does.

Figure 6.22

Object recognition These are examples of moderately complex shapes to which inferotemporal cortical neurons can learn to respond. (Courtesy of Keiji Tanaka.)

➡ **What would be the effect of damage to the inferotemporal cortex on the recognition of these shapes?**

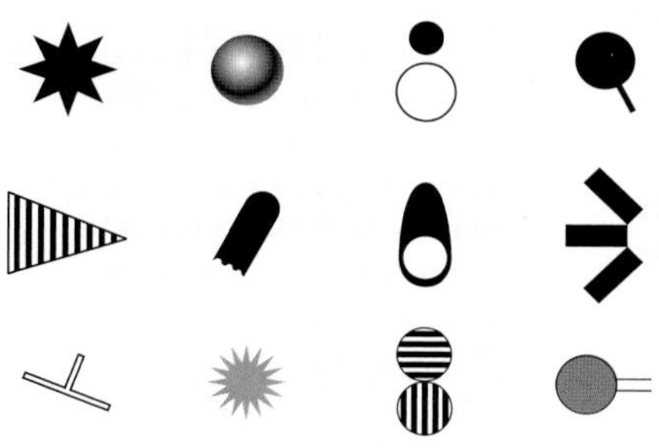

Prosopagnosia is a difficulty in recognizing familiar faces (*prosopon* is Greek for "person"). People with prosopagnosia have problems identifying familiar faces and may even be unable to recognize their own face. For example, a prosopagnosic patient will bump into a mirror and say "Excuse me," mistaking his or her own image for another person. People with prosopagnosia are able to discriminate faces normally (i.e., recognize that one face is different from another) and can usually recognize faces as faces;

they just cannot identify whose face they are viewing. They eventually learn to use extrafacial cues such as hair length, height, sound of voice, or distinguishing birthmarks to identify people whose faces they cannot recognize.

An individual with prosopagnosia is described in minute detail in the cover story of *The Man Who Mistook His Wife for a Hat,* by Oliver Sacks (1987). The source of the book's title was an event that occurred during Sacks's first meeting with Dr. P., the man with the problem. Assuming that the examination was over, Dr. P. searched for his hat. "He reached out his hand and took hold of his wife's head, tried to lift it off, to put it on. He had apparently mistaken his wife for a hat! His wife looked as if she was used to such things" (p. 11).

Autopsies of people with prosopagnosia have revealed damage to the inferior prestriate area and adjacent portions of the inferotemporal cortex or inferotemporal pathway (Damasio, 1990). In particular, the damaged area involved in prosopagnosia appears to be the fusiform face area in the right hemisphere (Barton & others, 2002; Rossion & others, 2003; Wada & Yamamoto, 2001). Wada and Yamamoto used MRI to examine the brain of a 67-year-old man who had developed prosopagnosia following a brain hemorrhage. MRI revealed damage limited primarily to the right fusiform area. Barton and colleagues found that patients with prosopagnosia, if their brain damage included the right fusiform face area, were severely impaired in discriminating changes in faces with altered spatial location of features.

Recognition in people with prosopagnosia occurs on an unconscious level. Tranel and Damasio (1988) measured the electrodermal skin conductance response (e.g., a change in sweatiness of the palms, which alters the ability of the skin to conduct electrical currents) in four prosopagnosic patients while they were shown pictures of either familiar or unfamiliar faces. The familiar faces triggered significantly larger and more frequent skin conductance responses than did the unfamiliar faces. Bauer and Verfaellie (1988) extended this work by demonstrating that the electrodermal discrimination occurred only for famous faces and not for unfamiliar faces.

Checkpoint

Explain how a person with visual agnosia could recognize a batch of freshly baked cookies. What evidence is there for unconscious facial recognition in a person who has prosopagnosia?

REVIEW

- The recognition of objects in our environment is aided by lateral inhibition, which sharpens the edges between an object and its background (its surround).
- If the object is brighter than the surround (or vice versa), the activity of ganglion cells at the boundary of the object and the surround increases or decreases, depending on the presence or absence of lateral inhibition from adjacent receptors.
- The receptive field of a visual system cell is a region of the retina that, when stimulated, causes a change in the activity (firing rate) of the cell.
- The receptive fields of bipolar cells, ganglion cells, LGN cells, and cortical cells in layer IV of the primary visual cortex have a center-surround configuration, with a central excitatory region and a peripheral inhibitory region, or vice versa.
- X ganglion cells have smaller receptive fields than Y ganglion cells, and they also respond to color.
- Simple cells of the striate cortex respond to lines or edges with a specific orientation and location in the visual field; they may receive input from several LGN cells.
- Complex cells in striate and prestriate cortex are sensitive to a specific line stimulus that moves in a particular direction anywhere in the visual field; they may receive input from several simple cells with the same line orientation but slightly different locations.
- Hypercomplex cells have receptive fields like those of complex cells, except the length of the line stimulus is critical: If it is too long, they do not respond.
- Spatial-frequency theory suggests that cells in the primary visual cortex respond not to lines or moving lines but to sine-wave gratings.

monocular depth cue A depth cue requiring only one eye for detection.

- Research on the effects of early visual deprivation indicates that there is a critical period for development of the visual system. Lack of appropriate early experience disrupts innate connections and pathways.
- Damage to the pathway from the primary visual cortex to the prestriate cortex and then to the inferotemporal cortex leads to visual agnosia, an inability to recognize objects visually.
- Prosopagnosia is a form of visual agnosia in which the person has difficulty recognizing familiar faces. The disorder is particularly associated with damage to the right fusiform face area.

The Perception of Depth, Movement, and Color

Alan, the young man with drusen, is an ardent professional football fan. His favorite team is about to appear on television, and Alan is preparing to watch the game. At the moment, he has opened his refrigerator and is looking inside for a bottle of his favorite beer. He spots it on a shelf on the door. Alan's visual system not only recognizes the bottle but perceives its three-dimensional form, its movement as he lifts it from the shelf, and its beautiful amber color. In this section we discuss how the visual system provides us (and Alan) with all this information.

A major pathway from the primary visual cortex to the secondary visual cortex, the one that extends through the prestriate cortex to the posterior parietal cortex, is responsible for detecting the location and movement of objects through space (see the blue arrow in Figure 6.8). We examine this pathway before turning to the mechanisms involved in perceiving color and, finally, the ways in which the brain combines all this information into a unified perception.

Depth Perception

After the weighty discussion in the last section, it is time to take a break. Look at the photographs in Figure 6.23. Each photo illustrates important depth cues—in this case, **monocular depth cues,** or cues that require only one eye in order to be detected. For example, in the highway scene, even though the picture is two-dimensional, you perceive the mountains to be in the background, far from the stretch of highway in the foreground. In other words, something about the picture gives it a three-dimensional quality. Your visual system enables you to perceive depth in the picture and, of course, in the world around you. If you could not see in three dimensions, you could not, for example, recognize how far your hand is from a pen that you want to pick up, and you would take much longer to retrieve it successfully.

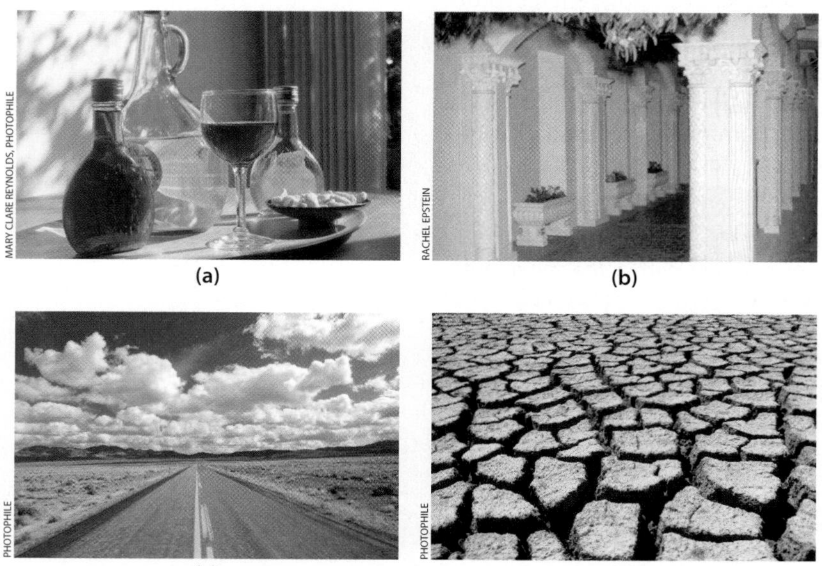

Figure 6.23
Four examples of monocular depth cues (a) Interposition, (b) relative brightness, (c) linear perspective, and (d) gradient of texture.

→ **What areas of the brain are responsible for depth perception?**

We use a number of cues to recognize depth, some of which are illustrated in Figure 6.23. *Relative size* is a monocular depth cue: Objects that produce a larger image on the retina are usually closer to us than objects that produce a smaller image. Additional monocular cues include *interposition* (an object that covers or partially covers another object is perceived as closer), *gradient of texture* (coarser objects are perceived as closer than finer-grained objects), *relative height* (objects higher in the visual field are perceived as farther away), *linear perspective* (the greater the convergence, the farther away the object is), and *relative brightness* (brighter objects are perceived as closer than dimmer objects).

Binocular depth cues are provided by both eyes (see Figure 6.6). Because our eyes are separated on our face, each eye has a slightly different view of the world. Our brain compares these two images, and the difference, or *retinal disparity*, provides an important depth cue: The greater the disparity in the two images, the closer the object is to us.

The brain detects cues, such as the slight differences in retinal images and the convergence of parallel lines that recede from us, and uses them to create our perception of depth. As described earlier, cells in the primary visual cortex respond to lines or edges or perhaps to sine-wave patterns and communicate what they have "seen" to the secondary visual cortex, which is responsible for detecting the form of objects. Research evidence suggests that cells in the primary visual cortex also react to depth cues. For example, some cells respond when each eye sees an object in a slightly different position—that is, when there is retinal disparity (Gonzales & others, 2001; Poggio, 1995). Some of these neurons are sensitive to slight differences in retinal disparity, and others are sensitive to greater differences in the input from each eye (Poggio).

Input from the neurons in the primary visual cortex travels to the prestriate cortex, then to the middle temporal cortex and the medial superior temporal cortex, and finally to the posterior parietal lobe (see the blue arrow in Figure 6.8). Neurons in this pathway respond to depth cues, where input is perceived as differences in depth.

The *Scientific American* Spotlight, "Seeing Is Believing," provides information about shading and depth perception. In the article, we learn that the brain makes assumptions about conditions of viewing, such as that a single source of light illuminates what we see. This makes perfect sense when you remember that we evolved on a planet revolving around a single sun, that is, with one source of light. Whether we see the disks as eggs or cavities depends on where we are in relation to the source of light. The article highlights the importance of the study of visual illusions for helping us understand visual perception.

binocular depth cue A depth cue provided by both eyes.

component direction-selective neuron A neuron in striate cortex that responds to movement in one direction.

pattern direction-selective neuron A neuron in the middle temporal cortex that combines the information arriving from the primary visual cortex to recognize the direction in which an object is moving.

Movement Detection

Information about movement, like information about depth, is first sent to neurons in the primary visual cortex from Y ganglion cells (via magnocellular neurons in the LGN). This information is then transmitted to the prestriate cortex, then to the MT cortex, the MST cortex, and finally the posterior parietal cortex (see the blue arrow in Figure 6.8). As in shape and depth detection, neurons in the pathway from striate cortex to the posterior parietal lobe are selectively sensitive—in this case, to movement. Research using fMRIs reveals that neurons in the MT or MST cortex are activated when people look at moving objects (Tootell & others, 1995), and similar results have been found in monkeys (Vanduffel & others, 2001). These movement-detecting neurons are not responsive to just any movement but are selectively sensitive to one of three types: horizontal, vertical, or motion perpendicular to one axis of orientation. For example, a specific neuron can detect whether an object is moving right or left, but not up or down. Movshon and his colleagues refer to the two types of movement-detecting neurons as **component direction-selective neurons,** or neurons that respond to movement in one direction (Gizzi & others, 1990; Movshon, 1990). To illustrate the functioning of these neurons, suppose an object is moving up and to the left. One neuron detects the "up" (vertical) movement and another detects the "to the left" (horizontal) movement. The third type of neuron, in the MT cortex, is a **pattern direction-selective neuron:** It combines the information from the two earlier neurons to recognize that the object is moving both up and to the left.

Neurons in the MST cortex also can detect the speed at which an object is moving (Movshon, 1990; Recanzone & Wurtz, 1999). This information is extracted from

Scientific American Spotlight

Seeing Is Believing

V. S. Ramachandran & D. Rogers-Ramachandran

The visual image is inherently ambiguous: an image of a person on the retina would be the same size for a dwarf seen from up close or a giant viewed from a distance. Perception is partly a matter of using certain assumptions about the world to resolve such ambiguities. We can use illusions to uncover what the brain's hidden rules and assumptions are. In this column, we consider illusions of shading.

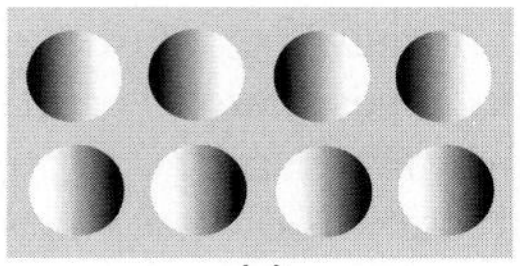
(a)

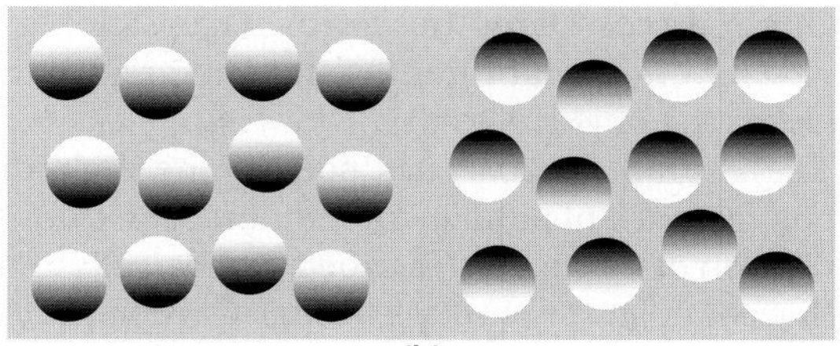
(b)

In (a), the disks are ambiguous; you can see either the top row as convex spheres or "eggs," lit from the left, and the bottom row as cavities—or vice versa. This observation reveals that the visual centers in the brain have a built-in supposition that a single light source illuminates the entire image, which makes sense given that we evolved on a planet with one sun. By consciously shifting the light source from left to right, you can make the eggs and cavities switch places.

In (b), the image is even more compelling. Here the disks that are light on the top (left) always look like eggs, and the ones that are light on the bottom (right) are cavities. So we have uncovered another premise used by the visual system: it expects light to shine from above. You can verify this by turning the page upside down. All the eggs and cavities instantly switch places.

Amazingly, the brain's assumption that light shines from above the head is preserved even when you rotate your head 180 degrees. Ask a friend to hold this page right side up for you. Then bend down and look between your legs at the page behind you. You will find that, again, the switch occurs, as if the sun is stuck to your head and shining upward from the floor. Signals from your body's center of balance—the vestibular system—guided by the positions of little stones in your ears called otoliths, travel to your visual centers to correct your picture of the world (so that the world continues to look upright) but do not correct for the location of the sun.

From this experiment we learn that despite the impression of seamless unity, vision is actually mediated by multiple parallel information-processing modules in the brain. Some of the modules connect to the vestibular system; however, the one that handles shape from shading does not. The reason might be that correcting an image for placement in so-called world-centered coordinates would be too computationally expensive and take too much time. Our ancestors generally kept their heads upright, so the brain could get away with this shortcut (or simplifying assumption). That is, our progenitors were able to raise babies to maturity often enough that no selection pressure acted to produce vestibular correction.

If you look at (c), you find that you can almost instantly mentally group all the eggs and segregate them from the cavities. As visual scientists discovered decades ago, only certain elementary features that are extracted early during visual processing "pop out" conspicu-

the firing pattern of neurons in the MT cortex, with a higher rate of firing signaling a faster-moving object.

These motion-sensitive neurons respond mainly to movement and are virtually insensitive to the identity of the object (Albright, 1992). For example, a motion-sensitive cell responds equally to a small or large object moving in the same direction. People with damage to this area of the cortex were found to have difficulty assessing the speed of an object, but their ability to detect the contrast of moving objects was unaffected (Greenlee & others, 1995).

How do we use this information about the movement of objects in our environment? Neural impulses from the MT and MST cortex travel directly to the brain stem and then to the cerebellum, where *pursuit eye movements,* or eye movements that track a moving object, are controlled. Thus, information from motion-sensitive neurons enables us to follow (visually) moving objects. The magnocellular pathway that detects movement also projects to the posterior parietal cortex, often called the *visual motor area,* which guides body movements toward objects. For example, a batter uses information from this part of the visual system to swing the bat

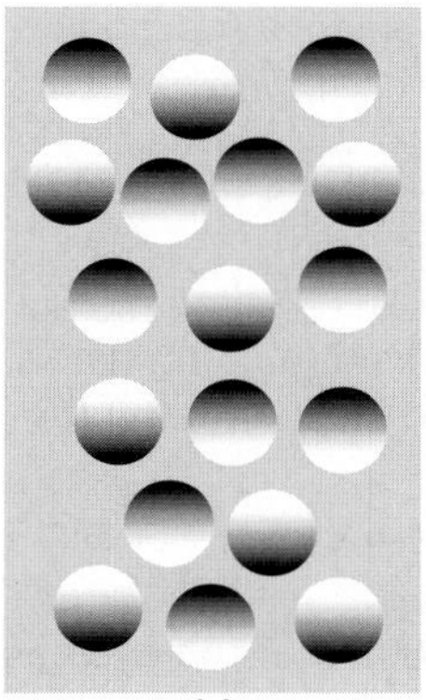
(c)

(d)

ously and can be grouped in this manner. For example, your brain can discern a set of red dots in a background of green ones but cannot group smiles scattered among a backdrop of frowns. Color is thus a primitive feature that is extracted early, whereas a smile is not. (It makes survival sense to be able to piece together fragments of similar color. A lion hidden behind a screen of green leaves is visible merely as gold fragments, but the visual brain assembles the pieces into a single gold lion-shaped form and warns: "Get out of here!" On the other hand, objects are not made up of smiles.)

The fact that you can group the eggs in (c) implies that shading information, like color, is extracted early in visual processing [see "Perceiving Shape from Shading," by Vilayanur S. Ramachandran; Scientific American, August 1988]. This prediction was verified in recent years by recording activity in the neurons of monkeys and by conducting brain-imaging experiments in humans. Certain cells in the visual cortex fire when the observer sees eggs; others respond only to cavities. In (d), where the circles have the same luminance polarities as in (c), you cannot perceive the grouping; this fact suggests the importance of perceived depth as a cue that is extracted early in visual processing.

Of course, over millions of years, evolution has "discovered" and taken advantage of the principles of shading that researchers have explored only lately. Gazelles have white bellies and dark backs—countershading—that neutralize the effect of sunshine from above. The result reduces pop-out so that gazelles are not as conspicuous; they also appear skinnier and less appetizing to a predator. Caterpillars have countershading, too, so they more closely resemble the flat leaves on which they munch. One caterpillar species has reverse countershading—which did not make sense until scientists realized that the insect habitually hangs upside down from twigs. One type of octopus can even invert its countershading: if you suspend the octopus upside down, it uses pigment-producing cells called chromatophores in the skin, which are controlled by its vestibular input, to reverse its darker and lighter areas.

Charles Darwin noticed a striking example of nature's use of shading in the prominent eyelike spots on the long tails of argus pheasants. With the tail feathers at horizontal rest, the orbs are tinged from left to right. During the bird's courtship display, however, the tail feathers become erect. In this position, the spots are paler on top and duskier at bottom, so the disks seem to bulge out like shiny metallic spheres—the avian equivalent of jewelry.

That a few simple shaded circles can unveil the underlying assumptions of our visual systems—and even how such principles have played a role in shaping evolutionary adaptations—shows the power of visual illusions in helping us to understand the nature of perception.

From: *Scientific American Mind,* vol. 14(1), pp. 100–101

at the moment when he or she is most likely to hit the ball. This visual pathway also allows us to shake hands with someone. These examples, swinging a bat and shaking hands, are but two of the many ways in which movement information guides our behavior.

➤Checkpoint

If you were blind in one eye, how would you be able to perceive depth? What disability might result from damage to the posterior parietal cortex?

REVIEW

- Several types of cues provide information about the spatial location of a stimulus, or depth perception.
- Monocular cues include relative size, interposition, gradient of texture, relative height, linear perspective, and relative brightness.
- The difference in visual images from the two eyes, or retinal disparity, provides a binocular depth cue.
- Specific neurons in the primary visual cortex react to gradient of texture and retinal disparity.

Young-Helmholtz trichromatic theory The theory that color perceptions come from a pattern of stimulation of three sets of color receptors in the eye.

opponent-process theory The theory that there are three receptor complexes operating in opponent fashion to yield a perception of color and brightness.

negative afterimage The brief perception of a complementary color after extended stimulation with a particular color.

color constancy The perception that the color of an object remains the same even under different lighting conditions.

- Component direction-selective neurons in the MT or MST respond to movement in one direction. Pattern direction-selective neurons in the MT cortex combine information from separate component direction-selective neurons to recognize the actual direction in which an object is moving.
- The magnocellular visual pathway controls pursuit eye movements and body movements toward objects in the environment.

Color Perception

You have already learned how the stimulation of cones is involved in color vision. Now we address how colors are perceived. We focus on the two (of the many) theories of color vision that have received the most support.

The Young-Helmholtz Trichromatic Theory

English physician and physicist Thomas Young proposed in 1802 that the eye has three types of receptors and that different patterns of stimulation of these receptors result in the perception of different colors. In 1852, Hermann Ludwig von Helmholtz revived and slightly modified Young's theory, suggesting that the eye has three different types of fibers: one that responds to red, a second to green, and a third to blue or violet. Different patterns of stimulation of the fibers enable us to see all the colors of the spectrum. For example, a yellow object equally activates both the green and the red fibers, creating the perception of yellow. This theory is known as the **Young-Helmholtz trichromatic theory.**

Hering's Opponent-Process Theory

Problems with the trichromatic theory soon became evident, and competing theories were proposed. For example, critics of the Young-Helmholtz theory pointed out that the most common color defect in people is an inability to distinguish red from green. If it is true, as Helmholtz argued, that yellow results from the equal activation of red receptors and green receptors, then a person with a red-green defect should also have problems detecting yellow—but this is not so.

The most successful of the color vision theories that were designed to compete with the trichromatic theory was proposed in 1874. Ewald Hering's **opponent-process theory** suggests that three receptor complexes operate in opponent fashion: a red-green complex, a blue-yellow complex, and a black-white complex, the latter accounting for brightness perception. For example, a red-green complex would be a retinal unit whose activity increased when stimulated by the color red and decreased when stimulated by green, or vice versa. Similarly, a blue-yellow complex would be activated by blue and inhibited by yellow, or vice versa.

Opponent-process theory is better than trichromatic theory at accounting for color defects. For one thing, color defects come in pairs, with red-green defects being most common and blue-yellow defects relatively rare. Because of the paired nature of color defects, Hering's theory has no problem accounting for the perception of yellow by a person with a red-green defect. To test your color vision, look at Figure 6.24. Also, note that we have been careful to use the term *color defect* rather than the more common and generally erroneous term, *color blindness.* True color blindness is associated with *albinism,* a genetic condition in which a person lacks an enzyme needed to form the pigment normally found in the skin, hair, and eyes. As a result, the hair is white and the eyes and skin are pink. Albinism is rare, whereas color defects, particularly red-green defects, are relatively common, occurring in about 8% of males and 1% of females of European descent.

Figure 6.24

A test of color vision If you cannot see the number in the figure, you may have a red-green color defect.

➜ **What areas of the brain recognize colors?**

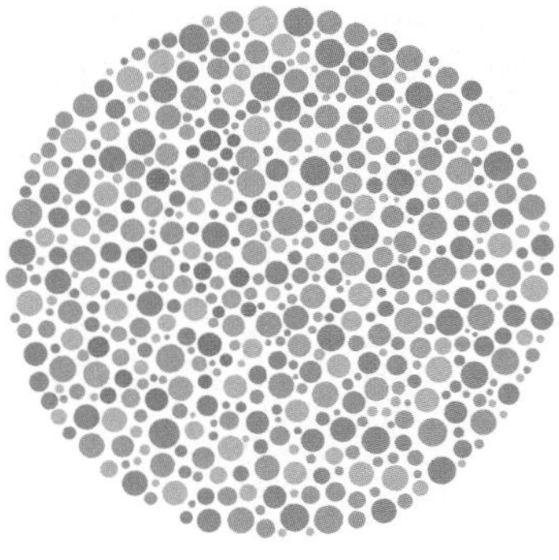

One phenomenon that Hering's theory was designed to explain is the **negative afterimage,** the brief perception of a complementary or opposite color after extended stimulation with a particular color. For example, if you stare for a couple of minutes at a picture of a red car and then glance over at a white wall or piece of white paper, for a few seconds you will see a ghostly green car. The explanation for the negative afterimage is that you have fatigued the red half of the red-green complex, and

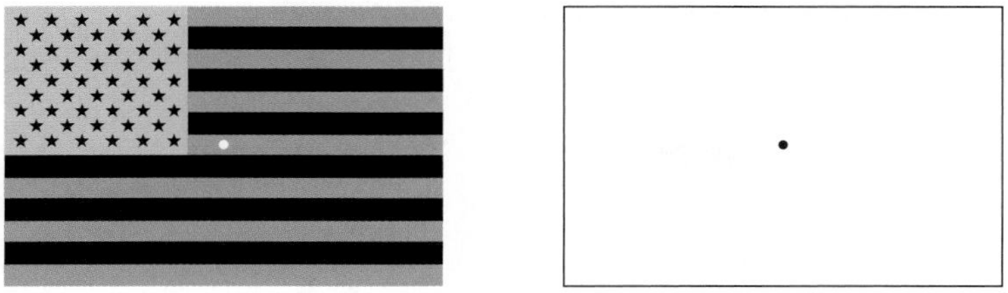

Figure 6.25

Negative afterimages You can demonstrate the phenomenon of a negative afterimage by staring at the flag for 2 minutes, then looking at the white rectangle. You should see a normal red, white, and blue flag.

What would be the negative afterimage of a blue flower with green leaves?

the afterimage represents the green half briefly accounting for more of the activity of the complex. Use Figure 6.25 to demonstrate negative afterimages for yourself.

Based on our discussion of color vision theories to this point, you probably have concluded that opponent-process theory presents the more accurate view of color vision. However, using microspectrophotometry, a technique for measuring the absorption spectrum of a single photoreceptor cell, Brown and Wald (1964) demonstrated that Young and Helmholtz were correct: There are three different types of cones. Brown and Wald found some cones sensitive to short wavelengths of light, some sensitive to medium wavelengths, and some sensitive to long wavelengths (Figure 6.26).

But this is not the end of the story. Beyond the level of the photoreceptors, where the findings support trichromatic theory, research has demonstrated what we would expect to find from opponent-process theory. For example, when X ganglion cells are stimulated with spots of colored light, the familiar center-surround receptive field appears—but with a twist: The central excitatory area is activated by red and inhibited by green, and vice versa, or activated by blue and inhibited by yellow, and vice versa (Dacey, 1996). Figure 6.27 illustrates four types of ganglion cells in terms of color responsiveness. Similar results have been found in parvocellular neurons in the LGN: They respond in opponent-process fashion (De Valois & others, 1966, 2000).

Figure 6.26

The relative absorption of different wavelengths of light by three types of cones and by rods A short-wavelength cone is maximally responsive to 419 nm light, a medium-wavelength cone to 531 nm light, and a long-wavelength cone to 559 nm light.

Which theory of color vision receives greatest support from three types of cones?

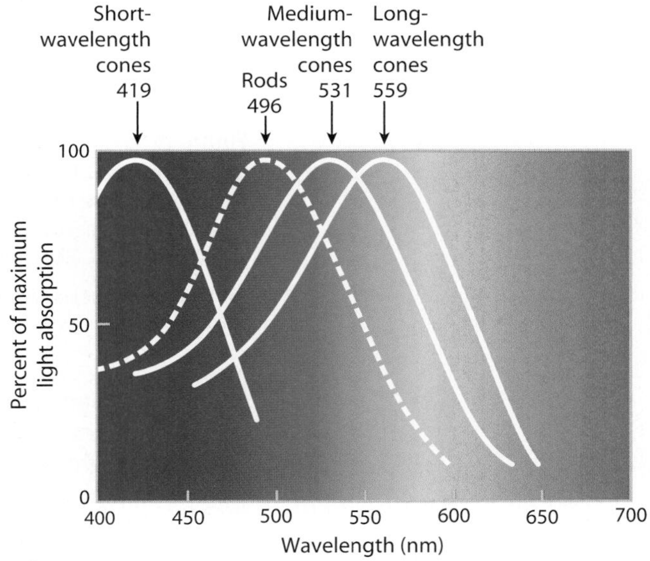

There apparently are three types of cones, as predicted by trichromatic theory, as well as the appropriate types of ganglion cells and LGN cells to satisfy the predictions of opponent-process theory. In 1974, Hurvich and Jameson introduced a simple diagram to suggest how three different cones might be "wired" to higher-level visual cells (bipolar cells) to produce opponent responses. Figure 6.28 is a simplified illustration of how different wavelengths of light could stimulate three types of cones to produce an opponent-process outcome. Note that bipolar, horizontal, and amacrine cells are not included.

Information about color travels from the LGN to the primary visual cortex, which contains cells sensitive to color (Gegenfurtner & Kiper, 2003). The cells in the striate cortex react in the same way as ganglion and LGN cells; that is, activity is increased by one color and decreased by its opposing color. By contrast, cells in the secondary visual cortex respond only to very specific colors.

As you probably have observed, the perception of a color is affected by its context. To illustrate this effect, look at Figure 6.29. Although the crossed lines in each pair of panels appear to be dramatically different colors, they are the same color. The background changes your perception of the color of the crossed lines. The action of cells in the prestriate cortex is believed to be responsible for this contrast effect. For example, one cell sensitive to green may react one way if red is also present in the visual field and another way if yellow is present.

It has also been suggested that cells in the prestriate cortex are responsible for a phenomenon known as **color constancy,** in which an object retains its known color despite changes in lighting conditions. Color constancy enables us to perceive a white car as white even when we look at it through

Figure 6.27

The color responsiveness of four types of ganglion cells Each ganglion cell is stimulated in the center by one color and inhibited in the surround by its opponent color.

The existence of ganglion cells that respond in opponent fashion supports which theory of color vision?

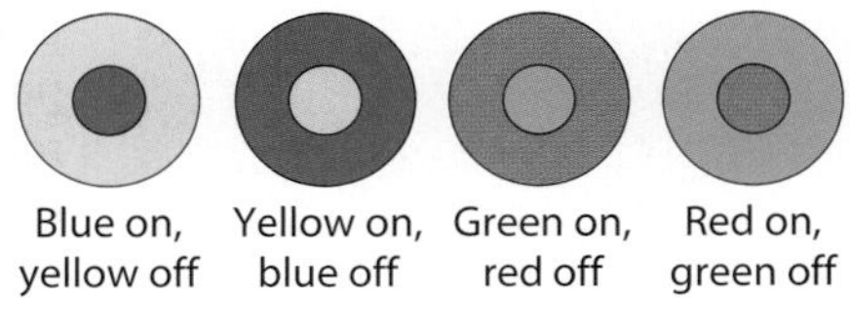

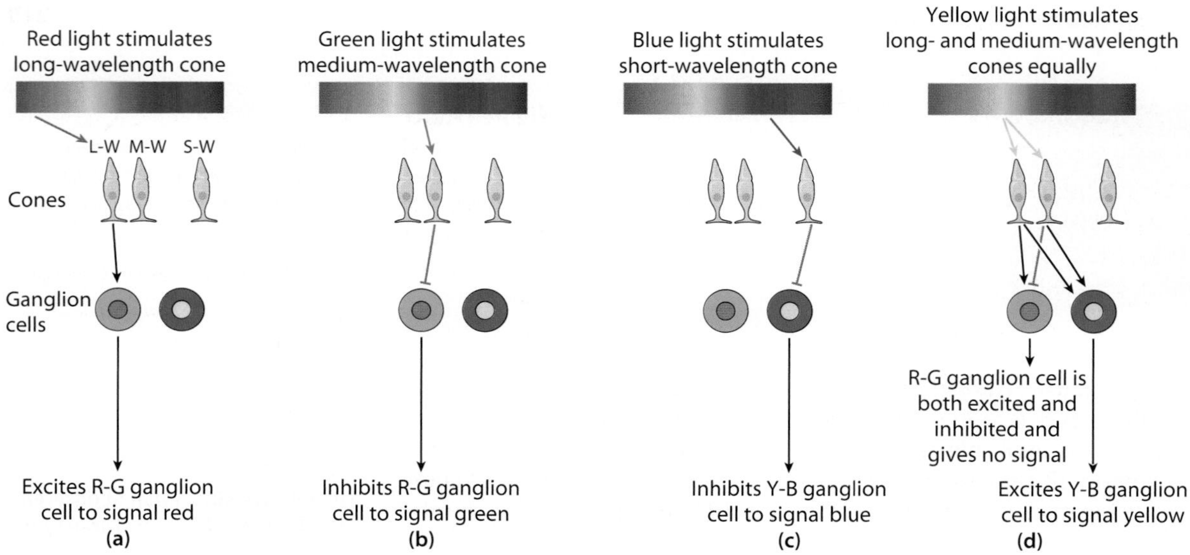

Figure 6.28

From trichromatic stimulation to opponent-process responding

(a) Long-wavelength cone stimulation excites the red-green (R-G) ganglion cell to produce the sensation of red.
(b) Medium-wavelength cone stimulation inhibits the red-green ganglion cell to produce a green sensation.
(c) Short-wavelength cone stimulation inhibits the yellow-blue (Y-B) ganglion cell to produce a blue sensation.
(d) Equal stimulation of long-wavelength and medium-wavelength cones results in no change in activity of the red-green ganglion cell, but stimulation of the yellow-blue ganglion cell produces a yellow sensation.

→ **Where are the cones located?**

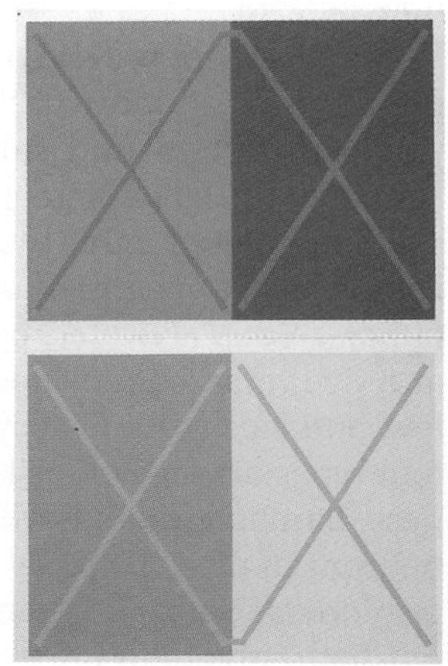

JOSEF ALBERS FOUNDATION/YALE UNIVERSITY PRESS

Figure 6.29

Contrast effects This painting by Josef Albers shows the influence of context on color. The crossed lines in each of the attached pairs of panels are actually the same color, although they appear different against different backgrounds. (Photo courtesy of the Josef Albers Foundation.)

→ **Which area of the brain is believed to be responsible for such contrast effects?**

green-tinted sunglasses. Studies with monkeys have shown that animals with prestriate cortex lesions have color constancy deficits while retaining the ability to discriminate slight wavelength differences—that is, they can still make fine color discriminations, but not under changing lighting conditions (Kulikowski & others, 1994; Walsh & others, 1993).

Checkpoint

Most people with defective color vision are unaware of their defect. Can you suggest how a person might be able to compensate for a red-green defect?

The Binding of Visual Features

One question remains: How does the visual system combine the information from the visual pathways that detect shape, color, and motion and depth into one visual perception? This is an example of the **binding problem**—how the brain combines information to form a unified perception. In 1982, Ungerleider and Mishkin proposed dual cortical visual systems, one dorsal and the other ventral. Reexamine Figure 6.8. You will see that the two pathways entering the temporal lobe carry information about the shape and color of the object; this is sometimes called the *ventral stream,* because it turns downward as it leaves the primary visual cortex, or the "what" pathway, because it answers the question, What is it? The second pathway, traveling upward to the parietal lobe, is the *dorsal stream,* or the "where" pathway, because it answers the question, Where is it? Because of the wide separation of these two visual streams, one suggestion is that their coordinated activity comes from temporally correlated neural activation in a variety of cortical structures (Gray & others, 1992; Singer & Gray, 1995). In other words, this view holds that no *single* structure or area combines the information about the shape, structure, and spatial location of an object into a unified perception of the object.

However, further research has indicated that the binding of the different pieces of visual information involves a particular location in the parietal lobe (Corbetta & others, 1995; Friedman-Hill & others, 1995; Kim & Robertson, 2001; Robertson & others, 1997). Much of the evidence for this binding site has come from studies of patients with parietal lobe damage. For example, Friedman-Hill and colleagues found that neurological patient R. M., who had bilateral parietal-occipital lesions, made frequent illusory conjunctions, joining together features and objects he had not seen. For example, if shown a red X and a blue O simultaneously, he might confidently report having seen a red O and a blue X. He was much less impaired when the stimuli were presented sequentially, implicating his spatial deficit in the binding problem. R. M. had greater difficulty binding the information presented simultaneously because of the lack of usable spatial information caused by his parietal damage.

Kim and Robertson (2001) also studied patient R. M. and concluded that the parietal-occipital section of the dorsal stream is necessary for conscious awareness of space. Although R. M. retained an ability to represent spatial configurations at an implicit level, he exhibited severe explicit spatial deficits. In addition, his implicit representations were inadequate for the normal binding of such object features as color and shape.

Corbetta and colleagues (1995) used PET scans to measure changes in regional cerebral blood flow while subjects studied visual displays for targets defined by motion or color or by the conjunction of motion and color. The greatest change in blood flow occurred in the superior parietal lobe during the conjunction task, providing further evidence for the involvement of this cortical area in the binding problem, at least for visual information.

Research by Goodale and his associates (e.g., Goodale & Milner, 1992; Goodale & Humphrey, 1998) suggests that designation of the dorsal stream as the "where" stream may be incomplete, that in fact the dorsal stream answers the question of "how" as well as "where." Like Ungerleider and Mishkin (1982), Goodale and coworkers view the ventral stream as the source of the perception of objects and their relations. These occipitotemporal pathways mediate the conscious visual experience of the world. By contrast, the dorsal stream, or occipitoparietal pathways, are involved in usually unconscious, visually guided responses to the perceived environment, a function that is obviously more than just detecting where an object is located.

Although the two systems interact extensively under normal circumstances, we can see their separate influences in people who have sustained injury to one of the systems. For example, patients with visual agnosia caused by damage to the ventral stream may be unable to recognize common objects or familiar faces but still be able to negotiate their everyday visual environment with skill. Goodale and Humphrey (1998) described one such person, D. F., a young woman with a severe visual form agnosia caused by anoxia from carbon monoxide poisoning. D. F. cannot visually identify friends and relatives and even fails to discriminate simple geometrical shapes such as triangles and circles. Despite such deficits, D. F. can perform visually guided movements with accuracy. During testing, although she was completely unable to indicate the width of a rectangular block by holding her thumb and index finger an appropriate distance apart, when she was simply asked to reach out and pick up the block, she was able to do this as well as a subject with normal vision. At the beginning of her movement, she automatically placed her thumb and index finger the correct distance apart for the thickness of the block.

By contrast, people with damage to the dorsal stream may have difficulty retrieving or pointing to visual targets that they are able to recognize (Goodale & Milner, 1992). Such damage can produce a condition known as Balint's syndrome, first described by Rudolf Bálint in 1909. **Balint's syndrome** is characterized by an inability to recognize two or more objects at the same time (*simultanagnosia*), an inability to reach correctly for an object (*optic ataxia*), and impaired control of eye

binding problem The problem of how the brain binds together information to form a unified perception.

Balint's syndrome A disorder caused by damage to the dorsal stream; characterized by difficulty in recognizing two or more objects that appear simultaneously, difficulty in visually guided reaching for objects, and impaired eye movements.

movements and visual scanning (*optic apraxia*) (Stasheff & Barton, 2001). Unlike D. F., individuals with optic ataxia have difficulty adjusting their grasp in response to the characteristics of an object, although their estimates of object size may be accurate (Goodale & Humphrey, 1998). Individuals with Balint's syndrome may also perceive the world as a series of single objects rather than as a continuous flow of objects and events (Rizzo & Vecera, 2002), again showing the importance of the dorsal stream for the binding problem.

Checkpoint

What is the binding problem, and where does the binding of visual information apparently occur? Describe the differences between the dorsal and ventral streams.

REVIEW

- The Young-Helmholtz trichromatic theory suggests there are three different types of fibers (receptors) in the eye: one that responds to blue, a second to green, and a third to red.
- Hering's opponent-process theory proposes three receptor complexes operating in opponent fashion: blue-yellow, green-red, and white-black.
- Cones can be classified into three types based on the range of wavelengths of light to which they are maximally responsive.
- Ganglion cells and LGN cells respond to color as predicted by opponent-process theory; some are excited by red and inhibited by green (and vice versa), some are excited by blue and inhibited by yellow (and vice versa), and some are excited by black and inhibited by white (and vice versa).
- Cells in the striate cortex react in a manner similar to ganglion and LGN cells, whereas cells in the prestriate cortex respond only to a narrow wavelength of light.
- Activity in prestriate cortex cells is affected by the presence of other colors in the visual field, so the perception of a color is determined by the context in which it is viewed. Cells in the prestriate cortex may also be responsible for color constancy.
- The binding of visual information may involve an area in the posterior parietal lobe.
- The dorsal stream is involved in visually guided actions, whereas the ventral stream mediates visual perception.

CHAPTER REVIEW

Key Terms

accommodation (p. 194)
across-fiber pattern coding (p. 193)
amacrine cell (p. 204)
aqueous humor (p. 194)
Balint's syndrome (p. 221)
binding problem (p. 220)
binocular depth cue (p. 215)
bipolar cell (p. 195)
blindsight (p. 200)
blind spot (p. 197)
blob (p. 199)
brightness (p. 202)
center-off, surround-on ganglion cell (p. 207)
center-on, surround-off ganglion cell (p. 207)
ciliary muscle (p. 194)
coding (p. 193)
color constancy (p. 219)
complex cell (p. 209)
component direction-selective neuron (p. 215)
cone (p. 196)
cornea (p. 194)
duplex theory (p. 196)
feature detector (p. 210)
fovea (p. 196)
fusiform face area (p. 212)
ganglion cell (p. 195)
horizontal cell (p. 204)
hue (p. 202)
hypercomplex cell (p. 209)
iris (p. 194)
labeled-line coding (p. 193)
lamella (p. 203)
lateral geniculate nucleus (LGN) (p. 198)
lateral inhibition (p. 206)
lens (p. 194)
magnocellular layer (p. 198)
monocular depth cue (p. 214)
negative afterimage (p. 218)

ocular dominance column (p. 209)
off ganglion cell (p. 204)
on ganglion cell (p. 204)
on-off ganglion cell (p. 204)
opponent-process theory (p. 218)
opsin (p. 203)
optic chiasm (p. 198)
optic disk (p. 197)
optic nerve (p. 198)
optic tract (p. 198)
orientation column (p. 209)
parvocellular layer (p. 198)
pattern direction-selective neuron (p. 215)
photopigment (p. 203)
photoreceptor (p. 194)
primary visual cortex (p. 199)
prosopagnosia (p. 212)
pupil (p. 194)
pursuit movement (p. 205)
receptive field (p. 207)
retina (p. 194)
retinal (p. 203)
retinal image (p. 194)
rhodopsin (p. 203)
rod (p. 196)
rod opsin (p. 203)
saccadic movement (p. 204)
saturation (p. 202)
secondary visual cortex (p. 201)
sense (p. 192)
simple cell (p. 208)
sine-wave grating (p. 210)
spatial-frequency theory (p. 210)
transduction (p. 192)
visual agnosia (p. 212)
visual field deficit (p. 200)
vitreous humor (p. 194)
X ganglion cell (p. 198)
Y ganglion cell (p. 198)
Young-Helmholtz trichromatic theory (p. 218)

Suggested Readings

De Valois, R. L., & De Valois, K. K. (1988). *Spatial vision.* New York: Oxford University Press.

Farah, M. J. (2000). *The cognitive neuroscience of vision.* Malden, MA: Blackwell.

Goodale, M. A., & Humphrey, G. K. (1998). The objects of action and perception. *Cognition, 67,* 181–207.

Hubel, D. H. (1988). *Eye, brain, and vision.* New York: Seventh American Library.

Wandell, B. A. (1995). *Foundations of vision.* Sutherland, MA: Sinauer.

Yantis, S. (Ed.) (2000). *Visual perception: Essential readings.* Philadelphia: Psychology Press/Taylor & Francis.

Zeki, S. (1992). The visual image in mind and brain. *Scientific American, 267*(3), 69–76.

Critical Thinking Questions

1. On spring break, Donna looked out of her hotel window at the beauty of Panama City. The water moved gently to the shore, and in the distance, a white sailboat approached. Donna and her friends were supposed to take a cruise in the afternoon on a sailboat, and she wondered if this was it. Explain the mechanism responsible for Donna's ability to recognize the moving object as a white sailboat.
2. Sheila mistakenly approached a stranger at the mall, thinking the person was her friend Heather. Suggest several possible reasons for Sheila's failure to distinguish between Heather and the other woman.
3. A TV ad shows star third baseman Alex Rodriquez watching the seams rotating on a baseball as it approaches him. (Keep in mind that major league pitchers can hurl a fastball at speeds approaching 100 mph.) Trace the image of the baseball through Rodriquez's visual sensory system, and explain a possible mechanism for the super acuity of his visual perception.

Fill-in-the-Blank Questions

1. The transformation of physical energy into a neural impulse is called ______.
2. The separate taste receptors for bitter and sweet are an example of ______ coding.
3. The recognition of a particular pattern of response from a number of visual receptors resulting in detection of a particular color is an example of ______ coding.
4. The transparent outer layer of the eye is the ______.
5. The ______ consists of bands of muscles covered by the colored tissue that gives the eye its color.
6. The change in the shape of the lens to maintain the focus of an image on the retina is called ______.
7. The image of an object focused on the retina is the ______.
8. ______ operate more effectively in bright light, and ______ are responsible for vision in dim light.
9. The differences between rods and cones are summarized in the ______ theory.
10. An object focused on the ______ of the eye cannot be seen.

11. The two optic nerves meet at the ______.
12. The parvocellular layers of the LGN receive input mostly from ______ ganglion cells.
13. Clusters of neurons in the primary visual cortex that are stained by the enzyme cytochrome oxidase are called ______.
14. An inability to see objects located in a particular part of the visual field is called a(n) ______.
15. ______ is the ability of a person to respond to objects in a missing part of the visual field without having a conscious awareness of seeing anything.
16. When we detect a specific wavelength of light, we perceive that wavelength as a specific ______, or ______.
17. ______, the photopigment found in rods, consists of the protein ______ and the lipid ______.
18. The cells in the retina that interconnect the photoreceptor cells and the bipolar cells are called ______ cells.
19. Hartline introduced the terms ______ for ganglion cells that respond when a light stimulus is turned on and ______ for cells that respond to a light stimulus being turned on and off.
20. The retinal process that sharpens the edges of an image is called ______.
21. The ______ of a cell in the visual system is that part of the retina that, when stimulated, causes a change in the activity of the cell.
22. According to Hubel and Wiesel, the three types of cells in the primary visual cortex are ______, ______, and ______.
23. ______ cells do not respond if the line stimulus extends beyond a specific point, and they are sometimes called end-stopped for this reason.
24. The ______ theory states that cortical cells respond to a complex pattern of light and dark.
25. In the condition known as ______, a person is unable to name an object presented visually but can identify it when it is presented in another sensory modality.
26. ______ is a disorder involving a difficulty in the recognition of faces.
27. ______ cues are cues to depth perception provided by both eyes.
28. According to the ______ theory of color vision, the colors we see come from different patterns of stimulation of three sets of color receptors in the eye.
29. Hering's ______ theory suggests there are three receptor complexes operating in opponent fashion.
30. The brief perception of a complementary color following extended stimulation with a particular color is called the ______.
31. ______ allows us to perceive objects as being the same color under different lighting conditions.
32. The way in which our disparate visual sensations are combined to give us a unified perception is the answer to the ______ problem.

Multiple-Choice Questions

1. The mechanism we use to transform environmental stimulation into information that the nervous system can use is a
   a. transducer.
   b. sense.
   c. code.
   d. perceiver.
2. The type of coding in which different receptors within a sensory system react to different stimulation is ______ coding.
   a. across-fiber pattern
   b. photoreceptor
   c. labeled-line
   d. transduction-pattern
3. Light passes through the ______, then the ______ and the ______ before it reaches the ______ of the eye.
   a. retina and iris, cornea, pupil, blind spot
   b. cornea, pupil, lens, retina
   c. pupil, iris, retina, optic nerve
   d. blind spot, optic tectum, cornea, lens
4. Great interest in a visual stimulus causes the pupils to
   a. dilate.
   b. constrict.
   c. darken.
   d. glow.
5. The two types of photoreceptors are the
   a. ganglion cells and bipolar cells.
   b. horizontal cells and amacrine cells.
   c. rods and bipolar cells.
   d. rods and cones.
6. Rods are more concentrated in the ______ of the retina, and cones are more concentrated in the ______ of the retina.
   a. periphery, center
   b. center, periphery
   c. center, surround
   d. surround, center
7. The blind spot at the back of the eye is also called the
   a. retina.
   b. optic nerve.
   c. optic disk.
   d. optic tectum.
8. Most fibers of the optic tract project to the
   a. primary visual cortex.
   b. lateral geniculate nucleus.
   c. secondary visual cortex.
   d. opposite side of the brain.
9. The ______ ganglion cells project to the parvocellular layers of the LGN.
   a. Y
   b. W
   c. Z
   d. X

10. A(n) ______ deficit is an inability to see objects in a particular place because of damage either to a portion of an occipital lobe or to the pathways leading to it.
   a. optic lobe
   b. visual field
   c. perceived-place
   d. visual agnosia

11. Following a gunshot wound, Amber is apparently blind in her right visual field. However, when asked to point to lights flashed in the right visual field, even though she says she cannot see them, Amber performs at a high level of accuracy, well above chance. She has
   a. visual agnosia.
   b. prosopagnosia.
   c. blindsight.
   d. sensory neglect.

12. Light can vary in terms of
   a. wavelength, frequency, and depth.
   b. wavelength, brightness, and saturation.
   c. length, depth, and height.
   d. brightness, depth, and movement.

13. The photopigment in rods is
   a. cyanopsin.
   b. porphyropsin.
   c. iodopsin.
   d. rhodopsin.

14. The photoreceptors and the bipolar cells are interconnected by ______ cells.
   a. amacrine
   b. horizontal
   c. vertical
   d. ganglion

15. Ganglion cells excited by a light stimulus are called ______ cells.
   a. off
   b. on-off
   c. on
   d. center

16. The first person to study single optic nerve fibers was
   a. Hubel.
   b. Kuffler.
   c. Wiesel.
   d. Hartline.

17. Rapid, jerky movements of our eyes are called ______ movements.
   a. saccadic
   b. pursuit
   c. fixation
   d. intoxicated

18. Decreased activity of a cell in the visual system caused by light stimulation of its neighbor is called
   a. mutual inhibition.
   b. lateral inhibition.
   c. lateral suppression.
   d. mutual suppression.

19. The limited, circular area of the retina to which a ganglion cell responds is called the ______ field.
   a. receptive
   b. visual
   c. on-center
   d. center

20. The general name for the type of receptive field configuration seen in ganglion cells and LGN cells is
   a. surround-center.
   b. on-off surround.
   c. off-on center.
   d. center-surround.

21. Which of the following has the smallest receptive field?
   a. X ganglion cell
   b. Y ganglion cell
   c. W ganglion cell
   d. Z ganglion cell

22. Hubel and Wiesel introduced the term ______ cells for cells in the visual cortex that appear to respond to lines or edges of light in a particular part of the visual field and with a particular orientation.
   a. simple
   b. complex
   c. hypercomplex
   d. spatial-frequency

23. End-stopped cells are also called ______ cells.
   a. simple
   b. complex
   c. hypercomplex
   d. spatial-frequency

24. The spatial-frequency theory was devised by
   a. De Valois and De Valois.
   b. Hubel and Wiesel.
   c. Horsley and Clark.
   d. Olds and Milner.

25. The various cortical cells that Hubel and Wiesel identified appear to be ______ detectors.
   a. spatial-frequency
   b. sine-wave grating
   c. feature
   d. Fourier-analysis

26. When Molly is shown a ball, she cannot name it. When she feels it in her hand, however, she correctly identifies it as a ball. Molly has
   a. a visual field deficit.
   b. visual agnosia.
   c. amnesia.
   d. partial blindness.

27. Prosopagnosia is a disorder in which people have difficulty
   a. seeing that a face is a face.
   b. recognizing a person's gender from facial cues.
   c. recognizing familiar faces, including their own face.
   d. identifying familiar objects by sight.

28. William started playing baseball 3 years ago, and he is a decent fielder but a poor hitter. His problem is that he always seems to swing too early, before the ball reaches him. The area of the brain responsible for this tendency is the ______ lobe.
   a. anterior parietal
   b. posterior parietal
   c. medial temporal
   d. anterior occipital

29. According to trichromatic theory, the three color receptors in the eye are maximally responsive to the colors
   a. blue, yellow, and green.
   b. red, blue, and yellow.
   c. blue, red, and white.
   d. green, blue, and red.

30. Neurons in the LGN respond to colors as predicted by the ______ theory.
   a. trichromatic
   b. specific-nerve
   c. opponent-process
   d. labeled-line

31. Which of the theories of color vision best accounts for the negative afterimage?
   a. labeled-line theory
   b. trichromatic theory
   c. opponent-process theory
   d. color-coding theory

32. We perceive pine trees as green even under different lighting conditions. This phenomenon is known as
   a. negative afterimage.
   b. color constancy.
   c. relative texture.
   d. linear perspective.

Answers can be found on the companion website at www.worthpublishers.com/klein.

7

Hearing, Balance, and the Cutaneous and Chemical Senses

An Unwelcome Call

It had been a bad day, make that a bad week. Working full-time and going to school in the evening was taking its toll. Heather was looking forward to relaxing in a scented bath, listening to some good music, and letting all the knots in her shoulders and lower back untie in the warmth of the water. While running the water, she poured herself a glass of lemonade. She loved the smell of lemonade and its just slightly tart taste.

When the steaming water had reached the ideal depth, Heather lowered herself gingerly into the bathtub, aware of a warmth that approached, but didn't quite reach, the level of pain. She lay back in the tub, supporting her head on the back rim, her right heel just grazing the drain's stopper. She retrieved her drink from the side of the tub and pressed the cold glass against her forehead, sighing from the pleasure of the chill. Life doesn't get much better than this, Heather thought.

At that instant, the phone rang two rooms away. Wondering yet again why she didn't own a cell phone, Heather climbed out of the tub, momentarily losing her balance as she did so. She wrapped a towel around herself and walked, dripping, to the kitchen.

She would have just let the phone ring and stayed in the tub, but she thought this might be an earlier-than-usual call from her sister, Kathy, who lived in another state. Kathy telephoned at least once a week with news of Sarah's latest antics. Sarah, Heather's niece, was just beginning to pull herself up in her playpen. Heather rarely saw her, but loved to keep up with news of her development. Kathy had told Heather the week before that she thought Sarah would take her first step at any moment—that could be today's news. Heather hoped their new puppy, Buddy, would stay out of the toddler's way when she did start walking. She knew this was a forlorn hope, however, and she could envision her little niece with a knot on her head from a spill caused by the puppy.

Heather snatched the receiver off the hook at the fifth ring and said "Hello" before she even got the phone to her ear. There was a pause at the other end of the line, and then a man asked, "Is Ms. Beasley there?"

"This is she."

"I'm calling from AF&G Services," the man began. "How are you today?" But he wasn't quick enough to get started on his spiel.

"I'm not interested," Heather almost shouted, slamming the receiver back into its cradle. The telemarketer's call, just as she was starting to unwind, was a fitting end to her horrible week. Things just had to get better after this.

sound Vibrations in a material medium, such as air, water, or metal.

pitch The perception of the frequency of a sound wave, measured in hertz (Hz).

loudness The perception of the amplitude of a sound wave, measured in decibels.

timbre The purity of a sound; the combination of frequencies that gives each sound its characteristic quality.

pinna The outer, visible portion of the ear.

tympanic membrane The membrane that divides the outer and middle parts of the ear; also called the eardrum.

malleus (hammer) The bone of the middle ear attached to the tympanic membrane and the incus.

incus (anvil) The bone of the middle ear attached to the malleus and stapes.

stapes (stirrup) The bone of the middle ear attached to the incus and the oval window.

oval window The part of the inner ear attached to the stapes.

BEFORE YOU BEGIN

- How was Heather able to hear the telemarketer's voice on the telephone?
- Which sense enabled Heather to feel the water dripping down her back as she walked to the kitchen?
- What is sound, and how is it received and processed by the auditory system?
- Which sense helps us to orient our bodies in space?
- How many types of touch receptors do we have, and what happens if one or more of them malfunctions?
- Which sense enabled Heather to taste her lemonade?
- What is the olfactory system, and how does it enable Heather to detect the smell of lemonade and of the perfumed crystals she put in her bathwater?

In this chapter, you will find the answers to these questions and many others.

The Auditory System

The auditory sense, or sense of hearing, was the sense most actively in use as Heather heard the phone ringing and then listened indignantly to the beginning of the telemarketer's spiel—annoying distractions when she was trying to relax. But consider the importance of hearing in Heather's life. And if you, like Heather, have normal hearing, imagine for a moment what life would be like without it. You would not be able to use a regular telephone, listen to your favorite music, or hear the soundtrack of a television show or movie. You would have to learn how to read lips and/or use sign language to communicate, and how to adapt to a life without auditory information of any kind.

In this section we describe how a normally functioning auditory system detects sounds and recognizes their meanings. **Sound** may be defined as vibrations in a material medium, such as air, water, or metal. When objects in the environment—such as your vocal cords—vibrate, they set air molecules in motion. The molecules are alternately condensed (pushed together) and rarified (moved apart) to create a wave of movement traveling away from the vibrating object. These waves are detected by auditory receptors in the ear and are ultimately perceived as particular sounds.

Sound waves vary along three dimensions: frequency, amplitude, and complexity (Figure 7.1). We perceive the *frequency* of a sound as **pitch.** Frequency refers to the number of vibrations per second and is measured in hertz (Hz), named for the 19th century German physicist Heinrich Hertz, or in kilohertz (kHz, 1,000 Hz). The human ear can detect sounds with frequencies between about 20 Hz (a low-pitched sound) and 20 kHz (a high-pitched sound). Some animals, such as elephants and whales, can hear slightly lower-pitched sounds, whereas others, such as bats and harbor seals, can hear sounds of 100 kHz or higher. Quite a few animals with which we share our immediate environment can hear higher-pitched sounds than we can. For example, Kathy's new puppy, Buddy, can hear sounds of up to 40 kHz.

Like ocean waves, sound waves also differ in their *amplitude* or height, which we perceive as **loudness.** The more intensely an object vibrates, the greater is the amplitude, or the change in condensation and rarefaction of the air molecules. Objects that produce small changes (small ripples) are perceived as soft sounds, objects that produce large changes

Figure 7.1
Wave forms for the three dimensions of a sound The three perceptual qualities of sound—pitch, loudness, and timbre—correspond to the frequency, amplitude, and complexity of a sound wave.

➡ **Name the dimension(s) used to differentiate a child's rendition of "Three Blind Mice" from a version by the Boston Pops Orchestra.**

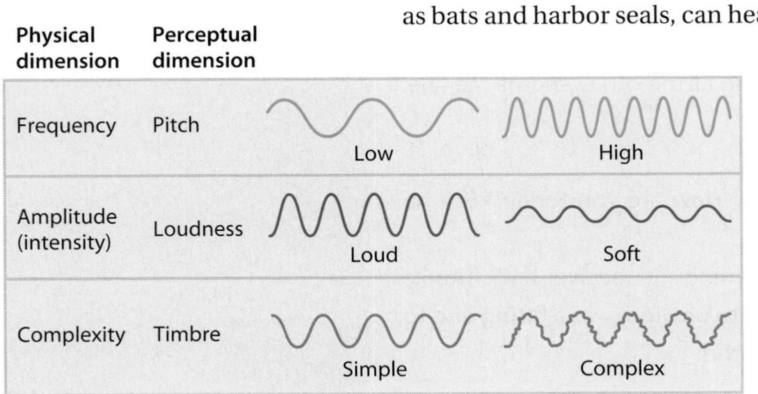

(large ripples) as loud sounds. The amplitude of a sound wave is measured in decibels (dB); the higher the decibel level, the louder the sound. Table 7.1 gives some examples of sounds of differing loudness, along with their potential for causing damage to the ear.

Some sounds are pure, consisting of a single frequency, but most are *complex,* consisting of multiple frequencies. The combination of frequencies gives each sound its characteristic quality, which we perceive as **timbre.** For example, a violin has sound that is different from that of a trumpet because the combinations of frequencies produced by each instrument are different.

Frequency, amplitude, and complexity are the physical qualities of a sound. The auditory receptors detect these qualities and transduce them into neural activity, which is ultimately interpreted by the auditory cortex as a sound of a certain pitch, loudness, and timbre.

Table 7.1
Amplitude and Damaging Effects of Various Sounds

Typical Decibel Level	Example	Exposure That Can Damage Hearing
0	Lowest audible sound	
30	Quiet library; soft whisper	
40	Quiet office; living room; bedroom away from traffic	
50	Light traffic at a distance; refrigerator; gentle breeze	
60	Air conditioner at 20 feet; conversation; sewing machine in operation	
70	Busy traffic; noisy restaurant	Some damage if continuous
80	Subway; heavy city traffic; alarm clock at 2 feet; factory noise	More than 8 hours
90	Truck traffic; noisy home appliances; shop tools; gas lawnmower	Less than 8 hours
100	Chain saw; boiler shop; pneumatic drill	2 hours
120	"Heavy metal" rock concert; sandblasting; thunderclap nearby	Immediate danger
140	Gunshot; jet plane	Immediate danger
160	Rocket launching pad	Hearing loss inevitable

Source: Martini, F. H. (1998). *Fundamentals of anatomy and physiology* (4th ed.). Upper Saddle River, NJ: Prentice-Hall.

The Ear

The visible portion of the ear is the **pinna.** Its unusual shape helps us detect where sounds originate, but it is not essential for hearing. Movable pinnae are even more useful for sound localization than our stationary ones. If you have lived with a dog or cat, you have undoubtedly observed how they direct their pinnae toward the source of a sound—sometimes directing each ear toward a different source. We will have more to say about sound localization later in the chapter. As you can see in Figure 7.2, the ear is divided into an outer ear (pinna to tympanic membrane), a middle ear (tympanic membrane to oval window), and an inner ear (cochlea and vestibular system).

Sound waves enter the pinna and travel down the external auditory canal until they reach the **tympanic membrane** or *eardrum,* which vibrates in response. The vibrations are transmitted by the three small bones, or auditory ossicles, of the middle ear, which are named for their shapes: **malleus (hammer), incus (anvil),** and **stapes (stirrup).** Attached to the tympanic membrane, the malleus vibrates with it, which causes corresponding movements of the incus and stapes and finally the **oval window,** to which the stapes is attached.

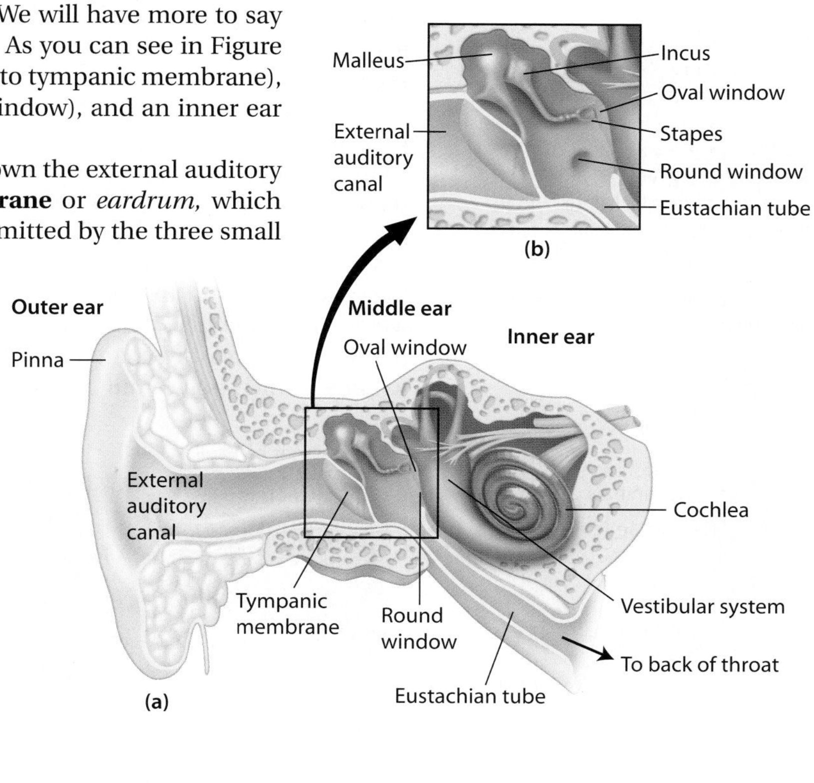

Figure 7.2
The ear (a) A cross-sectional view of the main structures of the ear. (b) The structures of the middle ear.

➜ **What causes the force of the vibrations to increase through the middle ear?**

eustachian tube A tube connecting the middle ear with the back of the throat.

cochlea A snail-shaped structure in the inner ear that contains the auditory receptors.

round window A membrane that bulges as a result of pressure on the fluid inside the cochlea, which results from the movement of the stapes against the oval window.

organ of Corti A structure inside the cochlea that contains the basilar membrane, the hair cells, and the tectorial membrane.

hair cell An auditory receptor involved in transducing eardrum vibrations into neural impulses.

basilar membrane A membrane in the organ of Corti to which auditory receptors are attached by Deiter's cells.

tectorial membrane A membrane in the organ of Corti in which hair cell cilia are embedded or with which cilia make close contact.

spiral ganglion An auditory structure containing bipolar neurons that synapse with hair cells of the inner ear.

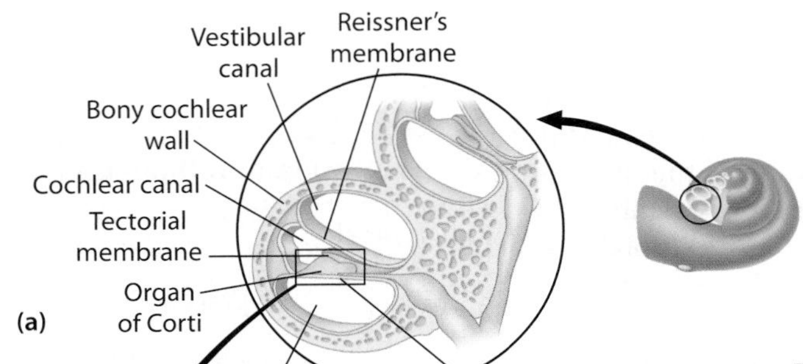

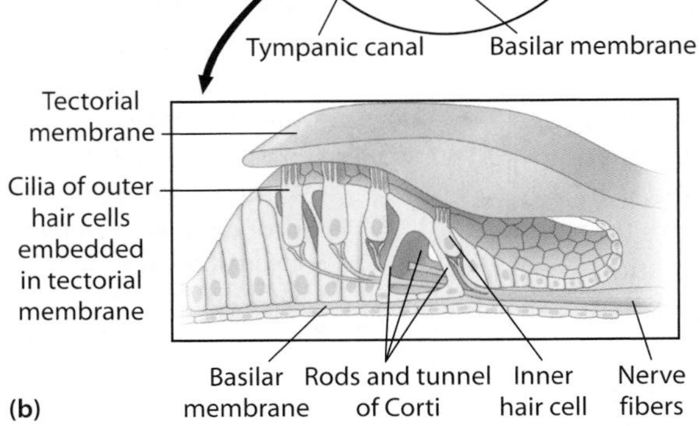

Figure 7.3

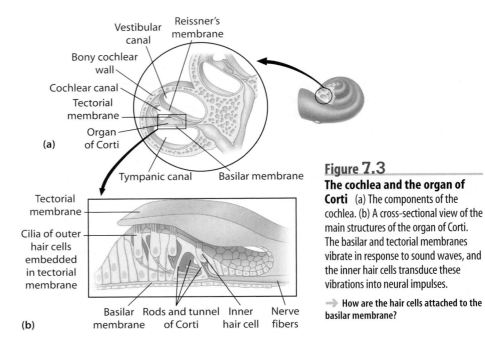

The cochlea and the organ of Corti (a) The components of the cochlea. (b) A cross-sectional view of the main structures of the organ of Corti. The basilar and tectorial membranes vibrate in response to sound waves, and the inner hair cells transduce these vibrations into neural impulses.

➡ How are the hair cells attached to the basilar membrane?

The tympanic membrane has a surface approximately 20 times larger than that of the oval window (see Figure 7.2), a difference that amplifies the force of the vibrations of the air molecules on the oval window. Further amplification comes from the three bones, which act like levers, and from the external auditory canal, which acts like a funnel. The increased force is necessary to carry the sound from a highly compressible medium (air) to one that is relatively noncompressible (the fluid inside the inner ear).

The **eustachian tube** connects the middle ear with the back of the throat (see Figure 7.2). Its purpose is to equalize air pressure on either side of the eardrum. The reason you are advised to chew gum or suck on hard candy when you are taking off and landing in a plane is to force air from outside, whose pressure is decreasing as the plane ascends rapidly, or increasing as the plane descends rapidly, into your middle ear. If you do not equalize this pressure in some way, or if you have an infection blocking the eustachian tube, the decreasing air pressure on the outside of the eardrum relative to the air pressure in the middle ear causes your eardrum to bulge outward, which can cause it to burst. One of our colleagues experienced this while flying with an ear infection and quite understandably refused to fly for many years afterward.

In the inner ear, behind the oval window, is a coiled structure called the **cochlea** (Latin for "snail shell"). The cochlea contains three long, fluid-filled chambers: the *vestibular canal,* the *cochlear canal,* and the *tympanic canal* (Figure 7.3a). The vestibular canal and the tympanic canal are connected through an opening called the *helicotrema* and are filled with a relatively noncompressible fluid similar to seawater, the *perilymph.* Vibrations of the oval window put pressure on the perilymph; the resulting pressure changes are transmitted through the cochlea to the **round window,** which bulges out as a result of the pressure on the fluid caused by the movement of the stapes (see Figure 7.2). The compressions of the oval window and the corresponding movements of the round window reflect the traveling wave in the perilymph, which continues to move as long as the stapes vibrates in response to a sound wave.

The cochlear canal is self-contained and is bounded by *Reissner's membrane* and the *basilar membrane. Endolymph,* the fluid in the cochlear canal, is thicker than perilymph and contains many potassium ions. A struc-

Figure 7.4

Auditory receptors (a) A cross-sectional view of an outer hair cell and an inner hair cell. (b) A photomicrograph of the cilia of inner and outer hair cells.

➡ What is the difference in the function of inner hair cells and outer hair cells?

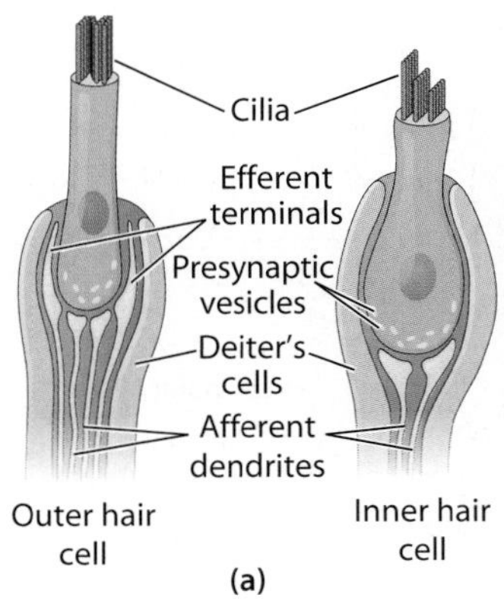

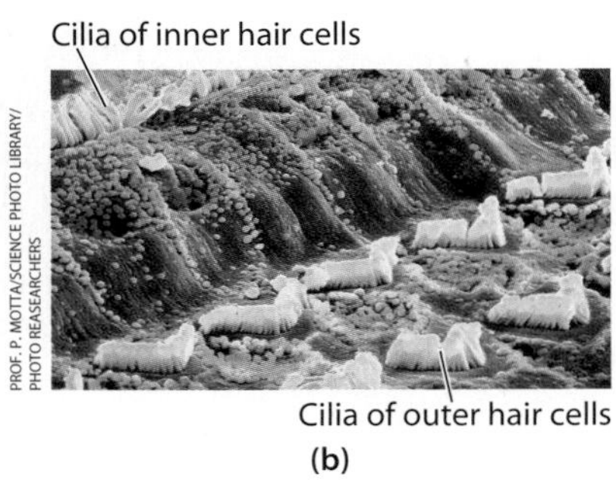

ture called the **organ of Corti,** at the bottom of the cochlear canal, consists of the basilar membrane, the hair cells, and the tectorial membrane (Figure 7.3b). The **hair cells** are the auditory receptors that transduce the vibrations that began in the tympanic membrane into neural impulses (Figure 7.4). Each ear has approximately 12,000 *outer hair cells* and 3,400 *inner hair cells;* the two types of hair cells are separated by the rods and tunnel of Corti. Both the outer and the inner hair cells are attached to the **basilar membrane** by *Deiter's cells.* The *cilia,* or hair-like outgrowths of the inner hair cells, come into close contact with the **tectorial membrane,** but do not actually touch it, whereas some cilia of the outer hair cells are embedded in the tectorial membrane. The traveling wave through the cochlea produces differential movement of the basilar and tectorial membranes, which causes the cilia of the hair cells to bend, thus activating the auditory hair cell receptors, primarily those of the inner hair cells (Figure 7.5).

Checkpoint

Describe the path of the sound of the telemarketer's voice from the telephone receiver to Heather's inner ear.

The Transduction of Sound Waves Into Neural Impulses

The inner hair cells have a resting potential of −60 mV (Hudspeth, 1997). When the cilia are at rest (Figure 7.5b), the probability of an ion channel being open is about 10%, which means that a small amount of K^+ and Ca^{2+} ions enter the cilium. When the cilia bend in the direction of the longest cilium (Figure 7.5c), the probability increases dramatically, and the membrane depolarizes. This depolarization leads to a rapid influx of Ca^{2+} ions into the hair cells, which results in the release of the neurotransmitter glutamate. As the cilia bend toward the shortest cilium (Figure 7.5a), the K^+ ion channels close, the membrane becomes hyperpolarized, and neurotransmitter release decreases.

Both inner and outer hair cells are innervated by neurons with cell bodies in a structure near the cochlea called the **spiral ganglion**. Approximately 95% of this innervation is of the inner hair cells, which gives you an idea of the relative importance of the two types of hair cells for audition. The more numerous outer hair cells vibrate at a rate corresponding to the frequency of the sound being heard. This vibration alters the physical properties of the basilar membrane, which affects how the inner hair cells respond to the vibrations of the membrane. As a further indication of the importance of the inner hair cells, studies have shown that a mutant strain of mice lacking inner hair cells is completely deaf (Deol & Gluecksohn-Waelsch, 1979). An average loss of 86% of the inner hair cells produced an elevation of the auditory threshold by an average of 40 dB relative to control animals (Sterbing & Schrott-Fischer, 2003). Figure 7.6 summarizes the steps in producing an auditory sensation.

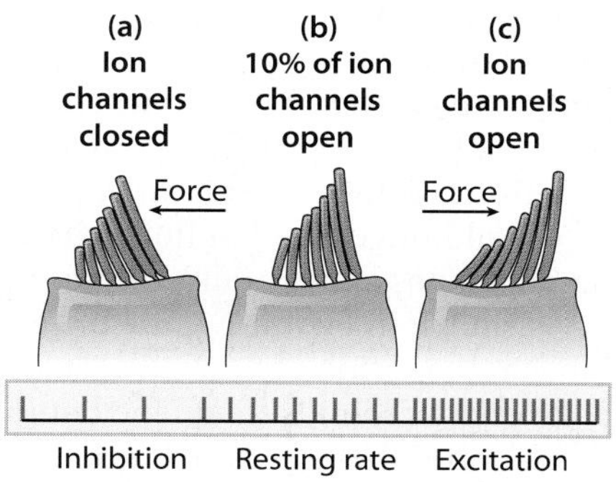

Figure 7.5

The activation of auditory receptors The central drawing (b) shows the cilia of an auditory receptor (hair cell) in the resting state. Movement of the cilia in the direction of the tallest one (c) increases the firing rate; movement away from the tallest one (a) decreases the rate.

What causes the movement of the cilia of the outer hair cells? Of the inner hair cells?

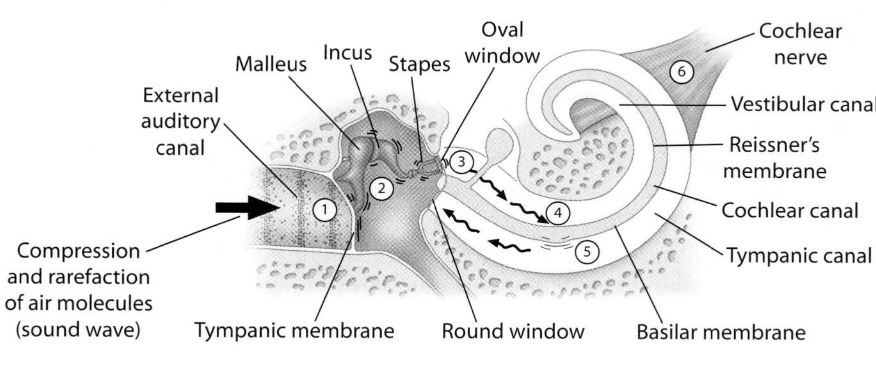

Figure 7.6

Steps in the production of an auditory sensation (1) A sound wave arrives at the tympanic membrane; (2) movement of the tympanic membrane causes displacement of the bones of the middle ear; (3) movement of the stapes at the oval window causes pressure waves in the vestibular canal; (4) the pressure waves, on their way to the round window of the tympanic canal, distort the basilar membrane; (5) vibration of the basilar membrane activates the auditory receptors (hair cells); (6) information about the sound is transmitted to the CNS via the cochlear nerve.

At what point in this pathway are sound waves converted into a neural impulse?

Pathways to the Auditory Cortex

As you might expect from the complexity of the auditory apparatus, the auditory pathways to and through the CNS are more complex than the main visual pathway (from the retina to the LGN to the striate cortex). First, hair cells synapse with the dendrites of bipolar cells in the spiral ganglion. Axons of the bipolar cells form the **cochlear nerve,** which is joined by fibers from the vestibular (balance) system (discussed later) to form the **auditory nerve,** also called the vestibulocochlear nerve, or cranial nerve VIII (Figure 7.7).

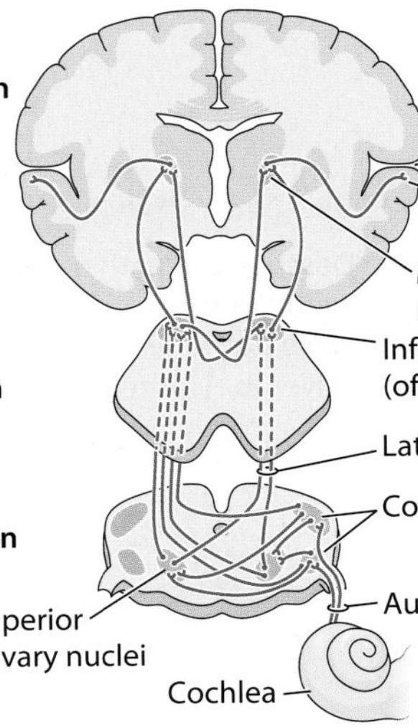

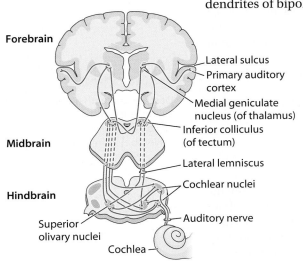

Figure 7.7
Auditory pathways Sound information passes from the hair cells through the auditory nerve to the primary auditory cortex.

➜ **Why does the left (or right) primary auditory cortex receive input from both ears?**

Cranial nerve VIII synapses with the **cochlear nuclei** of the medulla. Some of the axons leaving the cochlear nuclei cross the midline and synapse with the **superior olivary** ("olive-shaped") **nucleus** on the contralateral side of the brain, whereas other fibers synapse with the superior olivary nucleus on the ipsilateral side. Still other axons extend from the cochlear nuclei directly to the **inferior colliculus** of the tectum of the midbrain, which is also the destination of the fibers from the superior olivary nuclei. The pathway from the superior olivary nuclei to the inferior colliculus is called the *lateral lemniscus.*

Fibers from the inferior colliculus extend to the **medial geniculate nucleus (MGN)** of the thalamus (see Figure 7.7). As at earlier levels, some of the fibers cross over on their way from the inferior colliculus to the MGN, whereas others remain on the same side of the brain. Finally, the axons of the MGN neurons extend to the **primary auditory cortex (Heschl's gyrus**, which is part of the superior temporal gyrus). Because of the crossover of neurons in the auditory system, each primary auditory cortex receives information from both ears, with an emphasis on contralateral representation. In other words, although Heather holds the telephone to her right ear, the auditory cortex on both sides of her brain receives neural input from the telemarketer.

As shown in Figure 7.7, the primary auditory cortex is located in the temporal lobe on the inside of the lateral sulcus. The primary auditory cortex detects characteristics of sounds (frequency, amplitude, complexity) from the neural impulses that begin with the auditory receptors, and it transmits this information to the **secondary auditory cortex,** which surrounds the primary auditory cortex.

As we indicated in Chapter 6, after the striate cortex, the cortical visual system splits into a dorsal "where" stream and a ventral "what" stream. This dual stream phenomenon—with one stream mediating "where" or spatial information, and the other mediating "what" or information allowing recognition of auditory patterns—appears to hold true for the auditory system as well. Rauschecker (1998) hypothesized the presence of a dual system in the macaque monkey, and MRI and PET studies in humans have supported the hypothesis. Using microelectrode recording and anatomical tracing of tracts, Romanski and colleagues (1999) found that the anterior auditory cortex is connected to nonspatial frontal areas, whereas the posterior auditory cortex is connected to spatial areas. Similarly, from their study of the cortical auditory system of monkeys, Rauschecker and Tian (2000, 2004) concluded that the system is divided into at least two streams: a pattern stream originating in the anterior portion of the superior temporal gyrus and a spatial stream coming from the posterior part of the gyrus.

In Chapter 6, we saw how the amygdala receives visual information and how this is used in fear conditioning to a visual stimulus. Not surprisingly, the same is true for the auditory system: The amygdala receives input from the auditory thalamus and uses this information in fear conditioning to an auditory stimulus (Campeau & Davis, 1995a, 1995b). We next explore how the auditory system recognizes what a sound is and where it originates.

➤Checkpoint

Construct a flow chart depicting the path of auditory input from the organ of Corti to the primary auditory cortex. Why can you still hear sounds from all around you even if you lose the hearing in one ear?

REVIEW

- The auditory system detects sound waves produced by objects vibrating in a material medium.
- Sound waves differ in three ways: frequency (perceived as pitch), measured in cycles per second, or hertz (Hz); intensity (perceived as loudness), measured by the amplitude of the wave, or decibels (db); and complexity (perceived as timbre).
- Sound waves enter the outer ear and travel to the end of the external auditory canal, where they cause the tympanic membrane (eardrum) to vibrate.
- Eardrum vibrations are transmitted by the bones of the middle ear to the oval window, which vibrates and causes a traveling wave in the fluid in the cochlea; this wave moves from the oval window to the round window.
- In the inner ear, the fluid movement causes vibrations in the basilar and tectorial membranes, which bend the cilia of the inner and outer hair cells, with the inner hair cells functioning as auditory receptors.
- The auditory receptors synapse with neurons of the cochlear nerve, which project to the cochlear nuclei of the medulla.
- Most axons leaving the cochlear nuclei cross the midline to synapse with the contralateral superior olivary nucleus, but some synapse with the ipsilateral superior olivary nucleus.
- The auditory pathways continue by way of the lateral lemniscus to the inferior colliculus of the midbrain, and from there to the MGN of the thalamus, and finally to the primary auditory cortex.
- From the primary auditory cortex, the auditory system splits into two streams, one mediating "where," or spatial information, and the other mediating "what," or the recognition of auditory patterns.

Pitch Perception

How can you tell the difference between the sound of your cell phone's ring tone and that of your friend's? How can Heather immediately tell the difference between the telemarketer's relatively low-pitched voice and her sister's higher-pitched voice? As noted earlier, *pitch perception* depends on the frequency of vibration of the material medium, with a direct relationship between frequency and pitch.

The Early Research

In the 19th century, Hermann Ludwig von Helmholtz proposed that different parts of the basilar membrane respond to different frequencies of sound. (Recall the Young-Helmholtz trichromatic theory from Chapter 6.) According to Helmholtz's auditory theory, the activation of a nerve fiber located at a specific place on the basilar membrane produces the perception of a sound of a specific pitch. This **place theory of pitch perception** suggested that high-pitched sounds, such as Sarah's cries, activate the nerve fibers at the base of the membrane, near the oval window, whereas low-pitched sounds, such as the sound of a foghorn on a river, stimulate nerve fibers at the opposite end (apex) of the basilar membrane.

As it turns out, the details of Helmholtz's theory are incorrect, but there is a great deal of experimental support for a place theory of pitch perception. For example, exposure to damaging sounds of a particular frequency can impair the ability of an individual to detect that frequency (Smith, 1974). As the frequency of the damaging sound increases, damage to the basilar membrane moves closer to its base.

The damage to hair cells that is sometimes caused by high doses of antibiotic drugs, such as kanamycin and neomycin, is not random; instead, hair cell death

cochlear nerve A nerve formed by the axons of bipolar cells in the spiral ganglion that synapse with the hair cells.

auditory nerve Cranial nerve VIII, the nerve that extends from the merging of the cochlear nerve and vestibular nerve.

cochlear nucleus The first neurons in the medulla that receive neural messages from auditory receptors via the auditory nerve.

superior olivary nucleus A group of neurons in the medulla that receives neural messages from the cochlear nuclei.

inferior colliculus An area of the tectum of the midbrain that receives neural messages from both the cochlear nucleus and the superior olivary nucleus.

medial geniculate nucleus (MGN) A group of neurons in the thalamus that receives neural impulses from the inferior colliculus.

primary auditory cortex (Heschl's gyrus) The part of the superior temporal gyrus that detects characteristics of sound (frequency, amplitude, complexity).

secondary auditory cortex The area of the temporal lobe surrounding the primary auditory cortex, where pitch, loudness, and timbre are perceived and specific sounds are recognized.

place theory of pitch perception The view that different sounds activate nerve fibers at different locations on the basilar membrane.

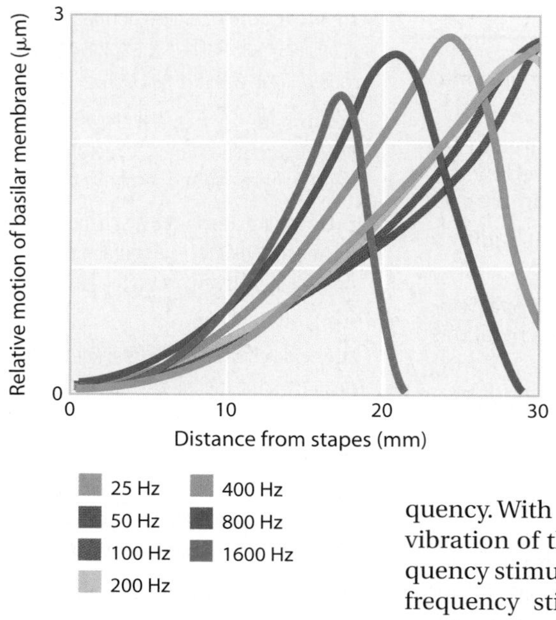

Figure 7.8

Evidence for the place theory of pitch perception The location of maximal vibration on the basilar membrane moves closer to the stapes as the frequency of the sound increases. (Adapted from von Békésy, 1960.)

→ **What other evidence supports the place theory of pitch perception?**

begins at the base of the basilar membrane and progresses toward the apex. Researchers have found that a cat given high doses of neomycin progressively lost the ability to detect pitch, matching the progressive death of the hair cells of the animal. Further, the hearing loss generally proceeded from highest to lowest frequencies (Shepherd & Clark, 1985).

The strongest support for a place theory of pitch perception comes from the work of Hungarian-born physiologist Georg von Békésy. Von Békésy (1960) studied the movement of the basilar membrane of recently deceased humans and other animals in response to sounds of different frequencies. After drilling a small "observation window" into the cochlea, von Békésy sprinkled tiny silver particles onto the basilar membrane to make it visible through a microscope. He then stimulated the ear with different frequencies of sound, flashing a stroboscopic light onto the vibrating basilar membrane at a rate matching the sound frequency. With this ingenious set up, von Békésy could see that the point of maximal vibration of the membrane depended on the frequency of stimulation: High-frequency stimulation produced peaks near the base of the membrane, whereas low-frequency stimulation produced peaks at the apex (Figure 7.8). Von Békésy received the 1961 Nobel Prize in Physiology or Medicine for his work.

But place theory is not the end of the pitch-perception story. In 1886, physicist William Rutherford challenged Helmholtz's version of place theory by proposing that the basilar membrane vibrates in synchrony with the sound wave. According to Rutherford, a sound of 1,000 Hz would cause the membrane to vibrate 1,000 times per second, with the result that the auditory nerve would generate 1,000 nerve impulses per second; a tone of 500 Hz would cause the auditory nerve to fire 500 times per second, and so on. The brain would decipher pitch by the rate of firing in the auditory nerve, which would match the frequency of the sound. Rutherford's theory became known as the **frequency theory of pitch perception.**

Several decades later, American psychologists Ernest Glen Wever and Charles William Bray (1930) found what appeared to be definitive support for Rutherford's frequency theory. They discovered that electrical activity from the cochlea of a cat perfectly matched the stimulating sound, an activity they called the *cochlear microphonic,* because it seemed that the cochlea functioned like a microphone. However, they soon learned that the cochlear microphonic did not match what was happening in the auditory nerve.

Continuing to seek evidence for frequency theory, Wever (1949) recorded electrical activity from the auditory nerve and found that the firing rate matched sound frequencies up to approximately 4 kHz, well beyond the firing rate of individual neurons. Wever's explanation for how the firing rate in the auditory nerve could continue to match the frequency of the sound beyond the maximum rate of firing of individual neurons is based on his **volley principle:** The auditory nerve contains sets of neurons that fire in volleys, asynchronously. While one group is firing, another group is recovering from its previous activity, with the end result that the combined firing of all the groups matches the frequency of the sound (Figure 7.9).

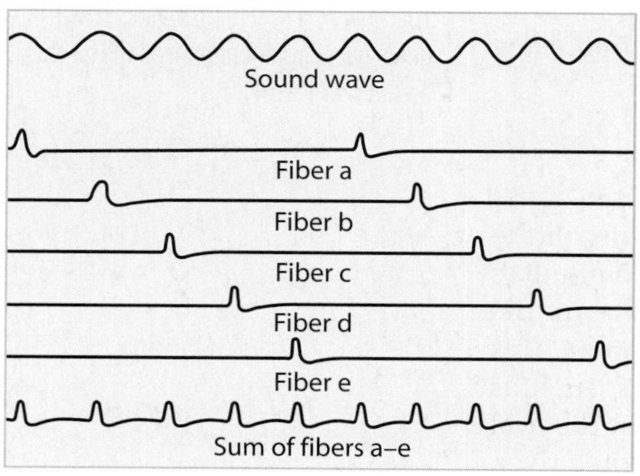

Figure 7.9

The volley principle and frequency matching in the auditory nerve Shown here is the sequence of firing of five fibers for a sound wave.

→ **How does the volley principle explain the differentiation of soft and loud sounds?**

Current Theory

The current theory of pitch perception uses a combination of mechanisms. From 20 Hz to about 400 Hz, Rutherford's frequency theory accounts for pitch perception: The firing rate of individual neurons in the auditory nerve directly matches the frequency of the sound. From 400 Hz to about 4 kHz, Rutherford's volley principle takes over, and beyond 4 kHz, von Békésy's place theory comes into play: The place of maximal vibration on the basilar membrane determines the pitch that we perceive. Actually, both place theory and the volley principle work for sounds from about 1 kHz to 4 kHz, which may explain our greater sensitivity to pitches within this range.

The evidence also indicates that individual neurons in the auditory pathways respond selectively to sounds of particular frequencies (J. P. Kelly, 1991). Further, a specific spiral ganglion cell is most responsive to the sound frequency that activates the auditory receptor that synapses with this spiral ganglion cell. Such specificity continues beyond the spiral ganglion. For example, Schwarz and colleagues (1993) measured the responses of individual neurons in the inferior colliculus of the chicken and found that the cells responded only to a narrow range of sound frequencies. A similar response selectivity has been observed in cells of the MGN that project to the anterior part of the auditory cortex and the "what" stream (Lennartz & Weinberger, 1992). In the auditory cortex, we find a more complex picture, however. Approximately 60% of the cells in the auditory cortex of the cat, for example, respond to pure tones; the remainder appear to respond to more complex sounds, such as clangs, noise bursts, or clicks (Coren & others, 1994). Similar functional specialization of areas of the auditory cortex has been found in monkeys (Tian & others, 2001).

Scheich and Zuschratter (1995), studying gerbils, found that neurons in different areas of the primary auditory cortex react to sounds of different frequency. Notice in Figure 7.10 that the orderly arrangement of neurons responding to particular sound frequencies in the basilar membrane carries through to the primary auditory cortex. This arrangement is called a **tonotopic distribution,** a pattern of neurons responding to specific tones in particular places throughout the auditory system. Tonotopic organization has been found in the auditory cortex of cats (Imaizumi & others, 2004), monkeys (Kosaki & others, 1997), and humans (Formisano & others, 2003; Weisz & others, 2004). Similar kinds of orderly distributions are found in other sensory mechanisms and in motor systems.

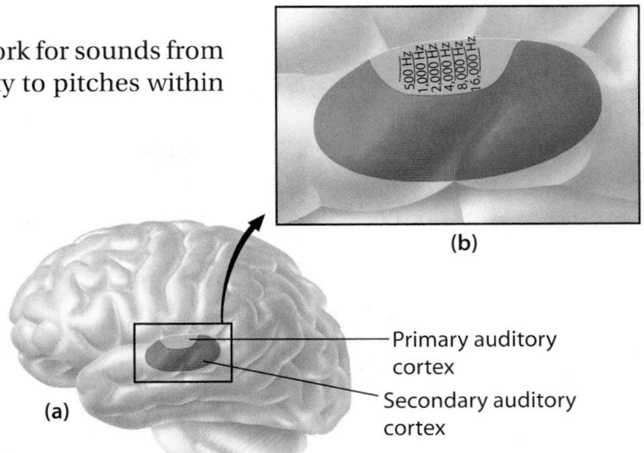

Figure 7.10

The auditory cortex and tonotopic distribution (a) The primary auditory cortex (blue) and secondary auditory cortex (red) are located almost entirely in the temporal lobe. (b) Tonotopic organization within the primary auditory cortex.

What would be the behavioral consequences of damage to the secondary auditory cortex?

Checkpoint

Compare and contrast place theory, frequency theory, and the volley principle. How do the theories complement one another?

Detection of Loudness

Despite, or perhaps because of, its great complexity, the auditory system is exquisitely sensitive to sound. For example, threshold-level sounds displace air molecules about one-tenth the diameter of the average air molecule (Coren & others, 1994). We now know that the hair cells respond (fire) when they move less than 100 picometers (100 trillionths of a meter) (Corwin & Warchol, 1991). In fact, in a very quiet environment, the auditory receptors can detect the sound of blood rushing through the arteries of the ear.

What about the ocean sound you hear when you hold a large seashell up to your ear? One explanation for this phenomenon is that you are hearing the echo of the blood rushing through the blood vessels in your ear. This cannot be the answer, however. If it were the case, then you would hear louder "ocean sounds" after exercising than before, but this does not happen. The most likely explanation is that you are hearing an amplification (by the seashell) of the noise around you. In fact, you can reproduce the same sound by holding an empty cup near your ear or even by using your cupped hand. If you experiment a little, you will find that the level of the sound varies depending on the angle of the cup to your ear or on its distance from you.

As we indicated in Chapter 4, the nervous system has two mechanisms for determining the intensity of a stimulus: the rate of firing of individual neurons and the number of neurons firing. The higher the firing rate, or the greater the number of neurons firing, the more intense the stimulus. For high-frequency sounds, the rate of firing indicates the loudness, with loud sounds producing a higher rate of firing than soft sounds. Pitch, as we have seen, is determined by which neurons

frequency theory of pitch perception The view that the firing rate in the auditory nerve matches the frequency of the sound.

volley principle The idea that groups of neurons in the auditory nerve fire asynchronously, in volleys, to match the frequency of the sound.

tonotopic distribution The pattern of neurons responding to specific tones in particular places throughout the auditory system.

are firing (place theory). For low-frequency sounds, particularly sounds for which pitch is determined by frequency theory, any increase in the rate of firing of individual neurons signals a different sound pitch. Thus, for low-frequency sounds, loudness must be signaled by the number of neurons firing rather than by their rate of firing, and the more neurons firing, the louder the sound.

Using fMRI, Jancke and colleagues (1998) studied the effect of auditory intensity on the cortex and found that the extent of activation of neurons in the superior temporal gyrus increased with increasing loudness. They hypothesized that auditory stimulus intensity is coded by the spread of excitation, or the number of neurons responding to the sound.

Detection of Sound Complexity

Pure tones are sounds of only one frequency, and complex sounds have two or more frequencies. The combination of frequencies produces what we perceive as the timbre of a particular sound. Timbre enables us to distinguish, for example, a middle C played on a flute and the same note played on a trumpet. Most of the sounds in our environment are complex rather than simple, pure sounds.

Each complex sound has a fundamental frequency and many harmonics (overtones), or multiples of the fundamental frequency. Thus, the complexity of the sounds of a musical instrument give the instrument its particular sound quality. Figure 7.11 shows a sound wave from a clarinet playing a specific note. The same type of Fourier analysis discussed in Chapter 6 in connection with spatial-frequency theory can also be used to break a complex sound wave into its component sine waves.

The particular area of the basilar membrane activated by a complex sound is determined by the fundamental frequency and its overtones. According to place theory, because each sound frequency activates a specific part of the basilar membrane, a complex sound produces a unique pattern of neural activity, enabling the listener to distinguish between the notes of a flute and a trumpet by the particular basilar membrane activity generated by each sound. The auditory cortex codes complexity information, and the processing of the meaning of complex sounds continues as the neural impulses travel through the ventral stream of the auditory pathway (Rauschecker & others, 1995).

Figure 7.11

A sound wave from a clarinet The clarinet produces a distinctive fundamental frequency and overtones.

➡ **How many waves would be shown in the Fourier analysis of a pure tone?**

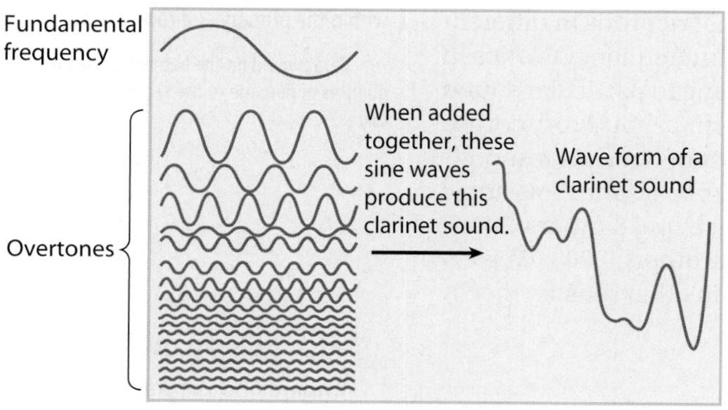

➤Checkpoint

Suggest why the rate of hair cell firing indicates the loudness of high-frequency sounds and the pitch of low-frequency sounds. Give an example from your own experience of a simple sound and a complex sound.

REVIEW

- ➤ Von Békésy's place theory of pitch perception suggests that the place of maximal vibration on the basilar membrane determines the pitch of the sound we hear.
- ➤ According to Rutherford's frequency theory of pitch perception, the rate of firing in the auditory nerve follows the frequency of the sound; Wever's volley principle carries the firing rate of the auditory nerve up to 4 kHz.
- ➤ The pattern of neurons responding to sound frequencies on the basilar membrane—a tonotopic distribution—is maintained throughout the auditory system.
- ➤ For low-frequency sounds, loudness is encoded by the number of neurons firing; for high-frequency sounds, loudness is encoded by the rate of responding: a higher rate for higher-intensity sounds.
- ➤ Each complex sound has one fundamental frequency and many overtones (multiples of the fundamental frequency).
- ➤ The auditory system identifies a sound, such as the sound of a specific instrument, by the unique pattern of basilar membrane activity it produces.

Sound Localization

While standing in line at the movie theater, you see a friend get out of her car and walk in your general direction, but it is obvious that your friend does not see you. You call her name, and she almost immediately spots you and comes to join you in line. This incident reveals your friend's ability to localize a sound. The auditory system uses different kinds of cues for sound localization, depending on whether the sound is low-pitched (less than 1.5 kHz) or high-pitched (more than 3 kHz). Intermediate-pitched sounds are difficult to localize, because the cues do not work well for such sounds. For both low-pitched sounds and high-pitched sounds, the cues to sound localization are based on differential time of arrival at the two ears. As long as the sound does not come from the median plane (a plane consisting of all the points directly in front of you, directly overhead, and directly behind you), the sound will arrive at one ear slightly before it gets to the other ear. As you can see in Figure 7.12a, a sound coming from the right of the head reaches the right ear before it reaches the left ear. As a result of differential activation of the basilar membrane of the two ears, the sound reaches the left and right medial superior olivary nuclei at slightly different times. Cells in these areas are sensitive to minute differences in the time of arrival of input from the two ears and can use these differences to locate where a sound is coming from (Tollin, 2003).

For relatively high-pitched sounds, like your voice, your friend uses **intensity differences** to detect where to look for you in line. Because your voice reaches one of your friend's ears slightly before it gets to her other ear, it is slightly louder in the closer ear. This intensity difference is detected by neurons in her lateral superior olivary nuclei (Tollin, 2003). Information from these neurons passes to the inferior colliculus (Fitzpatrick & others, 2002), where other neurons code the intensity differential.

In a microelectrode study of the responses of cortical neurons during a sound-localization task in monkeys, approximately 80% of the neurons in the auditory cortex were "spatially sensitive" (Recanzone & others, 2000). However, proportionally more of the neurons in the "where" stream had spatial sensitivity that matched the behavioral performance of the animals, suggesting their superiority for sound localization over other neurons in the primary auditory cortex (Recanzone, 2000).

A slightly different cue is involved in localizing low-pitched sounds, although this is still based on differences in arrival times at the two ears. As you can see from Figure 7.12b, low-pitched sounds reach the two ears at slightly different phases in their cycles of compression and rarefaction of air molecules; these **phase differences** are detected by the medial superior olivary nuclei.

intensity difference A cue to the localization of high-pitched sounds; a sound is louder in the ear closer to it than in the ear farther away.

phase difference A cue to localizing a low-pitched sound by the difference in the cycle of the sound wave when it reaches each ear.

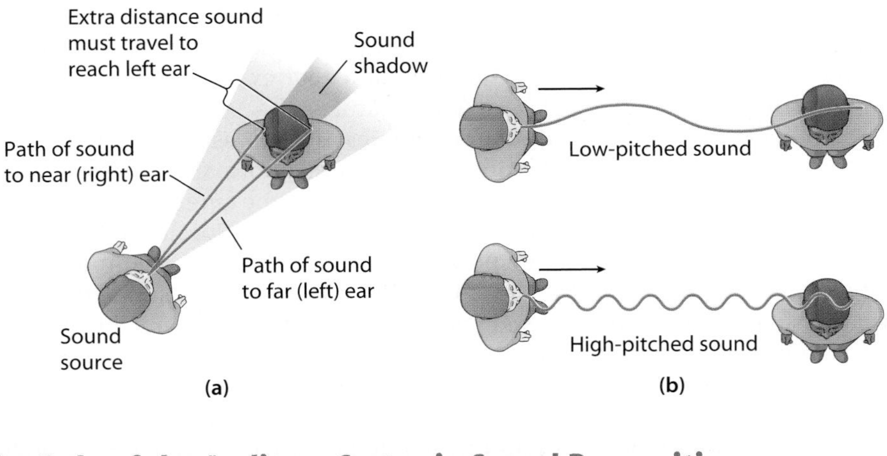

Figure 7.12
The use of timing and intensity cues in the location of a sound (a) Differential loudness is a cue for the localization of high-pitched sounds. (b) Phase differences of sound waves as they reach the ears are cues for the localization of low-pitched sounds; for high-pitched sounds, phase differences are less important for sound localization.

Which structures of the brain detect differences in the time of arrival of the input from the two ears?

The Role of the Auditory Cortex in Sound Recognition

Imagine that you are in an elevator with several other students when your cell phone rings. You flip it open and answer it softly. At the sound of the ring tones, some of the other people on the elevator looked in your direction, illustrating their

Box 7.1

Cochlear Implants and the Plasticity of the Auditory Cortex

Imagine for a moment that, having grown up with normal hearing, you suddenly can no longer hear any of the sounds around you. No sound of birds singing, no sound from your radio or television. You cannot hear friends talking to you. Music is lost to you, as well as the sound of your parents and friends on the telephone. This loss of hearing would represent a significant loss of contact with the world around you. It is perhaps not surprising that hearing loss is associated with paranoia (Sanchez Galan & others, 2000; Zimbardo & others, 1981).

Hearing aids can offer some help for people with partial deafness, but for many people, a hearing aid provides little or no benefit. For someone with profound hearing loss, whether congenital or acquired after birth, a cochlear implant may be a means for regaining some of the hearing that has been lost or was never there. A **cochlear implant** is a device that transmits electrical impulses along the auditory nerve to the brain (Figure 7.13). It consists of a microphone, a speech processor, a transmitter, a receiver, and an electrode array; the electrode array is surgically implanted into the cochlea of the inner ear (Nelson, 2000). Acoustic signals are picked up by a microphone that converts the sound into electrical signals. The speech processor filters out distracting noise and

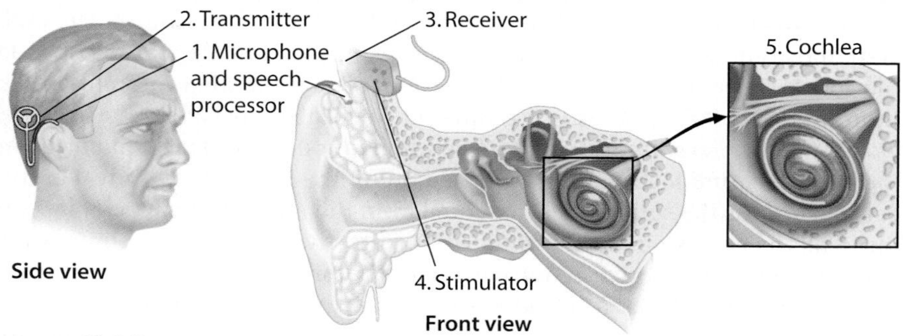

Figure 7.13

A multichannel cochlear implant A sound is received by the microphone and speech processor (1), which codes useful sounds and sends them to the transmitter (2). The transmitter sends codes to the receiver (3), which converts them to electrical signals and sends the signals to a stimulator (4), and from there to electrodes implanted in the cochlea (5). The electrodes stimulate the auditory nerve fibers, and the brain perceives the pattern of activity as sound.

➔ **What change occurs in the auditory cortex with long-term use of a cochlear implant?**

ability to localize sounds, but none of them answered their own cell phones. How could you tell that the call was for you, and how could the other elevator occupants tell that it was not for them?

Auditory receptors encode the frequency, intensity, and timbre of a sound and send this information to the primary auditory cortex. There, some neurons respond selectively to specific aspects of sounds, whereas other neurons react to more complex aspects of the sound stimulus. For example, in cats, Sutter and Schreiner (1991) observed that a specific combination of two or more tones of particular frequencies activated specific neurons in the primary auditory cortex, suggesting that some neurons in the primary auditory cortex react to the pattern of a complex sound rather than to its individual features.

The processing of a sound stimulus continues as it moves beyond the primary auditory cortex. The sound is identified as the neural information moves through the "what" stream, from the primary auditory cortex to the anterior part of the lateral surface of the superior temporal gyrus; the sound is localized as it moves through the "where" stream to the posterior part of the superior temporal gyrus and then to the parietal cortex. The study of humans who have suffered damage to various parts of the temporal and parietal lobes further supports the existence of two streams of auditory processing (Clarke & others, 2002).

Damage to Wernicke's area and surrounding areas, which are part of the secondary auditory cortex in the hemisphere controlling language (usually the left hemisphere, as we discuss in Chapter 13), often produces an inability to understand language, which is known as Wernicke's aphasia (Brookshire, 1997). A person with Wernicke's aphasia can recognize sounds, such as a siren, but not words. This finding suggests that Wernicke's area and the surrounding areas are respon-

cochlear implant A device that transmits electrical impulses along cranial nerve VIII to the brain.

sends the resulting electrical signals to an external transmitter, similar to a behind-the-ear hearing aid. From there, an internal magnetic coil, implanted under the skin beneath the external transmitter, picks up the signals and stimulates the implanted electrodes (Hegde, 2001). The electrodes stimulate the nerve endings of the auditory nerve, which transmits the neural impulses to the brain, where they are perceived as sound.

A cochlear implant is much more limited than the normal auditory system, which can detect more than 10,000 different frequencies. The surgeon has to implant up to 24 electrodes, each of which responds to a particular frequency band in the cochlea (Nelson, 2000). However, despite their limited function, cochlear implants do improve speech perception as a function of changes in the central auditory system (Purdy & others, 2001). Improvements in psychological well-being have also been found (Knutson & others, 1998). Nishimura and colleagues (2000) used PET to study the cortical responses of short-term and long-term cochlear implant users simultaneously listening to words and watching sign language. In short-term implant users, the auditory cortex was inactive, whereas in long-term users, it was fully engaged—a feat presumably accomplished by neural plasticity in the mature auditory cortex.

The effectiveness of cochlear implants depends on factors such as age at the onset of deafness, age at implantation, and the condition of the auditory nerve. Implantation in prelingual children under 6 years old has the best results in speech reception and production, suggesting a critical period of auditory neural plasticity (Manrique & others, 2004). In addition, studies of age-related evoked potentials (Chapter 1) indicate that, without normal auditory stimulation, some aspects of the central auditory system fail to mature; a cochlear implant can provide enough stimulation of the auditory system to restore some of the maturation that would have occurred with normal hearing (Ponton & others, 1999).

The U. S. Food and Drug Administration approved the use of cochlear implants for adults in 1985 and for children in 1990. More than 59,000 adults and children from all over the world have received such implants. The estimated cost for surgery, postoperative adjustments, and training is $60,000. Fortunately, the cost is frequently covered by health insurance.

A recent recipient of a cochlear implant is the talk show host Rush Limbaugh, who lost his hearing as a result of an autoimmune inner ear disorder. Shortly after undergoing the implantation procedure, Limbaugh claimed that he felt great, and he has subsequently returned to his radio show.

sible for detecting the combination of sounds we recognize as specific words. Clarke and colleagues (2000) found that unilateral damage to the secondary auditory cortex can lead to **auditory agnosia,** or an inability to recognize both language and nonlanguage sounds. If Kathy (from our opening vignette) had this type of damage, she might not be able to recognize Sarah's voice or the sound of a car horn at the same time that she could detect features of either sound. Thus, the "what" stream of the secondary auditory cortex is responsible for determining the meaning of the wide range of sounds that are detected by the auditory receptors and transmitted to the primary auditory cortex.

Assuming that the neural areas for sound detection and recognition are intact, is there anything that can be done to provide some auditory ability to a person with complete hearing loss because of damage to the organ of Corti? Box 7.1 describes the use of cochlear implants for people with profound hearing loss.

Checkpoint

What are the mechanisms that your auditory system uses for sound localization? Why are intermediate pitches difficult to locate? What is auditory agnosia and what kind of brain lesion would produce it?

REVIEW

- Sound localization depends on time-of-arrival cues, intensity differences, and phase differences.
- Neurons in the primary auditory cortex respond selectively to frequency, intensity, and complexity.
- The recognition of the meaning of a sound is the function of the "what" stream beyond the primary auditory cortex. Damage to the secondary auditory cortex can lead to auditory agnosia, the inability to recognize sounds.

auditory agnosia An inability to recognize language and nonlanguage sounds because of damage to the secondary auditory cortex.

◆ The Vestibular Sense

When Heather (from the opening vignette) hurriedly got out of the bath to answer the telephone, she momentarily lost her balance, nearly falling against the tub. But what exactly do we mean when we say "she lost her balance"? What is balance? How does your body maintain its orientation in space? Maintaining balance is the responsibility of the **vestibular sense** (from the Latin *vestibulum,* "an entrance hall"). *Vestibular* refers to the passageway leading to the cochlea from the semicircular canals (Figure 7.14). Our highly developed vestibular sense enables us to walk on two feet, keep our head upright, and adjust our eye movements to compensate for our head movements.

Figure 7.14

Components of the vestibular system (a) Location of the vestibular system within the head. (b) Hair cells in the vestibular sacs are stimulated by passive movements of the head. Hair cells in the semicircular canals are stimulated by rotations of the head.

→ **Where are the vestibular hair cells located?**

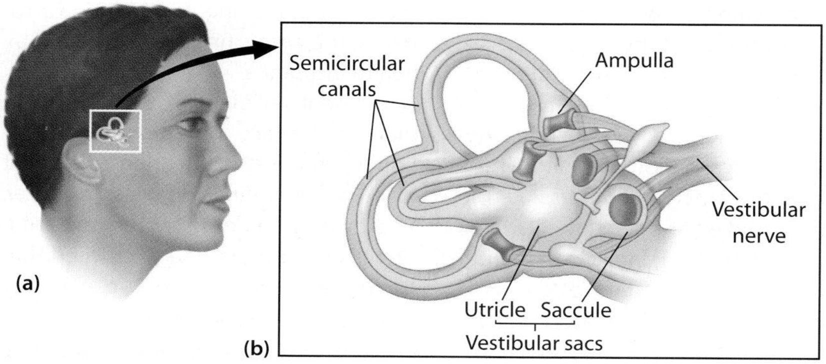

Components of the Vestibular System

The vestibular system has two parts: the semicircular canals and the vestibular sacs (Figure 7.14b). The **vestibular sacs** provide information about the position of the head relative to the body. The semicircular canals provide information related to head movements or rotations. Take another look at Figure 7.2; you will see that the vestibular system is part of the inner ear and is attached to the cochlea.

The two vestibular sacs are the **utricle** and the **saccule,** which contain the vestibular receptor cells, or hair cells. Some vestibular hair cells are located on the "floor" of the utricle and others on the "wall" of the saccule when the head is in an upright position. These hair cells are embedded in a gelatinous (jelly-like) mass, on top of which are small crystals of calcium carbonate, called *otoliths* (Figure 7.15a).

The vestibular system has three **semicircular canals,** each filled with endolymph and containing an enlarged area, the *ampulla,* which contains a structure

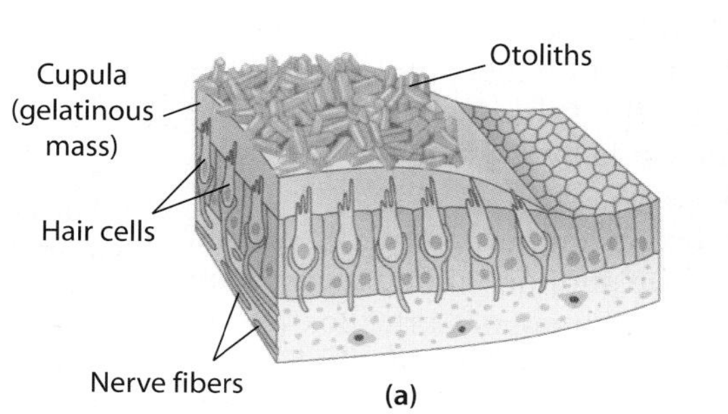

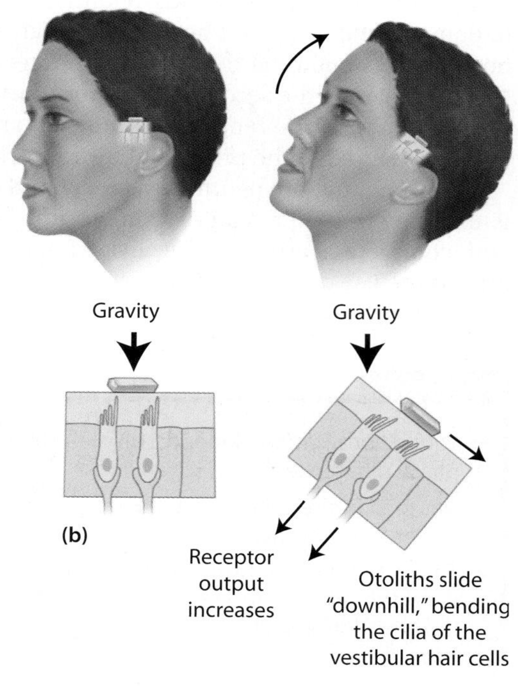

Figure 7.15

Receptors of the vestibular system and their response to head movement (a) Vestibular hair cells are embedded in the gelatinous mass of the vestibular sacs (saccule and utricle). (b) Movement of the head causes the otoliths and the gelatinous mass in which they are embedded to shift, which bends the cilia of the vestibular hair cells. Depending on the direction of head movement, the hair cell membrane is either depolarized or hyperpolarized.

→ **How does passive head movement affect balance?**

called the *crista*. The crista, like the vestibular sacs, contains hair cells embedded in a gelatinous mass, the *cupula*. The semicircular canals are oriented in the three major planes—sagittal, coronal, and horizontal (see Figure 2.4).

Vestibular Hair Cells

The hair cells of the vestibular system look much like the hair cells of the auditory system (compare Figures 7.3b and 7.4 with Figure 7.15a). The hair cells in the vestibular sacs are stimulated by passive movement of the head, which causes the cupula to shift position because of the weight of the otoliths. This shifting causes bending of the cilia of the hair cells and either depolarization or hyperpolarization of the hair cell membranes, depending on which way the cilia move (Figure 7.15b). Depolarization increases neurotransmitter release from the hair cells, and hyperpolarization decreases neurotransmitter release.

Similarly, any rotation of the head stimulates the vestibular hair cells in the cristae of the semicircular canals. A shift in the flow of the fluid in the semicircular canals, in response to changed orientation (or rotation) of the head, causes movement of the cupula, bending of the hair cell cilia, and depolarization or hyperpolarization of the hair cell membranes. In summary, the vestibular hair cells convert information about passive head movement (in the vestibular sacs) and active head rotation (in the cristae of the ampullae) into an increase or decrease in neurotransmitter release.

Vestibular Pathways

Like the rods and cones of the visual system, and like the auditory hair cells, vestibular hair cells synapse with bipolar neurons. The cell bodies of these bipolar cells form the **vestibular ganglia,** and their axons, clustered together, become the **vestibular nerve.** Vestibular nerve fibers combine with cochlear nerve fibers to form the auditory nerve (cranial nerve VIII).

Most vestibular nerve fibers synapse with **vestibular nuclei** in the medulla; others connect directly with neurons in the cerebellum. The vestibular nuclei project to other areas of the medulla, as well as to the pons, the cerebellum, the spinal cord, the red nucleus, the superior colliculus, and the temporal cortex. The projections of the vestibular nuclei to the spinal cord (vestibulospinal tracts) and cerebellum influence the coordination of balance, changes in body position, and body movement. Vestibular nuclei that project to other areas of the medulla and to the pons coordinate head and eye movements—movement of the eyes to compensate for head movements. This coordination is accomplished through the stimulation of cranial nerves III, IV, and VI for eye movements and XI for head movements (see Table 2.1). The projections to the temporal cortex are not well understood, but they may produce conscious feelings of dizziness and imbalance.

Have you ever taken a long boat ride? If so, you may have experienced the dizziness and nausea of **motion sickness.** There are two main kinds of motion sickness, both of which occur when the body is moved passively without motor activity and the corresponding feedback to the brain. The first kind of motion sickness occurs when the vestibular system detects movement, but motor actions that could have produced the movement have not occurred. This inconsistency between the information from the vestibular system and the motor system results in the type of motion sickness one experiences when riding on a boat, in a plane, or in a car.

The second kind of motion sickness results when the vestibular system senses movement inconsistent with the information about movement sensed by the eyes: Passive movement causes the vestibular system to report motion, but the eyes register no motion. This inconsistency produces **nystagmus,** or rapid side-to-side eye movements—the attempt by the visual system to compensate for the report of movement by the vestibular system. Again, the inconsistency of motion cues from the vestibular and visual systems can cause motion sickness. It is generally believed that stimulation of brain stem structures produces the nausea and

vestibular sense The sense responsible for maintaining balance.

vestibular sac The part of the vestibular system that provides information about the position of the head relative to the body.

utricle, saccule The two vestibular sacs containing the vestibular receptor cells, or hair cells.

semicircular canal One of three fluid-filled canals in the vestibular system.

vestibular ganglion A group of bipolar neurons that receive input from vestibular hair cells.

vestibular nerve Axons of the vestibular ganglion neurons.

vestibular nucleus The part of the medulla with which most vestibular nerve fibers synapse.

motion sickness The feelings of dizziness and nausea that occur when the body is moved passively without motor activity and corresponding feedback to the brain.

nystagmus The rapid side-to-side eye movements caused by inconsistent information from the visual and vestibular systems.

vomiting of motion sickness, whereas temporal cortex stimulation causes the dizziness.

As a child, you may have experienced the second type of motion sickness by spinning yourself around rapidly with your eyes closed and then stopping suddenly and opening your eyes. You would have experienced nystagmus—without knowing its name, of course—and dizziness, perhaps with mild nausea.

"Home" or "folk" remedies for preventing or treating motion sickness abound, despite a lack of scientific evidence for their effectiveness. For example, ginger has long been touted as a cure, but evidence supporting its efficacy is mixed. In one study of motion sickness produced by a rotating chair, scopolamine, a standard pharmacological remedy, was significantly more effective than a placebo, but ginger, in several different doses and forms, was completely ineffective (Stewart & others, 1991). By contrast, Lien and colleagues (2003) found ginger quite effective against motion sickness induced by rotation in volunteers with a history of motion sickness. Schmid and coworkers (1994) tested the efficacy of seven commonly used drugs for preventing seasickness. Ginger root was just as effective as the other substances, and scopolamine was the least effective of the chemicals tested.

Another popular remedy for motion sickness involves acupressure, a type of Oriental medicine related to acupuncture. With acupressure, points on the surface of the skin are pressed rather than punctured with needles. Wrist bands with a plastic button designed to press against a crucial pressure point on the wrist are supposed to work against the nausea and vomiting associated with motion sickness. Although acupressure has been found to reduce nausea and vomiting from such disparate causes as combat, pregnancy, chemotherapy, and surgery, it does not appear to work against motion sickness (Bruce & others, 1990; Warwick-Evans & others, 1991).

In addition to motion sickness, certain types of stimulation of the vestibular system can result in visual/vestibular illusions that can produce disorientation, with a potentially fatal outcome. One such illusion occurs in conditions of poor visibility. Called the *false climb illusion,* the vestibular system perceives acceleration as occurring with the plane in a nose-up position (Burden, 2000). The problem is that both acceleration and the head tilted backward (as it would be in a steep climb) produce the same effect on the vestibular apparatus. Thus, with the head in a vertical position, acceleration makes the pilot feel as though the plane were climbing rather than flying level. With poor visibility, the pilot may attempt to compensate for the illusion by lowering the nose of the airplane. This increases the acceleration of the plane, which increases the illusion, which leads to further lowering of the nose, etc. As you might imagine, the result can be a high-speed crash into water or the ground. John F. Kennedy, Jr., who died in a plane crash along with his two passengers in 1999, may have been a victim of this illusion ("JFK Jr.," 2000).

➤Checkpoint

What element(s) of the vestibular system must be especially fine-tuned in a tightrope walker? Compare the auditory hair cells with the vestibular hair cells.

REVIEW

- The vestibular system, consisting of the vestibular sacs (the saccule and utricle) and the semicircular canals, maintains balance, helps keep the head in an upright position, and adjusts eye movements to compensate for head movements.
- Head movement resulting from changes in body position causes the calcium carbonate crystals and the gelatinous mass in the utricle and saccule to shift, which in turn causes bending of the cilia of the hair cells embedded in the mass. This bending initiates activity in the vestibular nerve.
- Vestibular hair cells are also embedded in the cupula, a gelatinous mass inside the cristae of the three semicircular canals, and the cilia of these hair cells are bent by rotation of the head.
- Vestibular hair cells synapse with vestibular nerve fibers, which combine with cochlear nerve fibers to form the auditory nerve.

> ➤ Vestibular nerve fibers project to the medulla and pons, which coordinate head and eye movements; to the spinal cord and cerebellum, which coordinate balance, body position, and body movement; and to the temporal cortex, which may produce conscious awareness of dizziness and imbalance.

somatosense The skin sensations of touch, pain, temperature, and proprioception.

proprioception The somatosense that monitors body position and movement, acts to maintain body position, and ensures the accuracy of intended movements.

Pacinian corpuscle The largest type of skin receptor, found in both hairy and hairless skin; detects high-frequency vibrations.

The Somatosenses

Have you ever had this experience? It is a class day, and you go outside to find snow and ice on your windshield. You try in vain to wipe it off with your bare hand. You would rather be inside your warm apartment, having a leisurely cup of coffee and reading the paper, but you have to get to school. And you cannot drive your car if you cannot see through the windshield. With your hands feeling nearly frozen, you decide to go back inside to look for your gloves and for something to use as a scraper. Before you go inside, you get into the car and start the motor. Leaving the car idling, you hurry back into the building.

The feeling of cold is one example of a skin sensation, or **somatosense.** A decrease in temperature is the stimulus that produces the sensation of cold. The feeling of warmth caused by an increase in temperature is another somatosense, and touch and pain are further examples. Touch is actually a response to two different stimuli: pressure, caused by a deformation of the skin, and vibration, caused by skin moving across a rough surface. Many different stimuli can produce pain; most of them reflect excessive sensory stimulation or cause tissue damage to the skin. The senses of cold, warmth, touch, and pain are sometimes called the *cutaneous senses.*

Another example of a somatosense is **proprioception,** which monitors body position and movement, acts to maintain body position, and ensures the accuracy of intended movements. The proprioceptive receptors are located in the muscles, tendons, and joints. Receptors in the skeletal muscles report changes in muscle length, and receptors in the tendons measure the force the muscles exert on the tendons. Receptors in the joints record the magnitude and duration of limb movement.

Information from the proprioceptive receptors is essential to the control of movement. For example, if the receptors in your elbows were not working, you would have trouble holding this book and turning its pages. We focus here on the cutaneous senses, and will examine the role of the proprioceptive system in the control of movement in Chapter 8.

In a chapter in *The Man Who Mistook His Wife for a Hat,* neurologist Oliver Sacks (1987) recounts the story of a young woman who, while awaiting surgery, lost her sense of proprioception. Over time, with great determination and practice, the "disembodied lady," as Sacks called her, was able to replace her normal sense of body position with visually guided reflexes. Although she was able to return to her normal life, she was anything but normal, telling Sacks that she felt "pithed," her core or sense of herself removed.

Skin Receptors

The components of the skin, and the different types of somatosensory skin receptors, are shown in Figure 7.16. The skin has two layers, the dermis and the epidermis. Its appearance can range from hairy and rough to smooth and hairless (glabrous). The functions of the skin include protecting the internal organs from injury; helping regulate body temperature by producing sweat, which cools the body when it becomes too hot; and providing a first line of defense against invading microorganisms.

The largest of the somatosensory receptors of the skin are the **Pacinian corpuscles,** which are found in both hairy and hairless skin, as well as in the joints, tendons, muscles, external genitalia, mammary glands, and some internal organs. Pacinian corpuscles are approximately 0.5 mm wide by 1.0 mm long—the largest sensory receptors in the body.

A Pacinian corpuscle consists of a terminal button of a single myelinated axon enclosed within 70 layers of collagen fibers, wrapped like an onion. These receptors

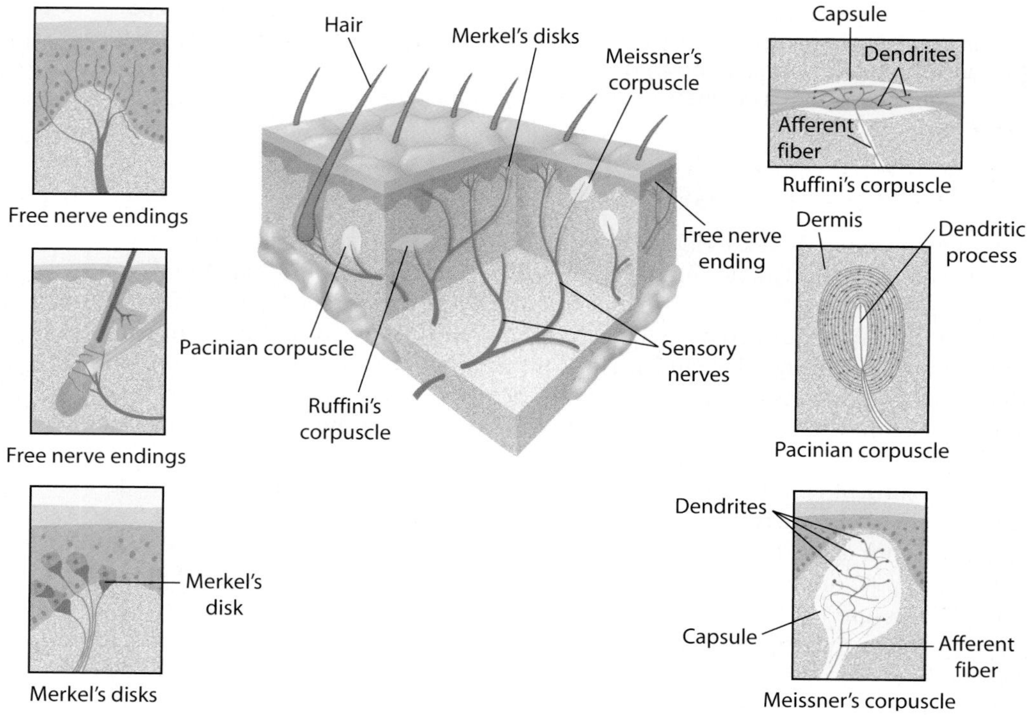

Figure 7.16
The somatosensory receptors of the skin

➡ To what types of stimuli is the Pacinian corpuscle sensitive?

are sensitive to touch stimulation, primarily to high-frequency vibrations (200 to 300 Hz) such as might be produced by running your fingers across a rough towel. The vibrations cause the tip of the axon in the Pacinian corpuscle to bend, which then causes Na^+ ion channels in the membrane to open, allowing Na^+ ions to enter and depolarize the cell. If the depolarization reaches the threshold, an action potential is generated.

Pacinian corpuscles have quite large receptive fields, which means that stimulating a small part of the hand produces feeling in a much wider area. As you can see from Figure 7.17, a rough tactile stimulus applied to the tip of your middle finger will feel as if your entire finger is being touched.

Free nerve endings, another type of somatosensory skin receptor, are located just below the surface in both hairy and hairless skin. Temperature change is one type of stimulus detected by free nerve endings; they increase their firing rate whether the temperature change comes from touching a cold or a hot object or from the atmosphere. The greater the increase in firing rate, the greater the sensation of coolness or warmth. The specific free nerve endings that detect hot and cold differ in how far beneath the skin they lie: Receptors for coolness lie close to the surface, and those for warmth are located farther down (Sinclair, 1981). This difference explains why it would take your hands much longer to feel warm (once you found your gloves and put them on) than to feel cold (when you first went outside to start your car).

Figure 7.17
Receptive fields and adaptation rates of touch receptors Meissner's corpuscles have small receptive fields and adapt quickly; Merkel's disks have small receptive fields and adapt slowly; Pacinian corpuscles have large receptive fields and adapt quickly; and Ruffini's corpuscles have large receptive fields and adapt slowly. (Adapted from Vallbo & Johansson, 1984.)

➡ Why do the receptive fields and adaptation rates of the skin receptors differ?

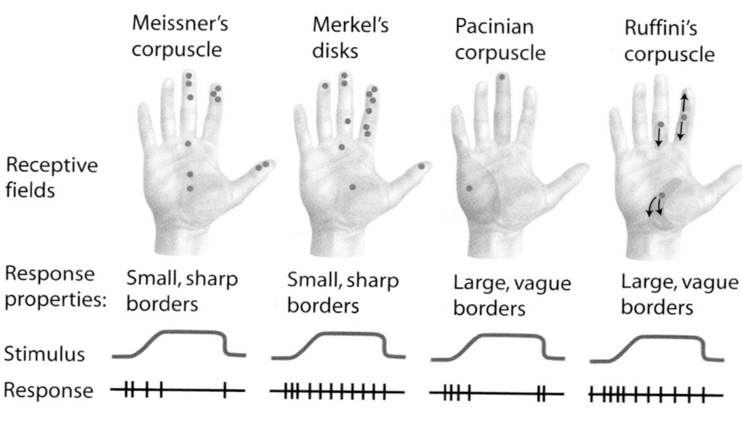

As you may realize from your own experience, sensations of warmth and coolness are relative. A temperature of 30 degrees Fahrenheit might feel quite cold to someone from Florida but not at all cold to someone from Alaska. Similarly, 90 degrees Fahrenheit might be sensed as hot by a Minnesotan but not by someone living in Arizona.

Free nerve endings also serve as pain receptors. Low-threshold free nerve endings detect touch rather than pain, but direct pressure stimulation of high-threshold free nerve endings signals a painful stimulus. Called **fast pain** or *prickling pain,* this kind of pain is produced by experiences such as an injection or a deep cut. The sensations of pain are carried over myelinated axons called type A fibers and quickly reach the spinal cord (Martini, 1998). From the spinal cord, the neural messages travel to the primary somatosensory cortex, where a conscious perception of localized pain is experienced. We provide more detail about this pathway later.

A second, more roundabout way of producing painful sensations is through cell damage. Damaged or injured cells synthesize prostaglandins, hormones that increase the sensitivity of free nerve endings to histamine. Histamine, also released by the injured cells, activates the free nerve endings, producing the sensation of pain. Messages about this type of pain, called **slow pain** or *burning and aching pain,* travel by unmyelinated type C fibers. Sensations are of an awareness of pain, with only a general awareness of the area damaged.

Pain can also be elicited by "pepper-hot" foods, such as chili peppers, although the painful sensation may enhance the accompanying flavors for some (Rozin & others, 1982). In this case, the free nerve endings are sensitive to **capsaicin,** the ingredient that gives chili peppers their "bite." Capsaicin (pronounced cap-say-uh-sin) causes neurons to release substance P, a peptide neurotransmitter (Chapter 4), which is involved in pain. (The involvement of substance P in pain is easy to remember—just think of "P" for pain.) Capsaicin also stimulates heat receptors in the mouth to produce the burning sensation you experience when eating hot peppers. Interestingly, after the hot sensation wears off from capsaicin, a period of anesthesia follows, and this characteristic has been used in topical treatments for arthritis and several other types of pain. Capsaicin has only limited effectiveness when used by itself but has a greater effect when used in conjunction with other analgesic drugs (Watson, 1994). In mice, the analgesic effect of capsaicin was enhanced by inflammation-induced activation of the receptors for capsaicin (Menendez & others, 2004). The gene for the capsaicin receptor, the *vanilloid* receptor, has been determined, and mice lacking this receptor respond normally to noxious mechanical stimuli but fail to respond to either painful heat or capsaicin (Caterina & others, 2000).

Meissner's corpuscles, found only in hairy skin, are located in the elevations (papillae, or "nipples") of the dermis into the epidermis (Figure 7.16). These receptors respond to pressure on the skin and to low-frequency vibrations (50 Hz)—such as might be produced by a smooth cotton shirt—with touch sensations. Unlike Pacinian corpuscles, Meissner's corpuscles have small receptive fields (Figure 7.17), which means that when a smooth tactile stimulus is applied to the tip of your middle finger, you will feel it only on your fingertip.

Merkel's disks, receptors located at the base of the epidermis near the sweat ducts, are sensitive to pressure but not to vibrations, and have small receptive fields; **Ruffini's corpuscles,** located just below the surface of the skin, respond to low-frequency vibrations but not to pressure, and they have large receptive fields (Figure 7.17). Both Merkel's disks and Ruffini's corpuscles respond to even lower-frequency vibrations than those that activate Meissner's corpuscles, vibrations such as might be produced by the smooth surface of your pen.

Some touch receptors (Meissner's corpuscles, Pacinian corpuscles) adapt quickly to stimulation and react only to stimulus change (see the response traces in Figure 7.17). Moderate, constant stimulation of the skin does not continue to produce sensations in these touch receptors. Consider what happens when you put on a shirt or blouse. You feel the pressure on your skin at first, but after a few seconds, you no longer notice the sensation produced by the garment. The advantage of touch receptor adaptation is obvious: If the receptors did not adapt, you would constantly be sensing the clothes you were wearing, and as a result, you would have difficulty attending to other aspects of your environment. Because touch receptors adapt quickly, an object can be identified by the skin senses only when it is moved along the skin. Movement causes vibrations and allows identification of the object by the touch receptors (Pacinian corpuscles, Meissner's cor-

free nerve ending A type of skin receptor located just below the surface in both hairy and hairless skin; detects temperature and pain stimuli.

fast pain The type of pain carried by myelinated type A fibers that quickly reaches the spinal cord.

slow pain The type of pain propagated by unmyelinated type C fibers that slowly reaches the spinal cord.

capsaicin The ingredient that gives chili peppers their hot taste by causing free nerve endings to release substance P.

Meissner's corpuscle A type of skin receptor in hairy skin, located in the elevations of the dermis into the epidermis; responds to pressure and low-frequency vibrations.

Merkel's disk A type of skin receptor in the base of the epidermis near the sweat ducts; sensitive to pressure.

Ruffini's corpuscle A type of skin receptor just below the surface; detects low-frequency vibrations.

puscles) that adapt quickly to touch sensations. Merkel's disks and Ruffini's corpuscles do not adapt quickly but continue to respond as long as the stimulus remains present. Thus, you continue to feel the pen while holding it, but you do not continue to feel the clothing you are wearing.

➤Checkpoint

What skin receptors provide the sensation of hot? Cold? Touch? Why do some skin receptors adapt more quickly than others?

REVIEW

- ➤ Somatosenses include the detection of touch, temperature, and pain as well as proprioception.
- ➤ Pacinian corpuscles are the largest of the skin receptors; they are sensitive to touch stimulation, particularly high-frequency vibrations.
- ➤ Free nerve endings, located just below the surface of the skin, detect changes in temperature and painful stimulation.
- ➤ Some other skin receptors are Meissner's corpuscles, which are sensitive to pressure and low-frequency vibrations; Merkel's disks, sensitive to pressure; and Ruffini's corpuscles, sensitive to low-frequency vibrations.

dorsal column–medial lemniscal system A somatosensory pathway that begins in the spinal cord and transmits information about touch and proprioception to the primary somatosensory cortex.

dorsal column nucleus A group of neurons in the medulla that receives neural messages about touch and proprioception via the dorsal column–medial lemniscal system.

medial lemniscus A ribbon-like band of fibers in the dorsal column–medial lemniscal system that conveys neural messages from the dorsal column nuclei to the ventral posterolateral thalamic nuclei.

Somatosensory Pathways

The axons of the skin receptors project to the CNS either through the cranial nerves of the face and head (see Table 2.1) or through the spinal nerves (see Figure 2.10). Once information from the skin reaches the CNS, the neural message travels through one of three somatosensory systems: the dorsal column–medial lemniscal system, the anterolateral system, or the spinocerebellar system (Figure 7.18).

The **dorsal column–medial lemniscal system,** which transmits information about touch and proprioception (Figure 7.18a), projects to the medulla, where it synapses with the two **dorsal column nuclei**. One of the dorsal column nuclei, the medial nucleus gracilis, receives dorsal column projections from the lower body, and the other, the lateral nucleus cuneatus, receives projections from the upper body. At this point, the two dorsal columns cross over to the other side of the brain and form a ribbon-like band of fibers, the **medial lemniscus** (the Greek

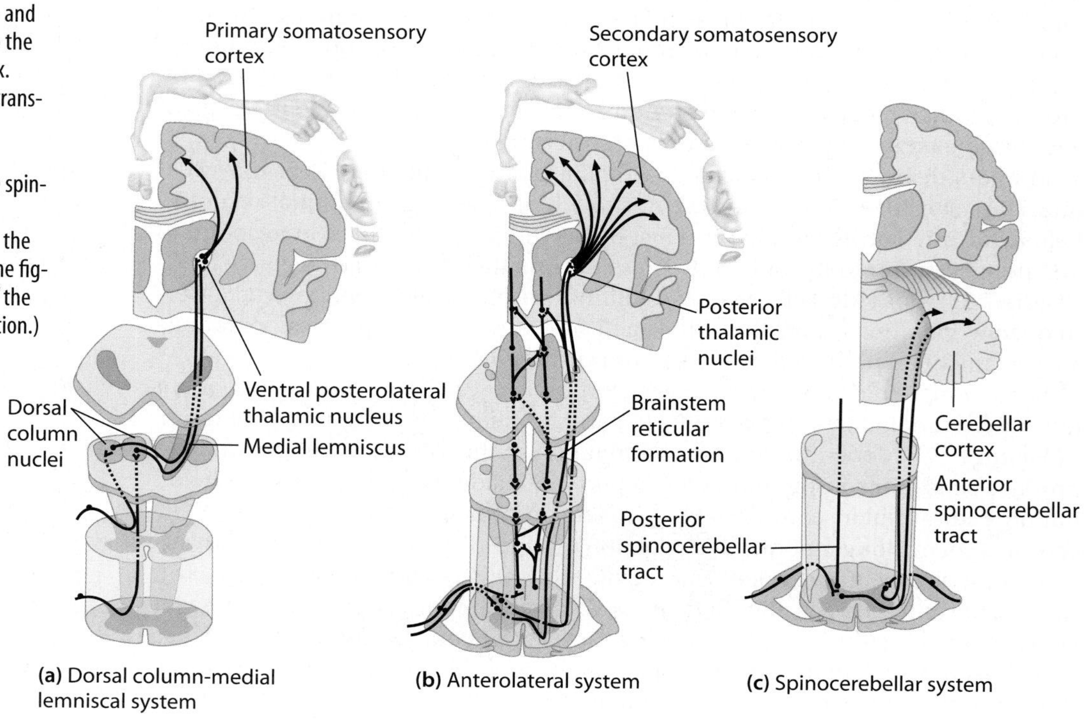

Figure 7.18
Somatosensory pathways
(a) The dorsal column-medial lemniscal system transmits touch and proprioceptive information to the primary somatosensory cortex. (b) The anterolateral system transmits temperature and pain information to the secondary somatosensory cortex. (c) The spinocerebellar system transmits proprioceptive information to the cerebellum. (Dotted lines in the figure represent the approach of the pathway from behind the section.)

➜ **Which pathways transmit information about body movements and position?**

lemniskos means "ribbon"). Both dorsal columns synapse with the **ventral posterolateral thalamic nucleus.** Information about touch and proprioceptive stimulation is then transmitted from the thalamus to the **primary somatosensory cortex.**

After crossing over at the spinal cord, many fibers of the **anterolateral system,** which transmits information about temperature and pain, project to the ventral posterolateral thalamic nucleus and the **posterior thalamic nucleus** (Figure 7.18b). Other fibers terminate in the brain stem reticular formation. From the thalamus, some anterolateral system fibers extend to the primary somatosensory cortex and others to the **secondary somatosensory cortex,** an area of the cortex lateral and slightly posterior to the primary somatosensory cortex.

Fibers of the **spinocerebellar system,** which transmit information about proprioception, enter the CNS through the dorsal root ganglia and synapse with the interneurons in the spinal cord (Figure 7.18c). Some axons of these interneurons cross over at the spinal cord level to form the anterior spinocerebellar tract; others do not cross over, and these become the posterior spinocerebellar tract. Both tracts project directly to the cerebellar cortex.

Checkpoint

Describe the path of touch sensation from your fingertips to your primary somatosensory cortex.

Locating Input to the Somatosensory System

In 1973, Canadian neurologist Wilder Penfield mapped the primary somatosensory cortex in humans (Figure 7.19). He found that when he stimulated areas of the postcentral gyrus or the primary somatosensory cortex in conscious patients before surgery, the patients reported feeling sensations from various parts of the body. Penfield observed that, like the visual and auditory systems, the somatosensory system is topographically organized. Adjacent places on the skin activate adjacent neurons in the primary somatosensory cortex, but the cortical organization is upside down. Sensory input from the feet goes to the top of the primary somatosensory cortex, which is actually down in the longitudinal fissure separating the left and right hemispheres, and input from the head goes to the bottom of the primary somatosensory cortex. As seen in the *somatotopic map,* or somatosensory homunculus ("little man in the brain") (Figure 7.19), not all body parts are equally represented. The greatest representation is for areas such as the hands, lips, and tongue, involved in fine tactile discrimination.

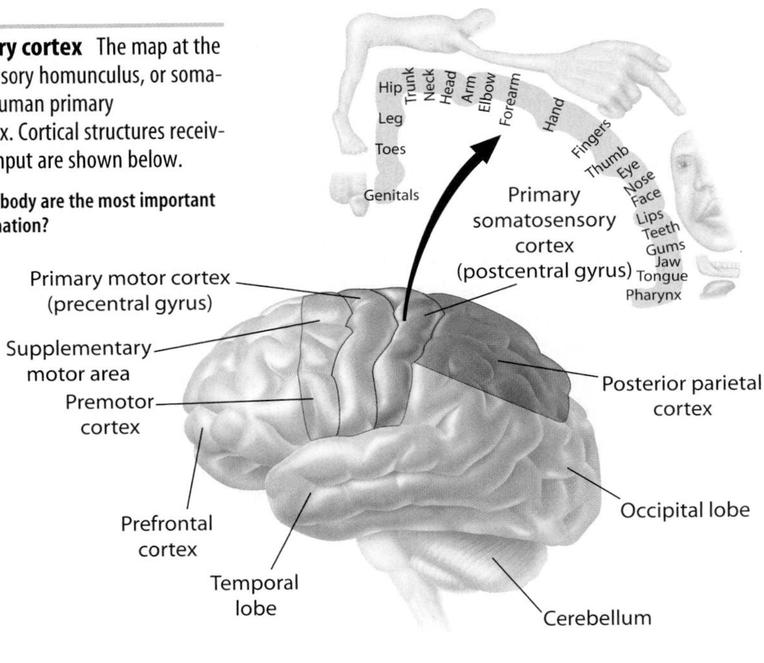

Figure 7.19

The somatosensory cortex The map at the top is the somatosensory homunculus, or somatotopic map of the human primary somatosensory cortex. Cortical structures receiving somatosensory input are shown below.

What parts of the body are the most important in fine tactile discrimination?

ventral posterolateral thalamic nucleus A group of neurons that receives information about touch and proprioception via the dorsal column–medial lemniscal system and about temperature and pain via the anterolateral system.

primary somatosensory cortex An area in the cortex that receives information about touch, proprioception, temperature, and pain.

anterolateral system The somatosensory pathway that begins in the spinal cord and transmits information about temperature and pain to the brain stem reticular formation and the primary and secondary somatosensory cortices.

posterior thalamic nucleus A group of neurons in the thalamus that receives information about temperature and pain via the anterolateral pathway.

secondary somatosensory cortex An area of the cortex, lateral and slightly posterior to the primary somatosensory cortex, that receives information from the skin senses.

spinocerebellar system The somatosensory pathway that begins in the spinal cord and transmits proprioceptive information to the cerebellum.

gate-control theory of pain The view that input from pain receptors will produce the perception of pain only if the message first passes through a "gate" in the spinal cord and lower brain stem structures.

periaqueductal gray (PAG) An area of the midbrain that is the origin of a descending fiber tract that synapses with inhibitory interneurons in the lower brain stem and spinal cord to block messages about pain.

The primary somatosensory cortex has four parallel columns (Kaas & others, 1981). Each column has its own topographic organization, and most neurons in each column are sensitive to specific somatosensory input. For example, neurons in one column respond to touch, neurons in another column to temperature.

Like the primary somatosensory cortex, the secondary somatosensory cortex is topographically organized. It receives most of its input from the primary somatosensory cortex (Pons & others, 1987). Moreover, there appear to be separate somatotopic maps for each type of somatosense; that is, separate areas in the secondary somatosensory cortex receive neural impulses from rapidly adapting touch receptors, from slow-adapting touch receptors, from temperature receptors, from pain receptors, and from proprioceptive receptors (Dykes, 1983).

The Experience and Control of Pain

As one of our somatosenses, pain is both a curse and a blessing. Chronic, intractable pain can be the bane of a person's existence. But under ordinary circumstances, pain is extremely useful, both warning us of potential injury and, if an injury occurs, inducing us to seek appropriate treatment. You only have to touch a hot stove to recognize the utility of pain; without the sensation that triggers a withdrawal reflex, you would suffer serious burns to the part of your body in contact with the stove. To imagine what life would be like without pain, consider the rare cases of people who apparently have been born without this sensory mechanism: A woman with this disorder died at age 29 from infections caused by years of repeated injuries to her skin, bones, and joints (Melzack & Wall, 1982).

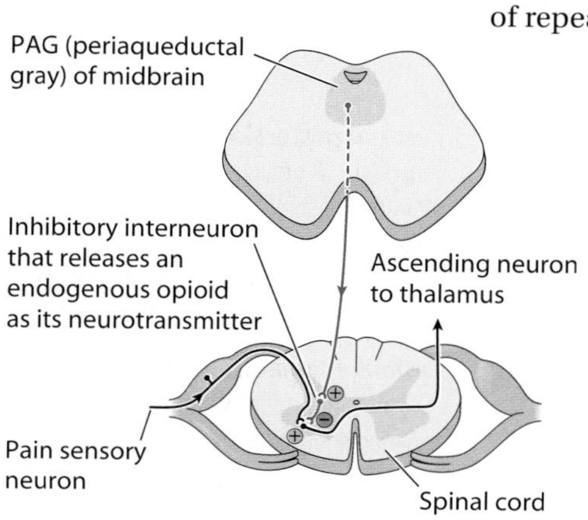

Figure 7.20
The periaqueductal gray fiber tracts
The descending fibers from the PAG inhibit sensory pain messages at the spinal cord and lower brain stem.

➡ **How do the neurons of the PAG "close the gate" to pain messages?**

For many years, the most widely accepted theory of pain has been one proposed in 1965 by Canadian psychologist Ronald Melzack and British physiologist Patrick Wall: the **gate-control theory of pain.** According to this idea, a group of nerve cells in the spinal cord acts as a sort of gate, either blocking pain messages or allowing them to travel to the brain, where we actually experience the pain. Melzack and Wall (1965) identified a descending fiber tract that begins in the **periaqueductal gray (PAG)** of the midbrain and synapses with inhibitory interneurons in the spinal cord and lower brain stem (Figure 7.20). These inhibitory neurons synapse with ascending sensory neurons that carry messages about pain. Activity in the PAG activates the inhibitory interneurons, which then block the pain messages from entering the CNS.

The spinal cord "gate" can be controlled either from above (the brain) or from below. The gate is opened from below by impulses from small pain fibers, which can then send their messages on to the brain to be interpreted as pain. However, the gate can also be closed from below by large fibers bringing messages about pressure and other types of sensations. That is why vigorously rubbing your elbow after bumping your "funny bone" can relieve your pain; the rubbing stimulates the large fibers that close the gate and do not allow the pain messages from the elbow, traveling by small fibers, to pass on to the brain.

By emphasizing that messages from the brain can also open or close the spinal cord gate, the gate-control theory helps us understand the psychological nature of pain. The theory provides a mechanism to account for why our sensation of pain can be so affected by our thoughts and feelings. If we are anxious about a particular experience that might involve pain, for example, that anxiety opens the gate from above, and the pain comes flooding through. But if we are convinced that a procedure will not involve pain, the gate is likely to be closed.

Focusing on pain, attending to it, and talking about it constantly—all of this probably keeps the pain gate open and intensifies the discomfort. Distraction, such as in an athletic contest, closes the gate, which explains the experience we have all had of injuring ourselves but not realizing it until long after the damage was done, when we are no longer distracted and the wound begins to hurt or we notice blood on ourselves. You may also have read about long-distance runners who injured themselves seriously in marathons, even broke bones in some cases, and yet were able to finish the race without pain. This example brings up one of the mechanisms by which the gate can be closed from above: the release of endogenous opioids, or endorphins.

Several investigators believe that endorphins released in response to a painful stimulus stimulate neurons in the PAG and thereby close the gate to incoming pain messages (Basbaum & Fields, 1984; Vasquez & Vanegas, 2000). For example, Basbaum and Fields reported that small amounts of the opiate drug morphine, which has an agonistic effect on the opiate receptors of the brain, relieve pain when injected into the PAG. The same amount of morphine injected into other brain areas did not produce any analgesic effect. Furthermore, Reynolds (1969) found that electrical stimulation of the PAG produced enough anesthesia to allow him to do abdominal surgery on animals without giving them any drugs. These observations suggest that opiates such as morphine block pain by stimulating the PAG.

Another way to stimulate the PAG and close the spinal cord gate is to use *acupuncture,* a pain control technique employed in China for more than 2,000 years, in which fine needles are inserted into the skin in different parts of the body (Figure 7.21). Acupuncture has been used successfully in a variety of medical procedures, including oral surgery (Lao & others, 1999), and during childbirth (Smith & others, 2003). Acupuncture probably relieves pain by stimulating endorphin release (Han, 2004), thereby closing the gate to incoming pain messages. The points at which the acupuncture needles are inserted are close to the somatosensory pathways that conduct pain sensations (Chen & others, 1986). As further evidence for the acupuncture-endorphin connection, Ulett and colleagues (1998) found that administration of naloxone, an endorphin antagonist, blocked the analgesic effect of acupuncture.

As powerful as the gate-control theory has been in accounting for pain phenomena, Melzack has supplemented it with what he calls the **neuromatrix theory of pain** (Melzack, 1999, 2001). Melzack's addition to pain theory is designed to account for types of pain that gate-control theory has difficulty explaining. For example, gate-control theory cannot explain severe, chronic pain existing in the absence of injury or disease. In one such case, an architect fractured his shoulder at a construction site, and although the injury was surgically repaired, he was continuously plagued with incapacitating pain that robbed him of sleep and forced him to give up his profession. Doctors have found nothing to explain his torment (Gawande, 1998).

Melzack's idea is that we have a neural representation of our body and body parts, which he calls the neuromatrix. Somewhere in the neocortex, a group of nerve cells forms the representation of your right hand, for example. Your consciousness of having a right hand, its shape, its position at the end of your right arm, and so on, resides in that specific group of cells. Suppose you lose your right hand in an accident. Even though the hand is gone, the nerve cells that constitute your awareness of that hand are still there, and if something activates them abnormally, you are likely to experience pain in the missing limb, a phenomenon known as **phantom limb pain.**

Phantom Limb Pain and Neuroplasticity in the Adult Brain

Like chronic pain in the absence of an injury or disease, phantom limb pain is a phenomenon that gate-control theory has difficulty explaining. In up to 70% of cases, people who lose a limb to injury or disease continue to experience the limb as still being attached and often have the sensation of pain coming from the limb. Some hand amputees experience the missing hand as being clenched and aching. Because the hand is no longer there, there is no way for them to straighten it out and relieve the tension.

V. S. Ramachandran, director of the Center for Brain and Cognition at the University of California, San Diego, is particularly fascinated by amputees with phan-

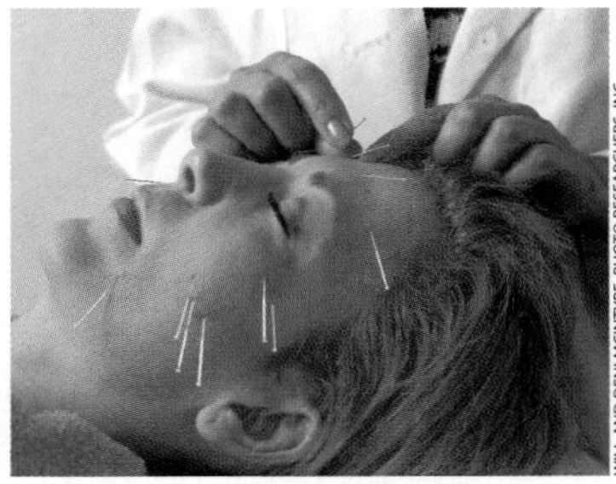

Figure 7.21

Acupuncture The practitioner inserts fine needles to treat pain.

➜ **What structure of the CNS is acupuncture believed to stimulate?**

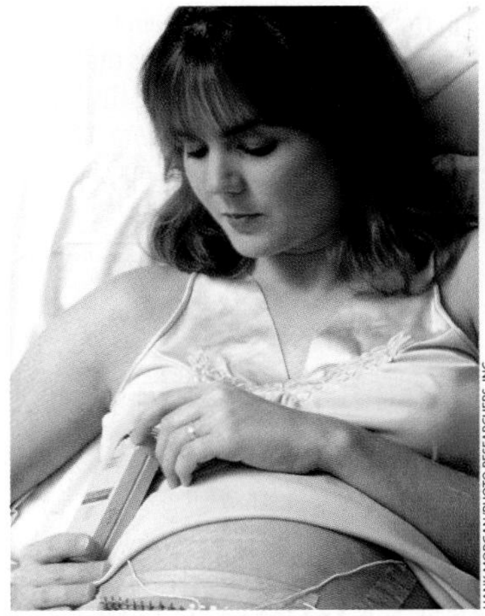

Transcutaneous electrical nerve stimulation (TENS), the gentle electrical stimulation of the skin, is another way of treating pain—in this case, the pain of labor contractions. The patient controls the rate and intensity of the electrical stimulation.

neuromatrix theory of pain A theory that accounts for types of pain unexplained by the gate-control theory of pain.

phantom limb pain The sensation of pain in a missing limb experienced by up to 70% of people who lose a limb.

Figure 7.22

A treatment for phantom limb pain People with a phantom limb often report sensation in the missing limb—for example, a person may feel that a missing hand is tightly clenched and aching. Looking at a mirror image of the normal limb—here, the right arm—the person sees the image as the missing limb. By relaxing the fist, he has the sensation that the phantom hand has unclenched, and the pain may be reduced.

→ **What causes phantom limb pain?**

tom limbs. In one study, Ramachandran and his colleagues (1995) tried to alleviate pain in a missing hand by requiring five phantom limb patients to view their intact limb in a mirror in such a way that it appeared to be the missing hand (Figure 7.22). When the patients were told to make a fist and then open their normal hand, all but one of them had the sensation that the phantom hand was also opening and relaxing, with a subsequent decrease in phantom limb pain.

In an episode of *Nova,* on public television, Ramachandran discussed some of his more interesting clinical cases. In case 2, for example, the physician studied touch sensitivity on various parts of the body of a man who had lost most of an arm in a car accident. Amazingly, Ramachandran found a topographic representation of the man's phantom hand on his face and another of the same hand on his left upper arm just above the amputation. The explanation for this phenomenon is **remapping,** a modification of neurons (in this case, in the somatosensory cortex) after they no longer receive input from the body part they once represented.

The *Scientific American* Spotlight, "Quieting Phantom Limbs," highlights a study of arm amputees. As expected, painful phantom sensations involved activity in the area of sensory cortex that would normally be operating if the limb were intact. Nonpainful sensations, on the other hand, engaged cortical areas involved with body image; one area helps us tell that a part of our body actually belongs to us and the other area assesses conflicting sensory or motor information. The author of the study, neuropsychologist Herta Flor, believes that the information will assist her group in developing treatments for the phantom sensations.

Remapping had been recognized earlier in studies of monkeys by Pons and his colleagues (Ergenzinger & others, 1998; Jones & Pons, 1998; Woods & others, 2000). For example, Jones and Pons reported that following long-term denervation of an upper limb in monkeys, the face representation in the somatosensory cortex enlarged and "took over," or remapped, what had previously been the representation of the hand of the animal, with corresponding enlargement of the face area in the ventral posterior thalamic nuclei. Ergenzinger and colleagues also found an enlargement of receptive fields in the somatosensory thalamus in monkeys following the suppression of neuronal activity in the somatosensory cortex. As the researchers concluded, this change in the thalamus resulting from lack of cortical

Scientific American Spotlight

Quieting Phantom Limbs

Chris Jozefowicz

Dealing with a missing limb is bad enough. But often amputees must also struggle with confusing sensations that seem to indicate that an arm or leg is still present or that can cause disabling pain. To find out why, a team led by Herta Flor, a professor of neuropsychology at the University of Heidelberg in Germany, tested people who had had an arm amputated. The results contradict the simple assumption that phantom sensations arise from the same brain pathways that processed sensory information when the limb was intact.

Because of a physiological quirk known as passive stimulation, present in a small fraction of people, Flor was able to deliberately induce phantom sensations in five amputees by stimulating other parts of their body. Previous studies had shown that when phantom sensations amount to pain, the region of the sensory cortex that is active is the one that would normally be operating if the limb were intact. But when Flor induced nonpainful sensations—described by patients as tingling or hot—that same region was not especially active. Instead two regions thought to be involved with body image were engaged. One region, the posterior parietal cortex, helps people feel that part of their body is their own, rather than some inanimate thing. The other region processes conflicting sensory or motor information.

"The activation patterns are pretty clear," Flor says, adding that the findings will help her group try to develop treatments for phantom sensations, possibly electrical stimulation or drugs. As many as 70 percent of amputees suffer some form of phantom pain.

From: *Scientific American Mind*, vol. 14(1), p. 5

feedback suggests that alterations in higher areas of the brain can trigger changes in the receptive field characteristics of neurons lower down in the sensory pathway. Pons's work with monkeys reveals a remarkable plasticity in cortical neurons and their associated subcortical areas in adult animals. The clinical cases in Ramachandran's notebook indicate that this neuroplasticity also extends to adult humans.

remapping The modification of neurons after they no longer receive input from the body part they once represented.

The neuroplasticity of the adult brain is not confined to the somatosensory system, however. For example, tinnitus provides evidence for cortical remapping in auditory areas. *Tinnitus* is a ringing or whistling sound experienced but not triggered by sound from the environment. Using magnetoencephalographic recordings, Muhlnickel and colleagues (1998) compared 10 tinnitus subjects with 15 controls and found that the tinnitus sound frequency was dramatically shifted in the tinnitus subjects relative to its normal tonotopic location. Further, the subjective strength of the tinnitus and the amount of cortical reorganization were highly related, leading the researchers to suggest that tinnitus might be the auditory equivalent of a phantom limb.

Adult neuroplasticity has also been found in the visual system. For example, the activity level in the primary visual cortex is elevated in blind subjects relative to sighted controls, both at rest and during tactile or auditory tasks, suggesting that this area of the brain can perform nonvisual functions. Sadato and colleagues (2004) used fMRI to measure neural activity during tactile discrimination tasks in sighted subjects and in subjects recently blinded who were naive to braille. The occipital cortex of the blind subjects was activated during a tactile discrimination task, but it remained inactive in the sighted subjects.

Cohen and colleagues (1997) provided evidence for the importance of visual cortical areas for tactile discriminations in blind braille readers. Using transcranial magnetic stimulation to disrupt cortical functioning in blind subjects attempting to identify braille or embossed Roman letters, these researchers found that stimulation of the occipital cortex led to errors in both tasks. By contrast, the same stimulation in sighted subjects had no effect on tactile performance.

Further, using fMRI, Burton and colleagues (2002) found robust activation of the visual cortex in blind subjects reading braille nouns and generating verbs in response. This result reveals significant language-processing abilities in the visual cortex of blind people.

In another illustration of cortical reorganization in blind subjects, Van Boven and colleagues (2000) examined tactile spatial resolution in blind braille readers. Compared with sighted control subjects, the blind subjects exhibited significantly greater spatial acuity in both their braille-reading fingers and their nonreading fingers. The researchers concluded that this superior ability may be an adaptive correlate of cortical neuroplasticity.

➤Checkpoint

Describe the role of the PAG in inhibiting the perception of pain. How could you use PET scans to examine phantom limb phenomena in amputees?

REVIEW

- ➤ Skin receptor fibers project to the CNS through the cranial nerves or the spinal nerves. Information from the skin receptors travels along one of three pathways: the dorsal column–medial leminiscal system, the anterolateral system, or the spinocerebellar system.
- ➤ The dorsal column–medial lemniscal system transmits information about touch and proprioceptive sensations to the dorsal column nuclei, then to the ventral posterolateral thalamic nuclei, and finally to the primary somatosensory cortex.
- ➤ The anterolateral system transmits information about temperature and pain sensations to the brain stem reticular formation, or the ventral posterolateral thalamic nuclei and the posterior thalamic nuclei, and then to the primary and secondary somatosensory cortices.
- ➤ The spinocerebellar system carries information about proprioception to the cerebellar cortex.

- The somatosensory cortex is organized topographically, with adjacent areas of the skin represented by adjacent areas of the somatosensory cortex. Input from the feet is transmitted to the "top" of the primary somatosensory cortex, and input from the head is transmitted to the "bottom."
- According to the gate-control theory of pain, sensory input from pain receptors produces the perception of pain only if the message first passes through a "gate" in the spinal cord and lower brain stem structures.
- The periaqueductal gray (PAG) is a midbrain structure that synapses with inhibitory interneurons in the lower brain stem and spinal cord to block messages about pain.
- Designed to explain such pain phenomena as phantom limb pain and continuing pain after an injury has healed, the neuromatrix theory describes a neural representation of body parts in cortical neurons.
- Remapping, or the reorganization of cortical neurons, may result in tinnitus, visual cortex involvement in auditory or tactile discrimination and language, and greater tactile acuity in blind braille readers.

The Chemical Senses

Think back to the last time you had a pizza delivered to your apartment. Remember how good the pizza smelled before you even opened the box. The aroma and taste of food are part of what make eating such an enjoyable activity. Our senses of taste and smell play significant roles in our lives. In this section, we examine the biology of the gustatory (taste) and olfactory (smell) systems. Although we have separated the two senses for this discussion, taste and smell are inextricably intermingled in our eating experiences. In fact, much of what we report as the taste of food actually comes from its odor, as you probably realize from your experience of eating when you have a cold.

It is important to note here, too, that the experience of eating is based on a great deal more than the food's *flavor,* defined as its taste and smell (Bartoshuk, 1991). For example, the mouth is quite sensitive to touch, and texture is an important element of our experience of food. You may prefer smooth mashed potatoes, whereas your friend likes her potatoes lumpy. Or, you may like your cereal to be crisp, but your roommate prefers soggy flakes. The visual characteristics of food also can play an important role in the enjoyment of a meal. Although you may like eggs and ham, the thought of "green eggs and ham" may make you queasy. The temperature of your food or drink may be important, and, as indicated earlier, pain and a sensation of heat from capsaicin can be important components in the enjoyment of certain types of food.

Gustation

One piece of candy tastes sweet, and another tastes sour. A peanut might taste salty, but it also might taste bitter. No matter how many different foods or liquids we ingest, their tastes can be classified according to four primary sensations: sweet, sour, bitter, and salty. The sense of taste is referred to in clinical terms as the **gustatory sense** (from the Latin *gustare,* "to taste").

In order to impart sweetness, bitterness, or any other flavor, the molecules in the food first must dissolve in the saliva in the mouth and stimulate the taste receptors on the tongue. Although each taste receptor is sensitive to all four tastes, it is maximally sensitive to just one. For example, the taste receptors that respond most to the hydrogen ions (H^+) found in all acids are maximally responsive to sour tastes, and receptors most sensitive to sodium chloride (table salt) detect salty tastes. A bitter taste is detected by receptors maximally responsive to alkaloid compounds, and a sweet taste by receptors maximally sensitive to sugars.

Although we normally think of taste from the standpoint of the enjoyment it brings, the ability to detect different tastes is important to our survival. Because

gustatory sense The sense of taste.

papilla A small, visible bump on the tongue that contains taste buds.

taste bud A cluster of taste receptors that lie either near or within a papilla.

many foods become acidic when they spoil, avoiding sour foods can prevent illness. Also, many plants contain bitter-tasting alkaloids that are poisons. Sweating can deplete the body of sodium chloride, leading to a salt craving that impels us to eat salty foods and drink fluids to replenish our salt level. In addition, sweet foods usually contain sugars needed for cell metabolism. Thus, humans and nonhuman animals generally avoid bitter and sour tastes and seek out sweet and salty ones. As much as Heather enjoyed the tartness of lemonade, she almost certainly would not enjoy a glass of lemon juice without sugar or some other sweetener added.

Taste Receptors

The tongue contains many small bumps, called **papillae** (Figure 7.23). (To see them, drink a colored liquid and then inspect your tongue in the mirror.) **Taste buds** lie either near or within the papillae. In humans, three different kinds of papillae contain taste buds: foliate, circumvallate, and fungiform (Figure 7.24). The tongue, with the palate, pharynx, and larynx, contains about 10,000 taste buds when we are young, but the number decreases with age. As a result of this decrease, foods we may have disliked when young often become more appetizing to us as we get older, so the next time someone offers you squash or broccoli (or whatever you found most distasteful as a child), give it a try. Taste receptors are individual cells located in the taste buds, which contain 20 to 50 taste receptors apiece. At the end of each receptor are microvilli that protrude through the pore of the taste bud and into the saliva coating the tongue. Molecules in the saliva stimulate the receptors, which have a relatively short life span—the tongue's population of receptors is completely replaced within 2 weeks (Farbman, 1997).

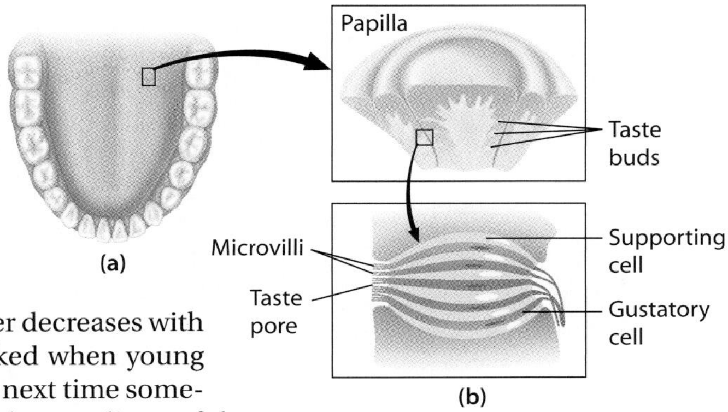

Figure 7.23
Taste receptors (a) Location of taste buds in the papillae of the tongue. (b) Components of a taste bud.

→ How are the taste receptors stimulated?

You may have encountered in some textbooks drawings of the tongue that show a distribution of taste receptors: the tip with receptors most sensitive to sweet and salty tastes, the sides with receptors maximally sensitive to sour tastes, and the back with receptors sensitive to bitter tastes. But noted taste researcher Linda Bartoshuk (1993) has called this distribution a "scientific myth." In fact, as you can see from Figure 7.24, neuroscientists have found that taste receptors for the four basic tastes occur anywhere on the tongue and that the areas of the tongue do not differ greatly in sensitivity to the basic tastes (Bartoshuk).

Umami, the taste for monosodium glutamate (MSG), may be the fifth basic taste. The word comes from the Japanese for "good taste." Lugaz and colleagues (2002) examined the ability of 109 subjects to discriminate between the taste of NaCl (salt) and of MSG. They found that 73% of the subjects exhibited a specific sensitivity to MSG, but the remaining 27% did not. Halpern (2000) reported that the effects of MSG on the flavor of food are different from the effects of salt, although the two flavors often interact. Umami is probably transduced by either an NMDA receptor or a metabotropic glutamate receptor, or both, within the taste bud (Brand, 2000; Lin & Kinnamon, 1999).

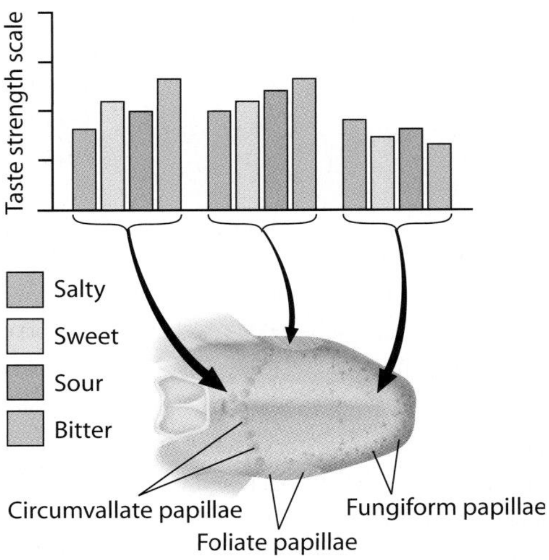

Figure 7.24
Types of papillae and distribution of taste receptors The graph shows that all four types of taste receptors are found in each type of papilla.

→ How does a salty food activate its taste receptor?

The Genetics of Taste

Perhaps you really enjoy bitter-tasting foods, or perhaps you have a sweet tooth. Bartoshuk and her colleagues have found that people differ in their sensitivity to bitter and some sweet tastes, such as saccharin (Bartoshuk & Beauchamp, 1994; Bartoshuk & others, 1998). These individual differences appear to be at least partly related to the number of taste buds on the tongue. Supertasters, comprising about 25% of people, have the most taste buds (averaging 425 per square centimeter on the tongue tip). Women are more likely to be supertasters, as are people from

South America, Asia, and Africa. The 50% of people classified as medium tasters have about 184 taste buds per square centimeter, and the remaining 25%, the nontasters, have about 96 per square centimeter.

The differences in taste sensitivity appear to be genetically determined. For example, nontasters cannot taste two bitter tastes: phenylthiocarbamide (PTC) and 6-*N*-propylthiouracil (PROP). The gene for tasting PTC and PROP has been identified, and one form of this gene is present in tasters but absent in nontasters (Matsunami & others, 2000).

Sensitivity to bitter tastes has important implications for taste preferences and diet. For example, in studies of adult female supertasters of PROP, the women had lower acceptance scores for foods such as Brussels sprouts, broccoli, spinach, and some soy products—all foods believed to have significant cancer-fighting potential (Drewnowski & others, 2000, 2001; Kaminski & others, 2000). Keller and colleagues (2002) reported similar taste preferences in preschool children supertasters.

Although the avoidance of some foods with bitter tastes may have undesirable consequences for supertasters, such individuals may have at least some degree of protection against alcoholism (Intranuovo & Powers, 1998). When asked about their drinking habits, nontasters reported consuming significantly more beer than did supertasters when they first started drinking.

However, genetic sensitivity to PROP is apparently not related to likes and dislikes for sweetened dairy products containing varying amounts of sugar and fat, at least in women (Drewnowski & others, 1998). Although sensitivity to bitterness does not appear to contribute to a "sweet tooth," differential sensitivity to sweet tastes may do so (Max & others, 2001). This differential sensitivity has a genetic basis, and researchers have developed sweet-sensitive and sweet-insensitive strains of mice. Montmayeur and colleagues (2001) have found a taste receptor gene in mice, near the genetic locus for the ability to taste certain sweet substances. This taste receptor gene is expressed in the taste cells of taste papillae. A similar gene has been found in humans (Liao & Schultz, 2003; Matsunami & others, 2000).

The Mechanisms of Taste Reception

The mechanism by which foods activate taste receptors differs for each of the four basic tastes. For example, a salty food activates a taste receptor by causing Na^+ ions to move through the Na^+ ion channels in the cell membrane of the taste receptor, depolarizing the receptor membrane and thus releasing neurotransmitter (Avenet & Lindemann, 1989). The saltier the food, the greater the Na^+ ion influx into the cell and the greater the depolarization and the neurotransmitter release.

Hydrogen ions in sour foods and sugar molecules in sweet foods close the K^+ ion channels in receptor membranes, preventing K^+ ions from leaving the cell; the accumulation of K^+ ions depolarizes the taste receptors, which leads to the release of neurotransmitter (Avenet & Lindemann, 1989; Kinnamon & others, 1988). As was true of salty foods, the sweeter or more sour the food, the greater the depolarization and the neurotransmitter release.

Alkaloid compounds that give bitter foods their bite trigger the movement of calcium ions into the cytoplasm from storage sites in the taste receptor. The increase in Ca^{2+} ions in the receptor cytoplasm increases the release of neurotransmitter (Akabas & others, 1988). The more bitter the food, the greater the Ca^{2+} ion influx into the cytoplasm and the neurotransmitter release.

Gustatory Pathways

Recall from Chapter 6 that labeled-line coding is a characteristic of taste; that is, each of the basic taste qualities is carried by its own particular group of taste fibers. Evidence for this type of coding comes from the identification of "best" taste fibers (Frank, 1985; Hyman & Frank, 1980). In keeping with the idea of four basic taste qualities, Frank and his colleagues have described sucrose-best, NaCl-best, HCl-best, and quinine-best fibers, corresponding to sweet, salty, sour, and bitter tastes, respectively.

chorda tympani A branch of cranial nerve VII that conveys taste information from the posterior tongue and the palate and throat to the nucleus of the solitary tract.

nucleus of the solitary tract A group of neurons in the medulla that receives information from taste receptors.

ventral posteromedial thalamic nucleus A group of neurons that receives taste information from the nucleus of the solitary tract and then transmits it to the primary gustatory cortex.

primary gustatory cortex An area located just ventral and rostral to the area representing the tongue in the somatosensory cortex.

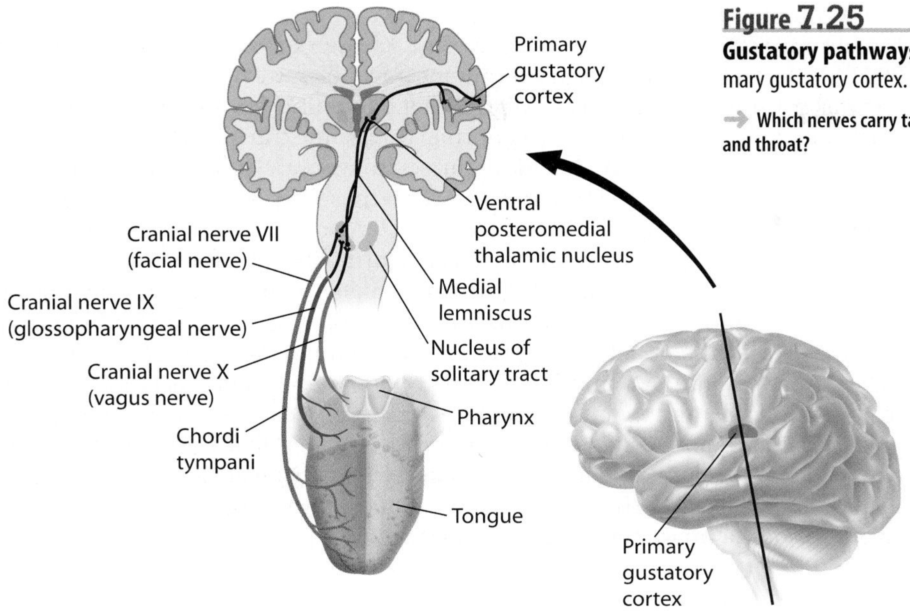

Figure 7.25

Gustatory pathways Pathways from the taste receptors to the primary gustatory cortex. (Adapted from Kandel et al., 1991.)

→ **Which nerves carry taste information from the posterior tongue, palate, and throat?**

Axons of taste receptors (taste fibers) become branches of cranial nerves VII, IX, and X and transmit neural impulses about taste to the CNS (Figure 7.25). Taste sensations originating in the anterior two-thirds of the tongue are carried by the **chorda tympani,** a branch of cranial nerve VII. Branches of cranial nerves IX and X convey taste information from the posterior tongue and from the palate and throat, respectively. Cutting the glossopharyngeal nerve (cranial nerve IX) in rats leads to a loss of quinine-triggered rejection responses; these responses recover with the regeneration of the cut nerve (King & others, 2000). Similarly, salt-discrimination ability recovers following regeneration of transected chorda tympani nerves in rats (Kopka & others, 2000).

Nerve fibers that transmit information from the taste receptors first synapse with the **nucleus of the solitary tract,** an area in the medulla. From there, axons synapse with neurons in the **ventral posteromedial thalamic nucleus,** which project to and synapse with neurons in the **primary gustatory cortex,** located just ventral and rostral to the tongue area in the somatosensory cortex. The reward value of taste seems to involve the orbitofrontal cortex, which contains the secondary taste cortex (Kringelbach, 2004; Rolls, 2004a). According to Rolls, neuroimaging studies have shown that this area of the human brain is activated by a variety of affective stimuli, such as pleasant or painful touch, taste, smell, and winning or losing money.

Given the undeniably pleasurable aspects of eating, we would have to assume that taste is tied in with the reward areas of the brain and with the neurotransmitters dopamine and the endogenous opioids, which are involved in virtually all aspects of reinforcement (Chapter 5). In fact, a variety of evidence implicates activity in the nucleus accumbens and surrounding structures as critical for positive responses to pleasant sensations, such as sweet tastes (Berridge, 2003; Pecina & Berridge, 2000). For example, Pecina and Berridge found that microinjections of opioid agonists (e.g., morphine) into the nucleus accumbens of rats increased both eating behavior (i.e., "wanting" food) and facial reactions consistent with "liking" food. Berridge (2000) has argued for a phylogenetic continuity in the appearance of taste-related positive reactions in such disparate species as humans, nonhuman primates, and rats. It makes good sense from a phylogenetic standpoint for survival behaviors such as food-seeking and eating to be tied into reward areas of the brain. Obtaining a sufficient supply of food definitely enhances survival of the individual and ultimately of the species.

This couple is about to eat their picnic lunch. In addition to the taste and smell of the food, their enjoyment of the meal will be influenced by factors such as their emotions, their mood, and their experience with similar outings in the past.

BANANA STOCK/ALAMY

Dopamine seems to be primarily involved in the "wanting" aspect of the reinforcing properties of a sweet taste (Pecina & others, 2003; Salamone & Correa, 2002). Pecina and colleagues used mutant mice to study the role of dopamine in natural rewards involving taste. Mice with a dopamine transporter mutation that leaves the animals with 10% of the normal dopamine transporters used in the reuptake of dopamine have a 70% increase in synaptic dopamine levels. When trained on a runway task for a sweet reward, these hyperdopaminergic mice exhibited enhanced performance (e.g., left the start area sooner, were more resistant to distractions, and required fewer trials to learn). On a taste reactivity test, however, the mutant mice failed to show higher "liking" reactions. This enhanced incentive motivation, without a change in the "liking" response to the sweet taste, is consistent with the conclusions reached by Salamone and Correa. According to these investigators, low to moderate doses of dopamine antagonists and decreases in dopamine in the nucleus accumbens decrease learned responding for food while leaving other aspects of reinforcement, such as "liking" of the reward, unchanged. Our discussion here and in Chapter 5 further clarifies the nature of addiction by suggesting that craving food reflects "wanting" but not necessarily "liking" food (or anything else a person craves).

What Taste Is It?

Life would be pretty boring if all we could taste were sweet, sour, bitter, and salty flavors. How do we distinguish particular tastes? Other than by color and texture, how can we distinguish between a Granny Smith apple and a Gala apple?

As we have indicated, taste receptors react maximally to one of the four primary tastes, and axons of the taste receptors synapse with neurons in the nucleus of the solitary tract, whose axons then synapse with cells in the ventral posteromedial thalamic nucleus. The structure of neurons in the nucleus of the solitary tract is related to their sensitivity to particular tastes (Renehan & others, 1996), and these neurons are organized into taste-sensitive clusters—that is, neurons sensitive to a particular taste are grouped together. A similar clustering of neurons occurs in the primary gustatory cortex, and the activity of these neurons is believed to be responsible for the perception of a specific taste.

Our taste perception is not determined solely by the molecules acting on the tongue at the moment we ingest a food or beverage. Past experiences also influence our taste sensations. A wine considered bitter by a novice, for example, might be perceived as sweet by an expert.

Some foods can alter the taste experience of other foods. Drinking orange juice after brushing your teeth, for example, will leave a bitter taste in your mouth, which is another good reason for brushing *after* you eat or drink rather than before. Normally, orange juice tastes sweet, but the sodium lauryl sulfate in most toothpastes increases the perceived bitterness of the juice and decreases its sweetness (DeSimone & others, 1980). The sodium lauryl sulfate prevents the sugar molecules from binding to sweet receptors, thus decreasing the perceived sweetness of the juice. Another example: Artichokes, which contain the chemical theophylline, reduce the perceived bitterness of foods (Bartoshuk, 1988). Many people report that water and most other liquids taste much sweeter after eating artichokes.

Taste perception also can be altered by the miracle berry, a plant native to West Africa. Although the miracle berry itself has no taste, it contains the protein *miraculin* that causes acids to stimulate sweetness receptors in humans (Bartoshuk & others, 1974) and in chimpanzees (Hellekant & others, 1998). After you chew a miracle berry, acids will taste sweet for about half an hour. Hellekant and colleagues used this property of miraculin to study a group of taste fibers in the chimpanzee that respond primarily to sweet tastes. After the animals ingested miraculin, the fibers responded to acids as well as to sweeteners, providing evidence for labeled-line coding in the taste system. Earlier work by the same researchers had shown that taste in chimpanzees is similar to that in humans (Hellekant & others, 1996).

Another protein of interest to taste researchers is *circulin,* which has a sweet taste. After circulin is held in the mouth for 3 minutes and its sweet taste has diminished, either deionized water or a mild citric acid solution applied to the tongue tastes sweet (Yamashita & others, 1995). Neither substance would have tasted sweet before pretreatment with circulin; the water would have had no taste and the acid would have tasted sour.

You can experience the contextual effects of taste by performing a simple experiment with a slice of lemon, a sugar cube, and a glass of water. Suck on the lemon slice for a few seconds and then take a sip of water. The water should taste sweet. Now eat the sugar cube. A sip of water should now taste sour. The taste of a particular food or drink is affected by more than just the activity of the taste receptors.

Checkpoint

Describe the pathway of the taste of a nectarine, from the moment you bite into it to the perception of taste by the primary gustatory cortex. Explain why your roommate likes the taste of broccoli and you hate it (or vice versa).

REVIEW

- Although many factors influence our enjoyment of a meal, the gustatory system distinguishes among just four basic tastes: sweet, sour, bitter, and salty.
- Taste receptors are found in taste buds located near or within papillae in the tongue, palate, pharynx, and larynx; these receptors respond to molecules dissolved in the saliva.
- Umami receptors detect monosodium glutamate.
- Genetic differences in the number of taste buds on the tongue determine whether people are supertasters, medium tasters, or nontasters in terms of sensitivity to certain tastes such as PTC and PROP.
- Salty foods open Na^+ ion channels in taste receptors. Hydrogen ions in acidic foods (sour taste) and sugar molecules (sweet taste) close K^+ ion channels. Alkaloid compounds (bitter taste) increase cytoplasmic Ca^{2+} ion levels.
- Neural messages pass from the taste receptors through cranial nerves VII, IX, and X to the nucleus of the solitary tract of the medulla, to the ventral posteromedial thalamic nucleus, then to the primary gustatory cortex, which is located near the area representing the tongue in the somatosensory cortex.
- Neurons in both the ventral posteromedial thalamic nucleus and the primary gustatory cortex respond differentially to each of the four basic tastes.
- Taste is associated with the reward areas of the brain and with such neurotransmitters as dopamine and the endogenous opioids.

Olfaction

Have you ever gone into a public restroom that badly needed cleaning? If so, you were undoubtedly struck by the particularly pungent and foul odor. The **olfactory sense**—our sense of smell—plays a significant role in daily life. For example, we use odor to detect and avoid spoiled food, and the smell of smoke can alert us to the danger of fire. Nonhuman animals use odors to detect predators and track prey, and odors are often a crucial factor in the recognition of other individuals of the species and in reproduction. We have more to say about the role of olfaction in reproductive activities in Chapter 11.

We can detect many different odors, some of them pleasant (like the fragrance of flowers or perfumes) and others unpleasant (like the dirty public restroom). With both pleasant and unpleasant odors, you may have noticed an interesting olfactory phenomenon: You rapidly "get used to" smells. For example, suppose you use a new bar of soap with a particularly fragrant odor. While you are taking a shower with the soap, you smell it quite strongly at first, but toward the end of the shower you no longer detect it. This *sensory adaptation* is caused by decreased responding by receptors when they are exposed to the same stimulus for a continued period of time. If you continue to use the same soap day after day, you will find

olfactory sense The sense of smell.

olfactory epithelium The mucous membrane in the top rear of the nasal passage, lined by olfactory receptors.

olfactory bulb A structure at the base of the brain that receives information about odor from olfactory receptors.

olfactory tract Axons of olfactory bulb neurons that project to the primary olfactory cortex.

primary olfactory cortex An area in the pyriform cortex in the limbic system that gives odors an emotional component.

that your awareness of its odor decreases to the point where you no longer detect it at all. At this point, you will have habituated to the odor. *Habituation,* decreased responding after repeated exposure to an innocuous stimulus, is a form of learning discussed in Chapter 14. Habituation occurs with other senses as well.

Odors are also important in human kin recognition. For example, Porter (1998–1999) found that children could differentiate the smell of their siblings from the odors of unfamiliar children and that mothers could differentiate between the odors of their own and other children. Weisfeld and colleagues (2003) found that mothers could recognize the odors of their own children but not those of their stepchildren, and that preadolescent children could identify their full siblings but not their half-siblings or stepsiblings. Further, Weisfeld and colleagues found that olfactory aversion occurred between fathers and daughters and between brothers and sisters, suggesting a possible mechanism for the development of incest avoidance. Studies have even shown that people can separate a T-shirt they have worn from T-shirts worn by others (Lord & Kasprzak, 1989). In addition, people are able to discriminate gender reliably on the basis of odor. Women are better than men at this discrimination, and superior to men overall at odor identification (Ship & Weiffenbach, 1993; Yousem & others, 1999).

The stimuli detected by the olfactory system, *odors* or smells, are molecules of volatile substances in the air. Humans are quite sensitive to these molecules (although not nearly as sensitive as many nonhuman animals). As an indication of this sensitivity, people can detect the unpleasant smell of ethyl mercaptan in concentrations as low as 1 part in 50 billion parts of air (Engen, 1982). Our extreme sensitivity to mercaptan is the reason it is added to odorless natural gas so that we can detect gas leaks.

The Genetics of Olfaction

Although mammals have receptors for nearly 1,000 different odors (Mori, 2003), we cannot describe odors in the way we can describe colors or sounds. For example, we can distinguish between two brands of perfume but have great difficulty *describing* the difference between the smells. Part of the problem is that our language contains few words to describe what we smell, although this lack of vocabulary may merely reflect the problem rather than cause it.

Our diverse odor recognition abilities are mediated by odorant receptor (OR) genes, which form the largest gene families in mammals. Since the discovery of the OR genes in the early 1990s, mapping of the human genome has given us a rough draft of the OR repertoire (Mombaerts, 2001). This repertoire consists of approximately 1,000 sequences, about half of which are *pseudogenes,* or genes without function. In a comparison of the OR gene repertoires of mice and 10 different primate species, Rouquier and colleagues (2000) found no pseudogenes in the mouse, virtually none in New World monkeys (e.g., spider monkeys and marmosets), approximately 27% in Old World monkeys (e.g., baboons and macaques), and approximately 50% in hominids (humans and the great apes). The researchers concluded that the percentage of pseudogenes in the OR repertoire might be indicative of the evolution of the decreased olfactory sense in primates.

Olfactory Receptors

The olfactory receptors line the **olfactory epithelium,** a mucous membrane in the top rear of the nasal passage (Figure 7.26). Odor molecules sometimes reach the olfactory receptors passively, but at other times, a sniff is needed to move the air to the back of the nasal passage so we can detect its odor. Proteins present in the fluids of the olfactory epithelium transport the odor molecules to olfactory receptors (Farbman, 1994). Each olfactory receptor contains cilia, or olfactory hair cells, that extend into the olfactory epithelium. We have approximately 50 million olfactory receptors that detect smell, yet we are rather low on the scale of mammalian olfactory sensitivity. Kathy's dog, Buddy, for example, may have up to 20 times as

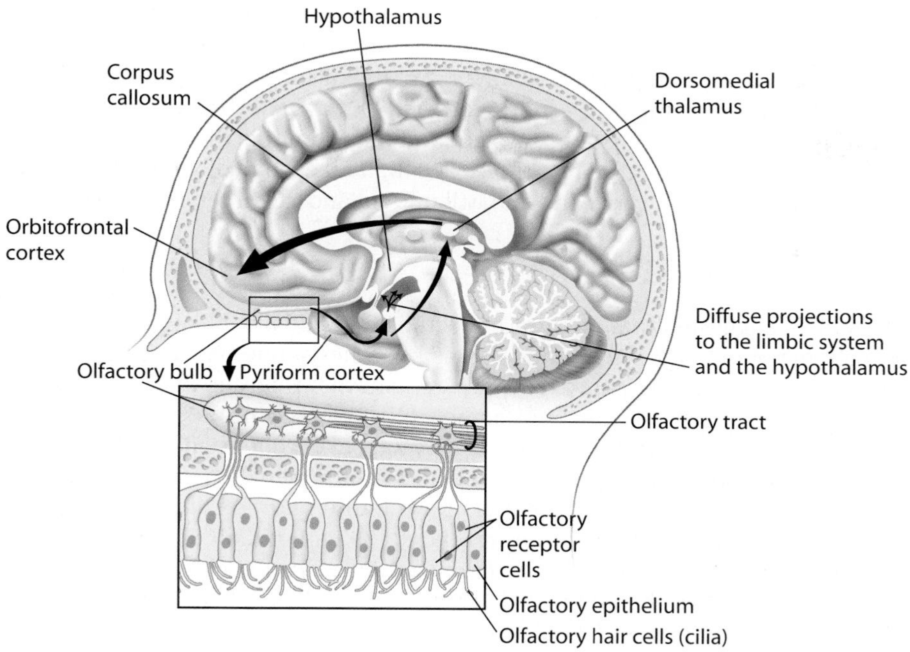

Figure 7.26
Olfactory receptors and pathways
Pathways from the olfactory receptors to the primary olfactory cortex (located in the pyriform cortex), then to other structures in the limbic system, the dorsomedial thalamus, and the orbitofrontal cortex.

→ **Which part of the olfactory system makes possible the strong emotional response to some smells?**

many receptor cells as Kathy, with each cell having more than 10 times as many cilia (Coren & others, 1994).

Odor molecules dissolve in the fluid covering the mucous membrane and stimulate a protein (G_{olf}) in the olfactory receptors (Touhara, 2002). G_{olf} then activates an enzyme that catalyzes the synthesis of cyclic adenosine monophosphate (cyclic AMP), a second messenger that influences synaptic transmission (Chapter 4). In olfactory receptors, cyclic AMP opens the Na^+ ion channels and depolarizes the receptor membrane. Sufficient depolarization causes transmission of the message along the axon of the olfactory receptor directly to the brain.

Olfactory Pathways

Axons of olfactory receptors enter the skull and synapse with cells of the **olfactory bulbs,** which lie at the base of the brain (Figure 7.26). Axons of the cells in the olfactory bulbs form the **olfactory tract.** Some of the olfactory tract fibers project to neurons on the ipsilateral side of the brain, others synapse with the olfactory bulb on the contralateral side. Fibers from the olfactory bulb extend to the **primary olfactory cortex,** which is in the pyriform cortex at the base of the temporal lobe, and to the amygdala. Both the pyriform cortex and the amygdala are part of the limbic system.

Because the primary olfactory cortex is part of the limbic system and projects to other parts of the limbic system, odors have an emotional component, which explains our strong responses to particular smells. When you enter a filthy public restroom, you experience both the sensation of the foul odor and the emotion of disgust. In addition, you have probably noticed that smells can be associated with memories, particularly if there is an emotional component to the memory. Having spent time in Europe, one of your authors now associates the smell of diesel fumes in the early morning with pleasurable experiences; it reminds him of standing on a street corner in Paris or driving behind a diesel-powered truck on the highway along the French Riviera.

Olfactory messages are transmitted from the primary olfactory cortex to the hypothalamus. These messages are important in motivating approach or avoidance behavior related to food or drink, as well as to potential mates. Other olfactory messages are transmitted to the dorsomedial thalamus and then to the orbitofrontal cortex (Figure 7.26), which is thought to be responsible for odor identification. In one study using PET, patients with head injuries that resulted in severe anosmia (loss of the sense of smell) showed lowered metabolism in the orbitofrontal cortex relative to control subjects (Varney & others, 2001). The orbitofrontal cortex also receives input from the gustatory system and may combine the taste and the odor of a food into its perceived flavor (Rolls, 2004b). (Take a bite of your favorite candy bar while holding your nose, and you will understand the difference between taste and flavor.)

What Odor Is It?

Axel (1995) suggested that an odor molecule is shaped like a "key" that fits into a specific receptor "lock." According to this hypothesis, one type of odor molecule activates one type of olfactory receptor, and another type activates a different olfactory receptor. As we indicated earlier, olfactory receptors contain a protein (G_{olf}) activated by odor molecules. Using molecular genetic methods, Buck and Axel (1991) identified 18 different members of a large gene family that code for receptor proteins, and other researchers have found additional olfactory receptor proteins (Mombaerts, 1999; Raming & others, 1993). (For their discoveries of odorant receptors and their work on the organization of the olfactory system, Richard Axel and Linda Buck shared the 2004 Nobel Prize in Physiology or Medicine.) The olfactory receptors are widely distributed in the nose, but in the olfactory bulbs they are highly organized into a fine spatial map (Nagao & others, 2002; Ressler & others, 1994). Further, the maps of similar molecules tend to be similar, suggesting that odors are encoded by spatial patterns of activation in the bulbs (Belluscio & Katz, 2001; Rubin & Katz, 1999).

Looking deeper into the olfactory system, Takagi (1984) reported that, in monkeys, half of the neurons in the olfactory area of the orbitofrontal cortex respond to a single odor. Other neurons react to two, three, or four odors, but none respond to five or more odors. Thus, our recognition of a specific odor may result from the combined activity of specific olfactory system neurons.

Odor identification can be impaired by brain lesions, particularly damage to the orbitofrontal cortex (Levy & others, 1999). Head injuries in general are often accompanied by damage to the olfactory system, as the olfactory nerve is easily torn in humans. Early studies suggested a 4% to 7% incidence of anosmia after head trauma, with more recent studies showing a higher incidence that may reach 60% in severe head injuries (Shen & Ryan, 2003). Of course, these are cases of anosmia or complete loss of the sense of smell; some impairment may occur in a much higher percentage of cases. Impaired odor identification has also been seen in such neurological disorders as Alzheimer's disease and Huntington's disease (Bacon & others, 1999), and these deficits have been suggested as early indicators of Alzheimer's disease (Nordin & Murphy, 1998). Using MRI scans, Murphy and colleagues (2003) found a strong correlation between medial temporal lobe volume and measures of olfactory functioning in subjects with suspected early Alzheimer's disease, further supporting the idea that olfactory measures may be useful in diagnosing Alzheimer's disease. Olfactory deficits may also occur in people with Parkinson's disease, HIV infection, chronic alcoholism and Korsakoff's psychosis (loss of recent memory with confabulation), and schizophrenia (Pantelis & others, 2001).

One final point: As we indicated in Chapter 6, the visual system combines different wavelengths of light to form synthetic colors from the three primary colors. By contrast, the auditory system distinguishes different sounds even when they are presented simultaneously, and that is why you can pick out the sounds of different instruments in an orchestra. The olfactory system has the ability to do both: pick out an individual odor from an array *and* synthesize a smell from a mixture of odors. For example, the smell of coffee alone is actually a mixture of several hundred different odor molecules. When coffee is brewing and eggs are frying, our olfactory system combines these hundreds of molecules so that we can smell the coffee and still distinguish the aroma of the cooking eggs. This suggests that some of our sensory systems operate by combining stimuli (vision), others by detecting individual stimuli (audition), and still others by a combination of both activities (olfaction).

Checkpoint

Why are dogs more sensitive than people to odors? Where in the brain are specific odors probably identified? Describe how the odor and taste of spaghetti sauce combine to form its flavor.

REVIEW

- Olfactory receptors are sensitive to airborne molecules of volatile substances.
- Mapping of the human genome indicates that about half of the odor receptor genetic sequences are pseudogenes, or genes with no function. The increasing percentage of pseudogenes may parallel a decreased importance of olfactory sensory ability from New World monkeys to Old World monkeys to hominids.
- Each olfactory receptor contains cilia that extend into the mucous membrane of the olfactory epithelium that lines the nasal passage. Odor molecules dissolve in the mucus and activate the olfactory receptors, opening Na^+ ion channels, depolarizing the cell membrane, and sending an odor message.
- Axons of olfactory receptors synapse with cells in the olfactory bulbs, and fibers from these cells form the olfactory tracts, which project to the primary olfactory cortex, an area of the limbic system. Olfactory messages pass from the primary olfactory cortex to the hypothalamus and to the dorsomedial thalamus.
- The orbitofrontal cortex receives information from the dorsomedial thalamus and from the gustatory system, and may be responsible for combining input about taste and odor into a perceived flavor.
- The orbitofrontal cortex seems to be important for odor identification, which is defective in such neurological disorders as Alzheimer's disease and Huntington's disease.

CHAPTER REVIEW

Key Terms

anterolateral system (p. 247)
auditory agnosia (p. 239)
auditory nerve (p. 232)
basilar membrane (p. 231)
capsaicin (p. 245)
chorda tympani (p. 255)
cochlea (p. 230)
cochlear implant (p. 238)
cochlear nerve (p. 232)
cochlear nucleus (p. 232)
dorsal column–medial lemniscal system (p. 246)
dorsal column nucleus (p. 246)
eustachian tube (p. 230)
fast pain (p. 245)
free nerve ending (p. 244)
frequency theory of pitch perception (p. 234)
gate-control theory of pain (p. 248)
gustatory sense (p. 252)
hair cell (p. 231)
incus (anvil) (p. 229)
inferior colliculus (p. 232)
intensity difference (p. 237)
loudness (p. 228)
malleus (hammer) (p. 229)
medial geniculate nucleus (MGN) (p. 232)
medial lemniscus (p. 246)
Meissner's corpuscle (p. 245)
Merkel's disk (p. 245)
motion sickness (p. 241)
neuromatrix theory of pain (p. 249)
nucleus of the solitary tract (p. 255)
nystagmus (p. 241)
olfactory bulb (p. 259)
olfactory epithelium (p. 258)
olfactory sense (p. 257)
olfactory tract (p. 259)
organ of Corti (p. 231)
oval window (p. 229)
Pacinian corpuscle (p. 243)
papilla (p. 253)
periaqueductal gray (PAG) (p. 248)
phantom limb pain (p. 249)
phase difference (p. 237)
pinna (p. 229)
pitch (p. 228)

place theory of pitch perception (p. 233)
posterior thalamic nucleus (p. 247)
primary auditory cortex (Heschl's gyrus) (p. 232)
primary gustatory cortex (p. 255)
primary olfactory cortex (p. 259)
primary somatosensory cortex (p. 247)
proprioception (p. 243)
remapping (p. 250)
round window (p. 230)
Ruffini's corpuscle (p. 245)
saccule (p. 240)
secondary auditory cortex (p. 232)
secondary somatosensory cortex (p. 247)
semicircular canal (p. 240)
slow pain (p. 245)
somatosense (p. 243)
sound (p. 228)
spinocerebellar system (p. 247)
spiral ganglion (p. 231)
stapes (stirrup) (p. 229)
superior olivary nucleus (p. 232)
taste bud (p. 253)
tectorial membrane (p. 231)
timbre (p. 229)
tonotopic distribution (p. 235)
tympanic membrane (p. 229)
utricle (p. 240)
ventral posterolateral thalamic nucleus (p. 247)
ventral posteromedial thalamic nucleus (p. 255)
vestibular ganglion (p. 241)
vestibular nerve (p. 241)
vestibular nucleus (p. 241)
vestibular sac (p. 240)
vestibular sense (p. 240)
volley principle (p. 234)

Suggested Readings

Axel, R. (1995). The molecular logic of smell. *Scientific American, 273,* 154–159.

Bartoshuk, L. M., & Beauchamp, G. K. (1994). Chemical senses. *Annual Review of Psychology, 19,* 419–449.

Buck, L. B. (1996). Information coding in the vertebrate olfactory system. *Annual Review of Neuroscience, 19,* 517–544.

Ehret, G., & Romand, R. (1997). *The central auditory system.* New York: Oxford University Press.

Goldstein, E. B. (1999). *Sensation and perception* (5th ed.). Belmont, CA: Wadsworth.

McLaughlin, S., & Margolskee, R. F. (1994). The sense of taste. *American Scientist, 83,* 538–545.

Melzack, R. (1992). Phantom limbs. *Scientific American, 266,* 120–126.

Critical Thinking Questions

1. Bill awakened to the sound of his daughter crying. It was his turn to feed the baby, so he forced himself out of bed. How was Bill able to hear his daughter crying? What process enabled him to distinguish her crying from other night sounds?
2. Janis felt the reassuring touch of her father's hand on her shoulder as she worked to fine-tune her résumé. His touch made her feel confident that she would do well at her interview. Trace the neural circuit from the sensory receptors to the primary somatosensory cortex that allowed Janis to feel her father's reassuring touch.
3. Tim is looking forward to his trip, as the sights and sounds of Paris are incomparable. For Tim, the best part of Paris is the food. On this trip, Tim is planning to eat at Aux Lyonnais, where he plans to sample such house specialties as dandelion salad, with crisp potatoes, bacon, and silky poached egg, and watercress soup poured over parsleyed frogs' legs. Explain the process that will enable Tim to experience the culinary delights of this four-star Paris restaurant. How are the taste and odor of dandelion salad combined into its particular flavor?

Fill-in-the-Blank Questions

1. ______ may be defined as vibrations in a material medium such as air, water, or metal.
2. We perceive the amplitude or height of a sound wave as ______.
3. The combination of frequencies gives each sound its characteristic quality, which we perceive as ______.
4. The eardrum transmits its vibrations to the bones called the ______, the ______, and the ______.
5. The ______ connects the middle ear with the back of the throat.
6. The coiled structure of the inner ear is called the ______.
7. The organ of Corti lies on top of the ______ membrane.
8. The cilia of the hair cells are either embedded in or nearly touch the ______ membrane.
9. Hair cells synapse with bipolar cells in the ______.
10. Cranial nerve VIII synapses with the ______ nuclei of the medulla.
11. In the auditory pathway, fibers from the inferior colliculus travel to the ______ nucleus.

12. Like the visual system, the cortical auditory system splits into a(n) ______ stream and a(n) ______ stream.
13. According to the ______ theory of pitch perception, high-frequency sounds activate the basal end of the basilar membrane and low-frequency sounds activate the opposite end.
14. According to the ______ theory of pitch perception, the rate of firing in the auditory nerve matches the frequency of the sound.
15. The pattern of neurons responding to specific tones in particular places throughout the auditory system is called a(n) ______ distribution.
16. Two types of cues that the auditory system uses to identify the location of a sound are ______ for high-pitched sounds and ______ for low-pitched sounds.
17. An inability to recognize both language and nonlanguage sounds is called ______.
18. A(n) ______ involves the surgical implantation of a device that transmits electrical signals along cranial nerve VIII to the brain.
19. The vestibular system consists of the ______ and the ______ canals.
20. The ______ are calcium carbonate crystals that respond to the change in fluid flow when we shift the position of our head.
21. Vestibular ganglia are clustered together to become the ______.
22. The feeling of cold is one example of a skin sensation, or ______.
23. The ______ system monitors body position and movement, acts to maintain body position, and ensures the accuracy of intended movements.
24. ______ is the substance that gives chili peppers their hot, painful sensation.
25. Found only in hairy skin, ______ respond to pressure on the skin and to low-frequency vibrations, such as might be produced by a smooth cotton shirt.
26. The most widely accepted theory of pain is the ______ theory, proposed by Melzack and Wall, which Melzack later supplemented with the ______ theory of pain.
27. ______ is ringing in the ears that may be the auditory equivalent of a phantom limb.
28. The ______ and ______ of a food combine for the perception of its flavor.
29. Taste receptors are located near or within the ______ on the tongue.
30. Taste sensations originating in the anterior two-thirds of the tongue are carried by the ______, a branch of cranial nerve VII.
31. The primary olfactory cortex is the only primary cortex located outside the cerebral cortex; it is located in the ______ of the limbic system.

Multiple-Choice Questions

1. The three dimensions along which sound waves vary are
   a. frequency, amplitude, and complexity.
   b. amplitude, complexity, and intensity.
   c. frequency, pitch, and timbre.
   d. loudness, amplitude, and pitch.
2. The ossicles of the middle ear transmit vibrations to the
   a. round window.
   b. triangular window.
   c. semicircular canals.
   d. oval window.
3. The ______ of hair cells respond to the movement of fluid through the organ of Corti.
   a. nerves
   b. membranes
   c. nuclei
   d. cilia
4. The ______ hair cells are the most important hair cells for our auditory ability.
   a. inner
   b. outer
   c. medial
   d. lateral
5. The cochlear nerve fibers join with fibers from the vestibular system to form the
   a. auditory nerve.
   b. vestibular nerve.
   c. primary visual cortex.
   d. organ of Corti.
6. In the medulla, the main auditory structures are the cochlear nuclei and the
   a. inferior colliculi.
   b. medial geniculate nuclei.
   c. superior olivary nuclei.
   d. lateral geniculate nuclei.
7. Beyond the primary auditory cortex, the auditory system splits into two streams:
   a. a high-pitched stream and a low-pitched stream.
   b. an anterior stream and a posterior stream.
   c. a "what" stream and a "where" stream.
   d. a reality stream and a memory stream.
8. Helmholtz advocated a(n) ______ theory of pitch perception, and von Békésy won a Nobel Prize for his modern version of the theory.
   a. frequency
   b. volley
   c. intensity
   d. place
9. Von Békésy's theory best explains our ability to detect pitches within the range of
   a. 4 kHz to 20 kHz.
   b. 20 Hz to 100 Hz.
   c. 100 Hz to 4 kHz.
   d. 1 kHz to 4 kHz.

10. The arrangement in which neurons responding to specific tones are located in specific places throughout the auditory system is called a(n) ______ distribution.
a. tonotopic
b. topographic
c. phototopic
d. audiotopic

11. For low-frequency sounds, loudness is determined by
a. only rate of firing.
b. only number of neurons firing.
c. both rate and number of neurons firing.
d. the location of neurons stimulated on the basilar membrane.

12. A complex sound consists of the ______ and its ______.
a. fundamental frequency, amplitude
b. amplitude, overtones
c. pure tone, frequency
d. fundamental frequency, overtones

13. For relatively high-pitched sounds, the main cue to sound localization is ______ differences.
a. phase
b. intensity
c. frequency
d. complexity

14. The inability to recognize both language and nonlanguage sounds is called
a. Broca's aphasia.
b. Wernicke's aphasia.
c. auditory agnosia.
d. universal agnosia.

15. The area of the brain responsible for detecting the combinations of sounds that we recognize as specific words is
a. Broca's area and surrounding areas.
b. Wernicke's area and surrounding areas.
c. the primary auditory cortex.
d. the medulla.

16. The vestibular sacs consist of the
a. cochlea and semicircular canals.
b. ampulla and cupula.
c. utricle and saccule.
d. utricle and stapes.

17. Receptor cells in the vestibular system, which are much like receptor cells in the auditory system, are called
a. otoliths.
b. oval windows.
c. hair cells.
d. ossicles.

18. Wanda generally experiences extreme nausea when she flies. Her motion sickness is caused by unusual activity in her ______ system.
a. auditory
b. vestibular
c. gustatory
d. olfactory

19. The largest of the skin's somatosensory receptors are the
a. free nerve endings.
b. Pacinian corpuscles.
c. Merkel's disks.
d. Ruffini's corpuscles.

20. ______ detect temperature change and also serve as pain receptors.
a. Pacinian corpuscles
b. Free nerve endings
c. Meissner's corpuscles
d. Ruffini's corpuscles

21. The first time William bit into a chili pepper, he screamed in pain and immediately drank half a glass of water. His pain was caused by the release of the neurotransmitter
a. epinephrine.
b. histamine.
c. substance P.
d. serotonin.

22. When we examine the somatosensory homunculus, we see that the greatest representation is for
a. the largest areas of the body, such as the trunk and legs.
b. the body areas with the most hair, such as the top of the head, the armpits, and the groin.
c. areas such as the hands, lips, and tongue that have fine tactile discrimination.
d. the body parts that are normally clothed.

23. Fibers from the ______ act to reduce the perception of pain.
a. primary somatosensory cortex
b. medial lemniscus
c. secondary somatosensory cortex
d. periaqueductal gray

24. Acupuncture probably relieves pain by stimulating the release of
a. dopamine.
b. acetylcholine.
c. naloxone.
d. endorphin.

25. Melzack's later addition to his theory about pain perception is the ______ theory of pain.
a. gate-control
b. phantom limb
c. neuromatrix
d. endorphin-release

26. The finding of a phantom hand represented on a person's face suggests there has been a
a. loss of facial representation in the cortex.
b. loss of hand representation in the cortex.
c. spread of facial representation into a cortical area that previously represented the missing hand.
d. spread of hand representation into a cortical area that previously represented the face.

27. Humans and nonhuman animals generally avoid
a. salty and sweet tastes.
b. salty and sour tastes.
c. bitter and sweet tastes.
d. sour and bitter tastes.

28. The number of taste buds we have
a. increases with age.
b. decreases with age.
c. stays roughly the same throughout our lives.
d. at first decreases and then later increases as we age.

29. Umami receptors enable you to tell the difference between
a. spoiled food and fresh food.
b. salt and MSG.
c. sweet and bitter tastes.
d. the taste of red wine and white wine.

30. Andrea was born with the genetic ability to taste PROP. Because of this ability, she hates the taste of
a. grapefruit juice and Brussels sprouts.
b. sweet tea and apples.
c. oranges and blackeyed peas.
d. grape juice and cauliflower.

31. Found in miracle berries, the protein miraculin causes
a. sweet foods to taste sour.
b. salty foods to taste sweet.
c. sour foods to taste sweet.
d. bitter foods to taste salty.

32. One of Katie's fondest memories is going to her grandmother's house. She can still remember the wonderful aroma of her grandmother's chocolate chip cookies. What area of the brain is primarily responsible for Katie's fond memories?
a. cerebellum
b. limbic system
c. thalamus
d. pituitary gland

33. An inability to identify odors may be an early symptom of
a. Alzheimer's disease.
b. myasthenia gravis.
c. multiple sclerosis.
d. depression.

Answers can be found on the companion website at www.worthpublishers.com/klein.

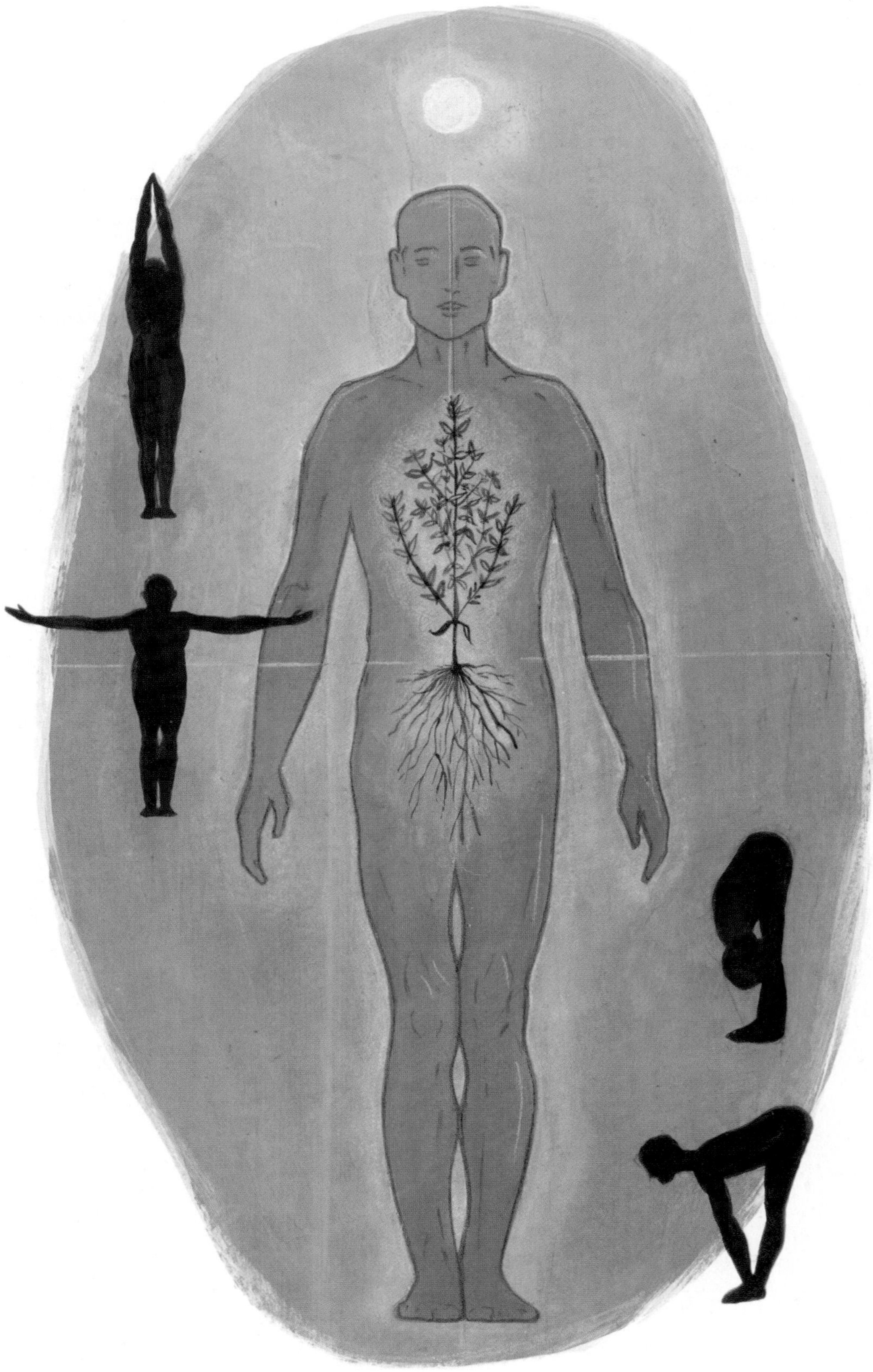

8

The Neurological Control of Movement

An Awkward Feeling

Putting together the machine had been easy; now came the hard part—actually using it. But Sam was determined to give it a try. After all, Tanya had paid plenty for the cross-country ski machine, and the DVD that came with it showed a man about Sam's age with washboard abs and essentially no body fat. Sam, however, saw a different sight when he looked in his mirror. He remembered wistfully a time when his stomach had been as flat as that of the man in the DVD, and he was determined to get back in shape.

He climbed aboard the ski machine, planting his running shoe-clad feet into the slots on the rail. He leaned into the waist pad, grasped the handles at each end of the rope, took a deep breath, took the first step—and nearly ruptured himself. With his legs farther apart than he thought they could go, Sam yelled for Tanya.

Tanya ran into the room, looked at her husband hanging onto the ski machine for dear life, and cracked up. After helping him return to the starting position, she decided to stay in the room until he got the hang of the machine. Sam slipped and slid and generally made a fool of himself in that first session, as Tanya tried hard to contain her laughter. Finally, after nearly falling for perhaps the tenth time, and sweating profusely, Sam said, "Try it yourself if you think it's so easy!"

Tanya mounted the machine, placed her feet in the ski slots, grabbed the handles, and after a few minutes of awkwardness, began to make the movements Sam had seen in the videotape. It reminded him of the few times they had gone dancing; Sam had two left feet, whereas Tanya always performed like a pro. Watching his wife moving so effortlessly on the machine, Sam vowed to master the ski machine or die trying.

For several weeks, Sam thought the machine would kill him, but eventually he began to feel some improvement. Although he frequently felt awkward and off balance, his coordination slowly improved until he could move his arms and legs in a smooth rhythm. Because he had been concentrating on getting the hang of the exercise, Sam hadn't really been thinking about his weight or physical condition. Thus, it came as a surprise when he stepped on the scales one morning and found he'd lost 10 pounds. He also noticed that his mirror image was beginning to look more like the mental picture he had of himself in his youth. Come to think of it, he was feeling better, too.

BEFORE YOU BEGIN

- **Why were Sam's movements on the ski machine so awkward?**
- **What neural changes enabled him to become proficient on the exercise equipment?**
- **What nervous system mechanisms control Sam's muscle movements?**

➢ **How does the nervous system prevent Sam from moving too quickly and falling off the ski machine?**

➢ **What structures in Sam's brain enable him to start and stop muscle movements on the ski machine?**

➢ **What brain structure gradually converts Sam's clumsiness on the machine into a skilled action?**

➢ **What neurological problems could cause Sam to lose his ability to control his muscle movements?**

In this chapter, you will find the answers to these questions and many others.

Levels of Control of Movement

Sam's gradual transition from awkward, slow movements to coordinated, rapid movements is typical of many physical learning experiences—learning to walk, swim, tie shoelaces, play the piano, or perform any other coordinated movement. In this chapter we discuss the biological control of **movement,** a change in the place or position of the body or any part of the body. We examine the neural structures that control movement and the neural processes responsible for Sam's transition from hesitant and clumsy to rapid and coordinated. Sometimes the neural control of movement fails, resulting in such movement disorders as myasthenia gravis, movement apraxia, and amyotrophic lateral sclerosis (ALS, or Lou Gehrig's disease) (see Boxes 8.1, 8.2, and 8.3, later in the chapter), and Huntington's disease and Parkinson's disease. These disorders demonstrate the importance of nervous system control of arm and leg movements.

Not all movements are as complex as exercising on a ski machine, an acquired skill involving the coordination of many different muscles. The simplest movements are reflexive reactions, such as sneezing when dust activates a sensory receptor in your nose or blinking when something rapidly approaches your eyes (see Chapter 2 for a discussion of reflexes). Movements more complex than simple reflexes but less complex than many other skills include maintaining posture and making postural changes (e.g., standing, sitting), locomotion (walking, running), sensory orientation (eye movement, head turning), and species-typical *fixed action patterns* (a complex sequence of behaviors that runs to completion when triggered by an innate releasing mechanism; examples include courtship and grooming behaviors).

Movement is stimulated by the motor neurons of the CNS. The neural control of a particular movement operates on several different levels (Figure 8.1), the most basic of which is the *spinal cord.* In spinal reflexes, the spinal cord alone controls movement. Promptly removing your hand from a hot stove is an example of a withdrawal reflex, one of the spinal reflexes. Higher neural structures operate through the cranial or spinal nerves to produce the movements we would use to turn off the stove.

The next level of control involves *brain stem* structures in the hindbrain and midbrain. Control of movement can originate in these structures and be transmitted via the cranial and spinal nerves. One example of such movement is the visual pursuit of a light stimulus (Chapter 6). Brain stem structures also receive input from higher brain structures and transmit commands to the spinal cord.

The highest level of movement control involves the *cerebral cortex.* In the cortex, the *dorsolateral prefrontal cortex* and the *secondary motor cortex* are responsible for the planning and preparation for movement. The *primary motor cortex* (and other cortical areas as well, such as somatosensory cortex) initiates movement by transmitting signals through brain stem structures and the spinal cord. Input from other cortical structures is crucial to movement. For example, the *posterior parietal cortex* provides the visual, auditory, and somatosensory informa-

movement A change in the place or position of the body or a body part.

cerebral palsy A congenital neurological motor disorder characterized by postural instability and extraneous movement.

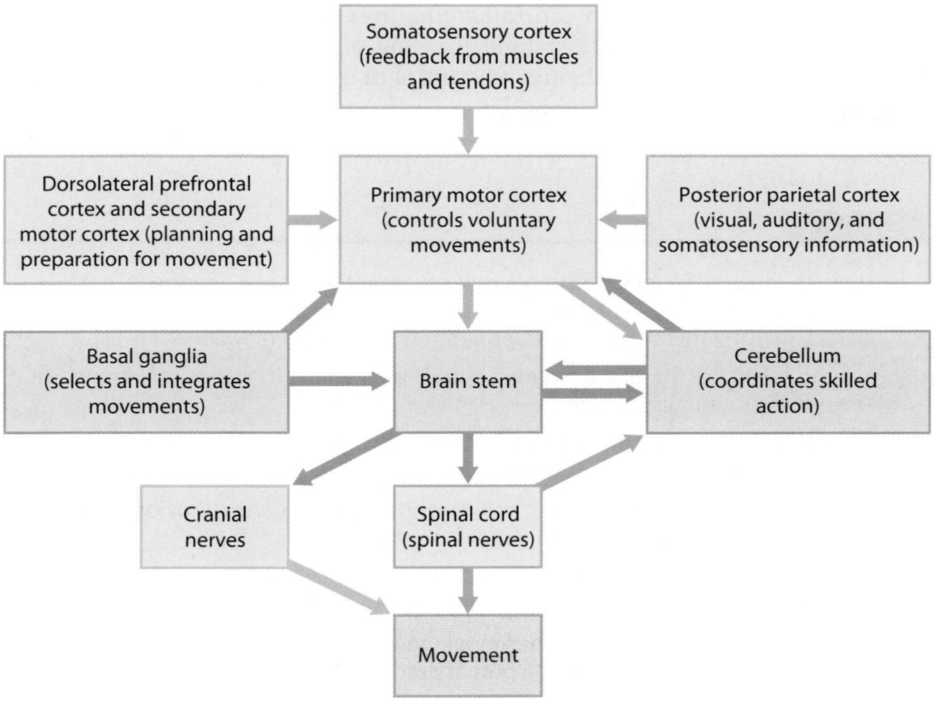

Figure 8.1

Key components in the control of movement Arrows indicate the directions of major influence. Cortical components are shaded green, subcortical components purple.

What is the role of the basal ganglia in movement?

tion needed to guide movement. Feedback from the muscles and tendons through the *somatosensory cortex* provides information about the current state of the motor system. The somatosensory cortex and primary motor cortex are so densely interconnected that they are sometimes referred to as the *sensorimotor cortex.*

The basal ganglia and the cerebellum are also important in movement control. As Figure 8.1 shows, both structures influence the activity of the brain stem structures and the primary motor cortex. The *basal ganglia* influence movement by smoothing out and refining it. In other words, the basal ganglia get rid of extraneous movement and act to ensure that the selected movement occurs with sufficient, but not excessive, force. The basal ganglia are also responsible for the muscle tone and postural adjustments that enable the body to perform normal movements. Some persons with **cerebral palsy,** a congenital neurological motor disorder, must struggle to do even a simple task. Damage to the basal ganglia can produce the postural instability and extraneous movement seen in these individuals. The term "cerebral palsy" actually refers to any of a group of movement disorders, and symptoms reflect the part or parts of the motor system that are damaged. The effects of cerebral palsy range all the way from a slight awkwardness of movement to essentially no muscle control.

The *cerebellum* plays a central role in translating an otherwise uncoordinated movement into a skilled action. (Although not apparent to Sam, his cerebellum was hard at work when he first stepped on the ski machine.) This development of skilled actions is accomplished through cerebellar control of the learning of neural motor programs. Sam sees the same type of control developing in his son Danny, who is learning to hit a baseball in Little League. The cerebellum also receives feedback from the sensory receptors that monitor movement and the brain stem structures that initiate movement. The cerebellum predicts the sensory changes that will result from the intended movement (controlled by the brain stem) and then compares its prediction (the *efference copy*) with the actual movement (detected by sensory neurons). The cerebellum can then make adjustments to ensure that intent and action coincide.

ERIK DRYER/GETTY

Muscles at work.

Checkpoint

Describe what happens neurologically when Sam decides to get off the ski machine at the end of his workout. Begin with the planning of movement by the dorsolateral prefrontal cortex. (Refer to Figure 8.1 as a guide.)

As you can see from this brief introduction, the control of movement is a complex process. To help you understand the "big picture," we begin by showing how muscles work and how the neural control of movement occurs at the cellular level.

REVIEW

- Types of movement include simple reflexes, maintenance or change in posture, locomotion, sensory orientation, fixed action patterns, and complex learned behaviors, such as operating exercise equipment or riding a bicycle.
- In some cases, the spinal cord alone controls movement; in others, movement involves higher neural structures.
- Control of movement can originate in brain stem structures, or information from higher brain structures passes through the brain stem to the spinal cord.
- The dorsolateral prefrontal cortex and secondary motor cortex provide the planning and preparation for voluntary movement
- Neurons from the primary motor cortex and other cortical areas initiate movement through signals transmitted via the brain stem and spinal cord.
- The posterior parietal cortex guides movement by providing visual, auditory, and somatosensory information to the primary motor cortex.
- The somatosensory cortex sends information to the primary motor cortex about the current state of the motor system.
- The basal ganglia integrate movement and regulate postural adjustments.
- The cerebellum coordinates movement and receives feedback from sensory neurons and brain stem structures.

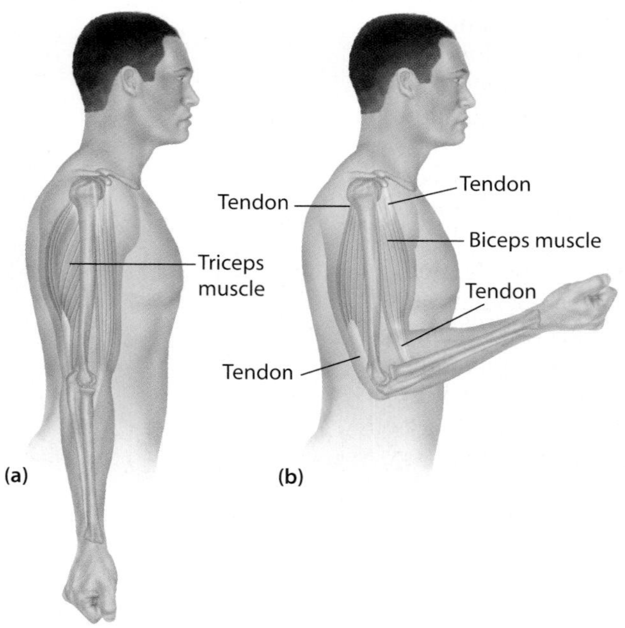

Figure 8.2
Opposing muscle movements
(a) Contraction of the triceps muscle causes extension of the arm. (b) Contraction of the biceps muscle causes flexion of the arm.

➜ **Which muscle lengthens when the arm is extended? When the arm is flexed?**

The Mechanics of Movement Control

When you run to catch a bus, you are using all three types of muscle tissue in your body. Your *smooth muscles* are controlling the movement of your internal organs, although you are not aware of this; your *cardiac muscles* (heart muscles) are actively working to pump blood through your circulatory system; and, as you are most keenly aware, your *skeletal muscles* are hard at work. **Skeletal muscles** enable us to perform the movements necessary to exercise and to engage in other activities. Because skeletal muscles are attached to bones by **tendons,** strong bands of connective tissue, contraction of these muscles causes the movements of bones. Many skeletal muscles work in opposing pairs; when one muscle of a pair contracts or shortens, the other must lengthen in order for the bone to move.

The opposing action of skeletal muscles is well illustrated in the extension and flexion of a limb (Figure 8.2). As you can tell from its name, contraction of an **extensor muscle** produces *extension* of the limb, its movement away from the body. For example, as the triceps (an extensor muscle) contracts and the biceps lengthens (relaxes), the arm moves away from the body. Muscles that work in opposition to each other, such as the biceps and triceps, are called *antagonistic muscles;* muscles whose contraction results in the same movement are called *synergistic muscles.*

Contraction of a **flexor muscle,** such as the biceps, causes *flexion,* which brings the extended arm back toward the body. Of course, at the same time that the biceps contracts, the triceps relaxes.

Complex movements such as walking require coordinated sequences of excitation and inhibition of different flexor and extensor muscles. When you walk, you extend one leg while flexing the other, then flex the first leg and extend the second, and so on. The CNS coordination of walking is so efficient that for the most part, you are unaware of it. In fact, if you try to think about the individual muscle extensions and flexions, your walking becomes uncoordinated.

To illustrate, try the following: Ask someone to watch you walk from one end of a room to the other. Now, as you walk back, try consciously to flex and extend your leg muscles. When you are through, ask the observer to describe the difference. To help you understand how the CNS provides the coordination you need to walk across the room smoothly, which you were able to do when you were not thinking about it, you first need to learn about the anatomy of the muscle and how it works.

skeletal muscle A type of muscle that produces the movements of bones.

tendon A strong band of connective tissue linking a muscle to a bone that causes the bone to move when the muscle contracts.

extensor muscle A muscle that produces movement of a limb away from the body.

flexor muscle A muscle that produces movement of a limb toward the body.

muscle fiber One of the units comprising a skeletal muscle.

myofibril One of the units comprising a muscle fiber.

The Anatomy of a Muscle

A skeletal muscle (Figure 8.3) consists of many individual **muscle fibers.** Each muscle fiber, about 10 to 100 micrometers (microns) in diameter, is in turn composed of many **myofibrils,** cylindrical structures about 1 to 2 micrometers across. (The prefix *myo* means "muscle.") A myofibril contains two kinds of

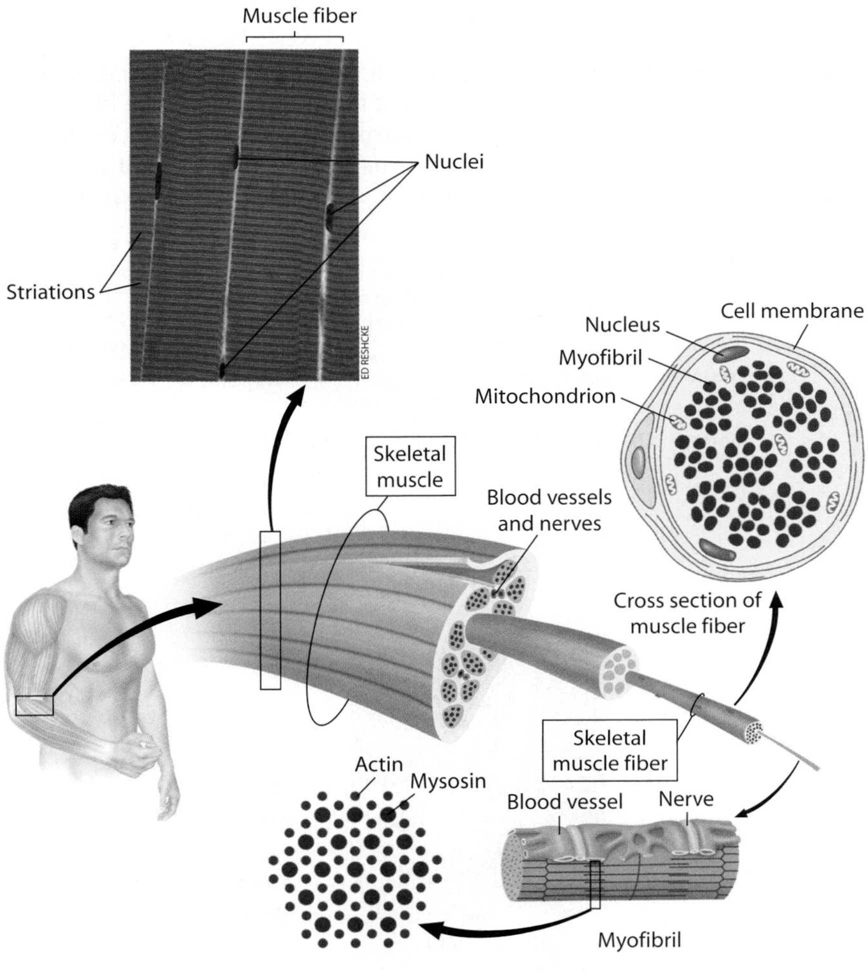

Figure 8.3
Major components of skeletal muscle Skeletal (or striated) muscle consists of many individual muscle fibers (muscle cells), which are composed of myosin and actin myofilaments.

➜ **Which type of protein is found in thick myofilaments?**

myofilaments: One is made of the protein **myosin** and the other of the protein **actin.** Myosin myofilaments are thicker than actin myofilaments; because of this difference in diameter, myosin myofilaments also are called thick filaments and actin myofilaments are called thin filaments (Figure 8.4). A myosin molecule has a distinct head end and tail end. The myosin head, also called a cross bridge, plays an important role in muscle contraction, as we will see shortly.

The actin and myosin molecules within the myofibrils are organized into functional units called **sarcomeres.** In each sarcomere, the overlapping bands of thick myosin filaments and thin actin filaments give skeletal muscles a striated, or striped, appearance, as you can see in Figure 8.4. For this reason, these muscles are sometimes called *striated muscles.*

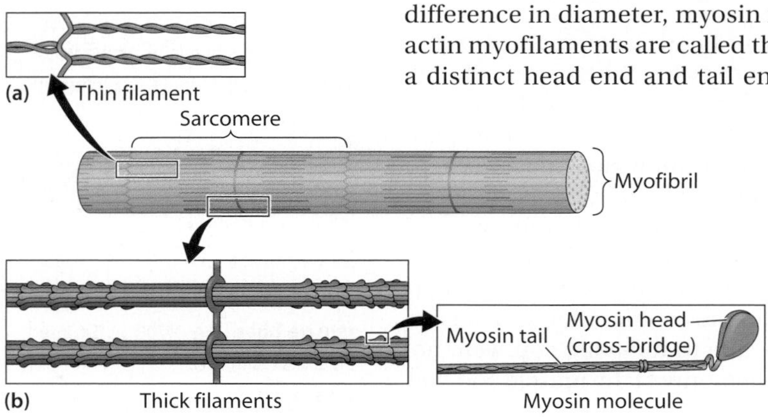

Figure 8.4
Thin and thick myofilaments (a) A thin (actin) myofilament. (b) A thick (myosin) myofilament and a myosin molecule, with its distinct head and tail ends.

➜ **Why are skeletal muscles sometimes called striated muscles?**

The Neural Control of Muscle Contraction

As indicated earlier (Chapter 2), the motor neurons of the peripheral nervous system control the skeletal muscles. The cell bodies of motor neurons are located in the gray matter of the ventral horn of the spinal cord and in different parts of the brain stem. Most motor neurons have long axons that leave the brain stem or the ventral root of the spinal cord and synapse with individual muscle fibers. Such motor neurons, called **alpha motor neurons,** are among the largest neurons in the body. Their axons must conduct information rapidly, often at a speed of more than 220 m/sec.

The muscle fiber controlled by an alpha motor neuron is called an **extrafusal muscle fiber.** The alpha motor neuron and the extrafusal muscle fiber connect at a highly specialized synapse called a **neuromuscular junction** (Figure 8.5). The presynaptic terminal of the alpha motor neuron flattens to form the **motor end plate** at the point where the motor neuron and muscle fiber synapse.

myofilament A component of a myofibril.

myosin The protein component of thick myofilaments.

actin The protein component of thin myofilaments.

sarcomere The functional unit of a myofibril, consisting of overlapping bands of thick myosin filaments and thin actin filaments.

alpha motor neuron A motor neuron with a long axon that leaves the ventral root of the spinal cord or brain stem and synapses with individual muscle fibers.

extrafusal muscle fiber A muscle fiber controlled by an alpha motor neuron.

neuromuscular junction A specialized synapse between an alpha motor neuron and an extrafusal muscle fiber.

motor end plate The flattened area of an extrafusal muscle fiber where a motor neuron and the muscle fiber synapse.

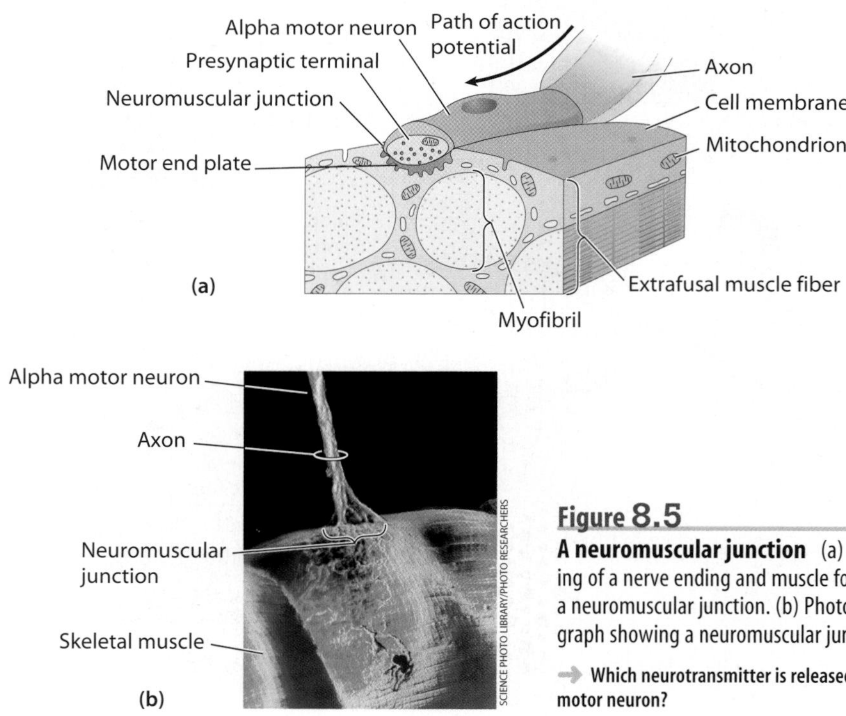

Figure 8.5
A neuromuscular junction (a) Drawing of a nerve ending and muscle forming a neuromuscular junction. (b) Photomicrograph showing a neuromuscular junction.

➜ **Which neurotransmitter is released by the motor neuron?**

Box 8.1
Myasthenia Gravis

Myasthenia gravis is a neuromuscular disorder caused by a reduction in cholinergic receptors (receptors for ACh) at neuromuscular junctions. The first signs of the disease usually involve the cranial nerves, with the patient experiencing double vision, drooping eyelids, weakness of speech, problems chewing or swallowing, or difficulty holding up the head. The primary symptom, however, is severe muscular fatigue after exercise. Muscle weakness may occur shortly after exercise begins, or after a period of work, or even following a long conversation. The fatigue of myasthenia gravis is distinguishable from normal fatigue following exercise or work by its sudden onset.

Although myasthenia gravis can develop at any age, it typically becomes apparent in the third decade of life, and it is more often seen in women than in men. In some people, the symptoms are relatively mild, whereas in others the symptoms can be severe or even life-threatening because of respiratory paralysis (Kolb & Whishaw, 2003). Aristotle Onassis, the Greek shipping tycoon who married Jacqueline Kennedy, the widow of assassinated President John F. Kennedy, was one of the most well-known victims of the disease.

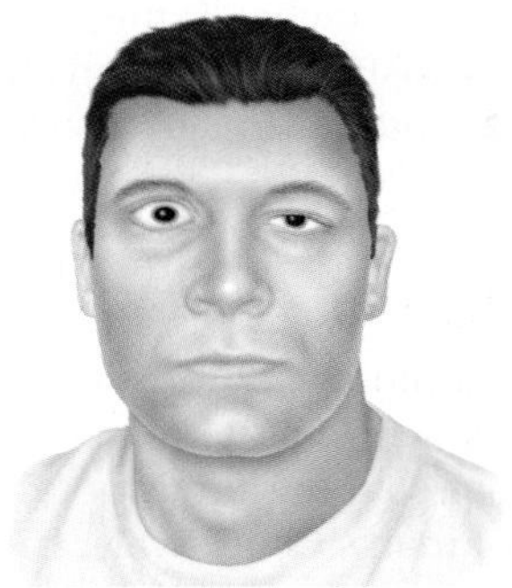

Eyelid droop is the most common symptom of myasthenia gravis seen by ophthalmologists.

Myasthenia gravis is a rare disorder, affecting about 3 people per 100,000 in the United States. No muscle tissue abnormalities are associated with the disorder. Rather, because cholinergic receptors are destroyed by antibodies, fewer messages reach the muscles from the cranial or spinal nerves. The responsiveness of the remaining cholinergic receptors is reduced (Lindstrom, 2000; Nicolle, 2002). We do not know why the antibodies form or how they attack the receptors. Also, for some unknown reason, muscle weakness does not occur equally in all muscles, as you might expect from a disease that eliminates cholinergic receptors.

The long-term treatment of myasthenia gravis is aimed at halting the disease process by reducing the destruction of cholinergic receptors. Thus, patients may undergo *thymectomy,* removal of the thymus gland, to decrease the production of antibodies to the receptors. In one study of the effectiveness of this treatment, almost 70% of the patients had a positive response (Remes-Troche & others, 2002). Factors associated with a poor prognosis include age at treatment (patients older than 60 had a poorer prognosis), the use of steroid treatment before surgery, and time elapsed between diagnosis and surgery. Patients with myasthenia gravis also take drugs to suppress the immune system. In a follow-up study of patients on high-dose immunosuppressive therapy, Heckmann and colleagues (2001) found a significant increase in remission and reduced mortality rates.

For relief of the immediate symptoms of myasthenia gravis, patients take drugs such as physostigmine that block the action of acetylcholinesterase (AChE). As noted in Chapter 4, the synaptic action of ACh is terminated by AChE. A drug that decreases the activity of AChE increases the ACh available at the neuromuscular junction. In a healthy person, physostigmine causes uncontrollable muscle contractions, but in someone with myasthenia gravis, it reduces muscle weakness. Immune system suppression and AChE therapy are an effective treatment approach for myasthenia gravis.

In Chapter 4 we discussed the transmission of neural impulses from one neuron to another. The transmission of a neural impulse from a motor neuron to a muscle fiber at the neuromuscular junction is similar. The motor neuron releases acetylcholine (ACh) into the synaptic cleft, and the ACh binds to receptor proteins on the postsynaptic membrane (the muscle fiber). Excitatory postsynaptic potentials (EPSPs) are produced. Box 8.1 discusses a disorder—myasthenia gravis—that is caused by a decrease in postsynaptic receptors at the neuromuscular junction.

myasthenia gravis A neuromuscular disorder characterized by muscle fatigue following exercise.

Figure 8.6 shows the role of myofilaments in muscle contraction. With sufficient excitation, an action potential is generated at the postsynaptic membrane. As the action potential travels down the muscle fiber, it increases the permeability of the fiber membrane to

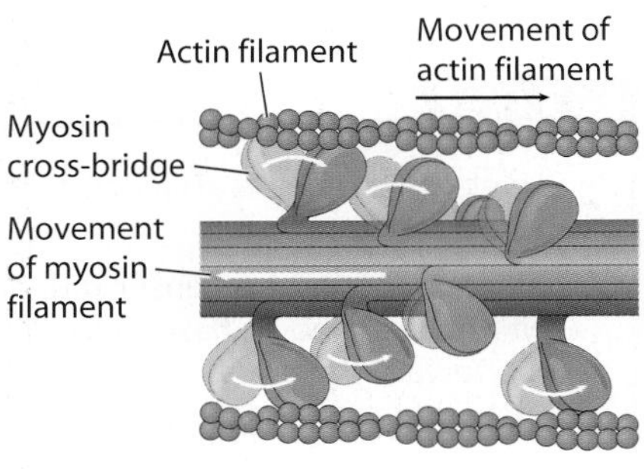

Figure 8.6
The role of actin filaments and myosin cross-bridges in muscle contraction

How does the movement of myofilaments lead to muscle contraction?

Checkpoint

The flexor muscles of the knee, located in the thigh, are the hamstrings and the sartorius; the knee extensors are collectively known as the quadriceps. Describe what happens to these muscles when you bend your knee. In your answer, use the terms *alpha motor neuron, extrafusal muscle fiber,* and *neuromuscular junction.*

calcium ions. Entry of Ca^{2+} ions into the cell causes myosin heads to form cross bridges with actin filaments. The myosin heads then pivot, causing the myosin and actin filaments to slide past one another. The cross bridges then detach and reattach at a new position, in a sort of rowing motion, with the result that the sarcomere, and thus the entire muscle fiber, shortens. In other words, the muscle contracts, the attached bone(s) moves, and the limb moves. When the muscle relaxes, the myosin and actin myofilaments slide back to their initial positions, and the muscle fiber returns to its original length.

The Motor Unit

Some alpha motor neurons have axons with only a few branches, whereas others have axons with many branches. Each branch of an axon synapses with a single muscle fiber, so some alpha motor neurons control just a few muscle fibers, and others control many. Collectively, an alpha motor neuron and all the muscle fibers it controls form a **motor unit.** Some motor units contain a few muscle fibers and others contain many.

When the axon of an alpha motor neuron has few branches and controls only a few muscle fibers, fine motor control is possible. For example, using a pen requires the precise control of our finger movements. By contrast, gross limb movements require the activation of many muscle fibers. Such movement is possible because the axons of some alpha motor neurons have many branches and control many muscle fibers.

motor unit An alpha motor neuron and all the muscle fibers it controls.

slow-twitch muscle A muscle fiber that contracts and fatigues slowly.

fast-twitch muscle A muscle fiber that contracts and fatigues quickly.

intermediate-twitch muscle A muscle fiber that contracts at a lower rate than fast-twitch and a higher rate than slow-twitch muscles.

Muscle Adaptation

A long-distance runner needs to move steadily for a long time, whereas a sprinter must move exceptionally quickly but only for a short time. Different types of muscles facilitate these diverse abilities. For the long-distance runner, **slow-twitch muscles** (type 1) produce slower contractions that can be maintained for long periods without fatiguing. By contrast, the sprinter is aided by **fast-twitch muscles** (type 2), which produce rapid contractions, but tire quickly. **Intermediate-twitch muscles** produce contractions of moderate speed and duration.

Obviously, the different types of muscles have not evolved just for sprinters and long-distance runners. We use primarily slow- or intermediate-twitch muscles when we stand or walk, and when we run at full speed we use fast-twitch muscles. The distribution within the body of the different types of muscles plays an important role in the success of world-class sprinters and long-distance runners. For example, a research group has shown that aerobic endurance training leads to a shift from fast- to slow-twitch muscle fibers (Thayer & others, 2000). Individuals with a decade or more of endurance training had 70.9% slow-twitch fibers, compared with just 37.7% in nontrained subjects. This group also found that the remaining fast-twitch fibers in the trained runners had significantly less oxidative capacity than such fibers in the nontrained group. World-class sprinters, by contrast, have many more fast-twitch fibers than slow-twitch fibers, at least in part because of their training in rapid running of short distances.

Checkpoint

Continuing the process you began in the first Checkpoint, explain what happens when Sam decides to step back on the ski machine. Begin at the level of the alpha motor neuron. Describe the effect on the target muscle of acetylcholine release at the neuromuscular junction.

REVIEW

- Skeletal muscles are attached to bones by tendons; bones move when skeletal muscles contract.
- The contraction of extensor muscles produces limb extension, moving the limb away from the body; flexor muscle contraction produces limb flexion, drawing the limb toward the body.
- Muscle fibers are composed of myofibrils, consisting of sarcomeres, with overlapping bands of myosin and actin proteins.

- Skeletal muscles are controlled by alpha motor neurons of the spinal cord, which synapse with extrafusal muscle fibers at neuromuscular junctions.
- Acetylcholine, the neurotransmitter at the neuromuscular junction, excites extrafusal muscle fibers.
- As the action potential travels down a muscle fiber, the permeability of the cell membrane to Ca^{2+} ions increases.
- Movement of Ca^{2+} ions into the cell causes the two types of myofilaments to move relative to each other, shortening the muscle fiber and moving the bone.
- As the muscle relaxes, it lengthens, and the bone returns to its original position.
- A motor unit consists of an alpha motor neuron and all the muscle fibers it controls. Some motor units control only a few muscle fibers, whereas others control many.
- Precise control of movement requires smaller motor units; gross limb movements depend on larger motor units.
- Fast-twitch, slow-twitch, and intermediate-twitch muscles produce contractions of varying speed and duration.

patellar reflex A reflex in which tapping the tendon of the knee stretches one of the muscles that extends the leg, and the resulting muscle contraction causes the leg to kick outward.

monosynaptic stretch reflex A spinal reflex with a single synapse between the sensory receptor and the muscle effector.

muscle spindle A structure embedded within an extrafusal muscle fiber that enables the CNS to contract a muscle to counteract the stretching of the extrafusal muscle fiber.

intrafusal muscle fiber A muscle fiber within the muscle spindle that is surrounded by annulospiral endings.

annulospiral ending A sensory receptor in the central part of an intrafusal muscle fiber.

Reflex Control of Movement

It is time for your physical, and, at the moment, you are seated on the examination table in the doctor's office. The doctor taps the tendon just below your kneecap with a small rubber hammer, and your leg kicks outward. This kick is a reflex—a simple, automatic response to a sensory stimulus. We described this **patellar reflex,** or knee-jerk reflex, in our discussion of spinal reflexes in Chapter 2 (see Figure 2.16). Although the brain controls many movements, including several reflexes, most reflexes are produced by the spinal cord without involvement of the brain. In other words, the spinal cord usually mediates reflexive reaction to the input from sensory receptors.

The Monosynaptic Stretch Reflex

The **monosynaptic stretch reflex** (Figure 8.7) is a spinal reflex with a single synapse between the sensory receptor and the muscle effector. Suppose you want to get off the examination table and stand, which requires you to extend your legs away from your body. When you stand, gravity exerts pressure on your legs. If this force were not counteracted, your legs would buckle, and you would fall. However, as you get off the table, stretching the muscles that extend your legs produces an opposing muscle contraction of the type you experienced when the doctor tapped your knee. The patellar reflex enables you to remain standing rather than fall.

Embedded within the extrafusal muscle fibers is a structure called the **muscle spindle**, which contains **intrafusal muscle fibers;** these fibers extend the length of the muscle spindle. The central portion of an intrafusal muscle fiber lacks myofibrils and has sensory receptors, the **annulospiral endings,** wrapped around it. When the extrafusal muscle fibers are stretched, so are the intrafusal fibers,

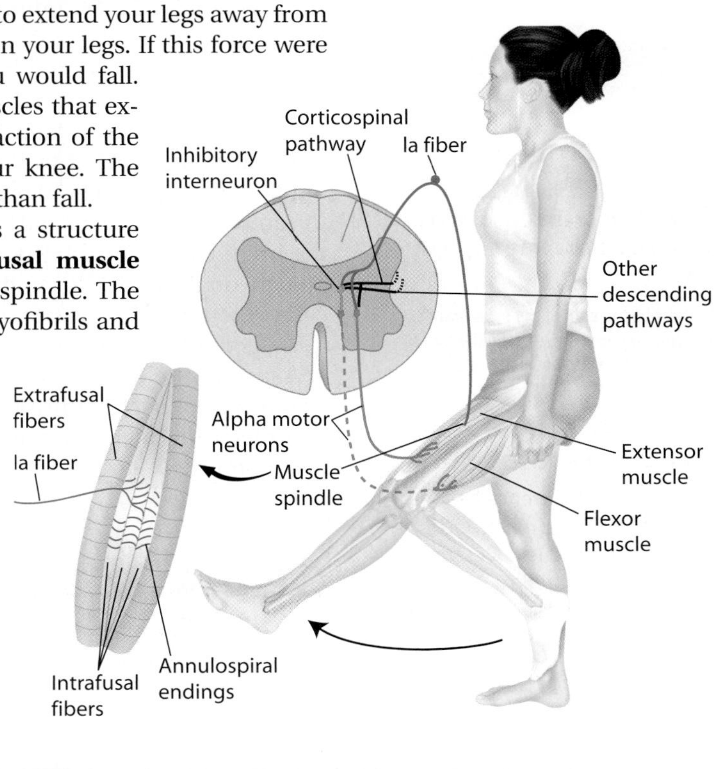

Figure 8.7
Components of the monosynaptic stretch reflex Stretching the muscle spindle activates the annulospiral endings of the spindle. Axons from the annulospiral endings (Ia fibers) enter the dorsal root of the spinal cord and synapse with alpha motor neurons. Stimulation of the alpha motor neurons causes the extrafusal muscle fibers to contract. (Adapted from Kandel & others, 1991.)

→ **What causes the intrafusal muscle fibers to stretch?**

Ia fiber An axon from an annulospiral ending that enters the dorsal root of the spinal cord and synapses with an alpha motor neuron.

polysynaptic reflex A spinal reflex with more than one synapse between the sensory receptor and the muscle effector.

withdrawal reflex The automatic withdrawal of a limb from a painful stimulus.

which stimulates the annulospiral endings. (Actually, the annulospiral endings are always active to some degree, which produces muscle tone.) Stretching the intrafusal muscle fibers causes the annulospiral endings to fire more rapidly. This increased neural activity travels along the axons, called **Ia fibers,** of the annulospiral endings; these axons enter the dorsal root of the spinal cord and synapse with alpha motor neurons. The Ia fibers have an excitatory influence on alpha motor neurons, causing the extrafusal muscle fibers to contract.

How does this process keep a person standing despite the force of gravity? Gravity stretches the extrafusal and intrafusal muscle fibers of both legs. The annulospiral endings detect this stretching, and the Ia fibers convey this information to the spinal cord. There, the Ia fibers stimulate the alpha motor neurons that contract the extensor muscles, so the legs straighten and the person remains standing. Contracting the extrafusal muscle fibers also causes the intrafusal muscle fibers to contract. This contraction decreases the firing rate of the annulospiral endings, unless the conditions that led to the stretching of the intrafusal muscle fibers continue, which is the case as long as the person remains standing.

The response to stretching the extrafusal muscle fibers is almost instantaneous. Like alpha motor neurons, Ia fibers transmit information rapidly; for example, a patellar reflex can be elicited in about 50 milliseconds.

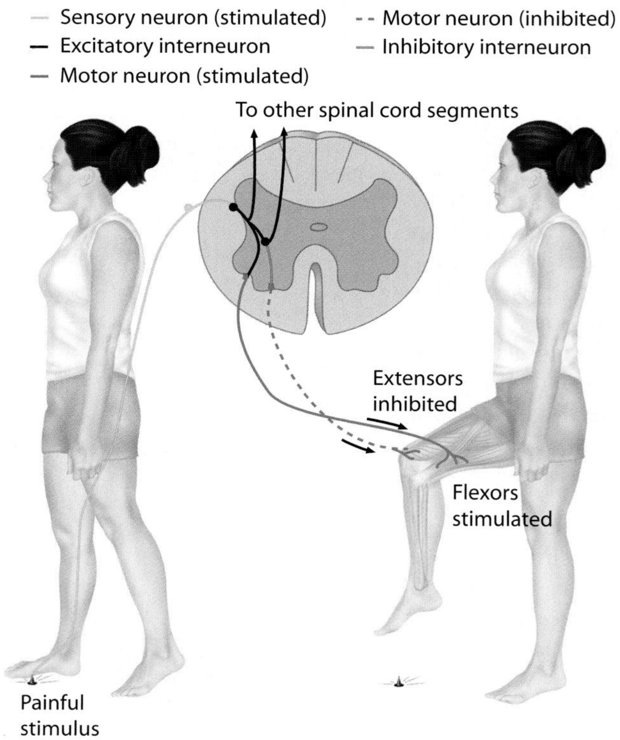

Figure 8.8

A polysynaptic reflex The withdrawal reflex is one example of a polysynaptic reflex.

→ **Describe the path of the polysynaptic reflex from the time you step on the tack to the time you lift your foot.**

The Polysynaptic Reflex

A **polysynaptic reflex** is a spinal reflex with more than one synapse between the sensory receptor and the muscle effector. Polysynaptic reflexes are more common than monosynaptic reflexes, and they vary greatly in complexity. Some are relatively simple reflexes in which the sensory neuron enters the spinal cord at the same level that the motor neuron exits; within the spinal cord, the two are connected by one or more interneurons. Other polysynaptic reflexes are more complex, with neurons entering and exiting the spinal cord at different levels and with connections to many interneurons.

Consider the following example: Suppose you are walking barefoot in the basement of your house and step on a tack (Figure 8.8). In addition to reflexively withdrawing your foot—the **withdrawal reflex**—you also make some postural changes to control your balance, such as extending your arms or reaching out for something to hold onto to keep from falling.

Although reflexes usually occur without any mediation from brain structures, the brain can influence the execution of polysynaptic reflexes. Suppose the only object you can reach for to maintain your balance is a very hot water pipe. In this case, you probably will not use the pipe to keep your balance; instead, your brain inhibits the reflex that would extend your arm to grab the pipe. Your brain sends a message to the interneurons in the part of the spinal cord containing the alpha motor neurons that control arm extension, and this message prevents the motor neurons from causing you to reach out and grab the pipe. The spinal cord can also inhibit reflexes—to prevent damage to our muscles, for example.

➤Checkpoint

What is the difference between a monosynaptic reflex and a polysynaptic reflex? Describe a monosynaptic reflex. What part of the muscle spindle is responsible for muscle tone?

REVIEW

➤ In the monosynaptic stretch reflex, a muscle contracts in response to stretching. Stretching of the intrafusal muscle fibers then activates annulospiral endings, sending a neural message to the spinal cord through Ia fibers, which synapse with alpha motor neurons. Firing of these neurons causes the extrafusal muscle fibers to contract.

- Simple polysynaptic reflexes involve only a sensory neuron and an alpha motor neuron at the same spinal level, and one or two interneurons; complex polysynaptic reflexes consist of sensory and motor neurons entering and exiting the spinal cord at different levels, involving many interneurons.
- Some polysynaptic reflexes occur without input from the brain; others are controlled by higher neural structures.
- Either the brain or the spinal cord can inhibit spinal reflexes.

Golgi Tendon Organs

While pitching in a Little League game, the son of one of your authors broke a bone in his arm. Apparently, on one throw the force of the pitch was so great that the muscles in the boy's arm contracted too much, snapping the bone. According to the son's physician, pitching a baseball is an unnatural motion, and many pitchers, at all levels of competition, have damaged their muscles, tendons, and bones. Of course, pitchers do not break bones every time they pitch, thanks to a mechanism that enables the motor system to control the extent of muscle contraction.

This mechanism is a set of receptors known as **Golgi tendon organs,** neurons located among the fibers of the tendons (Figure 8.9). Golgi tendon organs measure the amount of force the muscle exerts on the bone to which the tendon is attached. The strength of muscle contraction reflects the force exerted by the muscle on the bone: the greater the contraction of the muscle fibers, the greater the force on the bone. Under normal circumstances (i.e., nonmaximal muscle contraction), the Golgi tendon organs supply the central nervous system with continuous information about muscle tension.

When muscles exert too much force, a protective function of the Golgi tendon organs comes into play. A neural message travels along the Golgi tendon organ axons, known as **Ib fibers,** to the spinal cord, where they synapse with interneurons. The interneurons inhibit the alpha motor neurons, reducing the contraction of extrafusal muscle fibers. As a result, the muscle exerts less pressure on the tendon and bone.

Golgi tendon organs have a higher activation threshold than the sensory receptors in the muscle spindle, which enables the muscles to contract under normal-force conditions. Only when the force exerted is too great are Golgi tendon organs activated and the extrafusal muscle fibers inhibited. Of course, there are times when people want to exert more force than their muscles (and Golgi tendon organs) will allow. Olympic weightlifters, for example, lift enormous weights. To prevent their Golgi tendon organs from defeating their efforts, weightlifters have been known to inject local anesthetics into

As this weight lifter performs curls, the Golgi tendon organs in the tendon attached to her biceps muscle prevent her from applying excessive force to the bones in her forearm. Eventually, if she keeps lifting long enough, the firing of Renshaw cells (discussed on the next page) will cause the firing of the alpha motor neurons to stop, and the weight lifter will be unable to do another curl.

Figure 8.9

Golgi tendon organs Excessive contraction of extrafusal muscle fibers activates Golgi tendon organs. Axons from the Golgi tendon organs enter the dorsal root of the spinal cord, where they synapse with inhibitory interneurons, which synapse with alpha motor neurons. Activation of the inhibitory interneurons thus inhibits the alpha motor neurons. (Adapted from Kandel & others, 1991.)

What is the other name for the axons of the Golgi tendon organs?

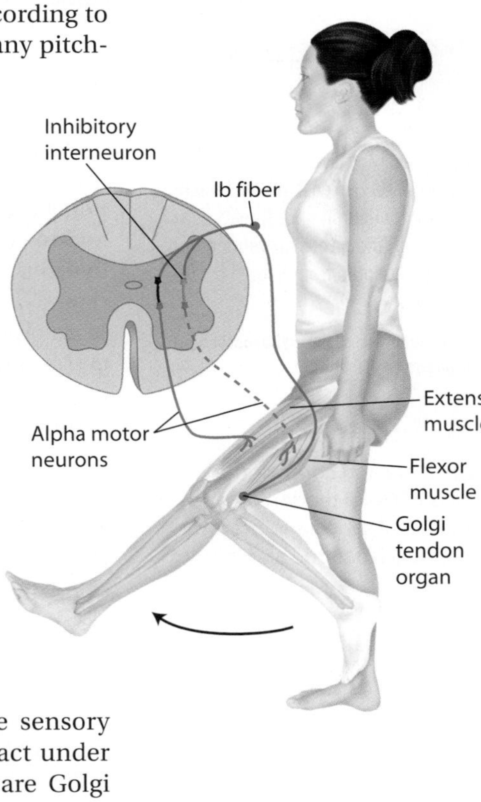

Golgi tendon organ A receptor located among the fibers of tendons that measures the total amount of force exerted by the muscle on the bone to which the tendon is attached.

Ib fiber An axon of a Golgi tendon organ that extends to the spinal cord and synapses with an interneuron that inhibits alpha motor neurons.

their tendons to block the action of the Golgi tendon organs. Although now able to lift more weight, the weightlifter is also more likely to damage the muscle, tear the tendon, or break a bone.

Renshaw Cells

Muscle damage can also result from fatigue, particularly if the muscles have contracted so often in a short period of time that they no longer work properly. To combat this fatigue, the nervous system has a set of inhibitory interneurons called **Renshaw cells.** Each alpha motor neuron has a collateral branch that turns back within the spinal cord to synapse with its Renshaw cell. The axon of the Renshaw cell circles around to the dendrites of the same alpha motor neuron, forming a circuit (Figure 8.10). The more the alpha motor neuron fires, the more its Renshaw cell fires, and when the inhibitory influence of the Renshaw cell on the alpha motor neuron reaches a threshold level, the alpha motor neuron stops firing, preventing excessive contraction of the muscle fiber.

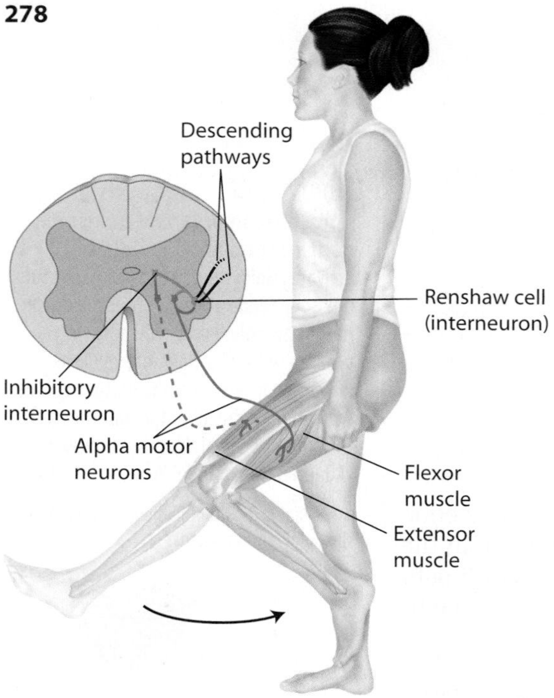

Figure 8.10
Renshaw cells A Renshaw cell inhibits its alpha motor neuron once it reaches a certain rate of firing, thus preventing muscle fatigue. (Adapted from Kandel & others, 1991.)

➡ **Is the inhibition of the alpha motor neuron long term or short term?**

A muscle contains many muscle fibers, and the alpha motor neurons innervating the fibers fire at different rates. Only the neurons that exceed the threshold for Renshaw cell inhibition stop firing; other alpha motor neurons continue to fire and to contract some muscle fibers. With the ability to inhibit some alpha motor neurons, a muscle can maintain prolonged contraction without becoming fatigued or damaged. Because it is controlled by a negative feedback loop, inhibition of an alpha motor neuron by its Renshaw cell is short-lived. Thus, as soon as the alpha motor neuron stops firing, the excitatory influence on its Renshaw cell ceases, which ends the inhibitory effect and allows the alpha motor neuron to resume firing.

➤Checkpoint

Compare and contrast the roles of Golgi tendon organs and Renshaw cells in preventing muscle fatigue and injury.

The Neural Control of Opposing Muscle Pairs

Recall that muscles occur in pairs. In order for one muscle of a pair to contract, the opposing muscle must relax, or lengthen, which means that its contraction must be actively inhibited. The process by which one muscle is excited and its opposing muscle is inhibited is similar to the action of the Golgi tendon organs.

Let us return to your barefoot encounter with the tack. Suppose you step on the tack with your right foot. In order to withdraw your right foot, you must contract the flexor muscles in your right leg and relax the opposing extensor muscles. Further, in order to keep from falling, you need to contract the extensor muscles in your left leg and relax the opposing flexor muscles. Sensory pain receptors in your right foot provide one stimulus for these actions. Axons from the pain receptors form four branches in the spinal cord (Figure 8.11). One branch synapses with the alpha motor neurons that contract the flexor muscles in the right leg, and a second branch synapses with the interneurons that inhibit the alpha motor neurons going to the extensor muscles of the same leg. The third branch synapses with the alpha motor neurons that contract the extensor muscles of the left leg, and the final branch synapses with the interneurons that inhibit the alpha motor neurons to the flexor muscles in the left leg. Activation of this complex polysynaptic reflex enables you to lift your right leg while maintaining your balance by straightening your left leg.

The Gamma Motor System

You have learned how stimulation by alpha motor neurons causes muscle contraction, producing movement. But muscle contraction does not always lead to movement. In fact, all of our muscles remain tense (or contracted) even when

Renshaw cell An inhibitory interneuron excited by an alpha motor neuron that causes it to stop firing, preventing excessive muscle contraction.

gamma motor neuron A neuron that synapses with intrafusal muscle fibers to produce continuous muscle tension.

muscle tone The resting tension of skeletal muscles caused by the activity of gamma motor neurons.

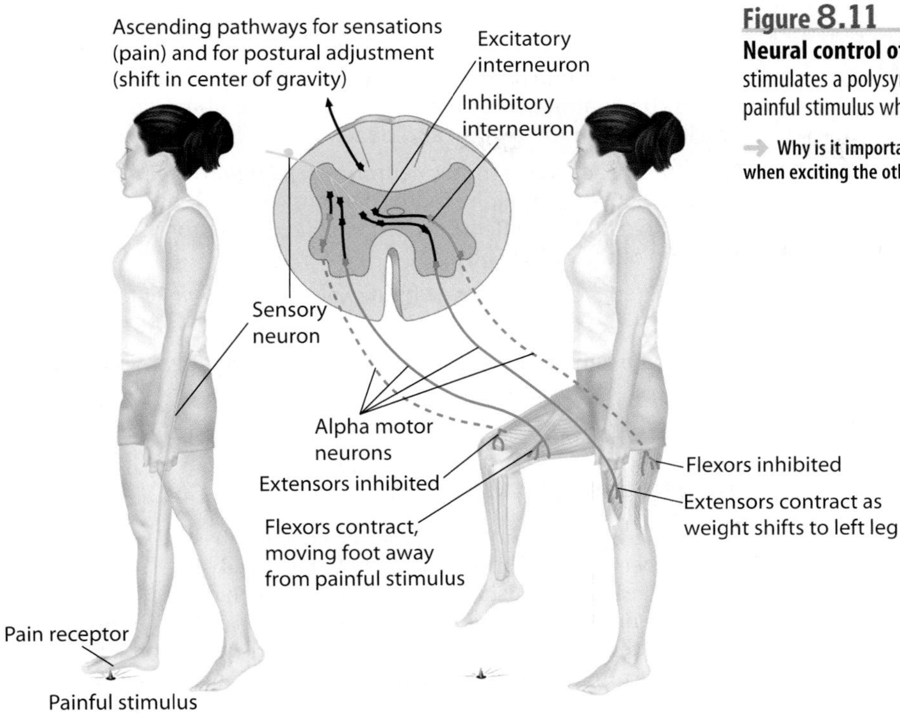

Figure 8.11

Neural control of opposing muscle pairs Stepping on a tack stimulates a polysynaptic reflex. The foot withdraws from the painful stimulus while the person maintains balance.

→ **Why is it important to inhibit one member of an opposing muscle pair when exciting the other?**

no movement is occurring. Because movement starts from a contracted muscle rather than a relaxed muscle, continuous muscle tension allows the rapid movement characteristic of spinal reflexes. This background of muscle tension is caused by **gamma motor neurons,** collectively known as the gamma motor system (Figure 8.12). Continuous activity of the gamma motor neurons produces a constant contraction of the extrafusal muscle fibers, or **muscle tone.** Muscle tone is maintained at all times, except during a stage of sleep called REM (Chapter 9).

Gamma motor neurons originate in the spinal cord, exit through its ventral root, and synapse with the intrafusal muscle fibers of the muscle spindle (see Figure 8.7). Gamma motor neurons are smaller than alpha motor neurons (which innervate the extrafusal muscle fibers) and thus conduct neural impulses more slowly. Contraction of the intrafusal muscle fibers following gamma motor neuron stimulation stretches the middle of the muscle spindle. This stretching activates the annulospiral endings and causes the extrafusal muscle fibers to contract.

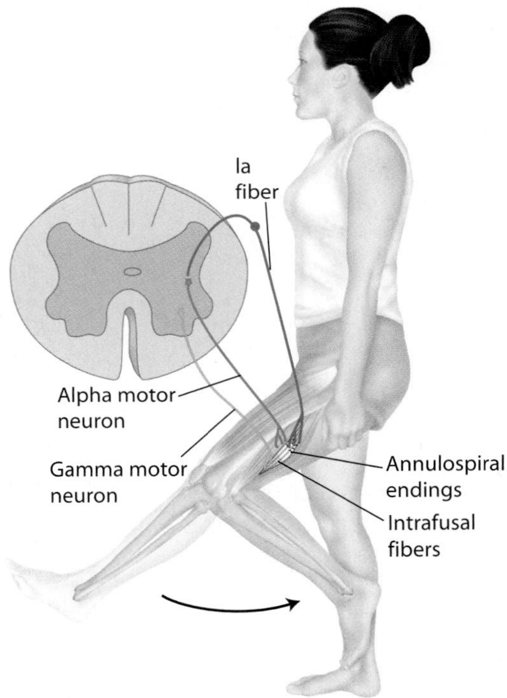

Figure 8.12

Gamma motor neurons Continuous gamma motor neuron activation produces constant contraction of extrafusal muscle fibers, or muscle tone.

→ **Why is it important for muscles to be tense when at rest?**

In addition to maintaining muscle tone, the gamma motor system gives us the ability to anticipate certain movements and react quickly. For example, when a player is at bat, he or she must be ready to swing at a ball that is over the plate and to withhold the swing if the ball is outside the strike zone. The extensor muscles in the player's arms and legs need to be primed for action. This readiness is accomplished by increased activity in the gamma motor neurons controlling the muscles that swing the bat and move the player's front leg forward. Such increased activity increases contraction of the appropriate muscles and enables the ballplayer to prepare to hit the ball.

So far, we have discussed reflexive movement and how the muscles are readied for such instructions as to swing or not swing at a ball. How the brain communicates instructions to our muscles so that we can engage in voluntary movements—how the neural mechanisms in the brain translate intention into action—is the topic of the next section.

Checkpoint

Why is it important for muscles to maintain a resting state of tension?

REVIEW

- When a muscle exerts too much force, the Golgi tendon organ is activated and ultimately reduces the contraction of the extrafusal muscle fibers, decreasing the force the muscle exerts on the tendon and bone.
- A collateral branch of each alpha motor neuron synapses with an inhibitory Renshaw cell, which synapses with alpha motor neurons. When alpha motor neuron activity reaches a threshold, the Renshaw cell inhibits the neuron, preventing excessive contraction of the muscle fiber.
- A complex polysynaptic reflex enables withdrawal of one leg while the other leg maintains balance.
- The gamma motor system produces muscle tone by keeping the muscles continually active.

Brain Control of Movement

Rhea is taking golf this semester as her elective in physical education. She hasn't been playing golf for long, but she already loves the game. She particularly enjoys using her driver to hit the ball off the tee and watching the ball sail 200 yards down the fairway. Hitting a crisp iron shot and seeing the ball settle on the green is almost equally satisfying. At the beginning of the semester, Rhea's skills matched Sam's on his ski machine. And like Sam, Rhea found that the proper motions didn't come naturally to her. In the beginning, she would often "top" the ball, sending it dribbling down the fairway. Even when she got the hang of swinging lower, she often hit "worm burners," shots that never rose more than a foot or two off the ground. With time and lots of practice, however, Rhea improved her wood and iron play, and she now feels good about her drives and approach shots to the greens. She's not sure whether she'll ever be a good putter, as she still finds it difficult to hit the ball just hard enough with the right line to get it in the hole. She's hoping that practice will do for her putting what it did for the other parts of her game.

Golf involves both powerful movements (the drive) and controlled movements (the putt). The brain has the amazing capacity to direct both types of movement, as well as the thousands of others we perform each day. Here we examine the neural structures responsible for drives, putts, and all the other voluntary movements of which we are capable.

As you will see, at least three principles govern the system responsible for our voluntary movements. First, it is hierarchically organized, beginning with the dorsolateral prefrontal cortex, which appears to be the decision maker after assessing external stimuli. The dorsolateral prefrontal cortex initiates the program. Sensory input is a second important principle by which the system operates. This input is primarily integrated by the posterior parietal cortex. The third principle is that learning changes the locus of control over the movements. As an illustration of this principle, consider the difference between your movements when you are just beginning to acquire a particular skill, such as riding a bicycle, and after you have a great deal of experience. At first your movements are awkward, reflecting your need for constant sensory input and feedback and nearly continuous motor adjustments. With practice, your movements become more economical, with little wasted motion, reflecting their subcortical control.

Dorsolateral Prefrontal Cortex

In nonhuman primates and humans, the **dorsolateral prefrontal cortex** (or *dorsolateral prefrontal association cortex*) seems to function as the top executive in the perception-action cycle (Fuster, 2004; Koechlin & others, 2003; Otani, 2002). Specifically, cells in this region integrate sensory information across time with

dorsolateral prefrontal cortex The top executive in the perception-action cycle; cells in this area integrate sensory information across time with motor actions needed to deal with the information.

secondary motor cortex A cortical area consisting of the supplementary motor area and the premotor cortex; involved in the planning and sequencing of voluntary movements.

supplementary motor area A part of the secondary motor cortex that receives input from the posterior parietal cortex and the somatosensory cortex.

premotor cortex A part of the secondary motor cortex that receives input mostly from the visual cortex.

mirror neuron Neuron in the primate premotor cortex that is activated by performing an action or by watching another monkey or person performing an action.

motor actions needed to deal with the information. As an illustration of this ability, Fuster and colleagues (2000) trained monkeys to associate sounds and colors (low-pitched tone with green, high-pitched tone with red) separated by a short delay (10 seconds) for reward. The researchers recorded from cells in the dorsolateral prefrontal cortex of the animals and found that a given neuron typically responded both to the sound and the color associated with it according to the task requirements. In trials in which a monkey chose the wrong color, there was no correlation between the response to the tone and the reaction of the monkey to the appropriate color.

The integrative function of the dorsolateral prefrontal cortex is well supported by its anatomical connections with other cortical areas (Fuster & others, 2000). For example, it receives information from sensory cortices and in particular from the posterior parietal cortex (Figure 8.13). In addition, the prefrontal area sends projections to the secondary motor cortex as well as to the primary motor cortex.

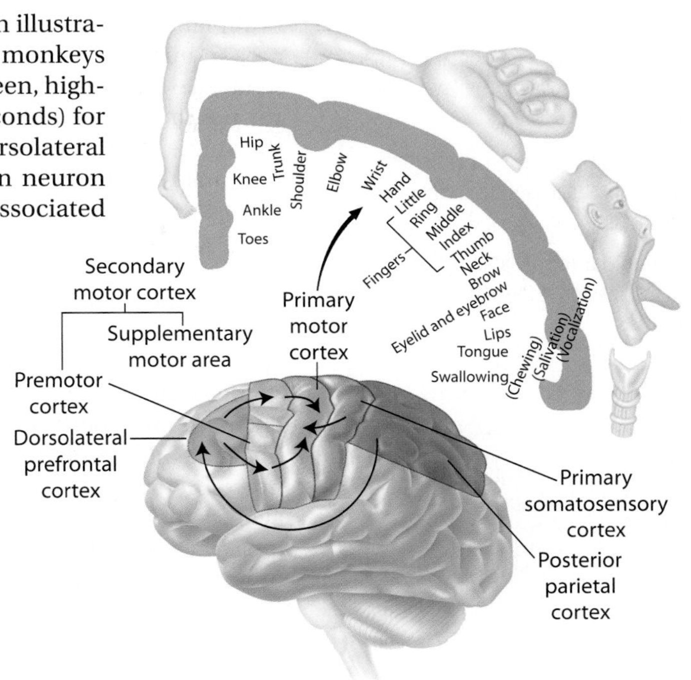

Figure 8.13

The cortical control of movement

The primary cortical structures involved in controlling movement are shown in the bottom drawing. Arrows represent input to the dorsolateral prefrontal cortex, secondary motor cortex, and primary motor cortex. The somatotopic map of the human primary motor cortex is shown above.

→ **What role does the posterior parietal cortex play in the initiation of voluntary movement?**

Secondary Motor Cortex

The **secondary motor cortex** consists of the supplementary motor area and the premotor cortex (see Figure 8.13). Both areas are involved in the planning and sequencing of voluntary movements, and both receive input from the dorsolateral prefrontal cortex, as indicated above. The **supplementary motor area** also receives input from the posterior parietal cortex and the somatosensory cortex, and the **premotor cortex** receives input mostly from the visual cortex. Many neural connections link the supplementary motor area and the premotor cortex, which allows the integration of information arriving from other cortical areas.

Apparently, there are differences in the movements planned and sequenced by the premotor cortex and by the supplementary motor area (Luft & others, 2002; Schubotz & von Cramon, 2001). The supplementary motor area seems to plan and sequence movements guided by internally generated stimuli (or intentions), whereas the premotor cortex does the same for externally guided movements. Most movements are guided by both intentions and external stimuli, and the connections between the supplementary motor area and the premotor cortex coordinate movement planning.

The role of the secondary motor cortex in sequencing movement is evident in monkeys trained to push a peanut through a hole with a finger of one hand and catch it in the palm of the other hand. Although a normal monkey has no difficulty with this task, an animal with unilateral damage to the supplementary motor area or to the premotor cortex typically fails to catch the peanut, because of an inability to coordinate the actions of the two hands (Brinkman, 1984). Generally, the hands of the brain-damaged monkey tend to perform the same action rather than sharing the task between them; that is, instead of one hand pushing while the other catches, both hands attempt to push the peanut and the monkey cannot catch it.

One of the most exciting findings in neuroscience involves neurons in the premotor cortex called mirror neurons. Discovered in monkeys, **mirror neurons** are activated both when the animal performs a movement and when it watches another monkey or person perform that movement (Rizzolatti & Craighero, 2004). Some mirror neurons in the monkey brain respond to both the sight and the sound of an action being performed (Keysers & others, 2003). Mirror neurons are found in the ventral part of the premotor cortex, in an area of the monkey

primary motor cortex An area in the precentral gyrus of the frontal lobe that plays a major role in voluntary movements.

precentral gyrus An area in the frontal lobe that contains the primary motor cortex.

pyramidal cell A large, pyramid-shaped neuron in the primary motor cortex.

brain labeled F5, which is considered to be the monkey counterpart of Broca's area in humans (Ferrari & others, 2003). Many of the studies of mirror neurons in monkeys have looked at hand actions, but Ferrari and colleagues studied mirror neurons in area F5 that coded mouth actions—again, responding either to the animal's own mouth movements or to those of another monkey. Some of the neurons responded most vigorously to the sight of communicative mouth gestures, such as lip smacking, which suggests that these neurons might play a role in communicative behaviors in monkeys, as do the neurons in Broca's area in humans.

A mirror neuron system also seems to exist in people (Avikainen & others, 2002; Blakemore & Frith, 2005; Buccino & others, 2004; Gangitano & others, 2004). Buccino and colleagues, for example, described an fMRI study that found that watching actions performed with the hand, mouth, or foot activated different parts of Broca's area, depending on the body part performing the action. These results strongly support an execution-observation matching system, or mirror neuron system, involved in action recognition. The primary motor cortex also seems to be part of the mirror neuron system, and mirror neurons in this area have been found to respond to the observation of tool use (Jarvelainen & others, 2004). Both nonhuman primates and humans learn many actions through observing and imitating the actions of others, and the mirror neuron system provides a mechanism through which observation can be translated into action.

Primary Motor Cortex

The **primary motor cortex,** located in the **precentral gyrus** of the frontal lobe (see Figure 8.13), is primary in the sense of being directly involved in the control of motor neurons, not in terms of its importance for motor functioning. In fact, rather than being the highest level of cortical movement processing, the primary motor cortex is the lowest level of such processing. A great deal of movement—locomotion, obtaining food, and so forth—is still possible without the primary motor cortex. Stimulation of the primary motor cortex results in movements involving groups of muscles, not individual muscles.

Organization of the Primary Motor Cortex

Two things are evident from the somatotopic map shown in Figure 8.13: First, the movement of different body parts is elicited by stimulation of different regions of the primary motor cortex. Second, as in the somatosensory map (see Figure 7.22), there is greater cortical representation of some body parts than of others. For example, body parts that produce precise movements, such as the hands and mouth, have greater representation in the primary motor cortex than do parts of the body that produce gross movements, such as the arms and legs.

The homunculus ("little man") drawing in Figure 8.13 is based on early work involving low-intensity electrical stimulation of the cortex. More recent work, using contemporary investigation methods (e.g., PET, fMRI), has supported the separation of functional areas within the primary motor cortex, such as an arm area separate from a hand area, but has not supported the precise segregation of body part functions suggested by the drawing (Sanes & Donoghue, 2000). Instead, the neurons representing any particular body part appear to be widely distributed, resulting in overlapping functional representation.

There are significant structural differences between the primary motor cortex and other cortical areas. For example, the small granular (or seed-like) cells found in layer IV of other cortical areas are absent in the primary motor cortex, along with layer IV itself. Because of the absence of these granular cells, cortical motor areas are sometimes called *agranular cortex.* Motor cortex layer V contains large neurons called **pyramidal cells,** or sometimes Betz cells after their discoverer, which make the primary motor cortex thicker than other cortical tissue. In humans, for example, the primary motor cortex is 3.5 to 4.0 mm thick, compared with the 1.5 to 2.0 mm thickness of the primary visual cortex.

The axons of the pyramidal cells leave the primary motor cortex in columns perpendicular to the cortical surface, which are organized into colonies of motor cortex neurons (Ghez & others, 1991). Within each colony, the neurons control different parameters of a movement, such as its direction and force. To study the neuronal control of the direction of a specific movement, Georgopoulos and colleagues (1993) trained monkeys to reach in eight different directions for objects and then measured the activity of hundreds of individual motor cortex neurons during each movement. Although each motor cortex neuron responded to a particular direction, no single neuron responded to the exact direction of an arm movement. However, the researchers found a strong relationship between the activity of several hundred motor cortex neurons and the specific direction of an arm movement, and the activity of different colonies corresponded to different movement directions. In other words, neural activity in a specific colony increased when the arm moved in one direction but not when it moved in other directions.

Evidence also suggests that the activity of individual neurons and groups of neurons in the primary motor cortex is related to the force of a movement (Ashe, 1997; Taira & others, 1996). For example, Taira and colleagues studied the effect on primary motor cortex cells of both the direction and force of arm movements in monkeys. The direction of movement had a significant effect on the activity of nearly 79% of the cells studied, force had a significant effect on 7%, and both direction and force significantly affected the remaining 14%. The researchers concluded that direction of movement can be controlled independently of force and that the specification of direction is particularly prominent in cells of the primary motor cortex.

Activity in clusters of neurons in the primary motor cortex is also related to hand movements designed to intercept a moving target (Lee & others, 2001). Two monkeys were trained to intercept a target that varied in the direction from which it appeared, the speed at which it traveled, and its acceleration. Single-cell recording from neurons in the arm area of primary motor cortex revealed that the activity of most neurons was closely related to the parameters of the animals' hand movements. The activity of some neurons, however, conveyed additional information needed for successful task performance, such as the intervals between successive movements and the initial velocity of the target. The researchers suggested that the transformation of information about target motion into movement-related signals occurs in a group of cortical areas that includes the primary motor cortex.

Plasticity of the Primary Motor Cortex

Being a typical experimental psychologist, one of your authors frequently observed his oldest son's efforts to learn to write. Although the boy's early attempts to write letters legibly often were unsuccessful, his handwriting improved considerably over a period of months, and his letters became increasingly easier to discern. This improvement highlights the flexibility of motor behavior.

This flexibility is also present in adult mammals, including humans (Sanes & Donoghue, 2000; Ungerleider & others, 2002). At least part of the reason for the flexibility is the lack of precise topography in the primary motor cortex, as indicated earlier. Rather than the point-to-point representation implied by the motor homunculus, representation for any particular body part is multiple and widely distributed. In addition, extensive experimental evidence confirms the plasticity of neurons in the primary motor cortex.

For example, Sanes and colleagues (1992) found that changing the forelimb position in anesthetized rats altered the representation of the forelimb area in the primary motor cortex. The researchers interpreted the change as an expansion of the representation of the forelimb and as further support for the flexibility of representations in the primary motor cortex.

Donoghue and colleagues (1990) examined the extent of functional reorganization in the primary motor cortex following transection of the forelimb motor nerve in adult rats. Within hours of the transection, they observed forelimb motor responses comparable to those seen before the transection. In addition, when the researchers reexamined the primary motor cortex after cutting the nerve, they found that the forelimb boundary had shifted from its original territory to invade cortical territory that formerly mediated activity in part of the snout of the animal. This may remind you of Ramachandran's finding that a man's phantom hand was remapped on his face and upper arm (Chapter 7). The explanation there, and here, is that cortical neurons have changed in response to a loss of information they once received.

Although we know that the primary motor cortex shows plasticity in its response to sensory and motor changes, we do not yet understand the precise synaptic processes underlying this modifiability. One possibility that has been investigated is a learning-type phenomenon called *long-term potentiation (LTP),* a long-lasting increased excitability in a specific neural circuit caused by repetitive stimulation (discussed in more detail in Chapter 14).

LTP is considered important because it may represent learning at the cellular level. Working with slices of rat motor cortex, Aroniadou and Keller (1995) were able to induce LTP in a high percentage of cells. Other researchers observed a similar potential for inducing enhanced responsivity, or LTP, within a specific neural circuit in the motor cortex cells of anesthetized cats (Kimura & others, 1994). The induction of LTP in primary motor cortex neurons illustrates activity-dependent plasticity—that is, the repetitive stimulation of neurons alters their responsivity. Practicing movements also leads to a use-dependent plasticity of the human primary motor cortex and enhanced performance of the movement. A study of the mechanisms of this use-dependent plasticity in humans revealed that it is dependent on NMDA receptor activation and $GABA_A$ receptor inhibition (Butefisch & others, 2000). Other researchers have found that use-dependent plasticity is weakened by the drug scopolamine, indicating involvement of a cholinergic influence (Sawaki & others, 2002).

Such use-dependent plasticity of the motor cortex has relevance for our everyday lives and particularly for the development of skilled motor behaviors. Jancke and colleagues (2000) used fMRI to study neuronal activity in the primary and secondary motor cortex of two professional pianists and two nonmusician control subjects during one-hand and two-hand tapping tests. Both cortical areas were much less activated during the bimanual task in the pianists, revealing a greater efficiency in the use of their motor cortical neurons. The researchers assumed that this decreased activation of the motor cortex to produce a specific movement permits greater control over a greater number of movements.

The use-dependent plasticity of the motor cortical areas suggests a greater potential for functional recovery from brain damage than has generally been assumed. For example, Jones and coworkers (1999) and Chu and Jones (2000) studied the effect of complex motor skills training (the acrobat task, which required traversing a series of obstacles, such as a ladder with widely spaced rungs, a grid platform, and a rope) on behavioral recovery and structural changes in rats following unilateral damage to the forelimb sensorimotor cortex. On tests of coordinated forelimb use, the rats given acrobat training performed better than control animals. In addition, the animals with training exhibited increased synapse-to-neuron ratios. Such findings in animals suggest that appropriate experiences in humans following a stroke or accidental injury could hasten the reorganization of the remaining undamaged motor cortical areas (Hallett, 2001; Nudo, 2003; Nudo & others, 2001).

Primary Somatosensory Cortex

As you might expect, the primary motor cortex does not operate independently of other cortical areas. In fact, it receives information from four different cortical structures, a cooperative action that enables the primary motor cortex to initiate successful movements. Let us consider Rhea's golf game. One type of information she requires—the amount of force she must exert to produce a particular swing, such as a putt—comes from her primary somatosensory cortex. The posterior parietal cortex supplies a second type of information—the present position of the golf ball—so that Rhea can move the club to hit the ball. Finally, the dorsolateral prefrontal cortex and secondary motor cortex provide the planning and sequencing of her swing.

The sensory receptors in the muscles and joints send information about the physical environment to the somatosensory cortex and ultimately to the posterior parietal cortex. From there, it goes to the dorsolateral prefrontal cortex, the secondary motor cortex, and then to the primary motor cortex. This input makes the primary motor cortex aware of the current status of the muscles that must be activated and the location of the body parts that must be moved in order to exert the right amount of force. Suppose Rhea wants to hit a 50 foot chip shot to the green. If she hits the ball too hard, it may sail 75 yards, but if she exerts too little force, it may go only a few feet. Her arms must not be too tight against her body, but they cannot be too far away either. Feedback from her muscles and joints enables Rhea's primary motor cortex to send the correct message to her muscles so that she moves her arms with sufficient force to hit the ball onto the green, preferably near the hole.

Posterior Parietal Cortex

Suppose Rhea hits an errant shot and finds her golf ball under a tree. To hit the ball without also hitting the tree, she must limit the backward extension of her arms. Input from her visual system enables her to swing her arms just enough to hit the ball but not the tree.

As discussed in Chapter 6, we rely heavily on our visual sense to guide our movements. At the same time, other senses also play important roles in directing movement. Suppose you enter a dark room and need to locate the light switch on the opposite wall. You might use your tactile sense to guide you to the switch, touching the walls and furniture as you walk across the room. Alternatively, you might be able to use your sense of hearing to locate the light switch, if you know there is a ticking clock next to it.

The **posterior parietal cortex** integrates input from the visual, auditory, and skin senses (see Figure 8.13) and relays it to the dorsolateral prefrontal cortex, which uses the information to guide our movements (Andersen & Buneo, 2002). The specific posterior parietal lobe area active during movement depends on the type of movement. For example, one set of neurons in the posterior parietal cortex becomes active when Rhea reaches for a golf ball, but a different set reacts when she holds it.

Individuals with damage to the posterior parietal cortex (typically in the right hemisphere) have difficulty responding to visual, auditory, or somatosensory stimuli presented to the contralateral side of the body (Driver & Vuilleumier, 2001; Pisella & Mattingley, 2004). This sensory-motor disturbance is called **contralateral neglect.** The following case history of a woman with stroke-produced damage to the right posterior parietal lobe illustrates contralateral neglect:

> She has totally lost the idea of "left," with regard to both the world and her own body. Sometimes she complains that her portions are too small, but this is because she only eats from the right half of the plate—it does not occur to her that it has a left half as well. Sometimes, she will put on lipstick and make up the right half of her

posterior parietal cortex A cortical area that integrates input from the visual, auditory, and skin senses and relays it to the primary motor cortex.

contralateral neglect A disturbance in the ability to respond to visual, auditory, or somatosensory stimuli on the left side of the body, generally caused by damage to the right posterior parietal cortex.

Box 8.2
Apraxia

Apraxia (literally, "no action") is a disorder characterized by missing or inappropriate actions that are not the result of paralysis or any other motor impairment. People with apraxia have problems organizing purposeful movements. Although they can sometimes spontaneously perform a movement, they cannot repeat the movement if asked to do so.

In 1866, English neurologist John Hughlings Jackson observed that some of his patients were unable to perform some voluntary movements, even though he could find no evidence of muscle weakness. Near the beginning of the 20th century, Hugo Liepmann investigated apraxia intensively and later proposed that it is caused by damage to the left cerebral hemisphere or the corpus callosum. He suggested that the left frontal lobe plans voluntary movements executed by the left parietal lobe; therefore, damage to the left frontal lobe would produce apraxia of the limbs on the right side of the body.

However, a person with apraxia can show impaired movement on both sides of the body. To account for this, Liepmann proposed that the left parietal cortex controls motor behavior on the same side of the body by sending a message to the left frontal cortex and then on to the right frontal cortex through the corpus callosum. In this way, apraxia could occur bilaterally.

According to Kolb and Whishaw (2003), one problem with Liepmann's model is that humans have several different motor systems, not all of which are located in the left frontal lobe, and damage to each motor system produces a different subtype of apraxia. For example, damage to the right parietal lobe causes **constructional apraxia,** in which individuals have difficulty drawing pictures or assembling objects. However, they show no impairment of other skilled movements of their arms or hands: They can pick up a cup when requested to do so but cannot draw the cup. Impairment in the voluntary use of a limb, **limb apraxia,** can be caused by damage to the left parietal lobe or to the corpus callosum. People with **apraxia of speech** have great difficulty speaking clearly but do not have a language impairment (aphasia). Their language is grammatically correct; only the production of speech is impaired. Apraxia of speech is generally thought to be caused by damage limited to Broca's area in the left frontal lobe. Apraxia of speech should not be confused with Broca's aphasia. As we will see in Chapter 13, Broca's aphasia, with labored speech and grammar problems, requires damage beyond the cortical region known as Broca's area.

A second problem with Liepmann's model is that it ignores the role of subcortical areas in movement. The basal ganglia and the thalamus are the major routes for messages from the primary motor cortex to the muscles. Damage to both subcortical and cortical motor areas produces more severe impairment than damage restricted to the cortical areas. Severe apraxia appears to involve the entire motor system, not just the left frontal lobe.

The treatment goal for any of the apraxias is to restore volitional control of the muscles (Melfi & Garrison, 2004). The treatment can be provided by a speech-language pathologist for apraxia of speech or by a physical or occupational therapist for the other apraxias. Treatment involves establishing a planned sequence of movements. For example, a speech-language pathologist teaches a series of exercises that result in a sequenced production of speech sounds in a person with apraxia of speech. As the patient learns simple sounds and words, more difficult sounds and words are attempted. Although treatment can be long and arduous, most people with apraxia do regain voluntary control of the affected movement.

> face, leaving the left half completely neglected: it is almost impossible to treat these things, because her attention cannot be drawn to them. . . (Sacks, 1990, p. 77)

Box 8.2 describes some other types of movement disorders, the apraxias, which are caused by damage to areas of the brain involved in the control of movement.

Returning to the golf example: Feedback from somatosensory receptors to the posterior parietal cortex enables Rhea to swing the golf club just enough to hit the ball and not the tree. However, swinging a golf club involves several movements, including gripping the club, moving the arms backward, and then moving the arms forward so that the club head makes contact with the ball. These movements require the planning and sequencing of all the muscles involved in the swing; the planning and sequencing are the functions of the secondary motor cortex. (Figure 8.14 summarizes the role of the posterior parietal cortex and other cortical structures in controlling movement.)

Checkpoint

What changes in a person's behavior would you expect to occur following damage to the dorsolateral prefrontal cortex? Describe how the posterior parietal cortex, the somatosensory cortex, and the secondary motor cortex work together to enable Rhea to lift her golf bag onto her shoulder.

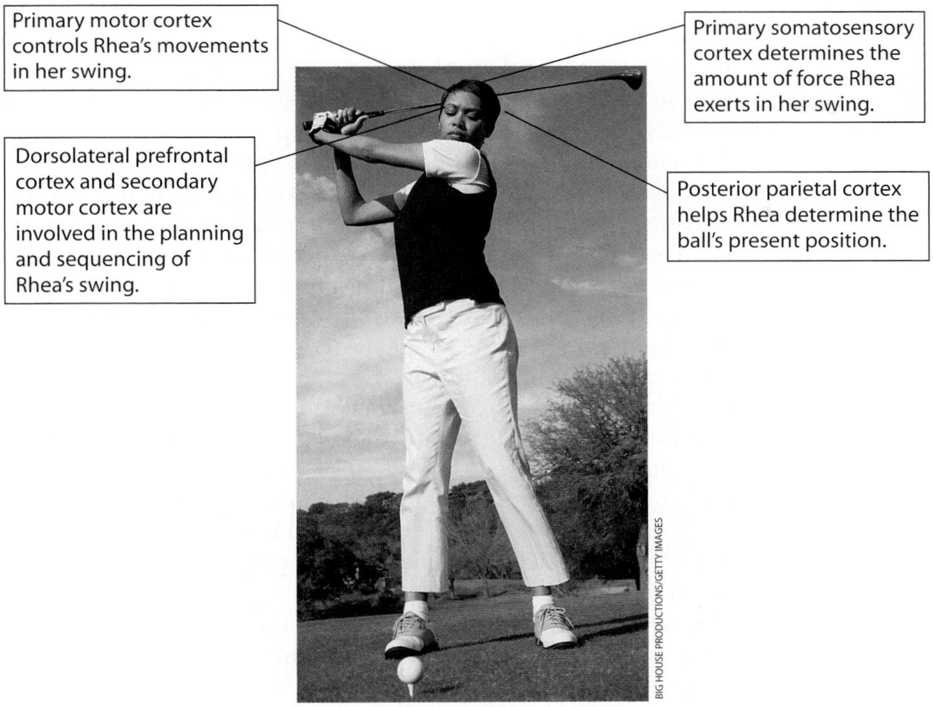

Primary motor cortex controls Rhea's movements in her swing.
Dorsolateral prefrontal cortex and secondary motor cortex are involved in the planning and sequencing of Rhea's swing.
Primary somatosensory cortex determines the amount of force Rhea exerts in her swing.
Posterior parietal cortex helps Rhea determine the ball's present position.
BIG HOUSE PRODUCTIONS/GETTY IMAGES

Figure 8.14
Rhea hitting a fairway iron

➡ **What is meant by the "activity-plasticity" of the primary motor cortex? The "use-plasticity"?**

REVIEW

- The dorsolateral prefrontal cortex and secondary motor cortex (supplementary motor area and premotor cortex) plan and sequence voluntary movements.
- The mirror neuron system provides a mechanism through which primates can learn by imitating the actions of others.
- The primary motor cortex receives information from the primary somatosensory cortex about muscle status and the movement of the body, and it plays a major role in voluntary movements, including the precise movement of the hands and mouth.
- Several findings—functional reorganization following nerve transection, the induction of LTP, and use-dependent plasticity—demonstrate the plasticity of the primary motor cortex.
- The posterior parietal cortex integrates input from the visual, auditory, and skin senses and relays it to the dorsolateral prefrontal cortex.

Motor Pathways

The posterior parietal cortex, somatosensory cortex, and secondary motor cortex provide information to the primary motor cortex, which uses this input to initiate movement. Two fiber tracts originate in the primary motor cortex (and other cortical areas) and travel through the midbrain and hindbrain before connecting with the PNS for the production of movement. Additional fiber tracts begin in subcortical areas in the midbrain and hindbrain and descend to the PNS.

Tracts Originating in the Motor Cortex

Both the corticospinal tract and the corticobulbar tract originate mainly in the primary motor cortex. Fibers of the **corticospinal tract** control movements of the fingers, hands, and arms, and of the trunk, legs, and feet. Fibers of the **corticobulbar tract** control movements of the face and tongue.

apraxia A movement disorder characterized by missing or inappropriate actions not caused by paralysis or any other motor impairment.

constructional apraxia A disorder characterized by difficulty drawing pictures or assembling objects.

limb apraxia An impairment in the voluntary use of a limb caused by damage to the left parietal lobe or the corpus callosum.

apraxia of speech A disorder characterized by difficulty speaking clearly, caused by damage limited to Broca's area.

corticospinal tract A motor pathway that controls movements of the fingers, hands, arms, trunk, legs, and feet.

corticobulbar tract A motor pathway that controls movements of the face and tongue.

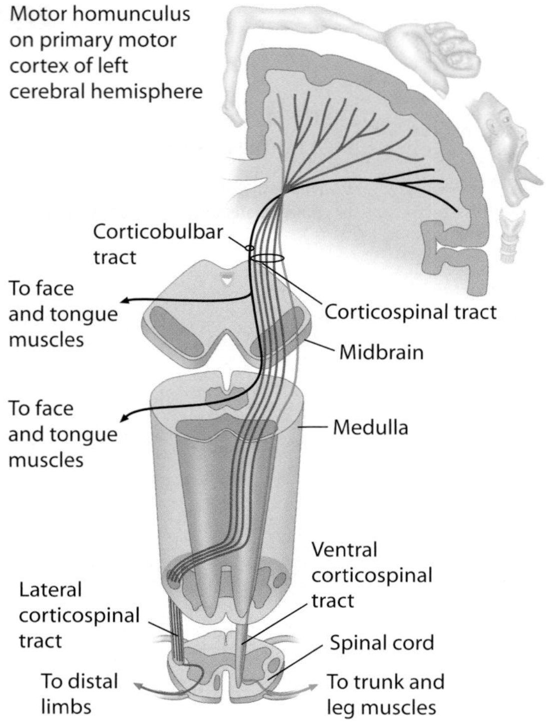

Figure 8.15

Fiber tracts that originate in the primary motor cortex Notice how the lateral corticospinal tract fibers cross over in the medulla before entering the spinal cord, whereas the ventral corticospinal tract fibers do not cross over. Corticobulbar tract fibers synapse with cranial nerves and extend to the face and tongue.

➔ **Describe the path of the lateral corticospinal tract from the motor cortex to the spinal cord.**

Most of the fibers in the corticospinal tract originate in the large pyramidal cells of the motor cortex, although some come from the premotor cortex and the somatosensory cortex. The axons of neurons in the corticospinal tract are quite long, typically 3 to 4 feet. After leaving the cerebral cortex, the axons travel through the midbrain and hindbrain to the spinal cord (Figure 8.15).

Most axons in the corticospinal tract cross over in the medulla to connect to the opposite side of the spinal cord. These crossing axons comprise the *lateral corticospinal tract,* which synapses with alpha motor neurons in the spinal cord that control movements of the fingers, hands, arms, lower legs, and feet. Because of this crossing over, the right side of the brain controls the movement of the left hand, fingers, arm, lower leg, and foot, and the left hemisphere controls the same musculature on the right side of the body. The noncrossing axons comprise the *ventral corticospinal tract.* These axons synapse with alpha motor neurons that control movements of the trunk and upper legs.

The importance of the corticospinal tract in precise movements is confirmed by studies of damage to this motor pathway in laboratory animals. For example, Lawrence and Kuypers (1968a) severed both the lateral and the ventral corticospinal tracts in monkeys and found that the animals, after an initial loss of ability, quickly regained the ability to reach for and then grasp an object. Although they had no impairments in posture or locomotion, the monkeys were permanently unable to use their fingers independently to pick up small pieces of food or release food once they were holding it.

The cell bodies of the corticobulbar tract neurons are in the primary motor cortex. Their axons descend through the midbrain and hindbrain to synapse with the motor neurons of the cranial nerves that control movements of the facial muscles and tongue muscles (see Figure 8.15). In Box 8.3, we examine amyotrophic lateral sclerosis, a degenerative neuromuscular disease that targets the corticospinal and corticobulbar tracts and the anterior horns of the spinal cord.

Box 8.3

Amyotrophic Lateral Sclerosis

Amyotrophic lateral sclerosis (ALS) is a degenerative neuromuscular disease caused by the deterioration of the corticospinal and corticobulbar tracts and the anterior (ventral) horns of the spinal cord (Charles & Swash, 2001; Jackson & Bryan, 1998). This disorder is sometimes called Lou Gehrig's disease, after the famous baseball player who died of ALS in 1941 at the age of 37. Gehrig was a star player for the New York Yankees from 1923 until his retirement in 1939. One of his most remarkable accomplishments was his record of 2,130 consecutive games played, a record finally broken in 1995 by Cal Ripken of the Baltimore Orioles.

Slightly more than 5,000 people in the United States are diagnosed with ALS each year. The first symptoms are usually feelings of weakness in a limb or problems in speaking or swallowing, and almost all voluntary muscle control is eventually affected. Because ALS is a progressive disorder, the muscular weakness and atrophy increase over time; most patients die within 2 to 5 years of diagnosis. However, some individuals die within a few months, whereas others live for many years. The famous physicist Stephen Hawking, author of *A Brief History of Time,* was diagnosed with ALS shortly after his 21st birthday and is still alive today, more than 40 years later.

At this time, the cause of ALS is unknown. Theories about contributing factors include free-radical oxidative stress, glutamate excitotoxicity, the accumulation of neurofilaments, and autoimmune disease (Shaw & others, 2001). Although there are currently no effective treatments for ALS, some researchers have found that the length of survival is correlated with psychological well-being (McDonald & others, 1994), but others have not (del Aguila & others, 2003). Individuals with ALS who feel depressed or hopeless have significantly shorter survival times than those with a more positive outlook (McDonald & others).

Tracts Originating in the Subcortex

The four ventromedial tracts and the rubrospinal tract originate in the subcortex (Figure 8.16). The **ventromedial tracts** begin in different subcortical areas and control movements of the trunk and limbs. The **vestibulospinal tract** originates in the vestibular nuclei of the brain stem and synapses with alpha motor neurons in the spinal cord that produce lower trunk and leg movement and play a central role in posture. The **tectospinal tract** begins in the superior colliculi and synapses with alpha motor neurons that control upper trunk (shoulder) and neck movements. The coordination of head and trunk movements, especially in the visual tracking of stimuli, is the main function of the tectospinal tract. The **lateral reticulospinal tract** starts in the medullary reticular formation and synapses with alpha motor neurons that activate the flexor muscles of the legs. The **medial reticulospinal tract** begins in the reticular formation in the pons (the pontine reticular formation) and synapses with alpha motor neurons that activate the extensor muscles of the legs. The coordinated activity of the lateral and medial reticulospinal tracts controls walking and running.

As you may have guessed from the descriptions of their functions, damage to the ventromedial tracts impairs posture and leg movements. For example, when Lawrence and Kuypers (1968b) severed the ventromedial tracts in monkeys, the animals had great difficulty standing and could not take more than a few steps without falling.

The **rubrospinal tract** originates in the red nucleus (*ruber* is Latin for "red") and synapses in the spinal cord with alpha motor neurons that control movements of the hands (but not the fingers), lower arms, lower legs, and feet (Figure 8.16). Axons in the rubrospinal tract are completely crossed and thus control arm and leg movements on the contralateral side of the body. In their study of monkeys with motor system damage, Lawrence and Kuypers (1968b) observed that monkeys with severed rubrospinal tracts had difficulty reaching for and holding food.

amyotrophic lateral sclerosis (ALS) A degenerative neuromuscular disease caused by degeneration of the corticospinal and corticobulbar tracts and the anterior horns of the spinal cord.

ventromedial tract One of four motor pathways originating in different parts of the subcortex that control movements of the trunk and limbs.

vestibulospinal tract A ventromedial tract that plays a central role in posture.

tectospinal tract A ventromedial tract that controls upper trunk (shoulder) and neck movements and coordinates the visual tracking of stimuli.

lateral reticulospinal tract A ventromedial tract that activates the flexor muscles of the legs.

medial reticulospinal tract A ventromedial tract that activates the extensor muscles of the legs.

rubrospinal tract A motor pathway that controls movements of the hands, lower arms, lower legs, and feet.

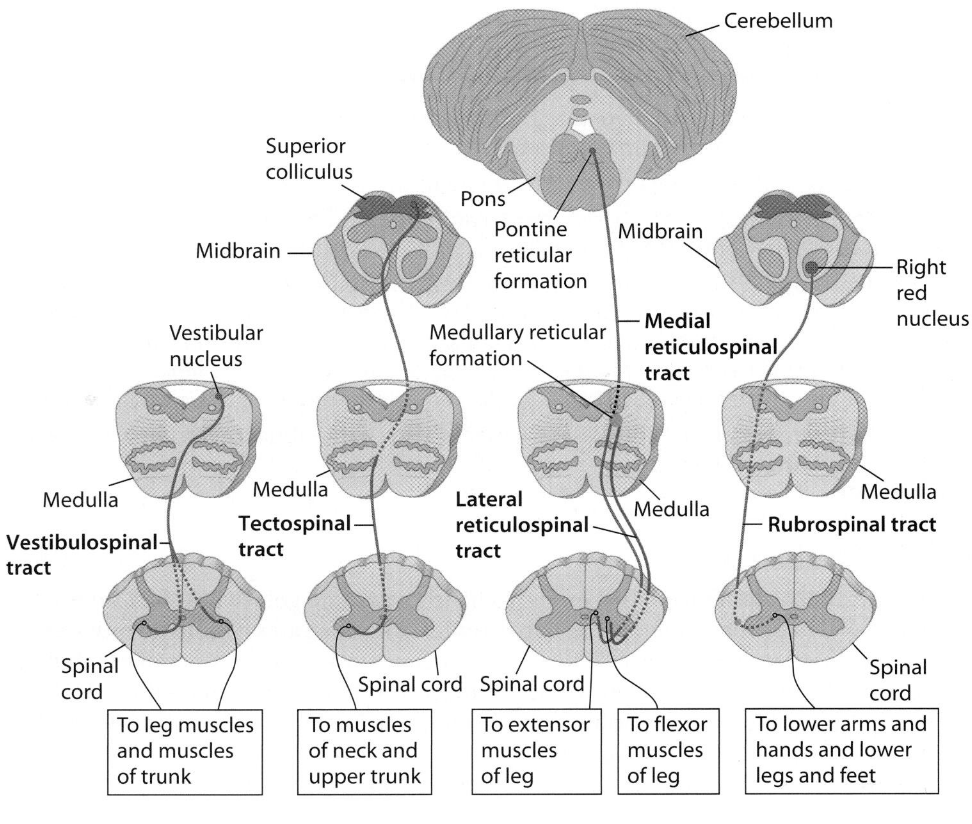

Figure 8.16
Fiber tracts that originate in subcortical areas The ventromedial tracts (vestibulospinal, tectospinal, and lateral and medial reticulospinal tracts) control movements of the trunk and limbs. The rubrospinal tract controls movements of the lower arms and hands and the lower legs and feet.

→ **What impairments result from damage to the ventromedial tracts? The rubrospinal tract?**

Table 8.1
Major Motor Pathways

Motor Tract	Point of Origin	Muscles Controlled
Corticospinal Tracts		
Lateral corticospinal tract	Finger, hand, arm, lower leg, and foot region of primary motor cortex	Fingers, hands, arms, lower legs, and feet
Ventral corticospinal tract	Trunk and upper leg region of primary motor cortex	Trunk and upper legs
Corticobulbar Tract	Face region of primary motor cortex	Face and tongue
Ventromedial Tracts		
Vestibulospinal tract	Vestibular nuclei of brain stem	Lower trunk and legs
Tectospinal tract	Superior colliculi	Neck and upper trunk
Lateral reticulospinal tract	Medullary reticular formation	Flexor muscles of legs
Medial reticulospinal tract	Pontine reticular formation	Extensor muscles of legs
Rubrospinal tract	Red nucleus	Hands (not fingers), lower arms, feet, and lower legs

Table 8.1 summarizes the major motor pathways, their points of origin, and the muscles they control. At one time, biological psychologists thought that motor functions were controlled by two independent motor systems: the pyramidal motor system, originating in the primary motor cortex and mediating voluntary movements, and the extrapyramidal motor system, beginning in subcortical areas and controlling involuntary movements. The evidence now indicates extensive interaction between the tracts that originate in motor cortex and those that originate in subcortical areas. The interaction is mediated by collateral axons of corticospinal tract neurons that synapse with the ventromedial and rubrospinal tracts. These connections help coordinate the motor functions required for everyday activities.

Checkpoint

Using what you know about the various motor circuits, describe which parts of the body would be affected by a stroke in the right motor cortex.

REVIEW

- Originating mainly in the primary motor cortex, the corticospinal tract controls the fingers, hands, arms, trunk, legs, and feet.
- The corticobulbar tract controls movements of the face and tongue.
- Control of most of the body's musculature is contralateral; trunk and upper leg muscles are controlled ipsilaterally.
- Beginning in the vestibular nuclei, the vestibulospinal tract controls lower trunk and leg movements and plays a central role in posture. The tectospinal tract controls the upper trunk and neck and coordinates head and trunk movements, especially visual tracking. The lateral reticulospinal tract activates the flexor muscles of the legs; the medial reticulospinal tract controls the extensor muscles of the legs.
- The rubrospinal tract controls movements of the hands (but not the fingers), lower arms, legs, and feet.

The Cerebellum

With extensive practice, Rhea executes nearly the same golf swing each time she is faced with a particular shot. The consistent swing illustrates a **ballistic movement,** a movement that is a well-practiced habit, occurs rapidly, and is not dependent on sensory feedback. Ballistic movements are controlled by the cerebellum, the brain area responsible for developing rapid, coordinated responses or habits (Lalonde & Botez-Marquard, 1997; Nixon, 2003).

ballistic movement A habitual, rapid movement that does not depend on sensory feedback.

Components of the Cerebellum

The cerebellum (from the Latin meaning "little brain") is located behind and beneath the cerebral cortex. It consists of two hemispheres, with an outer surface that is extremely convoluted, like the cerebral cortex (Figure 8.17). Representing just 10% of the mass of the brain, the cerebellum contains more than half of its neurons.

Input to (and output from) the cerebellum is conveyed by large bundles of axons known as *peduncles,* coming from several neural structures. The bundles of axons pass through the pons into the white matter of the cerebellum and then into the cerebellar cortex, bringing information from the primary motor cortex, about motor activity; the vestibular system, about balance and the position of the head in space; and the spinal cord, about the position of the limbs (proprioception) and the extent of muscle contraction. The cerebellum integrates all this information and determines whether ongoing movements are deviating from their intended course.

If movements begin to deviate, the cerebellum can correct them by sending signals to other movement-related structures. For example, within the white matter, **deep cerebellar nuclei** (see Figure 8.17) project to the ventral lateral thalamus, which in turn projects to the premotor cortex and the primary motor cortex. Axons of the deep cerebellar nuclei also project to the red nucleus and to the descending reticular formation, and both of these structures are connected to the alpha motor neurons of the spinal cord.

The process the cerebellum uses for coordinating ballistic movements is complex. The cerebellar cortex has several different cell types (Figure 8.18). Input to the cerebellar cortex comes from neurons called *climbing fibers* and *mossy fibers,* which have an excitatory influence on their targets, the Purkinje cells and granule cells, respectively. Additional cell types in the cerebellar cortex include Golgi cells and stellate cells, both of which have inhibitory effects that moderate the input to and output from the cerebellum. The axons of the granule cells are called *parallel fibers.*

Output from the cerebellar cortex is transmitted by **Purkinje cells,** which use GABA and thus have an exclusively inhibitory effect (Pugh & Raman, 2005). An

deep cerebellar nucleus A group of neurons that correct movements in progress.

Purkinje cell An output cell from the cerebellar cortex, which has an exclusively inhibitory effect.

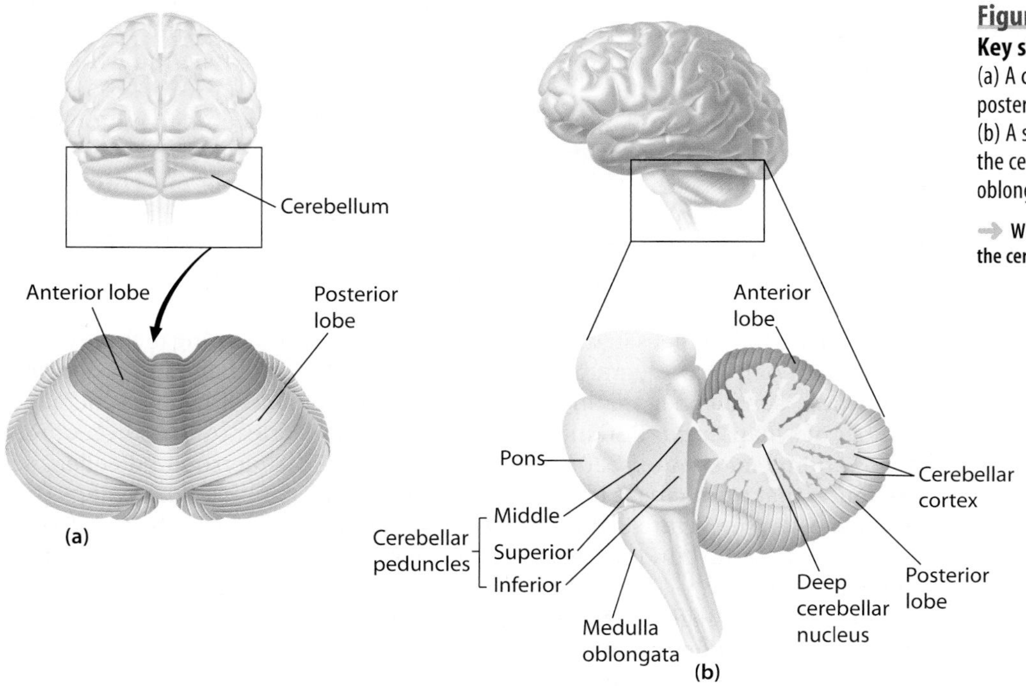

Figure 8.17

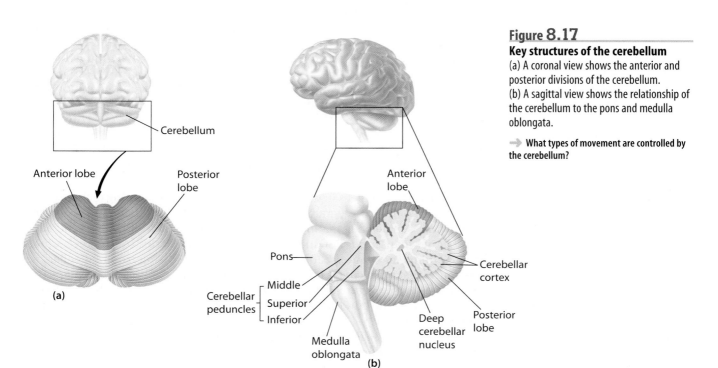

Key structures of the cerebellum

(a) A coronal view shows the anterior and posterior divisions of the cerebellum.

(b) A sagittal view shows the relationship of the cerebellum to the pons and medulla oblongata.

What types of movement are controlled by the cerebellum?

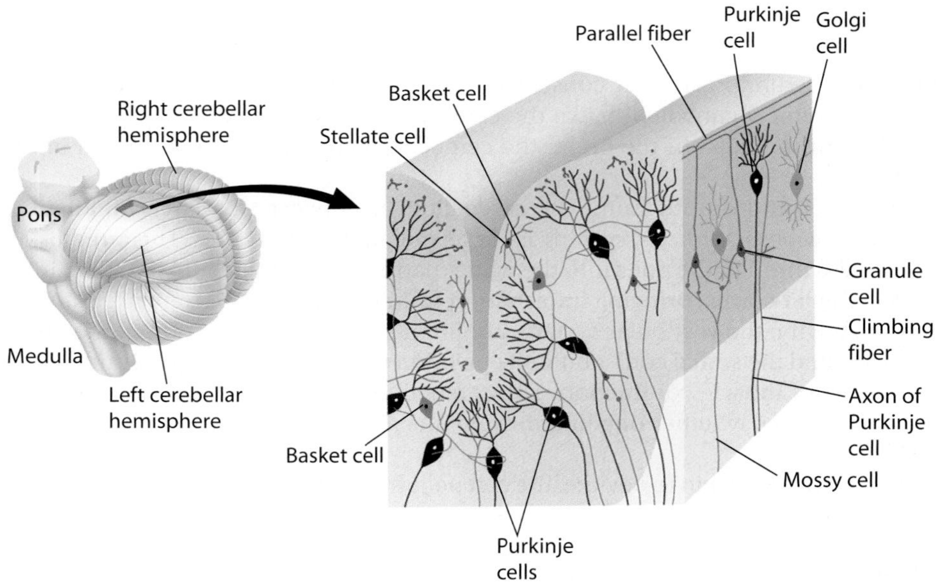

Figure 8.18
The cellular structure of the cerebellar cortex Messages enter the cerebellar cortex through the climbing and mossy fibers and exit through the Purkinje cells. Other cells in the cerebellar cortex (granule cell, Golgi cell, basket cell, and stellate cell) act to moderate the input to and output from the cerebellum.

➡ **Are the mossy fibers inhibitory or excitatory?**

active Purkinje cell inhibits neighboring Purkinje cells, as well as surrounding **basket cells,** which have an inhibitory influence on Purkinje cells. Through the combination of excitation and inhibition, Purkinje cells fire at a high rate, producing a continual state of inhibition in the deep cerebellar nuclei. Thus, the extensive circuitry of the cerebellar cortex produces its effect on movement through inhibition and disinhibition.

Plasticity of the Cerebellum

As noted earlier, structural (synaptic) changes in the primary motor cortex are responsible for the changes in a movement as it is repeated, whereas the primary motor cortex plays only a minor role in the changes that occur with the sequencing of movements and when movement is associated with sensory stimuli. The cerebellum has a complementary role: Structural changes within the cerebellum allow for movement changes during sequencing movements or when associating a movement with an environmental event (motor skill learning), but the cerebellum plays little role in improvements in movement with repetition (Kleim & others, 1997).

Extensive evidence exists for the central role of the cerebellum in motor learning. For example, cerebellar damage makes it difficult to develop conditioned motor habits (Bracha & others, 2000) and to combine simple movements into complex ones (Laforce & Doyon, 2001). Although movement is still possible after such damage, it is neither rapid nor coordinated. The direction, force, velocity, aim, and/or timing of the movement can be impaired (Baizer & others, 1999; Diedrichsen & others, 2005; Timmann & others, 1999).

The structural changes in the cerebellum during motor learning include the establishment of motor programs or circuits (Ito, 2000). Rats trained on a complex motor task, such as negotiating an elevated obstacle course, have an increased number of synapses per Purkinje cell in the cerebellar cortex (Anderson & others, 1996; Federmeier & others, 2002; Kim & others, 2002). Anderson and colleagues also found that the increase involved parallel fiber and climbing fiber synapses on Purkinje cells (see Figure 8.18). Activation of the parallel fibers enhances the responsiveness of the Purkinje cell and allows it to trigger the motor response (Federmeier & others).

Other studies suggest that motor planning from the cerebral cortex and feedback about ongoing movement from the spinal cord affect the mossy fiber neurons, which activate granule cells and ultimately Purkinje cells (Braitenberg & others, 1997; Heck & Sultan, 2002). The output from the Purkinje cells results in

basket cell A cerebellar neuron that has an inhibitory influence on Purkinje cells.

basal ganglia A group of three structures that integrates voluntary movements; consists of the caudate nucleus, the putamen, and the globus pallidus.

motor behaviors such as Rhea's swing to hit the golf ball. Specific changes within synapses enable the cerebellum to create neural motor programs, as we discuss in more detail in Chapter 14.

Consequences of Cerebellar Damage

Individuals with cerebellar damage can have difficulty maintaining a stable posture, making movements such as walking unsteady. Speech can be slurred and eye movements uncoordinated. Focusing on an object may be difficult because of problems in coordinating the angle and position of the lens, which is controlled by fine ciliary muscles, or because of impaired saccadic eye movements (Chapter 6), which normally shift the eyes from one fixation point to the next.

Persons suspected of driving while intoxicated may be asked by a police officer to shut their eyes, hold one arm straight out, and then touch their nose—something most people can do easily. An intoxicated person may move the finger too far and in the wrong direction and poke himself or herself in the eye. Neurons in the cerebellum are sensitive to alcohol, and alcohol intoxication can lead to signs of cerebellar malfunction (Figure 8.19).

Studies of individuals with cerebellar damage suggest that the cerebellum may play a significant role in cognitive behaviors in addition to its role in the fine-tuning of motor movements and in motor learning. For example, a study of two young adult twins who had sustained cerebellar stroke damage revealed linguistic difficulties such as comprehension deficits, aggrammatism, and reading and writing disorders (Fabbro & others, 2004). Both twins also showed relatively poor performance on a visuospatial short-term memory task (copying a figure from memory). Defective attention has been suggested to be the common denominator in the cognitive deficits seen in people with cerebellar damage, and some recent studies have supported this idea (Allen & Courchesne, 2003; Golla & others, 2005).

The *Scientific American* Spotlight, "Probing Cerebellar Function," describes experiments that show that the cerebellum may play a role in processing sensory information in addition to its functions in controlling movement and in cognitive activities.

Figure 8.19
Field sobriety tests target cerebellar function

➔ **Why might cerebellar damage be confused with alcohol intoxication?**

The Basal Ganglia

The **basal ganglia,** a group of structures that integrates movement and controls postural adjustments and muscle tone, consist of three subcortical nuclei located close to the thalamus: the *caudate nucleus,* a long, curving structure; the oval-shaped *putamen,* adjacent to the caudate nucleus; and the *globus pallidus* or "pale globe" (Figure 8.20). In cross section, the caudate nucleus and putamen appear striped because of the heavily myelinated axons running through them and

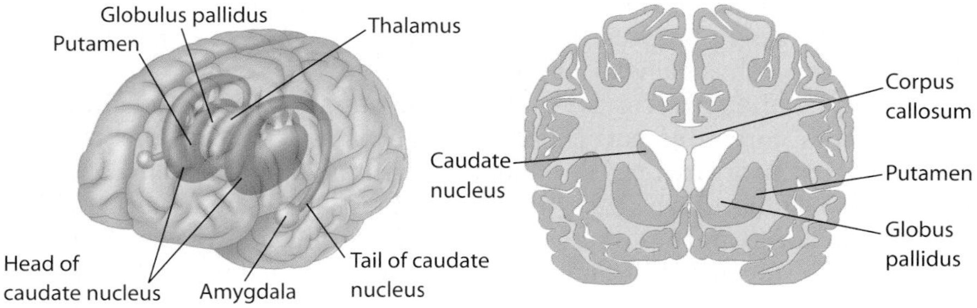

Figure 8.20
The basal ganglia The basal ganglia are involved in the control of movement.

➔ **Which structures form the corpus striatum?**

Scientific American Spotlight

Probing Cerebellar Function

James M. Bower and Lawrence M. Parsons

To discriminate between the cerebellum's possible roles in coordinating movement and integrating sensory input, we devised a four-part experiment. We used a technique called functional magnetic resonance imaging to reveal brain activity in the cerebellum of six healthy people while they were either sensing a stimulus on their fingers without moving them or picking up and dropping small objects. In the first scenario, we immobilized a subject's hands and rubbed pieces of sandpaper gently across their fingertips (a). Sometimes they were asked to compare the coarseness of two different types of sandpaper (b). Both were purely sensory tasks, but the latter one required each person to discriminate between what they were feeling on each hand.

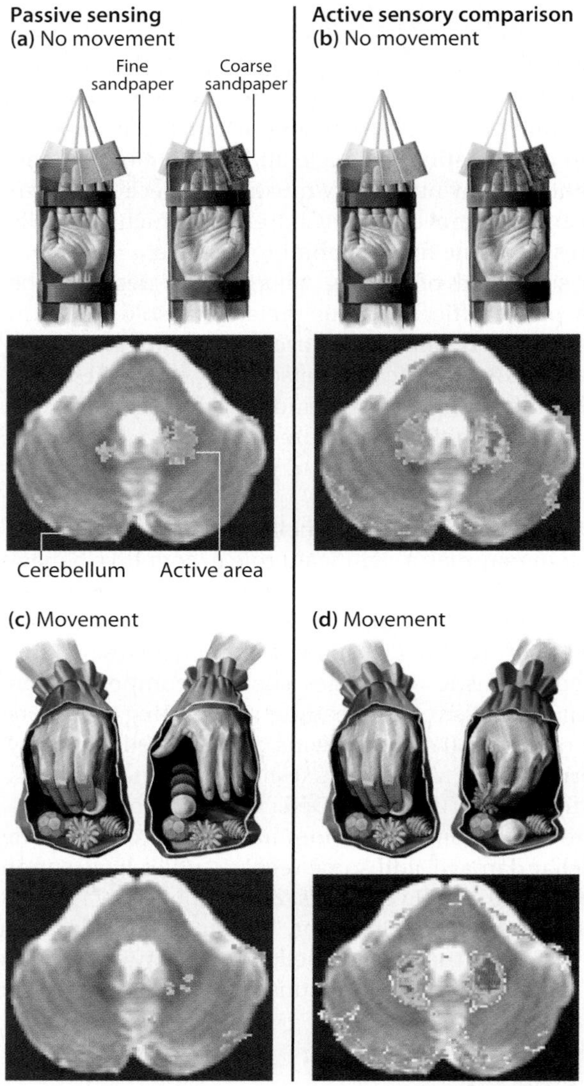

The second scenario involved both sensory and motor aspects. A volunteer placed his or her hands into separate bags that contained small wooden balls of different shapes and textures. In the first task (c), the person was told to randomly pick up and drop the balls, paying little heed to their shapes. In the second task (d), the individual was asked to compare the shape and feel of two balls every time he or she picked one up in each hand.

The cerebellum showed very little activity during the task that simply required picking up and dropping balls (c). In general, it was most active when the subjects were evaluating what they were sensing, either while moving (d) or still (b). These findings and others support our hypothesis that the cerebellum's main role is in processing sensory information rather than in controlling movement.

From: *Scientific American*, vol. 289(2), p. 56

are often collectively referred to as the **corpus striatum,** meaning "striped body." Because the caudate nucleus and putamen are phylogenetically newer (evolved later) than the globus pallidus, they are also called the *neostriatum* to differentiate them from the globus pallidus, or *paleostriatum.*

The corpus striatum receives input from the *substantia nigra* and from all areas of the cerebral cortex, but particularly from the primary motor cortex and the primary somatosensory cortex. The caudate nucleus and putamen are connected to the globus pallidus, which sends messages to the thalamus and then on to the primary motor cortex and brain stem structures controlling movement. As a unit, the basal ganglia integrate movement through interconnections with the primary motor cortex, the cerebellum, and other motor centers in the brain, including the

corpus striatum The part of the basal ganglia consisting of the caudate nucleus and putamen.

substantia nigra and red nucleus (Figure 8.20). They control postural adjustments and muscle tone through the ventromedial tracts.

The effects of damage to the basal ganglia provide information about their role in the integration of movement (Abbruzzese & Berardelli, 2003; Ring & Serra-Mestres, 2002). Individuals with damaged basal ganglia may show impaired muscle tone, postural instability, and poorly integrated movements, and they may have difficulty performing voluntary movements such as standing or walking. You may recognize these symptoms as somewhat characteristic of Parkinson's disease, which is caused by abnormally low levels of dopamine in the circuit connecting the substantia nigra to the basal ganglia and the degeneration of dopaminergic synapses in the basal ganglia. Huntington's disease also results from damage to the basal ganglia. This degenerative neurological disorder is characterized by rapid, uncontrolled movements of the limbs and facial muscles. As the disease progresses, individuals lose the ability to walk or speak.

In addition to their motor functions, basal ganglia structures play a role in emotion, reinforcement, and cognition (Haber, 2003; Postle & D'Esposito, 1999, 2003). For example, Postle and D'Esposito used fMRI to show that the human caudate nucleus is involved in spatially coded memory. Other nonmotor functions are evident from the study of people with degenerative neurological disorders. Although Parkinson's disease is considered primarily a movement disorder, it can also entail cognitive impairments and deficits in emotional processing (Zgaljardic & others, 2003). For example, neuropsychiatric problems seen in Parkinson's patients include dementia, depression, and anxiety disorders, with panic attacks being particularly prevalent (Lauterbach, 2004). The cognitive deficits, however, may reflect disordered connections between the corpus striatum and the frontal lobes (Lewis & others, 2003).

In a study comparing 31 patients with degenerative diseases of the cerebellum, 21 with Huntington's disease, and 29 neurologically healthy subjects, the individuals with Huntington's disease and those with cerebellar degeneration had a high rate of psychiatric and cognitive disorders (Leroi & others, 2002). Again, the cognitive disorders may reflect pathology involving the connections in the frontal lobe with the corpus striatum (Watkins & others, 2003). Psychiatric and cognitive disorders also occur in neurologically asymptomatic carriers of the Huntington's disease gene, who were found to have significantly worse recognition memory and more irritability than healthy controls (Berrios & others, 2002). The basal ganglia may be selectively involved in identifying the emotion of disgust. Wang and colleagues (2003) found that Chinese patients with Huntington's disease were severely impaired in recognizing facial expressions of that particular emotion.

Another function of the basal ganglia may be to select the appropriate action from among those considered by the cortex, as suggested by an influential model of basal ganglia functioning proposed by Gurney and his colleagues (Gurney & others, 2001a, 2001b). Gurney's response-selection model ties in well with evidence indicating that activity in dopamine neurons provides a reinforcement signal for the learning of sensorimotor associations in the corpus striatum (Hollerman & others, 2000; Suri & others, 2001). The model also easily accounts for the lack of action displayed by people with Parkinson's disease. Gurney and coworkers (2004) have described in detail the features and advantages of their modeling approach and have used robotic implementation to test the response-selection characteristics of the model successfully (Girard & others, 2003).

Checkpoint

Describe the role of Purkinje cells in the control of movement. What are the effects of cerebellar damage?

REVIEW

- The cerebellum contains more than half the neurons in the brain, enabling it to produce rapid, coordinated, skilled movements.
- The cerebellum receives information about motor activity from the primary motor cortex, about balance and head position from the vestibular system, and about

Parkinson's disease A degenerative neurological disorder characterized by rigidity of the limbs and muscle tremors.

bradykinesia A movement disorder characterized by slowed movement.

festination A tendency in a movement disorder to speed up a walking pace to running.

the position of the limbs and the extent of muscle contraction from the spinal cord. It sends information first to the ventral lateral thalamus and then to the primary motor cortex, as well as to the red nucleus and the descending reticular formation.

- The cerebellum plays a central role in motor learning, which is accompanied by structural (synaptic) changes.
- The basal ganglia consist of the caudate nucleus and putamen, collectively called the corpus striatum, and the globus pallidus; they integrate movement, control postural adjustments and muscle tone, and may be involved in selecting appropriate actions.
- The corpus striatum receives input from the primary motor cortex and the primary somatosensory cortex, and from the substantia nigra. The corpus striatum is connected to the globus pallidus, which sends information to the thalamus and then to the primary motor cortex or to the brain stem structures involved in movement.

Damage to the Motor System: Parkinson's Disease and Huntington's Disease

Now that you have learned about the neurological basis of movement, you can appreciate more fully how damage to the motor system can lead to the severe motor impairments experienced by individuals with Parkinson's disease or Huntington's disease.

Parkinson's Disease

Parkinson's disease, which we talked about in several previous chapters, was first described by English physician James Parkinson. Parkinson wrote in 1817 that people with the disorder displayed such symptoms as "involuntary tremulous motion," bent posture, and a tendency to progress from walking to running, without any apparent sensory or mental impairment. The tremors are the most visible symptom of Parkinson's disease; they occur intermittently and worsen when a limb is resting, hence the phrase "tremor at rest." One type of tremor is called *pill-rolling,* or movement as if a pill were being rolled between the thumb and fingers.

Parkinson's disease is also characterized by increasing rigidity of the limbs caused by increased muscle tone in both flexor and extensor muscles. When a limb is moved passively, an initial resistance to movement gives way to some movement, followed by a return of resistance. This stop-start type of activity is called *cogwheel rigidity.*

Posture and locomotion are also impaired. When the individual is sitting, the head may be drooped forward; when standing, the body is usually stooped (Figure 8.21). Another characteristic is slowed movement called **bradykinesia,** causing the person to have great difficulty taking the first step from a stationary position. Once the person starts walking, the footsteps are short, with a wide base because of impaired balance, and often become faster and faster until the person is running. This tendency to speed up walking to the point of running is called **festination.** Normal movements such as brushing the teeth, buttoning a coat, or tying shoelaces take more and more effort. Difficulty in speaking also occurs, with the voice becoming weak and monotonous. Lack of facial expression and lack of spontaneous blinking are commonly seen.

Figure 8.21
The stooped posture of Parkinson's disease

➡ **Damage to what area of the brain results in the stooped posture of a person with Parkinson's disease?**

Most people with Parkinson's disease do not have all these symptoms, and the actual symptoms experienced vary widely. For example, in one person tremors may predominate, whereas rigidity and bradykinesia are the main symptoms experienced by another person. In fact, a substantial percentage of Parkinson's disease patients experience only slight tremor or none at all.

Although the symptoms of Parkinson's disease usually begin at around age 50 or 60, the disease can appear much earlier. Actor Michael J. Fox (star of the film *Back to the Future* and the television series *Spin City*) was diagnosed with Parkinson's disease in his early thirties. Fox's autobiography, *Lucky Man: A Memoir,* was published, with all profits from the sale of the book slated to go to The Michael J. Fox Foundation for Parkinson's Disease Research (Fox, 2002). The first sign of the disease may be a tremor in one hand or some stiffness in the muscles of a leg. Over time, the tremors and rigidity worsen, and movement becomes increasingly impaired. The motor disturbances are caused by the degeneration of the dopamine-producing cells of the substantia nigra that synapse with the basal ganglia. Damage to this nigrostriatal dopaminergic system leads to the bradykinesia, whereas the rigidity and tremors are thought to result from excessive activity in a neural loop extending from the ventrolateral thalamus to the primary motor cortex and back again.

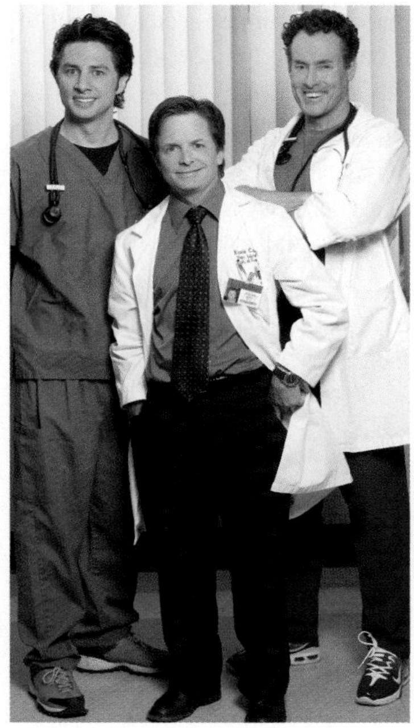
ABC/TOUCHSTONE PICTURES

Following his appearance on the NBC comedy *Scrubs,* Michael J. Fox poses with two of the show's lead actors.

Although James Parkinson did not think that the people with this disorder suffered from impaired intellect, cognitive deficits do occur in approximately 40% of cases (Emre, 2003). The cognitive deficits, which may reflect impairments in the striatal connections with the frontal lobes, include problems with learning, memory, attention, and judgment, and people with Parkinson's often display apathy and social withdrawal. Not surprisingly, Parkinson's disease is associated with atrophy of the hippocampus (Camicioli & others, 2003).

A variety of causes have been suggested for Parkinson's disease (Schapira, 2001; Siderowf, 2001; Siderowf & Stern, 2003). For example, an attack of encephalitis can lead to Parkinson's disease, as evidenced in the movie *Awakenings,* which was based on a book by Oliver Sacks, a clinical neurologist. As Sacks reported, some victims of a 1916–1917 encephalitis epidemic underwent remarkable recovery following the administration of a drug used to treat patients with Parkinson's disease. Other possible causes of Parkinson's include arteriosclerosis, carbon monoxide or manganese poisoning, trauma to the head, and syphilitic damage to the brain. Unfortunately, in many cases the origin of the disease is unknown.

Research evidence for a genetic basis for Parkinson's disease has been accumulated recently (Chung & others, 2003; Muthane & others, 2001). Chung and colleagues, for example, discuss 10 genetic loci that have been linked to hereditary forms of the disease. According to Muthane and colleagues, epidemiological studies have uncovered significant variations in the prevalence of the disorder across populations, with the highest rates exhibited by populations of European origin.

One disease characteristic that may be associated with a specific gene is age at onset, and the gene that may be involved is one also associated with Alzheimer's disease, the apolipoprotein E (APOE) gene (Zareparsi & others, 2002). Other researchers, however, found that the APOE gene is not related to age at onset but is possibly related to dementia associated with Parkinson's disease (Parsian & others, 2002). In a population study in the Netherlands, Harhangi and colleagues (2000) found that one specific allele of the APOE gene increases the risk of Parkinson's disease, and particularly Parkinson's disease with dementia. A study of Alzheimer's patients reported that a variant of the APOE gene is significantly associated with cell loss in the substantia nigra, which would provide a neurological basis for the development of Parkinson's disease (Camicioli & others, 1999).

Important evidence indicates that at least some cases of Parkinson's disease involve environmental toxins. For example, Lewin (1985) reported that in a Canadian study examining the relationship between the incidence of Parkinson's disease in nine different regions of Quebec Province and the level of pesticide use in these regions, the correlation was a staggering .967. Further, there is a close chemical similarity between the herbicide paraquat and a substance known as MPTP, which was a contaminant in synthetic heroin injected by several young people in southern California in 1983. As a result of the injections, each of these individuals developed a severe form of Parkinson's disease (Ballard & others, 1985; Langston & others, 1983).

Since the discovery of the "frozen addicts," neuroscientists have learned that the contaminant MPTP is converted to MPP+, a chemical selectively toxic to dopaminergic neurons in the substantia nigra (Snyder & D'Amato, 1986). As subsequent

levodopa (L-dopa) A drug converted to dopamine in the brain; used to treat Parkinson's disease.

thalamotomy A psychosurgical treatment for Parkinson's disease that relieves tremors and improves rigidity but does not relieve bradykinesia.

pallidotomy A psychosurgical treatment for Parkinson's disease that reduces tremors, rigidity, and bradykinesia.

research has found, monkeys injected with MPTP provide researchers with an excellent animal model of Parkinson's disease (e.g., Heimer & others, 2002; Jan & others, 2000; Raz & others, 2001).

Since his diagnosis with Parkinson's disease, Michael J. Fox's therapy has been the drug Sinemet, which is a combination of levodopa (dihydroxyphenylalanine), or L-dopa, and carbidopa. **Levodopa (L-dopa)** is the mainstay of the treatment of Parkinson's disease and the drug Oliver Sacks gave to the victims of the encephalitis epidemic. L-dopa is a precursor of dopamine that can be converted into dopamine in the brain, thereby increasing the dopamine levels depleted by the disease. However, if L-dopa is administered by itself, much of it does not reach the brain; it is destroyed by enzymes in the intestine and blood plasma or converted to dopamine in the PNS, leading to nausea (Standaert & Young, 1996). The solution has been to combine L-dopa with carbidopa, which prevents the conversion of L-dopa to dopamine in the PNS, but not in the CNS.

L-dopa is highly effective in decreasing rigidity and improving movement, but it is less effective in reducing tremors (Julien, 2005). Side effects include nausea and vomiting, hypotension (low blood pressure), and cardiac dysrhythmias (abnormal heart activity). Unfortunately, the effectiveness of the drug declines as the destruction of dopaminergic neurons in the substantia nigra progresses (Kolb & Whishaw, 2003). Increasing the dosage has risks, such as the development of schizophrenic symptoms. Two dopaminergic agonists, bromocriptine mesylate and pergolide, can be substituted for L-dopa as its effectiveness begins to wane. Both drugs directly stimulate striatal dopaminergic receptors, but neither is as effective as L-dopa, and they have more negative side effects (Hughes, 1997).

Despite continuing to take Sinemet, Michael J. Fox noticed that his symptoms, especially the tremors, increased over the 7 years between receiving his diagnosis and revealing it to the public. His treatment at that point was a psychosurgical procedure called **thalamotomy,** in which the ventrolateral thalamus is excised. Thalamotomy was a common surgical intervention for Parkinson's disease in the 1950s and 1960s, as was pallidotomy, introduced in the late 1930s (Meyers, 1942). Pallidotomy decreased tremors and rigidity, but unlike thalamotomy, it also reduced bradykinesia (Lang & others, 1999). In **pallidotomy,** selected areas of the globus pallidus are destroyed, with damage to the posterior and ventral medial globus pallidus producing the most desirable effects.

Thalamotomy and pallidotomy—forms of psychosurgery—were more or less abandoned in the late 1960s following the introduction of drug treatments for Parkinson's disease. However, as the limitations of L-dopa and other dopaminergic agonists became apparent, psychosurgery reemerged as a viable treatment. There is considerable evidence for the effectiveness of both thalamotomy (Ohye & others, 2002; Zesiewicz & Hauser, 2001) and pallidotomy (Eskandar & others, 2000; Schrag & others, 1999) as treatments for Parkinson's disease patients. As you might expect, both psychosurgical procedures involve risk, with speech difficulties and concentration problems being the most likely side effects. The procedures are recommended only as the effectiveness of drug treatment diminishes. At this time, thalamotomy is the psychosurgery of choice when the predominant complaint is tremor, and pallidotomy is recommended for other patients (Krack & others, 2000).

Deep brain stimulation is a recently introduced alternative to thalamotomy (Benabid, 2003; Chan & others, 2001). The procedure involves high-frequency stimulation of the thalamus, and the effects are similar to those of L-dopa and thalamotomy, with fewer complications (Pahwa & others, 2001). By contrast, pallidal stimulation does not appear to be an effective alternative to pallidotomy (Tronnier & others, 1997).

Unfortunately, neither drug therapy nor psychosurgery cures Parkinson's disease. At their best, the psychosurgical treatments have the effect of turning the clock back 4 or 5 years for a Parkinson's disease patient. A newer procedure, the transplantation of fetal tissue into the corpus striatum, offers the promise of a cure

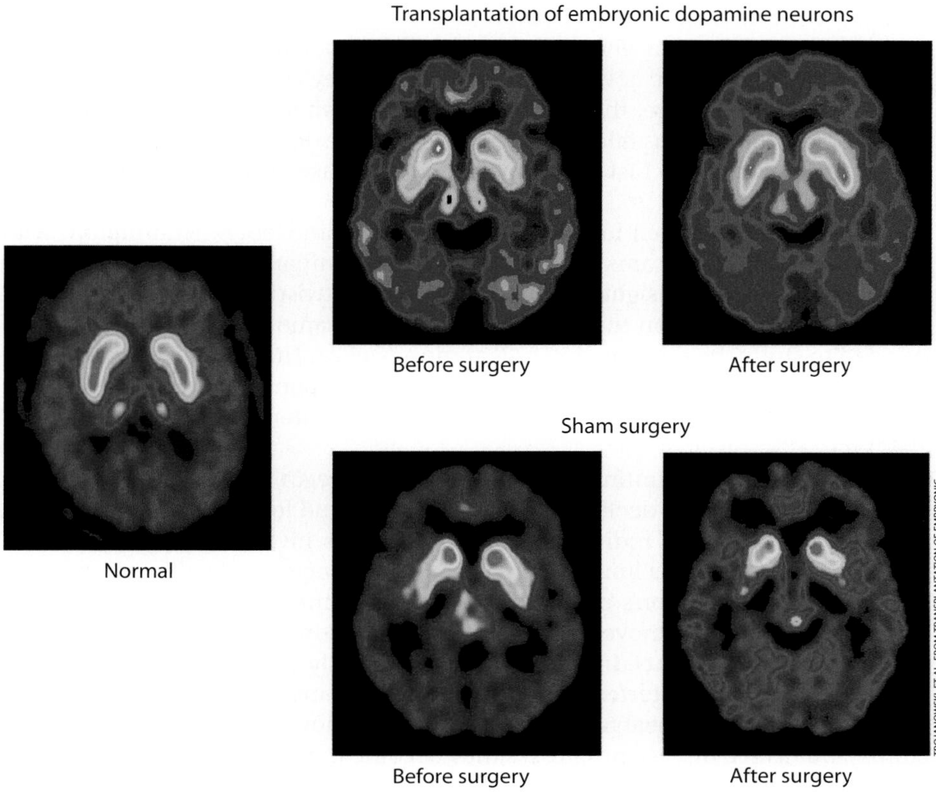

Figure 8.22
Fetal tissue implants and Parkinson's disease PET scans show the essentially normal appearance of activity in the basal ganglia of a Parkinson's disease patient following transplantation of embryonic dopamine neurons. No change is apparent following sham surgery.

➡ What is the implication of increased activity in the basal ganglia of a person with Parkinson's disease following implantation of fetal tissue?

(Figure 8.22), but the use of fetal tissue is controversial. Preliminary results have been encouraging, with an observed growth of dopaminergic neurons and enhanced synaptic connections, as well as an improvement in motor function (Borlongan & Sanberg, 2002; Lindvall, 2000). These results are preliminary, however, and further research is needed to demonstrate whether this is a viable treatment for Parkinson's disease.

As we have noted, treatment with L-dopa is at best a temporary solution for relieving Parkinson's symptoms. Recently, studies have shown that the drug deprenyl (also called selegiline) delays the need for patients to begin L-dopa therapy (Knoll, 2000). Deprenyl appears to postpone the onset of symptoms requiring L-dopa treatment, and patients taking L-dopa plus deprenyl live longer than those taking L-dopa alone. Deprenyl also may improve cognitive functions in Parkinson's disease patients (Dixit & others, 1999).

Deprenyl appears to protect dopaminergic neurons by preventing *apoptosis,* a form of cellular suicide. Cells are genetically programmed to die when they receive the appropriate signal, and a great deal of neuronal cell death occurs normally during development (Chapter 3). When apoptosis occurs in the adult, however, the result can be a neurodegenerative disease such as Parkinson's. Naoi and colleagues (2000) found that deprenyl protects dopaminergic neurons from apoptotic DNA damage. This protection occurred even after the deprenyl was removed from the experimental preparation, suggesting that it had initiated a process that prevented apoptotic neuronal destruction. Further research into the potentially beneficial effects of deprenyl in treating Parkinson's disease is clearly warranted.

Huntington's Disease

As we discussed in Chapter 3, **Huntington's disease** is an inherited neurological disorder caused by a dominant, defective gene on the short arm of chromosome 4. Individuals with Huntington's disease undergo a slow, progressive deterioration

Huntington's disease An inherited neurological disorder characterized by a slow, progressive deterioration of motor control, cognition, and emotion.

of motor control, cognition, and emotion (Bonelli & Hofmann, 2004; Kent, 2004). With the discovery of the genetic basis of this disorder, people with a family history of Huntington's can now determine whether they carry the gene before they have children. Of course, the ability to determine whether a person carries the gene leads to the obvious dilemma: Knowing that the disease is currently untreatable, if you had a family history of Huntington's disease, would you want to know if you had the gene?

The disorder is named for the American physician George Huntington, who first observed the symptoms as a child when he accompanied his physician father on hospital rounds. The sight of two tall, thin women twisting and grimacing made such a big impression on the boy that, when he became a physician himself, he decided to study the disorder. In 1872, at the age of 22, Huntington wrote the first complete description of the disease. One of the most famous victims of Huntington's disease was the American folksinger and songwriter, Woody Guthrie (1912–1967).

The symptoms of Huntington's disease usually begin between the ages of 30 and 50, typically with a decline in physical activity and loss of interest in worldly activities (apathy). The individual soon experiences involuntary movements of whole limbs or parts of a limb, which may appear dance-like, leading to the alternative name, Huntington's chorea (from the Greek meaning "choral dance"). At first, these involuntary movements are slight and inconsistent, but over time they become more pronounced and constant, eventually involving the head, face, trunk, and limbs, and interfering with such voluntary movements as walking, writing, swallowing, and speaking. Initially, voluntary movements become slow and clumsy, but as the disease progresses they become impossible.

Cognitive deficits produced by Huntington's disease—which may reflect frontal lobe dysfunction rather than damage to the basal ganglia—include impaired storage and later retrieval of information, deficits in visuospatial problem solving, poor abstract reasoning, and diminished cognitive flexibility. Severe dementia is also a characteristic. Not surprisingly, anxiety and depression are common in people with Huntington's. They experience a gradual reduction in the ability to carry out daily living activities and difficulties in social communication and judgment, and they tend to withdraw from social activities. The symptoms of Huntington's disease worsen over 15 years or so, and death eventually results from a loss of muscle control.

Autopsy studies of the brains of people with Huntington's disease reveal massive pathology (Halliday & others, 1998; Harris & others, 1992). There is shrinkage and thinning of the cerebral cortex as well as substantial decreases in the number of small neurons of the caudate nucleus and putamen and large neurons of the globus pallidus, as revealed by gross atrophy of the basal ganglia (Figure 8.23).

GABA and ACh, the neurotransmitters of the basal ganglia, normally act to inhibit dopaminergic neurons in the nigrostriatal tract, which extends from the substantia nigra to the basal ganglia. The death of neurons in the basal ganglia causes a significant decrease in GABA and ACh levels, resulting in increased activity in the nigrostriatal dopaminergic pathway and the appearance of the involuntary movements that characterize Huntington's disease. This model of Huntington's disease is supported by the observation that the administration of L-dopa, which increases dopamine in the brain, exacerbates the symptoms of the disease. In addition, Parkinson's patients may develop Huntington-like symptoms if they receive an excess of L-dopa to treat their motor symptoms (Walters & others, 1990). Large doses of the antipsychotic drug clozapine, which decreases dopaminergic activity,

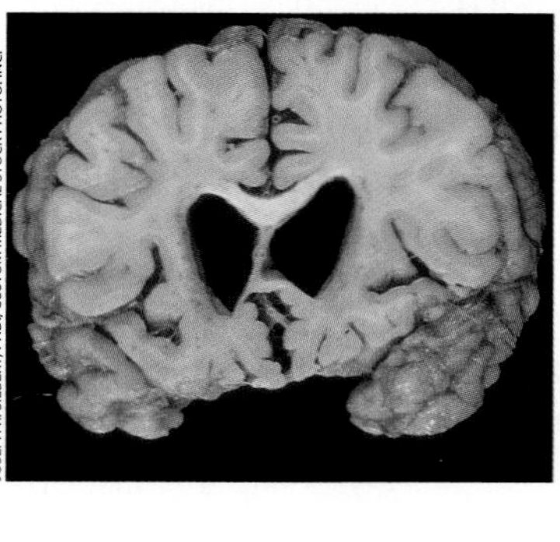
JOSEPH R. SIEBERT, PHD./CUSTOM MEDICAL STOCK PHOTO, INC.

Figure 8.23

The corpus striatum and Huntington's disease The death of neurons in the caudate nucleus and putamen leads to substantial enlargement of the lateral ventricles, as seen clearly in this coronal section of the brain.

→ **Why does neuron death in the corpus striatum cause enlargement of the lateral ventricles?**

may be of benefit in managing the motor impairments caused by the disease (Factor & Friedman, 1997).

Additional medications may be prescribed to help control movement and emotional symptoms. For example, antidepressants are often used to treat depression and obsessive-compulsive behavior. Tranquilizers, such as the benzodiazepines (Xanax, Valium), may be prescribed to treat anxiety and chorea (irregular, jerky movements), and botulinum toxin is sometimes used to treat symptoms such as jaw clenching. Mood stabilizers, such as lithium, may be given if the Huntington's patient experiences mania or bipolar disorder.

Checkpoint

What is the prognosis for individuals with Parkinson's disease? Huntington's disease? Contrast the effects on the nigrostriatal pathway of Parkinson's disease and Huntington's disease.

REVIEW

- The motor impairments of Parkinson's disease (slowed movement, impaired posture) are caused by the degeneration of dopaminergic cells of the substantia nigra that synapse with the basal ganglia; damage to the neural circuit between the ventral thalamus and the motor cortex causes the rigidity and tremors at rest.
- Drug treatments for Parkinson's disease include levodopa (L-dopa), converted by dopaminergic neurons into dopamine, and carbidopa, which prevents the destruction of L-dopa by enzymes in the intestine and blood plasma and the conversion of L-dopa in the PNS. Deprenyl apparently protects against neuronal apoptosis, delays the need for L-dopa treatment, and improves cognitive and motor functioning.
- Psychosurgical treatments for Parkinson's include thalamotomy, which relieves tremors and improves rigidity without affecting bradykinesia, and pallidotomy, which reduces tremors, rigidity, and bradykinesia. Fetal tissue implantation has also been tried as a treatment for Parkinson's disease.
- In Huntington's disease, atrophy of the cerebral cortex and basal ganglia causes an inability to control voluntary movements. The loss of inhibitory GABA and cholinergic neurons in the basal ganglia increases activity in the nigrostriatal dopaminergic pathways.

Chapter Review

Key Terms

actin (p. 272)
alpha motor neuron (p. 272)
amyotrophic lateral sclerosis (ALS) (p. 288)
annulospiral ending (p. 275)
apraxia (p. 286)
apraxia of speech (p. 286)
ballistic movement (p. 290)
basal ganglia (p. 293)
basket cell (p. 292)
bradykinesia (p. 296)
cerebral palsy (p. 269)
constructional apraxia (p. 286)
contralateral neglect (p. 285)
corpus striatum (p. 294)
corticobulbar tract (p. 287)
corticospinal tract (p. 287)
deep cerebellar nucleus (p. 291)
dorsolateral prefrontal cortex (p. 280)
extensor muscle (p. 270)
extrafusal muscle fiber (p. 272)
fast-twitch muscle (p. 274)
festination (p. 296)
flexor muscle (p. 271)
gamma motor neuron (p. 279)
Golgi tendon organ (p. 277)
Huntington's disease (p. 299)
Ia fiber (p. 276)
Ib fiber (p. 277)
intermediate-twitch muscle (p. 274)
intrafusal muscle fiber (p. 275)
lateral reticulospinal tract (p. 289)
levodopa (L-dopa) (p. 298)
limb apraxia (p. 286)
medial reticulospinal tract (p. 289)
mirror neurons (p. 281)
monosynaptic stretch reflex (p. 275)
motor end plate (p. 272)
motor unit (p. 274)
movement (p. 268)
muscle fiber (p. 271)
muscle spindle (p. 275)

muscle tone (p. 279)
myasthenia gravis (p. 273)
myofibril (p. 271)
myofilament (p. 272)
myosin (p. 272)
neuromuscular junction (p. 272)
pallidotomy (p. 298)
Parkinson's disease (p. 296)
patellar reflex (p. 275)
polysynaptic reflex (p. 276)
posterior parietal cortex (p. 285)
precentral gyrus (p. 282)
premotor cortex (p. 281)
primary motor cortex (p. 282)
Purkinje cell (p. 291)
pyramidal cell (p. 282)
Renshaw cell (p. 278)
rubrospinal tract (p. 289)
sarcomere (p. 272)
secondary motor cortex (p. 281)
skeletal muscle (p. 270)
slow-twitch muscle (p. 274)
supplementary motor area (p. 281)
tectospinal tract (p. 289)
tendon (p. 270)
thalamotomy (p. 298)
ventromedial tract (p. 289)
vestibulospinal tract (p. 289)
withdrawal reflex (p. 276)

Suggested Readings

Fox, M. J. (2002). *Lucky man: A memoir.* New York: Hyperion.

Kandel, E. R., Schwartz, J. H., & Jessell, T. M. (2000). *Principles of neural science* (4th ed.). New York: McGraw-Hill.

Rothwell, J. (1994). *Control of human voluntary movement* (2nd ed.). London: Chapman and Hall.

Sacks, O. (1999). *Awakenings.* New York: Vintage.

Sanes, J. N., & Donoghue, J. P. (2000). Plasticity and primary motor cortex. *Annual Review of Neuroscience, 23,* 393–415.

Tanji, J. (2001). Sequential organization of multiple movements: Involvement of cortical motor areas. *Annual Review of Neuroscience, 24,* 631–651.

Thach, W. T. (1998). A role for the cerebellum in learning movement coordination. *Neurobiology of Learning and Memory, 70,* 177–188.

Critical Thinking Questions

1. Sonja is about to run the most important race of her life. She moves to the starting block, her left foot almost touching the line, and her right leg bent so that the foot rests against the block. As she waits for the signal, Sonja can feel her muscles tense. When the gun fires, she leaps forward and flies down the track. What neural process enables Sonja to be ready to run this race? What neural mechanism is responsible for the initiation of her movements down the track?
2. Although John has taken lessons for years, he still does not play the piano well. His sister, Sybil, plays the piano very well, but she is a weaker tennis player than John. What neural systems control movements such as playing the piano and playing tennis? Suggest some neurological reasons why John and Sybil differ in their abilities.
3. Theresa's father had suffered from an undiagnosed motor disorder, for which he was institutionalized during the last several years of his life. Now in her thirties, Theresa is starting to drop things and to experience occasional dance-like movements that she cannot control and cannot explain. In his late fifties, Dennis is beginning to experience some slowness of movement and rigidity, and tremors in his hands when they are at rest that resemble pill-rolling movements. What neurological disorders might be causing Theresa's and Dennis's symptoms? Explain the neurological deficits responsible for their motor problems.

Fill-in-the Blank Questions

1. Movement is stimulated by the ______ neurons of the central nervous system.
2. The contraction of ______ muscles enables Sam to operate the ski machine.
3. Skeletal muscles are attached to bones by ______.
4. Contraction of a(n) ______ muscle causes the movement of a limb away from the body.
5. Each muscle fiber is composed of many ______, which contain two kinds of myofilaments, one made of the protein ______ and the other of the protein ______.
6. The muscle fiber controlled by an alpha motor neuron is called a(n) ______.
7. The ______ is the part of the extrafusal muscle fiber where the muscle fiber synapses with the motor neuron.
8. In ______, the immune system produces antibodies that destroy the cholinergic receptors at neuromuscular junctions.
9. A motor neuron and all the muscle fibers it controls are known as a(n) ______.

10. The ______ muscles produce the fastest contractions, the ______ muscles produce the slowest contractions, and the ______ muscles produce contractions that fall in between.

11. The knee-jerk reflex is also called the ______.

12. The muscle spindle contains muscle fibers known as ______.

13. The axons of the annulospiral endings are called ______ fibers.

14. Reflexes involving more than one synapse are called ______ reflexes.

15. The ______ measure the total amount of force exerted by the muscle on the bone to which its tendon is attached.

16. Each alpha motor neuron has a collateral branch that turns back within the spinal cord to synapse with its ______, which provides a mechanism to prevent muscle fatigue.

17. The resting tension of skeletal muscle, known as ______, is lost during REM sleep.

18. Because of the size of the ______ cells, the primary motor cortex is much thicker than other cortical tissue.

19. The sensory receptors in the muscles and joints send information about the physical environment to the ______ cortex.

20. Patients with the disorder ______ have damage to the posterior parietal cortex that results in difficulty responding to visual, auditory, or somatosensory stimuli presented to the contralateral side of the body.

21. Apraxia of speech is thought to be caused by damage limited to ______ area.

22. The two areas of the secondary motor cortex are the ______ and the ______.

23. The two major motor tracts originating in the primary motor cortex are the ______ tract and the ______ tract.

24. The two major motor pathways originating in the subcortex are the ______ and the ______.

25. The ______ tract begins in the reticular formation in the pons and synapses with alpha motor neurons that activate the extensor muscles of the legs.

26. Degeneration of the corticospinal and corticobulbar tracts and the anterior horns of the spinal cord causes ______, also known as Lou Gehrig's disease.

27. Rhea's golf swing illustrates a(n) ______ movement, a movement that is a well-practiced habit, occurs rapidly, and is not dependent on sensory feedback.

28. Output from the cerebellar cortex is transmitted by the ______ cells.

29. The basal ganglia consist of three subcortical structures: the ______, ______, and ______.

30. ______ disease is an inherited motor system disorder caused by a defect in a gene on the short arm of chromosome 4.

31. The slowed movement in a person with Parkinson's disease is called ______; the person's tendency to speed up a walking pace until running is called ______.

32. The two types of brain surgery sometimes used to treat Parkinson's disease are ______, in which the ventrolateral thalamus is lesioned, and ______, in which selected areas of the globus pallidus are damaged.

Multiple-Choice Questions

1. Movement can be controlled at the
   - **a.** spinal cord, brain stem, or cerebral cortex.
   - **b.** spinal cord, muscles, or bones.
   - **c.** brain stem, muscles, or cerebral cortex.
   - **d.** brain stem, spinal cord, or bones.

2. The contraction of a(n) ______ muscle produces extension; the contraction of a(n) ______ muscle produces flexion.
   - **a.** skeletal, cardiac
   - **b.** skeletal, flexor
   - **c.** extensor, flexor
   - **d.** extensor, smooth

3. The two proteins that make up muscle fibers are
   - **a.** myofibril and myofilament.
   - **b.** actin and myosin.
   - **c.** sarcomere and windomere.
   - **d.** alpha and beta.

4. The alpha motor neuron and the extrafusal muscle fiber synapse at the
   - **a.** neurotransmitter receptor site.
   - **b.** myofibril junction.
   - **c.** neuromuscular junction.
   - **d.** sarcomere gate.

5. When an action potential is generated in a motor neuron, the influx of Ca^{2+} ions causes the ______ to form cross bridges with the ______.
   - **a.** myosin heads, actin filaments
   - **b.** actin filaments, sarcomeres
   - **c.** myofibrils, myosin heads
   - **d.** sarcomeres, myofibrils

6. The shortening of a muscle during muscle contraction is caused by the pivoting of the ______, causing the entire ______ to shorten.
   - **a.** actin filaments, myofibril
   - **b.** myosin heads, flexor
   - **c.** myosin heads, sarcomere
   - **d.** actin filaments, sarcomere

7. Myasthenia gravis is caused by
   a. too little ACh.
   b. too few nicotinic receptors at the neuromuscular junctions.
   c. too much ACh.
   d. too few muscarinic receptors at the neuromuscular junctions.

8. Collectively, a motor neuron and all the muscle fibers it controls are known as a(n)
   a. sarcomere. c. motor unit.
   b. myosin head. d. actin filament.

9. Carlos is a world-class sprinter. He almost certainly has ______ fast-twitch muscles and ______ slow-twitch muscles than the average man.
   a. more, more c. fewer, more
   b. more, fewer d. fewer, fewer

10. The reflex experienced when a doctor taps your knee with a rubber hammer is called the ______ reflex.
    a. patellar c. muscle spindle
    b. polysynaptic d. fast-twitch

11. The sensory nerve endings surrounding the central part of the intrafusal muscle fiber are the
    a. extrafusal muscle fibers. c. Ia fibers.
    b. intrafusal endings. d. annulospiral endings.

12. Phillip accidentally touched a hot burner on the stove and reflexively withdrew his finger, illustrating the ______ reflex.
    a. patellar c. heat removal
    b. withdrawal d. Babinski

13. The mechanism that enables the motor system to control the extent of muscle contraction is the
    a. Golgi tendon organ. c. muscle spindle organ.
    b. patellar reflex. d. annulospiral ending.

14. The nervous system combats the excess contraction of muscles and the resulting fatigue through a type of inhibitory interneuron called a(n)
    a. Golgi tendon organ. c. annulospiral ending.
    b. Renshaw cell. d. extrafusal fiber.

15. The part of the precentral gyrus that plays a major role in voluntary movement is the
    a. primary motor cortex. c. pons.
    b. cerebellum. d. medulla.

16. The ______ and the ______ are overrepresented in the homunculus of the primary motor cortex.
    a. hands, feet c. chest, face
    b. hands, face d. chest, feet

17. The primary motor cortex receives information from four cortical structures: the primary somatosensory cortex, the secondary motor cortex, the dorsolateral prefrontal cortex, and the ______ cortex.
    a. anterior prefrontal c. posterior parietal
    b. pyriform d. occipital

18. The ______ cortex integrates input from the visual, auditory, and skin senses and relays it to the primary motor cortex.
    a. somatosensory c. posterior parietal
    b. secondary motor d. tertiary motor

19. Regina has had a stroke on the left side of her brain and now consistently ignores the right side of her body. She is likely to be diagnosed with
    a. motor apraxia. c. contralateral neglect.
    b. Huntington's disease. d. ipsilateral neglect.

20. Difficulty performing voluntary movements that is not the result of paralysis is a manifestation of
    a. apraxia. c. Parkinson's disease.
    b. ALS. d. motor neuron disease.

21. Damage to the right parietal lobe produces ______, in which individuals have difficulty drawing pictures or assembling objects.
    a. limb apraxia
    b. constructional apraxia
    c. assembling and artistic apraxia
    d. contralateral neglect

22. The two major motor pathways originating in the primary motor cortex are the
    a. corticospinal tract and corticobulbar tract.
    b. corticospinal tract and cerebellar tract.
    c. neurospinal tract and corticobulbar tract.
    d. rubrospinal tract and cerebellobulbar tract.

23. Neurons in the ventral corticospinal tract control the movement of the
    a. facial muscles and tongue muscles.
    b. fingers, hands, and arms.
    c. lower legs and feet.
    d. trunk and upper legs.

24. The rubrospinal tract extends from the ______ to the spinal cord.
    a. substantia nigra c. cerebellum
    b. red nucleus d. basal ganglia

25. Julia's grandfather has ______, a neuromuscular disease caused by degeneration of the corticospinal and corticobulbar tracts and the anterior horns of the spinal cord.
    a. apraxia
    b. Parkinson's disease
    c. amyotrophic lateral sclerosis
    d. Huntington's disease

26. Ballistic movements are governed by the
    a. primary motor cortex. c. thalamus.
    b. basal ganglia. d. cerebellum.

27. The ______ of the cerebellum produce continuous movement in a specific muscle and prevent movement in an opposing muscle.
    a. mossy fibers c. Purkinje cells
    b. climbing fibers d. basket cells

28. The two structures of the basal ganglia that comprise the corpus striatum are the
a. globus pallidus and putamen.
b. globus pallidus and caudate nucleus.
c. putamen and caudate nucleus.
d. putamen and amygdala.

29. The motor disturbances of ______ are caused by decreased production of dopamine, whereas the motor disturbances of ______ are the result of increased dopaminergic activity caused by the death of GABAergic and cholinergic neurons.
a. Parkinson's disease, Huntington's disease
b. Huntington's disease, Parkinson's disease
c. myasthenia gravis, Huntington's disease
d. Parkinson's disease, amyotrophic lateral sclerosis

30. Dwayne's grandmother exhibits bradykinesia and festination; several years ago, she was diagnosed as having
a. Huntington's disease.
b. myasthenia gravis.
c. ALS.
d. Parkinson's disease.

Answers can be found on the companion website at www.worthpublishers.com/klein.

Landy.

9

Wakefulness and Sleep

Jet Lag

For weeks, Sheila had been planning her trip to Paris. Although she'd been to Quebec and New Orleans with her parents, she was still looking forward to an authentic French experience. She found it hard to contain her excitement at the prospect of going to the City of Light.

Although her trip was related to her profession—she was a researcher for a large pharmaceutical company and was attending an international meeting in Paris—she had planned it so she'd have some time for sightseeing. By leaving Boston on Friday evening, she would get to France on Saturday morning, Paris time. That would give her half of Saturday and all Sunday to see as many sights as possible. The trick was to sleep on the plane and arrive in Paris rested and ready to go.

Once in the air, Sheila quickly realized the impossibility of this first part of her plan. The plane's vibrations, the drone of the engines, the sounds of the family behind her, and all the other stimuli during the flight prevented her from settling into even a light sleep. Still, when she arrived at Orly Airport at 9 a.m. local time, she felt more excited than tired. She retrieved her luggage, found a cab, and using her college French, directed the driver to take her to the convention hotel. By 10:30, she was walking down the Champs Elysées toward the Louvre.

Sheila was awestruck by what she saw in the museum and raced from one magnificent collection to another. She soon realized, of course, that she'd be able to see only a small fraction of the Louvre's more than 6,000 paintings. Her spirits and energy flagging, Sheila dragged herself back to the hotel around 4 p.m. She decided to take a short nap before going out to find something for dinner. Perhaps she would be hungry when she woke up; at the moment, her stomach felt unsettled from the events of the day.

Sheila had planned to sleep for just an hour or so, but when she awakened, it was dark outside. Her reset watch read 2:30 a.m. She felt tired and achy and hoped she wasn't getting sick. Her attempts to get back to sleep failed, so she propped herself up in bed to read her travel guide. When she found herself reading the same sentence over and over, she wondered what was wrong with her. Then she remembered the warnings about jet lag and decided that was her problem. She just hoped she'd feel better when daylight arrived, as she still wanted to see more of the sights Paris had to offer.

BEFORE YOU BEGIN

- ➤ Why was Sheila able to function well enough to find the Louvre, even though she had had no sleep on the flight?
- ➤ What caused the disruption of her sleep schedule?
- ➤ What is jet lag, and why does it occur?

jet lag The fatigue and sleep disturbance caused by traveling across several time zones.

circadian cycle A change in biological and behavioral functioning that occurs over a 24 hour period.

circadian rhythm The intrinsic process that controls the circadian cycle.

lark A person who is active and alert in the morning and becomes drowsy and inattentive in the evening.

- How do people eventually adjust to new time zones?
- What purpose does sleep serve?
- What are dreams, and when do they happen?
- Why do we dream?
- We all know there is such a thing as too little sleep; is it possible to get too much sleep?

In this chapter, you will find the answers to these questions and many others.

Biological Rhythms

Our biological rhythms cause us to sleep and awaken at certain times. The disruption of these rhythms when we travel across several time zones is known as **jet lag.** In flying from Boston to Paris, Sheila has crossed several time zones—Paris time is 6 hours ahead of Boston time—therefore, the Paris time does not match her biological clock. She may need several days to adjust to the new time, so, on this short trip, she will probably begin to feel normal just when she is scheduled to return home. In this chapter, we discuss the biological patterns of wakefulness and sleep and how we can make adjustments that will enable us to function in a new time zone.

Humans and nonhuman animals experience regular fluctuations in the timing of bodily processes. Some fluctuations occur over several minutes, others over hours or days. For example, humans have a 90 minute cycle of activity and drowsiness (Duchniewska & Kokoszka, 2003; Shono & others, 2001). Other examples are the 28 day menstrual cycle in human females and a similar, but less obvious, cycle of sex hormone secretion in males (Hirschenhauser & others, 2002). Cycles can even be as long as a year, and some people experience significant mood changes based on the seasons during the year (Sher, 2000, 2004). This atypical/abnormal pattern of mood changes, called seasonal affective disorder (SAD), is discussed later in the chapter.

The 90 minute, 28 day, or yearly cycles generally have only a modest effect on human behavior, but daily (24 hour) cycles have profound behavioral effects. Fluctuations in biological processes during a 24 hour period are governed by circadian rhythms.

Figure 9.1

Behavioral and biological changes during two successive 24 hour periods Alertness and body temperature are highest during the day and lowest at night. By contrast, blood plasma levels of growth hormone and cortisol are lowest during the day and highest at night.

→ **As descriptions of activity patterns, what is the difference between a lark and an owl?**

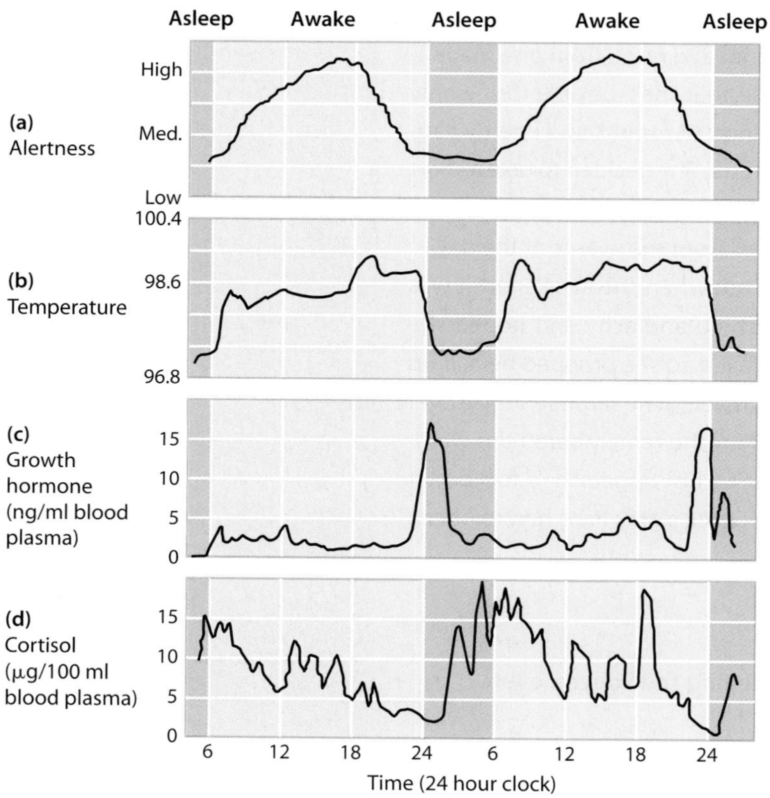

The Circadian Cycle

A **circadian cycle** (from the Latin, *circa*, "about," and *dies*, "day") is a change in biological and behavioral functioning over a 24 hour period. For example, we have different activity levels throughout the day; the levels typically increase until midday then decline until the evening when we sleep. Our alertness, or attentiveness to environmental stimuli, also fluctuates (Figure 9.1a). An intrinsic rhythm, or **circadian rhythm,** controls the biological and behavioral changes during a circadian cycle.

Akerstedt and Froberg (1976) introduced the term **larks** for people who are active and alert in the morning and drowsy and inattentive in the evening, and the term **owls** for those who are drowsy and inattentive in the morning and active and alert in the evening. These alertness patterns correspond to changes in epinephrine levels: Larks typically have peak epinephrine levels in the morning, owls in the evening, and others in the middle of the day. About 10% of the population are extreme larks and 10% extreme owls, with the rest of us falling somewhere in the middle.

owl A person who is drowsy and inattentive in the morning and active and alert in the evening.

suprachiasmatic nucleus (SCN) An area in the brain that regulates the circadian cycle.

Apparently, being a lark or an owl can affect behavior. For example, Guthrie and colleagues (1995) reported that student larks obtained higher grades on examinations in morning courses than in evening courses, whereas student owls did better on examinations in evening courses than in morning courses. The old saying "early to bed and early to rise makes a man healthy, wealthy, and wise" does not seem to hold true for larks, however, as Gale and Martyn (1998) found no evidence that larks were wealthier than people with different sleeping patterns. To find out which type of "bird" you are, answer the questions in Table 9.1.

Body temperature also changes over a 24 hour period. For most people, body temperature is lowest during the early morning hours and highest in the late afternoon or early evening (Figure 9.1b). Not surprisingly, the peak body temperature of larks occurs earlier than the peak temperature of owls (Bailey & Heitkemper, 2001). Body temperature at a particular time is related to mood and to whether the person is a lark or an owl (Kerkhof, 1998).

Hormone levels also change throughout the day. As you can see in Figure 9.1c, growth hormone secretion is highest in the middle of the night. Cortisol secretion by the adrenal gland and melatonin secretion by the pineal gland also peak at night (Figure 9.1d). The cortisol peaks earlier in larks than in owls (Bailey & Heitkemper, 2001).

Table 9.1
Are You a Lark or an Owl?

Respond to each of the following items by circling either "Day" or "Night."

1.	I feel most alert during the	Day	Night
2.	I have most energy during the	Day	Night
3.	I prefer to take classes during the	Day	Night
4.	I prefer to study during the	Day	Night
5.	I get my best ideas during the	Day	Night
6.	When I graduate, I would prefer to find a job during the	Day	Night
7.	I am most productive during the	Day	Night
8.	I feel most intelligent during the	Day	Night
9.	I enjoy leisure-time activities most during the	Day	Night
10.	I prefer to work during the	Day	Night

Note: If you answer "Day" to eight or more of these questions, you are probably a lark. If you answer "Night" to eight or more, you are probably an owl.

From Wallace, B. (1993). Day persons, night persons, and variability in hypnotic susceptibility. *Journal of Personality and Social Psychology, 64,* 827–833.

The Role of the Suprachiasmatic Nucleus

In 1967, Curt Richter reported that large lesions of the medial hypothalamus in rats disrupted activity-related changes in their circadian cycle. Soon, two research teams identified the **suprachiasmatic nucleus (SCN),** located above the optic chiasm in the medial hypothalamus, as the area responsible for the circadian cycle (Moore & Eichler, 1972; Stephan & Zucker, 1972). The researchers found that SCN lesions eliminated activity changes over a 24 hour cycle and also affected hormone-release cycles and sleep-wake cycles. Figure 9.2 shows the location of the SCN in humans.

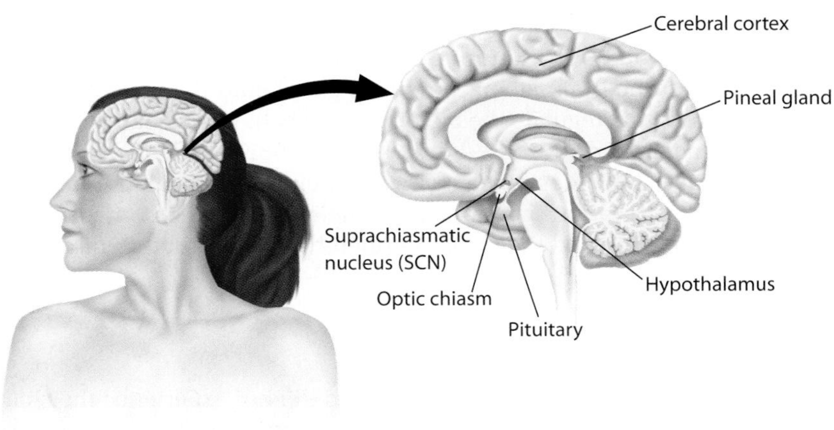

Figure 9.2
A sagittal view of the suprachiasmatic nucleus (SCN) and the pineal gland in the human brain The SCN controls the circadian cycle; the pineal gland secretes the hormone melatonin, which reduces activity and produces fatigue.

What is the significance of the location of the SCN in the brain?

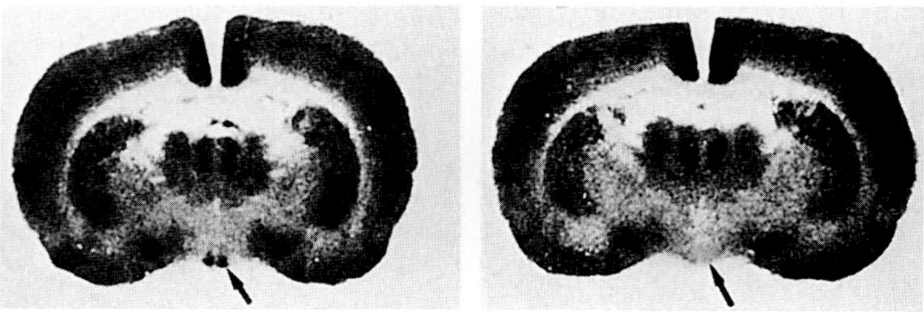

COURTESY OF WILLIAM J. SCHWARTZ

Figure 9.3

The activity of the SCN These autoradiographs of the brain of a rat record the absorption patterns of radioactive 2-deoxyglucose by the SCN (arrows). The patterns indicate greater SCN activity during the day (left) than at night (right).

➡ **Does the SCN control circadian activity directly?**

Moore (1982) reported that SCN neurons in a rat show circadian cycles of electrical and biochemical activity, with all activities being significantly greater during the day than at night. To observe activity in the SCN of rats, Schwartz and Gainer (1977) administered radioactive 2-deoxyglucose (2-DG) and found that the SCN absorbs more 2-DG during the day than at night (Figure 9.3). Curiously, this same SCN activity pattern has been observed in both nocturnal and diurnal animals. **Nocturnal animals,** such as most rodents, sleep by day and are active at night, whereas **diurnal animals,** such as humans, are awake by day and sleep at night.

The observation that SCN activity is highest during the day and lowest at night for both nocturnal and diurnal animals suggests that the SCN keeps track of day and night but does not directly control the activity of the animal. Instead, the day-night monitoring by the SCN affects other neural structures that are responsible for the activity changes. In other words, the SCN establishes the length of the circadian cycle, but other structures determine the activities of the animal during the cycle.

Further investigations found that lesions that isolate the SCN from other CNS structures did not affect cyclical changes in SCN activity (Groos & Hendriks, 1982) but did cause the 24 hour circadian cycle to increase to a 25 hour cycle. (The reason for this change will be apparent shortly.) In another study, transplantation of the SCN from hamsters with a 20 hour cycle into hamsters with a 24 hour cycle produced a 20 hour cycle in the 24 hour cycle hamsters; the opposite effect was observed when the SCN was transferred from 24 hour to 20 hour hamsters (Ralph & others, 1990). These results suggest that the SCN is genetically programmed to have a specific circadian rhythm, which is unaffected by other structures.

In humans, changes in the timing of sleep and wakefulness commonly occur with age. This is also true for Syrian hamsters in which the *free-running rhythm*—a daily rhythm that continues under constant conditions, such as continuous light or dark—shortens with age. Viswanathan and Davis (1995) found that transplants of fetal SCN into older hamsters that had had their SCNs removed restored the younger free-running rhythm, measured by continuous records of wheel-running activity. With time, however, the free-running rhythms became shorter, indicating that age-related changes in the SCN are responsible for the shortening of the free-running rhythm that occurs with age.

The SCN of a rat contains approximately 10,000 densely packed, small neurons (Meijer & Rietveld, 1989). These neurons, which contain a large amount of rough endoplasmic reticulum (a network of channels involved in intracellular transport), are clustered around capillaries (Moore & others, 1980). Hormones are released from the SCN into the capillaries and carried by the circulatory system throughout the body. The neurons of the SCN also project to other areas of the hypothalamus, the brain stem, the pineal gland, and the pituitary gland—all of which are areas that regulate the biological and behavioral changes occurring during the circadian cycle (Moore-Ede & others, 1982). More recently, Aston-Jones and colleagues (2001) described a circuit for circadian regulation of arousal consisting of the SCN, various hypothalamic nuclei (e.g., the dorsomedial and the paraventricular nuclei), and the locus coeruleus (a brain structure discussed later in the chapter).

nocturnal animal An animal that sleeps during the day and is awake at night.

diurnal animal An animal that remains awake during the day and sleeps at night.

A 25 Hour Day?

What would happen if we lived in a cave and did not experience the change from the darkness of night to the light of day? How would we know when to go to sleep and when to wake up? Moore-Ede and colleagues (1982) set out to answer these

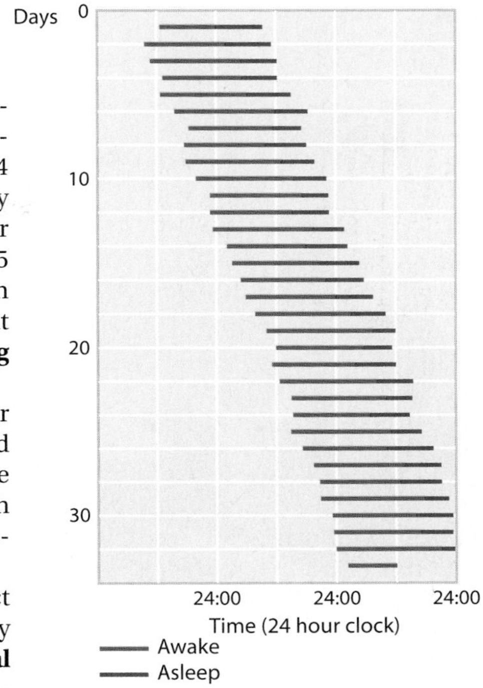

Figure 9.4

The human sleep-wake cycle in the absence of external time cues This subject went to sleep a little over an hour later each day, producing a typical free-running circadian sleep-wake cycle of approximately 25 hours.

→ **Why do we usually maintain a 24 hour cycle?**

questions by studying a group of people who volunteered to live in an environment without external time cues—no windows, clocks, radios, televisions—and only artificial light. Most of the individuals shifted from a 24 hour day to a 25 hour day during the first days or weeks of the study. They would wake up and go to sleep an hour later each day (Figure 9.4). Other bodily functions, such as activity and temperature, also shifted to the 25 hour cycle. After several days or weeks, the cycle had increased to as much as 36 hours in some individuals. The 25 hour (or more) sleep-wake cycle that develops in the absence of natural light-dark cycles is called a **free-running rhythm.**

Many conditions in nature, such as the position of the sun and the outdoor temperature, operate on a 24 hour cycle. These 24 hour conditions, called **zeitgebers** (pronounced "TSITE-gay-burs"), which in German means "time givers," reset the biological clock of an organism every 24 hours. Although nature has many zeitgebers, studies have suggested that intense broad-spectrum light is the critical stimulus that resets our circadian rhythm.

In Chapter 6, we discussed how the photoreceptors in the eye detect light, which is transduced into a neural impulse. The vertebrate eye actually contains two classes of photoreceptors (Vigh & others, 2002): the **visual photoreceptor,** which codes features of a light stimulus that are later detected and analyzed by cortical areas, and the **nonvisual photoreceptor,** which detects the daily dawn-dusk cycle. Evidence for the two photoreceptor types is provided by studies on a strain of mice in which the visual rods and cones degenerate postnatally, and the mice become blind. However, this blind strain has circadian cycles identical to those in other strains of mice, suggesting that nonvisual photoreceptors continue to operate normally (Foster & others, 1993; Provencio & others, 1994). Research with blind humans has shown that most have free-running rhythms, with recurrent insomnia and daytime sleepiness (Sack & others, 2000).

Information from the nonvisual photoreceptors about the light-dark cycle travels via the **retinohypothalamic tract** to the suprachiasmatic nucleus, which is reset by the information. One piece of evidence for this resetting is that damage to the connections between the retina and the SCN produces a 25 hour biological cycle (Johnson & others, 1988). Electrical stimulation of the SCN has an effect similar to pulses of light (Rusak & Groos, 1982), and glutamate injections also mimic the effect of light stimuli (Meijer & others, 1988), suggesting that light activates SCN cells by triggering the release of the neurotransmitter glutamate.

In addition to resetting the body's biological clock, exposure to intense broad-spectrum light influences the secretion of **melatonin** by the **pineal gland** (see Figure 9.2). As you will recall from Chapter 2, the pineal gland and melatonin secretion play a role in reproductive readiness in seasonally breeding mammals. Melatonin also has a sedative effect (Ebadi & others, 1998; Pang & others, 1998), and high levels reduce the activity of the animal and produce fatigue. SCN activity, caused by exposure to light, inhibits melatonin release; a lack of SCN activity, as experienced under dim lighting conditions, increases melatonin release.

Richard J. Wurtman and his colleagues have found that low doses of melatonin, given to healthy volunteers, decrease the time to fall asleep (sleep latency) without altering sleep architecture (sleep stages, as described later) and without producing a "hangover effect" (Zhdanova, 2004; Zhdanova & Tucci, 2003; Zhdanova & Wurtman, 1997; Zhdanova & others, 1996). Similarly, sleep efficiency in insomniac subjects over 50 years old was improved by low doses of melatonin (Zhdanova & others, 2001). Low melatonin doses also promoted sleep and reduced motor activity in children with Angelman syndrome, a genetic disorder characterized by severe developmental delay, impaired or absent speech, movement or balance disorder, and increased motor activity (Zhdanova & others, 1999). That is, melatonin even worked to improve sleep in the case of a genetic disorder in which the children have other problems as well. Wurtman and his colleagues have concluded that melatonin has a dual effect on sleep: acute sleep promotion within an

free-running rhythm A 25 hour (or more) sleep-wake cycle that develops in the absence of natural light-dark cycles.

zeitgeber An external time cue that resets an animal's biological clock every 24 hours.

visual photoreceptor A type of photoreceptor that codes the features of a light stimulus.

nonvisual photoreceptor A type of photoreceptor that detects the daily dawn-dusk cycle.

retinohypothalamic tract A fiber tract that conveys information about the daily dawn-dusk cycle to the SCN.

melatonin A hormone secreted by the pineal gland in response to daylight and darkness.

pineal gland A structure of the epithalamus that controls seasonal rhythms in behavior through its release of melatonin.

This woman is using a light box, which provides artificial light, to combat the symptoms of SAD; light therapy works by reducing melatonin release.

hour of oral administration and alteration of the underlying circadian pacemaker with repeated administrations (Zhdanova & others, 1997; Zhdanova & Wurtman, 1997). They have also found a similar sleep-promoting effect of melatonin in nonhuman primates, providing an animal model for the investigation of melatonin secretion and sleep (Zhdanova & others, 1998; Zhdanova & others, 2002).

Fewer hours of daylight occur during the winter months than during the other seasons. This reduced light can produce a form of depression called **seasonal affective disorder (SAD).** People with SAD have altered melatonin levels (Srinivasan, 1997) and feel tired no matter how much sleep they get. Fortunately, **light therapy,** which involves an increase in intense broad-spectrum light during the winter months by the use of artificial light, reduces melatonin release and produces increased activity and enhanced mood in most SAD sufferers (Saeed & Bruce, 1998). In addition, low doses of melatonin in the afternoon may be beneficial in treating winter depression (Lewy & others, 1998), and Leppamaki and colleagues (2003) found that controlled-release melatonin improved sleep and well-being in adults with subclinical SAD.

Genetic Regulation of the Circadian Cycle

Although researchers had identified the genetic basis for circadian rhythms in the fruit fly *Drosophila,* a favorite animal for the analysis of heredity, not until the early 1990s was a similar mechanism determined in mammals (Roenneberg & Merrow, 2003). In their search for the genetic basis, Vitaterna and colleagues (1994) used a classic approach called *forward genetics,* in which large numbers of animals are screened for mutant characteristics, and when a mutation is found, the underlying genetic difference is determined. These researchers identified 1 mouse in about 300 whose circadian rhythm was more than an hour longer than normal, a seemingly small difference but actually six standard deviations away from the average. The researchers then determined that the characteristic was inherited as a mutant gene, which they called *Clock.* In constant darkness, *Clock* mice first developed circadian periods of 27 to 28 hours; circadian rhythmicity completely disappeared in about 2 weeks of darkness. The researchers mapped the *Clock* gene to the midportion of mouse chromosome 5, which has considerable similarity to human chromosome 4.

Since the discovery of the *Clock* gene, significant progress has been made in understanding the genetic regulation of the circadian rhythm in mammals (King & Takahashi, 2000; Shimomura & others, 2001). According to the current model, the circadian clock consists of genes for proteins that alternately stimulate and inhibit a subset of the same genes. The expression of one or several of the *Clock* genes results in protein(s) that inhibit, by a negative feedback loop, the expression of the same gene(s). With removal of the inhibitory proteins, expression of the *Clock* genes resumes. The cycle takes approximately 24 hours, giving rise to the circadian rhythm.

Shimomura and coworkers (2001) have discovered at least 16 different genetic loci that affect circadian rhythms in mice, all of which differ from the 9 previously known *Clock* genes. These investigators concluded that multiple genes control the circadian rhythm and that several different *Clock* genes control different aspects of the circadian cycle, such as its free-running rhythm and activity levels.

The circadian rhythm of humans appears to be quite similar to that of other mammals (Czeisler & others, 1999; Wager-Smith & Kay, 2000). In addition, the

seasonal affective disorder (SAD) A form of depression caused by reduced daylight during the winter months.

light therapy An increased exposure to intense broad-spectrum light that enhances mood in people with SAD.

Clock genes have now been identified in humans (King & Takahashi, 2000). Thus, as we learn more about the genetic basis of the circadian cycle in nonhuman mammals, this knowledge most likely will translate into further characterization of the genes involved in a variety of human conditions and behaviors that are affected by circadian rhythms, such as sleep disturbances and affective disorders.

Checkpoint

Are you a lark or an owl? Explain the mechanism by which exposure to bright light might help Sheila overcome her jet lag in time for her Monday morning meetings.

Phase-Sequence Problems

For some people, the biological clock gets out of synchrony with natural day-night fluctuations in activity, forcing them to try to stay awake when their body is ready to sleep and to try to sleep when their body wants to stay awake. Jet lag can produce this asynchrony, as can shift work—different hours of work during different weeks.

People who work the late shift, usually midnight to 8 a.m., must stay awake when they normally would be asleep, and 20% of American workers rotate shifts, sometimes working at night and other times working during the day (Moorcroft, 1987). A significant percentage of workers report that shift work causes health problems, interferes with social life, and increases the risk of accidents (Garbarino & others, 2002). Automobile accidents from sleepiness are more common among shift workers than in the general population (Stutts & others, 2003), and sleepiness is especially evident during night shift work and while driving home from work (Horne & Reyner, 1999; Steele & others, 1999). Shift work is also related to higher rates of stress-related problems such as heart disease, ulcers, cigarette smoking, and adverse pregnancy outcomes (Nicholson & D'Auria, 1999; Scott, 2000).

Czeisler and colleagues (1982) have suggested one approach to reduce the adverse effects of shift work. On the standard schedule, or **phase-advance shift** rotation, each week the worker rotates to an earlier shift. Czeisler and colleagues studied a group of industrial workers on the phase-advance shift schedule who in the first week worked midnight to 8 a.m., the second week 4 p.m. to midnight, and the third week 8 a.m. to 4 p.m. (Figure 9.5a). This shift rotation shortens the day, because each week the worker rotates to a shift during which he or she would still have been sleeping on the previous rotation. Another group of workers in the study, on a **phase-delay shift** schedule, rotated to a later shift each week, rotating from a midnight start, to an 8 a.m. start, and finally to a 4 p.m. start (Figure 9.5b). This shift rotation lengthens the day, because each week the worker starts the new shift after having been awake longer than on the previous rotation. Relative to the phase-advance shift workers, the phase-delay shift workers reported greater job satisfaction, had fewer health problems, and experienced a lower turnover rate.

Figure 9.5

Easing the burden of shift work

(a) Phase-advance shift workers rotate to an earlier shift each week. (b) Phase-delay shift workers rotate to a later shift each week.

→ **Which type of shift rotation do workers prefer?**

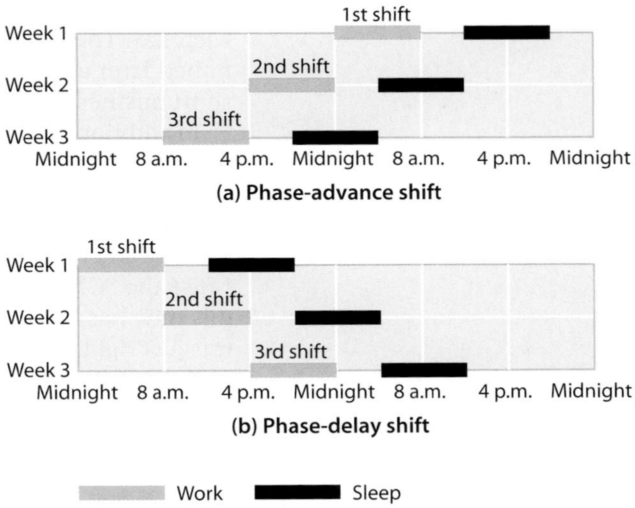

Earlier we noted that without the normal zeitgebers, the body has a tendency to shift to a 25 hour or longer circadian cycle. The difficulty with the typical phase-advance shift rotation is that it works against this natural tendency, because workers must shorten their day (go to sleep earlier) as the new rotation begins. By contrast, the phase-delay rotation works with the circadian rhythm by requiring workers to lengthen their day.

Sheila's symptoms after traveling eastward across time zones from Boston to Paris are typical of jet lag, another phase-sequencing problem. In addition to the symptoms Sheila notices, there may be other, less-apparent symptoms. For example, athletes have been found to have diminished anaerobic power and capacity, as well as reduced dynamic strength, as part of jet lag (Hill & others, 1993), and

phase-advance shift A schedule that shortens the day by requiring a worker to start on the late shift and then rotate to an earlier shift the following week.

phase-delay shift A schedule that lengthens the day by requiring a worker to rotate to a later shift each week.

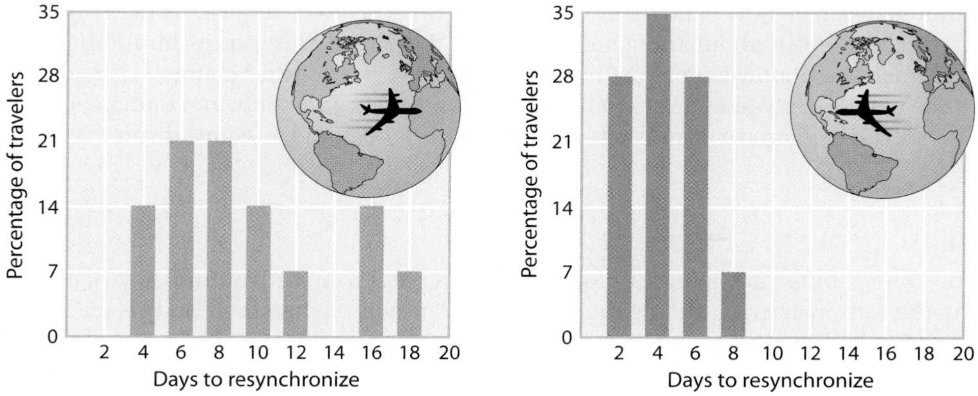

(a) Eastbound (phase advance) **(b) Westbound (phase delay)**

Figure 9.6

Disturbances in the sleep-wake cycle caused by jet lag Air travelers generally experience greater difficulty adjusting to (a) eastbound travel than to (b) westbound travel.

➡ **What can you do before traveling to diminish the jet lag problem?**

even brief air travel (across two time zones) can influence team performance (Bishop, 2004). Such effects ease after several days, not nearly soon enough to salvage a victory in a close athletic contest.

When Sheila returns to Boston, she will experience jet lag again, although her body will adjust more quickly this time. As with shift work, it is easier on your body to lengthen your day by flying west (phase delay) than to shorten your day by flying east (phase advance). Lemmer and colleagues (2002) have reported that flyers generally adjusted more quickly to westbound than to eastbound travel (Figure 9.6).

One thing Sheila could have done to diminish her jet lag would have been to shift her activities toward the new time zone several days before the trip. For her eastbound trip to Paris, she could have gone to bed earlier and gotten up earlier each day. Then, to prepare for her westbound flight home, she could have gone to bed later and gotten up later—although this would not be feasible on such a short business trip.

In addition, high-protein foods help people stay awake, whereas high-carbohydrate foods can hasten sleep. Before the trip Sheila could have changed to a diet consisting of a high-protein breakfast and lunch and a high-carbohydrate dinner. Sheila's walk to the Louvre helped in resetting her biological clock, as it provided exercise and exposed her to bright sunlight (Parry, 2002; Shiota & others, 1996). Because the SCN is insensitive to light in the middle of the day, exposure to light at this time has little effect (Moore-Ede, 1993); therefore, Sheila's midmorning jaunt was just right.

Earlier we pointed out that melatonin, secreted by the pineal gland in the absence of SCN activity, has a sedative effect. Several studies have reported that taking synthetic melatonin on the day of arrival in a new time zone can reduce or prevent the symptoms associated with jet lag (Lino & others, 1993; Takahashi & others, 2000). A combination of bright light and melatonin may also alleviate jet lag (Takahashi & others; Zisapel, 2001). Appropriately timed bright light and melatonin administration may also be useful for helping workers adapt to night-shift jobs (Burgess & others, 2002).

The *Scientific American* Spotlight, "From Bulimia to Jet Lag," describes how bright light from light boxes may be useful in treating disorders other than SAD that appear to have developed from disrupted circadian rhythms. In addition to bulimia and jet lag, the article highlights difficulties caused by sleep delay and shift workers forced to change shifts.

Having discussed the circadian cycle, we still need to address the question of how the central nervous system controls our activity and alertness levels. In the next section, we explain why most of us are more alert for a 10 a.m. class than for a 4 p.m. class.

➤Checkpoint

Describe a phase-advance shift and a phase-delay shift for air travel and for shift work. What can Sheila do on Sunday, Monday, and Tuesday to ease the jet lag she will experience after returning to Boston on Wednesday?

Scientific American Spotlight

From Bulimia to Jet Lag

Ulrich Kraft

Light therapy has succeeded in fending off seasonal affective disorder—and with virtually no side effects. Though not a miracle cure, it is helping people overcome other challenging conditions:

Bulimia. This binge-eating disorder, which primarily afflicts young women, is associated with serious psychological maladies. But psychologist Raymond Lam of the University of British Columbia in Vancouver realized that many of his patients fared worse in January than in June. He has conducted studies in which he has bulimic women sit in front of light boxes every day, and after only a couple of sessions both their psychological and eating difficulties seemed to ease.

Sleep delay. Some people cannot fall asleep until very late at night and often cannot get moving again until 10 or 11 A.M. The reason: their internal clocks are out of phase with the natural day-night cycle. In some cases, extended bouts can inexplicably reverse: sufferers crash by early evening and end up waking hours before dawn. Scott Campbell, a chronobiologist at New York Presbyterian Hospital/Weill Cornell Medical Center, has had some success correcting this phase problem; people who fall asleep too late are exposed to light in the early morning, whereas the early risers will get the light at night.

Shift workers. One week they work 8 A.M. to 4 P.M.; the next week their schedule is from midnight to eight in the morning. Almost no shift worker escapes the consequences of this circadian whiplash. At a minimum, many become fatigued and have trouble concentrating when working nights. Although their inner clocks can adjust, the transition takes several days, and then almost immediately they must switch back. Researchers have found that shift workers make the transition much more easily when the workplace is bathed in at least 1,200 lux of light—what would be found in a bright office. Often, however, occupational safety laws require only 500 lux or so.

Jet lag. After a trip across many time zones, an individual's circadian clock usually needs several days to reset. The most obvious symptoms are sleep problems. Researchers disagree about whether light therapy can speed the reset process, but doctors nonetheless urge long-distance travelers to get as much daylight or bright light as possible during the first few days. Some hotels now offer in-room light boxes or special lamps that simulate sunrise to help the jet-lagged adjust.

From: *Scientific American Mind,* vol. 16(3), p. 81

REVIEW

- The circadian rhythm regulates biological and behavioral changes during a 24 hour circadian cycle.
- Changes in alertness occur over the course of the day; larks are most active and alert in the morning, whereas owls are most active and alert in the evening. Body temperature and hormone release also change over a 24 hour period.
- The suprachiasmatic nucleus (SCN) of the brain controls the circadian cycle; without external light cues, the SCN sets a circadian cycle of 25 (or more) hours.
- In dim lighting, melatonin release from the pineal gland increases and the individual experiences reduced activity and increased fatigue. Small doses of melatonin may be beneficial in treating insomnia.
- Intense broad-spectrum light can reset the biological clock by activating the SCN.
- Beginning with the discovery of a *Clock* gene, great progress has been made in understanding the genetic regulation of circadian rhythms in mammals.
- The biological clock of shift workers is out of synchrony with the natural day-night fluctuations in light, resulting in fatigue, sleep problems, and higher rates of accidents and stress-related diseases. Fatigue and sleep disturbances also are caused by jet lag.
- Adjusting to phase-sequence discontinuity is easier when the day is lengthened (phase-delay shift) than when it is shortened (phase-advance shift).

Wakefulness

Sheila has to attend her conference meetings on Monday morning, no matter how tired or groggy she feels. What determines degree of alertness or wakefulness, and how can the level of wakefulness be measured? Researchers use cortical EEG patterns to determine whether a person is awake or asleep and the different types and levels of wakefulness and sleep.

Figure 9.7

Three distinct EEG patterns Beta activity (18 to 24 Hz) is associated with being awake and alert; alpha activity (8 to 12 Hz) with being awake and relaxed, with eyes closed; and delta activity (1 to 4 Hz) with being asleep.

→ **Describe the awake state in which alpha waves predominate.**

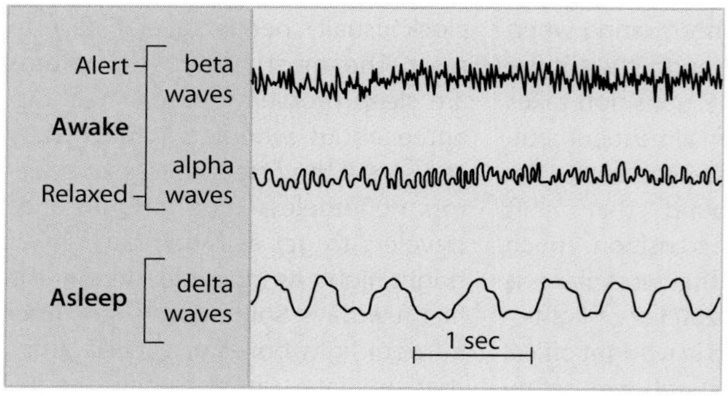

Levels of Arousal

The ability to study levels of arousal is generally attributed to Hans Berger's discovery and recording of the electrical potential of the brain. Berger spent years trying to establish relationships between various physiological measures and psychological states. While studying heartbeat, respiration, and brain temperature, he placed electrical recording equipment on the scalp and recorded the first electroencephalogram (EEG). This was in 1929, and just 15 years later, a review of research cited approximately 450 references to the use of EEG (Lindsley, 1944). Unlike virtually everyone else, Berger credited the much earlier research of Richard Caton on rabbits and monkeys as being the first recording of the electrical activity of the brain (Finger, 1994).

When we are awake and active, our brain-wave EEG shows a rapid, desynchronized pattern of small-voltage changes (approximately 18 to 24 Hz; recall that 1 Hz = 1 cycle per second) (Figure 9.7). This EEG pattern is called **beta activity** (or *beta waves*). **Alpha activity** (or *alpha waves*) is observed when we relax with our eyes closed; the frequency of activity decreases to between 8 and 12 Hz, and alpha waves are larger and more synchronized than beta waves. Alpha activity stops when we open our eyes and resume normal activity, or when we become so relaxed that we drift off to sleep (*delta waves*). We discuss EEG activity during different stages of sleep later.

Brain Mechanisms Controlling Arousal

One of the most influential early hypotheses on wakefulness and sleep was that sleep is caused by a lack of sensory input to the higher areas of the brain, the so-called deafferentation hypothesis. Although the hypothesis was later found to be incorrect, it seemed to receive support from the lesion work that Belgian neurophysiologist Frédéric Bremer conducted on cats. Bremer misinterpreted his work, but it is worth discussing because it eventually led to the correct answer as to what produces wakefulness and sleep.

In his **cerveau isolé preparation** (isolated forebrain preparation), Bremer made a cut between the inferior colliculi and the superior colliculi, depriving the higher brain areas of the sensory information arriving through the spinal cord and brain stem structures (Figure 9.8). Cats that had undergone this operation slept contin-

beta activity A rapid, desynchronized EEG pattern of small voltage changes (18 to 24 Hz) that occurs when a person is awake and active.

alpha activity An EEG pattern of waves that are larger and more synchronized (8 to 12 Hz) than beta waves, which occurs when an individual is relaxed with eyes closed.

cerveau isolé preparation An experimental preparation depriving higher brain areas of sensory information arriving from the spinal cord and brain stem; used to identify brain areas controlling arousal.

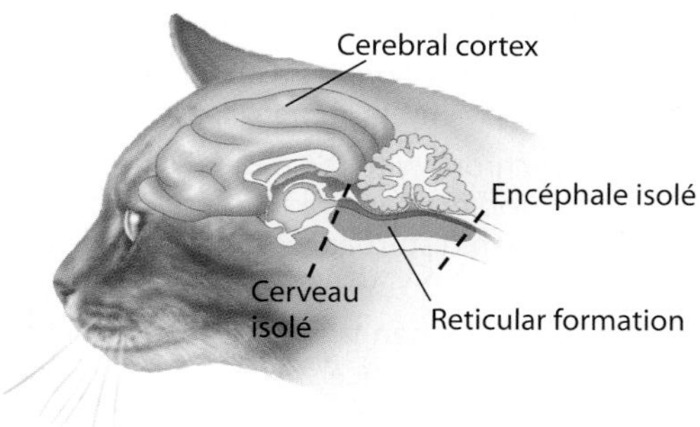

Figure 9.8

Cerveau isolé and encéphale isolé preparations in a cat brain Animals receiving the cerveau isolé operation sleep continuously. By contrast, animals with the encéphale isolé operation have normal sleep-wake cycles. The dashed lines show the location of each cut.

→ **What important connection does the cerveau isolé operation sever?**

uously, at least in short-term experiments; later studies showed that over a longer term, cats with the cerveau isolé preparation had a desynchronized EEG pattern (Gottesmann, 1988). Bremer concluded that sleep is produced by the lack of sensory input to the cerebral cortex, with wakefulness resulting from sensory stimulation. When he made the cut through the brain just above the spinal cord, the **encéphale isolé preparation** (isolated brain preparation), cats had normal sleep-wake cycles (see Figure 9.8). Bremer considered this further support for his sensory stimulation hypothesis of sleeping and waking, as the higher brain areas of the cats with the encéphale isolé receive more sensory information than do the cortical areas in cats with the cerveau isolé preparation.

encéphale isolé preparation An experimental preparation depriving higher brain areas of sensory information arriving from the spinal cord; used to identify brain areas controlling arousal.

reticular activating system (RAS) A diffuse network of neurons originating in the hindbrain and extending through the midbrain; stimulation produces cortical arousal and behavioral alertness.

Guiseppe Moruzzi and Horace Magoun (1949) provided an alternative explanation for Bremer's findings. Between Bremer's two cuts lies much of the reticular formation, which, after Moruzzi and Magoun's work, became known as the **reticular activating system (RAS).** The reticular formation is a network of nuclei and pathways beginning in the hindbrain and extending through the midbrain (Chapter 2). Moruzzi and Magoun reported that electrically stimulating the RAS produced beta-wave EEG arousal and behavioral alertness, similar to the effects of environmental stimulation. They also found that disruption of RAS functioning produced a low level of alertness and the large-wave synchronized EEG recordings characteristic of sleep. When the reticular formation in the midbrain was damaged, animals appeared to be in a continuous state of sleep, whereas lesions at the same level that damaged ascending sensory pathways did not affect sleep or wakefulness, providing evidence against Bremer's sensory hypothesis.

However, Moruzzi and Magoun's version of a unitary, nonspecific RAS began to unravel with further experimentation. For example, in the latter part of the 1950s, Moruzzi and his colleagues found that if they transected the brain stem of cats at the midpontine level (through the middle of the pons), which is only slightly posterior to Bremer's cerveau isolé transection, the animals were unable to sleep (D. D. Kelly, 1991b). This suggests that the caudal brain stem, below the new transection, contains an area necessary for inducing sleep. One possible site for this sleep-inducing area is the raphé nucleus, which we discuss in the section on sleep.

Although the reticular formation is no longer considered a unitary, nonspecific system, and has even been subdivided into as many as five specific cell groups (e.g., Marrocco & others, 1994), its function as an RAS is still considered valid (Steriade, 1996). The midbrain reticular formation receives nonspecific sensory input from all sensory systems and arouses the cerebral cortex via projections through thalamic nuclei. In this way, the RAS influences cortical excitability to incoming sensory information carried by the classical pathways (Figure 9.9). Specific evidence for an arousal function of the midbrain reticular formation has come recently from a PET study of regional cerebral blood flow (rCBF) in human volunteers that revealed activation of the midbrain reticular formation and a thalamic area when the participants went from a relaxed state to one requiring arousal and vigilance (Kinomura & others, 1996).

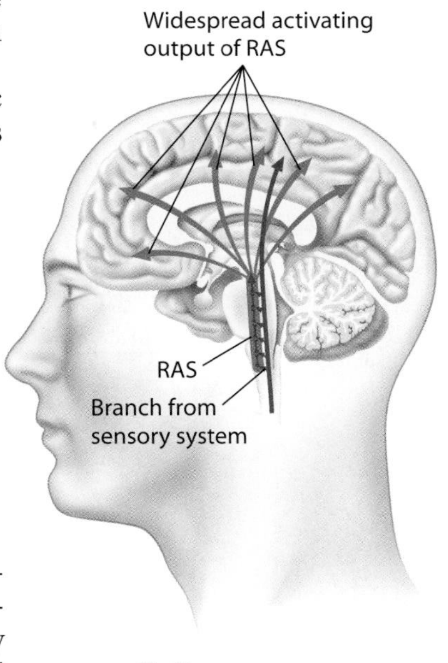

Figure 9.9

The reticular activating system The blue arrows represent input from specific sensory systems. The red arrows indicate the general activating effect of output from the RAS.

What are the two main functions of the reticular activating system?

Let us consider an example to illustrate the influence of the RAS. Suppose that on Monday Sheila is listening to a dull presentation while sitting in a comfortable chair; her environment is relatively devoid of perceptually arousing stimulation. Under these conditions, her RAS is not activated, little beta-wave EEG activity is occurring, and she becomes drowsy. Although sensory information (the sound of the lecturer's words) is reaching her cerebral cortex, because her RAS is not activated, she is not aware of the information.

Now, let us suppose it is Tuesday and Sheila is listening to a fascinating presentation. Stimulated by the content of the lecture, her RAS arouses her cerebral cortex, and she sits erect in her seat and attends to the speaker's every word. However, this exciting presentation produces only a moderate level of RAS activation. Considerably greater RAS activation may be induced if Sheila happens to think about

locus coeruleus A group of neurons within the reticular formation important for cortical activity and behavioral alertness.

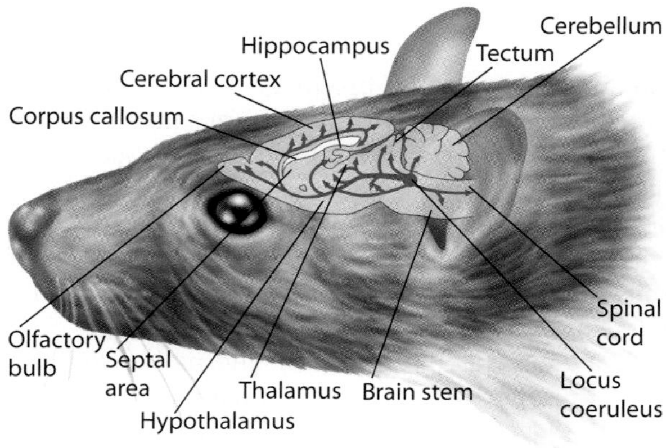

Figure 9.10
The locus coeruleus in a rat brain This sagittal view shows the location of the locus coeruleus, a key structure in determining the level of alertness, and its projections throughout the brain (blue arrows). (Adapted from Moore, 1979.)

➔ **In what brain structure is the locus coeruleus located?**

her upcoming flight home. This thought produces intense cortical arousal and behavioral alertness, with perhaps a tinge of anxiety.

Within the RAS is a group of neurons called the **locus coeruleus,** which is important for cortical activity and behavioral alertness (and also for REM sleep, as discussed later). The locus coeruleus (named for its bluish color) has widespread connections to other CNS areas, including the thalamus, hippocampus, and cerebral cortex (Figure 9.10). As evidence of its role in cortical activity and behavioral alertness, destruction of this structure produces increased sleep and decreased wakefulness (Jones & others, 1969). Inactivation of the anterior portion of the locus coeruleus by cooling was found to induce various sleep stages in the cat, whereas electrical stimulation invariably produced wakefulness (Cespuglio & others, 1982). In addition, locus coeruleus activity is highly correlated with level of wakefulness in the monkey (Rajkowski & others, 1994): the greater the activity, the higher the level of behavioral activity. The same study showed that the firing rate of locus coeruleus neurons increases as an animal awakens and declines when it goes to sleep (Figure 9.11). Further, the longer the animal is awake, the higher the activity in the locus coeruleus; activity declines to almost nothing when the animal goes to sleep.

Figure 9.11
Locus coeruleus activity during wakefulness and sleep in a rat The level of activity decreases as the animal goes to sleep and increases when it awakens.

➔ **In what stage of the sleep-wake cycle does the lowest level of locus coeruleus activity occur? What does this suggest?**

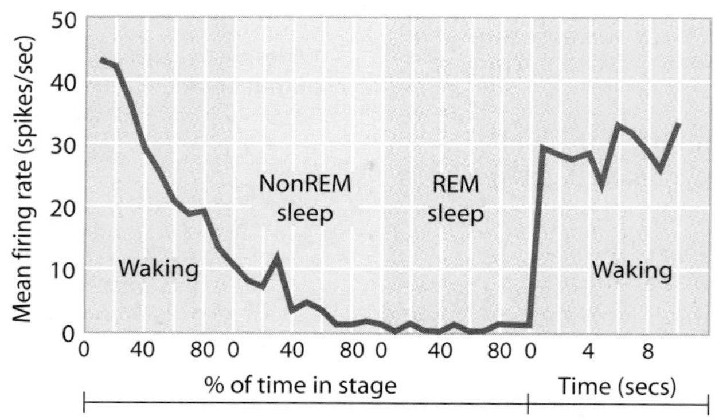

Other researchers have suggested that locus coeruleus activity influences an animal's attention to environmental stimuli (Aston-Jones & others, 1991). They observed that when animals are grooming or drinking sweetened water, locus coeruleus activity is low, but when they are attending to important environmental events, the activity is high.

Norepinephrine is the neurotransmitter in the locus coeruleus, and its release seems to have a gating effect. Stimuli that would normally be below threshold can trigger threshold neuronal responses when the locus coeruleus is stimulated either electrically or with injections of norepinephrine. This gating effect of norepinephrine can lead to increased attention to environmental stimulation (Waterhouse & others, 1988). More recently, a variety of studies in animals have shown that the effects of stimulants (e.g., amphetamine) on reinforcement processes and locomotor activity are mediated by dopaminergic effects at the nucleus accumbens, whereas their effects on cognitive behaviors (e.g., delayed responding, working memory) are mediated by adrenergic pathways from the locus coeruleus to the prefrontal cortex (Solanto, 1998).

In summary, RAS activity influences cortical arousal and behavioral functioning, and cortical arousal plays a vital role in our behavior when we are awake. Sleep also serves a valuable purpose, and disruption of the sleep-wake cycle, such as sleep deprivation, can have serious consequences—as we discuss in the next section.

➤Checkpoint
When does your brain engage in alpha activity? Beta activity? What are the consequences of RAS stimulation by the sensory systems?

REVIEW

- Beta activity, the awake EEG pattern, is characterized by rapid, desynchronized, small-voltage changes. Slower, alpha activity occurs during a relaxed state.
- Activation of the reticular activating system (RAS) by environmental stimuli produces cortical arousal and behavioral alertness.
- The locus coeruleus, an area in the RAS with widespread connections throughout the brain, determines levels of cortical activity and behavioral alertness. Damage to this structure produces increased sleep and decreased wakefulness.

Sleep

As Sheila found out on her trip to Paris, and as you have learned from your own experience, sleep is essential to our well-being. Before going into detail about why this is so, let us look at how researchers study sleep. Again, macroelectrode recording of the cortical EEG is the tool for assessing the state and level of sleep (Figure 9.12).

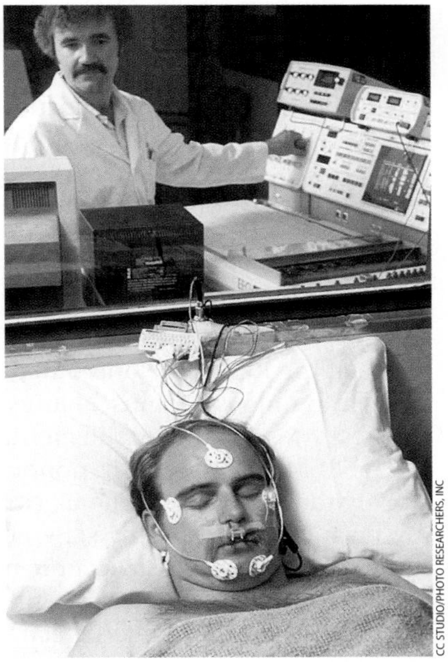

Figure 9.12
Sleep research Studies of sleeping humans have revealed much about the nature of sleep.

What type of recording is used to monitor sleep?

Levels and Stages of Sleep

Based on EEG patterns, we can divide sleep into several stages. When we first fall asleep, we are in **stage 1 sleep** or light sleep, characterized by mostly **theta activity** (or *theta waves*), with a frequency of 4 to 7 Hz. Next comes **stage 2 sleep,** which consists of theta activity with the addition of **sleep spindles,** 1 to 2 second bursts of 12 to 14 Hz activity, and **K complexes,** consisting of a single large negative wave (upward spike) followed by a single large positive wave (downward spike). **Stage 3 sleep** is characterized by the addition of **delta activity** (or *delta waves*), with a frequency of 1 to 4 Hz. After stage 3, the sleeper may enter an even deeper level of sleep, called **stage 4 sleep,** in which delta waves predominate. Collectively, these four stages of sleep are known as **nonREM (NREM) sleep,** based on the EEG differences between these stages and REM sleep, discussed below. Stages 3 and 4 are also called **slow-wave sleep (SWS),** because the rate of activity in the EEG is slower than in waking states. The EEG patterns typically seen in the four NREM stages and the cycling of sleep stages during a night's sleep are shown in Figure 9.13.

As we go to sleep, our brain activity slows, then increases, then slows again, and so on. This transition from being awake to being asleep is probably responsible for sleep spindles and K complexes. As sleep deepens, the bursts of increased activity stop and the brain remains relatively calm. Although deepening sleep makes people increasingly more difficult to awaken, if roused from stage 4 sleep, they are likely to report that they just fell asleep, even though this stage usually occurs 45 minutes into the first or second sleep cycle.

Until the early 1950s, biological psychologists assumed that sleep consisted entirely of NREM sleep. Another sleep stage was discovered by Eugene Aserinsky, a graduate student working in the laboratory of the sleep researcher Nathaniel Kleitman. Aserinsky noted that every 90 minutes or so, the EEG patterns of the sleeper would change from the slow waves characteristic of sleep to fast, low-amplitude beta waves usually indicative of an awake state (Aserinsky & Kleitman, 1953). This

stage 1 sleep The first stage of light sleep, characterized by mostly theta activity.

theta activity An EEG pattern during light sleep, characterized by synchronized waves that are larger in amplitude (4 to 7 Hz) than beta and alpha waves.

stage 2 sleep The second stage of sleep, characterized by sleep spindles and K complexes in addition to theta activity.

sleep spindle A 1 to 2 second burst of activity of 12 to 14 Hz that occurs during stage 2 sleep.

K complex A single large negative wave (upward spike) followed by a single large positive wave (downward spike) that occurs during stage 2 sleep.

stage 3 sleep The third sleep stage, characterized by the addition of delta activity.

delta activity An EEG pattern during deep sleep characterized by synchronized waves that are larger in amplitude (1 to 4 Hz) than theta waves.

stage 4 sleep The deepest stage of sleep, in which delta activity predominates.

nonREM (NREM) sleep Sleep stages 1 to 4, in which the EEG patterns are markedly different from those in REM sleep.

slow-wave sleep (SWS) Stages 3 and 4 of nonREM sleep.

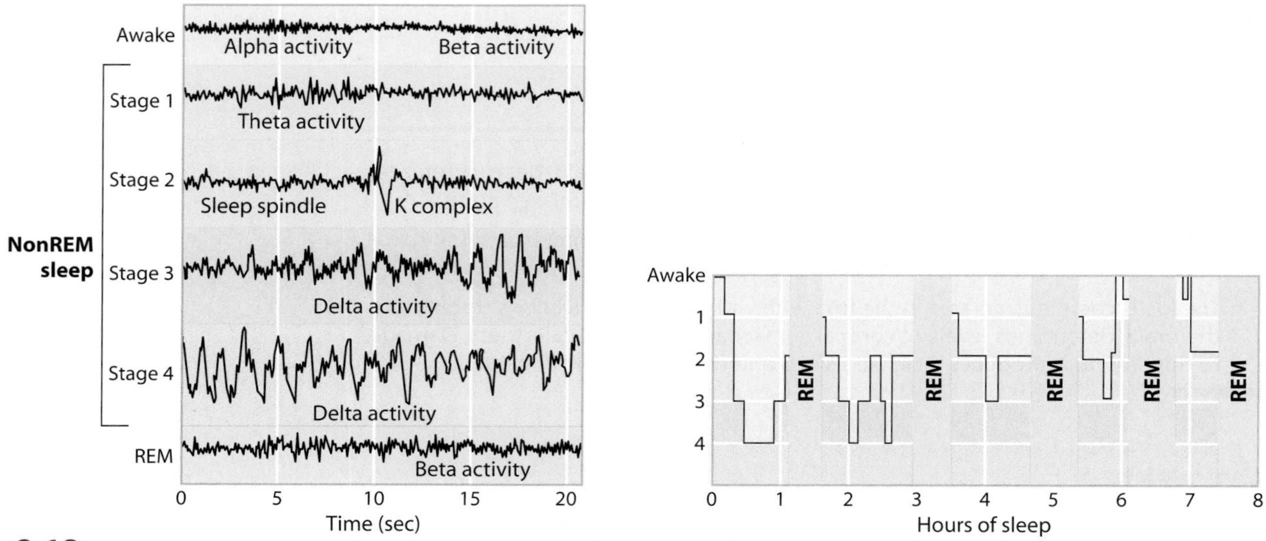

Figure 9.13

EEG patterns during waking and sleeping, and a typical night's sleep Over the course of the night, the depth of sleep lessens and the length of time in light sleep increases. The duration of a REM sleep cycle also increases as the night progresses.

What other stage of the sleep-wake cycle has a wave pattern similar to that of REM sleep? What are the two major types of sleep?

sleep stage is called **rapid eye movement (REM) sleep,** because of the accompanying eye movements, most of which are not actually rapid; it is also called *paradoxical sleep,* because of the waking pattern of EEG activity observed in a sleeping state (see Figure 9.13). Despite the waking pattern, nonhuman animals and humans are harder to arouse during this stage than during any other. Dreaming is typically associated with REM sleep, although people report dreams when awakened from other sleep stages as well. The difference is that REM-sleep dreams are generally more vivid and detailed than NREM dreams. Another major difference between the REM state and other sleep stages is that REM sleep is accompanied by a profound loss of muscle tone, which prevents the sleeper from acting out or physically responding to the mental activity reflected in the alert EEG.

The REM EEG pattern in nonhuman animals also shows **PGO waves,** spikes of activity that begin in the pons, continue to the LGN of the thalamus, and end in the occipital cortex, hence the acronym PGO (pons-geniculate-occipital). Presumably PGO waves also occur in humans and may provide the foundation for the visual imagery we experience in dreams, although a confirmation of this would require the insertion of microelectrodes into the brain, which for obvious reasons has not been done.

Checkpoint

Why is REM sleep sometimes called paradoxical sleep? Describe the differences in brain activity in the various sleep stages.

The Function of Sleep

All of us have stayed up long past our usual bedtime at one time or another. By the end of the following day, we find ourselves tired and irritable, so we fall asleep early and feel rested the next morning, having "made up" the lost sleep. Because of this type of experience, we tend to assume that the function of sleep is to restore biological resources consumed while we are awake. Another view is that sleep plays a crucial role in learning and memory. And a third view, based on evolutionary theory, is that sleep enhances the survival of a species by keeping animals inactive during the hours when food is scarce and there is more danger from predators.

A Restorative Function

As we noted in Chapter 1, Aristotle thought the mind was located in the heart. Another of his ideas was that poisonous substances accumulate in the body while we are awake and are eliminated by sleep. Scientists have not confirmed a poisonous buildup during the day, but sleep researchers have determined that valuable substances are manufactured during sleep (Anch & others, 1988). For example, the highest levels of growth hormone secretion occur during NREM sleep, and protein synthesis in the brain is greatest during REM sleep. This suggests we need NREM sleep for normal growth and REM sleep for nervous system development.

rapid eye movement (REM) sleep The phase of sleep in which the EEG pattern resembles the waking state, the eyes move behind closed lids, and muscle tone is absent.

PGO wave A brief burst of neural activity during REM sleep that begins in the pons, is transmitted to the LGN, and ends in the occipital lobe.

J. Allan Hobson (1995) has suggested that one important function of sleep might be to replace neurotransmitters depleted during the day, particularly transmitters such as norepinephrine and serotonin. With the lack of activity in areas such as the locus coeruleus during REM sleep, the neurotransmitters made in the cells can be replenished. "The fact is that the aminergic neurons, thought to be crucial to attentive learning and memory, *do* rest in sleep and do so most decidedly in the REM phase. And that has got to be of some functional interest" (p. 192).

Additional evidence for a restorative function for sleep has come from studies of individuals who engage in unusually high activity levels during their waking hours. For example, people who have performed strenuous exercise, such as running a marathon, generally have increased sleep time after the activity (Kubitz & others, 1996). Interestingly, exercise increases total time spent asleep and in NREM sleep, but time in REM sleep *decreases* (Driver & Taylor, 2000).

Horne and Wilkinson (1985) provided further support for a restorative view of sleep. They found that individuals who reduced their sleep time reported increased fatigue and fell asleep faster than regular sleepers, but once allowed to sleep, they recovered quickly.

Sleep stages 3 and 4 appear especially important for restoring depleted biological systems. Studies of people whose overall sleep time was reduced, a technique called partial deprivation, showed that they engaged in as much stage 3 and stage 4 sleep as the control subjects, who were allowed normal sleep time (Webb & Agnew, 1970). Other research suggests that stage 1 sleep has little recuperative value (Wesensten & others, 1999).

In modern society, significant deficits in the amount of sleep an individual needs may begin in adolescence. In one major study, more than 3,000 high school students were surveyed about their sleep patterns and behaviors presumably affected by those patterns (Wolfson & Carskadon, 1998). Total sleep times decreased by 40 to 50 minutes from age 13 to 19, primarily as a function of later bedtimes. On weekends, these later bedtimes produced a phase shift in adolescent sleep patterns, as the students went to sleep later but slept later in the morning. With early school times during the week, however, the later bedtimes produced major sleep deficits.

The sleep deficits definitely affected behavior. Students with higher grades tended to sleep longer and to have more regular sleep habits than students with lower grades. Breaking their sample into students with adequate sleep habits and those with less than adequate sleep habits, Wolfson and Carskadon (1998) found that the students in the inadequate group reported more behavioral difficulties. Such difficulties included problems getting up, being late to class, greater feelings of depression, and, not surprisingly, greater daytime sleepiness. The researchers concluded, "most of the adolescents surveyed do not get enough sleep, and their sleep loss interferes with daytime functioning" (p. 875).

William C. Dement is one of the world's leading authorities on sleep, sleep deprivation, and sleep disorders and is the founder of the first sleep disorders clinic, at Stanford University. Dement (1999) has estimated that 80% of college students are "dangerously sleep deprived." The effect of this deprivation is irritability, fatigue, difficulty concentrating, reduced productivity, and increased mistakes. Dement has also suggested that the brain keeps track of lost sleep, or sleep debt, and this deficit must be made up. In a review of the effects of sleep deprivation on performance, Himashree and colleagues (2002) reported such detrimental effects on psychological performance as slowing of thinking ability, memory impairment, and decreases in vigilance and sustained attention. The effects of sleep deprivation on physical performance included a decline in the ability to exercise at a maximum level and an increase in the perceived exertion of exercise.

College students often adopt a strategy of studying all night before a major examination; however, this approach may be self-defeating. For example, a comparison of the cognitive abilities of college students after either 24 hours of sleep deprivation or approximately 8 hours of sleep found that deprivation significantly reduced cognitive ability (Pilcher & Walters, 1997). In addition, the sleep-deprived subjects rated their concentration and cognitive abilities higher than did nonde-

REM rebound A greater proportion of sleep time spent in REM sleep after a period of REM-sleep deprivation.

microsleep A brief period during which a person appears to be awake, but the EEG patterns resemble stage 1 sleep.

prived subjects, indicating a lack of awareness of the effect of the deprivation. A similar lack of awareness of cognitive deficits following chronic sleep restriction was seen in a sleep-restriction study involving 48 healthy adults (Van Dongen & others, 2003). The battery of tests used with the sleep-deprived subjects included a sustained-attention reaction time test, a digit symbol substitution task, and a serial addition/subtraction task; subjective sleepiness was self-rated with the 7-point Stanford Sleepiness Scale. Chronic restriction of sleep to 6 hours or less a night for 2 weeks resulted in impairment on the cognitive performance tasks equal to up to 2 nights of total sleep deprivation. Another study found that 36 hours of sleep deprivation in male undergraduates had a significantly negative effect on several factors related to cognitive ability (McCarthy & Waters, 1997).

Researchers used fMRI to study the effects of sleep deprivation on mental arithmetic performance in normal volunteers (Drummond & others, 1999). After the subjects had a normal night of sleep, fMRI revealed activity localized in the prefrontal cortex, the parietal lobes, and the premotor areas. This activity was markedly reduced after sleep deprivation, and the subjects' performance on the task also declined (Figure 9.14). Similarly, using PET, researchers found global decreases in brain activity following short-term sleep deprivation (24 hours), with significantly larger activity reductions in the thalamus, prefrontal cortex, and the posterior parietal cortex (Thomas & others, 2000). Alertness and cognitive performance (serial addition/subtraction task) declined in conjunction with the reductions in brain activity.

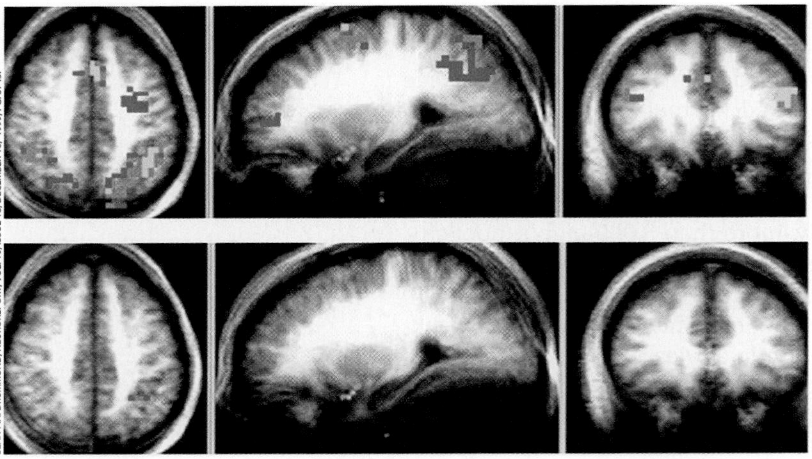

Figure 9.14

Sleep deprivation and cognitive ability fMRI showing activation of different parts of the brain during a mental arithmetic task. The top row shows activation following a normal night of sleep, the bottom row following sleep deprivation. Yellow represents the most intense activation.

➡ **Why is the activity diminished in the brain areas for mental arithmetic after sleep deprivation?**

Sleep researchers have also studied the effects of selective deprivation of REM sleep (Dement, 1974). To achieve REM-sleep deprivation, subjects are awakened briefly throughout the night whenever their EEG indicates REM sleep. Control subjects are awakened from NREM sleep the same number of times as their REM-deprived counterparts. The REM-deprived subjects report feeling tired, lacking concentration, and being irritable, and with continued deprivation, show more and more attempts at REM sleep. Further, subjects who have been deprived of REM sleep spend a greater proportion of sleep time in REM sleep when no longer deprived, a process called **REM rebound.** Increased REM time may last for several days or even weeks following REM deprivation (Hobson, 1995), an observation that indirectly indicates that REM sleep is regulated separately from NREM sleep. There is also more direct evidence for this, which we provide later in describing the neural structures controlling REM sleep and NREM sleep.

In 1965, Randy Gardner, a San Diego high school student, stayed awake for 264 hours (11 days) in order to break the world record for sleeplessness (Gulevich & others, 1966). He accomplished this feat by watching television, talking to family and friends, and playing pinball. Although he became tired and was sometimes confused, he showed no severe or permanent impairment from his sleep loss. Randy recovered rapidly: He slept 15 hours the first night, 10 hours the second, and between 8 and 9 hours the third night, failing to make up nearly 67 hours of lost sleep. Not all sleep stages were made up equally, however. Higher percentages of recovery occurred for stage 4 and REM sleep, suggesting their greater importance in any restorative function. In a sleep laboratory, subjects have great difficulty staying awake beyond 3 or 4 days, and after 3 days they exhibit periods of **microsleep** in which they appear to be awake but their EEG patterns resemble stage 1 sleep.

Because people can, at least temporarily, function without sleep, it may appear that sleep does not serve any critical purpose. However, the effects of sleep deprivation can be quite serious, especially for people with such occupations as driving a bus, flying an airplane, or performing brain surgery. Maas (1998) reported that about 30% of deaths on Australian highways could be attributed to drivers falling asleep, and research at the Stanford Sleep Disorders and Research Center concluded that sleep deprivation and alcohol intoxication had equally negative effects on reaction times and driving performance (Powell & others, 2001). In a study of 10 U.S. Air Force pilots, continuous wakefulness led to significant declines in CNS activation, mood, cognition, and, not surprisingly, flight skills, with the most severe deficits appearing after 25 hours of sleep deprivation (Caldwell & others, 2004). Even though we may not be entirely sure of the function of sleep, we certainly hope our bus drivers, airline pilots, and brain surgeons have had enough of it when we put ourselves in their hands.

Some adverse effects are clearly evident in this man who has been deprived of sleep.

The Role of Sleep in the Plasticity Underlying Learning and Memory

Another possible role for sleep, or particular stages of sleep, is its importance for brain plasticity and, in the adult brain, for learning and memory. Extensive evidence indicates that sleep is involved in memory consolidation (Chapter 14), the specific neural changes that change a memory trace from a short-term, easily disrupted state to a long-term, relatively permanent condition (Ficca & Salzarulo, 2004; Maquet, 2001; Stickgold & others, 2001). For example, Rauchs and colleagues (2004) found that selective REM-sleep deprivation impaired memory of an episodic event (event located in time and space). The researchers concluded that human memory consolidation of episodic events mainly involves REM sleep. Additional research reported that REM sleep was particularly important in the formation of emotional memories in humans (Wagner & others, 2001).

Further supporting the idea that REM sleep is involved in memory consolidation is the finding that REM sleep increases after training in several different experimental situations (Maquet, 2001). This is true for both nonhuman animals and humans; in animals, the REM-sleep time returns to normal with task mastery.

Despite the wealth of evidence supporting the role of REM sleep in memory consolidation, Vertes and Eastman (2000) have argued against such a function. According to the researchers, clinical evidence in humans indicates that REM sleep can be profoundly reduced with little or no disruption of learning and memory. For example, a few patients have survived bilateral lesions of the pons that essentially abolished REM sleep. These individuals reportedly led normal lives. In addition, the major antidepressant drugs all produce marked reductions in REM sleep, again with little effect on learning and memory. Vertes and Eastman suggest that the primary function of REM sleep is to arouse the brain periodically in order to maintain appropriate levels of CNS activity during sleep. According to this proposal, the brain uses REM sleep to facilitate recovery from sleep.

This is not the end of the story, however. As we noted in Chapter 2 and explore more extensively in Chapter 14, the hippocampus plays an important role in learning and memory. Different experiences activate distinct neural circuits within the hippocampus, and research indicates that neural circuits activated during a learning experience are reactivated during sleep. For example, in studies on rats, Lee and Wilson (2002) reported that hippocampal neurons that were active during the acquisition of a spatial learning task exhibited the same sequential activity during NREM sleep that they had exhibited during the daytime experience. Other researchers also have found that the firing pattern of the hippocampal cells of rats during waking experiences (e.g., spatial learning, running in an activity wheel) is duplicated during sleep (Louie & Wilson, 2001; Nadasdy & others, 1999).

As we discuss in Chapter 14, changes in synaptic responsivity are associated with memory storage and recall. Observation of such changes in single neurons in the hippocampus during REM sleep suggests that specific neural circuits are restructured during this stage by strengthening recent memories and weakening earlier ones (Poe & others, 2000).

Of perhaps greater importance than the animal research is the preliminary work with humans that suggests the hippocampal populations used in learning are reactivated during sleep (Staba & others, 2002). In extensive research by Maquet and colleagues (Maquet, 2001; Maquet & others, 2000), data from PET scans and rCBF measurements indicated that several areas of the brain active during a particular task were significantly more active during REM sleep in trained subjects than in untrained ones. These results support the idea of REM-sleep processing of memory traces in humans (Maquet & others, 2003) but contradict the writings of Vertes and Eastman (2000) in opposition to that idea. Future research will undoubtedly be needed to resolve this controversy.

An Evolutionary Perspective

Webb (1988, 1992) suggested that sleep evolved in order to force animals to conserve energy at a time when they would be less efficient in obtaining resources. According to this idea, animals sleep when food is scarce and when there is more danger from predators. If this evolutionary perspective were valid, the amount of time spent asleep should be related to the amount of danger the animal faces; therefore, species with few predators should sleep more than species with many predators. Animal species do differ in the amount of time they sleep (Figure 9.15), and a comparison of animals in each category is consistent with the evolutionary theory. Animal species with many predators, such as sheep and goats, sleep little, whereas animal species with few predators, such as cats and armadillos, sleep a lot. Animals that graze most of the day, such as horses and cows, sleep little, perhaps because they have to spend an enormous amount of time eating in order to meet their energy needs. By contrast, predatory animals that eat one large meal a day, such as cats, tend to sleep a lot.

Hauri (1979) noted problems with Webb's evolutionary perspective. One unanswered question is why sheep and goats sleep at all, given that they are constantly in danger. The evolutionary perspective alone does not explain sleep in these highly preyed upon species.

We have discussed evidence for three possible functions of sleep: restoration, cognition, and protection. In its restorative role, sleep may foster the development of specific substances, such as hormones and neurotransmitters, depleted during the day. Another possibility is that sleep might have a more general restorative function, such as replenishment of the body's energy reserves. In its cognitive function, sleep may play a role in learning and memory. In its protective role, sleep may have evolved in order to force organisms to be inactive during a time when they would be more subject to predation. Of course, these possible functions are not mutually exclusive; it is entirely possible, even likely, that sleep may play all three roles. It is also possible that sleep has other major functions that have not yet been discovered.

Figure 9.15
Daily hours of sleep for various mammals Animals that have many predators sleep little. By contrast, animals with few predators sleep a lot.

➔ Would dogs sleep more or less than rabbits? Wolves more or less than cattle?

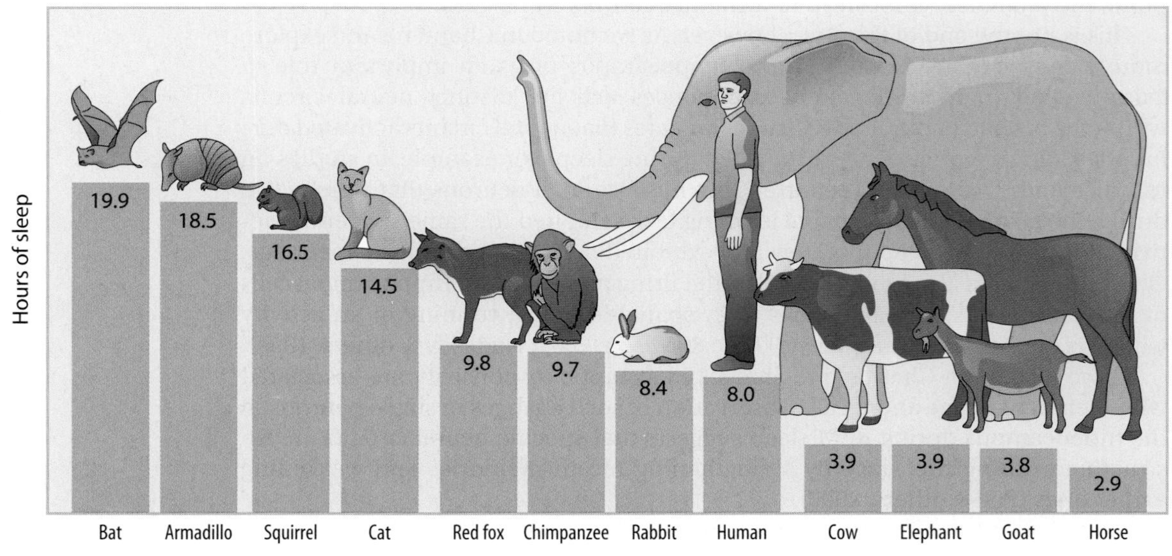

Developmental Changes in Sleep Patterns

The changes in time spent in REM sleep with age support the idea that REM sleep plays an important role in brain development. Roffwarg and colleagues (1966), for example, reported that the amount of time humans spend in REM sleep decreases steadily from infancy to adulthood (Figure 9.16). By contrast, NREM sleep time increases slightly from infancy to age 6, then declines slightly until adulthood. Adult NREM sleep time is only slightly less than that of infants. These observations suggest that the significance of REM sleep decreases as we get older, whereas NREM sleep continues to be important throughout our lives.

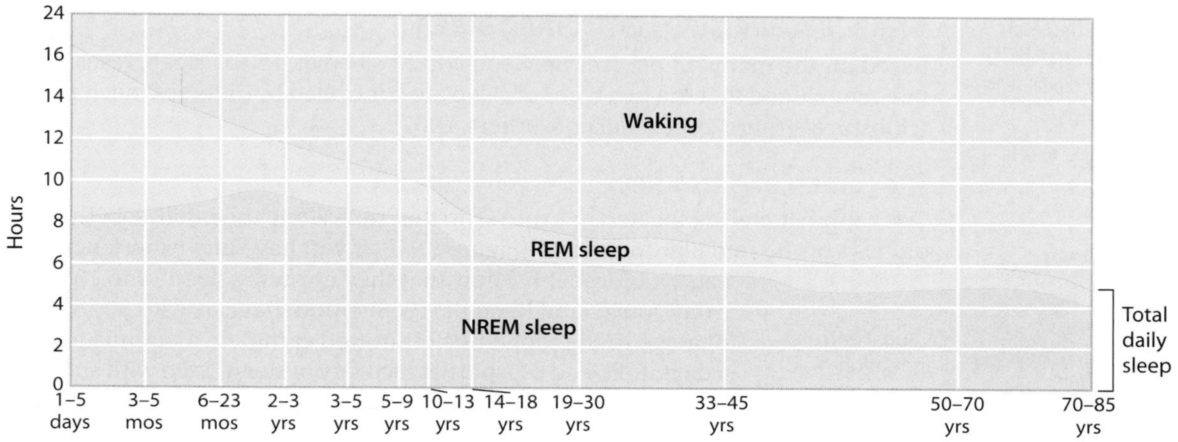

Figure 9.16

Time spent in NREM sleep and REM sleep at various ages The amount of NREM sleep time remains relatively constant throughout life, but the length of time spent in REM sleep each night decreases as we get older. (Adapted from Roffwarg & others, 1966.)

➜ Why do infants spend more time than adults in REM sleep?

Apparently, infants spend so much time in REM sleep because it enhances brain development (Marks & others, 1995). As we noted in Chapter 3, neural activity is essential to neural development; REM sleep in the infant may stimulate the brain in order to keep it from being inactive for much of the day. This idea is supported by the finding that premature infants spend even greater amounts of time in REM sleep than full-term newborns. The brains of premature infants are developing at a rapid rate, and the higher levels of cortical activity during REM sleep may facilitate this process. In addition, newborn cats and dogs have proportionally longer REM-sleep time than newborn cows and horses, perhaps because cows and horses have more highly developed brains at birth than dogs and cats.

Total sleep time is reduced in the elderly. Older adults also tend to sleep less soundly than young adults, which is consistent with a reduction in deep stage 4 sleep. There is also a reduction in REM sleep, although the difference is not nearly as great as the reduction that occurs from infancy to childhood (see Figure 9.16).

➤Checkpoint

Explain how partial sleep deprivation might have helped Sheila reduce the effects of jet lag. Suggest why rabbits sleep so much more than goats.

REVIEW

- The two distinct phases of sleep are nonREM (NREM) sleep and rapid eye movement (REM) sleep.
- The four stages of NREM sleep are characterized by high-amplitude, slow-wave, synchronized EEG patterns. In stage 1, EEG patterns show theta activity (4 to 7 Hz); in stage 2, theta activity, sleep spindles, and K complexes. Delta activity (1 to 4 Hz) is added in stage 3 and predominates in stage 4.
- REM sleep is characterized by low-amplitude, fast-wave EEG activity resembling that of the waking state, with rapid lateral eye movements and loss of muscle tone.
- PGO waves during REM sleep are brief bursts of neural activity that begin in the pons and travel to the LGN and then to the occipital lobe.

- The restorative view of sleep suggests that biological reserves depleted during the day are restored during sleep. Sleep deprivation results in fatigue, reduced concentration, greater irritability, and decreased motivation; symptoms are usually alleviated by a few extra hours of sleep.
- Sleep may also play an important role in memory consolidation.
- The evolutionary view of sleep argues that sleep evolved in response to the scarcity of food and an increased danger from predators during certain hours.
- REM-sleep time decreases as people age, whereas the amount of NREM sleep remains relatively constant throughout life.

Brain Mechanisms Controlling Sleep

Based on the many differences between NREM sleep and REM sleep, researchers have concluded that the two types of sleep are controlled by different mechanisms (Hobson & others, 2000; Walker & others, 2002).

The Control of NREM Sleep

The **raphé nuclei** are located in a thin strip that runs along the midline in the caudal part of the reticular formation (Figure 9.17). If you have any experience with cats, you probably know that they normally sleep 14 to 15 hours a day. Jouvet and Renault (1966) found that cats with 80% to 90% damage to the raphé nuclei showed complete insomnia for 3 or 4 days, followed by a partial recovery of sleep. Even with some recovery, cats with substantial raphé nuclei damage never slept more than 2.5 hours per day.

Figure 9.17
Structures that regulate NREM and REM sleep in a cat brain The basal forebrain initiates NREM sleep, and the raphé nuclei maintains it. The caudal reticular formation initiates REM sleep.

➡ **How does damage to the raphé nuclei affect a cat's sleep pattern?**

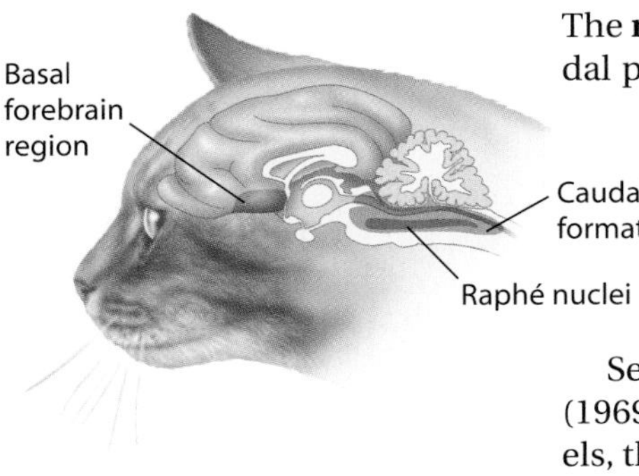

Serotonin is one of the neurotransmitters in the raphé nuclei. When Jouvet (1969) gave rats parachlorophenylalanine (PCPA), which decreases serotonin levels, the animals displayed a dramatic decrease in NREM sleep, and not until more than 10 days later did their sleep time return to normal (Figure 9.18). Injections of 5-hydroxytryptophan (5-HTP), a serotonin precursor, restored normal sleep patterns within a few minutes in cats that had received PCPA. This 5-HTP-induced pattern of sleep lasted 6 to 10 hours and was followed by another bout of continuous wakefulness until the PCPA effects wore off. Jouvet (1974) also noted that damage to the raphé nuclei lowered the overall serotonin level in the brain. He observed that the amount of serotonin loss was highly correlated with the amount of sleep loss; that is, the lower the amount of serotonin produced following raphé nuclei damage, the less the cats slept. Jouvet concluded that activation of the serotonergic raphé nuclei initiates and maintains NREM sleep.

Although no one has challenged Jouvet's conclusion about the raphé nuclei and NREM sleep, subsequent research indicates that he may have been wrong about the raphé nuclei *initiating* NREM sleep. For example, reexamination of the effects of raphé lesions in cats suggests that the nucleus seems to be involved in arousal processes rather than in promoting sleep directly (Arpa & De Andres, 1993). In addition, raphé stimulation does not cause an awake animal to go to sleep (Kostowski & others, 1969). Instead, stimulation of the **basal forebrain region,** an area anterior to the hypothalamus that includes the preoptic area (see Figure 9.17), has been shown to induce sleep in laboratory animals, and damage to this area has produced sleeplessness (McGinty & Szymusiak, 2003). McGinty and Szymusiak suggest that GABAergic neurons in the basal forebrain are responsible for the sleep-inducing functions of the area.

Figure 9.18
Serotonin and NREM sleep in rats The effects of parachlorophenylalanine (PCPA) administration (green line) and 5-HTP administration (red line) on time in NREM sleep, as percentage of control measurements (i.e., percentage of time spent in NREM sleep after injection relative to animals that have not been injected). (Adapted from Jouvet, 1969.)

➡ **The sleep of rats with substantial raphé nuclei damage is reduced by how many hours?**

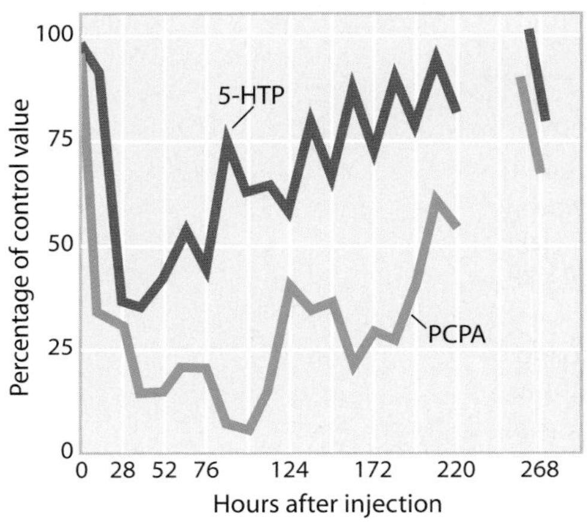

Further evidence for involvement of the preoptic area in NREM sleep comes from the observation that people become sleepier in warmer weather. As we indicated in Chapter 7, thermoreceptors in the skin transmit temperature information to the preoptic area of the hypothalamus. Research indicates that the preoptic area contains temperature-sensitive neurons; warming the neurons promotes NREM sleep in animal subjects (Alam & others, 1996; Guzman-Marin & others, 2000; Methippara & others, 2003).

PET imaging studies of NREM sleep typically reveal a global pattern of deactivation throughout the brain relative to the waking state or to REM (Hobson & others, 1998). However, despite the overall lack of activity, research has found specific regions of deactivation during NREM sleep in the same areas where activity is believed to produce REM sleep, as we discuss below.

raphé nucleus Nucleus located in a thin strip of neurons running along the midline in the caudal part of the reticular formation; damage to this area produces insomnia.

basal forebrain region A brain area anterior to the hypothalamus and including the preoptic area; stimulation produces sleep and damage produces sleeplessness.

caudal reticular formation An area within the reticular formation that produces REM sleep.

The Control of REM Sleep

Earlier, we implicated the locus coeruleus in cortical arousal and behavioral alertness. Jouvet (1967) suggested that this structure also governs REM sleep, but more recent research has shown that locus coeruleus activity is associated with an absence of REM sleep, and that REM sleep occurs when the locus coeruleus is not active (Payne & others, 2002; Singh & Mallick, 1996). For example, Singh and Mallick found that locus coeruleus stimulation in rats significantly reduced REM sleep and produced a REM sleep rebound during the poststimulation period. Decreased locus coeruleus activity removes the inhibition of the **caudal reticular formation,** which then initiates REM sleep (see Figure 9.17).

PET scans and rCBF have provided a comprehensive description of cerebral activity during REM sleep in humans. Maquet and colleagues (1996) found that rCBF was positively correlated with REM sleep in the pontine tegmentum (i.e., the caudal or pontine reticular formation), the left thalamus, the amygdala bilaterally, the anterior cingulate cortex, and an area in the right parietal lobe. REM sleep was negatively correlated with rCBF in several areas, including much of the prefrontal cortex. The researchers concluded that the amygdaloid activation is consistent with earlier observations of amygdaloid involvement in the formation and consolidation of memories, particularly memories involving emotional stimuli. We have already noted evidence that REM sleep is involved in some kinds of memory consolidation (e.g., Rauchs & others, 2004). In addition, the combined activation of the amygdaloid area and the cingulate cortex, both regions of the limbic system, could be responsible for the frequently experienced emotional aspects of dreams associated with REM sleep. (In Maquet and coworkers' study, all subjects awakened after REM sleep recalled dreams.) Finally, the deactivation of the prefrontal lobes during REM sleep could explain such characteristics of dreams as time distortions, illogical reasoning, and rapid forgetting upon awakening (Hobson & others, 1998).

Although REM sleep and dreaming are closely associated, Solms (2000) has argued that the two are actually controlled by different brain mechanisms. REM sleep is controlled by cholinergic brain stem mechanisms (Hobson, 1992)—that is, the caudal reticular formation—whereas dreaming requires the mediation of a forebrain mechanism that probably involves dopaminergic pathways. Evidence in support of this idea includes the finding that dreaming can be altered by dopamine agonists and antagonists without affecting REM sleep, and it can be induced by forebrain stimulation during nonREM sleep (Solms).

Checkpoint

How do GABAergic neurons mediate the transition from wakefulness to sleep? What neural structures control NREM and REM sleep?

Dreams

People have always been fascinated by dreams, often investing them with great significance as portents of the future. At least 70 passages in the Old Testament describe dreams. As early as 5000 B.C.E., the ancient Babylonians were recording dreams on clay tablets. The Egyptians built temples to Serapis, the god of dreams. In the early 13th century, Francis of Assisi was rebuffed by the Pope until the Pope had a dream that convinced him of the friar's validity.

Until fairly recently, the only way to study dreams was to rely on people's recollections of the dreams either soon after they occurred or at some later date. Because such recollections can be unreliable for a variety of reasons, including perceptual biases and selective forgetting, their validity was always questionable. Fortunately, Dement and other modern sleep researchers have developed better ways to investigate dreams (e.g., Dement, 1998). In contemporary studies of dreaming, EEGs of participants are continuously monitored to indicate their sleep stage, then subjects are awakened at various times during the sleep period and asked whether they have been dreaming. If they have been dreaming, the researchers ask further questions about the dream content.

The Content of Our Dreams

A **dream** is an altered state of consciousness in which remembered images and fantasies are confused with external reality. Dreams usually take place in familiar settings and are about objects or events in the life of the dreamer. Misfortune is more likely than success to be a part of our dreams (Figure 9.19). Although you might think sex would be a common theme, only 1% of dreams involve overt sexual activity. People known to the dreamer are the most common characters; bizarre creatures and monsters rarely appear.

Wake up, Dear. You're having another McNightmare.

Figure 9.19
The meaning of a dream Our dreams typically are about objects or events in our lives.

➔ **What is the definition of a dream?**

People have about four to six dreams each night (Dement, 1969), with the first dream usually beginning after about 90 minutes of sleep. Dreams generally last about as long as would the scenes in real life, and we experience about 1 to 2 hours of dream time each night. As noted earlier, dreams are most likely to be remembered following REM sleep. Dement found that subjects awakened during REM sleep reported 70% of the time that they had been dreaming, whereas subjects awakened during NREM sleep reported just 30% of the time that they had been dreaming. Most NREM sleep dreams seem to consist of a single thought, image, conversation, or emotion, rather than having the story-like aspect of REM dreams.

Do you believe that you do not dream? You almost certainly do dream (Faraday, 1974), but you may not remember your dreams upon awakening. The ability to recall a dream decreases the longer after REM sleep you are awakened (Dement & Kleitman, 1957). A lack of recall is more probable than the absence of dreaming.

We have defined a dream as an altered state of consciousness. Dreams differ from conscious experiences in at least two significant ways: First, the setting of a dream can change instantaneously. For example, you might be dreaming one moment about sailing on a lake and the next about climbing a mountain. Second, dreams can be set in the present, past, or future, and can involve people long dead from our own past or from a past we have never experienced.

The Function of Dreams

A variety of hypotheses have been put forward to explain why we dream. Sigmund Freud (1938), for example, suggested that dreams represent an acceptable release of sexual and aggressive instincts. Although Freudian theory has been remarkably influential in Western society, in recent years Freud's notions have been criticized so severely that we should consider them of historical, rather than scientific, interest (e.g., Crews, 1996). Here we examine two main views of the role of dreaming. (Table 9.2 summarizes these ideas about the function of dreams.)

Table 9.2
Hypotheses of the Function of Dreams

View	Central Idea
Freudian	Dreams represent acceptable release of sexual and aggressive instincts.
Cognitive	Dreams are a way to deal with life's problems, perhaps by previewing them. Also, dreams are involved in memory storage.
Activation-Synthesis	Dreams have no inherent meaning and result from mental interpretation of neural activity during sleep.

A Cognitive View of Dreams. Cognitive psychologists have suggested that dreams are a way of dealing with life's problems, perhaps by previewing them (Antrobus, 1991; Domhoff, 1996). According to this view, dreams involve everyday experiences and often occur just before a related important event. For example, you might dream about starting a new job the night before you accept the position. (Maybe the hen in Figure 9.19 knows it is headed for McDonald's.) The **cognitive perspective** also suggests that dreams may help store certain memories and discard or forget others. As already indicated, we do know that REM sleep enhances the consolidation or storage of recent experiences (Chapter 14).

Anecdotal reports suggest that remarkable scientific insights may occur following sleep. In Chapter 1, for example, we discussed Otto Loewi's experiments with frog hearts in which he demonstrated that at least one form of synaptic transmission is chemical. Loewi's idea for the experiment came to him in a dream. The first time he had the dream, he scribbled some notes on the idea when he awoke during the night. Unfortunately, he was unable to decipher his notes the next morning, and the idea seemed lost. When he had the same dream the following night, Loewi got out of bed, went to his laboratory, and did the experiment that eventually won him a Nobel prize (Loewi, 1960). Recent work shows that such sleep-related insights can actually be quantified (Stickgold & Walker, 2004; Wagner & others, 2004). For example, Wagner and colleagues first trained subjects on a complex procedure for a mathematical task. After the initial training, the subjects were retested on the task after a period of waking or after a night of sleep. The subjects who had slept used the procedure to solve the task 16.5% faster than before; subjects who did not sleep before retesting averaged less than 6% improvement. More importantly, nearly 60% of the subjects who had a night of sleep between training and retesting discovered a "shortcut" that enabled them to cut their average time to solution by more than 70%! This shortcut was recognized by no more than 25% of the subjects who did not sleep. Thus, sleeping may facilitate the insight process, although exactly how this occurs is unknown.

dream An altered state of consciousness in which remembered images and fantasies are confused with external reality.

cognitive perspective In dream research, the view that dreams help solve everyday problems and may help store certain memories and discard other memories.

activation-synthesis theory The view that dreams are a mental interpretation of the neural activity that occurs during sleep.

lucid dream A dream in which the person is conscious that he or she is dreaming.

Activation-Synthesis Theory. Hobson and McCarley (1977) proposed that dreams have no inherent meaning. Instead, according to their **activation-synthesis theory,** dreams are a mental interpretation of the neural activity that occurs during sleep. During REM sleep, the brain produces a great deal of neural activity, with activation of sensory areas and inhibition of motor areas. Because this neural activity involves random areas, our brain attempts to synthesize it in such a way that it makes sense. As an illustration, our motor systems are almost completely paralyzed during REM sleep. People commonly dream of being either locked up or tied up, which perhaps represents the brain's interpretation of the suppression of muscle tension.

Another characteristic of REM sleep is the activation of the vestibular system (Chapter 7), the system responsible for balance. Stimulation of the vestibular organs while we are lying down would thus be expected to create sensations of falling, floating, or flying—which are indeed frequent themes of dreams.

Hobson (1988) suggested a reason why REM sleep and dreaming do not occur throughout the night. The neurons of the pons that initiate REM sleep fire in unrestrained bursts, but they do not contain unlimited ammunition: They must reload before refiring, and this, according to Hobson, is why we do not dream continuously. Consistent with this idea, a depletion of ACh, the neurotransmitter used by the pontine neurons, is associated with the end of a period of REM sleep, and the next period of REM begins when the neurons have replenished their ACh. Drugs that stimulate cholinergic neurons produce REM sleep (e.g., Gann & others, 2001; Kubin, 2001), whereas cholinergic antagonists reduce REM sleep (e.g., Mavanji & Datta, 2002; Schafer & Greulich, 2000). Further, increased REM sleep has been found in rats selectively bred for cholinergic hyperactivity (Benca & others, 1996; Greco & others, 1998). Of the various ideas about the role of dreaming, the activation-synthesis theory has the greatest experimental support.

Lucid Dreams

Have you ever had a dream in which you realize you are dreaming? If so, you have experienced a **lucid dream,** a dream in which the sleeper is conscious of being in a dream state (Blackmore, 1991; LaBerge, 1993). In surveys on this topic, about half of all respondents, and sometimes more, report having had at least one lucid dream (Gackenbach & LaBerge, 1988). The lucid dream has two components: the dream content and the conscious awareness of dreaming.

Of course, being aware that you are dreaming may simply mean that you are not really asleep. However, research by Stephen LaBerge and his associates indicates that many lucid dreams begin with the high level of cortical activity and high autonomic nervous system activity at the beginning of a REM sleep period (LaBerge, 1993). In one examination of physiological correlates of lucid dreaming, LaBerge and colleagues (1986) found decreased finger pulse amplitude, increased breathing rate and irregularity, and increased eye-movement activity compared with normal REM sleep. As a further illustration that lucid dreaming is a real phenomenon, a study of a lucid dreamer who was able to signal to researchers during dream episodes revealed that the muscles of his body displayed small movements that corresponded to the actions he was performing in a dream (Schatzman & others, 1988). Gackenbach and LaBerge (1988) suggested that one way to tell we are dreaming and not awake when having a lucid dream is the inconsistency of the dream content with reality. For example, your dog talking in perfect English might be a clue that you are dreaming.

One of the most interesting aspects of lucid dreaming is that some people can learn to experience lucid dreams (Gackenbach & LaBerge, 1988) and thus control their dream content. LaBerge and his associates (1983) tested a woman who had developed the ability to dream lucidly at will and could direct her dreams to create sexual experiences. Using physiological recordings, the researchers found that her dream orgasms were matched by real orgasms.

Recent research on lucid dreaming suggests that the time required for specific tasks in lucid dreams and the waking state depends on the task (Erlacher & Schredl, 2004). The time needed for counting was the same in both states, whereas the time required for a motor activity (performing squats) was longer in the dream state than in the waking state. In addition, the induction of lucid dreaming has been found to be a useful treatment for recurrent nightmares, possibly because it gives the dreamer the ability to change dream content (Tanner, 2004; Zadra & Pihl, 1997). Based on his research, Watanabe (2003) concluded that most people probably have the capacity to have lucid dreams, if an appropriate training method can be found to reinforce their private self-consciousness.

Checkpoint

Exhausted from her afternoon in Paris, Sheila falls asleep and dreams she is in the Louvre and Mona Lisa is trying to tell her something. She tries to move closer, but a guard sees her approach the painting and begins to chase her. She runs and runs but cannot seem to get away. Briefly interpret Sheila's dream according to the cognitive perspective and the activation-synthesis theory.

REVIEW

- NREM sleep is maintained by the raphé nuclei. The transition from wakefulness to sleep most likely involves GABAergic neurons in the basal forebrain region, including the preoptic area of the hypothalamus.
- The caudal reticular formation initiates REM sleep. Decreased activity in the locus coeruleus removes the inhibition of the caudal reticular formation, initiating REM sleep.
- In a dream, remembered images and fantasies are confused with external reality. Dreams are more likely to occur during REM sleep than during NREM sleep.
- The cognitive perspective suggests that dreams represent a means of solving problems we may be facing in our lives. The activation-synthesis theory proposes that a dream is a mental interpretation of the essentially random neural activity that occurs during REM sleep.
- In a lucid dream, the sleeping person is aware of dreaming.

Sleep Disorders

Walter saw a notice for a Colorado ski trip during spring break. He'd have to share a room with someone he didn't know, but Walter had lived with many different roommates and thought he could handle anything. But that was before he met Paul, one of the school's chaperones who accompanied the students on the trip.

Paul was a nice enough guy, although he was old enough to be Walter's father. He was also quite large, and Walter was grateful they did not have to share a bed. The first night at the lodge, Walter turned in around 1:00 a.m. When he got to the room, he found that Paul had already gone to bed and was sleeping soundly. Trying to be as quiet as possible, Walter slid under the covers as the clock on the nightstand showed 1:15. He dropped off to sleep quickly.

Less than an hour later, Walter struggled to consciousness, aware only of a deafening rasping sound. Was it an avalanche? Earthquake? Walter threw off the covers, rolled out of bed, and ran into the hall—but the noise was gone. Total silence greeted him as he slipped back into his room. He got back under the covers, rolled into his sleeping position, closed his eyes . . . and the noise started again. It was Paul, making the loudest snoring sounds Walter had ever heard. He thought his father was a loud snorer, but now he knew better. Paul must be the king of snorers.

As suddenly as the noise had started, it stopped again, and Walter realized that Paul wasn't breathing. He held his own breath in sympathy for 10 . . . 20 . . . 30 agonizing seconds, before the rasping began again. What in the world was wrong with the man?

insomnia A sleep disorder characterized by a long-term inability to obtain adequate sleep.

Paul suffers from sleep apnea, one of the many types of sleep disorder. Although there are other ways to categorize them, most sleep disorders can be grouped into two broad categories: insomnia, or not enough sleep (which includes sleep apnea), and hypersomnia, or too much sleep.

Insomnia

You probably have trouble falling asleep sometimes, tossing and turning for what seems like hours before finally nodding off. When you awaken the next morning, you still feel tired. After a few nights like this, you might wonder whether you have a sleeping problem. Unless you have a good situational reason for your sleep difficulties, like Walter did with his snoring roommate, you may suffer from **insomnia,** a long-term inability to get enough sleep. Insomnia can involve taking a long time to fall asleep, frequent waking during the night, and/or awakening several hours before the normal rising time.

Insomnia is a common disorder. Dement (1986) suggested that if we consider insomnia in all its forms, it may well be the most common medical problem. Insomnia is a persistent problem for about 10% of the population in the United States (Walsh, 2004). Not all people are equally likely to suffer from insomnia; for example, it is more prevalent in older adults and in women (Walsh). Widowed, divorced, or separated people also are more likely to experience insomnia than married or single, never-married people. A too-noisy environment, an uncomfortable bed, or new surroundings can also produce insomnia. (See Box 9.1 for tips on overcoming mild insomnia.)

Insomnia is often more apparent than real. Most people who complain of chronic sleeplessness actually require only about 30 minutes to fall asleep, and they frequently sleep as much as other adults. For example, Weitzman (1981) examined the EEG records of people who reported they slept little, if at all, and found they usually slept for 6 or 7 hours a night.

Anxiety and depression are important contributors to insomnia (Soldatos & Kales, 1986). Individuals who are anxious about their daily problems often have difficulty falling asleep. Some people worry so much about being unable to fall asleep that they have greater difficulty doing so, creating a vicious cycle. Some depressed people have no trouble falling asleep but wake up too early and then cannot get back to sleep, whereas others simply have difficulty falling asleep. Insomnia caused by psychological problems can be treated along with the psychopathology (Soldatos & Kales).

Not surprisingly, stimulants such as caffeine and/or nicotine can make falling asleep difficult (Chapter 5). Although people often consume alcohol to help them fall asleep, excessive alcohol use can actually lead to insomnia, which then persists even with lower levels of drinking (Brower, 2003).

Taking sedatives or tranquilizers is a popular way to treat insomnia. However, a sedative reduces the time needed to fall asleep by an average of only 15 minutes,

Box 9.1
Treating Mild Insomnia

Brief, minor insomnia often can be overcome without therapy, by following the following guidelines:

- Do not nap during the day, as this can reduce your need for sleep and make it harder for you to fall asleep at night.
- Go to bed and get up at the same time each day, to establish a regular sleep-wake cycle.
- Avoid sleeping in a room that is either too warm or too noisy. The ideal temperature seems to be between 65 degrees and 70 degrees. If outside noise is a problem, a "sleep machine" that produces a constant sound (e.g., soothing sound or "white noise") may be the answer to your insomnia problem.
- Read something pleasant or relaxing, take a warm bath, or get a massage before going to sleep. Peaceful stretching or relaxation exercises may be helpful.
- Avoid stimulants, such as caffeine or nicotine, especially in the evenings.
- Try drinking a cup of chamomile tea half an hour before bedtime.
- Tryptophan-rich foods eaten before bedtime may be useful, as they tend to raise the levels of serotonin and melatonin. Foods high in tryptophan include dairy products such as milk, cottage cheese, yogurt, and ice cream, chicken, tuna, cashews, soy beans, and bananas. Be sure you have only a light snack of tryptophan-rich foods before bedtime, as a large, heavy meal may produce insomnia rather than alleviating it.
- Do not do anything stimulating before bedtime. This includes exercising, watching an exciting movie or television program, and reading an exciting book.
- Do not use alcohol, sedatives, or over-the-counter sleeping pills to help you fall asleep.
- Some people find visualization useful. For example, you might focus all your attention on your toes or visualize lying in the warm sand on a peaceful beach. It may also help to think of something mindless or repetitive.
- If you still cannot get to sleep, do not lie in bed worrying about it. Get up, leave the bedroom, and read, do some work, or watch television until you feel drowsy.

and the total extra sleep time produced is only about half an hour (Mendelson, 1987). Some sedatives enable people to fall asleep but the effect wears off before morning and the person awakens early (Kales & others, 1983). Other sedatives may last too long, causing sleepiness the next day, which the person may try to alleviate by taking stimulants. Still other sedatives reduce REM sleep time, which causes the person to awaken still tired (Gottesmann, 1996). The benzodiazepine zolpidem, which does not appear to disrupt the natural progression and duration of sleep stages, has become a popular treatment for insomnia (Besset & others, 1995).

The long-term use of sedatives can cause greater difficulty sleeping, as the individual becomes tolerant to the drug and is forced to continue its use just to fall asleep. **Drug-dependent insomnia** is a disturbance of sleep that can occur when a person stops taking a sleeping medication or takes a lower-than-normal dose. This insomnia produced by withdrawal from a sleeping medication is perceived as worse than that experienced before the medication was initially taken, and it can develop after just one night of medication (Merlotti & others, 1991). Fortunately, *rebound insomnia* can be prevented by using the lowest effective dose of the medication and discontinuing drug treatment gradually (Roehrs & others, 1990). Because of the problems sleeping medication can produce, its use in general appears to be unwise.

Sleep apnea, the type of insomnia affecting Paul, is a repeated interruption of sleep caused by the cessation of breathing (apnea). Individuals with sleep apnea fall asleep and, while sleeping, stop breathing for periods of up to a minute. Breathing stops because of the obstruction of airflow in the throat, which occurs when the upper throat muscles relax, closing the airway in the back of the mouth. The person then makes a loud snorting sound when gasping for air. This cycle of breathing cessation followed by gasping for air may take place up to several hundred times each night. No wonder Walter was unnerved by Paul's sleep apnea and had such difficulty sleeping in the same room. Amazingly, Paul probably has no recollection of his many awakenings during the night and knows only that he feels tired every morning when he gets up.

drug-dependent insomnia A sleep disorder that occurs when a person attempts to sleep without previously used sleep medication or takes a lower-than-normal dose.

sleep apnea A sleep disorder characterized by repeated interruptions of sleep caused by the cessation of breathing.

Sleep apnea is a serious problem that lowers the quality of life of the sufferer (Moyer & others, 2001; Yang & others, 2000) and is a major factor in death in the elderly because of its association with cardiovascular problems and increased risk of traffic accidents (Quinnell & Smith, 2004). The disorder is strongly associated with obesity and is at least twice as common in men as in women (Jordan & McEvoy, 2003; Kapsimalis & Kryger, 2002). Studies of people with sleep apnea have also revealed numerous cognitive deficits associated with the disorder, such as reduced memory span, difficulty initiating new mental processes and inhibiting automatic ones, and problems with verbal and visual learning abilities (Engleman & others, 2000; Naegelé & others, 1995). Therapies include weight loss, oral appliances, surgery, and continuous positive airway pressure (CPAP), in which a small compressor delivers a steady stream of air through a mask worn over the nose (Hoekema & others, 2004) (Figure 9.20). CPAP treatment also can alleviate the cognitive problems seen with sleep apnea (Malhotra & others, 2000).

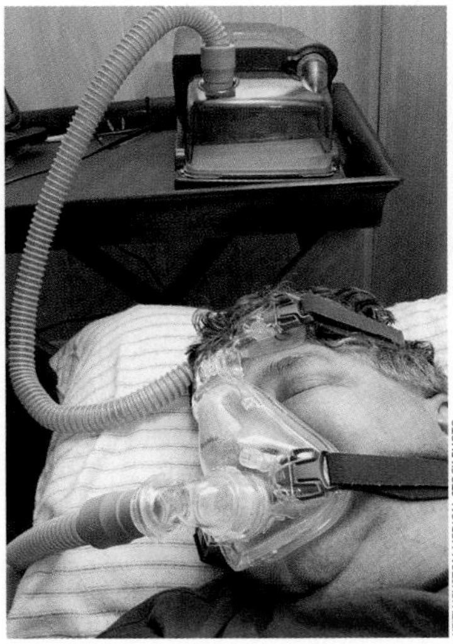

KEITH/CUSTOM MEDICAL STOCK PHOTO

Figure 9.20

Treatment of sleep apnea This man is using continuous positive airway pressure (CPAP) to treat his sleep apnea. The CPAP device employs a mask that fits over the patient's nose and mouth and forces air through the nasal and oral passages.

What are some of the symptoms of sleep apnea?

Hypersomnia

People who suffer from **hypersomnia** get too much sleep. NREM sleep disorders and REM sleep disorders are two categories of hypersomnia.

NREM Sleep Disorders

REM behavior disorder, in which dreams are acted out, should not be confused with sleepwalking. **Sleepwalking,** or *somnambulism,* occurs during NREM sleep and is not related to dreaming. Sleepwalking is most common in children, who usually outgrow the problem. In a typical episode—which usually occurs during the first 3 hours of sleep, when sleep stages 3 and 4 are most common—the child gets out of bed and walks around the room for up to half-an-hour (Masand & others, 1995). Although the sleepwalker often walks in a poorly coordinated manner, he or she may perform such actions as opening a door or going to the bathroom. While sleepwalking, the child is not responsive to others and will either return to bed and continue sleeping or awaken in a confused state. On waking, the child generally has little or no recollection of having sleepwalked. Management of this disorder involves implementing appropriate safety measures such as locking windows and doors.

Night terror, or *pavor nocturnus,* is an abrupt awakening from NREM sleep accompanied by intense autonomic arousal and feelings of panic. A person experiencing a night terror typically emits a piercing cry, sits upright in bed, and stares into space. The panic fades quickly, and the person goes back to sleep. A night terror attack should not be confused with a *nightmare,* which is an anxiety-induced dream; the individual experiencing night terror typically does not recall any dream. Night terrors are most common in children, especially between the ages of 3 and 8 years, and they usually outgrow them. Treatment is generally unnecessary.

Bedwetting, or *nocturnal enuresis,* is another NREM sleep disorder. Bladder control during the night develops as a child matures, and by 4 or 5 years of age, most children do not wet the bed. One way to treat chronic bedwetting is by using a commercial device that establishes an association between bladder tension and awakening. When the child begins to urinate, an alarm rings and awakens the child; this forms an association between the need to urinate and the alarm. With repeated trials, the child will awaken rather than wet the bed. This treatment, which is a type of conditioning, usually is effective (Glazener & others, 2003). If relapse occurs, reconditioning is achieved quickly and often cures bedwetting permanently. (For more on conditioning, see Chapter 14.)

REM Sleep Disorders

Narcolepsy is characterized by sudden, uncontrollable sleep attacks, usually initiated by monotonous activity and lasting 2 to 4 minutes, or sometimes up to 15 minutes. After a sleep attack, the person awakens feeling refreshed. The danger of narcolepsy is that the sleep attacks can happen at any time, without warning. A person with narcolepsy could thus fall asleep while crossing the street, driving a

hypersomnia A sleep disorder characterized by too much sleep.

sleepwalking Getting out of bed and walking during NREM sleep.

night terror An abrupt awakening from NREM sleep, accompanied by intense autonomic arousal and feelings of panic.

bedwetting An NREM sleep disorder characterized by lack of bladder control during sleep.

narcolepsy A sleep disorder characterized by a sudden, uncontrollable sleep attack, usually initiated by monotonous activity.

cataplexy A sudden, complete lack of muscle tone that sometimes accompanies narcolepsy.

sleep paralysis A brief paralysis that occurs when a person with narcolepsy is going to sleep or awakening.

REM behavior disorder A sleep disorder in which the person acts out a dream, because of a failure to lose muscle tone during REM sleep.

car, or swimming in a pool. Imagine how your activities would be restricted if you could fall asleep at any moment.

Three additional symptoms sometimes experienced by people with narcolepsy are cataplexy, sleep paralysis, and hallucinations. **Cataplexy** is a sudden, complete lack of muscle tone. During a cataplectic attack, the person suddenly wilts, falls to the ground, and lies paralyzed, unable to move for several seconds to several minutes. Whatever causes sleep attacks probably also produces the loss of muscle tone, which is characteristic of REM sleep. Exhibited by most people with narcolepsy, cataplexy is almost always triggered by intense situations, such as being in a highly emotional state or engaging in strenuous physical activity.

Sleep paralysis is a brief paralysis that occurs when the individual with narcolepsy is falling asleep or awakening. Another person often can interrupt the paralysis by touching the sleeper or saying his or her name. Sleep paralysis is less common than cataplexy; only 20% of individuals with narcolepsy experience it.

Some people with narcolepsy also dream or experience hallucinations (recall that most remembered dreams occur during REM sleep). These are often unpleasant, alarming, and sometimes terrifying. Hallucinations can occur during sleep paralysis, when the person is either going to sleep or awakening.

Narcolepsy appears to involve the intrusion of REM sleep into wakefulness, and an analysis of EEG records has revealed that most people with narcolepsy show REM sleep patterns during their attacks (Wilson & others, 1973). People with narcolepsy go directly from a waking state to REM sleep, which lasts 10 to 20 minutes (Figure 9.21). If the person remains asleep, REM sleep is followed by a slow progression through stages 1 through 4 of NREM sleep.

As an indication of the major role of genetics in narcolepsy, family studies suggest that the incidence of narcolepsy is 20 to 40 times higher in first-degree relatives of someone with the disorder than in the general population (Chabas & others,

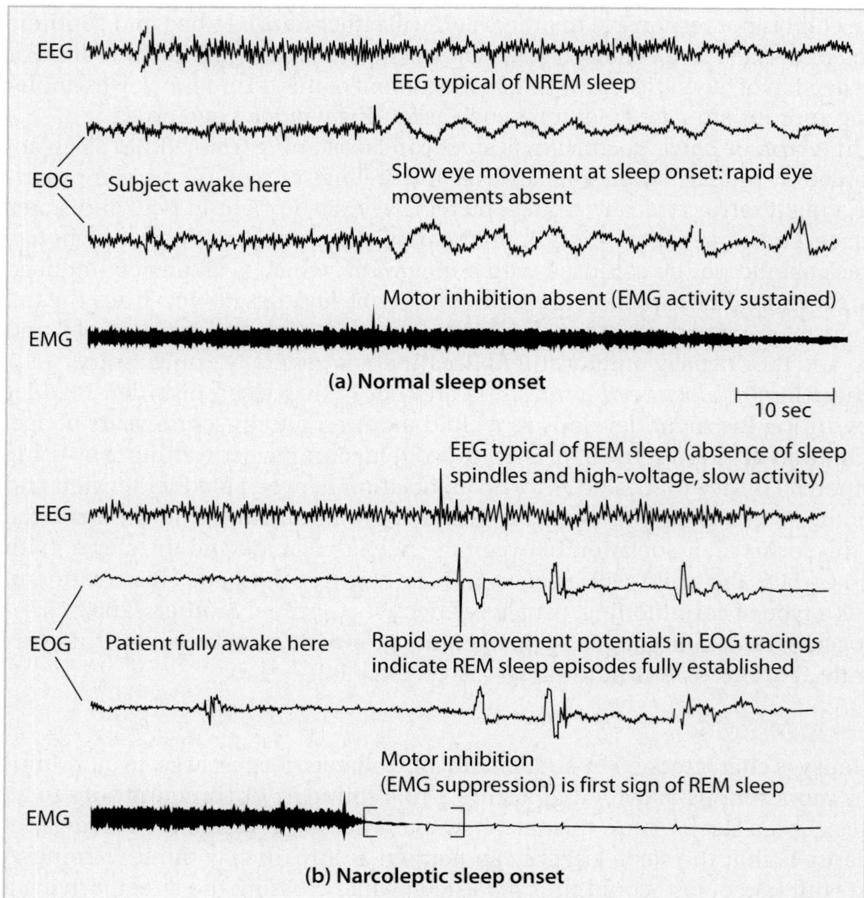

Figure 9.21

Narcolepsy and sleep onset (a) In normal sleep onset, the waking state is followed by NREM sleep. These tracings show that REM sleep is not present immediately after sleep begins. (b) A person with narcolepsy can enter REM sleep from the waking state. EOG and EMG refer to measurement of eye movements (two tracings, one from each eye) and muscular activity, respectively.

➡ **What is the significance of the sleep differences between normal sleepers and people with narcolepsy?**

2003). In addition, the human leukocyte antigen (HLA) is strongly associated with narcolepsy, which suggests that the disorder has an autoimmune basis (Chabas & others; Lin & others, 2001; Nishino & others, 2000). Further research indicates that narcolepsy is associated with the autoimmune destruction of lateral hypothalamic neurons containing the peptide hypocretins (orexins) (Lin & others).

Biologists have bred a line of dogs with narcolepsy, which have long been used in the study of the disorder (Figure 9.22). Research with the canine model has concluded that narcolepsy is caused by a problem with the hypocretin (orexin) receptor 2 gene, which results in a deficiency in hypocretin neurotransmission (Lin & others, 1999; Taheri & Mignot, 2002; Taheri & others, 2002). Additional evidence for the importance of orexin in sleep and wakefulness comes from work on mice without the orexin gene, which can be used as a model for human narcolepsy (Chemelli & others, 1999).

Hypothalamic neurons containing orexin send their axons throughout the brain, including to the major structures involved in sleep regulation (Chemelli & others, 1999). One of those structures is the locus coeruleus, which is densely innervated by orexin neurons (Bourgin & others, 2000). As we indicated earlier, activity in the locus coeruleus inhibits REM sleep. Bourgin and colleagues found that administration of one of the orexins into the locus coeruleus suppressed REM sleep and increased wakefulness, which led the researchers to suggest that the orexin receptor in the structure is a key target for regulating REM sleep and is possibly involved in narcolepsy. Dysfunction in the locus coeruleus may cause an intrusion of REM sleep into the waking state, which is experienced as narcolepsy.

Therapeutic naps and medications are two approaches for treating narcolepsy (Vgontzas & Kales, 1999). For example, catecholamine agonists such as amphetamine (Chapter 5) can keep a person with narcolepsy awake. The drugs probably work by activating noradrenergic receptors in the locus coeruleus. Antidepressant drugs such as imipramine appear to reduce cataplexy, sleep paralysis, and hallucinations in people with narcolepsy by increasing activity in neurons that use serotonin, norepinephrine, and dopamine as neurotransmitters. The finding that different drugs affect different systems suggests that the structures that produce the sleep attacks are different from those that produce the other narcoleptic symptoms. Usually, both types of drugs are prescribed in treating narcolepsy. In keeping with the research evidence implicating the hypocretins in the pathophysiology of narcolepsy, hypocretin agonists are being developed as potential therapeutic agents in the disorder (Dauvilliers & others, 2003).

Given that monotonous activities such as driving can cause a sleep attack in a person with narcolepsy, avoiding such activities reduces the probability of an attack. In addition, people susceptible to cataplexy can learn to control the intensity of their emotions in order to reduce the likelihood of an attack.

Another type of REM sleep disorder is **REM behavior disorder,** or *REM without atonia,* in which the person acts out the events in a dream (Ferini-Strambi & Zucconi, 2000). As the alternative name suggests, people with REM behavior disorder fail to lose muscle tone during REM sleep and thus can perform their REM sleep actions. The following case illustrates the danger in this disorder:

> I was a halfback playing football, and after the quarterback received the ball from the center he lateraled it sideways to me and I'm supposed to go around end and cut back over tackle and—this is very vivid—as I cut back over tackle there is this big 280-pound tackle waiting, so I, according to football rules, was to give him my shoulder and bounce him out of the way, supposedly, and when I came to I was standing in front of our dresser and I had knocked lamps, mirrors and everything off the dresser, hit my head against the wall and my knee against the dresser. (Schenck & others, 1986, p. 294)

Similar disorders have been produced in laboratory animals. For example, when Jouvet (1972) damaged the brains of cats in the area caudal to the dorsolateral pons, they would carry out different behaviors during REM sleep periods, in the absence of external stimulation. For example, a cat might play with a dream mouse or attack a dream enemy.

Lesions of the dorsolateral pons, which are known to produce an apparent REM behavior disorder in cats (Jouvet, 1972), disrupt the neural connection from the

© CATHERINE KARNOW

Figure 9.22

Narcoleptic dog From the excitement of discovering some food, this Doberman has succumbed to narcolepsy, with cataplexy, a complete lack of muscle tone.

→ **What can studies on narcoleptic dogs tell us about narcolepsy in humans?**

dorsolateral pons to a structure called the magnocellular nucleus in the medial medulla (Sakai, 1980). The magnocellular nucleus is active during REM sleep (Kanamori & others, 1980), and damage to this structure produces REM without atonia (Schenkel & Siegel, 1989). These observations suggest that the neural connection between the dorsolateral pons and the magnocellular nucleus inhibits muscle tone during REM sleep and that malfunctioning of this pathway leads to REM behavior disorder.

REM behavior disorder typically occurs in older men, and its incidence in the general population is thought to be around 0.5% (Fantini & others, 2005). The disorder often precedes Parkinson's disease, and the converse is also true—some persons with Parkinson's disease subsequently develop REM behavior disorder (Ferini-Strambi & Zucconi, 2000; Lai & Siegel, 2003; Montplaisir, 2004). REM behavior disorder may also be associated with other neurodegenerative diseases, such as multiple system atrophy (originally known as Shy-Drager syndrome; main symptoms are parkinsonism and autonomic failure) and dementia with Lewy bodies (the second most common cause of dementia in the elderly; it is characterized by abnormal structures—Lewy bodies—in certain areas of the brain) (Abad & Guilleminault, 2004). Nightingale and colleagues (2005) found a much stronger than expected association between REM behavior disorder and narcolepsy.

➤Checkpoint

What is the difference between REM behavior disorder and sleepwalking? What is the difference between night terrors and nightmares?

REVIEW

- The two major classes of sleep disorders are insomnia, or failing to get enough sleep, and hypersomnia, or getting too much sleep.
- A person with insomnia may take a long time to get to sleep, awaken frequently during the night, and/or awaken several hours before normal rising time.
- Anxiety and depression are major causes of insomnia, along with stimulating drugs and noisy or unfamiliar environments.
- In sleep apnea, a type of insomnia, an obstruction in the airway causes a cessation of breathing during sleep.
- Disorders of NREM sleep include sleepwalking, walking around while asleep for up to 30 minutes; night terrors, an abrupt awakening from NREM sleep accompanied by intense autonomic nervous system arousal and feelings of panic; and bedwetting.
- Narcolepsy, a type of hypersomnia, is characterized by sudden, uncontrollable sleep attacks that can last from 2 to 15 minutes. It results from dysfunction of the locus coeruleus, which allows REM sleep to occur in the waking state.
- Other symptoms of narcolepsy include cataplexy, a complete loss of muscle tone initiated by intense circumstances; sleep paralysis, a brief paralysis that occurs when the person is going to sleep or awakening and is accompanied by high levels of anxiety; and hallucinations.

Chapter Review

Key Terms

activation-synthesis theory (p. 329)
alpha activity (p. 316)
basal forebrain region (p. 326)
bedwetting (p. 333)
beta activity (p. 316)
cataplexy (p. 334)
caudal reticular formation (p. 327)
cerveau isolé preparation (p. 316)
circadian cycle (p. 308)
circadian rhythm (p. 308)
cognitive perspective (p. 328)
delta activity (p. 319)
diurnal animal (p. 310)
dream (p. 328)
drug-dependent insomnia (p. 332)
encéphale isolé preparation (p. 317)
free-running rhythm (p. 311)
hypersomnia (p. 333)

insomnia (p. 331)
jet lag (p. 308)
K complex (p. 319)
lark (p. 308)
light therapy (p. 312)
locus coeruleus (p. 318)
lucid dream (p. 329)
melatonin (p. 311)
microsleep (p. 322)
narcolepsy (p. 333)
night terror (p. 333)
nocturnal animal (p. 310)
nonREM (NREM) sleep (p. 319)
nonvisual photoreceptor (p. 311)
owl (p. 309)
PGO wave (p. 320)
phase-advance shift (p. 313)
phase-delay shift (p. 313)
pineal gland (p. 311)
raphé nucleus (p. 326)
rapid eye movement (REM) sleep (p. 320)
REM behavior disorder (p. 335)
REM rebound (p. 322)
reticular activating system (RAS) (p. 317)
retinohypothalamic tract (p. 311)
seasonal affective disorder (SAD) (p. 312)
sleep apnea (p. 332)
sleep paralysis (p. 334)
sleep spindle (p. 319)
sleepwalking (p. 333)
slow-wave sleep (SWS) (p. 319)
stage 1 sleep (p. 319)
stage 2 sleep (p. 319)
stage 3 sleep (p. 319)
stage 4 sleep (p. 319)
suprachiasmatic nucleus (SCN) (p. 309)
theta activity (p. 319)
visual photoreceptor (p. 311)
zeitgeber (p. 311)

Suggested Readings

Dement, W. C. (1992). *The sleepwatchers.* Stanford: Stanford Alumni Association.

Hobson, J. A. (1995). *Sleep.* New York: Scientific American Library.

Hobson, J. A., Pace-Schott, E. F., & Stickgold, R. (2000). Dreaming and the brain: Toward a cognitive neuroscience of conscious states. *Behavioral and Brain Sciences, 23,* 793–1121.

King, D. P., & Takahashi, J. S. (2000). Molecular genetics of circadian rhythms in mammals. *Annual Review of Neuroscience, 23,* 713–742.

Maquet, P. (2001). The role of sleep in learning and memory. *Science, 294,* 1048–1052.

Moorcroft, W. H. (1993). *Sleep, dreaming, and sleep disorders* (2nd ed.). Lanham, MD: University Press of America.

Webb, W. (1992). *Sleep: The gentle tyrant* (2nd ed.). Boston: Anker Publishing.

Critical Thinking Questions

1. Heather is planning a trip from California to Australia. Describe the biological consequences she is likely to experience as a result of her trip (the time difference is 17 hours). What might Heather do to minimize the effects of jet lag?
2. Sven lives in northern Finland. During the winter, he experiences several days with no sunlight. What might be the effects of these "endless nights"? How might Sven avoid or alleviate these effects?
3. Carolyn dreamed she was being chased by a lion. Interpret Carolyn's dream from the perspective of the activation-synthesis theory.

Fill-in-the-Blank Questions

1. ______ is a pattern of mood changes based on the seasons.
2. People who are most alert in the morning are referred to as ______ and those most alert in the evening as ______.
3. A(n) ______ is a change in biological and behavioral functioning over a 24 hour period.
4. The brain area responsible for the circadian cycle is the ______.
5. ______ animals sleep by day and are active at night; ______ animals are awake by day and asleep at night.
6. The sleep-wake cycle that occurs in the absence of external time cues is called a(n) ______.
7. ______ are conditions in nature that operate on a 24 hour cycle and reset an organism's biological clock.
8. The ______ photoreceptor detects the dawn-dusk cycle.
9. In ______, a person receives intense broad-spectrum light to treat seasonal affective disorder.
10. Two examples of phase-sequence problems are ______ and ______.

11. In waking subjects, the active EEG pattern is called ______ activity, and the relaxed EEG pattern is called ______ activity.
12. Bremer made a cut between the inferior colliculi and the superior colliculi in the ______ preparation, and a cut just above the spinal cord in the ______ preparation.
13. Following the classic study of Moruzzi and Magoun, the reticular formation became known as the ______.
14. The area within the reticular formation responsible for cortical activity and behavioral alertness is the ______.
15. The two distinct EEG patterns observed during stage 2 sleep are ______ and ______.
16. Stages 3 and 4 sleep are also called ______.
17. Spikes of neural activity that begin in the pons, continue to the LGN, and end in the occipital cortex are called ______.
18. People deprived of REM sleep spend a greater proportion of their sleeping time in REM sleep when they are no longer being deprived; this phenomenon is called ______.
19. After 3 days of sleep deprivation, people exhibit periods of ______ in which they appear to be awake but their EEG patterns resemble stage 1 sleep.
20. The ______, located in a thin strip along the midline of the reticular formation, control the length of slow-wave sleep; REM sleep is initiated by the ______.
21. A(n) ______ is an altered state of consciousness in which remembered images and fantasies are temporarily confused with external reality.
22. According to the ______ view of dreams, dreaming is a way of dealing with life's problems.
23. According to the ______ theory, dreams are a mental interpretation of the essentially random neural activity that occurs during sleep.
24. A dream in which you realize you are dreaming is called a(n) ______ dream.
25. A repeated interruption of sleep caused by the cessation of breathing is called ______.
26. ______ is a disturbance of sleep that occurs when a person who has been taking sleep medication attempts to sleep without medication or takes a lower-than-normal dose.
27. An abrupt awakening from NREM sleep accompanied by autonomic arousal and feelings of panic is characteristic of ______.
28. The main characteristic of ______ is sudden, uncontrollable sleep attacks.
29. ______ is a brief paralysis that occurs when a person with narcolepsy is either going to sleep or awakening.
30. In ______, a person maintains muscle tone during REM sleep.

Multiple-Choice Questions

1. A change in biological functioning over a 24 hour period is called a
   a. circadian cycle.
   b. circannual pattern.
   c. circular pattern.
   d. cyclical rhythm.
2. The circadian rhythm is controlled by
   a. the locus coeruleus.
   b. the suprachiasmatic nucleus.
   c. the reticular activating system.
   d. raphé nuclei.
3. You would expect ______ to make higher grades in morning courses than in evening courses and ______ to perform better in the evening.
   a. owls, larks
   b. larks, owls
   c. owls, robins
   d. robins, owls
4. "Zeitgeber" means
   a. sleep giver.
   b. time taker.
   c. time giver.
   d. sleep taker.
5. If you lived in a cave and did not experience the change from the darkness of night to the light of day, you would develop a
   a. diurnal cycle.
   b. nocturnal cycle.
   c. free-running rhythm.
   d. zeitgeber.
6. Information from the nonvisual photoreceptors travels to the SCN by way of the
   a. arcuate fasciculus.
   b. reticular activating system.
   c. spinothalamic tract.
   d. retinohypothalamic tract.
7. Reduced daylight can produce ______ in some individuals.
   a. seasonal affective disorder
   b. pavor nocturnis
   c. REM behavior disorder
   d. phase-sequencing disorder
8. In people who work rotating shifts, a ______ is more manageable than a ______.
   a. night shift, swing shift
   b. phase-delay shift, phase-advance shift
   c. day shift, swing shift
   d. phase-advance shift, phase-delay shift
9. Maria feels tired and groggy after her flight to London from Atlanta. The best thing for her to do is to
   a. go to bed and sleep until her normal waking time.
   b. take a short nap.
   c. take a walk in the sunshine.
   d. tour a dark museum.

10. The EEG pattern characterized by a rapid, desynchronized pattern of small voltage changes (about 18 to 24 Hz) is called _____ activity.
a. alpha **c.** beta
b. theta **d.** gamma

11. Wanda can hardly keep her eyes open as she watches a *Friends* rerun. If we could record her EEG activity, it would probably show a predominance of _____ waves.
a. beta **c.** delta
b. alpha **d.** theta

12. The part of the brain that controls arousal is the
a. pineal gland. **c.** frontal lobe.
b. reticular activating system. **d.** cerebellum.

13. Bremer found that cats with an encéphale isolé preparation
a. displayed normal sleep-wake cycles.
b. slept continuously.
c. died from lack of sleep.
d. slept continuously at first, but then had a desynchronized EEG pattern.

14. The five levels of sleep are
a. alpha, beta, theta, delta, and gamma.
b. stage 1, stage 2, stage 3, stage 4, and REM sleep.
c. alpha, beta, theta, delta, and REM.
d. stage 1, stage 2, stage 3, stage 4, and nonREM sleep.

15. REM sleep is also called paradoxical sleep because
a. the person appears to be wide awake, but the EEG pattern resembles stage 4 sleep.
b. the person appears to be sound asleep, but the muscles twitch constantly.
c. the person is obviously asleep, but the EEG pattern resembles the waking state.
d. the EEG shows alpha rhythms, but the person's muscles are paralyzed.

16. Most of our vivid and bizarre dreams occur during
a. stage 1 sleep. **c.** stage 4 sleep.
b. nonREM sleep. **d.** REM sleep.

17. PGO waves proceed from the _____ to the _____ to the _____.
a. pons, LGN, oculomotor nerve
b. parietal lobe, LGN, occipital cortex
c. pons, LGN, occipital cortex
d. parietal cortex, MGN, optic chiasm

18. The idea that we need sleep to replenish our biological resources is called
a. the restorative theory. **c.** the cognitive theory.
b. the evolutionary perspective. **d.** the activation-synthesis theory.

19. According to the _____, dreams are a mental interpretation of the neural activity that occurs during sleep.
a. cognitive perspective **c.** evolutionary theory
b. activation-synthesis theory **d.** lucid dream theory

20. People deprived of sleep for 3 days or more begin to exhibit periods of
a. REM sleep. **c.** lucid dreaming sleep.
b. nonREM sleep. **d.** microsleep.

21. Which of the following decreases steadily from infancy to adulthood?
a. SWS **c.** nonREM sleep
b. REM sleep **d.** stage 4 sleep

22. Locus coeruleus activity is associated with an absence of
a. REM sleep. **c.** SWS.
b. nonREM sleep. **d.** stage 4 sleep.

23. We are said to be having a _____ when we are conscious of our dream state.
a. flashback **c.** hallucination
b. pavor nocturnis **d.** lucid dream

24. A person whose sleep is frequently interrupted by a cessation of breathing probably has
a. narcolepsy. **c.** REM without atonia.
b. insomnia. **d.** sleep apnea.

25. Which of the following sleep disorders is often more apparent than real?
a. sleep apnea **c.** hypersomnia
b. insomnia **d.** narcolepsy

26. Sonia sometimes sits bolt upright during the night and screams. She then quickly falls back to sleep and has no recollection of her panic when she wakes up in the morning. Sonia probably has
a. pavor nocturnis. **c.** REM behavior disorder.
b. somnambulism. **d.** narcolepsy.

27. In addition to sleep attacks, three symptoms often observed in narcoleptics are
a. cataplexy, sleep paralysis, and hallucinations.
b. cataplexy, lucid dreams, and REM sleep.
c. insomnia, sleep paralysis, and hallucinations.
d. insomnia, lucid dreams, and hallucinations.

28. Sleepwalking and night terrors both occur during
a. REM without atonia. **c.** lucid dreams.
b. REM sleep. **d.** nonREM sleep.

29. While sleeping, Michael injured his right shoulder attempting to tackle a large armoire in his bedroom. He probably has
a. schizophrenia. **c.** pavor nocturnis.
b. REM behavior disorder. **d.** lucid dreaming.

Answers can be found on the companion website at www.worthpublishers.com/klein.

10

The Biology of Eating and Drinking

- Eating
- The Neural Control of Eating Behavior
- The Nonneural Control of Eating Behavior
- *Scientific American* **Spotlight** The Diet That Fits
- The Long-Term Regulation of Body Weight
- Drinking

Out of Control

After his visit to the Student Health Center for his annual physical, Chris was discouraged. The doctor had made a big issue of Chris's weight; she said he really needed to get it under 250 pounds. At the moment, it was perilously close to 300. When Chris asked about a pill to melt away his pounds, the doctor instead sent him to the dietitian. The dietitian gave him a diet and exercise program that seemed easy enough: During the first month, he was supposed to eat normal meals, exercise for an hour 4 days a week, cut out all between-meal snacks, and keep a record of everything he ate or drank. "Piece of cake," he thought, then remembered the carrot cake he was planning to have for dessert that evening.

Chris had known since his early adolescence that he had a weight problem. He'd tried several prescription weight-loss medications and over-the-counter diet aids. He'd also tried several fad diets. Some of them worked temporarily, but he'd always regained his "lost" weight.

As Chris walked back to his car, he stopped at a small bakery and bought an energy bar to give him strength for his exercise program. He avoided looking at the nutritional information on the wrapper, which said each bar had 632 calories. He also bought a couple of chocolate chip cookies, one of which he ate before he got to his car. Strapped in, he was halfway through the second cookie when he remembered he was supposed to give up between-meal snacks. Might as well finish it, he thought, licking the crumbs from his fingers. He'd get a fresh start on the diet the next day.

For a week, Chris avoided snacks and dutifully wrote down everything he ate and drank. He even went for long walks. By the weekend, he was sure he'd lost several pounds, and to celebrate, he went to his favorite Italian restaurant, just off campus. His plan was to get a small salad, a small pizza, a bowl of spaghetti, and a glass of the house wine. With a nod to his diet, he rejected the foccacia (Italian bread) served with olive oil.

It was amazing how the wine stimulated his appetite and dissolved his good intentions. The second glass *really* worked on his appetite; Chris had ordered it after he'd finished the salad, asked for a second pizza, and wolfed down the bowl of spaghetti. When dessert time came, he couldn't resist the chocolate cream pie topped with Italian ice cream. As he took the last bite, he felt stuffed—and knew he'd blown any progress he had made on his diet and exercise program.

On his way home, Chris decided it was all the doctor's fault for not giving him the short-term prescription for something that would have taken his pounds off in a hurry. Maybe stomach stapling was the answer. He'd ask the doctor at his next visit.

BEFORE YOU BEGIN

- **Why does Chris find it so hard to stick to a diet?**
- **What is it about food that he finds so satisfying?**
- **What behavioral changes does he need to make to lose weight?**
- **What biological processes make Chris hungry when he enters the restaurant and thirsty after he eats the first pizza?**
- **What processes satisfy his hunger and thirst?**
- **How are his hunger for the pizza and his thirst for the wine related physiologically?**
- **What central nervous system structure(s) control his eating and drinking behavior?**
- **What mechanism made him feel full after he finished his dessert in the Italian restaurant?**
- **What are the psychological and biological bases of eating disorders such as anorexia nervosa and bulimia nervosa, and how can they be treated?**

In this chapter, you will find the answers to these questions and many others.

Eating

Although we rarely think about it in countries where food is plentiful, our ability to survive depends on the effectiveness of the biological systems that control eating, the means by which we obtain energy. These systems protect us against starvation by initiating eating when we need food, and under most conditions they act to suppress eating when we are full, or reach **satiety** (pronounced sa-TI-eh-tee). Such suppression is desirable because excessive weight gain can lead to metabolic disturbances that threaten our health. Excessive amounts of food may be consumed under certain conditions, such as when animals (and sometimes people) gorge themselves when food is available in order to maximize the benefits of an infrequent food source. If you have ever owned a dog, you have undoubtedly observed examples of behavior that led to the phrase "wolfing it down." The control mechanisms that govern eating behavior lie within the CNS (Logue, 1991), but information gathered from peripheral biological systems is also important for maintaining an ideal body weight.

But before we consider these central and peripheral systems, we must discuss the processes they control. We will look into what happens to Chris's body when he consumes that plate of spaghetti, then discuss the neural and nonneural mechanisms that control when he starts and stops eating and how much he eats.

The Body's Energy Needs and the Digestive Process

The operation of our biological functions requires energy from three types of nutritional substances: carbohydrates, fats, and proteins. Normally, we have only limited reserves of these energy sources, so we consume food to correct any depletion and restore energy supplies to the level necessary for optimal physiological functioning.

When Chris puts a forkful of spaghetti into his mouth, he chews it, mixing it with saliva and breaking it up into a small mass called a bolus; the enzymes in his saliva begin the breakdown of carbohydrates. Chris then swallows the bolus, and it passes through the esophagus into the stomach, where stomach acid and enzymes continue the digestion process with the breakdown of proteins. The food then passes to the small intestine, where most digestion occurs. Enzymes break down the food molecules into smaller molecules that can be absorbed by the small intestine (Figure 10.1). Anything not absorbed here passes into the large intestine in preparation for elimination.

satiety The state of feeling full or satisfied, relative to hunger or thirst.

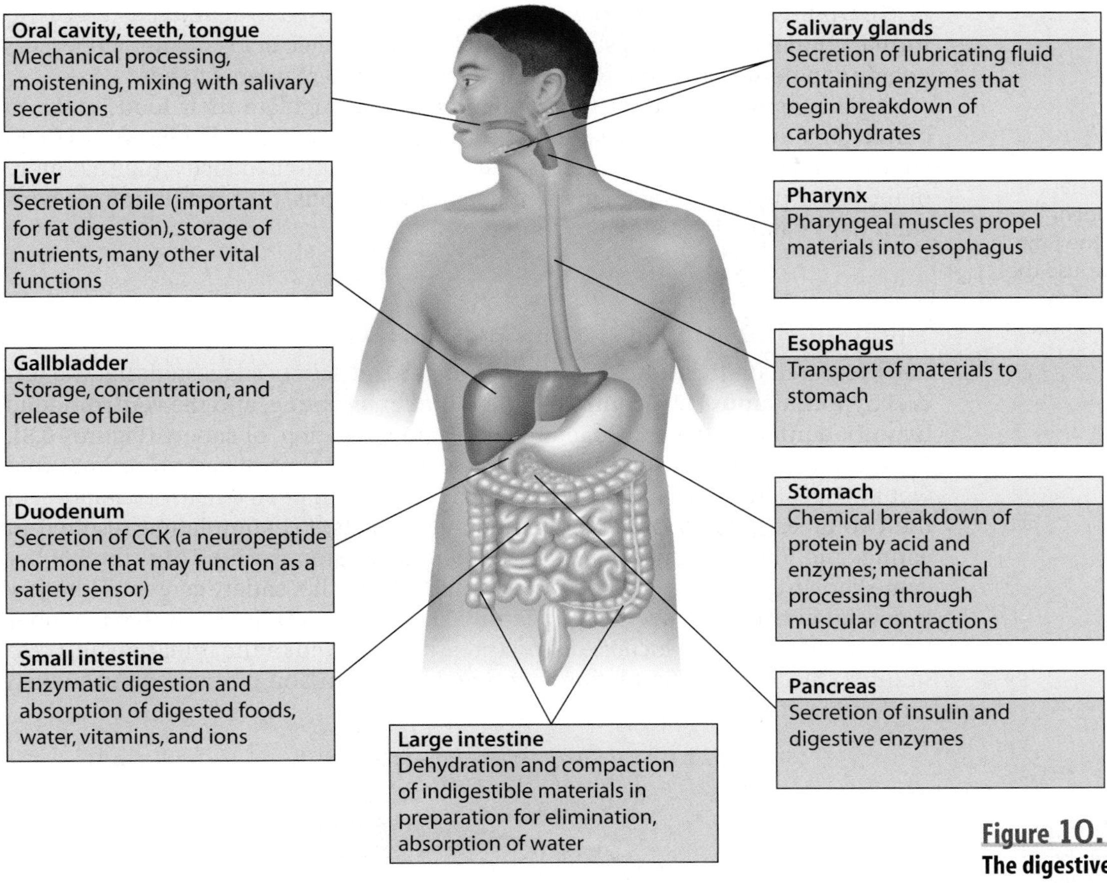

Figure 10.1
The digestive system

➜ **Where in the digestive system does digestion begin?**

When carbohydrate, in the form of glucose, is absorbed by the small intestine, the blood glucose level rises. Elevated blood glucose triggers release of the hormone insulin from the pancreas. Insulin increases glucose uptake from the blood into the liver, where glucose not needed for immediate energy needs is converted into glycogen and stored. Stored glycogen can later be converted back to glucose and distributed to the cells to supply energy for metabolism. Any excess glucose not stored as glycogen is stored as fat in adipose tissue.

Figure 10.2 summarizes the metabolism of nutrients. Energy nutrients (carbohydrates, fats, proteins) are broken down into simpler compounds (glucose, fatty

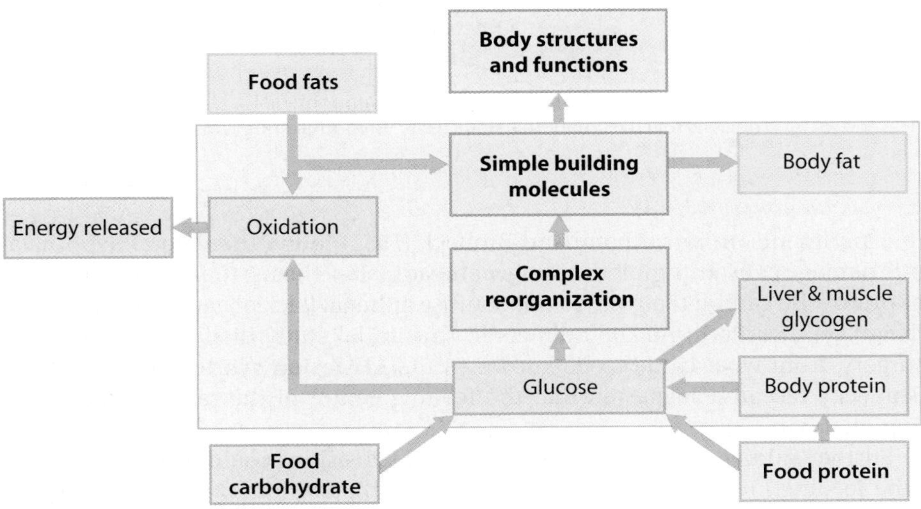

Figure 10.2
Energy nutrients Carbohydrates, fats, and proteins are the sources of the materials and energy needed for the structures and functions of the body.

➜ **Which nutrient provides the most readily available source of energy?**

acids, amino acids). The simpler compounds can be used to generate energy or to form essential compounds such as proteins and nucleic acids. Again, any excess energy can be stored as fat, which is available for future energy needs.

Organisms monitor their nutritional levels and regulate their food intake to correct any nutritional deficiencies. For example, Johnson and colleagues (1986) showed that when rats are fed diets that vary in nutritional density, they eat more of the lower density foods than the higher density foods, thus maintaining a constant daily caloric intake.

Checkpoint

Describe what happens to the energy bar that Chris eats after leaving the Student Health Center, from the time he takes the first bite; use the terms chewing, salivation, bolus, breakdown, absorption, and glycogen.

The Hypothalamus in Hunger and Satiety

Early research on the brain's control of hunger and satiety suggested that the **lateral hypothalamus (LH)** controlled the initiation of eating, and the **ventromedial hypothalamus (VMH)** controlled the inhibition of eating, or satiety (Figure 10.3). Lesion studies on rats found that damage to the LH produced an animal that would not eat, whereas damage to the VMH caused a rat to overeat. Stimulation of the two areas produced the complementary effects: LH stimulation resulted in eating, and VMH stimulation caused an animal to stop eating. Thus, the LH became known as the "hunger center," and the VMH as the "satiety center." This view is now known to be an oversimplification. More recent studies show that two fiber tracts, rather than two localized structures, are involved in the initiation and cessation of feeding. But first let us examine the information that was accumulated on the role of the LH and VMH.

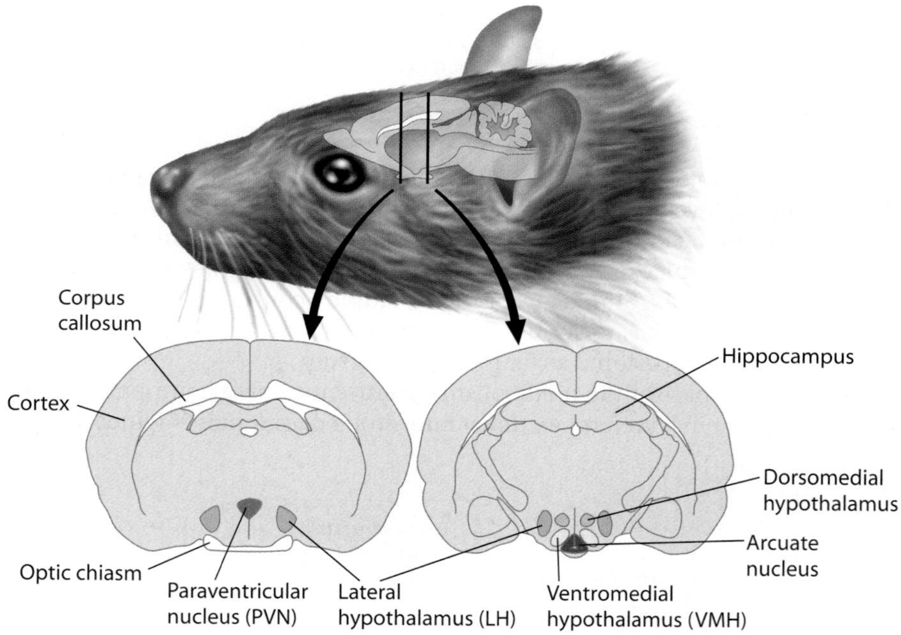

Figure 10.3
The hypothalamus and eating behavior The lateral hypothalamus (LH), paraventricular nucleus (PVN), ventromedial hypothalamus (VMH), and arcuate nucleus are involved in the control of eating behavior.

➜ What happens to eating behavior when the lateral hypothalamus is destroyed?

The LH-Lesion Syndrome

In experiments on rats, Anand and Brobeck (1951) found that lateral hypothalamic damage caused complete **aphagia** and **adipsia**—that is, the rats no longer ate or drank. (Be careful that you do not confuse aphagia [lack of eating] with aphasia [language disorder].) All the animals in this initial study died within a week of surgery, from what came to be known as the **LH-lesion syndrome.** Anand and Brobeck's research suggested that the feeding center of the rat is in the lateral hypothalamus.

Further studies soon showed that rats with LH lesions could be kept alive with tube feeding (Teitelbaum & Stellar, 1954), and that with appropriate treatment, some LH-lesioned animals recovered the ability to regulate their body weight on

lateral hypothalamus (LH) A hypothalamic area once thought to be the "hunger center."

ventromedial hypothalamus (VMH) A hypothalamic area once thought to be the "satiety center."

aphagia The absence of eating.

adipsia The absence of drinking.

LH-lesion syndrome The pattern of aphagic and adipsic behavior exhibited by rats following damage to the lateral hypothalamus.

Table 10.1
Stages of Recovery in Animals With the LH-Lesion Syndrome

	Stage I: Adipsia/Aphagia	Stage II: Adipsia/Anorexia	Stage III Adipsia/ Dehydration-Adipsia	Stage IV: "Recovery"
Eats wet palatable foods	No	Yes	Yes	Yes
Regulates food intake and body weight on wet palatable foods	No	No	Yes	Yes
Eats dry foods (if hydrated)	No	No	Yes	Yes
Drinks water; survives on dry food and water	No	No	No	Yes

Source: Teitelbaum, P., & Epstein, A. M. (1962). The lateral hypothalamic syndrome: Recovery of feeding and drinking after lateral hypothalamic lesions. *Psychological Review, 69,* 74–90. Copyright 1962 by the American Psychological Association. Reprinted by permission.

a standard laboratory diet, although they typically maintained a weight considerably below the preoperative level (Teitelbaum & Epstein, 1962).

Teitelbaum and Epstein (1962) described four stages in the recovery from LH damage, as summarized in Table 10.1. In stage I, the rat neither eats nor drinks and will die unless force-fed through a tube into its stomach. Approximately 20 days after surgery, the rat enters stage II, during which it cannot regulate its food intake to meet its needs. During stage III, which begins about 40 days after surgery, the rat recovers the ability to regulate its food intake to meet its nutritional needs, as long as it is given wet food; it still exhibits adipsia. In stage IV, the LH-lesioned rat begins to drink water again and thus can survive on a regimen of dry lab chow and water.

Note in Table 10.1 that stage IV is labeled "Recovery." The reason for this qualification is that the stage IV LH-lesioned rat is still not normal—not restored to its preoperative behavior. For example, although it exhibits **prandial drinking,** or drinking while eating, it will not drink without eating even after being deprived of water. In addition, the rat is extremely sensitive to taste and will reject food that does not taste good no matter how food-deprived it is. Finally, the rat never regains the weight lost during the initial stages of the LH-lesion syndrome; it eats only enough to maintain its "recovered" weight. Figure 10.4 compares the physical appearance and body weight of aphagic, normal, and hyperphagic rats. (**Hyperphagia** is excessive food intake; we discuss this later in the chapter.)

The pattern of recovery of eating and drinking in LH-lesioned animals resembles the developmental sequence of eating and drinking in normal animals (Teitelbaum & others, 1969). Newborn rats drink milk (a wet, palatable food) but refuse water, a pattern of behavior that resembles stage II. A slightly older animal eats dry food and drinks water while eating, but will not drink without eating even after it has been deprived of water, a pattern resembling stage III. Teitelbaum and colleagues noted that the newborn rat is essentially a decerebrate animal, because of its undeveloped cerebral cortex. As the cortex develops, the rat acquires the ability to maintain its energy requirements through eating and drinking—and the same thing appears to happen in the LH-lesioned rat.

The VMH-Lesion Syndrome

Other researchers found that damage to the ventral hypothalamus that did not involve the pituitary gland produced a dramatic increase in food intake of the rats, which typically led to a large weight gain (Hetherington & Ranson, 1942). Subsequent lesion studies implicated the VMH in this hyperphagia and obesity (e.g., Brobeck & others, 1943). Along with certain other behavioral anomalies that we explore next, the hyperphagia and obesity seen after VMH damage became known as the **VMH-lesion syndrome.**

Brobeck and colleagues (1943) reported that the eating and obesity in VMH-lesioned rats occurred in two stages. First, the animals were in a dynamic stage of

prandial drinking Drinking while eating.

hyperphagia Excessive food intake; overeating.

VMH-lesion syndrome The pattern of hyperphagia and obesity typically exhibited by rats following damage to the ventromedial hypothalamus.

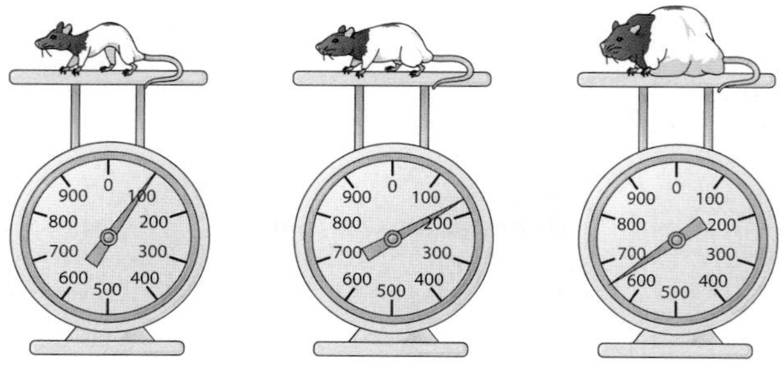

hyperphagia, with food intake sometimes reaching four times the normal level and weight rising steadily to peak at two to four times the normal weight about 40 days following surgery (Figure 10.4). In the second stage, or static stage, the rats decreased their food intake to just enough to maintain the weight they had reached during the dynamic phase. Interestingly, a similar change was reported in the eating behavior of human patients with pathology (e.g., a tumor) in the VMH area. Like the VMH-lesioned rats, they exhibited hyperphagia and obesity (Bray & Gallagher, 1975).

Figure 10.4

A comparison of aphagic, normal, and hyperphagic rats Before lesioning of the lateral hypothalamus (LH) or ventromedial hypothalamus (VMH), these rats weighed the same. In their present condition, the aphagic rat weighs 100 grams, the normal rat weighs 175 grams, and the hyperphagic rat weighs 650 grams.

➜ **Describe the VMH paradox.**

In addition to their hyperphagia and obesity, the VMH-lesioned rats were finicky eaters (Teitelbaum, 1955). They would not eat any bad-tasting food, such as stale chow or food mixed with quinine—which normal rats will eat if it is the only food available. Rats with VMH lesions would eat a greater amount of sweet-tasting or highly palatable food than normal rats. Other researchers found that VMH-lesioned rats were less willing to work for food as their weight increased (Miller & others, 1950), and once obese, the rats were considerably less motivated than normal to obtain food. This characteristic of the VMH-lesioned rat became known as the **VMH paradox**—on the one hand, the animal appears more motivated for food because it overeats and becomes obese, but on the other hand, it appears less motivated because it will not tolerate adulteration of its food and will not work to obtain it. In addition, a VMH-lesioned animal is less active than a nonlesioned animal in a quiet environment but more active in a noisy one (e.g., during animal maintenance) (Gladfelter & Brobeck,1962). Finally, many studies of VMH-lesioned animals described them as hyperirritable—hard to handle (Anand & Brobeck, 1951; Kaelber & others, 1965; Wheatley, 1944). All these results suggested to some (e.g., Schachter, 1971) that the environment is more influential in VMH-lesioned animals than in normal animals in determining the level of activity.

Cephalic Reflexes

When a human or nonhuman animal is exposed to food, it exhibits **cephalic reflexes,** responses that prepare it to digest, metabolize, and store the food once it has been consumed (Giduck & others, 1987; Powley, 2000). A reflex is considered cephalic when input to the brain originates in the head region, output to the periphery goes to the autonomic nervous system and endocrine system, and the CNS mediates the input and output. Triggered by the taste and smell of food, cephalic reflexes include the secretion of saliva in the mouth, gastric juices in the stomach, pancreatic enzymes into the small intestine, and insulin into the bloodstream.

The intensity of cephalic reflexes is directly related to the palatability of a food: The more palatable the food, the greater are the cephalic responses and the amount of food consumed. Table 10.2 summarizes the magnitude of cephalic response as a function of the sensory characteristics of different foods. As you can see, in these studies a self-selected meal stimulated nearly twice as much gastric secretion as gruel, and the sight and smell of a banana split or pizza triggered approximately seven times as much saliva as did an unappealing pizza (Powley, 1977). Chris's cephalic reflexes were undoubtedly maximally stimulated by the meal at the Italian restaurant.

The smell or taste of food, or even the sight of food, activates the LH feeding system, suggesting lateral hypothalamic involvement in the cephalic reflexive regulation of eating (Figure 10.5). The LH receives input from the olfactory and gustatory systems (Nakamura & others, 1989), and the intensity of the response to this input is directly related to the palatability of the food (Fukuda & others, 1986). In addition, LH activation enhances the cephalic reflexes, which, in a positive feedback loop, maintain the activation of the LH feeding system (Anand & others, 1962)—thus, the eating behavior continues.

VMH paradox In VMH-lesioned rats, a motivational inconsistency between overeating in some situations and a reluctance to eat in others.

cephalic reflex A response that prepares an animal to digest, metabolize, and store food; controlled by the CNS.

Table 10.2
Cephalic Response Magnitude as a Function of the Sensory Quality of Food

Cephalic Responses and Sensory Stimuli	Foods Compared	Subjects
Salivary secretion:		
Sight of food	Pickled plum > orange > apple > biscuits (approx. 6:3.4:1.2:1)	Man (Japanese)
Sight and smell of food	Banana split or pizza > unappealing pizza (approx. 7:1)	Man
Gastric secretion:		
Sham feeding	Self-selected meal > hospital meal > gruel (approx. 1.8:1.4:1)	Man
Sham feeding	Meat > milk > bread (approx. 7:6:1)	Dog
Sham feeding	Fish > meat (approx. 1.8:1)	Man (Russian)
Sham feeding	Meat > milk > bread (approx. 2.2:2:1)	Dog
Pancreas secretion:		
Sight and smell of food	Usual French breakfast > beefsteak at breakfast (approx. 4:1)	Man (French)
Sham feeding	Dog food > rat chow	Rat

Adapted from: Powley, T. L. (1977). The ventromedial hypothalamic syndrome, satiety, and a cephalic phase hypothesis. *Psychological Review, 84,* 89–126.

An additional set of cephalic responses explains the active rejection of food. Doty (1968) found that taste cues from unpalatable food could trigger a rejection reflex consisting of ejection, gagging, and vomiting. This rejection reflex results from stimulation of the feeding system in the presence of unpalatable foods (Robinson & Mishkin, 1968).

Powley (1977) proposed that one major function of the VMH satiety system is to control the intensity of the cephalic responses to food (Figure 10.5). The satisfaction of nutritional needs activates the VMH, which inhibits the LH, thereby stopping the eating behavior. According to Powley, destruction of the VMH satiety system eliminates VMH inhibition and causes exaggerated cephalic responses to food. In a VMH-lesioned animal, palatable foods produce a heightened preparatory response, thereby increasing food intake; unpalatable foods increase the cephalic rejection response and cause increased avoidance of the unpleasant food. In this way, Powley explained both the excessive eating and the finickiness of VMH-lesioned animals.

Support for Powley's idea of heightened cephalic responding in VMH-lesioned rats came from the work of Louis-Sylvestre and colleagues (1980), who measured insulin release in VMH-lesioned and normal rats. They found that the insulin response of VMH-lesioned animals was much greater than that of normal animals, if the rats had been allowed to taste and ingest a small amount of glucose. Other

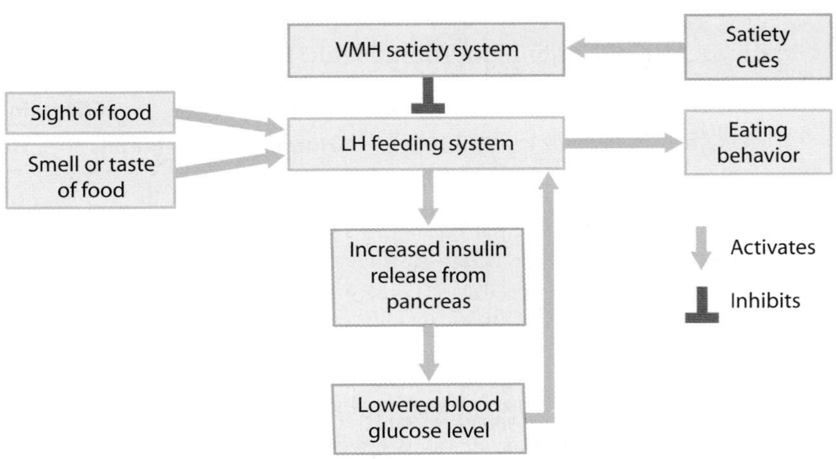

Figure 10.5
The lateral hypothalamus (LH) feeding system and cephalic reflexes
The sight of food or its smell and taste can activate the LH feeding system, which then elicits eating. Stimulation of the LH also causes the pancreas to release insulin, which acts to lower blood glucose level and thus continues the stimulation of the LH. Eating continues until the satiety cues activate the ventromedial hypothalamus (VMH) satiety system, which in turn inhibits the LH feeding system and causes eating behavior to end.

Which area of the hypothalamus is involved in regulating cephalic reflexes?

researchers found that VMH-lesioned animals had a significantly larger secretion of gastric acid (Tominaga & others, 1993). Also, a comparison of food intake and weight gain in VMH-lesioned and nonlesioned animals exposed to either a palatable or a relatively unpalatable diet showed that the unpalatable diet produced minimal cephalic responding, whereas the palatable diet led to high cephalic responding (Powley, 1977). None of the animals overate or gained weight on the unpalatable diet, but the VMH-lesioned animals became hyperphagic and gained weight over a 2-week period on the palatable diet. When returned to the unpalatable diet, the VMH-lesioned animals reduced their intake and stopped gaining weight, suggesting that one reason such animals overeat is their overresponsiveness to palatable foods.

Comparative Psychology Applied to Eating Behavior

In 1971, social psychologist Stanley Schachter published an intriguing comparison of the eating habits of obese and normal-weight subjects (humans and nonhuman animals), which reviewed studies on the effect of a VMH lesion in animals and the behavioral characteristics of obese humans—college students at Columbia University. Schachter presented his comparison of behaviors as a "batting average," a ratio of the number of studies that showed differences between groups to the total number of studies. For example, he found that nine out of nine studies reported that VMH-lesioned animals ate more than nonlesioned animals, and two out of three studies found that obese humans ate more than normal-weight participants. In addition, he expressed the average percentage difference between the behavior of obese and normal participants as a "fat-to-normal" (F/N) ratio. For example, he found that VMH-lesioned animals ate (on average) 1.19 times more than nonlesioned animals and that obese human subjects ate (on average) 1.16 times more than normal-weight subjects (Table 10.3).

Schachter (1971) concluded that, compared with their normal counterparts, both VMH-lesioned animals and obese humans eat more food during a day, eat fewer meals per day, eat more per meal, eat faster, show a greater preference for good-tasting food, and have an exaggerated dislike of bad-tasting food. In addition, like VMH-lesioned animals, if food cues are not prominent (e.g., sandwiches are in a refrigerator rather than on a table in front of the obese person) obese humans will not work as hard for their food as their normal-weight counterparts. For example, when offered almonds either in the shell or already shelled, the obese subjects ate fewer of the unshelled almonds but more of the shelled almonds than normal-weight subjects. Furthermore, obese humans and hyperphagic rats continued to eat with a full stomach, whereas control animals and normal-weight humans generally did not eat with a full stomach. Note in Table 10.3 that the F/N ratios are quite similar in human and nonhuman animals.

Table 10.3
Eating Habits of Nonhuman Animals and Humans

	Batting Average		F/N ratio	
	Animals	Humans	Animals	Humans
Amount of food eaten	9/9	2/3	1.19	1.16
Number of meals per day	4/4	3/3	0.85	0.92
Amount eaten per meal	2/2	5/5	1.34	1.29
Speed of eating	1/1	1/1	1.28	1.26
Good taste	5/6	2/2	1.45	1.42
Bad taste	3/4	1/2	0.76	0.84

Note: Batting average is the ratio of the number of studies showing a difference to all studies conducted: F/N refers to the ratio of behavior in fat (obese) subjects to behavior in normal subjects.

Source: Schachter, S. (1971). Some extraordinary facts about obese humans and rats. *American Psychologist, 26,* 129–144. Copyright 1971 by the American Psychological Association. Reprinted by permission.

VMH-lesioned animals and obese humans also share characteristics unrelated to eating: Compared with their unlesioned or normal-weight counterparts, both are more reactive to external stimulation and more sensitive to pain. The remarkable similarities between obese humans and VMH-damaged animals led Schachter (1971) to speculate that the physiological locus of human obesity might be a malfunctioning ventromedial hypothalamus.

Checkpoint
Describe the components of cephalic reflexes that caused Chris to feel hungry when he entered the Italian restaurant.

REVIEW

- The main function of eating is to regulate energy balance and maintain an optimal body weight.
- In experimental studies on rats, damage to the lateral hypothalamus (LH) produced a loss of appetite and weight loss; damage to the ventromedial hypothalamus (VMH) caused overeating and obesity.
- Cephalic reflexes, such as salivation, gastric juice release, and insulin release, are detected by the LH, which acts to maintain eating behavior. The VMH controls the intensity of the cephalic reflexes.
- Obese humans and VMH-lesioned animals exhibit similarities such as an overreaction to taste, excessive eating, less motivation to work for food, and a hypersensitivity to high-prominence environmental cues.

The Neural Control of Eating Behavior

Despite the elegance and simplicity of the VMH as the satiety center and the LH as the hunger center of the brain, research soon revealed that the two hypothalamic areas could not be the sole agents of hunger and satiety and that several other hypothalamic areas are critically involved. Evidence against the exclusive involvement of the lateral hypothalamus in hunger begins with a consideration of the nigrostriatal pathway. A dopaminergic system originating in the substantia nigra, passing through the lateral hypothalamus, and continuing to the basal ganglia, the **nigrostriatal pathway** (Figure 10.6) is involved in voluntary behavior (Chapter 8). Eating and drinking, essential to the survival of an organism, are examples of such behavior. Damage to the nigrostriatal bundle of laboratory animals without involving the LH virtually eliminated voluntary activities, including eating and drinking; that was followed by gradual recovery and maintenance of a body weight considerably lower than that of control animals (Stricker & Zigmond, 1984). Thus, damage to the nigrostriatal pathway outside the LH reproduced many symptoms of the LH-lesion syndrome. The nigrostriatal lesion effect may not have been specific to hunger, however. Instead, the animals seemed less aroused in general, which suggests that a greater than normal stimulus for hunger is needed to trigger their feeding response.

Figure 10.6
The nigrostriatal system of the rat brain The nigrostriatal pathway extends from the substantia nigra through the lateral hypothalamus to the basal ganglia.

What type of behavior is controlled by this pathway?

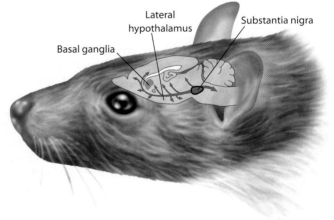

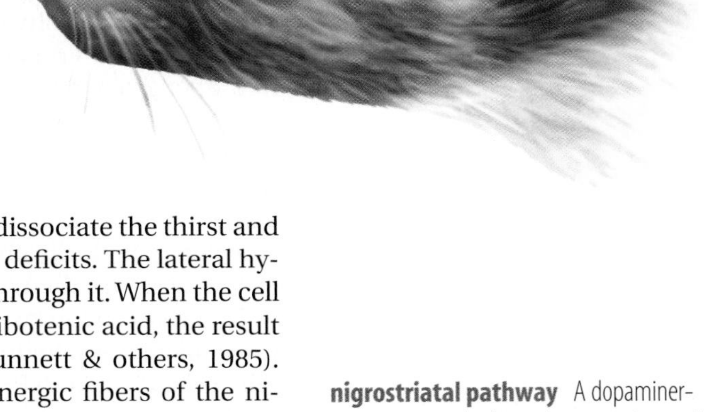

Subsequent research demonstrated that it is possible to dissociate the thirst and hunger defects of the LH syndrome from the sensorimotor deficits. The lateral hypothalamus has both cell bodies and nerve fibers passing through it. When the cell bodies are selectively destroyed with a neurotoxin such as ibotenic acid, the result is aphagia and adipsia without sensorimotor deficits (Dunnett & others, 1985). Injections of 6-hydroxydopamine, which destroy dopaminergic fibers of the nigrostriatal pathway, produce marked sensorimotor problems that may produce disturbances in feeding behavior as a secondary consequence of the sensorimotor defects. In a similar experiment, Lenard and colleagues (1988) applied either kainic acid, ibotenic acid, or 6-hydroxydopamine to the lateral hypothalamus of rats and

nigrostriatal pathway A dopaminergic system involved in voluntary eating and drinking behavior; begins in the substantia nigra, passes through the lateral hypothalamus, and ends in the basal ganglia.

paraventricular nucleus (PVN) A hypothalamic area where damage may produce the VMH-lesion syndrome.

nucleus of the solitary tract A structure in the medulla that influences the amount of food consumed.

dorsal motor nucleus of the vagus A group of neurons in the medulla that regulates insulin release by the parasympathetic nervous system.

neuropeptide Y (NPY) A peptide neurotransmitter involved in hunger.

arcuate nucleus A hypothalamic nucleus that produces neuropeptide Y and releases it into the PVN and the lateral hypothalamic area.

found that either cellular microlesions of the LH or damage to the dopaminergic fibers of the nigrostriatal pathway resulted in feeding disturbances. These researchers concluded that the LH and the nigrostriatal pathway are part of a common system involved in hunger motivation.

Although the VMH as the hypothalamic satiety center remained the focus of research interest for many years, there were frequent problems with its preeminent status. For example, Gold (1973) showed that damage to the ventral noradrenergic bundle may be involved in the VMH-lesion syndrome.

The Paraventricular Nucleus—An Integrating Center

Later studies suggested that damage to the **paraventricular nucleus (PVN)** of the hypothalamus (see Figure 10.3) could also produce the VMH-lesion syndrome (Bray & York, 1998). Fibers from the PVN travel through the outer edges of the ventromedial hypothalamus en route to two structures in the medulla—the **nucleus of the solitary tract** and the **dorsal motor nucleus of the vagus**—both of which are involved in food intake and metabolism. The nucleus of the solitary tract influences the amount of food consumed, especially foods high in carbohydrates (Chris's pizza and spaghetti), and the dorsal motor nucleus of the vagus regulates insulin release by the parasympathetic nervous system. The nucleus of the solitary tract receives messages from the PVN and also meal-related satiety information by way of the vagus nerve. We review meal-related satiety information later.

Apparently, damage to the fiber tracts extending to the nucleus of the solitary tract and dorsal motor nucleus of the vagus from the PVN or VMH causes the VMH-lesion syndrome. Sclafani (1971) observed that lesions lateral to the VMH produced overeating, a result that Gold and colleagues (1977) attributed to the destruction of connections leaving the VMH and the PVN. Lesions that sever PVN connections to the nucleus of the solitary tract and the dorsal motor nucleus of the vagus without damaging the VMH also produce overeating (Kirchgessner & Sclafani, 1988).

To determine what would happen with stimulation of the paraventricular nucleus, Leibowitz and colleagues (1985) injected norepinephrine directly into the PVN and observed increased consumption of carbohydrates, little or no change in ingestion of fats, and sometimes a suppression of protein intake. The researchers suggested that the PVN noradrenergic system might play a specific role in carbohydrate ingestion.

Drugs such as clonidine that activate certain adrenergic receptors also produce overeating when injected into the PVN, whereas drugs that block these adrenergic receptors (e.g., AMPT) suppress eating. In fact, continuous injection of clonidine into the PVN caused rats to become fat, primarily because of an increased consumption of carbohydrates; the ingestion of both fats and proteins was suppressed. Continuous AMPT administration led to a loss of weight (Yee & others, 1987).

Similarly, Stanley and colleagues (1989) found that repeated PVN stimulation with **neuropeptide Y (NPY),** a neurotransmitter involved in hunger, triggered increased daily carbohydrate and fat intake and dramatic weight gain in female rats. Neurons in the **arcuate nucleus** of the hypothalamus (see Figure 10.3) produce neuropeptide Y, and energy deficits, such as those caused by food deprivation, activate these neurons to release the neuropeptide Y into the PVN and the lateral hypothalamic area (Williams & others, 2000, 2001). Kalra and Kalra (2003) concluded that the NPY network in the hypothalamus is the primary neural pathway associated with appetite-stimulating impulses. Predictably, the NPY neurons are hyperactive in genetically obese mice and rats (Williams & others, 2001), and finding a way to decrease their activity may hold the key to treating obesity.

The same neurons in the arcuate nucleus that produce NPY also manufacture and release a neurotransmitter with the improbable name agouti-related protein (AGRP). Like NPY, agouti-related protein is a powerful stimulator of food intake. Another group of neurons in the arcuate nucleus produces two substances that induce an anorexic (appetite-suppressing) response—pro-opiomelanocortin (POMC), which is the precursor of α-melanocyte-stimulating hormone (α-MSH), and cocaine- and amphetamine-regulated transcript (CART).

In addition to its connections with the PVN, the arcuate nucleus has reciprocal connections with other hypothalamic areas, including the dorsomedial hypothalamic nucleus, the ventromedial hypothalamic nucleus, and the lateral hypothalamic area. Its location at the base of the hypothalamus effectively places the arcuate nucleus outside the blood-brain barrier, which means that its neurons have ready access to circulating messengers related to nutritional status, such as glucose, insulin, and leptin, a hormone secreted by fat cells in mammals, which we discuss in detail later. Thus, changes in these messengers can readily affect the release of NPY/AGRP and POMC/CART. Figure 10.7 shows one simplified model of how the arcuate nucleus affects eating through its response to changes in circulating levels of leptin, which is directly related to fat deposits in the body. Circulating leptin levels increase with increases in body fat and fall with decreases in body fat from such events as deprivation (e.g., dieting) and starvation.

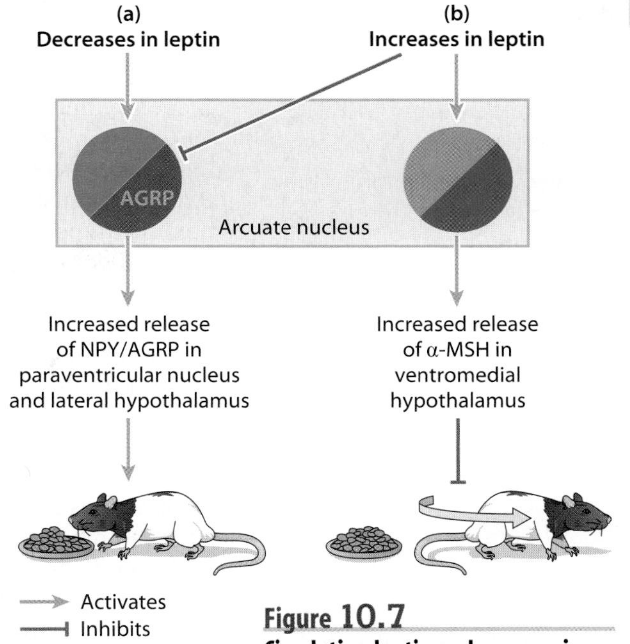

Figure 10.7

Circulating leptin and neurons in the arcuate nucleus (a) Decreased leptin causes the release of neuropeptide Y/agouti-related protein (NPY/AGRP) from the arcuate nucleus and increased eating. (b) Increases in leptin both inhibit the NPY/AGRP neurons and stimulate the release of pro-opiomelanocortin/cocaine- and amphetamine-regulated transcript (POMC/CART), which results in an inhibition of eating. Note: α-MSH, α-melanocyte-stimulating hormone.

→ **What might cause leptin levels to fall?**

In addition to neuropeptide Y and agouti-related protein, the peptides orexin-A and orexin-B (sometimes called hypocretin-1 and -2), produced by the LH, stimulate food intake in rats (Williams & others, 2001). Of the two, orexin-B has much less of an effect on feeding than orexin-A and is more likely involved in arousal. (You may recall from Chapter 9 that narcolepsy is associated with damage to LH neurons containing the orexins.) Further, an orexin receptor antagonist reduces food consumption in genetically obese mice (Haynes & others, 2002) and in normal rats (Ishii & others, 2004). Orexin concentrations in human blood plasma are related to body weight and nutritional status. Komaki and colleagues (2001) found that levels of orexin-A significantly increased during fasting in nonobese females. Adam and colleagues (2002) found that orexin-A levels were significantly lower in obese participants, and concluded that this peptide is involved in regulating energy metabolism.

If damage to the PVN reproduces the dramatically increased food consumption of the VMH-lesion syndrome, stimulating the area should lead to less consumption, not more. So why does stimulation by clonidine, NPY, and the orexins *increase* consumption? The answer apparently lies in two different types of adrenergic receptors. According to Wellman and colleagues (1993), descending fibers from the PVN act to stimulate or inhibit "satiety" cells in the VMH, resulting in either satiety or feeding, respectively. Several researchers have suggested that the PVN contains two classes of adrenergic receptors: α_1 and α_2 (e.g., Wellman, 2000), and thus input to the PVN can have two different effects: First, activation of the α_1 receptors suppresses eating, presumably by stimulating the VMH satiety cells (Figure 10.8a); consistent with this idea, feeding is suppressed by α_1-adrenergic agonists (Cheng & Kuo, 2003). Second, stimulation of the α_2-adrenergic receptors increases food intake (Figure 10.8b).

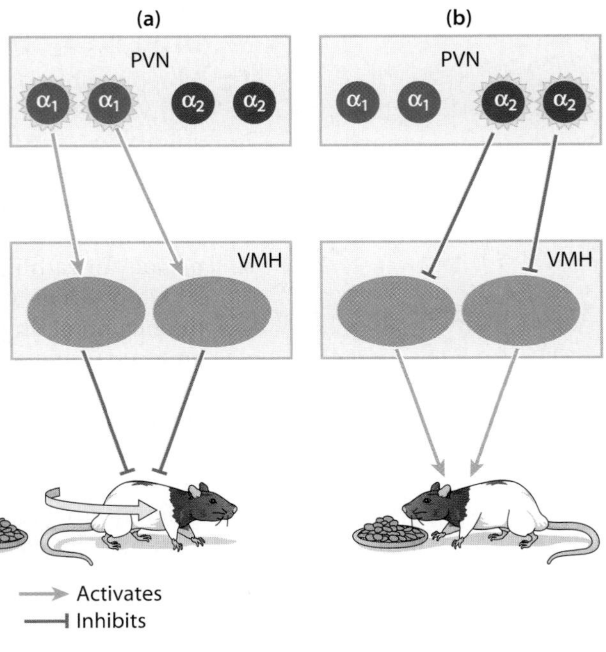

Figure 10.8

The role of the paraventricular nucleus (PVN) in feeding and satiety (a) When α_1-adrenergic receptors in the PVN are stimulated, the "satiety" neurons in the ventromedial hypothalamus (VMH) are stimulated, thereby decreasing feeding behavior. (b) When α_2-adrenergic receptors are stimulated, the "satiety" neurons are inhibited, which results in increased feeding.

→ **Describe some evidence supporting this model of how the PVN works to either increase or decrease feeding.**

ingestional neophobia A reluctance to eat novel foods.

fen-phen A drug combination of fenfluramine and phentermine, once used in treating obesity.

Indeed, eating behavior is enhanced by α_2-adrenergic agonists (Capuano & others, 1992) and inhibited by α_2-adrenergic antagonists (Alexander & others, 1993).

In order for substances such as NPY to have an effect on feeding through the PVN, they must be associated with norepinephrine. Matos and colleagues (1996) demonstrated that injection of NPY into the ventricles of rats results in increased extracellular levels of norepinephrine and dopamine without altering the level of serotonin. The NPY injections also increased feeding in the animals, and the researchers concluded that NPY-induced feeding is associated with activation of the hypothalamic catecholaminergic system.

The presence of two adrenergic receptor types in the PVN may be associated with the reluctance of animals to eat novel foods, an instinct for avoidance called **ingestional neophobia.** This response sometimes occurs in babies encountering strained vegetables for the first time. As the food becomes more familiar, the avoidance response fades and consumption of the food increases. Presumably, the α_1-adrenergic receptors suppress the intake of a novel food, then, following repeated exposure to the food, the α_2-adrenergic receptors release the inhibited eating behavior.

In summary, "the PVN is an integrating center, on which converge many neural pathways that influence energy homeostasis" (Williams & others, 2001, p. 684). As we have indicated, the PVN receives axons from the arcuate nucleus that release the substances NPY/AGRP and POMC/CART, which have appetite-stimulating and appetite-suppressing effects, respectively. The PVN also receives orexin neurons from the lateral hypothalamus and contains terminals that supply appetite-modifying neurotransmitters such as norepinephrine, serotonin, the opioid peptides, and α-MSH. The PVN also has reciprocal connections with the VMH, which you would expect given the similarity in the effects of lesions of the two structures. Finally, the PVN is connected to two brain stem structures (the nucleus of the solitary tract and the dorsal motor nucleus of the vagus) that are involved in food intake and metabolism. Table 10.4 summarizes the hypothalamic neurochemicals involved in hunger and satiety; Figure 10.9 shows the major hypothalamic hunger-related areas and some of their interconnections.

Table 10.4
Neurochemicals Involved in Hunger and Satiety

Neuropeptide Y (NPY)	Stimulates eating
Agouti-related protein (AGRP)	Stimulates eating
Pro-opiomelanocortin (POMC)	Anorexic effect
Cocaine- and amphetamine-regulated transcript (CART)	Anorexic effect
Orexin-A (hypocretin-1)	Stimulates eating
Serotonin (5-HT)	Anorexic effect
Norepinephrine	Anorexic effect (α_1 receptors) Stimulates eating (α_2 receptors)
α-Melanocyte-stimulating hormone (α-MSH)	Anorexic effect

Drug Treatments for Weight Loss

Norepinephrine is not the only neurotransmitter that affects neurons in the PVN and VMH. Serotonin, or drugs that increase serotonin release, inhibit food consumption—carbohydrate much more than fat or protein intake. This phenomenon is mediated, at least in part, by serotonin receptors in the medial hypothalamus (Leibowitz & Alexander, 1998). Injecting drugs that either inhibit serotonin synthesis or block serotonin receptors increases food consumption, especially of carbohydrates (Stallone & Nicolaidis, 1989).

Many drugs with adrenergic or serotonergic action have an important influence on eating and weight control. For example, such adrenergic agonists as amphetamine, or such serotonergic agonists as fenfluramine, have a strong appetite-suppressing (anorexic) effect and have been used in treating obesity (Bray, 1999). This anorexic effect apparently results from the drugs' influence on the PVN's α_1-adrenergic receptors (Figure 10.8a), which suppresses or prevents eating.

You may have heard of the drug **fen-phen,** which is a combination of two different drugs: *fenfluramine,* a serotonergic agonist, and *phentermine,* a dopaminergic agonist. Both drugs were approved by the U.S. Food and Drug Administration (FDA) as appetite suppressants in treating obesity—phentermine in 1959

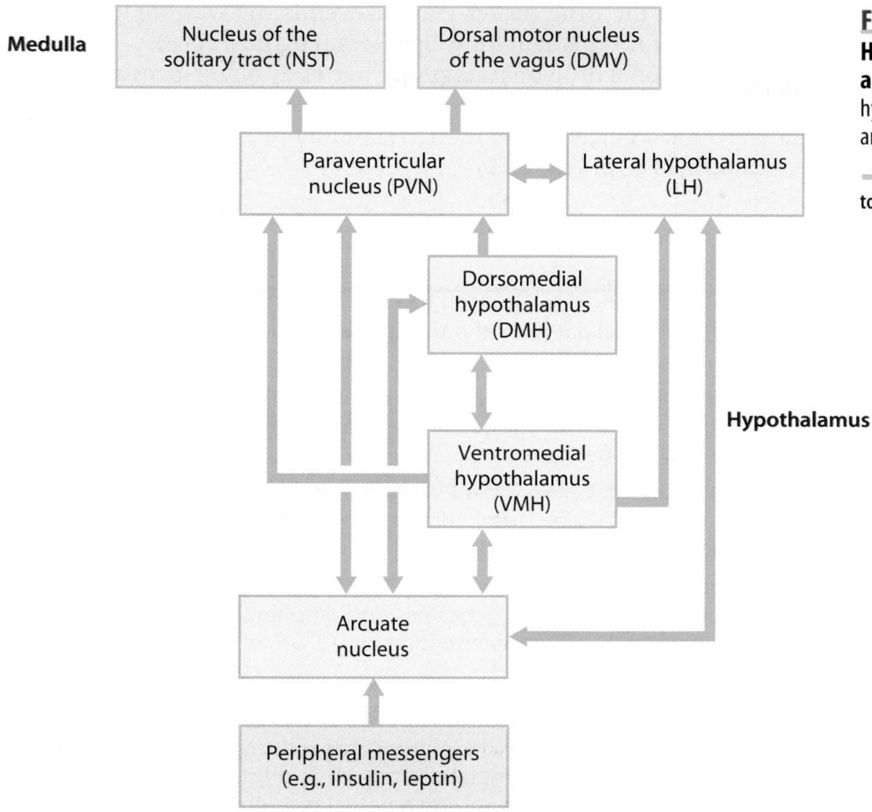

Figure 10.9

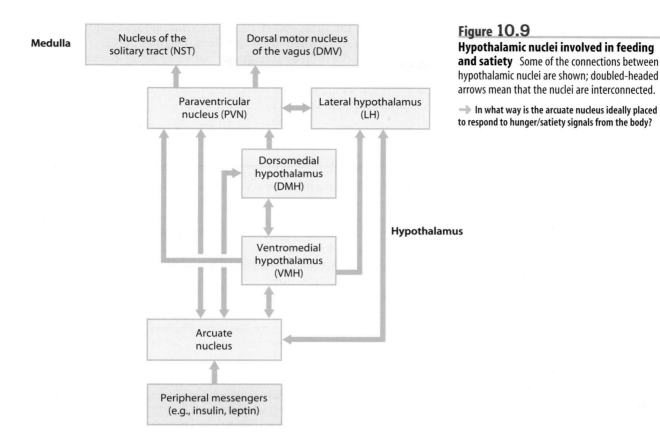

Hypothalamic nuclei involved in feeding and satiety Some of the connections between hypothalamic nuclei are shown; doubled-headed arrows mean that the nuclei are interconnected.

→ In what way is the arcuate nucleus ideally placed to respond to hunger/satiety signals from the body?

and fenfluramine in 1973. In the early 1990s, the two drugs were combined, and clinical research found that fen-phen, combined with behavioral management techniques, produced significant, long-term weight loss in most obese people (Atkinson & others, 1997; Wangsness, 2000). The success of fen-phen in treating obesity led to its skyrocketing use, but the FDA had never approved the use of the two drugs together, and some people developed heart valve disease after long-term use. In 1997, the FDA recommended that people stop taking fen-phen, and fenfluramine has been withdrawn from the market (Campfield & others, 1998).

Drug treatments for obesity can be categorized as drugs that reduce food intake, drugs that alter metabolism, and drugs that increase thermogenesis (heat production) (Bray, 2000a). In the first category, sibutramine, which is a norepinephrine and serotonin reuptake inhibitor, has been approved for long-term weight control. In the second category, orlistat (Xenical), which received FDA approval for the treatment of obesity in adolescents in late 2003, decreases fat absorption. Both sibutramine and orlistat can cause weight loss of between 5% and 10% over 2 years or more. Although this is not a great deal more weight loss than produced by a placebo, research has shown that even this modest loss can significantly reduce the incidence of diabetes in the obese (Halford, 2004).

Recall from Chapter 5 that the active ingredient in marijuana, THC, has been used to treat nausea and stimulate appetite in cancer patients. Recent research has demonstrated that a brain receptor that responds to THC, the cannabinoid-1 (CB_1) receptor, plays a role in regulating appetite (Black, 2004). Further, when mice with diet-induced obesity, an animal model widely used in the study of human obesity, are treated with a CB_1 antagonist, they exhibit a substantial and sustained reduction of body weight (20%) and body fat (50%) (Ravinet Trillou & others, 2003). A similar effect has been demonstrated in humans in two year-long studies (Després & others, 2005; Van Gaal & others, 2005).The CB_1 antagonist, rimonabant, remains in phase III clinical trials as a treatment for human obesity (Bays, 2004) and as an aid to smoking cessation (Fernandez & Allison, 2004). In February 2006, the

Checkpoint

Describe the nigrostriatal pathway, and explain why early researchers concluded that the lateral hypothalamus was the feeding center. Describe the paraventricular system, and explain why early researchers concluded that the ventromedial hypothalamus was the satiety center.

FDA disappointed the drug maker (Sanofi-Aventis) by withholding blanket approval of the use of rimonabant for weight loss (Fogoros, 2006).

Although additional drug treatments are currently being investigated, any new medicines that are developed will undoubtedly work best as adjuncts to fitness-related behavioral changes rather than as stand-alone solutions to the problem of obesity (Campfield & others, 1998).

REVIEW

- Both the nigrostriatal pathway and the LH are involved in hunger motivation.
- The VMH is part of a feeding/satiety system that controls the expression and suppression of eating behavior. Other major hypothalamic structures in the system include the paraventricular nucleus (PVN), arcuate nucleus, dorsomedial nucleus, and lateral hypothalamic area.
- Descending fibers travel from the PVN to the nucleus of the solitary tract, which elicits eating, especially of carbohydrates, and to the dorsal motor nucleus of the vagus, which regulates insulin secretion.
- Neurochemicals, such as neuropeptide Y (NPY), agouti-related protein (AGRP), pro-opiomelanocortin (POMC), cocaine- and amphetamine-regulated transcript (CART), and orexin-A, influence food intake.
- Activation of α_1-adrenergic receptors suppresses feeding behavior and insulin release. Activation of α_2-adrenergic receptors increases food intake.
- Drug treatments for obesity include drugs that reduce food intake, such as sibutramine, and drugs that alter metabolism, such as orlistat. Rimonabant acts as an appetite suppressant by antagonizing a neural receptor for the active ingredient of marijuana.

The Nonneural Control of Eating Behavior

The brain alone cannot control eating behavior. The CNS control mechanisms that initiate and suppress eating must rely on other biological systems for information about the nutritional condition of the body. For example, Chris's hunger system may have initiated his eating the spaghetti and the pizza, but prior stimulation of various sensory systems is what made him decide he needed to get something to eat. In this section, we examine how information from other parts of the body reaches the CNS to let Chris know when he is hungry and when it is time to stop eating.

The survival of an organism depends on its ability to maintain an adequate energy balance and an optimal body weight. Energy balance is regulated in the short term, from meal to meal, whereas body weight control occurs over the long term, from day to day. Any depletion detected by these regulatory systems produces the perceptual experience of hunger, leading the organism to eat to satisfy its needs (Logue, 1991). First we examine the internal changes that are perceived as hunger, changes categorized as peripheral cues or metabolic cues, then some effects of environmental factors on eating behavior.

Peripheral Cues

Two classes of peripheral cues, oral sensations and stomach cues, have long been associated with hunger and eating, and have even been related to satiety and the suppression of eating.

Oral Sensations

Although the taste quality of food does not initiate eating, it does appear to control the continuation of eating. The pizza that Chris could not stop eating is a good example of the influence of taste on feeding behavior. Snowdon (1969) demonstrated the effect of oral sensations on the maintenance of feeding. Using a technique developed by Teitelbaum and Epstein (1962), Snowdon implanted a tube into the rat's head that coursed through its nose and into its stomach (Figure 10.10). Rats first were trained to press a bar for oral food ingestion, then trained to press a bar to deliver liquid food directly to the stomach (intragastric feeding), bypassing oral sensations. During oral feeding of a liquid diet, by increasing meal sizes rats were able to maintain a constant daily nutrient intake despite dilutions of the diet up to 75% with distilled water. In addition, during oral feeding, the rats' weights increased steadily, as would occur in normally fed rats of this age.

The rats required special training to learn to feed intragastrically, but once this training had occurred, the animals were able to maintain a constant daily nutrient intake even with dilution of the liquid diet. However, the body weights of the intragastrically fed rats remained stable rather than increasing. In addition, intragastrically fed rats exhibited licking, chewing, and swallowing movements while feeding, illustrating the importance of oral sensations for normal eating. Snowdon (1969) concluded that oral sensations "are of great importance in motivating and sustaining feeding behavior at optimal levels" (p. 98).

In a study of voluntary intragastric feeding in humans, Jordan (1969) observed good regulation of food intake without the normal oral factors in feeding. However, the subjects did not find intragastric feeding as satisfying as oral ingestion, and when they received both oral feeding and intragastric feeding, they overate and the overeating did not decrease with practice. This shows that oral factors take precedence over gastric factors, as the subjects were unable to decrease their intragastric intake enough to compensate for the amount of the liquid diet ingested orally.

Oral signals are also involved in suppressing food intake. For example, Janowitz and Grossman (1949) cut the esophagus of a dog and manipulated the cut end to the outside of the body so that when the animal ate, the swallowed food fell to the ground. Initially, the esophagotomized dog ate only slightly more than a normal dog would eat, but the suppression of eating was short-lived, and the animal soon began eating again. Without the normal satiety signals from the stomach, the dog resumed eating as soon as the oral sensations dissipated.

Figure 10.10

Oral sensations and eating behavior

When the rat presses the bar, a machine delivers liquid nutrients through the tube directly into its stomach, bypassing the mouth.

➜ Why was it difficult to train this rat to press the bar?

Stomach Cues

In 1934, the well-known Harvard physiologist Walter B. Cannon proposed a peripheral theory of hunger, associating stomach contractions with hunger and cessation of contractions with satiety. In a classic experiment in which human volunteers swallowed a balloon that recorded stomach contractions, Cannon and Washburn (1912) had found a close correlation between stomach contractions and the subjective experience of hunger. However, later evidence indicated that gastric factors do not play a significant role in hunger. For example, removing the stomach did not alter daily food intake by rats, although the animals did eat more frequent and smaller meals (Tsang, 1938). This is also true for human patients whose stomachs have been removed for medical reasons, suggesting that information from the stomach is not what makes human and nonhuman animals hungry.

Stomach cues are involved in satiety. Researchers have found, for example, that preloading the stomach of a rat produces a significant reduction in eating. (**Preloading** is filling the stomach with food before making food available to an experimental subject.) In addition, although food is broken down in the mouth, stomach, and small intestine, the nutrients in the food are not metabolized until they have been absorbed into the bloodstream and distributed to the cells. Because satiety occurs *before* this absorption, the cessation of feeding must depend not on metabolic changes but on peripheral cues.

preloading An experimental procedure in which food is placed in the stomach before food becomes available to the subject.

Two events take place in the stomach that cause the rat to stop eating. First, food distends the stomach, and this distention suppresses eating by activating pressure detectors. As an illustration of this factor, when either a liquid food or a salt solution

insulin A pancreatic hormone that lowers blood glucose levels.

glucostatic theory A theory that hunger is caused by low blood glucose levels.

glucoreceptor A specialized receptor that monitors blood glucose levels.

diabetes mellitus A disorder in which the pancreas makes too little insulin or insulin is unable to act effectively to remove glucose from the blood.

was injected directly into the stomachs of hungry rats, the animals ate less than animals with empty stomachs (Berkun & others, 1952). Second, the stomach has nutrient detectors. When liquid food, rather than saline, was injected into the stomach of a rat, a smaller volume suppressed eating (Janowitz & Hollander, 1953).

Research evidence suggests that the paraventricular satiety system, which receives input from the gastric region via the vagus nerve, is involved in the suppression of eating produced by preloading the stomach. Monitoring of electrical activity in the VMH area as a balloon in the stomach was filled with water revealed that the pressure detectors of the stomach activate the VMH area to produce satiety (Sharma & others, 1961).

In a further examination of how gastric factors contribute to the inhibition of eating, rats deprived of food for 15 hours were allowed to consume a high-calorie liquid diet for 30 minutes, then 5 ml of the stomach contents were removed through an implanted tube. When the animals were permitted to eat again, they ate only enough to compensate for the calories in the 5 ml that had been removed (Deutsch & Gonzalez, 1980). Deutsch (1983) reported that such compensation occurred only with familiar food, and suggested that feedback from the metabolic consequences of a particular food enables the brain to recognize the nutritional value of the signals coming from the stomach. Without this information, the organism cannot use stomach cues to recognize when to stop eating. Assuming this is true for humans as well as for rats, we are more likely to overeat a new food that our brain has not "digested."

Checkpoint

What evidence suggests that stomach contractions do not make us hungry?

Metabolic Cues

So far we have suggested that the delicious taste of pizza and spaghetti stimulates Chris to keep eating, and that ordinarily he knows to stop eating when his stomach is full. (Dieting can lead to binge eating, or excessive overeating, as we discuss later.) But why does he start eating? We have seen that hunger can be experienced without signals from the stomach; therefore, something else must be responsible. Experimental evidence suggests that a deficiency in energy-rich substances, such as sugar and fat, is what provides the hunger signal; when the CNS detects these deficiencies, it initiates eating.

The Glucostatic Theory

A great deal of evidence suggests that the amount of sugar in the blood—the blood glucose level—is somehow involved in hunger. For example, MacKay and colleagues (1940) found that the administration of a form of **insulin,** which lowers blood glucose levels, stimulated eating in nonhuman animals, and the same appears to be true in humans. Observations of this type led Jean Mayer (1953) to propose the **glucostatic theory:** Hunger is caused by a low blood glucose level, which stimulates specialized **glucoreceptors** in the CNS (probably in the hypothalamus) to initiate eating. The elevation of blood glucose after eating produces satiety.

Normally, *hyperglycemia,* an elevation of blood glucose, stimulates the pancreas to release insulin into the bloodstream. Insulin lowers blood glucose by stimulating glucose uptake by cells and storage of excess glucose as glycogen in the liver and muscle, or its conversion to fat (Figure 10.11). As you are undoubtedly aware, many people have too little insulin or a defect in the action of insulin whereby glucose is not removed from their blood effectively—a condition called **diabetes mellitus,** which means "sweet-tasting urine." (You can imagine how testing for diabetes was done in the days before modern techniques became available.)

Figure 10.11

The influence of insulin on blood glucose level An elevated blood glucose concentration (hyperglycemia) stimulates the pancreas to release insulin, which lowers blood glucose by promoting its removal from the bloodstream and its storage as glycogen in the liver and muscle, or its conversion to fat.

➜ Why does the administration of insulin increase food intake?

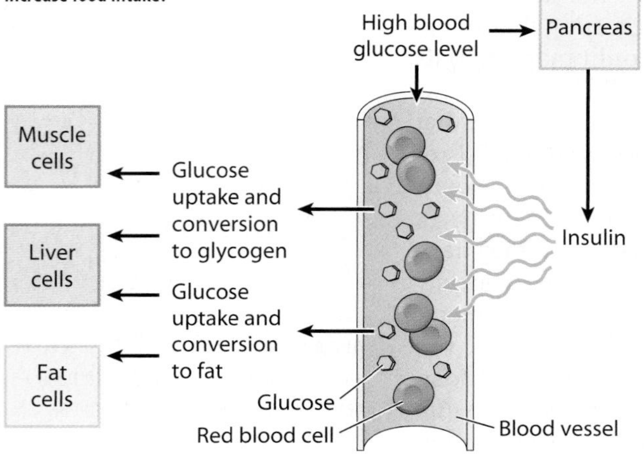

Further evidence for Mayer's glucostatic theory comes from experiments by Louis-Sylvestre and Le Magnen (1980), in which they continuously measured blood glucose levels in rats and found that the levels fell several minutes before each meal. This result shows a correlation between blood glucose level and the initiation of feeding, but it does not prove that a lowered blood glucose level *causes* eating. Campfield and Smith (1990) reviewed research that, among other things, demonstrated that each meal was preceded by a transient decline in blood glucose, that experimentally induced transient decreases in blood glucose led to the initiating of eating, and that raising blood glucose levels by injection of glucose actually postponed eating in rats, which again supports the idea that decreases in blood glucose are related to hunger and increases to satiety (Figure 10.12). Note that in the figure, the meal does not begin at the lowest point of the blood glucose decline, but about 7 minutes later, when the blood glucose level has returned almost to its normal, baseline level.

glucagon A pancreatic hormone that increases blood glucose levels.

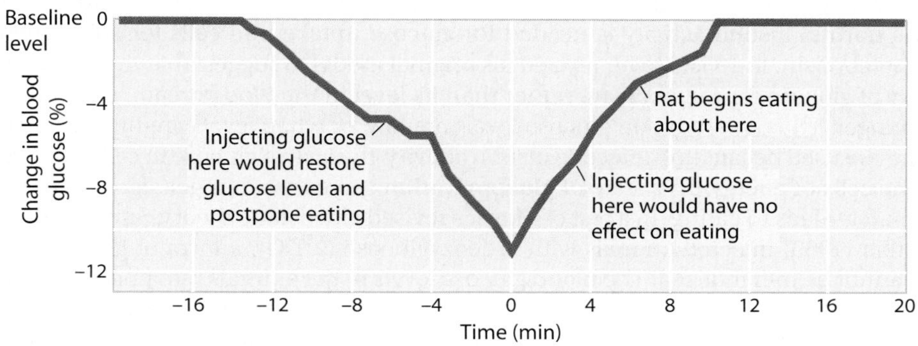

Figure 10.12

The correlation between a fall in blood glucose level and eating behavior The blood glucose level falls to its minimum level (at time zero) approximately 7 minutes before the animal begins to eat. Injecting glucose to restore the normal blood level before, but not after, the low point would suppress eating.

→ **What is glucoprivation?**

In a series of studies, Judith Rodin and her associates preloaded human subjects with liquid containing either glucose or fructose, then measured their caloric intake at a "buffet" meal (Rodin, 1990; Rodin & others, 1988). Although both substances are sugars, glucose produces a stronger insulin release and greater drop in blood glucose level than does fructose. Mayer's theory would predict that the subjects with the glucose preload would eat more than those with the fructose preload, because of the larger drop in blood glucose in the first group. This is what the experimenters observed. As a practical matter, these studies suggest that if you are on a weight-reduction diet, snacking on a piece of fruit (high in fructose) is a better choice than a piece of cake (high in glucose); the fruit is also much lower in fat content.

Research also supports the suggestion by Mayer that the increase in blood glucose that follows feeding activates glucoreceptors that suppress eating, leading to satiety. Injection of **glucagon,** a pancreatic hormone that increases blood glucose levels, produces a rapid decrease in both stomach contractions and reported hunger in human subjects (Stunkard & others, 1955). Mayer (1955) also found that glucagon injections suppress food intake in food-deprived animals. Figure 10.13 summarizes the influence of glucagon on blood glucose level.

As you might expect, the paraventricular system responds to increased blood glucose by suppressing eating. For example, a rise in blood glucose coincides with increased electrical activity in the VMH area and with a decrease in eating (Anand & others, 1962). However, evidence indicates that the satiety glucoreceptors are not located in the VMH or even in the brain. Stricker and colleagues (1977) injected insulin in rats to produce *hypoglycemia,* a low blood glucose level. Subsequent infusion

Figure 10.13

The influence of glucagon on blood glucose level When the blood glucose level is low (hypoglycemia), glucagon is released from the pancreas and stimulates the conversion of glycogen in the liver into glucose and the release of glucose into the bloodstream for use as an energy source.

→ **Why would the administration of glucagon suppress food intake?**

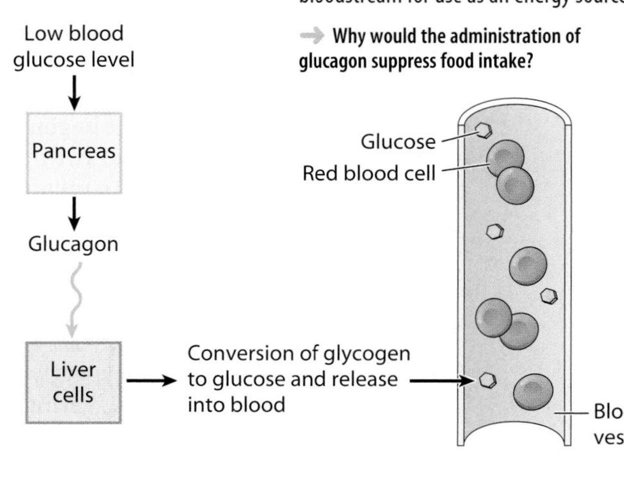

glucoprivation The unavailability of glucose as an energy source.

of fructose prevented a hypoglycemia-induced feeding response—that is, it inhibited eating in response to the lowered blood glucose. Fructose cannot cross the blood-brain barrier, so if the glucoreceptors were located in the brain, the animal should have remained hungry after fructose injections. Thus, we must conclude that the receptors are not located in the brain.

Russek (1971) injected glucose into either the hepatic portal vein (the blood supply to the liver) or the jugular vein (the blood supply to the brain) in a food-deprived dog. Administration into the hepatic portal vein suppressed eating, whereas administration into the jugular vein had no effect on eating. From this experiment, Russek concluded that the satiety glucoreceptors are located in the liver.

Challenges to the Glucostatic Theory

One obvious problem with the glucostatic theory, as Mayer (1953) originally proposed it, is that people with diabetes mellitus experience excessive hunger despite high blood glucose levels. The explanation for this apparent anomaly is that untreated people with diabetes cannot convert their high blood glucose into energy, as normal insulin activity is needed for glucose uptake into cells for subsequent metabolism. In 1955, Mayer revised his original model to suggest that the *availability* of glucose for metabolism, rather than its level in the bloodstream, determines hunger. Thus, when blood glucose levels are low, or when levels are high but cannot be used because of defective insulin activity, the lack of glucose in cells deprives the cells of energy. This state of **glucoprivation** serves as a hunger signal and ultimately leads to eating. In a test of Mayer's revised glucostatic theory, Smith and Epstein (1969) injected animals with 2-deoxyglucose (2-DG), a form of glucose that cannot be metabolized. The blood glucose levels in the animals remained high, but they overate. Like people with diabetes, they were both hungry *and* hyperglycemic.

Let us return to Chris's visit to the Italian restaurant. A low blood glucose level caused Chris to feel hungry and to begin eating the pizza and spaghetti. One possible reason for his low blood glucose is deprivation, defined as the time since he last ate. However, animals often eat when their deprivation level is insufficient to cause a depletion in their nutritional resources, and from what we know about Chris, he does not really need the Italian meal to replenish diminished energy stores. What, then, triggered his low blood glucose level and his hunger? Studies by Campfield and Smith (1990) showed that the decreased blood glucose levels that precede eating are caused by a brief, 50% rise in insulin secretion from the pancreas. These researchers suggested that signals from the brain cause this release of insulin—which takes us back to the CNS.

Mayer (1953) had suggested that the glucoreceptors that respond to decreases in blood glucose are located in the brain and probably in the hypothalamus. However, some evidence indicates that the glucoreceptors are located in the liver and in the hindbrain, but not in the hypothalamus (Penicaud & others, 1990; Tordoff & others, 1991). For example, rats began eating sooner and ate more when a substance similar to fructose (a fructose analogue) was injected into the hepatic portal vein rather than into the jugular vein. In addition, severing the branch of the vagus nerve serving the liver blocked the eating response to injections of the fructose analogue (Tordoff & others). Both results indicate that a signal to initiate feeding behavior begins in the liver.

Ritter and coworkers (1981) infused 5-thioglucose (5-TG), a glucose analogue with effects similar to those of 2-DG, into either the lateral ventricles of the forebrain or the fourth ventricle of the hindbrain. In both cases, hyperglycemia and increased feeding resulted. However, when the researchers blocked the cerebral aqueduct, which connects the fourth ventricle with the forebrain ventricles, 5-TG caused hyperglycemia and feeding only when it was infused into the fourth ventricle; when 5-TG was forced to remain in the forebrain, which includes the hypothalamus, hyperglycemia and increased feeding did not occur. In other words, the receptors triggering the increased hyperglycemia and feeding response are in the hindbrain, not in the hypothalamus.

At this point, we can conclude that glucoreceptors in the liver and in the hindbrain detect either a reduced blood glucose level or a reduced glucose availability, which might be caused by an insufficient insulin activity. On detection of one of these states, a message is sent to the hypothalamic system, activating it and triggering feeding behavior.

In the glucostatic theory, satiety results when an increase in blood glucose stimulates the glucoreceptors in the liver, which send the appropriate message to the paraventricular system. In support of this idea, Schmitt (1973) found that an infusion of glucose into the liver increased neural activity in the VMH. Presumably, the paraventricular system continues to inhibit eating as long as blood glucose levels are above the threshold level for hunger.

cholecystokinin (CCK) A neuropeptide hormone that may serve as a satiety sensor.

Checkpoint

Compare and contrast the effects of glucagon and insulin on blood glucose levels. How do you know that glucoreceptors are located in the liver and/or in the hindbrain?

Hormonal Satiety Cues

The neuropeptide hormone **cholecystokinin (CCK)** also may serve as a satiety sensor, monitoring food intake and inhibiting eating when a sufficient amount of food has been consumed (Bray, 2000b). When food enters the duodenum (the first section of the small intestine after the stomach), the intestinal lining secretes CCK, and the CCK limits the rate at which food passes from the stomach into the small intestine, ensuring proper digestion. In addition, research suggests that CCK produces satiety and suppresses eating, as CCK injections into the PVN have been found to decrease food intake in rats (Helm & others, 2003). In humans, MacIntosh and colleagues (2001) found that CCK infusions produced greater food intake suppression in older individuals than in younger ones and suggested that increased CCK activity may in part explain the anorexia associated with aging. Further, high-fat or high-protein diets in rats increased circulating CCK levels relative to low-fat diets, which led to reduced sensitivity over time to the satiating effects of CCK (Covasa & others, 2001). This effect of the diets on CCK release and sensitivity might explain dramatic initial weight loss in obese humans on such diets followed by a decreased effect as the diet continues.

Further indirect evidence for the role of CCK in regulating food intake comes from studies of genetically obese mice and from humans with eating disorders. For example, several researchers have reported much lower brain levels of CCK in genetically obese mice compared to control animals (Cain & others, 1997; Wang & others, 1998). In women with bulimia nervosa, an eating disorder characterized by eating binges and purging, CCK secretion following a meal is abnormally low, but it is normal in people with either anorexia nervosa or hyperphagia associated with seasonal depression (Devlin & others, 1997; Geracioti & others, 1989; Geracioti & Liddle, 1988; Geracioti & others, 1992). In addition to a decreased CCK release, Devlin and colleagues found that women with bulimia have increased gastric capacity and delayed gastric emptying, which perhaps contribute to their impaired satiety response.

Two different mechanisms of CCK action have been suggested. According to the first proposal, activation of peripheral CCK receptors in the stomach and small intestine stimulates the vagus nerve, which transmits the satiety message to the hypothalamus through the nucleus of the solitary tract. In support of this idea, several studies have found that severing the vagus nerve blocks the satiety effect of CCK (Crawley & Kiss, 1985; Reidelberger & others, 2004). In addition, drugs that counteract the effect of CCK on peripheral receptors increase food intake in a variety of experimental situations (Salorio & others, 1994). Salorio and colleagues further found that the satiating effects of CCK were age dependent in rats, inhibiting food intake in a dose-related fashion in adult animals but having less of an effect in younger rats. Similarly, administration of a CCK antagonist had no effect on food intake in younger animals while significantly increasing consumption in older animals. The researchers concluded that adolescent rats are relatively insensitive to CCK, because they are in a period of high food intake and rapid growth.

The second way CCK may produce satiety is by activating CCK receptors in the brain. In keeping with the idea of the paraventricular system and the importance

ghrelin A gastrointestinal peptide with an appetite-stimulating effect.

of the VMH in satiety, CCK receptors are found in the VMH as well as in the PVN (Heidel & Davidowa, 1998; Monnikes & others, 1997). To demonstrate that peripherally released CCK activates CCK receptors in the brain, Dourish and coworkers (1989) administered a drug that specifically antagonizes the CCK receptors in the brain, and observed that food intake increased in animals that previously had been partially satiated, and the animals ate for a longer period. The investigators then turned the experiment around, selectively antagonizing the peripheral CCK receptors; they found a much smaller effect than when the brain CCK receptors were blocked. These observations suggest that CCK produces satiety through the activation primarily of brain CCK receptors.

However, some of the effect of CCK injections may be caused by nausea rather than by satiety. Animals were found to develop *taste aversion conditioning* to a flavor paired with CCK—that is, they avoided it after the pairing—which suggests that the CCK injections were aversive to the animals (Mosher & others, 1996, 1998). Further, the inhibitory effect of CCK on eating could be decreased by an injection of a drug that suppresses nausea, indicating that the effects of exogenous CCK, administered by injection, are quite different from the effects of endogenous (naturally occurring) CCK (Moore & Deutsch, 1985). In other words, the experimenter-administered CCK may produce nausea, which causes the apparent satiating effects. Further evidence for such an effect came from experiments in which the same neurochemical, oxytocin, was released from the pituitary following either drug-induced nausea or the injection of CCK (Stricker & Verbalis, 1991). The problem is that the exogenously administered CCK doses in animal studies may not correspond to the amount released endogenously by food reaching the duodenum, and evidence indicates that CCK is a physiological satiety factor in humans (Beglinger, 2002; Degen & others, 2001).

Unlike CCK, which tends to promote satiety, a gastrointestinal peptide has recently been discovered that has an appetite-stimulating effect. It is called **ghrelin,** which is short for growth hormone (GH) *releasin.* Not surprisingly, ghrelin also plays a role in the release of growth hormone. Blood levels of ghrelin increase shortly before a meal in humans (Cummings & others, 2001), and the effect of the peptide on the initiation of a meal is apparently through NPY/AGRP neurons in the arcuate nucleus (Nakazato & others, 2001).

The *Scientific American* Spotlight, "The Diet That Fits," discusses the possibility that many diseases, including obesity, may simply be metabolic syndromes. Thus, metabolic testing may lead to the tailoring of treatment more precisely to the individual. What works for you may not work for someone else, and metabolic testing may provide the answer people have been looking for.

➤Checkpoint

Describe how energy balance (level of glucose) is maintained in the short term. Using what you have learned about glucoprivation, explain why fad diets that lack a particular type of nutrient probably will not work in the long run.

REVIEW

- ➤ Oral sensations do not initiate feeding, but they are necessary for its continuation.
- ➤ Cues from the stomach are involved in satiety, through the activation of both pressure detectors and nutrient detectors.
- ➤ Food deprivation lowers the blood glucose level, which stimulates eating behavior.
- ➤ The glucostatic theory suggests that hunger is caused by low glucose availability, as detected by glucoreceptors in the liver and hindbrain. Satiety occurs when an increase in blood glucose stimulates the glucoreceptors in the liver, which send the message to the paraventricular system.
- ➤ The peripheral release of CCK may produce satiety by stimulating the vagus nerve (which transmits the satiety message to the hypothalamus), by stimulating the paraventricular system directly, or by producing nausea.
- ➤ Ghrelin is a gastrointestinal peptide that may be involved in the initiation of feeding, probably by its stimulation of NPY/AGRP neurons in the arcuate nucleus.

Scientific American Spotlight

The Diet That Fits

Analyzing Metabolism for Personalized Nutrition

Gunjan Sinha

No single diet works for everyone. Some people can slurp cabbage soup for a week and lose only a few ounces, while others on the same spartan regimen lose 10 pounds. But what if you could measure your metabolism and get a prescription for a customized diet?

Metabonomics may do just that. It is one of the latest offshoots of the "-omics" revolution—after genomics (genes) and proteomics (proteins). With the understanding that some diseases such as obesity are metabolic syndromes in which multiple biochemical pathways interact to cause complex symptoms, metabolic testing offers a way to gauge health over a lifetime. What is more, metabonomic technology might identify disorders before they produce symptoms. Such testing could help people choose diet and exercise regimens that are tailored to their individual metabolic states.

Alan J. Higgins of Icoria, a company based in Research Triangle Park, N.C., that is applying its metabonomic technology to human health, explains that "metabonomics gives you the functional component" that is not always evident from a genetic or protein analysis. Changes in gene expression do not necessarily affect health, because the body's homeostatic mechanisms may compensate. Moreover, genes and proteins interact and only sometimes cause net changes in metabolic pathways. Metabonomics attempts to unify genomics and proteomics by examining an organism as a system. "We pick up those changes on the downstream end," Higgins adds.

At any given moment, the human body excretes thousands of metabolites that can be measured in urine, plasma and various body tissues. Conventional technology such as mass spectrometry and nuclear magnetic resonance can measure such components—that is how biochemists test the toxicity of drugs or environmental pollutants on human cells. The challenge, however, has been interpreting the reams of data generated. The bioinformatics boom has helped solve that problem. Scientists can now analyze metabolites in greater detail and also conduct more informative comparative studies. For example, three years ago London-based Metabometrix demonstrated that high-frequency radio waves bounced off a blood sample could identify atherosclerosis. The radio waves measure the sample's magnetic properties, and computer software generates a telltale pattern.

Comfort food: In a new field called metabonomics, you eat (and drink) what you are.

Profiling metabolic disease before symptoms appear may also be possible. Researchers at BG Medicine, based in Waltham, Mass., examined mice genetically engineered to develop atherosclerosis if placed on a high-fat diet. Scientists fed the mice a moderate-fat diet and after nine weeks measured lipid molecules in their livers and plasma. Compared with levels in a control group, certain lipid metabolites were elevated in the transgenic mice, even though they appeared perfectly healthy.

Of course, biochemical markers that flag disease, such as high cholesterol, already exist, but they are not sufficient. "A single biomarker gives information," says Jan van der Greef of BG Medicine, "but typically biomarker patterns are necessary to tell the complete story." Van der Greef suspects that many diseases have metabolic signatures that technology can detect even before a marker such as cholesterol would be elevated—the challenge is to identify the patterns. That is no small task: there is not yet a clear understanding of normal human metabolism, let alone abnormal metabolism.

Relatively speaking, "gene sequencing is so easy," says José M. Ordovas, director of the Nutrition and Genomics Laboratory at Tufts University. He notes that sequencers have to cope with only four components (A, C, T and G), whereas "in metabonomics you have different [technology] platforms that measure things in different ways. We are talking about thousands of components."

To move forward, scientists would like to see a human metabonome established—an equivalent of the human genome for metabolism. But the field lacks coordination and money, says Ordovas, who estimates that it might take analyses of half a million people or more to accomplish the task.

Ordovas is, however, inching his way ahead. In a joint project with Metabometrix, he is examining a few thousand subjects, some who have severe cases of metabolic diseases such as obesity and some who are healthy, to identify how extremes differ from the norm. He will also investigate whether diet and exercise tailored to a person's unique metabolic profile can bring weight down to normal and prevent a premature slide into bad health. In the future, instead of scanning food labels for calories, fats and carbs, we might be matching labels to our metabolic type.

From: *Scientific American*, vol. 292(3), pp. 22–23.

Environmental Influences on Eating Behavior

In addition to such peripheral cues as oral sensations and stomach contractions, and such metabolic cues as blood levels of glucose, environmental cues, such as the sight and smell of delicious food, can affect our hunger and satiety.

Conditioned Hunger

Has the sight of a cream puff in the window of your local bakery ever made you feel hungry, even if you had just eaten (Figure 10.14)? Rolls and colleagues (1976, 1980) found that neurons in the lateral hypothalamic region of a monkey changed their rate of firing when the monkey looked at food. The neurons did not respond to nonfood objects or to simple visual stimuli, and they failed to respond to olfactory stimuli or when the monkey ate in the dark. The researchers concluded that the activity of the neurons was associated with the sight of food. For people, just the thought of a delicious food is often sufficient to trigger **conditioned hunger**—hunger resulting from something in the environment and produced by conditioning.

JEAN LUC MORALES/GETTY IMAGES

Figure 10.14
Conditioned hunger Attractive foods can elicit a strong insulin response and intense hunger. Only a strong conditioned satiety response could enable a person with a sweet tooth to resist the baked goods shown here.

→ **Where in the CNS does the sight of your favorite food provoke the greatest response?**

The motivation for an animal to eat is intensified during eating because the cephalic reflexes (salivation, gastric secretions, etc.) elicited by food stimulate the hunger system and maintain eating until the satiety cues occur (Powley, 1977). Palatable foods produce greater cephalic responses than unpalatable foods, and the enhanced cephalic responses can become conditioned.

In *classical conditioning,* a stimulus (the sight of a cream puff) is paired with a biologically significant stimulus (the taste of a cream puff) a sufficient number of times for the novel stimulus to elicit the behavior, a *conditioned response (CR),* that was originally elicited only by the biologically significant stimulus, an *unconditioned response (UCR).* In Ivan Pavlov's view, the sight of the food is the *conditioned stimulus (CS)* and its taste is the *unconditioned stimulus (UCS).* (In Chapter 14 we discuss Pavlov and classical conditioning in greater detail.)

In studies on rats, Weingarten and Powley (1981) found that a light and a sound (the CS) paired with a high-fat food (the UCS) eventually stimulated the release of a gastric acid (the CR) in the absence of the food. Detke and colleagues (1989) found that a contextual stimulus (the CS) paired with food (the UCS) produced insulin release as the CR, as well as enhancing the movement of an animal toward a source of food in a Skinner box. In human participants, food or even the thought of food stimulates insulin release and produces feelings of hunger (Rodin, 1985). These studies suggest that environmental cues associated with palatable foods can elicit the cephalic feeding responses.

Schachter's research, discussed earlier in this chapter, underscores the importance of environmental cues in initiating eating by obese humans. Moreover, other researchers found that VMH-lesioned rats showed more conditioned responding than unlesioned rats (Kramer & others, 1983; Powley, 1977). And because of Schachter's observation of greater responsivity to food-related cues in obese humans, we would also expect to see a comparatively stronger conditioned response in humans—which has been confirmed by Sjostrom and coworkers (1980), who observed that obese women have a stronger insulin response than normal-weight women to food-related cues.

Conditioned Satiety

conditioned hunger Hunger resulting from environmental factors, produced by conditioning.

conditioned satiety Satiety resulting from stimuli at the end of a meal, producing a short-term inhibition of eating.

Suppose you take two bites of pecan pie and feel full. This is probably because of **conditioned satiety.** Booth (1990) proposed that stimuli at the end of a meal are associated with the nutritional changes that occur after eating (e.g., glucagon release triggered by food in the stomach). These conditioned stimuli (CSs) then elicit a conditioned satiety response (CR), producing a short-term inhibition of eating. The unconditioned nutritional changes (UCRs) maintain the inhibition until the next meal. This observation that human and nonhuman animals stop eating before experiencing the nutritional effects of eating supports the idea that classical conditioning is involved in satiety.

As an illustration of conditioned satiety, Booth (1972) provided rats with both a dilute diet of one flavor and a rich diet of a different flavor. At first, the animals ate an equal amount of each diet, showing the same preference for each flavor. During the course of the study, however, the animals ate less of the rich diet and more of the dilute diet. Booth proposed that the rich diet produced a greater conditioned satiety response (e.g., glucagon release stimulated by a little food in the stomach) because it produced a stronger unconditioned satiety effect (a greater increase in blood glucose following eating). In support of this proposal, Booth found that when the flavor of the rich diet was switched to that of the dilute diet, the rats ate small amounts of both diets and lost weight; switching the flavor of the dilute diet to that of the rich diet caused the animals to eat large amounts of both diets and gain weight. Using a two-bottle choice test, Gibson and Booth (2000) found that rats drank more of fluid with a novel odor than they did of fluid with an odor that had been presented in the later part of meals. The researchers considered this evidence that the rats had developed conditioned satiety to the odor associated with the later part of meals. Booth and colleagues (1976) observed a similar phenomenon in human participants, further supporting Booth's idea that conditioned satiety plays a role in regulating food intake.

Nonhuman animals typically eat only a single type of food at a time, which enables them to learn the flavors linked to satiety. For humans, the wide variety of foods eaten during a meal is partly responsible for overeating. Similarly, rats eat more and become obese when allowed access to high-fat, high-sugar, or "cafeteria" diets (Louis-Sylvestre & others, 1984). The researchers concluded that good taste and variety are sufficient to overcome the normal regulatory mechanisms of rats. Perhaps we could regulate our eating more easily if we limited the number of foods consumed in a single meal.

Conditioned Taste Aversion

Although Chris very much enjoys his food, he will not touch mushrooms and he will not eat at the burger place closest to the campus. Most of us have some food we will not eat or a restaurant we avoid (Figure 10.15), often because we once experienced illness after eating a particular food or dining at a particular place, and now we associate the food or the place with the illness through classical conditioning. Such an experience creates a conditioned aversion to the taste (or smell or sight) of the food or the place where we ate it.

In some classical studies, John Garcia and his associates demonstrated that animals learn to avoid a flavor associated with illness (Garcia & others, 1955; Garcia & others, 1961). Although rats will consume large quantities of saccharin even when not food deprived, a rat will not subsequently drink saccharin if the consumption is followed by illness, induced by agents such as x-ray irradiation or lithium chloride injections. Conditioned taste aversion learning is quite rapid, with significant avoidance occurring after only a single pairing of flavor with illness.

If there is a particular food you avoid eating, perhaps you can identify the cause of your aversion to it. Garb and Stunkard (1974) found in a survey that 38% of 696 subjects reported at least one strong taste aversion. Of these, 89% could identify a specific instance in which they became ill after eating the food. Even though the illness generally did not begin until several hours after eating the food, they still avoided the food in the future. The survey also indicated that people are more likely to develop aversions between the ages of 6 and 12 than at any other age.

More systematic experimentation has further documented the establishment of people's taste aversions (Logue, 1991). For example, Bernstein (1978) found that children in the early stages of cancer acquired an aversion to a distinctively flavored ice cream eaten before toxic chemotherapy targeting the gastrointestinal (GI) tract. After the therapy, instead of eating ice cream with the same flavor, the

Figure 10.15

Food aversion Food aversion conditioning results when we associate an incidence of illness with eating a certain food. In this photograph, the man has developed an aversion to green jello because he once ate some and was sick afterwards.

In the case of food aversion, is the food the conditioned stimulus, the unconditioned stimulus, or the conditioned response?

children preferred either to play with a toy or to eat ice cream of another flavor. By contrast, children who had received the chemotherapy without first eating the ice cream, as well as children who had been given the ice cream before receiving chemotherapy that did not involve the GI tract, ate the ice cream after the therapy.

Women receiving chemotherapy for breast cancer were found to develop conditioned taste aversions (Jacobsen & others, 1993), and cancer patients receiving radiation therapy often lose weight (Beaver & others, 2001). Cancer patients also show an aversion to foods eaten before chemotherapy (Schwartz & others, 1996). Further, chemotherapy patients experience anticipatory nausea before their second and subsequent treatments (Stockhorst & others, 1998), and this anticipatory nausea is associated with the persistence of nausea and distress among survivors of Hodgkin's disease (Cameron & others, 2001). Conditioning principles are currently being tested to determine whether the conditioned nausea and reduced appetite can be prevented in cancer patients receiving chemotherapy (Stockhorst, Wiener, & others, 1998).

➤Checkpoint

You have just had a huge meal at a restaurant. Walking down the street to your apartment, you pass your favorite ice cream shop. Suddenly, your mouth begins to water, and you feel the need for a double chocolate fudge ice cream cone. Describe the role of classical conditioning in producing your hunger response.

REVIEW

- ➤ Hunger can be classically conditioned.
- ➤ Stimuli at the end of a meal can be associated with nutritional changes after eating to produce conditioned satiety.
- ➤ Animals and humans quickly learn to associate a food or a place with illness in conditioned taste aversion.
- ➤ Conditioned taste aversion can explain much of the weight loss associated with cancer treatment.

◆ The Long-Term Regulation of Body Weight

So far we have focused on how an animal maintains an adequate energy balance, but in order to survive, the animal must also maintain an optimal body weight. In this section, we consider how body weight is regulated over the long term.

The Lipostatic Theory

The glucostatic theory provides an explanation for hunger and satiety based on a short-term, meal-to-meal mechanism. The **lipostatic theory** accounts for weight regulation through a long-term, day-to-day mechanism based on fat deposits. Mayer (1955) was among the first to propose the lipostatic theory.

A decreased blood level of **lipids,** or fatty acids, as a cause of hunger is firmly established. (Note that the term "lipid" includes both fat, as ingested or as stored in the body, and fatty acids, which are components of fat.) For example, injections of mercaptoacetate, which blocks the ability to metabolize fatty acids without affecting glucose levels, produce an increase in food consumption (Swithers & McCurley, 2002). The lack of availability of lipids (both in the diet and stored) as a source of energy is called **lipoprivation.**

The increased food intake resulting from mercaptoacetate administration can be eliminated by administering capsaicin, a neurotoxin found in red peppers that destroys fine-diameter, unmyelinated PNS axons that carry information from internal organs to the brain, or by cutting the vagus nerve where it enters the abdominal cavity (Scharrer, 1999). These observations suggest that the receptors that detect low lipid availability are in the abdominal cavity and that information about hunger travels via unmyelinated axons from this area to the brain.

The mammalian hormone **leptin,** secreted by fat cells, seems to provide the brain with feedback about the level of stored fat (Woods & others, 2000). Consi-

lipostatic theory A theory that proposes a relationship between fat deposits and hunger.

lipid A fat or fatty acid; fatty acid levels in the blood are involved in hunger.

lipoprivation The unavailability of fats or fatty acids as an energy source.

leptin A hormone secreted by fat cells that appears to provide the brain with feedback about the level of stored fat in the body.

dine and colleagues (1996) have found that leptin levels are much higher in obese people than in normal-weight people and are highly correlated with body fat percentage, suggesting that obese people are insensitive to their leptin concentrations. Moreover, Keim and colleagues (1998) found that leptin levels declined in response to a moderate energy deficit in a group of healthy women, and the decline was associated with an increase in hunger—supporting the idea that leptin is a physiological regulator of hunger during energy deficits (dieting) in humans.

Receptors for leptin are found in several areas within the hypothalamus, including the arcuate nucleus, the ventromedial nucleus, the dorsomedial nucleus, and the paraventricular nucleus (Baskin & others, 1999). Neurons in the arcuate nucleus project to the PVN, an area of the brain that releases neuropeptide Y. Leptin receptors in the arcuate nucleus react to the lower levels of leptin caused by low body fat by increasing NPY release (Williams & others, 2004). As we described earlier in the chapter, increased NPY in the PVN increases food intake (Kalra & others, 1988) and decreases energy expenditure.

Although you can find literally thousands of advertisements on the Internet for miracle weight-loss products based on leptin, the reality is that such products are unlikely to work for most overweight people. As we indicated, the majority of obese people already have high levels of circulating leptin that is not curbing their appetites. According to Proietto and Thorburn (2003), clinical trials have shown that leptin works to suppress food intake only in people who overeat because of low leptin levels. The problem is that most obese people are insensitive to the leptin their fat cells are making in excess, and adding more leptin to the system does not help. A better approach may be to look for agents that will attack the leptin insensitivity of the obese person.

DONNA DAY/GETTY IMAGES

Combined with snacking, sedentary activities such as watching television may lead to obesity.

Set-Point Theory

Related to lipostatic theory is the idea that animals maintain a constant body weight by having a critical level of stored fat, which Keesey and Powley (1986) called the **critical set point.** Set point is related to **homeostasis,** Harvard physiologist Walter B. Cannon's term for an inherent tendency of an animal to maintain a stable, or steady, internal state. When the stored fat of an animal falls below the set point, the hunger system activates food-seeking behaviors and remains active until the animal's body weight returns to the set point. Similarly, when the amount of stored body fat exceeds the critical set point, the paraventricular system inhibits further eating. As you can see, the set-point theory is one explanation for why Chris has such trouble losing weight—his body's set point is higher than the weight he would like to achieve on his diet.

A normal animal deprived of food for several days will regain the lost weight when it again has access to food. Because of short-term satiety, the animal does not eat enough at one time to regain all the lost weight, but instead gains weight over several days by eating more frequent meals.

Keesey and Powley (1986) used their set-point theory to explain the dramatic weight loss seen in LH-lesioned animals; they suggested that the LH damage resets the set point of the animals to a lower level than before the operation. In order for an LH-lesioned animal to begin eating postoperatively, its body weight must drop to the new set point. To test their theory, Powley and Keesey (1970) first deprived rats of food preoperatively, reducing their body weight below the presumed new set

critical set point The critical level of stored fat that either activates or inhibits food-seeking behaviors.

homeostasis A tendency of an animal to maintain a constant internal state.

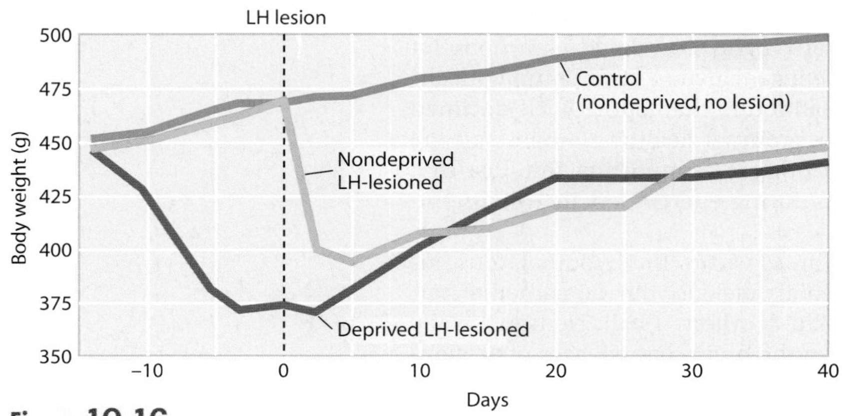

Figure 10.16

The effect of preoperative starvation on the LH-lesion syndrome Animals deprived before LH lesioning do not lose weight following the operation, but instead regain weight to the level seen in nondeprived LH-lesioned animals.

➡ **What is the set-point theory?**

point that would be produced by LH damage (Figure 10.16). After LH lesioning, these animals lost no more weight. In fact, some animals that had smaller lesions began eating in order to bring their weight up to the level achieved by starvation of preoperatively nondeprived LH-lesioned rats. This result suggests that LH lesions lower the set point rather than directly causing aphagia, which is actually a side effect of the lowered set point induced by the lesion.

Powley and Keesey (1970) also suggested that VMH damage might raise the critical set point. According to this idea, the VMH-lesioned animal becomes obese because it eats until it has stored enough fat to satisfy the new, higher set point. This hypothesis also satisfies Hoebel and Teitelbaum's finding (1966) that VMH-lesioned rats did not overeat postoperatively if before surgery they were made obese by force-feeding. According to the set-point theory, the fat stores of these obese rats were already at or above the higher critical set point, and so after VMH lesioning, their satiety systems inhibited further excessive eating. In addition, once the rats became obese from their lesion-induced hyperphagia, they defended this higher weight by starving if they were made heavier by force-feeding or by ravenous eating if they were food-deprived to a lower weight (Figure 10.17).

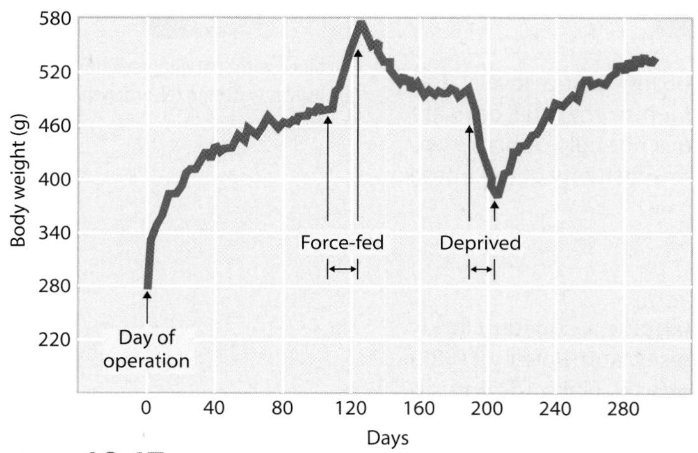

Figure 10.17

The effect of postoperative force-feeding and starvation on VMH-lesioned animals The animals gain weight if force-fed and lose weight if deprived, but return to their previous weight after the force-feeding or deprivation ends.

➡ **How is this figure relevant to set-point theory? Justify your answer.**

Rohner-Jeanrenaud (2000) has suggested that neuropeptide Y and leptin provide the links that allow set-point mechanisms to operate, and their importance in this regard has been corroborated in research with humans (Hallschmid & others, 2004). Changes in NPY and leptin levels in the blood maintain normal body homeostasis. Fasting causes decreases in leptin and corresponding increases in hypothalamic NPY levels, increases in food intake, and subsequent weight gain. This weight gain leads to increased leptin release, decreased NPY, decreased eating, and either a stabilized weight level or weight loss. However, at least one study with rats found that increasing leptin levels in the blood immediately before the end of a period of food restriction did not prevent the animals from regaining the weight they had lost (Velkoska & others, 2003), which suggests that leptin might have little value in helping dieters *maintain* their weight loss. Hypothalamic damage disrupts the leptin/NPY regulation of body weight and leads to the LH- or VMH-lesion syndrome.

The idea of a body-weight set point as a homeostatic mechanism is an interesting concept, with some explanatory potential, at least for understanding the feeding behavior of laboratory animals under certain conditions (e.g., following LH or VMH damage). However, when we begin to consider the real-world eating behavior and weight regulation of human beings from a homeostatic standpoint, questions soon arise. For example, why does the body-weight set point of many adults seem to rise as they get older, and why is it so markedly different in people of the same height and general body type? Why is there so much cultural variation in set point? Attempted answers to these and other questions may lie in the concept of allostasis, introduced by Sterling and Eyer (1988).

Allostasis is the maintenance of stability (homeostasis) through change. Although Sterling and Eyer (1988) introduced the term "allostasis" to describe how

allostasis The maintenance of stability through change.

allostatic load The cumulative cost to the body of repeated cycles of allostasis.

the cardiovascular system adjusts to different bodily states (e.g., rest, activity), the concept can be applied to other physiological mechanisms as well, such as the secretion of cortisol and catecholamines in response to stress. (The stress reaction is discussed at length in Chapter 12.) When adaptive systems are turned on and off efficiently and infrequently, they help the body cope with stressors that otherwise might not be survivable (McEwen, 1998). Repeated allostasis, however, such as changes in cortisol and catecholamine secretion in response to stress, affects **allostatic load,** which is the general wear and tear on the body from repeated cycles of allostasis. Specific examples of allostatic load include the atrophy of nerve cells in the hippocampus, the loss of bone minerals (osteoporosis), and the accumulation of abdominal fat (McEwen, 2000a).

How are allostasis and allostatic load related to obesity in humans? Population studies have shown that adrenal stress hormones, such as cortisol, are strongly associated with the deposition of body fat around the waist and with obesity (Bjorntorp, 2001). Other adrenal hormones, the glucocorticoids, increase food intake and leptin-resistant obesity, perhaps by altering the balance between leptin and neuropeptide Y to favor the latter. Recall that NPY acts on the PVN to increase hunger and eating. According to Bjorntorp, the ultimate result of continued glucocorticoid exposure might be "stress eating."

Extending the concept of allostatic load, McEwen and Wingfield (2003) discuss allostatic *overload.* In one type of allostatic overload, the consumption of either enough or too much energy (e.g., excessive intake of calories) is accompanied by social conflict (e.g., society's preoccupation with the desirability of thinness). Allostatic overload can lead to serious pathophysiology, such as obesity and its concomitant effects (e.g., hypertension, diabetes). McEwen and Wingfield note that this type of allostatic overload can be overcome only through learning and changes in the social structure.

Genetics and Obesity

Evidence clearly exists for genetic contributions to obesity (Williams & others, 2001). For example, genetic mutations have produced several inbred strains of obese mice and rats, including *ob/ob* mice, *db/db* mice, and *fa/fa* Zucker rats. In these animals, leptin deficiencies lead to overactive neuropeptide Y neurons and the hyperphagia and obesity that are metabolically similar to the syndromes seen after VMH or PVN damage. This similarity suggests that leptin may have its metabolic effects through these two hypothalamic centers (Bray & York, 1998).

The genetic mutations in *db/db* mice and *fa/fa* Zucker rats cause defects in leptin receptors (Beck, 2000). In *fa/fa* Zucker rats, leptin has little effect on food intake, suggesting that the obesity may at least partly result from the inability of leptin to inhibit neuropeptide neurons in these animals (Woods & others, 1998).

By contrast, *ob/ob* mice have intact leptin receptors but are unable to synthesize leptin. These mice respond to the satiety effect of leptin, and small amounts of leptin administered into the brains of *ob/ob* mice reverse the hyperphagia-obesity syndrome (Woods & others, 1998).

Instead of injecting *ob/ob* mice with exogenous leptin, another approach to treating the hyperphagia and obesity caused by a lack of leptin might be to manipulate the genes to make the animals deficient in neuropeptide Y. Palmiter and colleagues (1998) used this approach to show that without NPY, *ob/ob* mice were less obese and also less affected by endocrine-related disorders. In another approach to the leptin problem, Muzzin and colleagues (2000) introduced a gene coding for leptin into the cerebral ventricles of obese *fa/fa* Zucker rats. As a result, the animals temporarily produced high levels of leptin, reduced their food intake, and lost weight—supporting the hypothesis that impaired sensitivity to leptin might be overcome in *fa/fa* rats by producing high endogenous levels of leptin.

Like NPY/AGRP, orexin-A stimulates feeding, but unlike NPY/AGRP it does not cause obesity (Williams & others, 2001). In fact, orexin-A levels are significantly lower in the hypothalamic nuclei, such as the LH and the PVN, of *ob/ob* mice than in those of lean animals (Stricker-Krongrad & others, 2002). As we indicated earlier, blood plasma levels of orexin-A are significantly lower in obese than in normal-weight humans. Adam and colleagues (2002) have suggested that orexin-A is involved in regulating energy metabolism. Although orexin-A does not have a direct role in obesity, manipulation of the orexin system may be a potential treatment for obesity. Haynes and colleagues (2002) found that repeated administration of an orexin receptor antagonist to *ob/ob* mice led to reduced food intake and lower body weight. The treatment also reduced fasting blood glucose levels, and the researchers concluded that their study provides the first demonstration that orexin receptor antagonists might have potential for use as antidiabetic and antiobesity drugs.

In addition to mutation-induced genetic changes that cause obesity, animals can become obese because of their diets (Hassanain & Levin, 2002; Levin & Dunn-Meynell, 2000, 2002; Levin & others, 2004; Ricci & Levin, 2003). Levin and his associates have found that approximately half of a particular strain of rats fed a diet high in fat and calories (a high-energy diet) develop diet-induced obesity (DIO); the other half are resistant to becoming obese (DR). DR rats gain weight and fat at the same rate as rats eating normal lab chow. Further, Levin and colleagues (1997) found that selective breeding of high DIO weight gainers resulted in DIO animals that, by the fifth generation, gained more than 90% more weight than selectively bred DR rats on the high-energy diet. They also gained substantially more weight than DR rats even on a low-fat chow diet. The researchers suggested that the DIO and DR tendencies result from a polygenic inheritance pattern that results in reduced sensitivity to leptin.

According to Levin (2000), once a genetically predisposed individual becomes obese, the increased body weight is strongly defended against caloric restrictions, which probably explains why restrictive diets are hard to maintain. Animals genetically predisposed to obesity exhibit neural abnormalities that encourage obesity given the right diet; after the animals become obese, the neural abnormalities mostly disappear, suggesting that obesity may be the normal state for the animals. Levin suggests that new neural circuits mediating energy homeostasis are created in the obese animals to make their elevated body weight nearly impervious to change. This neuroplasticity, or change in neural circuits, can occur either during nervous system development or during adult life.

Using DIO and DR rats, Levin and Keesey (1998) found evidence that DIO animals fed the high-energy diet develop a higher body-weight set point that is then defended against dietary changes (e.g., by lowering metabolic rate). In this study, after becoming obese on the high-energy diet, DIO rats maintained their high body weight when they were returned to the normal lab chow diet. When they received a diet restricted to 60% of their prior intake of lab chow, the body weight of the obese DIO rats returned to normal levels within 2 weeks. When the dietary restriction was removed, however, the body weight returned to prerestriction obese levels within 2 weeks.

Although the DR rats do not become obese on the high-energy diet, they do become obese when fed a highly palatable diet (Levin & Dunn-Meynell, 2002; Levin & Keesey, 1998). When returned to a lab chow diet, their food intake decreased 60% compared with intake before obesity, and their body weight returned to normal levels within 6 weeks. Thus, in contrast to the DIO rats that developed a higher body-weight set point and defended it against changes in diet, the set point of the DR animals was not changed by their diet-induced obesity. These experimental results show that genetic predisposition, dietary composition, and food palatability interact to determine body weight.

The Role of Metabolism in Eating and Satiety

Metabolic rate is the number of calories required to fuel an organism's metabolic processes at a particular moment in time, and it appears to be genetically influenced. For example, Roberts and coworkers (1988) measured the metabolic rate of

18 infants at ages 3 months and 1 year. Despite eating the same amount of food, at 3 months the babies who became overweight by 1 year (half of the babies born to overweight mothers) generated 21% less energy (had a lower metabolic rate) than the babies of normal-weight mothers. The researchers concluded that lowered energy expenditure at 3 months was an important factor in the excessive weight gain exhibited by some of the infants born to overweight mothers.

To Diet or Not to Diet?

Obesity is associated with numerous medical problems, including diabetes, heart disease, arthritis, asthma, sleep apnea, and various cancers (Gale & others, 2004). This association between chronic health problems and obesity is greater than the association between such conditions and either smoking or excessive drinking (Sturm, 2002). Because of the health risks associated with obesity, obese and overweight people, like Chris, often go on diets. They find losing weight difficult and almost always gain back any weight they have lost (McInnis, 2000). The difficulty in losing weight and the inability to keep it off are partly caused by metabolic differences between obese and normal-weight people.

A metabolic disturbance produces elevated insulin levels or insulin resistance in obese humans (Steinbaum, 2004), in VMH-lesioned rats (Valensi & others, 2003), and in DIO rats (Levin & others, 1997), and this increased insulin or insulin resistance produces low blood glucose levels and a constant state of hunger. As long as their food is tasty, these obese animals usually eat whatever is placed before them; however, their obesity often prevents them from working to obtain food that is not easily available (Schachter, 1971). If a VMH-lesioned rat is prevented from becoming fat, it will be as motivated to work for food as is a normal-weight animal (King, 1980; Sclafani & Kluge, 1974).

Freidman and Stricker (1976) suggested that a VMH-lesioned animal eats because food intake is its only available source of energy. The elevated insulin level in these animals promotes the storage of digested food as glycogen and fat, while preventing the animals from effectively using their fat reserves as an energy source.

VMH-lesioned rats kept at normal weight have an elevation in blood insulin level shortly after receiving the lesion (Tannenbaum & others, 1974). These nonobese VMH-lesioned animals will gain weight even on a restricted diet: Their elevated insulin level causes them to store more of their ingested food as fat than do normal animals (Han & Liu, 1966).

As you know, obese and overweight people quickly regain the weight they have lost by dieting (McInnis, 2000). Given that nonobese VMH-lesioned animals store more food as fat than do normal animals, the weight gain seen in obese humans after they stop dieting may similarly reflect an inherent tendency of obese people to store more of their ingested food as fat. Thus, unless the food intake of the obese person is severely restricted, additional methods must be used to maintain weight loss.

Leptin levels may also be crucial to regaining lost weight by obese humans. Mavri and colleagues (2001) measured leptin levels in 30 obese women before dietary intervention, after 12 weeks of intervention, and after 5 months. The dietary restriction produced a lower body mass index (measure of obesity) and lower serum levels of leptin. At the 5 month follow-up, 12 women had regained weight, and 18 had maintained their weight reduction. Weight regainers had significantly lower baseline levels of leptin than maintainers, suggesting that differences in leptin resistance might influence the success of dieting by obese women.

To Exercise or Not to Exercise?

Mayer (1978) suggested that exercise must be an integral part of a successful weight-reduction program. He compared obese adolescents and adults to static-stage hyperphagic animals: After reaching their maximal weight, they eat only enough to maintain it. Obese people are typically less active than normal-weight people, and exercise would enable them to use their excess calories rather than storing them as fat.

Mayer (1978) reported successfully implementing a weight-loss program involving diet and exercise in the public school system of a large city. The obese children were placed on a balanced but not restrictive diet and were given psychological counseling on how to improve their dress, their walk, and their general appearance. They attended special physical education classes and followed an independent exercise program on weekends and holidays. Mayer found improvement in the majority of the children in his program: Their activity increased and they lost weight. More recent studies continue to find an association between exercise and an initial weight loss, plus the maintenance of that weight loss among both adults and children (McInnis, 2000; Sothern, 2001). Exercise is important in the maintenance of weight loss (Jakicic, 2002; Votruba & others, 2000).

The influence of exercise on metabolic rate appears to be a big factor in its success as part of a weight-loss program. Research has found that dieting lowers the metabolic rate of women, which tends to counteract any weight loss that might result from the restricted food intake (McCargar, 1996). However, combining dieting with moderate physical exercise, which either increases the metabolic rate or at least does not lower it as much as dieting alone (Thompson & others, 1996), may be beneficial for long-term weight loss and maintenance.

Checkpoint

What is the role of leptin in satiety and body weight? What happens when the fat stores of an animal fall below its critical set point? Rise above its critical set point? What is allostasis and how might it be related to food intake and obesity?

REVIEW

- Lipostatic theory accounts for long-term weight regulation with a mechanism based on fat deposits. Leptin appears to provide feedback to the brain about the level of stored fat; low leptin levels lead to an increase in hunger and food intake.
- Set-point theory proposes that animals maintain a constant body weight by having a critical level of stored fat; if the stored fat falls below the set point, the hunger system induces eating until the set point is reestablished. If the stored fat rises above the set point, the paraventricular system inhibits eating until the set point is reached.
- Allostasis is the maintenance of stability through change; allostatic load is the cumulative wear and tear on the body through allostasis. Allostasis may be related to obesity through the stress hormones, which increase food intake, cause fat deposition around the middle of the body, and may alter the balance between leptin and NPY in favor of the latter.
- Genetic mutations in mice and rats that lead to defects in the role of leptin in controlling eating behavior produce obese animals. Like NPY/AGRP, the orexins stimulate feeding; unlike NPY/AGRP-induced eating, this does not result in obesity.
- A high-energy diet can produce obesity, particularly in animals with a genetic predisposition to become obese. The gain in body weight results in a higher body-weight set point that is then defended against change.
- A person's metabolic rate appears to be genetically influenced. Obese people tend to have a lower metabolic rate than normal-weight people, and VMH-lesioned rats have a lower metabolic rate than normal rats.
- Obese people and VMH-lesioned hyperphagic rats also have elevated insulin levels, causing more food to be stored as fat, even on a restricted diet.
- A combination of exercise (which increases metabolic rate) and dieting reduces weight and helps maintain a healthy body weight.

Eating Disorders

Jerry spotted the article about his ex-girlfriend as soon as he picked up the campus paper. The headline was hard to miss: Sophomore Found Dead in Dormitory Room. Jerry was shocked—yet found himself skimming through the article to find the cause of her death, to confirm what he already knew. But the article said Shannon had died of cardiac arrest, and further investigation was ongoing. I warned her, he thought. What else could he have done? He knew there was no reason to blame himself, but he felt guilty anyway.

He remembered the first time he'd caught her; they had eaten a special meal prepared by his roommate. After stuffing herself, Shannon had gone to the bathroom. When he heard muffled noises that sounded like vomiting, Jerry burst into the bathroom to see whether there was anything he could do. Shannon was on her knees in front of the toilet, her face turned toward the door, too startled to remove the fingers she had thrust down her throat.

When they talked about it later, Shannon told him how guilty she felt about her "shame," about her secret battle to keep from gaining weight. She told Jerry about the binges, when she'd eat gallons of ice cream, whole pies, and once an entire three-layer carrot cake. And it wasn't just vomiting, she admitted; she also used laxatives and exercised for hours at a time.

Jerry was stunned by what she told him. He really cared for Shannon. He urged her to talk to her parents, to get help. But after the constant secrecy and the lying and repeated relapses of her illness, it became too much. He broke off their relationship, despite her protestations that she finally had the disorder under control. Jerry heard this as another of Shannon's lies.

Now he saw he'd been right, but it didn't make him feel any better. Such a waste, he thought. He began to cry as he reread the terrible headline.

anorexia nervosa An eating disorder in which adolescents or young adults diet and lose as much as 35% of their body weight, yet still feel fat.

Shannon suffered from bulimia nervosa, an eating disorder. This disease, and the related disorder anorexia nervosa, involves an intense dissatisfaction with body image.

American society glorifies thinness and scorns heaviness, even though half of all adults in the United States are either overweight or obese. Social psychologists have found that heavy people are generally considered unattractive, not only because of their physical appearance but also because of what others perceive as a lack of self-control (Crandall & Martinez, 1996). Overweight and obese children are frequently tormented by their peers, and, although the scorn is more subtle, obese adults are fully aware that others think poorly of them. The obese person is frequently discriminated against at school and at work, and jokes about fat people are the mainstay of many comedians. Our culture's obsession with thinness has contributed to the prevalence of anorexia nervosa, bulimia nervosa, and a newly recognized illness, binge eating disorder.

Figure 10.18

Anorexia nervosa The extreme thinness of this woman is typical of people who suffer from anorexia nervosa.

→ **Why is anorexia nervosa so difficult to treat?**

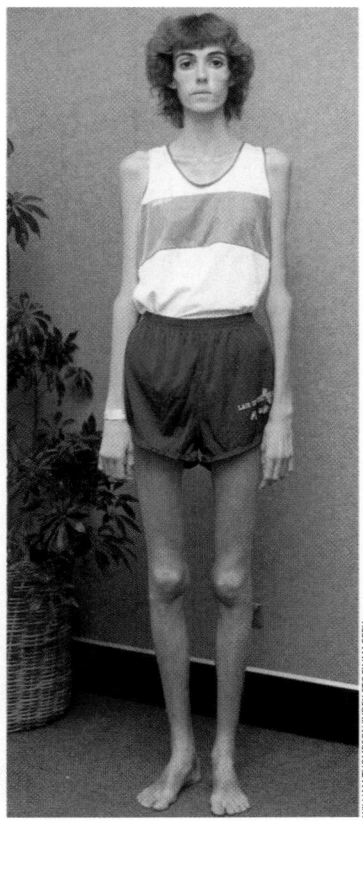

WILLIAM THOMPSON/INDEX STOCK IMAGERY

Anorexia Nervosa

Some people go to extraordinary lengths to avoid being overweight. You may know someone (most likely a young woman) who diets constantly even though she is already thin. She perceives herself as fat, always needing to lose several pounds in order to be more attractive. In fact, she may be suffering from **anorexia nervosa,** a psychological eating disorder considered to be a consequence of society's obsession with thinness (Bruch, 1980). Although people with anorexia frequently are slightly overweight before the disorder develops, they rarely are obese and sometimes are thin. Once they develop anorexia, they lose an average of 35% of their body weight, often weighing as little as 60 to 80 pounds (Figure 10.18). Even after they lose so much weight, they still feel fat, and when they look in the mirror, they still see a fat person.

Anorexia nervosa is most common in adolescent girls and young women (Becker & others, 1999), but as many as 10% of anorexics are males. In fact, anorexia may be underdiagnosed in young men because of the general belief that it is exclusively a female disorder. One study has noted the similarity in a variety of characteristics between females with anorexia and male athletes who are described as "obligatory runners" (Yates & others, 1983). For example, both obligatory runners and women with anorexia tend to inhibit anger, have high self-expectations, tolerate physical discomfort, and deny serious debility, and are preoccupied with food and having a lean body. Thus, some male obligatory runners may have anorexia but be undiagnosed. Among female runners, those

bulimia nervosa An eating disorder characterized by recurrent episodes of binge eating, followed by self-induced vomiting and other forms of purging.

who run more than 30 miles a week may be at high risk for developing anorexia nervosa (Estok & Rudy, 1996).

In addition to their preoccupation with food and with not becoming fat, people with anorexia seem unaware of hunger and feel full after only a few bites. If they binge eat, which happens occasionally, they usually attempt to purge the ingested food. The significant weight loss in people with anorexia produces such physiological effects as loss of menstrual cycles, cardiac arrhythmias, and extremely low blood pressure. The mortality rate from the disorder is quite variable across studies, but is generally found to be high (Steinhausen, 2002). The singer Karen Carpenter was a victim of anorexia; she died from complications related to the disorder in 1983, at the age of 32. Christy Henrich, a ranked gymnast, also died of anorexia-related complications, at the age of 22. Henrich weighed just 47 pounds at the time of her death from multiple organ failure in 1994. According to her family, her battle with anorexia began shortly after she joined the U. S. national gymnastics team.

According to Hilde Bruch (1980), the fear of becoming fat is the major force precipitating anorexia. Bruch's therapeutic approach deemphasizes the importance of body size for self-esteem and strives to enhance the patient's feelings of self-worth and self-initiative. Bruch has found that changes in self-esteem can lead to normal eating behavior.

Other investigators have suggested that anorexia is caused by a physiological or chemical disturbance (Patrick, 2002). One piece of evidence for a physiological basis is the strong genetic predisposition found for anorexia: In twin studies, the concordance rate (if one twin has the disorder, the other does also) tends to be higher for identical twins (44%) than for fraternal twins (13%) (Kipman & others, 1999).

Although the exact origin of anorexia remains unknown, cognitive-behavior therapy has been used with some success (Bowers, 2001). For example, hospitalized patients rewarded for eating by receiving a weekend pass or an opportunity to socialize with friends gained 20 to 30 pounds during the 2 to 10 weeks of treatment (Garfinkel & others, 1973).

Treating anorexia with selective serotonin reuptake inhibitors (SSRIs) appears to be promising. For example, fluoxetine (Prozac) may be useful in preventing relapse after weight has been restored (Kim, 2003), and compared to a control group of patients with anorexia, sertraline produced a significant improvement in depressive symptoms, perfectionism, and lack of bodily self-awareness in 14 weeks of treatment in an outpatient program (Santonastaso & others, 2001). Some researchers, however, have reported that fluoxetine is ineffective in treating anorexia (e.g., Attia & others, 1998).

Many people with anorexia also suffer from depression, and serotonergic agonists, such as the SSRIs, are effective in treating depression (Chapter 15). The antidepressant effect of serotonergic agonists, rather than their effect on appetite, is probably responsible for the weight gain in people with anorexia. In fact, serotonergic agonists tend to cause weight loss in obese people. Unfortunately, the serotonergic agonists have not been effective in changing attitudes of people with anorexia about weight, and thus these medications have not been successful in preventing relapse. Because of the difficulty in changing a person's body image, anorexia nervosa is a difficult disorder to treat (Hsu, 2004).

A person with bulimia nervosa may consume thousands of calories in a single sitting.

OMNI PHOTO COMMUNICATIONS/INDEX

Bulimia Nervosa

As you learned from Shannon's story, **bulimia nervosa** is characterized by recurrent episodes of binge eating followed by purging, most often by self-induced vomiting; other methods of purging include the use of laxatives, excessive exercise, and dieting. As with anorexia, the vast majority of people with bulimia are young women. In binge eating, a person with bulimia consumes vast quantities of food, even thousands of calories at a time. A meal consisting of a whole fried chicken, a jar of peanut butter, a giant bag of potato chips, a loaf of bread, and a gallon of ice cream would not be unusual for such a person.

Binge eating and purging can cause a variety of physiological problems. Repeated vomiting can erode tooth enamel, produce chronic inflammation of the esophagus, and cause a loss of potassium, which in turn may produce cardiac arrhythmias and cardiac arrest. This is undoubtedly what killed Shannon.

Like anorexia, bulimia involves a dissatisfaction with body image (Gowers & Shore, 2001; van den Berg & others, 2002). But unlike people with anorexia, who are too successful at dieting, bulimics are unsuccessful at controlling their food intake and a substantial minority diet only after binge eating (Grilo & Masheb, 2000). Also in contrast to those with anorexia, people with bulimia recognize the abnormality of their eating behavior and hide it from others. And because there are fewer outward physical signs of a problem (people with bulimia tend to have a normal or slightly elevated weight), bulimia is easy to hide. Both anorexia nervosa and bulimia nervosa appear to have a familial basis (Lilenfield & others, 1998; Strober & others, 2000).

A hormonal imbalance is another possible cause of bulimia. People with bulimia secrete abnormally low levels of CCK in response to a meal, which may lead to less satiation than normal (Devlin & others, 1997). However, given that, following treatment with an antidepressant, CCK levels return to normal in response to a meal, the abnormally low CCK levels before treatment are most likely a result of this disorder rather than a cause.

Bulimia often begins following a period of stringent dieting (Brewerton & others, 2000), and several studies have found that dieting can lead to overeating (Fedoroff & others, 1997, 2003; Field & others, 2003). (Remember Chris's spaghetti and pizza at the Italian restaurant after his week of restrained eating?) Polivy and Herman (1993) studied the causes of binge eating in restrained eaters (dieters) versus unrestrained eaters (nondieters). When the restrained eater, who normally can inhibit eating, eats even a small amount of food, the inhibition is reduced, and the formerly restrained eater consumes greater amounts than the unrestrained eater. As Figure 10.19 shows, even the smell of pizza or thoughts about pizza caused restrained eaters to consume more than unrestrained eaters (Federoff & others, 1997).

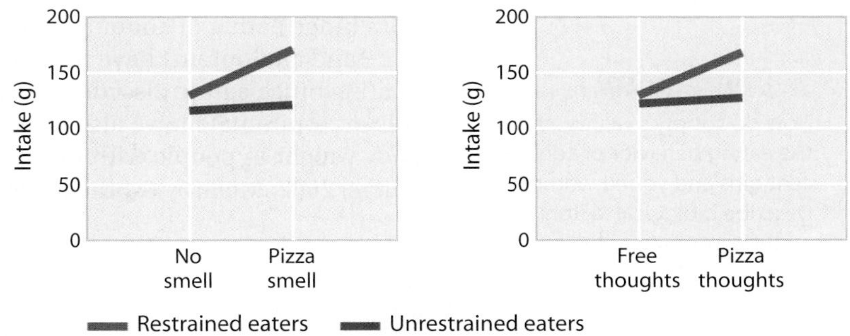

Figure 10.19
The influence of preexposure to food cues on the amount consumed by restrained (dieting) and unrestrained (nondieting) human subjects Exposure to an olfactory food cue (pizza smell) or to thoughts of food (pizza thoughts) increases consumption in restrained eaters but has little effect in unrestrained eaters.

→ **Why does dieting often precede the development of bulimia?**

A study by Fedoroff and associates (2003) illustrates why it is so difficult for dieters to stay on a restrictive diet. Restrained eaters (dieters) and unrestrained eaters were preexposed to one of three olfactory cues: the smell of pizza, the smell of cookies, or no smell. Preexposure to the olfactory cues increased food intake, but only in the restrained eaters and only when they were allowed to eat the specific food they had smelled. The preexposure also increased the craving for the cued food item, again, only in the restrained eaters. The researchers concluded that preexposure to the food cues produced an urge to eat and craving in the restrained eaters, but only for a highly specific food. With the easy availability of so many types of food in our society, such a craving would make it difficult to remain on a restrictive diet.

Conditioning has proved a viable way to treat bulimia. When confronted with forbidden food, the individual with bulimia initially experiences anxiety, which motivates eating to distract from the negative feelings. Unfortunately, the binge eating increases the negative emotions, and purging seems to be the only effective way to reduce the anxiety that results from overeating. Using a group therapy setting, Gray and Hoage (1990) reported that forced exposure to forbidden foods and then prevention of purging reduces the likelihood that people will continue binge eating and purging. Anxiety about eating is eliminated as a result of consuming forbidden food and *not* purging.

binge eating disorder An eating disorder characterized by recurrent episodes of binge eating without such compensatory weight-loss methods as vomiting, use of laxatives, and excessive exercise.

Drug therapy with SSRIs is another promising approach in treating bulimia. Earlier in the chapter, we noted that fenfluramine is effective in reducing eating and promoting weight loss in obese humans. Fenfluramine also reduces binge eating in bulimic patients (Stunkard & others, 1996). Another SSRI, fluoxetine (Prozac), is an effective treatment for bulimia in patients in a primary care setting (Walsh & others, 2004) and also for patients who have not responded well to psychological treatment (Walsh & others, 2000). A third SSRI, sertraline, can significantly reduce the frequency of binges and is well tolerated by people with bulimia (McElroy & others, 2000).

As with anorexia, the SSRIs may help treat bulimia because of their mood-improving effects rather than any direct effect on the eating disorder. Ferguson and Pigott (2000) have observed that long-term treatment for bulimia is most effective when it combines cognitive-behavioral therapy that modifies eating habits, a diet and exercise program to manage weight, and the use of an antidepressant medication, such as fluoxetine.

Binge Eating Disorder

Another type of eating disorder, **binge eating disorder,** is defined as recurrent episodes of binge eating without such compensatory weight-loss methods as vomiting, use of laxatives, and excessive exercise. In addition, binge eating disorder is likely to include such symptoms as eating until uncomfortably full, eating when not physically hungry, eating alone, and feelings of depression or guilt; depression and personality disorders are common in people with binge eating disorder. Because the disorder tends to be associated with obesity, sufferers often seek treatment for weight control rather than for the underlying binge eating disorder (de Zwaan, 2001).

Cognitive-behavioral therapy and interpersonal psychotherapy have been used with some success in treating binge eating disorder, producing rates of abstinence from binge eating of about 50% (de Zwaan, 2001). Although the SSRIs (e.g., fluoxetine and citalopram) have received the most study as pharmacological agents in treating binge eating disorder, the antiobesity agent sibutramine and the anticonvulsant topiramate have also been found to significantly reduce binge eating and body weight in people with this disorder (Appolinario & McElroy, 2004; Arnold & others, 2002; McElroy & others, 2003).

➤Checkpoint

How do society's values affect the eating behavior of adolescent girls and young women? Describe biological factors that might contribute to bulimia.

REVIEW

- ➤ Anorexia nervosa is an eating disorder characterized by self-starvation and a distorted body image. Genetic predisposition and social pressure are contributing factors, but the direct physiological cause is unknown.
- ➤ Bulimia nervosa is characterized by recurrent episodes of binge eating followed by purging. In bulimics, lower CCK levels may intensify binge eating, and anxiety about gaining weight elicits purging; the reinforcing aspects of purging and the fear of eating fattening foods may contribute to the binge-purge cycle.
- ➤ Binge eating disorder is characterized by recurrent episodes of binge eating without the use of purging or other weight-loss measures.
- ➤ SSRIs have shown some promise in treating bulimia, binge eating disorder, and, to a lesser extent, anorexia.

◆ Drinking

Rosa is addicted to salty foods—the saltier, the better. Today, she saw a special on shelled peanuts at the grocery store. She bought several bags of the fully salted variety, because the reduced-sodium and no-sodium nuts taste like cardboard to her, and she ate several handfuls on the way home. As she unloaded the groceries, Rosa could think of nothing but how thirsty she was. When she opened the refrigerator to put away the milk and juice, a diet soda beckoned. She grabbed the can, popped the tab, and guzzled it down. The soda tasted great, and her thirst was soon quenched. Now she could finish putting away the groceries.

secondary drinking Drinking that anticipates a bodily need.

primary drinking Drinking in response to loss of intracellular or extracellular fluid.

As you know from your own experience, eating salty food makes you extremely thirsty, and drinking soda will satisfy your thirst. But what produces the thirst in this and other types of situations? In this section, we explain the mechanisms of thirst, from the standpoint of what is happening to your body fluids and what happens in your brain.

The Body's Fluid Needs

Believe it or not, the human body consists of about 70% water. Approximately two-thirds of this body water is inside cells (intracellular), and the other third is outside the cells (extracellular), in the interstitial fluid (26%) and blood (7%). Maintaining a constant fluid level is essential for effective metabolic functioning, and any change activates compensatory mechanisms that restore optimal fluid levels.

Usually, we drink more water than we need, and our kidneys excrete the excess. This kind of drinking in anticipation of a need is called **secondary drinking.** Drinking in response to a loss of intracellular or extracellular fluid is called **primary drinking.** Although most drinking is actually secondary drinking, most of the research on thirst deals with primary drinking.

When your fluid levels are lower than they should be, two things happen: First, systems are activated that concentrate the urine—that is, decrease the amount of water lost through urination. Second, specific brain receptors are stimulated to create thirst, which causes you to drink fluids in order to restore the optimal level of body water (Logue, 1991).

Thirst

Several different conditions can produce thirst and motivate drinking behavior. Although thirst is often caused by a biological need, it can, like hunger, also result from a psychological need.

The "Dry Mouth" Theory

In 1934, Walter B. Cannon proposed that we become thirsty and drink when our mouth is dry and that wetting the tissues of the mouth quenches the thirst. Although this may strike you as a good hypothesis, the evidence does not support it. For example, just a few sips of water eliminate a dry mouth, but we usually drink much more to satisfy our thirst. In addition, neither the removal of the salivary glands, which causes a permanently dry mouth, nor the administration of drugs that cause excessive salivation has any influence on the amount of water consumed when thirsty. Sham drinking studies, in which an animal drinks but the water does not reach its stomach, indicate that wetting the mouth only temporarily reduces thirst. Thus, factors other than a dry mouth appear to determine the amount of water we drink.

Osmotic Thirst

Body fluids contain a small amount of sodium chloride (NaCl, or table salt). Increases in salt intake (as when Rosa eats the nuts) affect the extracellular fluids first, so that the NaCl concentration outside the cells becomes greater than the concentration inside the cells (Figure 10.20a). This greater NaCl concentration creates a higher osmotic pressure outside than inside the cells; the pressure draws water from the cells to decrease the concentration of NaCl in the extracellular fluid, thereby equalizing the osmotic pressure (Figure 10.20b). The resulting *cellu-*

Figure 10.20

Osmotic thirst (a) Eating salty food increases the NaCl concentration (shown by the colored dots) in the extracellular fluid, which thus develops a higher osmotic pressure than the intracellular fluid. (b) As a result, water is drawn out of the cell to equalize the osmotic pressure across the cell membrane, and the cell shrinks.

Is osmotic thirst caused by a decreased level of intracellular fluid or extracellular fluid?

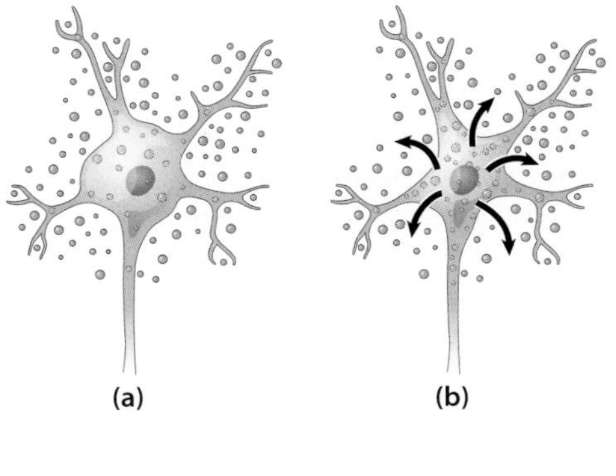

osmotic thirst A condition of thirst caused by increased osmotic pressure that results from increased salt levels in the extracellular fluid.

antidiuretic hormone (ADH) A hormone secreted by the posterior pituitary that causes fluid retention by the kidneys.

osmoreceptor A neuron that monitors osmotic pressure.

subfornical organ (SFO) A structure outside the blood-brain barrier that contains osmoreceptors; plays a role in thirst.

organum vasculosum lamina terminalis (OVLT) A structure outside the blood-brain barrier that contains osmoreceptors; plays a role in thirst.

lar dehydration activates two processes that work to restore normal intracellular water levels: The kidneys concentrate the urine, and the animal becomes thirsty and drinks fluids. The type of thirst caused by increased osmotic pressure because of increased salt levels in the extracellular fluid is called **osmotic thirst.**

Verney's classic experiment (1947) investigated the changes that occur when NaCl is injected into the bloodstream. In response, the posterior pituitary secretes **antidiuretic hormone (ADH),** which causes the kidneys to retain more water (i.e., to concentrate the urine). Verney also noted that the NaCl injections caused rats to drink excessive amounts of water, demonstrating osmotic thirst. In order to explain osmotic thirst, Verney suggested that the heightened osmotic pressure, caused by increased extracellular NaCl from the saline injections, stimulates special **osmoreceptors** (neurons sensitive to changes in osmotic pressure) in the hypothalamus; this produces the sensation of thirst and causes the posterior pituitary to release ADH.

Early studies suggested that osmoreceptors were located in the lateral preoptic area (LPO) of the hypothalamus (Blass & Epstein, 1971; Peck & Novin, 1971). For example, injections of hypertonic saline (a solution with a greater concentration of NaCl than is normally found in blood) into the LPO caused drinking in satiated rats, whereas injections of distilled water caused thirsty animals to stop drinking (Blass & Epstein). Damage to the LPO altered the drinking behavior of the rats in response to cellular dehydration. However, the amount of drinking produced by hypertonic saline injections into the LPO was relatively small, whereas intravenous injections of hypertonic saline caused rats to consume great quantities of water. These results suggest that most osmoreceptors are located somewhere other than in the LPO.

After a series of studies with rats receiving infusions of hypertonic solutions, Schoorlemmer and colleagues (2000) concluded that the osmoreceptors are in the head but outside the blood-brain barrier. Bourque and colleagues (1994) suggested that several structures in and around the hypothalamus contain osmoreceptors—for example, the medial preoptic area, the median preoptic nucleus, and the supraoptic nucleus—but the leading contenders appear to be two areas outside the blood-brain barrier: the **subfornical organ (SFO)** and the **organum vasculosum lamina terminalis (OVLT).** Figure 10.21 shows the location of these two structures relative to the third ventricle.

Supporting the idea of the SFO and the OVLT as the location of osmoreceptors is the finding that systemic infusions of hypertonic saline activated neurons almost exclusively in parts of the SFO and the OVLT (McKinley & others, 1998). Water deprivation also activated cells in these areas, along with cells in several other hypothalamic regions (De Luca & others, 2002; Morien & others, 1999).

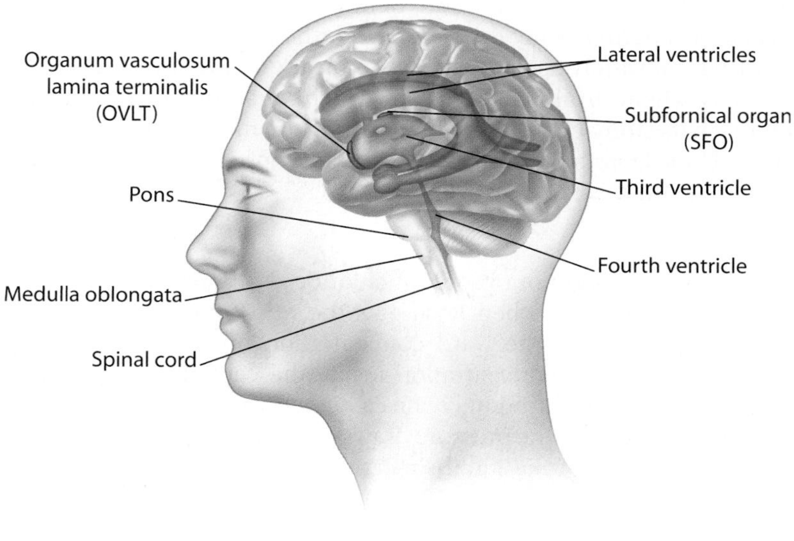

Figure 10.21
Brain locations of osmoreceptors
Osmoreceptors in the SFO and the OVLT detect increased osmotic pressure, thereby regulating thirst and drinking behavior.

➔ **Why are the SFO and the OVLT more sensitive than the lateral preoptic area of the hypothalamus to changes in salt concentration?**

Hypovolemic Thirst

Another type of thirst, **hypovolemic thirst,** occurs when we lose extracellular fluid. Fluid loss results from sweating during exercise (sweat is salty because both salts and fluids are lost), diarrhea, or bleeding, either from an injury or from heavy menstrual flow. Like osmotic thirst, hypovolemic thirst activates internal changes that cause both water retention and increased fluid intake.

Hypovolemia (decreased blood volume) can be produced by injecting drying agents under the skin of laboratory animals. Such chemicals as formaldehyde (embalming fluid) and polyethylene glycol draw fluids out of the body to produce hypovolemia, which lowers blood pressure. The lowered blood pressure stimulates mechanoreceptors, called baroreceptors, in large blood vessels, which in turn signal the brain to release ADH, thus stimulating the kidneys to concentrate urine.

The lowered blood pressure also stimulates receptors in the kidneys to release the enzyme renin, which is involved in converting the protein angiotensinogen into the hormone **angiotensin.** (There are different forms of angiotensin, but the only form that seems to affect thirst is angiotensin II. Here, angiotensin refers to angiotensin II.) Angiotensin, in turn, stimulates the adrenal cortex to release **aldosterone,** a hormone that causes increased NaCl and water retention by the kidneys. Figure 10.22 summarizes the hormonal changes that result from lowered blood pressure.

As we have already noted, the loss of extracellular fluid produces hypovolemic thirst. Early physiological evidence suggested that angiotensin activates neurons in the preoptic and anterior areas of the hypothalamus that detect hypovolemic (or volumetric) thirst, and this activation motivates drinking. For example, when Epstein and colleagues (1970) injected angiotensin into the preoptic and anterior hypothalamic areas of rats, they observed drinking even in satiated animals. Moreover, increasing the quantity of injected angiotensin caused the rats to drink more. These results suggest that under natural conditions, the amount of fluid consumed corresponds to the amount lost, because the level of angiotensin released is proportional to the amount of depleted extracellular fluid.

The loss of body fluids creates both thirst and a craving for substances, such as NaCl, that are lost as a result of hypovolemia. Salt-deprived rats develop a preference for salty tasting solutions, preferring salty fluids to salty foods (Bertino & Tordoff, 1988). In humans, salt depletion causes moderate sensory changes (e.g.,

hypovolemic thirst A type of thirst caused by a loss of extracellular fluid.

angiotensin A hormone that stimulates the adrenal cortex to release aldosterone.

aldosterone A hormone released by the adrenal cortex that causes increased water and salt retention by the kidneys.

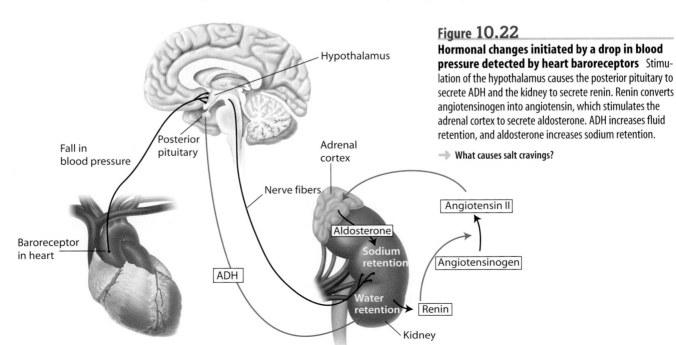

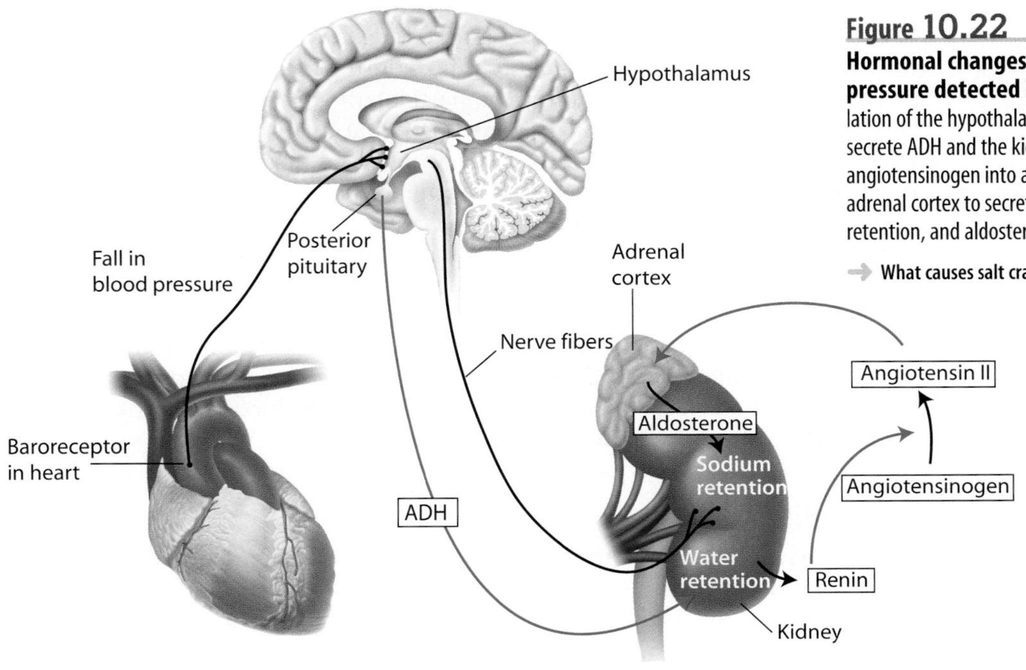

Figure 10.22

Hormonal changes initiated by a drop in blood pressure detected by heart baroreceptors Stimulation of the hypothalamus causes the posterior pituitary to secrete ADH and the kidney to secrete renin. Renin converts angiotensinogen into angiotensin, which stimulates the adrenal cortex to secrete aldosterone. ADH increases fluid retention, and aldosterone increases sodium retention.

→ **What causes salt cravings?**

nucleus medianus A group of neurons in the brain involved in osmotic and hypovolemic thirst.

increased sensitivity to the taste of salt) and an increased preference for salty foods (Beauchamp & others, 1990). Aldosterone and angiotensin both contribute to this salt craving. Treatments that either increased aldosterone secretion or decreased it in rats increased or decreased the desire for salty foods, respectively (Stricker, 1983). Further, angiotensin injections increased sodium appetite in rats (Dalhouse & others, 1986). Experiments with rats in which the adrenal gland has been removed, which also depletes the aldosterone in the animals, reveal the synergistic relationship between angiotensin and aldosterone in the sodium appetite of the rats (Sakai & Epstein, 1990).

A Common Neural Circuit

Osmotic thirst and hypovolemic thirst generally occur together, and experimental evidence points to a common neural circuit for the two types of thirst. Earlier we mentioned the SFO and the OVLT as leading candidates for the brain structures that contain osmoreceptors and play a role in osmotic thirst. The same areas also appear to be important for hypovolemic thirst. For example, injections of angiotensin into the SFO of laboratory animals led to increased fluid consumption (Gutman & others, 1989); damaging the SFO reduced the response to hypovolemic thirst in both rats (Simpson & others, 1978) and pigeons (Massi & others, 1986). Similarly, lesions of the OVLT reduced angiotensin-induced drinking (Caputo & Scallet, 1995).

The SFO sends neural input to the **nucleus medianus,** a structure near the anterior and ventral part of the third ventricle. Like the SFO and the OVLT, the nucleus medianus seems to be involved in both osmotic and hypovolemic thirst. For example, both hypertonic saline and polyethylene glycol injections failed to cause drinking after nucleus medianus damage when the animals were tested during the day, but normal drinking responses to both substances occurred when the animals were tested at night (Gardiner & Stricker, 1985). According to the researchers, the lesions appeared to disrupt circadian influences on drinking behavior.

A Good Meal Can Make You Thirsty

Most of us drink fluids when eating a meal (Kraly, 2004). One way that eating causes thirst is by diverting water from the rest of the body to the stomach and small intestine for use in the digestive process. This fluid movement causes hypovolemia, and the resulting angiotensin release stimulates drinking. In support of this idea, Kraly and colleagues (1995) found that an angiotensin antagonist inhibited drinking during eating in rats. Also, Starbuck and Fitts (2001) reported that SFO lesions in rats delayed drinking after eating; the researchers concluded that the SFO is involved in initiating water intake during meals.

Foods that contain protein may be particularly dehydrating. Rats on a high-carbohydrate diet were found to consume equal quantities of water and food, whereas animals on a high-protein diet consumed approximately 1.5 times as much water as food (Fitzsimons & Le Magnen, 1969). Although these results suggest that rats (and perhaps people) drink as much as they need to compensate for the dehydrating effect of eating, drinking during a meal—for reasons other than to eliminate a dry mouth and convert water into urine—is probably learned. Evidence for this comes from an experiment in which animals learned to drink a sufficient amount of fluid before eating to prevent dehydration (Oatley & Toates, 1969). Because most of our drinking is secondary drinking, or drinking in anticipation of need, we, like rats, can anticipate impending thirst and drink enough to counteract future dehydration.

Satisfying Thirst

The factors that cause us to stop drinking have not been defined as clearly as those that initiate drinking. In fact, rigid control over drinking cessation is not nearly as important as the regulation of thirst that leads to drinking, because any excess fluid consumed is easily eliminated. Research suggests that the amount of ingested fluid plays an important role in the inhibition of drinking, with the mouth functioning as a meter to suppress further fluid intake after a sufficient amount has been drunk. However, our oral meter is not a perfect regulatory device.

In an early study of the importance of oral factors in thirst, Bellows (1939) found that esophagotomized dogs drank twice as much water as their bodies needed before they stopped drinking. (Recall that in esophagotomized animals, swallowed material falls out of the cut esophagus to the ground.) These results suggest that oral factors do contribute to the suppression of drinking but that other factors are also involved.

Water in the duodenum seems to be another important factor in the inhibition of drinking. For example, Maddison and colleagues (1980) studied water-deprived monkeys that had chronic cannulae (tubes) implanted both in the stomach and in the duodenum. When both cannulae were closed, the monkeys drank an average of 137 mL of water. With the stomach cannula open, the animals consumed an average of 878 mL of water, and the monkeys also dramatically overdrank with the duodenal cannula open (634 mL). This pattern of nearly continuous sham drinking suggests that oropharyngeal stimulation by itself is not sufficient to halt drinking, nor is drinking curtailed in response to the added stimulation of either the stomach or the first part of the duodenum. The researchers found, however, that infusions of water into the duodenum (25 to 100 mL) slowed or stopped sham drinking. Infusions of isotonic saline, a solution having the same NaCl level as the blood plasma, did not suppress drinking. This result indicates that receptors in the portion of the duodenum beyond the duodenal cannula monitor water intake and signal whether or not fluid needs have been met.

Receptors in the liver also may have a role in regulating fluid consumption. For example, infusion of fluid into the hepatic portal vein, which connects the stomach to the liver, decreases fluid intake (Kozlowski & Drzewiecki, 1973).

Satisfaction of salt cravings also occurs in salt-deprived animals, and the liver appears to be the site of receptors that detect the blood sodium level. In a study of salt hunger, slow infusion of a saline solution into the hepatic portal vein of sodium-deprived rats significantly reduced drinking of the salt solution (Tordoff & others, 1987). By contrast, a salt solution infused into the jugular vein, which connects to the head rather than the liver, did not affect subsequent drinking.

Checkpoint

Why did the nuts make Rosa so thirsty? Describe how the soda quenched Rosa's thirst.

REVIEW

- Eating salty foods causes an increased salt concentration in the extracellular fluid and thus an increased osmotic pressure, which causes water to move out of the cells. This cellular dehydration produces osmotic thirst.
- Loss of extracellular fluid lowers blood pressure, leads to increased levels of angiotensin and aldosterone in the blood, and causes hypovolemic thirst.
- Both osmotic thirst and hypovolemic thirst stimulate the release of ADH from the pituitary gland, which acts on the kidneys to conserve water and causes drinking behavior.
- Angiotensin increases water retention, and aldosterone increases salt retention.
- Receptors in areas adjacent to the third ventricle—the SFO and the OVLT—appear to detect increased osmotic pressure, and in response produce thirst and drinking. The stimulation of neurons in the SFO and the OVLT also produces a craving for salt.
- Drinking activates satiety receptors for water in both the stomach and the liver; satiety receptors for salt are found only in the liver.

Chapter Review

Key Terms

adipsia (p. 344)
aldosterone (p. 377)
allostasis (p. 366)
allostatic load (p. 367)
angiotensin (p. 377)
anorexia nervosa (p. 371)
antidiuretic hormone (ADH) (p. 376)
aphagia (p. 344)
arcuate nucleus (p. 350)
binge eating disorder (p. 374)
bulimia nervosa (p. 372)
cephalic reflex (p. 346)
cholecystokinin (CCK) (p. 359)
conditioned hunger (p. 362)
conditioned satiety (p. 362)
critical set point (p. 365)
diabetes mellitus (p. 356)
dorsal motor nucleus of the vagus (p. 350)
fen-phen (p. 352)
ghrelin (p. 360)
glucagon (p. 357)
glucoprivation (p. 358)
glucoreceptor (p. 356)
glucostatic theory (p. 356)
homeostasis (p. 365)
hyperphagia (p. 345)
hypovolemic thirst (p. 377)
ingestional neophobia (p. 352)
insulin (p. 356)
lateral hypothalamus (LH) (p. 344)
leptin (p. 364)
LH-lesion syndrome (p. 344)
lipid (p. 364)
lipoprivation (p. 364)
lipostatic theory (p. 364)
neuropeptide Y (NPY) (p. 350)
nigrostriatal pathway (p. 349)
nucleus medianus (p. 378)
nucleus of the solitary tract (p. 350)
organum vasculosum lamina terminalis (OVLT) (p. 376)
osmoreceptor (p. 376)
osmotic thirst (p. 376)
paraventricular nucleus (PVN) (p. 350)
prandial drinking (p. 345)
preloading (p. 355)
primary drinking (p. 375)
satiety (p. 342)
secondary drinking (p. 375)
subfornical organ (SFO) (p. 376)
ventromedial hypothalamus (VMH) (p. 344)
VMH-lesion syndrome (p. 346)
VMH paradox (p. 346)

Suggested Readings

Becker, A. E., Grinspoon, S. K., Klibanski, A., & Herzog, D. B. (1999). Eating disorders. *New England Journal of Medicine, 340,* 1092–1098.

Bray, G. A. (2000). Afferent signals regulating food intake. *The Proceedings of the Nutrition Society, 59,* 373–384.

Bray, G. A., Brouchard, C., & James, P. T. (1997). *The handbook of obesity.* New York: Dekker.

Levin, B. E. (2000). The obesity epidemic: Metabolic imprinting on genetically susceptible neural circuits. *Obesity Research, 8,* 342–347.

Logue, A. W. (1991). *The psychology of eating and drinking* (2nd ed.). New York: Freeman.

Stricker, E. M. (1990). *Handbook of behavioral neurobiology. Vol. 10. Neurobiology of food and fluid intake.* New York: Plenum Press.

Woods, S. C., Schwartz, M. W., Baskin, D. G., & Seeley, R. J. (2000). Food intake and the regulation of body weight. *Annual Review of Psychology, 51,* 255–277.

Critical Thinking Questions

1. John has gained 20 pounds over the last few months. He believes that his habit of eating while watching many hours of television is responsible for his weight gain. Could he be right? Describe a mechanism that could cause overeating while watching television. Suggest several alternative explanations for the weight gain. What could John do to lose weight?

2. Karen has just run a 10K race and is extremely exhausted and thirsty. Describe two biological processes that contribute to her thirst. What might she have done before the race to prevent her thirst after the race, and what should she do now to eliminate her thirst?

3. Your friend Shondra is extremely thin. Although she is preoccupied with food, she never seems hungry, and when she does eat, she eats very little. You are concerned about her health. Suggest several possible causes for Shondra's physical appearance and eating habits. Do you have any suggestions that might help her?

Fill-in-the-Blank Questions

1. ______ is the absence of eating, and ______ is the absence of drinking.
2. Early research suggested that the hunger center in the rat was the ______, and its satiety center was the ______.
3. The failure of rats to either eat or drink after hypothalamic damage became known as the ______ syndrome.
4. Drinking only while eating is called ______ drinking.
5. Hyperphagia and obesity seen in rats following hypothalamic damage became known as the ______ syndrome.
6. The tendency of hyperphagic and obese rats to reject adulterated food and not to work for food is called the ______.
7. The responses that prepare an organism to digest, metabolize, and store food once it has been consumed are the ______ reflexes.
8. The ______, which originates in the substantia nigra, passes through the lateral hypothalamus, and proceeds to the basal ganglia, is involved in the control of feeding behavior.
9. The ______, which originates in the paraventricular nucleus of the hypothalamus, passes through the ventromedial hypothalamus (VMH), and proceeds to two hindbrain structures, is involved in the control of satiety.
10. A reluctance to eat novel foods is called ______.
11. The weight-control drug ______, formed by combining ______, a serotonergic agonist, and ______, a dopaminergic agonist, was removed from the market because it caused heart valve disease in some patients.
12. The idea that a low level of blood glucose stimulates glucoreceptors to produce the sensation of hunger is known as the ______ theory.
13. Injections of ______, a pancreatic hormone that increases blood glucose levels, produces a rapid decrease in stomach contractions and hunger.
14. The deprivation of energy in cells caused by a lack of glucose is known as ______.
15. When food enters the duodenum, it triggers the release of ______, which may serve as a satiety sensor.
16. The ability of a factor in the environment to cause hunger through conditioning is called ______ hunger.
17. According to the ______ theory, a decreased level of fatty acids can cause hunger.
18. The lack of availability of fatty acids as a source of energy is called ______.
19. ______, a peptide produced by fat cells, appears to provide feedback to the brain about the level of stored fat in the body.
20. According to the ______ theory, each organism has a weight that it actively maintains, either by initiating eating behavior when weight falls below this level or by suppressing eating behavior when weight rises above this level.
21. A combination of ______ and ______ is the most successful way to lose weight and keep it off.
22. ______ is an eating disorder characterized by tremendous weight loss and a preoccupation with food and with body weight.
23. A person who goes on binges of overeating and then induces vomiting to get rid of the food suffers from ______.
24. Drinking in anticipation of a need is called ______ drinking, and drinking in response to a physiological need is called ______ drinking. Most of the research on thirst deals with ______ drinking.
25. Increased osmotic pressure caused by increased salt levels in extracellular fluids produces ______ thirst.
26. In response to either type of thirst, the posterior pituitary gland secretes ______, which causes the kidneys to concentrate urine.
27. Two structures outside the blood-brain barrier that probably contain many of the osmoreceptors of the brain are the ______ and the ______.
28. The type of thirst that results from the loss of extracellular fluid without changing osmotic pressure is called ______ thirst.
29. Renin is involved in converting angiotensinogen into the hormone ______, which stimulates the adrenal cortex to release ______, a hormone that increases salt and water retention by the kidneys.
30. The subfornical organ sends neural input to the ______, a structure near the anterior and ventral part of the third ventricle that appears to be involved in both osmotic and hypovolemic thirst.

Multiple-Choice Questions

1. The three classes of nutritional substances that can provide energy for bodily processes are
   a. carbohydrates, fats, and proteins.
   b. lipids, carbohydrates, and fats.
   c. meat, dairy products, and vegetables.
   d. fats, carbohydrates, and insulin.
2. Early brain lesion research on hunger and satiety suggested that two hypothalamic structures were responsible for initiating feeding and stopping feeding: the ______ and ______, respectively.
   a. LH, SFO
   b. LH, VMH
   c. VMH, LH
   d. SFO, LH

3. Rats with damage to the hypothalamic "hunger center" exhibited
   a. hyperphagia and obesity.
   b. anorexia and bulimia.
   c. aphagia and adipsia.
   d. euphoria and analgesia.
4. When Jason was a child, his parents took him to a fast-food restaurant at least three or four times a week. As an adult, Jason is obese, is very finicky about what he eats, and will not eat nuts if he has to shell them. Jason's behavior is similar to that of rats with ______ lesions.
   a. LH
   b. VMH
   c. DVM
   d. LGN
5. Which of the following is *not* a characteristic of the VMH-lesion syndrome?
   a. hyperphagia and obesity
   b. picky eating
   c. unwillingness to work for food
   d. inability to drink
6. Triggered by the taste and smell of food, the secretion of saliva, gastric juices, and insulin are examples of
   a. cephalic reflexes.
   b. spinal reflexes.
   c. gastrointestinal reflexes.
   d. rejection reflexes.
7. Schachter found that hyperphagic rats were quite similar behaviorally to
   a. LH-lesioned rats.
   b. obese humans.
   c. college sophomores.
   d. professional baseball players.
8. The two hindbrain structures considered part of the paraventricular satiety system are the ______ and the ______.
   a. substantia nigra, VMH
   b. substantia nigra, paraventricular nucleus
   c. nucleus of the solitary tract, lateral hypothalamus
   d. nucleus of the solitary tract, dorsal motor nucleus of the vagus
9. The PVN may contain two different adrenergic receptor types because rats need
   a. to be both hungry and thirsty.
   b. to eat both salty and sweet foods.
   c. to have an instinct to avoid novel foods.
   d. to eat both fats and proteins.
10. The drug fen-phen was removed from the market because
    a. it did not cause weight loss.
    b. it caused heart disease in some people.
    c. it was highly addictive.
    d. it caused some people to develop eating disorders.
11. People who have had their stomach removed
    a. become aphagic and adipsic.
    b. are never hungry.
    c. become hyperphagic and obese.
    d. experience hunger and eat more often than normal.
12. An individual who has high levels of blood glucose but is unable to use the glucose because of too little insulin activity has a disorder called
    a. diabetes mellitus.
    b. anorexia nervosa.
    c. bulimia nervosa.
    d. hypoglycemia.
13. Whenever Evelyn thinks about food, her pancreas releases ______ and her blood sugar level ______.
    a. insulin, increases
    b. insulin, decreases
    c. glucagons, increases
    d. glucagons, decreases
14. ______ removes glucose from the blood; ______ increases blood glucose levels.
    a. Glucagon; insulin
    b. Glycogen; insulin
    c. Insulin; glycogen
    d. Insulin; glucagon
15. The satiety glucoreceptors appear to be located in the
    a. LH.
    b. liver.
    c. pancreas.
    d. stomach.
16. Genetically obese mice may overeat because they have only one-third the amount of the gut hormone ______ relative to their nonobese littermates.
    a. glucagon
    b. insulin
    c. CCK
    d. PVN
17. When we avoid a food that has previously made us ill, we are exhibiting
    a. anorexia.
    b. a conditioned aversion.
    c. bulimia.
    d. a conditioned stimulus.
18. Booth proposed that stimuli at the end of a meal are associated with the nutritional changes that occur after eating; this is
    a. conditioned taste aversion.
    b. conditioned satiety.
    c. conditioned hunger.
    d. conditioned ingestional neophobia.
19. The peptide produced by fat cells that appears to give the brain feedback about the body's levels of stored fat is
    a. CCK.
    b. insulin.
    c. glucagon.
    d. leptin.
20. Tanisha has a family history of obesity and is obese herself. She probably has a(n) ______ insensitivity.
    a. glucagon
    b. insulin
    c. CCK
    d. leptin
21. Powley and Keesey's ______ theory suggests that an organism has a particular weight that it will defend, either by eating to bring its weight up or by fasting to bring its weight down.
    a. set-point
    b. critical-weight
    c. homeostatic
    d. ideal body weight
22. Exercise would probably help Chris keep off lost weight by
    a. occupying his time so that he does not eat.
    b. taking his mind off hunger.
    c. producing a feeling of nausea.
    d. increasing his metabolic rate.

23. A person who loses 35% of body weight, is preoccupied with food, and eats very little may be suffering from
a. bulimia nervosa. **c.** adipsia.
b. hypoglycemia. **d.** anorexia nervosa.

24. Anorexia nervosa is considered a particularly difficult disorder to treat because
a. it is difficult to change a person's body image.
b. no therapeutic drugs are available.
c. metabolic changes make weight gain nearly impossible.
d. binge eating is hereditary.

25. Keshia sometimes eats large quantities of food and then purges herself by vomiting. In response to a meal, she probably has an abnormally low secretion of
a. glucose. **c.** CCK.
b. insulin. **d.** glucagon.

26. A person who consumes excessive amounts of food, which is then purged, is suffering from
a. hypoglycemia. **c.** anorexia nervosa.
b. adipsia. **d.** bulimia nervosa.

27. Like anorexia nervosa, bulimia nervosa is often helped by treatment with
a. dopaminergic agonists. **c.** serotonergic antagonists.
b. adrenergic antagonists. **d.** serotonergic agonists.

28. The thirst produced by increased sodium chloride levels in extracellular fluid is called ______; the thirst produced by a decreased volume of extracellular fluid is called ______.
a. dry mouth; hypovolemic thirst
b. hypovolemic thirst; osmotic thirst
c. osmotic thirst; dry mouth
d. osmotic thirst; hypovolemic thirst

29. Drinking in anticipation of a need is called ______ drinking.
a. prandial **c.** primary
b. osmotic **d.** secondary

30. Antidiuretic hormone has its effect on thirst by
a. forcing the person to drink.
b. causing the kidneys to retain more fluid.
c. stimulating osmoreceptors in the liver.
d. producing hypovolemic thirst.

31. Renin is involved in the conversion of angiotensinogen into
a. aldosterone. **c.** ADH.
b. CCK. **d.** angiotensin.

Answers can be found on the companion website at www.worthpublishers.com/klein.

11

Sexual Development and Sexual Behavior

- Sexual Development
- Human Sexual Behavior
- Gender Identity and Sexual Preference
- *Scientific American* **Spotlight** What's Smell Got to Do With It?
- Sexual Dysfunction

What Happened to the Joy of Sex?

Paula sat at the kitchen table, her hands drawing warmth from a mug of steaming cocoa. Through the window she could see her husband raking leaves in the backyard and the children playing: 10-year-old Ryan was chasing 8-year-old Sarah toward the pile of leaves Doug had collected. As Paula watched, both children jumped into the pile, scattering leaves everywhere. Doug appeared to be laughing rather than scolding them.

Paula sighed, wishing she felt as happy as Doug apparently did. She couldn't remember the last time she and Doug had enjoyed each other sexually, and, in her mind at least, the absence of decent lovemaking was tearing their marriage apart. Strangely, Doug didn't seem to share her feelings about this—he certainly didn't talk about it.

Things had been going well until Doug was laid off from the auto plant. Before that, he had always been the family's main breadwinner, with Paula working part time to supplement the family income. Now, Doug had drawn his last unemployment check and had apparently given up his job search, so Paula was working full time and they were living on her salary.

At least Doug did a lot around the house. He took the children to school, picked them up from band practice, took Ryan to soccer practice, and drove them to the mall with their friends when they asked him to. For the last several months, Doug had done the grocery shopping and most of the cooking; he also cleaned the house and washed the clothes. He had even started making the beds in the morning, something Paula had not always been diligent about doing.

Doug was a good father, and a good husband in many ways, but Paula needed more than that. She needed the passion they'd had when they were dating and for most of their married life. The problem started when Doug lost his job. The first time they tried to have sex after that, he was unable to maintain an erection. After a couple more attempts, he had quit trying, and now he wouldn't even talk about it. Paula had seen Doug with an erection while he was sleeping, so she was sure the problem was in his head. But how could she get him to see a therapist when he wouldn't even admit anything was wrong? She decided to call their family physician and see whether he had any thoughts about the situation.

BEFORE YOU BEGIN

- **What biological process(es) determined that Paula and Doug's first child would be a boy and their second a girl?**
- **When does sexual development begin?**
- **What is the biological basis of sexual arousal and intercourse?**

sex-determining gene The gene on the short arm of the Y chromosome that determines the biological sex of an individual.

> ➤ **Physiologically, what is the cause of Doug's erectile dysfunction?**
> ➤ **What effect do hormones have on sexual arousal in women? In men?**
> ➤ **Is there a biological basis for sexual preference?**
> **In this chapter, you will find the answers to these questions and many others.**

Sexual Development

We begin by looking at what determines whether a zygote—a fertilized egg—develops into a male or a female organism. Although environmental factors are important to sexual development, in the beginning, genetics plays the primary role.

The Genetics of Sexual Development

Recall from Chapter 3 that at conception, the human zygote, or fertilized egg, has 23 pairs of chromosomes, a total of 46. Paula and Doug's children received one chromosome of each pair from Paula and the other from Doug. For Ryan, like all typical human males, each chromosome pair consists of two similar members, with one exception: the sex chromosomes. There are two types of sex chromosomes: X and Y. Thus, Ryan and his father have one X chromosome and one Y chromosome in each cell. Sarah and her mother, along with all typical human females, have two X chromosomes in each of the cells in their bodies.

You will also remember from Chapter 3 that the sperm and the egg (the gametes) have half the number of chromosomes found in other cells. Each of Paula's eggs has a single X chromosome, but Doug's sperm cells have either an X or a Y chromosome. Ryan received an X chromosome from Paula and a Y chromosome from Doug; Sarah received an X chromosome from each parent (Figure 11.1). Thus, genetic sex is determined at conception by the type of sperm that fertilizes the egg.

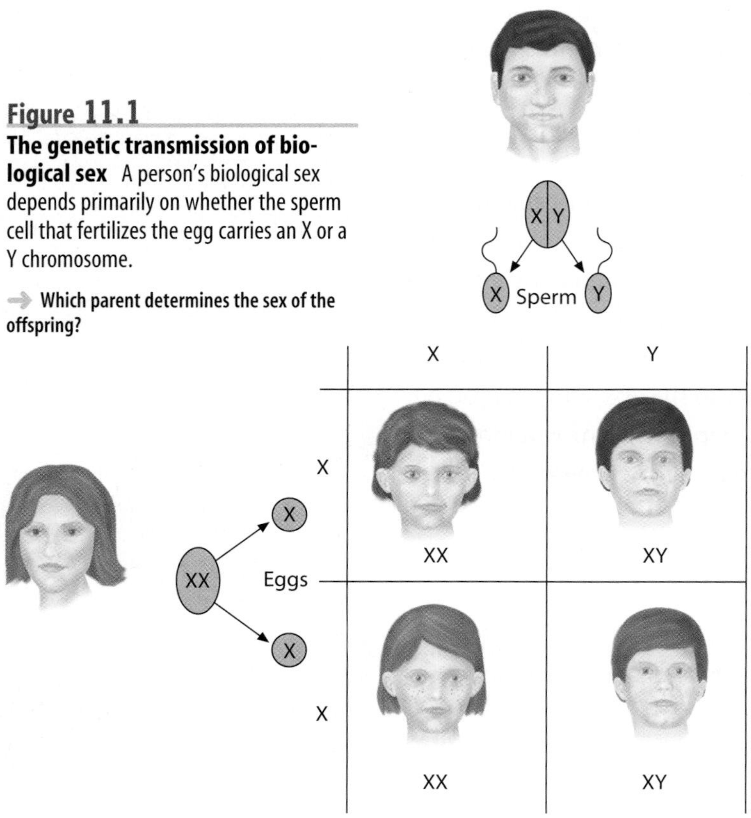

Figure 11.1
The genetic transmission of biological sex A person's biological sex depends primarily on whether the sperm cell that fertilizes the egg carries an X or a Y chromosome.

➡ **Which parent determines the sex of the offspring?**

But the presence of an XX or XY pair does not, by itself, determine the sex of the offspring. Regardless of its genetic makeup, the zygote is capable of developing as either a female or a male. Early research suggested that biological sex depends on the activity of a **sex-determining gene** located in the middle of the short arm of the Y chromosome (Gubbay & others, 1990). This gene is called *SRY* in humans and *Sry* in mice; *SRY* stands for sex-determining region of Y. *SRY* is involved in testicular development and appears to contribute to both the physical and the behavioral aspects of sexual differentiation. More recent research suggests that *SRY* is probably not the original mammalian sex-determining gene, as it appears to have been derived from a brain-determining gene rather than a sex-determining one, and it has been lost entirely in at least two rodent species (mole-voles, genus *Ellobius*) (Graves, 2001, 2002a, 2002b). Evidence is accumulating, in fact, that the development of the testes depends on the correct functioning of *SRY* and several genes on other chromosomes (Mittwoch, 2004; Sinisi & others, 2003).

By 6 weeks of development, the human embryo has formed crude, primordial reproductive structures (Figure 11.2). No evidence of

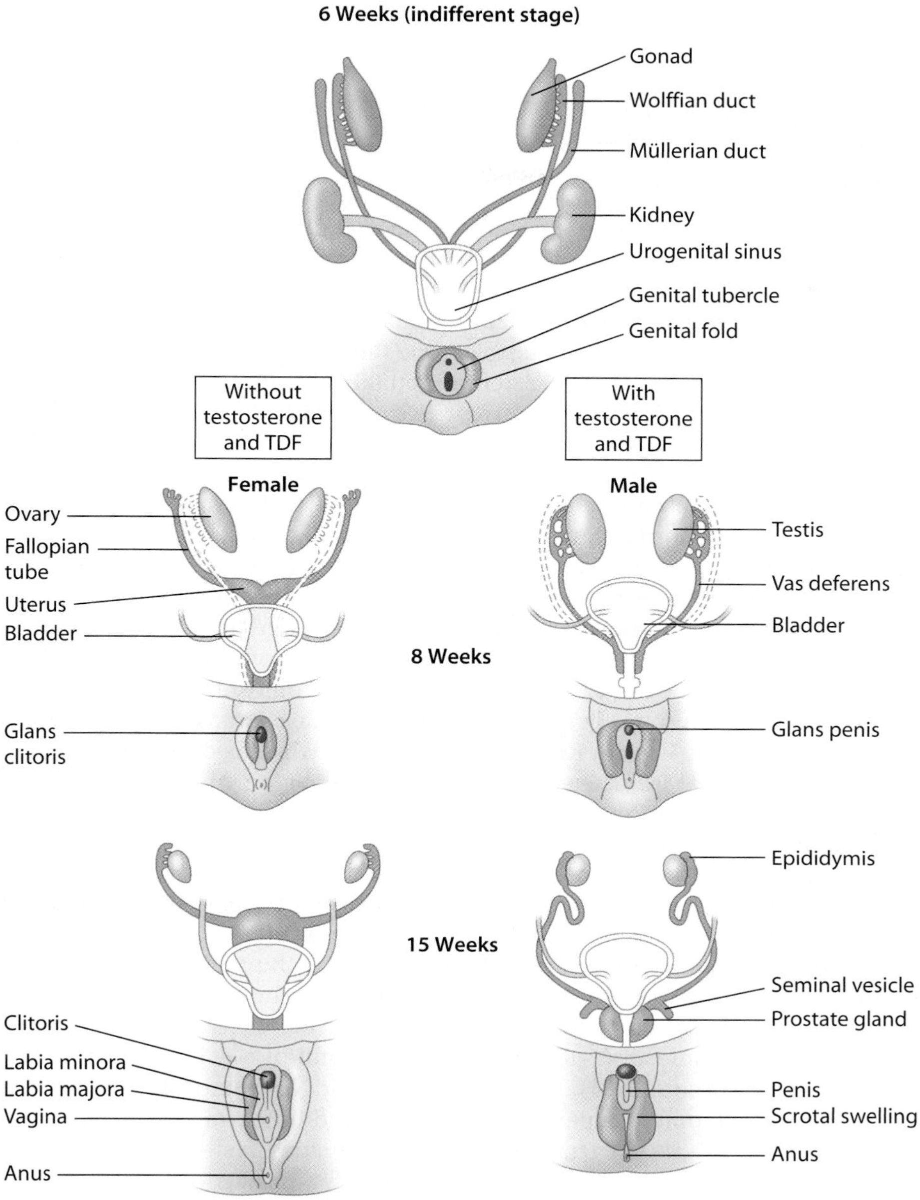

Figure 11.2

Development of the human reproductive structures Changes occurring at 6 weeks in the as yet undifferentiated reproductive system produce either a female or male reproductive system, shown here at 8 and 15 weeks of development.

What hormones determine whether the reproductive system develops as male or female?

the sex of the individual is visible at this time, and embryologists call this the "indifferent stage" (Puerta-Fonolla, 1998). Among the primitive reproductive structures are two sets of ducts known as the Müllerian ducts and the Wolffian ducts, a pair of simple gonads, and early genital structures. The **Müllerian system** will later form some of the female reproductive structures, and the **Wolffian system,** some of the male structures. At 6 weeks, the primitive gonad is neither ovary nor testis, but the cortex (outer core) of each gonad has the potential to develop into a female ovary, and the medulla (inner core) has the potential to develop into a male testis. The early genital structures will eventually develop into the familiar female or male external anatomy.

During week 6 of development of an XY embryo, *SRY,* with assistance from several other genes, produces **testis-determining factor (TDF),** which causes the undifferentiated gonads to become testes (Koopman & others, 1991; O'Neill & O'Neill, 1999). The testes later secrete testosterone and manufacture sperm. The Wolffian ducts mature into the *seminal vesicles* and *prostate gland,* which produce the fluid in which sperm cells are ejaculated, and the *vas deferens,* the passage through which the sperm cells travel from the testis to the urethra (Figure 11.2). While the Wolffian system is developing into these male reproductive structures, the Müllerian system is degenerating as a result of **Müllerian-inhibiting substance (MIS),** a

Müllerian system A set of ducts in the human embryo that develops into parts of the female reproductive system.

Wolffian system A set of ducts in the human embryo that develops into parts of the male reproductive system.

testis-determining factor (TDF) An enzyme that causes the undifferentiated gonads to become testes.

Müllerian-inhibiting substance (MIS) A hormone released by the testes that helps prevent the development of the female reproductive system.

Klinefelter syndrome A condition in which a person has an XXY genotype and is phenotypically male, but has small external genitals, sparse pubic and armpit hair, and a tendency to be infertile.

Turner syndrome A condition in which a person is born with one X chromosome and no other sex chromosome; the female reproductive system develops only partially.

hormone released by the testes that helps prevent the development of female reproductive structures. Beginning in week 7, testosterone from the embryonic testis is responsible for the development of the external genitals, the *penis* and *scrotum.*

In the XX embryo, which has neither TDF nor MIS, the gonads become ovaries, which secrete estrogen and progesterone and manufacture eggs. The Müllerian ducts mature into the internal female reproductive system: the *uterus* and upper part of the *vagina,* and the *fallopian tubes,* through which eggs travel from the ovaries to the uterus (see Figure 11.2). "Wolffian-inhibiting substance" is unnecessary, because in the absence of testosterone the Wolffian ducts do not continue to develop; instead the female external genitals develop. Without something extra—TDF—the individual develops female external genitals. Clearly, the default pattern of sexual development in humans is female.

To demonstrate that the presence of the Y chromosome rather than the absence of a second X chromosome causes an embryo to develop as a male, Koopman and colleagues (1991) performed a study, using mice, in which the segment of the Y chromosome containing the sex-determining gene (*Sry*) was attached to one of the X chromosomes of a female mouse. As a result, a male reproductive system developed in the genetically female mouse, indicating that *Sry* (and perhaps other genes on the attached segment) causes the development of the male reproductive system.

Additional evidence for the importance of the Y chromosome, rather than lack of a second X chromosome, in the development of male characteristics in humans comes from individuals with **Klinefelter syndrome,** which is caused by a second X chromosome. That is, instead of having an XY genotype, men with Klinefelter syndrome have an XXY genotype. Rather than developing as females because of the second X chromosome, individuals with Klinefelter syndrome develop as males but are likely to have small testicles and penis, sparse pubic and armpit hair, enlarged breasts, and infertility. Testosterone therapy benefits the condition in many ways, although the individual is usually still infertile.

Figure 11.3

Turner syndrome A person with Turner syndrome, showing the characteristic short stature and arms that turn out slightly at the elbow.

→ **Why are individuals with Turner syndrome infertile?**

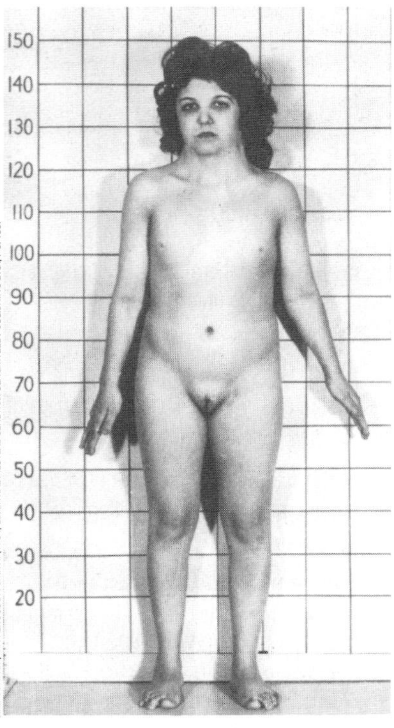

J.M. CONNOR; M.A FERGUSON-SMITH. (1984) *ESSENTIAL MEDICAL GENETICS.* BLACKWELL PUBLISHING LTD., PG. 135.

Studies of people with **Turner syndrome** (Figure 11.3) provide further support for the critical role of the Y chromosome in determining biological sex. In this disorder, a person has one intact X chromosome and a complete or partial absence of the other X chromosome; this is usually the result of a defect in the father's sperm (Soares & others, 2001). If the lack of a second X chromosome determined male sexual development, a person with Turner syndrome would have a male reproductive system. In fact, the female reproductive system develops—to a point. Because two X chromosomes are needed for the ovaries to produce eggs, individuals with Turner syndrome are incapable of having children. Characteristic physical features of this syndrome include a webbed neck, short stature, and arms that turn out slightly at the elbows. In addition to reproductive system involvement, Turner syndrome may affect organ systems throughout the body, including the cardiovascular system, the renal system, and the gastrointestinal system (Halac & Zimmerman, 2004), showing that X chromosomes are critical for far more than sexual development.

Additional evidence for the critical role of the Y chromosome comes from cases in which a person with male characteristics is found to have two X chromosomes and no Y chromosome, or an individual with female characteristics to have an X and a Y chromosome. How can this happen? The answer lies in the crossing over process (D. D. Kelly, 1991a). In Chapter 3, we noted that crossing over occurs during gamete formation, when a segment of one member of a chromosome pair is exchanged with a segment from its partner during meiosis. In sperm formation, if the sex-determining gene on the Y chromosome is

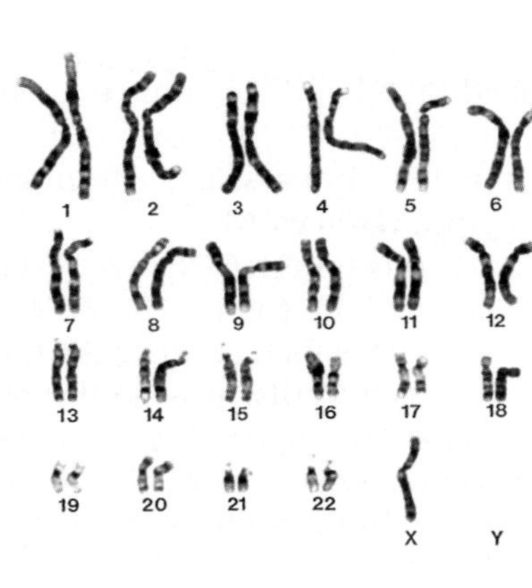

SCIENCE PHOTO LIBRARY/PHOTO RESEARCHERS, INC.

transferred to the X chromosome during crossing over, the resulting sperm will carry an X chromosome that produces TDF, and, following fertilization, the offspring will be a biological male with two X chromosomes. The sperm with the Y chromosome that lost the sex-determining gene will produce an offspring that is a biological female with one X and one Y chromosome—like the mouse produced experimentally by Koopman and coworkers (1991). Human males with two X chromosomes and females with an X and a Y chromosome are extremely rare, occurring in fewer than 2 out of 10,000 live births (Sax, 2002).

At this point, because the terms are sometimes used interchangeably, we want to distinguish between *sex* and *gender*. We have just discussed the biology of sexual development. Humans are classified sexually as female or male, as determined by their external sex organs, their internal sex organs, and the secondary sexual development that occurs at puberty. **Gender** refers to culturally defined roles, attitudes, and responsibilities for females and males that are learned, may change with time, and vary among and within societies. Although typically the sex of a person (female or male) does not change, the gender of the person (feminine or masculine) may change as her or his socially constructed role evolves. In summary, sex is biological; gender, cultural.

gender A set of culturally defined roles, attitudes, and responsibilities for females and males that are learned, may change with time, and vary among and within societies.

testosterone The male sex hormone that influences the sexual development of the brain and plays a significant role in male sexual arousal.

Checkpoint

Explain this statement: The occurrence of an XX male or an XY female cannot be attributed to any defect in the mother's egg.

REVIEW

- The sex-determining gene on the Y chromosome is essential for male sexual differentiation: If the gene is absent, the embryo typically develops as a female; if present, it typically develops as a male.
- Testis-determining factor (TDF) causes the undifferentiated embryonic gonads to become testes.
- Testicular testosterone causes the Wolffian system to develop into the male reproductive system; Müllerian-inhibiting substance (MIS), also released from the testes, causes the Müllerian system to degenerate.
- Without TDF and MIS, the primordial gonad becomes an ovary, and the Müllerian system develops into the female reproductive system—the default pattern of human sexual development.

The Plasticity of the Developing Brain

You probably will not be surprised to learn that the brains of females and males are different. But why is this so? What effect does biological sex have on the brain? The pattern of hormone release by the anterior pituitary gland and by the gonads, as well as the hormones that stimulate the hypothalamus to produce sexual responsivity, are different for males and females. This suggests that differences in male and female brains are determined by variations in the early hormonal environment, and these variations affect male and female differences in sexual behavior. In fact, several studies suggest that testosterone in the prenatal or early postnatal period is responsible for a masculinized brain; without testosterone, a female brain develops (Gorski, 2002).

Note that hormones have both *organizational* and *activational* effects on development. For example, the organizational function of testosterone is what makes the developing brain a male brain. When the individual matures, the activational effect of the testosterone determines sexual responsivity.

The Importance of Testosterone

In order for a male rodent to develop the structures and functions characteristic of its sex and species, its brain must be subjected to testicular hormones, such as testosterone, during a critical period of development (Gorski, 2002; Negri-Cesi & others, 2004). An early study of rats provided convincing evidence for the organizing influence of **testosterone** on the sexual development of the brain (Pfeiffer,

lordosis A female copulatory posture in which the hindquarters are raised to facilitate insertion of the penis by the male.

1936). When Pfeiffer removed the ovaries (which manufacture and secrete estrogen) of newborn female rats and the testes (which manufacture and secrete testosterone) of newborn male rats, on reaching adulthood both genetic females and genetic males exhibited a female pattern of gonadotropic hormone release (see Table 4.1 for a summary of endocrine glands and the hormones they release). In contrast, transplanting testes into newborn female rats with or without ovaries caused the genetic females to display the male gonadotropic hormone release pattern. Again, we find that the basic pattern for both sexual and brain development is female; without testosterone, the female pattern develops. With testosterone, the male pattern develops, even in females with ovaries.

The presence or absence of prenatal or early postnatal exposure to testosterone determines not only the type of hormonal cycle (female or male) that emerges but also the behavioral responsivity to sex hormones. Exposure to testosterone early in development is necessary to produce a brain that responds to testosterone. To demonstrate the effect of early testosterone exposure on the brain, researchers injected testosterone into pregnant guinea pigs and removed the ovaries (ovariectomy) of the female offspring shortly after birth (Phoenix & others, 1959). Once these offspring had matured, the researchers injected them with testosterone and found that these females exhibited a significantly greater number of male-typical mounting behaviors than did ovariectomized adult females not exposed to testosterone prenatally. Apparently the organizational effect of the prenatal testosterone exposure produced a masculinized brain that caused the females to display male-typical sexual behavior when later exposed to the activational effect of testosterone. These masculinized females also exhibited less female-typical sexual responding following estrogen and progesterone injections. Figure 11.4 shows the typical rodent male and female sexual behaviors: The male rat mounts the female, who displays the **lordosis,** or copulatory, posture by raising her hindquarters to facilitate insertion of the penis.

Figure 11.4
Copulation in rats The female rat raises her hindquarters and deflects her tail to facilitate insertion of the penis by the male rat, which here is exhibiting characteristic mounting behavior.

➡ **What is the effect of castration or removal of the ovaries on these male-typical and female-typical sexual behaviors?**

Thus, early testosterone exposure, either prenatally or postnatally, can increase the male-typical behaviors and decrease the female-typical behaviors of a genetic female. To examine the effect on males of a lack of early testosterone exposure, male rats were castrated shortly after birth (without their testes, the animals were not exposed to testosterone) (Grady & others, 1965). When these animals received testosterone injections as adults, they failed to exhibit normal male sexual behavior. But estrogen and progesterone injections produced greater female-typical sexual behavior in these male rats than in noncastrated animals. Again, we see reversion to the female pattern without the early organizing effects of testosterone.

A Critical Period of Development

Testosterone or its absence during the prenatal and early postnatal period clearly affects brain development and subsequent sexual behavior. Researchers have found that there is a *critical period* for the testosterone organizational effect, after which exposure has no effect. To determine when the critical period ends, male rats were castrated shortly after birth and then exposed to testosterone at different times during their first 14 days of life (Beach & others, 1969) (Figure 11.5). If testosterone was administered within 4 days after birth, the adult rats would display nearly normal male sexual behavior following testosterone exposure. However, the activational effect of testosterone administration on adults decreased rapidly as the time between castration and first exposure increased. If neonatally castrated rats were first exposed to testosterone at days 13 and 14 after birth, it had little effect, and testosterone administered to these rats once they were adults triggered little male sexual behavior.

Figure 11.5
The critical period for sexual development of the rat brain The graph shows the percentage of neonatally castrated male rats ejaculating or displaying lordosis as a function of the time when testosterone was administered.

➡ **What is the effect of testosterone administration after the end of the critical period?**

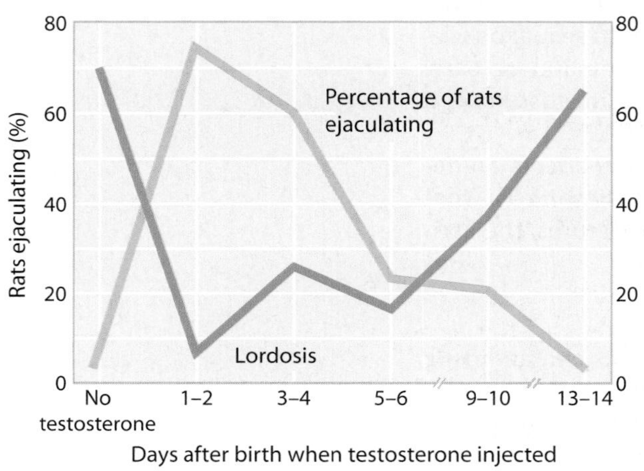

How do you think the presence or absence of testosterone during the critical period affected the female-like behavior of these castrated rats? When testosterone was administered during the critical period of the sexual development of the brain (1 to 6 days following birth), castrated male rats, as adults, exhibited little female sexual behavior (Figure 11.5). In contrast, if the rats received no postnatal testosterone or if it was withheld until they were 13 or 14 days old, the adult rats exhibited female sexual behavior when they were injected with estrogen and progesterone.

Note the importance of this research for our understanding of the development of male or female sexual behavior in rats. If castrated males are exposed to testosterone within a critical period after birth (the first 6 days), then they exhibit male sexual behavior as adults when given testosterone. Without this early postnatal exposure, they exhibit little male sexual behavior as adults when primed with testosterone. Instead, priming with estrogen and progesterone leads to female sexual behavior in the male rats.

Structural Differences in the Brain

As the animal studies demonstrated, an animal develops a "female brain" unless exposed to testosterone, in which case a "male brain" develops. But what do we mean by a "female brain" or a "male brain"? Are there structural differences in the brains of the two sexes? In fact, such differences have been noted. For example, a nucleus in the preoptic area of the hypothalamus—the *sexually dimorphic nucleus* (SDN-POA)—is several times larger in male rats than in female rats (Gorski & others, 1980; Jacobson & Gorski, 1981; Rhees & others, 1990). Swaab and colleagues (1995) reported that a structure in the preoptic area of the human brain, which they called the SDN although it may not correspond to the SDN-POA of rats, is more than twice as large in young adult men as in women and contains about twice as many cells. At least two additional hypothalamic structures differ in males and females, as we shall see: the bed nucleus of the stria terminalis and the interstitial nucleus of the anterior hypothalamus (INAH).

Just as there is a critical period for testosterone injections to produce male sexual behavior in castrated male rats, so there is a critical period for the development of structural differences in the preoptic area. Rhees and colleagues (1990) found that the critical period for such differences is the first 5 postnatal days; on day 6 and beyond, testosterone injections in either intact females or castrated male rats had no effect on the size of the SDN-POA.

Note that the experiment of Rhees and coworkers involved exogenously administered testosterone. Subsequent research suggested there might be a different critical period for an effect on SDN size resulting from the removal of *endogenously* produced testosterone. Davis and colleagues (1995) castrated male rats at various ages and found that the loss of endogenously produced testosterone continued to have an effect on the SDN size for at least 29 days postnatally. The investigators suggested the possibility of multiple critical periods for the sexual differentiation of the SDN, depending on the source of the testosterone.

Not surprisingly given the difference in life spans, the development of the SDN in humans occurs over a much longer postnatal period than it does in rodents. Swaab and coworkers (1995) reported that the SDN at birth contains only about 20% of the cells that are present between 2 and 4 years of age. Further, the rate of cell formation is equivalent in girls and boys until that age. Between ages 2 and 4, however, cell number in the SDN decreases in girls but not in boys, which leads to the sexual differentiation of the structure. There is also a much later change in the SDN, as the number of cells declines dramatically in men after age 50 (Zhou & Swaab, 1999).

Prenatal stress has also been found to reduce the size of the SDN and to lower sexual activity in the adult male rat (Kerchner & Ward, 1992; Rhees & others, 1999). However, some of the prenatally stressed animals exhibited sexual activity, and some of the nonstressed males did not, and there was a strong positive correlation

estradiol A form of estrogen; a hormone similar to testosterone, thought to be responsible for masculinization of the brain.

estrogen The female sex hormone.

alpha-fetoprotein A protein synthesized by the fetal liver and present in the bloodstream of both male and female fetuses that binds to and deactivates circulating estradiol.

between SDN size and sexual activity in both stressed and nonstressed animals: Male rats with large SDNs were sexually active; male rats with small SDNs were sexually inactive. Prenatal stress also affected sexual activity in female rats but in the opposite direction; stressed females showed dramatically increased receptivity to males relative to nonstressed females (Gutierrez & others, 1989; Rojo & others, 1986).

The particular type of prenatal stress affected the adult sexual behavior. Pregnant rats were subjected to either immobilization stress (the type of stress used in the previously cited studies), REM sleep deprivation, unavoidable foot shocks, or immersion in cold water (Velazquez-Moctezuma & others, 1993). Immobilization stress impaired male-typical behavior in genetic male offspring; REM sleep deprivation caused even greater impairment than immobilization; electric shocks had little effect on male-typical behavior; and water immersion actually increased several aspects of male-typical behavior.

Another widely reported structural difference in humans involves the corpus callosum and particularly its posterior portion, the splenium. In a number of studies, using widely varying methodologies, the splenium has been found to be larger in females (e.g., Dubb & others, 2003; Holloway & others, 1993). Dubb and colleagues also found that males had a larger genu (anterior portion) of the corpus callosum. However, the finding of a larger female splenium is controversial. In a meta-analysis of 49 studies, Bishop and Wahlsten (1997) concluded that the idea that women have a larger splenium than men (and thus, perhaps, think differently from men) is invalid. More recently, MRI measurements of the corpus callosum of neurologically normal males and females revealed no significant sex differences, although subtle differences in shape were found (Luders & others, 2003). Another MRI study comparing 51 healthy men and 41 healthy women reported that the corpus callosum was larger in men than in women relative to brain size (Sullivan & others, 2001). Using ultrasonographs, Hwang and colleagues (2004) studied the corpus callosa of neonates and found no significant gender differences in overall size, although some of the measurements did differ. For example, the average male corpus callosum was taller than that of the female, whereas the female splenium tended to be thicker than the male splenium. The controversy over size differences in the corpus callosum of men and women continues.

The Influence of Estradiol

Testosterone is not the only hormone that affects brain development. A male-like brain also can result from exposure to androstenedione, estradiol, or diethylstilbestrol (D. D. Kelly, 1991a). These other hormones produce a male-like brain because of the chemical similarities between testosterone and **estradiol,** which is a form of the female sex hormone **estrogen** that is present in the bloodstream of a mature female. After testosterone crosses the blood-brain barrier, *aromatase enzymes* in the brain cells add a benzene ring to each molecule of testosterone to produce estradiol. Thus, estradiol, rather than testosterone, is actually responsible for masculinization of the brain and activation of male sexual behavior (Balthazart & others, 2004; Balthazart & Ball, 1998, 2004; Kelly).

Why does the estradiol circulating in a mother's body during pregnancy fail to masculinize her daughter's brain? **Alpha-fetoprotein,** a protein synthesized by the fetal liver and present in the bloodstream of both female and male fetuses, binds to and deactivates any circulating estradiol in the fetal system (D. D. Kelly, 1991a). Once deactivated, estradiol cannot masculinize the developing female brain. Testosterone is not affected by alpha-fetoprotein, however, so the testosterone manufactured by fetal testicles enters the brain of the male offspring and is converted to estradiol by the steroid-sensitive neurons that take it up. In this form, the estradiol is safe from the deactivating effects of alpha-fetoprotein and can masculinize the developing fetal brain.

A Range of Sex-Typical Behaviors?

At this point, you may have concluded that the brain is either completely female-like or completely male-like. Although we can understand why you have come to this conclusion, it is completely wrong. There is strong evidence for intermediate levels of both feminization and masculinization (D. D. Kelly, 1991a). These normal variations are responsible for the range of sexual behaviors among genetically normal female and male animals.

According to D. D. Kelly (1991a), there is considerable variability in the amount of testosterone to which a developing fetus is exposed. Exposure to the lower levels early in development will increase the female-like characteristics and decrease the male-like characteristics of the brain. Early exposure to lower testosterone levels also increases the prevalence of the cycles and behaviors typical of the female and decreases the prevalence of male-typical hormonal cycles and sexual behaviors.

For example, after examining testosterone levels in the blood of mouse fetuses and in the surrounding amniotic fluid, vom Saal and Bronson (1980) concluded that the testosterone levels depended on the position of the fetus in the uterus. A female fetus has a higher testosterone concentration in its blood and in its surrounding amniotic fluid when it is between two male fetuses than when it is between a male and a female or two female fetuses. As adults, the female mice positioned between two males displayed erratic changes in female-typical hormonal patterns, began to mate later, and ceased bearing young earlier than did adult female mice that developed between two females. Male mice positioned between two female fetuses developed smaller testes that weighed less, and the testosterone dose necessary to produce sexual responsivity in a castrated male of this type was higher, compared with male mice that had been positioned between two males. However, males prenatally positioned between two females were also more sexually active as adults and less aggressive (vom Saal & others, 1983). These observations support the idea that normal variations in sex hormone cycles and sexual behavior among males and females may reflect differences in levels of prenatal testosterone exposure.

A more recent study investigated the effects of intrauterine position of either rats or mice on a variety of measures related to sexual development and behavior (Nagao & others, 2004). The researchers concluded that intrauterine position did not affect growth of the reproductive organs, sexual maturation, or behavior. Intrauterine sex hormone diffusion may have an organizing effect on other measures, however, such as opioid receptor density in mice (Morley-Fletcher & others, 2003) and tooth crown size in humans (Dempsey & others, 1999).

Comparable research in humans is made more difficult by the relative rarity of multiple births. However, some researchers have studied twins and have found that certain masculine and feminine traits may be affected by the intrauterine hormonal environment (Cohen-Bendahan & others, 2004, 2005; Resnick & others, 1993; Ryan & Vandenbergh, 2002). For example, one experiment reanalyzed Sensation Seeking Scale scores from an earlier study of 422 British twin pairs, of which 51 were opposite-sex pairs (Resnick & others). Because sensation seeking is typically higher in men than in women, the researchers hypothesized an increase in sensation seeking in the female members of opposite-sex pairs, who would have been exposed in utero to higher levels of testosterone than the female members of same-sex pairs. The reanalysis confirmed the hypothesis.

Researchers in the Netherlands compared the lateralization of verbal function in girls from same-sex and opposite-sex twin pairs (Cohen-Bendahan & others, 2004). "Lateralization" refers to the differentiation of functions between the cerebral hemispheres, with boys typically showing a more lateralized pattern of verbal processing than girls. That is, boys are more likely to have their language functions confined to the left hemisphere, whereas girls tend to have some language functions in the right hemisphere as well. Cohen-Bendahan and colleagues found that girls from opposite-sex twin pairs were more like males in their

➤Checkpoint

Using what you have learned about genetics, hormones, and CNS development, describe the development of Paula and Doug's daughter, Sarah, from the moment the sperm fertilized the egg until the moment of birth. Then do the same for Ryan.

cerebral lateralization than were girls from same-sex twin pairs, suggesting that the intrauterine hormonal environment affected their language lateralization. We have more to say about cerebral lateralization in Chapter 13.

REVIEW

- Without testosterone during the prenatal or early postnatal period, development produces a female brain, which controls the female-typical hormonal cycle and behavior.
- Testosterone produced by the testes in the prenatal or early postnatal period masculinizes the brain. The male brain controls the male-typical hormonal cycle and behavior.
- The critical period in rats for the development of the male brain ends shortly after birth.
- Testosterone acts on the brain to increase the size of and the number of neurons in the sexually dimorphic nucleus (SDN) of the preoptic area of the hypothalamus.
- The SDN is larger in males than in females. Prenatal stress can affect the size of the SDN-POA in male rats and generally leads to a decrease in male-typical sexual activity, although the effect depends on the nature of the stressor.
- Testosterone in the brain is converted by the aromatase enzyme to estradiol, a form of the female sex hormone estrogen. This estradiol is responsible for masculinizing the male brain.
- In female fetuses during the critical period, estradiol (from the mother) is deactivated by alpha-fetoprotein, preventing females from developing a masculinized brain.
- Intermediate levels of feminization and masculinization of the brain, resulting from varying testosterone levels during the critical period, are responsible for the normal range of sexual behaviors in females and males.

Human Sexual Behavior

So far we have discussed how sexual behavior is affected by testosterone, primarily in nonhuman animals. But many other factors also affect sexual behavior, especially in humans. Consider, for example, what might be affecting Paula and Doug's sexual relationship.

What exactly do we mean by sexual behavior? We usually think first about the human sexual response, the physiological changes that occur when a woman or a man is sexually aroused. During sexual stimulation, individuals are aware of some of the biological structures involved but are not particularly concerned at that moment with how they work, or how hormones and psychological factors (mediated biologically, of course) are contributing to sexual arousal. Yet these structures, hormones, and psychological factors are essential aspects of sexual behavior. Psychological factors in Doug's situation might include the stress of being unable to find a job, guilt from having relinquished his role as the family's chief bread-winner, and loss of self-esteem caused by (and contributing to) his erectile dysfunction.

vasocongestion A dilation and filling of blood vessels that produces erection of the penis or clitoris, nipple erection, and sexual flush.

myotonia The rhythmic contraction of muscles, as in the male and female genital organs during orgasm; also causes erection of the nipples.

orgasm The climax of the sexual response.

The Physiology of Sexual Behavior

William H. Masters and Virginia E. Johnson (1966) conducted a 12-year study of sexual behavior in 382 women and 312 men, in which they recorded more than 10,000 cycles of sexual arousal and orgasm, providing a detailed picture of the human sexual response. This research revealed four phases in the human sexual response: excitement, plateau, orgasm, and resolution (Figure 11.6). Although some features of the four-phase model have been confirmed, more recent evidence suggests that a unitary model may be too restrictive (Levin, 1998). Levin

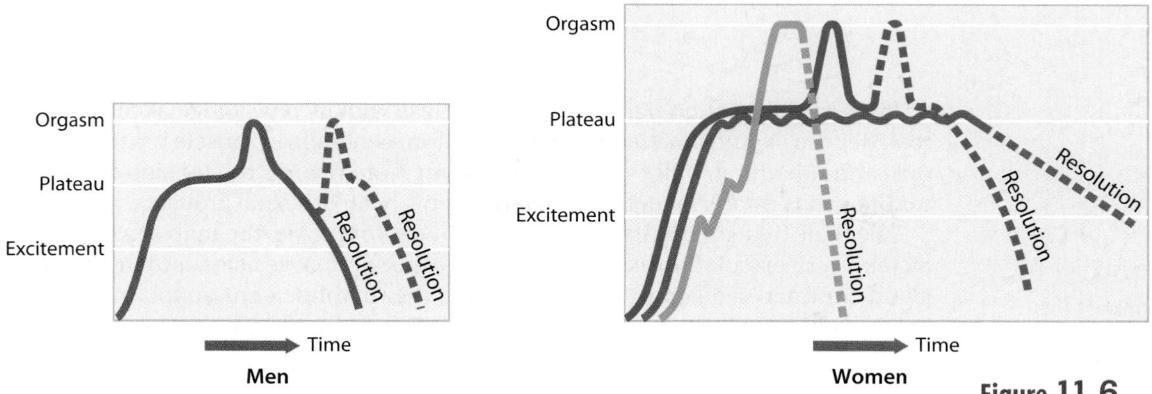

Figure 11.6

The four phases of the human sexual response The male response always goes through the four phases. The female response may include only one orgasm (green line), more than one orgasm (blue line), or no orgasm (red line).

→ **How does the resolution phase differ in men and women?**

(2002), for example, suggested a slightly altered sequence of stages (desire, excitation, orgasm, and resolution), with the desire stage split into two components: D1 for the spontaneous activation of desire and D2 for desire triggered by sexual excitation. Still, the Masters-Johnson model continues to provide a useful description of the sexual response.

Phases of the Female Sexual Response

Most women experience the basic sexual response pattern described by Masters and Johnson, with excitement, plateau, orgasm, and resolution phases. When sexually stimulated, the woman experiences physiological changes that include, during the *excitement* phase, dilation or filling of the blood vessels (**vasocongestion**) in the clitoris and fluid seepage through the vaginal walls. (Figure 11.7 shows the male and female reproductive systems.) These changes provide the vaginal lubrication that facilitates intercourse. In addition, the rhythmic contraction of muscles (**myotonia**) causes the nipples to become erect, and vasocongestion causes them to swell. The vasocongestion of the clitoris is analogous to the erection of the penis. The sexual flush, a reddening of the neck and chest, begins, and heart rate and blood pressure increase.

Vasocongestion and myotonia reach their peak during the *plateau* phase, reflecting a high level of sexual arousal in response to continued sexual stimulation. The physiological changes in this phase produce both the subjective feeling of sexual arousal and the tension necessary for **orgasm,** the climax of the sexual response. In fact, some women mistake the arousal of the plateau phase for an orgasm.

The intense, rhythmic muscle contractions during orgasm occur at approximately 0.8 second intervals. A mild orgasm may have three or four contractions, whereas a strong, prolonged orgasm may produce as many as a dozen. The female orgasm has been described as a sensation that spreads from the clitoris throughout the whole pelvic region (Hyde & Delamater, 2000).

Orgasm is followed by the *resolution* phase, during which the arousal level of the woman diminishes. Unlike in men (see below), there is no refractory period following orgasm, and with sufficient stimulation, a woman can experience another orgasm immediately. Some women do not experience distinct plateau and orgasm phases, instead having a series of sustained orgasms (Figure 11.6). Other patterns include a move from excitement to orgasm without any plateau phase, or a shift from plateau to resolution without an orgasm.

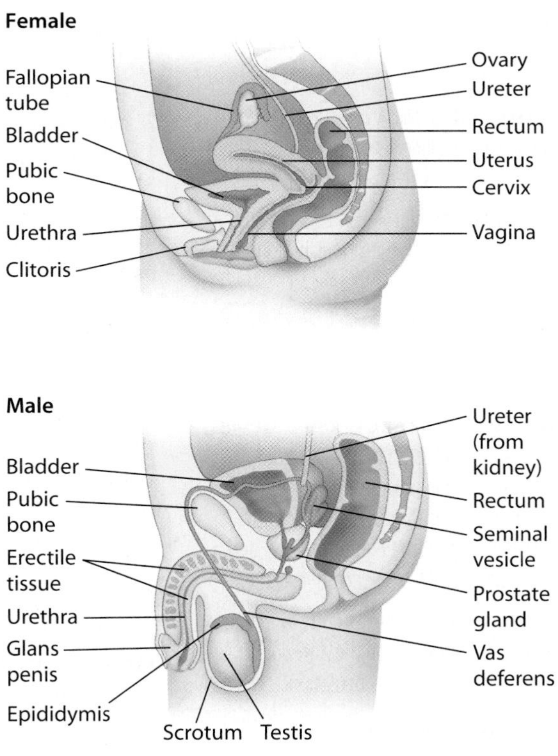

Figure 11.7

Female and male reproductive systems, shown in sagittal sections

→ **Where in the female's body does myotonia occur? Where in the male's body does vasocongestion occur?**

Phases of the Male Sexual Response

In the *excitement* phase, the penis fills with blood a few seconds after stimulation, producing an erection. As noted above, the increased blood flow to the pelvic area is caused by vasocongestion. Nipple erection and sexual flush may also occur in some men during the excitement phase.

If sexual stimulation persists, sexual arousal, with its physiological changes, intensifies during the *plateau* phase. In addition, generalized muscle tension develops, and breathing, pulse rate, and blood pressure rise. As the tension necessary for orgasm is established, the man reaches his peak of sexual arousal.

The male orgasm occurs in two stages. In the first stage, the man senses the inevitability of ejaculation as the vas deferens, the seminal vesicles, and the prostate gland contract (see Figure 11.7). Myotonia, the rhythmic contraction of muscles, occurs in the genital organs to force the ejaculate (fluid) into the urethra. In the second stage, the urethra and the penis contract rhythmically, at intervals of 0.8 seconds, forcing the semen out of the urethra. The intensely pleasurable aspects of orgasm are experienced in this second stage.

Orgasm is followed by a return to the nonaroused state in the *resolution* phase, during which there is a loss of sexual responsivity. In this *refractory period,* men usually cannot be sexually aroused and are often incapable of having an erection. The length of the resolution phase varies, lasting only a few minutes for some men and up to 24 hours for others.

Checkpoint

Compare and contrast the phases of the female sexual response and the male sexual response. Suggest why the female sexual response phases are so much more variable than those of the male sexual response. Which phase(s) of the human sexual response seem(s) to be missing from Doug and Paula's sexual activities since Doug lost his job?

REVIEW

- The four phases of the human sexual response are excitement, plateau, orgasm, and resolution.
- Vasocongestion of the genitals occurs in both men and women during the excitement phase. Myotonia, the rhythmic contraction of muscles during orgasm, contributes to sexual pleasure.
- Most women experience the basic sexual response pattern, but some have multiple orgasms, move directly from excitement to orgasm, or do not experience an orgasm at all.
- Men generally experience all phases of the human sexual response, with a loss of sexual responsivity (refractory period) during the resolution phase that varies from a few minutes to 24 hours.

Biological Systems Controlling Sexual Behavior

The ability to experience the four phases of the human sexual response depends on the effective functioning of several biological systems, which involve both hormonal and neural mechanisms. These biological systems have two effects: They provide a general sensitivity to sexually related environmental cues, and they produce sexual arousal and motivate behaviors. In discussing these systems, we will be referring to both human and nonhuman animal studies.

Hormonal Influences in Females

Levels of female sex hormone change dramatically but regularly during the **menstrual cycle** in humans and some other primates and the **estrous cycle** in other mammals. For example, estrogen levels are high in the middle of each cycle, but low at the beginning and end. For most mammals, female sexual arousal and behavior occur only when the estrogen level is high, revealing the activational role of the hormone; the intense sexual arousal during this period is called estrus, or more commonly, **heat.** However, in humans and certain other primate species, females respond sexually throughout the menstrual cycle, indicating that estrogen does not play the same major role in sexual motivation that it does in other species.

Estrous and menstrual cycles are divided into the *follicular phase* and the *luteal phase.* In women, each phase lasts approximately 14 days. However, the timing of ovulation varies from individual to individual, and even from cycle to cycle in the same person. At the beginning of the follicular phase, the anterior pituitary gland begins secreting **follicle-stimulating hormone (FSH).** FSH

menstrual cycle A cycle of changes in the level of female sex hormones in humans and some other primates.

estrous cycle A cycle of changes in the level of female sex hormones in nonhuman mammals.

heat A period of intense sexual arousal when estrogen levels peak in estrous mammals; also called estrus.

follicle-stimulating hormone (FSH) A hormone secreted by the anterior pituitary gland that causes one or several ovarian follicles to grow into a mature Graafian follicle, the egg to mature, and the Graafian follicle to secrete estrogen.

luteinizing hormone (LH) In females, a hormone secreted by the anterior pituitary gland that causes ovulation.

progesterone A female sex hormone manufactured by the corpus luteum; with estrogen, it prepares the lining of the uterus for implantation of the fertilized egg.

endometrium The inner lining of the uterus.

menstruation The expulsion of the uterine lining in menstrual animals.

ovariectomy The surgical removal of the ovaries.

has several effects: One or several *ovarian follicles,* the small spheres of cells surrounding the egg (ovum), grow into a mature *Graafian follicle,* the egg matures, and the Graafian follicle secretes estrogen (Figure 11.8).

The released estrogen also has several effects: First, in a negative feedback loop, high estrogen levels inhibit the further release of FSH. Second, estrogen stimulates the anterior pituitary to release **luteinizing hormone (LH).** Thus, as the estrogen level rises, the FSH concentration falls and LH concentration rises. Third, estrous animals experience intense sexual arousal when the estrogen level peaks.

Toward the end of the follicular phase, the follicle containing the mature egg becomes embedded in the surface of the ovary. When the LH level is at its highest, the walls of the follicle rupture, pushing the egg through the wall of the ovary into the fallopian tube. The release of the egg is called *ovulation.*

After ovulation, the luteal phase begins. LH causes the ruptured follicle to become a corpus luteum ("yellow body") (see Figure 11.8). The corpus luteum begins to secrete estrogen and another sex hormone, **progesterone,** which together prepare the lining of the uterus for implantation of a fertilized egg. This stage involves the growth of the **endometrium,** the inner lining of the uterus. If fertilization occurs, the corpus luteum continues secreting estrogen and progesterone to maintain the endometrium until the *placenta* (an organ that contains and sustains the embryo or fetus) assumes this role in the third month. However, if the egg is not fertilized, the uterine lining is reabsorbed in estrous animals or is expelled in menstrual animals in the process of **menstruation** (menses). In another negative feedback loop, progesterone also inhibits LH release. If the egg has been fertilized, progesterone secretion continues, but if the egg has not been fertilized, progesterone secretion stops, the luteal phase ends, and the next cycle begins.

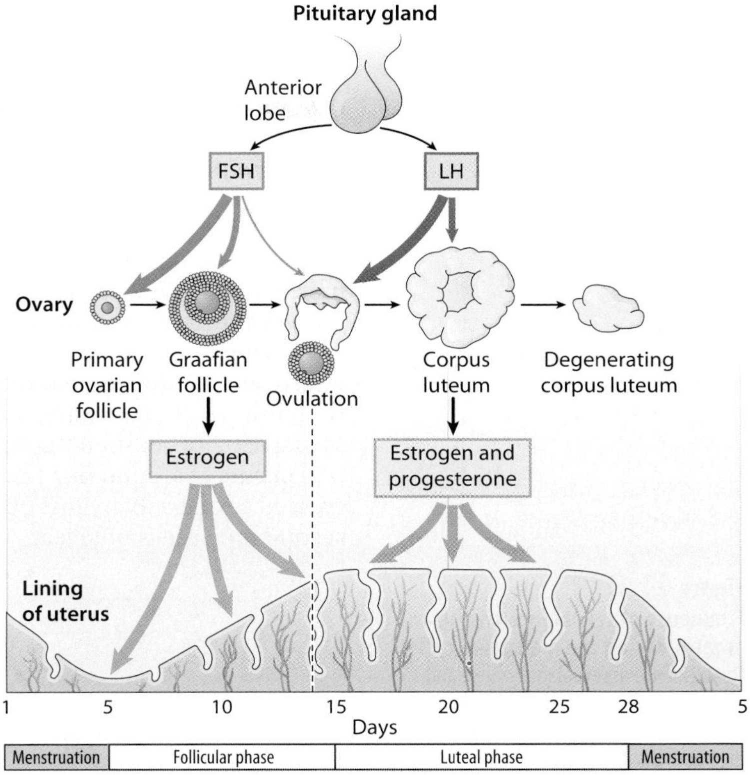

Figure 11.8

Changes in the pituitary hormones, ovaries, and uterine wall during the menstrual cycle The widths of the arrows are proportional to the level of the hormone at that time of the cycle, and their direction shows the cause-effect relationships. (From E. P. Volpe, 1979.)

What is the function of the Graafian follicle?

The influence of sex hormones on female sexual arousal and sexual behavior can be assessed by correlating the incidence of sexual behavior with hormonal changes, or, experimentally, by administering hormones during periods when they are absent in the body, and by removing the ovaries and observing the subsequent effects on sexual behavior. Considered together, the results of these studies, some of which we summarize here, reveal how sex hormones affect female sexual behavior.

Evidence for a link between estrogen level and sexual behavior comes from studies in which estrogen was administered at a time in the estrous cycle when it was normally low. Beach (1947) found that estrogen injections in female rats produce intense sexual receptivity identical to that normally occurring before ovulation. Such motivation lasts only as long as the estrogen level remains high, however. By contrast, **ovariectomy,** or surgical removal of the ovaries, produces a rapid, permanent loss of sexual receptivity that can be reversed by estrogen replacement therapy.

The influence of estrogen on sexual receptivity is not as significant in many nonhuman primates as it is in estrous animals, but it is still important. Although females of many primate species will engage in sexual activity throughout the cycle (Ford & Beach, 1951), the highest incidence occurs during the few

Some of the contraceptives now available. Note the disparity in the number of contraceptives for women compared with the number for men.

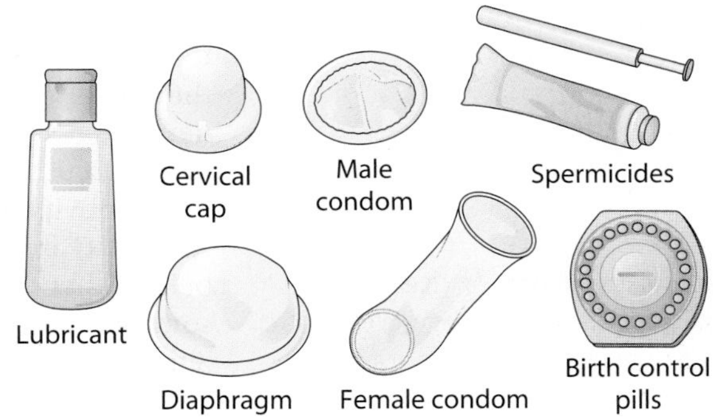

days before ovulation. This is when female behaviors that solicit mounting behavior in the male are most likely to occur (Baum & others, 1977). Genital swelling and vaginal pheromone secretion, two other effects of high estrogen levels, also increase the attraction of the male primate to the female and contribute to increased sexual activity when estrogen levels are high.

The importance of estrogen also is evident in studies of ovariectomized primates. For example, Zehr and colleagues (1998) reported virtually no female initiation of sexual activity in ovariectomized rhesus monkeys. Estrogen replacement significantly increased sexual initiation by the monkeys. In the common marmoset (a small New World monkey), however, female receptivity persists even after both ovariectomy and adrenalectomy (Dixson, 2001).

Although estrogen affects the sexual activity of the human female, its effect is clearly less significant and more variable than in nonhuman primates (Money & Ehrhardt, 1972). For example, Udry and Morris (1968) found a sharp increase in sexual activity between the end of menstruation and ovulation (recall that ovulation occurs at around day 14). The researchers also noted that women showed increased sexual activity just before menstruation (Figure 11.9). The reason for this second increase is not clear.

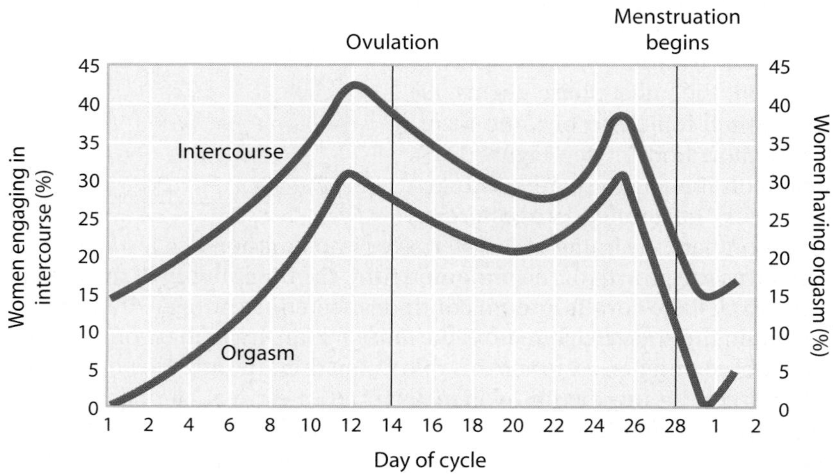

Figure 11.9

Frequency of sexual intercourse and orgasm during the menstrual cycle

The incidence of sexual intercourse and orgasm increases as estrogen level increases, up to the middle of the cycle; then both decline as estrogen declines. Note the rapid rise in sexual activity and orgasm at the end of the cycle.

→ **How does the relationship between estrogen level and sexual activity differ in estrous and menstrual animals?**

Although sexual activity is less frequent in women at some times in the menstrual cycle than at others, it does occur throughout the cycle. Obviously, factors other than estrogen influence human female sexual behavior; for many women, sexual motivation is not diminished by ovariectomy or by menopause, when estrogen production by the ovaries stops naturally. After a hysterectomy-ovariectomy or following menopause, some women receive testosterone therapy, which increases their sexual responsivity. The reason for this testosterone effect is that women (before menopause) secrete an adrenal androgen hormone similar to testosterone, called **androstenedione.** Produced continuously at low levels by the adrenal gland, androstenedione affects the sexual motivation and frequency of sexual activity of women. Removal of the adrenal gland results in a loss of or a sharp decrease in androstenedione and a subsequent reduction in sexual motivation, which can be restored by testosterone therapy (Michael, 1980). Testosterone therapy also restored several aspects of sexual function in women who had undergone both hysterectomy and oophorectomy (removal of the ovaries) (Floter & others, 2002).

Sensitivity to androstenedione provides a hormonal basis for female sexual responsivity throughout the menstrual cycle. Many primatologists (e.g., Hrdy, 1979) believe that the evolution of continuous sexual responsivity enabled humans and some nonhuman primates (such as gibbons) to establish stable pair bonding. Similarly, Wallen and Zehr (2004) have suggested that the uncoupling of fertility and sexual motivation in female primates has allowed sexual activity to be used

androstenedione An adrenal androgen hormone similar to testosterone that affects the sexual motivation of a premenopausal woman.

A human family and a gibbon family. Bonding between male and female of a mating pair helps ensure the success of raising offspring.

for social purposes, such as social attraction and the cohesion of pair bonds. Evolutionary theory holds that the stability of pair bonds promotes the care and protection of offspring.

Checkpoint

Explain how removal of the ovaries affects a female's sexual motivation.

Hormonal Influences in Males

Manufactured in the Leydig cells of the testes, testosterone plays a significant role in the arousal necessary for male sexual behavior. This is the activational role of the hormone; we discussed its organizational function earlier. Testosterone production is controlled by the hypothalamus, which releases gonadotropic-releasing hormone into the hypophyseal portal system (see Figure 2.21) and stimulates the anterior pituitary to manufacture and release luteinizing hormone (LH) into the bloodstream. LH stimulates the testes to produce and release testosterone. In mammalian adults, testosterone levels fluctuate slightly, but the adult male, human or nonhuman, remains sensitive to environmental events, such as a receptive female, that can initiate sexual behavior.

The importance of testosterone becomes apparent when it is eliminated, as in **castration.** When the testes are removed, testosterone levels plummet. This loss of testosterone typically renders a male less able, or completely unable, to be sexually aroused, which suggests that testosterone has a significant influence on a male's desire to engage in sexual activity.

The rapidity of the loss of sexual motivation after castration varies considerably among members of a species. For example, Davidson (1966) discovered that although most male rats lost their sexual interest within a few weeks of castration, some remained sexually motivated for months. Humans also show a variable loss of sexual drive and behavior following castration (Money & Ehrhardt, 1972). Bremer (1959) observed 157 Norwegian men who had agreed to be castrated to reduce the length of their prison terms for sex-related offenses. Nearly 50% showed a rapid loss of sexual motivation, 18% lost their interest within a year, and the rest continued to experience sexual motivation for several years. The data for male rats and male humans are comparable if we consider the different life spans of each species: Because the average life span of a rat is approximately 2 years, a rat retaining sexual motivation 5 months after castration is comparable to a human retaining this motivation for several years.

If testosterone loss eliminates sexual motivation, then testosterone administration should restore it, and in castrated human and nonhuman males it does indeed produce a rapid return of sexual responsivity. For example, Grunt and Young (1952) found that male guinea pigs typically showed a gradual reduction in sexual behavior over the 16 weeks following castration (Figure 11.10). Subsequent testosterone injections then produced a steady increase in sexual motivation, reaching the level of uncastrated control animals within approximately 6 to 9 weeks. Without

castration The removal of the testes.

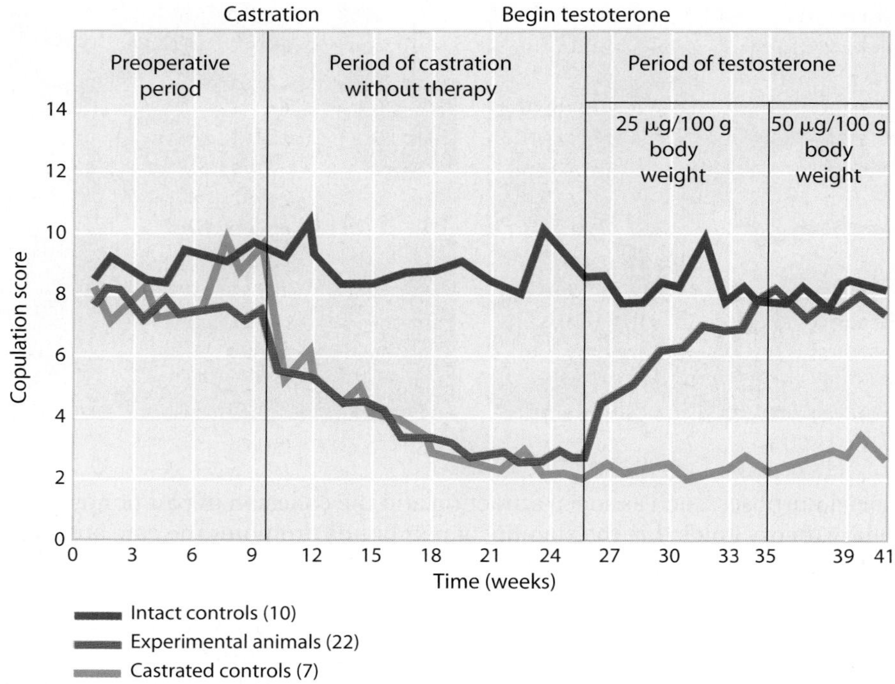

Figure 11.10
The effects of castration and subsequent testosterone administration on the sexual activity of male guinea pigs Both experimental and castrated control animals showed a decline in copulation after castration. Testosterone replacement led to a resumption of sexual activity in the experimental animals.

➡ **Is the effect of testosterone replacement therapy the same in humans and guinea pigs?**

testosterone injections, castrated control animals showed no resumption of sexual behavior. Similar increases in sexual motivation, as indicated by performance of sex-related activities, follow hormone replacement therapy in castrated male hamsters (Havens & Rose, 1992), rats (Everitt & Stacey, 1987), and humans (Money, 1961).

Interestingly, doubling the effective dose of testosterone did not increase sexual motivation further in castrated guinea pigs (Grunt & Young, 1952), or in castrated men (Bermant & Davidson, 1974). Apparently, a critical level of testosterone is necessary to produce sexual motivation, but once this level is reached, more testosterone has no additional effect.

➤Checkpoint

Describe how castration affects a male's sexual motivation.

Pheromones and Reproductive Activity

As we indicated earlier, estrogen levels peak just before ovulation in estrous mammals. This peak corresponds to a defined period of sexual receptivity that lasts for several days before ovulation. The receptive female secretes vaginal **pheromones,** chemicals released into the external environment, that make her attractive to males. Once a male is attracted, the estrous female readily accepts his advances. When the female is not in heat, she does not produce pheromones and thus does not attract males. Any male that mistakenly makes sexual advances outside the estrous period is rebuffed.

Pheromones also play a role in regulating reproductive cycles. For example, in the absence of a male, the estrous cycles of group-housed female mice are suppressed, a phenomenon called the *Lee-Boot effect* (van der Lee & Boot, 1955). Exposure to either a male mouse or his urine restores cycling in the female—the *Whitten effect* (Bronson & Whitten, 1968); and the presence of a strange male (or his urine) terminates pregnancy in female mice—the *Bruce effect* (Bruce, 1960). All of these phenomena depend on a structure close to the olfactory bulbs, the vomeronasal organ, which we discuss further below.

An apparent synchrony in reproductive cycles of women living in close proximity, such as students in women's dormitories, was first reported more than 3 decades ago (McClintock, 1971). Since that time, there have been many similar reports (McClintock, 1998). For example, menstrual synchrony has been reported in a group of women working together (Weller & others, 1999a), among sisters and

pheromone A chemical released into the external environment for communication within a species; can be used to signal reproductive readiness.

close friends (Weller & others, 1999b), and among a group of Bedouin women (members of nomadic desert tribes of the Middle East and North Africa) in nuclear families (Weller & Weller, 1997).

Despite these reports of menstrual synchrony, the phenomenon remains controversial. Critics generally cite methodological artifacts, such as cycle variability and recall biases, which they contend, if taken into account, would rule out menstrual synchrony (Arden & Dye, 1998; Schank, 2000, 2002). From an evolutionary standpoint, one might argue that synchrony of cycles should be avoided, as it puts females in direct competition with each other in their attempts to mate with high-quality males (Schank, 2001a, 2001b, 2004). As you would expect, those who find evidence for menstrual synchrony have defended their findings against such criticism (Graham, 2002; Weller & Weller, 2002a, 2002b). Obviously, this is an area that will benefit from further research.

If menstrual synchrony does exist, what is its likely mechanism? It could be produced by substances in axillary (underarm) secretions. Preti and colleagues (1986) exposed women to axillary extract from a group of female donors and found that the time of menses onset in the exposed women shifted toward the donor cycle; this change did not occur in women exposed to blank/ethanol samples (samples with the odor only of the ethanol base).

Another cycle-related phenomenon observed in women is that the menstrual cycle becomes more "regular" if a woman has weekly sexual activity with a man than if she does not. This increased regularity was also observed in sexually inactive women if they were exposed to axillary extract from donor males, but not in control women exposed to blank/ethanol samples (Cutler & others, 1986). More recently, Preti and colleagues (2003) observed that male axillary extracts stimulated the release of LH in women, which affects the length and timing of the menstrual cycle. The pheromonal extracts also reduced tension in the women and increased their feelings of relaxation.

Oxytocin and Reproductive Activity

Oxytocin is a neuropeptide manufactured in the paraventricular and supraoptic nuclei of the hypothalamus and stored in and released from the posterior pituitary gland (Chapter 2). Oxytocin stimulates the birth process (labor) and milk secretion from the breasts; in males, it stimulates contractions of the prostate gland (Chapter 4).

In addition to its release into the bloodstream, oxytocin is also released into the brain. Evidence from a wide range of animal studies has implicated this release of oxytocin into the CNS in reproductive behaviors, such as sexual arousal, orgasm, and nest building, and in such specifically maternal behaviors as suckling and bonding with offspring (Anderson-Hunt & Dennerstein, 1995). For example, administering oxytocin directly into the brain resulted in maternal and reproductive activities in rats placed in a state of reproductive readiness with gonadal steroids, and the administration of oxytocin antagonists or creation of hypothalamic lesions blocked such behaviors (Insel, 1992). Caldwell and Moe (1999) found that infusions of a combination of oxytocin and estradiol into the medial preoptic area in the anterior hypothalamus or the medial basal hypothalamus significantly increased the sexual receptivity of rats.

Oxytocin has also been found to affect reproductive activities in male rodents. Rao (1995) cited reports of the potent effect of oxytocin on male activities, such as penile erection, mounting behavior, and side-by-side contact with other animals.

Oxytocin apparently plays a major role in the formation of long-lasting pair bonds in monogamous prairie voles (Young, 1999; Young & others, 2001). Compared with the nonmonogamous animals, the monogamous prairie voles have a greater density of oxytocin receptors in the nucleus accumbens (Young & others), a structure that we discussed in Chapter 5 in connection with reward circuits in the brain. When the receptors of prairie vole females are blocked by oxytocin antagonists, the animals fail to establish long-lasting pair bonds with

oxytocin A posterior pituitary hormone that plays a role in reproductive activities, such as sexual arousal, orgasm, nest building, suckling, and bonding with offspring.

males. Because of the location of the oxytocin receptors, the researchers hypothesized that oxytocin facilitates social attachment through its effect on the reward pathways.

➤Checkpoint

What are pheromones and how are they related to reproductive activities?

REVIEW

- ➤ The ability of the male to be aroused depends primarily on the sex hormone testosterone.
- ➤ In animal studies, pheromones affect reproductive cycles in female mammals in the Lee-Boot effect, the Whitten effect, and the Bruce effect; similar phenomena have been observed in women.
- ➤ Oxytocin plays an important role in reproductive activities, such as sexual arousal, orgasm, nest building, suckling, and bonding with offspring.

Neural Influences in Females

The hypothalamus and the cerebral cortex have important functions in sexual receptivity and sexual behavior in females, both human and nonhuman (Figure 11.11). For example, the hypothalamus indirectly controls the release of the female sex hormones. Neural activity in the medial basal area of the hypothalamus

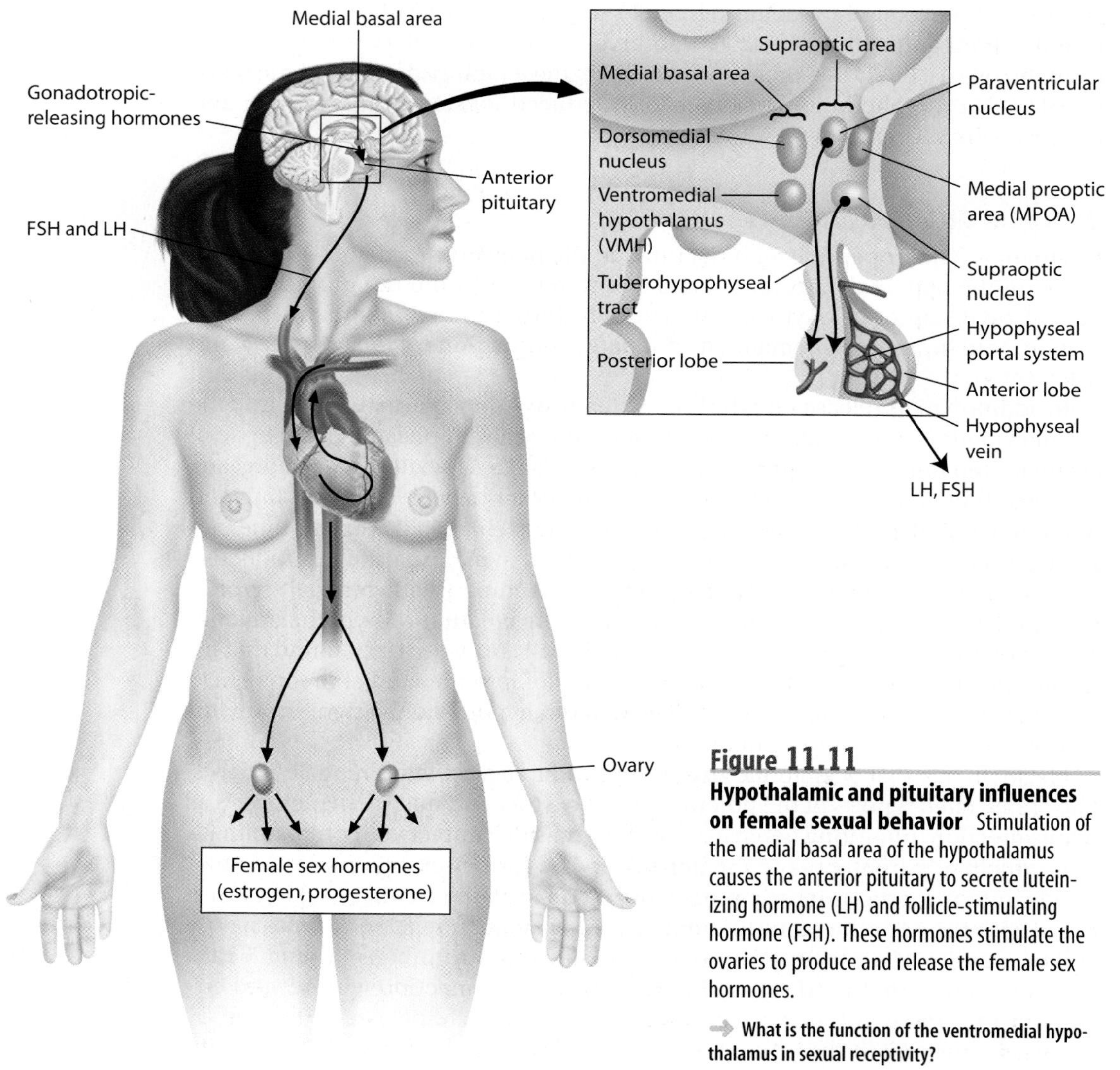

Figure 11.11

Hypothalamic and pituitary influences on female sexual behavior Stimulation of the medial basal area of the hypothalamus causes the anterior pituitary to secrete luteinizing hormone (LH) and follicle-stimulating hormone (FSH). These hormones stimulate the ovaries to produce and release the female sex hormones.

➡ **What is the function of the ventromedial hypothalamus in sexual receptivity?**

stimulates the anterior pituitary gland to release the gonadotropic-stimulating hormones LH and FSH into the bloodstream (Robison & Sawyer, 1987). LH and FSH stimulate the ovaries to produce and release the female sex hormones.

To test this role of the hypothalamus, Robison and Sawyer (1987) lesioned the medial basal area of the hypothalamus in female cats, completely eliminating both sex hormone production and sexual activity. Estrogen replacement therapy reinstated sexual motivation but not hormone production, providing further evidence for the role of the medial basal hypothalamus in releasing gonadotropic-stimulating hormones.

Given that estrogen replacement therapy reinstates sexual motivation in animals with a lesioned medial basal area, a different hypothalamic area must be responsible for the influence of estrogen on sexual behavior. Many studies indicate that this area is the **ventromedial hypothalamus (VMH)** (see Figure 11.11) (Kow & others, 1994). For example, estrogen acts on the VMH to promote the lordosis response in female rats, and estrogen treatment of the VMH actually increases dendritic spines in the structure (Flanagan-Cato & others, 2001). Electrical stimulation of the VMH increased sexual behavior in female rats, and sexual behavior was eliminated following damage to the VMH (Pfaff & Sakuma, 1979a, 1979b). Loss of sexual response after lesioning reflects the inability of the animals to detect estrogen, the hormone responsible for sexual arousal. The presence of estrogen-sensitive receptors in the VMH would account for this lack of response to estrogen administration in VMH-lesioned animals. Axons from the VMH project to the periaqueductal gray of the midbrain, which in turn projects to the spinal cord. The neural message from the VMH, activated by estrogen, triggers the lordosis response of the female (Pfaff, 1997).

The **medial preoptic area (MPOA),** located in the anterior hypothalamus (see Figure 11.11), seems to be involved in eliciting sexual behavior in females. Stimulating the MPOA with microinjections of galanin produces female-typical behavior (Bloch & others, 1996), and damage to the MPOA negatively affects mating behavior in female rats (Guarraci & others, 2004). MPOA activity stimulates the mesolimbic reinforcement system. Activity in this system is stimulated by reinforcing stimuli—in this case, by the presence of a sexually active male or copulation. Either significantly increases the release of dopamine in the nucleus accumbens of female rats (Pfaus & others, 1995), which helps explain why sexual behavior is so pleasurable. The MPOA is significantly smaller in females than in males, but the reason for this difference is not apparent.

The cerebral cortex seems to have a minimal effect on nonhuman female sexual behavior. For example, in one experiment with rats, lordosis behavior was retained in decorticated newborn females, although behaviors such as hopping, darting, and rejecting were almost entirely eliminated (Carter & others, 1982). The decorticated animals were mounted by males at least as often as were the intact-cortex controls.

The cortex does appear to provide some organization of female sexual behavior in nonhuman mammals. For example, the sexual response of cortically lesioned female rats, rabbits, cats, and dogs is less integrated than that of normal animals (Ford & Beach, 1951). Although the sexual behavior of the lesioned animals is organized well enough to permit copulation, they do not show the normal orderly sequence of sexual behaviors. There are no comparable data for the role of the cortex in the sexual behavior of female primates, human or nonhuman.

ventromedial hypothalamus (VMH) The hypothalamic area responsible for the effect of estrogen on sexual behavior.

medial preoptic area (MPOA) A group of neurons in the anterior hypothalamus that influences female sexual responsivity.

Neural Influences in Males

Sexual arousal and behavior in men does not result only from testosterone. CNS areas are also involved, including the hypothalamus, the amygdala, and the cerebral cortex. The hypothalamus influences sexual behavior indirectly by stimulating the manufacture and release of testosterone and directly by eliciting sexual behavior. Stimulation of the *medial basal area* causes the release of gonadotropic-releasing hormones that are transmitted to the anterior pituitary gland, where they trigger the release of LH and FSH into the bloodstream (Figure 11.12). LH

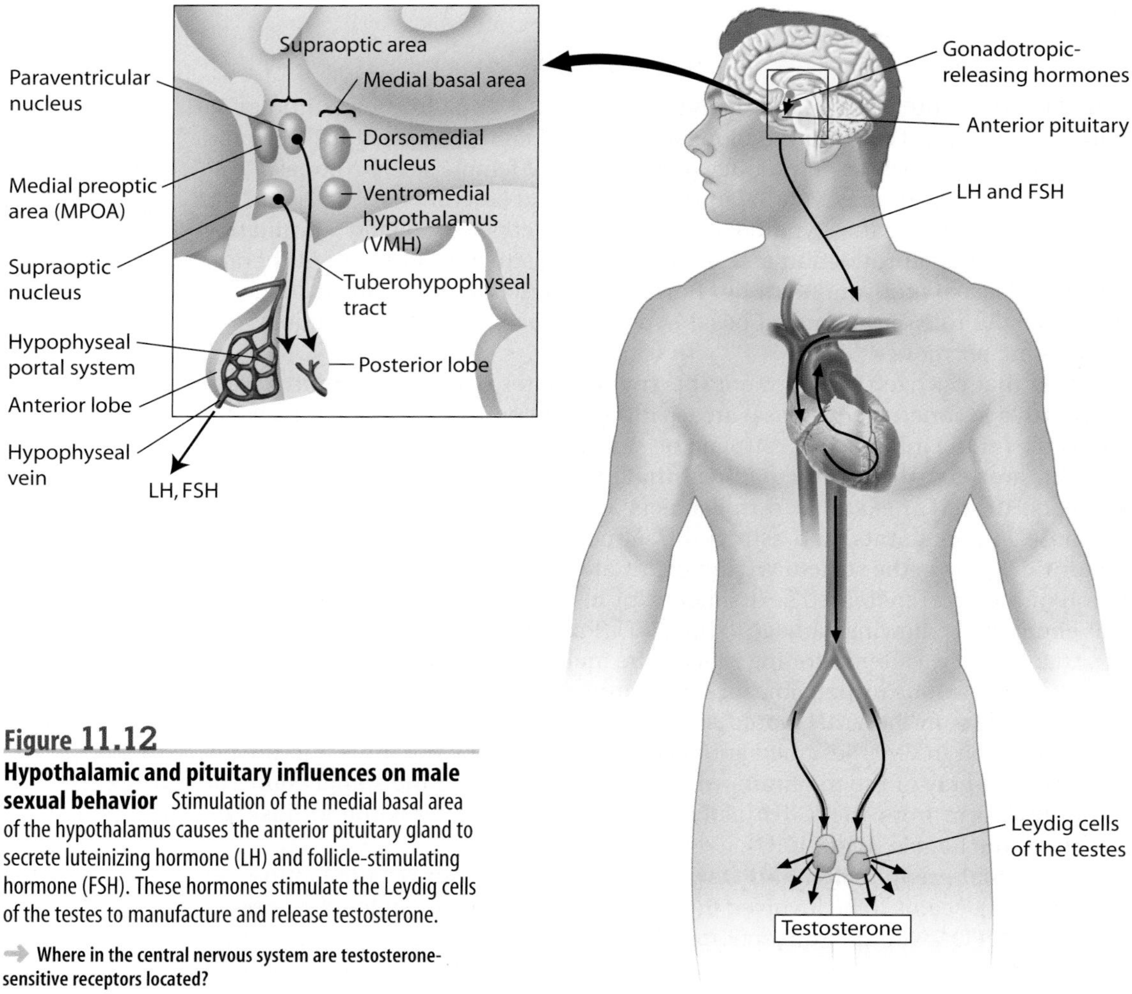

Figure 11.12

Hypothalamic and pituitary influences on male sexual behavior Stimulation of the medial basal area of the hypothalamus causes the anterior pituitary gland to secrete luteinizing hormone (LH) and follicle-stimulating hormone (FSH). These hormones stimulate the Leydig cells of the testes to manufacture and release testosterone.

➡ **Where in the central nervous system are testosterone-sensitive receptors located?**

affects the Leydig cells of the testes, stimulating them to synthesize and secrete testosterone; FSH is responsible for the production of sperm.

In males, as in females, the MPOA is involved in sexual activity. For example, the MPOA (see Figure 11.12) contains receptors stimulated by testosterone to produce sexual responsivity (Coolen & Wood, 1999), as has been confirmed in many studies. In addition, microinjections of the peptide neurotransmitter galanin into the MPOA of male rats increased male-typical mounting behavior (Bloch & others, 1998). Destruction of the MPOA had the opposite effect of stimulation, producing severe deficits in copulatory behavior (Liu & others, 1997; Paredes & others, 1998). In addition, Paredes and colleagues found that male rats with MPOA damage changed their partner preference postoperatively, preferring to spend more time with another male than with a receptive female. An androgen antagonist had different effects depending on the part of the MPOA in which it was implanted: Implantation into the anteroventral MPOA suppressed sexual behavior (copulation), whereas implantation into the posterodorsal MPOA reduced sexual motivation (partner preference) (McGinnis & others, 2002). The MPOA is apparently involved in the motivation of male sexual behavior rather than in the execution or regulation of such behavior (Paredes, 2003).

In the rat castration studies cited earlier, testosterone was injected into the bloodstream. To determine whether testosterone administration affects the hypothalamus, the hormone was injected directly into the anterior hypothalamus of castrated rats, and the animals regained sexual motivation (Davidson, 1980). Earlier studies on testosterone replacement therapy found that it did not reinstate sexual arousal in animals with anterior hypothalamic lesions, suggesting that such lesions make males insensitive to the hormone and thus incapable of responding to sexual stimulation (Heimer & Larsson, 1966/1967). These earlier studies provided evidence that the key hypothalamic area for sexual behavior is the anterior hypothalamus; more recent studies have narrowed it down to the MPOA.

Dopamine is one of the neurotransmitters in the MPOA, and sexual behavior has been associated with dopamine release in male rats (Putnam & others, 2003; Sato & others, 1995) and in female rats (Matuszewich & others, 2000). Dopamine agonists injected into the MPOA of rats facilitated male sexual behavior, whereas dopamine antagonists inhibited it (Dominguez & others, 2001). The same studies showed that damage to the medial amygdala, which sends olfactory information to the MPOA, impaired copulation in male rats; copulatory ability was restored by injection of a dopamine agonist into the MPOA.

The presence of a receptive female does not trigger dopamine release in castrated male rats, although there is evidence that dopamine has been synthesized normally and is available for release (Hull & others, 1997). Apparently, testosterone promotes nitric oxide synthesis in the MPOA, and this in turn facilitates dopamine release (Hull & others). In one study, dopamine release in the MPOA produced by testosterone injection was correlated with restored sexual behavior in castrated male rats (Putnam & others, 2001), which provides further evidence for the importance of the MPOA in male sexual behavior.

The MPOA normally triggers sexual behavior only if testosterone is available and a receptive female is detected. Testosterone-sensitive neurons in the MPOA react to the hormone, and several other brain structures send input to the MPOA about the presence of a receptive female. For example, receptors in the **vomeronasal organ,** a specialized sensory organ separate from the main olfactory system (Figure 11.13), detect pheromones released by a receptive female (Holy & others, 2000). Because the vomeronasal organ is separate from the olfactory system, the organ probably does not respond to airborne molecules; rather, it appears to react to compounds found in fluid substances, which would explain why the organ is involved in such rodent phenomena as the Bruce, Lee-Boot, and Whitten effects. The fluid substances are pumped into the organ whenever the animal is stimulated by a novel situation, which suggests that the organ may have functions beyond the communication of reproductive information (Meredith, 1994; Meredith & others, 1980).

The presence and possible functions of the vomeronasal organ in humans are poorly understood at the present time (Besli & others, 2004). Besli and coworkers performed nasal examinations on 346 adult subjects and on 21 cadaver heads and identified the organ in 32% of the subjects and 38% of the cadaver heads. Halpern and Martinez-Marcos (2003) cited anatomical studies indicating the presence of the organ in human adults and other reports suggesting that the system might be functional. However, it should be noted that critical components of the vomeronasal system found in nonprimate mammals are not present in adult humans, which indicates that the system in humans may not function in the same way as that of other mammals (Wysocki & Preti, 2004). These missing critical components include bipolar receptor cells and axonal projections to the brain from bipolar neurons (both present in the fetus but absent in adults) and an identifiable accessory olfactory bulb. After an extensive review, Meredith (2001) concluded that further research is needed to resolve the conflicting evidence for and against chemical communication in humans involving the vomeronasal organ. However, based on molecular phylogenetic studies, Keverne (2004) concluded that pheromones acting on the vomeronasal organ probably play little or no role in human sexual behavior.

In nonprimate mammals, the neurons of the vomeronasal organ project to the accessory olfactory bulb, which in turn sends information about a receptive female to the *medial amygdaloid nucleus* (Keverne, 1999). In support of this functional pathway is the finding in rats that the presence of a

vomeronasal organ A specialized sensory organ, separate from the main olfactory system, that detects pheromones released by a receptive female.

Figure 11.13

The vomeronasal system of a rodent (hamster) and a man As shown here, this system is completely separate from the olfactory system.

➡ In the male hamster, which part of the amygdala receives information about a receptive female?

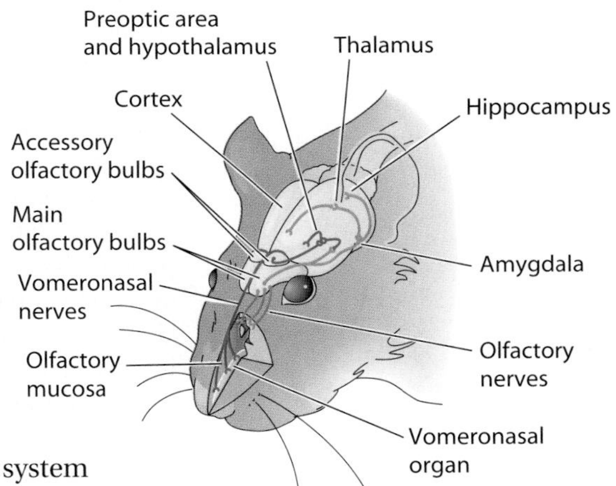

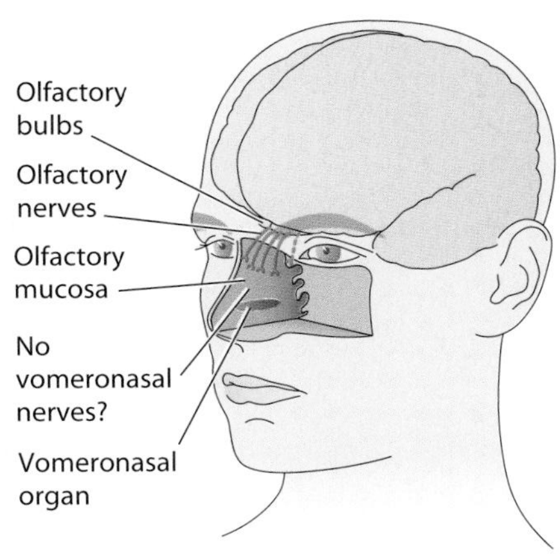

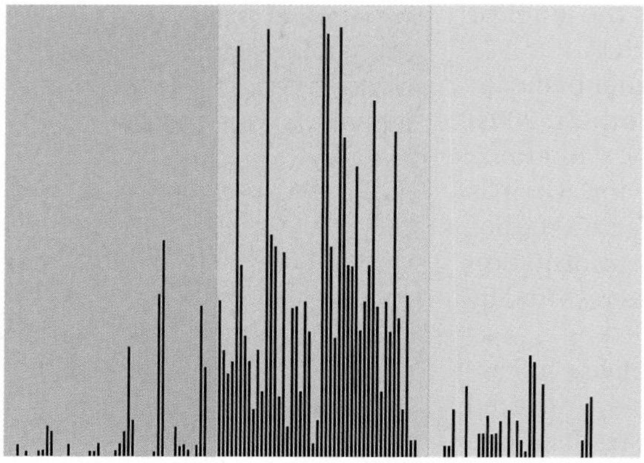

Figure 11.14
The role of the medial amygdaloid nucleus in male sexual behavior
This trace shows the level of activation of a cell in a male rat's medial amygdaloid nucleus before (blue), during (light red), and after (green) exposure to a receptive female rat (Minerbo & others, 1994). "C" indicates copulatory bouts.

→ **How does a receptive female rat activate the medial amygdaloid nucleus in a male rat?**

receptive female increases the rate of firing of cells in the medial amygdaloid nucleus of the male (Minerbo & others, 1994) (Figure 11.14). Electrical stimulation of the nucleus can elicit sexual behavior in male rats even in the presence of a nonestrous female (Stark & others, 1998); chemical stimulation produces increased levels of extracellular dopamine in the MPOA, which is associated with sexual behavior (Dominguez & Hull, 2001).

The medial amygdaloid nucleus is directly connected to the MPOA, and this connection conveys information about the odor of a receptive female to the MPOA (Wood, 1998). Axons from the MPOA project to the ventral midbrain via the medial forebrain bundle (MFB) fiber system, which is part of the mesolimbic reinforcement system (Chapter 5). Activity in this system is stimulated by reinforcing stimuli—in this case, by a receptive female. The ventral midbrain relays information from the MPOA to the basal ganglia, which initiates male-typical copulatory behavior.

Unlike the situation in females, the cerebral cortex plays an important role in male sexual behavior. One possible reason for this difference is that, in nonhuman mammals, the repertoire of the male requires more sensory and motor coordination than that of the female. In addition, male sexual arousal relies heavily on the sight and smell of a receptive female, whereas female sexual arousal depends mainly on her hormonal state.

In an early study reporting evidence for the involvement of the cerebral cortex in male sexual behavior, no animal exhibited copulatory behavior if more than 60% of its cortex were removed, but the loss of sexual activity appeared to be independent of where the damage occurred (Beach, 1940). Beach suggested that the cortex performs such functions as organizing the motor responses involved in sexual activity, detecting the sexual content of sensory information, and storing memories of past sexual experiences. A malfunctioning cortex can lead to either a misdirected sexual response or a failure to engage in sexual behavior. For example, large cortical lesions, especially in the frontal cortex, can result in a decline in sexual activity (Larsson, 1964). The more extensive the lesion, the greater the loss of sexual responsivity. More recently, experimenters have reported that medial prefrontal lesions profoundly affect sexual behavior in the male rat, at least temporarily (Agmo & others, 1995). The researchers suggested that the damaged area may be more important for initiating sexual behavior than for its execution. Hernandez-Gonzalez and colleagues (1998) provided further evidence for the involvement of the frontal cortex in the sexual activity of the male rat. The experimenters reported that frontal lobe activity, as shown in EEGs, is related to the animal's sexual behavior.

The temporal lobe, which receives sensory information and analyzes it to determine the availability of an appropriate sexual partner, is crucial to normal sexual behavior, in humans and other animals. When the temporal cortex functions normally, animals display sexual behavior only toward appropriate partners. However, temporal lobe defects can result in sexual behavior toward inappropriate objects (e.g., a member of another species or an inanimate object). In a classic study, Heinrich Klüver and Paul Bucy (1939) found that bilateral temporal lobectomies led to aberrant sexual behavior in male rhesus monkeys. The brain-damaged monkeys exhibited increased sexual activity by themselves and toward each other. In a later study, more circumscribed lesions of the temporal lobes were performed, destroying the amygdala and the pyriform cortex in cats (Schreiner & Kling, 1953). The researchers reported dramatic changes in sexual activity in the lesioned animals. In one case, as seen in a film made of the experiment, a cat attempted to copulate successively with a large dog, a chicken, and a monkey. When four lesioned male cats were placed together, the film shows what the experimenters dubbed "tandem copulation"—four cats, one atop the other.

Some human males with temporal lobe damage also show changes in sexual behavior. In 1955, Terzian and Ore reported that men with such damage exhibited a strong sexual response to inappropriate objects. Since then, the Klüver-Bucy syndrome has been observed in several men following temporal lobe damage, although this condition is apparently rare. Goscinski and colleagues (1997) reported the Klüver-Bucy syndrome in men with temporal lobe damage resulting from head trauma, and the syndrome also has been reported to result from temporal lobe damage associated with Alzheimer's disease, Pick's disease, and herpes encephalitis, as well as head trauma (Varon & others, 2003). A case of the syndrome has even been reported in a woman who sustained temporal lobe damage in an automobile accident (Salim & others, 2002). Finally, an early study reported a strong relationship between certain sexual behaviors, including fetishism, transvestitism, and voyeurism, and temporal lobe dysfunction (Kolarsky & others, 1967).

Checkpoint

Compare and contrast the roles of the hypothalamus and the cortex in the sexual behavior of female and male rats.

REVIEW

- The medial basal area of the hypothalamus governs hormone secretion.
- In human and nonhuman mammals, activity in the ventromedial hypothalamus (VMH) in females and the medial preoptic area (MPOA) of the anterior hypothalamus in males triggers sexual behavior.
- In female rats, the VMH projects to the periaqueductal gray of the midbrain, which projects to the spinal cord to stimulate the lordosis response.
- The influence of the cortex in women is unknown, but in nonhuman females it appears to organize the sexual response and inhibit sexual behavior.
- In male rats, the vomeronasal organ detects a pheromone secreted by a receptive female and sends this information to the medial amygdaloid nucleus, then to the MPOA, then via the medial forebrain bundle to the ventral midbrain, which sends information to the basal ganglia, the area responsible for integrating male-typical sexual behavior.
- In male mammals, the cerebral cortex organizes the motor responses involved in sexual activity, detects the sexual content of sensory information, and stores memories of past sexual experiences. The temporal lobe identifies sexually appropriate partners.

Psychological Processes Governing Sexual Activity

Sexual arousal and sexual behavior are controlled by psychological processes (mediated, of course, by biological processes) as well as by purely biological ones. Classical conditioning is one way in which a psychological process affects sexual activity. In this form of learning (Chapter 14), environmental stimuli acquire the ability to elicit sexual arousal and to motivate sexual behavior. For example, a situation (time, place, sounds, smells) in which a person has experienced sexual satisfaction in the past might more easily produce sexual arousal on subsequent occasions.

The Influence of Erotic Stimuli

Sexually explicit material, such as films or photographs, can affect sexual arousal. For example, Howard and colleagues (1971) showed male subjects an erotic movie and simultaneously recorded penis size changes as a measure of sexual arousal (Figure 11.15). During the first few minutes of the film, most of the men showed a rapid increase in penis size, and this sexual arousal continued throughout the 20 minute film. Penis size decreased

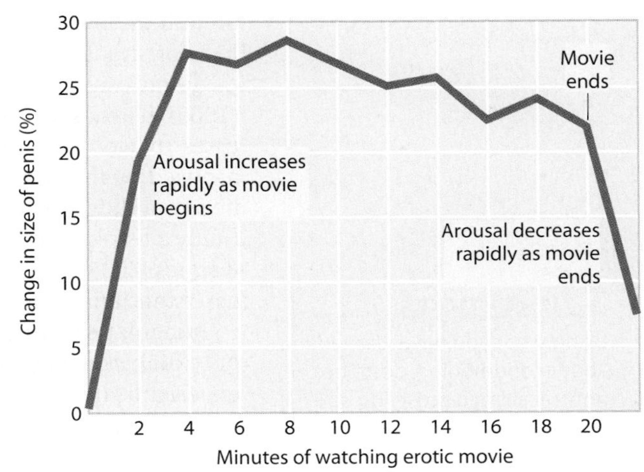

Figure 11.15
The sexual arousal of male subjects while watching an erotic movie
Sexual arousal increases rapidly when the movie begins and declines quickly after the movie ends.

→ **What nonvisual erotic stimuli can produce sexual arousal?**

acquired sexual motive A learned sexual response to a stimulus produced through conditioning.

rapidly when the movie ended. Similarly, when women were shown visual sexual stimuli, they responded with vaginal vasocongestion and self-reported sexual arousal (Laan & others, 1995). Both men and women became more sexually aroused when they paid close attention and became absorbed in the activities portrayed in erotic film segments than when they were distracted or perceived the stimuli as aversive (Koukounas & McCabe, 1997, 2001). Moreover, the perceived sexual arousal of the participants was positively related to the experienced entertainment and curiosity value of the stimuli and negatively related to boredom. Although these results applied to both sexes, the researchers reported that men experienced more arousal than women, and women were more likely to be disgusted by the content of some films.

Sexual arousal can also be produced by nonvisual stimuli. For example, listening to explicit sexual material produced intense sexual arousal in both female and male college students, whereas nonexplicit material had no effect (Heiman, 1975). An experiment that examined the arousing effects on men of different modes of presentation of erotic material found that film presentation produced the greatest arousal, with fantasy (subjects were told to fantasize sexual activities from a written script) producing the least (Julien & Over, 1988). Slides, spoken text, and written text produced intermediate levels of arousal and did not differ significantly from each other. Exposure to sexually arousing stimuli may also motivate sexual activity. For example, exposing men to erotic slides not only produced sexual arousal but also motivated sexual intercourse once the men returned home to their wives (Cattell & others, 1972).

Acquired Sexual Motives

Not everyone becomes aroused when viewing or hearing sexually explicit material, so the response might possibly be developed through conditioning. An **acquired sexual motive** is a learned sexual response to a stimulus that occurs through conditioning. Several studies indicate that neutral stimuli paired with sexual arousal in both nonhuman animals (Gutierrez & Domjan, 1997; Pfaus & others, 2003) and humans (Hoffmann & others, 2004; Plaud & Martini, 1999) acquire the ability to produce sexual arousal and motivate sexual behavior.

For example, researchers presented a red light to male Japanese quail as a receptive female quail approached (Domjan & others, 1986). The repeated pairing of the red light with the arrival of the receptive female eventually caused the male to become excited by the red light alone. Further, the presence of the red light led the male to copulate more readily with a receptive female, and the male quail even developed a preference for the area of the cage where the red light appeared. Sexual arousal and sexual behavior also could be conditioned in female quail, although the behaviors conditioned were different: approach in the male and squatting in the female (Gutierrez & Domjan, 1997). Zamble and coworkers (1986) found conditioning of sexual arousal in rats, and noted that this could provide the basis for an animal model of the conditioning of sexual arousal in humans to unusual objects or situations.

As an example of how such sexual arousal might be conditioned, Rachman (1966) instructed male subjects to view pictures of nude women together with pictures of women's shoes. After several conditioning trials, the subjects became aroused by the pictures of shoes alone. Although the origins of shoe fetishes may lie in conditioning experiences, the sexual arousal in Rachman's study was not actually a fetish: A fetish is a condition in which a person (or animal; Koksal and colleagues [2004] developed an animal model of fetishism with male Japanese quails) can experience sexual satisfaction only with the fetish object.

Imagination and reminiscence apparently play important roles in the strength of sexual arousal by a particular stimulus. When people replay a satisfying sexual experience in their minds, the ability of the conditioned stimulus to produce sexual arousal is enhanced.

➤Checkpoint

Using what you have learned about conditioning, describe how recalling a satisfying sexual experience with Doug could sexually arouse Paula.

REVIEW

- Sexually explicit material can positively affect sexual arousal in both women and men.
- Through classical conditioning, environmental stimuli such as a situation, object, or image associated with past sexual pleasure may produce sexual arousal.

Gender Identity and Sexual Preference

Heterosexuals engage in sexual activity with people of the opposite sex, whereas homosexuals are sexually attracted to same-sex partners (*hetero* means "different," *homo* means "same"). In one widely cited survey, Laumann and colleagues (1994) have suggested that the homosexuality rate in the United States is 2.8% for men and 1.4% for women. But how is sexual preference determined? Is it primarily the result of biological predisposition, or "nature," or mainly the result of environmental experiences from a young age, or "nurture"?

The Biological Basis of Gender Identity

Recall our earlier differentiation of the terms "gender" and "sex": *Gender* refers to learned roles, attitudes, and responsibilities of women and men, whereas *sex* refers to the different biological characteristics of men and women. We have discussed how and when sex is determined. But when does "gender" develop? And why, for some individuals, do their "assigned" gender and sex seem to diverge?

According to the well-known sex researcher John Money, given that gender/sexual identity is a social construction, "sex reassignment" is possible if done early enough, that is, before about 18 months of age (Money & Ehrhardt, 1972). If the change is made before this age, a biological male, for example, should be able to develop the sexual preference and gender identity of a biological female.

One widely publicized case of early sex reassignment, however (a case conducted by John Money at Johns Hopkins), argues strongly for the predominant influence of biological factors in the development of sexual preferences and gender identity (Colapinto, 2000; Diamond & Sigmundson, 1997). As an infant, Bruce/Brenda (later David Reimer) lost his penis in a botched circumcision. The parents were advised by Money to raise Bruce as a girl (Brenda). Because Bruce/Brenda had an identical twin brother with undamaged genitals, Money saw this as a golden opportunity to validate his theory of the social construction of gender identity.

Apparently, Brenda experienced a truly horrible childhood, ridiculed and socially isolated by her peers for her masculine behavior (Colapinto, 2000). On learning the truth at age 14, Bruce/Brenda immediately elected to become a boy. He stopped the hormonal treatments designed to make him more feminine and underwent mastectomy to remove the breasts the hormonal treatments had caused him to develop. After years of psychotherapy to help him deal with his childhood, David Reimer spent more than a decade trying to live a normal life as a man, with a wife and stepchildren. It was not to be, however, as Reimer lost his job, was separated from his wife and family, and, on May 24, 2004, committed suicide (Colapinto, 2004). He was 38 years old.

As a result of the Bruce/Brenda case and other similar ones (e.g., Phornphutkul & others, 2000), in 2000 the American Academy of Pediatrics (AAP) altered its recommendation about the sex rearing of infants born with ambiguous genitals. The AAP statement acknowledges the historical assumption that psychosexual development is largely the result of the rearing environment, but goes on to cite the recent evidence indicating that the effect of testosterone on the fetal brain may irreversibly determine male sexual orientation. Thus, the AAP suggests extreme caution before recommending a sex rearing different from the chromosomal sex of the child (American Academy of Pediatrics, 2000).

The Biological Basis of Sexual Preference

What causes sexual preference? Some theories have suggested that it is genetically determined; others have proposed that differences in sexual preference are mainly the result of hormonal differences or differences in brain structure(s) that arise during development. Of course, these possibilities may not be mutually exclusive, as hormones and brain structures are at least in part genetically determined. Developmental factors, too, have been suggested as responsible for differences in sexual preference. We present and evaluate evidence for these ideas below.

Genetic Factors in Sexual Preference

Biological explanations for differences in sexual preference include genetic factors. For example, Kallman (1952) reported a 100% concordance rate for sexual preference among identical (monozygotic) twins; that is, both twins were homosexual or both were heterosexual. Among fraternal (dizygotic) twins, the concordance rate was only 10%, the same as for any pair of siblings. In a study of monozygotic and dizygotic Australian twins, Kirk and colleagues (2000) also found a higher concordance rate for homosexuality, but at 50% to 60% for females and approximately 30% for males, the concordance rate in this study was considerably lower than the 100% rate of Kallman. Researchers also found evidence for a high concordance rate for sexual preference in twins, with greater resemblance between monozygotic than dizygotic twins (Kendler & others, 2000). Evidence for *heritability* (the degree to which a characteristic, such as homosexuality, is determined by genetics) has been found in female subjects taken from the Minnesota Twin Registry but not in men from the same source (Hershberger, 1997).

Is there evidence for a "homosexual" gene (or genes)? Research by molecular biologist Dean Hamer and colleagues (1993) suggested that there might be. To begin his search for a genetic contribution to sexual orientation, Hamer looked at the rate of homosexuality among the male relatives of 76 homosexual men. He found that the incidence of homosexual preference in these male family members was considerably higher than in his whole sample (114 families of homosexual men) and that there were more gay relatives on the mother's side of the family, suggesting that male homosexuality might be passed from one generation to the next through women. Hamer next studied a selected group of 40 families with pairs of gay brothers and no evidence for nonmaternal transmission. In this subgroup, the researchers found a high correlation between homosexual orientation and markers on the X chromosome (inherited, of course, from the mother) in 33 of the pairs of brothers tested. This genetic marker was on Xq28, a region of the long arm of the X chromosome.

Hamer and colleagues then extended their initial research by studying DNA linkages in two series of families with pairs of gay brothers or lesbian sisters (Hu & others, 1995). The linkage between the markers on Xq28 and sexual orientation was again found for the males, but not for the females. The researchers concluded that the Xq28 region has a locus influencing sexual orientation in men but not in women.

More recently, Hamer and his group have performed a full genome scan of male sexual orientation using a sample of 456 individuals from 146 families with two or more gay brothers (Mustanski & others, 2005). Although they found no linkage to Xq28 in the full sample, a reanalysis of the DNA from the families previously reported, in which the linkage had been found, again revealed the linkage. Other groups of researchers have failed to replicate the linkage to Xq28 (e.g., Rice & others, 1999).

From an evolutionary standpoint, we could argue that natural selection would quickly eliminate a gene for homosexuality, because most homosexuals do not have children (Pillard & Bailey, 1998). But a homosexual might enhance his or her own genetic success by assisting the reproductive efforts of siblings, who share a common genetic base—including, perhaps, genes linked to homosexuality, even if not expressed in these heterosexual siblings.

Hormones, Brain Structure, and Sexual Preference

Another biological theory proposes that homosexual behavior results from a hormonal imbalance such as, in men, a lower-than-normal testosterone level (Hyde & DeLamater, 2000). However, Money (1980) found no hormonal difference between homosexual and heterosexual men, and some attempts by psychiatrists to treat homosexuality with testosterone injections have been unsuccessful. The injections did not alter sexual preference, but they did sometimes increase the sex drive.

Gartrell and colleagues (1977) found that homosexual women had higher testosterone levels than heterosexual women, but Downey and coworkers (1987) were unable to reproduce these results. To complicate matters further, higher testosterone levels were found in "butch" lesbians relative to "femme" lesbians (Singh & others, 1999). Also, because testosterone merely increases sexual arousal, it is unclear how a high testosterone level could influence the sexual preference of homosexual women unless it reflects a prenatal difference as well.

Another biological approach looks for structural differences in the brains of heterosexuals and homosexuals. For example, LeVay (1991) performed postmortem measurements of four cell groups of the anterior hypothalamus of women, heterosexual men, and homosexual men, and found that the volume of the interstitial nucleus 3 (or $INAH_3$) was twice as large in heterosexual men as in homosexual men (Figure 11.16). The volume of the $INAH_3$ in the women was the same as in the homosexual men. As we noted earlier, in heterosexuals, a nucleus in the preoptic area of the hypothalamus, the SDN, is larger in men than in women. LeVay suggested that a larger $INAH_3$ is associated with sexual attraction to women, whereas a smaller nucleus is associated with attraction to men.

Figure 11.16
The interstitial nucleus 3 ($INAH_3$)
The average size of the $INAH_3$ in heterosexual men is twice that in homosexual men and heterosexual women.

→ **What are some criticisms of LeVay's (1991) study?**

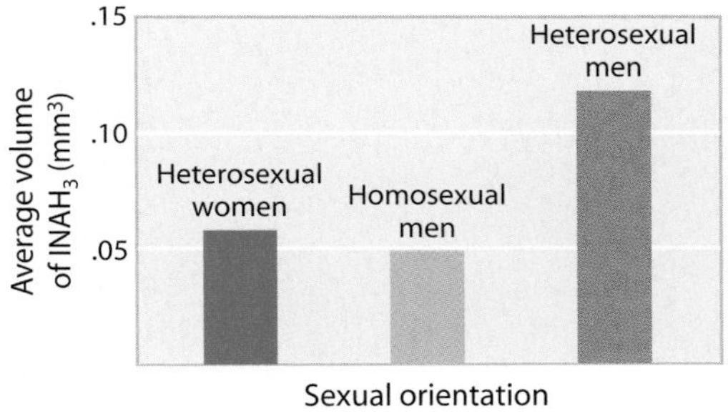

We should point out that LeVay's study (1991) can be criticized on methodological grounds. For example, the sample sizes were small (16 heterosexual men, 19 homosexual men, and 6 women), and some of the subjects had died of AIDS (all 16 homosexual men, 1 woman, and 6 heterosexual men), and an AIDS-related disease might have affected the brains of the study participants. In addition, there is no way to know whether the small size of the $INAH_3$ in the homosexual men caused their homosexual preferences or was the result of their sexual activities. In partial support for LeVay's report, Byne and colleagues (2000) found that men had a significantly larger $INAH_3$ than women, but Byne and colleagues (2001) failed to find a structural difference related to sexual orientation, although there was a trend in the right direction.

Rather than being *the* sexual orientation center, the $INAH_3$ neurons may be part of the neural pathway governing sexual behavior. Support for this view came from Allen and Gorski's apparent discovery (1992) that the *anterior commissure,* a fiber tract connecting the right and left hemispheres, is 34% larger in homosexual men than in heterosexual men and 18% larger than in heterosexual women. More recently, however, Lasco and colleagues (2002) found no difference in the size of the human anterior commissure in relation to such variables as age, gender, HIV status, or sexual preference.

The *Scientific American* Spotlight, "What's Smell Got to Do With It?," describes experiments that examined the effects of different odors on the neural activities of heterosexual and homosexual men and women. Evidence was found for sex-related differences in odor preferences.

Scientific American Spotlight

Olfaction: What's Smell Got to Do With It?

A. J. Minkel

Chemicals that seem to act as sex-specific signals tickle the brains of gay men and straight women in a similar way. Using brain scans, Swedish researchers had found that women getting a whiff of the steroid derivative androstadienone, found in sweat, experience increased blood flow in a part of their hypothalamus known to release sexual hormones. Male sniffers responded instead to an estrogen derivative. Now the group has observed that in gay men the same brain location, called the preoptic area, responds to androstadienone rather than the estrogen-like steroid. Further experiments are needed to conclude that these activation patterns reflect sexual attraction, as opposed to discriminating between genders, or that the responses are innate or learned, cautions Ivanka Savic of the Karolinska Institute in Stockholm, co-author of the report in the May 17 *Proceedings of the National Academy of Sciences USA.* Indeed, olfactory response may be more sensitive to sexual orientation than brain scanning can resolve. In the September *Psychological Science,* researchers from the Monell Chemical Senses Center in Philadelphia will report how they collected armpit sweat from straight and gay men and women. The outcomes were not as simple as "prefers men" or "prefers women." All groups except gay men preferred the scent of lesbians to that of gay men, for example. Still, the work adds evidence for sex-based differences in odor production and preference.

Developmental Factors and Sexual Preference

Perhaps structural brain differences between heterosexuals and homosexuals are caused by prenatal hormonal patterns. In fact, some studies have suggested that prenatal exposure to testosterone contributes to female homosexuality, and a lack of or abnormal pattern of such exposure may lead to male homosexuality.

The development of normal external genitals in an XY male requires both testosterone and dihydrotestosterone (DHT) (Sultan & others, 2001). DHT is produced from testosterone through the action of the 5-alpha-reductase type 2 enzyme, and a mutation in the gene(s) for this enzyme results in **5-alpha-reductase deficiency (5-ARD)**. Individuals with 5-ARD may have what appear to be normal female genitals, perhaps with a slightly enlarged clitoris. The clitoris is, in fact, a penis capable of ejaculation, and these individuals have testes, which are undescended, at least until puberty. They lack a uterus and Fallopian tubes, because of the normal action of Müllerian-inhibiting substance during development. Because the external genitals may be ambiguous at birth but usually appear more female than male, individuals with 5-ARD are usually raised as females. If the diagnosis of 5-ARD is made in infancy, the child can undergo surgery to make the genitals more typically female (Wilson, 2004). If the diagnosis is not made early, it becomes apparent at puberty, when the testes may descend, the voice deepens, and the penis enlarges. Often, such individuals change gender roles at this time (Imperato-McGinley & Zhu, 2002; Sultan & others, 2002; Wilson, 2001).

Adrenogenital syndrome, or *congenital adrenal hyperplasia,* occurs when the adrenal glands of the infant secrete too much androstenedione, resulting in genetically female (XX) humans with masculinized genitals and potentially masculinized brains. Money and colleagues (1984) studied 30 young women with this condition and found that 11 (37%) described themselves as homosexual or bisexual and 12 (40%) as heterosexual; the remainder would not discuss their sexual preferences. In a study in Germany, 34 female patients with adrenogenital syndrome were compared with 14 control sisters on measures of psychosexual development and sexual orientation (Dittmann & others, 1992). Nearly half of the patients over 21 either expressed an interest in or had had homosexual relationships; none of the sisters

5-alpha-reductase deficiency (5-ARD) A condition in which testosterone is not converted to dihydrotestosterone in a genetic male because of a deficiency of 5-alpha-reductase type 2 enzyme; the external genitals typically have a female appearance at birth.

adrenogenital syndrome A condition resulting from excess androstenedione secretion by the adrenal glands in a genetically female human, producing masculinized genitals.

androgen insensitivity syndrome (AIS) A condition in which a defective androgen receptor protein prevents normal testosterone action, causing a genetic male to develop female external genitals or ambiguous genitals.

expressed such an interest. Another German study compared 45 women with adrenogenital syndrome with 46 age-matched controls and found no evidence for increased homosexual preferences (Kuhnle & Bullinger, 1997).

More recently, Hines and colleagues (2004) studied 16 women and 9 men with adrenogenital syndrome and 15 unaffected female and 10 unaffected male relatives. The researchers found that women with the disorder showed increased male-typical play as children and a reduced heterosexual interest as adults; men with the disorder did not differ from those without. The women also reported less satisfaction with their assigned sex, and significantly more of them identified themselves as either homosexual or bisexual compared with the healthy controls. These results suggest that early fetal exposure to androstenedione in females may influence human sexual preference.

In other cases, genetic males (XY) who were insensitive to prenatal testosterone because of a defective androgen receptor protein developed external female genitals or ambiguous genitals. This condition is known as **androgen insensitivity syndrome (AIS)** (Figure 11.17). Disease characteristics generally include feminization (or undermasculinization) of the external genitals at birth, abnormal development of secondary sex characteristics at puberty, and infertility (Gottlieb & others, 2004).

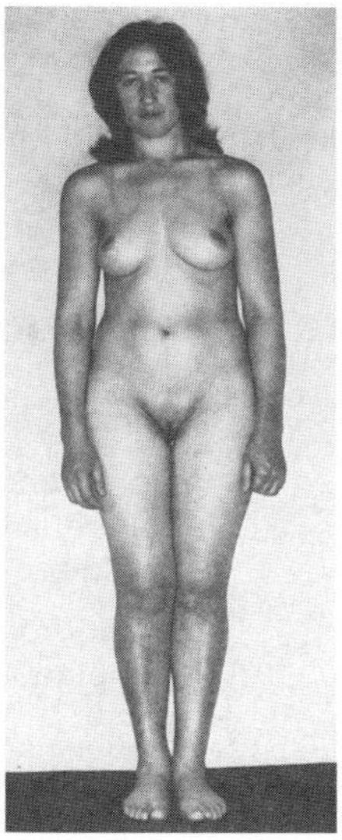

Figure 11.17
Androgen insensitivity syndrome This individual, an adult genetic male, shows the feminization characteristic of this syndrome.

➡ **What is adrenogenital syndrome?**

AIS is categorized into three subtypes: complete androgen insensitivity syndrome (CAIS), partial androgen insensitivity syndrome (PAIS), and mild androgen insensitivity syndrome (MAIS). In CAIS, the individual has normal female genitals and is raised as a female. The diagnosis is typically made when the person consults a doctor about inguinal masses, which are subsequently identified as undescended testes, or at puberty because of a lack of menstrual periods and sparse or absent pubic and axillary hair (Gottlieb & others, 2004). In a study of 14 adult women with CAIS, all were satisfied with having been raised as females and none wanted to change their sex to male (Wisniewski & others, 2000). In terms of sexual preferences, all reported a female heterosexual orientation in adolescence. One of the group developed a female homosexual orientation in adulthood.

In PAIS, the individual may have predominantly female external genitals, with signs of masculinization such as an enlarged clitoris; or ambiguous genitals; or predominantly male genitals. In cases of PAIS with predominantly female genitals, the situation is similar to that in CAIS, except that removal of the testes before puberty is recommended, as it helps the individual avoid the emotional discomfort of further enlargement of the clitoris at puberty (Gottlieb & others, 2004). Individuals with PAIS and predominantly male genitals are raised as males, as are those with MAIS and unambiguous male genitals.

A problem of sex assignment arises in cases of PAIS with genital ambiguity (e.g., small penis that looks like a clitoris, scrotum that appears to be labia majora). Whichever choice is made, it should be done with great care and as early as possible (Gottlieb & others, 2004).

The research on adrenogenital syndrome and androgen insensitivity syndrome points out an important difference between genetic sex and gender identity: A genetic male can have female genitals (as a result of androgen insensitivity syndrome) and a female gender identity, and a genetic female can have masculinized genitals (as a result of adrenogenital syndrome) and show preference for a male gender identity. Further, most research suggests that women with adrenogenital syndrome are more likely to express homosexual or bisexual preferences than women without the syndrome. However, most homosexual women do *not* have adrenogenital syndrome, and most men with androgen insensitivity syndrome are not homosexuals. Clearly, more research is needed to clarify the role of early testosterone exposure in homosexuality.

➤Checkpoint

Construct an experiment to test whether sexual preference is determined more by genetics, hormone levels, or structural differences.

REVIEW

- Genetic factors, hormonal imbalances, or structural brain differences may explain the basis of sexual preference, although the evidence is inconclusive.
- The interstitial nucleus 3 ($INAH_3$) of the anterior hypothalamus may be larger in heterosexual than in homosexual men.
- In 5-alpha-reductase deficiency, testosterone is not converted to dihydrotestosterone in a genetic male, and the external genitals typically have a female appearance at birth.
- In adrenogenital syndrome, the adrenal gland secretes too much androstenedione, and a genetically female human has masculinized genitals and often masculinized behavior.
- In androgen insensitivity syndrome, a genetic male develops female genitals or ambiguous genitals because of a defective androgen receptor protein.

Sexual Dysfunction

Many people have difficulty in engaging in sexual activity at times, because of temporary states such as anxiety, depression, or alcohol or drug intoxication. These experiences do not constitute a **sexual dysfunction,** which is a chronic failure to obtain sexual satisfaction. A complex phenomenon, sexual dysfunction has become a major problem in American society, affecting approximately 43% of women and 31% of men (Rosen, 2000). Sexual dysfunction is common in people treated with antidepressants, particularly the SSRIs (see Chapter 4) (Clayton & others, 2002, 2003, 2004; Worthington & Peters, 2003). Unfortunately, such dysfunction is typically underestimated by physicians (Clayton & others, 2002), and it can lead to patient dissatisfaction and decreased compliance with treatment (Labbate & others, 2003). Several antidepressants appear to produce less sexual dysfunction than the SSRIs, including bupropion, nefazodone, and reboxetine (Baldwin, 2004; Clayton & others, 2002, 2003; Labbate & others). Unlike the SSRIs, which specifically target serotonin, bupropion inhibits reuptake of dopamine and norepinephrine, nefazodone inhibits both serotonin and norepinephrine reuptake as well as blocking some serotonin receptors, and reboxetine inhibits the reuptake of norepinephrine.

Masters and Johnson (1970) reported that organic (i.e., biologically but not psychologically based) factors cause about 10% to 20% of sexual dysfunction cases, with psychological problems accounting for the rest. Here we briefly describe several forms of sexual dysfunction and their organic causes, and discuss Masters and Johnson's suggested treatments for each disorder, which, although introduced more than a quarter century ago, are still widely employed.

Types of Sexual Dysfunction

Erectile dysfunction, or *impotence,* was the most common form of male sexual disorder in Masters and Johnson's study (our discussion here refers to data from their 1970 report, unless noted otherwise). They reported that 54% of the 448 men with sexual dysfunction in their study suffered from a chronic inability to have an erection sufficient to achieve penetration, although most had been able to engage in intercourse on at least one occasion. In the general population, more recently, Rosen (2000) found an incidence of erectile dysfunction of 10% to 20%, with an increasing percentage as men age.

Erectile failure can result from serious illness such as coronary disease, Parkinson's disease, multiple sclerosis, or diabetes mellitus; from damage to the lower spinal cord area controlling erectile functions; and from severe stress or fatigue. Drugs can also cause sexual dysfunction (Long, 1984). For example, alcohol and

sexual dysfunction A chronic failure to obtain sexual satisfaction.

erectile dysfunction A chronic inability to have a penile erection sufficient to achieve penetration.

opiates impair erectile function, and anticholinergic drugs, primarily used in treating peptic ulcers and glaucoma, may cause erectile dysfunction by inhibiting the parasympathetic nerves that normally produce an erection. As we saw earlier, widely prescribed antidepressants, such as the SSRIs, can cause sexual dysfunction, including erectile failure.

Masters and Johnson (1970) found that 41% of their study's male subjects with sexual dysfunction experienced **premature ejaculation,** which they defined as the inability 50% of the time for a man to delay ejaculation during vaginal intercourse until he satisfies his partner. If by partner satisfaction we mean the partner has an orgasm, there is at least one obvious problem with this definition, as some women never achieve orgasm through vaginal intercourse. The current *Diagnostic and Statistical Manual* definition of premature ejaculation acknowledges the inability of the person to control his orgasm and the distress this lack of control causes. In the general population, premature ejaculation is the most common male sexual dysfunction, occurring in approximately 30% of men, according to most studies (Rosen, 2000). Premature ejaculation can result from the use of anti-adrenergic drugs prescribed to treat hypertension and other vascular disorders; these drugs block the sympathetic nerves that normally inhibit an ejaculation. But premature ejaculation is also generally considered often to have a psychological cause, such as the need to have a speedy orgasm because of an associated fear of discovery while masturbating or while having intercourse in a relatively unprotected location.

Retarded ejaculation, or an inability to ejaculate, is the third major form of male sexual dysfunction. Some men with this problem can ejaculate with manual stimulation, whereas others cannot. Although Masters and Johnson found this disorder to be rare (affecting only 4% of their male patients), others believe it is fairly common (Kaplan, 1974). There is an association between retarded ejaculation and Parkinson's disease.

Orgasmic dysfunction, the inability to have an orgasm, was by far the most prevalent form of sexual dysfunction in the women in Masters and Johnson's study, with 91% of 371 female patients reporting this problem. More than half of these patients (56%) never had an orgasm, and the others achieved orgasm only under certain conditions. In recent community-based studies, orgasmic dysfunction is commonly reported, with about 10% to 15% of women being affected (Rosen, 2000). Masters and Johnson reported that 9% of the sexual dysfunctions of their female patients were caused by involuntary contractions of the muscles surrounding the vagina, or **vaginismus.** These muscle contractions close the entrance to the vagina and prevent intercourse. Severe illness or fatigue can contribute to orgasmic dysfunction, and some disorders of the reproductive system can lead to vaginismus.

premature ejaculation The inability of a man to delay ejaculation until his partner achieves orgasm.

retarded ejaculation The inability to ejaculate during sexual intercourse.

orgasmic dysfunction The inability to have an orgasm.

vaginismus A condition in which muscle contractions close the vagina and prevent intercourse.

Treatment Methods

Treatment approaches for sexual dysfunction can be either biological or psychological. In many patients, sexual dysfunction can be eliminated by treating the underlying organic cause. For example, for a person with diabetes, insulin can manage both the disease and the sexual dysfunction it produces.

In other cases, drugs can be used to treat the sexual dysfunction itself. Cyclic guanosine monophosphate (cyclic GMP) plays a role in the penile response to stimulation. Sildenafil (Viagra) inhibits cyclic GMP breakdown in the corpus cavernosum, a body of erectile tissue in the penis. This prolongs the action of the cyclic GMP and increases the penile response. Clinical studies have shown that Viagra is a safe and effective treatment for erectile dysfunction (e.g., Guay & others, 2001). For example, in one experiment, Viagra or placebo was administered for 24 weeks to 532 men with erectile dysfunction, with different men receiving different doses of Viagra (25, 50, or 100 mg) (Goldstein & others, 1998). Higher doses of Viagra were associated with an improved ability to have and maintain an erection,

sex therapy The psychological approach to treating sexual dysfunction.

with the 100 mg group averaging a score of 4.0 (vs. 2.0 before treatment) on a question about achieving erections (maximum score of 5.0). In a dose-escalation study (the dose was increased over time to 100 mg), another 329 men were studied over a 12 week period. During the last 4 weeks, the men receiving Viagra were able to have intercourse successfully on 69% of their attempts, compared with only 22% for the men receiving a placebo.

William H. Masters and Virginia E. Johnson, pictured here in 1965, revolutionized Western thinking about sexuality and sexual disorders.

BETTMAN/CORBIS

Use of Viagra has some side effects, such as headaches and flushing, but it has proven to be safe and effective even for men with major disorders such as Parkinson's disease (Hussain & others, 2001; Raffaele & others, 2002) and cardiovascular disease (Cheitlin, 2003; Speakman & Kloner, 1999). In addition, Viagra users have reported enhanced emotional well-being and improved relationships with their sexual partners (Montorsi & Althof, 2004; Paige & others, 2001).

The psychological approaches to treating sexual dysfunction are collectively called **sex therapy.** In the initial stages of therapy, a patient receives factual information about human sexuality and the organic cause(s) of a particular sexual dysfunction; this helps correct many misconceptions about sexuality, and eliminating these misperceptions and giving the person a better understanding of his or her disorder often enhances sexual functioning.

As pioneers in sex therapy, Masters and Johnson developed a program that has been widely adopted. Exercises in which the patient learns to provide his or her partner with sensual pleasure other than through intercourse are an important part of this program. The exercises are structured to give people successful sexual experiences and to eliminate anxiety and the expectation of failure. The treatment of sexual dysfunction is often successful. For example, Masters and Johnson reported that their treatment approach alleviated symptoms in 65% to 90% of patients. In a 5 year follow-up study of 225 patients, only 7% had again become dysfunctional. Other psychologists have also reported the successful treatment of people with sexual dysfunction, which suggests that sex therapy can result in long-lasting behavioral change (Gupta & others, 1989; Segraves & Althof, 1998).

Checkpoint

Do you think Doug's sexual dysfunction has a biological or psychological basis?

REVIEW

- Sexual dysfunctions in men include erectile dysfunction, premature ejaculation, and retarded ejaculation. Women may experience orgasmic dysfunction or vaginismus.
- In 10% to 20% of cases, sexual dysfunction is caused by organic factors such as serious illness or neurological damage, or by the use of certain drugs.
- Erectile dysfunction can be treated with sildenafil (Viagra). Other sexual disorders are treated by sex therapy, which uses exercises to provide sensual pleasure without intercourse and specific techniques to treat specific sexual problems.

CHAPTER REVIEW

Key Terms

acquired sexual motive (p. 408)
adrenogenital syndrome (p. 412)
alpha-fetoprotein (p. 392)
androgen insensitivity syndrome (AIS) (p. 413)
androstenedione (p. 398)
castration (p. 399)
endometrium (p. 397)
erectile dysfunction (p. 414)
estradiol (p. 392)
estrogen (p. 392)
estrous cycle (p. 396)
5-alpha-reductase deficiency (5-ARD) (p. 412)
follicle-stimulating hormone (FSH) (p. 396)
gender (p. 389)
heat (p. 396)

Klinefelter syndrome (p. 388)
lordosis (p. 390)
luteinizing hormone (LH) (p. 397)
medial preoptic area (MPOA) (p. 403)
menstrual cycle (p. 396)
menstruation (p. 397)
Müllerian-inhibiting substance (MIS) (p. 387)
Müllerian system (p. 387)
myotonia (p. 395)
orgasm (p. 395)
orgasmic dysfunction (p. 415)
ovariectomy (p. 397)
oxytocin (p. 401)
pheromone (p. 400)
premature ejaculation (p. 415)
progesterone (p. 397)
retarded ejaculation (p. 415)
sex-determining gene (p. 386)
sex therapy (p. 416)
sexual dysfunction (p. 414)
testis-determining factor (TDF) (p. 387)
testosterone (p. 389)
Turner syndrome (p. 388)
vaginismus (p. 415)
vasocongestion (p. 395)
ventromedial hypothalamus (VMH) (p. 403)
vomeronasal organ (p. 405)
Wolffian system (p. 387)

Suggested Readings

Gerall, A. A., Moltz, H., & Wald, I. L. (1992). *Handbook of behavioral neurobiology: Vol. 11. Sexual differentiation.* New York: Plenum.

Gorski, R. A. (1997). Gonadal hormones and the organization of brain structure and function. In D. Magnusson (Ed.), *The lifespan development of individuals: Behavioral, neurobiological, and psychosocial perspectives: A synthesis* (pp. 315–340). New York: Cambridge University Press.

Levin, R. J. (1998). Sex and the human female reproductive tract—what really happens during and after coitus. *International Journal of Impotence Research, 10,* S14–S21.

Masters, W., & Johnson, V. (1966). *Human sexual response.* Boston: Little, Brown.

Masters, W., & Johnson, V. (1970). *Human sexual inadequacy.* Boston: Little, Brown.

Nelson, R. J. (1995). *An introduction to behavioral endocrinology.* Sunderland, MA: Sinauer.

Segraves, R. T., & Althof, S. (1998). Psychotherapy and pharmacotherapy of sexual dysfunctions. In P. E. Nathan & J. M. Gorman (Eds.), *A guide to treatments that work* (pp. 447–471). New York: Oxford University Press.

Critical Thinking Questions

1. While Charlotte is pregnant, she suffers from an illness in which her adrenal glands secrete abnormally high amounts of testosterone. This medical problem is eventually brought under control. Assuming the fetus is a genetic female, what impact might the prenatal testosterone exposure have on the child's development?
2. Simone has often been called a tomboy, but she can be quite feminine when she wishes. She is sexually attracted to men, and not to women. Suggest a possible reason for Simone's rough-and-tumble character.
3. Most people find sex extremely pleasurable. Describe the physiological changes that occur during sexual activity. Indicate the similarities and differences in the physiology of the sexual behavior of men and women. What biological system might be responsible for the pleasurable quality of sex?

Fill-in-the-Blank Questions

1. The ______ gene on the Y chromosome is responsible for determining the biological sex of the individual.
2. The ______ system of an embryo develops into male reproductive structures, and the ______ system develops into female structures.
3. The enzyme ______ causes the undifferentiated gonads of the embryo to become testes.
4. In the absence of testis-determining factor, the ______ system matures into a female reproductive system.
5. In ______ syndrome, a person is born with one X chromosome and no other sex chromosome.
6. In typical rodent sexual behavior, the female displays ______, or the copulatory posture.
7. Estradiol present in a female fetus is deactivated by ______ to prevent masculinization of the brain.
8. During sexual arousal, an increased blood flow to the pelvic area of both males and females occurs through ______, or blood vessel dilation.
9. The four phases of the human sexual response are ______, ______, ______, and ______.
10. ______, or rhythmic muscle contractions, of the male genital organs forces the ejaculate into the urethra.
11. A male's ability to become sexually aroused depends on the presence of the hormone ______; a female's ability to become aroused depends on the presence of the hormone ______.

12. Female sex hormones change dramatically during the ______ cycle in nonhuman mammals and the ______ cycle in humans.
13. The ______ released by the anterior pituitary gland stimulates the ovaries to release female sex hormones.
14. Estrogen and a second sex hormone, ______, prepare the lining of the uterus for implantation of a fertilized egg.
15. In their reproductive years, women secrete ______, an adrenal androgen hormone similar to testosterone.
16. In the ______ effect, the estrous cycles of group-housed female mice are suppressed in the absence of a male mouse; in the ______ effect, the cycles are reinstated by the odor of male urine.
17. The ______ is the anterior hypothalamic area that contains testosterone-sensitive receptors that produce sexual responsivity.
18. The ______ is a specialized sensory organ, separate from the main olfactory system, that detects pheromones released by a receptive female.
19. In a classic study, Klüver and Bucy found that bilateral ______ lobectomies led to aberrant sexual behavior in male monkeys.
20. Although significantly smaller in females than in males, the ______ of the hypothalamus is involved in eliciting sexual behavior in both sexes.
21. A(n) ______ is a learned sexual response to a stimulus that occurs through conditioning.
22. ______ engage in sexual activity with individuals of the opposite sex; ______ engage in sexual activity with individuals of the same sex.
23. ______, caused by the adrenal glands secreting too much androstenedione, produces a genetic female with masculinized genitals.
24. The most common form of male sexual disorder found by Masters and Johnson was ______.
25. The most prevalent form of female sexual dysfunction found by Masters and Johnson was ______.
26. In ______, muscle contractions close the opening to the vagina and prevent intercourse.
27. Several studies have found that the drug ______ is a safe and effective treatment for erectile dysfunction.
28. The psychological approaches to treating sexual dysfunction are called ______.

Multiple-Choice Questions

1. If the sex-determining gene is present, the individual develops as a ______; if it is absent, the individual develops as a ______.
   a. male, female
   b. female, male
   c. XX, XY
   d. XXY, XYY
2. Testosterone released from the testes causes the ______ to develop into the mature male reproductive system.
   a. Müllerian system
   b. Wolffian system
   c. penis
   d. TDF
3. Amy was born with only one X chromosome and no other sex chromosome. As a result she is infertile. She has been diagnosed as having ______ syndrome.
   a. Klinefelter
   b. Down
   c. Turner
   d. fragile X
4. The presence of ______ in the prenatal and early postnatal period is responsible for a masculinized brain.
   a. testosterone
   b. estrogen
   c. progesterone
   d. prolactin
5. In rats, the critical period for the sexual development of the brain is the ______ following birth.
   a. 6 hours
   b. 14 days
   c. 6 days
   d. 14 weeks
6. A nucleus in the preoptic area of the hypothalamus is
   a. more than twice as large in men as in women.
   b. more than twice as large in women as in men.
   c. responsible for the inhibition of sexual responsivity.
   d. six times larger in female rats than in male rats.
7. Alpha-fetoprotein deactivates circulating ______ in a fetus.
   a. testosterone
   b. estradiol
   c. diethylstilbestrol
   d. oxytocin
8. A male mouse that had been positioned between ______ in the uterus would have smaller-than-normal testes.
   a. two females
   b. two males
   c. a male and a female
   d. a male and the uterine wall
9. Heather often finds her boyfriend so sexy that she flushes when she sees him. This reveals that she is in the ______ phase of the human sexual response.
   a. excitement
   b. plateau
   c. orgasm
   d. resolution
10. The hypothalamus releases gonadotropic-releasing hormones, which in turn stimulate the anterior pituitary gland to release luteinizing hormone, which acts on the
    a. ovaries to produce androstenedione.
    b. ovaries to increase sex drive.
    c. testes to produce testosterone.
    d. penis to increase sex drive.
11. In human males, castration
    a. results in an immediate loss of sex drive.
    b. results in a decline in sex drive, which recovers to original levels as the man ages.
    c. produces variable changes in sex drive and behavior.
    d. generally has little effect on sex drive and behavior.

12. The period of intense sexual responsivity in female mammals occurs
a. at the beginning of the estrous cycle.
b. just before ovulation.
c. just after ovulation.
d. at the end of the estrous cycle.

13. The rhythm method of birth control has a high failure rate because of variability in
a. a woman's interest in sexual activity.
b. the time of ovulation.
c. the estrous cycle.
d. a man's fertility.

14. Removal of the ______ in an estrous animal ______ sexual behavior.
a. ovaries, increases
b. testes, increases
c. ovaries, decreases
d. testes, decreases

15. Estrogen and ______ prepare the uterine lining for implantation of a fertilized egg.
a. testosterone
b. androstenedione
c. estradiol
d. progesterone

16. In their reproductive years, women secrete ______, an adrenal hormone similar to testosterone.
a. progesterone
b. estradiol
c. androstenedione
d. vasopressin

17. Release of the neurotransmitter ______ in the MPOA is associated with sexual behavior.
a. norepinephrine
b. dopamine
c. acetylcholine
d. serotonin

18. The ______ organ is a sensory organ separate from the main olfactory system that detects pheromones released by a receptive female.
a. vestibular
b. vomeronasal
c. rhinonasal
d. pheromone-detecting

19. Klüver and Bucy observed dramatic changes in sexual behavior in male monkeys following bilateral removal of the ______ lobes.
a. frontal
b. temporal
c. parietal
d. occipital

20. The influence of the cortex on female sexual behavior in nonhuman mammals appears to
a. be extremely high.
b. be minimal.
c. decrease with age.
d. increase with age.

21. Sexual activity displayed in erotic film segments
a. has a greater effect on women than on men.
b. has an equal effect on men and women.
c. has a greater effect on men than on women.
d. invariably produces disgust in women.

22. The three factors proposed as the basis for sexual preference are
a. genetic factors, hormonal balance, and structural brain differences.
b. genetic factors, hormonal balance, and social experiences.
c. hormonal balance, structural brain differences, and social experiences.
d. genetic factors, social experiences, and structural brain differences.

23. Genetic males who lack testosterone receptors in their brain and develop external female genitals have a disorder called
a. adrenogenital syndrome.
b. congenital adrenal hyperplasia.
c. Turner syndrome.
d. androgen insensitivity syndrome.

24. Sean has Parkinson's disease and has recently begun to experience a sexual dysfunction. What is the most likely type of his dysfunction?
a. retarded ejaculation
b. premature ejaculation
c. impotence
d. orgasmic dysfunction

25. The most common form of male sexual disorder observed by Masters and Johnson was ______, whereas the most common disorder in the general population is ______.
a. erectile dysfunction, retarded ejaculation
b. premature ejaculation, erectile dysfunction
c. erectile dysfunction, premature ejaculation
d. premature ejaculation, retarded ejaculation

26. Recently wed, Myra finds sexual intercourse with her husband impossible, because muscle contractions close her vagina. Myra probably has
a. vaginismus.
b. vaginal hyperplasia.
c. urethral hypoplasia.
d. vaginal constriction syndrome.

Answers can be found on the companion website at www.worthpublishers.com/klein.

M T W
1 2
8 9 10
14 15 16 17
22 23 24
30
QUALLS

12

The Biology of Emotion and Stress

An Irreplaceable Loss

Stuart almost felt like whistling as he walked through Oak Memorial Grove on the way to his first class. The morning was clear and cool, with just a hint of the smell of food from a nearby cafeteria mingled with the odor of the trees. All was right in Stuart's world, until his cell phone rang. He expected it to be his girlfriend or his roommate, his most frequent callers.

"Stuart?" he heard. It was his stepmother, although her voice seemed to have an unfamiliar quaver. Bad connection, he thought.

"Horrible news, son. Your father had a massive coronary this morning while he was packing the car for our trip. I called 911, but he was gone by the time they got here."

"Gone?" he heard himself ask, stupidly, as he staggered to a bench beside the path. He could tell that his stepmother was crying as she tried to keep talking. He struggled to grasp the information. Memories of his father flooded over him: his smell, a mix of Old Spice and cigarettes; his gentle touch and comforting words when Stuart's mother died, just after his seventh birthday. Stuart and his father had a wonderful relationship. How could it be over?

"Too soon," he wanted to say. "I'm not ready. I haven't told him in years how much I love him." But it was too late now.

Somehow Stuart managed to say the appropriate things to his stepmother, to tell her he would be home on the first flight he could get. When she broke the connection, his hands shook so badly he dropped the phone, then angrily kicked it and buried his face in his hands.

BEFORE YOU BEGIN

- **What is the physiological basis of Stuart's shaking hands?**
- **What parts of the brain were responsible for Stuart's feelings of happiness as he walked through the grove of trees, then the grief when he learned of his father's death?**
- **What exactly is an emotion, and what process do we go through when experiencing one?**
- **When Stuart kicks his cell phone, what type of aggression is he experiencing? What other types are there?**
- **Can the news of his father's death be considered a stressor?**
- **What can Stuart do to decrease the effects of the stress caused by the death of his father?**

In this chapter, you will find the answers to these questions and many others.

emotion A feeling that differs from a person's normal state; includes a change in physiological arousal, an affective (feeling) component, and a behavioral response.

James-Lange theory of emotion The view that the physiological changes that occur in response to an event determine the experience of an emotion.

Defining Emotion

No doubt you have felt happy when you received an A on a tough exam or have been saddened by the ending of a movie. Perhaps your girlfriend or boyfriend has broken up with you, causing you to feel angry and hurt. Although each situation is different, all have a common characteristic: You had an emotional reaction. We feel many different and varied emotions—rage, disgust, fear, joy, annoyance, sorrow, anger, grief, terror, happiness, surprise, and amazement, to name just a few.

An **emotion** is a feeling that differs from a person's normal affective state and, like everything else we have considered, is a biological function of the nervous system (LeDoux, 1996). Emotions have three central attributes (Carlson & Hatfield, 1992):

- A change in physiological arousal, ranging from slight to intense.
- An affective response, feelings that are pleasant or unpleasant.
- The capacity to motivate a specific behavior.

Behavior is specifically linked to certain emotions (Lazarus, 1993). For example, anger motivates aggressive behavior, and fear usually motivates escape behavior.

Learning of the death of his father triggered an intense emotional reaction in Stuart. If we asked him what he was feeling, he would probably say that he was badly hurt, that his heart ached with longing for his father. Although Stuart's pain is quite different from the sensory pain discussed in Chapter 7, it is nevertheless real and has a strong physiological basis. In this chapter, we examine the physiological changes that underlie Stuart's feelings of loss, as well as the joy he will eventually be able to recapture as he remembers the good times he and his father shared.

Figure 12.1
The James-Lange theory of emotion
In this example, you perceive a man with a gun. This perception causes you to respond physiologically, and awareness of your physiological response gives you the experience of fear.

➔ **According to the James-Lange theory, how can we experience so many emotions?**

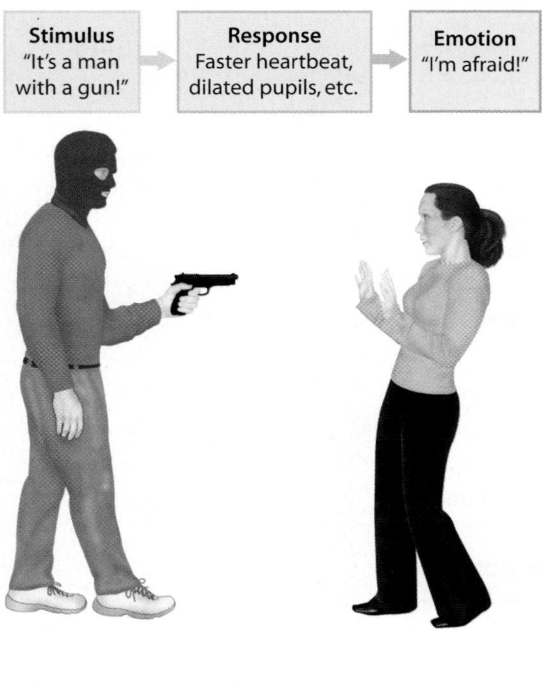

Theories About Experiencing an Emotion

Several major theories or models have been proposed to explain the nature of emotion, including the James-Lange theory, the Cannon-Bard theory, the Papez-MacLean model, and Schachter's cognitive model. The first three emphasize the role of physiological processes in an emotional experience, whereas the fourth suggests that cognitive processes are the determining factor in emotional responses.

The James-Lange Theory

The traditional way to think of an emotion is that a stimulus occurs (say, you see a man with a gun), you feel an emotion (fear), and then you have a response (accelerated heartbeat, dilated pupils). Independently, William James (1884) and Carl Lange (1885/1887) proposed over a century ago that the traditional view is simply wrong. Instead, they suggested that the physiological changes—the *expression* of an emotion—occur before the emotional feeling—the *experience* of an emotion (Figure 12.1).

The James-Lange theory is often paraphrased as "I run, therefore I am afraid." According to this view, the physiological changes—the emotional response—occur before the feeling of the emotion. The kinds of visceral changes (e.g., faster or slower heartbeat) and somatic changes (e.g., increased or decreased muscle tension) depend on the event; different situations cause different internal physiological responses. According to the **James-Lange theory of emotion,** we interpret these physiological changes to determine how we feel, or how we experience an emotion. The different visceral and somatic responses enable us to experience different emotions. For example, when Stuart learned of the death of his father, the knowledge triggered bodily reactions such as changes in his heart rate and blood pressure, he perhaps felt nauseated, and he began to cry. These responses characterized Stuart's expression of an emotion, and then his awareness of this expression produced his emotional experience of great sadness.

Consider the following examples. Your instructor announces an examination next week, and this frightens you. Alternatively, your instructor postpones a scheduled exam, giving you an extra week to study, and you feel relieved. According to the James-Lange theory, the announcement of the exam speeds up your heartbeat, elevates your blood pressure, and increases your breathing rate, among other things. By contrast, the postponement causes your heartbeat to slow down, your blood pressure to fall, and your breathing rate to decrease. These different internal responses produce the different emotions of fear and relief.

William James (1842–1910) and daughter in 1892, 2 years after publication of his monumental *Principles of Psychology*.

Some evidence suggests that subtle physiological differences exist between several emotional states. For example, more epinephrine than norepinephrine is released from the adrenal medulla in the case of fear, and the opposite happens with anger (Ax, 1953). In addition, the effects of norepinephrine and epinephrine on the body differ slightly. One example is that norepinephrine elevates diastolic blood pressure (pressure when the heart is relaxed and filling with blood; the "bottom" number—as the 70 in a blood pressure of 120/70), whereas epinephrine increases systolic blood pressure (pressure when the heart is pumping blood; the "top" number).

Autonomic activity, as assessed by such parameters as skin electrical conductance, skin blood flow, and skin temperature, differentiates basic emotions such as happiness, surprise, anger, and fear (Collet & others, 1997). Further, tears of sadness contain more protein than tears triggered by chopping raw onions (Frey & Langseth, 1985). Levenson and colleagues (1990) reported that voluntarily produced facial expressions result in different patterns of autonomic activity and that difficulty in producing the expressions did not account for emotion-specific heart rate changes (Levenson & Ekman, 2002). It has even been shown that the four basic taste sensations—salty, sweet, sour, and bitter—are associated with different patterns of autonomic nervous system activity related to how appealing the tastes are: Sweet produced the smallest autonomic response and bitter the largest (Rousmans & others, 2000).

Harvard physiologist Walter Cannon (1927) suggested several difficulties with the James-Lange theory. If, as the theory states, emotional experience follows emotional expression, then blocking emotional expression should prevent or at least decrease emotional experience; without expression, there should be no experience. However, in his review of studies on this topic, Cannon found evidence that emotional experience can occur without feedback from the internal organs, and several studies appeared to show that emotional feeling was unchanged following destruction of the spinal cord in dogs, cats, and humans.

More recent evidence based on humans with spinal cord injuries presents a mixed picture, with some of it supporting Cannon's criticism and some of it appearing to validate the James-Lange theory. For example, when 29 people with spinal cord injuries were asked about the intensity of their emotional experiences following their injuries, no evidence was found for a "decline in affective tone," which supports Cannon's criticism (Lowe & Carroll, 1985). By contrast, a clear inverse relationship was found between the level of the spinal cord injury (i.e., the position of cord damage) and the intensity of the person's feelings; patients with higher injuries (less visceral feedback) reported less intense emotions than patients with lower injuries, clearly supporting the James-Lange theory (Hohman, 1966). Comparing spinal cord–injured subjects with other disabled and nondisabled individuals, Chwalisz and colleagues (1988) supported both positions. The three groups differed on only one measure of emotional intensity: spinal cord–damaged individuals reported stronger fear after than before their injuries, just

Walter B. Cannon (1871–1945), Harvard colleague and friend of William James. Cannon attacked the James-Lange theory of emotion on several fronts in 1927.

the opposite of what the James-Lange theory would predict. However, Chwalisz and colleagues did find that the amount of autonomic feedback in the spinal cord–injured subjects was related to emotional intensity. For example, subjects with greater autonomic feedback tended to report more intense negative emotions than subjects with less feedback, which supports the James-Lange theory, because, according to this theory, autonomic feedback is primarily responsible for the emotional experience.

Another of Cannon's criticisms (1927) was that essentially the same autonomic responses occur in diverse emotions (e.g., both fear and anger stimulate the sympathetic nervous system), whereas the James-Lange theory contends that the internal physiological responses for each emotion should differ. In fact, subtle differences have been found in the physiological responses accompanying different emotional states, as noted above.

According to Cannon (1927), if emotional experience follows emotional expression, as the James-Lange theory contends, then the artificial creation of emotional expression should produce emotional experiences. Cannon argued that this did not happen. He reported studies in which people injected with epinephrine to stimulate autonomic arousal generally failed to report any emotional experience.

Although the failure of artificially created expression to trigger an emotional feeling appears to be a good argument against the James-Lange theory, there may be another way to interpret Cannon's observations, which we will consider when we discuss Schachter's work on emotions. At this point, let us examine the theory Cannon proposed to replace the James-Lange theory.

Checkpoint

According to the James-Lange theory, what physiological changes caused Stuart to experience grief in response to the death of his father? Using what you know about the James-Lange theory, suggest what Stuart could do to change his emotion from sorrow to happiness.

The Cannon-Bard Theory

Walter Cannon (1927) and Philip Bard (1934) proposed that visceral changes, somatic changes, and the emotional experience occur at the same time (Figure 12.2). According to the **Cannon-Bard theory of emotion,** an emotion-producing event stimulates the thalamus, which then stimulates the cerebral cortex to produce the emotional feeling, and the rest of the body to produce the visceral and somatic changes appropriate for the feeling. In other words, the emotional expression and experience take place simultaneously by way of thalamic stimulation. For Stuart, in the Cannon-Bard theory, the news of his father's death stimulated his thalamus, which then stimulated his cerebral cortex to produce the feeling of sadness and simultaneously stimulated his autonomic nervous system to trigger the bodily changes appropriate for the emotion.

Although Cannon and Bard presented experimental evidence to support their theory, the thalamus is not the only brain area controlling emotional expression and experience. Walter Papez (1937) and Paul MacLean (1949) argued for involvement of the limbic system and hypothalamus in the emotional response to an event.

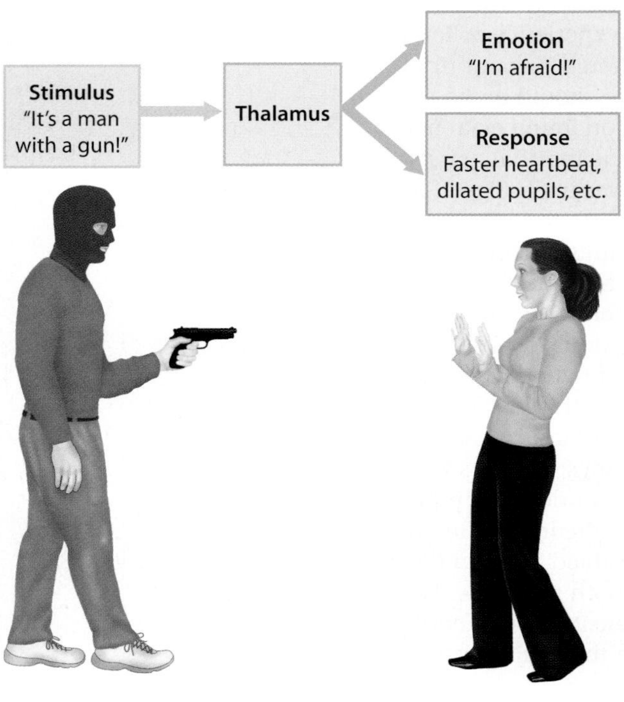

Figure 12.2

The Cannon-Bard theory of emotion Perception of the man with a gun activates the thalamus. The message from the thalamus is sent simultaneously to the cerebral cortex and the autonomic nervous system. Cortical stimulation produces the experience of fear, and stimulation of the autonomic system causes the physiological arousal needed to cope with the threatening situation.

→ **According to the Cannon-Bard theory, how are we able to experience so many different emotions?**

Papez and MacLean: The Limbic System

In 1937, Papez (rhymes with grapes) proposed that emotional expression and experience are mediated by a system of interconnected forebrain structures, which came to be known as the **Papez circuit** (Figure 12.3). The emotional circuit begins with the hippocampus, which is connected by the fornix to the mammillary bodies of the hypothalamus. From the mammillary bodies, the mammillothalamic tract travels to the anterior thalamic nuclei, which are connected to the cingulate gyrus. From there, the circuit returns to the hippocampus by way of the entorhinal cortex. According to Papez, the expression of emotion occurs through the hypothalamus, which, with its control of the autonomic nervous system, is ideally suited for this role. He suggested the cingulate gyrus as the neural area responsible for emotional experience. Papez's evidence for this circuit included the observation that certain stimuli, such as taste, smell, and pain, activate the structures of the circuit and thereby elicit strong emotional responses. In addition, he cited contemporary work reporting that monkeys were emotionally inactive following lesions of the mammillary bodies.

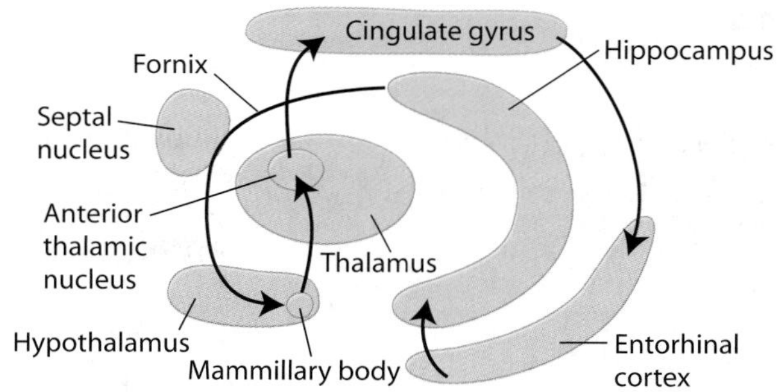

Figure 12.3
The Papez circuit, part of the limbic system According to Papez, the expression of emotion occurs through the hypothalamus, with emotional experience taking place in the cingulate gyrus.

→ **Why did MacLean call the Papez circuit and associated structures the limbic system?**

MacLean (1949, 1970) revised and expanded Papez's theory, calling the Papez circuit the **limbic system,** because it forms a border (limbus) around brain stem structures. He compared the sizes of the cerebral cortex and limbic system in several different animal species and noted that the size of the cortex is greater in monkeys than in cats and greater in cats than in rabbits (Figure 12.4). Because the relative size of the limbic system (i.e., size relative to cortex size) is approximately the same in each species, MacLean concluded that the limbic system must control the primitive functions shared by all mammalian species.

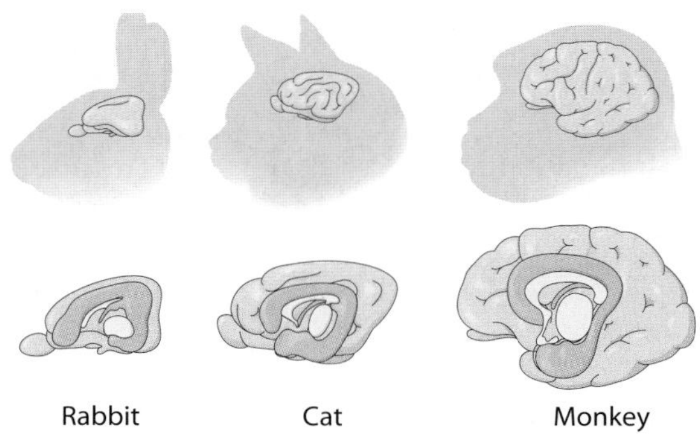

Figure 12.4
The limbic system in a rabbit, a cat, and a monkey The top drawings show lateral views of the cerebral cortex of each animal, and the bottom drawings show medial views, with the limbic system in blue.

→ **What is the significance of the relative sizes of the limbic system of these animals?**

MacLean identified three separate circuits in the limbic system, encompassing the amygdala, the hippocampus, the cingulate gyrus, the septum, the hypothalamus, and the thalamus. The first circuit includes the amygdala and the hippocampus and is involved in survival. The importance of this circuit is suggested by the observation that damage to the medial amygdala in wild rats led to decreased defensiveness without affecting flight behavior, whereas damage to medial structures that spared the medial nucleus did not affect defensiveness but did reduce flight behavior (Kemble & others, 1984). A later study by the same researchers found a dramatic reduction in flight behavior after damage to all major regions of the amygdala (Kemble & others, 1990).

Lesions of the amygdala have often been found to produce a drop in social dominance (e.g., Rosvold & others, 1954), which may be the result of a reduction in aggressive behavior and a failure to modify aggressive behavior on the basis of experience (Vochteloo & Koolhaas, 1987). Fonberg (1988) implicated the dorsal amygdala in dominance. Rats with damage to the central amygdala showed a reduction in experimentally induced anxiety similar to that seen following the ingestion of anxiety-reducing drugs (Moller & others, 1997). Damage to the amygdala in humans has been found to impair a person's enhanced perception of emotionally important events (Anderson & Phelps, 2001).

Stimulating specific regions in the amygdala can trigger emotions. For example, electrical stimulation of the medial amygdala facilitates defensive rage produced by stimulation of the medial hypothalamus and motivates aggressive behavior in cats (Shaikh & others, 1993; Siegel & others, 1997) and humans (Mark & Ervin, 1970). Destruction of the central amygdaloid nucleus blocked a fear-induced startle reaction in rats (Campeau & Davis, 1995b), and monkeys with similar damage exhibited less fear than control animals when confronted by either a snake or a human intruder (Kalin & others, 2004). Bilateral damage to the amygdala in humans impairs social perception, particularly the perception of fear and anger, and this occurs in both visual and auditory modalities (Scott & others, 1997).

Cannon-Bard theory of emotion The view that an event activates the thalamus, which stimulates the cerebral cortex to produce the feeling component (the experience) of the emotion and, at the same time, the rest of the body to produce the expression of the emotion.

Papez circuit A system of interconnected forebrain structures that are responsible for the expression and experience of an emotion.

limbic system The name MacLean gave to the Papez circuit.

kindling Repeated stimulation of the amygdala, causing an animal to be more susceptible to seizure activity.

Repeated stimulation of the amygdala in experimental animals produces long-term structural changes that make the animal more susceptible to seizure activity following one or a few stimulations. This phenomenon is called **kindling,** because it is considered analogous to starting a fire. Kindled seizure activity produces lasting behavioral changes in animals during the interictal period—the period between seizures (Adamec & Shallow, 2000; Kalynchuk & others, 1998, 1999). These changes involve increases in emotionality, which is similar to (or models) the between-seizure emotionality changes often seen in humans with temporal lobe epilepsy (Kalynchuk, 2000). The similarity between kindled seizure activity and certain types of epilepsy suggests that an epileptic seizure may be caused by a brief neural event that produces changes in the characteristics of neural circuits (Westbrook, 2000).

The second circuit in MacLean's model includes the cingulate gyrus, the septum, and some hypothalamic areas. Stimulation of this circuit produces pleasure, especially sexual pleasure (MacLean, 1970). As we discussed in Chapter 5, many researchers have found that stimulation of certain brain structures—especially the mesolimbic pathway, which includes the ventral tegmental area, the medial forebrain bundle fiber system, and the nucleus accumbens—is extremely reinforcing and is responsible for the pleasurable quality of some emotions.

The third circuit consists of parts of the hypothalamus and the anterior thalamus. This circuit is involved in the control of cooperative social behaviors that aid the survival of a species (MacLean, 1970).

Thus, according to the James-Lange theory, emotions result from distinct visceral responses, whereas in the Papez-MacLean model, activation of a specific neural system produces a specific emotion. In the Papez-MacLean model, Stuart's hearing about the death of his father activated one of the three neural systems to cause an experience of sadness because of memories of his father.

But what happens when we are aroused but cannot use our internal state to recognize how we feel? Under these circumstances, cognitive processes can provide the information we need to label our emotional state, as proposed in Schachter's cognitive model of emotion.

Primary and Secondary Emotions: Putting It All Together

In *Descartes' Error,* Antonio Damasio (1994) differentiates two types of emotion: primary and secondary. *Primary emotions* are built-in, hardwired, innate. As he puts it, "we are wired to respond with an emotion, in preorganized fashion, when certain features of stimuli in the world or in our bodies are perceived, alone or in combination" (p. 131). Examples of such "features of stimuli" include size (e.g., large animals or persons), type of movement (e.g., wriggling, as in snakes), certain sounds (e.g., loud noises, growling), and particular internal sensations (e.g., a crushing feeling in the chest). The limbic system and particularly the amygdala are primarily involved in the processing of these preorganized emotions, which Damasio also calls "Jamesian," because he believes the James-Lange theory successfully accounts for them.

Secondary emotions include the experience of an emotion, the feeling of it, and learning is involved. We develop secondary emotions by forming connections between certain situations (e.g., the death of someone close to us, winning the lottery) and primary emotions. According to Damasio (1994), the limbic system structures are not sufficient for the development of secondary emotions, although they are obviously involved in the expression of such emotions. For Damasio, the prefrontal areas and somatosensory cortices are added to the network in the case of secondary emotions. From this analysis, damage to the limbic system would be expected to impair the regulation of the primary emotions, and this is what we saw in our discussion of impairment following damage to the amygdala. By the same token, damage to the prefrontal areas would be expected to affect the processing of secondary emotions negatively, and we will present evidence for this later in the chapter.

Checkpoint

Which of the three Papez-MacLean circuits was activated when Stuart learned of the death of his father?

Schachter's Cognitive Model

In 1964, Stanley Schachter proposed an alternative model for emotional response. **Schachter's cognitive model of emotion** argues that when we become aware of internal tension or arousal, we seek to identify the cause of the arousal, and unless we know why we are aroused, we attribute our arousal to the prevailing environmental conditions. To return to our earlier example, the source of the arousal is the sight of a man with a gun (Figure 12.5). Or in Stuart's case, he had no difficulty attributing his internal arousal to the sad message he had just received. In another illustration, imagine you are at a party where the people around you are having a good time. You are internally aroused (or excited), and you attribute your arousal to the party and assume that you are also having a good time. If you experienced similar arousal while studying for a difficult exam, you might attribute your arousal to fear of performing poorly on the test. This illustrates an important aspect of Schachter's model: Internal arousal may not actually be produced by a particular environment but just experienced at that time in that particular setting. Thus, you may misattribute your arousal to the environment, when, in reality, something else is responsible. For example, you may attribute your bad time at a party to what is happening at the party, when, in fact, your negative arousal is caused by worries about an upcoming exam.

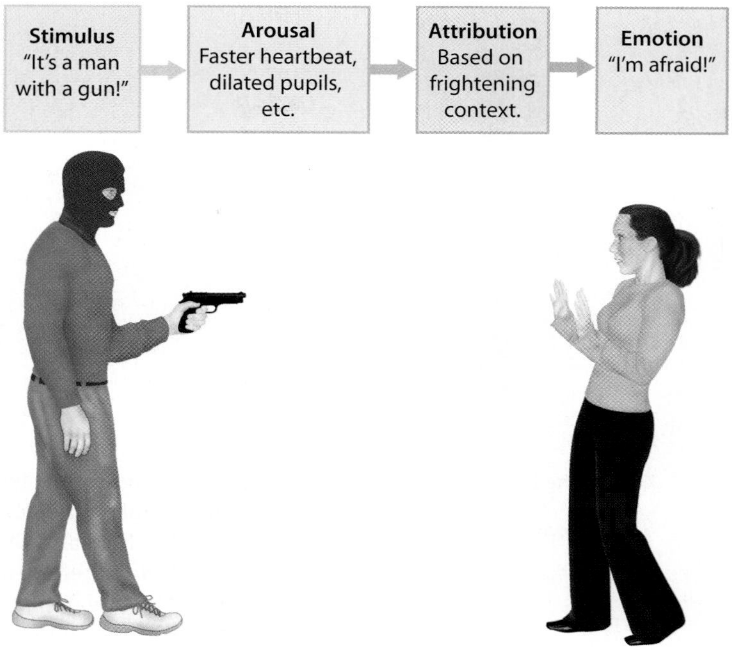

Figure 12.5
Schachter's cognitive model of emotion If you did not know why you were aroused, which is clearly not the case here, you would attribute your arousal to prevailing environmental conditions.

→ According to Schachter's model, is it possible that something other than the man with the gun made you afraid?

The Classic Schachter-Singer Study

In 1962, Schachter and Singer reported the results of an experiment that shows the importance of cognition to our emotional experience. The researchers told participants that the study was intended to evaluate the effects of a vitamin on visual skills. The participants received either a placebo injection or an injection of epinephrine, which produces autonomic arousal; they either were told what to expect physiologically (informed), were given no information about physiological changes (uninformed), or were misinformed about what to expect (i.e., given a list of possible side effects that would not be produced by an injection of epinephrine); and they were exposed to a euphoric confederate of the research team or to an angry confederate.

Although the results were not as clear cut as the experimenters might have hoped, they did tend to support Schachter's cognitive model. For example, in groups exposed to a euphoric confederate, participants either misinformed or uninformed about the physiological effects of the injection averaged higher scores on an activity index (a measure of the degree to which the subject engaged in activities modeled by the confederate) than either the placebo participants or the ones who were told what to expect from the epinephrine injection (Figure 12.6). Likewise, participants given epinephrine injections without being told what to expect averaged higher scores on an anger index (a coding method in which numbers were assigned on the basis of how the participant reacted to the comments of the angry confederate; positive values indicate the participant agreed with the confederate, negative values that the participant either disagreed with or ignored the confederate).

Note that in each case, the participants in the placebo group actually had higher average scores than those in the epinephrine-informed group (Figure 12.6). Schachter and Singer attributed this greater emotionality in the participants in the placebo group to arousal in some of the participants created by the actions of the confederate to whom they were exposed. When the placebo participants with indications of sympathetic arousal were factored out, the remaining participants in the placebo

Schachter's cognitive model of emotion The view that if unable to identify the cause of physiological arousal, a person will attribute it to environmental conditions.

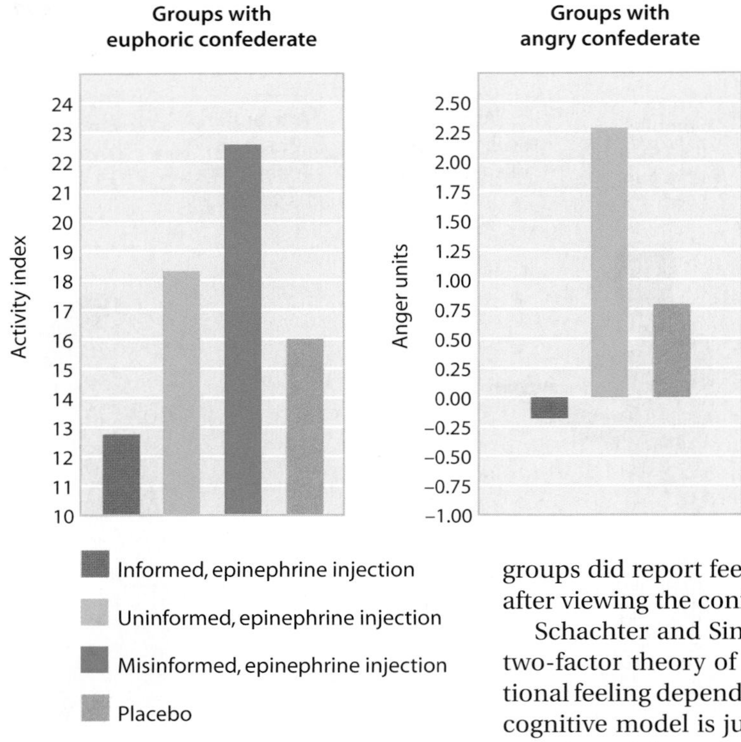

Figure 12.6

The outcome of the Schachter-Singer study on the attribution of emotions Participants who were uninformed about the cause of their arousal felt either euphoric or angry, depending on the actions of the confederate. Misinformed participants exposed to a euphoric confederate experienced their arousal as euphoria; there were no misinformed subjects in the "angry confederate" condition. Informed participants were little affected by the actions of the confederate.

➜ **Why were the placebo group scores higher than those of the informed group?**

group exhibited comparable emotional levels to the epinephrine-informed participants.

In summary, the participants who received the epinephrine injection were internally aroused and needed an explanation for their arousal. As predicted, participants told of the true effects of the injection attributed their arousal to the injection and were not influenced by the behavior of the confederate. But participants who were injected with epinephrine and were misinformed or uninformed about its effects needed to attribute their arousal to the environment, which in this case included the behavior of the confederate. Schachter and Singer found that the participants in these groups did report feeling more euphoric or angry than other participants after viewing the confederates' euphoric or angry behavior.

Schachter and Singer (1962) concluded that their results supported a two-factor theory of emotion: A stimulus causes arousal, and our emotional feeling depends on how we label the stimulus. Note that Schachter's cognitive model is just the James-Lange theory with attribution; the expression of the emotion precedes the experience. Presumably, participants in the reports that Cannon (1927) had reviewed failed to experience any emotion because their arousal from epinephrine injections took place in a neutral environment to which they were unable to attach a label.

Although many psychologists have criticized the Schachter and Singer study because of its methodological flaws—for instance, note the missing group in the anger-confederate condition in Figure 12.6—and lack of empirical evidence for some of its deductions (e.g., Reisenzein, 1983), other experiments have generally supported Schachter's two-factor theory of emotion (e.g., Palace, 1995). Let us consider one such study.

Are You in Love?

Imagine you are going on a first date. You know little about your date, and you have been anxiously awaiting the evening. As the hour approaches, your palms start to sweat and your heartbeat speeds up. When you finally meet your date, your mouth is dry and you feel incredibly tense. Of course, these are all symptoms of apprehension or anxiety, but if the evening goes well, you may erroneously attribute these feelings to falling or being in love.

To test the importance of adversity in producing the emotion of love, male subjects were asked to cross a long, narrow, flexible suspension bridge (Dutton & Aron, 1974) (Figure 12.7). The experience was terrifying for many of the participants, with the bridge swaying as the men crossed 200 feet above rocks and rapids. After crossing the bridge, each man met an attractive female experimenter who questioned him about his experiences. The woman approached the men either immediately

Figure 12.7

Are you in love? After crossing this suspension bridge, male participants met an attractive female experimenter. When the woman approached the men immediately after they crossed the bridge, many of them attributed their arousal to feelings of attraction for the female experimenter, not to having just crossed the bridge.

➜ **What is misattribution of arousal?**

after their crossing, when they were still aroused by their fearful experience, or 10 minutes later, when their arousal had diminished. After the interview, the woman gave each subject her telephone number and said he could call her to learn more about the study. Dutton and Aron predicted that if the men were attracted to the woman, they would call her. In fact, 65% of the men in the aroused condition—the ones approached immediately after crossing the bridge—telephoned the woman, compared with only 30% of the men in the nonaroused condition.

Misattribution of arousal also affects emotions other than love. Studies indicate that the misattribution of arousal can explain increased anger in hot environments (Anderson, 1989), increased sexual passion following an intense argument or frightening experience (Palace, 1995), and the increased edge experienced by successful athletes during competition (Christensen, 2000). These findings all demonstrate the significant role that cognitive processes play in the interpretation of emotions.

As you can see from our discussion, both physiological and psychological processes influence our emotional experiences. Emotions, in turn, have a powerful influence on our actions. When we feel happy, we might give a loved one a hug; when we feel angry, we might yell at that same loved one. Perhaps no other behavior is influenced as much by our emotions as is aggressive behavior. Aggression has been studied more than any other motivated behavior, and it is the topic of the next section.

Checkpoint

While rock climbing with a group of friends, you suddenly find yourself trapped on a ledge with a member of the group to whom you are attracted. Your heart is pounding and your stomach is churning—is it fear, or a response to being trapped together with this attractive person?

REVIEW

- An emotion is a feeling that differs from the normal affective state of a person.
- The three attributes of an emotion are a change in physiological arousal accompanying the emotional experience, an affective response, and the capacity to motivate a specific behavior.
- According to the James-Lange theory of emotion, an event causes a distinctive physiological response; interpretation of the internal physiological changes determines the experience of an emotion.
- According to the Cannon-Bard theory of emotion, each emotion-causing event activates the thalamus, which stimulates the cerebral cortex and the internal organs, so that visceral changes (the expression) and emotional experience occur at the same time.
- The Papez-MacLean model of emotion proposes that the limbic system influences the emotional reaction to an event. One neural circuit (including the amygdala and the hippocampus) controls survival, a second neural circuit (the cingulate gyrus, the septum, and some hypothalamic areas) is involved in the experience of pleasure, and a third circuit (part of the hypothalamus and anterior thalamus) controls cooperative social behavior.
- Primary emotions are innate and involve the limbic system; secondary emotions are acquired and involve prefrontal brain areas and somatosensory cortices in addition to the limbic system.
- Schachter's cognitive model of emotion proposes that when unable to identify the cause of physiological arousal, a person attributes it to the environmental conditions.

Emotions and Aggressive Behavior

Phillip had become increasingly worried about his wife's inability to control her temper. Darla's anger was often directed at their two daughters, and she had begun to punish them severely for even the slightest misbehavior. During a recent flare-up over spilled cereal, Darla slapped Tara, their older girl, as hard as she could across the face and then yelled at Phillip when he grabbed her hand to prevent her from slapping the girl again. After the incident, Phillip was able to talk with his wife, and she seemed to recognize that she had acted too harshly. She told Phillip then that although she believed the girls needed to be disciplined, she would try to do it without losing control of herself.

Phillip first noticed Darla's inability to control her temper after her recent promotion at the bank. Along with her new job responsibilities, Darla seemed to have a never-ending set of complaints from the patrons at the bank, and she frequently came home tired and irritable.

Tonight Darla really lost control. The girls were especially quarrelsome, fighting over coloring books and which TV programs to watch. Phillip noticed Darla's anger building but did not say anything for fear of triggering a reaction. In retrospect, that had been a mistake. When 5-year-old Jamie refused to go to bed, Darla snapped and yanked Jamie's arm so violently that she pulled it out of the shoulder socket. Jamie shrieked, and her arm hung loosely at her side. Darla froze for an instant, then fled into the bedroom and slammed the door, leaving Phillip to deal with the emergency.

He carried Jamie to the car with Tara at his side. At the emergency room, Phillip told the doctor that his daughter had fallen off a swing in their backyard, had tried to catch herself, and the arm had popped out of its socket. He could see the disbelief on the face of the doctor and was afraid she might have to report the injury as a possible case of child abuse.

What causes Darla's aggressive behavior, which is producing such intense physical and psychological pain for her family? Darla's inability to control her anger may reflect dysfunction in specific brain structures, or it may have other psychological and biological causes.

Defining Aggression

We often refer to behavior such as Darla's as aggressive, but what exactly do we mean by that? Table 12.1 presents a list of behaviors (and their possible consequences) that can be considered aggressive, but even a cursory glance at the list

Table 12.1
Potentially Aggressive Behaviors

1. A Boy Scout helping an elderly woman across the street accidentally trips, and she sprains her ankle.
2. An assassin attempts to kill the President, but the shot misses.
3. A housewife knocks a flowerpot off a fifth-story window ledge, and it hits a pedestrian.
4. A farmer kills a chicken for dinner.
5. In a debate, one person belittles another person's qualifications.
6. A soldier presses a button that fires a nuclear missile and kills thousands of people he cannot even see.
7. A police officer trying to break up a riot hits a rioter on the head with a club and knocks him unconscious.
8. A cat stalks, catches, tosses round, and eventually kills a mouse.
9. A wife accuses her husband of having an affair, and he retorts that after living with her anyone would have an affair.
10. A frightened boy, caught stealing and trying to escape, shoots his discoverer.
11. One child takes away a toy from another, making him cry.
12. A man unable to get into his locked car kicks in the side of the door.
13. A man pays $1 to beat an old car with an iron bar, which he does vigorously.
14. A football player blocks another player from behind and breaks his leg.
15. A businessman hires a professional killer to "take care of" a business rival.
16. A woman carefully plots how she will kill her husband, then she does so.
17. Two students get into a drunken brawl, and one hits the other with a beer bottle.
18. A businessman works vigorously to improve his business and drive out the competition.
19. On the Rorschach inkblot test, a hospitalized mental patient is scored as being highly aggressive, although he has never actually harmed anyone.
20. A young boy talks a lot about how he is going to beat up others but never does it.
21. A hired killer successfully completes his job.

Adapted from: Beck, R. C. (1990). *Motivation: Theories and principles* (3rd ed.). Englewood Cliffs, NJ: Prentice-Hall.

reveals the disparity between many of the behaviors. For example, an energetic executive trying to drive out competitors seems totally different from someone who works as a hired killer. Still, we consider both behaviors aggressive.

Psychologists have struggled for years to derive a single definition of aggression that encompasses all the aggressive behaviors listed in the table. The most frequent definition is that **aggression** is behavior intended to harm a living being or, under some conditions, an inanimate object (Klein, 1982). Thus, any behavior with malicious intent is considered aggressive (Figure 12.8).

Figure 12.8
Aggression In this Shoe cartoon, the pitcher is trying to decide how best to pitch to a strong batter. Determined not to give the batter a hit, the pitcher decides to throw at his head, definitely an aggressive act. (Tribune Media Services, Inc. All rights reserved. Reprinted with permission.)

➔ If there were no thought bubble in the final frame of the cartoon, how (according to Moyer) might you infer the pitcher's intent?

One difficulty with the definition is determining intent. We might, for example, try to determine someone's intent from verbal behavior. In the case of Phillip and Darla, Phillip might ask his wife why she slapped Tara or yanked Jamie's arm. Unfortunately, Darla's verbal response may not accurately reveal her intent, as she is unlikely to admit that she was deliberately aggressive toward her daughters. Also, because animals have no verbal behavior, we cannot use it to detect their intent. Kenneth Moyer (1976) suggested an indirect way to assess intent: We can infer aggressive intent by observing the persistence of an animal's (or human's) "destructive acts toward the same or similar stimulus objects at different times" (p. 2). In our example, Moyer would consider Darla's acts toward her daughters aggressive, because she persists in doing them.

Are All Aggressive Acts Alike?

As you can see from Table 12.1, many different behaviors can be considered aggressive, and aggressive acts can occur in a variety of situations. This tremendous disparity suggests that there might be several different types of aggression, with different neurological bases (Moyer, 1976). In his analysis, Moyer identified the following eight types of aggression: fear-induced, instrumental, intermale, irritable, maternal, predatory, sex-related, and territorial (Table 12.2).

Table 12.2
Eight Types of Aggression

Type	Description
Fear-induced	An animal cornered and unable to escape from danger becomes aggressive.
Instrumental	An animal emits an aggressive behavior to obtain a desired goal.
Intermale	A male threatens and then attacks a strange male of the same species.
Irritable	A frustrated or angry animal attacks another animal or object.
Maternal	A mother assaults a perceived threat to her young.
Predatory	An animal stalks, catches, and kills its natural prey.
Sex-related	A male becomes aggressive when encountering sex-related stimuli.
Territorial	An animal defends its territory against intrusion.

aggression A behavior motivated by the intent to harm a living being or an inanimate object.

Each type of aggression is characterized by a different pattern of aggressive behavior. For example, although a male animal will display aggressive behavior both toward its natural prey and toward an unfamiliar male of its own species, the form of its predatory response is quite different from the form of its aggressive response toward the strange male. In addition, evidence indicates that each type of aggressive behavior is controlled by a different genetic mechanism. For example, selective breeding for reduced levels of one type of aggression did not influence other types (Popova & others, 1993).

Moyer (1976) suggested that in nonhuman animals, the motivational system differs for each type of aggression. This is explained in part by the existence in nonhuman animals of separate biological systems for the various forms of aggression, with the exception of instrumental aggression (means to an end). (Note that in instrumental aggression, the behavior patterns are learned rather than involving a biological system built into the animal through evolution.) In addition, there is a specific releasing stimulus for each form of aggression, but the effectiveness of a particular releasing stimulus depends on the efficient functioning of the relevant physiological systems. For example, a releasing stimulus for predatory aggression (the presence of the prey) does not trigger predatory behavior unless the neural circuits in the lateral hypothalamus controlling predatory aggression are functioning effectively (Flynn, 1972).

Unlike nonhuman animals, humans do not appear to have different releasing stimuli or behavior patterns for different types of aggression. Consider a male debater who belittles the qualifications of an opponent. This could be one of several different kinds of aggression, including instrumental aggression (vying for the attention of a woman), fear-induced aggression (fear of the opponent's attack), and irritable aggression (anger at the opponent over an incident just before the debate). These observations indicate that in humans, different motives can produce the same form of aggressive behavior.

Let us take a closer look at two of Moyer's types of aggression: irritable aggression and fear-induced aggression. Our discussion focuses on the specific neural and hormonal systems that control each type and the powerful influence that emotions have on our actions.

➤Checkpoint

You and a friend are walking back to your car after seeing a movie, when a man runs up and grabs your friend's purse. As she screams for the man to stop, without thinking you chase after the purse snatcher, catch him, and throw him to the ground. According to Moyer's types of aggression, which type was exhibited by the purse snatcher? By your friend? By you?

REVIEW

- ➤ Aggression is behavior motivated by the intent to harm a living being or inanimate object.
- ➤ According to Moyer, the eight types of aggression are fear-induced, instrumental, intermale, irritable, maternal, predatory, sex-related, and territorial.
- ➤ In both human and nonhuman animals, each form of aggression, except for instrumental aggression, appears to have a particular physiological basis.

Irritable Aggression

As we know from reading the newspapers and watching news programs, **irritable aggression** is the most prevalent form of human aggression; it is also the most studied type of aggression. Moyer (1976) defined irritable aggression less by what it is than by what it is not—as aggression that does not fit any of the other specific types. According to Moyer, irritable aggression is aggression that involves attack without an attempt to escape. In fear-induced aggression, for example, an animal will escape if possible. Unlike predatory, intermale, and sex-related aggression, irritable aggression is inclusive: An irritably aggressive animal will attack anything, regardless of stimulus or intent. One of the most common examples of irritable aggression in humans is what we might also call *pain-elicited aggression,* or aggres-

irritable aggression An attack on almost anything without making attempts to escape.

sion triggered by a physically (or psychologically) painful injury. You have probably had the experience of injuring yourself in some way—hitting your thumb with a hammer, for example—and then lashing out at a friend or loved one who asked if you had hurt yourself.

In its mild form, irritable aggression might involve an overt display of annoyance, such as making a crude gesture toward a driver who has just cut you off in traffic or kicking a cell phone after learning of a death in your family, whereas extreme cases may involve destructive, uncontrollable rage such as a celebrity might direct toward paparazzi she thought were invading the privacy of her family. Several CNS structures have been identified as having a controlling influence on irritable aggression. Some brain systems arouse irritable aggressive behavior, others inhibit it. Several hormones also appear to play a role in the expression of irritable aggression.

Klüver-Bucy syndrome A disorder produced by temporal lobectomy, characterized by placidity, socially inappropriate sexual activity, compulsive orality, a decreased ability to recognize people, and memory deficits.

Neural Influences on Irritable Aggression

In 1939, Heinrich Klüver and Paul Bucy performed bilateral temporal lobectomies on rhesus monkeys and reported a variety of behavioral changes, including remarkable placidity. This classic study suggested that the temporal lobes might be involved in the initiation of certain types of aggression. On the basis of this work, some surgeons removed the temporal lobes of excessively aggressive people (e.g., Terzian & Ore, 1955). Although this surgical treatment did reduce aggressive behavior, it also produced negative side effects, including socially inappropriate sexual activity, compulsive orality, a decreased ability to recognize people, and memory deficits. The behavioral effects resulting from temporal lobectomies are known as the **Klüver-Bucy syndrome.**

In place of this radical surgical procedure, other, more limited treatments to reduce irritable aggressiveness are now used. (Note that any psychosurgical procedure is extreme and is recommended only when other treatments have proven ineffective.) Research has confirmed that aggressive behavior is associated with intense temporal lobe activity (Engel, 1992). Using *single photon emission computerized tomography (SPECT)* imaging, significant differences in brain activity were found between a group of participants who had displayed aggression in the 6 months before the examination and a group of psychiatric patients of similar age who had not exhibited such aggression (Amen & others, 1996). Compared with the nonaggressive subjects, the aggressive individuals had decreased activity in the prefrontal cortex and focal abnormalities in the left temporal lobe. Using MRI scans, researchers compared patients with epilepsy involving the temporal lobe who had a history of explosive aggression with individuals who had epilepsy involving the temporal lobe without such a history (van Elst & others, 2000). Overall the researchers found no evidence for greater sclerosis of the amygdala in the aggressive patients, but nearly half of them had either atrophy of the amygdala or other temporal lobe damage affecting the amygdala or periamygdaloid structures.

Inside the temporal lobe, the amygdala appears to influence the excitation and suppression of irritable aggression. The amygdala is divided into several functional areas, two of which seem to be most involved in emotions: the central nucleus and the lateral nucleus (Figure 12.9). An indication that the amygdala plays an important role in irritable aggression in humans is the observation that seizures (or excessive neural activity) originating here have been associated with violent behavior. During a seizure, the amygdala is extremely active, and irritable aggression can be intense. Mark and Ervin (1970) demonstrated a positive relationship between activity in the amygdala during a seizure and the occurrence of hostility in humans. For example, they reported the case of Julia, a young woman who had had an attack of encephalitis before age 2 and had begun having epileptic seizures at age 10. On several occasions, Julia had attacked people without apparent provocation. The most serious attack had occurred when

Figure 12.9
Key structures in the amygdala that are related to emotional behavior

→ **What evidence suggests that the amygdala plays a role in irritable aggression in humans?**

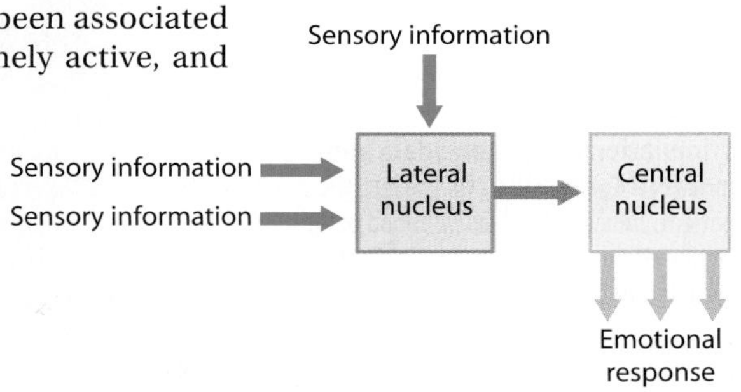

amygdalectomy A surgical procedure that treats extreme aggressiveness by destroying areas in the amygdala.

she was 18. At a movie theater with her parents, she had told them she felt one of her "racing spells" coming on and had gone to the women's lounge to wait for them. In the lounge, she looked into a mirror and had an hallucination in which she saw one side of her face and arm as disfigured and "evil." At the same moment, another woman accidentally bumped into her, triggering Julia to attack her with a small knife she carried. Julia's screams brought help quickly, and the person was saved.

Mark and Ervin (1970) implanted electrodes in Julia's amygdala and filmed her activities as they stimulated her brain. Figure 12.10 shows photographic stills from before and after stimulation of Julia's amygdala. In describing the last photograph, Mark and Ervin wrote, "Her spring toward the wall was sudden and quite unexpected . . . We were able to understand how victims of her attacks had not had the time to defend themselves!" (p. 104). After performing lesions in Julia's amygdala, Mark and Ervin reported that she had only two mild rage episodes in the first year after the operation and none the second year. The surgical procedure is called an **amygdalectomy.**

Other clinical observations also suggest that amygdalectomy is an effective treatment for excessive violence in some people. For example, of a group of 481 people with untreatable aggressiveness who received lesions of the amygdala, 76% initially showed either excellent or moderate improvement in their aggressiveness; a 3-year follow-up found that 70% still showed improvement (Ramamurthi, 1988). Similarly, 85% of 51 hostile people who had their amygdala lesioned showed a significant reduction in aggression (Narabayashi, 1972). Against this apparent success in other countries (Narabayashi in Japan, Ramamurthi in India), Valenstein (1980) reported a much lower success rate in the United States. According to his review of the research literature, fewer than 29% of the patients undergoing amygdalectomies for their aggressive behavior exhibited significant improvement. More recently, two patients were studied who had undergone bilateral amygdalotomy (cutting the connections to the amygdala) for intractable aggression (Lee & others, 1998). Although both showed reduced levels of autonomic arousal to stress and a reduction in aggressive outbursts, both continued to have problems controlling their aggression.

Irritable aggressive behavior also has been shown to be influenced by the hypothalamus in nonhuman animals. For example, cholinergic stimulation of the lateral hypothalamus facilitated predatory aggression in rats, which the researchers suggested might have been related to increases in irritable aggression in the animals (Yoburn & others, 1981). In another study, seizures produced by stimulation of either the pyriform cortex (an area in the medial temporal lobe) or the amygdala lowered the threshold for eliciting aggression by stimulation of the anterior hypothalamus in cats (Brutus & others, 1986).

One function of the ventromedial hypothalamus may be to suppress irritable aggressive behavior, as hyperirritability has been observed following VMH lesions

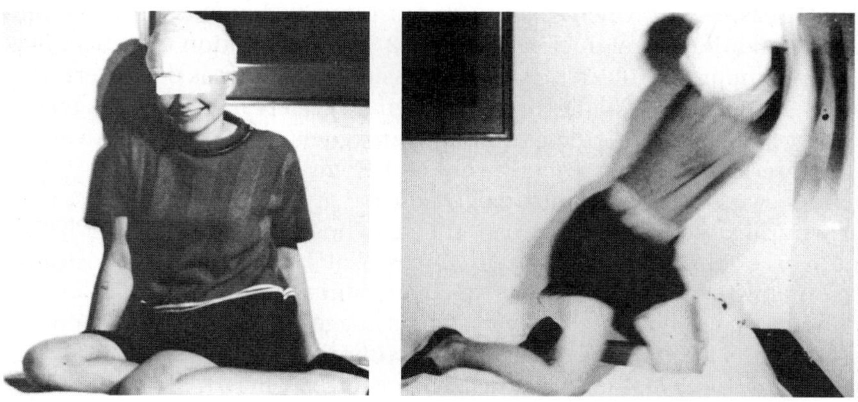

Figure 12.10

Stimulation of the amygdala and irritable aggression On the left, the patient, Julia, is in a pleasant mood before amygdala stimulation; on the right, after stimulation, Julia attacks the wall.

➡ **What type of surgery was used to treat this patient's rage episodes?**

in rats (Brayley & Albert, 1977; Grossman, 1972) and in cats (Wheatley, 1944). Hyperirritability also has been reported in humans with tumors in the VMH area (Haugh & Markesbery, 1983; Reeves & Plum, 1969; Tonkonogy & Geller, 1992). Some research suggests that the VMH inhibits irritable aggression in rats by directly suppressing activity in the lateral hypothalamus (Sclafani, 1971). When Sclafani cut the neural connections between the two areas, he observed hyperirritability similar to but less persistent than that produced by VMH lesions.

Both amygdalar and septal areas in cats facilitated aggression triggered by hypothalamic stimulation (Stoddard-Apter & MacDonnell, 1980). The facilitatory sites in the amygdala projected mainly to the VMH, and the septal sites to the paraventricular and dorsomedial hypothalamic nuclei. Further, the benzodiazepine receptor may modulate excitability in the amygdalo-VMH pathway (Adamec, 2000). Recall from Chapter 4 that the benzodiazepine receptor is part of the $GABA_A$ receptor complex, which is associated with CNS inhibition.

Disease and Irritable Aggression

Among other diseases, brain tumors and epilepsy have been found to intensify levels of irritability, hostility, and overt aggressiveness. Perhaps the best known example of aggression caused by a brain tumor is the case of Charles Whitman. In the summer of 1966, under the influence of a malignant brain tumor, Whitman first killed his wife and mother and then took a high-powered rifle with a telescopic sight to the top of the tower on the University of Texas campus in Austin. From there, he methodically shot 38 people, 14 fatally, before being killed by police. Autopsy revealed a malignant tumor that probably involved his temporal lobe; the neuropathologist could not determine the location of the tumor for certain because of the damage to Whitman's brain from gunshot wounds (Sweet & others, 1969). Other investigators have reported cases of violent, assaultive behavior in people with tumors in the temporal lobes (e.g., Malamud, 1967) and unusually aggressive behavior in children with such tumors (Guimaraes & others, 2004; Nakaji & others, 2003). Temporal lobe damage caused by viral encephalitis (recall the case of Julia) also has been associated with aggression (Greer & others, 1989).

Earlier we discussed the association between seizures initiated in the amygdala and irritable aggression, which, although rare, is a well-recognized problem (van Elst & others, 2000). Hindler (1989), for example, described the case of a 19-year-old girl who killed an infant during an epileptic attack, and Franzon and colleagues (2004) reported that aggressiveness was more likely to occur in younger children (under 6 years old) with temporal lobe epilepsy than in older children (6 to 18 years old). However, most people with epilepsy, rather than being angry and violent after a seizure, become frightened or depressed. The reason for these different behavioral responses is unknown, but past experience may affect an individual's reaction to a seizure.

Brain Activity and Irritable Aggression

Abnormal EEG activity also has been associated with violence. For example, Bayrakal (1965) reported that of 200 problem children (e.g., poor impulse control, hostility), 100 had abnormal EEGs. Among these 100 children, most showed disturbances in the temporal lobe and related subcortical areas. In another early study, 50% to 60% of children with behavioral problems showed EEG disturbances, compared with 5% to 15% of children without such problems (Monroe, 1970). More recently, in a review of the usefulness of the EEG in psychiatry, Hughes (1996) reported that nonspecific abnormalities are often seen in children with behavior disorders.

Individuals who commit impulsive crimes are also likely to have abnormal EEG patterns and abnormalities, particularly in the temporal lobes, detectable in CT scans (Wong & others, 1994). Computerized EEGs of male psychiatric inpatients revealed that violent behavior was related to increased delta activity and decreased alpha activity in the temporal and parieto-occipital areas (Convit & others, 1991).

Focal EEG abnormalities, particularly in the left hemisphere, were found to be related to violent offenses in a subgroup of defendants referred for psychiatric examination (Pillmann & others, 1999).

Hormonal Influences on Irritable Aggression

There is extensive evidence that the male sex hormone testosterone affects irritable aggression. First, researchers have found that testosterone level is high in groups selected for heightened aggressiveness (Archer, 1991; Banks & Dabbs, 1996). A high testosterone level in 4,462 male U.S. military veterans was related to a variety of antisocial behaviors, including past trouble with parents, teachers, and classmates; being assaultive toward other adults; and going AWOL (Dabbs & Morris, 1990). Further, men convicted of violent crimes such as murder had higher testosterone levels than men convicted of nonviolent crimes (e.g., burglary) (Dabbs & others, 1995). In an earlier study, the relationship between testosterone and violence was most pronounced at the extremes of testosterone distribution (Dabbs & others, 1987). Among inmates with the highest concentration, 91% had committed violent crimes; in inmates with the lowest concentration, 82% were nonviolent offenders.

Second, males of most species exhibit more aggressive fighting and threatening behavior than females, and this behavior is not limited to intermale aggression. For example, male domesticated animals, such as the bull and the stallion, are as aggressive with people who handle them as they are with other males of their own species (Moyer, 1976). In addition, men commit a significantly greater number of violent crimes than women (e.g., Correctional Service Canada, n.d.).

Third, the elimination of testosterone reduces displays of irritable aggression. Many studies have shown that domestic animals are docile following castration. Human studies have noted that castration of sex offenders can also reduce their aggressiveness (Moyer, 1976). In a study of normal men, researchers found that chemically suppressing gonadal function, which reduced serum testosterone levels, led to a decrease in outward-directed aggression in all subjects (Loosen & others, 1994).

Finally, testosterone administration reinstates the antisocial behavior of castrated males. Wagner and colleagues (1980) observed an increase in aggressive behavior of castrated mice following testosterone replacement (Figure 12.11); cessation of testosterone led to a reduced level of aggressiveness. More recently, researchers confirmed a restoration of aggressive behavior in castrated mice with testosterone replacement (Ogawa & others, 1996). Similarly, testosterone injections in castrated men reinstated aggressive behaviors, such as attacking children, instigating fights, breaking windows, and destroying property (Hawke, 1950). The irritable aggression decreased when testosterone was no longer administered.

Some researchers have suggested that estrogen enhances irritable aggression in females. For example, increased aggressiveness has been reported in sexually receptive female rhesus monkeys and baboons, and estrogen injections significantly increased the frequency of irritable aggressive behavior displayed by both species (Michael, 1969).

Figure 12.11
The effects of testosterone replacement on aggressive behavior The curves plot aggressive behavior toward a target in castrated and noncastrated mice receiving various levels of injected testosterone. The testosterone affects only the castrated mice.

➡ **What hormone(s) affect irritable aggression in females?**

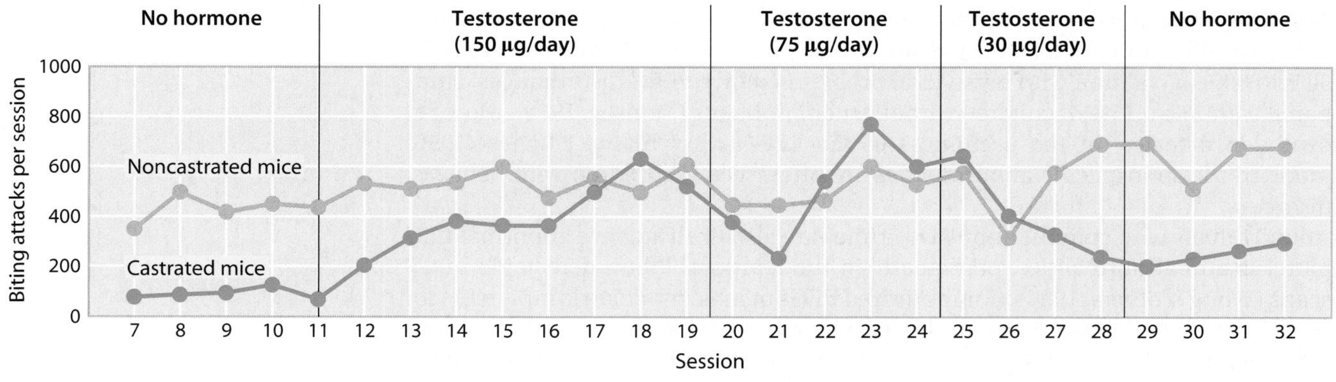

In contrast to estrogen, progesterone appears to inhibit irritable aggression. Irritability during the premenstrual phase of the menstrual cycle—known as **premenstrual syndrome (PMS)**—has been attributed to the progesterone decline that occurs at this time. Several studies have found that some women show increased irritable aggression during the premenstrual phase (e.g., Deuster & others, 1999; Van Goozen & others, 1996). For example, 58 women (18 in the follicular phase of the cycle, 40 in the premenstrual phase) were exposed to an anger-provoking situation (Van Goozen & others). Significantly higher systolic blood pressure and intensity of anger were noted for women in the premenstrual phase than for those in the follicular phase of the menstrual cycle, with some further differences found in anger intensity between women who before the study had reported suffering from premenstrual emotional lability and irritation and those who had not. Additional support for the relationship between PMS and aggression came from the finding that 49% of reported crimes committed by women occurred during the premenstrual phase of the offenders (Dalton, 1961). (Note that the premenstrual phase accounts for only 25% of the menstrual cycle.) Female vervet monkeys also show a heightened irritability during the premenstrual phase (Rapkin & others, 1995).

premenstrual syndrome (PMS) An irritability in human females during the premenstrual phase, attributed to a drop in progesterone level.

There is evidence that progesterone administration can decrease the irritable aggression of the premenstrual phase (Dalton, 1964). In one study, women who took oral contraceptives containing progesterone had much less premenstrual irritability than women who did not take them (Hamburg & others, 1968). Not surprisingly, women who experience PMS appear to have an abnormal response to progesterone (Roca & others, 2003), and recent reviews have found that progesterone treatment is ineffective in treating PMS (Freeman, 2004; Kouri & Halbreich, 1998).

Serotonin and Irritable Aggression

Although a high testosterone level is associated with aggressive behavior, testosterone alone does not produce irritable aggression (Bernhardt, 1997). Bernhardt observed that successful businessmen and male athletes who are no more aggressive than their less successful counterparts have higher testosterone levels; that is, testosterone level is correlated with the success of a man's actions as well as with his level of aggressive behavior. According to Bernhardt, high testosterone levels promote dominance-seeking behaviors in males. When attempts at dominance fail, the male experiences frustration. If serotonin levels in the amygdala are low, as is likely in a male with unsuccessful dominance-seeking behaviors, failure causes an extremely negative emotional frustration reaction and an intense aggressive response. In other words, high testosterone levels promote dominance-seeking behavior, and low serotonin levels produce aggression when the dominance-seeking behavior fails.

A great deal of evidence indicates that low serotonin levels are associated with male irritable aggression in both humans and nonhuman primates. In studies conducted in a natural environment, juvenile male monkeys with low cerebrospinal fluid (CSF) levels of a serotonin metabolite, 5-hydroxyindoleacetic acid (5-HIAA), showed high levels of risk-taking behavior, which included behaving aggressively toward older and larger male monkeys and leaping off tall trees (Higley & others, 1996a; Mehlman & others, 1995). The juvenile monkeys with low 5-HIAA levels exhibited low levels of social competence, which probably led to their earlier emigration from their birth groups (Mehlman & others). The researchers concluded that low CSF levels of 5-HIAA lead to excessive risk taking, aggression, and premature death (Higley & others) (Figure 12.12). Among female monkeys, the average CSF concentration of 5-HIAA was significantly lower in the animals that died during the study than in the animals that survived, and infants born

Figure 12.12
Serotonin level and survival in male monkeys Low CSF levels of 5-HIAA at age 2 lead to poor survival at age 6.

→ **How is serotonin level related to the level of risk-taking behavior?**

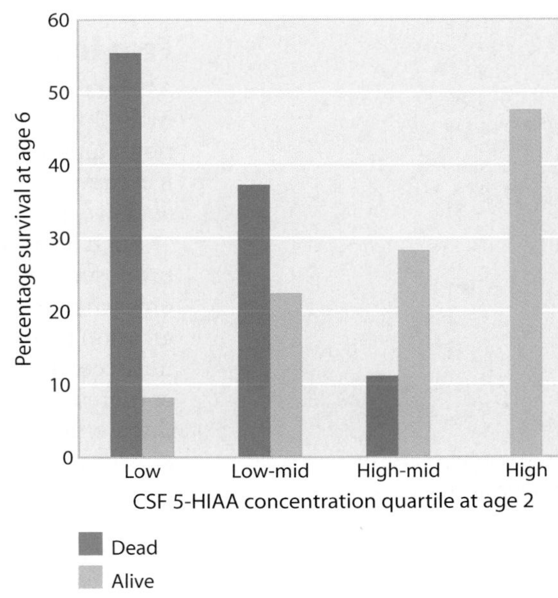

to mothers with higher 5-HIAA levels were more likely to survive (Westergaard & others, 2003). Finally, high CSF testosterone levels were correlated with competitive aggression, but this was not the type of unrestrained, impulsive aggression exhibited by monkeys with low CSF levels of 5-HIAA (Higley & others, 1996b).

In forensic psychiatric patients who had set fires or committed other violent crimes, low levels of 5-HIAA in the CSF were related to a family history of paternal alcoholism and violence (Virkkunen & others, 1996). In addition, men who repeated their offenses during a follow-up period after release from prison had lower 5-HIAA concentrations than nonrepeat offenders.

Although low serotonin levels are typically associated with increased aggressive behavior, the opposite has also been seen. For example, offenders who had aggressive personality disorder were compared with healthy control group participants on a measure of serotonin function (Dolan & others, 2002). Low-impulsive aggressive offenders had higher serotonin function than highly impulsive offenders and healthy control group participants. A possible explanation for this apparent discrepancy in serotonin levels and aggressive behavior will be presented at the end of the section on the genetics of aggression.

Checkpoint

What are the major differences between irritable aggression and other types of aggression? What area of the amygdala appears to be particularly involved in irritable aggression?

REVIEW

- Irritable aggression is an impulsive aggressive reaction elicited by anger and frustration, which can be directed toward the source of the annoyance or displaced to another object. Irritable aggressive behavior can range from mild to uncontrollable rage.
- Neural systems in the temporal lobes, the amygdala, and the anterior lateral hypothalamus initiate irritable aggressive behavior. The ventromedial hypothalamus may inhibit this behavior.
- Malfunctions in the excitatory areas of the temporal lobe and amygdala are related to violent behavior in humans; surgical destruction of these areas can be an effective treatment for hostile and destructive behavior.
- In males, high testosterone levels promote dominance-seeking behaviors, and if serotonin levels in the amygdala are low, failure of the dominance-seeking behaviors produces intense aggressiveness.
- In females, estrogen has been associated with irritable aggression, whereas progesterone appears to suppress irritable aggression.

Fear-Induced Aggression

As you undoubtedly know, a cornered animal can be quite dangerous. When animals (human and nonhuman) are exposed to dangerous environmental conditions, an intense state of fear is aroused. Fear motivates the attempt to escape, and if escape fails, aggression often arises. This aggressive behavior continues until the aversive event ends or the animal is no longer able to fight.

Such **fear-induced aggression** clearly differs from the other types of aggression proposed by Moyer. Fear-induced aggression is a defensive reaction that occurs only when the animal is threatened and perceives escape to be impossible. This aggression involves intense autonomic arousal and defensive threat display, which, if unsuccessful, is followed by an all-out attack. Thus, the aggressive behavior of a cornered or captured animal is a final, last-ditch effort to escape a perceived life-threatening situation. The worst thing you can do under such conditions is to make an animal perceive that it has no means of escape: You are likely to be attacked by even a normally nonaggressive animal.

fear-induced aggression An aggressive behavior that is a defensive reaction occurring only when the organism feels threatened and perceives escape to be impossible.

Klüver and Bucy's classic study (1939) of rhesus monkeys indicated that fearfulness was significantly reduced by bilateral temporal lobectomies, and Franzen and Myers (1973) found that a lesion of either the anterior third of the temporal lobes or the prefrontal cortex severely disrupted the fear-induced aggression of rhesus monkeys.

Observations of the behavior of albino rats following amygdalectomy provide a dramatic illustration of the importance of the amydala in motivating fear and fear-induced aggression (Blanchard & Blanchard, 1972). A normal albino rat typically freezes when it sees a cat and greatly reduces its activity as long as the cat is present. By contrast, an amygdalectomized rat shows no fear of cats. One of the animals climbed on the head of a cat and nibbled its ear. Even after being attacked and released by the cat, the rat reattached itself to the back of the cat. This lack of a normal fear reaction following amygdalectomy has also been reported in monkeys, agoutis (the agouti is a large Central American rodent), and lynxes (Schreiner & Kling, 1953).

Using the classical lesion method and neuroanatomical tracing techniques, LeDoux and colleagues (LeDoux, 1995; LeDoux & others, 1988; Nader & others, 2001) have shown that the amygdala plays a central role in fear conditioning. Specifically, the researchers have found that the lateral nucleus of the amygdala receives sensory information and is thus the input system; the central nucleus is the output system, through its projections to the motor systems, the autonomic nervous system, and the hypothalamic-pituitary axis, as shown in Figure 12.13. In the figure, the connection to the amygdala from the sensory thalamus (1) provides information for simple fear conditioning (e.g., making a fear response to a sound). The connection from the sensory association cortex (2) allows more complex conditioning (e.g., responding to one sound but not to another), and the connection from the hippocampus (3) is needed for conditioning to cues from the context in which the fear conditioning occurs (e.g., the sight or smell of the conditioning apparatus).

The input pathways to the amygdala may be divided on the basis of the complexity of the conditioned fear behavior (Yaniv & others, 2004). According to this view, the lateral amygdala receives information limited to a simple conditioned stimulus; more complex stimuli activate the basal amygdaloid nucleus.

The amygdala also influences the experience of fear in humans. For example, using fMRI, LaBar and colleagues (1998) observed increased blood flow to the amygdala when subjects were shown a light stimulus previously associated with electric shock. A tone associated with a loud noise produced a weak autonomic response in humans who had had the amygdala and surrounding tissues on one side of the brain lesioned to treat severe epileptic seizures (LaBar & others, 1995). Although damage to this area of the brain impaired their autonomic response, these individuals still knew that the tone predicted the loud noise.

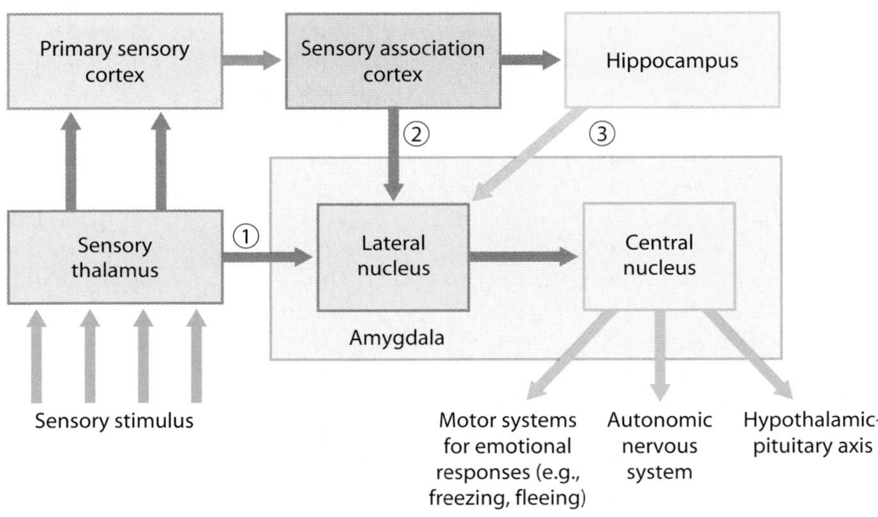

Figure 12.13

The role of the amygdala in fear conditioning Sensory input arrives at the lateral nucleus of the amygdala either directly (1) or indirectly (2). The hippocampus informs the lateral nucleus about the context of the frightening stimulus (3), and the lateral nucleus stimulates the central nucleus to produce emotional responses.

→ **What emotional responses would you expect to occur through the autonomic nervous system?**

(a)

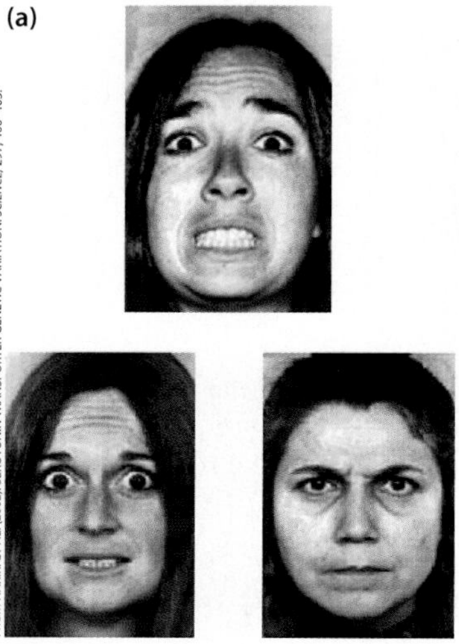

FROM HARIRI ET AL. (2002). SEROTONIN TRANSPORTER GENETIC VARIATION. *SCIENCE*, 297, 400–403.

(b)

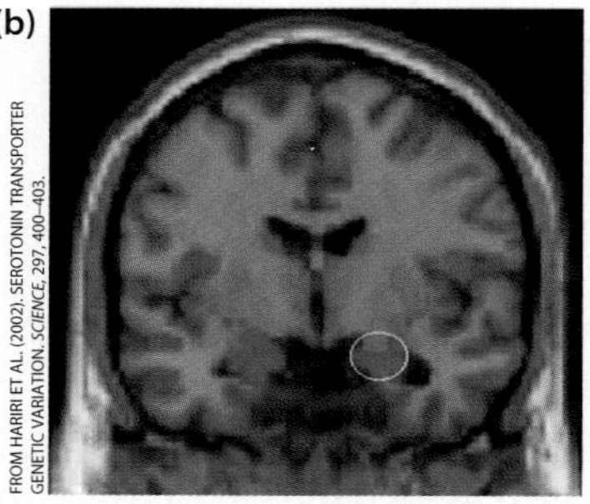

FROM HARIRI ET AL. (2002). SEROTONIN TRANSPORTER GENETIC VARIATION. *SCIENCE*, 297, 400–403.

Figure 12.14

Variation in the serotonin transporter gene and response of the amygdala to a frightening stimulus (a) Participants were asked to select the bottom picture that matched the emotion displayed in the top picture. (b) When matching pictures showing fear, participants with the gene for less serotonin transporter had an enhanced fMRI response (shown in red) in the amygdala (circled in white).

➜ **What effect might this enhanced response of the amygdala have for people with the gene for less serotonin transporter?**

In another study using fMRI, Hariri and colleagues (2002) found that a variation in the gene that codes for the serotonin transporter (a transporter that removes serotonin from the synapse) can affect how a person's amygdala responds to fearful stimuli. One inherited variation of the gene codes for less of the serotonin transporter protein. When subjects performed a facial emotion-matching task on a computer screen (Figure 12.14a), fMRI revealed that, while matching pictures of faces showing fear, those with the gene coding for less of the transporter exhibited greater activation of the amygdala than those with the gene coding for more of the transporter (Figure 12.14b). This suggests that the genetic variation contributes to differential excitability of the amygdala and thus to differential responses to fear- and anxiety-producing stimuli.

Further evidence has been found in humans for the involvement of the amygdala in both acquisition and extinction of conditioned fear (Phelps & others, 2001, 2004). Using fMRI, the researchers found that the left amygdala was activated in a threat condition (the subjects were told that they might be shocked) (Phelps & others, 2001). In a study of fear conditioning and extinction, activation of the amygdala was related to the conditioned response in both acquisition and the first part of extinction (Phelps & others, 2004).

Extensive research with people with brain damage has revealed the importance of the amygdala in the recognition of emotions and particularly in the recognition of fear. For example, SM, a woman with bilateral damage to the amygdala, was unable to recognize fear from facial expressions, although she could extract other information from the faces, such as the identity of a familiar person and the age and gender of an individual (Adolphs & others, 1994). When SM was asked to draw faces illustrating different emotions, she did quite well with faces showing all the basic emotions except fear (Adolphs & others, 1995). She initially refused to draw a fearful face, explaining that she could not imagine such a thing. When forced, she finally drew a cartoonish figure with hair standing on end (Figure 12.15).

In a study of nine individuals with bilateral damage to the amygdala, the individuals as a group were significantly impaired relative to controls in recognizing fear, although individually the performance ranged from severely impaired to normal (Adolphs & others, 1999). None of the individuals was impaired in recognizing happy expressions. In later research with SM, the researchers concluded that her failure to recognize facial expressions of fear was caused by impaired viewing of the faces (Adolphs & others, 2005). SM failed to fixate her gaze on the eyes in the pictures, although the eyes are the most important visual feature for recognizing

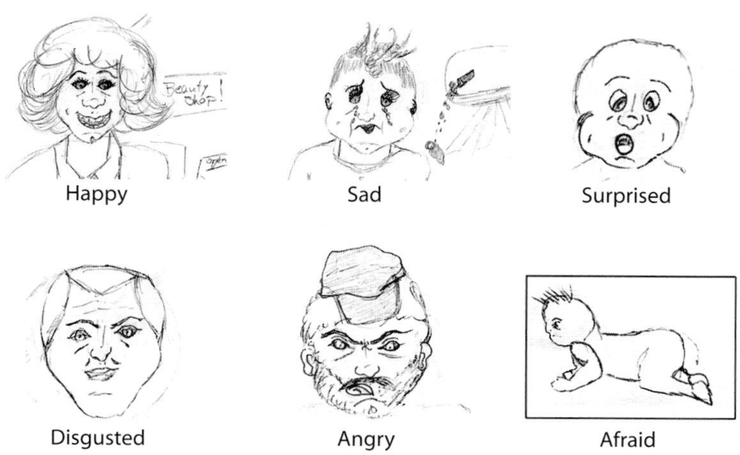

COPYRIGHT 1995 BY THE SOCIETY OF NEUROSCIENCE.

Figure 12.15

The amygdala and the detection of emotional facial expressions After drawing excellent representations of happy, sad, surprised, disgusted, and angry faces, SM, a woman with bilateral damage to the amygdala, was unable to draw a frightened face.

➜ **What simple change in her behavior enables SM to recognize fearful faces?**

fear. When SM was told specifically to focus on the eyes, her recognition of the fearful faces became normal.

Although they are impaired in recognizing fear from facial expressions, people with bilateral damage to the amygdala have little difficulty recognizing emotion in speech (Adolphs & Tranel, 1999; Adolphs & others, 2001). The ability to recognize emotional prosody seems to be a function of the right inferior frontal lobe (Buchanan & others, 2000). In fact, the right hemisphere in general appears to be more involved in emotional recognition than the left hemisphere. When individuals with unilateral temporal lobectomies were studied, those with damage to the right temporal lobe, but not those with left temporal lobe damage, were significantly impaired in recognizing fear from facial expressions (Adolphs & others, 2001). Similarly, individuals with right unilateral damage to the amygdala performed worse than those with left unilateral damage on a task requiring the identification of facial expressions of emotions other than fear (Adolphs & Tranel, 2004).

In addition to an impaired ability to detect fear in facial expressions, people with damage to the amygdala may also have deficits in detecting other negative emotions, such as sadness and anger. For example, individuals with bilateral damage to the amygdala were impaired in recognizing angry faces shown in isolation, frequently mistaking them for smiling faces, a mistake that was never made by a control (Adolphs & Tranel, 2003). In another study, persons with bilateral damage to the amygdala were specifically impaired in rating the intensity of emotional expression in sad faces, performing normally with happy faces (Adolphs & Tranel, 2004). Further, individuals with damage to the amygdala, whether unilateral or bilateral, were impaired relative to controls (brain-damaged or normal) in the detection of social emotions, such as guilt, admiration, and flirtatiousness (Adolphs & others, 2002). The researchers concluded that the human amygdala may be specialized to process complex social stimuli.

Located in the limbic system, the septal area is another brain area that may be involved in fear-induced aggression (Albert & Walsh, 1984). In classic studies, Brady and Nauta (1953, 1955) found that large septal lesions in rats induced a temporarily increased tendency to escape and an increased aggressive response to threat, and these observations have been repeated many times in a variety of contexts (e.g., Albert & Richmond, 1975; Latham & Thorne, 1974; Thorne, 1993). Although septally lesioned rodents readily bite and make frantic attempts to escape when restrained, such animals show little aggression in encounters with others of their species, which suggests an increase in fear-induced aggression (Slotnick & McMullen, 1972). Another possibility, however, is that animals with septal damage actually exhibit an increase in irritable as well as fear-induced aggression (Moyer, 1976; Wallace & Thorne, 1978).

The Genetics of Aggression

Researchers can breed mice that are either extremely aggressive or unaggressive (e.g., Brodkin & others, 2002). Further, the differences in aggressiveness appear to be related to alterations of the serotonin system (Miczek & others, 2001) and to manipulation of the environment in which the animals are raised (Nyberg & others, 2004).

As we indicated in Chapter 4, monoamine neurotransmitters, such as serotonin and norepinephrine, are degraded by monoamine oxidase (MAO). Genetic engineering methods have been used to develop mice that lack the gene that codes for one type of MAO, with the result that the animals have elevated brain levels of serotonin, norepinephrine, and dopamine (Shih & Chen, 1999; Shih & others, 1999a, 1999b). Such *knock-out mice* (so called because a particular gene has been "knocked out") exhibit aggressive behavior similar to that seen in human males lacking the same form of MAO. By contrast, genetically engineered mice lacking the serotonin transporter mechanism showed a reduction in aggressive behavior and activity relative to normal mice (Holmes & others, 2002).

The soluble gas neurotransmitter nitric oxide (NO) has also been implicated in aggressive behavior in mice (Chiavegatto & others, 2001; Kriegsfeld & others, 1997). For example, male mice lacking a form of the enzyme nitric oxide synthase, necessary for the synthesis of NO, exhibit extremely aggressive behavior relative to wild-type mice (Kriegsfeld & others). This was true only for males, however; females lacking the NO synthase displayed little or no aggression. Further, these researchers found that the aggression was testosterone-dependent. Castrated animals were not aggressive, and testosterone replacement restored aggression to precastration levels.

Evidence supporting Moyer's thesis (1976) of different types of aggression with different neurological bases comes from Gammie and coworkers (2000), who found that female mice lacking a form of the NO synthase gene exhibited impaired maternal aggression (i.e., failed to attack male intruders while nursing a litter of pups). Their male counterparts, by contrast, displayed increased aggression.

Research has also revealed a connection between the NO system, serotonin, and aggression in genetically engineered mice. For example, mice lacking the NO synthase gene exhibited increased impulsiveness and aggressiveness, which were caused by decreases in serotonin turnover and defective serotonin receptor function in neural areas controlling emotion (Chiavegatto & others, 2001). This defect can lead to an enhanced sensitivity of serotonergic receptors in aggressive animals (van der Vegt & others, 2001), which may account for some of the variability in results relating aggression to either low or high serotonin levels.

REVIEW

- Fear-induced aggression, occurring when an animal is cornered with no possible escape, involves intense autonomic arousal, defensive threat display, and if all else fails, attack.
- The amygdala plays a central role in fear conditioning, with the lateral nucleus receiving sensory information (input) and the central nucleus controlling output through its connections with the motor systems, the autonomic nervous system, and the hypothalamic-pituitary axis.
- In humans, the amygdala is important for the recognition of emotions and particularly in the recognition of negative emotions, such as fear.
- Genetic studies of aggression in mice demonstrate the involvement of the serotonin and nitric oxide neurotransmitter systems.

Stress

So far, we have discussed the physiological processes that determine how we feel and act. Some emotional responses are mild, others can be quite intense. Intense emotions, such as anger over an inconsequential event with a friend, are often evoked by stressful environmental events (e.g., an upcoming examination, difficulties in a relationship).

During our lives, we experience many different environmental events, some of which place unusual demands on us. A **stressor** is any event that either strains or overwhelms our ability to adjust to our environment (Taylor, 2003). *Physiological stressors* include extreme cold or heat, the invasion of dangerous microorganisms, and physical injury; the death of a relative or friend, an impending examination, and being fired from a job are *psychological stressors.* However, stressors are not always negative; for example, the anticipation of that first date we discussed earlier can be as stressful as an approaching deadline. Stress that is positive rather than negative is called eustress, which we discuss later.

stressor An event that either strains or overwhelms the ability of an organism to adjust to the environment.

Consider the following example: At the beginning of the semester, your biological psychology teacher assigns a research paper that is due by midterm. Before you know it, the deadline is just a week away, and you have only recently begun to work on your report. You are beginning to feel pressure to get it completed and are sure the tension will increase as the due date approaches. *Pressure* can be defined as an expectation (by yourself or others) to behave in a specific way within a particular time frame; a deadline that produces pressure is one example of a stressor. Other stressors are *conflict,* the inability to satisfy two or more incompatible motives, and *frustration,* the obstruction of achieving a goal.

Significant psychological and physiological changes, known as the *stress response,* occur when we encounter a stressor. These behavioral and biological responses determine whether we are able to adapt to the stressful experience. Our reactions to stressors are sometimes effective, sometimes ineffective.

The physiological consequences of experiencing a stressor are closely related to psychological processes. In other words, our perception of a stressful event influences our physiological response to the stressor. Jay Weiss and associates (1970) discovered that electric shocks that could be escaped or avoided by the subject (a rat) produced an elevation of norepinephrine in the animal's brain relative to norepinephrine levels in the brains of rats receiving uncontrollable shocks of equal duration and intensity. More recently, norepinephrine turnover (faster turnover results in lower norepinephrine levels and higher levels of a metabolite of norepinephrine) was examined in various brain areas in rats that spent either 3 hours or 6 hours in an avoidance-escape stress procedure (Tsuda & Tanaka, 1985). Experimental rats that were able to avoid or escape electric shock exhibited greater norepinephrine turnover in the hypothalamus, amygdala, and thalamus than yoked control animals that were unable to control the shock. After 21 hours of such stress, however, the yoked control rats showed greater norepinephrine turnover in the brain areas than the experimental rats. The researchers concluded that there is an increased norepinephrine response before the animals learn the coping response and a decreased norepinephrine response after the coping response is established.

The effects of controllable and uncontrollable footshock on monoaminergic (norepinephrine, dopamine, and serotonin) activity were studied in the frontal cortex of male and female rats (Heinsbroek & others, 1991). The researchers found that the activation of all three neurotransmitters was greater after uncontrollable than after controllable shock, with larger differences for females than males in norepinephrine and dopamine. Exposure to the experimental environment alone raised corticosterone levels in the blood of the animals, and there was a further elevation in response to the footshock. Corticosterone levels were independent of the controllability of the shock.

Checkpoint

After a long, frustrating day at the library working on your term paper, and after being stuck in traffic on the way home, you walk through the front door of your apartment and are greeted by the sight of your dog chewing up the newspaper, which you left on the table in the dining area. List the potential stressors in this scenario.

Biological Reactions to Stressors

In 1956, Hans Selye (SELL-yee), wrote that when we are exposed to a stressor we exhibit a general pattern of internal biological changes. Selye called this physiological stress response the **general adaptation syndrome (GAS),** and he observed that all stressors, whether physiological or psychological, produce this response. The GAS has three stages: alarm, resistance, and exhaustion (Figure 12.16).

The Alarm Stage

You start to give a speech in front of your class. During the speech, your voice quavers, your mouth is dry, your palms are sweating, and your hands are shaking. These biological responses are part of the **alarm stage** (also called the *alarm reaction*).

When we are exposed to a stressor, our sympathetic nervous system is aroused, resulting in an increased respiration rate, which enhances oxygen intake; an increased heart rate, which pumps more oxygen through the bloodstream; the release of stored red blood cells from the spleen to carry the increased oxygen; and

general adaptation syndrome (GAS) A pattern of physiological responses to a physiological or psychological stressor.

alarm stage The first stage in the GAS, characterized by intense sympathetic nervous system arousal; also called *alarm reaction.*

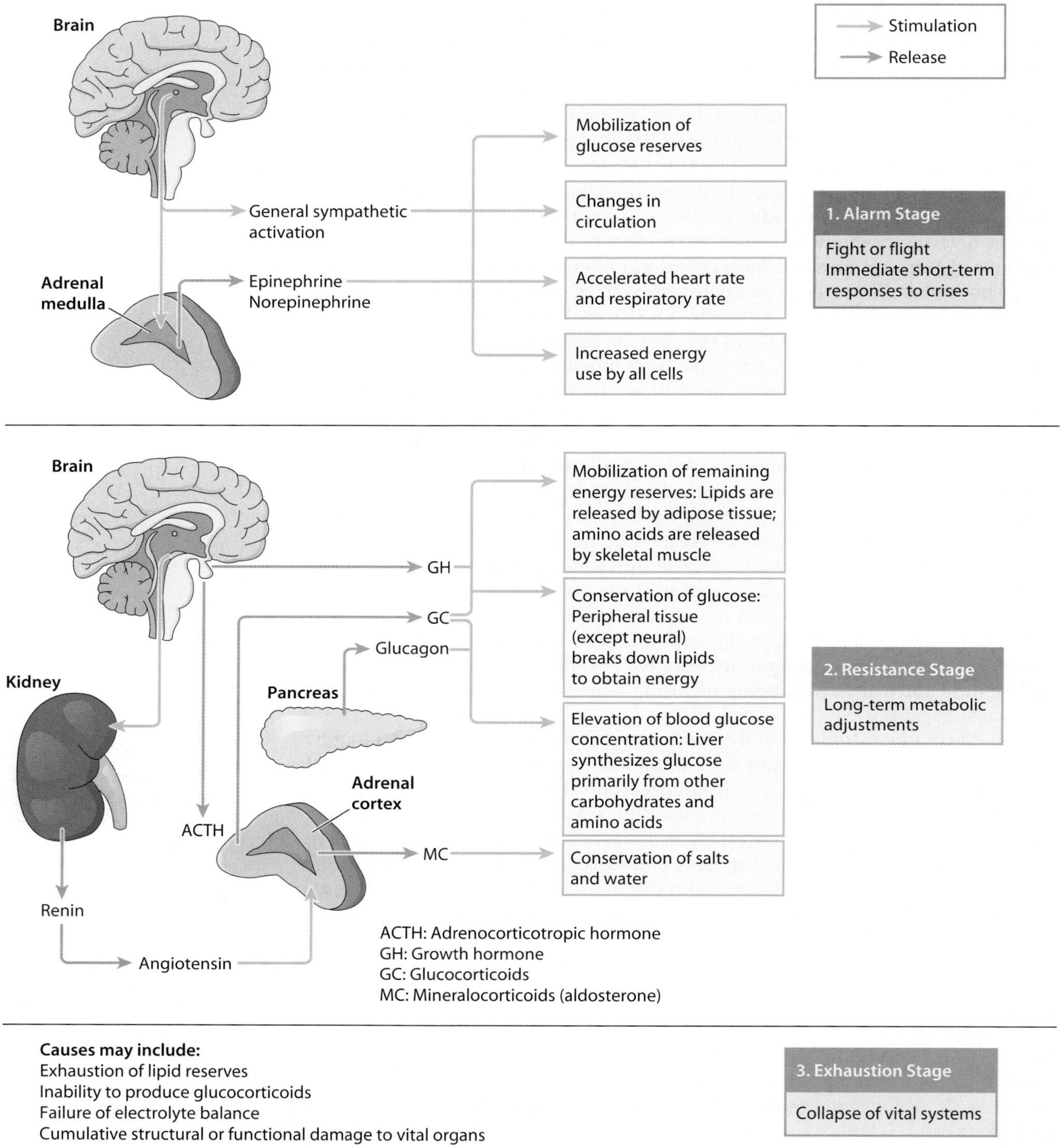

Figure 12.16

The general adaptation syndrome
Characteristic internal physiological changes occur at each stage of the GAS.

➜ **What conditions promote a change from the alarm stage to the resistance stage?**

a redistribution of the blood supply from the skin and internal organs to the brain and muscles. In addition, conversion of glycogen to glucose (sugar) is increased, followed by glucose release from the liver (the brain and muscles use glucose for energy). Epinephrine and norepinephrine are secreted from the adrenal medulla into the bloodstream; the pupils dilate, which enhances visual ability; and the reticular formation is activated to enhance alertness and attentiveness. In 1915, Cannon referred to these internal changes as our emergency reaction, which mobilizes our resources and prepares us for fight or flight, enabling us to cope behaviorally with stressful experiences.

Although the alarm reaction generally permits effective coping, it can be impairing. For example, many people "freeze" when confronted with an emergency such as an accident; their intense internal responses may prevent them from helping the injured. The inability to recall information during examinations is another example of an impairing stressor-produced reaction. An extreme stressor may even cause death.

Although it may seem like an eternity when you are standing in front of the class, the alarm reaction lasts for a relatively short time, several minutes to several hours. When the stressor ends, the parasympathetic nervous system takes over, restoring our physiological reserves to prestressor levels. For example, the parasympathetic nervous system increases the digestive process, quickly returning glycogen stores to prestress levels. However, if the stressor continues, we enter the second stage of the GAS, mobilizing all our physiological resources to cope with the stressor.

resistance stage The second stage of the GAS, characterized by the mobilization of physiological resources to cope with a prolonged stressor.

The Resistance Stage

In the **resistance stage,** a prolonged stressor continues the hypothalamic activation that began in the alarm stage, which causes an increased release of adrenocorticotropic hormone (ACTH) from the anterior pituitary gland (Figure 12.16). ACTH released into the bloodstream continues to stimulate the manufacture and release of glucocorticoid hormones from the adrenal cortex. This sequence of structures—hypothalamus, pituitary gland, adrenal cortex—is part of the *limbic-hypothalamic-pituitary-adrenal axis,* or the *stress axis.* Although Selye's work emphasized the parasympathetic nervous system responses, the sympathetic nervous system is also involved, as we indicated earlier. In this case, the stressor acts through the brain to stimulate the sympathetic nervous system to increase the release of epinephrine and norepinephrine from the adrenal medulla.

Glucocorticoid hormones such as hydrocortisone, corticosterone, and cortisol enable an animal to remain mobilized in its fight against a continued stressor by stimulating the conversion of nonsugars (fats, proteins) to sugars and by enhancing glycogen storage in the liver. This provides the continued energy supply needed to cope with the stressor. In addition, glucocorticoid hormones increase the effectiveness of epinephrine and norepinephrine, enabling us to continue to respond even with diminished levels of the latter two hormones. The glucocorticoid hormones act like a tune-up for an automobile, allowing its engine to run more efficiently and use less gas; the glucocorticoid hormones enable the body to use energy more effectively and thus to require less food.

During the resistance stage, as the internal systems described above are activated, all physiological systems not directly involved in stress resistance are inhibited. A prolonged stressor causes decreased secretion of thyroid-stimulating hormone (TSH) and growth hormone (GH). Sexual and reproductive physiology are also inhibited. For men, a prolonged stressor produces a decrease in sperm and testosterone levels. Women are likely to experience a suppressed menstrual cycle (suppressed estrus in nonhuman mammals), a lack of ovulation, an increased risk of miscarriage, and reduced lactation.

The glucocorticoid hormones also antagonize the inflammatory response of the immune system. This delays the growth of new tissue around a wound or foreign substance in the skin, inhibits antibody formation, decreases white blood cell formation, and reduces the effectiveness of the thymus gland and other lymphoid tissues. Psychological stress has been found to impair wound healing in rodents and humans (Detillion & others, 2004). For example, isolated Siberian hamsters had slower wound healing than socially housed animals. Isolated hamsters treated with oxytocin, a hormone associated with social contact and bonding, showed faster wound healing than untreated animals; socially housed hamsters treated with an oxytocin antagonist exhibited delayed wound healing. The researchers concluded that social isolation (a stressor) impairs wound healing, and oxytocin facilitates the healing in isolated animals. Studies of the impact of stressors on the immune system are an important part of the dynamic new field of *psychoneuroimmunology.*

Thus, glucocorticoid hormones provide the resources needed to cope with stressful events but simultaneously antagonize the body's defense against a stressor. Consequently, an added stressor such as a virus can result in an illness that might have been resisted in an organism not busy responding to the original stressor. Additional stressors may even result in death.

Many studies have shown that stressors can reduce the ability to fight illness. For example, Cohen and colleagues (1991) determined the level of life stress for 394 healthy volunteers in England and then administered nasal drops containing one of five different viruses. An additional 26 participants received saline nasal drops as a placebo. The participants reporting higher stress had greater rates of infection for all five viruses. Similarly, during periods of academic stress (e.g., during major examinations), the level of immune system response in first-year dental students declined (Jemmott & others, 1983). A link has even been reported between stress and upper respiratory illness (Cohen & others, 2002). Several anterior pituitary hormones (e.g., prolactin, growth hormone) are known to be involved in immunoregulation, perhaps as substances that counteract negative immunoregulatory factors produced in reaction to major stressors (Dorshkind & Horseman, 2001).

A neuropeptide has been discovered recently that may serve to decrease the stress response of the body during the resistance stage. *Nociceptin/orphanin FQ (N/OFQ)* blocks stress-induced loss of appetite in rats (Ciccocioppo & others, 2004), blocks defensive behaviors in mice in a highly stressful situation (Griebel & others, 1999), and is involved in the decreased neuroendocrine responses to stress in adult rats exposed to short periods of handling early in life (Ploj & others, 2001). Mice deficient in N/OFQ, produced by genetic engineering, are more reactive to stressful stimuli and have an impaired ability to adapt to acute and chronic stressors (Ouagazzal & others, 2003; Reinscheid & others, 2000).

The ability of N/OFQ to reduce the stress response may result in part from its effect on the lateral amygdala, where it inhibits glutamate and GABA release (Meis & Pape, 2001). The amygdala is part of the limbic-hypothalamic-pituitary-adrenal cortex axis. In studies on the interaction of N/OFQ and the stress axis in rats, the neuropeptide has been shown to play a role in the regulation of the stress response and is implicated in physiological and psychological well-being (Devine & others, 2001).

Recent studies with mice have provided evidence for genetic involvement in stress reactions. For example, following up on previous studies showing that mice deficient in corticotropin-releasing factor receptor 1 (CRFR1) have an impaired stress response and mice deficient in CRF receptor 2 (CRFR2) have an exaggerated stress response, Bale and coworkers (2002) developed mice deficient in both receptor types (double-mutant mice). Among other things, the double-mutant mice exhibited greater impairment of the limbic-hypothalamic-pituitary-adrenal stress response than CRFR1 mice. The study of mice with impaired CRF receptor functioning may hold the key to understanding the physiological bases of stress-related mental disorders, such as depression and anxiety (Gass & others, 2001; Urani & Gass, 2003).

The Exhaustion Stage

If the stressor continues indefinitely, an animal eventually depletes its physiological resources and enters the **exhaustion stage.** When no resources remain, the defense systems of the body fail and the animal dies. Stress can kill (see Figure 12.16).

Stress can also produce negative effects that fall short of killing the individual. One example of the exhaustion stage in humans is the overtraining syndrome, which is typically seen in endurance athletes. The **overtraining syndrome** is characterized by significantly reduced performance, chronic fatigue, and increased susceptibility to upper respiratory infections (Angeli & others, 2004; Budgett, 1998). As the name indicates, it is caused by strenuous training without sufficient rest (Kentta & Hassmen, 1998).

exhaustion stage The final stage of the GAS; when a stressor continues indefinitely, physiological resources are depleted, resulting in failure of the body's defense systems and eventually death.

overtraining syndrome Disorder caused by excessive training by athletes; characterized by decreased performance, mood changes, and evidence of a compromised immune system.

Stress in other areas of the individual's life may play a significant role in the development of the overtraining syndrome (Meehan & others, 2004). For example, the researchers reported that one individual experienced a change in his social life (his marriage broke up because of his excessive running) and in his employment (he was promoted to a position of greater responsibility) in the period before the onset of symptoms. Similarly, in the months before his symptoms began, another individual was fired from his job and had his first child, who had sleep difficulties that negatively altered the lifestyle of the exerciser.

disease of adaptation An illness caused by the efforts of the body to cope with stressors; examples are essential hypertension, gastric or peptic ulcers, and colitis.

Research indicates that the overtraining syndrome may be caused by cumulative alterations in metabolism from excessive training (Petibois & others, 2003). The process begins with a change in carbohydrate metabolism, followed by an alteration in lipid metabolism. These changes lead to a greater use of amino acids, probably from the breakdown of protein. Thus, the metabolic changes in the overtrained individual proceed from the use of the normal stores of energy for exercise (carbohydrates and lipids) to the use of proteins, which are normally not tapped to supply energy for the skeletal muscles used in exercise.

One hypothesized cause of the overtraining syndrome involves *cytokines,* which are proteins released by the white blood cells to facilitate communication among cells of the immune system and between immune system cells and the rest of the body (L. L. Smith, 2000, 2003). According to this hypothesis, excessive training produces muscle, skeletal, or joint trauma, or some combination of all three. The injury-related cytokines then trigger changes in the immune system that produce systemic inflammation. This leads to symptoms such as excessive fatigue, depressed mood, and disturbances in sleep patterns. The symptoms in turn lead to behavior changes designed to facilitate survival and recovery; specifically, the individual curtails his or her normal exercise routine. If the individual stops exercising excessively and pursues an appropriate regeneration plan, the symptoms usually go away within 6 to 12 weeks (Angeli & others, 2004). However, the symptoms may persist or recur if the athlete resumes a hard training regimen too quickly.

The *Scientific American* Spotlight, "Don't Stress," discusses the effects of long-term stress on neurological, physiological, and behavioral systems. Research has shown that early isolation of an individual increases the sensitivity of the stress response, with negative consequences throughout the brain and body. These negative consequences include such changes as the development of abdominal obesity, which is related to adult-onset diabetes and coronary artery disease; hypertension; depression; and suppression of the immune system.

Diseases of Adaptation

Long-term exposure to a stressor can wreak havoc on the body. Selye called diseases produced by the stress response **diseases of adaptation.** Note that such diseases differ from illnesses caused by external factors such as viruses, which are themselves considered stressors. Diseases of adaptation include essential hypertension (high blood pressure with no known physiological cause), gastric or peptic ulcers (small holes in the lining of the stomach or upper part of the small intestine caused by long-term excessive hydrochloric acid [HCl] secretion), and colitis (inflammation of the mucous membrane of the colon). Stress reactions can both cause these illnesses and intensify their severity. Let us examine ulcers as an example of a disease of adaptation.

Hans Selye (1907–1982), Austrian-born Canadian physician best known for his description of general adaptation syndrome. Selye is shown here on a 2000 Canadian postage stamp.

COURTESY OF CANADA POST

Early research indicated that a psychological stressor can cause increased HCl secretion (Mahl, 1950). Using eight male students who volunteered to swallow a tube that allowed him to assess HCl secretion, Mahl measured acid levels on nonstressful days either before or after the final exam period and on a stressful day during the final examination period when the student was scheduled to take what he considered to be a difficult examination. Based on interviews, Mahl divided the subjects into a low anxiety group (two) and a high anxiety group (six). Neither of the low anxiety participants showed an increase in HCl secretion before the exam,

Scientific American Spotlight

Don't Stress

Kristin Leutwyler

Most people do not share Chicken Little's fear of falling skies. Stress is, after all, largely subjective. Nevertheless, it does prompt a series of marked physiological changes: The adrenal gland cranks out steroids that mobilize sugars and fat reserves. Additional hormones curb growth, reproduction and other nonessential activities to conserve energy. And the brain produces more epinephrine to ready the heart and other muscles for action.

In the face of danger, this short-lived reaction helps you survive. If the stress response is regularly tripped for the wrong reasons, however, it has the opposite effect. Indeed, researchers have known for some time that chronic stress often leads directly to certain illnesses, including heart disease, hypertension, depression, immune suppression and diabetes. Recently they have discovered that stress also causes developmental abnormalities, unhealthy weight gain and neurodegeneration. Fortunately, some of these new insights suggest better means for combating excess stress.

An individual's susceptibility to undue stress seems to reflect, in part, early life experiences. Michael Meaney and his colleagues at the Douglas Hospital Research Center in Montreal examined levels of corticotropin-releasing hormone (CRH)—the master hormone choreographing the stress response—in baby rats. They found that when mother rats lick their offspring often, the pups produce less CRH. "The amount of maternal licking during the first 10 days of life is highly correlated with the production of CRH in the hypothalamus of the brain of the adult offspring," Meaney says.

In addition, Meaney discovered that, compared with isolated infants, licked rats develop more glucocorticoid receptors in the hippocampus. These receptors, when activated, inhibit the production of CRH in the hypothalamus and thus dampen the stress response. Licked rats also produce more receptors for the CRH-inhibiting neurotransmitter GABA in both the amygdala and locus coeruleus, brain regions associated with fear. "When the rat is raised in calm environments, regions of the brain that inhibit CRH are enhanced," Meaney summarizes. "But bad environments enhance areas that activate CRH production. So over the long term, these systems are biased to produce more or less base amounts of CRH." In effect, early experiences set the sensitivity of an individual's stress response.

Not only do orphaned rats generate fewer glucocorticoid and GABA receptors, they actually have fewer neurons in certain brain regions as well. Mark Smith of the Du Pont Merck Research Labs and researchers at the National Institute of Mental Health looked at patterns of programmed cell death—a normal pruning process—during development. They found that in orphaned pups, twice as many cells died in several brain areas, particularly in the hippocampus, a central structure in learning and memory. Smith suggests that a lack of tactile stimulation might bring about this cell death much the way that insufficient visual stimulation causes abnormal organization of the visual cortex in infants.

whereas five of the six high anxiety participants exhibited an increase. Mahl concluded that the experimental results supported an anxiety hypothesis of the cause of gastric ulcers.

In a study that revealed a link between stressors and ulcers, hungry rats had to cross a grid floor that delivered an electric shock in order to receive either food or water (Sawrey & others, 1956). These animals experienced conflict: The conflicting motives were hunger and thirst and fear of shock. The researchers employed a variety of controls and drew the following conclusions from their results: (1) Conflict contributes significantly to ulcer formation; (2) hunger and shock contribute significantly but only through their interaction; (3) thirst does not play a role; and (4) the weight loss observed in all groups is not related directly to ulcer formation. Similarly, a review of studies of gastric lesions in animals revealed that the degree of psychological conflict engendered in the animals was a major determining factor in whether or not they developed gastric ulcers (Tsuda & Hirai, 1976).

Early research indicated that the inability to control stress is a major cause of ulcers (Weiss, 1968). In one experiment, Weiss studied three groups of rats in restraint cages: In one group, a rat could avoid or escape electric shock by touching a metal plate with its nose or front feet; in a second group, a rat could not avoid or escape (i.e., control) the shock, which terminated independently of its behavior; and in the third group, rats did not receive a shock. Rats in the first and second

Mary Carlson of Harvard Medical School observed behavioral problems in socially isolated chimpanzees and suspected that the autisticlike symptoms stemmed from a lack of tactile stimulation. So she and her coworkers chose to study the adrenal stress steroid, a glucocorticoid (GC) called cortisol, in Romanian orphans, who often display similar behaviors. Half of the children Carlson studied had participated in a social and educational enrichment program, and half had not. Compared with family-reared children, all showed retarded physical and mental growth. But the enriched children had more normal levels of cortisol during the day and under stress than the most deprived children did. Those with the most irregular cortisol fluctuations suffered the most extreme behavioral and learning problems.

Over time, elevated levels of GCs cause other serious disorders. Studies done by Mary F. Dallman of the University of California at San Francisco indicate that persistently high levels of GCs interact with insulin to increase food intake and redistribute energy stores in the body. "The results may be very clinically relevant because sustained responsiveness of the stress program to new stimuli may be a root cause for abnormal cardiovascular events in highly stressed individuals," Dallman says. "In addition, the redistribution of energy stores from muscle to fat, particularly abdominal fat, may have a role in the development of abdominal obesity, which is strongly associated with increased incidence of adult-onset diabetes, coronary artery disease and stroke."

Robert M. Sapolsky of Stanford University has found that total lifetime exposure to GCs best determines the rate of neuron loss in the hippocampus and cognitive impairment during aging. Sapolsky reports that not only do chronically high GC levels kill off hippocampal neurons, they leave many others vulnerable to damage from epilepsy, hypoglycemia, cardiac arrest and proteins implicated in Alzheimer's disease and AIDS-related dementia. "Metaphorically, GCs make a neuron a bit lightheaded," Sapolsky explains, "and if that happens to correspond with the worst day of that neuron's life, the cell is much more likely to succumb to the stroke or seizure."

Sapolsky and his co-workers are developing gene therapies to protect stress weary neurons. But a simpler solution may come from work outside the laboratory. For 18 years Sapolsky has studied a population of wild baboons in the Serengeti. In stable hierarchies, subordinate animals have higher levels of GCs—as well as less "good" cholesterol and less robust immune and reproductive systems. The lowest levels of GCs occur in males with the strongest social networks. "These more socially savvy or socially affiliating personality styles appear to be lifelong and to predict more successful lifelong rank histories, life span and old age," Sapolsky adds. "The worst thing for an animal is to remain isolated."

From: *Scientific American*, vol. 278, pp. 28–29.

groups received the same number of shocks for the same amount of time. Weiss discovered that rats unable to control shocks developed more severe gastric lesions than rats that were able to perform a coping response. In another rat study, both the ability to control and the predictability of the stressor (shock) influenced ulcer formation (Tsuda & others, 1983).

Perhaps you noticed an apparent contradiction between the results of Sawrey and colleagues (1956) and those of Weiss (1968). If the rats in Sawrey and coworkers' study had control over whether they received a shock (they could have remained hungry, after all), why did they develop ulcers, whereas Weiss's rats that could control shocks did not develop ulcers? Gray (1972) suggested that the most severe ulcers developed in Sawrey and coworkers' study because the conflict over *both* motives (hunger and shock) is greater than that over just one of the motives (hunger or shock). Also, perceived control is probably lower in conflict situations than in nonconflict situations.

Stress and Neuroplasticity

Stress clearly can affect a variety of organ systems, and it can have dramatic effects on the brain and on the plasticity of certain brain structures in response to environmental events. For example, the dentate gyrus of the hippocampus undergoes structural remodeling throughout the life of an animal; the production of new granule cells (one of the cell types in the hippocampus; see Chapter 14) was observed in mammals ranging from rodents to primates (Gould & Tanapat, 1999). Further research has revealed that granule cell production is affected by the levels of circulating steroids secreted by the adrenal gland—in other words, by hormones released in reaction to stress. Chronic stress suppresses cellular proliferation and produces changes in the structure of the dentate gyrus, leading to changes in hippocampal function. Further, chronic stress leads to a shortening and loss of dendrites in another region of the hippocampus (McEwen, 1999, 2000b). MRI studies of the human hippocampus have revealed selective atrophy associated with several mental disorders and with aging; the loss of cells is probably caused by prolonged psychosocial stress (Hedges & others, 2003; McEwen & Magarinos, 2001; Vermetten & others, 2003).

Neurogenesis in the hippocampus plays a significant role in learning and memory (Chapter 14). By preventing the cellular changes that accompany memory, stressors can have a profound effect on the ability of an animal to learn and remember. Learned helplessness is a condition akin to depression produced by subjecting animals to inescapable shock (Chapter 15). Research has demonstrated that exposure to inescapable shock impairs a particular hippocampal cellular function that is related to plasticity and learning, and the experimenters concluded that a stress-induced reduction in neuronal plasticity is almost certain to have a profound effect on behavior (Shors & others, 1990).

Not all stress has negative consequences, of course, as we indicate later in our discussion of eustress. In fact, acute stress enhances both the immune system and the memory of potentially threatening events (McEwen, 2000c). Chronic stress, by contrast, suppresses the ongoing creation of new cells in one part of the hippocampus and remodels the dendrites in another part, as we have seen. Further, McEwen pointed out that psychosocial stressors—what animals do to each other—often have a much greater effect than stressors applied by experimenters.

➤Checkpoint

Philip, Darla, and the girls are sitting down to dinner when Jamie knocks over her glass of milk, which fills her plate and drips onto the floor. Darla perceives this as a stressor. Describe a possible pattern of biological reactions in Darla, using the three stages of the GAS. Explain how stress might cause Darla to develop an ulcer.

REVIEW

- ➤ A stressor is an event that either strains or overwhelms the ability of a person to adjust to the environment. Biological and behavioral responses to stressors determine whether someone can adapt to the stressful events.
- ➤ Pressure, one type of stressor, is experienced when a person is expected to behave in a particular way within a specific time frame. Conflict results from the impossibility of satisfying two or more competing motives. Frustration occurs when the ability to reach a goal is blocked.
- ➤ The general adaptation syndrome (GAS) is a pattern of internal changes—alarm, resistance, exhaustion—that results from exposure to a physiological or psychological stressor.
- ➤ The alarm stage consists of cortical arousal, produced by stimulation of the reticular formation, and activation of the sympathetic nervous system, mobilizing the resources and coping strategies of the body. The alarm stage stops when the stressor stops. The parasympathetic nervous system then becomes dominant, restoring biological reserves to prestressor levels.
- ➤ The resistance stage follows if the stressor continues; high levels of glucocorticoid hormones are released by the adrenal cortex to provide the energy needed to cope with long-term stressors. The release of glucocorticoid hormones also suppresses the inflammatory response, reducing the ability of the body to defend against stressors. Exposure to a new stressor can cause disease that would not have occurred if the body were not already coping with the first stressor.
- ➤ The neuropeptide nociceptin/orphanin FQ appears to reduce the stress response.
- ➤ If the stressor continues indefinitely, the resources of the body eventually become depleted, and the exhaustion stage begins; this may ultimately lead to death. The

overtraining syndrome, in which performance by an athlete engaging in excessive exercise diminishes, is an illustration of the exhaustion stage.

- Long-term exposure to stressors can lead to diseases of adaptation, such as essential hypertension, ulcers, and colitis.
- Chronic stress can adversely affect learning and memory through its effect on the hippocampus.

Coping With Stressors

Experiencing stress is part of life. Thus far we have discussed the negative effects of stress, but stress can have positive effects as well. In fact, Hans Selye's last major contribution to the stress literature was to distinguish between negative stress, or *distress*, and positive stress, or *eustress* (Szabo, 1998). Distress is what people are generally referring to when they talk about being "under stress" at work or in other aspects of their lives. The reactions to distress are what we have described to this point.

Eustress, or positive stress, by contrast, has beneficial effects. For example, suppose you are playing a board game, such as Scrabble, with a friend, and you win the game. The effect of winning is stressful, just as losing would be, but winning is an illustration of eustress. As another example, imagine that you are about to run in a race. Again, this is a form of stress, but it can be eustress if it enhances your competitive edge and helps you to do well in the event.

The physiological effects of eustress can be measured. Free radicals (highly reactive molecules capable of causing damage) in the blood have been associated with a variety of pathological conditions, such as aging, inflammation, and tumor formation, and their prompt removal is considered beneficial to health. The free-radical-scavenging ability of saliva was measured in 27 healthy volunteers before, during, and after they watched a 30 minute comic video (Atsumi & others, 2004). As a result of the eustress response to the video, the free-radical-scavenging ability of the saliva was significantly increased. The boost was greater in subjects who reported feeling "very good" while watching the video than in those who reported feeling merely "good," and greater in the latter subjects than in those who reported feeling "ordinary + dull." Similarly, the eustress of humor therapy may have beneficial effects on the immune system of healthy subjects. Men shown a humor video for an hour experienced significant increases in a variety of neuroimmune parameters, such as natural killer cell activity, activated T cells, and several immunoglobulins—all of which indicate improved immune function (Berk & others, 2001).

After exposure to the "exceptional eustress of bungee jumping," the levels of cortisol in the saliva and beta-endorphin immunoreactivity in the blood were examined in 12 novice jumpers (Hennig & others, 1994). Ratings of euphoria were dramatically elevated after the jump and were significantly correlated with beta-endorphin concentrations, which increased more than 200%. Although salivary cortisol increased after the jump, it was not correlated with the ratings of euphoria.

For students, examinations provide frequent stressful experiences, which can be distress for some and eustress for others. Although some students may develop a physical illness as a result of taking exams, most will not, and some will even find that the prospect of an exam helps them focus on their schoolwork and learn many things they would not have learned without the motivation of the exam. Different people respond differently to the same stressor. Some people have an intense alarm reaction to a stressor that causes only a low or moderate reaction in other people. These responsivity differences influence disease development; the more you respond physiologically to a stressor, assuming that it provides distress rather than eustress, the more likely you are to develop a stress-related illness. In the next section we examine support for the idea that how we respond to a stressor affects our susceptibility to disease. In Box 12.1 we describe one successful approach to coping with the stress response.

Box 12.1

Managing the Stress Response

Overreacting to stressors can have seriously adverse consequences. Fortunately, there are ways we can reduce our responses to stress to acceptable levels (Lehrer & others, 1994; Smith & Baum, 2003). Some of these methods directly inhibit the stress response, and others decrease the perceived aversiveness of stressful experiences. Stress-sensitive people can use these techniques to minimize their susceptibility to physical or psychological disease, or to curtail disease that has already developed. Here we discuss one successful stress management method.

Richard Lazarus (Lazarus, 1993; Lazarus & Lazarus, 1994) suggested that exposure to a stressor causes people to evaluate the impact of the event on their lives. Lazarus called this evaluation **cognitive appraisal,** and it can either increase or decrease reactions to stressors (Figure 12.17).

Lazarus (1993) identified two stages in the cognitive appraisal process. The first stage is an evaluation of the degree to which environmental events represent a threat or challenge, and the appraisal can occur either consciously or unconsciously. This stage, *primary appraisal,* can indicate that a stressor represents either a serious threat to well-being, an interesting new challenge, or little or no threat. The physiological reaction to an event can be either intensified (if the event is viewed as more threatening) or reduced (if the event is viewed as less threatening) by the cognitive appraisal process.

After determining whether the stressor represents a challenge or a threat, people then evaluate their ability to respond to the situation. In this *secondary appraisal* stage, people determine whether they have the resources to cope with the stressor. The coping method determined by the secondary appraisal process is then tried and its success evaluated. The success of both primary and secondary appraisal determines the strength or intensity of the stress response. Failure to adapt to the stressor may lead to additional attempts to cope with it or to withdraw from it.

To help people learn how to alter the steps of the cognitive appraisal process so that they can cope more effectively with stressors, Meichenbaum (1996) described a three-stage technique called **stress inoculation training.** Let us assume a celebrity with an anger-management problem, such as Russell Crowe, learns to use this technique. In the first stage, the educational stage, Crowe learns to recognize stressful situations and to link his behavioral responses to the situations. For example, he could learn that he reacts violently to criticism by another person. The educational stage also involves learning that reactions to stressors are

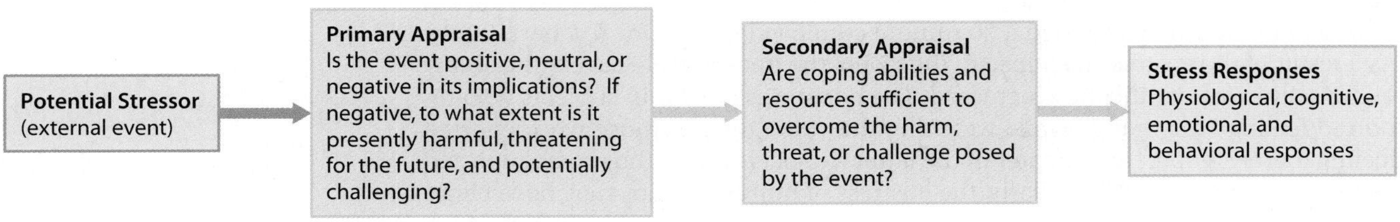

Figure 12.17

The cognitive appraisal process According to Lazarus, on exposure to a stressful event, an individual first evaluates whether the stressor represents a threat or a challenge. After this primary appraisal, the person determines whether he or she has the capacity to cope with the stressor (secondary appraisal), then responds biologically and psychologically to the event. [From Kolb B., & Whishaw, I. Q. (1996). Human neuropsychology (4th ed.). New York: W. H. Freeman.]

→ **What is stress inoculation?**

cognitive appraisal A cognitive evaluation of an event to determine its effect on one's life.

stress inoculation training A technique to alter the cognitive appraisal process by recognizing stressful situations, linking behavioral responses to situations, understanding that reactions to stressors are determined by the appraisal of the situation, and then learning new ways to appraise the situation.

◆ Coping Behaviors: Type A, Type B, and Hardiness

Carlos is walking briskly to the library to work on a term paper that is due in 2 weeks. As he walks, his thoughts are focused on all the things he has to do today. After he spends 2 hours working on the paper, he will meet Amy, his girlfriend, for lunch, for which he has budgeted 45 minutes. Then, he will go to class for an hour, although he knows he will not listen to the lecture. He usually sits in the back of the classroom and reads news magazines while listening to music on his headphones. After class, Carlos will hurry back to his fraternity house for a meeting with the other officers of his fraternity, probably catch a bite to eat, and then get his car so that he can race over to Amy's apart-

determined by the appraisal of the situation. In our example, Crowe would discover that he appraises criticism as a threat to self-esteem and that he has developed attack as a coping response to that threat. In the last part of the educational stage, Crowe learns new ways to appraise the situation, called *cognitive reappraisal*. For example, he could learn to view criticism as constructive rather than as an attack on self-esteem.

The second stage of stress inoculation training involves rehearsal. Crowe practices the ways of appraising the situation (cognitive reappraisals) by verbalizing them. Some examples of phrases designed to reduce the physiological reaction to stressors are: "I can work out a plan to handle this" and "It's not worth it to get so angry." The rehearsal stage also involves practicing muscle relaxation to reduce physiological arousal.

In the third stage, application, Crowe uses cognitive reappraisals in actual stressful situations. Table 12.3 presents some examples of cognitive reappraisals, called coping self-statements, that can be used before, during, and after stressful experiences.

Table 12.3

Examples of Coping Self-Statements

Preparation

I can develop a plan to deal with it.

Just think about what I can do about it. That's better than getting anxious.

No negative self-statements, just think rationally.

Confrontation

One step at a time; I can handle this situation.

This anxiety is what the doctor said I would feel; it's a reminder to use my coping exercises.

Relax; I'm in control. Take a slow, deep breath. Ah, good.

Coping

When fear comes, just pause.

Keep focus on the present; what is it I have to do?

Don't try to eliminate fear totally; just keep it manageable.

It's not the worst thing that can happen.

Just think about something else.

Self-reinforcement

It worked; I was able to do it.

It wasn't as bad as I expected.

I'm really pleased with the progress I'm making.

From: Meichenbaum, D. H. (1977). *Cognitive behavior modification: An integrative approach.* New York: Plenum.

Stress inoculation training has proven quite successful. For example, Awalt and colleagues (1997) found that the treatment was an effective way to manage anger in patients treated for substance abuse. Stress inoculation training also helped first-year law students deal with the stress of law school (Sheehy & Horan, 2004). A meta-analysis of 37 studies involving 1,837 participants concluded that stress inoculation training effectively reduces performance anxiety and enhances actual performance under stress (Saunders & others, 1996).

Despite some limitations, stress inoculation training and other cognitive approaches have also proved useful in managing pain and anxiety associated with self-pain or the pain of others (Weisenberg, 1998). For example, the technique reduced the pain experienced by athletes during rehabilitation following knee surgery and the length of that rehabilitation (Ross & Berger, 1996). Law and colleagues (1994) found that stress inoculation training reduced pain from a dental procedure, but only in patients with a high desire for control over their pain and low perceived self-control. Jay and Elliott (1990) found that stress inoculation training helped parents better cope with their children's painful medical procedures. Parents given the training reported lower anxiety scores and higher positive self-statement scores than parents who participated in a child-focused intervention group.

ment off campus and spend some time with her (she has complained lately that he does not give her enough attention, and Carlos remembers that his previous girlfriend had a similar complaint before she broke up with him). Although Carlos tries not to think about it, Amy has also complained lately that he never really listens to her when she tries to have a conversation with him. Carlos realizes there is some truth to this complaint, as he often pretends to listen to Amy when really he is thinking of all the things on his schedule. Lately he has begun to think that Amy talks too slowly, and he catches himself finishing her sentences and wanting to tell her to spit it out already, to get on with what she has to say. After all, he does not have all day to listen to her and what are, usually, just trivial concerns.

Does Carlos have too many things on his schedule? While driving, would Carlos be more likely to pay attention to traffic or talk on his cell phone, shave when he stops at a traffic light, and fidget impatiently while he waits for an older person to cross the street? Someone who regularly acts in this manner is exhibiting some aspects of type A behavior. California cardiologists Meyer Friedman and Ray Rosenman (1974) noted that many of their cardiac patients were agitated and impatient. Closer observation revealed that the patients showed an excessive competitive drive, high aggressiveness, and an intense sense of time urgency—characteristics the cardiologists called the **type A behavior pattern (TABP).** By contrast, individuals with the type B behavior pattern are relatively relaxed, patient, and easygoing.

Suspecting that TABP might be involved in coronary artery disease, Friedman and Rosenman (1974) examined 3,000 individuals over an 8.5 year period. Controlling for risk factors such as obesity, smoking, and hypertension, they reported that people with TABP ("type As") were twice as likely to have a heart attack as "type Bs" (Figure 12.18). A later study found that type As were more likely than type Bs to have moderate to severe coronary blocking, even when the researchers controlled for risk factors such as age, sex, smoking, blood pressure, and blood cholesterol level (Blumenthal & others, 1978). The investigators concluded that the type A behavior pattern is an independent risk factor for developing coronary heart disease.

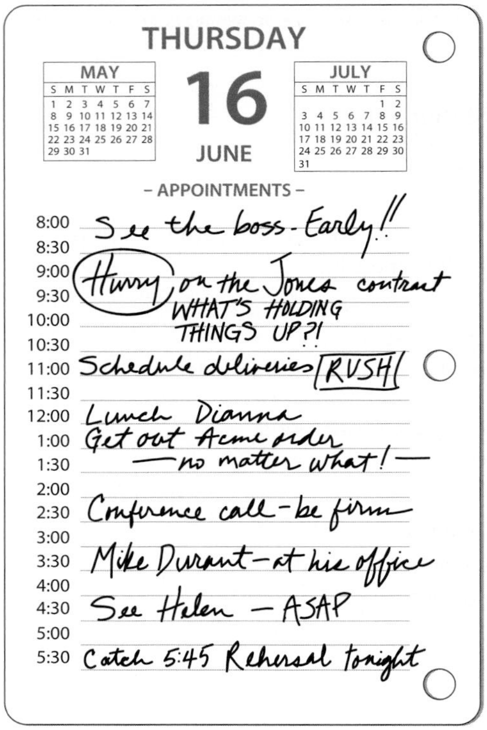

THURSDAY
MAY
16
JUNE
JULY
- APPOINTMENTS -
8:00 See the boss - Early!!
9:00 Hurry on the Jones contract
WHAT'S HOLDING THINGS UP?!
11:00 Schedule deliveries RUSH!
12:00 Lunch Dianna
1:00 Get out Acme order
— no matter what! —
2:30 Conference call - be firm
3:30 Mike Durant - at his office
4:30 See Helen - ASAP
5:30 Catch 5:45 Rehersal tonight

Figure 12.18
The type A behavior pattern Type A people are impatient and experience an extreme sense of time urgency. These feelings are vividly apparent on this page from an appointment calendar.

➡ **In addition to impatience and an intense sense of time urgency, what behaviors do type As exhibit?**

In part, type As are more at risk for coronary disease because they are significantly more reactive to stressors than type Bs (Krantz & Manuck, 1984). For example, higher heart rates and blood pressure were found in type As during a task that measured reaction times to visually presented stimuli (Dembroski & others, 1977). Also, type As displayed higher norepinephrine levels than type Bs when exposed to a challenging task (Friedman & others, 1975). In particular, type As showed greater cardiovascular reactivity than type Bs in situations involving positive or negative feedback, verbal harassment or criticism, and the kind of time pressure found in playing video games (Lyness, 1993).

This greater norepinephrine release in type As may play an important role in coronary disease development (Glass, 1977). For example, researchers reported that norepinephrine release can accelerate arterial damage, enhance blood clot formation, and produce cardiac arrhythmias (Eliot, 1979; Haft, 1974). Further, relative to type Bs, type As smoke more, sleep less, and drink more caffeinated drinks, all behaviors associated with an increased risk of coronary disease (Hicks & others, 1983).

Not all people with TABP develop coronary disease, however, and some people without TABP do. In fact, some studies have not found TABP to be a coronary disease risk factor (Houston & Snyder, 1988; Matthews & Haynes, 1986). Some of these inconsistencies may result from the difficulty of identifying type As (Dimsdale, 1988), as not all type A people show extreme levels of all the behaviors associated with the pattern: For example, a person can be both easygoing and competitive. An alternative explanation is that physiological and psychological differences between type As and type Bs do not occur in all situations. Glass (1977) reported that his subjects showed the extreme responsivity typical of TABP only when given a challenging task or when exposed to an uncontrollable stressor. In nonstressful situations, the two types did not differ. A final factor is that exposure to intense and prolonged stressors can lead to disease. Many individuals with coronary disease who do not show type A behavior may have experienced extremely stressful events for prolonged periods.

type A behavior pattern (TABP) A set of behaviors that includes an excessive competitive drive, high aggressiveness, and an intense sense of time urgency.

Hostility and quick-tempered anger are often components of TABP, and a meta-analysis of studies on hostility and health concluded that hostility is an independent risk factor for coronary heart disease (Miller & others, 1996). To illustrate, in a study of 58 women, participants who suppressed their anger had greater cardiovascular reactivity (e.g., changes in their systolic blood pressure) than those who expressed their anger assertively (Anderson & Lawler, 1995). Recently, expressions of anger and hostility in men have been found to be related to a type of heartbeat irregularity that can lead to blood clots or a stroke (Eaker & others, 2004). In a study of nearly 13,000 black and white men and women, in participants with normal blood pressure, proneness to anger was a significant risk factor for coronary heart disease death (Williams & others, 2000). Further, the subjects most at risk were those who responded angrily with little or no provocation (Williams & others, 2001).

People differ in their responsivity to stressors, and the potential for hostility makes people susceptible to coronary disease. Yet many people cope well both behaviorally and biologically despite being exposed to extreme stressors. The question is, why do some people thrive in the face of adversity?

Hardiness may explain why some individuals thrive despite being raised in extremely dysfunctional circumstances, whereas others fail even in the most advantageous environments. According to Suzanne Kobasa and others, people with hardiness are less responsive biologically to stressors and cope better with stressors than other people (Clark, 2002; Eid & others, 2004; Kobasa, 1979; Kobasa & others, 1983).

hardiness An ability to cope effectively with stressors, because of a high level of commitment, a perception that change is a challenge rather than a threat, and a sense of control over events.

People with the trait of hardiness show a higher level of commitment than nonhardy people, which leads to greater involvement in tasks and a greater tendency to perceive these tasks as meaningful. They view change as a challenge rather than as a burden or threat. And they have a greater sense of control than other people over events in their lives. The importance of these characteristics was illustrated in a study of middle- and upper-level executives at a large company (Kobasa, 1979). Some of the executives had become physically ill following a stressful event (e.g., divorce, job transfer, inferior job performance evaluation) in the previous 3-year period, whereas others had not become ill after experiencing comparable stressors. Kobasa found that the executives who did not become ill exhibited more hardiness, which included having a greater sense of purpose, a stronger commitment to self, and an internal locus of control.

In a study of 67 caregivers of disabled older adults, hardiness was inversely related to depression and fatigue; caregivers with low hardiness experienced more depression than those higher on the trait (Clark, 2002). In a study of adaptation to the stress of caring for a child with developmental difficulties, both hardiness and social support predicted adaptation (Weiss, 2002). Finally, Eid and colleagues (2004) studied hardiness and individual coping of submarine crewmembers during an exercise simulating a sunken submarine. Not surprisingly, crewmembers higher in hardiness experienced less emotional stress.

Checkpoint

Are you a type A or a type B person? What are the three characteristics of hardiness? Do you consider yourself a hardy or a nonhardy individual?

REVIEW

- Stress with positive effects is called eustress, whereas stress with negative effects is called distress.
- People with the type A behavior pattern (TABP) show an excessive competitive drive, high aggressiveness, great impatience, and an intense sense of time urgency, as well as a stronger biological reaction to stressors than people with a type B behavior pattern.
- One aspect of TABP, the potential for hostility or suppressed anger, has been associated with a heightened susceptibility to heart disease.
- Hardy people are better able to cope with stressors, because they have a high level of commitment to goals, view change as a challenge rather than a threat, and have a greater sense of control over the events in their lives.

Chapter Review

Key Terms

aggression (p. 431)
alarm stage (p. 443)
amygdalectomy (p. 434)
Cannon-Bard theory of emotion (p. 424)
cognitive appraisal (p. 452)
diseases of adaptation (p. 447)
emotion (p. 422)
exhaustion stage (p. 446)
fear-induced aggression (p. 438)
general adaptation syndrome (GAS) (p. 443)
hardiness (p. 455)
irritable aggression (p. 432)
James-Lange theory of emotion (p. 422)
kindling (p. 426)
Klüver-Bucy syndrome (p. 433)
limbic system (p. 425)
overtraining syndrome (p. 446)
Papez circuit (p. 425)
premenstrual syndrome (PMS) (p. 437)
resistance stage (p. 445)
Schachter's cognitive model of emotion (p. 427)
stress inoculation training (p. 452)
stressor (p. 442)
type A behavior pattern (TABP) (p. 454)

Suggested Readings

Aggleton, J. (Ed.). (1992). *The amygdala: Neurobiological aspects of emotion, memory, and mental dysfunction.* New York: Wiley-Liss.

LeDoux, J. E. (1996). *The emotional brain: The mysterious underpinnings of emotional life.* New York: Simon & Schuster.

McEwen, B. S. (2000c). The neurobiology of stress: From serendipity to clinical relevance. *Brain Research, 886,* 172–189.

Moyer, K. E. (1976). *The psychobiology of aggression.* New York: Harper & Row.

Stan, N. L., Leventhal, B., & Travasso, T. (Eds.) (1990). *Psychological and biological approaches to emotion.* Hillsdale, NJ: Erlbaum.

Taylor, S. (2003). *Health psychology* (5th ed.). New York: McGraw-Hill.

Critical Thinking Questions

1. Having just ended a long-term dating relationship, Joan feels sad and cannot stop crying. Use the James-Lange, Cannon-Bard, and Schachter theories of emotion to explain the basis of Joan's emotional response to the end of the relationship.
2. Several months have gone by, and Joan is still upset. What physiological changes might have taken place over the last few months? What are the dangers if Joan continues to be troubled by the break-up? How might Joan cope better with this situation?
3. Joan has just learned that her ex-boyfriend is now dating her best friend. What emotions might this knowledge produce in Joan? How might she respond to this information? What factors might cause her response to be aggressive?

Fill-in-the-Blank Questions

1. A(n) ______ is a feeling that differs from an individual's normal state.
2. The physiological changes accompanying an emotion-producing stimulus constitute the ______ of an emotion; the emotional feeling is the ______ of an emotion.
3. According to the ______ theory of emotion, expression of the emotion comes first, and the awareness of this expression is the emotional feeling.
4. According to the ______ theory of emotion, we experience visceral changes, somatic changes, and the emotional experience simultaneously.

5. In the Papez circuit, the expression of emotion occurs through the ______, with the ______ gyrus responsible for emotional experience.
6. Paul MacLean called the Papez circuit the ______ system.
7. Repeated stimulation of the amygdala makes an animal more susceptible to seizure activity, in a phenomenon called ______.
8. According to ______ model of emotions, when we notice we are internally aroused, we attribute our arousal to the prevailing environmental conditions.
9. In the classic Schachter-Singer study, participants who received epinephrine injections and either were not told or were misinformed about what to expect tended to attribute their emotional response to the ______.
10. ______ is behavior motivated by an intent to harm a living being or an inanimate object.
11. ______ identified eight different types of aggression, each with a different physiological base.
12. Aggression triggered by a painful injury of some sort is an example of ______ aggression.
13. The constellation of effects resulting from temporal lobectomies in primates is the ______ syndrome.
14. Mark and Ervin developed the surgical procedure called a(n) ______ to treat people with a history of violence associated with ______ malfunction.
15. Autopsy of Charles Whitman, the young man who shot 38 people from the top of the University of Texas tower, revealed a tumor that probably involved his ______ lobe.
16. Female irritability during the premenstrual period has been attributed to the decline in the hormone ______ that occurs during this time.
17. ______ aggression is a defensive reaction triggered by a threatening situation with no way to escape.
18. A(n) ______ is any event that strains or overwhelms our ability to adjust to our environment.
19. Selye called the physiological responses to exposure to a stressor the ______.
20. The GAS has three stages: ______, ______, and ______.
21. Selye called diseases produced by the stress response ______ diseases.
22. Friedman and Rosenman called the pattern of behavior characterized by an excessive competitive drive, high aggressiveness, and a sense of time urgency the ______.
23. Many researchers believe that the ______ associated with TABP is the single most important risk factor for coronary disease.
24. People who have a high level of commitment, who view change as a challenge rather than as a threat, and who have a greater sense of control over their lives are strong in a trait known as ______.
25. The cognitive evaluation of the impact of an event on one's life is called ______.
26. Meichenbaum's method of altering the cognitive appraisal process to cope more effectively with stress is ______.

Multiple-Choice Questions

1. According to the James-Lange theory, we experience
   a. the physiological changes, then the emotion.
   b. the emotion, then the physiological changes.
   c. the physiological changes and the emotions simultaneously.
   d. differing emotional responses depending on our hardiness.
2. Jonelle has just gotten back her biological psychology test and learned that she failed it. Her heart rate speeds up, her blood pressure increases, and she feels slightly nauseated. Becoming aware of these physiological changes, she experiences fear. This illustrates the ______ theory of emotion.
   a. Schachter **c.** James-Lange
   b. Cannon-Bard **d.** Papez-MacLean
3. According to the Cannon-Bard theory, an emotion-producing event stimulates the ______, which then stimulates the cortex to produce the feeling and the rest of the body to produce the response.
   a. hypothalamus **c.** amygdala
   b. thalamus **d.** hippocampus
4. The major structures in the Papez circuit are the
   a. thalamus, frontal lobe, parietal lobe, and hippocampus.
   b. frontal lobe, midbrain, and brain stem.
   c. thalamus, hypothalamus, cingulate gyrus, and hippocampus.
   d. hypothalamus, cingulate gyrus, cerebellum, and amygdala.
5. Because it forms a border around brain stem structures, MacLean called the Papez circuit the
   a. reticular formation. **c.** corpus striatum.
   b. border structure. **d.** limbic system.

6. According to MacLean, the three separate circuits in the limbic system are responsible for
   a. anger, worry, and euphoria.
   b. survival, pleasure, and cooperative social behaviors.
   c. anger, pleasure, and cooperative social behaviors.
   d. survival, euphoria, and competitive sexual behaviors.
7. Repeated stimulation of the amygdala in animals makes them more susceptible to seizure activity, demonstrating a phenomenon called
   a. epileptogenic focus. c. kindling.
   b. induced aggression. d. hardiness.
8. Schachter's model of emotions is just the James-Lange theory with the addition of
   a. attribution. c. anger.
   b. euphoria. d. cognition.
9. In the experiment in which male subjects crossed a suspension bridge over a high gorge, what were the men in the high-arousal condition more likely to do than the men in the diminished-arousal condition?
   a. go back across the bridge because of the pleasure of the experience
   b. call the woman who interviewed them after the crossing
   c. call Schachter to see how they were supposed to feel after the experience
   d. go back across the bridge because that was the only way they could get to their cars
10. Behavior motivated by the intent to harm a living creature or inanimate object is called
    a. stress. c. aggression.
    b. anger. d. burnout.
11. Mike accidentally hit his thumb with the hammer while he was trying to hang a picture for his wife. When she asked if he had hurt himself, he yelled at her. According to Moyer, Mike's behavior illustrates ______ aggression.
    a. fear-induced c. instrumental
    b. irritable d. sex-related
12. Attack of virtually any stimulus without making an attempt to escape is characteristic of ______ aggression.
    a. predatory c. irritable
    b. fear-induced d. instrumental
13. After sustaining major damage to both of his temporal lobes, Harry explores everything visually and orally, displays inappropriate sexual behavior, and has memory problems. He has the classic ______ syndrome.
    a. Papez-MacLean c. Cannon-Bard
    b. Klüver-Bucy d. James-Lange
14. Julia, a young woman who sometimes attacked people without provocation, benefited from a(n) ______ performed by Mark and Ervin.
    a. prefrontal lobotomy c. amygdalectomy
    b. cingulectomy d. temporal lobectomy
15. The hormones thought to stimulate aggressive behavior in men and women are ______, respectively.
    a. testosterone and estrogen
    b. testosterone and progesterone
    c. estrogen and prolactin
    d. norepinephrine and estrogen
16. Which of the following appears to inhibit irritable aggression?
    a. prolactin c. progesterone
    b. estrogen d. androstenedione
17. The premenstrual syndrome has been attributed to the decline in ______ that occurs at this time.
    a. estrogen c. progesterone
    b. prolactin d. androgen
18. High levels of ______ promote dominance-seeking behaviors in males, and if ______ levels in the amygdala are low, the failure of dominance-seeking behavior produces intense aggressiveness.
    a. testosterone, dopamine c. testosterone, serotonin
    b. epinephrine, norepinephrine d. ACTH, acetylcholine
19. In studies of juvenile male monkeys, animals with low levels of ______ showed high levels of risk-taking behavior and were more likely to die young.
    a. 5-HIAA c. serotonin
    b. testosterone d. GABA
20. The defensive reaction exhibited by an animal when it perceives there is no escape is called ______ aggression.
    a. irritable c. instrumental
    b. fear-induced d. territorial
21. One of Blanchard and Blanchard's rats, after having a(n) ______, climbed on the head of a cat and nibbled its ear.
    a. cingulectomy c. prefrontal lobotomy
    b. hippocampectomy d. amygdalectomy
22. The three stages of the general adaptation syndrome are
    a. the alarm reaction, the defensive reaction, and the exhaustion stage.
    b. the defensive reaction, the resistance stage, and the exhaustion stage.
    c. the defensive reaction, the resistance stage, and death.
    d. the alarm reaction, the resistance stage, and the exhaustion stage.
23. An excessive competitive drive, high aggressiveness, and sense of time urgency are characteristics of the
    a. type B behavior pattern. c. third stage of the GAS.
    b. type A behavior pattern. d. second stage of the GAS.

24. A person who is less biologically responsive than others to stressors is said to exhibit
    a. TABP.
    b. hardiness.
    c. stress inoculation training.
    d. type B behavior pattern.

25. The characteristic of TABP that seems to be the single most important risk factor for developing heart disease is
    a. hard-driving competitiveness.
    b. anger and hostility.
    c. lack of time urgency.
    d. cynicism and pessimism.

26. A classic workaholic, Jesse continually sets deadlines for herself. She walks, talks, and eats rapidly because of her sense of time urgency. She also has a lot of hostility and reacts aggressively at the slightest provocation. Jesse exhibits ______ behavior.
    a. type A
    b. type B
    c. type C
    d. type D

27. The three stages of stress inoculation training are
    a. the educational stage, rehearsal, and application.
    b. cognitive reappraisal, rehearsal, and performance.
    c. the educational stage, adjustment, and application.
    d. cognitive reappraisal, application, and rejection.

Answers can be found on the companion website at www.worthpublishers.com/klein.

they cannot
rom its s
and
from the
each of these
may be
together
most
being
the

13

Language and Lateralization

- Language
- Hemispheric Lateralization
- *Scientific American* **Spotlight** Same Brain for Speech and Sign
- Communicative Disorders: The Aphasias
- Other Communicative Disorders
- Communicative Disorders: Diagnosis and Recovery
- **Box 13.1** Treatment Approaches for Aphasia

The Stroke

John was in his biological psychology class when his cell phone rang. Heads swiveled, and the instructor nailed him with a dirty look as he struggled to turn the thing off before it could ring again. Whoever was calling could leave a message, and he would check it when class was over.

Outside the building, John listened to the message and was alarmed to hear his father's voice telling him to call as soon as he could. Why in the world would his father be calling in the middle of the day? John sat on a bench near the psychology building and dialed the number his father had left; it wasn't a number he recognized, and that was even more alarming. The number turned out to be a hospital automated message center, and John punched in the extension number his father had supplied. Two rings, and his father answered.

"Grandmother Springer had a stroke this morning," his father said without preamble. "The doctor told us it was caused by the rupture of a blood vessel in her brain. It's pretty serious at her age, but she's expected to live. We'd like you to come home this weekend if possible. Ashley will be coming, too."

Ashley, John's sister, had met him at the station, and now they were in the elevator on their way to their grandmother's hospital room. John's father had told him a little about his grandmother's condition; she was paralyzed on her right side and couldn't speak, although she appeared to understand what was said to her. Ashley now told him that the doctor said it might be weeks or even months before they would know the extent of any permanent deficits.

John had e-mailed his biological psychology teacher to tell her the reason for the phone call and had asked her what she could tell him about the stroke's effect. "Your grandmother's stroke must have occurred on the left side of her brain," his teacher had replied. "If it had been on the right side, she would be paralyzed on the left side of her body, and she would be able to talk."

As John and Ashley neared the room, John was wondering whether his grandmother would recognize him. Would she understand him when he tried to talk to her? Had she regained any ability to speak in the time since he'd talked to his father? Although John enjoyed his biological psychology course, he hadn't expected to see such an immediate connection between real life and what he was learning. He wished the new, personal lesson didn't involve someone in his family.

Ashley, too, was thinking about the ability to speak, but at the moment she wasn't thinking about her grandmother. Instead, she was thinking about her 2-year-old son, Mickey, waiting in the hospital lobby with her husband, Harry. Mickey was just learning to use language, and when she left the lobby, Harry was trying to teach the boy to say "hospital."

BEFORE YOU BEGIN

- **What happened to the brain of John's grandmother that impaired her movement and language abilities?**
- **What part of her brain was damaged, and why did the injury produce these specific impairments in functioning?**
- **What is language?**
- **What areas of the brain are responsible for producing and understanding language?**
- **What do split-brain studies tell us about how the two cerebral hemispheres function?**
- **How is lateralization between the hemispheres studied in humans?**
- **Which functions differ between the two cerebral hemispheres?**
- **What is apraxia? Alexia? Agnosia? What characteristics distinguish these disorders, and what do they have in common with other communicative disorders?**
- **What causes language disorders, and how can they be treated?**

In this chapter, you will find the answers to these questions and many others.

Language

Mickey and his friend Gil, both 2 years old, are playing with bubbles on Mickey's front porch on a warm summer afternoon. Their mothers dip plastic wands into jars of bubble soap and blow out streams of bubbles, which the two little boys delightedly chase after and pop. Gil suddenly seizes the jar of soap from his mother, spilling it and covering both himself and the porch floor with a sticky mess.

Gil's mother takes him inside the house to clean him up. As they go, Mickey observes to Ashley, "Gil spill bubboo." He then thinks for a moment before adding a further comment: "Mickey no spill bubboo."

At age 2, Mickey is already able to produce original sentences that clearly express his thoughts; he can also vary his sentences in understandable ways. He does this spontaneously, effortlessly, and, as it sometimes seems to Ashley, continuously. In this chapter we examine the aspects of the human brain that are responsible for this seemingly miraculous ability to communicate, an ability that, given normal development, all children possess, mostly without any special effort by their parents to teach them. We explore what is known about the perhaps uniquely human ability to express ourselves using words, and how we understand what is being said to us, even when it is expressed imperfectly. (How did you know Mickey meant "bubbles"?)

language A system of words, word meanings, and rules for combining words into phrases and sentences.

phoneme The simplest functional speech sound.

morpheme The smallest meaningful unit of language.

phrase A group of two or more related words that expresses a single thought.

sentence Two or more phrases that convey an assertion, question, command, wish, or exclamation.

phonology The study of the sound system of a language that prescribes how phonemes can be combined into morphemes.

syntax The system of rules for combining words into meaningful phrases and sentences.

When you compare Mickey's first attempts at talking to the smooth flow of words from your biological psychology instructor, you can begin to appreciate the complexity of this form of communication we call language. **Language** is a system of words, word meanings, and rules for combining words into phrases and sentences. For example, consider the sentence, *The dog bit the man.* You understand it because you know the meanings of the individual words—*dog, bit,* and *man*—and because you understand the grammatical structure of the English language: You know the sentence is about a dog who did something to a man. Each of the thousands of human languages has its own system for arranging sounds into meaning. Almost any human being can learn to communicate in any human language.

To appreciate the important role of language in our lives, try to ask your roommate, without saying a word or writing anything, if he or she would like to go out for pizza. This will make obvious the first of the three functions of language: the communication of ideas, a function that allows people to work and play together and form social bonds. A second, less obvious function is that language facilitates the thinking process. Although thought can occur without language, the system of interrelated symbols and rules that makes up language greatly enhances our ability to learn concepts and solve problems. For example, nonhuman animals can understand the structure of their environment without language (Dickinson, 1989); however, our use of language gives us greater opportunities (going out for pizza) than are available to nonhuman animals. The third function of language is that it enables us to write down our experiences and ideas, or to record them in other ways, thereby helping us both to retain knowledge of past events and to overcome the limitations of our memory system.

Checkpoint

What aspects of your life would be different if you did not have language? What aspects would be the same?

The Structure of Language

Spoken language is made up of four main structural units: phonemes, morphemes, phrases, and sentences. The simplest functional element of language is a **phoneme,** or speech sound. For example, the word *bone* contains three phonemes: the *b* sound, the long *o* sound, and the *n* sound. The word *light* also contains three: the *l,* the long *i,* and the *t.* Each language uses a different number of sounds or phonemes. English has 45 basic sounds; languages can have as few as 15 or as many as 85 (Mills, 1980). Because different languages use different numbers and types of sounds, people are often unable to discriminate between phonemes that do not exist in their own language. (Rather than having phonemes, written language has *graphemes,* which are the written letters that represent the sounds of a language.)

The smallest meaningful unit of language is a **morpheme,** which is the simplest combination of sounds, or phonemes, with meaning. Words are examples of morphemes, as are prefixes and suffixes. For example, the word *unavailable* contains three morphemes: *un, avail,* and *able.*

Words are rarely used alone in language. Instead, we combine them into a phrase. A **phrase** is two or more related words that, when combined, express a single thought. We then put two or more phrases together to form a **sentence,** two or more phrases that convey an assertion, question, wish, command, or exclamation. For example, the sentence *The couple bought the house* consists of two major phrases: the noun phrase *the couple* and the verb phrase *bought the house.*

Because different languages use different sounds, people often find it difficult if not impossible to discriminate between sounds that do not exist in their own language.

Rules of Language Usage

Phonemes cannot be combined in just any order to form words, nor can words be combined randomly to form phrases or phrases combined randomly into a sentence. *Fnag* is not an English word, although all its phonemes occur in English; nor is *dog cat fish* an English phrase. Rules govern how phonemes are grouped to form words and how words are combined to form phrases and sentences.

Not all possible phoneme combinations are permissible in a particular language. **Phonology,** the study of the sound system of a language, prescribes how phonemes can be combined into morphemes. Each language places its own restrictions on these phoneme combinations. As with phonemes, words cannot be combined randomly into phrases or phrases into sentences. Rules of **syntax** indicate the acceptable ways that words can be combined into meaningful phrases and sentences. No speaker of Standard English would say, *Table is back on the* or *Newspaper the read I.*

Checkpoint

Write a sentence in any language in which you are fluent. Describe how the four main units of language work together to produce the sentence.

semantics The linguistic analysis of the meaning of language.

The Meaning of Language

Although syntax tells us how to combine words into phrases and sentences, it does not tell us the meaning of these word combinations. To determine the meaning of a sentence, we turn to **semantics,** the linguistic analysis of the meaning of language. A sentence contains a "doer" (the agent) and a something or someone that is "done-to" (the object). Consider the sentence *The boy hit the ball.* In this sentence, the boy, the agent, did something to the ball. How do we know this is the meaning of the sentence? According to Bever (1970), one approach we can use to analyze meaning is the "first-noun-phrase-did-it" strategy. In this strategy, a sentence is assumed to be in the active voice; the first noun phrase is assumed to be the agent and the second noun phrase is assumed to be the object. In other words, the sentence means that the boy (the agent) did something to the ball (the object). This strategy works much of the time, because most of our sentences are in the active voice. Because the sentence *The boy hit the ball* is in the active voice, Bever's strategy works and we understand the sentence.

Suppose we change the sentence to *The ball was hit by the boy.* This sentence in the passive voice has a different syntax than the other sentence, but the same meaning. If we use the "first-noun-phrase-did-it" strategy, we will misinterpret the sentence. Fortunately, some clues indicate that a sentence is not in the active voice. For example, the words *was* and *by* indicate that the sentence is in the passive voice and therefore the "first-noun-phrase-did-it" strategy is not appropriate. Although we need more time to understand a sentence in the passive voice (Slobin, 1966), recognizing when sentences are in the passive voice prevents us from misinterpreting them. Slobin's finding was part of a broader study in which he looked at both active versus passive and active negative versus passive negative statements. The study required children of four different ages (6, 8, 10, and 12 years) and adults (average age about 20 years) to match sentences of four types (active, passive, negative, passive negative) with pictures of the action taking place. Although sentences in the passive voice are grammatically more complex than negative sentences (e.g., *The boy did not hit the ball*), Slobin found that negative sentences took significantly longer to evaluate than passive sentences, and passive negative sentences (e.g., *The ball was not hit by the boy*) were the most difficult of all.

➤Checkpoint

What are the two essential parts of a sentence? Why do we take longer to understand a sentence in the passive voice than in the active voice?

REVIEW

- ➤ Language is a system of words, word meanings, and the rules for combining words into phrases and sentences.
- ➤ The three functions of language are the communication of ideas, the facilitation of thought, and the recording of ideas in written or other form to transcend the limits of our memories and help retain knowledge of past events.
- ➤ Spoken language consists of phonemes (sounds), morphemes (words), phrases, and sentences.
- ➤ Phonology, the study of the sound system of language, prescribes how phonemes can be combined in morphemes. Syntax dictates the ways that words can be combined into phrases and sentences.
- ➤ Semantics is the study of the meaning of language.

Language as an Instinct

Impressed with how easily young children learn their native language, Noam Chomsky (Chomsky & Lightfoot, 1990) presented what he called an instinctive view of human language acquisition. He described the universal sequence of language development from nonsense sounds to the generation of complex sentences and, on the basis of his observations, suggested that children are born with a language-generating mechanism, which he dubbed the **language acquisition device (LAD).** The LAD "knows" the universal aspects of language, and this knowledge allows children to grasp the syntax relevant to their native language readily. In Chomsky's view, however, this biological preparedness does not result in automatic language acquisition; a child must be exposed to language to learn it. Usually, parents eager for their child to start talking provide a more than adequate exposure, using prompts such as "Say 'da da.'"

language acquisition device (LAD) An innate mechanism that allows children to readily grasp the syntax relevant to their native language.

Chomsky's view received a considerable amount of support during the 1960s and 1970s. For example, one researcher argued that language acquisition is an innate, species-specific characteristic, and its expression depends only on physical maturation and minimal exposure to language (Lenneberg, 1969, 1993). Language is acquired in a fixed order and at a particular rate. Lenneberg found that a period of nonsense jargon (lengthy, fluent speech that makes little or no sense) is always followed by one-word speech, which develops into the use of two-word structures, followed by telegraphic speech, and then the use of complex sentences. Language is acquired in the same sequence by all children, even when maturation is abnormally slow, as in the case of children with Down syndrome, in whom language develops at a slower rate.

Although only minimal exposure is necessary for language acquisition, the earlier the experience the better. Johnson and Newport (1989) evaluated the ability of Korean and Chinese immigrants to the United States to accurately identify 276 English-language sentences as grammatically correct or incorrect. Each immigrant had been living in the United States for approximately 10 years. Even though the length of exposure to English was the same for all the immigrants, those who had arrived before age 8 understood grammar as well as native speakers, but the accuracy declined to approximately 80% when the age at immigration was 11 to 15 years and to about 75% when the age at immigration was 17 to 39 years. Although immigrants who arrive in the United States after age 8 can master basic words and how to use them, Johnson and Newport's study suggests that these older immigrants are unlikely to become as fluent as individuals born in the United States in producing and comprehending subtle grammatical differences.

Deaf children also appear to need only minimal exposure to learn sign language (Petitto, 2000a, 2000b). According to Petitto, deaf children with deaf, signing parents learn to sign at the same age as hearing children learn to speak. However, deaf children who are not exposed to sign language in early childhood never become as fluent in signing as deaf children exposed to language at an early age. The late-exposed deaf children also have a difficult time producing and comprehending the subtle aspects of language. These observations support the idea that early language exposure is necessary for a person to become proficient in a language, and failure to gain this experience has permanent effects. Petitto's work also stresses the fundamental similarities between spoken and signed languages and their development in children.

IMAGE100/SUPERSTOCK

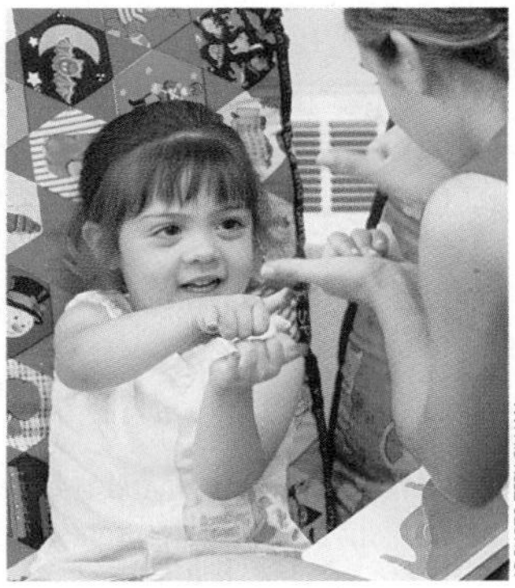

AP PHOTO/TERY GILLIAM

The timing and progress of linguistic development are fundamentally similar in all children, whether learning spoken or signed language.

All of this information suggests that language acquisition in humans is a biologically based form of learning that occurs during a sensitive period of development, which is the first 13 years of life (Komarova & Nowak, 2001). Presumably, language ability has evolved in humans because it enhances biological fitness: Better communicators generate more offspring (Nowak & others, 1999). Further, children inherit a strategy for language learning—Chomsky's LAD—from their parents. This LAD permits them to acquire the grammar of their parents' language merely by hearing sample sentences, which suggests they are born with preformed expectations (Komarova & others, 2001). Komarova and Nowak (2003) called the mecha-

Williams syndrome A rare genetic disorder in which relatively intact language ability is coupled with mild to moderate mental retardation.

arcuate fasciculus A bundle of nerve fibers in the brain that connects Wernicke's area and Broca's area.

Wernicke-Geschwind model A model of language processing in which language is comprehended in Wernicke's area before messages are passed to Broca's area for speech production.

angular gyrus An area of the parietal lobe with connections to Wernicke's area; involved in comprehending written language.

nism that children use to evaluate the sample sentences and extract a grammar from them *universal grammar,* and suggested that this universal grammar cannot be learned but must be in place before the learning process begins.

Some psychologists have argued that language acquisition is not a unique ability and merely reflects cognitive strategies translated into language (Rice, 1989). If language acquisition merely reflects an extension of our cognitive abilities, then there should be a high level of correspondence between cognitive abilities and language proficiency. Although such a high correspondence usually is found, some researchers have noted that cognitive development and linguistic development can be uncoupled (Dronkers & others, 2000). For example, Cromer (1994) described the case history of a young woman with both hydrocephaly (see Chapter 2 for a discussion of this disorder) and spina bifida (Chapter 3). She has excellent verbal language skills despite being severely retarded in virtually all other cognitive abilities. This separation of linguistic ability from other cognitive abilities ties in well with Howard Gardner's idea of multiple intelligences, one of which is linguistic (Gardner, 1983, 2003).

Williams syndrome is another possible example of the uncoupling of cognitive and linguistic ability. This rare genetic disorder is caused by the deletion of about 20 genes on chromosome 7 (Mervis, 2003). Individuals with the syndrome have relatively intact language abilities with mental retardation (Bellugi & others, 1988), and the syndrome is often cited as evidence for "functional modules" in the brain. Other characteristics of the syndrome include hypersociability (an intense desire to meet and interact with strangers) and distinct facial features, growth deficiencies, and a heart defect (Hirota & others, 1996). The hypersociability is often a major concern for the parents of children with Williams syndrome (Bellugi, Adolphs, & others, 1999; Doyle & others, 2004).

Individuals with Williams syndrome tend to exhibit mild to moderate mental retardation (Bellugi & others, 2000; Mervis & Klein-Tasman, 2000). Their strengths include auditory rote memory, communication ability, and socialization skills; weaknesses include impaired daily living and motor skills and a profound deficit in visuospatial construction (e.g., drawing a reasonable representation of a house). Because of their impaired daily living skills, most individuals with the syndrome do not achieve independent living.

Although children with Williams syndrome are excellent communicators who use affective prosody (rhythm, accent, intonation) much more frequently than normally developing children of the same mental age (Bellugi, Adolphs, & others, 1999), Karmiloff-Smith and associates believe that their language skills are deficient and that the syndrome may not support the existence of independent, innate brain modules (Grant & others, 2002; Karmiloff-Smith & others, 1997, 1998, 2003). For example, on a simple task examining the syntax of relative clauses, older children and adults with Williams syndrome performed at about the level of 5-year-old cognitively healthy controls (Grant & others). Further, adults with Williams syndrome showed clear-cut deficits on tasks that focused on expressive or receptive language (Karmiloff-Smith & others, 1997). The researchers concluded that the language learning of people with Williams syndrome may turn out to be more like learning a second language than the normal acquisition of native language.

Studies of the brains of individuals with Williams syndrome provide neurophysiological evidence that may account for their deficits and strengths. For example, one experiment found such cellular anomalies as an exaggerated horizontal organization of neurons, particularly in striate cortex; increased density of cells throughout brain areas; and abnormally clustered neurons (Galaburda & others, 1994). Researchers have also noted that posterior forebrain areas (posterior parietal lobe, occipital lobe) are quite small, which might explain the visuospatial deficit typically seen (Galaburda & Bellugi, 2000). MRI studies show a relative sparing of frontal and limbic structures, and an abnormal functional organization of areas that mediate language and process information about faces has been found (Bellugi, Lichten-

Children with Williams syndrome have characteristic facial features, sometimes referred to as "elfin" features.

COURTESY OF REBECCA TROSPER

berger, & others, 1999). Both results might help account for the strengths in language and facial recognition seen in Williams syndrome.

Checkpoint

What is the significance of Chomsky's view of language acquisition? Relate this view to the age at which most American students in English-language families are exposed to a second language.

The Anatomy of Language

Did you try the little challenge posed earlier—to ask your roommate to go out for pizza, without using language? If so, chances are good that it failed, and after 5 minutes of playing charades you gave up and resorted to language to convey your message. When John asked his roommate, Gary, this question, Gary asked, "Where do you want to go?" John's question and his roommate's response are just one of many linguistic interactions people have every day. How is Gary able to respond to John's question? He must hear and understand the words, decide on an answer, and produce that answer—all in a split second. What brain structures enable John to understand and respond to Gary's question? The following model of language organization provides us with the beginning of an answer.

Norman Geschwind (1991, 1992) proposed that the comprehension of spoken language is the function of Wernicke's area in the left hemisphere (Figure 13.1a). (Although Norman Geschwind died in 1984, his writings continue to have enough relevance to be reprinted in collections of readings and elsewhere. In addition, throughout this discussion, we will almost always be referring to language areas in the left hemisphere of the brain and particularly to the neocortex of the left hemisphere.) Recall from Chapter 1 that German physician Carl Wernicke first recognized the significance of this brain area in 1874 (see Figure 1.6). Wernicke's area is located in the dorsal part of the left temporal lobe in the posterior superior temporal gyrus.

Geschwind (1991) suggested that once the meaning of spoken language is understood, Wernicke's area generates a representation of a verbal response, which could be an auditory neural image of the response. This neural representation is then transferred to the **arcuate fasciculus,** a bundle of fibers that connects Wernicke's area and Broca's area (Figure 13.1b). In Chapter 1, we briefly discussed the significance of Broca's area (described by French physician Paul Broca in 1861) for speech production. Broca's area is in the left frontal area in the posterior third frontal convolution anterior to the primary motor cortex (see Figure 1.6).

Studies in monkeys reveal few direct connections between the structures we call Broca's and Wernicke's areas (Aboitiz & Garcia, 1997). Instead, they suggest that the connection between the areas may be through ventral parietal structures, a connection that would tie in with working memory (Chapter 14). Aboitiz and Garcia hypothesize that language processing is intimately related to working memory and that the major language areas evolved from a working memory network for linguistic production.

Language can be communicated visually (reading/writing) as well as orally (speaking/listening). According to the **Wernicke-Geschwind model** (Geschwind, 1991), the secondary visual cortex and the **angular gyrus** are responsible for comprehension of the written word (Figure 13.1b). Located in the parietal lobe, the angular gyrus borders the left occipital lobe and has connections to Wernicke's area. Damage to the connection between the angular gyrus and Wernicke's area has been associated with an impaired ability to comprehend written words, which suggests that Wernicke's area is important for comprehending both spoken and written language.

Figure 13.1

The Wernicke-Geschwind model of language (a) The location of key areas in language comprehension and speech production, according to the Wernicke-Geschwind model. (b) The neural routes for responding verbally to a heard question and for reading a word aloud.

→ **Outline the route of the visual and auditory responses to reading this question aloud.**

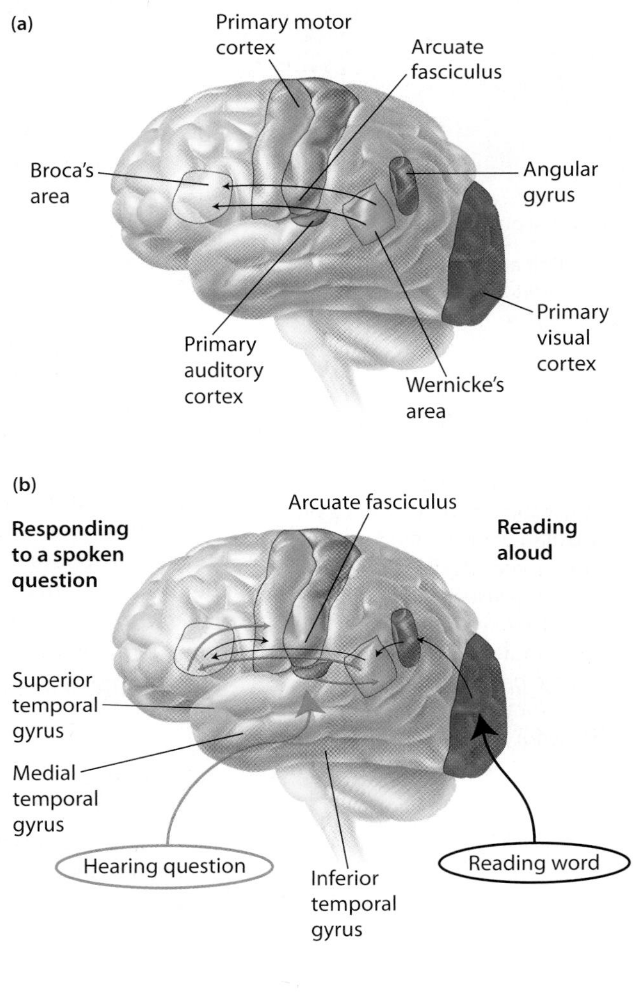

Research suggesting that brain regions other than Wernicke's area are important in the comprehension of speech has been reported (Davis, 1993), however. The syntactic and semantic comprehension of language is the responsibility of the secondary auditory cortex, located in the posterior part of the superior and middle temporal gyrus (including Wernicke's area), and the **temporoparietal cortex.** The temporoparietal cortex includes the supramarginal gyrus and the angular gyrus. Damage to these areas can produce **neologistic jargon,** lengthy, fluent, nonsensical speech. The occurrence of neologistic jargon in individuals suffering damage to the secondary auditory cortex and the temporoparietal cortex points to an important role for these areas in language comprehension (Perecman & Brown, 1981).

The Wernicke-Geschwind model of the functions of Broca's area has also been challenged. True Broca's aphasia, with labored speech, missing verbs and connecting words (e.g., conjunctions, articles), and defective repetition, requires damage beyond the cortical region known as Broca's area (Dronkers & others, 2000). Damage restricted just to Broca's area produces a condition known as *Broca area aphasia,* which is both milder and shorter lasting than true Broca's aphasia.

Extensive analysis of a large number of left-hemisphere stroke patients with language comprehension difficulties cast further doubt on the status of the key structures of the Wernicke-Geschwind model (Dronkers & others, 2004). Subjects in the study were required to select a line drawing from a set of three or four that best illustrated the content of a sentence presented orally. Analysis of the patients' lesions revealed several cortical areas involved in this language task, but damage to Broca's or Wernicke's areas was not significantly related to the measure of language comprehension examined.

Figure 13.2

Systems controlling language perception and production Lateral view of the left human neocortex, showing the major areas currently thought to be involved in language. Structures shown in red comprise the implementation system; the green areas surrounding the implementation system are part of the mediational system; the conceptual system is not shown.

➡ **What is the effect of damage restricted to Broca's area?**

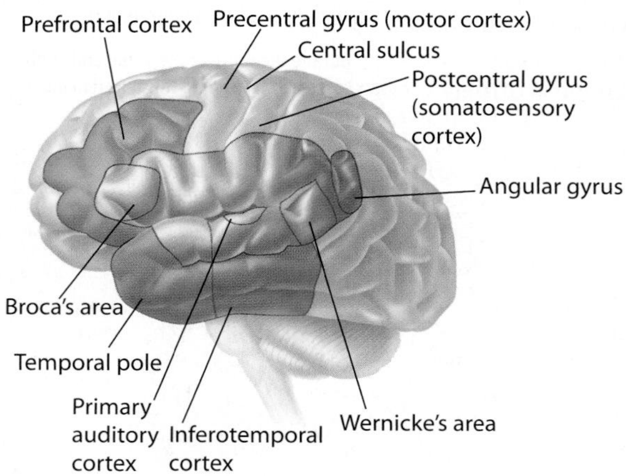

Although the relative simplicity of the Wernicke-Geschwind model is intuitively appealing (see Figure 13.1), research in the last decade has suggested a much broader framework (Damasio & Damasio, 2000). At this point, you may be asking yourself why we have spent so much time on the Wernicke-Geschwind model if it has been superseded by more recent research. In addition to its historical relevance, the model has played an important role both in directing research on language and the brain and helping to organize and interpret research results once they have been obtained. The current theoretical framework for the anatomical control of language envisions three systems acting in concert for language perception and production (Dronkers & others, 2000). The *language implementation system* includes Broca's and Wernicke's areas as well as parts of insular cortex (cortex beneath the temporal and frontal lobes) and the basal ganglia (Figure 13.2). The anterior and posterior parts of the implementation system (Broca's and Wernicke's areas, respectively) are bidirectionally connected by the arcuate fasciculus and surrounding tissue (Matsumoto & others, 2004). The implementation system analyzes incoming auditory signals and ensures that outgoing responses are grammatical and well articulated.

The implementation system is surrounded by the *mediational system,* which consists of separate regions in the temporal, parietal, and frontal association areas (Figure 13.2). This system acts as a go-between for the implementation system and the *conceptional system,* which Dronkers and colleagues (2000) define as "a collection of regions throughout the remainder of higher-order association cortices, which support conceptual knowledge" (p. 1175).

➤Checkpoint

You and your roommate go to a pizza parlor. The two of you must share a menu. You begin reading choices aloud to your roommate. Describe the path of all the visual and auditory input involved, beginning with your seeing the words on the page, and ending with your roommate comprehending your spoken morphemes.

REVIEW

- Chomsky suggested that children are born with a language-generating mechanism called the language acquisition device (LAD) and are thus instinctively prepared for the development of language skills.

- Individuals with Williams syndrome have mild to moderate mental retardation, relatively intact language skills, and hypersociability.
- According to the Wernicke-Geschwind model of language production, Wernicke's area comprehends spoken language and sends a neural representation of the verbal response through the arcuate fasciculus to Broca's area, which is responsible for expressing the verbal response.
- The Wernicke-Geschwind model assumes that the secondary visual cortex and the angular gyrus are responsible for the comprehension of written language.
- Recent research suggests that the Wernicke-Geschwind model is too simple and that a broad array of cortical and subcortical structures is involved in language comprehension and production. The current framework consists of a language implementation system, a mediational system, and a conceptual system.

temporoparietal cortex A brain area encompassing the supramarginal gyrus and angular gyrus; involved in language comprehension.

neologistic jargon A passage of lengthy, fluent, nonsensical speech.

hemispheric lateralization The differentiation of functions between the right and left sides of the brain.

Hemispheric Lateralization

In earlier chapters, we have discussed such important functions as hunger, thirst, sleep, and vision as if they originated in the brain as a whole, or as if the two cerebral hemispheres were mirror images of each other—much like other structures that exist in pairs, such as our ears or our eyes, which do indeed work this way. However, as we have also indicated, there are major differences, both structural and functional, between the two hemispheres of the brain. Severe impairments can result from damage to a part of one cerebral hemisphere, even if the other hemisphere remains intact, and numerous studies have shown that in most people some functions differ between hemispheres. One of the most important of such functions is language, which has two components: expression, more commonly in the form of speech, and perception, or an understanding of what is being said. This differentiation of functions is called **hemispheric lateralization.**

Recall from Chapter 2 that the cerebral cortex has two hemispheres connected by a series of cerebral commissures, the largest of which is the *corpus callosum* (Figure 13.3). The commissures are composed of axons carrying information from one hemisphere to the other, and most interhemispheric information exchange occurs here. Much of our knowledge about lateralization of function comes from research by Roger Sperry, who conducted a series of experiments on cats in the 1950s in which he severed the commissures, as well as the optic chiasm, eliminating most communication between the hemispheres. Called the **split-brain preparation,** Sperry's technique and the results it generated are the focus of the following discussion.

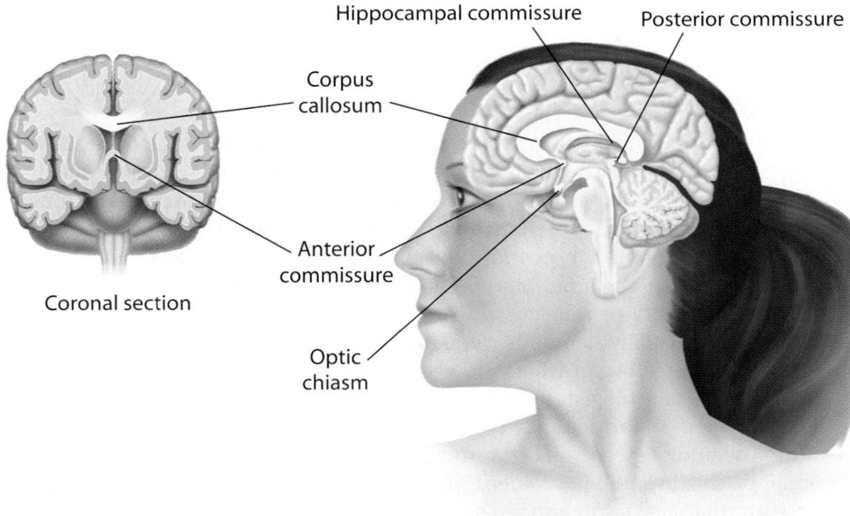

Figure 13.3
The cerebral commissures The corpus callosum, anterior commissure, hippocampal commissure, and posterior commissure allow information to be exchanged between the left and right hemispheres of the brain.

What happens if the cerebral commissures are damaged?

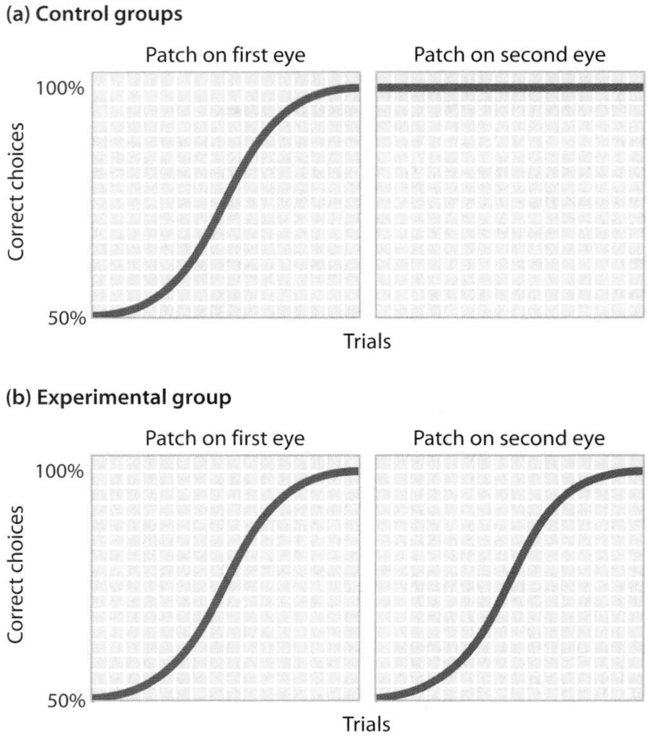

Figure 13.4

Performance on a simple visual discrimination task in Myers and Sperry's split-brain study in cats With a patch on one eye, all animals learned a visual discrimination task at the same rate and to the same final performance level. (a) Control animals (cats with either corpus callosum or optic chiasm severed, or both intact) continued to perform perfectly when the patch was switched to the other eye. (b) Experimental animals (cats with both corpus callosum and optic chiasm severed) performed at a chance level when the patch was switched to the other eye and took as long to relearn the task as they had taken to learn it originally.

→ **How do the above results show that separate memories can be stored in each hemisphere?**

Split-Brain Studies in Cats

Sperry (1961) reported that "split-brain" cats, animals whose cerebral commissures and optic chiasm had been cut, showed no evidence that information stored in one hemisphere was available to the other hemisphere. (Hippocampal commissures are not affected by the split-brain preparation, and they provide some information exchange, which we discuss later.) Further, behaviors learned by one hemisphere could not be performed by the other hemisphere. In fact, split-brain animals could learn different behaviors in each hemisphere, suggesting the cats were functioning as if they had two separate "brains" (Myers & Sperry, 1958; Sperry & others, 1956).

In one study, cats were trained to perform a discrimination task, discriminating between visual stimuli with a patch over one eye (Myers & Sperry, 1953). (In a discrimination task, responding to one visual stimulus, such as a round light, is rewarded, whereas responding to the other visual stimulus, such as a square light, is not.) In experimental animals with severed cerebral commissures and optic chiasm, the patch limited visual information to one hemisphere. Visual information was available to both hemispheres in control animals with a patch—cats with intact cerebral commissures and optic chiasm or cats with either severed cerebral commissures or severed optic chiasm, but not both. Myers and Sperry reported that experimental and control animals learned the visual discrimination at the same rate and to an equal level of performance. After the initial training, the patch was switched to the other eye. The transfer did not affect performance in the control animals (Figure 13.4a), but it profoundly affected the experimental subjects. Following the switch, the performance of the experimental animals dropped to a chance level (i.e., results governed by chance alone) (Figure 13.4b), and the cats relearned the task at the same rate as naive (untrained) animals. There was absolutely no evidence for any previous learning in the split-brain cats.

Checkpoint

What was the purpose of Sperry's experiments with cats? Summarize their results.

Split-Brain Studies in Humans

Yoko has a an epileptic seizure disorder that is now well controlled. However, before she began taking medicine to manage the seizures, each attack proceeded as follows: A feeling of extreme dread preceded a tonic phase, in which Yoko's muscles would contract powerfully. Her body would become rigid for about 15 seconds, and then she would begin to jerk violently during the seizure's clonic phase. The convulsions lasted about 30 seconds, with the intensity of the muscle contractions slowly diminishing. After the seizure, Yoko usually slept for several hours.

Yoko's seizures began when she was a child. The pediatrician referred her parents to a neurologist, who ordered an electroencephalogram (EEG). The EEG revealed abnormal activity in Yoko's temporal lobes. After ruling out a tumor or other disease as the cause of the abnormal activity producing her epileptic seizures, the neurologist prescribed phenytoin (Dilantin), a CNS depressant that acts as an anticonvulsant. Yoko has responded well to the drug, and her seizures are now fewer and less severe.

If Yoko had been born before the advent of effective seizure control with drugs such as Dilantin, she might have been a candidate for a surgical procedure to cut her cerebral commissures, as this was used successfully to treat seizure disorders in a number of patients. Roger Sperry and his colleagues began the study of these patients, which continues today.

Sperry's animal research suggested that each hemisphere can process information independently. Sperry also was interested in extending his observations to humans, which an experimental surgical treatment developed by surgeons Phillip Vogel and Joseph Bogen allowed him to do.

Vogel and Bogen, of the California College of Medicine, decided to try **commissurotomy,** or cutting the cerebral commissures, as a treatment for otherwise uncontrollable seizures in human patients. The surgeons hoped the operation would reduce the intensity of the seizure activity by limiting the seizures to just one hemisphere. In fact, the operation was more beneficial than that, and some commissurotomized patients never had another seizure.

Beginning in 1961 with the first patient to undergo this procedure, Sperry and various associates, particularly Michael Gazzaniga, studied the patients postoperatively to try to learn as much as possible about the function of the corpus callosum and about the different functions of the two hemispheres. As was readily apparent, the split-brain persons experienced little change in temperament, personality, and general intelligence. Proving that his sense of humor was still intact, one of the first patients, upon awakening from anesthesia, told the surgeons that he had a "splitting headache" (Gazzaniga, 1967).

Research with Vogel and Bogen's patients shows that the two cortical hemispheres do indeed have different functions (Sperry, 1982). Language and analytical functions are lateralized to (located in) the left hemisphere, and nonverbal, visual-spatial functions are lateralized in the right hemisphere.

split-brain preparation A surgical technique that severs the cerebral commissures and the optic chiasm (only in nonhuman animals), eliminating most communication between the hemispheres.

commissurotomy A surgical cutting of the cerebral commissures to treat otherwise uncontrollable seizures.

Left-Hemisphere Language Functions

To study the behavior of Vogel and Bogen's split-brain patients, Sperry used a special piece of equipment called a *tachistoscope* to present information very briefly (for a second or less; the Greek *tachistos* means "swiftest") to the right or left visual field. (Recall that a visual field is the part of the visual world to the right or left of a point of fixation. Be careful not to confuse what you see with your left [or right] eye with your left [or right] visual field. Look at Figure 13.5, and you will see that each eye receives input from both halves of the visual field.) In Chapter 6, we explained how information presented to the right visual field goes to the left hemisphere, and information presented to the left visual field to the right hemisphere (Figure 13.5). (Note that, unlike in the experimental animals in Sperry's studies, the optic chiasm was not cut in the split-brain patients.)

In a typical study, the split-brain patient sat at a table facing a small screen on which images were projected from behind by a tachistoscope. The experimenter then showed different stimuli to the patient and asked him or her to identify each object *verbally.* When the information was presented in the right visual field (traveling to the left hemisphere), both normal (intact-brain) and split-brain patients accurately and rapidly identified the object. For example, if a picture of a fork were flashed in the right visual field, the person would say *fork.* For images flashed in the left visual field (information traveling initially to the right hemisphere), normal subjects could verbally identify objects but split-brain subjects could not (Figure 13.6). However, the mute right hemisphere could inform the experimenter that it saw a fork by retrieving the fork with the split-brain patient's left hand, which it controls.

In an interesting variation of the research, a split-brain patient was shown the word *HEART* in such a way that *HE* appeared in the

Figure 13.5

The route of visual input from the right and left visual fields to the right and left hemispheres Although input from the right visual field goes initially to the left visual cortex and input from the left visual field goes initially to the right visual cortex, when the corpus callosum is intact, the information is available to both hemispheres.

→ Trace the route of visual input from the right visual field to both eyes and then into the cerebral cortex.

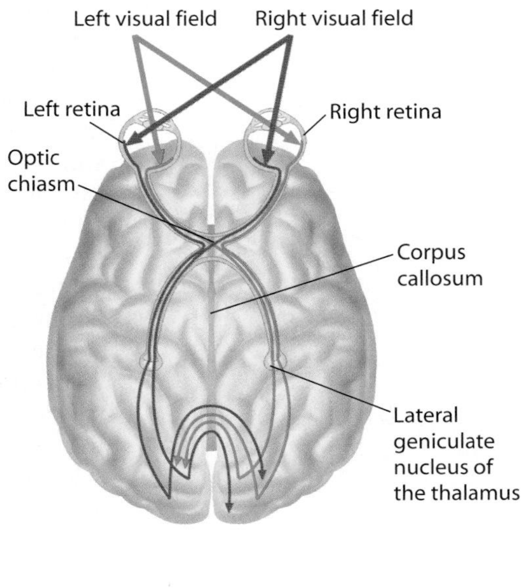

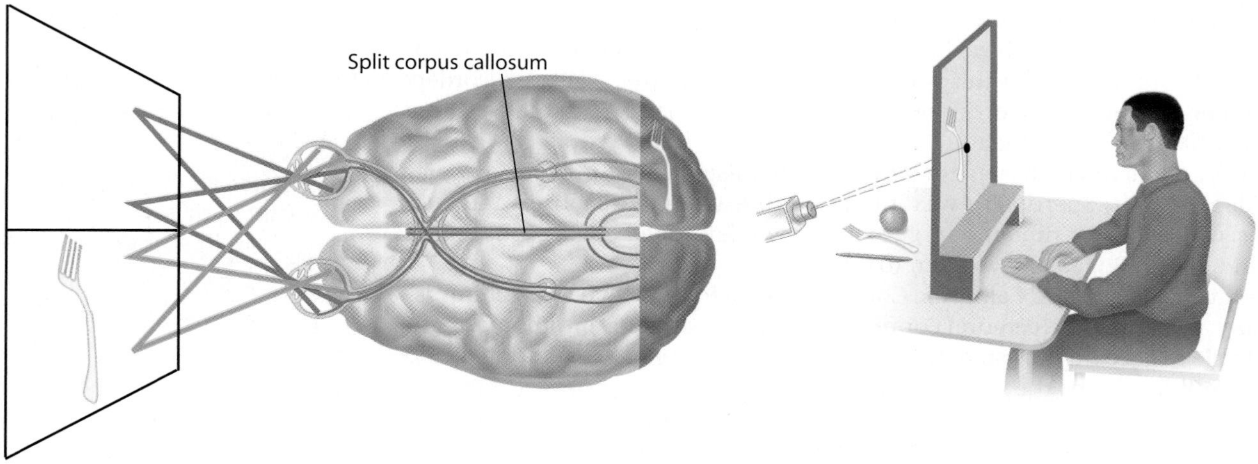

Figure 13.6
The difference between normal (intact-brain) and split-brain individuals When a fork is presented to the left visual field of a normal individual, the person can verbally identify the object because the information from the right visual cortex is available to the left (speaking) hemisphere through the corpus callosum. However, when the same object is presented to the left visual field of a split-brain patient, he cannot identify it verbally.

➡ **Why is it that the split-brain patient cannot verbally identify the fork presented to the right hemisphere? How could the right hemisphere tell the experimenter that it saw a fork?**

left visual field (information traveling to the right hemisphere) and *ART* in the right visual field (to the left hemisphere). Sperry and his associates found that the split-brain patient would verbally report seeing only the word *ART* (Figure 13.7).

Extensive evidence indicates that the left hemisphere is more active than the right when an unimpaired person is engaged in verbal activities. Some examples: Blood flow velocity is greater in the left than in the right hemisphere during verbal tasks (Hartje & others, 1994; Vingerhoets & Stroobant, 1999). Single-unit neural activity appears earlier in the left hemisphere than in the right during a rhyming verbal task (Schwartz & others, 2000). Neural activity as measured by fMRI is greater for the left hemisphere than the right when an unimpaired person is engaged in a verbal task (Buchanan & others, 2000). In another fMRI study, Opitz and colleagues (2000) reported that the left prefrontal cortex is more active than the right when people are retrieving verbal information. All these observations suggest that the ability to name objects is a function of the left hemisphere, and they explain why John's grandmother could not speak following the stroke affecting her left hemisphere. Although the split-brain patients in the *HEART* experiment described above could not verbalize it, they could point to the word *HE* with the left hand, which is controlled by the right hemisphere (see Figure 13.7).

Right-Hemisphere Language Functions

Sperry's research suggested that the left hemisphere controls speech functions, but that does not mean that the right hemisphere has no language ability. All we can say at this point in our discussion is that the right hemisphere is almost always mute. Sperry and his associates sought the answer to the question of the right hemisphere's language ability in their studies of split-brain patients (Gazzaniga, 1967, 1977, 1983, 1995; Gazzaniga & others, 1977; Gazzaniga & Sperry, 1967). Before considering their research, keep several things in mind: (1) Items flashed to the left visual field travel to the right hemisphere, and vice versa. (2) The control of Broca's area for speech resides in the left hemisphere, so when a split-brain person is asked a question requiring a verbal response, the left hemisphere answers. (3) The neural systems controlling voluntary motor responses are mostly crossed, which means the right hemisphere controls the left hand and the left hemisphere the right hand. This control is not absolute, however, as there is some limited ipsilateral control (Springer & Deutsch, 1998). Still, one way to ensure that the right hemisphere is responding to a question is to require the split-brain person to answer by using his or her left hand.

In one experiment, split-brain patients were shown a picture of a specific object (say a fork) in the left or right visual field (Gazzaniga, 1983). They were then asked to reach under a curtain with the left hand (controlled by the right hemisphere) and select the pictured object from among several other objects (see Figure 13.6). The split-brain patients could pick out the correct object with the left hand when a pic-

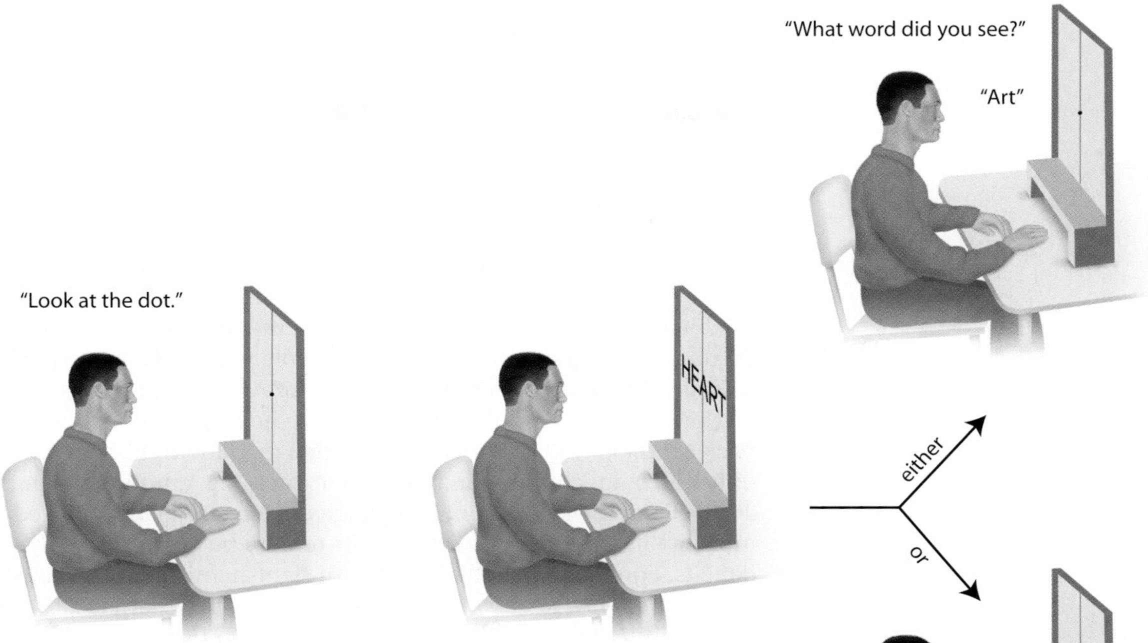

"What word did you see?"

"Look at the dot."

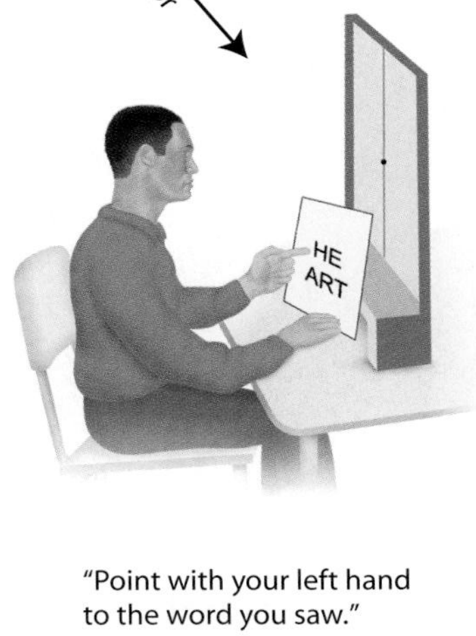

HE
ART
"Point with your left hand
to the word you saw."

Figure 13.7
The lack of information transfer between hemispheres in a split-brain individual The word *HEART* is flashed on a screen. *HE* goes to the right hemisphere and *ART* to the left hemisphere. The split-brain patient verbally reports seeing *ART*. However, he points to the word *HE* with his left hand.

→ **Why can the split-brain patient verbally report the word ART, but not HE? Why does he point to the word HE with his left hand?**

ture of the object was shown to the left visual field, but not when the picture was shown to the right visual field. Of course, for presentation to the right visual field, they were able to either name the object or pick it out with their *right* hand.

The stimulus projected to the left visual field could be a picture of an object (picture of a fork), the word for the object ("fork"), or a phrase about the use of the object (e.g., "used to eat a piece of cake") (Gazzaniga, 1983). After exposure to any of these stimuli, the split-brain patients could select a fork with their left hand. However, they could not verbally identify the object in their left hand as long as they could not see it, and they would deny exposure to a visual stimulus. These results indicate that although the right hemisphere cannot name objects, because it usually lacks control of Broca's area, it can understand the meaning of a word or simple phrase. Some research suggests that the right hemisphere can comprehend vocabulary at the level of a 13-year-old and sentence structure at the level of a 5-year-old (Code & Rowley, 1987). However, the early work with split-brain patients suggested more language ability in the right hemisphere than has been found in subsequent patients (Gazzaniga, 1998).

Nevertheless, the right hemisphere does have an important language function (Ornstein, 1997). For example, using PET and rCBF (regional cerebral blood flow; a measure of blood flow in a specific part of the brain), Bottini and colleagues (1994) concluded that the right hemisphere plays a special role in the appreciation of figurative or nonliteral aspects of language, such as metaphors. This finding was recently corroborated by Sotillo and colleagues (2005). Further, in comparisons among brain-damaged patients, individuals with left-hemisphere damage performed better than those with right-hemisphere damage in tests involving metaphoric alternative meanings of words, again suggesting the right hemisphere plays a vital role in the comprehension of metaphors (Brownell & others, 1995). Ornstein argued that without the ability to recognize the figurative aspects of language, a person with right-hemisphere damage has difficulty understanding complex human discourse.

Damage to the right hemisphere can also produce difficulties in comprehending and expressing humor (Lehman, 2003). For example, persons with right hemisphere damage have difficulty integrating incongruous elements of a joke (the punch line) with the rest of the joke. This difficulty is related to a deficit in interpreting nonliteral utterances, statements that are not meant to be taken literally (Kaplan & others, 1990). In one study, event-related brain potentials were recorded in healthy adults as they read "punch words" to one-line jokes or nonjoke control words, presented to the left or the right hemisphere (Coulson & Williams, 2005). (An example of a stimulus joke, with the joke/nonjoke endings: "I still miss my ex-wife, but I am improving my aim/ego.") Semantic activation differed in the two hemispheres, with right hemisphere activation enabling comprehension of the jokes.

The right hemisphere also may provide an understanding of the context of language (Ornstein, 1997). Consider the ambiguous sentence, *We saw her duck.* This sentence could mean either that we saw a woman's pet duck or that we saw a person lower her head, with the meaning determined by the context. Obviously, a person may be able to recognize the words in an ambiguous sentence even when unable to appreciate the meaning of a sentence because of the lack of an appropriate frame of reference (context). People with right-hemisphere damage have difficulty recognizing context and therefore the rich meaning of language.

Nonverbal communication appears to be a right hemisphere function (Brumback & others, 1996). For example, damage to the right hemisphere can produce difficulties in comprehending and expressing emotional language (Lehman, 2003). Expressive emotional language deficits are evident as reduced emotional intensity in speech, and such deficits tend to be greater than the comprehension deficits. For example, individuals with right-hemisphere damage are deficient in speech prosody relative to people without brain damage (Gandour & others, 1995). Similarly, Mitchell and colleagues (2003) used fMRI to show that the right hemisphere is important for processing emotional prosody. Also, right-brain-damaged individuals show less emotional expression when recalling emotional and nonemotional experiences than either left-brain-damaged or normal adults (Montreys & Borod, 1998). And people with right-hemisphere damage have difficulty interpreting the emotional tone of other people's speech (Tucker, 1981) and their emotional facial expressions (Mandal & others, 1999). For example, they would be unable to tell whether Yoko is sad or angry when she describes her experience with epilepsy.

The *Scientific American* Spotlight, "Same Brain for Speech and Sign," examines how the brains of deaf people process their use of sign language. The title provides the conclusion: The same parts of the cerebral cortex process language no matter what the sensory channels (vision in sign language, hearing in speech). Further research using fMRI revealed right hemisphere activity as well as left hemisphere activity in the use of sign language in people born deaf who grew up using American Sign Language (ASL) and in people who were raised bilingually with both English and ASL.

Checkpoint

How does split-brain surgery relieve seizures? What does this treatment suggest about the way the two halves of the brain work together? When the answer to a question must be given orally, which hemisphere answers the question? Which hemisphere is usually better at determining the meaning of verbal metaphors? At understanding the context of language?

Right-Hemisphere Use of Visual-Spatial Information

Visual-spatial abilities, the coordination of visual and motor functions, appear to be lateralized in the right hemisphere, and the right hemisphere also enables us to recognize and react to complex visual stimuli. Once again, the best way to evaluate these functions is when they are absent. Individuals with right-hemisphere damage may have difficulty finding their way between physical locations in their environment, and they often have trouble recognizing faces.

In a study providing evidence for right-hemisphere control of visual-spatial activities, split-brain patients were instructed either to draw a representation of an observed object or to assemble blocks into a specific design (Gazzaniga & Sperry, 1967). The split-brain persons could reproduce an object or assemble blocks correctly with their left hand (right hemisphere) but not with their right hand (left hemisphere). Figure 13.8 shows the difference in drawings produced by the right and the left hemispheres. Note that the split-brain patient was right-handed, which explains the crudeness of the drawings produced with the left hand—but not the nonrepresentational quality of the drawings made with the right hand.

Jerre Levy and her colleagues also studied the lateralization of visual-spatial abilities (Levy, 1985; Levy & others, 1972). In this research, split-brain patients

Scientific American Spotlight

Same Brain for Speech and Sign

Jens Lubbadeh

How does the brain process sign language? In the 1980s neuroscientist Ursula Bellugi of the Salk Institute for Biological Studies in San Diego made some of the first attempts to answer that question. It had been well established that Wernicke's region of the brain was largely responsible for understanding speech and that Broca's region was the main player in the production of words and sentences. Bellugi studied deaf subjects with injuries to many different brain regions.

Some patients seemed to suffer from symptoms comparable to Wernicke's aphasia—they could sign fluently but had trouble understanding signs from others. Bellugi found that they indeed had damage in Wernicke's area. Other patients had difficulties that paralleled Broca's aphasia—they struggled to form sign-language hand positions even though other fine-motor skills posed no problems. Sure enough, Bellugi found lesions in their Broca's area. The work by Bellugi and others provided evidence that although signing uses completely different sensory channels—vision instead of hearing—it is processed in the same brain regions.

Neuroscientists have since concluded that certain parts of the cerebral cortex are reserved for language processing, no matter what sensory channel brings in the linguistic input. For many researchers, this finding was evidence that the ability to speak is innate. People are born into the world with a speech center and then learn one or more tongues, whether they are English, Japanese, American Sign Language (ASL) or French Sign Language.

Recent observation of a secluded group of deaf children in Nicaragua supports this thesis. The children were never taught any sign language and had therefore simply created their own, and it had grammatical structures that were strikingly similar to those of spoken languages.

Further research has delved into whether the left or right hemisphere of the brain is dominant. The answer had been hard to determine until the advent of functional magnetic resonance imaging allowed scientists to more or less watch the brains of signers in conversation. Using this technique, Helen Neville and Aaron Newman of the University of Oregon and David Corina of the University of Washington compared brain activity in three groups: people born deaf who had grown up using ASL, hearing people who had grown up speaking English and could not sign, and hearing people who had grown up with deaf parents and were raised bilingually with English and ASL.

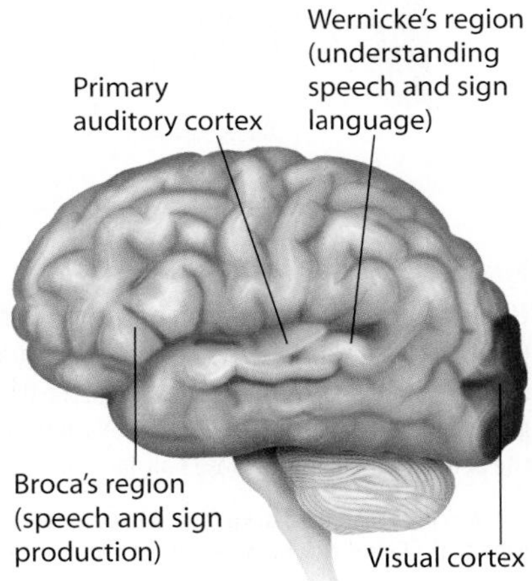

All the subjects were presented with sentences in written English and with videos of signers presenting sentences in ASL. The right hemisphere was hard at work among the deaf subjects but did little for the hearing people who did not know ASL—for them the left side dominated. Yet the right hemisphere was highly active in the subjects who were bilingual in oral and sign language. This result suggests that the activity in the right hemisphere is characteristic of sign language itself and is not, for instance, a side effect of being deaf. Just what the right hemisphere contributes to sign language is not yet clear, but researchers are looking for answers.

From *Scientific American Mind*, vol. 16(2), pp. 86–87.

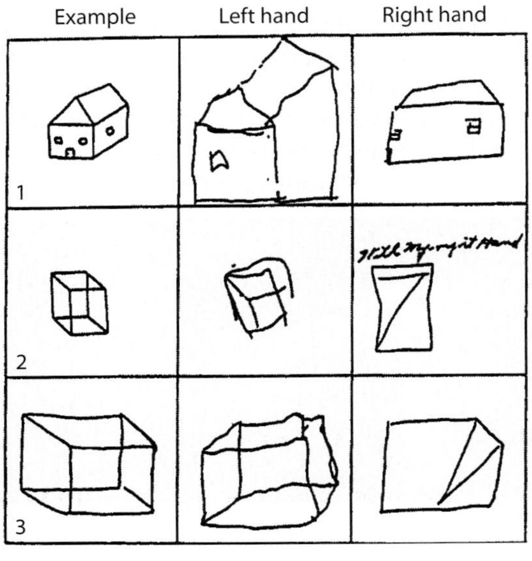

COURTESY OF DR. MICHAEL GAZZANIGA

Figure 13.8

Drawings by a split-brain patient The patient was asked to reproduce the three designs in the left column. Drawings made by the right hand bear little resemblance to the example; in contrast, the drawings made by the left hand look fairly similar to the example. (The drawings were made by a right-handed person, and artwork by the nondominant hand is less than perfect.)

→ **Why does the split-brain patient draw good representations of the original design with the left hand but not with the right hand?**

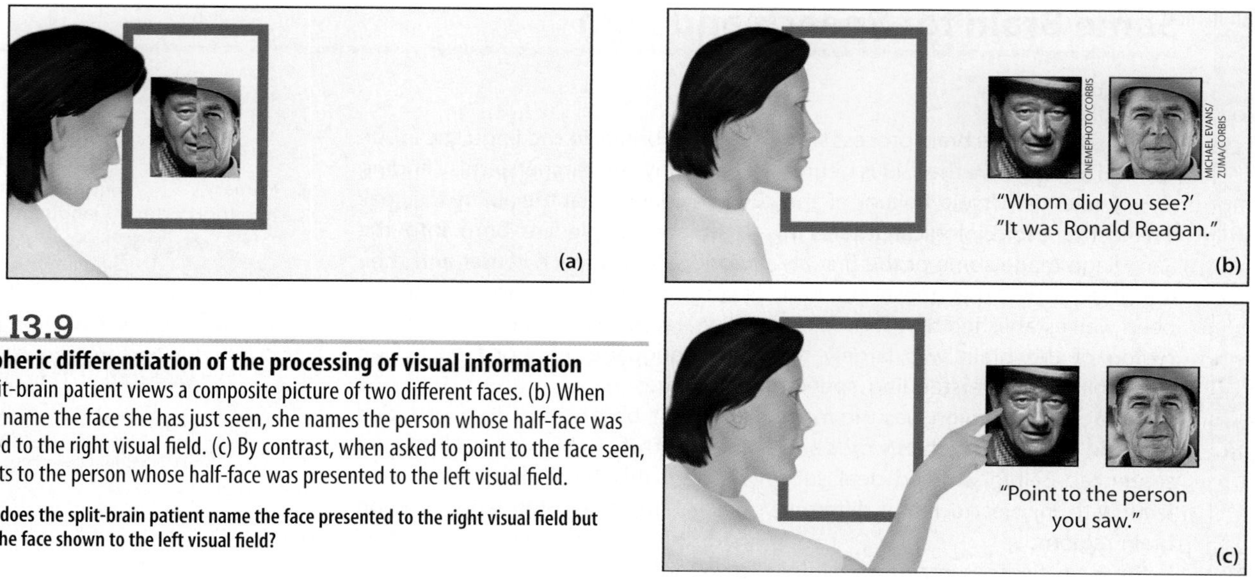

Figure 13.9

Hemispheric differentiation of the processing of visual information
(a) A split-brain patient views a composite picture of two different faces. (b) When asked to name the face she has just seen, she names the person whose half-face was presented to the right visual field. (c) By contrast, when asked to point to the face seen, she points to the person whose half-face was presented to the left visual field.

➜ **Why does the split-brain patient name the face presented to the right visual field but point to the face shown to the left visual field?**

were asked to focus on the center of a screen and were then shown a *chimeric face,* composed of one half of one person's face and the other half of another person's face (Figure 13.9a). (In Greek mythology, a chimera was a monster with a lion's head, a goat's body, and a serpent's tail.) The split-brain patients then viewed several normal faces, including the two whole faces corresponding to the two halves of the chimeric face, and were asked to identify the face they had seen previously. When verbally identifying the face, the split-brain patients named the face presented to the right visual field (Figure 13.9b), but when asked to point to the face they had previously seen, they pointed to the face seen by the right hemisphere (Figure 13.9c).

If you study Figure 13.9c carefully, you will notice that the subject is pointing to the picture of John Wayne with her right hand, presumably controlled by her left hemisphere, even though her right hemisphere is answering the question. Why this apparent discrepancy? The answer is twofold. First, as we noted above, motor control is not completely crossed. According to J. Levy (personal communication, November 29, 2001), by about 6 months after their operation, split-brain patients gain some ipsilateral motor control of their hands, and this control is certainly great enough to perform a movement as simple as pointing to a picture. Second, both hemispheres see the choices, and when the person is asked to point to the face he or she saw, the right hemisphere controls the eye movements, with the result that the gaze of the split-brain person focuses on the picture of John Wayne. Seeing this choice, the left hemisphere can direct the right hand to point to the appropriate picture.

As we noted earlier, brain activity is greater in the left hemisphere than in the right when a person with intact cerebral commissures is engaged in a verbal task. As you can probably guess, a variety of studies using different techniques (e.g., fMRI, event-related potentials) reveal increased neural activity in the right hemisphere in men during spatial tasks such as block design or mental rotation, providing further support for the concept of hemispheric lateralization (Johnson & others, 2002; Rilea & others, 2004; Trojano & others, 2002). We should note that

Figure 13.10

PET scans showing differences in hemispheric functioning The left hemisphere shows more activity when language is processed, whereas the right hemisphere shows more activity when music is processed.

➜ **How do these PET scans demonstrate hemispheric lateralization?**

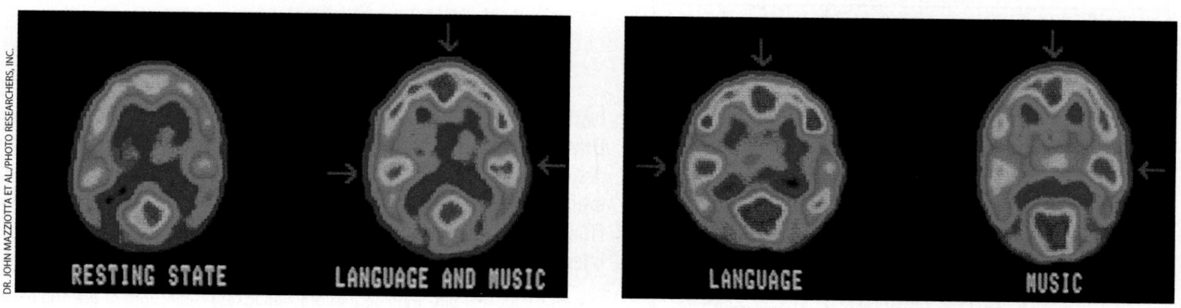

women often show bilateral hemispheric representation on spatial tasks (Johnson & others; Rilea & others).

There are other differences in function between the two hemispheres. Lateralization of the perception of music has often been reported, for example, with evidence frequently supporting right-hemisphere localization. In a PET study, automatic phonetic processing was observed in the left hemisphere and musical processing in the right (Tervaniemi & others, 2000) (Figure 13.10). A study using intracarotid sodium amytal to anesthetize one or the other hemisphere provided evidence for a specific role of the right temporal lobe in memory for music (Plenger & others, 1996). Using rCBF, Alfredson and colleagues (2004) found that emotional music activated the right temporal lobe and deactivated the right prefrontal cortex. However, this right-hemispheric lateralization for music breaks down when trained musicians are compared with nonmusicians (e.g., Altenmuller, 2001). When popular melodies were presented to both ears, musicians exhibited a right-ear (left-hemisphere) advantage in melody identification, whereas nonmusicians had a left-ear (right-hemisphere) advantage (Messerli & others, 1995).

Finally, in keeping with its differential ability to recognize and react to complex visual stimuli, the right hemisphere seems to be more involved in the global assessment of a visual stimulus (e.g., detecting the forest); the left, in local assessment (detecting the trees). In a study of this difference, healthy adult participants viewed figures showing a letter at a global level made up of different letters at a local level (Fink & others, 1996). An example of such a letter is shown in Figure 13.11. Using rCBF as a measure of brain activity, the researchers found that global assessment (detecting the *W*) activated the right hemisphere, whereas local assessment (detecting the *c*) activated the left hemisphere. Thus, the left hemisphere excels at processing the focal details of a scene and the right hemisphere at getting the big picture.

Table 13.1 summarizes some of the many other important differences in function between the two hemispheres, too numerous to discuss here.

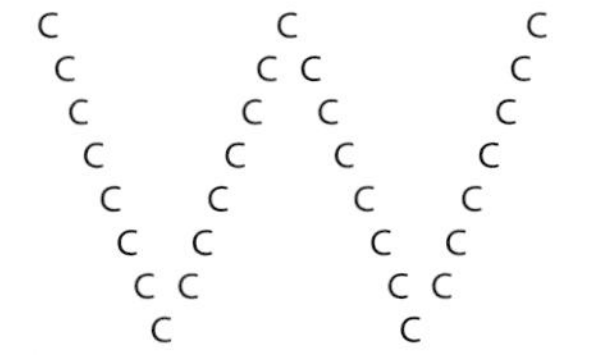

Figure 13.11

Type of picture used to assess global and local processing Activity increases in the right hemisphere when the individual concentrates on the large letter (*W*) but in the left hemisphere when the individual concentrates on the small component letters (*c*).

→ **Which hemisphere is more involved in spatial processing?**

Checkpoint

Which side of your brain is more active when you are listening to music? When looking intently at the face of a friend? When reading a book?

Table 13.1

Lateralization of Function of the Left and Right Hemispheres

Function	Left Hemisphere	Right Hemisphere
Visual system	Letters, words	Complex geometric patterns Faces
Auditory system	Language-related sounds	Nonlanguage environmental sounds Music
Somatosensory system	?	Tactile recognition of complex patterns Braille
Movement	Complex voluntary movement	Movements in spatial patterns
Memory	Verbal memory	Nonverbal memory
Language	Speaking Reading Writing Arithmetic	Emotional intonation Prosody?
Spatial processes		Geometry Sense of direction Mental rotation of shapes

Note: Functions of the respective hemispheres that are predominantly mediated by one hemisphere in right-handed people.
Source: Adapted from Kolb, B., & Whishaw, I. Q. (2003). *Fundamentals of human neuropsychology* (5th ed.). New York: Worth.

REVIEW

- The largest of the cerebral commissures, the corpus callosum consists of many axons interconnecting the cerebral hemispheres and allowing them to communicate.
- Hemispheric lateralization is the differentiation of functions between the two hemispheres of the brain. Much of the evidence for lateralization has come from studies by Roger Sperry and his associates on people who had their corpus callosum cut as a treatment for epilepsy.
- In most people, the left hemisphere processes the phonetic, syntactic, and semantic aspects of language.
- The right hemisphere interprets the intonational, emotional, and nonliteral aspects of language, such as metaphors and humor; it also controls visual-spatial functions.

Do We Have Two Brains?

In the middle of the 19th century, Gustav Fechner (1801–1887), the founder of psychophysics—and some would say of experimental psychology—predicted that if the corpus callosum were cut, the result would be two separate minds. Vogel and Bogen's operations and Sperry's investigations of their patients allowed Fechner's speculation to be tested. As we have seen, Sperry's work suggests that our two cerebral hemispheres have several different functions and responsibilities, but does this mean we actually have two brains in our head? To answer this question, we will let Sperry speak for himself:

> Each hemisphere . . . has its own . . . private sensations, perceptions, thoughts, and ideas, all of which are cut off from the corresponding experiences in the opposite hemisphere. Each left and right hemisphere has its own private chain of memories and learning experiences that are inaccessible to recall by the other hemisphere. In many respects each disconnected hemisphere appears to have a separate "mind of its own." (Sperry, 1974, p. 7)

To this point, we have described in some detail the operation of the brain(s) in split-brain individuals. In unimpaired people, the connection between the two hemispheres allows the two to work together rather than independently. The integration of the activities of the two hemispheres permits higher mental processes than could be achieved by the two hemispheres working independently (Levy, 1985). For example, this integration allows the expression of the creativity and intelligence characteristic of humans.

The importance of hemispheric cooperation can be seen in people whose brain has failed to develop a corpus callosum. Normally, the corpus callosum develops during the first 5 to 10 years of life, and it is one of the last brain structures to mature. Like other CNS structures, the corpus callosum develops mainly through the retention of some axons and the atrophy of others (Chapter 3). This selection process results in functional neural connections between the two hemispheres, but in a few individuals, for some unknown reason, the corpus callosum fails to mature and establish the appropriate interhemispheric connections.

Observations of *acallosal* people, people with *callosal agenesis,* show them to be quite different from split-brain individuals (Chiarello, 1980). For example, acallosal individuals can verbally identify objects presented to either the right or the left visual field. Apparently, humans can compensate to some extent for the missing corpus callosum by using other forebrain connections (e.g., anterior commissures, hippocampal commissures).

However, acallosal individuals do exhibit language and motor impairments. For example, they have greater difficulty understanding passive voice sentences—for example, *The ball was hit by the bat*—than normal individuals (Sanders, 1989). Children with callosal agenesis have impaired phonological reading (reading in which unfamiliar words are sounded out to identify them), suggesting that the corpus callosum may be necessary for the normal development of this skill (Temple & others, 1990).

Acallosal individuals also tend to be slow and clumsy at motor tasks, such as coordinating their hands to tie their shoelaces (Sauerwein & others, 1981). People with callosal pathology (i.e., acallosal or split-brain patients) show deficits on all tasks requiring the transfer of motor and visual-spatial skills and on some tasks involving the integration of tactile and visual information across the body's midline (Lassonde & others, 1995). This sensory and motor impairment may be produced by conflicting information from each hemisphere, a conflict easily resolved when the two hemispheres can readily communicate with each other.

Checkpoint

What do the abilities of individuals without a corpus callosum tell us about the way the two halves of the brain work together?

The Purpose of Lateralization

According to our discussion so far, the left hemisphere is lateralized for language and the right hemisphere for visual-spatial functions. Why did this lateralization evolve? What is its purpose?

Sperry (1982) suggested that each hemisphere controls a different type of thinking. The left hemisphere interprets experiences in a logical, analytical fashion, much as a computer processes information. It detects conspicuous features of events and interprets experiences in an orderly, sequential fashion. Because it is structured sequentially and lends itself to analytical interpretation, language is a left-hemisphere function. By contrast, the right hemisphere operates in a more complex, or synthetic (combining), mode, tending to view experiences in their totality rather than interpreting isolated units. For example, the right hemisphere recognizes a ball as a specific object rather than as a collection of curved lines. The Gestalt view of perception, which argues that the whole is different from the sum of its parts, suggests the importance of synthetic thinking (Westheimer, 1999).

To understand the distinction between the two modes of thinking better, consider the difference between the word *cup* and the object *cup*. The word *cup* exists as three separate letters recognized as a word by a sequential analysis of the letters; analysis is a left-hemisphere process. By contrast, as an object, a cup exists only as a whole-stimulus configuration, not as something that can be broken down into its constituent elements. Our recognition of a cup as a cup is a synthetic, or right-hemisphere, process.

To evaluate the validity of Sperry's idea that each hemisphere has a different mode of thinking, Kosslyn and colleagues (reported in Kosslyn, 1987) presented a series of stimuli to the left or right visual fields of college students (in experiments based on the assumption that visual stimuli presented to one visual field will go more strongly to the contralateral hemisphere). The stimuli consisted of a dot either on or off the outline of a blob (Figure 13.12). The students were required to judge whether the dot was on or off the line (analytical task) or whether the distance from the dot to the line was more or less than 2 mm from the outline of the blob (synthetic task). Kosslyn found that judgments were more rapid for the analytical task if the stimulus was presented to the right visual field (projecting more strongly to the left hemisphere), but more rapid for the synthetic task if the visual stimulus was presented to the left visual field (projecting more strongly to the right hemisphere).

Studies of the Japanese language provide additional evidence for the analytical-synthetic dichotomy between the left and right hemispheres. There are two forms of Japanese written language: *kanji,* based on Chinese ideographs in which one symbol conveys an entire idea; and *kana,* based on phonetic symbols that can be used for writing foreign words, such as scientific terms. Apparently, Japanese children and adults process the phonetic-based *kana* in the left hemisphere and the picture-based *kanji* in both the left and right hemispheres (Springer & Deutsch, 1998). Using fMRI, Matsuo and colleagues (2000) found that an area in the right parietal lobe was extensively activated during a task in which volunteers copied *kanji* ideographic characters, whereas Broca's area in the left hemisphere was activated during a writing task involving phonological information.

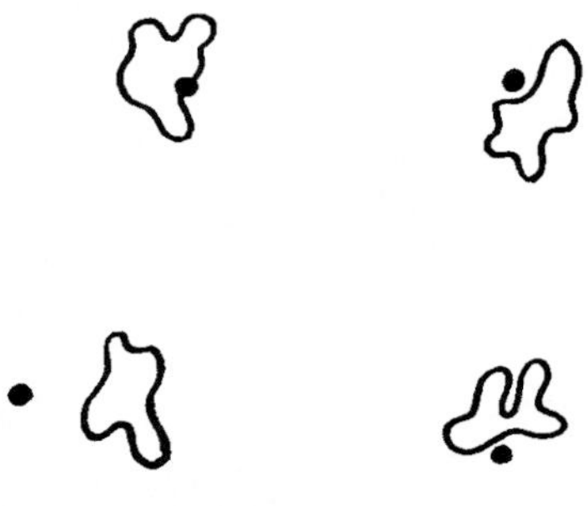

Figure 13.12

Stimuli for assessing hemispheric thinking In a study reported by Kosslyn (1987), participants were asked whether the dot was on or off the outline (analytical task) or whether the dot was more than 2 mm from the outline (synthetic task).

How does this study assess analytical and synthetic thought processes in the brain?

Experience teaches us that a task is sometimes accomplished more efficiently when two people separately do part of the work and then later combine their efforts. Perhaps hemispheric lateralization evolved for a similar reason—to allow parallel processing of information and to provide a mechanism for hemispheric sharing of that information (Hellige, 1993). For example, the left hemisphere usually is dominant for processing the phonetic, syntactic, and semantic aspects of language, whereas the right hemisphere is usually dominant for processing intonational and pragmatic aspects of language. Although both aspects of language are important, it may be more efficient to process the different aspects separately and then combine them through the cerebral commissures. In fact, based on an MRI study of the brains of 30 men, Hellige and colleagues (1998) suggested that the size of the corpus callosum is related to the degree of functional isolation of the two hemispheres: A bigger corpus callosum may be indicative of greater functional isolation. When we are listening to someone, the left hemisphere processes what is actually said and the right hemisphere processes the way the speaker presents the message, which may be important for the way we interpret it. For example, suppose the doctor gives John the following message about his grandmother: "She's improving." Depending on the tone of the doctor's voice, John may interpret the statement to mean, "She is improving, but will never be the same," or, "She has made great progress toward a full recovery." Information from both hemispheres is required to understand what the doctor is really saying.

The extensive evidence for lateralization revealed by the split-brain research ties in with a "modular model" of brain function—that is, the historical idea of localization of function that we introduced in Chapter 1 (Gazzaniga, 1998). Rather than acting like "a general problem-solving device whose every part is capable of any function," the brain is really "a collection of devices that assists the mind's information-processing demands" (p. 53). One of the most intriguing modules of the left hemisphere, according to Gazzaniga, is an area that tries to explain, among other things, the sometimes inexplicable behaviors produced by the right hemisphere in the split-brain patient.

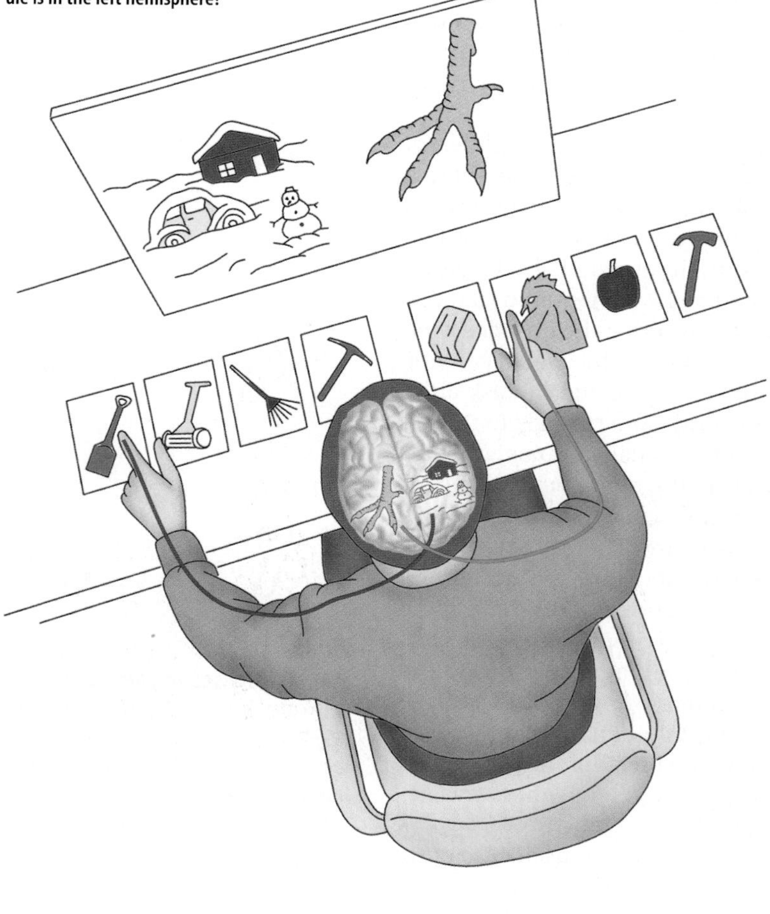

Figure 13.13

The action of the left-hemisphere "interpreter" module A split-brain patient sees a snow scene in the left visual field (to right hemisphere) and a chicken claw in the right visual field (to left hemisphere). When asked to point to a picture that goes with what he saw, the subject points with his right hand to a chicken and with his left hand to a snow shovel. When asked why he pointed to the snow shovel, the left hemisphere, which has information only about a chicken, answers, "To shovel chicken 'waste.'"

➡ **How do we know the "interpreter" module is in the left hemisphere?**

The "interpreter" module was discovered from the results of the following experiment (Gazzaniga & LeDoux, 1978). A split-brain patient was first shown two pictures, one in the left visual field (a snow scene) and the other in the right visual field (a chicken claw) (Figure 13.13). Then, asked to point to the picture that goes with what he had just seen, the person's left hand pointed to the snow shovel, and his right hand pointed to the chicken. When the subject was asked why the left hand was pointing to the shovel, the left hemisphere (which answered the question but has no way of knowing the answer) quickly came up with an explanation: The shovel would be used to clean chicken "waste." The "interpreter" module continually tries to make sense out of the conscious and unconscious input it receives; "it tries to bring order and unity to our conscious lives" (Gazzaniga, 1989, p. 947).

Rather than seeing lateralization as an evolutionary *addition,* it is possible that at least some of the lateralized phenomena required the affected hemisphere to lose a function (Gazzaniga, 1998). Perhaps the location of the analytical aspects of language in the left hemisphere means that the left hemisphere has lost visual-spatial abilities.

> In what must have been fierce competition for cortical space, the evolving primate brain would have been hard-pressed to gain new faculties without losing old ones. Lateralization could have been its salvation. Because the two hemispheres are connected, mutational tinkering with a homologous cortical region could give rise to a new function—yet not cost the animal, because the other side would remain unaffected. (Gazzaniga, 1998, p. 55)

Checkpoint

What does Kosslyn's dot and blob experiment suggest about the way each half of the brain processes information? Name some evidence for a "modular model" of how the brain works.

Lateralization and Neuroplasticity

Although the right hemisphere has some important language abilities, for most people the left hemisphere mediates the receptive and expressive aspects of language. Damage to language areas in the left hemisphere, however, sometimes leads to development of right-hemisphere language abilities that would not otherwise have occurred. For example, in a study of six children, ages 7 to 14, who had had their left hemisphere removed as treatment for Rasmussen's syndrome (a rare disorder characterized by seizures, inflammation of the brain, and mental deterioration), by a year after surgery, the children's receptive language functions were at least as good as they had been before the operation (Boatman & others, 1999). Expressive functions were not as well recovered; the speech of the children was limited mainly to single words. The investigators attributed the remarkable recovery of receptive functions to plasticity in the right hemisphere that persists beyond the period (6 years of age) usually considered critical for development of such functions.

In another study of a child with Rasmussen's syndrome, fMRI was used to map the language networks of the child before and after removal of the left hemisphere (Hertz-Pannier & others, 2002). The first fMRI study was performed at the age of 6 years, 10 months, about a year after the child developed the syndrome. At that time, the language networks were lateralized to the left hemisphere. Surgery at age 9 resulted in profound aphasia and alexia (disorders discussed later in the chapter), followed by rapid recovery of receptive language abilities, with much less recovery of expressive abilities. Functional MRI 18 months after surgery revealed a shift of the language networks to the right hemisphere during both receptive and expressive tasks. The right-hemisphere regions that were activated had not been evident before surgery, but mirrored the left-hemisphere areas activated preoperatively. This study dramatically illustrates the plasticity of the young brain and the ability of the right hemisphere to mediate language functions, even when the damage to the left hemisphere occurs at a relatively late age.

The neuroplasticity seen in children who have had their left hemisphere removed is remarkable, but there are limits to the ability to develop language skills following early brain damage (Chilosi & others, 2001; Dick & others, 2004; Thal & others, 1991; Vicari & others, 2000). For example, in a study of sentence comprehension skills in typically developing children, children with language impairment, or children with focal brain injuries that occurred around birth, the children with brain injury and the children who were language-impaired were profoundly developmentally delayed (Dick & others). Whether the damage was to the left hemisphere or the right hemisphere was not related to the degree of impairment of the children with brain damage. By contrast, in another study of children with congenital focal brain lesions, those with left-hemisphere damage were more delayed in their development of vocabulary and grammar than were the children with right-hemisphere damage (Chilosi & others). Thal and colleagues, however, found that children with focal lesions to the left hemisphere were slightly *better* in vocabulary comprehension than children with right-hemisphere damage. Finally, in children with early focal brain lesions who were studied during the first development stage of word production, those with left-hemisphere injuries showed greater delays in developing expressive vocabulary than those with right-hemisphere damage (Vicari & others). Clearly, the results of these studies are too variable to allow us to conclude whether left-hemisphere or right-hemisphere damage has a more negative effect on subsequent language development, but it is apparent that the neuroplasticity of the young brain is not great enough to prevent early focal damage from producing some language impairment.

Checkpoint

What do the brain-imaging studies of children treated for Rasmussen's syndrome tell us about laterality and neuroplasticity?

REVIEW

- According to Sperry, the left hemisphere interprets experiences in a logical, analytical fashion, whereas the right hemisphere operates in a more complex, synthetic mode, interpreting experiences in their totality rather than as isolated units.
- Lateralization may exist to allow for the parallel processing of information by the hemispheres in their different modes, and the subsequent sharing of processed information.
- Damage to left-hemisphere language areas sometimes leads to right-hemisphere language abilities that would not otherwise have developed, as can be seen in children treated for Rasmussen's syndrome.

Handedness and Hemispheric Language Dominance

Given that the left hemisphere tends to be dominant for language and generally controls the motor functioning on the right side of the body, why is it that not everyone writes with the right hand? For that matter, which hemisphere is dominant for language in the 10% of the population classified as left-handed? More than 95% of right-handed people showed left-hemisphere dominance for language in one large study, but approximately 70% of left-handed people also displayed left-hemisphere dominance (Rasmussen & Milner, 1977). The remaining left-handed individuals were equally split between equal dominance and right-hemisphere dominance. More recently, in a group of patients undergoing a diagnostic work-up before surgery for epilepsy, 77% had exclusive left-hemisphere language representation, 2% exclusive right-hemisphere language, and the remaining 21% bilateral language representation (Loring & others, 1990). Of the bilateral group, 59% had more left-hemisphere representation than right-hemisphere. In the total group, only 6% had either exclusive right-hemisphere representation or right-hemisphere-dominant language. There was no breakdown in terms of handedness.

Despite the left-hemisphere dominance for language for the majority of left-handed people, damage to either hemisphere impairs language in most left-handed people, whereas right-handed people may show no obvious language impairment following damage to the right hemisphere (Satz, 1979). This finding demonstrates partial control by both hemispheres in most left-handed people—that is, less strict laterality in left-handed than in right-handed people. Habib and colleagues (1991) used a handedness questionnaire to divide 35 men and 18 women into consistent right-handed subjects (CRH; used right hand for all activities) and nonconsistent right-handed (NCRH; used left hand for at least one activity). Using MRI, the researchers found that the anterior half of the corpus callosum was significantly larger in NCRH subjects, and particularly in males. Another part of the callosum was enlarged in CRH females. This greater size may promote more communication between the hemispheres, leading to the partial control of language by both hemispheres seen in many left-handed men and in women.

Several interesting hypotheses have been proposed to account for handedness or, more specifically, for left-handedness. Genetics appears to be involved, as the likelihood of being left-handed increases with the number of left-handed parents: With one left-handed parent, individuals are 2.3 times more likely to be left handed than someone with two right-handed parents; with both parents left-handed, the likelihood is 3.4 times greater (Springer & Deutsch, 1998). Of course, the environment created by two left-handed parents may bias a child to develop left-handed preferences.

In a different genetic approach, Marion Annett developed the "right shift" theory of handedness (Annett, 1999, 2003; Annett & Alexander, 1996). Instead of a gene for handedness per se, there is a dominant gene (rs^+) for developing language in the left hemisphere, which increases the chance of greater right-handed skills. The recessive form of the gene (rs^-) is related to an absence of systematic bias either way, which means that environmental factors would determine the degree and direction of laterality in the person with two copies of this allele. Assuming both alleles occur equally often in the population, and assuming random mating, then 50% of the population would be rs^+/rs^-, 25% rs^+/rs^+, and 25% rs^-/rs^-. Individuals in the first two categories would show a right shift, with left-hemisphere language and right-handedness, whereas those in the third category (rs^-/rs^-) would have handedness and language dominance determined by the environment. Without a strong environmental bias, we would expect about half of the last group to be right-handed and half left-handed, or about 12.5% of the population to be left-handed—which is close to what actually occurs.

Geschwind and Galaburda (1987) have proposed a handedness model that emphasizes the male sex hormone testosterone. The idea of a link to testosterone began when Geschwind found an association between left-handedness and a variety of autoimmune disorders, such as migraine headaches, allergies, and thyroid problems. This association led Geschwind and Galaburda to propose that testosterone is responsible for both left-handedness and immune disorder susceptibility. According to the model, testosterone exposure in the uterus slows the maturation of parts of the left hemisphere, which allows corresponding right-hemisphere structures to develop more rapidly. At the same time, the testosterone exposure is assumed to affect immune system development, increasing the susceptibility to immune system disorders. Because male fetuses are exposed to more testosterone than females, males would tend to have a greater shift to right-hemisphere participation in both language and handedness and would also tend to have enhanced right-hemisphere skills such as map reading and pictorial representation. The greater prevalence of left-handedness in males than in females supports Geschwind and Galaburda's view, as does the observation of a higher incidence of autoimmune diseases in the families of left handers compared to right handers (Morfit & Weekes, 2001). In addition, the sex hormones do play a role in the immune response, with estrogens serving as enhancers and testosterone and progesterone as suppressors (Cutolo & others, 2002, 2004). Unfortunately, some of the predictions of the Geschwind-Galaburda model are not supported by the data (Springer & Deutsch, 1998). For example, the model's predicted association between handedness and autoimmune disorders is supported by the data for some autoimmune disorders (e.g., left-handed people are at greater risk for such disorders as allergies and asthma), but not by the data for other disorders (e.g., right-handers are more at risk for arthritis and myasthenia gravis).

Although many of the proposed models of handedness specify a relationship between handedness and language, the association may not be causal. Rather, similar processes may affect both handedness and language.

Checkpoint

The stroke that John's grandmother suffered caused paralysis on her right side, and she lost the ability to speak. Can you determine from this information whether she is right-handed or left-handed? Why or why not?

REVIEW

- In one major study, more than 95% of right-handed people and 70% of left-handed people showed left-hemisphere dominance for language. The remaining 30% of left-handed people were equally split between equal dominance and right-hemisphere dominance for language.
- Genetic hypotheses and a model emphasizing the effect of testosterone have been proposed to account for left-handedness.

Communicative Disorders: The Aphasias

Because it gave him a lot of time to study, Ken liked working the "graveyard shift" at the convenience store. But sometimes he worried that some of the rougher characters who came into the store during the early morning hours might give him trouble. Tonight, for example, a jittery youth had been cruising the aisles for several minutes without picking anything up.

"Can I help you?" Ken asked, when the kid rounded the cold-drink aisle and approached the register where Ken was sitting, his finger marking the place in his psychology textbook. Ken's voice sounded unnaturally loud in the silent store.

"You sure can," the youth said, pulling a gun so small and shiny it looked like a toy. "Just empty the drawer in a sack and toss it over. No false moves or you're dead meat."

Ken had the irrational (hysterical?) urge to tell the robber he couldn't be "dead meat" because he was a vegetarian, but this wasn't the time for humor. "The sacks are under the counter," he said. "I'll just get one and fill it up." As he pulled out a sack with his right hand, he pressed the silent alarm with his left forefinger.

Working as swiftly as he could, Ken retrieved all the cash from the drawer and dumped it into the sack. The kid with the gun kept glancing toward the door, and Ken prayed silently that no one would come in; he thought any change in the situation would cause the kid to panic and start shooting.

"I hope this is enough," he said as he held out the sack. He tried to smile at the kid, who took one more look at the door, snatched the sack, and pulled the trigger. Ken's world went black.

Ken awoke in a hospital bed, in intense pain. He tried to call out, to ask where he was. All he could say was something that sounded to him like "urk." He tried again, and produced a second "urk." With that, he gave up.

As the doctor explained to Ken's parents, the bullet struck their son on the left side of his brain, in an area that is responsible for speech production. It was difficult to know the extent of the damage from the size of the wound. They would do CT scans in a day or two to get a better idea. Ken's speech might return to normal in a few days, or the impairment might be permanent.

Communicative disorders are impairments in speech, hearing, and/or language. Some communicative disorders resulting from neurological damage include aphasia, an acquired impairment in the use of language; apraxia of speech, an inability to plan and sequence the movements involved in speech production (Chapter 8); auditory-verbal agnosia, an inability to identify spoken words but not other auditory stimuli (Chapter 7); alexia, an inability to read; and agraphia, an inability to write. It is worth noting here that the prefix "a" means "without," so that "alexia" means "without the ability to read" and "agraphia," "without the ability to write." The prefix "dys" means "abnormal" or "impaired," so that "dyslexia" refers to an impaired reading ability and "dysgraphia," to an impaired ability to write.

Ken's **aphasia** is caused by traumatic damage to neural areas involved in receiving (understanding) and/or expressing (producing) language. The impairment produced by aphasia is limited to language, leaving nonverbal processes such as reasoning and memory intact, hence an aphasic person should be able to use nonverbal communication. For example, when you enter his room, Ken might indicate he recognizes you by greeting you with a smile, without being able to say *hello*. People with aphasia, however, may have additional, nonlanguage-related impairments resulting from damage to brain structures other than the ones controlling language.

Neurological disorders such as schizophrenia and Alzheimer's disease also involve language impairments, but the language deficits are secondary to the primary characteristics of the disease; therefore, someone with schizophrenia or Alzheimer's disease should not be described as having aphasia. In fact, the language disturbances caused by aphasia are qualitatively different from those caused

aphasia An acquired impairment in the use of language.

nonfluent aphasia A difficulty producing fluent, well-articulated, and self-initiated speech.

fluent aphasia An inability to understand the language of others and the production of less meaningful speech than normal.

Broca's aphasia A communicative disorder caused by damage to the left cerebral hemisphere rostral to the base of the primary motor cortex; an inability to initiate well-articulated conversational speech.

agrammatical speech Speech that is deficient in grammar.

Table 13.2
Sites of Lesion and Characteristics of Nonfluent and Fluent Aphasias

Disorder	Site of Lesion	Spontaneous Speech	Speech Comprehension	Repetition	Naming
Broca's aphasia	Left frontal cortex rostral to base of motor cortex	Nonfluent	Relatively intact	Poor	Poor
Global aphasia	Anterior and posterior language areas	Nonfluent	Poor	Poor	Poor
Transcortical motor aphasia	Areas of premotor cortex anterior and superior to Broca's area	Nonfluent	Relatively intact	Intact	Poor
Wernicke's aphasia	Posterior part of superior and middle left temporal gyrus and left temporoparietal cortex	Fluent	Poor	Poor	Poor
Conduction aphasia	Left temporoparietal region, above and below posterior Sylvian fissure	Fluent	Relatively intact	Poor	Intact
Anomic aphasia	Left temporo-occipital junction	Fluent	Relatively intact	Intact	Poor
Transcortical sensory aphasia	Areas surrounding and including Wernicke's area	Fluent	Poor	Intact	Poor

by schizophrenia or Alzheimer's disease (Davis, 1993). In addition, the treatments for aphasia and the other disorders differ. We discuss the treatment of aphasia in Box 13.1, and we examine the language impairments caused by schizophrenia and Alzheimer's disease in Chapters 14 and 15.

The aphasias can be categorized as **nonfluent aphasias,** difficulty producing fluent, well-articulated, and self-initiated speech, and **fluent aphasias,** the inability to understand the language of others and the production of less meaningful speech than normal (Davis, 2000). Each category has different subtypes, with characteristic behaviors and sites of brain damage (as summarized in Table 13.2). Keep in mind throughout our discussion of the aphasias that they are not as easy to understand as Geschwind, and Wernicke before him, had thought.

Nonfluent Aphasias

Ken's difficulty producing fluent, well-articulated, and self-initiated speech indicates that he suffers from a nonfluent aphasia. The three types of nonfluent aphasia are Broca's aphasia, global aphasia, and transcortical motor aphasia.

Broca's Aphasia

Broca's aphasia is the most prevalent type of nonfluent aphasia. In 1861, Paul Broca proposed that this language disorder was caused by a lesion (or dysfunction) in the left frontal lobe area rostral to the base of the primary motor cortex (Figure 13.1a). **Broca's aphasia** is characterized by an inability to initiate well-articulated conversational speech. Damage limited to Broca's area produces what has been called "baby Broca's aphasia" (Mohr, 1980). More widespread damage including areas adjacent to Broca's area produces "big Broca's aphasia," characterized by slow, labored, and telegraphic or **agrammatical speech** (speech that omits grammatical morphemes, such as articles—*a, an,* and *the*—and verb tense endings) as well as difficulties with intonation (the melody of language), stress pattern (the emphasis on syllables and words), and articulation (production of speech sounds). CT scans of a patient with Broca's aphasia (someone like Ken?) are shown in Figure 13.14.

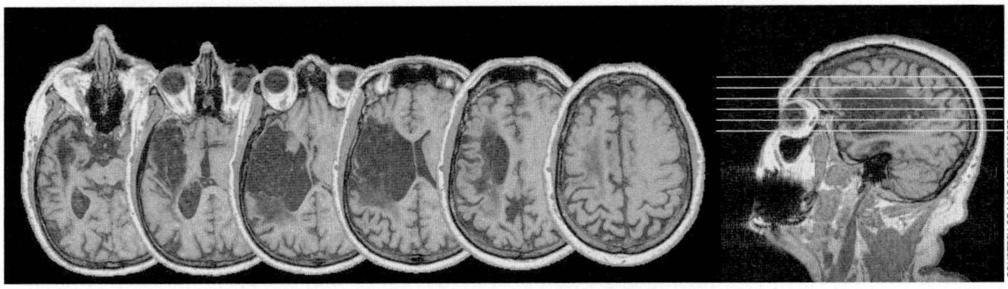

COURTESY OF MARGARET NAESER

Figure 13.14
MRI scans of a patient with Broca's aphasia Damage to the anterior left hemisphere is evident as a darkened area.

→ **Why would damage to the anterior left hemisphere lead to Broca's aphasia?**

The following example illustrates the communication problems associated with Broca's aphasia. When asked to describe what is going on in the picture in Figure 13.15, taken from the Boston Diagnostic Aphasia Examination (Goodglass & others, 2001a, 2001b), a test used to diagnose aphasia and determine its severity, one patient said:

> "Water dripping. Boy" (pointing to girl) "Girl" (pointing to boy)
> Okay. Okay. . . . Mother. . . . Mother."
> ([Examiner asks] What's going on?) "No."
> (Goodglass & others, 2001a, p. 64)

GOODGLASS, ET AL (2001) BDAE STIMULUS CARDS (3RD ED.): LIPPINCOTT WILLIAMS & WILKINS.

Figure 13.15
A picture from the Boston Diagnostic Aphasia Examination The patient with an aphasia is asked to describe what is happening in the picture; his or her response can be used to diagnose specific types of aphasia.

→ **What are the primary characteristics of Broca's aphasia?**

As is obvious from this extract, the person is having an extremely difficult time communicating his thoughts. He had suffered a stroke that left him with a severe language disorder. Before his stroke, he could speak fluently.

A person with Broca's aphasia also has poor handwriting, with the written communication resembling the nonfluent speech (Figure 13.16). Like other aphasias, Broca's aphasia includes anomia, difficulty selecting the correct word in either written or spoken language. More specifically, patients with Broca's aphasia often have more difficulty retrieving verbs than nouns (Damasio & Damasio, 2000). Despite the extreme difficulty in initiating speech that can be understood easily by others, language comprehension is relatively intact.

Global Aphasia

People suffering from **global aphasia** experience a severe depression of all language functioning. They have poor speech comprehension and difficulty repeating words or remembering names. Speech may be limited to a jargon (nonsense) phrase repeated in all contexts or to a phrase used inappropriately. Words are rarely used in a functional or meaningful way. The limited functional speech does not mean that people with global aphasia cannot communicate at all; they can, for example, communicate their feelings and wishes through facial, vocal, and other physical gestures.

In addition to an inability to produce meaningful language, people with global aphasia do not understand the language of others. The characteristics of this aphasia suggest that damage extends beyond Broca's area (Davis, 2000). In fact, as revealed by CT scans, global aphasia results from both anterior (including Broca's area) and posterior (including Wernicke's area) lesions (Murdoch & others, 1986). Although the person with global aphasia cannot understand language, this aphasia is categorized as a nonfluent aphasia because of the limited speech.

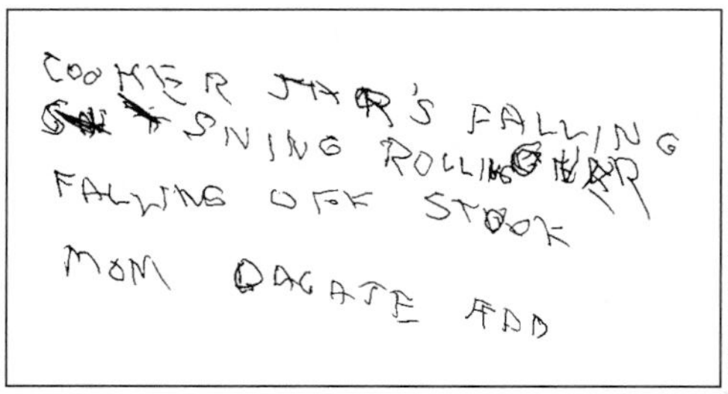

GOODGLASS, ET AL (2001) BDAE STIMULUS CARDS (3RD ED.): LIPPINCOTT WILLIAMS & WILKINS.

Figure 13.16
The handwriting of a person with Broca's aphasia The individual was asked to describe the cookie theft picture shown in Figure 13.15. The poor handwriting and agrammatical construction are evident in this sample.

→ **Why does a person with Broca's aphasia show similar defects in speech and writing?**

Transcortical Motor Aphasia

A person with **transcortical motor aphasia** usually does not initiate speech and often speaks only if strongly encouraged. When speech does occur, it tends to be nonfluent and agrammatical. Utterances typically consist of only one or two words, and complete sentences are rare. In contrast to the sparseness of self-initiated speech, however, the person can repeat long and complex sentences fluently. As in Broca's aphasia, the person has relatively good language comprehension. The disorder is caused by damage to regions of the premotor cortex anterior and superior to Broca's area, which is not damaged. The relatively intact language comprehension reflects the lack of involvement of such language-related structures as the arcuate fasciculus and Wernicke's area.

Checkpoint

What characteristics do all the nonfluent aphasias have in common? In what general ways do they differ? How could a person with a nonfluent aphasia communicate?

REVIEW

- An aphasia is an acquired language impairment caused by damage to the areas of the brain that control language functioning.
- The three types of nonfluent aphasia are Broca's aphasia, global aphasia, and transcortical motor aphasia.
- The primary characteristics of Broca's aphasia, in which the left frontal lobe area rostral to the base of the primary motor cortex is damaged, are the inability to initiate well-articulated, conversational speech and the production of agrammatical speech.
- Global aphasia is caused by damage to the anterior and posterior language areas of the left hemisphere; all language functioning is severely depressed.
- Transcortical motor aphasia is caused by damage to areas anterior and superior to Broca's area; speech is nonfluent and agrammatical and naming is poor, but comprehension is relatively intact and repetition is fluent.

Fluent Aphasias

The fluent aphasias, in which speech is easily produced but frequently meaningless, are Wernicke's aphasia, conduction aphasia, anomic aphasia, and transcortical sensory aphasia.

Wernicke's Aphasia

Damage to the posterior portion of the left hemisphere's superior and middle temporal gyrus and the temporoparietal cortex produces a language disorder called Wernicke's aphasia (Figures 13.1a and 13.17). Unlike the nonfluency of people with Broca's aphasia, the person with Wernicke's aphasia can speak fluently. However, although syntactic structure is preserved, the speech is less meaningful. The person produces jargon, leaving out key words, substituting words, and including extra words.

A person with Wernicke's aphasia may also substitute verb tenses or have difficulty using the correct pronoun or preposition. This is **paragrammatical speech,** the use of inappropriate morphemes. For example, the person may say *to you* rather than *for you* or *he* rather than *she* and might also substitute or transpose sounds, saying, for example, *pork* for *fork* or *pesnal* for *pencil.* Speech often takes the form of jargon, and attempts to repeat something produce speech dissimilar to the original.

anomia A difficulty selecting the correct word for either written or spoken language.

global aphasia A severe depression of all language functioning.

transcortical motor aphasia Sparse, self-initiated speech with relatively good language comprehension.

Wernicke's aphasia A communicative disorder caused by damage to the posterior portion of the superior and middle temporal gyrus and the temporoparietal cortex; an inability to comprehend language.

paragrammatical speech Speech characterized by the use of inappropriate morphemes.

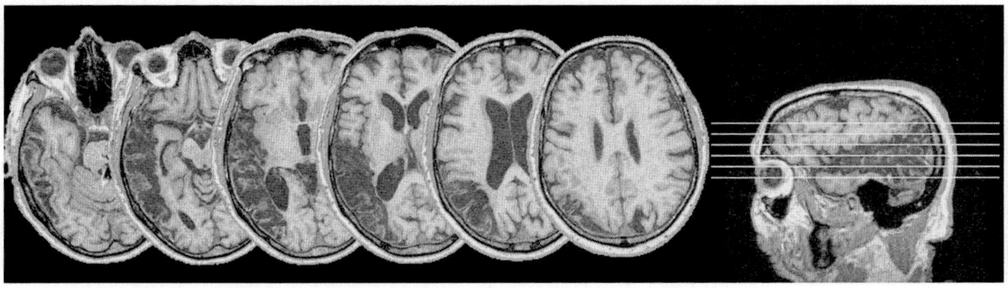

Figure 13.17

MRI scans of a patient with Wernicke's aphasia Damage to the posterior left hemisphere is visible as a darkened area.

Why would damage to the posterior left hemisphere lead to Wernicke's aphasia?

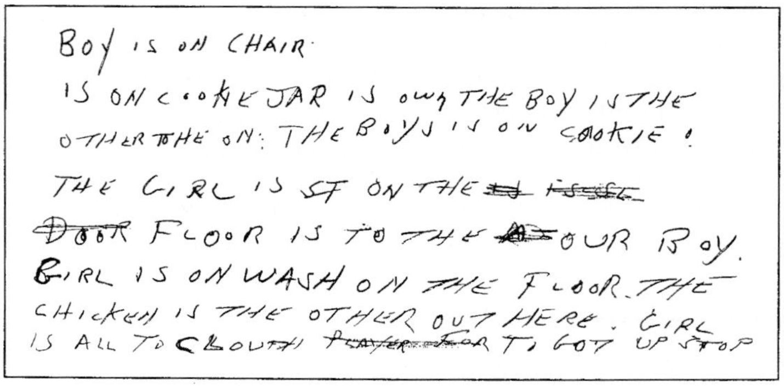

HELM-ESTABROOKS, N., AND ALBERT, M.L. (2004) MANUAL OF APHASIA AND APHASIA THERAPY (2ND EDITION) AUSTIN, TX: PRO-ED. PAGE 74.

Figure 13.18

The handwriting of a person with Wernicke's aphasia This attempted description of the cookie theft picture shown in Figure 13.15 provides a good illustration of the impaired meaning of the person's writing.

➜ **Why does a person with Wernicke's aphasia show similar defects in speech and writing?**

Here is how a patient with Wernicke's aphasia described the cookie theft scene in Figure 13.15:

> And their falling is scooting that over just getting ready when they have apparently when they want to get it. . . .
>
> He was, he was doing usual, but he has been following water all over the place over here, pushing over that, and the process of doing that, he's sitting on it and all that sort of stuff, but it wasn't a bother. (Goodglass & others, 2001a, p. 68)

Now reread the paragraph, pretending you have not seen Figure 13.15. Would you be able to figure out what is being described?

Individuals with Wernicke's aphasia often do not realize their speech is meaningless and are surprised by the puzzled looks of the people they are talking to. These puzzled looks may be all the person has to go on, because the disorder produces not only speech that lacks meaning but also deficient understanding. In addition, reading comprehension is poor, and writing may be unintelligible (Figure 13.18).

The symptoms of Wernicke's aphasia demonstrate the importance of language; without it, people are cut off from their social environment. Those with a severe form of the disorder can neither understand the language of others nor communicate their thoughts to others. However, once they are convinced their speech is unintelligible, people with Wernicke's aphasia, like other aphasics, can communicate with facial expressions or motor gestures.

Conduction Aphasia

A person with **conduction aphasia** has great difficulty repeating orally presented information, and the degree of impairment depends on the length of the phrase to be repeated. With short, familiar phrases, the person may repeat accurately or may have a single phonemic paraphasia. A **paraphasia** is an error in speaking, and a *phonemic paraphasia* is the substitution of a similar sounding word—saying *pike* instead of *pipe,* for example. With longer, less familiar phrases, the number of phonemic paraphasias may increase until speech contains none of the originally spoken words. Despite the impairment in repetition, language comprehension is relatively good, and conversational speech is only mildly impaired.

Because the arcuate fasciculus connects Wernicke's area to Broca's area, Wernicke (1874) suggested that damage to the arcuate fasciculus would produce a conduction aphasia. Evidence from CT scans shows that damage to the left temporoparietal region, above and below the Sylvian fissure (which includes the arcuate fasciculus), causes conduction aphasia, but damage limited to the arcuate fasciculus does not appear to be associated with the disorder (Shuren & others, 1995). In addition, researchers stimulated the posterior superior temporal gyrus of an epileptic patient and observed the symptoms of conduction aphasia in the patient, suggesting that cortical dysfunction by itself may produce the disorder (Anderson & others, 1999). A study using a variation of MRI has revealed a previously undescribed pathway that runs parallel to the arcuate fascicus and also interconnects Broca's and Wernicke's areas (Catani & others, 2005). Conduction aphasia could reflect a short-term memory problem, which would explain the repetition impairment, or a deficiency in selecting phonemes during speech production, which would explain the paraphasias.

Anomic Aphasia

Earlier, we defined anomia as a difficulty selecting the correct word for written or spoken language. You have probably experienced this problem at one time or another, but if you are like most people, anomia occurs only occasionally. A person with **anomic aphasia** has consistent difficulty finding names and often substitutes indefinite nouns and pronouns for substantive words. The impairment in language caused by anomic aphasia can be seen vividly in the following description of driving a car by a 27-year-old subject:

> When you get into the car, close your door. Put your feet on those two things on the floor. So, all I have to do is pull . . . I have to put my . . . You just put your thing which I know of which I cannot say right now, but I can make a picture of it . . . you put it in . . . on your . . . inside the thing that turns the car on. You put your foot on the thing that makes the stuff come on. It's called the, uh . . . . (Davis, 2000, p. 8)

The speaker has good language comprehension and the speech is fluent and grammatical, but the absence of crucial words makes it difficult to follow what the person is saying. Verbal communication is possible for people with anomic aphasia, but only when the context indicates the specific words to which the indefinite words, such as *thing,* refer.

Perhaps because of the very few cases of pure anomic aphasia, the identification of a specific area of dysfunction has proven difficult. In fact, at least one researcher has suggested that anomic aphasia may actually be a mild form of Wernicke's aphasia (Brookshire, 2003). Supporting this suggestion, Takeda and colleagues (1999) used MRI and cerebral blood flow imaging to study a patient with pure anomic aphasia whose disorder was caused by a subcortical hemorrhage in the left temporoparieto-occipital lobe, which had presumably produced a lesion at the left temporo-occipital junction.

conduction aphasia Difficulty repeating verbal information.

paraphasia An error in speaking.

anomic aphasia A consistent difficulty finding names, and substituting indefinite nouns and pronouns for substantive words.

transcortical sensory aphasia Fluent speech, poor comprehension, and anomia, along with an unusual tendency to repeat verbal stimuli.

echolalia A repetition of something someone has just said.

Transcortical Sensory Aphasia

A person with **transcortical sensory aphasia** has impairments similar to those of Wernicke's aphasia (fluent speech, poor comprehension, anomia), along with an unusual tendency to repeat verbal stimuli. This tendency, called **echolalia,** is a repetition of something someone has just said, causing the person to repeat a question endlessly instead of answering it.

Damage to areas that surround and include Wernicke's area may produce this disorder (Boatman & others, 2000). Boatman and colleagues produced transcortical sensory aphasia by transient electrical interference with areas adjacent to and including Wernicke's area. They also found that areas producing phonological decoding of speech sounds and word-meaning processing remained functional, suggesting that transcortical sensory aphasia is the result of a disruption of the flow of information from the area decoding phonological information to the area determining the meaning of the sound. Thus, a person with transcortical sensory aphasia can repeat a sound without understanding it.

Checkpoint

Compare the communication problems of a person with fluent aphasia and the difficulties of a person with nonfluent aphasia. Describe a conversation between a person with Broca's aphasia and a person with anomic aphasia.

REVIEW

- The four types of fluent aphasia are Wernicke's aphasia, conduction aphasia, anomic aphasia, and transcortical sensory aphasia.
- In Wernicke's aphasia, the posterior portion of the superior and middle left temporal gyrus and the left temporoparietal cortex are usually damaged; speech is fluent, but comprehension, repetition, and naming are poor.
- The primary characteristic of conduction aphasia, typically caused by damage to the left temporoparietal region, is difficulty in repeating verbal information (poor repetition).
- The primary characteristic of anomic aphasia, in which the temporo-occipital junction is generally damaged, is consistent difficulty finding names for objects.
- In transcortical sensory aphasia, the area surrounding and including Wernicke's area is damaged; comprehension and naming are poor, but speech is fluent, and the person tends to repeat everything just said (echolalia).

Other Communicative Disorders

Much of Ken's ability to speak has returned in the days following his gunshot wound, although one problem persists: He often fails to produce the correct sound for the word he is trying to say. This evening, for example, his mother visited him in the hospital, and as she was leaving, Ken wanted to tell her to bring ChapStick on her next visit, as his lips have been too dry.

"Can I get you anything?" his mother asked.

"Please bring me a *chumpstitch,*" he said.

"What's that, dear?" his mother asked.

"A *chumpstitch,*" he said, realizing the word wasn't right. "*Chumpstitch,*" he said again.

His mother shook her head. "I didn't get it," she said.

Taking deep breaths to calm himself, Ken tried again, more slowly this time. "*Ch–ump–stitch.*"

His mother smiled helplessly.

Ken could hear the word in his mind, but he knew he would never be able to say it, at least not tonight. Retrieving a plastic knife from his tray, he held it by the blade, circling his hand in front of his face, with the knife's handle near his lips.

"Oh, ChapStick?" his mother asked, and Ken nodded gratefully.

The communicative disorders other than aphasias affect speech, reading, and/or writing in a variety of ways (Table 13.3), and each type can occur with or without accompanying aphasia.

Table 13.3
Sites of Lesion and Characteristics of Nonaphasic Communicative Disorders

Disorder	Site of Lesion	Characteristics
Apraxia of speech	Third frontal convolution anterior to primary motor cortex (Broca's area)	Inability to voluntarily sequence speech production
Auditory-verbal agnosia	Connections from primary auditory cortex and secondary auditory cortex	Inability to identify spoken words as meaningful
Alexia/dyslexia	Connections from primary visual cortex to angular gyrus	An inability to read/ difficulty in reading
Agraphia/ dysgraphia	Inferior parietal lobe and superior temporal lobe	An inability to write/ difficulty in writing

Apraxia of Speech

Apraxia of speech is a language disorder caused by a dysfunction in the frontal lobe area (including Broca's area) that is responsible for the planning and programming of speech production. In Chapter 8, we defined *apraxia* as a serious impairment in the ability to organize voluntary movement; apraxia of speech is an inability to voluntarily control the muscle movement necessary for speech production. Like Ken, the individual has no muscle weakness, and no difficulty in using the lips, tongue, or pharynx for nonspeaking purposes such as chewing and swallowing food. The impairment becomes evident only when the person starts to speak. He or she has great difficulty producing the correct sound for a specific word, saying, for example, *spork* instead of *fork* (or *chumpstitch* for *ChapStick*).

Several types of articulation errors in apraxia of speech have been identified (Brookshire, 2003). For example, although the individual substitutes incorrect sounds for correct sounds, most of the phoneme substitutions resemble the correct sound. The failure to articulate the correct sound is not consistent; the person may articulate the same phoneme correctly on one occasion and incorrectly on another.

Context is an important influence on whether the correct sound is produced. For example, a person with apraxia of speech may correctly articulate the *d* sound in *dishes* when the same phoneme is repeated in *Don did the dishes,* but misarticulate the same sound when contrasting phonemes occur, as in *Don bought the dishes.* As an illustration, the person might say, *Don bought the bishes.* Further, the person is more likely to articulate sounds correctly in a natural setting than in an artificial setting, saying *goodbye* correctly when she says it spontaneously while leaving but not when she is asked to say *goodbye.* The person is aware of the misarticulations and may become upset by the failure to say the correct sound.

apraxia of speech An inability to plan and sequence movements for producing speech.

Apraxia of speech most often occurs along with Broca's aphasia, because of the close proximity of the motor cortex controlling speech and Broca's area. A patient with apraxia of speech and Broca's aphasia will have difficulty articulating sounds and will produce agrammatical speech. (The agrammatism is a characteristic of aphasia, not apraxia.) The following is a description by a patient with Broca's aphasia and apraxia of speech of the attempted assassination of President Ronald Reagan:

> Um . . . Reagan . . . um . . . President . . . Reagan . . . shod . . . was . . . um . . . yesterday . . . um . . . um . . . New Yoak Cidy . . . uh . . . hospidal . . . be oh-kay . . . nod bad . . . . (Brookshire, 1992, p. 278)

As this selection clearly shows, the patient is misarticulating words as well as leaving out "function" words such as articles, conjunctions, and prepositions. These omissions give the speech a "telegraphic" character accentuated by incorrect sound articulations.

auditory-verbal agnosia An inability to identify spoken words but not other auditory stimuli.

visual-verbal agnosia An inability to recognize printed words, but not spoken words; results from damage that isolates the visual cortex from cortical language areas.

alexia An inability to read.

agraphia An inability to write.

pure alexia An inability to read, with no difficulty writing; caused by a separation of the angular gyrus from visual input; also called alexia without agraphia.

Auditory-Verbal Agnosia

A person with *agnosia* is unable to identify an object by using a specific sensory modality, but the object can be recognized through other modalities (Chapters 6 and 7). Sensory deficits with agnosia can be limited to language. For example, a person with an **auditory-verbal agnosia,** or *pure word deafness,* cannot identify spoken words because he or she does not recognize them as meaningful, but other auditory stimuli such as bells and whistles are recognized. In addition, auditory-verbal agnosia does not affect reading comprehension; for example, the person can read the word *dog,* either silently or aloud, but is unable to say the word *dog* upon hearing it spoken. Damage that severs the connections between the primary and secondary auditory cortices bilaterally is associated with auditory-verbal agnosia. **Visual-verbal agnosia** is an inability to recognize printed words, but not spoken words, which results from damage that isolates the visual cortex from cortical language areas. Both types of verbal agnosia are quite rare.

Alexia and Agraphia

More than a century ago, Dejerine (1891) discovered that damage to the angular gyrus, an area of the cerebral cortex located in the posterior parietal lobe (Figure 13.1), is associated with **alexia** and **agraphia,** the inability to read and write, respectively. Reading and writing require integrated input from the visual, auditory, and body senses (e.g., touch). Deaf (either at birth or from an early age) high school graduates rarely achieve more than a fourth-grade reading level (Paul, 1998, 2001), and one reason is their inability to associate written symbols with sounds (King & Quigley, 1985). The angular gyrus receives information from each of these senses, making it ideally suited to control reading and writing; therefore, damage to this area would be expected to produce reading and writing deficits. In support of this view, a professional musician who suffered a stroke localized to the left angular gyrus developed alexia with agraphia for both language and musical scores (Kawamura & others, 2000).

Damage that causes alexia does not always cause agraphia. For example, Dejerine (1892) noted that one of his patients, following a lesion to the left occipital lobe and the posterior end of the corpus callosum, could not read but had no difficulty writing. This patient suffered from **pure alexia,** or *alexia without agraphia.* He could still write but could not read what he had written.

As we discussed in Chapter 6, a person with visual agnosia cannot recognize objects and thus cannot name them. By contrast, a person with pure alexia can identify and name objects but cannot read. Visual agnosia is caused by bilateral damage to the secondary visual cortex, whereas pure alexia occurs when the angular gyrus does not receive input from the visual cortex (Damasio & Damasio, 1992).

Dyslexia and Dysgraphia

Unlike individuals with alexia, people with **dyslexia** can read, but they have difficulty doing so. Dyslexia can become apparent when a child is learning to read (*developmental dyslexia*) or can develop later, in people who already know how to read, as a result of brain damage (*acquired dyslexia*).

Dyslexia occurs in at least two forms. Someone with *word-form dyslexia* does not immediately recognize words but, if given sufficient time to sound them out, is able to read. By contrast, someone with *phonological dyslexia* can identify familiar words but is unable to sound out and read unfamiliar words, even if given plenty of time.

The two dyslexias are closely associated with the two methods of reading—whole-word reading and phonetic reading. In whole-word reading, we recognize a specific word by its shape and pronunciation, whereas in phonetic reading we read a word by sounding out its letters. Whole-word reading is used with familiar words, and people with word-form dyslexia have difficulty with these words. Phonetic reading is used with unfamiliar words, and people with phonological dyslexia cannot decipher such words.

Using fMRI, researchers have examined differences in brain activity between people with dyslexia and nondyslexic controls. People with dyslexia show less activity in posterior regions of the brain (Wernicke's area, angular gyrus, and primary visual cortex) than do people without dyslexia (Shaywitz & others, 1998). The same pattern of reduced neural activity has also been found in children with developmental dyslexia (Shaywitz & others, 2002). Less activation has been observed in the primary visual cortex of dyslexics relative to controls, as well as reduced activation of several other cortical areas (Demb & others, 1998). The lower level of neural activity in the posterior areas of the brain, where sounds (auditory) and symbols (visual) are associated, undoubtedly is related to the reading difficulties of people with dyslexia.

Analogous to alexia, the inability to read, and to dyslexia, a difficulty in reading, are agraphia, an inability to write, and **dysgraphia,** a difficulty with writing. Difficulty in using visually based writing (or in visually imaging whole words) is found in people with *orthographic dysgraphia;* these individuals can spell out regular words such as *won* that sound the way they are spelled (where they can use phonetics) but not irregular words such as *one* (where the pronunciation must be in memory). By contrast, someone with *phonological dysgraphia* can write familiar words such as *car* but cannot write unfamiliar words such as *automobile* that must be sounded out phonetically.

Orthographic and phonological dysgraphia apparently have different neurological bases: Orthographic dysgraphia is associated with damage to the inferior parietal lobe, and phonological dysgraphia with damage to the superior temporal lobe (Benson & Geschwind, 1985). These observations suggest that different neural circuits mediate whole-word writing and phonetic writing, as is true for whole-word reading and phonetic reading.

Clearly, the many different types of language disorders have overlapping characteristics, which means that differentiating and diagnosing them can be tricky.

➤Checkpoint

What do alexia and agraphia tell us about reading and writing as distinct from speaking and listening?

REVIEW

- ➤ Apraxia of speech, the loss of voluntary control of the muscles necessary for speech production, most commonly occurs with Broca's aphasia, because of the close proximity of the motor cortex to Broca's area.
- ➤ In auditory-verbal agnosia, also called pure word deafness, the person cannot identify spoken words but can recognize other auditory stimuli. Visual-verbal agnosia is the inability to recognize the printed word, with no impairment in speech comprehension.
- ➤ Alexia is the inability to read, and agraphia the inability to write. They usually occur together.

➤ Dyslexia is difficulty in reading. In word-form dyslexia, the person does not immediately recognize words but can read them if given sufficient time to sound them out; in phonological dyslexia, the person can identify familiar words but cannot sound out unfamiliar ones. Dysgraphia is difficulty in writing; agraphia, an inability to write.

dyslexia A difficulty with reading.

dysgraphia A difficulty with writing.

Communicative Disorders: Diagnosis and Recovery

Although the causes of aphasia are quite varied, many are similar to the causes of brain damage described in Chapter 2. Recall that John's grandmother developed aphasia following a stroke. Strokes, or cerebrovascular accidents, are the third leading cause of death in the United States (National Center for Health Statistics, 2003), and brain damage from a stroke is the most common cause of aphasia.

Head trauma is another leading cause of aphasia. The consequences of Ken's gunshot wound illustrate the effect of a penetrating head wound that damages the language areas. A closed-head injury, which can result from events such as a motorcycle or automobile accident, blows received during a fight, or a fall from a high place, also can cause aphasia.

Several insidious processes can cause language problems. For example, a tumor growing within a language area can produce aphasia, which worsens as the tumor enlarges and affects more neural areas. Aphasia can also result from an infection of the brain. Exposure to toxic substances can lead to language disturbances. Long-term exposure to heavy metals (lead, mercury) or to certain chemical compounds can slowly damage the brain, including the language areas, producing a gradual onset of aphasic symptoms. Metabolic disorders such as hypoglycemia and thyroid disorders can cause CNS dysfunction and aphasia, and language disorders can also result from nutritional deficiencies. Obstructive hydrocephalus (literally "water head," but the "water" is cerebrospinal fluid) increases intracranial pressure and is yet another cause of aphasia.

Diagnosing the Aphasias

Determining whether a person suffers from Broca's or Wernicke's aphasia might appear to be relatively easy, but many individuals with language impairments cannot be placed into a single diagnostic category. One reason is that a person can have multiple or extensive lesions that produce symptoms of several different aphasias. In addition, the aging process may produce language disturbances characteristic of more than one type of aphasia.

The diagnostic classification of patients with communicative disorders may focus too much attention on differences rather than similarities (Darley, 1982). Treatment approaches should be selected based on specific behaviors rather than a specific diagnosis. For example, the same treatment for difficulties in naming would be appropriate for patients with Broca's aphasia or global aphasia, even though in other respects treatments for these two types of aphasia would be different. The treatment of aphasia is discussed in Box 13.1.

Benson's (1993) evaluation of individuals with language impairments suggests that a diagnosis of type of aphasia can be made in only about half of aphasia cases, so the incidence of each type of disorder is unclear. For patients with a clear diagnosis, Benson found that 65% of the cases were evenly distributed among Broca's, Wernicke's, and anomic aphasias. About 10% of the diagnoses were of global and conduction aphasias, and the remaining 25% included transcortical aphasias and modality-specific disorders such as auditory-verbal agnosia and alexia.

The situation has not changed appreciably in the past 25 years. Goodglass and colleagues (2001a) noted that the diagnostic categories are just clusters of symptoms that recur in roughly similar form. Depending on how strictly or loosely the definitions of different disorders are applied, the proportion of unambiguous classifications can range from 30% to 80%.

➤Checkpoint

A 70-year-old man has had a stroke. Testing reveals fluent speech, relatively intact comprehension, and little difficulty naming objects shown to him on flash cards. However, he has trouble repeating phrases spoken to him. How would you diagnose this patient's aphasia?

Box 13.1

Treatment Approaches for Aphasia

Speech-language pathologists provide treatment to improve the communication skills of people with aphasia and other language disorders. There are two schools of thought about aphasia, each of which calls for a different treatment (Brookshire, 2003). Some researchers consider aphasia an access problem; that is, the language is still there but cannot be retrieved. Others believe aphasia is a loss of language, and language needs to be retaught.

Experts who believe aphasia is an access or retrieval disorder advocate a *stimulation approach* to treatment. For example, some early researchers argued that sensory stimulation is the only method available for making complex events happen in the brain and that auditory stimulation is crucial in the retrieval of language processes (Schuell & others, 1964). The use of other skills, such as reading and writing, is also encouraged, but the main treatment component is intensive auditory stimulation. According to this approach, the patient's responses should be elicited, not forced or corrected. If the desired response does not occur, the patient is given more stimulation to retrieve it, but is not corrected or given information about why a response is inadequate.

Auditory stimulation tasks can involve listening, speaking, or both. Listening tasks include completing "point to" tasks, in which the therapist says a word and asks the patient to point to the correct word or object in a grouping; following verbal directions by the therapist to perform a task; and providing answers to yes/no questions. Speaking tasks—which also involve listening—include repeating words spoken by the therapist; completing a phrase begun by the therapist, who provides the first sound, first syllable, or meaning; engaging in verbal association, in which the therapist provides a word and the patient supplies another word through free association, opposites, or rhyming, depending on instructions; responding to words given by the therapist by supplying definitions or appropriate sentences; and retelling stories the therapist has read aloud (Figure 13.19).

Experts who believe aphasia results from a loss of language and that language needs to be relearned promote a *programmed approach* to treatment (Sarno, 1998), which uses behavior-modification techniques. The activities themselves may not differ significantly from those used in the sensory stimulation approach. Programmed therapy focuses on particular goals (e.g., sentence production), specifies the stimuli to use (e.g., pictures), and indicates how the therapist should record a response (e.g., response latency, completeness of sentence). The therapist gives the patient feedback by indicating whether each response is correct or incorrect.

A programmed approach to treatment includes the following steps: (1) determining the baseline rate of the behavior to be changed; (2) using behavior-modification techniques and applying reinforcement and punishment to change the rate of the baseline behavior; (3) extending the situations that elicit speech. In the last step, the therapist attempts to transfer the behavior from the highly structured clinical setting to more spontaneous and natural situations. This may require altering reinforcement schedules and the types of reinforcement to make the contingencies more like those the patient will encounter in the "real world."

In the speech-language clinic, practitioners frequently use some combination of the stimulation and programmed approaches (Brookshire, 2003). With any treatment method, the clinician and patient must determine whether the technique is proving effective. One difficulty

REVIEW

- Some of the many causes of communicative disorders are strokes, head trauma, infectious disease, tumor, exposure to toxic substances, and metabolic disorders.
- In practice, the different types of language disorders can be difficult to distinguish from one another and thus to diagnose.
- Treatment approaches should be based on symptoms/behaviors rather than on specific diagnosis.

Recovery: Evidence for Neuroplasticity of the Language Areas

Extensive evidence supports the idea that speech-language training after brain damage facilitates a neural reorganization that leads to the recovery of some linguistic ability. For example, researchers took 12 consecutive measurements of rCBF in four patients with aphasia caused by left-hemisphere stroke damage to Wernicke's area (Musso & others, 1999). The patients received intensive language comprehension training in the intervals between measurements. Performance improved significantly in all patients, and one of the brain areas in which activity

Figure 13.19
Auditory stimulation A patient with aphasia receives individual therapy from a speech-language pathologist. Group therapy can also be effective.

➡ **What is the likely prognosis for this patient with aphasia?**

is that many aphasic individuals spontaneously recover language functioning, and the spontaneous improvement may be misinterpreted as a response to treatment. However, most spontaneous recovery occurs within the first 3 months following brain damage. To show treatment effectiveness, language recovery must be greater than would be expected from spontaneous recovery alone.

Studies of treatment effectiveness indicate that language recovery is indeed enhanced following treatment for aphasia (Brookshire, 2003). For example, one large-scale clinical study found that patients undergoing early treatment (treatment between 1 and 4 months after the onset of their symptoms) showed greater improvement than did those receiving late treatment (treated between 4 and 12 months post onset): 78% of the patients receiving immediate treatment showed significant improvement in language skills, whereas only 46% of patients in the late treatment group improved (Poeck & others, 1989). Amazingly, 68% of the subjects in a "chronic" group that started an intensive treatment regimen 12 months post onset of symptoms showed significant improvement, which shows that progress can occur even after the first year of symptoms.

Although many persons with aphasia are helped by treatment, for some adults, language skills do not improve even with therapy. These latter patients probably have large lesions affecting Wernicke's area. Using CT scans, investigators found that extent of improvement by therapy was negatively correlated with the size of the lesion, and patients with damage to the temporobasal regions showed less improvement than others (Goldenberg & Spatt, 1994). However, given that treatment can be effective, we know that language skills impaired by other types of brain damage (e.g., smaller amounts of damage, damage that does not involve temporal and parietal areas in and around Wernicke's area) can be recovered or relearned.

changes best correlated with the training-induced improvement was the right superior temporal gyrus—that is, the right-hemisphere region corresponding to the damaged Wernicke's area.

Functional recovery of language abilities lost after brain damage probably involves the activation of areas in the right hemisphere corresponding to left-hemisphere language areas (e.g., Broca's area, Wernicke's area), or of undamaged left-hemisphere language areas, or both (Thompson, 2000). Thompson noted that as early as the late 19th century, researchers observed that language functions that had been recovered after a left-hemisphere stroke disappeared following a subsequent stroke in the right hemisphere. This is evidence for functional takeover by the right hemisphere following left-hemisphere damage. Also, as we indicated earlier, studies of left-hemispherectomized patients provide evidence for the ability of the right hemisphere to mediate some aspects of language.

Research using brain imaging techniques has also revealed the neuroplasticity of the right hemisphere in functional recovery after damage to left-hemisphere language areas, and an increased activation of undamaged left-hemisphere language structures. For example, researchers used PET to measure rCBF in six right-handed patients who had recovered from Wernicke's aphasia following a left-hemisphere stroke and six unimpaired right-handed volunteers (Weiller & others, 1995). As expected, during a language task the unimpaired subjects showed large rCBF increases in the posterior part of the left superior and middle temporal gyrus (Wernicke's area). By contrast, during the same language task the recovered aphasics had large rCBF increases in right-hemisphere areas corresponding to Wernicke's area and greater rCBF increases in undamaged left-hemisphere language areas than the unimpaired subjects.

Heiss and colleagues (1999) used PET scans to study aphasic patients 2 and 8 weeks after stroke. Patients with temporal lobe damage showed some improvement in word comprehension at 8 weeks, along with activation of the right-hemisphere areas roughly corresponding to Broca's area and Wernicke's area. More recently, investigators used fMRI to study neural changes in two patients with Broca's and Wernicke's aphasia caused by left hemisphere damage (Abo & others, 2004). After speech therapy, both patients showed complete recovery on a repetition task, and fMRI results showed activation of only right hemisphere compensatory areas during performance of the task.

Successful recovery following damage to left-hemisphere language areas does not necessarily involve remodeling of right-hemisphere regions, however. Cornelissen and colleagues (2003) used a specific training method to treat anomia in three chronic aphasics with left-hemisphere damage. All patients improved their ability to name trained items, and all showed training-induced changes in the activity of an area in the left inferior parietal lobe, which is close to the damaged area producing their aphasia. There was no evidence for activity changes in the right hemisphere.

Thus, the studies we have reviewed here support the adaptation of corresponding areas in the right hemisphere and the remodeling of language areas in the left hemisphere during functional recovery from aphasia. The expansion of language activities in undamaged regions of the left hemisphere is analogous to the cortical remapping following denervation of a limb and the cortical reorganization in tinnitus patients and in blind persons that we discussed in Chapter 7. It is important to note that many patients with aphasia show little or no recovery of function and few experience complete recovery.

REVIEW

- Studies of treatment effectiveness have shown that recovery of language abilities is enhanced in many patients who undergo treatment in the first several months after damage.
- The recovery of some language ability is probably mediated by the activation of right-hemisphere areas corresponding to the damaged left-hemisphere areas and/or by increased activation of undamaged left-hemisphere language areas.

CHAPTER REVIEW

Key Terms

agrammatical speech (p. 485)
agraphia (p. 491)
alexia (p. 491)
angular gyrus (p. 467)
anomia (p. 487)
anomic aphasia (p. 489)
aphasia (p. 484)
apraxia of speech (p. 490)
arcuate fasciculus (p. 467)
auditory verbal agnosia (p. 491)
Broca's aphasia (p. 485)
commissurotomy (p. 471)
conduction aphasia (p. 488)
dysgraphia (p. 492)
dyslexia (p. 492)
echolalia (p. 489)
fluent aphasia (p. 485)
global aphasia (p. 486)
hemispheric lateralization (p. 469)
language (p. 462)
language acquisition device (LAD) (p. 465)
morpheme (p. 463)
neologistic jargon (p. 468)
nonfluent aphasia (p. 485)

paragrammatical speech (p. 487)
paraphasia (p. 488)
phoneme (p. 463)
phonology (p. 463)
phrase (p. 463)
pure alexia (p. 491)
semantics (p. 464)
sentence (p. 463)
split-brain preparation (p. 469)
syntax (p. 463)
temporoparietal cortex (p. 468)
transcortical motor aphasia (p. 486)
transcortical sensory aphasia (p. 489)
visual-verbal agnosia (p. 491)
Wernicke-Geschwind model (p. 467)
Wernicke's aphasia (p. 487)
Williams syndrome (p. 466)

Suggested Readings

Brookshire, R. H. (2003). *An introduction to neurogenic communication disorders* (6th ed). St. Louis: Mosby.

Davis, G. A. (2000). *Aphasiology: Disorders and clinical practice.* Boston: Allyn and Bacon.

Gazzaniga, M. S. (1998). The split brain revisited. *Scientific American, 279,* 50–55.

Geschwind, N., & Galaburda, A. M. (1987). *Cerebral lateralization: Biological mechanisms, associations, and pathology.* Cambridge, MA: MIT Press.

Goodglass, H., Kaplan, E., & Barresi, B. (2001a). *The assessment of aphasia and related disorders* (3rd ed.). Philadelphia: Lippincott Williams & Wilkins.

Hellige, J. B. (1993). *Hemispheric asymmetry.* Cambridge, MA: Harvard University Press.

Springer, S. P., & Deutsch, G. (1998). *Left brain, right brain* (5th ed.). New York: W. H. Freeman.

Thompson, C. K. (2000). Neuroplasticity: Evidence from aphasia. *Journal of Communication Disorders, 33,* 357–366.

Critical Thinking Questions

1. Susan has especially good verbal skills but cannot draw, whereas Marta is an accomplished artist but is not articulate. Discuss evidence that the disparities in Susan's and Marta's abilities reflect hemispheric differences.
2. Richard rushed to the hospital after being told his wife had had a stroke. When he got there, he learned the stroke had damaged the dorsal part of his wife's left temporal lobe. Based on what you have learned, what changes in his wife's language abilities is Richard likely to notice?
3. Jaime was shot in a hunting accident last year. His wounds have healed, but he continues to experience difficulty in initiating well-articulated conversational speech. He understands others very well, but he often omits articles and verb tense endings, and other people have difficulty understanding him. What area of Jaime's brain was probably damaged in the accident?

Fill-in-the-Blank Questions

1. ______ is a system of words, their meanings, and rules for combining words into phrases and sentences.
2. The simplest functional unit of a language is a speech sound, also called a(n) ______.
3. The smallest meaningful unit of language is a(n) ______.
4. A(n) ______ is two or more phrases that convey an assertion, question, wish, command, or exclamation.
5. In any language, ______ dictates how phonemes can be combined into morphemes.
6. The rules of ______ dictate how words are combined into meaningful phrases.
7. The linguistic analysis of the meaning of language is called ______.
8. Chomsky thought all children were born with a language-generating mechanism that he called the ______.
9. The bundle of association fibers that connects Wernicke's area and Broca's area is the ______.
10. According to the Wernicke-Geschwind model of language, the secondary visual cortex and the ______ are responsible for comprehension of the written word.
11. Lengthy, fluent, nonsensical speech is called ______ jargon.
12. The differentiation of function between the cerebral hemispheres is called ______.
13. Working with cats, Sperry cut the cerebral commissures and the optic chiasm to produce the ______ preparation.
14. Using an operation called a(n) ______, Vogel and Bogen cut the cerebral commissures as a treatment for uncontrollable epilepsy.
15. The ______ hemisphere of the brain is more important for the emotional expression of language.

16. In the middle of the 19th century, ______ predicted that cutting the corpus callosum would result in two separate minds in the same head.
17. The left hemisphere generally operates in a logical, sequential fashion, whereas the right hemisphere operates in a(n) ______ mode.
18. According to Gazzaniga, the ______ module of the brain tries to make sense out of otherwise inexplicable information.
19. Geschwind found a link between ______ handedness and autoimmune disorders such as migraine headaches and allergies.
20. An acquired impairment of language is a(n) ______.
21. A(n) ______ is an inability to identify spoken words but not other auditory stimuli.
22. In ______ aphasia, the person is unable to produce well-articulated, self-initiated speech.
23. A difficulty selecting the correct word for either written or spoken language is called ______.
24. A person with ______ has a severe depression of all language functioning.
25. ______ speech uses inappropriate morphemes.
26. ______ aphasia causes great difficulty in repeating verbal information.
27. A person who repeats a question endlessly instead of answering it is exhibiting ______.
28. A person with a(n) ______, or pure word deafness, cannot identify spoken words but does recognize other auditory stimuli such as bells and whistles.
29. ______ is an inability to read; ______ is an inability to write.
30. People with ______ can read, but they have difficulty doing so.
31. Experts who believe aphasia is a retrieval problem advocate a(n) ______ approach to treatment.

Multiple-Choice Questions

1. The simplest functional element of language is a
   a. morpheme.
   b. phoneme.
   c. syllable.
   d. phrase.
2. How many phonemes does the word *dish* contain?
   a. one
   b. two
   c. three
   d. four
3. The smallest meaningful language unit is a
   a. morpheme.
   b. phoneme.
   c. syllable.
   d. phrase.
4. How many morphemes does the word *distrust* have?
   a. one
   b. two
   c. three
   d. four
5. The acceptable ways in which words can be combined into sentences are dictated by the rules of
   a. semantics.
   b. phonetics.
   c. morphology.
   d. syntax.
6. The linguistic analysis of the meaning of language is
   a. semantics.
   b. syntax.
   c. grammar.
   d. phonetics.
7. Which of the following is a noun phrase?
   a. swims quickly
   b. is able
   c. the little boy
   d. to commit an error
8. ______ suggested that children are born with a language acquisition device.
   a. Herbert Terrace
   b. Paul Broca
   c. Noam Chomsky
   d. Gustav Fechner
9. Susan loves meeting strangers and is a marvelous storyteller, yet she has an IQ of only 54. Susan is most likely to have
   a. Down syndrome.
   b. Williams syndrome.
   c. Tay-Sachs disease.
   d. Fragile X syndrome.
10. According to the Wernicke-Geschwind model, the comprehension of spoken language is the function of
    a. Broca's area.
    b. the arcuate fasciculus.
    c. the angular gyrus.
    d. Wernicke's area.
11. Tyrus recently had a stroke and is unable to understand what his family tells him. In addition, they are unable to understand what Tyrus says, although he speaks fluently. Tyrus's stroke probably damaged
    a. Broca's area.
    b. the arcuate fasciculus.
    c. the angular gyrus.
    d. Wernicke's area.
12. The differentiation of functions between the cerebral hemispheres is called
    a. split-brain preparation.
    b. hemispheric lateralization.
    c. the Wernicke-Geschwind model.
    d. hemispheric differentiation.
13. Commissurotomy is an effective treatment for patients with uncontrolled seizures because it
    a. removes the seizure focus area of the brain.
    b. prevents seizure activity from intensifying.
    c. increases the effectiveness of drug therapy.
    d. punishes the seizure activity so much that the person stops having it.
14. The purpose of Sperry's experimental split-brain preparation was to
    a. prevent seizures in cats.
    b. investigate the visual system of cats.

c. block communication between hemispheres.
d. prevent cats from communicating with each other.

15. Sperry's research with cats showed that
a. the cerebral hemispheres can process information separately.
b. epilepsy originates in the corpus callosum.
c. visual discrimination is located in the right hemisphere.
d. split-brain subjects can no longer learn new tasks.

16. Sperry used a tachistoscope in his studies of split-brain patients in order to
a. present stimuli to the front and back of the cortex simultaneously.
b. present information to only one visual field at a time.
c. observe their language behavior.
d. distinguish them from normal subjects.

17. Although the right cerebral hemisphere generally cannot name objects, it can control
a. use of the right hand to select objects presented to it.
b. verbal identification of objects in the left visual field.
c. most other language skills.
d. use of the left hand to select objects presented to it.

18. If the word *forearm* is flashed to a split-brain person so that *fore* is in the left visual field and *arm* is in the right visual field, the person will
a. say she saw the word *fore.*
b. say she saw the word *arm.*
c. indicate she saw the word *arm* by pointing to the word with her left hand.
d. say she saw nothing.

19. Last fall, Leon was hit in the head by the backswing of the golfer he was caddying for. He seems to have fully recovered from the injury, except that he no longer finds anything funny in the punch line of a joke. Leon probably suffered damage to his
a. right hemisphere.
b. left hemisphere.
c. corpus callosum.
d. hippocampus.

20. MRI scans have shown that Shannon has damage to the left hemisphere of her brain. She appears perfectly normal to most observers, but in tests of language ability she has difficulty interpreting sentences in the passive voice. She is also slow and clumsy at motor tasks such as tying her shoes. The damaged area probably includes
a. the amygdala.
b. the corpus callosum.
c. the hippocampus.
d. Broca's area.

21. Chester has difficulty finding his way from one physical location to another. He has probably suffered damage to his
a. corpus callosum.
b. right hemisphere.
c. left hemisphere.
d. brain stem reticular formation.

22. When shown a chimeric face constructed from half of one person's face and half of another person's face, split-brain patients
a. named the face presented to the left visual field.
b. pointed to the face presented to the right visual field.
c. could not name either face.
d. pointed to the face presented to the left visual field.

23. Which of the following is an example of a synthetic mode of thinking?
a. defining the word *ball*
b. writing and reading the word *ball*
c. recognizing different spherical objects as balls
d. comparing the diameters of two different balls

24. Most of the brain structures important in language comprehension are located in the
a. left parietal lobe.
b. left frontal lobe.
c. left temporal lobe.
d. corpus callosum.

25. The handedness model proposed by Geschwind and Galaburda emphasizes the importance of
a. the number of left-handed parents a person has.
b. the "right shift" theory.
c. testosterone and autoimmune disorders.
d. brain damage at birth.

26. Broca's aphasia is an example of
a. fluent aphasia.
b. pure alexia.
c. global aphasia.
d. nonfluent aphasia.

27. A person with transcortical motor aphasia usually cannot
a. initiate speech.
b. repeat long, complex sentences.
c. understand speech.
d. read and write.

28. A common symptom of Wernicke's aphasia is
a. agrammatical speech.
b. anomic aphasia.
c. dyslexia.
d. paragrammatical speech.

29. An aphasic patient who has great difficulty repeating spoken information may be diagnosed as having ______ aphasia.
a. anomic
b. global
c. Wernicke's
d. conduction

30. Apraxia of speech most often occurs together with
a. Broca's aphasia.
b. Wernicke's aphasia.
c. conduction aphasia.
d. visual-verbal agnosia.

31. Following an accident in which she sustained brain damage, Alison can no longer write. She has been diagnosed as having
a. alexia.
b. micrographia.
c. dyslexia.
d. dysgraphia.

Answers can be found on the companion website at www.worthpublishers.com/klein.

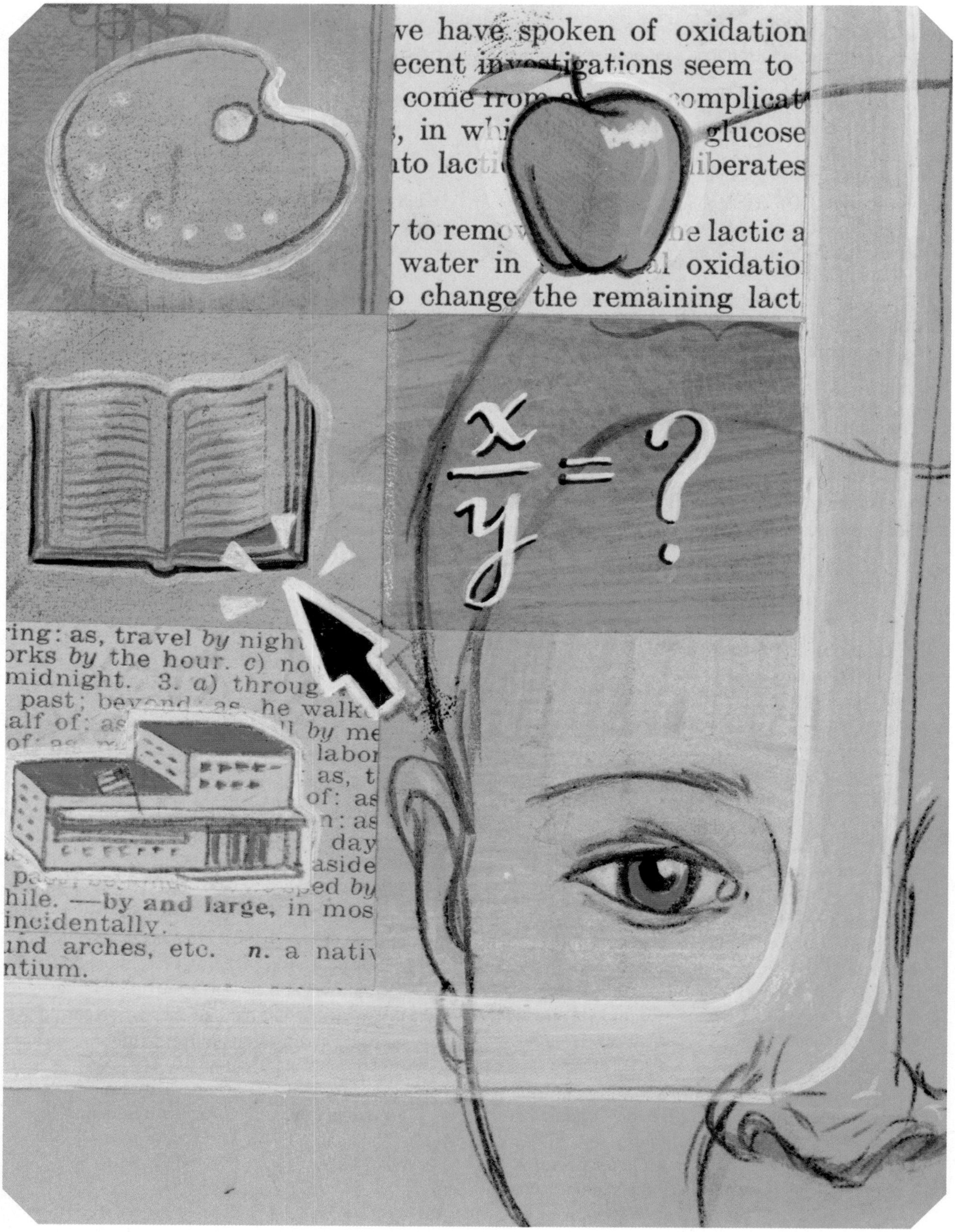
ve have spoken of oxidation
ecent investigations seem to
come from
complicat
, in wh
glucose
nto lac
iberates
to remo
e lactic a
water in
oxidatio
o change the remaining lact
ring: as, travel by night
orks by the hour. c) no
midnight. 3. a) throug
past; beyond: as, he walke
alf of: as
by me
labor
as, t
of: as
n: as
day
aside
hile. —by and large, in mos
incidentally.
und arches, etc. n. a nativ
ntium.

14

The Biology of Learning and Memory

- ➤ Types of Learning
- ➤ Models of Memory Storage and Retrieval
- ➤ Types of Memories
- ➤ The Memory Consolidation Process
- ➤ The Cellular Basis of Learning and Memory
- ➤ The Anatomy of Learning and Memory
- ➤ Alzheimer's Disease
- ➤ *Scientific American* Spotlight Senile Words
- ➤ Box 14.1 Treating Alzheimer's Disease

If You Can't Remember, Make Something Up

"Chester," the woman said to the carelessly dressed man sitting at a table in the dining room, "I want you to meet some students from the med school. You don't mind if we chat awhile, do you?"

"Of course not, Pamela," Chester said, brightening at the sight of his visitors. "I've been wondering when you would come see me again." He lowered his voice and winked conspiratorially. "Particularly after our last date."

Dr. Angela Sauers blushed, as the students giggled behind her.

"Look again, Mr. Hawthorne," she said. "You've mistaken me for someone else. Now do you know who I am?"

"I thought you were Pamela Cartwright," Chester said, "the girl who sits behind me in Spanish. But you're dressed like a doctor, although I've never seen a woman doctor before."

"What year is this, Mr. Hawthorne?" Angela asked.

"Why, it's 1957." Chester's mobile face showed his surprise at the question.

"And do you know who I am?"

"Can't say as I've had the pleasure. I would surely remember someone as pretty as you, Doc—if you really are a doctor."

"Oh, I'm a doctor, Mr. Hawthorne," Angela said, resisting the urge to add, "and we've met many times before." After all, the man could do nothing about his memory problems. Nor could the hospital. "Do you know where you are?"

Chester looked around the almost empty dining room, appearing to see it for the first time. "It looks like a cafeteria of some sort."

"And do you know what you had for breakfast?" Angela asked. The students knew Chester had not yet eaten.

For an instant, a look of bewilderment flashed across Chester's features. But only for an instant. "Eggs Benedict," he said, "with a rasher of bacon." He paused, as though savoring the exquisite flavors. "Four slices of toast slathered with real butter, not the fake oleo they sometimes try to pawn off on you in the high school cafeteria. And then there was some freshly squeezed orange juice, and the whole shebang was followed by the best cup of coffee money can buy." Another grin and wink: "With just a drop of Irish whiskey in it."

"And that's Mr. Hawthorne's problem," Angela said to the students after they had left the dining room. "He has Korsakoff's syndrome, which can follow chronic alcoholism. We don't know much about his previous life, but I'm willing to bet he drank many of his meals. Alcohol has lots of calories, so alcoholics often don't feel hungry. This can lead to improper nutrition and a vitamin B_1 deficiency."

BEFORE YOU BEGIN

- What caused Chester's severe memory impairment?
- What parts of his brain were affected by the lack of vitamin B_1 caused by his drinking?
- Why can Chester remember the name of the girl who sat behind him in high school but not the name of his physician?
- Can anything be done to improve Chester's memory?
- What is the relationship between learning and memory?
- How is the memory of Chester stored in Angela's brain?
- What physical changes take place in the brain when a memory is stored?
- What brain structures are involved in the storage and retrieval of memories?
- What conditions improve the chance that a specific memory will be retained?

In this chapter, you will find the answers to these questions and many others.

Throughout this text we have frequently referred to learning and memory. Here we will focus on the biological bases of these processes—or how a normally functioning CNS enables you to read the words on this page and recognize at least some of them when your instructor springs a surprise quiz. And we will consider, too, what happens in the brain to cause these processes to break down, as has happened to Chester.

Learning is a long-term change in behavior as a function of experiences, and **memory** is the capacity to retain and retrieve the experiences. We begin this chapter with a brief introduction to learning and memory, then continue with a detailed examination of how neural processes change as the result of an experience, allowing the formation of memories—which, when he was healthy, would have enabled Chester to remember the name of his doctor, whether he had had breakfast, and, if so, what he had eaten.

learning A long-term change in behavior as a function of experiences.

memory The capacity to retain and retrieve past experiences.

habituation A decrease in response following repeated exposure to a non-threatening stimulus.

sensitization An increase in reactivity to a stimulus following exposure to an intense event.

Pavlovian conditioning A type of learning in which a neutral stimulus is paired with a stimulus that elicits a reflex response until the neutral stimulus elicits the reflex response by itself.

unconditioned stimulus (UCS) A stimulus that involuntarily elicits a reflexive response.

unconditioned response (UCR) A reflexive reaction to an unconditioned stimulus.

conditioned stimulus (CS) An initially neutral stimulus that eventually elicits a conditioned response after pairing with a UCS.

conditioned response (CR) A learned reaction to a conditioned stimulus.

◆ Types of Learning

Consider the following scenarios, each of which illustrates one kind of learning:

1. Amy selects a pair of jeans from her closet, removes them from the hanger, and puts them on. At first she feels the denim against her skin, but after a while, she is no longer aware of this sensation.
2. Trisha is studying intently for an exam. Her roommate quietly enters the room, walks up behind Trisha, and touches her on the shoulder to get her attention. Trisha jumps from her chair as if she had been shot out of a cannon.
3. Theo is having dinner with an attractive partner. The lights are dim, soft music is playing, and candles are flickering on the table. In this romantic setting, Theo becomes sexually aroused.
4. Ali and a group of friends drive to a nearby casino. At the first quarter slot machine that becomes available, Ali drops in some money and almost instantly wins $325.

The first scenario illustrates **habituation,** a decrease in response following repeated exposure to an innocuous (nonthreatening) stimulus. (Note that habituation is not the same as *sensory adaptation,* which is a decrease in response to a stimulus because of changes in the responsivity of the sensory receptor; sensory adaptation occurs at the receptor level, whereas habituation involves central nervous system processes.) Amy initially reacts to the feel of the jeans on her skin, but with continued exposure she no longer feels the fabric. The same type of learning explains her rapid loss of awareness of the smell of the soap she uses to bathe, the perfume she applies in the morning, and the ordinary sounds around her when she sits down to read the paper. The benefit of this type of learning is obvious—imagine what it would be like if you were constantly aware of the clothes touching your skin, the odors around you, or the myriad sounds in your world. If you lost the ability to habituate to innocuous stimuli, you would have difficulty reading the words on this page because of all the distractions, much less learning anything from them.

The second scenario illustrates **sensitization,** an increase in reactivity to a stimulus following exposure to an intense event, such as studying for an examination. While Trisha is aroused for studying, her sensitivity to other stimuli is heightened, which causes her increased startle reaction to her roommate's touch. Another less obvious example, which may seem more like common sense than sensitization, is an increased reluctance to eat new foods when you are ill.

Ivan Pavlov (center) and some of his associates with one of their experimental dogs (1904).

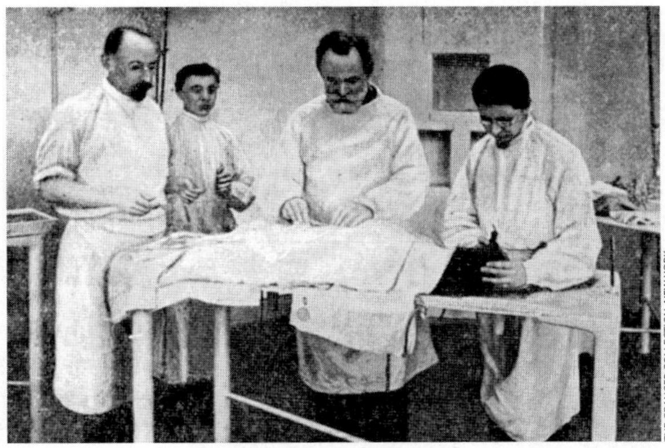

THE GRANGER COLLECTION, NEW YORK

The third scenario illustrates Pavlovian conditioning, a type of learning first studied by the Russian physiologist Ivan Pavlov at the beginning of the 20th century. Pavlovian conditioning is also called classical conditioning, which we introduced in the context of conditioning associated with hunger in Chapter 10. In **Pavlovian conditioning,** an initially neutral stimulus is paired with a stimulus that elicits a reflex response, and the neutral stimulus by itself eventually elicits the response. Pavlov began by studying the digestive process in dogs, research for which he won the Nobel Prize in Physiology or Medicine in 1904. While working on the digestive system, he discovered that dogs began to salivate before having food placed in their mouths, merely as a result of being removed from their cages or seeing an experimenter. Pavlov recognized that the animals had transferred a response (salivation) originally triggered by food to a stimulus—such as the sight of an experimenter—that had not initially caused them to salivate. He was so fascinated by this phenomenon that he talked about these *conditioned reflexes* at Stockholm when he received his Nobel Prize, and he devoted the rest of his career to their study.

To explain his observations, Pavlov began with the idea that animals (including humans) have instinctual or *unconditioned reflexes.* An unconditioned reflex consists of an **unconditioned stimulus (UCS),** which elicits an involuntary **unconditioned response (UCR).** For example, the UCS in many of Pavlov's studies was the taste of food, and the UCR was salivation. As the result of repeated pairings of an environmental event, such as the sight of food or of the experimenter, with the unconditioned stimulus, the environmental event becomes a **conditioned stimulus (CS)** and begins to elicit a learned or **conditioned response (CR)**—salivation without the taste of food. Classical conditioning creates a preparatory/anticipatory response that alerts the learner that something important is about to happen.

In our scenario, as a result of Theo's previous association of the attractive person and the romantic setting with sexual pleasure (the UCS), the person becomes a conditioned stimulus (CS) eliciting sexual arousal as the conditioned response (CR). Other examples of Pavlovian conditioning would be your fear (CR) of driving at night in the rain (CS) as a result of pain experienced after an automobile accident under similar road conditions; feeling nauseated (CR) when seeing a particular food (CS) that previously made you ill; and lowering your head (CR) when going downstairs to the basement (CS), because of an earlier bump on the head. Advertisers often try to take advantage of classical conditioning to sell their products (Figure 14.1).

Figure 14.1

Classical conditioning In this automobile advertisement, the car's manufacturer pairs the woman's legs (UCS) with its product, a red sports car (CS).

➜ **What are the UCR and CR in this example of classical conditioning?**

IMAGE SOURCE/SUPERSTOCK

Figure 14.2
Operant conditioning Gambling is a vivid example of the powerful effect of reinforcement on human behavior.

Why do people spend hours playing a slot machine?

The fourth scenario illustrates **operant conditioning,** which is learning how to behave to obtain reinforcement, such as coins flowing from a slot machine (Figure 14.2), or how to behave to avoid punishment. Another way to say this is that you learn an association between a behavior (something you do) and its consequences. **Reinforcers** are events or activities (the jackpot) that increase the frequency of the behavior that precedes an event or activity (putting a quarter in the machine and pulling the lever). Other instances of operant behavior producing reinforcement include fishing (if the person can cast freely), dating (if the person can ask out as many people as he or she wants), calling a friend on your cell phone, and checking the Web site of a professor for your exam grade.

Punishers are events or activities that decrease the frequency of the behavior that precedes them. Examples of punishers are the loss of privileges for the 10-year-old child who refuses to do her homework; a verbal reprimand for a habitually tardy student; a fine for driving at 80 mph in a 55 mph zone; and being excluded from playing in a flag football game after breaking team rules. The punisher is applied to decrease the future occurrence of the undesirable behavior.

B. F. Skinner in his laboratory (1933).

Operant conditioning is associated with B. F. Skinner (1938), who extensively investigated the influence of reinforcement on behavior, using a simple structured environment that became known as the Skinner box; Skinner himself called it an "operant conditioning apparatus." The typical **Skinner box** is an enclosed chamber with a small bar on the inside wall, which, when pressed by a rat or other small animal, causes release of a reinforcer. The operant chamber can be modified to accommodate many different animal species. Pigeons, for example, peck a key rather than pressing a bar.

A central concept in operant conditioning is **contingency,** a specified relationship between behavior and reinforcement or punishment. According to Skinner (1980), the environment determines contingencies between behavior and reinforcement or punishment, and people must perform the appropriate behavior to obtain reinforcement or avoid punishment. Other researchers have shown that animals are sensitive to contingencies between behavior and punishment and that behavior is suppressed because of previous punishment (Arbuckle & Lattal, 1992; Leclerc, 1985).

Checkpoint

You are driving through an intersection in which you recently had an accident. You hear the sound of a car horn, and you slam on the brakes. Which type(s) of learning are you exhibiting? What are the main differences among habituation, sensitization, Pavlovian conditioning, and operant conditioning?

REVIEW

- The four types of learning are habituation, sensitization, Pavlovian conditioning, and operant conditioning.
- Habituation is a decrease in response following repeated exposure to a nonthreatening stimulus.
- Sensitization is an increase in response to additional events following or during exposure to an intense event.
- Pavlovian conditioning establishes an association between a neutral stimulus and a stimulus that triggers a reflex response.
- Operant conditioning is learning how to behave to obtain reinforcement or to avoid punishment or learning an association between a behavior and its consequences.

Models of Memory Storage and Retrieval

You now know something about the several ways in which we learn. But how do we remember what we have learned? How does Dr. Angela Sauers recall what she has learned about her patient, Chester Hawthorne? A variety of models have been proposed to account for memory storage and retrieval.

The Atkinson-Shiffrin Model

According to the **Atkinson-Shiffrin model** (Atkinson & Shiffrin, 1968, 1971; Estes, 1999; Izawa, 1999), memory storage has three stages (Figure 14.3). Consider what happens when you look up the telephone number of your study partner. The external input (the telephone number) is initially stored in your **sensory register** for a brief time, usually 0.5 to 1 second, which should be long enough for you to punch the number. Information in the sensory register is an initial impression of the environment in the form of an exact duplicate of external stimuli (the 7 or 10 numbers on the page of the directory). However, not all information from the external environment is stored in the sensory register (you do not store all the phone numbers on the page, for example). Information decays rapidly after leaving the sensory register and is lost unless transferred into the short-term store; you will probably have to look up the number again the next time you need to call.

The **short-term store** is a temporary storage site for our experiences, in which memories can remain for 5, 10, or 15 seconds, or even longer. The length of time information remains in the short-term store depends on two variables: rehearsal and the amount of information. First, input such as the phone number must be rehearsed, or repeated, in order to be held in the short-term store. Without such repetition, the phone number can be lost before it is stored. Rehearsal also organizes the information in the short-term store, enhancing the likelihood you will be able to recall the phone number later, perhaps by associating the name of your study partner with the telephone number. Second, only a limited amount of information can be retained in the short-term store: If new information comes in, old information may be forced out. For example, if you have just looked up a phone number and someone runs in yelling the score of a basketball game you are interested in, old information such as the phone number is kicked out—unless the short-term store has enough room for both the old and the new. Rehearsal can prevent the game score from bumping the telephone number from the short-term store.

Some information in the short-term store is transferred automatically into the **long-term store,** the site of permanent memory storage. Atkinson and Shiffrin

operant conditioning A type of learning in which a response either produces reinforcement or avoids punishment.

reinforcer An event that increases the frequency of the behavior that precedes it.

punisher An event that decreases the frequency of the behavior that precedes it.

Skinner box An enclosed chamber invented by B. F. Skinner to train an animal through operant conditioning.

contingency The specified relationship between a behavior and its reinforcement or punishment.

Atkinson-Shiffrin model A model of memory storage in which an experience is sequentially stored in the sensory register, the short-term store, and the long-term store.

sensory register In the Atkinson-Shiffrin model, the initial storage site where a memory is held for a brief time without modification.

short-term store In the Atkinson-Shiffrin model, a temporary site where information is held before storage in permanent memory.

long-term store The site of permanent memory storage.

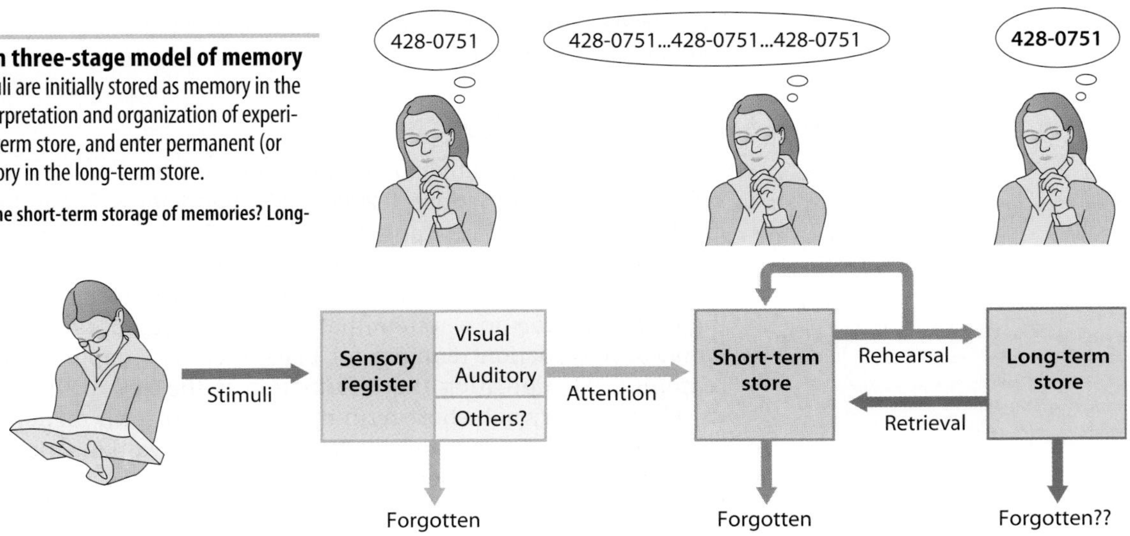

Figure 14.3

The Atkinson-Shiffrin three-stage model of memory storage External stimuli are initially stored as memory in the sensory register. The interpretation and organization of experiences occur in the short-term store, and enter permanent (or nearly permanent) memory in the long-term store.

➡ **What events trigger the short-term storage of memories? Long-term storage?**

interference An inability to recall a specific memory because of other memories.

memory attribute An aspect of an event that can stimulate memory retrieval.

rehearsal systems approach An alternative to the Atkinson-Shiffrin model in which Baddeley argued that memories go directly from the sensory register to long-term storage.

working memory A system that permits the temporary storage and manipulation of information required for tasks such as comprehension, learning, and reasoning.

(1971) suggested that information can be lost from the long-term store through decay, but the issue of whether long-term memory is ever lost has not been settled. Most research indicates that if information gets into the long-term store it stays there permanently (Spear & Riccio, 1994). However, some research suggests that decay does cause some memories to be lost (Staddon, 1998).

Storage of the telephone number in the long-term store does not guarantee you will be able to recall it tomorrow or next week, as two processes may hinder such recall. First, other memories in the long-term store may prevent recollection of a particular experience; this recall failure because of other memories is called **interference.** Second, failure to recall a memory from the long-term store may result from the lack of a specific stimulus to trigger retrieval (Morgan & Riccio, 1998).

People use notable aspects of an event, called **memory attributes** (cues), to help them remember the event. For example, a visit from a friend may remind you of a past experience with her. Or, returning to a place that you have not visited for several years may cause you to remember something you once did there. The presence of your friend or the place you revisit is the memory attribute that enables you to retrieve the memory of your earlier experiences. A memory attribute can even be an internal stimulus, such as an emotion (Bower & Forgas, 2001). When you are feeling sad, for example, you might remember the death of a beloved grandparent, because sadness is the memory attribute for your grandparent's funeral. You also might remember that painful day every time you pass the funeral home. Without these environmental events, you are less likely to recall the memory of your grandparent's death.

The Atkinson-Shiffrin model suggests that the analysis or organization of an experience can occur even after the memory has been transferred to the long-term store. When a memory is retrieved from the long-term to the short-term store, it can receive additional processing that may facilitate its later recall. As an example, after beginning a new class, you might be able to recall the name of your professor only after hearing it a second time. Processing can also alter the memory, making it more logical, consistent, or appealing. For instance, you may recall that a particular friend was at a party, when, in fact, the person *should* have been there but was not. Thus, memories that have been retrieved and further processed may not accurately reflect the actual experience (Loftus, 2003). For example, in relating an exciting event you experienced to a friend, you may include some details that did not really occur. Later, when you attempt to retrieve the memory for another telling, you may mistakenly retrieve the memory that included false details, and this scrambled memory then becomes your memory of the episode rather than the "real" one. As another example, your memory of your grandparent's funeral, especially if you were very young when the death occurred, may be shaped more by overheard recollections of family members than by your own memory of what happened at the funeral.

Alternative Models

One significant alternative to the Atkinson-Shiffrin model is Baddeley's **rehearsal systems approach** (Baddeley, 2000, 2001; Baddeley & Logie, 1999). Baddeley argued that memories are transferred directly from the sensory register to permanent or long-term storage. Experiences can be retained in sensory systems for analysis, which is the function of working memory. According to Baddeley, **working memory** refers to a system that permits the temporary storage and manipulation of information required for tasks such as comprehension, learning, and reasoning. Manipulating the information is the key to the difference between working memory and short-term memory; short-term memory primarily maintains the information for memorization, whereas working memory maintains the information in order to perform complex cognitive tasks with it or upon it. Working memory shares the attributes of the short-term store; that is, it has a limited capacity and duration, and rehearsal enhances organization and increases retrieval. When we discuss memory consolidation later in the chapter, we will look at evidence that permanent memory storage occurs soon (within a few seconds) after an experience.

In a second alternative to the Atkinson-Shiffrin model, Craik and Lockhart (1972; Lockhart & Craik, 1990) argued that rather than existing in different storage levels, memories differ in the extent to which they have been processed. The more completely a memory has been processed, the more likely a person is to remember it later. As an illustration of different levels of memory processing, consider the last movie you saw. Shallow processing might enable you to recall only that you saw a movie, but not any of its details. At a deeper level, you might remember surface details, such as the length of the movie, one or two of its major actors, and whether or not you liked it. With further processing, you might remember the main plot of the movie and a few of its more surprising moments. Finally, with deep processing, you remember virtually everything about the film, including other films that are similar in some way, perhaps other movies by the same director or starring the same actors, and so on. Lockhart and Craik's view of memory storage is not necessarily inconsistent with either Baddeley's view or the Atkinson-Shiffrin model; it may simply describe different aspects of memory storage.

episodic memory The memory of temporally related events experienced at a particular time and place.

semantic memory The memory of knowledge concerning the use of language and the rules, formulas, or algorithms for the development of concepts or solutions to problems.

Checkpoint

Using what you have learned about the Atkinson-Shiffrin model, indicate where in the model Chester's memory deficit most likely originates.

REVIEW

- The Atkinson-Shiffrin model proposes that the three stages of memory storage are the sensory register, the short-term store, and the long-term store. The sensory register is the initial storage site; the short-term store rehearses and organizes experiences; and the long-term store is the site of permanent memory storage.
- Baddeley's rehearsal systems approach proposes that memories are transferred directly from the sensory register to long-term storage, and the process involves working memory.
- In Lockhart and Craik's model, memories differ only in the extent to which they have been processed, not in their storage level.

Types of Memories

In our discussion of memory storage, we have used simple, commonplace examples of the types of memories that might be stored. You may be wondering whether all memories are treated the same. Are they all stored in the same place? Is recalling a place you have visited the same sort of process as remembering that telephone numbers have at least seven digits? And why can Chester remember the name of a friend from grade school but not the name of the physician he now sees almost every day?

Episodic Versus Semantic Memories

In 1972, Endel Tulving suggested two types of long-term memory: episodic and semantic. An **episodic memory** consists of information about temporally related events, such as an event you experienced at a particular time and place. A **semantic memory** contains information about words and symbols, and the rules, formulas, or algorithms for the development of concepts or solutions to problems. Episodic memories are your memories of the events in your life; semantic memory is filled with facts and rules about how to do things like counting and driving a car and speaking the English language. For example, your memory that you ate pancakes for breakfast is an episodic memory, whereas your memory that the sentence "I ate pancakes for breakfast" is constructed with a noun and a verb is a semantic memory. Your memory of what a pancake is and how to make it is also an example of a semantic memory.

Memory retrieval from the episodic system is deliberate and often requires conscious effort, whereas the recall of information from the semantic system is automatic, occurring without conscious knowledge (Tulving, 1983). Although we can be aware of knowledge contained in both memory systems, we interpret episodic memories as part of our personal past and semantic memories as part of the impersonal present. Thus, we use the word *remember* when referring to episodic memories and the word *know* to describe semantic memories. When you say you have learned something, such as how to conjugate a verb, you are referring to semantic memory. According to Tulving, semantic memories are retrieved unchanged, whereas episodic memories are often changed on retrieval, making the episodic system much more vulnerable to distortion than the semantic system. Table 14.1 lists important differences between episodic and semantic memory.

Table 14.1
Characteristics of Episodic Memory and Semantic Memory

Episodic Memory	Semantic Memory
Stores events	Stores ideas or concepts
Organized temporally	Organized conceptually
Based on personal belief	Based on social agreement
Reported as remembrance	Reported as knowledge
Access is deliberate	Access is automatic
Affect relatively important	Affect relatively unimportant
Very susceptible to amnesia	Relatively unsusceptible to amnesia
Stored late in childhood	Stored early in childhood

Source: Adapted from Tulving, E. (1983). *Elements of episodic memory.* Oxford: Clarendon Press/Oxford University Press.

The difference between episodic and semantic memory is greater than just the difference in types of information stored in each system (Tulving, 1998, 2002). In fact, Tulving believes the two systems are anatomically distinct, and recent studies provide extensive support for this distinction. For example, in a recent study participants studied 20-word lists and then performed either episodic or semantic retrieval tasks while undergoing PET scans (Duzel & others, 2001). The scans during episodic retrieval revealed increased blood flow in the right frontal lobe and left medial temporal lobe, the latter increase when the subject retrieved old (vs. new) items. Semantic retrieval led to greater activity in the left frontal lobe and the anterior cingulate gyrus when the individual retrieved living (vs. nonliving) items.

In addition, the effect of brain damage on episodic and semantic memory depends on the brain area(s) involved. For example, researchers studied remote memory in 25 patients with unilateral temporal lobe epilepsy and in 22 unimpaired controls (Viskontas & others, 2000). The patients exhibited impaired personal episodic memory, as measured by the Autobiographical Memory Interview (Kopelman & others, 1989), but were unimpaired in their personal semantic memory. The researchers concluded that even slight damage to the medial temporal lobes impaired autobiographical episodic memory. Further, despite amnesia for all episodes of "everyday life," three patients with bilateral hippocampal pathology as revealed by MRI demonstrated enough semantic memory ability to show levels of language competence, literacy, and factual knowledge within the normal range (Vargha-Khadem & others, 1997). Based partly on this research, Mishkin and coworkers (1999) hypothesized that the cortical areas below the hippocampus are needed for both episodic and semantic memory, whereas episodic (but not semantic) memory depends on processing by the hippocampus itself.

➤Checkpoint

You are walking home from the library looking at the stars, and suddenly the trick that helped you learn the names of the planets pops into your head—along with the image of your third-grade teacher reciting it to the class: "My very educated mother just served us nine pickles." Is this an example of episodic memory or semantic memory?

Procedural Versus Declarative Memories

Perhaps, like many people, on entering adulthood you embraced the automobile as a means of transportation and put away your bicycle. You probably had a lot of experience riding a bicycle when you were younger, and you probably have not lost the skills required to ride one now even though it may have been years since you last rode one. Your memories of how to ride a bicycle, which are in your long-term store, illustrate procedural memory.

procedural memory Skill memory, or the memory of highly practiced behavior.

According to Larry Squire (1986; Squire & Zola, 1996), **procedural memory** (also called *nondeclarative memory*) is skill memory (Table 14.2). Procedural memories

Table 14.2
Characteristics of Declarative Memory and Procedural Memory

Procedural Memory	Declarative Memory
Stores skills and procedures	Stores facts, episodes, and data
Is learned incrementally	Can be learned in a single trial
Contained within processing systems (e.g., sensory, motor)	Available to many processing systems
Information is modality specific	Information is modality general
Phylogenetically primitive	Phylogenetically late
Developmentally early	Developmentally late
Preserved in amnesia	Impaired in amnesia
Inaccessible to conscious recollection	Accessible to conscious recollection

Source: Adapted from Squire, L. R. (1984). The neuropsychology of memory. In P. Marler & H. Terrace (Eds.), *The biology of learning* (pp. 667–685). Berlin: Springer-Verlag.

are not accessible to conscious awareness, and evidence for these memories can be gained only through observations of performance. For example, you may not be able to describe how to play Mozart's Piano Sonata in C major, but you can demonstrate your ability to play it. Procedural memories represent knowledge of how to do things, such as drive a car, tie shoelaces, play a slot machine, or ride a bicycle, that is stored as a result of operant conditioning experiences (recall Ali's visit to the casino). Procedural memories also can represent emotional reactions to environmental events, such as becoming fearful before driving over a high bridge or sad when thinking of a deceased friend. These emotional reactions are stored through Pavlovian conditioning. As an illustration, the thought of your dead friend is a CS that triggers the emotional reaction of sadness, which is a CR.

Declarative memory, by contrast, is memory of facts. For example, you quickly learn at the start of the fall television season that your favorite show is on at 8:30 p.m. on Tuesday. The time and day of the show are facts stored as declarative memories (Table 14.2). Other examples of declarative memory are knowing how to spell *schizophrenia* and remembering what happened at the last football game you attended.

declarative memory Factual memory, or the memory of specific events.

Facts that are independent of context, such as how to spell your name, London is the capital of England, or that 6 times 5 is 30, make up semantic memory. Memories (or facts) that are dependent on context, such as what you had for breakfast this morning, what you did on your last birthday, or events at your grandfather's funeral, constitute episodic memory. As you can see, declarative memory consists of episodic and semantic memory (Figure 14.4).

In contrast to procedural memories, we are consciously aware of declarative memories. According to Squire (1986), a declarative memory can exist as a verbal thought or as a nonverbal image. Thus, you are verbally aware of when your favorite television show is on, whereas knowledge of your route to school may exist only as a nonverbal image. Although a declarative memory can be formed in a single experience, practice can enhance our ability to recall it. Like episodic memories, declarative memories are more susceptible to interference than procedural memories.

Procedural and declarative memories may also differ in an evolutionary sense (Squire, 1986). Procedural memories are found even in simple invertebrates, whereas declarative memories are found only in advanced vertebrates, which makes them the phylogenetically more recent (more advanced) type. This difference in the types of memory suggests that they

Figure 14.4
Types of long-term memory

→ What are some additional examples of each of the memory types from your own experience?

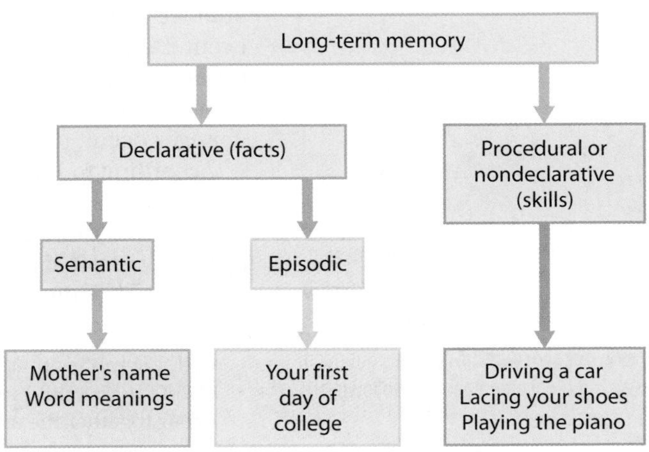

are anatomically distinct (Squire & Zola, 1996). Declarative memories appear to be formed in the medial temporal lobe and in structures of the diencephalon, whereas procedural memories are established in the cerebral cortex (or cerebral neocortex), basal ganglia, and cerebellum (Poldrack & Gabrieli, 1997). Further, procedural memories are stored early in development and across the lifetime of a person, whereas storage of declarative memories begins later in development (DiGiulio & others, 1994). A similar distinction has been made for semantic memories (stored early in childhood) and episodic memories (stored later in childhood) (Tulving, 1998). Thus, you remember how to ride a tricycle without being able to remember the specific experience at the age of 4 when you acquired the ability, or you know how to construct a sentence without being able to recall when you learned how to do so. Both declarative and procedural (nondeclarative) memories, as well as semantic and episodic memories, are part of long-term memory storage (Figure 14.4).

➤Checkpoint

Try to describe how to drive a car or ride a bike. Why is this descriptive task so difficult?

REVIEW

- ➤ Episodic memory is the temporally organized, deliberate recall of past events.
- ➤ Semantic memory is the automatic recall of ideas or concepts organized conceptually.
- ➤ Procedural memory is skill memory and is not accessible to conscious thought.
- ➤ Declarative memory is memory of facts and is accessible to conscious thought.

◆ The Memory Consolidation Process

We now begin to look at the workings of memory at the cellular level. This subject has long intrigued neuroscientists. Almost all agree that memory initially involves short-term mechanisms and that these are followed by long-term storage that occurs through a process of consolidation.

Hebb's Cell Assemblies

Donald Olding Hebb (1949), in *The Organization of Behavior,* presented one of the most interesting conceptual suggestions about learning and memory. He proposed that our experience of an event activates a neural circuit in the CNS. The activity *reverberates,* or continues to circulate, through this circuit even after the event ends, and one function of this reverberatory activity is to provide temporary storage and a record of the event until it can be consolidated (modified and stored) into a permanent memory. Hebb called the neural circuit a **cell assembly.**

Hebb also suggested that physiological changes occurring in a cell assembly after we experience an event represent the way the brain permanently records the event. Because these physiological changes take place relatively slowly, the **reverberatory activity** must be maintained until the storage process is completed. If the activity is disrupted, the consolidation process stops, and no further physiological changes occur. (Can you see how this fits with the Atkinson-Shiffrin model?)

According to Hebb, the cell assembly is the basic memory unit. Simple psychological processes, such as reflexive behaviors, are controlled by a single cell assembly, whereas more complex processes, such as voluntary behaviors, are governed by interconnected assemblies. Cell assemblies become interconnected into a *phase sequence,* all activated at the same time. Hebb (1972) described how cell assemblies become connected in order to control complex processes:

> Cell assemblies that are active at the same time become interconnected. Common events in the child's environment establish assemblies, and then when these events occur together the assemblies become connected (because they are active together).

cell assembly A circuit of neurons that become active at the same time; serves as the site of permanent memory.

reverberatory activity The continued reactivation of a neural circuit following an experience.

> When the baby hears footsteps, let us say, an assembly is excited; while this is still active, "footsteps assembly" becomes connected with the "face assembly" and the "being-picked-up assembly." (p. 67)

The strength of a memory depends on the length of time the stimulus was initially experienced (Hebb, 1949). Disruption of reverberatory activity early in the consolidation process produces a weak or nonexistent permanent memory of an event. However, disruption late in the process usually has little impact: Because the permanent physiological changes have almost been completed, the permanent memory is strong, and recall of the event is probable.

In summary, Hebb's model suggests that an experience triggers reverberatory neural activity, and this activity is essential for storing a memory in a permanent form. The reverberatory activity is followed by physiological changes in the cell assembly that produce a relatively permanent record of the event.

In support of Hebb's cell-assembly model, Burns (1958) isolated a section of cortical tissue in the cat by cutting its neural connections to other parts of the brain. In the isolated section, he electrically stimulated selected areas and recorded bursts of neural activity in the area of stimulation that continued following termination of the stimulus. Although reverberation seems to be the most reasonable explanation for the continued neural activity, Burns took the study a step further. He reasoned that if all the neurons in the circuit were stimulated simultaneously, then the sustained activity would stop when all the neurons were in the refractory period. (Recall from Chapter 4 that the *absolute refractory period,* when a neuron will not fire another action potential no matter how intense the stimulus, is followed by the *relative refractory period,* when the neuron will fire but only in response to a more intense stimulus than normal.) To test this hypothesis, Burns delivered a single intense shock to the center of the isolated section of cortical tissue. This produced initial activity throughout the neural tissue, followed by complete cessation of neural activity, as he had predicted.

Verzeano and Negishi (1960) produced additional support for Hebb's model. Electrodes were implanted close together (30 to 200 micrometers apart), arranged in a row, to record electrical activity in adjacent neurons. Brain stimulation produced neural activity that began with the stimulated neurons and continued sequentially in adjacent neurons, and the activity occurred in recurring waves of neural impulses throughout the neural circuit. The researchers also observed that the pattern of neural activity depended on the stimulus, implying that different reverberatory circuits are activated by different events. For example, the activation of different neural circuits presumably accounts for our ability to remember several telephone numbers.

More recent work provides additional support for Hebb's concept of cell assemblies. For example, evidence from studies of evoked potentials supports a cell-assembly model of language and other higher cognitive activities (Pulvermueller, 1996). In a study of changes in synaptic strength in slices of adult rat hippocampus, the alterations confirmed the Hebb memory model (Bains & others, 1999). Also, Leisman and Koch (2000) have discussed a mathematical model of memory consistent with Hebb's cell-assembly concept, and Bailey and colleagues (2000a) have concluded that Hebbian mechanisms are used primarily for short-term memory and for learning, not for long-term memory. Finally, long-term potentiation (LTP)—a lasting change in synaptic responsivity in a particular pathway caused by a brief series of electric impulses applied to it—is another phenomenon that supports Hebb's memory model; we discuss LTP at length later in the chapter.

Checkpoint

Use Hebb's cell-assembly model to describe how the telephone number of your study partner is recorded in your CNS. Do you think the telephone number would be represented by a single cell assembly or by multiple assemblies?

Is Reverberatory Activity Essential for Memory Storage?

If event encoding in the long-term store requires reverberatory activity, then disrupting activity early in the consolidation process should prevent memory formation. To test the critical role of reverberatory activity in memory consolidation,

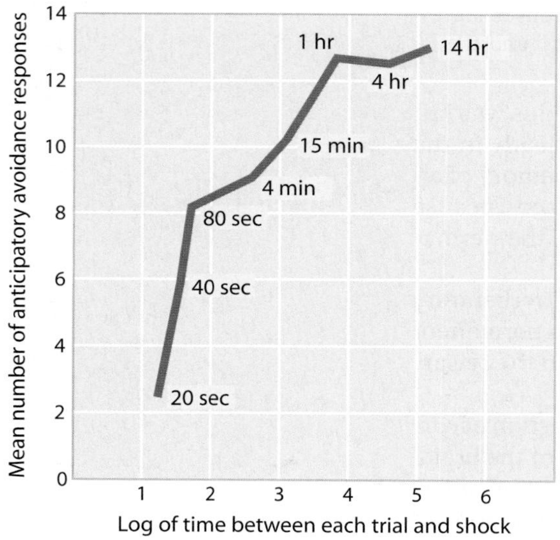

Figure 14.5

Time required for memory consolidation Adapted from Duncan (1949), this graph shows active-avoidance performance as a function of the interval between avoidance training and ECS. Anticipatory responses are trials in which the animal avoids shock. The results suggested, perhaps incorrectly, that the amnesic influence of ECS declines as the interval between training and ECS increases.

➜ **What is an alternative explanation for Duncan's results, other than a failure of memory consolidation?**

researchers in the 1940s and 1950s used *electroconvulsive shock (ECS)* to disrupt the consolidation of memory for active-avoidance conditioning trials (an animal learns to make a response in order to avoid an aversive stimulus) and other learning situations (e.g., maze learning, visual discrimination) (Duncan, 1949; Thompson & Dean, 1955). In general, the ECS appeared to produce **retrograde amnesia,** an inability to recall events that precede a traumatic event, resulting in a failure to show the learned avoidance behavior in later trials. In Duncan's experiment, rats learned to run from a dark chamber with a grid floor through which shock could be passed, into a lighted safe compartment with a wire mesh floor. After 10 seconds in the safe chamber, the rats were removed and then given ECS at varying intervals after the learning trial, or no ECS if they were control animals. Consolidation seemed to occur relatively quickly, as rats given electroshock after longer intervals (1, 4, and 14 hours) did not differ from a control group that had the training without receiving electroshock (Figure 14.5). Retrograde amnesia following ECS was also reported in human patients undergoing ECS therapy for otherwise untreatable depression (Cronholm & Molander, 1957, 1961, 1964), and this side effect continues to be a concern today (e.g., Rami-Gonzalez & others, 2001), although some types of memory (e.g., declarative) are clearly more affected than others.

However, the aversiveness of ECS was a major methodological flaw in these early studies. Using multiple ECS applications may have inadvertently caused the animals to associate the aversive properties with the environment in which the ECS was administered. For example, an acquired aversiveness to the chamber the animal entered before receiving ECS might have produced poor avoidance behavior, but not because of a disruption of memory consolidation, as Duncan (1949) assumed. Instead, the poor performance may have simply reflected avoidance of the situation in which the ECS was experienced. The positive correlation between performance and the length of time between the training trial and ECS, attributed to greater memory consolidation, may instead have resulted from less aversive conditioning produced by a longer delay between the end of the training trial and the administration of ECS.

In fact, ECS has aversive properties and can actually improve some learning (Coons & Miller, 1960). The researchers first trained rats to run from a dark chamber into a lighted chamber to escape footshock, essentially replicating Duncan's (1949) results. In a second experiment, the researchers again trained rats in the active avoidance response, but this time, after the animals had learned to avoid the shock, it was introduced into the formerly safe, lighted chamber. Thus, the new contingency required the animals to withhold their avoidance response in order to avoid the shock in the lighted chamber (passive avoidance). If the ECS had disrupted consolidation of the memory of the shock in the lighted chamber, then the animals given ECS closer to the shock should have shown poor passive avoidance. In fact, just the opposite occurred: The rats learned the passive avoidance situation faster the *sooner* the ECS followed each shocked trial. Coons and Miller concluded that the aversiveness of the ECS added to the fear from footshock in the lighted chamber to produce superior passive avoidance learning.

To minimize aversive conditioning from ECS, studies since the 1950s have tended to use a single ECS (e.g., Chorover & Schiller, 1965; Lewis, 1979). In addition, the experiments have used passive-avoidance tasks, in which *not responding* prevents a painful stimulus, rather than active-avoidance tasks, which require a response in order to prevent a painful stimulus. Because of this difference, any aversive qualities of ECS would cause the subject to take longer to respond, thus improving performance in the passive-avoidance situation. If ECS disrupts memory consolidation, then the animal will respond quickly, exhibiting poor passive avoidance.

retrograde amnesia The inability to recall events that preceded a traumatic event.

Chorover and Schiller (1965) used a step-down apparatus to train rats to avoid electric shock passively (Figure 14.6). Placed on the platform, rats quickly stepped down, received a footshock through the grid floor, and, if they were in the experimental groups, received an ECS following delays ranging from 0.5 to 60 seconds after the end of the footshock. Animals in the control group received either shock without ECS, or neither shock nor ECS. When tested the next day, control rats that had not received ECS after training remembered being shocked and refused to leave the platform. The control animals that received neither shock nor ECS readily stepped off, as did rats that received ECS within 10 seconds after passive-avoidance training. This suggests that ECS administered after training disrupted consolidation of the memory of the footshock. ECS was ineffective when given more than 10 seconds after training, implying that memory consolidation occurs within seconds (Figure 14.7). Thus, the longer time intervals during which the consolidation process appeared to be occurring observed in earlier studies may have been caused by processes other than memory consolidation.

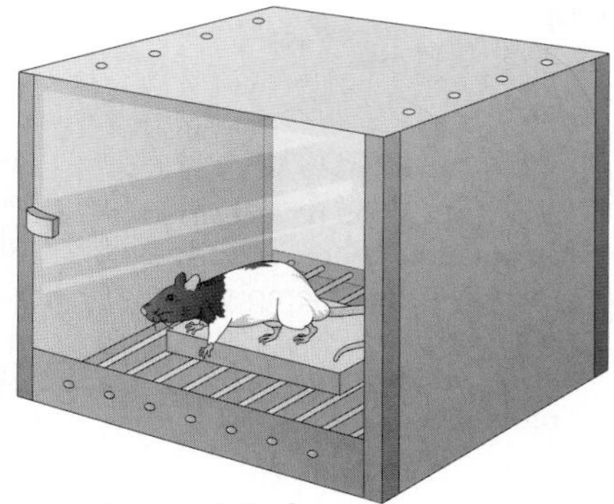

Figure 14.6

A step-down apparatus used for passive-avoidance training When the animal steps off the platform, it receives an electric footshock. The reluctance of the animal to step off the platform on later trials indicates the level of conditioning of the passive-avoidance response.

→ **Distinguish between active-avoidance and passive-avoidance training.**

The most likely such process appears to be memory retrieval. To study the effect of ECS on memory retrieval, researchers trained thirsty rats to lick water from a glass tube in a specially constructed lick chamber (Misanin & others, 1968). On the first treatment day, animals were placed individually into the chamber, and after 47 seconds, the conditioned stimulus, an 80 decibel white noise, was presented for 10 seconds and immediately followed by a 3 second footshock. All of the animals except those in group 1 were then returned to their home cages; group 1 rats received ECS immediately after the footshock. On the next day, the rats were placed into a distinctive box inside the lick chamber and received the following treatments: Group 2 animals received 2 seconds of the CS, followed immediately by ECS; groups 3 and 4 received only the CS or the ECS, respectively; and groups 1 and 5 received nothing. Twenty-four hours later, animals were returned to the lick chamber and allowed to lick water until 100 licks occurred; after this, the CS came on and remained on until an animal made 10 more licks or 10 minutes elapsed, whichever came first. Analysis of the first 100 licks data indicated that group 1 animals, which had received ECS immediately after the fear-conditioning trial, licked at a higher rate than the other animals, which did not differ. This result supports previous studies finding that ECS given soon after fear conditioning produces amnesia for the event and also reinforces the idea that ECS disrupts memory consolidation.

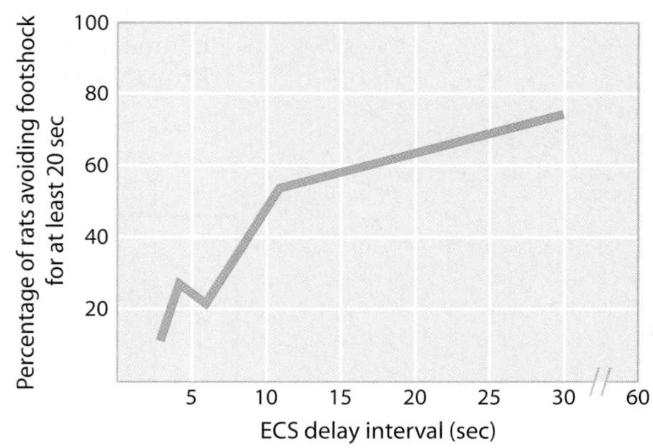

Figure 14.7

The timing of memory consolidation Shown here are the results for rats in Chorover and Schiller's (1965) experimental group that received a footshock followed by ECS.

→ **Chorover and Schiller found that rats that received ECS within 10 seconds of passive-avoidance training readily stepped off the platform. What does this finding suggest?**

However, in the analysis of lick rates after the CS came on, group 2 animals did not differ from group 1 animals and both licked at significantly higher rates than the other animals. Thus, in group 2 animals, even though the ECS came 24 hours after the original CS-footshock pairing, it still produced amnesia for the fear conditioning when it followed a brief CS reminder presentation. Given that consolidation of the memory of the CS-footshock pairing must have been completed within 24 hours, the retrograde amnesia could not have resulted from disruption of memory consolidation. Retrograde amnesia is produced only when a memory is active; that is, ECS can interfere with retrieval, but only when the memory is being transferred from stored to active memory. Thus, Misanin and colleagues suggested that the CS reactivated the memory of original training, and the ECS produced interference and subsequent amnesia.

If, as Misanin and colleagues (1968) and others showed, a CS reminder stimulus can reinstate a memory apparently lost after ECS, then the initial amnesia cannot have been caused by a failure of consolidation. If consolidation had not occurred, then the memory would have been irretrievably lost. In lengthy review papers, both Miller and Springer (1973) and Lewis (1979) concluded that memories

Checkpoint

Using what you have learned so far about memory, do you think Chester's memory problem is one of storage or retrieval? How could you prove it?

are consolidated in a fraction of a second rather than in seconds or longer. Further, both concluded that ECS or other forms of brain intervention (e.g., chemicals, physical trauma) affect memory retrieval rather than memory storage.

The Conditioning (Plasticity) of Neural Circuits

So far we have covered evidence supporting Hebb's reverberatory cell assemblies—although these neural circuits may be more involved in memory retrieval than in memory consolidation. We now turn to the evidence for the physiological changes that occur in memory consolidation.

Richard F. Thompson and his associates have identified the neural circuit that mediates the conditioning of the *nictitating membrane* of the rabbit, which is involved in the eyeblink response of the animal (Krupa & Thompson, 1997; Krupa & others, 1993; Tracy & others, 1998). The nictitating membrane is a tough inner eyelid found in many mammals (but not humans), birds, reptiles, amphibians, and fish.

When an unconditioned stimulus (UCS), such as a puff of air, threatens the eye of the animal, the nictitating membrane moves laterally to cover the eye (the unconditioned response, UCR). When the UCS is paired with a neutral stimulus (CS), such as a tone, the CS produces a conditioned eyeblink response (CR).

Using a corneal air puff UCS and a tone CS, Thompson and colleagues used such methods as microstimulation of localized neurons, localized infusions of neurotransmitter agonists and antagonists, localized lesions, and reversible inactivation of neurons through cooling or short-acting chemicals to determine the neural circuitry in the conditioned eyeblink response of the rabbit (Thompson & Krupa, 1994). Figure 14.8 shows a simplified version of this circuitry.

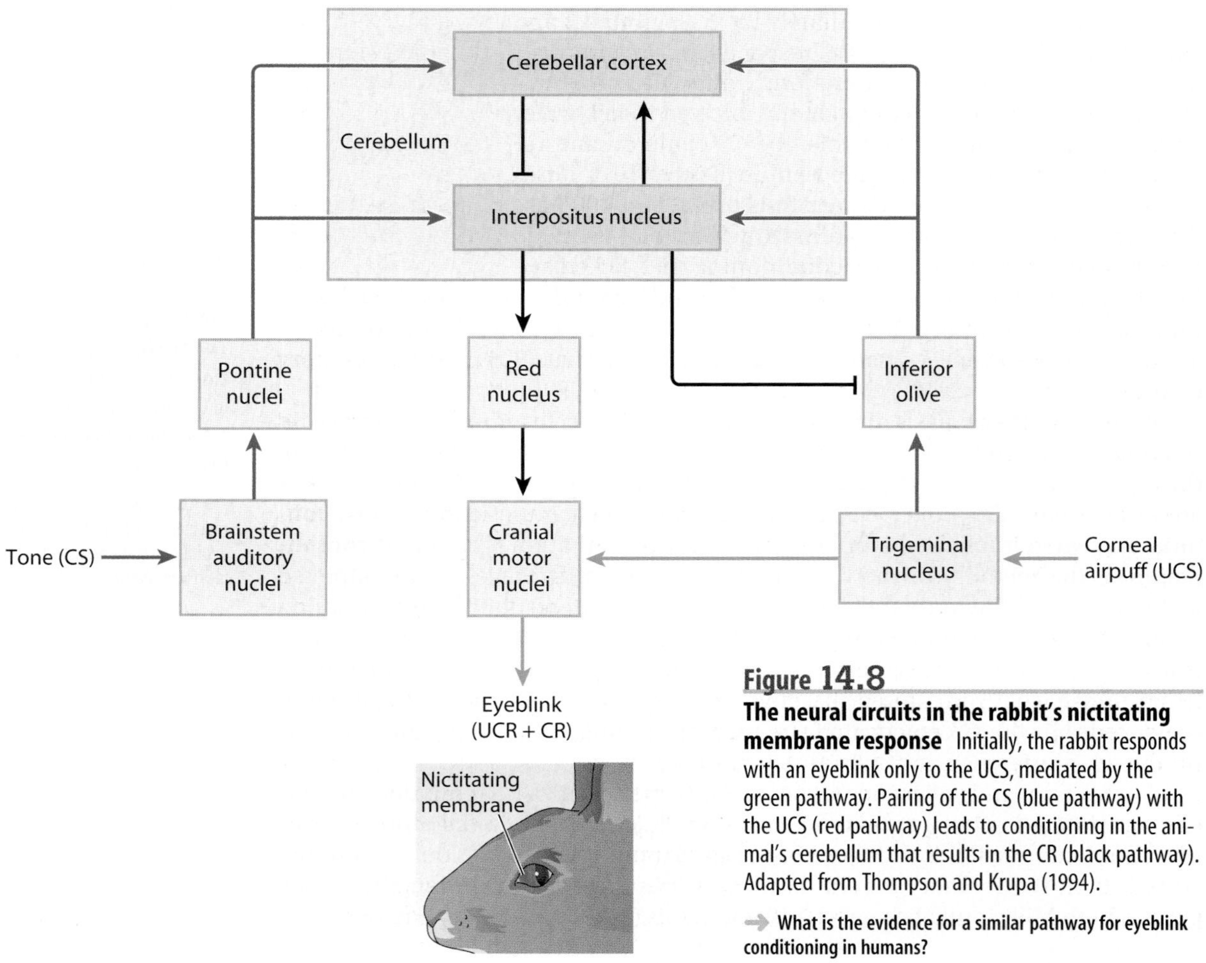

Figure 14.8

The neural circuits in the rabbit's nictitating membrane response Initially, the rabbit responds with an eyeblink only to the UCS, mediated by the green pathway. Pairing of the CS (blue pathway) with the UCS (red pathway) leads to conditioning in the animal's cerebellum that results in the CR (black pathway). Adapted from Thompson and Krupa (1994).

➔ **What is the evidence for a similar pathway for eyeblink conditioning in humans?**

interpositus nucleus The area of the brain central to the conditioning of the nictitating membrane response.

Before conditioning, there is only the animal's eyeblink reflex, shown in green in Figure 14.8; the air puff to the cornea (UCS) stimulates the trigeminal nucleus, which activates the cranial motor nuclei to produce the nictitating membrane response (UCR). Information about the UCS also goes to the inferior olive of the brain stem and from there to the cerebellum, specifically to the cerebellar cortex and the interpositus nucleus (red pathway). The axons carrying this information into the cerebellum are called *climbing fibers.* The tone (CS) information travels to the brain stem auditory nuclei and from there to the pontine nuclei, which send axons (*mossy fibers)* into the cerebellum (blue pathway).

After repeated pairings of the tone and the corneal air puff, the tone alone begins to elicit a nictitating membrane response, traveling along the pathway from the interpositus nucleus to the red nucleus and from there to the cranial motor nuclei for the eyeblink response (black pathway).

Before conditioning, the tone had no effect on the eyeblink response. Because of the plasticity or modifiability (see Chapter 3) of the neural circuits of the rabbit, conditioning established and then strengthened a connection between the sensory receptors detecting the tone (CS) and the muscles producing the nictitating membrane response (CR). The cerebellum is essential in this conditioning because of its role in situations that require learning about the temporal relationship between successive events (i.e., between the tone and the airpuff) (Ivry, 1997; Salman, 2002).

To investigate the brain circuitry connecting nuclei in the pons and the cerebellar interpositus nucleus further, experimenters paired direct electrical stimulation of the pontine nuclei (CS) with a corneal air puff (UCS) (Tracy & others, 1998). Following eyeblink conditioning, the threshold of stimulation necessary to elicit the CR with pontine stimulation decreased dramatically and then returned to baseline after extinction training. By contrast, the stimulation threshold of the interpositus nucleus remained the same throughout training and extinction. This lack of change in the interpositus nucleus suggests that further conditioning of the CR does not occur in the pathway efferent to the cerebellar structure, which argues for localization of the memory trace in the cerebellum. Tracy and colleagues concluded that the pons relays CS information to the cerebellum, where the essential connection between the CS and the CR is formed.

The **interpositus nucleus** is central to conditioning the nictitating membrane response (Bao & others, 2000). Thompson and colleagues found no evidence of conditioning when the interpositus nucleus was reversibly inactivated with the GABA agonist muscimol (Krupa & others, 1993; Krupa & Thompson, 1997). (Recall from Chapter 4 that GABA is an inhibitory neurotransmitter.) Despite repeated CS-UCS pairings, the CS failed to elicit the nictitating membrane response while the nucleus was inactivated, and the CS was equally ineffective after the muscimol effect wore off, indicating that conditioning had not occurred. However, without the inactivation of the nucleus, conditioning proceeded at a rate comparable to that in rabbits with no previous experience. Inactivating the red nucleus, by contrast, prevented the CS from eliciting the CR without preventing conditioning. After the effect of the muscimol ended, the CS elicited the nictitating membrane response without further CS-UCS pairings. These results indicate that the neural circuit must be fully functional for the CS to elicit the nictitating membrane response, and the cerebellar interpositus nucleus is where conditioning of the nictitating membrane occurs.

Further study of the cerebellar interpositus nucleus in eyeblink conditioning confirms that GABA is the neurotransmitter involved (Nolan & others, 2002; Ramirez & others, 1997). For example, infusion of the $GABA_B$ agonist baclofen into the interpositus nucleus of male rabbits abolished the eyeblink conditioned response without affecting the unconditioned response (Ramirez & others). Further, naive animals given interpositus infusions during training could not be conditioned. Nolan and coworkers studied both excitatory eyeblink conditioning and conditioned inhibition of the eyeblink response in male rats. Picrotoxin (a $GABA_A$ receptor antagonist) infusions into the interpositus nucleus and lateral pontine nuclei impaired excitatory conditioning but had no effect on inhibitory conditioning. This suggests that GABA mediates the expression of conditioned excitation of the eyeblink reflex but not its conditioned inhibition.

At this point, you may be asking yourself why so many researchers have devoted so much time and effort to the study of the classical conditioning of the nictitating membrane response of the rabbit. As we pointed out at the beginning of the chapter, Pavlovian or classical conditioning is one of the major forms of learning studied by psychologists, and many examples can be given of human behaviors acquired through this form of conditioning. In addition, because of the acceptance of the concepts of organic evolution, it is assumed that the processes of learning are the same wherever the phenomenon is found in the animal kingdom. That is, if we can understand the brain structures and processes that underlie the classical conditioning of a response in the rabbit, then our understanding should transfer to humans.

In fact, research on humans suggests a comparable neural circuit responsible for eyeblink conditioning. For example, measurement of neural activity with PET scans revealed increased activity in the cerebellum and red nucleus during the conditioning of an eyeblink response, along with increased activation of the hippocampus and corpus striatum (Logan & Grafton, 1995). Further, people with damage to the cerebellum have impaired eyeblink conditioning (Woodruff-Pak & others, 1996), and this is also true for an animal model of human fetal alcohol syndrome. Adult rats given binge-like exposure to alcohol as newborn animals exhibit impaired eyeblink conditioning (Green, 2004).

Checkpoint

What do Thompson's experiments suggest about the relationship between learning and memory? What effect on the conditioned eyeblink reflex would you expect to observe following damage to the cerebellar cortex? To the pathway connecting the pontine nuclei and the cerebellum?

REVIEW

- Hebb proposed that the experience of an event activates a neural circuit, or cell assembly, in the CNS, and reverberatory activity in the cell assembly is responsible for consolidating permanent memory. Simple processes are controlled by single-cell assemblies, and complex processes by multiple assemblies.
- In Hebb's model, the strength of a memory depends on the amount of time the initial experience or stimulus is available.
- Subsequent testing of Hebb's model has supported the existence of reverberatory circuits, the rapid consolidation of memory, and the role of reverberatory circuits in memory retrieval rather than in consolidation.
- Studies of nictitating eyelid conditioning in rabbits have demonstrated that specific neural circuits have the plasticity that allows them to be modified by experience; the conditioning occurs in the interpositus nucleus of the cerebellum. A comparable neural circuit appears to be involved in eyeblink conditioning in humans.

The Cellular Basis of Learning and Memory

What were you doing on the morning of September 11, 2001? Like most people, you were probably glued to a television set watching the shocking events unfold in New York City and Washington, DC. Your memory of these events is strong and will stay that way for the rest of your life. The question that interests us here is: As you watched the events transpire, what physical changes were occurring in your brain that would enable you to remember these events forever? Researchers have proposed that learning changes neural responsiveness, a view of the neuroplasticity of the brain called the **cellular modification theory** (Bailey & others, 2004; Lynch, 2004). These changes can reflect either the enhanced functioning of existing neural circuits or the establishment of new neural connections. We examine first the effect of experience on synaptic responsivity, and then the structural changes in neurons that result from experience. To begin, we introduce a simple animal that has proved invaluable in studies of the neural basis of learning.

cellular modification theory The view that learning permanently enhances the functioning of existing neural circuits or establishes new neural connections.

Learning in *Aplysia californica*

Nobel Prize–winner Eric Kandel and his associates have investigated learning-related changes in synaptic responsivity in the sea slug *Aplysia californica,* a shell-less marine mollusk (Antonov & others, 2001; Bailey & others, 2000b; Hawkins & others, 1998; Kandel, 2000a). *Aplysia* (Figure 14.9) has external organs—the gill and the siphon—that retract, or withdraw, when either the mantle shelf or the siphon is touched. This defensive withdrawal response can be either sensitized or habituated by experience and is analogous to the withdrawal responses found in almost all higher animals. An example would be your reaction to touching a hot burner on a stove. What makes *Aplysia* so suitable for learning studies is its withdrawal reflex and its neural simplicity: Researchers can separate out individual synapses from their neighbors and study them intensively to determine the processes that account for such learning phenomena as habituation, sensitization, and conditioning.

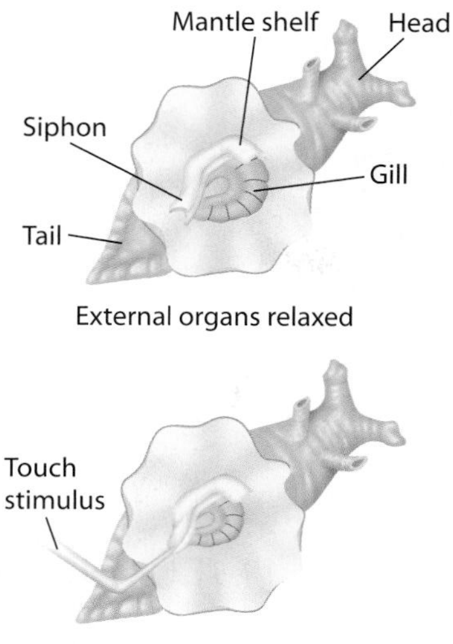

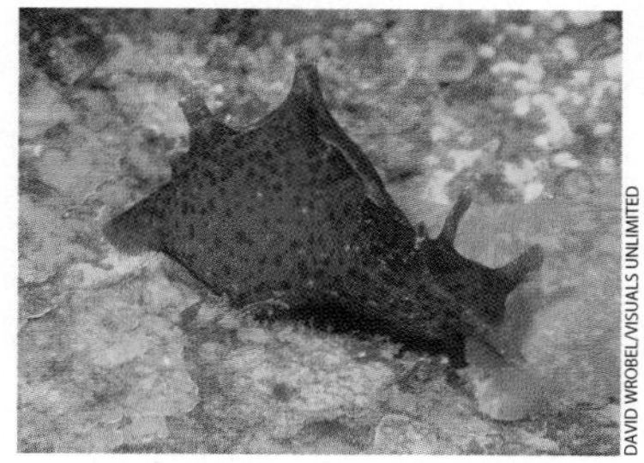

Figure 14.9

Aplysia californica *Aplysia*'s breathing apparatus (gill) is contained in a respiratory chamber covered by a protective sheet (mantle shelf), which ends in a spout (siphon). Touching either the siphon or the mantle shelf elicits a defensive retraction of the gill.

➡ ***Aplysia*'s gill withdrawal reflex is analogous to what behavior in higher animals?**

Repeatedly presenting a weak tactile stimulus to *Aplysia* decreases the strength of its defensive withdrawal reaction (Figure 14.10), which satisfies our earlier definition of a type of learning called habituation—recall Amy's habituation to the feel of the jeans she is wearing. Habituation of *Aplysia*'s defensive response is stimulus-specific; that is, the decreased withdrawal reaction occurs only in response to a weak touch on a particular part of the animal's body. Similarly, Amy's habituation to the feel of the jeans is specific to that stimulus; if she changed pants, she would feel the new pair initially but would soon habituate to them as well.

If the tail of *Aplysia* is electrically shocked before its siphon is touched, the result is an exaggerated defensive reaction because of sensitization—an increase in the innate reactivity to a stimulus following exposure to an intense stimulus. Here you will recall Trisha's exaggerated startle reaction to the touch of her roommate. Unlike habituation, which occurs in response to a specific stimulus, the sensitizing effect is nonspecific. After exposure to an electric shock, any stimulus, even a weak one, will trigger a strong defensive reaction in *Aplysia.* Presumably, Trisha would also have had a greater reaction than normal to the sound of the telephone ringing.

The defensive reaction of *Aplysia* can be conditioned, and the conditioning is controlled by the same variables that affect all conditioned responses. For example, when a light touch to the mantle or siphon (CS) is paired with a strong electric shock to the tail (UCS), after several pairings, the light touch alone elicits the strong withdrawal response produced by the shock to the tail (CR) (Carew & others, 1983). In addition, when the CS precedes the UCS by a short time (0.5 seconds), conditioning proceeds rapidly (Hawkins & others, 1986), but the CR does not develop if the CS precedes the UCS by 2, 5, or 10 seconds or if the UCS precedes the CS (backward conditioning). Further, the CS produces a conditioned response that is the same as the unconditioned withdrawal response to the UCS (Hawkins & others, 1989).

Habituation of the defensive reaction of *Aplysia* lowers the responsivity of the synapses between the sensory and motor neurons involved in withdrawal (Hawkins & others, 1993) (Figure 14.10). This decrease reflects a decreased calcium (Ca^{2+}) ion influx into the sensory neuron and a reduced neurotransmitter release from its presynaptic membrane. In other words, habituation occurs through a decrease in neurotransmitter release at the synapse.

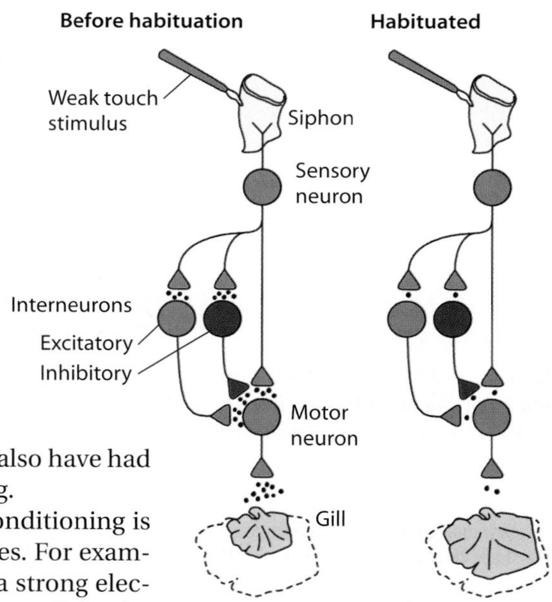

Figure 14.10

Habituation of the gill withdrawal response in Aplysia Repeated exposure to a weak tactile stimulus leads to a reduced withdrawal reaction (habituation). The neural circuit that mediates the habituation of the gill withdrawal response includes the sensory neuron, excitatory and inhibitory interneurons, and the motor neuron.

➡ **What is the mechanism for habituation?**

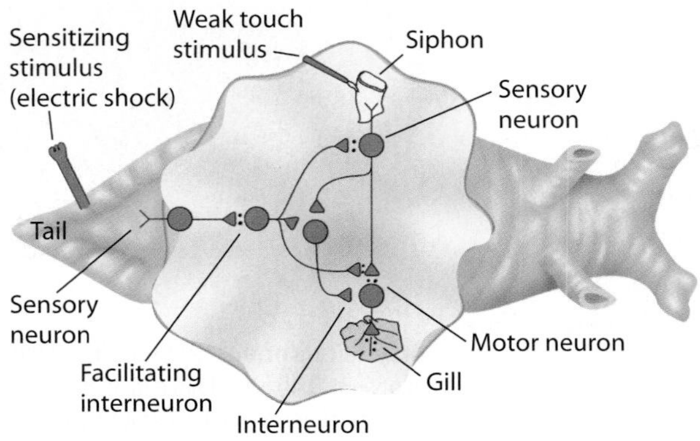

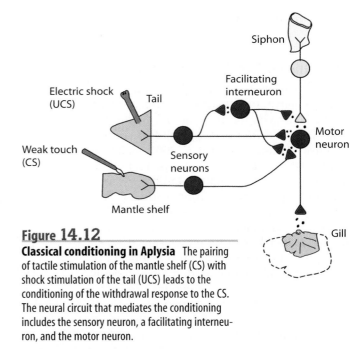

Figure 14.11
Sensitization of the gill withdrawal response in Aplysia Exposure of the tail to an intense electric shock leads to an increased withdrawal reaction to a weak tactile stimulus (sensitization). The neural circuit that mediates the sensitization includes the sensory neuron, a facilitating interneuron, and the motor neuron.

➡ **What is the mechanism for sensitization?**

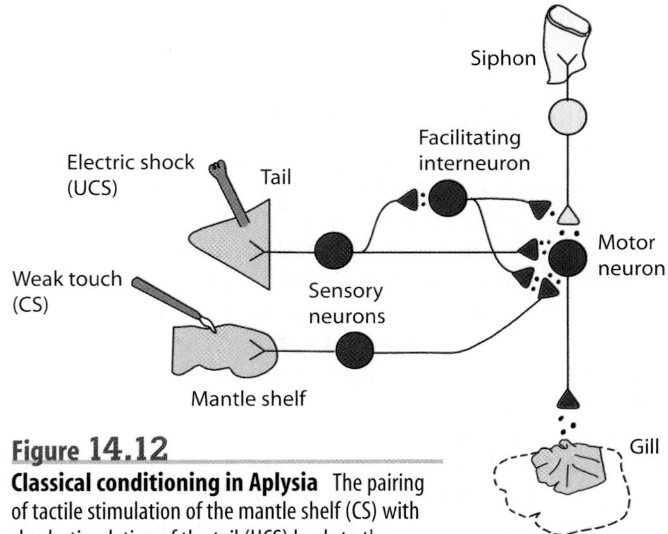

Figure 14.12
Classical conditioning in Aplysia The pairing of tactile stimulation of the mantle shelf (CS) with shock stimulation of the tail (UCS) leads to the conditioning of the withdrawal response to the CS. The neural circuit that mediates the conditioning includes the sensory neuron, a facilitating interneuron, and the motor neuron.

➡ **What is the mechanism for Pavlovian conditioning?**

Figures 14.11 and 14.12 show diagrammatically what happens during sensitization and conditioning of *Aplysia*'s defensive reflex (Hawkins & others, 1993). In either case, there is an increase in the responsivity of the synapses between the sensory and motor neurons of the reflex, which is caused by increased neurotransmitter release from the sensory neuron and increased activity in the motor neuron. The increased motor neuron activity is caused by presynaptic facilitation.

Kandel and his associates have identified the mechanism of synaptic facilitation in *Aplysia* (Bao & others, 1998). Some of the interneurons modulating the defensive reflex are serotonergic. When released from a facilitatory interneuron, serotonin increases the duration of the action potential in the sensory neuron by prolonging the closure of potassium (K^+) ion channels (Hawkins & others, 1993). Recall from Chapter 4 that during an action potential, K^+ ions leave the cell shortly after sodium (Na^+) ions enter. With reduced K^+ ion movement out of the cell as a result of the closed K^+ ion channels, the action potential lasts longer (Figure 14.13); this leads to greater Ca^{2+} ion movement into the presynaptic membrane of the sensory neuron, and thus greater neurotransmitter release into the synapse between the sensory and motor neurons. The same facilitation of neurotransmitter release from the sensory neuron occurs in either sensitization or conditioning. In summary, serotonin release from the facilitatory interneuron causes a decreased movement of K^+ ions from the sensory neuron, which increases the duration of the action potential, causing more Ca^{2+} ions to enter and more neurotransmitter to be released for uptake by the motor neuron—all of which strengthens the withdrawal response.

Figure 14.13
Changes in K^+ ion movement during an action potential (a) The typical sequence of ion movement; (b) the slower exit of K^+ ions from the cell caused by presynaptic facilitation.

➡ **How could a prolonged action potential play a role in memory storage and retrieval?**

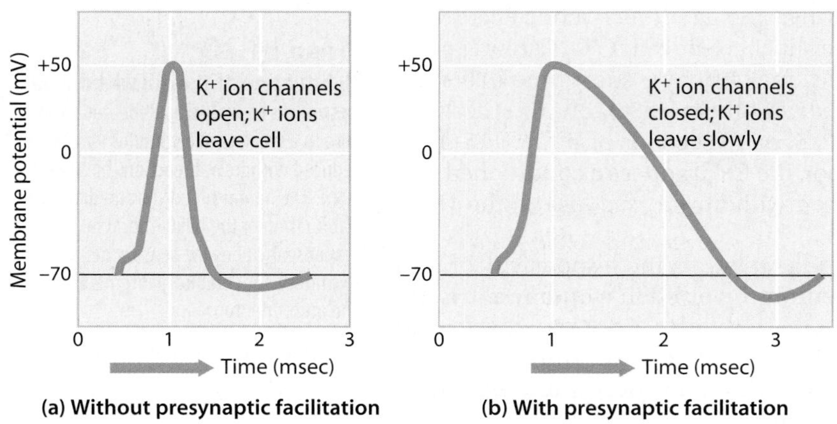

Although we have only scratched the surface in our description of it, Kandel's celebrated research shows that experience can alter the synaptic functioning of defensive reactions in *Aplysia.* This evidence for synaptic plasticity has implications far beyond the sea slug.

Assuming the mechanisms for habituation, sensitization, and conditioning are basically the same throughout the animal kingdom, as Darwinian evolution proposes, then Kandel's work with *Aplysia* suggests that learning in higher organisms will turn out to involve increases and decreases in neurotransmitter release.

Structural Changes and Storing Experiences

Gary Lynch found that experience enhances Ca^{2+} ion entry into hippocampal neurons and that the Ca^{2+} ions activate the enzyme *calpain* (e.g., Lynch, 1986; Lynch & Baudry, 1984). Calpain breaks down *fodrin,* a protein that coats the dendrites, exposing more glutamate receptors to stimulation from other neurons (Figure 14.14a, b)—that is, making the postsynaptic neuron more sensitive. With continued experience, more receptors are exposed, resulting in even greater sensitivity.

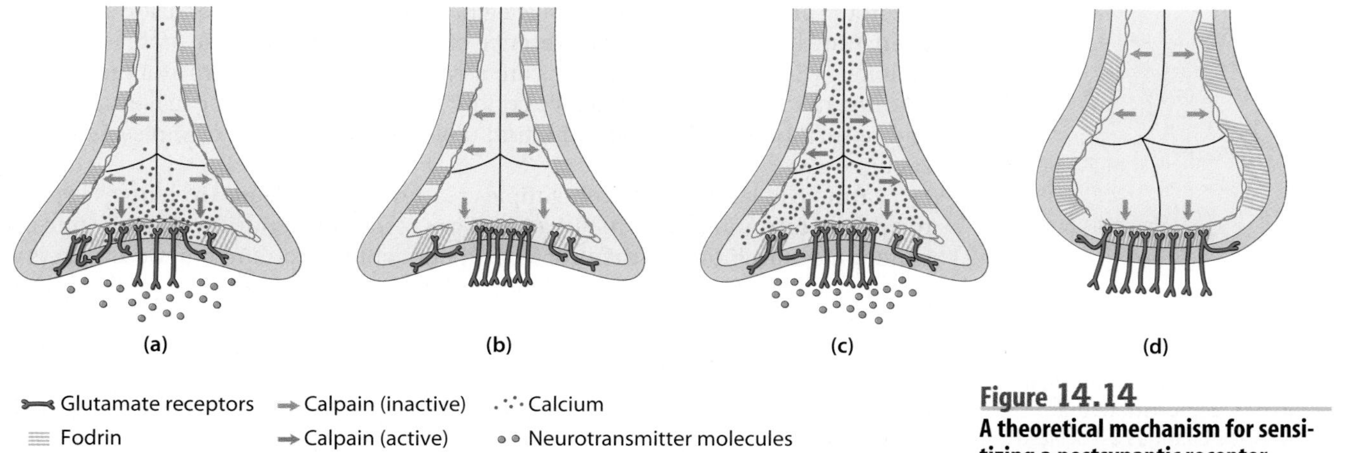

Figure 14.14
A theoretical mechanism for sensitizing a postsynaptic receptor (a) Neurotransmitter release causes an increase in Ca^{2+} ions inside the receptor; this activates calpain, which degrades fodrin and exposes more glutamate receptors. (b) Ca^{2+} ions are removed, which inactivates calpain, but the additional exposed glutamate receptors remain. (c) Repeated activity causes more Ca^{2+} ion entry because of the added receptors. This activates more calpain, which causes more degradation of fodrin and eventually a change in the shape of the receptor. (d) Ca^{2+} ions are removed, but the shape change and added receptors remain.

Where in the brain is this hypothetical activity assumed to occur?

Lynch and Baudry (1984) also theorized that repetitive stimulation causes further breakdown of the fodrin coating and eventually shape changes in the terminal button, which might be the mechanism for the permanence of long-term memory storage (Figure 14.14c, d). In Lynch's view, this change in sensitivity of new neural connections may be the biological basis of learning and memory. For example, Lynch and Baudry trained rats to find food in an eight-arm radial maze of the type shown in Figure 14.15. In this *spatial-learning* problem, food (as reinforcement) is placed in all eight arms, and the task of the rat is to visit each arm only once; if it goes down an already-visited arm, it finds no food at the end. The

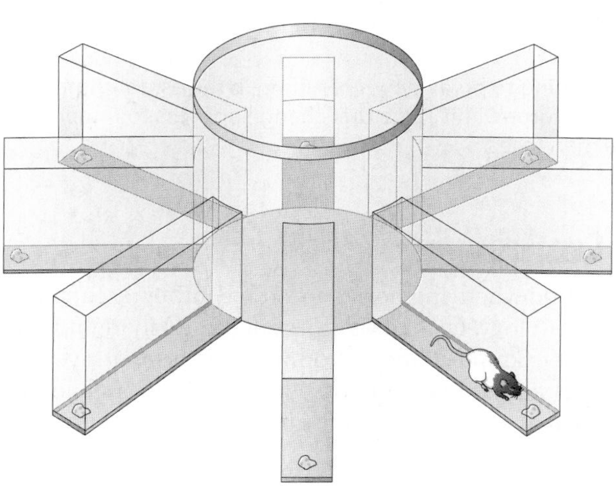

Figure 14.15
Use of a radial maze in studies of spatial learning and memory Reinforcement (food) is placed in each arm of the maze, and rats are trained to visit each arm without returning to a previously visited arm.

What is the effect of leupeptin on the performance of this task?

medial temporal lobe A brain area containing the hippocampus and surrounding cortical areas; involved in storing experiences.

anterograde amnesia An inability to recall events after injury to the brain.

rats quickly learned the task, and then, in the experimental rats, the researchers implanted a pump that infused the peptide leupeptin into cannulae in the lateral ventricles of the animal. Leupeptin inhibits the breakdown of fodrin and presumably prevents the establishment of new neural connections and spatial memories. The researchers found that although the leupeptin-treated rats showed obvious memory for their earlier training when placed in the radial maze, they made significantly more errors (re-entering an arm in which the food had already been consumed) than control animals.

As we noted in Chapter 3, early synaptic connections are formed during prenatal development by the attraction of spine-like extensions from the growth cones of developing neurons (filopodia) to chemicals (neurotrophins) released by target cells that guide the developing axon. A similar process seems to be involved in the establishment of new synaptic connections formed as a result of experience. For example, in rats, a type of neurotrophin called a neural cell adhesion molecule (NCAM) is produced both during nervous system development and beginning 6 to 8 hours after learning (Murphy & Regan, 1998). Increases in dendritic spine frequency are associated with the presence of the NCAMs, and these increases in the dentate gyrus of the hippocampus are associated with long-term storage of such learning tasks as passive avoidance conditioning, spatial learning in a water maze, and reward-based odor discrimination (Foley & others, 2003; O'Malley & others, 2000).

Learning, at least in relatively simple creatures, clearly leads to changes in neuronal structure and function. But going from sprouting dendrites and synaptic facilitation or inhibition to the processes that enable us to remember our past is a quantum leap. Moreover, the evidence indicates that memories are not stored in any specific location in the brain. The noted psychologist Karl Lashley (1950) failed to locate the *engram*—a memory trace, or the physical location of a memory—following decades of work with rats subjected to brain lesions either before or after they had been trained on some sort of task (Chapter 1). Lashley concluded, not entirely tongue-in-cheek, "I sometimes feel, in reviewing the evidence on the localization of the memory trace, that the necessary conclusion is that learning is just not possible" (pp. 477–478). Learning is possible, of course, and in the next section, we look at the evidence for the neural structures primarily involved.

➤Checkpoint

Why have researchers working with mammals not been able to demonstrate the synaptic changes associated with learning that Kandel has examined in *Aplysia*? What evidence do we need to show that the cellular modification theory holds for mammals?

REVIEW

- Reflecting the neuroplasticity of the brain, the cellular modification theory argues that learning can modify the responsivity of specific neurons and can produce structural changes in neurons.
- Studies on *Aplysia californica* have demonstrated that habituation, sensitization, and conditioning can result from specific chemical reactions at the synapse; habituation decreases neurotransmitter release, whereas sensitization and conditioning increase neurotransmitter release.
- Experience causes dendrite coating to break down, resulting in the establishment of new connections between neurons. This structural change appears to underlie the permanent storage of experiences.

◆ The Anatomy of Learning and Memory

Although Lashley (1950) failed to find where memories are stored, other researchers, often using Lashley's lesion methodology, have been more successful in identifying learning and memory systems. For example, Robert Thompson, who spent a year in Lashley's laboratory when he was a graduate student, sought to identify a learning/memory system in subcortical areas, which Lashley had avoided (Thompson, 1993).

Larry Squire and his colleagues have developed a model detailing the structures involved in declarative memory (Squire, 1998; Squire & others, 2004; Teng & others, 2000; Zola-Morgan & Squire, 1993) (Figure 14.16). They proposed that information initially processed in the cortical sensory areas is sent first to structures in the **medial temporal lobe** for further processing. Key structures in the medial temporal lobe include the hippocampus and surrounding cortical areas (perirhinal, entorhinal, and parahippocampal cortices), structures that provide for our recognition of the familiarity of recent events (Squire, 1998). Projections from these structures then convey information to diencephalic areas, such as the mammillary nuclei, the anterior thalamic nuclei, and the mediodorsal thalamic nuclei, where the information receives further processing before relay to the frontal lobe.

The frontal lobe plays a crucial role in the planning, execution, and control of behavior. The medial temporal lobe structures and the medial thalamus jointly may be essential for the formation of long-term memory, and connections between these structures and the frontal lobe may provide a route by which memories can influence behavior (Zola-Morgan & Squire, 1993). Long-term memory itself is formed elsewhere, presumably in the neocortex. Procedural or nondeclarative memories, of which habit learning is one example, involve the neocortex and the neostriatum. In particular, the caudate nucleus and putamen, structures in the basal ganglia, are needed for procedural learning (Squire, 1998). Finally, as we have seen in the work of Richard Thompson and his colleagues, classical conditioning of reflexes depends on the cerebellum (Swain & Thompson, 1993).

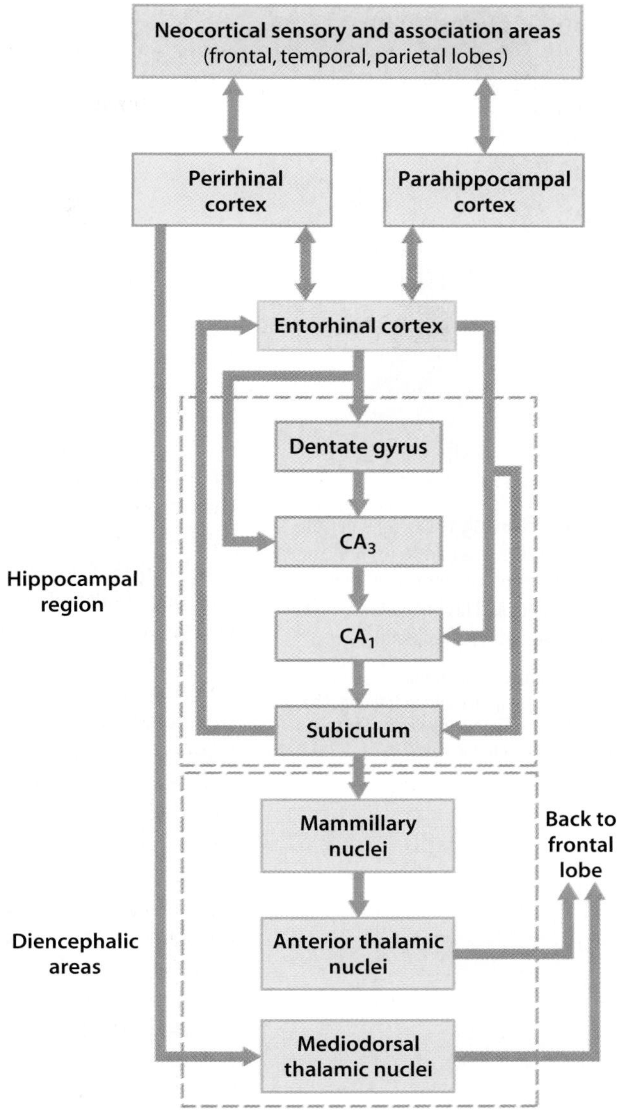

Figure 14.16

Key brain structures involved in declarative memory storage and retrieval Information travels from neocortical sensory and association areas to the medial temporal lobe (hippocampus and adjacent areas) and then to the diencephalic areas for further processing, before returning to the frontal lobe.

→ **What is the function of the connections between the memory structures located deep within the brain and the frontal lobe?**

The Medial Temporal Lobe

The Case of H.M.

In the annals of clinical cases contributing to our knowledge of brain function, probably none is more cited than the famous case of H.M. In 1953, H.M. had his medial temporal lobes (including the hippocampus, amygdala, and surrounding cortical tissue) removed as a treatment for severe epilepsy. Although the operation alleviated H.M.'s seizure problem, the unfortunate side effect was profound memory impairment. H.M. is good-natured and cooperative, and many researchers have examined his memory disorder over the years (e.g., Corkin, 2002; Kensinger & others, 2001; O'Kane & others, 2004; Scoville & Milner, 1957).

H.M.'s greatest impairment is **anterograde amnesia,** an inability to recall events that have occurred since the operation. For example, on each visit to the hospital, he has to be reintroduced to his doctors. H.M. also cannot recall events that took place in the several years leading up to his operation, but he can clearly remember events older than that, much like Chester in the opening vignette of this chapter. H.M. is fully aware of the extent of his memory loss:

> Every day is alone in itself, whatever enjoyment I've had, and whatever sorrow I've had. . . . Right now, I'm wondering. Have I done or said anything amiss? You see, at this moment everything looks clear to me, but what happened just before? That's what worries me. It's like waking from a dream; I just don't remember. (Milner, 1970, p. 37)

(a)

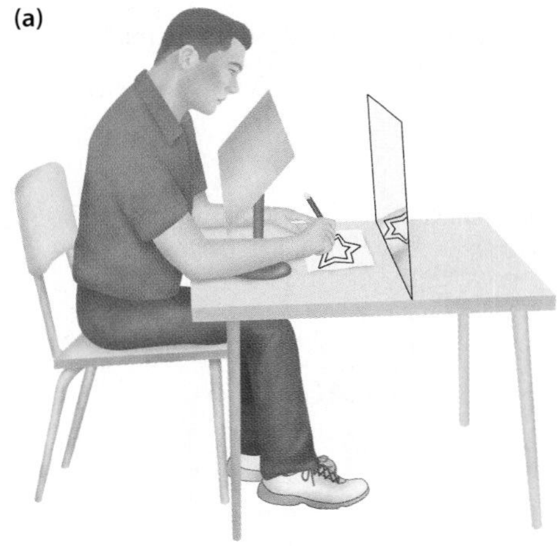

(b)

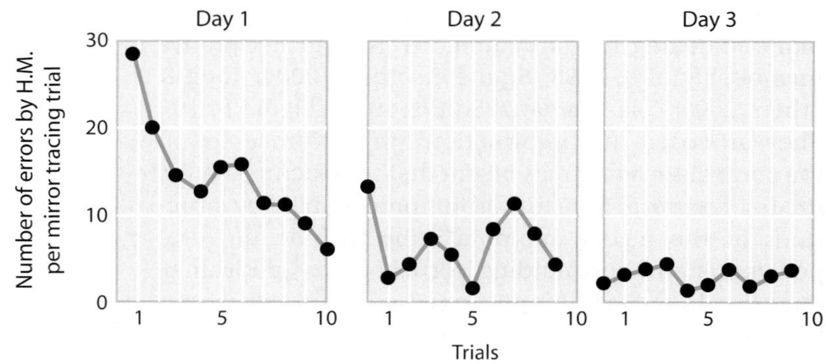

Figure 14.17

The mirror tracing task (a) A person traces a star seen in a mirror. (b) H.M. made fewer errors on this task during each day of training, and his improvement was retained over 3 days of training.

➡ **How could H.M.'s performance on the mirror tracing task improve during training if he could not remember having performed this task from one day to the next?**

Despite his severe memory impairment, some areas of H.M.'s memory remain intact. For example, although he cannot store declarative memories, he can store and recall procedural memories (Squire, 1987). Further, even though recent episodic memories are lost, semantic memories are not affected by his brain damage. H.M.'s language ability is intact and he can still read and write, but his speech contains no words introduced into the English language since his surgery (Gabrieli & others, 1988). For example, H.M. defined *flower child* as *a young person who grows flowers.* This failure to learn new terms further reflects his inability to store new facts (declarative memories).

Brenda Milner's work (1965) with H.M. clearly shows he can acquire new skills (procedural memories). In one study, H.M. participated in a mirror tracing task (Figure 14.17a), which involves tracing an object while looking at it in a mirror, without looking down at one's hand or the paper. Because the subject must draw in a direction opposite to the one indicated by the visual stimulus (the reflection in the mirror), the task is difficult and requires practice. H.M.'s performance improved over a series of trials each day. In addition, as you can see from Figure 14.17b, his improvement was maintained over 3 days of training, indicating that a memory of the task was formed. Despite his obvious retention of a procedural memory over days, however, H.M. was unable to remember participating in the task from one day to the next.

The reason for this discrepancy between an intact procedural memory and amnesia for the task itself is that tracing the figure is a visual-motor skill that involves procedural memory, which appears to be unaffected by damage to the medial temporal lobe (Squire, 1998; Squire & others, 2004). By contrast, awareness of having traced the figure is an episodic memory, and this type of memory storage does appear to be affected by medial temporal lobe damage.

Surprisingly, recent work with H.M. indicates that he has been able to acquire some knowledge of the world in the half-century following his surgery. Researchers used forced-choice and cued-recall recognition tasks to examine whether H.M. has any knowledge of people who have become famous since the onset of his amnesia (O'Kane & others, 2004). With first names as cues, H.M. recalled the corresponding famous last name for more than a third of such postoperatively famous personalities as Lyndon Johnson, Ray Charles, Sophia Loren, and Woody Allen. H.M. did even better on a task in which he was asked to identify the famous person of a pair that included a name selected from the Baltimore telephone directory. He correctly chose 88% of the names of people who had become famous after his surgery, a score that was not significantly different from the accuracy achieved by age-matched controls (H.M. was 76 at the time of testing). The researchers concluded that this latest work with H.M. shows that some semantic learning can occur through the use of structures beyond the hippocampus itself.

Although the case of H.M. is the most widely studied, it is not an isolated one; additional cases of amnesia following medial temporal lobe damage have been documented. For example, in a study of eight psychiatric patients whose medial temporal lobes had been removed in an attempt to reduce their behavioral problems, all experienced severe anterograde amnesia (Scoville & Milner, 1957).

The Importance of the Hippocampus

As a great deal of evidence suggests, of all the brain structures that are damaged by removal of the medial temporal lobe, the hippocampus is the key memory structure (e.g., Squire & others, 2004). For example, lesions to the hippocampus (including the dentate gyrus and the subicular complex) and surrounding areas in monkeys (perirhinal, entorhinal, and parahippocampal cortices) produce deficits in learning a simple object discrimination (Teng & others, 2000). Damage to the hippocampus, with minimal destruction of the perirhinal, entorhinal, and parahippocampal cortex, produced long-lasting impairment in monkeys on a delayed nonmatching-to-sample task, described below (Alvarez & others, 1995). Further, damage limited to the hippocampus produces less memory impairment than damage that includes adjacent areas such as the entorhinal and parahippocampal cortices (Alvarez & others; Zola-Morgan & others, 1994).

In a *delayed nonmatching-to-sample task,* the subject (a monkey) is shown a stimulus (the sample) and, after varying time intervals, is shown the sample and a second stimulus. The monkey must select which of the two stimuli is *not* the sample shown previously. Animals with hippocampal damage can identify the stimulus that is not the sample if the retention interval is short, but not if the interval is long. Further, the level of memory impairment is influenced by the extent of hippocampal damage, with some impairment when damage is confined to the hippocampus and greater deficits when the destruction also includes areas surrounding the hippocampus (Alvarez & others, 1995).

Researchers examined the memory of patient R.B., a 52-year-old man with coronary disease (Zola-Morgan & others, 1986). R.B. had suffered a cardiac arrest that caused a temporary loss of blood to his brain; the resulting lack of oxygen (anoxia) produced brain damage and profound anterograde amnesia. R.B. died 5 years after his cardiac arrest, and histological examination of his brain revealed a significant degeneration of hippocampal tissue (Figure 14.18). Damage to the hippocampus also has been linked to memory deficits in other patients (Rempel-Clower & others, 1996). For example, a high-resolution MRI of several patients with severe memory impairment revealed significant reduction in the size of the hippocampus in each case (Squire & others, 1990). An MRI performed on H.M. showed that most of his hippocampus and all of his entorhinal and parahippocampal cortices were absent bilaterally (Corkin & others, 1997) (Figure 14.19). In addition, in a study of six amnesic patients with damage limited to the hippocampus, as determined by a postmortem neurohistological analysis, all six exhibited significantly impaired recognition memory (Reed & Squire, 1997).

Although H.M. is unable to store most new declarative memories, he can retrieve such memories acquired before his surgery. This suggests that the hippocampus is involved in storing declarative memories but is not the site of storage. Researchers have pointed to the frontal and temporal lobes as the declarative memory storage sites (Gabrieli, 1998; Tulving, 1998), and Gabrieli has suggested that any particular type of knowledge, such as for words or for pictures, is confined to a specific, but widespread, network of neurons. Activation of such a network enables us to recall a past experience. In support of Gabrieli's and Tulving's suggestion

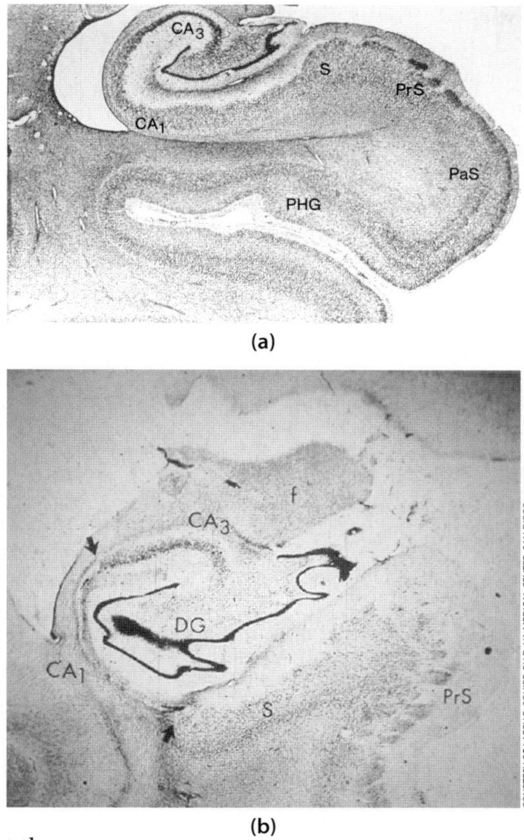

COURTESY OF LARRY R. SQUIRE, PH.D. VA MEDICAL CENTER, SAN DIEGO

Figure 14.18

The normal and damaged hippocampus These photomicrographs show (a) normal hippocampal structures and (b) the degeneration of hippocampal pyramidal cells in field CA_1 caused by a lack of oxygen.

➔ **What were the effects of degeneration of hippocampal cells on R.B.'s memory?**

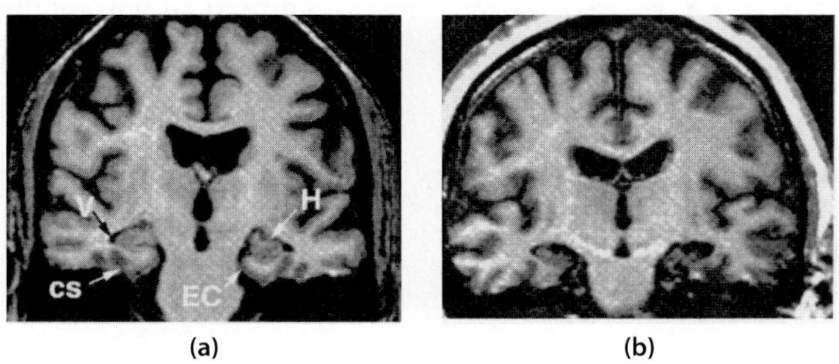

COURTESY OF SUZANNE CORKIN

Figure 14.19

MRI scans of the normal and damaged hippocampus The hippocampus (H) and entorhinal cortex (EC) (a) in a normal brain and (b) absent bilaterally in H.M.'s brain.

➔ **What were the consequences of bilateral removal of H.M.'s hippocampus?**

Checkpoint

Describe H.M.'s plight in your own words. What does this case imply about the role of memory in the ability to learn something new? What evidence suggests that damage to the medial temporal lobe affects declarative and episodic memory but leaves procedural and semantic memory intact?

of localization of declarative memory, PET scan studies have found that the frontal and temporal lobes of both hemispheres become active during the retrieval of past events (Nyberg & others, 1996; Tulving & Markowitsch, 1997). Nyberg and colleagues also found evidence for differential hemispheric encoding and retrieval processes, with episodic encoding primarily engaging the left frontal areas and episodic retrieval the right frontal regions.

In summary, the hippocampus and surrounding structures are critical for storing new declarative memories. We look next at how experience can modify the functioning of hippocampal neurons.

Long-Term Potentiation in the Hippocampus

As Kandel's elegant studies of *Aplysia* have demonstrated, experience can change synaptic responsivity in the sensory neurons controlling the animal's defensive withdrawal response (Antonov & others, 2001, 2003; Bao & others, 1998). Evidence for similar changes have been found in specific hippocampal pathways of rats (Lei & others, 2003; Wang & others, 2004). A brief, intense series of electrical impulses is applied to the afferent neurons in one of three pathways into the hippocampus: the perforant fiber, mossy fiber, and Schaffer collateral fiber pathways (discussed below). This stimulation causes increased synaptic responding when a test stimulus is later applied to the same pathway. Seen as an increase in the amplitude and duration of excitatory postsynaptic potentials (EPSPs) in response to the test stimulus, this increased responsivity is called **long-term potentiation (LTP).** Figure 14.20 shows a synaptic wave, or summation of EPSPs from a population of neurons, generated in response to a test stimulus before and after exposure to an intense potentiating stimulus. As you can see, the synaptic wave is as strong at 96 hours as it was at 1 hour following the intense electrical stimulation—hence the name *long-term* potentiation.

Figure 14.20
Long-term potentiation in the hippocampus These traces represent a summation of the EPSPs of a population of neurons in the dentate gyrus before and after application of a potentiating stimulus. Notice that increased synaptic responsivity persists for 96 hours following exposure to intense electrical stimulation.

➔ **How does the LTP phenomenon help us understand the physiological basis of learning and memory?**

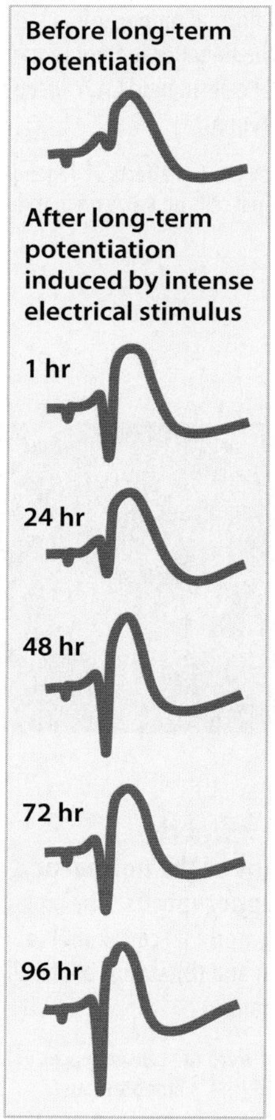

Neurons in the **perforant fiber pathway** (the red pathway in Figure 14.21), the most widely studied of the hippocampal pathways, are situated in the entorhinal cortex and connect to granule cells in the dentate gyrus. A brief series of intense electrical stimuli to the entorhinal cortex produces an increased reactivity of the neurons in the dentate gyrus. The other pathways in which LTP occurs are the **mossy fiber pathway** (green pathway), which begins in granule cells in the dentate gyrus and connects to the pyramidal cells in the CA_3 field of the hippocampus, and the **Schaffer collateral fiber pathway** (blue pathway), which begins in the hippocampal pyramidal cells of field CA_3 and connects to the pyramidal cells of hippocampal field CA_1. (CA stands for *cornu Ammonis,* which refers to the horn of Ammon, or horn of the ram; Ammon was an ancient Egyptian god.)

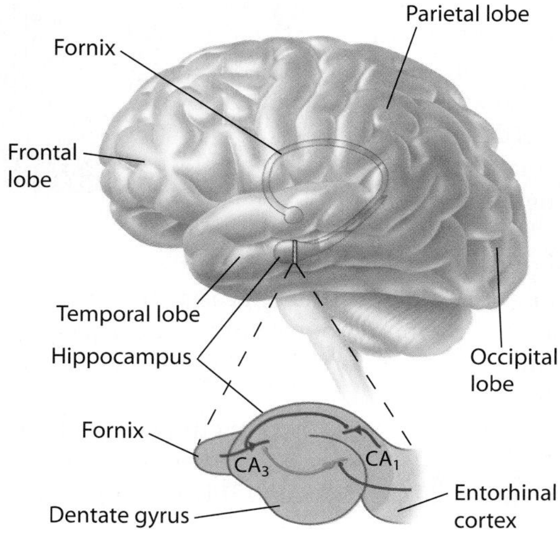

Figure 14.21
LTP and three neural circuits in the hippocampus LTP results from brief, intense stimulation of neurons in the perforant (red), mossy fiber (green), and Schaffer collateral (blue) pathways to the hippocampus. (Adapted from Kandel & others, 2000.)

➔ **Why does LTP separately affect the three hippocampal pathways?**

LTP has several key characteristics:

1. A brief sensitizing stimulus is sufficient to produce LTP, which demonstrates that hippocampal neurons can change synaptic responsivity following a single event.
2. The LTP-changed synaptic responsivity is confined to a specific neural pathway. For example, LTP induced in perforant fiber pathway neurons does not alter the synaptic responsivity of neurons in other hippocampal pathways.
3. LTP can be produced either by a single stimulus or by the convergence of stimuli that individually would not produce LTP. Analysis of an experience generally requires input from multiple sources. With the ability of several inputs to produce LTP, convergence of inputs to a specific pathway can modify synaptic responsivity.
4. LTP can last for days or weeks, which suggests that it is not just a temporary change in synaptic responsivity.

The increased synaptic responsivity of hippocampal neurons can be conditioned, which supports the idea that changes in neural activity underlie learning and memory. To demonstrate this conditioning, experimenters implanted stimulating electrodes into different fibers in hippocampal slices from the Schaffer collateral pathway of a rat brain, and administered two different weak stimuli and a strong stimulus through three separate electrodes (Kelso & Brown, 1986). Forward pairings of the weak stimuli or presentations of the strong stimulus by itself failed to produce associative LTP, as did backward pairings of the weak and strong stimuli. Forward pairings of the weak and strong stimuli resulted in associative LTP, and the researchers concluded that the mechanism that produces this plasticity in hippocampal neurons probably participates in conditioning.

LTP appears to occur through a modification in the NMDA (*N*-methyl-D-aspartate) receptor in the perforant and Schaffer collateral pathways (Kandel, 2000a). The **NMDA receptor** is sensitive to the neurotransmitter glutamate. By itself, glutamate does not produce an action potential at the NMDA receptor, because magnesium (Mg^{2+}) ions block the ion channels of the NMDA receptor and glutamate by itself cannot dislodge them (Figure 14.22). In order for the NMDA receptor to be activated, it must already have been partially depolarized by nearby EPSPs from several afferent axons by the time the glutamate reaches the postsynaptic membrane. When the Mg^{2+} ions are expelled, Ca^{2+} ions can now enter through the receptor channels. Earlier we described how calpain breaks down fodrin, a coating on dendrites, to expose more receptor sites to stimulation. As it turns out, calpain release is activated by the influx of Ca^{2+} ions into NMDA receptors, altering the reactivity and ultimately the structure of the postsynaptic membrane. This alteration is responsible for LTP and increased synaptic responsivity. Kandel refers to the type of LTP in the perforant and Schaffer collateral pathways as *associative*. In associative learning, the organism learns a relationship between two stimuli (classical conditioning) or between behavior and the consequences of that behavior (operant conditioning).

In the mossy fiber pathway, glutamate is released from the granule cells onto the target pyramidal cells in the CA_3 field, and the glutamate binds to both NMDA and non-NMDA receptors (Kandel, 2000a). In this case, however, the NMDA receptors play only a minor role in synaptic plasticity. LTP apparently depends not on Ca^{2+} influx into the postsynaptic receptor but on Ca^{2+} influx into the presynaptic cell after the LTP-inducing stimulus. Kandel refers to the LTP in the mossy fiber pathway as *nonassociative;* in nonassociative learning, the organism learns about the properties of a single stimulus. Habituation and sensitization are examples of this type of learning.

After this long discussion about LTP, you may be wondering how we know that this phenomenon is involved in learning. Microinfusions of agonists and antagonists of neurotransmitter receptors were used to study memory of avoidance

long-term potentiation (LTP) An increased neural responsivity that follows a brief, intense series of electrical impulses to neural tissue.

perforant fiber pathway The most widely studied of three pathways into the hippocampus; intense stimulation of its neurons produces LTP.

mossy fiber pathway One of the afferent pathways into the hippocampus; intense electrical stimulation of its neurons produces LTP.

Schaffer collateral fiber pathway One of the afferent pathways into the hippocampus; intense electrical stimulation of its neurons produces LTP.

NMDA receptor A receptor that is sensitive to the neurotransmitter glutamate.

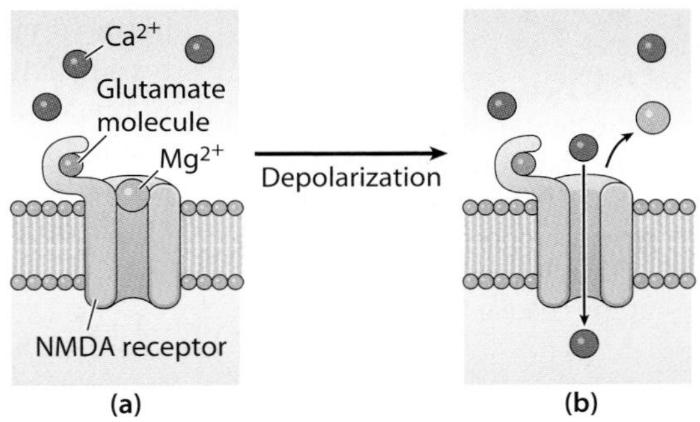

Figure 14.22
Ion changes at the NMDA receptor that result in LTP (a) When Mg^{2+} ions block the ion channel, glutamate cannot activate the NMDA receptor. (b) Depolarization of the postsynaptic membrane as a result of activation of non-NMDA receptors causes Mg^{2+} ions to leave the channel. Glutamate can now activate the NMDA receptor, allowing Ca^{2+} ions to pass through the ion channel into the postsynaptic membrane.

What is the role of the NMDA receptor in LTP?

retrograde messenger A chemical sent from the postsynaptic membrane to the presynaptic membrane to maintain neurotransmitter release.

long-term depression (LTD) A persistent activity-dependent reduction in synaptic effectiveness.

conditioning and habituation to a novel environment in rats (Izquierdo, 1995). Izquierdo concluded that his results provided evidence for memory mediation by LTP in such areas of the brain as the hippocampus, amygdala, and entorhinal cortex (Izquierdo & Medina, 1993). In addition, injection of drugs that block NMDA receptors impairs spatial learning (Shapiro, 2001). For example, in the radial maze test, animals receiving drugs that block NMDA receptors repeatedly go to arms that do not contain food or fail to return consistently to arms where food is located. These results suggest that LTP in the NMDA receptors of the hippocampus is crucial to the ability of an animal to learn about its spatial environment.

LTP is produced not only by changes in postsynaptic responsivity but also by changes in presynaptic responsivity—by an increase in presynaptic neurotransmitter release. Several studies have reported increased glutamate release following exposure to a potentiating stimulus (Goussakov & others, 2000; Maguire & others, 1999; Manahan-Vaughan & others, 1999). Such increases may be maintained over time by the action of a **retrograde messenger,** sent from the postsynaptic membrane back to the presynaptic membrane to maintain neurotransmitter release. Studies have shown that the soluble gas nitric oxide (NO) is a retrograde messenger for LTP (Arancio & others, 1996; Hawkins & others, 1994; Ko & Kelly, 1999). For example, the administration of an NO inhibitor blocked LTP (Ko & Kelly), and the application of NO to hippocampal slices produced a rapid and long-lasting increase in the size of synaptic potentials, but only if the application occurred at the same time as weak stimulation of the presynaptic fibers (Hawkins & others). Carbon monoxide (CO), another soluble gas, also seems to act as a retrograde messenger for LTP (Fin & others, 1995; Hawkins & others).

In summary, an intense stimulus can produce an increased synaptic reactivity in the hippocampus, a long-term potentiation. This causes increased postsynaptic responsivity and enhanced neurotransmitter release from the presynaptic membrane, which maintains LTP until permanent changes in the NMDA receptors can occur. LTP is interesting to neuroscientists because it may be an example of learning at the cellular level. Presumably H.M. has lost many of the cells required for LTP and is thus unable to form most new memories.

➤Checkpoint

How do the characteristics of LTP suggest that it might be related to learning? What evidence supports the idea that LTP is a learning phenomenon at the cellular level?

Long-Term Depression in the Hippocampus

As we have indicated, long-lasting, activity-dependent increases in the effectiveness of synaptic transmission (LTP) in the hippocampus may play an important role in learning and memory. Not surprisingly, the opposite process also appears to be involved. **Long-term depression (LTD)** is a persistent, activity-dependent reduction in synaptic effectiveness. It can be induced by repeated low-frequency stimulation, and LTD in the CA_1 region of the hippocampus has been reported to be involved in novelty acquisition in rats and in their reaction to stressful situations (Braunewell & Manahan-Vaughan, 2001).

Like long-term potentiation, LTD seems to involve changes in postsynaptic glutamate receptors (Blitzer & others, 2005), with NMDA receptors (Shapiro, 2001) and AMPA receptors (Bredt & Nicoll, 2003; Malenka, 2003; Malinow & Malenka, 2002) particularly affected. The persistence of LTP and LTD over long periods requires gene transcription (DNA to RNA) and translation (RNA to protein) (Blitzer & others) to produce changes in postsynaptic receptor density, although presynaptic changes may also play a role. Such LTP and LTD can last for minutes or hours and may be the basis of learning and memory storage (Vickery & others, 1997).

Deficits in LTD, like deficits in LTP, are associated with impaired learning and memory (Lee & others, 2003). In one experiment, mice were created with mutations in their $GluR_1$ phosphorylation sites ($GluR_1$ is a subunit of the AMPA glutamate receptor, and phosphorylation—the addition of a phosphate group to a molecule—is necessary for many forms of synaptic plasticity). The resulting mice were defective in both LTD and LTP and had memory deficits in spatial learning tasks. The researchers concluded that phosphorylation of $GluR_1$ is crucial for both LTD and LTP and the retention of memories (Lee & others). Further, mice deficient in calcineurin (a calcium-dependent protein phosphatase, which removes a phosphate from a molecule) had diminished LTD at Schaffer collateral CA_1 synapses (Zeng & others, 2001). As a result, the animals were impaired on hippocampus-dependent episodic memory problems, such as the radial maze task.

neuroplasticity The modifiability of the brain that allows adaptation to changing environmental conditions.

Neuroplasticity in the Hippocampus

The hippocampus and surrounding areas clearly are vitally involved in learning and memory, particularly of new information. Recent work on rodents indicates that learning that involves the hippocampus enhances the survival of new hippocampal neurons (Ambrogini & others, 2000; Leuner & others, 2004; Gould & others, 1999; Shors & others, 2001). We first mentioned this research in Chapter 3, in the context of *neurogenesis,* the formation of new neurons, which helps provide for **neuroplasticity,** or the modifiability of the brain to help in adaptation to changing environmental conditions. This work has revealed that several thousand hippocampal cells are formed daily and many of them die within a few weeks. Elizabeth Gould and colleagues reported that learning tasks that involve the hippocampus—such as Pavlovian trace conditioning, in which the animal must associate stimuli separated by time (temporal-based learning)—doubled the number of surviving neurons in the dentate gyrus. By contrast, learning tasks that did not involve the hippocampus had no effect on the survival of new neurons.

As further evidence for the importance of newly created hippocampal cells for learning, treatments that reduced the number of newly generated hippocampal neurons impaired learning that involves the hippocampus, but had no effect on learning that does not involve the hippocampus, such as conditioning involving two simultaneous stimuli (Shors & others, 2001). In addition, in research using a hippocampus-dependent spatial-learning task based on activity in a water maze, individual learning was found to be correlated with the new-cell survival rate (Ambrogini & others, 2000). Individual differences in associative learning appear to predict the survival rate of new neurons, which survive well beyond the time they are required in retention tests (Leuner & others, 2004).

New hippocampal neurons may participate in the formation of memories by the hippocampus; that is, they may become part of neural circuits established by a temporal-based learning experience (Shors & others, 2001). This is why a reduced production of new cells impairs hippocampus-dependent learning and the recovery of neuron production allows such learning. For example, age-related impairments in the ability of a rat to learn a hippocampus-dependent task (the water maze) were related to hippocampal neurogenesis, with unimpaired aged rats having a higher level of new-cell formation than age-impaired animals (Drapeau & others, 2003).

A series of studies that began in the late 1950s demonstrated that enriching the environment in which rats develop, by group housing the animals and including a variety of stimulating objects in their living quarters, increased the size of the animals' brains, their levels of cortical ACh, and their learning ability (e.g., Rosenzweig & Bennett, 1996). As more recent studies have shown, enriched environments can also increase hippocampal neurogenesis, and the effect occurs even in adult animals (Duffy & others, 2001; Nilsson & others, 1999; Williams & others, 2001). For example, Nilsson and colleagues found that the number of new cells in the dentate gyrus of adult rats was greatly increased by 4 weeks of environmental enrichment, and the animals also showed improved performance in a spatial-learning task. Duffy and colleagues demonstrated that environmental enrichment in mice resulted in improved memory for fear conditioning and enhanced LTP in hippocampal slices.

The Role of Genetics in LTP

As we have indicated, a change in the synaptic plasticity of specific neurons in the hippocampus is responsible for temporal-based learning and memory. Kandel has suggested that the establishment of long-term synaptic plasticity is regulated by specific genes (e.g., Nguyen & others, 2000; Pittenger & Kandel, 1998). Pittinger and Kandel, for example, have identified an activator (ApCREB1) and a repressor (ApCREB2) for genes that control the late phase of synaptic facilitation in *Aplysia.*

Levels of a protein involved in gene expression (cyclic AMP-responsive element-binding protein, or CREB) increase during LTP in the rat hippocampus (Kasahara & others, 2001). Phosphorylation of CREB was significantly reduced in a strain of genetically altered mice, and these animals had impaired long-term memory (Kang & others, 2001).

Researchers have provided additional evidence for a genetic control of synaptic plasticity in LTP (Wilson & others, 1999). They created a mouse strain deficient in endothelial nitric oxide synthase. (Recall that NO is a retrograde messenger for LTP, and NO is synthesized by NO synthase.) Stimulation of a region of the hippocampus that would normally produce LTP failed to produce LTP in these genetically altered mice.

➤Checkpoint

What parallels exist between synaptic responsivity in *Aplysia* and LTP in rats?

REVIEW

- ➤ Information is first processed in the cortical sensory areas, then travels to the medial temporal lobe and on to the mediodorsal thalamus for further processing.
- ➤ In the medial temporal lobe, key areas responsible for memory are the hippocampus and its surrounding structures, which are intricately connected to the frontal lobe and to the mammillary bodies of the hypothalamus.
- ➤ Damage to the medial temporal lobe causes anterograde amnesia, an inability to recall events subsequent to the damage, that is limited to episodic and declarative memory.
- ➤ Long-term potentiation (LTP), or increased synaptic responsivity, can be produced by a single stimulus or a series of stimuli. It is confined to the pathway that receives the stimulus, and it may last for days or weeks.
- ➤ LTP may result from presynaptic facilitation or increased postsynaptic responsivity.
- ➤ Long-term depression (LTD), or a decrease in synaptic effectiveness, is also thought to be involved in learning and memory.
- ➤ Experience enhances neurogenesis in the hippocampus, and the new cells participate in establishing neural circuits to mediate the learning and memory—an illustration of the neuroplasticity of the brain.

The Role of the Mediodorsal Thalamus

To this point, we have discussed the effects on memory of damage to structures in the medial temporal lobe, particularly the hippocampus and associated areas. Damage to the medial thalamus—specifically, the **mediodorsal thalamus**—has also been associated with profound memory impairment (Li & others, 2004; Van der Werf & others, 2003). For example, one study found that monkeys with lesions restricted mostly to the posterior portion of the mediodorsal thalamus performed poorly on a test of memory that detects human amnesia but showed no impairment on a skill-based task (Zola-Morgan & Squire, 1985). In other words, like the medial temporal lobe, the mediodorsal thalamus appears to be involved in the memory of facts (declarative memories) not skills (procedural memories). However, although extensive damage to the medial thalamus resulted in severe deficits in recent memory, more selective damage produced only mild memory deficits, not severe amnesia like that observed following hippocampal damage (Aggleton, 1986).

Memory impairments have also been seen in humans following mediodorsal thalamic nuclei damage (Halliday & others, 1994; Zoppelt & others, 2003). For example, people with thalamic lesions with or without involvement of the mediodorsal nucleus were assessed on a word list discrimination task for their recollection and sense of familiarity with the material. Lesions that included the mediodorsal thal-

mediodorsal thalamus A brain structure associated with profound memory impairment.

amus produced recollection deficits, with some evidence that the nucleus contributes to familiarity (Zoppelt & others).

In addition to memory loss caused by strokes, severe memory impairment is also common in chronic alcoholics. This memory loss was first described by Russian neurologist Sergei Korsakoff in 1889. His alcoholic patients failed to recall past events, and if an event recurred, they showed no evidence of having experienced it previously. This disorder is now known as **Korsakoff's syndrome**—Dr. Sauer's diagnosis of Chester's condition in the opening vignette.

Korsakoff's syndrome A severe memory impairment usually seen in chronic alcoholics.

confabulation A tendency to make up stories to fill in gaps in memory.

Alcohol contains a lot of calories, so chronic alcoholics often drink rather than eat, resulting in poor nutrition. Korsakoff's syndrome is caused by a thiamine deficiency. Thiamine (vitamin B_1) is needed to metabolize glucose, and a thiamine deficiency leads to the atrophy of brain cells, especially in the mammillary bodies of the hypothalamus (Squire & others, 1990). Recall that the mammillary bodies are part of the Papez circuit (Chapter 12). Using MRI, Squire and colleagues found that alcoholic Korsakoff's syndrome was associated with barely detectable mammillary bodies, whereas the temporal lobes and associated structures (hippocampus, etc.) were normal sized. By contrast, patients with amnesia but without Korsakoff's syndrome had markedly reduced hippocampal formations, with much less reduction in the size of their mammillary bodies.

Although undersized mammillary bodies are frequently seen in patients with Korsakoff's syndrome, (e.g., Shear & others, 1996; Visser & others, 1999), the extent of the reduction is not always associated with the extent of the anterograde amnesia. For example, using MRI, Shear and coworkers found both mammillary body and cerebellar shrinkage in chronic alcoholics, but the shrinkage did not differentiate between patients with amnesia and patients without amnesia. Also using MRI, Visser and coworkers found that the amnesia of Korsakoff's syndrome was associated with shrinkage in the midline thalamic nuclei but not with atrophy of either the mammillary bodies or the hippocampus and associated structures. However, compared with alcoholics without amnesia and with control subjects, the alcoholics with Korsakoff's syndrome had reductions in the size of their hippocampus, thalamus, and mammillary bodies.

Many alcoholics also have atrophy of cells in the mediodorsal thalamic nuclei and the anterior thalamic nuclei. For example, in a study of various diencephalic areas (thalamus, hypothalamus) in both amnesic and nonamnesic alcoholics, substantial neuronal degeneration was found in the mammillary bodies and in the mediodorsal thalamic nuclei in both alcoholic groups, but only the alcoholics with Korsakoff's syndrome had consistent neuronal loss in the anterior thalamic nuclei (Harding & others, 2000). In an earlier paper, these researchers had reported cell loss in both the mediodorsal thalamic nuclei and the anterior thalamic nuclei in alcoholic patients with Korsakoff's syndrome (Halliday & others, 1994).

Like H.M., individuals with Korsakoff's syndrome have profound anterograde amnesia. The memory impairment in Korsakoff's syndrome involves a loss of declarative rather than procedural memory. For example, tests of Korsakoff's syndrome patients on a skill-learning task (mirror reading) and a verbal recognition task found that they had great difficulty recognizing the words but learned the mirror reading task itself normally (Martone & others, 1984). These results suggest that the patients retained knowledge of the contingency between behavior and reinforcement (procedural memory) but forgot the actual words they had seen (declarative memory).

Although people with mediodorsal thalamic damage show memory deficits similar to those seen in medial temporal lobe damage, there are important differences between the two groups. For example, individuals (like H.M.) with medial temporal lobe damage are aware of their memory deficits. By contrast, those with Korsakoff's syndrome, from whatever source, are unaware of their memory loss. They use **confabulation,** the making up of stories, to fill in the gaps in their memories (Benson & others, 1996; Inagaki & others, 2003). Think of what Chester told the doctor about his breakfast, and you will have a good example of confabulation.

Emotion is generally intact following medial temporal lobe damage, whereas individuals tend to be emotionally flat and apathetic after mediodorsal thalamic damage. The confabulation and lack of insight in Korsakoff's syndrome patients are probably caused by frontal lobe damage (Benson & others, 1996; Demery & others, 2001; Inagaki & others, 2003). For example, Benson and colleagues used single-photon emission CT (SPECT) to study the brain of a 32-year-old woman with alcohol-induced Korsakoff's syndrome. During an early examination, the woman exhibited severe amnesia with confabulation; her SPECT showed reduced activity in the orbital and medial frontal lobe areas, along with depressed activity in the medial diencephalic region. Later examination showed continued amnesia without confabulation; activity in the frontal lobe had returned to normal, but there was little change in the diencephalic scans. The mediodorsal thalamus projects to the prefrontal cortex, and individuals with Korsakoff's syndrome have impairments similar to those occurring with prefrontal damage.

Checkpoint

If you could examine Chester's brain, would you expect to find more shrinkage in his mammillary bodies, his mediodorsal thalamic nuclei, or his anterior thalamic nuclei? Contrast the effects of mediodorsal thalamic damage and medial temporal lobe damage.

The Caudate Nucleus-Putamen Memory System

Squire (1998) proposed two separate memory systems: (1) the hippocampal-mediodorsal thalamic system, which mediates temporal-based episodic (declarative) memories; and (2) the caudate nucleus-putamen system, which controls skill (procedural) memories. We have already discussed one piece of evidence supporting this differentiation—the finding that Korsakoff's syndrome patients are significantly impaired in episodic memories, but their ability to learn habits (procedural memory) is relatively intact (Martone & others, 1984).

Research also points to the *corpus striatum*—the *caudate nucleus* and *putamen*—as the brain structures that control the ability to develop procedural memories (Packard & Teather, 1997; Setlow & McGaugh, 1999). For example, Packard and Teather trained rats on either a spatial task, which tests the recognition of places previously visited, or a cued task, which involves learning a habitual response to a cue. The rats were then injected with saline (controls) or with an NMDA antagonist into the hippocampus or the dorsal part of the corpus striatum. Hippocampal injection of the antagonist impaired memory in the spatial task without affecting cued-task performance, whereas injection of antagonist into the corpus striatum impaired memory in the cued task without affecting spatial learning. Given that the corpus striatum is involved in integrating movements to eliminate extraneous actions (Chapter 8), it is not surprising that these basal ganglia structures are also involved in the control of the acquisition and memory of motor skills.

The Amygdala and Memory

Perhaps you have noticed that you are more likely to recall memories acquired under stressful conditions. Stress enhances memory, and the effect of stress on memory involves the amygdala (McGaugh & others, 1996; Packard & Cahill, 2001).

McGaugh and colleagues (1996) described several lines of evidence for the memory-modulating effects of the amygdala. For example, in rats, infusions into the amygdala of epinephrine and glucocorticoids (stress-related substances) enhance memory for a learned task, whereas lesions of the amygdala or the injection of beta-adrenergic blocking agents block the memory-enhancing effects of epinephrine and the glucocorticoids. In addition, these investigators indicated that research on humans is consistent with animal research in demonstrating that blocking agents decrease the effects of emotional arousal on memory. The recall of emotional material is highly related to activation of the right amygdala during encoding of the memory for the material, as observed by PET.

Damage to the areas controlling memory, as described thus far, can result from such conditions as chronic alcoholism, stroke, or other events that limit blood flow to key brain structures, as well as from head trauma. In the next section, we discuss another major cause of memory impairment: Alzheimer's disease, a progressive, debilitating disorder for which there currently is no cure.

dementia A loss or impairment of mental functioning.

Alzheimer's disease (AD) A type of dementia characterized by progressive neurological degeneration and a profound deterioration of mental functioning.

REVIEW

- Damage to the mediodorsal thalamus is associated with anterograde amnesia and with Korsakoff's syndrome. Atrophy of the mammillary bodies also is associated with Korsakoff's syndrome.
- The mediodorsal thalamus projects to the prefrontal cortex, and individuals with damage to the thalamus, like people with prefrontal lobe damage, confabulate and show a lack of insight into their condition.
- The corpus striatum (caudate nucleus and putamen) mediates the storage and retrieval of skill or procedural memories.
- The amygdala modulates the memory of emotional experiences.

Alzheimer's Disease

"It's nothing to worry about, Beth," Greg had told his wife in the early days of her problem. "We're just getting older, and all our friends report the same kind of forgetfulness."

Well, not quite the same. Beth seemed unusually forgetful. She would park her car at the mall and be unable to find it, or she would get lost on the way home from their daughter's house, a drive she had made hundreds of times. In addition, there were changes in emotionality. She would fly off the handle at trivial things, screaming and cursing over a dropped plate, then she was filled with remorse afterwards.

As the months went by, Beth's forgetfulness worsened. A careful bookkeeper, she had always maintained the family's finances. Then one day she confessed to Greg that she could no longer reconcile their checking account. "I just don't know what to do with it anymore, Greg," she said tearfully. "I know there are some steps to follow, but I just can't remember them."

With the urging of Greg and their adult children, Beth finally consented to see her doctor. A standard physical examination revealed nothing that could account for her symptoms, and the physician strongly urged further tests and said he suspected Alzheimer's disease. Perhaps because she had lived with the problem so long, Beth didn't seem particularly upset, but Greg was horrified. He knew that Alzheimer's would destroy the woman he had known and loved for 47 years, leaving only a shell of a person to be cared for until she died.

Beth suffers from dementia of the Alzheimer's type, or Alzheimer's disease. **Dementia,** a term derived from two Latin words meaning "away" and "mind," is a loss or impairment of mental functioning. In **Alzheimer's disease (AD),** the impairment occurs in language (e.g., anomia or word-finding problems, as discussed in Chapter 13); in memory (e.g., forgetting how to prepare a meal); in visual-spatial orientation (e.g., becoming lost in a familiar area); and in judgment (e.g., wearing a bathrobe on a shopping trip to the mall).

Although several conditions can lead to dementia, Alzheimer's disease is the most common. First described by the German physician Alois Alzheimer in 1907, its symptoms can become apparent as early as age 40 but are more likely to occur at more advanced ages. For many years, AD was considered a rare form of dementia that only affected relatively young people between the ages of about 40 and 60. In the last few decades, neuroscientists have recognized that the hallmark neuronal pathologies characterizing AD are the same in both young sufferers and the elderly. Thus, AD, far from being a rare form of dementia, is now known to be relatively common, affecting about 4.5 million people in the U.S. population in 2000, with a predicted increase to more than 13 million in 2050 (Hebert & others, 2003).

neurofibrillary tangle An unusual triangular and looped fiber in the cytoplasm of neurons that is a hallmark of AD.

senile plaque A granular deposit of amyloid beta protein and the remains of degenerated dendrites and axons; found in large numbers in the brains of people with AD.

amyloid beta protein A protein that accumulates in neural tissue and is thought to cause the degeneration of neural fibers and disruption of neural connections in specific brain areas that are characteristic of AD.

Although AD is more common in women, this may simply reflect the fact that women live longer than men (Hebert & others, 2001). AD is also more common in elderly African Americans than in non-Hispanic whites; estimates of the difference between the two populations range between 14% and 100%, according to the Alzheimer's Association. AD is characterized by a gradual onset and, at later stages, a progressive deterioration of mental functioning. Because the neuropathology does not involve brain areas necessary for life, it is more appropriate to say that people die with AD than that they die from the disease.

When the symptoms of AD appear before age 65, the person is likely to be diagnosed as having early-onset Alzheimer's, as opposed to the "normal," or late-onset, form of the disease. Research is focused on differentiating early-onset from late-onset cases because of the greater evidence supporting a genetic basis for the former than for the latter.

Well-established risk factors for AD include increasing age, a familial clustering of cases, and Down syndrome. Another widely studied predisposing factor is the presence of a particular form of the apolipoprotein E gene (ApoE) on chromosome 19. Additional factors sometimes associated with the disorder are a low educational level, depression, head injury, hypertension, and aluminum in the water supply. In recent years, epidemiological studies have indicated a protective role against AD for such things as nonsteroidal anti-inflammatory drugs (NSAIDs) used to treat arthritis; estrogen use by postmenopausal women; a diet high in vitamins B_6, B_{12}, and folate; and red wine in moderate quantities (McDowell, 2001).

The Stages of Alzheimer's Disease

For diagnostic purposes, AD can be divided into three stages according to the severity of deficits in functioning (Table 14.3). Mild anterograde amnesia characterizes *stage I* (*early* or *mild AD*). For example, a person in this stage of the disease forgets where he or she has left the car keys or parked the car. Beth, from our opening vignette, is in stage 1. In *stage II* (*middle* or *moderate AD*), the person begins to lose memory of all recent events. In *stage III* (*late* or *severe AD*), in addition to having a much impaired recent memory, the person cannot recognize family members or remember distant events, such as those that occurred in childhood.

The amnesia associated with AD is different from that of Korsakoff's syndrome. People with AD lose semantic and procedural memories as well as episodic and declarative memories, and they do not use confabulation to fill in the gaps. Beth's inability to reconcile the checking account illustrates the loss of procedural memory.

Table 14.3
Characteristics of the Three Stages of Alzheimer's Disease

	Other Terms	Intelligence	Personality	Language
Stage I	Early Mild	Forgetful Disoriented Careless	Apathetic Anxious Irritable	Comprehension nearly normal Vague words in talk Naming may be impaired
Stage II	Middle	Recent events forgotten Math skills reduced	Restless	Comprehension reduced Paraphasias, jargon Naming becomes wordy Poor self-monitoring
Stage III	Late	Recent events fade fast Remote memory impaired Family not recognized	Unresponsive Withdrawn	Unresponsive Mute

Source: Adapted from Davis, G. A. (1993). *A survey of adult aphasia and related language disorders* (2nd ed.). Boston: Allyn & Bacon. All rights reserved. Adapted with permission.

Language functioning is also defective, and the impairment worsens as the disease progresses (Table 14.3). Language impairment in stage I involves *anomia,* or naming problems, and vague or unclear words are used in conversation. In addition, the person typically displays a reduced word frequency (e.g., fewer words are used to answer a question). Comprehension and repetition are generally good in the first stage but significantly reduced in stage II. Also, jargon words, or *paraphasias* (speaking errors), become prominent; anomia is pronounced, with many words needed to identify an object; and conversation makes little sense. In stage III, language is lost completely, and the person becomes mute and unresponsive.

The *Scientific American* Spotlight, "Senile Words," looks at a study of a group of 700 retired Midwestern nuns, some of whom developed Alzheimer's disease and some of whom did not. In a comparison of early writing styles, the nuns who later developed dementia displayed a much simpler writing style than those who did not. Because the life of the nuns was remarkably similar after their early 20s, this difference in writing styles suggests that the factors that lead to the development of Alzheimer's are determined at an early age.

A man with Alzheimer's disease and his caregiver.

DAVID YOUNG-WOLFF/PHOTOEDIT

People with AD may also display personality changes, ranging from apathetic, anxious, and irritable in stage I (remember Beth's irritability?) to restless in stage II, and withdrawn and unresponsive in stage III. Loss of visual-spatial orientation and poor judgment are also seen. People with AD usually remain in good physical health until the later stages of the disease, when their ability to participate in physical activities declines dramatically, and they become increasingly susceptible to illnesses such as pneumonia (Miller, 2000).

The Cellular Basis of Alzheimer's Disease

Despite extensive efforts to develop a definitive test for AD in living persons, a conclusive diagnosis of the disorder requires the identification of distinct neurological changes in the brain, which can be confirmed only by examination of brain tissue after death—just as in Alois Alzheimer's day (Coll & others, 2003; Perl, 2000). The main characteristics of the disease, as Alzheimer reported in 1907, are neurofibrillary tangles and senile plaques. **Neurofibrillary tangles** are unusual triangular and looped fibers in the cytoplasm of neurons (Figure 14.23); **senile plaques** are granular deposits of a protein known as amyloid beta protein and the remains of degenerated dendrites and axons, which increase in number as the disease progresses (as is evident from autopsy studies of patients who died at various stages of AD).

Amyloid beta protein deposits are thought to cause the degeneration of neural fibers and a disruption of neural connections within specific areas of the brain. As would be expected from the memory deficits, senile plaques are pronounced in granular layers II and IV of the inferior temporal lobe; both layers have connections to the hippocampus. Senile plaques also form in the temporal lobe, especially in Wernicke's area, causing the characteristic language impairments. Further, senile plaques are found in the posterior association areas of the cerebral cortex and pyramidal layers III and V of the parietotemporal lobe, again in areas controlling memory and language.

Figure 14.23

Neurofibrillary tangles and senile plaques This postmortem brain tissue sample is from a person with Alzheimer's disease. The neurofibrillary tangles appear as twisted fibers (the dark squiggles) that make the cells seem blackened. Senile plaques (the large masses) contain amyloid beta protein and degenerated axons and dendrites.

→ **What behavioral changes are associated with Alzheimer's disease?**

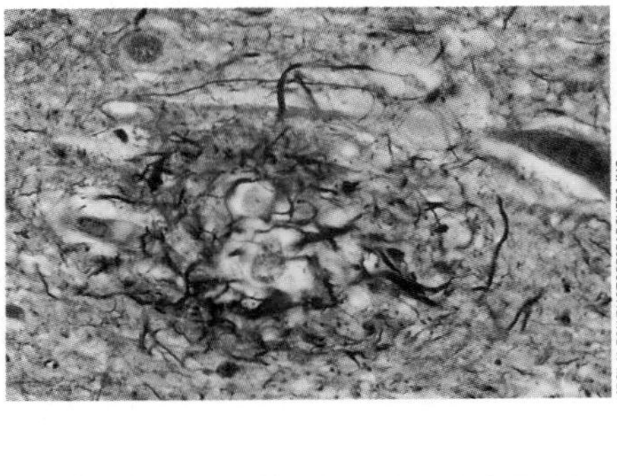

CECIL H. FOX/PHOTORESEARCHERS, INC

People with Down syndrome (Chapter 3) who live to middle age are likely to develop AD (Lott & Head, 2005; Neve & others, 2001). Until fairly recently, because of their susceptibility to serious cardiac and respiratory diseases, individuals with Down syndrome were unlikely to reach middle age; thus, the connection to AD was not recognized. But medical advances have now increased the average life expectancy for people with Down syndrome to 55 years (National Association for Down Syndrome, 2005). Postmortem examinations of people with Down syndrome and AD reveal significant accumulations of senile plaques and neurofibrillary tangles, and some senile plaques and neurofibrillary tangles are also found in Down syndrome

Scientific American Spotlight

Senile Words

Susceptibility to dementia may be apparent at an early age

Paul Wallich

Alzheimer's disease destroys the memory. It kills many older people. Their brains contain so-called senile plaques. Yet some senior citizens, passed over by this capricious angel of death, die at advanced ages with their faculties intact and neural connections free of the ailment's proteinaceous tangles. The root cause of the disease is still unknown.

An ongoing study of some 700 retired midwestern nuns, however, appears to have uncovered an odd correlation between writing style at an early age and senile dementia decades later. All the novices who wrote autobiographical essays in very simple sentences died with symptoms of Alzheimer's (*A*), but none of those whose prose style was more complex succumbed to the disease (*B*).

(*A*) "I attended the public school until the fifth grade. I started St. John's school when I was in the fifth grade. On September 1, 1925 following graduation, I entered as junior. I reentered on August 29th, 1927. On account of ill health I was a novice for two years."

(*B*) "During my junior year I again thought of entering. My father himself gave me the opportunity to express this desire, when he asked me what I intended to make of myself. I told him, 'a Notre Dame.' To my surprise, he said, 'If it's your vocation go to it.' I went to it, with God's grace, and find myself, this very day, happily preparing to take Holy Vows—preparing to be 'a Notre Dame.' "

Susan J. Kemper of the University of Kansas, who studied the biographical essays, notes that measurements of "idea density" are surprisingly consistent and appear to correspond to some kind of general cognitive skill. Because all the nuns in the study belonged to the teaching order of the School Sisters of Notre Dame, and because many of them were educated in the same schools and classes, it seems reasonable that their preferred writing styles would be similar, Kemper explains. (Cohorts with some subjects brought up to emulate Ernest Hemingway and others nurtured on Anthony Trollope would show too much variability for such an effect to be noticeable.)

The nuns who wrote the simplest sentences probably did so, Kemper argues, because even around age 20, they did not have the short-term memory skills to juggle all the components of more complex wordings. She notes that many people tend to write less densely as they grow older, even while other aspects of their writing style remain the same.

patients who died in their teens or twenties. As we noted in Chapter 3, Down syndrome is caused by three copies of chromosome 21, which is the same chromosome that carries a gene that mutates to produce amyloid beta protein—further evidence that amyloid beta protein plays a critical role in producing AD.

The Degeneration of Neural Pathways

Biological psychologists have theorized that neural tissue degeneration in AD patients occurs in cholinergic neurons that originate in the basal forebrain in a structure called the *nucleus basalis of Meynert* and synapse in the neocortex and the hippocampus (Coyle & others, 1983). The degeneration of cholinergic neurons significantly decreases the levels of acetylcholine, choline acetyltransferase (the enzyme that synthesizes ACh), and acetylcholinesterase (AChE, the enzyme that inactivates ACh), all of which further depresses cholinergic transmission. In support of this theory, researchers used PET to measure the brain AChE activity of AD patients in a series of scans over time (Shinotoh & others, 2000). The detected changes suggested a progressive loss of the ascending cholinergic system from the nucleus basalis of Meynert. In addition, the investigators found a highly significant correlation between cholinesterase levels and scores on a measure of cognitive ability, further supporting the cholinergic hypothesis of AD.

An impaired cholinergic system can produce memory deficits in experimental animals (Levin, 1988), and the administration of cholinergic antagonists also leads to memory deficits. For example, taste recognition memory and learned taste aversion was studied in rats given microinfusions of different neurotransmitter antagonists in the perirhinal cortex (Gutierrez & others, 2004). Learned taste aversion was impaired only by the muscarinic antagonist infusions, and this was also true for the consolidation of taste recognition memory, suggesting that choliner-

One long-running hypothesis about Alzheimer's holds that people show signs of dementia only when brain damage has eroded their "cognitive reserve"—the smaller the reserve, the earlier the onset. If this extra brain capacity could somehow be enhanced or preserved, it might be possible to stave off the worst phases of Alzheimer's, says David A. Snowdon of the University of Kentucky, the director of the nun study. Martha Storandt, a psychologist at Washington University, notes that some of the subjects at whom she and her colleagues have looked died free of apparent cognitive impairment, but with at least some visible senile plaques in their brain. These elderly patients may have been reaching the end of their cognitive reserve.

Snowdon points out, however, that examinations of the brains of nuns who have died cast doubt on the cognitive reserve theory: those who suffered from dementia before death had numerous neural plaques and tangles characteristic of Alzheimer's; those who died unimpaired had almost none. If the theory were correct, he explains, one would expect to see roughly similar numbers of tangles in both cases.

Although the narrow slice of Midwestern population covered by the study makes it possible for researchers to see effects that would otherwise be hidden, it also prevents easy generalization. It appears that early in life something may be measurable that distinguishes those at high risk for Alzheimer's from those at low risk, but finding a way to detect it in the general population will be difficult.

Because the nuns have led remarkably similar lives since their early twenties—doing essentially the same work, often living in the same residences and eating the same food—it appears that whatever factors control susceptibility to Alzheimer's are probably fixed at an early age, Snowdon says. Recent studies of people who have tested positive for genes that mark a familial version of the ailment tell a parallel story: scans indicate differences in brain metabolism among subjects in their early fifties, long before any cognitive changes are apparent.

The researchers are currently investigating what is known of their subjects' prenovitiate life to see if any childhood or teenage factors seem to be correlated with the disease.

Scientific American, vol. 274, pp. 26–27.

gic neurotransmission in the perirhinal cortex is essential for both taste recognition memory and learned taste aversion. In another study, investigators injected either saline, scopolamine (cholinergic antagonist), or physostigmine (cholinergic agonist) into the CA_3 region of the hippocampus before training rats on a fear conditioning problem (Rogers & Kesner, 2004). Scopolamine disrupted encoding of the context of the problem (e.g., surroundings, lighting) but not retrieval, whereas physostigmine disrupted retrieval but not encoding. The researchers concluded that increased levels of ACh are needed for encoding spatial contexts, and retrieval of learned spatial contexts requires decreased levels of ACh.

Unfortunately, treating AD patients with drugs that increase ACh in the brain has not greatly improved outcomes. This suggests that the cognitive impairments may be caused at least in part by the degeneration of neurons that use other neurotransmitters. For example, experimenters observed a degeneration of the neurons that secrete glutamate in AD patients (Hyman & others, 1987). The degeneration of glutamate neurons may be particularly important, given our earlier discussion of the involvement of glutamate in LTP in the hippocampus. The researchers observed degeneration of glutamate-secreting neurons in the perforant pathway, which as you will recall is a major pathway involved in memory, beginning in the entorhinal cortex and synapsing in the dentate gyrus. Further, these researchers found an 83% reduction of glutamate levels in the dentate gyrus, an important structure for memory storage. Degeneration of this structure probably contributes to the anterograde amnesia of AD patients. Similarly, a marked decrease was reported in glutamate uptake sites in the cortical and hippocampal regions of people with AD, with no changes in subcortical areas (Hardy & others, 1987).

More recent evidence suggests that glutamate neurotoxicity may cause the neuronal death associated with AD (Arias & others, 1998; Hynd & others, 2004). Glutamate is normally taken up rapidly from the synaptic cleft by glutamate transporters, and the inhibition of this uptake is implicated in several neurodegenerative disorders, including AD. Researchers suspect that oxidative damage produced by the disease disrupts glutamate transporters, and the failure to clear glutamate from the synaptic cleft contributes to the degeneration of neurons in the affected areas; they have also found evidence implicating amyloid beta protein as a causative agent in the disorder (Lauderback & others, 2001).

Oxidative damage to amyloid beta protein creates protein fragments that are neurotoxic, inactivating the glutamate transporter mechanisms (Aksenov & others, 1997; Hensley & others, 1994). The oxidation of amyloid beta protein may be responsible for producing the amnesic effect of AD, and increasing evidence supports the idea that amyloid beta protein accumulation is the fundamental initiator of the disorder (Hardy & Selkoe, 2002; Selkoe, 2000). In studies of gerbils, researchers found that protein oxidation is greater in older than in younger animals and that memory is poorer in the older animals (Carney & Floyd, 1991). When the investigators administered a drug that inactivates the chemicals that oxidize proteins, they found that spatial memory in the older gerbils improved to the level seen in young gerbils. On the basis of this research, Selkoe (1992) has suggested that future treatment of AD patients might include methods of inhibiting the oxidation of amyloid beta protein or of preventing the entry of the protein into cerebral tissue.

Box 14.1

Treating Alzheimer's Disease

Efforts to enhance memory in people with Alzheimer's disease by administering drugs that increase brain levels of ACh have had limited success, at best. Early efforts involved the use of such precursors of ACh as choline and lecithin, which were ineffective in improving cognitive ability. Some researchers have suggested that these were the wrong precursors to use (Amenta & others, 2001). According to these investigators, intermediates in choline biosynthetic pathways such as CDP-choline and choline alphoscerate lead to greater availability of ACh than do choline and lecithin, and to modest improvement in cognitive dysfunction in AD patients. These results suggest that additional cholinergic precursors, and particularly choline alphoscerate, should be tried in large, carefully controlled clinical trials before the approach is abandoned.

At present, however, the treatment for AD tends to be drugs that increase CNS ACh by inhibiting cholinesterase activity at the synapse. For example, the cholinergic agonist tacrine (Cognex) has been prescribed to AD patients since the early 1990s, although it is no longer being actively marketed (Alzheimer's Disease Education & Referral Center, 2004). The cholinesterase inhibitors have a significant, but modest, impact on the cognitive functioning of people with mild to moderate AD (Grutzendler & Morris, 2001). Because of rather severe side effects from Cognex, a more selective, second-generation cholinesterase inhibitor, donepezil (Aricept), is often prescribed and has been found to have beneficial effects relative to a placebo, at least for periods up to a year (Birks & Harvey, 2003; Wolfson & others, 2002). Cholinesterase inhibitors more recently approved by the FDA for treating AD are galantamine (Reminyl) and rivastigmine (Exelon). Beth's physician will probably prescribe one of the newer cholinesterase inhibitors.

When Beth's AD progresses, her doctor may prescribe memantine (Namenda), which is an NMDA antagonist (Areosa & others, 2004). Memantine works by regulating glutamate, which, as we noted, is toxic to neurons in excess amounts. The drug appears to delay progression of some of the symptoms associated with moderate to severe AD, such as incontinence, that place an added burden on caregivers. Research has shown that the combination of a cholinesterase inhibitor in the mild to moderate stage of AD and memantine in the moderate to severe stage is significantly more effective than a cholinesterase inhibitor alone (Standridge, 2004).

In addition to efforts aimed at increasing neural ACh, clinical trials are underway to test compounds that may reduce neuronal damage by limiting oxidation, such as monoamine oxidase inhibitors (MAOIs), nonsteroidal anti-inflammatory drugs (NSAIDs), and antioxidants (Cutler & Sramek, 2001). Additional substances being tested for efficacy against AD include hormones (e.g., estradiol), herbs (e.g., *Ginkgo biloba*), lipid-lowering agents (e.g., statins), vitamins (e.g., E, B_{12}, folic acid), and antihypertensives (Doraiswamy, 2002). Another approach seeks to prevent the formation and accumulation of amyloid beta protein plaques.

Gene therapy combined with nerve growth factor (NGF) seems to be a promising approach for treating the loss of cholinergic neurons in AD (Blesch & Tuszynski, 2004; Tuszynski & Blesch, 2004; Tuszynski & others, 2002). Early clinical trials with a few patients had to be halted because of adverse effects when NGF was infused into the ventricles of patients; these were caused

The Role of Genetics in Alzheimer's Disease

As noted earlier, the connection between Down syndrome and Alzheimer's disease suggests a link between chromosome 21 and AD. The relationship between Down syndrome and AD has led to the discovery of a gene on chromosome 21 that is linked to the early-onset form of the disorder (Sorbi & others, 2001; St. George-Hyslop, 2000). This gene, along with a gene on chromosome 14 and another on chromosome 1, have been linked to increased levels of amyloid beta protein and early-onset AD (Hutton & others, 1998; St. George-Hyslop).

Researchers have identified another gene, *apolipoprotein E* or *ApoE* on chromosome 19, that is associated with increased amyloid beta protein levels and late-onset AD (Levy-Lahad & others, 1998; Zekanowski & others, 2004). There are several forms of *ApoE*, the most common being *ApoE2*, *ApoE3*, and *ApoE4*. Everyone has two copies (alleles) of the *ApoE* gene, but people with one or two *ApoE4* alleles have a much greater risk of developing late-onset AD. Researchers have shown that the product of *ApoE4* is not as effective an antioxidant for amyloid beta protein as are the products of the other alleles (Lauderback & others, 2002). This further points to the role of oxidative neuronal damage in AD and suggests a need to develop more effective methods to increase antioxidants in the brains of AD patients. We examine treatment methods further in Box 14.1.

Checkpoint

Based on what you have learned about the cellular, neurochemical, and genetic bases of Alzheimer's disease, propose a new method of treatment for this disease.

by the effects of NGF on nontargeted structures in the central and peripheral nervous systems (Blesch & Tuszynski). Subsequent research involving the targeted delivery of cells genetically modified to produce NGF has avoided these earlier problems, and the results of these studies seem promising.

For example, in a study with monkeys, researchers examined whether monkey cells that had been genetically modified to produce human NGF would prevent the degeneration of cholinergic neurons triggered by an injury (Tuszynski & others, 1996). Monkeys receiving grafts that produced NGF retained more than twice as many cholinergic neurons after 1 month as animals receiving control grafts. When the grafts were placed immediately adjacent to the injured neurons, the NGF-producing grafts provided up to 92% protection. A clinical trial with eight patients with mild AD employed the same approach used in the earlier nonhuman primate studies—the implantation of cells that had been taken from that individual and genetically modified to express human NGF (Tuszynski & others, 2005). After 22 months, no adverse effects of the treatment were found in six of the patients. Further, mental testing revealed an improvement in the rate of cognitive decline, and brain autopsy from one patient indicated that the NGF had produced robust neuronal growth responses.

In recent years, stem cells have been touted as possible agents in the treatment of a variety of neurological diseases, including AD (Rice & others, 2003). The use of embryonic stem cells, which requires the death of a human embryo, raises ethical concerns for many people (Rice & others), but stem cells can also be obtained from adults. Such cells can be cultivated in vitro and potentially used as transplant material in the person from whom they were taken (Oliveira & Hodges, 2005; Sugaya & Brannen, 2001). To show the efficacy of this approach, researchers injected cultivated human neuronal stem cells into the lateral ventricles of either 2-month-old rats or 24-month-old rats that had earlier been trained on a water maze (Qu & others, 2001; Sugaya, 2005). Four weeks after the transplants, the older rats showed dramatic cognitive improvement. Postmortem examination of the rat brains showed that the transplanted human cells had been extensively incorporated into the host brains.

Despite these promising approaches to treating neurodegenerative diseases, we do not yet have a way to halt the progression of AD and are a long way from a cure. Several interventions do seem to be helpful, however. For example, *mnemonic techniques,* which are memory aids that improve the storage and retrieval of information, can enhance memory in the early stages of the disease (Clare & Wilson, 2004). Mnemonic techniques rely on associative processes to link events. For example, suppose a person has difficulty remembering where he or she has left the car keys. The keys could be put in the same place every day, allowing the person to associate the keys with that place.

Reality orientation programs that enable AD patients to maintain awareness of who and where they are seem somewhat beneficial as well. Support groups can help families learn more about the disease and about methods of caring for a person with AD. Finally, treatment programs for caregivers of AD patients, such as Beth's husband, Greg, can enhance the well-being of both the family members and the loved one in their care (Mittelman, 2000).

REVIEW

- Alzheimer's disease is a progressive impairment in mental functioning that includes deficits in language, memory, visual-spatial orientation, and judgment.
- Stage I AD is characterized by mild forgetfulness and disorientation, sometimes accompanied by anxiety. Stage II is characterized by greater forgetfulness of recent events, reduced comprehension of language, and paraphasias. In stage III, the person has severe memory loss, nonrecognition of family members, unresponsiveness, and total loss of language skills.
- The characteristic neurological changes in AD are neurofibrillary tangles and senile plaques, as well as progressive degeneration of cholinergic and glutamatergic neurons in the neocortex and hippocampus.
- The oxidation products of amyloid beta protein may be toxic to glutamate transporters, causing the accumulation of neurotoxic glutamate in the synapse and the degeneration of neurons in the hippocampus and neocortex.
- Research into AD has revealed several genetic links, such as between genes on chromosomes 1, 14, and 21 and early-onset AD and between the ApoE gene on chromosome 19 and late-onset AD.
- Current treatments are aimed at increasing neural ACh or reducing neuronal degeneration by limiting oxidative damage.

Chapter Review

Key Terms

Alzheimer's disease (AD) (p. 531)
amyloid beta protein (p. 533)
anterograde amnesia (p. 521)
Atkinson-Shiffrin model (p. 505)
cell assembly (p. 510)
cellular modification theory (p. 516)
conditioned response (CR) (p. 503)
conditioned stimulus (CS) (p. 503)
confabulation (p. 529)
contingency (p. 504)
declarative memory (p. 509)
dementia (p. 531)
episodic memory (p. 507)
habituation (p. 502)
interference (p. 506)
Korsakoff's syndrome (p. 529)
interpositus nucleus (p. 515)
learning (p. 502)
long-term depression (LTD) (p. 526)
long-term potentiation (LTP) (p. 524)
long-term store (p. 505)
medial temporal lobe (p. 521)
mediodorsal thalamus (p. 528)
memory (p. 502)
memory attribute (p. 506)
mossy fiber pathway (p. 524)
neurofibrillary tangle (p. 533)
neuroplasticity (p. 527)
NMDA receptor (p. 525)
operant conditioning (p. 504)
Pavlovian conditioning (p. 503)
perforant fiber pathway (p. 524)
procedural memory (p. 508)
punisher (p. 504)
rehearsal systems approach (p. 506)
reinforcer (p. 504)
retrograde amnesia (p. 512)
retrograde messenger (p. 526)
reverberatory activity (p. 510)
Schaffer collateral fiber pathway (p. 524)
semantic memory (p. 507)
senile plaque (p. 533)
sensitization (p. 503)
sensory register (p. 505)
short-term store (p. 505)
Skinner box (p. 504)
unconditioned response (UCR) (p. 503)
unconditioned stimulus (UCS) (p. 503)
working memory (p. 506)

Suggested Readings

Cohen, N. J., & Eichenbaum, H. (1993). *Memory, amnesia, and the hippocampal system.* Cambridge, MA: MIT Press.

Cutler, N. R., & Sramek, J. J. (2001). Review of the next generation of Alzheimer's disease therapeutics: Challenges for drug development. *Progress in Neuropsychopharmacology & Biological Psychiatry, 25,* 27–57.

Gould, E., Tanapat, P., Hastings, N. B., & Shors, T. J. (1999). Neurogenesis in adulthood: A possible role in learning. *Trends in Cognitive Science, 3,* 186–192.

Rose, S. P. (1992). *The making of memory: From molecules to mind.* New York: Anchor Books/Doubleday.

Selkoe, D. J. (2000). Toward a comprehensive theory for Alzheimer's disease. Hypothesis: Alzheimer's disease is caused by the cerebral accumulation and cytotoxicity of amyloid beta-protein. *Annals of the New York Academy of Sciences, 924,* 17–25.

Shapiro, M. (2001). Plasticity, hippocampal place cells, and cognitive maps. *Archives of Neurology, 58,* 874–881.

Zola-Morgan, S., & Squire, L. R. (1993). Neuroanatomy of memory. *Annual Review of Neuroscience, 16,* 547–563.

Critical Thinking Questions

1. Sheryl was in an automobile accident but has no recollection of it. What process may be responsible for her inability to recall the accident?
2. Lori has difficulty remembering where she parked her car and what she had to eat this morning, yet she can readily recall the plot of a movie she saw as a child. Give some possible reasons for Lori's ability to remember some experiences but not others.
3. Rodrigo suffered a stroke last week. The stroke caused considerable bilateral damage to the medial temporal lobe and surrounding areas. What memory impairments might he experience as a result of the stroke? What memory functioning might remain intact?

Fill-in-the-Blank Questions

1. ______ is a long-term change in behavior that results from experience, and ______ is the capacity to retain and retrieve experiences.
2. ______ is a decrease in response after repeated exposure to an innocuous stimulus, and ______ is an increase in reactivity following exposure to an intense event.
3. In ______, a neutral stimulus paired with a stimulus that elicits a reflex response eventually elicits the response by itself.
4. ______ is learning how to respond to obtain reinforcement.
5. ______ are events or activities that increase the probability of repeating the behavior that preceded them; ______ are events or activities that decrease the frequency of the behavior that brought them about.
6. In operant conditioning, a specified relationship between a behavior and a reinforcement or punishment is called a(n) ______.
7. In the ______ model, memory is first stored in the sensory register, then in the ______, and finally in the ______.
8. Recall failure because of other memories is called ______.
9. According to Baddeley's ______, ______ has the attributes of the short-term store.
10. Memory of an event experienced at a particular time or place, accessed deliberately, is ______ memory.
11. A(n) ______ memory contains information about words and symbols and the rules for the development of concepts or solutions to problems.
12. Knowledge of facts as opposed to skills is referred to as ______ memory; skill memory is called ______.
13. Hebb's simple physical unit of memory is referred to as a(n) ______.
14. ______ is the continued activity in a circuit of neurons that must be maintained until the memory storage process is completed.
15. In Hebb's terminology, cell assemblies become interconnected into a(n) ______.
16. Amnesia for events that happened before an injury to the nervous system is ______ amnesia.
17. The ______ of the cerebellum is central to conditioning the rabbit's nictitating membrane response.
18. The view that learning changes neural responsiveness is called ______.
19. Lynch found that experience enhances Ca^{2+} ion entry into the neurons, where the Ca^{2+} ions activate the enzyme ______, which breaks down ______, a protein that coats the dendrites.

20. Squire suggested that the ______ structures (hippocampus and surrounding areas) and the ______ thalamus jointly establish long-term memory.
21. With damage to his temporal lobes, H.M.'s most profound deficit is ______ amnesia.
22. A brief, intense series of electrical impulses to neurons in one of three pathways into the hippocampus leads to long-term ______.
23. LTP appears to occur through a modification in the ______ receptor.
24. The soluble gas ______ is a(n) ______ messenger for LTP.
25. According to Elizabeth Gould and others, formation of new ______ is linked to associative learning tasks involving the hippocampus.
26. ______ is a form of severe memory impairment common in chronic alcoholics.
27. Making up stories to fill in gaps in memory is called ______.
28. According to Squire, the ______ memory system controls the ability to develop procedural memories.
29. ______ disease is the most common form of dementia.
30. The neuropathology of AD includes ______ tangles and ______.
31. People with ______ syndrome who live to middle age are likely to develop AD.
32. Current research suggests that deposits of ______ protein cause the degeneration of neural fibers and a disruption of connections within specific brain areas.

Multiple-Choice Questions

1. You no longer smell your cologne shortly after you apply it, because of the type of learning called
   a. sensitization. c. Pavlovian conditioning.
   b. habituation. d. operant conditioning.
2. While studying intently for an exam, you have an exaggerated startle reaction when your telephone rings. This is an example of
   a. sensitization. c. Pavlovian conditioning.
   b. habituation. d. operant conditioning.
3. Repeated pairing of a tone (______) with food (______) eventually allows the tone to elicit saliva (______).
   a. UCS, CS, CR c. CS, UCS, UCR
   b. CS, UCS, CR d. UCS, CS, UCR
4. A(n) ______ is an event that increases the probability of the behavior that brings it about; a(n) ______ is an event that decreases the frequency of the behavior that precedes it.
   a. punisher, operant c. punisher, reinforcer
   b. operant, reinforcer d. reinforcer, punisher
5. A specified relationship between a behavior and a reinforcement or punishment is a(n)
   a. operant. c. contingency.
   b. conditioned response. d. respondent.
6. The stages of the Atkinson-Shiffrin model are
   a. sensory register, long-term potentiation, long-term memory.
   b. sensory register, short-term memory, long-term memory.
   c. cell assembly, short-term memory, working memory.
   d. rehearsal, memory consolidation, memory transfer.
7. External input can stay in the sensory register
   a. for 0.5 to 1 second. c. for 5 to 15 seconds.
   b. for 1 to 4 seconds. d. indefinitely.
8. Recall failure because of other memories in the long-term store is known as
   a. consolidation. c. interference.
   b. memory decay. d. memory attributes.
9. Remembering your mother's birthday by recalling how you celebrated it last year is an example of the use of
   a. memory attributes. c. memory consolidation.
   b. memory transfer. d. rehearsal.
10. According to Lockhart and Craik, long-term memories are memories that are
    a. stored for the longest time.
    b. the result of long-term potentiation.
    c. the most elaborated.
    d. the most thoroughly processed.
11. Remembering how to drive your car is an example of ______ memory.
    a. procedural c. semantic
    b. declarative d. episodic
12. A man with bilateral hippocampal damage is likely to forget
    a. how to drive a car.
    b. how to speak in his native tongue.
    c. how to play the piano.
    d. how the accident occurred that damaged his memory.
13. ______ memories are not accessible to conscious awareness and the evidence for them comes only from observations of performance.
    a. Procedural c. Episodic
    b. Semantic d. Declarative
14. Jacques's recollection of the great dinner he had last night is an illustration of ______ memory.
    a. episodic c. declarative
    b. semantic d. procedural

15. Hebb's memory consolidation theory is based on the idea that reverberatory activity
    a. must precede the event to be remembered.
    b. is necessary for retrieval of information from memory.
    c. results in permanent physiological changes.
    d. is responsible for long-term potentiation.
16. The neural circuit through which activity reverberates to act as a memory store is, according to Hebb, a(n)
    a. cell assembly.
    b. phase sequence.
    c. consolidation unit.
    d. fodrin activator.
17. Following a closed-head injury that resulted from a fall, Stan cannot recall any events immediately preceding his accident. This illustrates ______ amnesia.
    a. anterograde
    b. retrograde
    c. trauma-induced
    d. temporary
18. The brain structure found to be central to nictitating membrane conditioning in rabbits is the
    a. lateral interpositus nucleus of the cerebellum.
    b. red nucleus of the midbrain.
    c. pontine nucleus.
    d. hippocampus.
19. Kandel has been particularly interested in studying conditioning in *Aplysia* because
    a. its complexity makes it a good model for primate behavior.
    b. it is a distant relative of primates and therefore of humans.
    c. its nervous system consists of only three neurons.
    d. its nervous system is simple enough that individual synapses can be studied.
20. According to Lynch, the biological basis of learning and memory lies in the
    a. buildup of the fodrin coating on dendrites.
    b. consolidation of the sensory register.
    c. establishment of new neural connections.
    d. development and release of novel neurotransmitters.
21. Karl Lashley spent decades searching for
    a. a credible theory of LTP.
    b. the engram.
    c. the site of nictitating membrane conditioning.
    d. evidence for Hebb's theory of brain function.
22. H.M. had his medial temporal lobes removed as a treatment for
    a. a severe memory problem.
    b. excessive aggressiveness.
    c. severe epilepsy.
    d. Korsakoff's syndrome.
23. H.M.'s most profound deficit is
    a. in procedural memory.
    b. retrograde amnesia.
    c. in semantic memory.
    d. anterograde amnesia.
24. An important characteristic of long-term potentiation is that
    a. it requires long-term stimulation.
    b. it occurs only in the mediodorsal thalamus.
    c. it is not a conditioned response but rather occurs naturally.
    d. the associated change in receptivity occurs in only a single pathway.
25. LTP appears to occur through a modification in the ______ receptor.
    a. acetylcholine
    b. NMDA
    c. dopamine
    d. serotonin
26. Nitric oxide functions as a(n) ______ messenger to maintain neurotransmitter release.
    a. retrograde
    b. anterograde
    c. first
    d. second
27. As the work of Elizabeth Gould and others has demonstrated, learning that involves the hippocampus
    a. decreases the survival of new hippocampal neurons.
    b. inhibits the formation of new hippocampal neurons.
    c. increases the survival of new hippocampal neurons.
    d. stimulates the formation of new neurons in areas other than the hippocampus.
28. People with mediodorsal damage, such as that caused by Korsakoff's syndrome, differ from people with medial temporal lobe damage in that they
    a. can describe what they are doing.
    b. are unaware of their memory deficit.
    c. can learn new tasks.
    d. have intact emotions.
29. Research points to the ______ as the brain structure(s) controlling the ability to develop procedural memories.
    a. hippocampal system
    b. medial temporal lobes
    c. corpus striatum
    d. anterior thalamic nuclei
30. Most people with ______ are likely to develop Alzheimer's disease if they live long enough.
    a. Korsakoff's syndrome
    b. Huntington's disease
    c. Down syndrome
    d. Parkinson's disease
31. Joan was recently diagnosed with Alzheimer's disease, and her physician prescribed the cholinesterase inhibitor Aricept. How much memory improvement can Joan expect?
    a. none
    b. modest improvement
    c. substantial improvement
    d. inconsistent improvement
32. Everyone has two copies (alleles) of the *ApoE* gene; people with one or two ______ alleles have a greater risk of developing late-onset AD.
    a. *ApoE1*
    b. *ApoE2*
    c. *ApoE3*
    d. *ApoE4*

Answers can be found on the companion website at www.worthpublishers.com/klein.

The Biological Basis of Affective Disorders and Schizophrenia

15

- **Affective Disorders**
- **Box 15.1 Electroconvulsive Therapy**
- **Schizophrenia**
- **Box 15.2 Preventing Relapse in Patients With Schizophrenia**
- ***Scientific American* Spotlight Fever In, Schizophrenia Out**

A Feeling of Hopelessness

Today was Rose's 50th birthday, but she didn't feel like celebrating. In fact, lately she hadn't felt much like doing anything. Her days always seemed the same: She would drag herself out of bed when Sidney's alarm went off, plod into the kitchen and fix breakfast, and then try to eat something so her husband wouldn't worry about her.

"This grapefruit is really good, Rose," he would say, and she would grunt noncommittally. Or, "I love these muffins. Don't you?" Another grunt.

"How'd you sleep?" Sidney asked this morning, after kissing her and wishing her a happy birthday. Forgetting that she didn't want to worry him, she responded, "Awful."

In truth, Rose couldn't remember the last time she'd had a good night's sleep. Invariably she would toss and turn, get up and take one of the Xanax the doctor had prescribed some months ago, then finally drop off at about 1:00 a.m.—only to wake up at 3:30 or 4:00, unable to get back to sleep. In those predawn hours she thought her darkest thoughts, thoughts of ending it all in the quickest, least messy way. Lately, her ruminations centered on poison, and it was all she could do on wash days to keep from drinking the bottle of bleach. But that would probably be painful and messy.

When she considered her life objectively, she knew she should be happier. She and Sidney had a good standard of living, nice cars, a house her friends envied, and grown-up children who were independent and a credit to their parents. Her first grandchild was on the way, and she should be looking forward to that. But she wasn't.

When she and Sidney became "empty nesters," at first it had seemed like a blessing—they were free to concentrate more on their own lives. Now, Rose thought of it as a curse. She was useless—that was the way she felt and thought about herself in those predawn hours.

This morning, after she said "Awful," Sidney suggested she see their family doctor again. "Find out if there's something physically wrong with you, Rose," was the way he put it. Rose just said, "What good would that do?" and continued her ruminations about killing herself.

BEFORE YOU BEGIN

- **What is the biological basis of Rose's depression?**
- **Would seeing her doctor do any good?**
- **Are all types of depression the same?**
- **What is bipolar disorder, and how can it be treated?**
- **Could genetics and/or experience have played a role in Rose's depression?**
- **How is Rose's depression affecting her sleep cycle?**
- **What are the symptoms of schizophrenia, and what causes them?**

affective disorder A mental disorder characterized by one or both of two mood states: depression and/or mania.

depressive disorder A type of affective disorder in which depression is the only mood state.

depression An affective disorder characterized by an intense, continuing feeling of sadness and worthlessness.

major depression A type of depressive disorder characterized by a depressed mood of at least 2 weeks' duration.

> **➤ Why are there so many different treatments for schizophrenia?**
>
> **In this chapter, you will find the answers to these questions and many others.**

Rose suffers from an affective disorder—an illness that has detrimental effects on the emotions, feelings, mood, or, as psychologists say, *affect,* of a person. Affective disorders are one group of the many types of mental disorders. In this chapter we focus on the affective disorders (depression, bipolar disorders) and schizophrenia—both of which can severely disrupt the ability to function in the everyday world—because these diseases have been extensively investigated and we know a great deal about their organic bases.

◆ Affective Disorders

A close friend announces she is quitting school, and although you try to talk her out of it, her mind is made up. Upset by the news, you are tempted to cut class—then you remember the instructor is supposed to return your last test, and you decide to go. When you get the test back, you find that you have received an A. The good grade not only raises your spirits but prompts you to think positively about the future. As we described in Chapter 11, both your sadness (about the impending departure of your friend) and your joy (about your good grade) are emotions that everyone experiences at one time or another. Usually, these changes of mood are part of a healthy emotional life. However, at times, the emotional state of a person interferes with normal functioning to such an extent that he or she may have one of the **affective disorders,** or *mood disorders.* These conditions are characterized by the persistence of high levels of one or both of two mood states: depression (sadness, loss of interest in things that previously brought pleasure, slowed movements) or mania (wild excitement, racing thoughts, exaggerated feeling of well-being).

There are two major categories of affective disorders: In depressive disorders depression is the only mood state; in bipolar disorders, the person experiences both mania and depression.

Depressive Disorders

Depressive disorders occur with much greater frequency worldwide than bipolar disorders (Sarason & Sarason, 2004). In fact, **depression,** an affective disorder characterized by an intense and continuing feeling of sadness and worthlessness, has been called the "common cold" of mental illness. No one is immune to the "blues"; each of us has felt "down" or depressed following a loss or disappointment or failure. Usually, however, these feelings quickly fade. A person with clinical depression, by contrast, feels "low" most or all of the time, for weeks or months on end. Wallace's classic account (1956) of the behavior of tornado victims in Worcester, Massachusetts, illustrates the typical healing power of time for someone who is not clinically depressed. Wallace noted that although the residents of Worcester functioned well immediately after a tornado hit their town, they were extremely distraught 24 to 48 hours later. They wandered about aimlessly or just sat in the rain. Within several days, however, most residents showed no evidence of their previous depression and were able to undertake the task of rebuilding their town. For some, unfortunately, the feelings of helplessness persisted, and they were unable to resume the normal tasks of daily life. Figure 15.1 shows a woman responding to a more recent disaster: Hurricane Katrina.

Figure 15.1

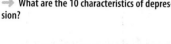

The face of depression Natural disasters such as hurricanes can be extremely distressing. The despair produced by the devastation of her home is evident in the face of this victim of Hurricane Katrina.

➜ What are the 10 characteristics of depression?

MARK WALLHEISER/REUTERS/CORBIS

A study of 3,258 adults in Canada found a lifetime risk of major depression of 8.6%, with 3.2% of the subjects depressed in any given 6 month period (Spaner & others, 1994). The worldwide incidence is about 5%, with approximately 8 million of the U.S. population affected at any given time (Kandel, 2000b). Many studies also have found that about twice as many women as men experience depression (e.g., Sloan & Kornstein, 2003).

People who are depressed, such as Rose in the chapter's opening vignette, are unable to cope with the stressors of life; their clinical disturbance prevents them from experiencing the pleasures available to other people and to themselves when they are not depressed. In one study, 85% of 380 individuals who initially recovered from a major depressive episode had at least one recurrence within 15 years, and 58% of 105 people who recovered and then remained well for at least 5 years had a recurrence of their disorder (Mueller & others, 1999). Although the risk of recurrence increases with each episode, the risk decreases with increasing length of recovery; that is, the longer a person goes without an episode, the less likely the person is to experience a recurrence of depression (Solomon & others, 2000).

The American Psychiatric Association's *Diagnostic and Statistical Manual of Mental Disorders* (*DSM-IV;* APA, 1994) identifies 10 symptoms of depression: (1) depressed mood (sadness); (2) loss of energy, or fatigue; (3) diminished ability to think or concentrate; (4) sleep disturbance (insomnia or hypersomnia); (5) weight loss, or change in appetite; (6) feelings of worthlessness or guilt; (7) diminished interest or pleasure in activities; (8) recurrent thoughts of death, including suicidal thinking; (9) agitation; and (10) psychomotor retardation (slowing of movements or speech). There are two types of depressive disorders: major depression and dysthymia.

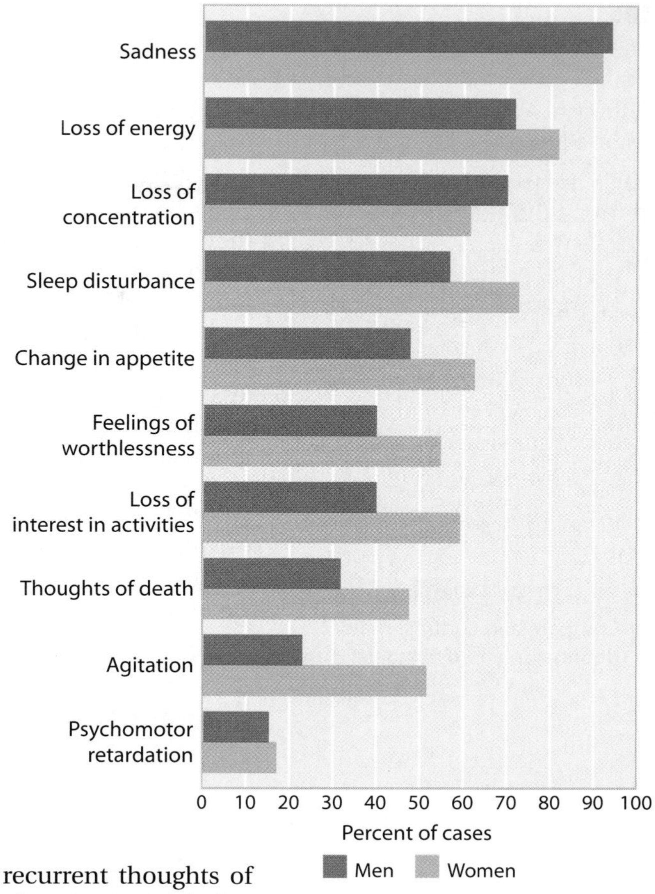

Figure 15.2
Percentage of men and women experiencing symptoms of major depression

➜ **What is the likelihood of recurrence of major depression?**

Major Depression

In all likelihood, Rose is suffering from **major depression,** which is characterized by depressed mood of at least 2 weeks' duration and by other symptoms such as weight loss (or weight gain), sleep difficulties, agitation or lethargy, difficulty concentrating, feelings of hopelessness, and suicidal thoughts. A depressive disorder is intense and incapacitating; if she does not get help, Rose may completely lose interest in the world around her and may indeed be tempted to end it all. The relative frequencies of the symptoms of major depression are shown in Figure 15.2.

The length of a major depressive episode is difficult to predict. It may last for only a few weeks or for as long as 6 months. Once the episode has ended, previous feelings and behavior patterns usually return. Unfortunately, as noted above, the vast majority of people who experience one major depressive episode will experience another (Mueller & others, 1999; Solomon & others, 2000). Many famous people are known to have suffered from major depression (Figure 15.3).

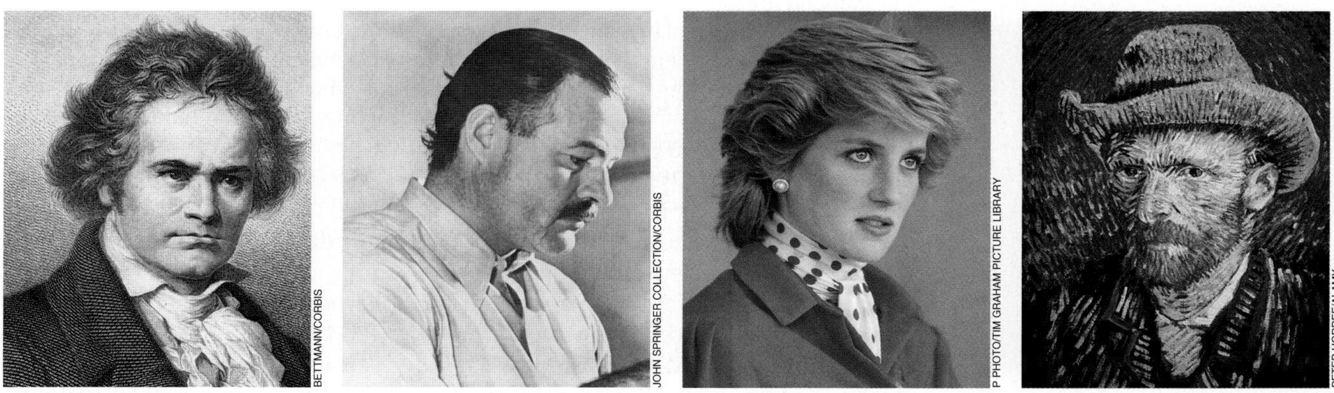

(a) (b) (c) (d)

Figure 15.3
Some famous people who suffered from a major mood disorder
(a) Ludwig van Beethoven, (b) Ernest Hemingway, (c) Princess Diana, (d) Vincent van Gogh.

➜ **What three factors influence the probability of recurrent episodes of mania and depression?**

dysthymia A chronic, usually low-level form of depression.

mania An elevated, expansive, or irritable mood and inflated self-esteem or grandiosity.

Dysthymia

Whereas people with major depression tend to experience a rapid onset of symptoms, others experience less intense symptoms of depression off and on for many years. During this time, these individuals are depressed for more days than not, and they have bad days and not-so-bad days. This kind of chronic, usually low-level, depression is called **dysthymia,** from the Greek *dys,* "bad," and *thymos,* "soul" or "life force." The dysthymic person experiences several of the symptoms of depression, such as difficulty with eating, sleeping, or concentrating, and may also suffer from low self-esteem and feelings of hopelessness. This form of depression tends to be less incapacitating than major depression, and most sufferers do not seek help. Instead, they try to live as well as they can with their distress, considering their condition an "I'm a sad person" personality trait rather than a disorder.

Dysthymia and major depression are clearly related disorders (Klein & Santiago, 2003). In one study, for example, approximately 75% of individuals with dysthymia reported having had a major depressive episode (Keller & others, 1995). In another report, the researchers concluded that nearly all persons with dysthymia eventually experience major depressive episodes (Klein & others, 2000).

➤Checkpoint

Compare and contrast major depression and dysthymia.

Bipolar Disorders

Henry and Martha live with their two school-age children in a comfortable, middle-class neighborhood. Unfortunately, they paid too much for their home and by the time they make their mortgage payment and the lease payments on two relatively new cars, there is not much left to cover normal living expenses. As a result, they seem to be sinking deeper and deeper into credit card debt, which made it a shock to Martha when Henry announced that he was taking off from work to take her and the kids shopping.

"We'll get all those things you've been talking about, honey," he said, and the excitement on his face was palpable. He seemed to be talking more rapidly than usual.

"What are you talking about, Henry? I really don't see how we can afford to buy anything extra this month," she said.

"What about that laptop I saw you looking at the other night at the mall, Martha? And you said yourself that the boys need new shoes and bedroom furniture. And they've got a special on garden furniture in the mall. And . . ."

Before he could continue, Martha asked, "But how are we going to pay for these things?"

"You know last night when I couldn't sleep? An idea came to me, and I got up and worked it all out," Henry said, producing a sheaf of pages from the desk. The print was single spaced, devoid of punctuation, with penned additions filling the margins.

"We can sell stuff on eBay, honey," Henry announced. "At first, it'll just be in our spare time and on weekends, but when the business takes off like I know it will, I'll tell them at the bank what they can do with their lousy job. In fact, I think I'll call Nancy [the bank president] and tell her right now what I think of her and the job."

When Henry reached for the telephone, Martha knew they were in trouble. She responded by grabbing her cell phone and calling their pastor. After she'd explained what was happening, the minister talked to Henry for a long time and persuaded him to check into a nearby residential facility. ("A little rest will do you a world of good, Henry," the minister told him.) There, Henry's extreme excitement over the planned business venture was quickly replaced by deep depression and feelings of the hopelessness of his life and career.

A person like Henry, with one of the bipolar disorders—either bipolar disorder or cyclothymia—experiences alternating episodes of mania and depression. **Mania** is a highly elevated, expansive, or irritable mood, probably more extreme than anything you have experienced. *DSM-IV* (APA, 1994) lists the following additional symptoms of a manic episode: (1) inflated self-esteem or grandiosity; (2) decreased need for sleep; (3) increased speech; (4) racing thoughts; (5) distractibility;

(6) increased activity or psychomotor agitation; and (7) excessive involvement in pleasurable activities, with a high potential for painful consequences (e.g., unrestrained buying sprees or sexual indiscretions). The symptoms of mania typically first appear during young adulthood (Fogarty & others, 1994). In their study of 3,258 randomly selected Canadian adults, Fogarty and colleagues found a lifetime risk of mania of 1.4% for men and 0.6% for women. A study in England reported that men seem to have an earlier age of onset of mania than women (Kennedy & others, 2005). As noted above, rather than occurring by itself, mania is usually one element of a cycle of mood swings known as a bipolar disorder.

bipolar disorder A type of affective disorder characterized by episodes of mania and depression that typically continue throughout the person's lifetime.

cyclothymia One of the bipolar disorders characterized by less intense episodes of mania and depression than are seen in bipolar disorder.

hypomania A milder form of mania in which occupational or social functioning is not impaired.

Bipolar Disorder

A psychiatrist may make a diagnosis of **bipolar disorder** for a person who has experienced only one manic episode and one depressive episode, but episodes of mania and depression typically continue throughout the lifetime of a person. A number of prominent individuals throughout history are thought to have suffered from bipolar disorder (Figure 15.3). About 1% to 3% of the U.S. population has bipolar disorder (Keck & others, 2001), with a worldwide prevalence of approximately 3% to 5% (Shastry, 2005). Bipolar disorder is equally common in males and females. In one study, the annual costs of the disorder in the United States were estimated to be slightly more than $45 billion in 1991 dollars (Kleinman & others, 2003), with hospitalization accounting for most of the direct costs of the illness. Indirect costs include lost time at work because of the disorder and premature mortality. There are also intangible costs such as impaired quality of life and being a burden on the family.

Bipolar disorder is a different disease than depression, presumably with a different neurological basis. The differences include the absence of a clear gender difference in rates of bipolar disorder, the stronger genetic component in bipolar disorder (e.g., Winokur & others, 1995b), and the different drugs used to treat the disorders. Lithium carbonate is the mainstay in the treatment of bipolar disorder, which is little helped by the antidepressants; the opposite is true for treatment of depression.

Three factors that influence whether a person will experience recurrent episodes of bipolar disorder have been identified (Ambelas & George, 1986). The probability is higher if the individual was young at the time of the first episode, if the first episode was precipitated by a minor stressor, and if a close family member has some kind of affective disorder. More recent studies have confirmed the influence of stressors as precipitators of bipolar episodes (Cohen & others, 2004; Hlastala, 2003).

Cyclothymia

Cyclothymia is similar to bipolar disorder, but the episodes of mania and depression are less intense. **Hypomania,** a milder form of mania, may involve any or all of the symptoms of mania (Sarason & Sarason, 2004). Although occupational or social functioning is not likely to be impaired in hypomania, functioning may be impaired during the depressive phase of cyclothymia, but not as severely as in major depression.

A diagnosis of cyclothymia is made when a person exhibits symptoms for at least 2 years. The symptoms usually first appear during adolescence or early adulthood, and, like bipolar disorder, there is no gender difference in rates of disease. Individuals with cyclothymia are likely to develop bipolar disorder later in life.

Checkpoint

What are the major differences between bipolar disorder and major depression? What differences suggest that the two mood disorders are different illnesses with different neurological bases?

REVIEW

- The two main categories of affective disorders—depressive disorders and bipolar disorders—are characterized by one or two extreme mood states: depression and mania.
- Symptoms of depression include depressed mood, diminished pleasure in activities, and feelings of worthlessness or guilt. Symptoms of mania include an elevated, expansive, or irritable mood and inflated self-esteem or grandiosity.

- The depressive disorders are major depression, characterized by depressed mood of at least 2 weeks' duration, and dysthymia, which is a chronic, low level of depression.
- The bipolar disorders, bipolar disorder and cyclothymia, consist of alternating episodes of mania and depression. In cyclothymia, the episodes are less intense but are likely to last longer than in bipolar disorder.

Neural Changes and Affective Disorders

What biological changes are probably associated with Rose's depression and with other affective disorders? Here we look at research that has detected changes in CNS structures, metabolic activity, and neurotransmitters.

Structural Abnormalities in the Brain

Affective disorders seem to be associated with specific structural abnormalities in the brain, according to recent brain imaging studies (Kanner, 2004). For example, using MRI, Lacerda and colleagues (2004) found that the volume of gray matter in the orbital frontal cortex of subjects with major depression was significantly reduced relative to matched healthy control individuals. Other researchers found significant gray matter reductions in the prefrontal cortex of persons with bipolar disorder relative to control individuals (Lopez-Larson & others, 2002). Reductions in the volume of brain tissue in persons with mood disorders have also been reported in such structures as the hippocampus, amygdala, entorhinal cortex, basal ganglia, and thalamic nuclei (Kanner). Drevets and colleagues (1998) found that the volume of gray matter ventral to the beginning of the corpus callosum was significantly reduced in people with familial affective disorders—major depression or bipolar disorder—irrespective of current mood state or treatment status. Drevets suggested there is an underlying pathology in the prefrontal cortical and striatal systems that normally regulate the limbic and brain stem structures that mediate emotional behavior, thus producing depressive symptoms. Based on the current evidence, it is impossible to tell which comes first: the depression or the neural pathology. Does the depression lead to the brain pathology, or does preexisting brain pathology cause depression? Only further research will enable us to answer this question.

Metabolic Activity in the Brain

During Rose's depressive episodes, she has difficulty initiating voluntary behavior, has problems concentrating, and withdraws socially. These symptoms suggest that cortical activity may be lower during her depressive episodes. The characteristics of mania (which Rose does not have), such as increased activity, unusual talkativeness, and rapid speech, suggest an abnormally high cortical activity.

As revealed by PET scans, measurements of overall brain activity confirm lower-than-normal activity during a depressive episode and higher-than-normal activity during a manic episode (Figure 15.4). Although depression is associated with reduced metabolic activity in a number of areas of the brain (Oda & others, 2003), the reduction is especially apparent in the left hemisphere, particularly in the left frontal cortex (Medved & others, 2001). Decreased blood flow and metabolism have also been found in the cingulate gyrus (Galynker & others, 1998) and the basal ganglia of depressed individuals (Soares & Mann, 1997).

Figure 15.4

PET scans revealing metabolic activity during depressive and manic episodes On May 17, this patient was depressed, and metabolic activity was low, as indicated by the darker colors (blue and green). He or she experienced a hypomanic mood on May 18, and metabolic activity in the brain increased, as indicated by the lighter colors (yellow and red). By May 27, the patient was again depressed and metabolic activity was low.

➡ **In which hemisphere are differences in activity especially noticeable during a depressive episode? Did this patient show the differences?**

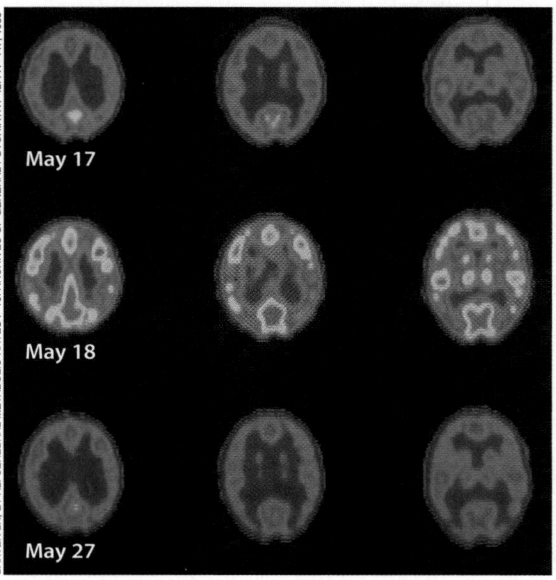

BAXTER LR, ET AL: CEREBRAL METABOLIC RATES F-18. ARCHIVES OF GENERAL PSYCHIATRY 42:441–447, 1985

Models of Depression: The Role of Neurotransmitters

Our discussion of the biological systems in the brain that are responsible for the structural abnormalities and dysfunctional metabolic activity seen in mood disorders focuses on the neurotransmitter systems involved in depressive and manic mood states.

The Monoamine Hypothesis of Depression: Reduced Monoamine Levels. A variety of evidence suggests that decreased activity in the monoamine neurotransmitter systems (the catecholamines and indoleamines; see Chapter 4) is involved in affective disorders (Nemeroff, 1998). As you will recall, the primary monoamine neurotransmitters in the brain are norepinephrine, dopamine, and serotonin. The finding that dopamine agonists, such as amphetamine and cocaine, are not effective treatments for depression suggests that dopamine is not involved, and the two monoamines thus implicated are norepinephrine (a catecholamine) and serotonin (an indoleamine). The idea that depression is caused by decreased activity at synapses where norepinephrine and serotonin are the neurotransmitters is called the **monoamine hypothesis of depression.**

monoamine hypothesis of depression The theory that depression is caused by decreased activity at monoaminergic synapses, particularly where serotonin and norepinephrine are the neurotransmitters.

The fact that dopamine agonists are generally not effective as antidepressants may strike you as counterintuitive. After all, you know that both cocaine and amphetamine, which increase dopamine release, produce euphoria in people who are not depressed. Surely such an effect in a depressed person would alleviate his or her depression. Sigmund Freud certainly thought this was the case, and he took it frequently to cure his "depression" (Jones, 1953). The typically prescribed antidepressants (e.g., MAOIs, tricyclics, SSRIs) have little or no effect on the reuptake of dopamine, which also suggests that dopamine is not involved in depression.

However, a sizable minority of depressed patients are not helped by any of the standard drug treatments, which leaves open the possibility that dopamine (or other neurotransmitters) may be involved in their depression (Warner, 2005). In this subset of patients, stimulants such as amphetamine may be beneficial, when used cautiously because of the potential for abuse (Nierenberg & others, 1998; Singh & Malone, 2001).

Early studies pointed to a deficiency in monoamine levels in depressed individuals. For example, the level of a serotonin metabolite (5-HIAA) was found to be lower than normal in people with major depression, which suggests that serotonin levels were low as well (Ashcroft & others, 1966). Low levels of 5-HIAA are also associated with a high risk of suicide (Asberg & others, 1976; Bourgeois, 1991; Mann & others, 1992; Ricci & Wellman, 1990). For example, in a sample of 68 depressed patients, Asberg and colleagues found a bimodal distribution of 5-HIAA levels. Patients in the low mode attempted suicide significantly more often than those in the high mode, and their methods were more violent. More recent evidence for an association between low CSF levels of 5-HIAA and high-lethality suicide attempters has been found (Placidi & others, 2001). Other studies found a lower-than-normal level of a norepinephrine metabolite (MHPG) in the cerebrospinal fluid, plasma, and urine of people with major depression (Maas & others, 1971, 1974) and that urinary levels of norepinephrine metabolites increased as subjects with bipolar disorder became manic and decreased as they became depressed (Bunney & others, 1972).

As further evidence for the monoamine hypothesis of depression, drugs that decrease brain monoamine levels have been found to induce depressive behavior. For example, reserpine reduces both serotonin and norepinephrine levels by making the neurotransmitter-containing synaptic vesicles leaky, and produces depression in some people taking it as a treatment for hypertension (Ban, 2001; Lemieux & others, 1956). Whether the depression is caused by reserpine's effect on the monoamines is debatable, however, and Baumeister and colleagues (2003) argue that reserpine does not produce depression and that the myth of its depressive effect is retained because of a reluctance by neuroscientists to discard the monoamine hypothesis of depression.

By contrast, drugs that elevate brain monoamine levels often decrease depressive symptoms, further suggesting the role of a monoamine deficiency in depression (Nutt, 2002). Research evaluating the effect of lithium carbonate on patients with bipolar disorder also supports the role of the brain monoamines in both mania and depression. As indicated earlier, norepinephrine metabolite levels in the urine increase during episodes of mania (Bunney & others, 1972). Because lithium carbonate decreases brain norepinephrine levels, it should provide an effective treatment for mania (Swann & others, 1987), and its clinical effectiveness is indeed well established (e.g., Baldessarini & others, 2002; Geddes & others, 2004; Goodwin & Geddes, 2003).

Refinements of the Monoamine Hypothesis: Receptor Sensitivity. Our discussion to this point suggests a simple relationship in which decreased norepinephrine and serotonin levels are associated with depression and increased levels with mania. However, more recent research indicates that the earlier studies may not have provided an accurate view of the biochemical basis of affective disorders. Studies using more sensitive measurements of MHPG (and thus norepinephrine) levels have reported that people with major depression have normal cerebrospinal fluid levels of norepinephrine (e.g., Geracioti & others, 1997). Other investigations have generally found increased plasma norepinephrine levels (e.g., Grossman & Potter, 1999). Mass spectroscopic measurements have revealed that depressed individuals have increased norepinephrine metabolite levels, and antidepressant drugs that successfully reduce depressive symptoms decrease cerebrospinal and plasma levels of MHPG (e.g., Sheline & others, 1997).

Thus, we find an apparent contradiction between the main idea of the monoamine hypothesis of depression and the results of studies of monoamine metabolite levels in people with depression. On the one hand, the monoamine hypothesis states that depression results from reduced activity at monoamine synapses, which suggests reduced levels of neurotransmitter, particularly norepinephrine and serotonin. On the other hand, many studies of monoamine metabolites have found *elevated* levels in people with depression and decreased levels during effective treatment. Further evidence against the monoamine hypothesis of depression, at least as originally stated, includes the observation that the major antidepressant drugs increase their target monoamines quickly, yet generally do not begin to produce an antidepressant effect for at least 2 weeks.

Because of these observations and others, the original monoamine hypothesis of depression has evolved into a hypothesis that stresses changes in monoamine receptor sensitivity rather than reductions in monoamine levels (Leonard, 1997). According to the receptor sensitivity idea, the delayed therapeutic effects of antidepressants result from time-dependent adaptational changes in the neurotransmitter receptors. The increased norepinephrine metabolite levels often seen in depressed people result from the attempt by the brain to compensate for the decreased receptor sensitivity by producing more norepinephrine.

Role of Norepinephrine and the Locus Coeruleus

Newer models of depression also stress the importance of the functioning of the *locus coeruleus,* a major site of norepinephrine synthesis that is located in the pons and connected to the hypothalamus, hippocampus, and cerebral cortex. Electrical stimulation of the locus coeruleus in primates produces intense arousal, hypervigilance, and suppression of exploratory activity (Aston-Jones & others, 1984). Exposure to threatening situations increases locus coeruleus activity, and the activity decreases during sleep, grooming, and feeding (Rajkowski & others, 1994).

The behaviors seen in primates when the locus coeruleus is stimulated are similar to behaviors seen in depressed humans, which suggests that excessive locus coeruleus activity may be involved in depression. In support of this idea, researchers have reported that antidepressant drugs decrease the firing rate in locus coeruleus neurons (Grant & Weiss, 2001; Szabo & Blier, 2001). And as we have indicated, antidepressant treatment reduces the levels of MHPG, a norepinephrine metabolite, in the CNS (Backman & others, 2000; Sheline & others 1997).

tricyclic compound A type of antidepressant drug that increases brain levels of norepinephrine and serotonin by interfering with neurotransmitter reuptake.

monoamine oxidase inhibitor (MAOI) A type of antidepressant drug that increases monoamine levels by preventing MAO from degrading excess monoamine neurotransmitters.

Role of GABA and Acetylcholine

In addition to norepinephrine and serotonin (and perhaps dopamine in some people), acetylcholine and GABA have been investigated as possible contributors to depression. For example, several studies have suggested that people with major depression may have hyperresponsive cholinergic systems (e.g., Janowsky & others, 1994; Risch & others, 1981). ACh stimulates certain receptors in the locus coeruleus, increasing the activity of this brain area in the rat (Adams & Foote, 1988). The cholinergic agonist nicotine activates noradrenergic neurons in the locus coeruleus of the rat (Erhardt & others, 2000).

Evidence for the possible involvement of GABA in depression includes the observation that many depressed people have low cerebrospinal fluid and plasma levels of GABA (Brambilla & others, 2003; Petty, 1994). Further, the administration of GABA agonists has been shown to have antidepressant effects (Brambilla & others). GABA inhibits the firing of noradrenergic neurons in the locus coeruleus of the rat (Van Bockstaele, 1998); therefore, a decrease in GABA levels would increase locus coeruleus activity, possibly leading to depression.

Checkpoint

Leo has decreased levels of norepinephrine, serotonin, and GABA. Based on what you have learned, would you expect him to exhibit symptoms of depression or mania?

REVIEW

- Brain activity is lower than normal during a depressive state and higher than normal during a manic state, with evidence implicating a dysfunction of the prefrontal cortex in people with depression.
- Relative to normal activity, the differences in brain activity during a depressive episode are most apparent in the left hemisphere and especially in the left frontal cortex.
- A variety of evidence supports the monoamine hypothesis of depression, which holds that depression is caused by decreased activity at synapses where norepinephrine and serotonin (and dopamine in some people) are the neurotransmitters.
- Newer models of depression stress the importance of the locus coeruleus; its increased activity produces intense arousal. Antidepressant drugs decrease the firing rate in the locus coeruleus.
- ACh stimulates certain receptors in the locus coeruleus, and the administration of cholinergic agonists can produce depression.
- GABA inhibits the firing of neurons in the locus coeruleus, and GABA levels may be abnormally low in depressed people.

Drug Treatments for Affective Disorders

Drugs that increase brain monoamine levels often have been found to decrease depressive symptoms. For example, two classes of drugs—tricyclic compounds and monoamine oxidase inhibitors (MAOIs)—increase brain monoamine levels and alleviate depression for many individuals. As explained in Chapter 4, **tricyclic compounds** increase norepinephrine and serotonin levels by interfering with their reuptake from the synapse after the neuron fires (Figure 15.5). Although the introduction of SSRIs (see below) has relegated the tricyclics to second choice in treating depression, tricyclics are as effective as the newer medications in treating mild to moderate depression and perhaps more effective in treating severe depression (Boyce & Judd, 1999).

Monoamine oxidase inhibitors (MAOIs) increase levels of norepinephrine and serotonin by preventing their breakdown (Figure 15.5), thus prolonging their effectiveness during neural transmission. An analysis of the available research concluded that MAOIs such as phenelzine and tranylcypromine are more effective than tricyclics in treating atypical depression—depression with symptoms such as overeating, excessive sleeping, and agitation—and are effective in treating depressed patients who do not respond to the tricyclics (Thase & others, 1995).

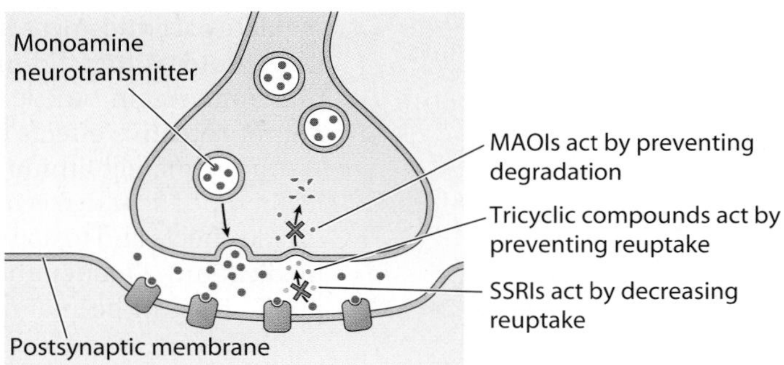
Monoamine neurotransmitter
Postsynaptic membrane
MAOIs act by preventing degradation
Tricyclic compounds act by preventing reuptake
SSRIs act by decreasing reuptake

Figure 15.5

The synaptic effects of three types of antidepressant drugs Tricyclic compounds block the reuptake of monoamines by the presynaptic membrane, monoamine oxidase inhibitors (MAOIs) prevent the breakdown of monoamines by monoamine oxidase, and serotonin-specific reuptake inhibitors (SSRIs) decrease the reuptake of the monoamine serotonin.

What is the monoamine theory of depression?

serotonin-specific reuptake inhibitor (SSRI) An antidepressant drug that increases the availability of serotonin by decreasing its reuptake.

Although tricyclic compounds and MAOIs are still prescribed, depressed patients are now more likely to take a **serotonin-specific reuptake inhibitor (SSRI),** such as fluoxetine (Prozac) or sertraline (Zoloft). In fact, Prozac is one of the most widely prescribed psychiatric drugs. As their name indicates, the SSRIs relieve depressive symptoms by decreasing serotonin reuptake (see Figure 15.5), thereby increasing serotonin levels. Clinical studies have shown that SSRIs are at least as effective in treating depression as tricyclics and MAOIs (Martin, 1998; Rahola, 2001). The advantage of SSRIs is that they have fewer and less serious side effects than either tricyclic compounds or MAOIs (Martin). The side effects of SSRIs are generally mild nausea or headache, whereas tricyclics may produce dizziness, drowsiness, blurred vision, rapid heart rate, dry mouth, and excessive sweating (Sarason & Sarason, 2004). These side effects can be so severe that the patient stops taking the medication or reduces it to an ineffective dose. MAOIs interact with tyramine, an amino acid derivative found in fermented foods, to produce a sometimes fatal increase in blood pressure. Because so many foods contain tyramine, such as cheese (the dramatic elevation of blood pressure caused by the MAOIs is sometimes called the "cheese effect"), wine, and pickles, MAOIs are used with extreme care and only for patients who do not respond to other antidepressants (Sarason & Sarason; Thase & others, 1995).

Lithium carbonate is clinically effective in treating patients with bipolar disorder (e.g., Baldessarini & others, 2002; Swann, 2005). For example, early research found that placebo group patients had a strong tendency to stop treatment and to be hospitalized, whereas the lithium carbonate group experienced a significant reduction in manic episodes (Prien & others, 1973). Lithium carbonate also reduces the intensity of depressive episodes in people with bipolar disorder. A recent meta-analysis of randomized controlled trials that compared lithium with placebo concluded that lithium was significantly more effective than placebo in preventing relapses and particularly those involving mania (Geddes & others, 2004).

Although much has been learned about how it affects the brain, exactly how lithium accomplishes its mood-stabilizing effect has not been determined. Part of the problem is that lithium affects many neural systems, and it may be that the beneficial effects of the drug require a complex combination of alterations. As just one illustration of the complexity of its effects, lithium influences the synthesis, release, or uptake of virtually every neurotransmitter studied, including dopamine, norepinephrine, serotonin, GABA, the neuropeptides, and glutamate (Jope, 1999; Lenox & Hahn, 2000).

After an extensive review, Jope (1999) concluded that three systems seem especially important in the therapeutic effects of lithium: (1) Lithium seems to alter neurotransmitter activities in a way that adjusts the balance between excitatory and inhibitory actions—to dampen the highs and elevate the lows. In addition, the decrease of glutamate activity by lithium appears to have a neuroprotective role and an antimanic effect (Shaldubina & others, 2001). (2) Lithium affects neuronal architecture through its actions on the structural proteins of the neurons. These architectural effects may also help lithium adjust the balance between excitatory and inhibitory influences on the brain. (3) Lithium regulates second-messenger signaling pathways (Chapter 4), transcription factors (proteins that aid in carrying out the instructions of a gene), and gene expression. Again, these effects contribute to the stabilizing influence and neuroprotective effects of lithium.

Unfortunately, lithium is far from an ideal therapeutic substance. For one thing, its therapeutic range is quite limited; too little has no effect, and too much results in side effects and toxicity that lead to noncompliance (the patient stops taking the medication). Frequent blood testing is needed in order for the appropriate therapeutic level to be maintained. In addition, like most other antidepressant and antipsychotic drugs, the therapeutic effect of lithium, if any, appears after a period of chronic treatment, suggesting that a complex and progressive biological process is involved (Detera-Wadleigh, 2001). Even at a therapeutic level, long-term lithium therapy can produce increased urination, cognitive deficits, and obesity (Julien, 2005; Keck & McElroy, 2003).

When drug treatment fails or becomes ineffective, a physician may prescribe electroconvulsive therapy for treatment of depression (Box 15.1). Another possibility for drug-resistant depressed patients is repetitive transcranial magnetic stimulation.

Checkpoint

Why might a particular antidepressant drug be effective for one patient but not for another?

REVIEW

- Antidepressant drugs (tricyclic compounds, MAOIs, SSRIs) are noradrenergic and serotonergic agonists.
- Lithium carbonate is clinically effective in treating patients with bipolar disorder.

The Role of Genetics in Affective Disorders

The symptoms of affective disorders are complex, often pervasive, and almost certainly have multiple causative factors. Genetics (family history) influences the development of these disorders. One common method of identifying the genetic basis of a particular characteristic, such as depression, is a twin study, in which identical (monozygotic) twins and fraternal (dizygotic) twins are examined to find the rate at which some characteristic of interest occurs in both members of the pairs—the **concordance rate.** If the concordance rate is much higher in identical twins than in fraternal twins, there is a strong likelihood of a genetic basis for the characteristic.

In a review of studies on concordance rates for bipolar disorder, the rate reported for identical twins ranged from approximately 20% to 75% (Craddock & Jones, 1999). This means that if one twin had bipolar disorder, the likelihood that the other twin also had this disorder was between 20% and 75%, depending on the study. By contrast, the rate for fraternal twins ranged from 0% to 8%. The concordance rate for other first-degree relatives, such as parent and child, was between 5% and 10%, which indicates that an individual has an increased risk of developing bipolar disorder if a close relative suffers from the disease. The likelihood that two unrelated people will both develop bipolar disorder is 0.5% to 1.5%. In a large Danish study, persons with a first-degree relative with bipolar disorder had a nearly 14 times greater risk of the disorder relative to persons without an affected relative (Mortensen & others, 2003).

Genetic factors also seem to contribute to major depression. For example, researchers found a concordance rate for identical twins of approximately 50% (Pauls & others, 1992) and a concordance rate for fraternal twins of about 20% (Tsuang & Faraone, 1990). In a Swedish sample, the concordance rate for affective disorders for identical twins was about twice as great as for fraternal twins: 48.2% versus 23.4%, or 69.7% versus 34.9%, depending on the stringency of the diagnostic criteria (Kendler & others, 1993). Early-onset major depression appears to have a stronger genetic component than later onset (Lyons & others, 1998; Pauls & others).

Adoption studies have provided further evidence of a genetic influence on the development of affective disorders (Ingraham & Wender, 1992; Taylor & others, 2002). One problem with studying the concordance rate for first-degree relatives is that they share the same environment, as well as sharing many of the same genes. Because they do not share the environment of their biological parents, the

concordance rate The rate at which any characteristic occurs in both members of a pair of relatives.

Box 15.1
Electroconvulsive Therapy

We have described three classes of antidepressant drugs—tricyclic compounds, MAOIs, and SSRIs—that are used for treating major depression, and there are many different drugs in each class. Unfortunately, a small but significant percentage of people with depression do not respond to any of the antidepressant medications, and some have such severe depression that there is a statistical probability they will commit suicide during the 2 week or longer period before an antidepressant medication begins to take effect. For these groups of patients, another treatment method that is both relatively old and quite controversial may help—**electroconvulsive therapy (ECT)** (Figure 15.6).

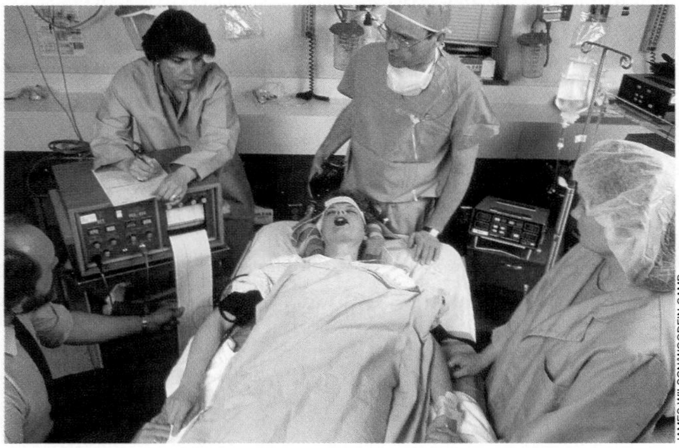

JAMES WILSON/WOODFIN CAMP

Figure 15.6
Use of electroconvulsive therapy (ECT) to treat major depression
ECT can be an effective antidepressant treatment in people with depression who do not respond to antidepressant medications.

➜ **What are the potential negative consequences of ECT?**

Introduced in 1934 for treating schizophrenia, ECT was quickly recognized to be an effective treatment for affective disorders (Fink, 2001). Its use declined in the 1950s and 1960s with the introduction of pharmacological medications, but ECT as a treatment for mental disorders never completely disappeared. According to Fink, ECT is both safe and effective in treating such disorders as major depression, bipolar disorder, and schizophrenia. Its major limitations include a high relapse rate, memory problems, and the mystery about its method of action, despite copious research. Still, ECT remains a worthwhile treatment for people with drug-resistant depression (Fink; McCall, 2001) and those with atypical affective disorders who do not respond to drug treatment (Ciapparelli & others, 2001).

In an ECT treatment, an electrical current is passed through the patient's head, to produce a tonic (rigid) and then clonic (shaking) seizure. To avoid the kind of serious injury that occasionally occurred in the early days of ECT treatment, the patient receives both anesthesia and a muscle relaxant before the current is applied (Figure 15.6).

One of the most serious problems with the use of ECT is the high relapse rate. For example, a review of the literature reported that the relapse rate in early studies was approximately 50% without follow-up treatment, and most relapses occurred in the first 6 months after treatment (Bourgon & Kelner, 2000). Of course, the high relapse rate is not surprising given that most ECT recipients are medication-resistant and that treatment is

---

concordance rate between an adopted child and the biological parents is a truer measure of the genetic influence. By the same token, the concordance rate between an adopted child and the adoptive parents is a truer measure of the environmental influence. Adoption studies generally show that the difference in concordance rates between identical and fraternal twins remains even when the twins are raised apart (e.g., DiLalla & others, 1996).

Although genetic factors appear to contribute to both major depression and bipolar disorder, the contribution may be greater for bipolar disorder. To evaluate the risks, researchers interviewed the relatives of 612 individuals hospitalized with symptoms of a mood disorder (Rice & others, 1987). The sample consisted of 2,225 parents, siblings, children, and spouses of the patients. The researchers found that 1.1% of the relatives of people with major depression showed symptoms of this disorder, and 5.7% of the relatives of people with bipolar disorder showed symptoms

electroconvulsive therapy (ECT) A treatment for depression in which an electric current is passed through the head to induce a seizure.

discontinued as soon as it becomes effective (McCall, 2001). Thus, maintenance ECT treatments may be the only way to prevent relapse for some patients.

Another major problem with the use of ECT is that it produces cognitive impairment, particularly retrograde amnesia (Chapter 14). In one study, the memory deficits after ECT were greater and more persistent for knowledge about the world (impersonal memory) than for knowledge about the self (personal memory), and bilateral ECT caused a greater amnesic effect than right unilateral ECT (Lisanby & others, 2000). Fortunately, right unilateral ECT at a high dose is just as effective at alleviating severe depressive symptoms as bilateral treatment, with less severe cognitive problems (Sackeim & others, 2000).

How ECT works to alleviate depressive symptoms remains both a mystery and a challenge (Fink, 2001). To respond to that challenge, researchers used single-photon emission computed tomography (SPECT) to measure the regional cerebral blood flow (rCBF) of depressed patients before and after ECT treatment (Milo & others, 2001). Before treatment, the depressed patients had decreased blood flow in their frontal lobes relative to controls. After ECT, patients with an excellent clinical response had rCBF changes toward normal blood flow, whereas those with a minimal to moderate clinical response showed no significant change in rCBF. These results suggest that ECT, when it works, normalizes blood flow in the frontal lobes.

In another study using SPECT to measure rCBF, clinically effective ECT resulted in a "highly significant increase" in GABAergic neurotransmission in drug-resistant depressed patients, suggesting that ECT increases the inhibitory effect of GABA on the locus coeruleus, decreasing its activity and alleviating depression (Mervaala & others, 2001). In a related experiment, researchers looked at changes in locus coeruleus activity in rats following the administration of various antidepressant drugs or ECT (Grant & Weiss, 2001). All of the treatments decreased locus coeruleus activity. Rather than being a mystery, ECT seems to produce changes that ultimately reduce locus coeruleus activity. The central question may now be, given that both ECT and the antidepressant drugs reduce locus coeruleus activity, why is ECT effective when drugs are not?

A relatively new alternative to electroconvulsive therapy is *repetitive transcranial magnetic stimulation* (rTMS). This treatment involves placing a magnet on the patient's head and stimulating the left prefrontal cortex with electromagnetic fields. Because evidence suggests that functioning in the left prefrontal cortex is generally depressed in depressive episodes and the prefrontal cortex is readily accessible to rTMS stimulation, major depression has been most frequently targeted with this treatment method (Electromagnetic Stimulation, 2000–2006). The treatment has also been tried for such diverse conditions as mania, post traumatic stress disorder, Parkinson's disease, and obsessive-compulsive disorder. One advantage of rTMS over ECT is that it does not require anesthesia, which means that patients can go about their normal routines before and after treatment and may even be able to drive themselves to and from the treatment facility (Dryden, 2004).

A meta-analysis of studies using rTMS concluded that the procedure produces measurable clinical improvement (Kozel & George, 2002). In addition, at least two reports from Taiwan have supported the effectiveness of rTMS for treating medication-resistant patients with major depression (Huang & others, 2005; Su & others, 2005). Finally, researchers in Germany compared the effectiveness of unilateral ECT and rTMS and found that rTMS was just as effective as ECT, without producing memory loss (Schulze-Rauschenbach & others, 2005).

of this disorder, suggesting that the genetic contribution is more than five times higher for bipolar disorder than for major depression. In addition, the relatives of people with bipolar disorder were more likely to show symptoms of an affective disorder than were the relatives of persons with major depression (Winokur & others, 1995a).

Researchers have attempted to identify the particular gene or genes responsible for the inheritance of an affective disorder. One study pointed to a dominant gene on the X chromosome as responsible for bipolar disorder (Cadoret & others, 1970). If this view is correct, then male children of a father with bipolar disorder and a mother without should not develop the disorder, because they receive their Y chromosome, not their X chromosome, from their father. An investigation of the family history of people with bipolar disorder reported no instances in which both father and son had been diagnosed with the disease (Winokur & others, 1969). By

learned helplessness A pattern of depression-like behavior produced by repeated exposure to an inescapable noxious event.

contrast, for father-daughter pairs, the researchers found a 13% concordance rate (one of the daughter's two X chromosomes comes from the father); mother-child pairs (mother-son and mother-daughter) had a 17% concordance rate (all children receive one X chromosome). These results support the idea that genes located on the X chromosome are responsible for transmitting bipolar disorder. In a later study, the researchers reported a pattern of risk for depressive illness incompatible with their genetic model for bipolar disorder (Cadoret & others, 1971). Although their simple genetic model was not supported, the results do provide further evidence for different types of affective disorder (bipolar and major depression).

In at least partial support for the X-chromosome idea of bipolar disorder, researchers presented evidence of an X chromosome location for bipolar disorder in Sephardic Jews (descendants of Jews who settled mainly in Spain, Portugal, and North Africa) but not for other populations (Baron & others, 1987). However, more recent research has found instances of father-son pairs diagnosed with bipolar disorder (e.g., Sham & others, 1992). Other studies have found no common genes on the X chromosomes of people with bipolar disorder (Vallada & others, 1998) and no support for genes for bipolar disorder on the X chromosome (Mors & others, 2001).

Other chromosomes also have been implicated in the transmission of affective disorders. For example, several researchers have pointed to a substantial genetic contribution to bipolar disorder on chromosome 13 (Badenhop & others, 2001; Shaw & others, 2003). Badenhop and colleagues (2002) also found evidence for bipolar susceptibility linkage to chromosomes 3, 9, 13, and 19, with possible additional susceptibility loci on chromosomes 8, 18, and 22.

In a review article, the authors described bipolar disorder as a complex genetic disorder, in which a single gene may occasionally play a major role in susceptibility (Craddock & Jones, 1999). More typically, however, bipolar disorder involves multiple genes or complex gene interactions. Craddock and Jones concluded that, given the amount of research interest in this area, bipolar susceptibility genes are almost certain to be identified in the next few years.

➤Checkpoint

Give a possible reason for the conflicting results in the search for a gene involved in the development of affective disorders. How would you go about determining whether there is a genetic basis for Rose's depression?

The Role of the Environment in Affective Disorders

Studies on the role of experience in the development of affective disorders have been conducted primarily on animals. Animal models are useful in making connections with the behavioral characteristics of human clinical depression.

For example, Martin Seligman (1975) found that repeatedly exposing animals to an inescapable noxious event produced a condition he called **learned helplessness.** In this condition, animals will fail to escape a new noxious event even when such escape is possible. They have learned to be passive in the face of uncontrollable events. Jay Weiss and his associates have produced evidence suggesting that learned helplessness may be responsible for the brain monoaminergic changes seen in depression (Weiss & others, 1985). These researchers have found that when rats are exposed to a series of inescapable shocks, they develop a pattern of behavior that reproduces many of the symptoms of human depression (Weiss & Simson, 1986).

Learned helplessness created in laboratory animals is accompanied by isolated decreases in norepinephrine in the locus coeruleus (Hughes & others, 1984; Weiss & Simson, 1986). The decreased norepinephrine level presumably reflects an increased sensitivity to the neurotransmitter. As noted earlier, antidepressant drugs decrease the firing rate of neurons in the locus coeruleus (Grant & Weiss, 2001) and reduce the level of the norepinephrine metabolite MHPG in the brain (Backman & others, 2000). If learned helplessness is a valid model of depression, then antidepressant drugs should decrease learned helplessness and reduce locus coeruleus activity. In fact, uncontrollable noxious events seem to produce heightened locus coeruleus activity, manifested as the behavioral changes associated with depression (Weiss & Simson).

Other animal models of depression include animals subjected to olfactory bulb removal (bulbectomy), animals given clomipramine as newborns, and animals deprived of their mothers while young (Norrholm & Ouimet, 2001). Clomipramine is structurally a tricyclic antidepressant, although Julien (2005) classifies it as a mixed serotonin-norepinephrine reuptake inhibitor because of its inhibitory effect on serotonin reuptake. Of the various treatments, olfactory bulbectomy appears to have received the greatest support as a valid animal model of depression, and the bulbectomy-induced behaviors seen in rats are consistent with behaviors associated with depression in humans. For example, researchers described the following behavioral changes in bulbectomized rats: hyperactivity in an enclosed area (similar to the agitation seen in people with depression); increased nocturnal activity (insomnia); and changes in food-motivated and conditioned taste aversion behavior (changes in eating habits) (Kelly & others, 1997).

Olfactory bulb removal reduces serotonin, norepinephrine, and dopamine levels in the frontal cortex (Redmond & others, 1997), and many of the behaviors and neurotransmitter changes produced by bulbectomy are lessened by long-term (but not short-term) treatment with antidepressant drugs (Cryan & others, 1999; Kelly & others, 1997). This reversal of bulbectomy-induced changes by antidepressant drugs apparently does not occur in the other animal models of depression, which makes the bulbectomy model even more promising (Jesberger & Richardson, 1985).

Further support for the rat bulbectomy model of depression comes from studies of olfactory sensitivity in humans with depression. For example, in one study, olfactory sensitivity was significantly reduced relative to control participants, and it increased following successful medical treatment (Pause & others, 2001, 2003).

Checkpoint

Why is it important to develop animal models of depression?

REVIEW

- Twin studies show that the probability of two people developing the same affective disorder increases as the closeness of their genetic relationship increases.
- The role of genetics is much stronger in bipolar disorder than in major depression.
- Investigators have identified several possible locations of the gene(s) for affective disorders, but no genetic mechanism has yet been identified.
- Repeated exposure to uncontrollable noxious events can produce learned helplessness in animals, which may be an animal model of human depression. Learned helplessness may be one factor responsible for the increased locus coeruleus activity associated with depression.
- The administration of antidepressant drugs decreases locus coeruleus activity and eliminates the behavioral deficits resulting from exposure to uncontrollable noxious events.
- The most promising animal model of depression is the olfactory bulbectomized rat, which shares several behavioral and physiological characteristics with depressed humans and responds similarly to antidepressant drugs.

Sleep and Depression

Sleep problems, such as insomnia and hypersomnia, are frequently reported by people suffering from depression. Several investigators have found that many depressed individuals show a disturbance in the typical sleep cycle (e.g., Berger & others, 2003; Seifritz, 2001). The same pattern of disturbances is also seen in

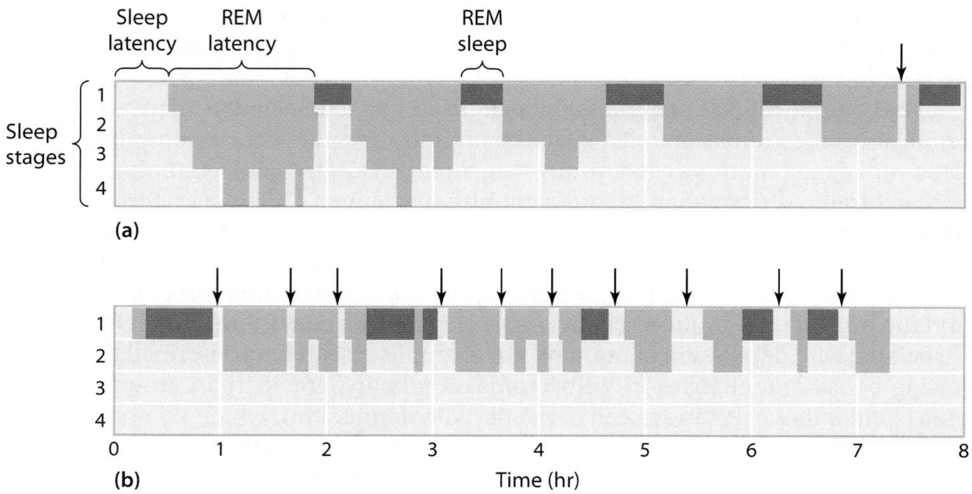

Figure 15.7
Depression and REM sleep (a) A normal sleep pattern and (b) the sleep pattern seen in many depressed people. Note that in (b), REM sleep occurs earlier in the sleep cycle, the duration of sleep is shortened, and there is no stage 3 or 4 sleep. (Arrows point to periods of wakefulness.)

➡ Why does REM sleep occur earlier in the cycle in depressed people?

people with bipolar disorder during the depression phase of their cycle (Riemann & others, 2002). REM sleep occurs earlier than normal (shorter REM latency), and total sleep time is shortened (Figure 15.7). Like Rose in the vignette, depressed people also experience greater difficulty falling asleep (increased sleep latency) and are more easily awakened during sleep.

As one explanation for the sleep disturbances, investigators suggested that REM sleep occurs earlier in the night to compensate for the hyperarousal of the locus coeruleus during the day (Gold & others, 1988). (Recall from Chapter 9 that REM sleep is associated with reduced locus coeruleus activity.) In agreement with this explanation, most antidepressant drugs tend to normalize the REM sleep pattern (Ott, 2001).

Altering the sleep-wake cycle can affect a person's depression. For example, research has shown that advancing the sleep-wake cycle by several hours (e.g., going to sleep at 5 p.m. and waking at 2 a.m.) can alleviate the symptoms of depression (Berger & others, 2003). On the basis of a review of the literature, Vogel and colleagues (1990) concluded that all drugs that produce arousal-type REM sleep deprivation improve depressive symptoms.

The disturbed sleep response of many people with depression can be produced in nondepressed people by shifting the onset of sleep from 10 p.m. to 10 a.m. (Weitzman & others, 1970). In addition, an experimentally altered sleep-wake cycle has been shown to trigger depression, hostility, and anxiety in some healthy individuals (Cutler & Cohen, 1979).

Sleep in some depressed persons resembles sleep in normal people with phase-advanced circadian rhythms (Wehr & others, 1979). Based on this observation, the researchers were able to bring a woman with a bipolar disorder out of her depression on two separate occasions by advancing her sleep cycle so that she went to sleep and arose 6 hours earlier than usual.

This relationship between an advanced sleep-wake cycle and depression may be influenced by genetic factors (Giles & others, 1998). For example, in a study of 14 people with early-onset depression, the risk for depression among relatives with reduced REM latency was nearly three times the risk in relatives with normal REM latency (Giles & others, 1988). The researchers also found that REM latency predicted major depression during a person's lifetime.

In addition, shortened REM latency following electroconvulsive therapy is associated with an increased tendency for a recurrence of depressive symptoms that have been alleviated by the ECT (Grunhaus & others, 1994, 1997). ECT has also been shown to improve sleep time, sleep continuity, and the structure of sleep, as indicated by increased stage 2 and REM sleep (Hoffmann & others, 1985).

hypercortisolism An abnormally high secretion (hypersecretion) of cortisol from the adrenal cortex; found in many people with major depression.

dexamethasone suppression test (DST) A test to determine whether the administration of dexamethasone suppresses ACTH and cortisol secretion; many depressed people have an abnormal response.

Advancing the time of REM sleep, although related to depression in some people, is only one of many factors involved in producing depression. Not all depressed people show a sleep disturbance, and an altered sleep-wake cycle does not always produce depression in nondepressed people. Clearly, there are different types and causes of depression.

Checkpoint

Explain why certain antidepressant drugs might delay the onset of REM sleep.

REVIEW

- In depressed people who experience sleep-wake cycle disturbances, REM sleep occurs earlier than normal, and total sleep time is shortened.
- The early onset of REM sleep may compensate for the hyperarousal of the locus coeruleus during the day. Antidepressant drugs restore the normal REM sleep pattern.
- Advancing the sleep-wake cycle by several hours can alleviate depression in some people.

A Biochemical Marker for Depression

Cortisol, which we encountered in Chapter 12 in the discussion of the stress reaction, is produced by the adrenal glands. The main function of cortisol is to mediate the body's response to stress. It is also involved in such functions as maintaining blood pressure, retarding the inflammatory response of the immune system, and maintaining arousal and a sense of well-being. Normally, the amount of cortisol produced by the adrenal glands is precisely regulated by the hypothalamus and the pituitary gland, operating in the following sequence: First, in the presence of stress the hypothalamus sends corticotropin-releasing factor (CRF) to the anterior pituitary, which responds by secreting adrenocorticotropic hormone (ACTH). ACTH stimulates the release of cortisol from the adrenal gland. Finally, completing the cycle, cortisol in the blood is a signal to the hypothalamus and the pituitary to decrease the secretion of ACTH. The hypothalamic-pituitary-adrenal axis is shown in Figure 15.8.

Many people with major depression have **hypercortisolism,** an abnormally high secretion of cortisol from the adrenal cortex (Gold & Chrousos, 1999). Dysfunctions in several CNS structures can produce hypercortisolism. For example, the anterior pituitary gland may secrete elevated amounts of ACTH, which in turn causes excessive cortisol secretion (Parker & others, 2003). The elevated ACTH levels may be caused by a hypothalamic dysfunction that leads to elevated levels of CRF. This dysfunction is revealed by the increased CRF levels in the cerebrospinal fluid of some depressed patients.

The abnormal response of depressed patients on the **dexamethasone suppression test (DST)** provides further evidence for a pituitary-adrenal system disorder. Dexamethasone, a synthetic glucocorticoid hormone, normally suppresses ACTH and cortisol secretion, but does not do so in many people with major depression (Figure 15.9). An abnormal response on the DST has been widely studied as a neuroendocrine marker for this disorder (Levine & others, 2001). Further, the DST validates the endogenous/nonendogenous categorization sometimes used for people with depression (endogenous means "coming from within") (Rush & others,

Figure 15.8

The hypothalamic-pituitary-adrenal axis Secretion of cortisol by the adrenal glands is regulated by a negative feedback loop. (+) = increased secretion, (−) = decreased secretion.

What is the evidence linking hypercortisolism with depression?

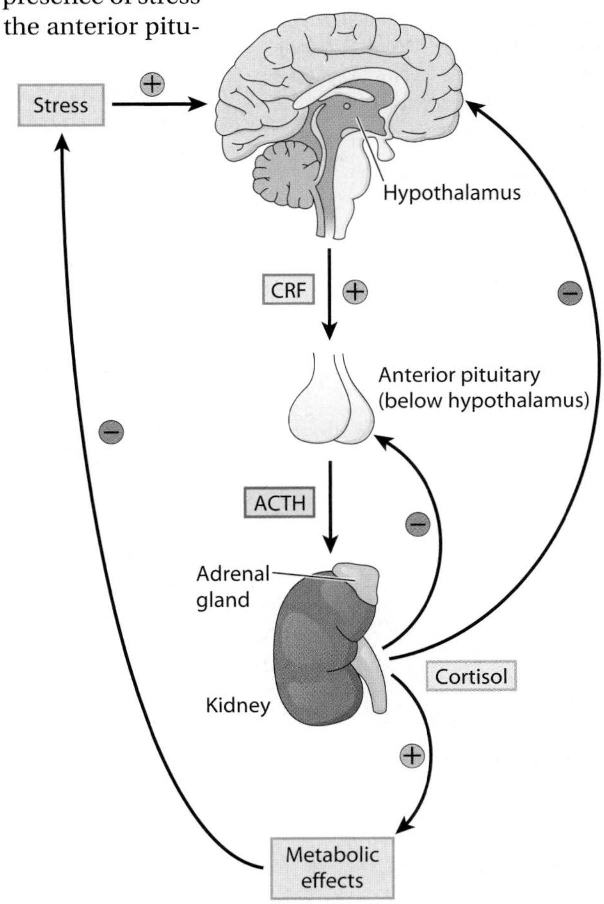

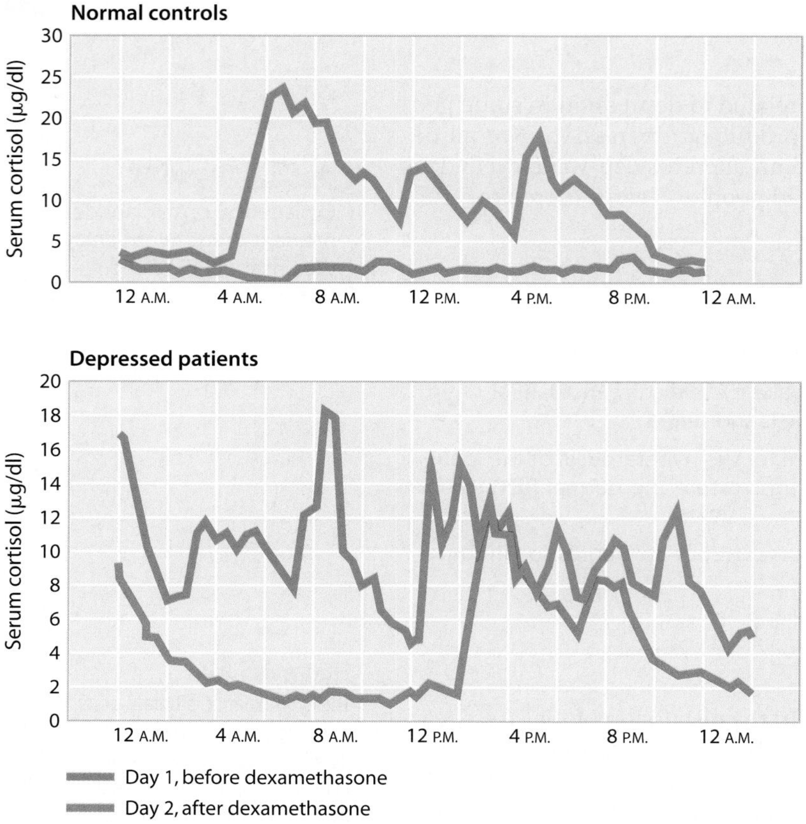

Figure 15.9

The dexamethasone suppression test Normally, dexamethasone suppresses the secretion of cortisol from the adrenal cortex; this suppression effect is absent or much reduced in many depressed people.

➔ **Why do depressed people respond to the DST as described here?**

1996). The mood disorder of a person with endogenous depression is not triggered by external events; rather, it is internally generated.

The effects of hypercortisolism can be severe, producing many of the symptoms associated with depression. For example, the direct administration of CRF into the central nervous system of rats resulted in changes such as decreased food intake, diminished sexual activity, sleep disturbances, and altered locomotor activity (Nemeroff, 1988)—all of which are symptoms of depression.

Chronic hypercortisolism causes Cushing's syndrome, which is strongly associated with major depression (Sonino & Fava, 2001, 2002). In fact, approximately half of all persons with Cushing's syndrome will also display symptoms of depression. Antidepressant drugs are generally ineffective in treating depression in patients with Cushing's syndrome (Sonino & Fava, 1998), and their symptoms often abate when they receive drugs that inhibit steroid production (Sonino & Fava, 2002). Because long-standing hypercortisolism often produces irreversible brain damage, Cushing's patients may still exhibit symptoms of depression after their cortisol levels have been normalized. In such patients, psychotherapy or drug therapy may be required for treating their depression (Sonino & Fava, 2001).

Additional support for pituitary-adrenal system involvement in major depression comes from studies of people with anorexia nervosa. Hypercortisolism is common in anorexic patients (Munoz & Argente, 2004; Seed & others, 2000), many of whom have strong family histories of major depression and suffer from depression themselves (Gucciardi & others, 2004; Rivinus & others, 1984).

We know that excessive locus coeruleus activity is associated with depression, and in addition to its effects on ACTH levels, CRF also increases the firing of neurons in the locus coeruleus (Conti & Foote, 1995, 1996). Continued exposure to stressors may produce both hypercortisolism and heightened locus coeruleus activity, which lead to depression (Gold & Chrousos, 1999).

People with major depression have a wide variation of symptoms. Some are hyperphagic (excessive eaters) rather than anorexic and experience hypersomnia instead of insomnia; some are agitated, others are not. Gold and Chrousos (1999) found evidence supporting their idea that these atypical symptoms are caused by a pathological suppression of both the CRF system and the locus coeruleus–norepinephrine system. Long-term exposure to stressors causes the inactivation of both systems and results in major depression characterized by hyperphagia and hypersomnia.

A connection has been made between depression and a combination of factors: a dysfunctional CRF system/locus coeruleus–norepinephrine system, childhood trauma, and genetic predisposition (Nemeroff, 1998). Nemeroff has put forward a hypothesis on how people who have a family history of affective disorders and had a troubled childhood subsequently develop depression—"the stress-diathesis model of mood disorders, in recognition of the interaction between experience (stress) and inborn predisposition (diathesis)" (p. 47). Several pharmaceutical manufacturers are working to develop blockers of CRF receptors to test their effectiveness as antidepressants.

➤Checkpoint

Describe the sequence of events that leads to hypercortisolism, beginning with the hypothalamus and including the terms hypothalamic CRF, anterior pituitary, ACTH, adrenal cortex, and cortisol.

REVIEW

- A hypothalamic dysfunction produces elevated levels of CRF, which increase ACTH secretion and stimulate the locus coeruleus.
- Hypercortisolism, an elevated cortisol secretion, and increased locus coeruleus activity are associated with major depression. Approximately half of the people diagnosed with Cushing's syndrome also have major depression.
- Anorexia nervosa also is correlated with both hypercortisolism and major depression.
- Some depressed people exhibit the atypical symptoms of hyperphagia, hypersomnia, and suppression of both the CRF system and the locus coeruleus–NE system.

schizophrenia A disabling mental disorder characterized by a loss of contact with reality and disturbances in perception, emotion, cognition, and motor behavior.

dementia praecox Kraepelin's name for the disorder now known as schizophrenia.

Schizophrenia

"Keep quiet. Don't answer. You stink. They know your thoughts. Fear is your worst enemy. Time is on your side." The voices came thick as leaves in fall, pelting Alice with their often nonsensical and contradictory messages. At one time she'd been aware they were self-generated, but by now this awareness had left her, along with most of her grasp on reality. She huddled in the back of her dorm room closet, listening to the voices that she was sure were planted by the Thought Patrol. The TP had gotten her wavelength a week ago and had beamed the thoughts incessantly ever since.

A knocking noise grew louder, more insistent. "Alice, are you in there?" a voice cried. The voice sounded familiar; it might belong to her roommate—or at least to the girl who claimed to be her roommate. Alice knew better. The girl who lived with her and spied on her all semester was a TP agent.

Alice pressed her body more tightly against the back of the closet, behind her dresses. The dresses reminded her of all the skin cells she had shed over her lifetime. Somehow they had coalesced into Alice replicas, and these now hung in front of her, shielding her real self from the perils outside.

Alice wasn't sure how long she had been in the closet, and she badly needed to go to the bathroom. Still, she didn't want to leave her sanctuary; the voices had been particularly insistent in their warnings.

"Hide in the closet, Alice," they had told her. "People don't want you around. You stink. Your professors are your enemies."

When Alice tried to argue, to tell them about a course she had enjoyed the few times she'd made it to class, the voices were ahead of her. "That teacher wanted to expose you in front of the class, Alice," they said. "He wanted to humiliate you."

Alice rocked on her haunches, humming loudly, trying to drown out the voices in her head. She was dimly aware of a crashing sound, of a girl, the hall monitor, saying "Oh, my God," and of her roommate telling where Alice was. Light streamed past her other selves, spotlighting her rocking form. Alice screamed, flailing out. She felt strong hands restraining her, a sharp prick on her shoulder, and then the voices and the room faded.

Alice suffers from auditory hallucinations, a symptom of schizophrenia. **Schizophrenia** is a disabling mental disorder characterized by a loss of contact with reality and by disturbances in perception, emotion, cognition, and motor behavior. As you might expect, schizophrenia is almost always associated with severe disruption of personal, social, and occupational functioning. People with schizophrenia usually have deficient social skills and few friends, impaired academic and work performance, and difficulty obtaining and keeping a job.

The behaviors characterizing schizophrenia were first described in 1883 by Emil Kraepelin, who called the disorder **dementia praecox,** the Latin for "premature insanity." The symptoms included delusions, hallucinations, attention deficits, and

neologism A meaningless word created by a person with schizophrenia.

delusion A false system of beliefs that a person defends against reality.

loosening of associations A tendency to make sentences containing several disconnected thoughts.

word salad A type of speech with no discernible links between the words.

hallucination A sensory experience in the absence of environmental stimulation.

bizarre motor behavior. Kraepelin believed that the illness began in adolescence (hence, prematurely) and involved an irreversible mental deterioration.

In 1911, Eugen Bleuler renamed this syndrome *schizophrenia,* from the Greek words *schizein,* meaning "to split," and *phren,* meaning "mind." Bleuler's rationale for changing the name was based on three observations: First, the deterioration does not always begin in adolescence but can begin later in life. Second, mental functioning may actually improve rather than deteriorate after the disorder is diagnosed. Finally, the disorder seems to reflect a splitting of the psyche's functions; that is, the person with schizophrenia experiences a dissociation of thought, emotion, and perception. The popular press and general public often confuse schizophrenia with "split personality" or "multiple personality disorder." A person with multiple personality disorder has two or more distinct personalities, whereas a person with schizophrenia has a single, rather unusual personality or one that is badly fragmented and split from reality.

Symptoms of Schizophrenia

Bleuler considered the cardinal symptoms of schizophrenia to be what he called the "four As": blunted affect (lack of or inappropriate emotions), loosening of associations (disordered thought patterns), ambivalence (inability to make decisions), and autism (withdrawal from the world outside, preoccupation with one's own thoughts). Today, we are more likely to categorize the symptoms of schizophrenia as disturbances in thought, disturbances in perception, disturbances in movement, and disturbances in affect. A person does not necessarily need to experience all categories of symptoms in order to be diagnosed with schizophrenia. For example, in a study of nearly 2,000 patients diagnosed with a schizophrenic-type illness, the most commonly reported symptoms were delusions (65%), hallucinations (52%), and conceptual disorganization (50%) (Breier & Berg, 1999). Most of the patients experienced one to three of the most common symptoms.

In order to be diagnosed as having schizophrenia, a person must satisfy a number of criteria. For example, the person must exhibit two or more characteristic symptoms, such as delusions, hallucinations, disorganized speech, disorganized behavior other than speech, or a negative symptom such as flattening of affect. Another criterion is social and/or occupational dysfunction. For example, the person with the disorder is unable to function in a work situation and/or exhibits a decreased ability to care for herself or himself. Duration of illness is important: To receive a diagnosis of schizophrenia, the person must have exhibited signs of disturbance for at least 6 months, with at least a month of the characteristic symptoms listed above.

Several disorders that resemble schizophrenia also must be ruled out before a definitive diagnosis can be made. Such disorders include a general medical condition caused by a substance such as a drug of abuse or a medication, a pervasive developmental disorder (e.g., autism), bipolar disorder, brief psychotic disorder, and various personality disorders (e.g., schizoid, paranoid).

Early symptoms of schizophrenia may be evident well before the first behavioral episode that leads to the diagnosis. For example, children with at least two family members suffering from schizophrenia may show signs of the illness as early as age 7 (Johnstone, 1998). These early signs include greater anxiety about acceptance, excessive inconsequential behavior (patients are active but in an aimless way), and high hostility. Attentional deficits and defects in information processing are also early signs of impending schizophrenia (Winters & others, 1991).

Disturbances in Thought

Because schizophrenia is characterized by disturbances in formal thought processes, it is often called a thought disorder, to distinguish it from affective (mood) disorders. *Tangentiality,* the inability to stick to one topic, is one example of a thought disturbance; people with schizophrenia often shift from one idea to another within a single sentence. Making up a meaningless word, a **neologism,** is another form of thought disturbance. Additional examples are the use of many rhyming words, the persistent use of particular words or ideas, and long pauses before completing a thought. All of these thought problems can make it difficult to understand the communication of a person with schizophrenia.

Persons with schizophrenia may also display disturbances in thought content. A **delusion,** or false system of beliefs that a person will defend against reality, is one example. Some of the most common delusions are *delusions of persecution,* the belief that other people are trying to inflict harm, as in Alice's case; *delusions of grandeur,* a person's belief that he or she is, say, Jesus Christ; and *delusions of influence,* the belief that one's thoughts or actions are being controlled by others.

As noted above, the speech of someone with schizophrenia is also likely to be impaired (DeLisi, 2001; Harvey & others, 1997). For example, a typical speech pattern may be rambling and disjointed. Sentences often contain several thoughts, which is called **loosening of associations,** one of Bleuler's cardinal symptoms. Such loosening of associations are often evident in paintings by individuals with schizophrenia (Figure 15.10). Because the person with schizophrenia often jumps from one idea to another when speaking, such speech is frequently incomprehensible. **Word salad,** with no discernible links between the words, is another characteristic.

MARTIN COHEN/WWW.FOUNTAINGALLERYNYC.COM

Figure 15.10
Work of an artist with schizophrenia The loosening of associations and distorted perceptions of a person with schizophrenia are evident in this painting.

→ **What additional symptoms of schizophrenia can you see in this piece of art?**

People with schizophrenia often do not understand why they may have been hospitalized or what is wrong with them. Investigators reported at least a moderate impairment in insight in 49.5% of patients with schizophrenia that they examined, and the impairment was highly related to severity of delusions, difficulty with abstract thinking, lack of social activities, and anxiety (Dickerson & others, 1997).

Disturbances in Perception

The most dramatic perceptual distortion experienced by a person with schizophrenia is an **hallucination,** a sensory experience in the absence of environmental stimuli. Auditory hallucinations are the most common—hearing a voice, hearing other people's thoughts, or hearing two other voices carrying on a conversation. Alice experiences this type of hallucination. People with schizophrenia may also see monsters or people that are not really there, feel bugs crawling on their skin, smell the poison gas they think their neighbors are pumping under their door, and so on. Hallucinations seem to occur in about half of cases of schizophrenia (Breier & Berg, 1999). Neural activity in the auditory cortex accompanying an hallucination has been observed during the brain imaging of people with schizophrenia. For example, functional magnetic resonance imaging (fMRI) detected increased blood flow in the primary auditory cortex of individuals with schizophrenia when they were experiencing auditory hallucinations (Dierks & others, 1999). Amazingly, their brains appear to have generated the perception of sound without external stimulation!

Disturbances in Movement

People with schizophrenia may have high levels of motor excitement, pacing constantly or flailing their limbs. They may also experience catatonic stupors or immobility, remaining in unusual positions, such as on one leg, for long periods

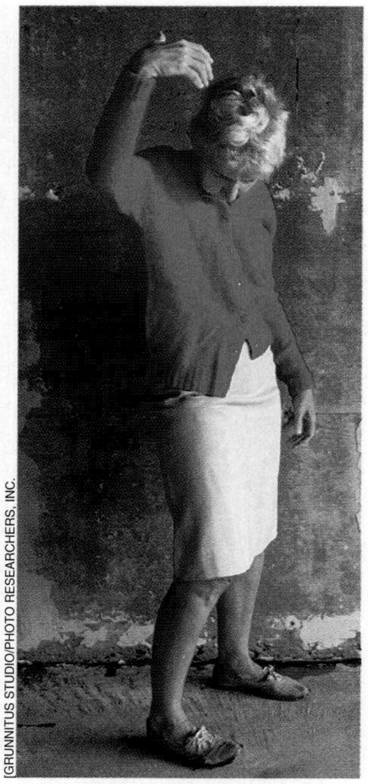

Figure 15.11
A motor disturbance in schizophrenia This woman shows the rigidity and bizarre posture characteristic of some people with schizophrenia.

➔ **What are two other types of motor disturbances experienced by people with schizophrenia?**

(Figure 15.11). Other motor disturbances include strange facial expressions or repetitive motor actions, such as head rubbing or paper tearing.

Disturbances in Affect

In addition to disordered thoughts, people with schizophrenia may exhibit either a blunted or flat affect or an inappropriate affect, another of Bleuler's cardinal symptoms. For example, a person with schizophrenia may exhibit no emotional response upon learning of the death of a family member, or may laugh when told that a friend has died. People with schizophrenia tend to use the same gestures and direct the same facial expression or gaze at the other person regardless of the emotions they are experiencing or describing (Alloy & others, 1999).

Social Withdrawal

Social withdrawal or emotional detachment is another type of symptom and also an early sign of schizophrenia (Alloy & others, 1999). People with schizophrenia often seem to be totally occupied with their own thoughts and uninterested in the world around them. Small talk is rare, and the schizophrenia sufferer often acts as if other people are not present.

Positive Versus Negative Symptoms

The symptoms of schizophrenia are sometimes categorized as positive or negative. **Positive symptoms** are behaviors not seen in normal people, such as delusions and hallucinations. **Negative symptoms** are normal behaviors such as emotions that fit the context and a desire for social contact that are absent in people with schizophrenia. Thus, a person with schizophrenia may exhibit flat affect and social withdrawal.

The Course of Schizophrenia

In many cases, schizophrenia follows a sequence of three phases (Comer, 2001). In the **prodromal phase,** which usually begins in adolescence or early adulthood (Kraepelin's dementia praecox), the person becomes socially withdrawn and school or work performance declines. The prodromal phase may be brief, or symptoms may develop gradually over a long period; the average length of this phase is about 5 years (an der Heiden & Hafner, 2000). In the **active phase,** the more acute symptoms of schizophrenia appear, such as delusions, hallucinations, or any of the other symptoms described earlier. A recovery of some functioning occurs in the **residual phase,** and the person may return to the social isolation of the prodromal phase or may continue to experience only the negative symptoms.

According to one report, in approximately 60% of cases the schizophrenia becomes chronic, whereas approximately 25% of people with schizophrenia recover within the first 5 to 6 years (an der Heiden & Hafner, 2000). Several factors affect the likelihood of recovery; poor adjustment before symptom onset, a low level of education, and negative symptoms are associated with a poor outcome (Lindstrom, 1996). Relapses are more likely to occur during times when multiple life events happen to individuals who are usually content with a low level of social integration; in one study, patients with a low level of social integration who wanted more were less likely to relapse (Hultman & others, 1997).

➤Checkpoint

Marco hears voices telling him his life is in danger; he alternates between pacing and immobility, and between hysterical laughter and unresponsiveness or stupor. Categorize Marco's symptoms according to the four general categories of disturbance, and then group them as positive or negative symptoms.

REVIEW

- Schizophrenia is a serious mental disorder characterized by disturbances in thought, perception, movement, and affect.
- Positive symptoms of schizophrenia are behaviors not seen in people without schizophrenia, such as delusions (false systems of belief) and hallucinations (false perceptions).
- Negative symptoms are normal behaviors (appropriate emotions, desire for social contact) that are absent in people with schizophrenia, as seen in social withdrawal and a flat affect.
- Schizophrenia usually goes through a prodromal phase, an active phase, and a residual phase.
- In the prodromal phase, the person becomes socially withdrawn. In the active phase, the more obvious symptoms of schizophrenia appear, such as delusions or hallucinations. Recovery of some functioning occurs in the residual phase.

positive symptom A behavior exhibited by a person with schizophrenia but absent in people without the disorder; examples are hallucinations and delusions.

negative symptom Normal behavior (e.g., appropriate emotions, desire for social contact) that is absent in people with schizophrenia, as seen in social withdrawal and a flat affect.

prodromal phase The phase of schizophrenia in which the person becomes socially withdrawn and school or work performance declines.

active phase The phase of schizophrenia in which the more acute symptoms of the disorder appear, such as hallucinations and delusions.

residual phase The phase of schizophrenia in which some recovery of functioning occurs.

dopamine hypothesis of schizophrenia The view that an excess of activity in the dopamine system results in the positive symptoms of schizophrenia.

The Dopamine Hypothesis and Drug Treatments for Schizophrenia

As we have indicated in earlier chapters, dopamine receptors are located throughout the brain and are involved in a variety of functions. Many biological psychologists have suggested that a disturbance in the dopaminergic receptors of the mesocortical dopamine system (Chapters 5 and 14) is responsible for such schizophrenia symptoms as hallucinations and delusions (e.g., Bennett, 1998). The *mesocortical dopamine system* begins in the ventral tegmental area (the bottom part of the midbrain) and projects to several forebrain regions of the cerebral cortex and limbic system (entorhinal, suprarhinal, and anterior cingulate cortex; lateral and medial frontal cortex). The **dopamine hypothesis of schizophrenia** states that an excess of dopamine activity in the mesocortical dopamine system produces the positive symptoms of schizophrenia.

Like some other important scientific breakthroughs, such as Olds's discovery of the reinforcement areas of the brain (Chapter 5), the involvement of dopamine in schizophrenia was ultimately revealed because of an accidental discovery. In 1950, French surgeon Henri Laborit noticed that antihistamine drugs reduced anxieties in his patients without producing mental confusion. Based on this observation, French chemist Paul Charpentier developed the antihistamine drug chlorpromazine and tested it on animals, noting its sedative effect. Laborit then reported that chlorpromazine also had a calming effect in humans. People with a variety of mental disorders received chlorpromazine (Thorazine), but it proved to be an effective treatment only for patients with schizophrenia, alleviating or eliminating their hallucinations and delusions (Delay & Deniker, 1952). Chlorpromazine and other antipsychotic drugs, such as haloperidol, have become an integral part of the treatment of schizophrenia.

In the 1960s, Arvid Carlsson reported a link between chlorpromazine, dopaminergic transmission, and schizophrenia. Chlorpromazine acts as a dopamine antagonist by blocking postsynaptic dopaminergic receptors (Figure 15.12), a finding that supports the dopamine hypothesis. The effectiveness of chlorpromazine and other antipsychotic medications in treating schizophrenia is primarily responsible for the dramatic decline in the number of patients in mental health care facilities.

Further support for the dopamine hypothesis has come from laboratory experiments showing that chlorpromazine

Figure 15.12

The synaptic effect of chlorpromazine Chlorpromazine, a dopaminergic antagonist, blocks transmission by attaching to dopamine receptors.

What is the dopamine hypothesis of schizophrenia and how is it supported by the actions of chlorpromazine?

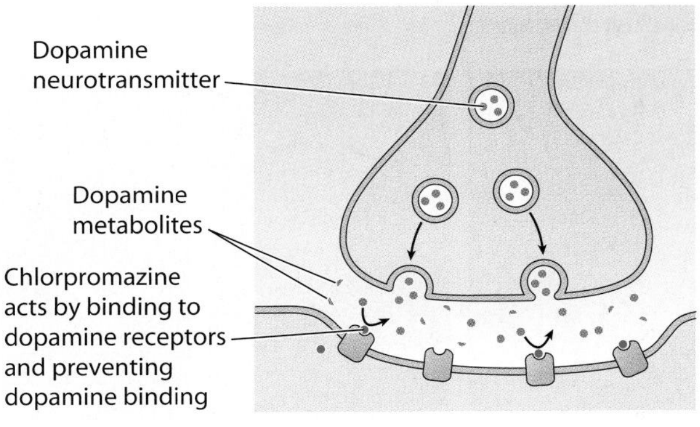
Dopamine neurotransmitter
Dopamine metabolites
Chlorpromazine acts by binding to dopamine receptors and preventing dopamine binding

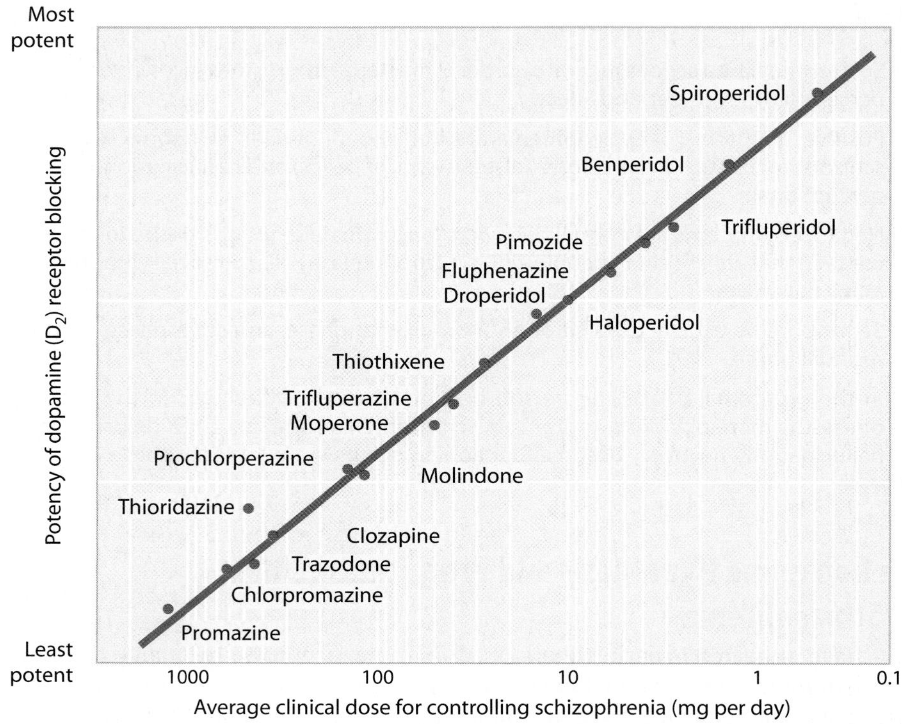

Figure 15.13

The clinical potency of antipsychotic drugs Therapeutic effectiveness is almost perfectly correlated with the ability of each drug to bind with dopamine (D_2) receptors. Note that the average clinically effective dose decreases from left to right, so the most clinically effective antipsychotic drugs are listed on the right of the graph.

➡ Which was the first-introduced antipsychotic drug? How does it compare with other antipsychotics in terms of clinical effectiveness?

and other antipsychotic drugs bind selectively to dopamine receptor sites (Creese & others, 1996). As this research demonstrates, the ability of the drugs to alleviate symptoms is highly correlated with their affinity for a particular group of dopamine receptors, the D_2 receptors; that is, the more tightly a drug binds to D_2 receptors, the more effective it is in reducing the positive symptoms of schizophrenia (Figure 15.13).

People with schizophrenia have sometimes been found to have abnormally high levels of dopamine metabolites in their blood plasma (Suzuki & others, 1994), although this is not always the case (Markianos & others, 1992; Oades & others, 2002). In addition, researchers found that the level of a certain type of dopamine metabolite was significantly higher in patients with schizophrenia in the poorest condition than in those in the best condition (Suzuki & others). These abnormal levels of dopamine metabolites presumably reflect greater synaptic activity in dopaminergic neurons and/or a greater number of dopamine receptors at each synapse. In fact, postmortem studies have revealed significantly more D_3 and D_4 receptors than normal in people with a history of schizophrenia (Marzella & others, 1997; Murray & others, 1995), whereas D_1 receptors are fewer than normal in prefrontal cortex (Okubo & others, 1997). This reduction was related to the severity of negative symptoms, such as emotional withdrawal. Some researchers found greater concentrations of D_4 receptors in the nucleus accumbens (Murray & others), and others reported more D_3 receptors in the corpus striatum (caudate nucleus and putamen; Figure 15.14) (Marzella & others).

Figure 15.14

Concentrations of dopamine (D_3) receptors in the corpus striatum Postmortem studies show greater concentrations of D_3 receptors in the nucleus accumbens (NA) of (a) an unmedicated person with schizophrenia than in (b) a person without schizophrenia or in (c) a person with schizophrenia who received antipsychotic medication. The lighter colors (red, orange, yellow) represent greater concentrations of D_3 receptors. Pu = putamen.

➡ What is the significance of the greater concentrations of D_3 receptors to the dopamine hypothesis of schizophrenia?

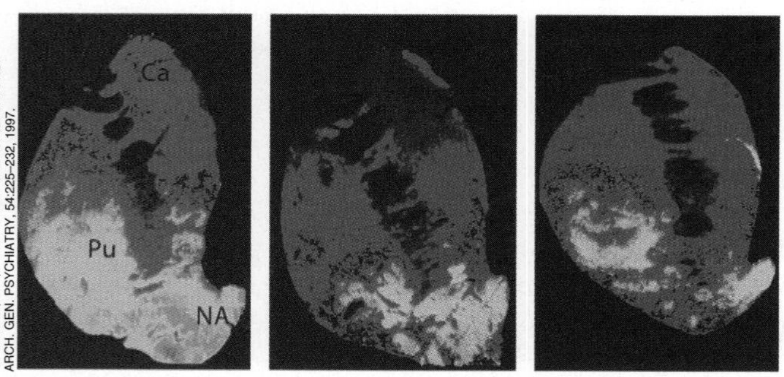

(a) (b) (c)

GUREVICH, E.V., ET AL: DOPAMINE D3 RECEPTORS. ARCH. GEN. PSYCHIATRY, 54:225–232, 1997.

Drugs that increase dopamine activity in the CNS, such as amphetamine and cocaine, can produce the positive symptoms of schizophrenia in people without the disorder (Harris & Batki, 2000; Yui & others, 2004), a finding that strengthens the dopamine hypothesis. Amphetamine use has also been shown to exacerbate positive symptoms in people already diagnosed with schizophrenia (Carlsson, 2001). Further indirect support for the dopamine hypothesis comes from the observation that L-dopa (which increases dopamine levels in the brain and is used to treat Parkinson's disease) can induce a psychosis that is responsive to such antipsychotic medications as clozapine (Fernandez & others, 1999; Meltzer & others, 1995). Thus, drugs such as the phenothiazines (e.g., chlorpromazine) that block dopaminergic activity reduce the positive symptoms of schizophrenia, whereas drugs that increase dopamine levels in the brain produce or exaggerate positive symptoms. Both of these observations support the dopamine hypothesis, at least for the positive symptoms.

Some evidence seems to be inconsistent at first glance with the dopamine hypothesis. For example, for perhaps as many as 30% of people with schizophrenia, their positive symptoms are not alleviated by treatment with chlorpromazine or other dopamine-blocking drugs (Baldessarini, 1996). However, the *atypical antipsychotic* drug clozapine (Clozaril) has proved clinically effective for patients unresponsive to treatment with the *phenothiazine antipsychotics,* such as chlorpromazine, or the *butyrophenone antipsychotics,* such as haloperidol (Pilowsky & others, 1992). Clozapine is a weak blocker of D_2 receptors, but a much more effective blocker of certain serotonergic receptors (Julien, 2005).

Further evidence against the exclusive role of the dopamine system in schizophrenia comes from research on other neurotransmitters. For example, a variety of studies have reported lower-than-normal levels of GABA and glutamate in the brains of people with schizophrenia (Cotter & others, 2002; Reynolds & others, 2001, 2004). Recall from Chapter 5 that PCP is a drug with hallucinogenic potential. Researchers have observed schizophrenic-like behaviors in primates treated with PCP (Jentsch & Roth, 1999). The symptoms of the animals were reversed with a dopamine-blocking antipsychotic drug, which supports the dopamine hypothesis. However, the mechanism of action of PCP also involves the NMDA glutamate receptor, providing further evidence for the involvement of glutamate in schizophrenia.

In fact, "schizophrenia may be a dopamine-related illness, but this relationship has not yet emerged as the neurological key to the disorder. Dopamine transmission may be a peripheral, or minor, component of the pathological mechanism itself. The nature of this mechanism remains elusive and indistinct" (Heinrichs, 1993, p. 225). At least one reason for the difficulty in elucidating the pathological mechanism in schizophrenia may be that researchers are dealing not with one illness but with several, each with a somewhat different neurological basis. This, of course, would help explain why no single antipsychotic drug is completely effective in treating schizophrenia.

As the search for the mechanism of the antipsychotic drugs continues, we will learn more about the role of dopamine and other neurotransmitters in producing the symptoms of schizophrenia. This should contribute to the development of drugs that are both more effective and more selective, without the sometimes debilitating side effects accompanying the long-term use of the major antipsychotics. Perhaps the worst side effect is **tardive dyskinesia** ("late-developing motor disorder"), characterized by facial tics and involuntary movements of the arms and legs, which may continue after a person stops taking the drug. The atypical antipsychotic medications, such as clozapine, do not have the same potential as earlier drugs for producing motor side effects.

The motor side effects that often result from long-term treatment of schizophrenia with typical antipsychotics remind us of the importance of the dopaminergic nigrostriatal system for movement and of the appropriate balance of the neurotransmitter dopamine and receptors for it for normal behavior. As we have indicated elsewhere (Chapters 4 and 8), the death of cells in the substantia nigra and the subsequent decrease of dopamine in the basal ganglia produce the motor symptoms of Parkinson's disease. Treatment of Parkinson's patients with L-dopa, which increases dopaminergic activity, has the potential to produce the symptoms of schizophrenia because of an excess of activity at dopaminergic receptors. By the same token, long-term treatment of patients with schizophrenia with

tardive dyskinesia A motor disorder with facial tics and involuntary limb movements; often appears after long-term use of antipsychotic medicines.

Box 15.2

Preventing Relapse in Patients With Schizophrenia

As we have indicated, antipsychotic medications such as the phenothiazines (e.g., chlorpromazine), the butyrophenones (e.g., haloperidol), and the newer, atypical antipsychotics (e.g., clozapine) alleviate the positive symptoms of schizophrenia, reducing or eliminating hallucinations and delusions. Unfortunately, under normal treatment conditions, half of patients with schizophrenia relapse within a year of their previous episode (Ayuso-Gutierrez & del Rio Vega, 1997). By 5 years after recovery from a first episode, nearly 82% of patients have relapsed (Robinson & others, 1999). Relapse in this case refers to a return of positive symptoms, and relapses appear to worsen the course of the disease—that is, the patient takes longer to recover from the relapse than would be expected from his or her treatment history.

Factors affecting relapse include failure to comply with a medication regimen (noncompliance), substance abuse, family dynamics and life events (e.g., stressors), and poor insight into the disease (Ayuso-Gutierrez & del Rio Vega, 1997; Lacro & others, 2002). Of these factors, medication noncompliance is the most important. For example, one study found that more than 70% of patients with schizophrenia who suffered a relapse requiring hospitalization had not complied with the treatment regimen (Ayuso-Gutierrez & del Rio Vega). Similarly, researchers found that medication noncompliance was associated with worsening symptoms, rehospitalization, and even homelessness, and that the patients at high risk for medication noncompliance were those who had a history of noncompliance, failed to recognize their own symptoms, and had a family that was not involved in their treatment (Olfson & others, 2000).

Patients with schizophrenia often stop taking their medication because of unpleasant side effects (Hudson & others, 2004; Marder, 1999). Given that the newer antipsychotic drugs have fewer such side effects, patients should have less likelihood of medication noncompliance and relapse. This has been confirmed in a comparison between the newer, atypical antipsychotic drug risperidone and an older drug, haloperidol (Csernansky & others, 2002). In another comparison between patients prescribed either risperidone or haloperidol, there was no difference in the percentage of patients who relapsed, but the time to relapse was shorter in the haloperidol group (deSena & others, 2003). In addition, the newer, atypical antipsychotics have a greater potential for alleviating the negative symptoms and cognitive deficits of schizophrenia, further increasing the likelihood of the successful rehabilitation of the patient (Naber, 2000).

---

antipsychotic drugs, most of which act by blocking dopaminergic transmission, has the potential of producing parkinsonian side effects.

Although antipsychotic drugs may reduce some of the negative symptoms of schizophrenia, a substantial number of patients do not experience any improvement in their negative symptoms in response to drug therapy (Goff & Evins, 1998). The negative symptoms, such as flat affect and social withdrawal, may result from brain damage, particularly to the frontal lobes. We have more to say about treating schizophrenia in Box 15.2.

➤Checkpoint

Compare and contrast the monoamine hypothesis of depression and the dopamine hypothesis of schizophrenia.

REVIEW

- ➤ According to the dopamine hypothesis of schizophrenia, excessive dopaminergic activity in the mesocortical dopamine system is responsible for producing the positive symptoms of the disease.
- ➤ Support for the dopamine hypothesis includes the abnormally high levels of dopamine metabolites in people with schizophrenia, the success of dopamine antagonists such as chlorpromazine and haloperidol in reducing or eliminating the positive symptoms, and the production of positive symptoms by dopamine agonists such as amphetamine and cocaine.
- ➤ Not all persons with schizophrenia have improvement in positive symptoms following treatment with the D_2 receptor-blocking drugs. These patients are often helped by clozapine, a weaker blocker of D_2 receptors but a more effective blocker of serotonergic receptors. The biochemical basis of the positive symptoms of schizophrenia remains unclear.

Brain Damage and Schizophrenia

The lateral ventricles of many people with schizophrenia are enlarged (Figure 15.15) (Copolov & Crook, 2000; Fannon & others, 2000). Larger spaces suggest less brain matter; enlarged ventricles have been attributed to smaller-than-normal neurons and increased neuronal density (Selemon & others, 1995) and the loss of neurons in structures near the ventricles, such as the amygdala and hippocampus (Marsh & others, 1994).

Postmortem examinations of the brains of people with schizophrenia have revealed differences in specific neural structures when compared with normal individuals without schizophrenia and those with other mental disorders. People with schizophrenia have a loss of dendritic material in the prefrontal cortex (Broadbelt & others, 2002), a reduced number of neurons in the mediodorsal and anteroventral/anteromedial nuclei of the thalamus (Young & others, 2000), a selective loss of hippocampal interneurons (Heckers & Konradi, 2002), and a decreased density of neurons in one layer of the cingulate cortex (Benes & others 2001). Further, neurons in the hippocampus and its extrinsic connections, particularly with the prefrontal cortex, are connected in a more disorganized fashion than normal (Figure 15.16) (Harrison, 2004), and the disorientation of hippocampal neurons has been found in both hemispheres, although they may be somewhat greater in the left hemisphere than in the right.

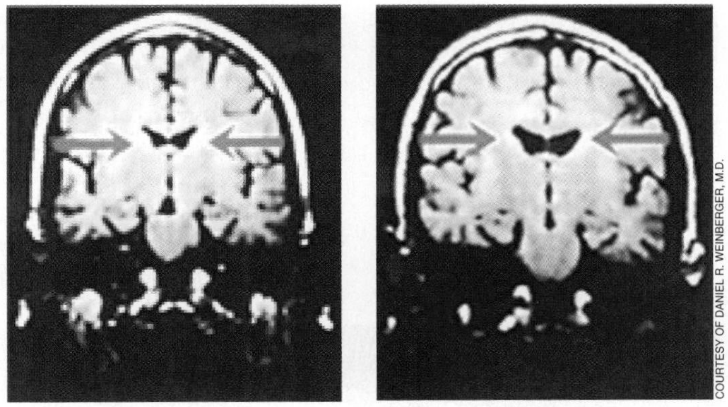

(a) (b)

Figure 15.15

MRI scans of the brains of twins discordant for schizophrenia (a) The twin without schizophrenia has smaller lateral ventricles than (b) his brother with schizophrenia.

➡ Which neural structures of patients with schizophrenia are different from those of normal individuals and of people with other mental disorders?

Neuronal disorganization in the cerebral cortex and the hippocampus may be caused by a failure of normal neural development (Chapter 3). In support of this view, researchers have found that the hippocampal disorganization in a person with schizophrenia is somewhat like that seen in mutant mice with disordered neurogenesis in the hippocampus (Scheibel & Conrad, 1993). Postmortem examinations of the prefrontal cortex of individuals with schizophrenia revealed that either abnormal neuronal migration or an alteration in the normal pattern of programmed cell death may have occurred during the fetal period (Akbarian & others, 1996). In addition, abnormal amounts of the neurotrophins that guide cell migration have been found in the brains of people with schizophrenia (Durany & others, 2001); this evidence could explain the disorganized orientation of neurons in the cerebral cortex and hippocampus.

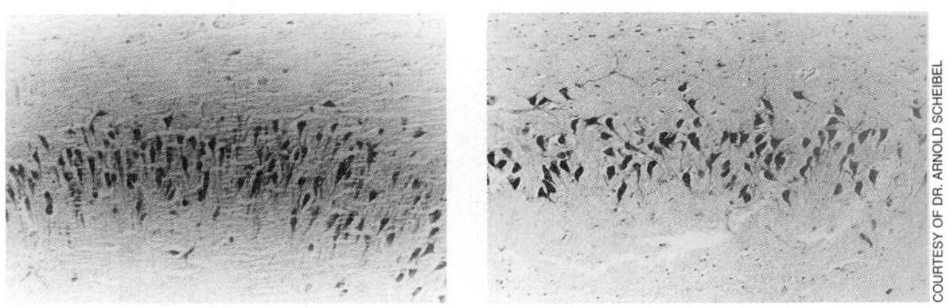

(a) (b)

Figure 15.16

The neuronal disorganization of schizophrenia These micrographs show the arrangement of hippocampal cells in (a) a normal individual and (b) a person with schizophrenia. The hippocampal cells are arranged in a more haphazard, disorganized fashion in the person with schizophrenia.

➡ What does the disorganization of brain cells suggest about the origin of schizophrenia?

Brain-imaging techniques—CT, MRI, and PET—also have revealed particular kinds of brain damage in people with schizophrenia. For example, using CT scans, researchers found a loss of neural tissue in the frontal and anterior temporal lobes and in the hypothalamus of 54 patients with schizophrenia when compared with age-matched controls (Bogerts, 1989), and other structural imaging studies have found a variety of subtle differences (Bogerts, 1999; Kotrla & Weinberger, 1995). In a comparison of the MRI scans of 15 sets of identical twins and 14 sets of same-sex fraternal twins discordant for schizophrenia (one twin with the disorder, the other without) with 29 matched healthy twin pairs, Baaré and colleagues (2001) found that the individuals with schizophrenia had smaller whole-brain volumes and larger lateral ventricles than their twins, who did not have schizophrenia (Figure 15.15). In a study of identical and fraternal twin pairs in which one twin in each pair had schizophrenia, smaller hippocampal volumes were found in the twins with schizophrenia (Narr & others, 2002). In the identical twins, however, there was no difference in hippocampal volume, even though one member of each pair was discordant for schizophrenia; that is, both had reduced hippocampal volume.

hypofrontality theory A theory that the negative symptoms of schizophrenia are caused by decreased activity in the prefrontal cortex.

This was not true for the fraternal twins, with only the twin with schizophrenia having reduced hippocampal volume. The researchers concluded that reduced hippocampal volume may be a marker for people with a genetic predisposition to develop schizophrenia.

Hypofrontality Theory

In studies using PET scans, people with schizophrenia show decreased metabolic activity in the frontal area of the brain (Figure 15.17), a condition called *hypofrontality* (Hazlett & Buchsbaum, 2001; Hazlett & others, 2000). The hypofrontality is also present in a first episode of psychosis, before the symptoms have actually progressed to schizophrenia (Molina & others, 2005). A **hypofrontality theory** might be able to account for the negative symptoms of schizophrenia, as damage to the prefrontal cortex in people with no history of schizophrenia is often associated with motivational difficulties, decreased speech content, a flat affect, social withdrawal, and cognitive impairment (Heinrichs, 1993). Other researchers also have concluded that the negative symptoms of schizophrenia reflect prefrontal cortex deficits (e.g., Wible & others, 2001).

Unfortunately for the hypofrontality theory, many persons with schizophrenia do not exhibit hypofrontality and some studies have failed to find it. For example, a review of PET findings reported that six studies found hypofrontality, three hyperfrontality, and five no differences (Buchsbaum, 1990). More recently, in a meta-analysis of 155 studies involving more than 4,000 people with schizophrenia, hypofrontality was exhibited by approximately half of the patients (Davidson & Heinrichs, 2003).

Recall from Chapter 2 that the prefrontal cortex plays an important role in the cognitive control of behavior (e.g., Braver & others, 1999; Miller & Cohen, 2001). Moreover, altered activity in the mesocortical dopamine neurons of the prefrontal cortex caused by brain damage may be associated with the cognitive deficits of schizophrenia (Cohen & Servan-Schreiber, 1992). These cognitive deficits are characterized by a difficulty in shifting between strategies when attempting to solve problems. On the Wisconsin Card Sorting Test, for example, a person with schizophrenia (or someone with prefrontal lobe damage) has difficulty shifting from one sorting strategy to another when a signal (oral feedback) indicates that the sorting rule has changed. Thus, a subject instructed initially to sort by shape (triangles, crosses, stars, or circles) may continue sorting by shape when the new sorting rule requires sorting by color. Continuing to sort by a rule that has changed is called *perseveration*.

Investigators used fMRI to study the prefrontal activity of people with schizophrenia relative to that of normal individuals when both groups were performing a working-memory task (Chapter 14) (Perlstein & others, 2001). Consistent with the hypofrontality theory, the subjects with schizophrenia exhibited deficient activity in the right dorsolateral prefrontal cortex during task performance, and those with the greatest dysfunction in this area were the most impaired. The researchers concluded that the working-memory deficits are probably caused by problems in the dorsolateral prefrontal cortex, which are associated with the cognitive disorganization seen in schizophrenia.

Using fMRI, researchers studied prefrontal cortex activity during a working-memory task in patients newly diagnosed with schizophrenia and not taking anti-

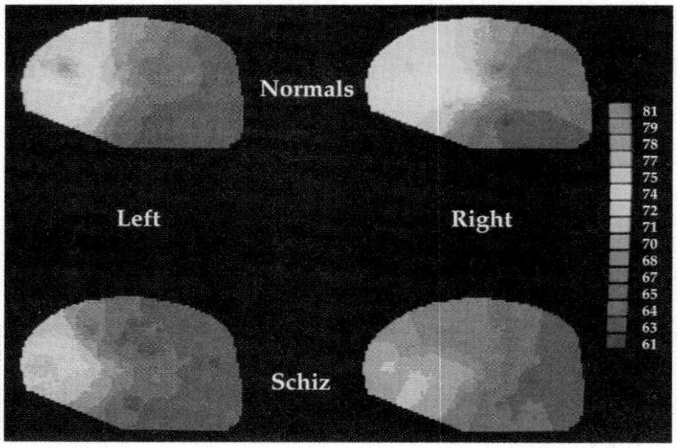

DR. KAREN FAITH BERMAN

(a) At rest

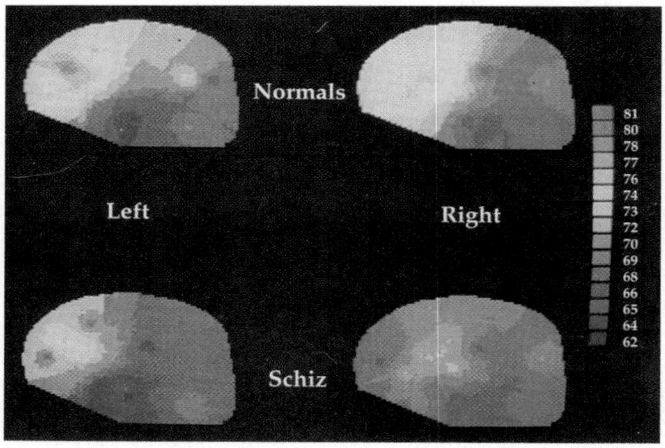

DR. KAREN FAITH BERMAN

(b) During card sort test

Figure 15.17
Hypofrontality in schizophrenia
The brain of a person without schizophrenia (top pair in each set of scans) shows much more activation in the frontal cortex both (a) at rest and (b) while performing a task that particularly employs the frontal cortex than that of a person with schizophrenia (bottom pair in each set). Areas of higher activation are shown in red, orange, and yellow.

➔ **Do people with schizophrenia show increased or decreased metabolic activity in the brain?**

psychotic medication (Barch & others, 2001). The fMRI showed deficits in dorsolateral prefrontal cortex activation but intact activation of other parts of the prefrontal cortex. Recall from Chapter 8 that the dorsolateral prefrontal cortex is the chief decision maker in deciding which movements to make on the basis of sensory information. Perhaps deficits in this neural area explain the often purposeless behavior exhibited by people with schizophrenia. The fMRI results indicate that the dorsolateral prefrontal cortex deficit is present at the beginning of the illness, before any exposure to antipsychotic medication. In addition, the deficit is specific to individuals with schizophrenia, as people with major depression did not exhibit the prefrontal dysfunction when both were tested on a working-memory task (Barch & others, 2003).

Dopamine Hypothesis and Brain Structures

Several pieces of research evidence support the idea that deficits in dopaminergic activity in the prefrontal cortex are responsible for schizophrenia-associated cognitive deficits. For example, in studies on rats, performance on cognitive tasks is impaired following destruction of the mesocortical dopaminergic neurons in the prefrontal cortex (Oades, 1981; Simon & others, 1980). In one experiment, investigators found that the level of cognitive impairment was equal to that observed when the entire prefrontal area was surgically ablated (Brozoski & others, 1979). They also reported that administering dopamine agonists after destruction of the mesocortical dopamine neurons restored cognitive functioning in their primate subjects. In addition, researchers found that in people with schizophrenia, levels of a dopamine metabolite in cerebrospinal fluid were correlated with activity levels in the prefrontal cortex during performance of a cognitive task: the lower the dopamine metabolite level, the greater the cognitive impairment (Weinberger & others, 1988). The metabolic hypofrontality in people with schizophrenia can be reversed by dopamine agonists (Geraud & others, 1987). More recent brain imaging research supports the idea of dysfunction of the prefrontal lobes, with dopaminergic involvement (Heinz & others, 2003).

No Neuropathological Smoking Gun

In summary, neither the dopamine hypothesis nor the hypofrontality theory provides a complete explanation for schizophrenia, although together they account for most of the disorder's symptoms. In schizophrenia, several different brain structures are dysfunctional and act together to produce the symptoms of the disorder. The effect of a dysfunction in a single area may be quite different from the effect when it is accompanied by dysfunctions in other areas. For example, the basal ganglia appear to be dysfunctional in people with schizophrenia, causing excessive dopamine activity in this area (Toru & others, 1988). In a more recent experiment that examined the L-dopa uptake rate in the basal ganglia of untreated patients with schizophrenia and healthy controls, no difference in the average uptake rate was found (Dao-Castellana & others, 1997). However, there was significantly greater variability in uptake values in the caudate nucleus and putamen of the people with schizophrenia. As you will recall from Chapter 8, the primary function of the basal ganglia is the integration of voluntary motor responses—but schizophrenia typically is not a disorder primarily of movement. Similarly, the hippocampus of people with schizophrenia also appears to be reduced in size relative to those of healthy persons (Suddath & others, 1990), and damage to the hippocampus is associated with memory loss—but schizophrenia is not a disorder of memory. It is possible that dysfunctions in the basal ganglia and the hippocampus produce different effects in people with and without schizophrenia.

In a different view of schizophrenia, Heinrichs (1993) has suggested that the frontal lobes, basal ganglia, and hippocampus may be dysfunctional in some people with schizophrenia, but these abnormalities are secondary to the disorder itself. According to Heinrichs, the "neuropathological smoking gun" that causes schizophrenia has not been found. As indicated earlier, Heinrichs also noted that

Checkpoint

Heinrichs has hired you to identify the neural structure(s) responsible for producing schizophrenia, and your report is due tomorrow. Using what you have learned so far in this chapter, propose a biological basis for schizophrenia.

schizophrenia may be several related disorders rather than a single one, citing the observations that some patients have prefrontal dysfunctions whereas others do not, and that dopamine antagonists help some patients but not others. As Heinrichs concluded, further research is needed to identify the neural structure or structures responsible for producing schizophrenia.

REVIEW

- Relative to healthy people, people with schizophrenia have fewer and smaller neurons in the cerebral cortex, dorsomedial thalamus, hippocampus, entorhinal cortex, parahippocampal cortex, and cingulate cortex. Neurons of the cerebral cortex and hippocampus are connected in a disorganized fashion, possibly caused by a failure of normal neural development.
- The observation of decreased activity in the prefrontal cortex in schizophrenia led to the theory of hypofrontality as a possible cause of the negative symptoms and cognitive deficits.
- In animal research, destruction of the mesocortical dopaminergic system, which influences activity in the prefrontal cortex, produces deficits in cognitive tasks, and administration of dopamine agonists restores the cognitive functioning.

The Role of Genetics in Schizophrenia

Because schizophrenia is relatively common, affecting about 1% of the U. S. population, and because it is so debilitating to sufferers and their families, scientists have devoted a great deal of research effort to trying to understand its causes. There is now significant evidence that genetic factors affect the likelihood of developing schizophrenia (Bassett & others, 2001).

Twin studies typically have found a much higher concordance rate for schizophrenia in identical twins than in fraternal twins; that is, the probability that a twin of someone with schizophrenia will also develop this disorder is much higher if the twin is identical (Barnes, 1987; Tsuang, 2000). As you can see in Figure 15.18, the risk of a person's developing schizophrenia seems to be directly related to the closeness of his or her relationship to a family member with schizophrenia, to his or her genetic relatedness (Gottesman, 1991). Another factor related to the risk of developing schizophrenia in identical twins is the subtype of the disorder with which the twin is diagnosed; some subtypes (e.g., unsystematic schizophrenia) have much greater concordance than others (Franzek & Beckmann, 1998).

By showing that the probability of an adopted child developing schizophrenia increases if one or both biological parents had schizophrenia, the results of adoption studies further support the theory of a genetic factor in schizophrenia (Gottesman, 1991; Plomin & others, 1997; Tsuang, 1998). The risk of developing schizophrenia is not increased by having an adoptive parent with

Figure 15.18
Family relationships and the risk of developing schizophrenia The risk increases with greater genetic relatedness.

➡ Is the risk of developing schizophrenia higher for a cousin or for a sibling of someone with the disorder?

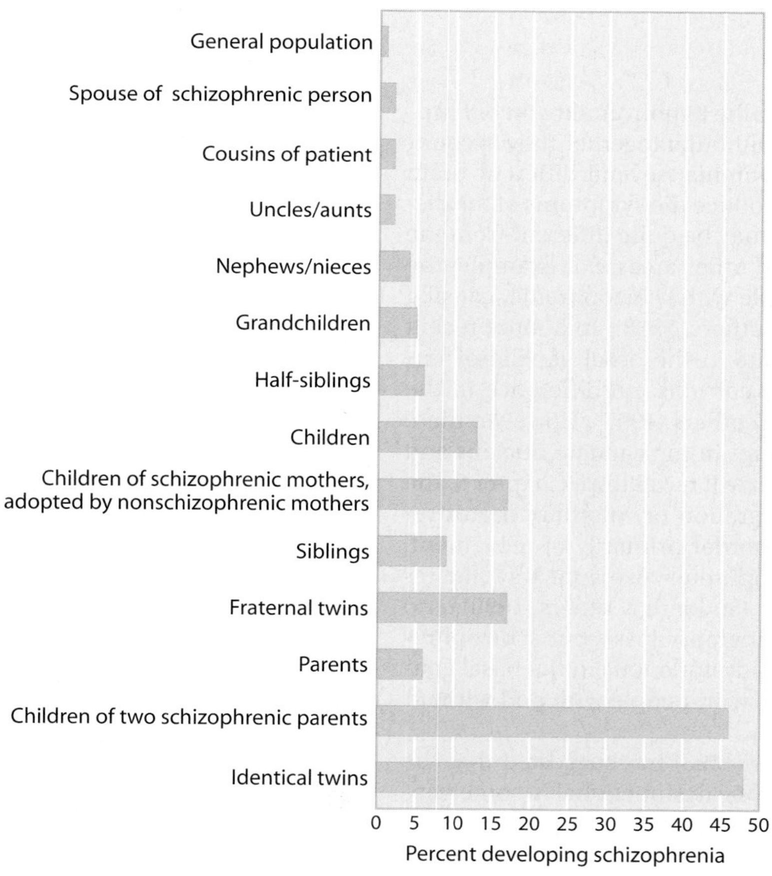

schizophrenia (Gottesman). Further, the approximately 50% chance of one twin developing schizophrenia when an identical twin has the disorder remains even when the twins are reared apart (Plomin & others) provides further evidence for a genetic basis.

One of the most interesting and widely reported case studies in the inheritance of schizophrenia is that of the Genain quadruplets (Figure 15.19). When they were born, in 1930, the quadruplets were celebrities, and as young children they performed song-and-dance routines in their hometown. As they grew to young adulthood, they began to show behaviors characteristic of schizophrenia. One of the twins dropped out of high school, and all had trouble holding jobs. Nora, the first-born quadruplet, was first hospitalized for schizophrenia at age 21, and Iris was hospitalized 7 months later. After the other two sisters, Myra and Hester, were diagnosed with schizophrenia in 1955, all four sisters spent the next 3 years being studied at the National Institute of Mental Health (NIMH).

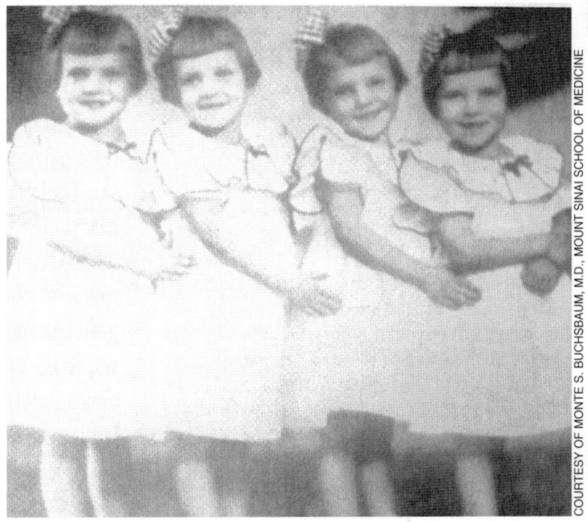

Figure 15.19

The inheritance of schizophrenia

Each of the Genain quadruplets developed schizophrenia in her 20s. The extent of the sisters' schizophrenia differed, suggesting a joint influence of heredity and environment in development of the disorder. The quadruplets first and last names are pseudonyms. *Genain* is from Greek words meaning "dire birth," and the first letters of the first names, Nora, Iris, Myra, and Hester, are from the letters NIMH, because the National Institute of Mental Health sponsored much of the research on the girls.

→ **What differences might lead the Genain quadruplets to differ in their ability to lead independent lives?**

The quadruplets were not the only members of their family to suffer from psychiatric disorders. The behavior of their father was often described as bizarre. He showed considerable hostility toward many people and refused to allow the quadruplets to play with other children. His brother, mother, and a paternal uncle were all hospitalized at some time with "nervous breakdowns," which was usually a euphemism for an affective disorder.

Although all four sisters suffered from schizophrenia, they differed in the severity and course of the disorder. Rosenthal's (1963) initial report on the quadruplets revealed that Nora and Myra were the more functional sisters. After leaving NIMH, Myra went to business school, worked as a secretary, and married and had children; Nora worked at least 7 years, mostly in government training programs. Hester and Iris both spent more than 15 years hospitalized in a state mental health care facility.

A follow-up study in 1981 at NIMH found that the quadruplets had normal CT scans but abnormal PET scans (Figure 15.20) (DeLisi & others, 1984; Mirsky & others, 1984). All four showed heightened activity in the visual areas of the brain when they were resting with their eyes closed, suggesting that they were hallucinating. Their brains also had less alpha activity, a sign of mental relaxation, than normal. The PET scans of Myra and Nora were closer to normal than those of their sisters—a predictable result, given their better adjustment and need for less antipsychotic medication.

Another follow-up investigation of the Genains in 1996, when they were 66 years old, revealed either stable neuropsychological test results compared with earlier testing or, for some measures, actually improved performance (Mirsky & others, 2000). This suggests that cognitive decline is not an inevitable feature of the disorder.

As our discussion suggests, what is inherited is only a susceptibility or *genetic predisposition* to

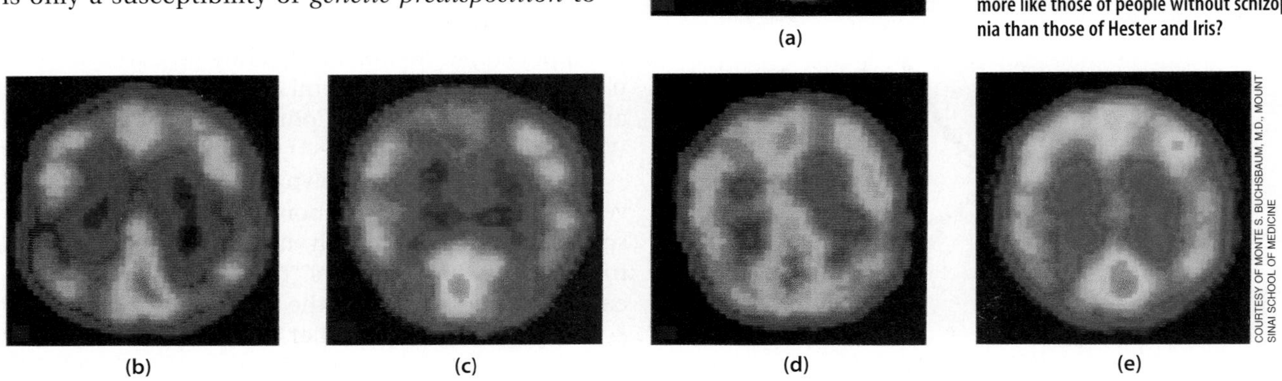

Figure 15.20

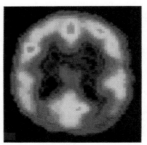

PET scans of the Genain quadruplets

The scans of all four Genain sisters (b through e) showed greater activity in the visual areas of the brain when the sisters rested with their eyes closed than is seen in (a) a person without schizophrenia, but the PET scans of (b) Myra and (c) Nora were closer to normal than those of (d) Hester and (e) Iris.

→ **Why were the PET scans of Myra and Nora more like those of people without schizophrenia than those of Hester and Iris?**

develop schizophrenia. The concordance rate for identical twins is not 100% but about 50% (Tsuang, 2000), indicating that a particular gene is not by itself sufficient to produce schizophrenia. Factors other than inheritance appear to contribute.

Another technique for determining genetic involvement is to locate the gene or genes responsible for producing schizophrenia. Unfortunately, nearly as many genes for schizophrenia have been identified as there have been studies seeking to find them. For example, a literature review found convincing evidence for susceptibility loci on chromosomes 1 and 13 (Bassett & others, 2001). In a study of a large sample of veterans, researchers found agreement on the role of chromosome 13 (Faraone & others, 2002). Evidence has also been found for susceptibility loci on chromosomes 3 and 5 for the combination of schizophrenia and bipolar disorder (Bailer & others, 2002; Sklar & others, 2004). Investigators reported a linkage of the core Kraepelin-identified dementia-praecox syndrome to chromosome 8, while ruling out linkages to chromosomes 5, 6, and 10 (Kendler & others, 2000). A linkage has been found between chromosome 15 and a subtype of schizophrenia called periodic catatonia, which is characterized by hyperkinetic and akinetic psychomotor disturbances (wild activity and complete lack of activity, respectively) (Stober & others, 2001, 2002). Despite a tremendous amount of work, research on the specific genetic abnormalities associated with schizophrenia is still in its initial stages. The search for the gene or genes controlling schizophrenia undoubtedly will continue to reveal more about the inheritance of the disorder and possibly its relationship to other psychoses, such as bipolar disorder.

Checkpoint

Suggest why data from adoption studies on schizophrenia might be skewed in favor of biological influence rather than environmental influence. (Adoptive parents are considered an environmental influence.)

Viral Infection and Schizophrenia

During an influenza epidemic, second-trimester fetuses have been found to have an increased risk of later developing schizophrenia (Izumoto & others, 1999; Limosin & others, 2003; Watson & others, 1999) (Figure 15.21). Izumoto and colleagues, for example, studied children born to mothers exposed to influenza in one of three different epidemics in 1957 in Kochi, Japan, whereas Limosin and colleagues examined children born to mothers exposed to influenza epidemics in France between 1949 and 1981. Watson and coworkers examined data gathered in the Helsinki Influenza Study and the Danish 40 year study. Despite these studies, some researchers have failed to find such a relationship (e.g., Crow & Done, 1992). However, in a study of the accuracy of retrospective reports of influenza during pregnancy, investigators found that the women tended to underreport their illnesses during pregnancy, which could account for the lack of a relationship reported by Crow and Done (Voldsgaard & others, 2002). Based on the time of fetal exposure to the virus, the risk of an individual later developing schizophrenia is proportional to the rate of influenza in the population. Often using animal models of schizophrenia, several researchers have found evidence supporting the idea that fetal exposure during the second trimester may contribute to the development of schizophrenia by causing the disorganization of hippocampal neurons frequently observed in people with the disorder (Fatemi & others, 2002; Pearce & others, 2000; Scheibel & Conrad, 1993; Zuckerman & Weiner, 2003).

Several studies have shown that individuals who develop schizophrenia are more likely to have winter-spring birth dates, which means that the second trimester of their mothers' pregnancy probably occurred during the peak of the year's flu season (Torrey & others, 1996; Torrey & others, 1997). As we have indicated, the flu season coincides with a greater probabil-

Figure 15.21

Viral infection and schizophrenia

The risk of a person's later developing schizophrenia is highest when the influenza rate (number of influenza cases per 1,000 population) was high during the 6th month of the mother's pregnancy (blue), moderate when the influenza rate was medium (red), and lowest when the rate was low (green).

→ How would exposure to the flu during the second trimester of pregnancy be a contributing factor to the development of schizophrenia?

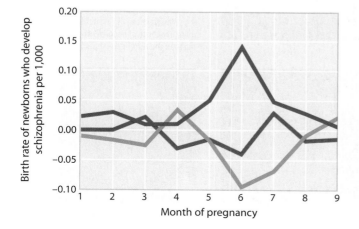

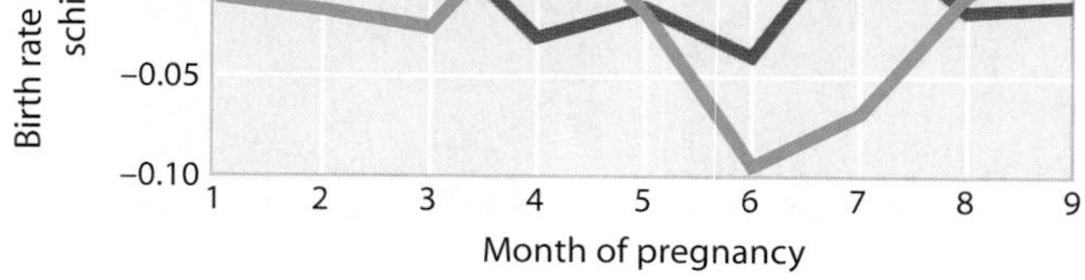

Scientific American Spotlight

Fever In, Schizophrenia Out

J. R. Minkel

Researchers had suspected that exposure to influenza during pregnancy raises the risk of offspring developing schizophrenia later in life but were dubious because the connection was based on dates of influenza outbreaks or mothers' recollections. Now a group at Columbia University and the New York State Psychiatric Institute has measured flu antibodies in 40-year-old blood samples from the mothers of schizophrenics and unaffected individuals. Those exposed to flu during the first half of pregnancy were three times more likely to develop schizophrenia, but those exposed during the second half had no increased risk, they found. (The average risk of schizophrenia is no more than 1 percent.) If the link is confirmed, further work might lead to preventive strategies against some cases of schizophrenia, says epidemiologist and senior author Ezra Susser, although he cautions that the evidence, based on only 200 offspring, is not yet solid enough for women to act on. Subtle brain damage from an inflammatory or autoimmune response to viral infection could be contributing to the disease, he speculates. See the August 2004 *Archives of General Psychiatry* for more.

Scientific American, vol. 291, p. 38.

ity of second-trimester fetuses developing schizophrenia later (Izumoto & others, 1999; Limosin & others, 2003; Watson & others, 1999). Perhaps genetics plays its role in the development of schizophrenia by creating a vulnerability to developing schizophrenia following prenatal exposure to a virus. Yet even when identical twins are exposed to a virus as fetuses and both develop schizophrenia, the severity of their disorder can differ. And in some cases, one twin develops schizophrenia and the other does not. The *Scientific American* Spotlight, "Fever In, Schizophrenia Out," discusses a study that provides additional support for the idea that prenatal exposure to influenza increases the likelihood of developing schizophrenia later in life, but only if the exposure comes during the first half of pregnancy.

Stressors have also been implicated as an important source of these different probabilities of developing schizophrenia (Tsuang, 2000). Identifying strategies to reduce the stress reactions of individuals who are genetically at increased risk for schizophrenia is a desirable goal (Koenig & others, 2002).

Checkpoint

Given a concordance rate for schizophrenia of about 50% among identical twins, suggest why all four Genain quadruplets developed the disorder.

REVIEW

- Twin studies provide evidence that some people may be genetically predisposed to develop schizophrenia.
- Family studies show that the risk of a person developing schizophrenia is directly related to how he or she is genetically related to a family member with schizophrenia: the closer the relationship, the greater the risk.
- Adoption studies have shown that the probability of an adopted child developing schizophrenia increases if a biological parent has schizophrenia.
- Several studies have identified chromosome sites as possible locations of the gene for schizophrenia, but none of these results have been confirmed.
- Fetal exposure to a viral infection during the second trimester of pregnancy is a possible contributing factor to developing schizophrenia.

Chapter Review

Key Terms

active phase (p. 564)
affective disorder (p. 544)
bipolar disorder (p. 547)
concordance rate (p. 553)
cyclothymia (p. 547)
delusion (p. 563)
dementia praecox (p. 561)
depression (p. 544)
depressive disorder (p. 544)
dexamethasone suppression test (DST) (p. 559)
dopamine hypothesis of schizophrenia (p. 565)
dysthymia (p. 546)
electroconvulsive therapy (ECT) (p. 554)
hallucination (p. 563)
hypercortisolism (p. 559)
hypofrontality theory (p. 570)
hypomania (p. 547)
learned helplessness (p. 556)
loosening of associations (p. 563)
major depression (p. 545)
mania (p. 546)
monoamine oxidase inhibitor (MAOI) (p. 551)
monoamine hypothesis of depression (p. 549)
negative symptom (p. 564)
neologism (p. 563)
positive symptom (p. 564)
prodromal phase (p. 564)
residual phase (p. 564)
schizophrenia (p. 561)
serotonin-specific reuptake inhibitor (SSRI) (p. 552)
tardive dyskinesia (p. 567)
tricyclic compound (p. 551)
word salad (p. 563)

Suggested Readings

Bennett, M. R. (1998). Monoaminergic synapses and schizophrenia: 45 years of neuroleptics. *Journal of Psychopharmacology, 12,* 289–304.

Bogerts, B. (1999). The neuropathology of schizophrenic diseases: Historical aspects and present knowledge. *European Archives of Psychiatry and Clinical Neuroscience, 249*(Supplement 4), 2–13.

Craddock, N., & Jones, I. (1999). Genetics of bipolar disorder. *Journal of Medical Genetics, 36,* 585–594.

Drevets, W. C. (2001). Neuroimaging and neuropathological studies of depression: Implications for the cognitive-emotional features of mood disorders. *Current Opinion in Neurobiology, 11,* 240–249.

Gold, P. W., & Chrousos, G. P. (1999). The endocrinology of melancholic and atypical depression: Relation to neurocircuitry and somatic consequences. *Proceedings of the Association of American Physicians, 111,* 22–34.

Heinrichs, R. W. (1993). Schizophrenia and the brain. *American Psychologist, 48,* 221–233.

McCall, W. V. (2001). Electroconvulsive therapy in the era of modern psychopharmacology. *International Journal of Neuropsychopharmacology, 4,* 315–324.

Nemeroff, C. B. (1998). The neurobiology of depression. *Scientific American, 278,* 42–49.

Critical Thinking Questions

1. Susan broke up with her boyfriend several weeks ago. She refuses to leave her house, does not want to see anyone, and is convinced that her life is over. Is Susan depressed? Discuss the biological processes that might be contributing to her behavior. What might be done to help her feel better?
2. Twin studies and adoption studies have been used to evaluate the contribution of genes to the development of depression and schizophrenia. Discuss the strengths and weaknesses of these approaches. What method would provide convincing evidence for a genetic contribution to the development of a behavior disorder?
3. Describe the symptoms of schizophrenia. What biological processes are known to be associated with schizophrenia? Evaluate what we know about the relationship between these processes and the symptoms of this disorder.

Fill-in-the-Blank Questions

1. An impairment in functioning caused by the persistence of high levels of depression or mania over a period of time is called a(n) ______ disorder.
2. ______ is the "common cold" of mental illness.
3. ______ is characterized by depressed mood of at least 2 weeks duration, sleep difficulties, and agitation or lethargy.
4. A chronic, usually low-level, depression is called ______.
5. ______ is an extremely elevated, expansive, or irritable mood.
6. ______ is a condition involving both mania and depression.
7. ______ is the milder form of mania occurring in a person with cyclothymia.
8. The ______ theory of depression holds that depression is caused by decreased activity at synapses where ______ and ______ are the neurotransmitters.
9. A person diagnosed with depression will probably first receive a prescription for a(n) ______, of which ______ is an example.
10. Excessive activity in the ______, a major site for the synthesis of norepinephrine, may be associated with depression.
11. ______ is a controversial treatment method sometimes used for depressed patients who do not respond to antidepressant drugs.
12. One of the most serious problems with the use of ECT in treating depression is the high ______ rate.
13. The ______ rate is the rate at which a characteristic of interest occurs in both members of a pair of subjects.
14. The genetic contribution to disease is significantly higher for ______ than for major depression.
15. Repeated exposure of an animal to an inescapable noxious event may produce ______, a condition that shares characteristics with human depression.
16. Of the animal models of depression, the one with the greatest support for its validity is the one involving removal of the ______.
17. In depressed people, REM sleep occurs ______ than normal in the sleep cycle, and total sleeping time is ______ than normal.
18. ______ is an abnormally high secretion of cortisol from the adrenal cortex.
19. Nemeroff has connected the dysfunctional CRF system/locus coeruleus-norepinephrine system, childhood trauma, and genetic predisposition to depression to create the ______ model of mood disorders.
20. ______ are sensory experiences in the absence of environmental stimuli.
21. A false system of beliefs that a person with schizophrenia defends against reality is called a(n) ______.
22. ______, in which there is no discernible link between the words spoken, is a speech characteristic of some people with schizophrenia.
23. The delusions and hallucinations experienced by people with schizophrenia are referred to as ______ symptoms.
24. The acute symptoms of schizophrenia appear in the ______ phase.
25. According to the ______ hypothesis, an excess of dopamine activity is responsible for the ______ symptoms of schizophrenia.
26. Drugs such as amphetamine and cocaine increase ______ activity in the CNS and can produce the positive symptoms of schizophrenia in people without the disorder.
27. People with schizophrenia who do not respond to the phenothiazines or to the butyrophenones may respond to the atypical antipsychotic drug ______.
28. ______ is a movement disorder characterized by facial tics and involuntary movements of the limbs, commonly occurring after long-term treatment with antipsychotic drugs.
29. Decreased metabolic activity in the prefrontal regions of the cerebral cortex, or ______, is associated with schizophrenia.
30. The concordance rate for schizophrenia in identical twins is about ______.
31. The more distant a person's relationship to a family member with schizophrenia, the ______ is the risk of the person developing the disorder.

Multiple-Choice Questions

1. The two major classes of affective disorders are
   a. dysthymia and cyclothymia.
   b. depressive disorders and manic disorders.
   c. depressive disorders and bipolar disorders.
   d. bipolar disorders and cyclothymia.
2. The following are among the 10 characteristics of depression:
   a. depressed mood, change in appetite, and sleep disturbances.
   b. blunted affect, change in appetite, and insomnia.
   c. disordered thought processes, fatigue, and inability to concentrate.
   d. hallucinations, delusions, and psychomotor agitation.

3. A depressed mood of at least 2 weeks' duration is characteristic of
   a. major depression.
   b. cyclothymia.
   c. bipolar disorder.
   d. dysthymia.
4. The following are symptomatic of a manic episode:
   a. inflated self-esteem, delusions, and hallucinations.
   b. decreased need for sleep, blunted affect, and distractibility.
   c. delusions, hallucinations, and blunted affect.
   d. increased speech, an elevated mood, and flights of fancy.
5. The first week in August, Melissa felt on top of the world. She was supremely optimistic, full of ideas, but was experiencing some sleep difficulties that she blamed on the constant ferment of thought in her mind. By the second week of the month, however, she was in the depths of despair. When she attempted to kill herself with an overdose of a prescribed sleeping aid, she was admitted to a residential treatment facility and diagnosed as having
   a. dysthymia.
   b. bipolar disorder.
   c. major depression.
   d. schizophrenia.
6. Which of the following is *not* a characteristic of bipolar disorder?
   a. Lithium carbonate is an effective treatment.
   b. Stress can be a precipitating factor.
   c. The genetic component is stronger than for major depression.
   d. Women are twice as likely to get it as men.
7. Which of the following classes of drugs is more effective at treating atypical depression?
   a. MAOIs
   b. tricyclics
   c. SSRIs
   d. atypical antidepressants
8. Prozac is an example of a(n)
   a. MAOI.
   b. tricyclic antidepressant.
   c. SSRI.
   d. ECT.
9. Which of the following antidepressants can be dangerous if tyramine is not restricted in the patient's diet?
   a. MAOIs
   b. tricyclic antidepressants
   c. SSRIs
   d. lithium carbonate
10. The tricyclic compounds and MAOIs provide clinical relief by
    a. increasing levels of norepinephrine in the brain.
    b. decreasing levels of norepinephrine in the brain.
    c. increasing levels of dopamine in the brain.
    d. decreasing levels of dopamine in the brain.
11. Which of the following antidepressant treatments would probably provide the quickest relief for a person with a high risk of suicide?
    a. MAOI
    b. ECT
    c. SSRI
    d. Prozac
12. The relapse rate among people with depression after ECT treatment without follow-up treatment is approximately
    a. 10%.
    b. 25%.
    c. 50%.
    d. 75% or higher.
13. After an effective ECT treatment, patients were found to have ______ blood flow in their ______ lobes.
    a. increased, temporal
    b. increased, frontal
    c. decreased, frontal
    d. decreased, temporal
14. A comparison between the rates of occurrence of a disorder in two related individuals is called the ______ rate.
    a. concordance
    b. twin
    c. gene
    d. adoption
15. Which of the following has received most support as a valid animal model of human depression?
    a. animals receiving clomipramine as newborns
    b. animals deprived of their mothers while young
    c. animals receiving locus coeruleus lesions
    d. animals undergoing olfactory bulbectomies
16. Mood was found to improve in depressed persons following which of the following treatments?
    a. They were awakened when entering slow-wave sleep.
    b. The sleep cycle was phase delayed by several hours.
    c. The sleep cycle was phase advanced by several hours.
    d. They were forced to sleep for 2 days.
17. The response of a healthy person to the dexamethasone suppression test would be
    a. suppression of ACTH and cortisol secretion.
    b. no effect on ACTH and cortisol secretion.
    c. increased ACTH and cortisol secretion.
    d. suppression of ACTH and dexamethasone secretion.
18. Schizophrenia is characterized by loss of contact with reality and
    a. disturbances in thought, perception, motor behavior, and emotions.
    b. alternation of depressive and manic episodes.
    c. multiple personalities.
    d. an inflated sense of self-worth.
19. Travis has schizophrenia. Which type of hallucination is he most likely to have?
    a. visual—he sees things that are not there
    b. gustatory—he tastes the poison his enemies are using to kill him
    c. olfactory—he smells the terrible odors leaving his body
    d. auditory—he hears voices telling him to do bad things
20. Defense of a false system of beliefs against reality is characteristic of a
    a. hallucination.
    b. neologism.
    c. delusion.
    d. word salad.
21. The positive symptoms of schizophrenia include
    a. hallucinations and delusions.
    b. lack of affect.
    c. social withdrawal.
    d. poverty of speech and blunted emotions.

22. The three stages of schizophrenia include
a. the preliminary phase, the active phase, and the residual phase.
b. the preliminary phase, the active phase, and the dormant phase.
c. the prodromal phase, the active phase, and the dormant phase.
d. the prodromal phase, the active phase, and the residual phase.

23. When he is not taking his medicine, André hears voices that tell him to kill his biological psychology teacher. During this time, an fMRI scan would probably show increased activity in André's ______ lobe and decreased activity in his ______ lobe.
a. temporal, parietal
b. frontal, temporal
c. temporal, frontal
d. parietal, temporal

24. Drugs that increase dopamine activity in the CNS can produce
a. the negative symptoms of schizophrenia.
b. the positive symptoms of schizophrenia.
c. depression.
d. bipolar disorder.

25. Long-term treatment with typical antipsychotic medications can cause
a. depression.
b. bipolar disorder.
c. tardive dyskinesia.
d. Alzheimer's disease.

26. According to one view, the negative symptoms of schizophrenia are caused by
a. excessive levels of dopamine.
b. overindulgence in drugs.
c. brain damage.
d. stress.

27. Kayla is thinking about adopting a child but is concerned about the possibility that the child might develop schizophrenia. She should be most worried if ______ has the disorder.
a. neither biological parent
b. neither adoptive parent
c. one or more adoptive parents
d. one or more biological parents

28. The concordance rate for schizophrenia in identical twins is about
a. 75%.
b. 50%.
c. 25%.
d. less than 10%.

29. Exposure of the fetus to a viral infection during the ______ of pregnancy increases the risk for development of schizophrenia.
a. the first week
b. the second trimester
c. the third trimester
d. the last week

Answers can be found on the companion website at www.worthpublishers.com/klein.

◆ Glossary

5-alpha-reductase deficiency (5-ARD) A condition in which testosterone is not converted to dihydrotestosterone in a genetic male because of a deficiency of 5-alpha-reductase type 2 enzyme; the external genitals typically have a female appearance at birth.

ablation The experimental destruction of neurons or the surgical removal of a part of the brain.

absolute refractory period The time during which the neuron is insensitive to further stimulation.

accommodation The change of the shape of the lens to maintain the focus of an image on the retina.

acetylcholine (ACh) A neurotransmitter synthesized from acetyl CoA and choline by the enzyme choline acetyltransferase.

acetylcholinesterase (AChE) An enzyme present in the synaptic cleft that quickly deactivates ACh after it is released.

acquired sexual motive A learned sexual response to a stimulus produced through conditioning.

across-fiber pattern coding The type of coding in which information about a stimulus is determined by the pattern of neural impulses.

actin The protein component of thin myofilaments.

action potential The changes that occur within the neuron in response to a stimulus; also called the spike potential or firing of the neuron.

activation-synthesis theory The view that dreams are a mental interpretation of the neural activity that occurs during sleep.

active phase The phase of schizophrenia in which the more acute symptoms of the disorder appear, such as hallucinations and delusions.

adipsia The absence of drinking.

adrenocorticotropic hormone (ACTH) An anterior pituitary hormone that stimulates the production and release of hormones by the adrenal cortex.

adrenogenital syndrome A condition resulting from excess androstenedione secretion by the adrenal glands in a genetically female human, producing masculinized genitals.

affective disorder A mental disorder characterized by one or both of two mood states: depression and/or mania.

afferent neuron A neuron that transmits messages from sensory receptors to the CNS, unless the receptors are already part of the CNS.

aggression A behavior motivated by the intent to harm a living being or an inanimate object.

agonist A drug that mimics or enhances the activity of a neurotransmitter.

agrammatical speech Speech that is deficient in grammar.

agraphia An inability to write.

alar plate A zone of cells in the dorsal portion of the neural tube that develops into the sensory neurons and the interneurons of the dorsal horn of the spinal cord.

alarm stage The first stage in the GAS, characterized by intense sympathetic nervous system arousal; also called *alarm reaction.*

alcohol Ethyl alcohol (ethanol); a powerful depressant that strongly influences consciousness and the ability to respond effectively to the environment.

alcoholism A dependence on alcohol.

aldosterone A hormone released by the adrenal cortex that causes increased water and salt retention by the kidneys.

alexia An inability to read.

allele An alternative form of a gene.

all-or-none law A principle stating that the strength of an action potential is independent of the intensity of the stimulus that elicits it.

allostasis The maintenance of stability through change.

allostatic load The cumulative cost to the body of repeated cycles of allostasis.

alpha activity An EEG pattern of waves that are larger and more synchronized (8 to 12 Hz) than beta waves, which occurs when an individual is relaxed with eyes closed.

alpha motor neuron A motor neuron with a long axon that leaves the ventral root of the spinal cord or brain stem and synapses with individual muscle fibers.

alpha-fetoprotein A protein synthesized by the fetal liver and present in the bloodstream of both male and female fetuses that binds to and deactivates circulating estradiol.

Alzheimer's disease (AD) A type of dementia characterized by progressive neurological degeneration and a profound deterioration of mental functioning.

amacrine cell A type of retinal neuron that receives neural messages from bipolar cells; synapses with and inhibits both bipolar and ganglion cells.

amphetamine A collective term for psychostimulant drugs typically used to treat attention deficit hyperactivity disorder and sleep disorders.

amygdala A limbic system structure at the base of the temporal lobe that processes the emotions of anger and fear.

amygdalectomy A surgical procedure that treats extreme aggressiveness by destroying areas in the amygdala.

amyloid beta protein A protein that accumulates in neural tissue and is thought to cause the degeneration of neural fibers and disruption of neural connections in specific brain areas that are characteristic of AD.

amyotrophic lateral sclerosis (ALS) A degenerative neuromuscular disease caused by degeneration of the corticospinal and corticobulbar tracts and the anterior horns of the spinal cord.

anandamide A naturally occurring THC-like substance.

anaxonic neuron A neuron without an axon.

androgen insensitivity syndrome (AIS) A condition in which a defective androgen receptor protein prevents normal testosterone action, causing a genetic male to develop female external genitals or ambiguous genitals.

androstenedione An adrenal androgen hormone similar to testosterone that affects the sexual motivation of a premenopausal woman.

anencephaly A neural tube defect that results when the brain or a major part of it fails to develop.

angiotensin A hormone that stimulates the adrenal cortex to release aldosterone.

angular gyrus An area of the parietal lobe with connections to Wernicke's area; involved in comprehending written language.

annulospiral ending A sensory receptor in the central part of an intrafusal muscle fiber.

anomia A difficulty selecting the correct word for either written or spoken language.

anomic aphasia A consistent difficulty finding names, and substituting indefinite nouns and pronouns for substantive words.

anorexia nervosa An eating disorder in which adolescents or young adults diet and lose as much as 35% of their body weight, yet still feel fat.

antagonist A drug that blocks the activity of a neurotransmitter.

anterior pituitary gland The part of the pituitary gland that manufactures and secretes releasing hormones; also called the adenohypophysis.

anterior Toward the front end.

anterograde amnesia An inability to recall events after injury to the brain.

anterograde degeneration The breakdown of an axon from the site of damage to the presynaptic terminals.

anterolateral system The somatosensory pathway that begins in the spinal cord and transmits information about temperature and pain to the brain stem reticular formation and the primary and secondary somatosensory cortices.

antidiuretic hormone (ADH) A posterior pituitary hormone that helps conserve bodily fluids by concentrating urine; also called vasopressin.

anxiolytic A sedative-hypnotic drug often used to reduce nervousness, anxiety, or fear.

aphagia The absence of eating.

aphasia An acquired impairment in the use of language.

apraxia A movement disorder characterized by missing or inappropriate actions not caused by paralysis or any other motor impairment.

apraxia of speech A disorder characterized by difficulty speaking clearly, caused by damage limited to Broca's area; an inability to plan and sequence movements for producing speech.

aqueous humor A clear fluid that fills the anterior chamber of the eye.

arachnoid mater A thin weblike sheet of tissue that is the middle layer of meninges.

arcuate fasciculus A bundle of nerve fibers in the brain that connects Wernicke's area and Broca's area.

arcuate nucleus A hypothalamic nucleus that produces neuropeptide Y and releases it into the PVN and the lateral hypothalamic area.

astrocyte A star-shaped glial cell that provides physical support for a neuron, transports nutrients into and waste products out of the neuron, regulates blood flow, and guides neural development.

Atkinson-Shiffrin model A model of memory storage in which an experience is sequentially stored in the sensory register, the short-term store, and the long-term store.

auditory agnosia An inability to recognize language and nonlanguage sounds because of damage to the secondary auditory cortex.

auditory nerve Cranial nerve VIII, the nerve that extends from the merging of the cochlear nerve and vestibular nerve.

auditory-verbal agnosia An inability to identify spoken words but not other auditory stimuli.

autonomic nervous system The division of the PNS containing the nerves that regulate the functioning of internal organs.

autoradiography The injection of radioactive chemicals into the bloodstream and subsequent analysis of neural tissue to determine where a specific chemical is found in the nervous system.

autoreceptor A presynaptic receptor whose stimulation decreases the amount of neurotransmitter released by that presynaptic neuron.

axoaxonic synapse A synapse between the axon of one neuron and the axon of another neuron.

axodendritic synapse A synapse between the axon of one neuron and the dendrite of another neuron.

axon A long, relatively thick fiber that transmits neural impulses away from the neural cell body.

axon hillock The part of the neuron where the axon and the action potential begin.

axosomatic synapse A synapse between the axon of one neuron and the cell body of another neuron.

Balint's syndrome A disorder caused by damage to the dorsal stream; characterized by difficulty in recognizing two or more objects that appear simultaneously, difficulty in visually guided reaching for objects, and impaired eye movements.

ballistic movement A habitual, rapid movement that does not depend on sensory feedback.

barbiturate A type of sedative-hypnotic drug that is a derivative of barbituric acid.

basal forebrain region A brain area anterior to the hypothalamus and including the preoptic area; stimulation produces sleep and damage produces sleeplessness.

basal ganglia A group of three structure that integrates voluntary movement; consists of the caudate nucleus, the putamen, and the globus pallidus.

basal plate A zone of cells in the ventral portion of the neural tube that develops into motor neurons and interneurons of the ventral horn of the spinal cord and the sympathetic and parasympathetic nervous systems.

basilar membrane A membrane in the organ of Corti to which auditory receptors are attached by Deiter's cells.

basket cell A cerebellar neuron that has an inhibitory influence on Purkinje cells.

bedwetting An NREM sleep disorder characterized by lack of bladder control during sleep.

behavior Anything that an organism does that involves action and response to stimulation.

behavior genetics The study of how inheritance affects the behavior of a species.

Bell-Magendie law The principle that the dorsal root of a spinal nerve carries sensory information to the spinal cord and the ventral root conveys commands to the muscles.

benzodiazepine A widely prescribed subclass of antianxiety drugs.

beta activity A rapid, desynchronized EEG pattern of small voltage changes (18 to 24 Hz) that occurs when a person is awake and active.

binding problem The problem of how the brain binds together information to form a unified perception.

binge eating disorder An eating disorder characterized by recurrent episodes of binge eating without such compensatory weight-loss methods as vomiting, use of laxatives, and excessive exercise.

binocular depth cue A depth cue provided by both eyes.

biological psychology The study of the influence of biological systems on behavior.

bipolar cell A cell between a photoreceptor and a ganglion cell in the retina.

bipolar disorder A type of affective disorder characterized by episodes of mania and depression that typically continue throughout the person's lifetime.

blind spot An area of the retina lacking photoreceptors, where no visual processsing occurs.

blindsight The ability of a person to respond to objects in a missing visual field without being conscious of seeing anything.

blob A cluster of neurons in the primary visual cortex that are sensitive to specific colors.

blood-brain barrier A barrier between the blood and the brain that prevents the free flow of substances between the two.

bradykinesia A movement disorder characterized by slowed movement.

brain The division of the CNS within the vertebrate skull, which interprets sensory messages and determines the appropriate behavioral response.

brain stem A group of structures consisting of the hindbrain (minus the cerebellum) and the midbrain.

brightness The intensity of a light stimulus.

Broca's aphasia A communicative disorder caused by damage to the left cerebral hemisphere rostral to the base of the primary motor cortex; an inability to initiate well-articulated conversational speech.

Broca's area An area in the frontal lobe of the left hemisphere of the brain that contributes to speech production.

bulimia nervosa An eating disorder characterized by recurrent episodes of binge eating, followed by self-induced vomiting and other forms of purging.

caffeine A psychostimulant found in various plants that increases alertness and decreases fatigue.

Cannon-Bard theory of emotion The view that an event activates the thalamus, which stimulates the cerebral cortex to produce the feeling component (the experience) of the emotion and, at the same time, the rest of the body to produce the expression of the emotion.

capsaicin The ingredient that gives chili peppers their hot taste by causing free nerve endings to release substance P.

castration The removal of the testes.

cataplexy A sudden, complete lack of muscle tone that sometimes accompanies narcolepsy.

catecholamine One of a subclass of monoamine neurotransmitters that includes epinephrine, norepinephrine, and dopamine.

caudal Toward the tail.

caudal reticular formation An area within the reticular formation that produces REM sleep.

cell assembly A circuit of neurons that become active at the same time; serves as the site of permanent memory.

cell-autonomous differentiation A process by which neurons develop without outside influence.

cell body (soma) The body of a neuron from which the dendrites and axon project.

cell membrane The structure that surrounds a cell and controls the flow of substances into and out of the cell.

cellular modification theory The view that learning permanently enhances the functioning of existing neural circuits or establishes new neural connections.

center-off, surround-on ganglion cell A type of ganglion cell stimulated when the surround is illuminated.

center-on, surround-off ganglion cell A type of ganglion cell stimulated when the center of the receptive field is illuminated.

central canal The chamber of the ventricular system that runs through the spinal cord.

central nervous system (CNS) The division of the nervous system that recognizes and analyzes the significance of sensory information, decides how to respond to that information, and sends the message to execute that response to the PNS.

central sulcus A deep groove that separates the anterior and posterior halves of the cerebral cortex.

cephalic reflex A response that prepares an animal to digest, metabolize, and store food; controlled by the CNS.

cephalization The evolutionary process of concentrating neurons in the head region; the fusion of many ganglion pairs to form an increasingly larger and more complex brain.

cerebellum A hindbrain structure located posterior to the medulla; develops and coordinates complex movement.

cerebral commissure A fiber tract that connects the two hemispheres of the brain.

cerebral cortex The outer layer of the forebrain that processes sensory information, controls thinking and decision making, stores and retrieves memories, and initiates motor responses.

cerebral palsy A congenital neurological motor disorder characterized by postural instability and extraneous movement.

cerebrospinal fluid (CSF) The clear fluid contained in the ventricular system and arachnoid space that supports and protects the CNS and provides it with nutrients

cerebrum The uppermost portion of the brain.

cerveau isolé preparation An experimental preparation depriving higher brain areas of sensory information arriving from the spinal cord and brain stem; used to identify brain areas controlling arousal.

channel protein A protein embedded in the cell membrane that provides a channel through which substances can pass from one side of the membrane to the other.

chemotropism The process by which a target cell releases chemicals that attract filopodia and guide the axon to its appropriate location in the nervous system.

cholecystokinin (CCK) A neuropeptide hormone that may serve as a satiety sensor.

cholinergic Describing a synapse or synaptic transmission with ACh as the neurotransmitter.

chorda tympani A branch of cranial nerve VII that conveys taste information from the posterior tongue and the palate and throat to the nucleus of the solitary tract.

choroid plexus A rich network of blood vessels in the ventricles that manufactures CSF.

chromatolysis The breakdown of a neuronal cell body following damage to the axon.

chromosome The structure in a cell that contains genes.

ciliary muscle One of several muscles that control the shape of the lens of the eye.

cingulate gyrus A limbic system structure involved in positive and negative emotional response.

circadian cycle A change in biological and behavioral functioning that occurs over a 24 hour period.

circadian rhythm The intrinsic process that controls the circadian cycle.

cocaine A psychostimulant extracted from the leaves of the coca plant that increases alertness, decreases fatigue, and produces a pleasurable emotional state.

cochlea A snail-shaped structure in the inner ear that contains the auditory receptors.

cochlear implant A device that transmits electrical impulses along cranial nerve VIII to the brain.

cochlear nerve A nerve formed by the axons of bipolar cells in the spiral ganglion that synapse with the hair cells.

cochlear nucleus The first neurons in the medulla that receive neural messages from auditory receptors via the auditory nerve.

codeine An alkaloid found in opium that is less potent than morphine.

coding A process involving a specific pattern of neural activity that contains information about stimuli in the environment.

cognitive appraisal A cognitive evaluation of an event to determine its effect on one's life.

cognitive neuroscience The study of the relationship between the nervous system and mental processes.

cognitive perspective In dream research, the view that dreams help solve everyday problems and may help store certain memories and discard other memories.

collateral sprouting A process by which neighboring neurons of a degenerating neuron sprout new axonal endings to connect to the receptor sites left vacant by the degenerated neuron.

color constancy The perception that the color of an object remains the same even under different lighting conditions.

commissurotomy A surgical cutting of the cerebral commissures to treat otherwise uncontrollable seizures.

comparative psychology The comparative study of the behavior of different species of animals, generally in a laboratory setting.

complex cell A neuron in striate or prestriate cortex that is sensitive to a line stimulus oriented in a particular direction and occurring anywhere in the receptive field.

component direction-selective neuron A neuron in striate cortex that responds to movement in one direction.

computerized axial tomography (CT) A technique that produces a static image of the brain by shooting a narrow beam of x-rays from all angles to produce a cross-sectional image, referred to as a CT scan or CAT scan.

conception The moment of fertilization of an egg by a sperm.

concordance rate The rate at which any characteristic occurs in both members of a pair of relatives.

conditioned hunger Hunger resulting from environmental factors, produced by conditioning.

conditioned response (CR) A learned reaction to a conditioned stimulus.

conditioned satiety Satiety resulting from stimuli at the end of a meal, producing a short-term inhibition of eating.

conditioned stimulus (CS) An initially neutral stimulus that eventually elicits a conditioned response after pairing with a UCS.

conduction aphasia Difficulty repeating verbal information.

cone A type of photoreceptor relatively concentrated in the center of the retina; detects fine details and colors in bright light.

confabulation A tendency to make up stories to fill in gaps in memory.

congenital disorder A disorder that is present at birth.

connexon A specialized protein channel through which ions move across gap junctions.

constructional apraxia A disorder characterized by difficulty drawing pictures or assembling objects.

contingency The specified relationship between a behavior and its reinforcement or punishment.

contralateral control The process by which one side of the brain controls movements on the opposite side of the body.

contralateral neglect A disturbance in the ability to respond to visual, auditory, or somatosensory stimuli on the left side of the body, generally caused by damage to the right posterior parietal cortex.

cornea The transparent outer layer of the eyeball.

coronal section A section of a structure as viewed from the front.

corpus callosum The largest of the cerebral commissures.

corpus striatum The part of the basal ganglia consisting of the caudate nucleus and putamen.

cortical plate A layer of daughter cells between the intermediate and marginal layers that develop into the neurons and glial cells of the cerebral cortex.

corticobulbar tract A motor pathway that controls movements of the face and tongue.

corticospinal tract A motor pathway that controls movements of the fingers, hands, arms, trunk, legs, and feet.

cranial nerve A group of axons that directly links sensory receptors to the brain, and the brain to certain muscles.

critical set point The critical level of stored fat that either activates or inhibits food-seeking behaviors.

crossing over The exchange of genetic material between chromosomes of a chromosome pair during meiosis.

cyclothymia One of the bipolar disorders characterized by less intense episodes of mania and depression than are seen in bipolar disorder.

cytoplasm The jellylike semiliquid substance inside a cell and the intracellular structures it contains; all cell contents other than the nucleus and cell membrane.

declarative memory Factual memory, or the memory of specific events.

deep cerebellar nucleus A group of neurons that correct movements in progress.

delta activity An EEG pattern during deep sleep characterized by synchronized waves that are larger in amplitude (1 to 4 Hz) than theta waves.

delusion A false system of beliefs that a person defends against reality.

dementia A loss or impairment of mental functioning.

dementia praecox Kraepelin's name for the disorder now known as schizophrenia.

dendrite A thin, widely branching projection from the cell body of a neuron that receives neural impulses.

dendrodendritic synapse A synapse between the dendrite of one neuron and the dendrite of another neuron.

dendrodendritic transmission Communication between anaxonic neurons from the dendrites of one neuron to the dendrites of another neuron.

deoxyribonucleic acid (DNA) A large, double-stranded molecule consisting of the nitrogen-containing bases adenine, guanine, cytosine, and thymine, which are attached to the sugar deoxyribose; the hereditary material that controls the production of RNA.

depolarization A reduction in electrical charge across the neuronal cell membrane.

depressant A type of psychoactive drug that acts on the CNS to slow down mental and physical functioning.

depression An affective disorder characterized by an intense, continuing feeling of sadness and worthlessness.

depressive disorder A type of affective disorder in which depression is the only mood state.

dermatome A segment of skin innervated by a spinal nerve from a particular segment of the spinal cord.

dexamethasone suppression test (DST) A test to determine whether the administration of dexamethasone suppresses ACTH and cortisol secretion; many depressed people have an abnormal response.

diabetes mellitus A disorder in which the pancreas makes too little insulin or insulin is unable to effectively remove glucose from the blood.

diencephalon The division of the forebrain containing the epithalamus, thalamus, hypothalamus, and the pituitary gland.

differentiation The creation of different cell types.

diffusion The tendency of molecules to move from areas of higher concentration to areas of lower concentration.

disease of adaptation An illness caused by the efforts of the body to cope with stressors; examples are essential hypertension, gastric or peptic ulcers, and colitis.

diurnal animal An animal that remains awake during the day and sleeps at night.

doctrine of specific nerve energies The theory that the message detected by the nervous system is determined by which nerve carries the message.

dominant allele The form of a gene that determines the expression of a physical characteristic, when either or both members of a pair of alleles are in that form.

dopamine A neurotransmitter synthesized from the amino acid tyrosine; closely related to norepinephrine.

dopamine hypothesis of schizophrenia The view that an excess of activity in the dopamine system results in the positive symptoms of schizophrenia.

dopaminergic Describing a synapse or synaptic transmission with dopamine as the neurotransmitter.

dorsal column nucleus A group of neurons in the medulla that receives neural messages about touch and proprioception via the dorsal column–medial lemniscal system.

dorsal column–medial lemniscal system A somatosensory pathway that begins in the spinal cord and transmits information about touch and proprioception to the primary somatosensory cortex.

dorsal motor nucleus of the vagus A group of neurons in the medulla that regulates insulin release by the parasympathetic nervous system.

dorsal Toward the back.

dorsolateral prefrontal cortex The top executive in the perception-action cycle; cells in this area integrate sensory information across time with motor actions needed to deal with the information.

Down syndrome A genetic disorder caused by an extra copy of chromosome 21; characterized by altered facial features, decreased mental functioning, and abnormalities in several internal organs.

dream An altered state of consciousness in which remembered images and fantasies are confused with external reality.

drug-dependent insomnia A sleep disorder that occurs when a person attempts to sleep without previously used sleep medication or takes a lower-than-normal dose.

dualism The idea that both body and mind exist.

duplex theory A theory of vision proposed by Max Schultze that summarizes the differences between rods and cones.

dura mater The thick, tough, and flexible outermost layer of the meninges.

dysgraphia A difficulty with writing.

dyslexia A difficulty with reading.

dysthymia A chronic, usually low-level form of depression.

echolalia A repetition of something someone has just said.

ectoderm The outermost layer of the embryo, which will become the nervous system, the skin, and parts of the eyes and ears.

efferent neuron A neuron that transmits messages from the CNS to skeletal muscles.

electrical synapse The junction between the dendrites of two neurons where localized depolarization or hyperpolarization is produced.

electroconvulsive therapy (ECT) A treatment for depression in which an electric current is passed through the head to induce a seizure.

electroencephalogram (EEG) A graphical record of the electrical activity of the cerebral cortex.

electrostatic pressure The attraction of opposite-polarity $(+/-)$ particles and the repulsion of same-polarity $(+/+$ or $-/-)$ particles.

embryo The human developmental stage for the first 8 weeks after conception.

emotion A feeling that differs from a person's normal state; includes a change in physiological arousal, an affective (feeling) component, and a behavioral response.

encéphale isolé preparation An experimental preparation depriving higher brain areas of sensory information arriving from the spinal cord; used to identify brain areas controlling arousal.

endocrine system The system of glands that releases hormones into the bloodstream, where they are carried to distant target areas.

endoderm The innermost layer of the embryo, which will form linings of the intestines, lungs, and liver.

endogenous opioid One of a class of neurotransmitters that have opiate-like characteristics.

endometrium The inner lining of the uterus.

engram A memory trace, or the physical location of specific memories.

enzymatic degradation Breakdown and thus deactivation of neurotransmitter molecules by an enzyme.

epinephrine A neurotransmitter closely related to norepinephrine; also called adrenalin (adrenaline).

episodic memory The memory of temporally related events experienced at a particular time and place.

epithalamus An area of the diencephalon above the thalamus; contains the pineal gland and the habenula.

equipotentiality The idea that any part of a functional area can carry out the function of that area.

erectile dysfunction A chronic inability to have a penile erection sufficient to achieve penetration.

estradiol A form of estrogen; a hormone similar to testosterone, thought to be responsible for masculinization of the brain.

estrogen The female sex hormone.

estrous cycle A cycle of changes in the level of female sex hormones in nonhuman mammals.

ethology The study of the behavior of animals, usually in their natural environments.

eustachian tube A tube connecting the middle ear with the back of the throat.

evoked potential A neural response to sensory stimulation introduced by an experimenter.

evolution The process by which succeeding generations of organisms change in physical appearance, function, and behavior through a process of natural selection.

excitatory postsynaptic potential (EPSP) The depolarization produced by neurotransmitter molecules acting on receptors on the postsynaptic membrane.

exhaustion stage The final stage of the GAS; when a stressor continues indefinitely, physiological resources are depleted, resulting in failure of the body's defense systems and eventually death.

experimental allergic encephalomyelitis A neurological disorder resembling MS produced by injecting myelin proteins into the bloodstreams of laboratory animals.

extensor muscle A muscle that produces movement of a limb away from the body.

extrafusal muscle fiber A muscle fiber controlled by an alpha motor neuron.

false transmitter A drug that prevents a neurotransmitter from binding to a receptor by attaching to the receptor on the postsynaptic membrane.

fast pain The type of pain carried by myelinated type A fibers that quickly reaches the spinal cord.

fast-twitch muscle A muscle fiber that contracts and fatigues quickly.

fear-induced aggression An aggressive behavior that is a defensive reaction occurring only when the organism feels threatened and perceives escape to be impossible.

feature detector A cell in the visual cortex that appears to respond to a specific feature of the visual scene.

fen-phen A drug combination of fenfluramine and phentermine, once used in treating obesity.

fertilization The fusion of an egg nucleus and sperm nucleus.

festination A tendency in a movement disorder to speed up a walking pace to running.

fetal alcohol syndrome (FAS) A disorder caused by alcohol consumption by the mother during pregnancy; characterized by low birth weight and diminished height, distinctive facial features, mental retardation, and behavioral problems (hyperactivity and irritability).

fetus The human developmental stage beginning at 8 weeks and continuing for the remainder of the pregnancy.

filopodia Spinelike extensions from the growth cone that pull the axon to the target cell.

flexor muscle A muscle that produces movement of a limb toward the body.

fluent aphasia An inability to understand the language of others and the production of less meaningful speech than normal.

follicle-stimulating hormone (FSH) A hormone secreted by the anterior pituitary gland that causes one or several ovarian follicles to grow into a mature Graafian follicle, the egg to mature, and the Graafian follicle to secrete estrogen.

forebrain The division of the brain containing the telencephalon and the diencephalon.

fovea The central region of the retina, where cones are most concentrated.

fragile X syndrome A disorder caused by a fragile gene at one site on the large arm of the X chromosome that can cause the chromosome to break; characterized by an abnormal facial appearance and mental retardation.

free nerve ending A type of skin receptor located just below the surface in both hairy and hairless skin; detects temperature and pain stimuli.

free-running rhythm A 25 hour (or more) sleep-wake cycle that develops in the absence of natural light-dark cycles.

frequency theory of pitch perception The view that the firing rate in the auditory nerve matches the frequency of the sound.

frontal lobe The lobe in the most anterior part of the cerebral cortex; responsible for executive functioning and the control of movement.

functional MRI (fMRI) A technique that uses high-powered, rapidly oscillating magnetic fields and powerful computation to measure cerebral blood flow in the brain and obtain an image of the neural activity in a specific brain area.

fusiform face area The region of the inferotemporal cortex most responsible for recognition of faces.

GABAergic Describing a synapse or synaptic transmission with GABA as the neurotransmitter.

gamma motor neuron A neuron that synapses with intrafusal muscle fibers to produce continuous muscle tension.

gamma-aminobutyric acid (GABA) An amino acid neurotransmitter, the most common inhibitory neurotransmitter in the brain.

ganglion A collection of neuronal cell bodies outside the CNS.

ganglion cell A cell in the third layer of cells in the retina.

gap junction The narrow space between the dendrites of two neurons; another name for an electrical synapse.

gate-control theory of pain The view that input from pain receptors will produce the perception of pain only if the message first passes through a "gate" in the spinal cord and lower brain stem structures.

gender A set of culturally defined roles, attitudes, and responsibilities for females and males that are learned, may change with time, and vary among and within societies.

gene A unit of heredity; a region of DNA that directs the making of a protein.

general adaptation syndrome (GAS) A pattern of physiological responses to a physiological or psychological stressor.

genetics The study of heredity or inheritance.

ghrelin A gastrointestinal peptide with an appetite-stimulating effect.

glial cell A nervous system cell that has a support function.

global aphasia A severe depression of all language functioning.

glucagon A pancreatic hormone that increases blood glucose levels.

glucoprivation The unavailability of glucose as an energy source.

glucoreceptor A specialized receptor that monitors blood glucose levels.

glucostatic theory A theory that hunger is caused by low blood glucose levels.

glutamate An amino acid neurotransmitter, the most common excitatory neurotransmitter in the CNS.

glutamatergic Describing a synapse or synaptic transmission with glutamate as the neurotransmitter.

glycoprotein A class of compounds in which a protein is combined with a carbohydrate group.

Golgi tendon organ A receptor located among the fibers of tendons that measures the total amount of force exerted by the muscle on the bone to which the tendon is attached.

gonadotropin An anterior pituitary hormone that regulates the activities of the gonads.

graded potential An EPSP or IPSP received by the dendrites and cell body that can have a different value at different times.

gray matter The cell bodies of neurons.

growth cone The swollen end of the developing neuron from which an axon emerges.

guidepost cell A cell that redirects the growth of the axon toward the target cell.

gustatory sense The sense of taste.

habenula A structure of the epithalamus with olfactory functions.

habituation A decrease in response following repeated exposure to a nonthreatening stimulus.

hair cell An auditory receptor involved in transducing eardrum vibrations into neural impulses.

half-life The amount of time it takes the body to eliminate half of a drug.

hallucination A sensory experience in the absence of environmental stimulation.

hardiness An ability to cope effectively with stressors, because of a high level of commitment, a perception that change is a challenge rather than a threat, and a sense of control over events.

heat A period of intense sexual arousal when estrogen levels peak in estrous mammals; also called estrus.

hemispheric lateralization The differentiation of functions between the right and left sides of the brain.

heroin A powerful semisynthetic opioid made by reacting acetic anhydride with morphine.

heterozygous Describing an allele pair in which the two alleles are different.

hindbrain The division of the brain just above the spinal cord that contains the medulla oblongata, the pons, the cerebellum, and the raphé system.

hippocampus A limbic system structure that processes or contributes to memory storage and retrieval.

homeostasis A tendency of an animal to maintain a constant internal state.

homozygous Describing an allele pair with identical alleles.

horizontal cell A type of retinal neuron that receives neural messages from photoreceptors; synapses with and has an inhibitory influence on bipolar cells.

horizontal section A section of a structure as viewed from above.

hormone A chemical produced by the endocrine glands that is circulated widely throughout the body via the bloodstream.

hue The color a particular wavelength of light is perceived to be.

Huntington's disease A progressive neurological disorder characterized by psychiatric symptoms, dementia, and a slow deterioration of muscle control; caused by a single dominant gene.

hydrocephalus A blockage of CSF flow from the brain.

hypercomplex cell A neuron that responds to visual stimuli of a particular orientation and a specific length in a relatively large receptive field.

hypercortisolism An abnormally high secretion (hypersecretion) of cortisol from the adrenal cortex; found in many people with major depression.

hyperphagia Excessive food intake; overeating.

hyperpolarized Having an electrical charge across the cell membrane that is more negative than normal.

hypersomnia A sleep disorder characterized by too much sleep.

hypofrontality theory A theory that the negative symptoms of schizophrenia are caused by decreased activity in the prefrontal cortex.

hypomania A milder form of mania in which occupational or social functioning is not impaired.

hypothalamus A forebrain structure that detects need states and controls pituitary hormone production and release.

hypovolemic thirst A type of thirst caused by a loss of extracellular fluid.

Ia fiber An axon from an annulospiral ending that enters the dorsal root of the spinal cord and synapses with an alpha motor neuron.

Ib fiber An axon of a Golgi tendon organ that extends to the spinal cord and synapses with an interneuron that inhibits alpha motor neurons.

incus (anvil) The bone of the middle ear attached to the malleus and stapes.

indoleamine One of a subclass of monoamine neurotransmitters that includes serotonin and melatonin.

induction A process in which neurons rely on the influence of other cells to determine their final form.

inferior Below a structure.

inferior colliculus An area of the tectum of the midbrain that receives neural messages from both the cochlear nucleus and the superior olivary nucleus and relays this auditory information.

ingestional neophobia A reluctance to eat novel foods.

inhalation The administration of a drug through the lungs.

inhibitory postsynaptic potential (IPSP) The hyperpolarization produced by neurotransmitter molecules acting on receptors on the postsynaptic membrane.

insomnia A sleep disorder characterized by a long-term inability to obtain adequate sleep.

insulin A pancreatic hormone that lowers blood glucose levels.

intensity difference A cue to the localization of high-pitched sounds; a sound is louder in the ear closer to it than in the ear farther away.

interference An inability to recall a specific memory because of other memories.

intermediate-twitch muscle A muscle fiber that contracts at a lower rate than fast-twitch and a higher rate than slow-twitch muscles.

interneuron A neuron that connects a sensory and a motor neuron or communicates with other neurons.

interpositus nucleus The area of the brain central to the conditioning of the nictitating membrane response.

intracerebral injection An injection of a drug directly into the brain.

intrafusal muscle fiber A muscle fiber within the muscle spindle that is surrounded by annulospiral endings.

intramuscular (IM) injection An injection of a drug into a muscle.

intraperitoneal (IP) injection An injection of a drug through the abdominal wall into the peritoneal cavity, or space surrounding major organs.

intravenous (IV) injection An injection of a drug into a vein.

intraventricular injection An injection of a drug into the cerebral ventricles in order to achieve widespread distribution in the brain and bypass the blood-brain barrier.

invertebrate An animal without a backbone.

ion A charged particle, such as a sodium (Na^+), potassium (K^+), or chloride (Cl^-) ion.

ionotropic receptor A receptor whose ion channels are rapidly opened by the direct action of a neurotransmitter.

iris Bands of muscles covered by the colored tissue of the eye.

irritable aggression An attack on almost anything without making attempts to escape.

James-Lange theory of emotion The view that the physiological changes that occur in response to an event determine the experience of an emotion.

jet lag The fatigue and sleep disturbance caused by traveling across several time zones.

K complex A single large negative wave (upward spike) followed by a single large positive wave (downward spike) that occurs during stage 2 sleep.

kindling Repeated stimulation of the amygdala, causing an animal to be more susceptible to seizure activity.

Klinefelter syndrome A condition in which a person has an XXY genotype and is phenotypically male, but has small external genitals, sparse pubic and armpit hair, and a tendency to be infertile.

Klüver-Bucy syndrome A disorder produced by temporal lobectomy, characterized by placidity, socially inappropriate sexual activity, compulsive orality, a decreased ability to recognize people, and memory deficits.

Korsakoff's syndrome A severe memory impairment usually seen in chronic alcoholics.

labeled-line coding The type of coding in which information about a stimulus is determined by the particular receptor reacting to the stimulus.

lamella In the eye, a thin membranous disc in the outer segment of a photoreceptor.

language A system of words, word meanings, and rules for combining words into phrases and sentences.

language acquisition device (LAD) An innate mechanism that allows children to readily grasp the syntax relevant to their native language.

lark A person who is active and alert in the morning and becomes drowsy and inattentive in the evening.

lateral Away from the midline.

lateral geniculate nucleus (LGN) A group of neurons in the thalamus that receives neural impulses from the ganglion cells of the retina and relays visual information to the cortex.

lateral hypothalamus (LH) A hypothalamic area once thought to control hunger and the initiation of eating.

lateral inhibition A decrease in activity of one neuron caused by the stimulation of its neighbors.

lateral reticulospinal tract A ventromedial tract that activates the flexor muscles of the legs.

lateral sulcus A deep groove that separates the temporal from the frontal and parietal lobes of the cerebral cortex.

lateralization of function The differentiation of the functions of the two hemispheres of the brain.

learned helplessness A pattern of depression-like behavior produced by repeated exposure to an inescapable noxious event.

learning A long-term change in behavior as a function of experiences.

lens A structure made of a series of transparent, onionlike layers of tissue that changes shape to focus images on the retina.

leptin A hormone secreted by fat cells that appears to provide the brain with feedback about the level of stored fat in the body.

levodopa (L-dopa) A drug converted to dopamine in the brain; used to treat Parkinson's disease.

LH-lesion syndrome The pattern of aphagic and adipsic behavior exhibited by rats following damage to the lateral hypothalamus.

light therapy An increased exposure to intense broad-spectrum light that enhances mood in people with SAD.

limb apraxia An impairment in the voluntary use of a limb caused by damage to the left parietal lobe or the corpus callosum.

limbic system A group of forebrain structures, surrounding the brain stem, that processes emotional expression and the storage and retrieval of memories; the name MacLean gave to the Papez circuit.

lipid A fat or fatty acid; fatty acid levels in the blood are involved in hunger.

lipoprivation The unavailability of fats or fatty acids as an energy source.

lipostatic theory A theory that proposes a relationship between fat deposits and hunger.

locus The location of a gene on a chromosome.

locus coeruleus A group of neurons within the reticular formation important for cortical activity and behavioral alertness.

longitudinal fissure A deep groove that separates the right and left hemispheres.

long-term depression (LTD) A persistent activity-dependent reduction in synaptic effectiveness.

long-term potentiation (LTP) An increased neural responsivity that follows a brief, intense series of electrical impulses to neural tissue.

long-term store The site of permanent memory storage.

loosening of associations A tendency to make sentences containing several disconnected thoughts, characteristic of people with schizophrenia.

lordosis A female copulatory posture in which the hindquarters are raised to facilitate insertion of the penis by the male.

loudness The perception of the amplitude of a sound wave, measured in decibels.

lucid dream A dream in which the person is conscious that he or she is dreaming.

luteinizing hormone (LH) In females, a hormone secreted by the anterior pituitary gland that causes ovulation.

lysergic acid diethylamide (LSD) A powerful synthetic psychedelic drug, also known as acid.

macroelectrode An electrode designed to record from many neurons at once.

magnetic resonance imaging (MRI) A technique that produces a static image of the brain by passing a strong magnetic field through the brain, followed by a radio wave, then measuring the radiation emitted from hydrogen atoms.

magnocellular layer One of the bottom two layers of the LGN, consisting of neurons with large cell bodies.

major depression A type of depressive disorder characterized by a depressed mood of at least 2 weeks' duration.

malleus (hammer) The bone of the middle ear attached to the tympanic membrane and the incus.

mania An elevated, expansive, or irritable mood and inflated self-esteem or grandiosity.

marijuana A drug obtained from a mixture of crushed leaves, flowers, stems, and seeds of the hemp plant, *Cannabis sativa.*

mass action Lashley's finding that the greater the brain area destroyed, the more severe the impact on learning.

MDMA The abbreviation for 3,4-methylenedioxymethamphetamine, a synthetic psychoactive drug, known as ecstasy, that induces a state of consciousness that facilitates communication.

medial Toward the midline.

medial forebrain bundle (MFB) A pathway of nerve fibers that interconnects structures in the limbic system with brain stem areas; considered part of the reinforcement system of the brain.

medial geniculate nucleus (MGN) A group of neurons in the thalamus that receives neural impulses from the inferior colliculus and relays auditory information to the cortex.

medial lemniscus A ribbon-like band of fibers in the dorsal column–medial lemniscal system that conveys neural messages from the dorsal column nuclei to the ventral posterolateral thalamic nuclei.

medial preoptic area (MPOA) A group of neurons in the anterior hypothalamus that influences female sexual responsivity.

medial reticulospinal tract A ventromedial tract that activates the extensor muscles of the legs.

medial temporal lobe A brain area containing the hippocampus and surrounding cortical areas; involved in storing experiences.

mediodorsal thalamus A brain structure associated with profound memory impairment.

medulla oblongata A hindbrain structure located just rostral to the spinal cord; controls essential functions such as respiration and heart rate.

meiosis The process by which gametes, sperm and egg cells with half the number of chromosomes found in other cells, are formed.

Meissner's corpuscle A type of skin receptor in hairy skin, located in the elevations of the dermis into the epidermis; responds to pressure and low-frequency vibrations.

melatonin A hormone secreted by the pineal gland in response to daylight and darkness.

memory The capacity to retain and retrieve past experiences.

memory attribute An aspect of an event that can stimulate memory retrieval.

meninges The three layers of tissue between the skull and brain and between the vertebral column and spinal cord.

menstrual cycle A cycle of changes in the level of female sex hormones in humans and some other primates.

menstruation The expulsion of the uterine lining in menstrual animals.

Merkel's disk A type of skin receptor in the base of the epidermis near the sweat ducts; sensitive to pressure.

mescaline The psychoactive ingredient in peyote.

mesencephalon Another name for the midbrain.

mesoderm The middle layer of the embryo, which will form the connective tissue, muscle, and blood and blood vessel linings.

mesolimbic reinforcement system (MRS) The brain reinforcement system traveling from the ventral tegmental area through the MFB to end in limbic structures, particularly the nucleus accumbens.

metabolite A component molecule of a drug, produced by enzymatic breakdown, that typically has little or none of the effect of the parent compound.

metabotropic receptor A receptor whose ion channels are opened indirectly by a second messenger.

metencephalon One of two divisions of the hindbrain; contains the cerebellum and the pons.

methadone An opioid drug with pleasurable effects similar to those of heroin, used to treat heroin addiction.

microdialysis A technique for identifying the neurotransmitter in a specific area of the nervous system by measuring the chemical constituents of fluid from neural tissue.

microelectrode An electrode designed to record the activity of one or a few neurons.

microglial cell A type of glial cell that removes the debris of dead neurons.

microsleep A brief period during which a person appears to be awake, but the EEG patterns resemble stage 1 sleep.

midbrain A division of the CNS that contains the tectum and the tegmentum.

mirror neuron Neuron in the primate premotor cortex that is activated by performing an action or by watching another monkey or person performing an action.

monism The idea that there is only one underlying reality, either body or mind.

monoamine One of a class of neurotransmitters that contain an amino group (NH_2); includes epinephrine, norepinephrine, dopamine, and serotonin.

monoamine hypothesis of depression The theory that depression is caused by decreased activity at monoaminergic synapses, particularly where serotonin and norepinephrine are the neurotransmitters.

monoamine oxidase (MAO) An enzyme that deactivates norepinephrine, dopamine, and serotonin.

monoamine oxidase inhibitor (MAOI) A type of antidepressant drug that increases monoamine levels by preventing MAO from degrading excess monoamine neurotransmitters.

monocular depth cue A depth cue requiring only one eye for detection.

monosynaptic stretch reflex A spinal reflex with a single synapse between the sensory receptor and the muscle effector.

morpheme The smallest meaningful unit of language.

morphine An extremely potent natural opioid that is the main alkaloid compound found in opium.

mossy fiber pathway One of the afferent pathways into the hippocampus; intense electrical stimulation of its neurons produces LTP.

motion sickness The feelings of dizziness and nausea that occur when the body is moved passively without motor activity and corresponding feedback to the brain.

motor cortex An area in the frontal lobe involved in the control of voluntary body movements.

motor end plate The flattened area of an extrafusal muscle fiber where a motor neuron and the muscle fiber synapse.

motor neuron A specialized neuron that carries messages from the CNS to muscles.

motor unit An alpha motor neuron and all the muscle fibers it controls.

movement A change in the place or position of the body or a body part.

Müllerian-inhibiting substance (MIS) A hormone released by the testes that helps prevent the development of the female reproductive system.

Müllerian system A set of ducts in the human embryo that develops into parts of the female reproductive system.

multiple sclerosis (MS) A progressive neurological disorder caused by the degeneration of the myelin sheath in the central nervous system.

muscle fiber One of the units comprising a skeletal muscle.

muscle spindle A structure embedded within an extrafusal muscle fiber that enables the CNS to contract a muscle to counteract the stretching of the extrafusal muscle fiber.

muscle tone The resting tension of skeletal muscles caused by the activity of gamma motor neurons.

myasthenia gravis A neuromuscular disorder characterized by muscle fatigue following exercise.

myelencephalon One of two divisions of the hindbrain; contains the medulla oblongata.

myelin A fatlike substance that surrounds and insulates the axons of certain neurons.

myelin sheath The segments of myelin covering certain axons; myelinated axons transmit a neural impulse faster than unmyelinated axons.

myofibril One of the units comprising a muscle fiber.

myofilament A component of a myofibril.

myosin The protein component of thick myofilaments.

myotonia The rhythmic contraction of muscles, as in the male and female genital organs during orgasm; also causes erection of the nipples.

naltrexone An opiate antagonist that binds to opiate receptors and blocks the action of heroin and other opiates.

narcolepsy A sleep disorder characterized by a sudden, uncontrollable sleep attack, usually initiated by monotonous activity.

negative afterimage The brief perception of a complementary color after extended stimulation with a particular color.

negative feedback loop The release of a substance that acts to inhibit its subsequent release.

negative symptom Normal behavior (e.g., appropriate emotions, desire for social contact) that is absent in people with schizophrenia, as seen in social withdrawal and a flat affect.

neologism A meaningless word created by a person with schizophrenia.

neologistic jargon A passage of lengthy, fluent, nonsensical speech.

nerve A collection of axons outside the CNS, within the PNS.

nerve net theory The idea that the nervous system consists of a network of connected nerves.

neural crest A specialized group of cells that migrate away from the neural tube to form several types of tissue, including the sensory and autonomic neurons of the PNS.

neural fold The lateral edge of the neural plate.

neural groove The space formed between the edges of the neural folds.

neural impulse The propagation of an action potential along an axon.

neural plate The thickened ectodermal layer of the embryo.

neural regeneration The regrowth of a neuron and the reestablishment of its connections to other neurons.

neural tube The closed space that is formed when the neural folds meet and close the neural groove.

neurofibrillary tangle An unusual triangular and looped fiber in the cytoplasm of neurons that is a hallmark of AD.

neurogenesis The formation of new neurons.

neuromatrix theory of pain A theory that accounts for types of pain unexplained by the gate-control theory of pain.

neuromodulator A type of chemical that modifies the sensitivity of groups of cells to neurotransmitters or the amount of neurotransmitter released.

neuromuscular junction A specialized synapse between an alpha motor neuron and an extrafusal muscle fiber; the point of contact between a neuron and a muscle.

neuron A nerve cell.

neuronal theory The idea that the nervous system is made up of individual nerve cells.

neuropeptide A peptide that functions as a neurotransmitter.

neuropeptide Y (NPY) A peptide neurotransmitter involved in hunger.

neuroplasticity The modifiability of the brain that allows adaptation to changing environmental conditions.

neuropsychology The study of the behavioral effects of brain damage in humans.

neuroscience The study of the nervous system.

neurotransmitter A chemical stored in the synaptic vesicles that is released into the synaptic cleft and transmits messages to other neurons, blood vessels, or muscles.

neurotransmitter reuptake The return of neurotransmitter to the presynaptic neuron.

neurotrophin A chemical released by a target cell that attracts the filopodia of a developing neuron.

nicotine A psychostimulant found in the leaves of the tobacco plant that increases alertness and decreases fatigue.

night terror An abrupt awakening from NREM sleep, accompanied by intense autonomic arousal and feelings of panic.

nigrostriatal pathway A dopaminergic system involved in voluntary eating and drinking behavior; begins in the substantia nigra, passes through the lateral hypothalamus, and ends in the basal ganglia.

nitric oxide (NO) A soluble gas neurotransmitter involved in such disparate functions as penile erection and learning.

NMDA receptor A receptor that is sensitive to the neurotransmitter glutamate.

nocturnal animal An animal that sleeps during the day and is awake at night.

node of Ranvier The space between myelinated segments of a myelinated axon.

nonbarbiturate sedative-hypnotic drug A type of sedative-hypnotic drug that is not derived from barbituric acid but has the same mode of action as barbiturates.

nonfluent aphasia A difficulty producing fluent, well-articulated, and self-initiated speech.

nonREM (NREM) sleep Sleep stages 1 to 4, in which the EEG patterns are markedly different from those in REM sleep.

nonvisual photoreceptor A type of photoreceptor that detects the daily dawn-dusk cycle.

noradrenergic (adrenergic) Describing a synapse or synaptic transmission with norepinephrine as the neurotransmitter.

norepinephrine A neurotransmitter synthesized from the amino acid tyrosine; sometimes called noradrenalin (noradrenaline).

nucleus (of cell) The part of a cell containing chromosomes, genes, and DNA.

nucleus (of CNS) A collection of neuronal cell bodies within the CNS.

nucleus medianus A group of neurons in the brain involved in osmotic and hypovolemic thirst.

nucleus of the solitary tract A group of neurons in the medulla that receives information from taste receptors and influences the amount of food consumed.

nystagmus The rapid side-to-side eye movements caused by inconsistent information from the visual and vestibular systems.

occipital lobe The lobe located in the most posterior part of the cerebral cortex; responsible for the analysis of visual stimuli.

ocular dominance column A column of cells in the visual cortex all having the same amount of dominance of input from either the left or the right eye.

off ganglion cell A type of ganglion cell excited when a light stimulus is removed.

olfactory bulb A structure at the base of the brain that receives information about odor from olfactory receptors.

olfactory epithelium The mucous membrane in the top rear of the nasal passage, lined by olfactory receptors.

olfactory sense The sense of smell.

olfactory tract Axons of olfactory bulb neurons that project to the primary olfactory cortex.

oligodendrocyte A type of glial cell that myelinates certain neurons in the CNS.

on ganglion cell A type of ganglion cell excited by bipolar cells in response to a light stimulus.

on-off ganglion cell A type of ganglion cell excited by both the presence and removal of a light stimulus.

operant conditioning A type of learning in which a response either produces reinforcement or avoids punishment.

opioid A drug derived from the opium poppy, or a drug that has an action comparable to that of drugs derived from the opium poppy.

opium A natural opiate drug obtained directly from the opium poppy.

opponent-process theory The theory that there are three receptor complexes operating in opponent fashion to yield a perception of color and brightness.

opsin The protein component of a photopigment.

optic chiasm The place where the two optic nerves meet and some or all of the optic nerve fibers cross to the opposite side of the brain.

optic disk The point at the back of the eye where axons from ganglion cells converge.

optic nerve A nerve formed by the axons of ganglion cells after leaving the optic disk.

optic tract The continuation of the optic nerve fibers beyond the optic chiasm.

oral ingestion The administration of a drug through the mouth.

organ of Corti A structure inside the cochlea that contains the basilar membrane, the hair cells, and the tectorial membrane.

organum vasculosum lamina terminalis (OVLT) A structure outside the blood-brain barrier that contains osmoreceptors; plays a role in thirst.

orgasm The climax of the sexual response.

orgasmic dysfunction The inability to have an orgasm.

orientation column A column of cells in the visual cortex all responding to the same orientation of a line stimulus (line-tilt).

osmoreceptor A neuron that monitors osmotic pressure.

osmotic thirst A condition of thirst caused by increased osmotic pressure that results from increased salt levels in the extracellular fluid.

oval window The part of the inner ear attached to the stapes.

ovariectomy The surgical removal of the ovaries.

overtraining syndrome Disorder caused by excessive training by athletes; characterized by decreased performance, mood changes, and evidence of a compromised immune system.

owl A person who is drowsy and inattentive in the morning and active and alert in the evening.

oxytocin A posterior pituitary hormone that plays a role in reproductive activities, such as sexual arousal, orgasm, nest building, suckling, and bonding with offspring. It stimulates uterine contractions and milk secretion in females and causes prostate gland contractions in males.

Pacinian corpuscle The largest type of skin receptor, found in both hairy and hairless skin; detects high-frequency vibrations.

pallidotomy A psychosurgical treatment for Parkinson's disease that reduces tremors, rigidity, and bradykinesia.

Papez circuit A system of interconnected forebrain structures that are responsible for the expression and experience of an emotion.

papilla A small, visible bump on the tongue that contains taste buds.

paragrammatical speech Speech characterized by the use of inappropriate morphemes.

paraphasia An error in speaking.

parasympathetic nervous system A division of the autonomic nervous system that is activated by conditions of recovery or the termination of stress.

paraventricular nucleus (PVN) A hypothalamic area where damage may produce the VMH-lesion syndrome.

parietal lobe The lobe of the cerebral cortex located between the central sulcus and the occipital lobe; responsible for the analysis of somatosensory stimuli.

Parkinson's disease A degenerative neurological disorder characterized by rigidity of the limbs and muscle tremors.

parvocellular layer One of the top four layers of the LGN, consisting of neurons with small cell bodies.

patellar reflex A reflex in which tapping the tendon of the knee stretches one of the muscles that extends the leg, and the resulting muscle contraction causes the leg to kick outward.

pattern direction-selective neuron A neuron in the middle temporal cortex that combines the information arriving from the primary visual cortex to recognize the direction in which an object is moving.

Pavlovian conditioning A type of learning in which a neutral stimulus is paired with a stimulus that elicits a reflex response until the neutral stimulus elicits the reflex response by itself.

perforant fiber pathway The most widely studied of three pathways into the hippocampus; intense stimulation of its neurons produces LTP.

periaqueductal gray (PAG) An area of the midbrain that is the origin of a descending fiber tract that synapses with inhibitory interneurons in the lower brain stem and spinal cord to block messages about pain.

peripheral nervous system (PNS) The division of the nervous system that detects environmental information, transmits that information to the CNS, and executes CNS decisions.

peyote A psychedelic drug obtained from the peyote cactus plant.

PGO wave A brief burst of neural activity during REM sleep that begins in the pons, is transmitted to the LGN, and ends in the occipital lobe.

phantom limb pain The sensation of pain in a missing limb experienced by up to 70% of people who lose a limb.

pharmacodynamics The study of the effects of a drug on the living organism, on the organs of the body.

pharmacokinetics The study of how a drug moves through the body, including absorption, metabolism, distribution to tissues, and elimination.

phase difference A cue to localizing a low-pitched sound by the difference in the cycle of the sound wave when it reaches each ear.

phase-advance shift A schedule that shortens the day by requiring a worker to start on the late shift and then rotate to an earlier shift the following week.

phase-delay shift A schedule that lengthens the day by requiring a worker to rotate to a later shift each week.

phencyclidine (PCP) A powerful synthetic psychedelic drug, also known as angel dust.

phenylketonuria (PKU) A genetic disorder involving the absence of an enzyme needed to break down phenylalanine; the resulting buildup of phenylalanine can lead to mental retardation.

pheromone A chemical released into the air, rather than into the bloodstream, that affects other members of a species; can be used to signal reproductive readiness.

phoneme The simplest functional speech sound.

phonology The study of the sound system of a language that prescribes how phonemes can be combined into morphemes.

photopigment A chemical molecule in the lamellae of the eye that absorbs light.

photoreceptor The receptor cell located at the back of the eye that transduces light into a neural impulse.

phrase A group of two or more related words that expresses a single thought.

phrenology Gall's "science of the mind," which assumed that mental functions are localized in certain brain areas and that the moral and intellectual character of a person can be determined by studying the bumps and indentations on the skull.

physiological psychology The study of the relationship between the nervous system and behavior by experimentally altering specific nervous system structures and observing the effects on behavior.

pia mater A thin membrane that adheres closely to the surface of the brain and is the innermost layer of the meninges.

pineal gland A structure of the epithalamus that controls seasonal rhythms in behavior through its release of melatonin.

pinna The outer, visible portion of the ear.

pitch The perception of the frequency of a sound wave, measured in hertz (Hz).

pituitary gland A gland located just ventral to the hypothalamus; divided into two lobes: the anterior pituitary gland and the posterior pituitary gland; also called the hypophysis.

place theory of pitch perception The view that different sounds activate nerve fibers at different locations on the basilar membrane.

polysynaptic reflex A spinal reflex with more than one synapse between the sensory receptor and the muscle effector.

pons A hindbrain structure located superior to the medulla; relays sensory information to the cerebellum and thalamus.

positive feedback loop The release of a substance that acts to promote its further release.

positive symptom A behavior exhibited by a person with schizophrenia but absent in people without the disorder; examples are hallucinations and delusions.

positron emission tomography (PET) A technique that measures the metabolic activity of a specific structure in the nervous system in order to determine neural functioning.

posterior Toward the rear end.

posterior parietal cortex A cortical area that integrates input from the visual, auditory, and skin senses and relays it to the primary motor cortex.

posterior pituitary gland The part of the pituitary gland, considered an extension of the hypothalamus, that produces and releases oxytocin and antidiuretic hormone; also called the neurohypophysis.

posterior thalamic nucleus A group of neurons in the thalamus that receives information about temperature and pain via the anterolateral pathway.

postsynaptic membrane The outer surface of a target cell that receives messages from the presynaptic membrane.

prandial drinking Drinking while eating.

precentral gyrus An area in the frontal lobe that contains the primary motor cortex.

prefrontal cortex An area in the anterior part of the frontal lobe that controls complex intellectual functions.

prefrontal lobotomy A surgical procedure that severs the connections of the prefrontal cortex to the rest of the brain.

preloading An experimental procedure in which food is placed in the stomach before food becomes available to the subject.

premature ejaculation The inability of a man to delay ejaculation until his partner achieves orgasm.

premenstrual syndrome (PMS) An irritability in human females during the premenstrual phase, attributed to a drop in progesterone level.

premotor cortex A brain area anterior to the primary motor cortex that includes Broca's area; damage results in agrammatical and awkward speech. A part of the secondary motor cortex that receives input mostly from the visual cortex.

pressure phosphene A visual sensation caused by pressure on the optic nerve.

presynaptic facilitation The enhanced release of neurotransmitter from the presynaptic membrane caused by the action of another neuron.

presynaptic inhibition A decrease in the release of neurotransmitter from the presynaptic membrane (despite the occurrence of an action potential) caused by the action of another neuron.

presynaptic membrane The outer surface of the presynaptic terminal, the site of release of neurotransmitters into the synaptic cleft.

presynaptic terminal A swelling at the end of an axon.

primary auditory cortex (Heschl's gyrus) The part of the superior temporal gyrus that detects characteristics of sound (frequency, amplitude, complexity). It receives auditory information from the thalamus.

primary drinking Drinking in response to loss of intracellular or extracellular fluid.

primary gustatory cortex An area located just ventral and rostral to the area representing the tongue in the somatosensory cortex.

primary motor cortex An area in the precentral gyrus of the frontal lobe that plays a major role in voluntary movements.

primary olfactory cortex An area in the pyriform cortex in the limbic system that gives odors an emotional component.

primary somatosensory cortex An area in the cortex that receives information about touch, proprioception, temperature, and pain.

primary visual cortex The area of the cerebral cortex (occipital lobe) that detects features of the visual environment; also called striate cortex. It receives visual information from the thalamus.

procedural memory Skill memory, or the memory of highly practiced behavior.

prodromal phase The phase of schizophrenia in which the person becomes socially withdrawn and school or work performance declines.

progesterone A female sex hormone manufactured by the corpus luteum; with estrogen, it prepares the lining of the uterus for implantation of the fertilized egg.

proprioception The somatosense that monitors body position and movement, acts to maintain body position, and ensures the accuracy of intended movements.

prosencephalon Another name for the forebrain, which divides into the telencephalon and the diencephalon.

prosopagnosia An impaired ability to recognize familiar faces visually.

psychedelic drug A drug that profoundly alters a person's state of consciousness.

psychoactive drug A drug that affects mental functioning.

psychopharmacology The study of the effects of psychoactive drugs on behavior.

psychophysiology The study of the relationship between behavior and physiology through the analysis of the physiological responses of human subjects engaged in various activities.

psychostimulant A drug that produces alertness by enhancing the functioning of the sympathetic nervous system and the reticular formation.

pump protein A protein in the cell membrane that exchanges one type of ion on one side of the membrane for another ion on the other side of the membrane.

punisher An event that decreases the frequency of the behavior that precedes it.

pupil The opening in the iris through which light passes.

pure alexia An inability to read, with no difficulty writing; caused by a separation of the angular gyrus from visual input; also called alexia without agraphia.

Purkinje cell An output cell from the cerebellar cortex, which has an exclusively inhibitory effect.

pursuit movement The smooth movement of the eyes following a moving object.

pyramidal cell A large, pyramid-shaped neuron in the primary motor cortex.

radial glial cell A glial cell that guides the migration of daughter cells during the embryonic development of the nervous system.

raphé nucleus Nucleus located in a thin strip of neurons running along the midline in the caudal part of the reticular formation; damage to this area produces insomnia.

raphé system A group of nuclei located along the midline of the hindbrain between the medulla and midbrain; controls the sleep-wake cycle.

rapid eye movement (REM) sleep The phase of sleep in which the EEG pattern resembles the waking state, the eyes move behind closed lids, and muscle tone is absent.

rate law A principle stating that the greater the stimulus intensity, the faster the rate of neural firing (up to the maximum rate possible for the neuron).

receptive field The part of the retina that, when stimulated, causes a change in the activity of the cell.

receptor protein A protein in the cell membrane that recognizes and binds a specific neurotransmitter.

recessive allele The form of a gene that can determine the expression of a specific physical characteristic only when both members of a pair of alleles are in that form.

red nucleus A structure in the tegmentum that controls basic body and limb movements.

reflex An involuntary response to a stimulus, caused by a direct connection between a sensory receptor and a muscle.

rehabilitation The process of developing compensatory behaviors that substitute for lost functions.

rehearsal systems approach An alternative to the Atkinson-Shiffrin model in which Baddeley argued that memories go directly from the sensory register to long-term storage.

reinforcer An event that increases the frequency of the behavior that precedes it.

relative refractory period The time following the absolute refractory period during which a neuron can be activated but only by a more intense stimulus than normal.

REM behavior disorder A sleep disorder in which the person acts out a dream, because of a failure to lose muscle tone during REM sleep.

REM rebound A greater proportion of sleep time spent in REM sleep after a period of REM-sleep deprivation.

remapping The modification of neurons after they no longer receive input from the body part they once represented.

Renshaw cell An inhibitory interneuron excited by an alpha motor neuron that causes it to stop firing, preventing excessive muscle contraction.

repolarization The process of recovery of the resting membrane potential.

residual phase The phase of schizophrenia in which some recovery of functioning occurs.

resistance stage The second stage of the GAS, characterized by the mobilization of physiological resources to cope with a prolonged stressor.

resting membrane potential The difference in polarity between the inside and the outside of the cell membrane when the neuron is at rest.

retarded ejaculation The inability to ejaculate during sexual intercourse.

reticular activating system (RAS) A diffuse, interconnected network of neurons originating in the hindbrain and extending through the midbrain; stimulation produces cortical arousal and behavioral alertness.

reticular formation A network of neurons that controls arousal and consciousness.

retina The interior lining at the back of the eye that contains the photoreceptors.

retinal The lipid component of a photopigment, synthesized from vitamin A.

retinal image The image focused on the retina; it is upside down and reversed relative to the stimulus that created it.

retinohypothalamic tract A fiber tract that conveys information about the daily dawn-dusk cycle to the SCN.

retrograde amnesia The inability to recall events that preceded a traumatic event.

retrograde degeneration The progressive breakdown of an axon between the site of the break and the cell body.

retrograde messenger A chemical sent from the postsynaptic membrane to the presynaptic membrane to maintain neurotransmitter release.

reverberatory activity The continued reactivation of a neural circuit following an experience.

rhodopsin The photopigment in rods; consists of rod opsin and retinal.

rhombencephalon Another name for the hindbrain.

ribonucleic acid (RNA) A single-stranded molecule consisting of four nitrogenous bases: adenine, guanine, cytosine, and uracil; directs the synthesis of proteins. It controls the manufacture of proteins, which regulate cell functioning.

rod A type of photoreceptor concentrated in the periphery of the retina; operates in low light.

rod opsin The form of opsin found in rods.

rostral Toward the head.

round window A membrane that bulges as a result of pressure on the fluid inside the cochlea, which results from the movement of the stapes against the oval window.

rubrospinal tract A motor pathway that controls movements of the hands, lower arms, lower legs, and feet.

Ruffini's corpuscle A type of skin receptor just below the surface; detects low-frequency vibrations.

saccadic movement The rapid, jerky movement of the eye from one point to another as the physical environment is scanned.

sagittal section A section of a structure produced by a plane that cuts the structure into left and right parts.

saltatory conduction The propagation of an action potential from node to node in myelinated axons.

sarcomere The functional unit of a myofibril, consisting of overlapping bands of thick myosin filaments and thin actin filaments.

satiety The state of feeling full or satisfied, relative to hunger or thirst.

saturation The purity of a light stimulus.

Schachter's cognitive model of emotion The view that if unable to identify the cause of physiological arousal, a person will attribute it to environmental conditions.

Schaffer collateral fiber pathway One of the afferent pathways into the hippocampus; intense electrical stimulation of its neurons produces LTP.

schizophrenia A disabling mental disorder characterized by a loss of contact with reality and disturbances in perception, emotion, cognition, and motor behavior.

Schwann cell A type of glial cell that myelinates certain neurons in the PNS.

seasonal affective disorder (SAD) A form of depression caused by reduced daylight during the winter months.

second messenger A chemical that causes changes inside the cell in response to a neurotransmitter that lead to ion channel changes.

secondary auditory cortex The area of the temporal lobe surrounding the primary auditory cortex, where pitch, loudness, and timbre are perceived and specific sounds are recognized.

secondary drinking Drinking that anticipates a bodily need.

secondary motor cortex A cortical area consisting of the supplementary motor area and the premotor cortex; involved in the planning and sequencing of voluntary movements.

secondary somatosensory cortex An area of the cortex, lateral and slightly posterior to the primary somatosensory cortex, that receives information from the skin senses.

secondary visual cortex The area of the cerebral cortex that combines visual features into a recognizable visual perception; also called prestriate cortex.

sedative-hypnotic drug A drug that has a calming (sedative) effect at low doses and a sleep-inducing effect at higher doses.

selective serotonin reuptake inhibitor (SSRI) A type of drug that increases the availability of serotonin by inhibiting its reuptake.

semantic memory The memory of knowledge concerning the use of language and the rules, formulas, or algorithms for the development of concepts or solutions to problems.

semantics The linguistic analysis of the meaning of language.

semicircular canal One of three fluid-filled canals in the vestibular system.

senile plaque A granular deposit of amyloid beta protein and the remains of degenerated dendrites and axons; found in large numbers in the brains of people with AD.

sense The mechanism we use to detect and react to stimuli, so as to transform environmental stimulation into information the nervous system can use.

sensitization An increase in reactivity to a stimulus following exposure to an intense event.

sensory neglect A condition resulting from parietal lobe damage (usually on the right side) in which a person shows clumsiness or neglect of the side of the body opposite the damage.

sensory neuron A specialized neuron that detects information from inside the body or from the outside world.

sensory register In the Atkinson-Shiffrin model, the initial storage site where a memory is held for a brief time without modification.

sentence Two or more phrases that convey an assertion, question, command, wish, or exclamation.

serotonergic Describing a synapse or synaptic transmission with serotonin as the neurotransmitter.

serotonin A neurotransmitter synthesized from the amino acid tryptophan; also known as 5-HT.

serotonin-specific reuptake inhibitor (SSRI) An antidepressant drug that increases the availability of serotonin by decreasing its reuptake.

sex-determining gene The gene on the short arm of the Y chromosome that determines the biological sex of an individual.

sex therapy The psychological approach to treating sexual dysfunction.

sexual dysfunction A chronic failure to obtain sexual satisfaction.

short-term store In the Atkinson-Shiffrin model, a temporary site where information is held before storage in permanent memory.

simple cell A neuron in the striate cortex that responds to lines (edges) in a specific part of the visual field having a specific orientation.

sine-wave grating The alternating lighter and darker intensities in a light stimulus.

skeletal muscle A type of muscle that produces the movements of bones.

Skinner box An enclosed chamber invented by B. F. Skinner to train an animal through operant conditioning.

skull The outer bony covering that protects the brain.

sleep apnea A sleep disorder characterized by repeated interruptions of sleep caused by the cessation of breathing.

sleep paralysis A brief paralysis that occurs when a person with narcolepsy is going to sleep or awakening.

sleep spindle A 1 to 2 second burst of activity of 12 to 14 Hz that occurs during stage 2 sleep.

sleepwalking Getting out of bed and walking during NREM sleep.

slow pain The type of pain propagated by unmyelinated type C fibers that slowly reaches the spinal cord.

slow-twitch muscle A muscle fiber that contracts and fatigues slowly.

slow-wave sleep (SWS) Stages 3 and 4 of nonREM sleep.

sodium-potassium pump A protein in the cell membrane that expels three Na^+ ions for every two K^+ ions it conveys into the cell.

soluble gas A class of neurotransmitters that includes nitric oxide and carbon monoxide.

somatic nervous system The division of the PNS containing sensory receptors that detect environmental stimuli and motor nerves that activate skeletal muscles.

somatosense The skin sensations of touch, pain, temperature, and proprioception.

somatosensory cortex An area in the anterior part of the parietal lobe that receives information about touch, pain, pressure, temperature, and body position from the thalamus.

somatotropin A growth-promoting hormone released by the anterior pituitary; also called growth hormone.

sound Vibrations in a material medium, such as air, water, or metal.

spatial summation The combined effects of neurotransmitters binding to different locations on the postsynaptic membrane at a particular moment in time.

spatial-frequency theory The theory that cells in the visual cortex are responding to spatial frequencies of lightness and darkness in a visual scene.

spina bifida A neural tube defect that results when some part of the neural folds fails to close.

spinal cord The division of the CNS located within the vertebrate spinal column, which receives sensory messages from the body below the head and sends motor commands to the PNS. Most sensory messages are sent to the brain and most motor commands originate in the brain.

spinal nerve A group of axons that transmits messages to and from the brain through the spinal cord.

spinal reflex A reflex in which afferent sensory input enters the spinal cord and then directly innervates an efferent motor neuron.

spinocerebellar system The somatosensory pathway that begins in the spinal cord and transmits proprioceptive information to the cerebellum.

spiral ganglion An auditory structure containing bipolar neurons that synapse with hair cells of the inner ear.

split-brain preparation A surgical technique that severs the cerebral commissures and the optic chiasm (only in nonhuman animals), eliminating most communication between the hemispheres.

stage 1 sleep The first stage of light sleep, characterized by mostly theta activity.

stage 2 sleep The second stage of sleep, characterized by sleep spindles and K complexes in addition to theta activity.

stage 3 sleep The third sleep stage, characterized by the addition of delta activity.

stage 4 sleep The deepest stage of sleep, in which delta activity predominates.

stapes (stirrup) The bone of the middle ear attached to the incus and the oval window.

stereotaxic apparatus A surgical instrument that allows a neuroscientist to create a lesion in a specific region of the brain.

stimulus-bound behavior Behavior motivated by brain stimulation in the presence of appropriate environmental stimuli.

stress inoculation training A technique to alter the cognitive appraisal process by recognizing stressful situations, linking behavioral responses to situations, understanding that reactions to stressors are determined by the appraisal of the situation, and then learning new ways to appraise the situation.

stressor An event that either strains or overwhelms the ability of an organism to adjust to the environment.

subarachnoid space The space between the arachnoid mater and pia mater that is filled with cerebrospinal fluid.

subcutaneous (SC) injection An injection of a drug under the skin.

subfornical organ (SFO) A structure outside the blood-brain barrier that contains osmoreceptors; plays a role in thirst.

substance abuse A pattern of drug use that results in negative effects.

substance dependence The compulsive use of a substance; also known as addiction.

substantia nigra A structure in the tegmentum that is involved in the integration of voluntary movements.

subventricular layer A layer of daughter cells between the intermediate and marginal layers that become either glial cells or interneurons.

superior Above a structure.

superior colliculus A structure in the tectum that relays visual information.

superior olivary nucleus A group of neurons in the medulla that receives neural messages from the cochlear nuclei.

supplementary motor area A part of the secondary motor cortex that receives input from the posterior parietal cortex and the somatosensory cortex.

suprachiasmatic nucleus (SCN) An area in the brain that regulates the circadian cycle.

supraesophageal ganglion A primitive brain above the esophagus, formed by the fusion of several ganglion pairs in certain invertebrates.

sympathetic nervous system A division of the autonomic nervous system that is activated by challenging, stimulating, or dangerous situations.

synapse The point of functional contact between a neuron and its target.

synaptic cleft The space between the presynaptic and postsynaptic membranes.

synaptic vesicle A sac within the presynaptic terminal that contains neurotransmitters.

syntax The system of rules for combining words into meaningful phrases and sentences.

tardive dyskinesia A motor disorder with facial tics and involuntary limb movements; often appears after long-term use of antipsychotic medicines.

target cell A cell with which a neuron establishes synaptic connections.

taste bud A cluster of taste receptors that lie either near or within a papilla.

tectorial membrane A membrane in the organ of Corti in which hair cell cilia are embedded or with which cilia make close contact.

tectospinal tract A ventromedial tract that controls upper trunk (shoulder) and neck movements and coordinates the visual tracking of stimuli.

tectum A midbrain structure that controls simple reflexes and orients eye and ear movements.

tegmentum A division of the midbrain that contains the substantia nigra, the red nucleus, and the reticular formation.

telencephalon The division of the forebrain that consists of the cerebral cortex, limbic system, and basal ganglia.

telodendron A branch at the end of an axon.

temporal lobe The lobe of the cerebral cortex that is ventral to the lateral sulcus; responsible for the analysis of auditory stimuli, language, and some visual information.

temporal summation The combined effects of neurotransmitter binding over time.

temporoparietal cortex A brain area encompassing the supramarginal gyrus and angular gyrus; involved in language comprehension.

tendon A strong band of connective tissue linking a muscle to a bone that causes the bone to move when the muscle contracts.

testis-determining factor (TDF) An enzyme that causes the undifferentiated gonads to become testes.

testosterone The male sex hormone that influences the sexual development of the brain and plays a significant role in male sexual arousal.

thalamotomy A psychosurgical treatment for Parkinson's disease that relieves tremors and improves rigidity but does not relieve bradykinesia.

thalamus A forebrain structure that relays information from sensory receptors to the cerebral cortex.

THC The abbreviation and commonly used name for delta-9-tetrahydrocannabinol, the psychoactive ingredient in marijuana.

theta activity An EEG pattern during light sleep, characterized by synchronized waves that are larger in amplitude (4 to 7 Hz) than beta and alpha waves.

threshold The level of cell membrane depolarization required for an action potential to occur.

thyroid-stimulating hormone (TSH) An anterior pituitary hormone that regulates the thyroid gland.

timbre The purity of a sound; the combination of frequencies that gives each sound its characteristic quality.

tolerance A decrease in the effects of a drug as a result of repeated use.

tonotopic distribution The pattern of neurons responding to specific tones in particular places throughout the auditory system.

tract A collection of axons within the CNS, outside the PNS.

transcortical motor aphasia Sparse, self-initiated speech with relatively good language comprehension.

transcortical sensory aphasia Fluent speech, poor comprehension, and anomia, along with an unusual tendency to repeat verbal stimuli.

transduction The conversion of physical energy into a neural impulse.

transmitter-gated ion channel An ion channel sensitive to a specific neurotransmitter.

transneuronal degeneration Damage to neurons with which a degenerating neuron has synaptic connections.

tricyclic compound A type of antidepressant drug that increases brain levels of norepinephrine and serotonin by interfering with neurotransmitter reuptake.

tumor An abnormal proliferation of cells.

Turner syndrome A condition in which a person is born with one X chromosome and no other sex chromosome; the female reproductive system develops only partially.

tympanic membrane The membrane that divides the outer and middle parts of the ear; also called the eardrum.

type A behavior pattern (TABP) A set of behaviors that includes an excessive competitive drive, high aggressiveness, and an intense sense of time urgency.

unconditioned response (UCR) A reflexive reaction to an unconditioned stimulus.

unconditioned stimulus (UCS) A stimulus that involuntarily elicits a reflexive response.

utricle, saccule The two vestibular sacs containing the vestibular receptor cells, or hair cells.

vaginismus A condition in which muscle contractions close the vagina and prevent intercourse.

vagusstoff Loewi's term for the chemical that acts to decrease the heart rate.

vasocongestion A dilation and filling of blood vessels that produces erection of the penis or clitoris, nipple erection, and sexual flush.

ventral Toward the belly.

ventral posterolateral thalamic nucleus A group of neurons that receives information about touch and proprioception via the dorsal column–medial lemniscal system and about temperature and pain via the anterolateral system.

ventral posteromedial thalamic nucleus A group of neurons that receives taste information from the nucleus of the solitary tract and then transmits it to the primary gustatory cortex.

ventricle One of four chambers of the ventricular system in the brain.

ventricular layer The innermost layer of the developing nervous system; its cells become daughter cells, some of which become neurons or glial cells.

ventricular system A series of interconnected hollow chambers in the brain and spinal cord that contain cerebrospinal fluid.

ventrolateral nucleus A structure in the thalamus that receives information from the cerebellum and relays this information to the motor cortex so the brain can determine whether its intended movement corresponds to the actual movement executed.

ventromedial hypothalamus (VMH) The hypothalamic area responsible for the effect of estrogen on sexual behavior; once thought to control the inhibition of eating, or satiety.

ventromedial tract One of four motor pathways originating in different parts of the subcortex that control movements of the trunk and limbs.

vertebral column The outer bony covering that protects the spinal cord; also called the spinal column, spine, or backbone.

vertebrate An animal with a protective covering over its spinal cord and brain.

vestibular ganglion A group of bipolar neurons that receive input from vestibular hair cells.

vestibular nerve Axons of the vestibular ganglion neurons.

vestibular nucleus The part of the medulla with which most vestibular nerve fibers synapse.

vestibular sac The part of the vestibular system that provides information about the position of the head relative to the body.

vestibular sense The sense responsible for maintaining balance.

vestibulospinal tract A ventromedial tract that plays a central role in posture.

visual agnosia A perceptual problem involving the inability to name an object when it is presented visually but not when it is presented in another sensory modality.

visual field deficit An inability to see objects in a specific part of the visual field, caused by damage to a region of the occipital lobe or the pathways leading to it.

visual photoreceptor A type of photoreceptor that codes the features of a light stimulus.

visual-verbal agnosia An inability to recognize printed words, but not spoken words; results from damage that isolates the visual cortex from cortical language areas.

vitreous humor A clear, jelly-like fluid between the lens and the retina.

VMH paradox In VMH-lesioned rats, a motivational inconsistency between overeating in some situations and a reluctance to eat in others.

VMH-lesion syndrome The pattern of hyperphagia and obesity typically exhibited by rats following damage to the ventromedial hypothalamus.

volley principle The idea that groups of neurons in the auditory nerve fire asynchronously, in volleys, to match the frequency of the sound.

voltage-gated ion channel An ion channel sensitive to changes in the cell membrane potential.

vomeronasal organ A specialized sensory organ, separate from the main olfactory system, that detects pheromones released by a receptive female.

Wernicke's aphasia A communicative disorder caused by damage to the posterior portion of the superior and middle temporal gyrus and the temporoparietal cortex; an inability to comprehend language.

Wernicke's area An area in the temporal lobe of the left hemisphere of the brain that contributes to understanding language and producing intelligible speech.

Wernicke-Geschwind model A model of language processing in which language is comprehended in Wernicke's area before messages are passed to Broca's area for speech production.

white matter Myelinated axons of neurons.

Williams syndrome A rare genetic disorder in which relatively intact language ability is coupled with mild to moderate mental retardation.

withdrawal reflex The automatic withdrawal of a limb from a painful stimulus.

withdrawal symptom A physical or psychological problem that results from stopping the use of a drug.

Wolffian system A set of ducts in the human embryo that develops into parts of the male reproductive system.

word salad A type of speech with no discernible links between the words.

working memory A system that permits the temporary storage and manipulation of information required for tasks such as comprehension, learning, and reasoning.

X ganglion cell A type of ganglion cell that originates mostly from the central part of the retina.

Y ganglion cell A type of ganglion cell that originates mostly from the peripheral part of the retina.

Young-Helmholtz trichromatic theory The theory that color perceptions come from a pattern of stimulation of three sets of color receptors in the eye.

zeitgeber An external time cue that resets an animal's biological clock every 24 hours.

zygote A single cell formed when the sperm fertilizes the egg.

◆ References

Abad, V. C., & Guilleminault, C. (2004). Review of rapid eye movement behavior sleep disorders. *Current Neurology and Neuroscience Reports, 4,* 157–163.

Abbott, N. J. (2002). Astrocyte-endothelial interactions and blood-brain barrier permeability. *Journal of Anatomy, 200,* 629–638.

Abbruzzese, G., & Berardelli, A. (2003). Sensorimotor integration in movement disorders. *Movement Disorders, 18,* 231–240.

Abel, E. L. (1995). An update on incidence of FAS: FAS is not an equal opportunity birth defect. *Neurotoxicology and Teratology, 17,* 437–443.

Abel, E. L. (1998). Fetal alcohol syndrome: The 'American Paradox'. *Alcohol and Alcoholism, 33,* 195–201.

Abo, M., Senoo, A., Watanabe, S., Miyano, S., Doseki, K., Sasaki, N., et al. (2004). Language-related brain function during word repetition in post-stroke aphasics. *NeuroReport, 15,* 1891–1894.

Aboitiz, F., & Garcia, R. (1997). The anatomy of language revisited. *Biological Research, 30,* 171–183.

Adam, J. A., Menheere, P. P., van Dielen, F. M., Soeters, P. B., Buurman, W. A., & Greve, J. W. (2002). Decreased plasma orexin-A levels in obese individuals. *International Journal of Obesity and Related Metabolic Disorders, 26,* 274–276.

Adamec, R. E. (2000). Evidence that long-lasting potentiation in limbic circuits mediating defensive behaviour in the right hemisphere underlies pharmacological stressor (FG-7142) induced lasting increases in anxiety-like behaviour: Role of benzodiazepine receptors. *Journal of Psychopharmacology, 14,* 307–322.

Adamec, R., & Shallow, T. (2000). Rodent anxiety and kindling of the central amygdala and nucleus basalis. *Physiology & Behavior, 70,* 177–187.

Adams, L. M., & Foote, S. L. (1988). Effects of locally infused pharmacological agents on spontaneous and sensory-evoked activity of locus coeruleus neurons. *Brain Research Bulletin, 21,* 395–400.

Adolphs, R., Baron-Cohen, S., & Tranel, D. (2002). Impaired recognition of social emotions following amygdala damage. *Journal of Cognitive Neuroscience, 14,* 1264–1274.

Adolphs, R., Gosselin, F., Buchanan, T. W., Tranel, D., Schyns, P., & Damasio, A. R. (2005). A mechanism for impaired fear recognition after amygdala damage. *Nature, 433,* 68–72.

Adolphs, R., & Tranel, D. (1999). Intact recognition of emotional prosody following amygdala damage. *Neuropsychologia, 37,* 1285–1292.

Adolphs, R., & Tranel, D. (2003). Amygdala damage impairs emotion recognition from scenes only when they contain facial expressions. *Neuropsychologia, 41,* 1281–1289.

Adolphs, R., & Tranel, D. (2004). Impaired judgments of sadness but not happiness following bilateral amygdala damage. *Journal of Cognitive Neuroscience, 16,* 453–462.

Adolphs, R., Tranel, D., & Damasio, H. (2001). Emotion recognition from faces and prosody following temporal lobectomy. *Neuropsychology, 15,* 396–404.

Adolphs, R., Tranel, D., Damasio, H., & Damasio, A. (1994). Impaired recognition of emotion in facial expressions following bilateral damage to the human amygdala. *Nature, 372,* 669–672.

Adolphs, R., Tranel, D., Damasio, H., & Damasio, A. R. (1995). Fear and the human amygdala. *The Journal of Neuroscience, 15,* 5879–5891.

Adolphs, R., Tranel, D., Hamann, S., Young, A. W., Calder, A. J., Phelps, E. A., et al. (1999). Recognition of facial emotion in nine individuals with bilateral amygdala damage. *Neuropsychologia, 37,* 1111–1117.

Aggleton, J. P. (1986). Memory impairments caused by experimental thalamic lesions in monkeys. *Revue Neurologique, 142,* 418–424.

Agmo, A., Villalpando, A., Picker, Z., & Fernandez, H. (1995). Lesions of the medial prefrontal cortex and sexual behavior in the male rat. *Brain Research, 696,* 177–186.

Aguayo, V. M., Scott, S., Ross, J., & PROFILES Study Group. (2003). Sierra Leone—investing in nutrition to reduce poverty: A call for action. *Public Health Nutrition, 6,* 653–657.

Akabas, M. H., Dodd, J., & Al-Awqati, Q. (1988). A bitter substance induces a rise in intracellular calcium in a subpopulation of rat taste cells. *Science, 242,* 1047–1050.

Akbarian, S., Kim, J. J., Potkin, S. G., Hetrick, W. P., Bunney, W. E., Jr., & Jones, E. G. (1996). Maldistribution of interstitial neurons in prefrontal white matter of the brains of schizophrenic patients. *Archives of General Psychiatry, 53,* 425–436.

Akerstedt, T., & Froberg, J. E. (1976). Interindividual differences in circadian patterns of catecholamine excretion, body temperature, performance, and subjective arousal. *Biological Psychology, 4,* 277–292.

Akinyinka, O. O., Adeyinka, A. O., & Falade, A. G. (1995). The computed axial tomography of the brain in protein energy malnutrition. *Annals of Tropical Paediatrics, 15,* 329–333.

Aksenov, M. Y., Aksenova, M. V., Carney, J. M., & Butterfield, D. A. (1997). Oxidative modification of glutamine synthetase by amyloid beta peptide. *Free Radical Research, 27,* 267–281.

Alam, M. N., McGinty, D., & Szymusiak, R. (1996). Preoptic/anterior hypothalamic neurons: Thermosensitivity in wakefulness and non rapid eye movement sleep. *Brain Research, 718,* 76–82.

Alberch, J., Perez-Navarro, E., & Canals, J. M. (2002). Neuroprotection by neurotrophins and GDNF family members in the excitotoxic model of Huntington's disease. *Brain Research Bulletin, 57,* 817–822.

Albert, D. J., & Richmond, S. E. (1975). Septal hyperreactivity: A comparison of lesions within and adjacent to the septum. *Physiology & Behavior, 15,* 339–347.

Albert, D. J., & Walsh, M. L. (1984). Neural systems and the inhibitory modulation of agonistic behavior: A comparison of mammalian species. *Neuroscience and Biobehavioral Reviews, 8,* 5–24.

Alberts, B., Bray, D., Lewis, J., Raff, M., Roberts, K., & Watson, J. D. (1994). *Molecular biology of the cell* (3rd ed.). New York: Garland.

Albright, T. D. (1992). Form-cue invariant motion processing in primate visual cortex. *Science, 255,* 1141–1143.

Alexander, J. T., Cheung, W. K., Dietz, C. B., & Leibowitz, S. F. (1993). Meal patterns and macronutrient intake after peripheral and PVN injections of the alpha 2-receptor antagonist idazoxan. *Physiology & Behavior, 53,* 623–630.

Alfredson, B. B., Risberg, J., Hagberg, B., & Gustafson, L. (2004). Right temporal lobe activation when listening to emotionally significant music. *Applied Neuropsychology, 11,* 161–166.

Allen, G., & Courchesne, E. (2003). Differential effects of developmental cerebellar abnormality on cognitive and motor functions in the cerebellum: An fMRI study of autism. *American Journal of Psychiatry, 160,* 262–273.

Allen, L. S., & Gorski, R. A. (1992). Sexual orientation and the size of the anterior commissure in the human brain. *Proceedings of the National Academy of Sciences of the United States of America, 89,* 7199–7202.

Alloy, L. B., Jacobson, N. S., & Acocella, J. (1999). *Abnormal psychology* (8th ed.). New York: McGraw-Hill.

Alper, K. R., Prichep, L. S., Kowalik, S., Rosenthal, M. S., & John, E. R. (1998). Persistent QEEG abnormality in crack cocaine users at 6 months of drug abstinence. *Neuropsychopharmacology, 19,* 1–9.

Altenmuller, E. O. (2001). How many music centers are in the brain? *Annals of the New York Academy of Sciences, 930,* 273–280.

Alvarez, P., Zola-Morgan, S., & Squire, L. R. (1995). Damage limited to the hippocampal region produces long-lasting memory impairment in monkeys. *The Journal of Neuroscience, 15,* 3796–3807.

Alvarez-Maubecin, V., Garcia-Hernandez, F., Williams, J. T., & Van Bockstaele, E. J. (2000). Functional coupling between neurons and glia. *The Journal of Neuroscience, 20,* 4091–4098.

Alzheimer's Disease Education & Referral Center. (2004). Alzheimer's disease medications fact sheet. Retrieved February 25, 2005, from http://www.alzheimers.org/pubs/medications.htm

Amass, L., Ling, W., Freese, T. E., Reiber, C., Annon, J. J., Cohen, A. J., et al. (2004). Bringing buprenorphine-naloxone detoxification to community treatment providers: The NIDA Clinical Trials Network field experience. *American Journal on Addictions, 13,* S42–S66.

Amato, L., Davoli, M., Ferri, M., & Ali, R. (2003). Methadone at tapered doses for the management of opioid withdrawal. *Cochrane Database of Systematic Reviews,* CD003409.

Ambelas, A., & George, M. (1986). Predictability of course of illness in manic patients positive for life events. *The Journal of Nervous and Mental Disease, 174,* 693–695.

Ambrogini, P., Cuppini, R., Cuppini, C., Ciaroni, S., Cecchini, T., Ferri, P., et al. (2000). Spatial learning affects immature granule cell survival in adult rat dentate gyrus. *Neuroscience Letters, 286,* 21–24.

Amen, D. G., Stubblefield, M., Carmichael, B., & Thisted, R. (1996). Brain SPECT findings and aggressiveness. *Annals of Clinical Psychiatry, 8,* 129–137.

Amenta, F., Parnetti, L., Gallai, V., & Wallin, A. (2001). Treatment of cognitive dysfunction associated with Alzheimer's disease with cholinergic precursors. Ineffective treatments or inappropriate approaches? *Mechanisms of Ageing and Development, 122,* 2025–2040.

American Academy of Pediatrics. (2000). Evaluation of the newborn with developmental anomalies of the external genitalia. *Pediatrics, 106,* 138–142.

American Psychiatric Association. (1994). *Diagnostic and statistical manual of mental disorders* (4th ed.). Washington, DC: Author.

American Psychological Association. (1992). Ethical principles of psychologists and code of conduct. *American Psychologist, 47,* 1597–1611.

an der Heiden, W., & Hafner, H. (2000). The epidemiology of onset and course of schizophrenia. *European Archives of Psychiatry and Clinical Neuroscience, 250,* 292–303.

Anand, B. K., & Brobeck, J. R. (1951). Hypothalamic control of food intake in rats and cats. *Yale Journal of Biology and Medicine, 24,* 123–140.

Anand, B. K., Chhina, G. S., & Singh, B. (1962). Effect of glucose on the activity of hypothalamic "feeding centers." *Science, 138,* 597–598.

Anch, A. M., Browman, C. P., Mitler, M. M., & Walsh, J. K. (1988). *Sleep: A scientific perspective.* Englewood Cliffs, NJ: Prentice Hall.

Andersen, R. A., & Buneo, C. A. (2002). Intentional maps in posterior parietal cortex. *Annual Review of Neuroscience, 25,* 189–220.

Anderson, A. K., & Phelps, E. A. (2001). Lesions of the human amygdala impair enhanced perception of emotionally salient events. *Nature, 411,* 305–309.

Anderson, B. J., Alcantara, A. A., & Greenough, W. T. (1996). Motor-skill learning: Changes in synaptic organization of the rat cerebellar cortex. *Neurobiology of Learning and Memory, 66,* 221–229.

Anderson, C. A. (1989). Temperature and aggression: Ubiquitous effects of heat on occurrence of human violence. *Psychological Bulletin, 106,* 74–96.

Anderson, I. M. (2000). Selective serotonin reuptake inhibitors versus tricyclic antidepressants: A meta-analysis of efficacy and tolerability. *Journal of Affective Disorders, 58,* 19–36.

Anderson, J. M., Gilmore, R., Roper, S., Crosson, B., Bauer, R. M., Nadeau, S., et al. (1999). Conduction aphasia and the arcuate fasciculus: A reexamination of the Wernicke-Geschwind model. *Brain and Language, 70,* 1–12.

Anderson, S. F., & Lawler, K. A. (1995). The anger recall interview and cardiovascular reactivity in women: An examination of context and experience. *Journal of Psychosomatic Research, 39,* 335–343.

Anderson-Hunt, M., & Dennerstein, L. (1995). Oxytocin and female sexuality. *Gynecologic and Obstetric Investigation, 40,* 217–221.

Andersson, K. E. (2003). Erectile physiological and pathophysiological pathways involved in erectile dysfunction. *The Journal of Urology, 170,* S6–S14.

Angeli, A., Minetto, M., Dovio, A., & Pacciotti, P. (2004). The overtraining syndrome in athletes: A stress-related disorder. *Journal of Endocrinological Investigation, 27,* 603–612.

Annett, M. (1999). Left-handedness as a function of sex, maternal versus paternal inheritance, and report bias. *Behavior Genetics, 29,* 103–114.

Annett, M. (2003). Cerebral asymmetry in twins: Predictions of the right shift theory. *Neuropsychologia, 41,* 469–479.

Annett, M., & Alexander, M. P. (1996). Atypical cerebral dominance: Predictions and tests of the right shift theory. *Neuropsychologia, 34,* 1215–1227.

Antonini, A., Leenders, K. L., & Eidelberg, D. (1998). [11C]raclopride-PET studies of the Huntington's disease rate of progression: Relevance of the trinucleotide repeat length. *Annals of Neurology, 43,* 253–255.

Antonov, I., Antonova, I., Kandel, E. R., & Hawkins, R. D. (2001). The contribution of activity-dependent synaptic plasticity to classical conditioning in Aplysia. *The Journal of Neuroscience, 21,* 6413–6422.

Antonov, I., Antonova, I., Kandel, E. R., & Hawkins, R. D. (2003). Activity-dependent presynaptic facilitation and hebbian LTP are both required and interact during classical conditioning in Aplysia. *Neuron, 37,* 135–147.

Antrobus, J. (1991). Dreaming: Cognitive processes during cortical activation and high afferent thresholds. *Psychological Review, 98,* 96–121.

Aou, S., Oomura, Y., Woody, C. D., & Nishino, H. (1988). Effects of behaviorally rewarding hypothalamic electrical stimulation on intracellularly recorded neuronal activity in the motor cortex of awake monkeys. *Brain Research, 439,* 31–38.

Appolinario, J. C., & McElroy, S. L. (2004). Pharmacological approaches in the treatment of binge eating disorder. *Current Drug Targets, 5,* 301–307.

Arancio, O., Kiebler, M., Lee, C. J., Lev-Ram, V., Tsien, R. Y., Kandel, E. R., et al. (1996). Nitric oxide acts directly in the presynaptic neuron to produce long-term potentiation in cultured hippocampal neurons. *Cell, 87,* 1025–1035.

Arbuckle, J. L., & Lattal, K. A. (1992). Molecular contingencies in schedules of intermittent punishment. *Journal of the Experimental Analysis of Behavior, 58,* 361–375.

Archer, J. (1991). The influence of testosterone on human aggression. *British Journal of Psychology, 82,* 1–28.

Arden, M. A., & Dye, L. (1998). The assessment of menstrual synchrony: Comment on Weller and Weller (1997). *Journal of Comparative Psychology, 112,* 323–324.

Areosa, S. A., McShane, R., Sherriff, F. (2004). Memantine for dementia. *Cochrane Database of Systematic Reviews,* (4), CD003154.

Arias, C., Becerra-Garcia, F., & Tapia, R. (1998). Glutamic acid and Alzheimer's disease. *Neurobiology (Budapest, Hungary), 6,* 33–43.

Arnold, L. M., McElroy, S. L., Hudson, J. I., Welge, J. A., Bennett, A. J., & Keck, P. E. (2002). A placebo-controlled, randomized trial of fluoxetine in the treatment of binge-eating disorder. *Journal of Clinical Psychiatry, 63,* 1028–1033.

Aroniadou, V. A., & Keller, A. (1995). Mechanisms of LTP induction in rat motor cortex in vitro. *Cerebral Cortex, 5,* 353–362.

Arpa, J., & De Andres, I. (1993). Re-examination of the effects of raphe lesions on the sleep/wakefulness cycle states in cats. *Journal of Sleep Research, 2,* 96–102.

Asanuma, H. (1989). *The motor cortex.* New York: Raven Press.

Asberg, M., Traskman, L., & Thoren, P. (1976). 5-HIAA in the cerebrospinal fluid: A biochemical suicide predictor? *Archives of General Psychiatry, 33,* 1193–1197.

Aserinsky, E., & Kleitman, N. (1953). Regularly occurring periods of eye motility, and concomitant phenomena, during sleep. *Science, 118,* 273–274.

Ashcroft, G. W., Crawford, T. B., Eccleston, D., Sharman, D. F., MacDougall, E. J., Stanton, J. B., et al. (1966). 5-hydroxyindole compounds in the cerebrospinal fluid of patients with psychiatric or neurological diseases. *Lancet, 2,* 1049–1052.

Ashe, J. (1997). Force and the motor cortex. *Behavioural Brain Research, 86,* 255–269.

Aston-Jones, G., Chen, S., Zhu, Y., & Oshinsky, M. L. (2001). A neural circuit for circadian regulation of arousal. *Nature Neuroscience, 4,* 732–738.

Aston-Jones, G., Chiang, C., & Alexinsky, T. (1991). Discharge of noradrenergic locus coeruleus neurons in behaving rats and monkeys suggests a role in vigilance. *Progress in Brain Research, 88,* 501–520.

Aston-Jones, G., Foote, S. L., & Bloom, F. E. (1984). Anatomy and physiology of the locus coeruleus neurons: Functional implications. In M. G. Ziegler & C. R. Lake (Eds.), *Norepinephrine. Frontiers of clinical neuroscience* (Vol. 2, pp. 92–116). Baltimore: Williams & Wilkins.

Atkinson, R. C., & Shiffrin, R. M. (1968). Human memory: A proposed system and its control processes. In K. W. Spence & J. T. Spence (Eds.), *The psychology of learning and motivation: Advances in research and theory* (Vol. 2, pp. 742–775). New York: Academic Press.

Atkinson, R. C., & Shiffrin, R. M. (1971). The control of short-term memory. *Scientific American, 225,* 82–90.

Atkinson, R. L., Blank, R. C., Schumacher, D., Dhurandhar, N. V., & Ritch, D. L. (1997). Long-term drug treatment of obesity in a private practice setting. *Obesity Research, 5,* 578–586.

Atsumi, T., Fujisawa, S., Nakabayashi, Y., Kawarai, T., Yasui, T., & Tonosaki, K. (2004). Pleasant feeling from watching a comical video enhances free radical-scavenging capacity in human whole saliva. *Journal of Psychosomatic Research, 56,* 377–379.

Attia, E., Haiman, C., Walsh, B. T., & Flater, S. R. (1998). Does fluoxetine augment the inpatient treatment of anorexia nervosa? *American Journal of Psychiatry, 155,* 548–551.

Avenet, P., & Lindemann, B. (1989). Perspectives of taste reception. *The Journal of Membrane Biology, 112,* 1–8.

Avikainen, S., Forss, N., & Hari, R. (2002). Modulated activation of the human SI and SII cortices during observation of hand actions. *Neuroimage, 15,* 640–646.

Awalt, R. M., Reilly, P. M., & Shopshire, M. (1997). The angry patient: An intervention for managing anger in substance abuse treatment. *Journal of Psychoactive Drugs, 29,* 353–358.

Ax, A. F. (1953). The physiological differentiation between fear and anger in humans. *Psychosomatic Medicine, 15,* 433–442.

Axel, R. (1995). The molecular logic of smell. *Scientific American, 273,* 154–159.

Axelrod, J., & Felder, C. C. (1998). Cannabinoid receptors and their endogenous agonist, anandamide. *Neurochemical Research, 23,* 575–581.

Ayuso-Gutierrez, J. L., & del Rio Vega, J. M. (1997). Factors influencing relapse in the long-term course of schizophrenia. *Schizophrenia Research, 28,* 199–206.

Baaré, W. F., van Oel, C. J., Hulshoff Pol, H. E., Schnack, H. G., Durston, S., Sitskoorn, M. M., et al. (2001). Volumes of brain structures in twins discordant for schizophrenia. *Archives of General Psychiatry, 58,* 33–40.

Backman, J., Alling, C., Alsen, M., Regnell, G., & Traskman-Bendz, L. (2000). Changes of cerebrospinal fluid monoamine metabolites during long-term antidepressant treatment. *European Neuropsychopharmacology, 10,* 341–349.

Bacon Moore, A. S., Paulsen, J. S., & Murphy, C. (1999). A test of odor fluency in patients with Alzheimer's and Huntington's disease. *Journal of Clinical and Experimental Neuropsychology, 21,* 341–351.

Baddeley, A. (2000). The episodic buffer: A new component of working memory? *Trends in Cognitive Sciences, 4,* 417–423.

Baddeley, A. D. (2001). Is working memory still working? *American Psychologist, 56,* 849–864.

Baddeley, A. D., & Logie, R. H. (1999). Working memory: The multiple-component model. In A. Miyake & P. Shah (Eds.), *Models of working memory: Mechanisms of active maintenance and executive control* (pp. 28–61). New York: Cambridge University Press.

Badenhop, R. F., Moses, M. J., Scimone, A., Mitchell, P. B., Ewen-White, K. R., Rosso, A., et al. (2001). A genome screen of a large bipolar affective disorder pedigree supports evidence for a susceptibility locus on chromosome 13q. *Molecular Psychiatry, 6,* 396–403.

Badenhop, R. F., Moses, M. J., Scimone, A., Mitchell, P. B., Ewen-White, K. R., Rosso, A., et al. (2002). A genome screen of 13 bipolar affective disorder pedigrees provides evidence for susceptibility loci on chromosome 3 as well as chromosomes 9, 13 and 19. *Molecular Psychiatry, 7,* 594–603.

Bailer, U., Leisch, F., Meszaros, K., Lenzinger, E., Willinger, U., Strobl, R., et al. (2002). Genome scan for susceptibility loci for schizophrenia and bipolar disorder. *Biological Psychiatry, 52,* 40–52.

Bailey, C. H., Giustetto, M., Huang, Y. Y., Hawkins, R. D., & Kandel, E. R. (2000a). Is heterosynaptic modulation essential for stabilizing Hebbian plasticity and memory? *Nature Reviews Neuroscience, 1,* 11–20.

Bailey, C. H., Giustetto, M., Zhu, H., Chen, M., & Kandel, E. R. (2000b). A novel function for serotonin-mediated short-term facilitation in Aplysia: Conversion of a transient, cell-wide homosynaptic Hebbian plasticity into a persistent, protein synthesis-independent synapse-specific enhancement. *Proceedings of the National Academy of Sciences of the United States of America, 97,* 11581–11586.

Bailey, C. H., Kandel, E. R., & Si, K. (2004). The persistence of long-term memory: A molecular approach to self-sustaining changes in learning-induced synaptic growth. *Neuron, 44,* 49–57.

Bailey, S. L., & Heitkemper, M. M. (2001). Circadian rhythmicity of cortisol and body temperature: Morningness-eveningness effects. *Chronobiology International, 18,* 249–261.

Bains, J. S., Longacher, J. M., & Staley, K. J. (1999). Reciprocal interactions between CA_3 network activity and strength of recurrent collateral synapses. *Nature Neuroscience, 2,* 720–726.

Baizer, J. S., Kralj-Hans, I., & Glickstein, M. (1999). Cerebellar lesions and prism adaptation in macaque monkeys. *Journal of Neurophysiology, 81,* 1960–1965.

Baker, D. A., & Kelly, J. M. (2004). Structure, function and evolution of microbial adenylyl and guanylyl cyclases. *Molecular Microbiology, 52,* 1229–1242.

Baker, K. A., Purdy, M. B., Sadi, D., Mukhida, K., & Mendez, I. (2002). A sequential intrastriatal dopaminergic graft strategy in the rodent model for Parkinson's disease: Implications for graft survival and targeting. *Cell Transplantation, 11,* 185–193.

Baldessarini, R. J. (1996). Drugs and the treatment of psychiatric disorders: Psychosis and anxiety. In J. G. Hardman, L. E. Limbird, P. B. Molinoff, R. W. Ruddon, & A. G. Gilman (Eds.), *Goodman and Gilman's the pharmacological basis of therapeutics* (9th ed., pp. 399–430). New York: McGraw-Hill.

Baldessarini, R. J., & Tarazi, F. I. (1996). Brain dopamine receptors: A primer on their current status, basic and clinical. *Harvard Review of Psychiatry, 3,* 301–325.

Baldessarini, R. J., Tondo, L., Hennen, J., & Viguera, A. C. (2002). Is lithium still worth using? An update of selected recent research. *Harvard Review of Psychiatry, 10,* 59–75.

Baldwin, D. S. (2001). Unmet needs in the pharmacological management of depression. *Human Psychopharmacology, 16,* S93–S99.

Baldwin, D. S. (2004). Sexual dysfunction associated with antidepressant drugs. *Expert Opinion on Drug Safety, 3,* 457–470.

Baldwin, E. (1993). The case for animal research in psychology. *Journal of Social Issues, 49,* 121–131.

Bale, T. L., Picetti, R., Contarino, A., Koob, G. F., Vale, W. W., & Lee, K-F. (2002). Mice deficient for both corticotropin-releasing factor receptor 1 (CRFR1) and CRF2 have an impaired stress response and display sexually dichotomous anxiety-like behavior. *The Journal of Neuroscience, 22,* 193–199.

Ball, G. F., & Balthazart, J. (2004). Hormonal regulation of brain circuits mediating male sexual behavior in birds. *Physiology & Behavior, 83,* 329–346.

Balla, A., Koneru, R., Smiley, J., Sershen, H., & Javitt, D. C. (2001). Continuous phencyclidine treatment induces schizophrenia-like hyperreactivity of striatal dopamine release. *Neuropsychopharmacology, 25,* 157–164.

Balla, A., Sershen, H., Serra, M., Koneru, R., & Javitt, D. C. (2003). Subchronic continuous phencyclidine administration potentiates amphetamine-induced frontal cortex dopamine release. *Neuropsychopharmacology, 28,* 34–44.

Ballabh, P., Braun, A., & Nedergaard, M. (2004). The blood-brain barrier: An overview: Structure, regulation, and clinical implications. *Neurobiology of Disease, 16,* 1–13.

Ballard, P. A., Tetrud, J. W., & Langston, J. W. (1985). Permanent human parkinsonism due to 1-methyl-4-phenyl-1,2,3,6-tetrahydropyridine (MPTP): Seven cases. *Neurology, 35,* 949–956.

Balthazart, J., Baillien, M., Cornil, C. A., & Ball, G. F. (2004). Preoptic aromatase modulates male sexual behavior: Slow and fast mechanisms of action. *Physiology & Behavior, 83,* 247–270.

Balthazart, J., & Ball, G. F. (1998). New insights into the regulation and function of brain estrogen synthase (aromatase). *Trends in Neuroscience, 21,* 243–249.

Ban, T. A. (2001). Pharmacotherapy of depression: A historical analysis. *Journal of Neural Transmission, 108,* 707–716.

Banks, T., & Dabbs, J. M., Jr. (1996). Salivary testosterone and cortisol in a delinquent and violent urban subculture. *Journal of Social Psychology, 136,* 49–56.

Bao, J. X., Kandel, E. R., & Hawkins, R. D. (1998). Involvement of presynaptic and postsynaptic mechanisms in a cellular analog of classical conditioning at Aplysia sensory-motor neuron synapses in isolated cell culture. *The Journal of Neuroscience, 18,* 458–466.

Bao, S., Chen, L., & Thompson, R. F. (2000). Learning- and cerebellum-dependent neuronal activity in the lateral pontine nucleus. *Behavioral Neuroscience, 114,* 254–261.

Barch, D. M., Carter, C. S., Braver, T. S., Sabb, F. W., MacDonald, A., 3rd, Noll, D. C., et al. (2001). Selective deficits in prefrontal cortex function in medication-naive patients with schizophrenia. *Archives of General Psychiatry, 58,* 280–288.

Barch, D. M., Sheline, Y. I., Csernansky, J. G., & Snyder, A. Z. (2003). Working memory and prefrontal cortex dysfunction: Specificity to schizophrenia compared with major depression. *Biological Psychiatry, 53,* 376–384.

Bard, P. (1934). On emotional expression after decortication, with some remarks on certain theoretical views. *Psychological Review, 41,* 309–329, 424–449.

Bardo, M. T. (1998). Neuropharmacological mechanisms of drug reward: Beyond dopamine in the nucleus accumbens. *Critical Reviews in Neurobiology, 12,* 37–67.

Barnes, D. M. (1987). Biological issues in schizophrenia. *Science, 235,* 430–433.

Baron, M., Risch, N., Hamburger, R., Mandel, B., Kushner, S., Newman, M., et al. (1987). Genetic linkage between X-chromosome markers and bipolar affective illness. *Nature, 326,* 289–292.

Barrett, B. T., Bradley, A., & McGraw, P. V. (2004). Understanding the neural basis of amblyopia. *Neuroscientist, 10,* 106–117.

Barry, U., & Zuo, Z. (2005). Opioids: Old drugs for potential new applications. *Current Pharmaceutical Design, 11,* 1343–1350.

Barton, J. J., Press, D. Z., Keenan, J. P., & O'Connor, M. (2002). Lesions of the fusiform face area impair perception of facial configuration in prosopagnosia. *Neurology, 58,* 71–78.

Bartoshuk, L. M. (1988). Taste. In R. C. Atkinson, R. J. Herrnstein, G. Lindzey, & R. D. Luce (Eds.), *Stevens's handbook of experimental psychology. Vol. 1: Perception and motivation* (pp. 461–499). New York: Wiley.

Bartoshuk, L. M. (1993). Genetic and pathological taste variation: What can we learn from animal models and human disease? In D. Chadwick, J. Marsh, & J. Goode (Eds.), *The molecular basis of smell and taste transduction* (pp. 251–267). New York: Wiley.

Bartoshuk, L. M., & Beauchamp, G. K. (1994). Chemical senses. *Annual Review of Psychology, 45,* 419–449.

Bartoshuk, L. M., Duffy, V. B., Lucchina, L. A., Prutkin, J., & Fast, K. (1998). PROP (6-n-propylthiouracil) supertasters and the saltiness of NaCl. *Annals of the New York Academy of Sciences, 855,* 793–796.

Bartoshuk, L. M., Gentile, R. L., Molkowitz, H. R., & Meiselman, H. L. (1974). Sweet taste induced by miracle fruit (*Synsepalum dulcificum*). *Physiology & Behavior, 12,* 449–456.

Basbaum, A. I., & Fields, H. L. (1984). Endogenous pain control systems: Brainstem spinal pathways and endorphin circuitry. *Annual Review of Neuroscience, 7,* 309–338.

Baskin, D. G., Schwartz, M. W., Seeley, R. J., Woods, S. C., Porte, D., Jr., Breininger, J. F., et al. (1999). Leptin receptor long-form splice-variant protein expression in neuron cell bodies of the brain and co-localization with neuropeptide Y mRNA in the arcuate nucleus. *The Journal of Histochemistry and Cytochemistry, 47,* 353–362.

Bassareo, V., & Di Chiara, G. (1999). Modulation of feeding-induced activation of mesolimbic dopamine transmission by appetitive stimuli and its relation to motivational state. *European Journal of Neuroscience, 11,* 4389–4397.

Bassett, A. S., Chow, E. W. C., Waterworth, D. M., & Brzustowicz, L. (2001). Genetic insights into schizophrenia. *Canadian Journal of Psychiatry, 46,* 131–137.

Bauer, R. M., & Verfaellie, M. (1988). Electrodermal discrimination of familiar but not unfamiliar faces in prosopagnosia. *Brain and Cognition, 8,* 240–252.

Baum, M. J., Everitt, B. J., Herbert, J., & Keverne, E. B. (1977). Hormonal basis of proceptivity in female primates. *Archives of Sexual Behavior, 6,* 173–192.

Bauman, A. L., Goehring, A. S., & Scott, J. D. (2004). Orchestration of synaptic plasticity through AKAP signaling complexes. *Neuropharmacology, 46,* 299–310.

Baumeister, A. A., Hawkins, M. F., & Uzelac, S. M. (2003). The myth of reserpine-induced depression: Role in the historical development of the monoamine hypothesis. *Journal of the History of the Neurosciences, 12,* 207–220.

Baumgardner, T. L., Green, K. E., & Reiss, A. L. (1994). A behavioral neurogenetics approach to developmental disabilities: Gene-brain-behavior associations. *Current Opinion in Neurology, 7,* 172–178.

Bayrakal, S. (1965). The significance of electroencephalographic abnormality in behaviour-problem children. *Canadian Psychiatric Association Journal, 10,* 387–392.

Bays, H. E. (2004). Current and investigational antiobesity agents and obesity therapeutic treatment targets. *Obesity Research, 12,* 1197–1211.

Beach, F. A. (1940). Effects of cortical lesions upon the copulatory behavior of male rats. *Journal of Comparative Psychology, 29,* 193–239.

Beach, F. A. (1947). A review of physiological and psychological studies of sexual behavior in mammals. *Psychological Review, 27,* 240–307.

Beach, F. A., Noble, R. G., & Orndoff, R. K. (1969). Effects of perinatal androgen treatment on responses of male rats to gonadal hormones in adulthood. *Journal of Comparative and Physiological Psychology, 68,* 490–497.

Beauchamp, G. K., Bertino, M., Burke, D., & Engelman, K. (1990). Experimental sodium depletion and salt taste in normal human volunteers. *The American Journal of Clinical Nutrition, 51,* 881–889.

Beauregard, M., & Bachevalier, J. (1996). Neonatal insult to the hippocampal region and schizophrenia: A review and a putative animal model. *Canadian Journal of Psychiatry, 41,* 446–456.

Beaver, M. E., Matheny, K. E., Roberts, D. B., & Myers, J. N. (2001). Predictors of weight loss during radiation therapy. *Otolaryngology and Head and Neck Surgery, 125,* 645–648.

Beck, B. (2000). Neuropeptides and obesity. *Nutrition, 16,* 916–923.

Becker, A. E., Grinspoon, S. K., Klibanski, A., & Herzog, D. B. (1999). Eating disorders. *New England Journal of Medicine, 340,* 1092–1098.

Beglinger, C. (2002). Overview. Cholecystokinin and eating. *Current Opinion in Investigational Drugs, 3,* 587–588.

Behrens, P. F., Franz, P., Woodman, B., Lindenberg, K. S., & Landwehrmeyer, G. B. (2002). Impaired glutamate transport and glutamate-glutamine cycling: Downstream effects of the Huntington mutation. *Brain, 125,* 1908–1922.

Békésy, G. von (1960). *Experiments in hearing.* New York: McGraw-Hill.

Bell, J., Byron, G., Gibson, A., & Morris, A. (2004). A pilot study of buprenorphine-naloxone combination tablet (Suboxone) in treatment of opioid dependence. *Drug and Alcohol Review, 23,* 311–317.

Bellows, R. T. (1939). Time factors in water drinking in dogs. *American Journal of Physiology, 125,* 87–97.

Bellugi, U., Adolphs, R., Cassady, C., & Chiles, M. (1999). Towards the neural basis for hypersociability in a genetic syndrome. *NeuroReport, 10,* 1–5.

Bellugi, U., Lichtenberger, L., Jones, W., Lai, Z., & St. George, M. (2000). I. The neurocognitive profile of Williams syndrome: A complex pattern of strengths and weaknesses. *Journal of Cognitive Neuroscience, 12,* 7–29.

Bellugi, U., Lichtenberger, L., Mills, D., Galaburda, A., & Korenberg, J. R. (1999). Bridging cognition, the brain and molecular genetics: Evidence from Williams syndrome. *Trends in Neuroscience, 22,* 197–207.

Bellugi, U., Sabo, H., & Vaid, J. (1988). Spatial deficits in children with Williams syndrome. In J. Stiles-Davis, M. Kritchevsky, et al. (Eds.), *Spatial cognition: Brain bases and development* (pp. 273–298). Hillsdale, NJ: Erlbaum.

Belluscio, L., & Katz, L. C. (2001). Symmetry, stereotypy, and topography of odorant representations in mouse olfactory bulbs. *The Journal of Neuroscience, 21,* 2113–2122.

Benabid, A. L. (2003). Deep brain stimulation for Parkinson's disease. *Current Opinion in Neurobiology, 13,* 696–706.

Benca, R. M., Overstreet, D. E., Gilliland, M. A., Russell, D., Bergmann, B. M., & Obermeyer, W. H. (1996). Increased basal REM sleep but no difference in dark induction or light suppression of REM sleep in flinders rats with cholinergic supersensitivity. *Neuropsychopharmacology, 15,* 45–51.

Benes, F. M., Vincent, S. L., & Todtenkopf, M. (2001). The density of pyramidal and nonpyramidal neurons in anterior cingulate cortex of schizophrenic and bipolar subjects. *Biological Psychiatry, 50,* 395–406.

Bennett, M. R. (1998). Monoaminergic synapses and schizophrenia: 45 years of neuroleptics. *Journal of Psychopharmacology, 12,* 289–304.

Benson, D. F. (1993). Aphasia. In K. M. Heilman & E. Valenstein (Eds.), *Clinical neuropsychology* (3rd ed., pp. 17–36). London: Oxford University Press.

Benson, D. F., Djenderedjian, A., Miller, B. L., Pachana, N. A., Chang, L., Itti, L., et al. (1996). Neural basis of confabulation. *Neurology, 46,* 1239–1243.

Benson, D. F., & Geschwind, N. (1985). Aphasia and related disorders: A clinical approach. In M. M. Mesulam (Ed.), *Principles of behavioral neurology* (pp. 193–238). Philadelphia: Davis.

Berg, B. J., Pettinati, H. M., & Volpicelli, J. R. (1996). A risk-benefit assessment of naltrexone in the treatment of alcohol dependence. *Drug Safety, 15,* 274–282.

Berger, M., van Calker, D., & Riemann, D. (2003). Sleep and manipulations of the sleep-wake rhythm in depression. *Acta Psychiatrica Scandinavica. Supplementum,* (418), 83–91.

Berk, L. S., Felten, D. L., Tan, S. A., Bittman, B. B., & Westengard, J. (2001). Modulation of neuroimmune parameters during the eustress of humor associated mirthful laughter. *Alternative Therapies in Health and Medicine, 7,* 74–76.

Berkun, M. M., Kessen, M. L., & Miller, N. E. (1952). Hunger-reducing effects of food by stomach fistula versus food by mouth measured by a consummatory response. *Journal of Comparative and Physiological Psychology, 45,* 550–554.

Bermant, G., & Davidson, J. M. (1974). *Biological bases of sexual behavior.* New York: Harper & Row.

Bernhardt, P. C. (1997). Influences of serotonin and testosterone in aggression and dominance: Convergence with social psychology. *Current Directions in Psychological Science, 6,* 44–48.

Bernstein, I. L. (1978). Learned taste aversions in children receiving chemotherapy. *Science, 200,* 1302–1303.

Berridge, K. C. (2000). Measuring hedonic impact in animals and infants: Microstructure of affective taste reactivity patterns. *Neuroscience and Biobehavioral Reviews, 24,* 173–198.

Berridge, K. C. (2003). Pleasures of the brain. *Brain and Cognition, 52,* 106–128.

Berrios, G. E., Wagle, A. C., Markova, I. S., Wagle, S. A., Rosser, A., & Hodges, J. R. (2002). Psychiatric symptoms in neurologically asymptomatic Huntington's disease gene carriers: A comparison with gene negative at risk subjects. *Acta Psychiatrica Scandinavica, 105,* 224–230.

Berry, D. S., & Pennebaker, J. W. (1993). Nonverbal and verbal emotional expression and health. *Psychotherapy and Psychosomatics, 59,* 11–19.

Bertino, M., & Tordoff, M. G. (1988). Sodium depletion increases rats' preferences for salted food. *Behavioral Neuroscience, 102,* 565–573.

Besli, R., Saylam, C., Veral, A., Karl B., & Ozek, C. (2004). The existence of the vomeronasal organ in human beings. *The Journal of Craniofacial Surgery, 15,* 730–735.

Besset, A., Tafti, M., Villemin, E., Borderies, P., & Billiard, M. (1995). Effects of zolpidem on the architecture and cyclical structure of sleep in poor sleepers. *Drugs Under Experimental and Clinical Research, 21,* 161–169.

Bever, T. G. (1970). The cognitive basis for linguistic structures. In J. R. Hayes (Ed.), *Cognition and the development of language* (pp. 279–362). New York: Wiley.

Bienkowski, P., Kostowski, W., & Koros, E. (1999). Ethanol-reinforced behaviour in the rat: Effects of naltrexone. *European Journal of Pharmacology, 374,* 321–327.

Birdsall, T. C. (1998). 5-hydroxytryptophan: A clinically-effective serotonin precursor. *Alternative Medicine Review, 3,* 271–280.

Birks, J. S., & Harvey. (2003). Donepezil for dementia due to Alzheimer's disease. *Cochrane Database of Systematic Reviews,* (3), CD001190.

Bishop, D. (2004). The effects of travel on team performance in the Australian national netball competition. *Journal of Science and Medicine in Sport, 7,* 118–122.

Bishop, K. M., & Wahlsten, D. (1997). Sex differences in the human corpus callosum: Myth or reality? *Neuroscience and Biobehavioral Reviews, 21,* 581–601.

Bjartmar, C., Wujek, J. R., & Trapp, B. D. (2003). Axonal loss in the pathology of MS: Consequences for understanding the progressive phase of the disease. *Journal of the Neurological Sciences, 206,* 165–171.

Bjorntorp, P. (2001). Do stress reactions cause abdominal obesity and comorbidities? *Obesity Reviews, 2,* 73–86.

Black, S. C. (2004). Cannabinoid receptor antagonists and obesity. *Current Opinion in Investigational Drugs, 5,* 389–394.

Blackmore, S. J. (1991). Lucid dreaming: Awake in your sleep? *Skeptical Inquirer, 15,* 362–370.

Blakemore, S. J., & Frith, C. (2005). The role of motor contagion in the prediction of action. *Neuropsychologia, 43,* 260–267.

Blanchard, D. C., & Blanchard, R. J. (1972). Innate and conditioned reactions to threat in rats with amygdaloid lesions. *Journal of Comparative and Physiological Psychology, 81,* 281–290.

Blass, E. M., & Epstein, A. N. (1971). A lateral preoptic osmosensitive zone for thirst in the rat. *Journal of Comparative and Physiological Psychology, 76,* 378–394.

Blesch, A., & Tuszynski, M. H. (2004). Gene therapy and cell transplantation for Alzheimer's disease and spinal cord injury. *Yonsei Medical Journal, 45,* 28–31.

Blitzer, R. D., Iyengar, R., & Landau, E. M. (2005). Postsynaptic signaling networks: Cellular cogwheels underlying long-term plasticity. *Biological Psychiatry, 57,* 113–119.

Bloch, G. J., Butler, P. C., Eckersell, C. B., & Mills, R. H. (1998). Gonadal steroid-dependent GAL-IR cells within the medial preoptic nucleus (MPN) and the stimulatory effects of GAL within the MPN on sexual behaviors. *Annals of the New York Academy of Sciences, 863,* 188–205.

Bloch, G. J., Butler, P. C., & Kohlert, J. G. (1996). Galanin microinjected into the medial preoptic nucleus facilitates female- and male-typical sexual behaviors in the female rat. *Physiology & Behavior, 59,* 1147–1154.

Blumenthal, J. A., Williams, R. B., Jr., Kong, Y., Schanberg, S. M., & Thompson, L. W. (1978). Type A behavior pattern and coronary atherosclerosis. *Circulation, 58,* 634–639.

Boatman, D., Freeman, J., Vining, E., Pulsifer, M., Miglioretti, D., Minahan, R., et al. (1999). Language recovery after left hemispherectomy in children with late-onset seizures. *Annals of Neurology, 46,* 579–586.

Boatman, D., Gordon, B., Hart, J., Selnes, O., Miglioretti, D., & Lenz, F. (2000). Transcortical sensory aphasia: Revisited and revised. *Brain, 123,* 1634–1642.

Bogerts, B. (1989). The role of limbic and paralimbic pathology in the etiology of schizophrenia. *Psychiatry Research, 29,* 255–256.

Bogerts, B. (1999). The neuropathology of schizophrenic diseases: Historical aspects and present knowledge. *European Archives of Psychiatry and Clinical Neuroscience, 249,* 2–13.

Bonelli, R. M., & Hofmann, P. (2004). A review of the treatment options for Huntington's disease. *Expert Opinion on Pharmacotherapy, 5,* 767–776.

Booth, D. A. (1972). Conditioned satiety in the rat. *Journal of Comparative and Physiological Psychology, 81,* 457–471.

Booth, D. A. (1990). Learned role of tastes in eating motivation. In E. D. Capaldi & T. L. Powley (Eds.), *Taste, experience, and feeding* (pp. 179–194). Washington, DC: American Psychological Association.

Booth, D. A., Lee, M., & McAleavey, C. (1976). Acquired sensory control of satiation in man. *British Journal of Psychology, 67,* 137–147.

Borlongan, C. V., & Sanberg, P. R. (2002). Neural transplantation for treatment of Parkinson's disease. *Drug Discovery Today, 7,* 674–682.

Bottini, G., Corcoran, R., Sterzi, R., Paulesu, E., Schenone, P., Scarpa, P., et al. (1994). The role of the right hemisphere in the interpretation of figurative aspects of language. A positron emission tomography activation study. *Brain, 117,* 1241–1253.

Bourgeois, M. (1991). Serotonin, impulsivity and suicide. *Human Psychopharmacology: Clinical and Experimental, 6,* 31–36.

Bourgin, P., Huitron-Resendiz, S., Spier, A. D., Fabre, V., Morte, B., Criado, J. R., et al. (2000). Hypocretin-1 modulates rapid eye movement sleep through activation of locus coeruleus neurons. *The Journal of Neuroscience, 20,* 7760–7765.

Bourgon, L. N., & Kellner, C. H. (2000). Relapse of depression after ECT: A review. *The Journal of ECT, 16,* 19–31.

Bourque, C. W., Oliet, S. H., & Richard, D. (1994). Osmoreceptors, osmoreception, and osmoregulation. *Frontiers in Neuroendocrinology, 15,* 231–274.

Bowd, A. D., & Shapiro, K. J. (1993). The case against laboratory animal research in psychology. *Journal of Social Issues, 49,* 133–142.

Bower, G. H., & Forgas, J. P. (2001). Mood and social memory. In J. Forgas (Ed.), *Handbook of affect and social cognition* (pp. 95–120). Mahwah, NJ: Erlbaum.

Bowers, W. A. (2001). Basic principles for applying cognitive-behavioral therapy to anorexia nervosa. *The Psychiatric Clinics of North America, 24,* 293–303.

Boyce, P., & Judd, F. (1999). The place for the tricyclic antidepressants in the treatment of depression. *The Australian and New Zealand Journal of Psychiatry, 33,* 323–327.

Bracha, V., Zhao, L., Irwin, K. B., & Bloedel, J. R. (2000). The human cerebellum and associative learning: Dissociation between the acquisition, retention and extinction of conditioned eyeblinks. *Brain Research, 860,* 87–94.

Brady, J. V. (1961). Motivational-emotional factors and intracranial self-stimulation. In D. E. Sheer (Ed.), *Electrical stimulation of the brain* (pp. 413–430). Austin: University of Texas Press.

Brady, J. V., & Nauta, W. J. (1953). Subcortical mechanisms in emotional behavior: Affective changes following septal forebrain lesions in the albino rat. *Journal of Comparative and Physiological Psychology, 46,* 339–346.

Brady, J. V., & Nauta, W. J. (1955). Subcortical mechanisms in emotional behavior: The duration of affective changes following septal and habenular lesions in the albino rat. *Journal of Comparative and Physiological Psychology, 48,* 412–420.

Braitenberg, V., Heck, D., & Sultan, F. (1997). The detection and generation of sequences as a key to cerebellar function: Experiments and theory. *The Behavioral and Brain Sciences, 20,* 229–245.

Brambilla, P., Perez, J., Barale, F., Schettini, G., & Soares, J. C. (2003). GABAergic dysfunction in mood disorders. *Molecular Psychiatry, 8,* 721–737.

Brand, J. G. (2000). Receptor and transduction processes for umami taste. *Journal of Nutrition, 130,* 942S–945S.

Braunewell, K. H., & Manahan-Vaughan, D. (2001). Long-term depression: A cellular basis for learning? *Reviews in the Neurosciences, 12,* 121–140.

Braver, T. S., Barch, D. M., & Cohen, J. D. (1999). Cognition and control in schizophrenia: A computational model of dopamine and prefrontal function. *Biological Psychiatry, 46,* 312–328.

Bray, G. A. (1999). Drug treatment of obesity. *Bailliere's Best Practice & Research. Clinical Endocrinology & Metabolism, 13,* 131–148.

Bray, G. A. (2000a). A concise review on the therapeutics of obesity. *Nutrition, 16,* 953–960.

Bray, G. A. (2000b). Afferent signals regulating food intake. *The Proceedings of the Nutrition Society, 59,* 373–384.

Bray, G. A., & Gallagher, T. F., Jr. (1975). Manifestations of hypothalamic obesity in man: A comprehensive investigation of eight patients and a review of the literature. *Medicine (Baltimore), 54,* 301–330.

Bray, G. A., & York, D. A. (1998). The MONA LISA hypothesis in the time of leptin. *Recent Progress in Hormone Research, 53,* 95–117.

Bray, G. M., Villegas-Perez, M. P., Vidal-Sanz, M., & Aguayo, A. (1987). The use of peripheral nerve grafts to enhance neuronal survival, promote growth and permit terminal reconnections in the central nervous system of adult rats. *Journal of Experimental Biology, 132,* 5–19.

Brayley, K. N., & Albert, D. J. (1977). Suppression of VMH-lesion-induced reactivity and aggressiveness in the rat by stimulation of lateral septum, but not medial septum or cingulate cortex. *Journal of Comparative and Physiological Psychology, 91,* 290–299.

Bredt, D. S., & Nicoll, R. A. (2003). AMPA receptor trafficking at excitatory synapses. *Neuron, 40,* 361—379.

Bregman, B. S., Kunkel-Bagden, E., Schnell, L., Dai, H. N., Gao, D., & Schwab, M. E. (1995). Recovery from spinal cord injury mediated by antibodies to neurite growth inhibitors. *Nature, 378,* 498–501.

Breier, A., & Berg, P. H. (1999). The psychosis of schizophrenia: Prevalence, response to atypical antipsychotics, and prediction of outcome. *Biological Psychiatry, 46,* 361–364.

Bremer, J. (1959). *Aesexualization.* New York: Macmillan.

Brewerton, T. D., Dansky, B. S., Kilpatrick, D. G., & O'Neil, P. M. (2000). Which comes first in the pathogenesis of bulimia nervosa: Dieting or bingeing? *The International Journal of Eating Disorders, 28,* 259–264.

Brinkman, C. (1984). Supplementary motor area of the monkey's cerebral cortex: Short- and long-term deficits after unilateral ablation and the effects of subsequent callosal section. *The Journal of Neuroscience, 4,* 918–929.

Broadbelt, K., Byne, W., & Jones, L. B. (2002). Evidence for a decrease in basilar dendrites of pyramidal cells in schizophrenic medial prefrontal cortex. *Schizophrenia Research, 58,* 75–81.

Brobeck, J. R., Tepperman, J., & Long, C. N. H. (1943). Experimental hypothalamic hyperphagia in the albino rat. *Yale Journal of Biology and Medicine, 15,* 831–853.

Broca, P. (1861). Remarques sur le siège de la faculté du langage articulé; suivies d'une observation d'aphémie (perte de la parole). *Bulletins de la Société Anatomique (Paris), 6,* 330–357, 398–407.

Brodkin, E. S., Goforth, S. A., Keene, A. H., Fosella, J. A., & Silver, L. M. (2002). Identification of quantitative trait loci that affect aggressive behavior in mice. *The Journal of Neuroscience, 22,* 1165–1170.

Brok, H. P., van Meurs, M., Blezer, E., Schantz, A., Peritt, D., Treacy, G., et al. (2002). Prevention of experimental autoimmune encephalomyelitis in common marmosets using an anti-IL-12p40 monoclonal antibody. *Journal of Immunology, 169,* 6554–6563.

Bronson, F. H., & Whitten, W. (1968). Estrus accelerating pheromone of mice: Assay, androgen-dependency, and presence in bladder urine. *Journal of Reproduction and Fertility, 15,* 131–134.

Brookshire, R. H. (1992). *An introduction to neurogenic communication disorders* (4th ed). St. Louis: Mosby.

Brookshire, R. H. (1997). *Introduction to neurogenic communication disorders* (5th ed.). St. Louis: Mosby.

Brookshire, R. H. (2003). *An introduction to neurogenic communication disorders* (6th ed). St. Louis: Mosby.

Brower, K. J. (2003). Insomnia, alcoholism and relapse. *Sleep Medicine Reviews, 7,* 523–539.

Brown, P. K., & Wald, G. (1964). Visual pigments in single rods and cones of the human retina. *Science, 144,* 45–52.

Brown, P. L., & Kiyatkin, E. A. (2004). Brain hyperthermia induced by MDMA (ecstasy): Modulation by environmental conditions. *European Journal of Neuroscience, 20,* 51–58.

Brown, T. M., & Fee, E. (2002). "Voodoo" death. *American Journal of Public Health, 92,* 1593–1596.

Brownell, H., Gardner, H., Prather, P., & Martino, G. (1995). Language, communication, and the right hemisphere. In H. S. Kirshner (Ed.), *Handbook of neurological speech and language disorders. Neurological disease and therapy* (Vol. 33, pp. 325–349). New York: Marcel Dekker.

Brozoski, T. J., Brown, R. M., Rosvold, H. E., & Goldman, P. S. (1979). Cognitive deficit caused by regional depletion of dopamine in prefrontal cortex of rhesus monkey. *Science, 205,* 929–931.

Bruce, D. G., Golding, J. F., Hockenhull, N., & Pethybridge, R. J. (1990). Acupressure and motion sickness. *Aviation, Space, and Environmental Medicine, 61,* 361–365.

Bruce, H. M. (1960). A block to pregnancy in the mouse caused by proximity of strange males. *Journal of Reproduction and Fertility, 1,* 96–103.

Bruch, H. (1980). Preconditions for the development of anorexia nervosa. *American Journal of Psychoanalysis, 40,* 169–172.

Bruck, W., & Stadelmann, C. (2003). Inflammation and degeneration in multiple sclerosis. *Neurological Sciences, 24,* S265–S267.

Brumback, R. A., Harper, C. R., & Weinberg, W. A. (1996). Nonverbal learning disabilities, Asperger's syndrome, pervasive developmental disorder—Should we care? *Journal of Child Neurology, 11,* 483–489.

Brutus, M., Shaikh, M. B., Edinger, H., & Siegel, A. (1986). Effects of experimental temporal lobe seizures upon hypothalamically elicited aggressive behavior in the cat. *Brain Research, 366,* 53–63.

Buccino, G., Binkofski, F., & Riggio, L. (2004). The mirror neuron system and action recognition. *Brain and Language, 89,* 370–376.

Buchanan, T. W., Lutz, K., Mirzazade, S., Specht, K., Shah, N. J., Zilles, K., et al. (2000). Recognition of emotional prosody and verbal components of spoken language: An fMRI study. *Brain Research. Cognitive Brain Research, 9,* 227–238.

Buchsbaum, M. S. (1990). The frontal lobes, basal ganglia, and temporal lobes as sites for schizophrenia. *Schizophrenia Bulletin, 16,* 379–389.

Buck, L., & Axel, R. (1991). A novel multigene family may encode odorant receptors: A molecular basis for odor recognition. *Cell, 65,* 175–187.

Budgett, R. (1998). Fatigue and underperformance in athletes: The overtraining syndrome. *British Journal of Sports Medicine, 32,* 107–110.

Bunney, W. E., Jr., Goodwin, F. K., & Murphy, D. L. (1972). The "switch process" in manic-depressive illness. 3. Theoretical implications. *Archives of General Psychiatry, 27,* 312–317.

Burden, G. (2000). Up, up and away! *The Medical Post, 36.* Retrieved from http://www.medicalpost.com/mpcontent/article.jsp?content=/content/EXTRACT/RAWART/3632/22A.html

Burgess, H. J., Sharkey, K. M., & Eastman, C. I. (2002). Bright light, dark and melatonin can promote circadian adaptation in night shift workers. *Sleep Medicine Reviews, 6,* 407–420.

Burkett, G., Yasin, S. Y., Palow, D., LaVoie, L., & Martinez, M. (1994). Patterns of cocaine binging: Effect on pregnancy. *American Journal of Obstetrics and Gynecology, 171,* 372–379.

Burns, B. D. (1958). *The mammalian cerebral cortex.* Oxford, England: Williams & Wilkins.

Burton, H., Snyder, A. Z., Diamond, J. B., & Raichle, M. E. (2002). Adaptive changes in early and late blind: A fMRI study of verb generation to heard nouns. *Journal of Neurophysiology, 88,* 3359–3371.

Bush, D. E., DeSousa, N. J., & Vaccarino, F. J. (1999). Self-administration of intravenous amphetamine: Effect of nucleus accumbens CCK_B receptor activation on fixed-ratio responding. *Psychopharmacology (Berlin), 147,* 331–334.

Butefisch, C. M., Davis, B. C., Wise, S. P., Sawaki, L., Kopylev, L., Classen, J., et al. (2000). Mechanisms of use-dependent plasticity in the human motor cortex. *Proceedings of the National Academy of Sciences of the United States of America, 97,* 3661–3665.

Bymaster, F. P., McNamara, R. K., & Tran, P. V. (2003). New approaches to developing antidepressants by enhancing monoaminergic neurotransmission. *Expert Opinion on Investigational Drugs, 12,* 531–543.

Byne, W., Lasco, M. S., Kemether, E., Shinwari, A., Edgar, M. A., Morgello, S., et al. (2000). The interstitial nuclei of the human anterior hypothalamus: An investigation of sexual variation in volume and cell size, number and density. *Brain Research, 856,* 254–258.

Byne, W., Tobet, S., Mattiace, L. A., Lasco, M. S., Kemether, E., Edgar, M. A., et al. (2001). The interstitial nuclei of the human anterior hypothalamus: An investigation of variation with sex, sexual orientation, and HIV status. *Hormones and Behavior, 40,* 86–92.

Cadoret, R. J., Winokur, G., & Clayton, P. J. (1970). Family history studies: VI. Depressive disease types. *Comprehensive Psychiatry, 12,* 148–155.

Cadoret, R. J., Winokur, G., & Clayton, P. J. (1971). Family history studies: VII. Manic depressive disease versus depressive disease. *British Journal of Psychiatry, 116,* 625–635.

Cain, B. M., Wang, W., & Beinfeld, M. C. (1997). Cholecystokinin (CCK) levels are greatly reduced in the brains but not the duodenums of Cpe(fat)/Cpe(fat) mice: A regional difference in the involvement of carboxypeptidase E (Cpe) in pro-CCK processing. *Endocrinology, 138,* 4034–4037.

Cain, M. E., Smith, C. M., & Bardo, M. T. (2004). The effect of novelty on amphetamine self-administration in rats classified as high and low responders. *Psychopharmacology (Berlin), 176,* 129–138.

Caldwell, J. A., Jr., Caldwell, J. L., Brown, D. L., & Smith, J. K. (2004). The effects of 37 hours of continuous wakefulness on the physiological arousal, cognitive performance, self-reported mood, and simulator flight performance of F-117A pilots. *Military Psychology, 16,* 163–181.

Caldwell, J. D., & Moe, B. D. (1999). Conjugated estradiol increases female sexual receptivity in response to oxytocin infused into the medial preoptic area and medial basal hypothalamus. *Hormones and Behavior, 35,* 38–46.

Caleo, M., Menna, E., Chierzi, S., Cenni, M. C., & Maffei, L. (2000). Brain-derived neurotrophic factor is an anterograde survival factor in the rat visual system. *Current Biology, 10,* 1155–1161.

Calford, M. B., Graydon, M. L., Huerta, M. F., Kaas, J. H., & Pettigrew, J. D. (1985). A variant of the mammalian somatotopic map in a bat. *Nature, 313,* 477–479.

Cameron, C. L., Cella, D., Herndon, J. E. 2nd, Kornblith, A. B., Zuckerman, E., Henderson, E., et al. (2001). Persistent symptoms among survivors of Hodgkin's disease: An explanatory model based on classical conditioning. *Health Psychology, 20,* 71–75.

Camicioli, R., Kaye, J., Payami, H., Ball, M. J., & Murdoch, G. (1999). Apolipoprotein E epsilon4 is associated with neuronal loss in the substantia nigra in Alzheimer's disease. *Dementia and Geriatric Cognitive Disorders, 10,* 437–441.

Camicioli, R., Moore, M. M., Kinney, A., Corbridge, E., Glassberg, K., & Kaye, J. A. (2003). Parkinson's disease is associated with hippocampal atrophy. *Movement Disorders, 18,* 784–790.

Campbell, F. W., & Robson, J. G. (1968). Application of Fourier analysis to the visibility of gratings. *Journal of Physiology, 197,* 551–566.

Campbell, G., Kitching, J., Anderson, P. N., & Lieberman, A. R. (2003). Different effects of astrocytes and Schwann cells on regenerating retinal axons. *Neuroreport, 14,* 2085–2088.

Campeau, S., & Davis, M. (1995a). Involvement of subcortical and cortical afferents to the lateral nucleus of the amygdala in fear conditioning measured with fear-potentiated startle in rats trained concurrently with auditory and visual conditioned stimuli. *The Journal of Neuroscience, 15,* 2312–2327.

Campeau, S., & Davis, M. (1995b). Involvement of the central nucleus and basolateral complex of the amygdala in fear conditioning measured with fear-potentiated startle in rats trained concurrently with auditory and visual conditioned stimuli. *The Journal of Neuroscience, 15,* 2301–2311.

Campfield, L. A., & Smith, F. J. (1990). Transient declines in blood glucose signal meal initiation. *International Journal of Obesity, 14,* 15–31.

Campfield, L. A., Smith, F. J., & Burn, P. (1998). Strategies and potential molecular targets for obesity treatment. *Science, 280,* 1383–1387.

Cancedda, L., Putignano, E., Sale, A., Viegi, A., Berardi, N., & Maffei, L. (2004). Acceleration of visual system development by environmental enrichment. *The Journal of Neuroscience, 24,* 4840–4848.

Cannon, W. B. (1915). *Bodily changes in pain, hunger, fear, and rage: An account of recent researches into the function of emotional excitement.* New York: Appleton-Century-Crofts.

Cannon, W. B. (1927). The James-Lange theory of emotions: A critical examination and an alternative. *American Journal of Psychology, 39,* 106–124.

Cannon, W. B. (1934). Hunger and thirst. In C. Murchison (Ed.), *A handbook of general experimental psychology* (pp. 247–263). Worcester, MA: Clark University Press.

Cannon, W. B. (1957). "Voodoo" death. *Psychosomatic Medicine, 19,* 182–190.

Cannon, W. B., & Washburn, A. L. (1912). An explanation of hunger. *American Journal of Physiology, 29,* 441–454.

Capuano, C. A., Leibowitz, S. F., & Barr, G. A. (1992). The pharmaco-ontogeny of the paraventricular alpha 2-noradrenergic receptor system mediating norepinephrine-induced feeding in the rat. *Brain Research. Developmental Brain Research, 68,* 67–74.

Caputo, F. A., & Scallet, A. C. (1995). Postnatal MSG treatment attenuates angiotensin II (AII) induced drinking in rats. *Physiology & Behavior, 58,* 25–29.

Carboni, E., Silvagni, A., Rolando, M. T., & Di Chiara, G. (2000). Stimulation of in vivo dopamine transmission in the bed nucleus of stria terminalis by reinforcing drugs. *The Journal of Neuroscience, 15,* RC102.

Cardinali, D. P., Brusco, L. I., Lloret, S. P., & Furio, A. M. (2002). Melatonin in sleep disorders and jet-lag. *Neuroendocrinology Letters, 23,* 9–13.

Carew, T. J., Hawkins, R. D., & Kandel, E. R. (1983). Differential classical conditioning of a defensive withdrawal reflex in Aplysia californica. *Science, 219,* 397–400.

Carlini, E. A. (2004). The good and the bad effects of (-) trans-delta-9-tetrahydrocannabinol (Delta 9-THC) on humans. *Toxicon, 44,* 461–467.

Carlson, J. C., & Hatfield, E. (1992). *Psychology of emotion.* Fort Worth: Harcourt Brace & Jovanovich.

Carlsson, A. (2001). Neurotransmitters—Dopamine and beyond. In A. Breier & V. P. Tran (Eds.), *Current issues in the psychopharmacology of schizophrenia* (pp. 3–11). Philadelphia: Lippincott Williams & Wilkins.

Carney, J. M., & Floyd, R. A. (1991). Protection against oxidative damage to CNS by alpha-phenyl-tert-butyl nitrone (PBN) and other spin-trapping agents: A novel series of nonlipid free radical scavengers. *Journal of Molecular Neuroscience, 3,* 47–57.

Carr, G. D., & White, N. (1986). Anatomical dissociation of amphetamine's rewarding and aversive effects: An intracranial microinjection study. *Psychopharmacology, 39,* 340–346.

Carreno, J. E., Alvarez, C. E., Narciso, G. I., Bascaran, M. T., Diaz, M., & Bobes, J. (2003). Maintenance treatment with depot opioid antagonists in subcutaneous implants: An alternative in the treatment of opioid dependence. *Addiction Biology, 8,* 429–438.

Carroll, C. R. (2000). *Drugs in modern society* (5th ed.). New York: McGraw-Hill.

Carroll, M. E., & Overmier, J. B. (Eds.). (2001). *Animal research and human health: Advancing human welfare through behavioral science.* Washington, DC: American Psychological Association.

Carskadon, M. A. (2000). In reply. *JAMA, 283,* 744.

Carter, A. J., O'Connor, W. T., Carter, M. J., & Ungerstedt, U. (1995). Caffeine enhances acetylcholine release in the hippocampus in vivo by a selective interaction with adenosine A_1 receptors. *The Journal of Pharmacology & Experimental Therapeutics, 273,* 637–642.

Carter, C. S., Witt, D. M., Kolb, B., & Whishaw, I. Q. (1982). Neonatal decortication and adult female sexual behavior. *Physiology & Behavior, 29,* 763–766.

Catani, M., Jones, D. K., & ffytche, D. H. (2005). Perisylvian language networks of the human brain. *Annals of Neurology, 57,* 8–16.

Caterina, M. J., Leffler, A., Malmberg, A. B., Martin, W. J., Trafton, J., Petersen-Zeitz, K. R., et al. (2000). Impaired nociception and pain sensation in mice lacking the capsaicin receptor. *Science, 288,* 306–313.

Cattell, R. B., Kawash, G. F., & DeYoung, G. E. (1972). Validation of objective measures of ergic tension: Response of the sex erg to visual stimulation. *Journal of Experimental Research in Personality, 6,* 76–83.

Cespuglio, R., Gomez, M. E., Faradji, H., & Jouvet, M. (1982). Alterations in the sleep-waking cycle induced by cooling of the locus coeruleus area. *Electroencephalography and Clinical Neurophysiology, 54,* 570–578.

Chabas, D., Taheri, S., Renier, C., & Mignot, E. (2003). The genetics of narcolepsy. *Annual Review of Genomics and Human Genetics, 4,* 459–483.

Chan, D. T., Mok, V. C., Poon, W. S., Hung, K. N., & Zhu, X. L. (2001). Surgical management of Parkinson's disease: A critical review. *Hong Kong Medical Journal, 7,* 34–39.

Chang, L., Cloak, C. C., & Ernst, T. (2003). Magnetic resonance spectroscopy studies of GABA in neuropsychiatric disorders. *Journal of Clinical Psychiatry, 64,* 7–14.

Charles, T., & Swash, M. (2001). Amyotrophic lateral sclerosis: Current understanding. *The Journal of Neuroscience Nursing, 33,* 245–253.

Cheitlin, M. D. (2003). Should the patient with coronary artery disease use sildenafil? *Preventive Cardiology, 6,* 161–165.

Chemelli, R. M., Willie, J. T., Sinton, C. M., Elmquist, J. K., Scammell, T., Lee, C., et al. (1999). Narcolepsy in orexin knockout mice: Molecular genetics of sleep regulation. *Cell, 98,* 437–451.

Chen, D. F., Schneider, G. E., Martinou, J. C., & Tonegawa, S. (1997). Bcl-2 promotes regeneration of severed axons in mammalian CNS. *Nature, 385,* 434–439.

Chen, G., Li, S., & Jiang, C. (1986). Clinical studies on neurophysiological and biochemical basis of acupuncture analgesia. *American Journal of Chinese Medicine, 14,* 86–95.

Chen, P., Hao, W., Rife, L., Wang, X. P., Shen, D., Chen, J., et al. (2001). A photic visual cycle of rhodopsin regeneration is dependent on Rgr. *Nature Genetics, 28,* 256–260.

Cheng, J. T., & Kuo, D. Y. (2003). Both alpha1-adrenergic and D(1)-dopaminergic neurotransmissions are involved in phenylpropanolamine-mediated feeding suppression in mice. *Neuroscience Letters, 347,* 136–138.

Chiarello, C. (1980). A house divided? Cognitive functioning with callosal agenesis. *Brain & Language, 11,* 128–158.

Chiavegatto, S., Dawson, V. L., Mamounas, L. A., Koliatsos, V. E., Dawson, T. M., & Nelson, R. J. (2001). Brain serotonin dysfunction accounts for aggression in male mice lacking neuronal nitric oxide synthase. *Proceedings of the National Academy of Sciences of the United States of America, 98,* 1277–1281.

Chilosi, A. M., Cipriani, P. P., Bertucelli, B., Pfanner, P. L., & Cioni, P. G. (2001). Early cognitive and communication development in children with focal brain lesions. *Journal of Child Neurology, 16,* 309–316.

Chiriboga, C. A. (2003). Fetal alcohol and drug effects. *Neurologist, 9,* 267–279.

Chomsky, N., & Lightfoot, D. (1990). Language and innateness. In W. G. Lycan (Ed.), *Mind and cognition: A reader* (pp. 627–659). Cambridge, MA: Basil Blackwell.

Chorover, S. L., & Schiller, P. H. (1965). Short-term retrograde amnesia in rats. *Journal of Comparative and Physiological Psychology, 59,* 73–78.

Christensen, D. S. (2000). Self-efficacy, cognitive interference, sport anxiety, and psychological coping skills as predictors of performance in intercollegiate golf. *Dissertation Abstracts International, 61*(3-B), 1629. (UMI No. AA199964244)

Chu, C. J., & Jones, T. A. (2000). Experience-dependent structural plasticity in cortex heterotop to focal sensorimotor cortical damage. *Experimental Neurology, 166,* 403–414.

Chung, K. K., Dawson, V. L., & Dawson, T. M. (2003). New insights into Parkinson's disease. *Journal of Neurology, 250,* iii15–iii24.

Chwalisz, K., Diener, E., & Gallagher, D. (1988). Autonomic arousal feedback and emotional experience: Evidence from the spinal cord injured. *Journal of Personality and Social Psychology, 54,* 820–828.

Ciapparelli, A., Dell'Osso, L., Tundo, A., Pini, S., Chiavacci, M. C., Di Sacco, I., et al. (2001). Electroconvulsive therapy in medication-nonresponsive patients with mixed mania and bipolar depression. *Journal of Clinical Psychiatry, 62,* 552–555.

Ciccocioppo, R., Cippitelli, A., Economidou, D., Fedeli, A., & Massi, M. (2004). Nociceptin/orphanin FQ acts as a functional antagonist of corticotropin-releasing factor to inhibit its anorectic effect. *Physiology & Behavior, 82,* 63–68.

Clare, L., & Wilson, B. A. (2004). Memory rehabilitation techniques for people with early-stage dementia. *Zeitschrift für Gerontopsychologie & Gerontopsychiatrie, 17,* 109–117.

Clark, N., Lintzeris, N., Gijsbers, A., Whelan, G., Dunlop, A., Ritter, A., et al. (2002). LAAM maintenance vs. methadone maintenance for heroin dependence. *Cochrane Database of Systematic Reviews,* (2), CD002210.

Clark, P. C. (2002). Effects of individual and family hardiness on caregiver depression and fatigue. *Research in Nursing and Health, 25,* 37–48.

Clarke, S., Bellmann Thiran, A., Maeder, P., Adriani, M., Vernet, O., Regli, L., et al. (2002). What and where in human audition: Selective deficits following focal hemispheric lesions. *Experimental Brain Research, 147,* 8–15.

Clarke, S., Bellmann, A., Meuli, R. A., Assal, G., & Steck, A. J. (2000). Auditory agnosia and auditory spatial deficits following left hemisphere lesions: Evidence for distinct processing pathways. *Neuropsychologia, 38,* 797–807.

Clayton, A. H., Pradko, J. F., Croft, H. A., Montano, C. B., Leadbetter, R. A., Bolden-Watson, C., et al. (2002). Prevalence of sexual dysfunction among newer antidepressants. *Journal of Clinical Psychiatry, 63,* 357–366.

Clayton, A. H., Warnock, J. K., Kornstein, S. G., Pinkerton, R., Sheldon-Keller, A., & McGarvey, E. L. (2004). A placebo-controlled trial of bupropion SR as an antidote for selective serotonin reuptake inhibitor-induced sexual dysfunction. *Journal of Clinical Psychiatry, 65,* 62–67.

Clayton, A. H., Zajecka, J., Ferguson, J. M., Filipiak-Reisner, J. K., Brown, M. T., & Schwartz, G. E. (2003). Lack of sexual dysfunction with the selective noradrenaline reuptake inhibitor reboxetine during treatment for major depressive disorder. *International Clinical Psychopharmacology, 18,* 151–156.

Cleary, M., & Walter, J. H. (2001). Assessment of adult phenylketonuria. *Annals of Clinical Biochemistry, 38,* 450–458.

Code, C., & Rowley, D. (1987). Age and aphasia type: The interaction of sex, time since onset and handedness. *Aphasiology, 1,* 339–345.

Cohen, A. N., Hammen, C., Henry, R. M., & Daley, S. E. (2004). Effects of stress and social support on recurrence in bipolar disorder. *Journal of Affective Disorders, 82,* 143–147.

Cohen, J. D., Barch, D. M., Carter, C., & Servan-Schreiber, D. (1999). Context-processing deficits in schizophrenia: Converging evidence from three theoretically motivated cognitive tasks. *Journal of Abnormal Psychology, 108,* 120–133.

Cohen, J. D., & Servan-Schreiber, D. (1992). Context, cortex, and dopamine: A connectionist approach to behavior and biology in schizophrenia. *Psychological Review, 99,* 45–77.

Cohen, L. G., Celnik, P., Pascual-Leone, A., Corwell, B., Falz, L., Dambrosia, J., et al. (1997). Functional relevance of cross-modal plasticity in blind humans. *Nature, 389,* 180–183.

Cohen, S. (1959). Purification and metabolic effects of a nerve-growth promoting protein from snake venom. *The Journal of Biological Chemistry, 234,* 1129–1137.

Cohen, S., Hamrick, N., Rodriguez, M. S., Feldman, P. J., Rabin, B. S., & Manuck, S. B. (2002). Reactivity and vulnerability to stress-associated risk for upper respiratory illness. *Psychosomatic Medicine, 64,* 302–310.

Cohen, S., Tyrrell, D. A. J., & Smith, A. P. (1991). Psychological stress and susceptibility to the common cold. *New England Journal of Medicine, 325,* 606–612.

Cohen-Bendahan, C. C., Buitelaar, J. K., Van Goozen, S. H., & Cohen-Kettenis, P. T. (2004). Prenatal exposure to testosterone and functional cerebral lateralization: A study in same-sex and opposite-sex twin girls. *Psychoneuroendocrinology, 29,* 911–916.

Cohen-Bendahan, C. C., van de Beek, C., & Berenbaum, S. A. (2005). Prenatal sex hormone effects on child and adult sex-typed behavior: Methods and findings. *Neuroscience and Biobehavioral Reviews, 29,* 353–384.

Colapinto, J. (2000). *As nature made him: The boy who was raised as a girl.* New York: HarperCollins.

Colapinto, J. (2004, June 3). Gender gap—What were the real reasons behind David Reimer's suicide? *Slate.* Retrieved November 30, 2004, from http://slate.msn.com/id/2101678/

Coll, P. P., Fortinsky, R. H., Kaplan, R., & Song, C. (2003). Diagnosis and management of Alzheimer's disease. *Connecticut Medicine, 67,* 505–510.

Collet, C., Vernet-Maury, E., Delhomme, G., & Dittmar, A. (1997). Autonomic nervous system response patterns specificity to basic emotions. *Journal of the Autonomic Nervous System, 62,* 45–57.

Colvin, M. K., Dunbar, K., & Grafman, J. (2001). The effects of frontal lobe lesions on goal achievement in the water jug task. *Journal of Cognitive Neuroscience, 13,* 1129–1147.

Comer, R. J. (2001). *Abnormal psychology* (4th ed.). New York: Worth.

Comer, S. D., Collins, E. D., Kleber, H. D., Nuwayser, E. S., Kerrigan, J. H., & Fischman, M. W. (2002). Depot naltrexone: Long-lasting antagonism of the effects of heroin in humans. *Psychopharmacology (Berlin), 159,* 351–360.

Comings, D. E., & Blum, K. (2000). Reward deficiency syndrome: Genetic aspects of behavioral disorders. *Progress in Brain Research, 126,* 325–341.

Considine, R. V., Sinha, M. K., Heiman, M. L., Kriauciunas, A., Stephens, T. W., Nyce, M. R., et al. (1996). Serum immunoreactive-leptin concentrations in normal-weight and obese humans. *New England Journal of Medicine, 334,* 292–295.

Conti, L. H., & Foote, S. L. (1995). Effects of pretreatment with corticotropin-releasing factor on the electrophysiological responsivity of the locus coeruleus to subsequent corticotropin-releasing factor challenge. *Neuroscience, 69,* 209–219.

Conti, L. H., & Foote, S. L. (1996). Reciprocal cross-desensitization of locus coeruleus electrophysiological responsivity to corticotropin-releasing factor and stress. *Brain Research, 722,* 19–29.

Convit, A., Czobor, P., & Volavka, J. (1991). Lateralized abnormality in the EEG of persistently violent psychiatric inpatients. *Biological Psychiatry, 30,* 363–370.

Cook, G., Tannahill, D., & Keynes, R. (1998). Axon guidance to and from choice points. *Current Opinion in Neurobiology, 8,* 64–72.

Cook, L. J. (2004). Educating women about the hidden dangers of alcohol. *Journal of Psychosocial Nursing and Mental Health Services, 42,* 24–31.

Coolen, L. M., & Wood, R. I. (1999). Testosterone stimulation of the medial preoptic area and medial amygdala in the control of male hamster sexual behavior: Redundancy without amplification. *Behavioural Brain Research, 98,* 143–153.

Coons, E. E., & Cruce, J. A. (1968). Lateral hypothalamus: Food current intensity in maintaining self-stimulation of hunger. *Science, 159,* 1117–1119.

Coons, E. E., & Miller, N. E. (1960). Conflict versus consolidation of memory traces to explain "retrograde amnesia" produced by ECS. *Journal of Comparative and Physiological Psychology, 53,* 524–531.

Copolov, D., & Crook, J. (2000). Biological markers and schizophrenia. *Australian & New Zealand Journal of Psychiatry, 34,* S108–S112.

Corbetta, M., Shulman, G. L., Miezin, F. M., & Petersen, S. E. (1995). Superior parietal cortex activation during spatial attention shifts and visual feature conjunction. *Science, 270,* 802–805.

Coren, S., Ward, L. M., & Enns, J. T. (1994). *Sensation and perception* (4th ed.). Fort Worth, TX: Harcourt Brace.

Corkin, S. (2002). What's new with the amnesic patient H.M.? *Nature Reviews. Neuroscience, 3,* 153–160.

Corkin, S., Amaral, D. G., González, R. G., Johnson, K. A., & Human, B. T. (1997). H. M.'s medial temporal lobe lesion: Findings from magnetic resonance imaging. *The Journal of Neuroscience, 17,* 3964–3979.

Cornelissen, K., Laine, M., Tarkiainen, A., Jarvensivu, T., Martin, N., & Salmelin, R. (2003). Adult brain plasticity elicited by anomia treatment. *Journal of Cognitive Neuroscience, 15,* 444–461.

Cornelius, M. D. (2003). Tobacco consumption during pregnancy and its impact on child development: Comments on Brennan, Fergusson and Fried. In R. E. Tremblay, R. G. Barr, & R. De V. Peters (Eds.), *Encyclopedia on early childhood development* [online, pp. 1–10]. Montreal, Quebec: Centre of Excellence for Early Childhood Development. Retrieved May 31, 2005, from http://www.excellence-earlychildhood.ca/documents/CorneliusANGxp.pdf

Cornelius, M. D., & Day, N. L. (2000). The effects of tobacco use during and after pregnancy on exposed children. *Alcohol Research & Health, 24,* 242–249.

Cornelius, M. D., Goldschmidt, L., Day, N. L., & Larkby, C. (2002). Alcohol, tobacco and marijuana use among pregnant teenagers: 6-year follow-up of offspring growth effects. *Neurotoxicology and Teratology, 24,* 703–710.

Correctional Service Canada. (n.d.). *The patterns of violent crime by women.* Retrieved January 7, 2005, from http://www.csc-scc.gc.ca/text/prgrm/fsw/fsw23/fsw23e01_e.shtml

Corrigall, W. A., & Coen, K. M. (1991). Cocaine self-administration is increased by both D_1 and D_2 dopamine antagonists. *Pharmacology, Biochemistry, and Behavior, 39,* 799–802.

Corwin, J. T., & Warchol, M. E. (1991). Auditory hair cells: Structure, function, development, and regeneration. *Annual Review of Neuroscience, 14,* 301–333.

Corwin, R. L., Gibbs, J., & Smith, G. P. (1991). Increased food intake after type A but not type B cholecystokinin receptor blockade. *Physiology & Behavior, 50,* 255–258.

Cotter, D., Landau, S., Beasley, C., Stevenson, R., Chana, G., MacMillan, L., et al. (2002). The density and spatial distribution of GABAergic neurons, labelled using calcium binding proteins, in the anterior cingulate cortex in major depressive disorder, bipolar disorder, and schizophrenia. *Biological Psychiatry, 51,* 377–386.

Coulson, S., & Williams, R. F. (2005). Hemispheric asymmetries and joke comprehension. *Neuropsychologia, 43,* 128–141.

Covasa, M., Marcuson, J. K., & Ritter, R. C. (2001). Diminished satiation in rats exposed to elevated levels of endogenous or exogenous cholecystokinin. *American Journal of Physiology. Regulatory, Integrative and Comparative Physiology, 280,* R331–337.

Cowey, A., & Stoerig, P. (1997). Visual detection in monkeys with blindsight. *Neuropsychologia, 35,* 929–939.

Cowey, A., & Stoerig, P. (2004). Stimulus cueing in blindsight. *Progress in Brain Research, 144,* 261–277.

Coyle, J. T., Price, D. L., & DeLong, M. R. (1983). Alzheimer's disease: A disorder of cortical cholinergic innervation. *Science, 219,* 1184–1190.

Craddock, N., & Jones, I. (1999). Genetics of bipolar disorder. *Journal of Medical Genetics, 36,* 585–594.

Craik, F. I. M., & Lockhart, R. S. (1972). Levels of processing: A framework for memory research. *Journal of Verbal Learning and Verbal Behavior, 11,* 671–684.

Crair, M. C., Gillespie, D. C., & Stryker, M. P. (1998). The role of visual experience in the development of columns in cat visual cortex. *Science, 279,* 566–570.

Crandall, C. S., & Martinez, R. (1996). Culture, ideology, and antifat attitudes. *Personality & Social Psychology Bulletin, 22,* 1165–1176.

Craufurd, D., Thompson, J. C., & Snowden, J. S. (2001). Behavioral changes in Huntington Disease. *Neuropsychiatry, Neuropsychology, and Behavioral Neurology, 14,* 219–226.

Crawley, J. N., & Kiss, J. Z. (1985). Paraventricular nucleus lesions abolish the inhibition of feeding induced by systemic cholecystokinin. *Peptides, 6,* 927–935.

Creese, I., Burt, D. R., & Snyder, S. H. (1996). Dopamine receptor binding predicts clinical and pharmacological potencies of antischizophrenic drugs. *The Journal of Neuropsychiatry and Clinical Neurosciences, 8,* 223–226.

Crews, F. (1996). The verdict on Freud. *Psychological Science, 7,* 63–68.

Critchley, H., Daly, E., Phillips, M., Brammer, M., Bullmore, E., Williams, S., et al. (2000). Explicit and implicit neural mechanisms for processing of social information from facial expressions: A functional magnetic resonance imaging study. *Human Brain Mapping, 9,* 93–105.

Cromer, R. (1994). A case study of dissociations between language and cognition. In Tager-Flusberg, H. (Ed.), *Constraints on language acquisition: Studies of atypical children* (pp. 141–153). Hillsdale, NJ: Erlbaum.

Crone, S. A., & Lee, K. F. (2002). The bound leading the bound: Target-derived receptors act as guidance cues. *Neuron, 36,* 333–335.

Cronholm, B., & Molander, L. (1957). Memory disturbances after electroconvulsive therapy: I. Conditions 6 hours after electroshock treatment. *Acta Psychiatrica et Neurologica (Kobenhavn), 32,* 280–306.

Cronholm, B., & Molander, L. (1961). Memory disturbances after electroconvulsive therapy. *Acta Psychiatrica et Neurologica (Kobenhavn), 36,* 83–90.

Cronholm, B., & Molander, L. (1964). Memory disturbances after electroconvulsive therapy. *Acta Psychiatrica Scandinavica, 40,* 212–216

Crow, T. J., & Done, D. J. (1992). Prenatal exposure to influenza does not cause schizophrenia. *British Journal of Psychiatry, 161,* 390–393.

Cryan, J. F., McGrath, C., Leonard, B. E., & Norman, T. R. (1999). Onset of the effects of the 5-HT_{1A} antagonist, WAY-100635, alone, and in combination with paroxetine, on olfactory bulbectomy and 8-OH-DPAT-induced changes in the rat. *Pharmacology, Biochemistry, and Behavior, 63,* 333–338.

Csernansky, J. G., Mahmoud, R., & Brenner, R. (2002). A comparison of risperidone and haloperidol for the prevention of relapse in patients with schizophrenia. *New England Journal of Medicine, 346,* 16–22.

Cummings, D. E., Purnell, J. Q., Frayo, R. S., Schmidova, K., Wisse, B. E., & Weigle, D. S. (2001). A preprandial rise in plasma ghrelin levels suggests a role in meal initiation in humans. *Diabetes, 50,* 1714–1719.

Cutler, N. R., & Cohen, H. B. (1979). The effect of one night's sleep loss on mood and memory in normal subjects. *Comprehensive Psychiatry, 20,* 61–66.

Cutler, N. R., & Sramek, J. J. (2001). Review of the next generation of Alzheimer's disease therapeutics: Challenges for drug development. *Progress in Neuropsychopharmacology & Biological Psychiatry, 25,* 27–57.

Cutler, W. B., Preti, G., Krieger, A., Huggins, G. R., Garcia, C. R., & Lawley, H. J. (1986). Human axillary secretions influence women's menstrual cycles: The role of donor extract from men. *Hormones and Behavior, 20,* 463–473.

Cutolo, M., Seriolo, B., Villaggio, B., Pizzorni, C., Craviotto, C., & Sulli, A. (2002). Androgens and estrogens modulate the immune and inflammatory responses in rheumatoid arthritis. *Annals of the New York Academy of Sciences, 966,* 131–142.

Cutolo, M., Sulli, A., Capellino, S., Villaggio, B., Montagna, P., Seriolo, B., et al. (2004). Sex hormones influence on the immune system: Basic and clinical aspects in autoimmunity. *Lupus, 13,* 635–638.

Czeisler, C. A., Duffy, J. F., Shanahan, T. L., Brown, E. N., Mitchell, J. F., Rimmer, D. W., et al. (1999). Stability, precision, and near-24-hour period of the human circadian pacemaker. *Science, 284,* 2177–2181.

Czeisler, C. A., Moore-Ede, M. C., & Coleman, R. H. (1982). Rotating shift work schedules that disrupt sleep are improved by applying circadian principles. *Science, 217,* 460–463.

Dabbs, J. M., Jr., Carr, T. S., Frady, R. L., & Riad, J. K. (1995). Testosterone, crime, and misbehavior among 692 male prison inmates. *Personality and Individual Differences, 18,* 627–633.

Dabbs, J. M., Jr., Frady, R. L., Carr, T. S., & Besch, N. F. (1987). Saliva testosterone and criminal violence in young adult prison inmates. *Psychosomatic Medicine, 49,* 174–182.

Dabbs, J. M., Jr., & Morris, R. (1990). Testosterone, social class, and antisocial behavior in a sample of 4,462 men. *Psychological Science, 1,* 209–211.

Dacey, D. M. (1996). Circuitry for color coding in the primate retina. *Proceedings of the National Academy of Sciences of the United States of America, 93,* 582–588.

Dalhouse, A. D., Langford, H. G., Walsh, D., & Barnes, T. (1986). Angiotensin and salt appetite: Physiological amounts of angiotensin given peripherally increase salt appetite in the rat. *Behavioral Neuroscience, 100,* 597–602.

Dalton, K. (1961). Menstruation and crime. *British Medical Journal, 5269,* 1752–1753.

Dalton, K. (1964). *The premenstrual syndrome.* Springfield, IL: Thomas.

Damasio, A. R. (1990). Category-related recognition defects as a clue to the neural substrates of knowledge. *Trends in Neuroscience, 13,* 95–98.

Damasio, A. R. (1994). *Descartes' error: Emotion, reason, and the human brain.* New York: Putnam.

Damasio, A. R., & Damasio, H. (1992). Brain and language. *Scientific American, 267,* 88–95.

Damasio, A. R., & Damasio, H. (2000). Aphasia and the neural basis of language. In M.-M. Mesulam (Ed.), *Principles of behavioral and cognitive neurology* (2nd ed., pp. 294–315). New York: Oxford University Press.

Damasio, H., Grabowski, T., Frank, R., Galaburda, A. M., & Damasio, A. R. (1994). The return of Phineas Gage: Clues about the brain from the skull of a famous patient. *Science, 264,* 1102–1105.

Dao-Castellana, M. H., Paillere-Martinot, M. L., Hantraye, P., Attar-Levy, D., Remy, P., Crouzel, C., et al. (1997). Presynaptic dopaminergic function in the striatum of schizophrenic patients. *Schizophrenia Research, 23,* 167–174.

Darley, F. L. (1982). *Aphasia.* Philadelphia: Saunders.

Darnton-Hill, I., & Coyne, E. T. (1998). Feast and famine: Socioeconomic disparities in global nutrition and health. *Public Health Nutrition, 1,* 23–31.

Darwin, C. (1874). *The descent of man, and selection in relation to sex* (2nd ed.). New York: A. L. Burt.

Darwin, C. (1958). *The origin of species, by means of natural selection or the preservation of favoured races in the struggle for life.* New York: New American Library. (Original work published 1859)

Datla, K. P., Ahier, R. G., Young, A. M., Gray, J. A., & Joseph, M. H. (2002). Conditioned appetitive stimulus increases extracellular dopamine in the nucleus accumbens of the rat. *European Journal of Neuroscience, 16,* 1987–1993.

Dauvilliers, Y., Billiard, M., & Montplaisir, J. (2003). Clinical aspects and pathophysiology of narcolepsy. *Clinical Neurophysiology, 114,* 2000–2017.

Davidson, J. M. (1966). Characteristics of sex behavior in male rats following castration. *Animal Behavior, 14,* 266–272.

Davidson, J. M. (1980). Hormones and sexual behavior in the male. In D. T. Krieger & J. C. Hughes (Eds.), *Neuroendocrinology* (pp. 232–238). Sunderland, MA: Sinauer Associates.

Davidson, L. L., & Heinrichs, R. W. (2003). Quantification of frontal and temporal lobe brain-imaging findings in schizophrenia: A meta-analysis. *Psychiatry Research, 122,* 69–87.

Davis, A. E. (2000). Mechanisms of traumatic brain injury: Biomechanical, structural and cellular considerations. *Critical Care Nursing Quarterly, 23,* 1–13.

Davis, E. C., Shryne, J. E., & Gorski, R. A. (1995). A revised critical period for the sexual differentiation of the sexually dimorphic nucleus of the preoptic area in the rat. *Neuroendocrinology, 62,* 579–585.

Davis, G. A. (1993). *A survey of adult aphasia and related language disorders* (2nd ed.). Englewood Cliffs, NJ: Prentice Hall.

Davis, G. A. (2000). *Aphasiology: Disorders and clinical practice.* Boston: Allyn and Bacon.

Davis, K. M., & Wu, J. Y. (2001). Role of glutamatergic and GABAergic systems in alcoholism. *Journal of Biomedical Science, 8,* 7–19.

De Luca, L. A., Jr., Xu, Z., Schoorlemmer, G. H., Thunhorst, R. L., Beltz, T. G., Menani, J. V., et al. (2002). Water deprivation-induced sodium appetite: Humoral and cardiovascular mediators and immediate early genes. *American Journal of Physiology. Regulatory, Integrative and Comparative Physiology, 282,* R552–R559.

de Sena, E. P., Santos-Jesus, R., Miranda-Scippa, A., Quarantini Lde, C., & Oliveira, I. R. (2003). Relapse in patients with schizophrenia: A comparison between risperidone and haloperidol. *Revista Brasileira de Psiquiatria, 25,* 220–223.

De Valois, R. L., Abramov, I., & Jacobs, G. H. (1966). Analysis of response patterns of LGN cells. *Journal of the Optical Society of America, 56,* 966–977.

De Valois, R. L., Cottaris, N. P., Elfar, S. D., Mahon, L. E., & Wilson, J. A. (2000). Some transformations of color information from lateral geniculate nucleus to striate cortex. *Proceedings of the National Academy of Sciences of the United States of America, 97,* 4997–5002.

De Valois, R. L., & De Valois, K. K. (1988). *Spatial vision.* New York: Oxford University Press.

de Zwaan, M. (2001). Binge eating disorder and obesity. *International Journal of Obesity and Related Metabolic Disorders, 25,* S51–S55.

Deacon, T., Schumacher, J., Dinsmore, J., Thomas, C., Palmer, P., Kott, S., et al. (1997). Histological evidence of fetal pig neural cell survival after transplantation into a patient with Parkinson's disease. *Nature Medicine, 3,* 350–353.

Degen, L., Matzinger, D., Drewe, J., & Beglinger, C. (2001). The effect of cholecystokinin in controlling appetite and food intake in humans. *Peptides, 22,* 1265–1269.

Dejerine, J. (1891). Sur un cas de cécité verbale avec agraphia, suivi d'autopsie. *Comtes Rendus des Séances de la Société de Biologie et de Ses Filiales, 3,* 197–201.

Dejerine, J. (1892). Des différentes variétés de cécité verbale. *Memories de la Société Biologique, 4,* 1–30.

del Aguila, M. A., Longstreth, W. T., Jr., McGuire, V., Koepsell, T. D., & van Belle, G. (2003). Prognosis in amyotrophic lateral sclerosis: A population-based study. *Neurology, 50,* 813–819.

Delay, J., & Deniker, P. (1952). Le traitement des psychoses par une method neurolytique derivée d'hibernothérapie; le 4560 RP utilisée seul un cure prolongée et continuée. *Comptes Rendus Congrès des Médicins Aliénistes et Neurologistes de France et des Pays de Lanque Française, 50,* 497–502.

DeLisi, L. E. (2001). Speech disorder in schizophrenia: Review of the literature and exploration of its relation to the uniquely human capacity for language. *Schizophrenia Bulletin, 27,* 481–496.

DeLisi, L. E., Mirsky, A. F., Buchsbaum, M. S., van Kammen, D. P., Berman, K. F., Caton, C., et al. (1984). The Genain quadruplets 25 years later: A diagnostic and biochemical followup. *Psychiatry Research, 13,* 59–76.

Demb, J. B., Boynton, G. M., & Heeger, D. J. (1998). Functional magnetic resonance imaging of early visual pathways in dyslexia. *The Journal of Neuroscience, 18,* 6939–6951.

Dembroski, T. M., MacDougall, J. M., & Shields, J. L. (1977). Physiologic reactions to social challenge in persons evidencing the type A coronary-prone behavior pattern. *Journal of Human Stress, 3,* 2–9.

Dement, W. C. (1969). The biological role of REM sleep. In A. Kales (Ed.), *Sleep physiology and pathology* (pp. 245–265). Philadelphia: Lippincott.

Dement, W. C. (1974). *Some must watch while some must sleep.* New York: W. H. Freeman.

Dement, W. C. (1986). Normal sleep, disturbed sleep, transient and persistent insomnia. *Acta Psychiatrica Scandinavica. Supplementum, 332,* 41–46.

Dement, W. C. (1998). The study of human sleep: A historical perspective. *Thorax, 53,* Supplement 3: S2–S7.

Dement, W. C. (1999). *The promise of sleep.* New York: Delacorte.

Dement, W., & Kleitman, N. (1957). Cyclic variations in EEG during sleep and their relation to eye movements, body motility, and dreaming. *Electroencephalography and Clinical Neurophysiology. Supplement, 9,* 673–690.

Demery, J. A., Hanlon, R. E., & Bauer, R. M. (2001). Profound amnesia and confabulation following traumatic brain injury. *Neurocase, 7,* 295–302.

Dempsey, P. J., Townsend, G. C., & Richards, L. C. (1999). Increased tooth crown size in females with twin brothers: Evidence for hormonal diffusion between human twins in utero. *American Journal of Human Biology, 11,* 577–586.

Dennett, D. C. (1995). *Darwin's dangerous idea: Evolution and the meanings of life.* New York: Simon & Schuster.

Deol, M. S., & Gluecksohn-Waelsch, S. (1979). The role of inner hair cells in hearing. *Nature, 278,* 250–252.

Descartes, R. (1972). *Treatise of man* (T. S. Hall, Trans.). Cambridge, MA: Harvard University Press. (Original work published 1662)

DeSimone, J. A., Heck, G. L., & Bartoshuk, L. M. (1980). Surface active taste modifiers: A comparison of the physical and psychophysical properties of gymnemic acid and sodium lauryl sulfate. *Chemical Senses, 5,* 317–330.

DeSousa, N. J., Bush, D. E., & Vaccarino, F. J. (2000). Self-administration of intravenous amphetamine is predicted by individual differences in sucrose feeding in rats. *Psychopharmacology (Berlin), 148,* 52–58.

DeSousa, N. J., & Vaccarino, F. J. (2001). Neurobiology of reinforcement: Interaction between dopamine and cholecystokinin systems. In R. R. Mowrer & S. B. Klein (Eds.), *Handbook of contemporary learning theories* (pp. 441–468). Mahwah, NJ: Erlbaum.

Després, J-P, Golay, A., & Sjöström, L. (2005). Effects of Rimonabant on metabolic risk factors in overweight patients with dyslipidemia. *New England Journal of Medicine, 353,* 2121–2134.

Detera-Wadleigh, S. D. (2001). Lithium-related genetics of bipolar disorder. *Annals of Medicine, 33,* 272–285.

Detillion, C. E., Craft, T. K. S., Glasper, E. R., Prendergast, B. J., & DeVries, A. C. (2004). Social facilitation of wound healing. *Psychoneuroendocrinology, 29,* 1004–1011.

Detke, M. J., Brandon, S. E., Weingarten, H. P., Rodin, J., & Wagner, A. R. (1989). Modulation of behavioral and insulin responses by contextual stimuli paired with food. *Physiology & Behavior, 45,* 845–851.

Deuster, P. A., Adera, T., & South-Paul, J. (1999). Biological, social, and behavioral factors associated with premenstrual syndrome. *Archives of Family Medicine, 8,* 122–128.

Deutsch, J. A. (1983). Dietary control and the stomach. *Progress in Neurobiology, 20,* 313–332.

Deutsch, J. A., & Gonzalez, M. F. (1980). Gastric nutrient content signals satiety. *Behavioral and Neural Biology, 30,* 113–116.

Devine, D. P., Watson, S. J., & Akil, H. (2001). Nociceptin/orphanin FQ regulates neuroendocrine function of the limbic-hypothalamic-pituitary-adrenal axis. *Neuroscience, 102,* 541–553.

Devine, D. P., & Wise, R. A. (1994). Self-administration of *morphine,* DAMGO, and DPDPE into the ventral tegmental area of rats. *The Journal of Neuroscience, 14,* 1978–1984.

Devlin, M. J., Walsh, B. T., Guss, J. L., Kissileff, H. R., Liddle, R. A., & Petkova, E. (1997). Postprandial cholecystokinin release and gastric emptying in patients with bulimia nervosa. *American Journal of Clinical Nutrition, 65,* 114–120.

Dewey, S. L., Brodie, J. D., Gerasimov, M., Horan, B., Gardner, E. L., & Ashby, C. R., Jr. (1999). A pharmacologic strategy for the treatment of nicotine addiction. *Synapse, 31,* 76–86.

Dewey, S. L., Morgan, A. E., Ashby, C. R., Jr., Horan, B., Kushner, S. A., Logan, J., et al. (1998). A novel strategy for the treatment of cocaine addiction. *Synapse, 30,* 119–129.

Di Sclafani, V., Tolou-Shams, M., Price, L. J., & Fein, G. (2002). Neuropsychological performance of individuals dependent on crack-cocaine, or crack-cocaine and alcohol, at 6 weeks and 6 months of abstinence. *Drug and Alcohol Dependence, 66,* 161–171.

Diamond, M., & Sigmundson, H. K. (1997). Sex reassignment at birth. Long-term review and clinical implications. *Archives of Pediatrics & Adolescent Medicine, 151,* 298–304.

Dick, F., Wulfeck, B., Krupa-Kwiatkowski, M., & Bates, E. (2004). The development of complex sentence interpretation in typically developing children compared with children with specific language impairments or early unilateral focal lesions. *Developmental Science, 7,* 360–377.

Dickerson, F. B., Boronow, J. J., Ringel, N., & Parente, F. (1997). Lack of insight among outpatients with schizophrenia. *Psychiatric Services, 48,* 195–199.

Dickinson, A. (1989). Expectancy theory in animal conditioning. In S. B. Klein & R. R. Mowrer (Eds.), *Contemporary learning theories* (pp. 279–308). Hillsdale, NJ: Erlbaum.

Dickson, B. J. (2002). Molecular mechanisms of axon guidance. *Science, 298,* 1959–1964.

Diedrichsen, J., Verstynen, T., Lehman, S. L., & Ivry, R. B. (2005). Cerebellar involvement in anticipating the consequences of self-produced actions during bimanual movements. *Journal of Neurophysiology, 93,* 801–812.

Dierks, T., Linden, D. E., Jandl, M., Formisano, E., Goebel, R., Lanfermann, H., et al. (1999). Activation of Heschl's gyrus during auditory hallucinations. *Neuron, 22,* 615–621.

DiGiulio, D. V., Seidenberg, M., O'Leary, D. S., & Raz, N. (1994). Procedural and declarative memory: A developmental study. *Brain & Cognition, 25,* 79–91.

DiLalla, D. L., Carey, G., Gottesman, I. I., & Bouchard, T. J., Jr. (1996). Heritability of MMPI personality indicators of psychopathology in twins reared apart. *Journal of Abnormal Psychology, 105,* 491–499.

Dimsdale, J. E. (1988). A perspective on type A behavior and coronary disease. *New England Journal of Medicine, 318,* 110–112.

Dittmann, R. W., Kappes, M. E., & Kappes, M. H. (1992). Sexual behavior in adolescent and adult females with congenital adrenal hyperplasia. *Psychoneuroendocrinology, 17,* 153–170.

Dixit, S. N., Behari, M., & Ahuja, G. K. (1999). Effect of selegiline on cognitive functions in Parkinson's disease. *The Journal of the Association of Physicians of India, 47,* 784–786.

Dixson, A. (2001). The evolution of neuroendocrine mechanisms regulating sexual behaviour in female primates. *Reproduction, Fertility, and Development, 13,* 599–607.

Dolan, M., Deakin, W. J., Roberts, N., & Anderson, I. (2002). Serotonergic and cognitive impairment in impulsive aggressive personality disordered offenders: Are there implications for treatment. *Psychological Medicine, 32,* 105–117.

Doly, M. (1994). Transduction of the light message: From the photon to the optic nerve. *Fundamental & Clinical Pharmacology, 8,* 147–154.

Domhoff, G. W. (1996). *Finding meaning in dreams: A quantitative approach.* New York: Plenum Press.

Dominguez, J., Riolo, J. V., Xu, Z., & Hull, E. M. (2001). Regulation by the medial amygdala of copulation and medial preoptic dopamine release. *The Journal of Neuroscience, 21,* 349–355.

Dominguez, J. M., & Hull, E. M. (2001). Stimulation of the medial amygdala enhances medial preoptic dopamine release: Implications for male rat sexual behavior. *Brain Research, 917,* 225–229.

Domjan, M., Lyons, R., North, N. C., & Bruell, J. (1986). Sexual Pavlovian conditioned approach behavior in male Japanese quail (*Coturnix coturnix japonica*). *Journal of Comparative Psychology, 100,* 413–421.

Donoghue, J. (2000). Antidepressant use patterns in clinical practices: Comparisons among tricyclic antidepressants and selective serotonin reuptake inhibitors. *Acta Psychiatrica Scandinavica. Supplementum, 403,* 57–61.

Donoghue, J. P., Suner, S., & Sanes, J. N. (1990). Dynamic organization of primary motor cortex output to target muscles in adult rats. II. Rapid reorganization following motor nerve lesions. *Experimental Brain Research, 79,* 492–503.

Doraiswamy, P. M. (2002). Non-cholinergic strategies for treating and preventing Alzheimer's disease. *CNS Drugs, 16,* 811–824.

Dorshkind, K., & Horseman, N. D. (2001). Anterior pituitary hormones, stress, and immune system homeostasis. *Bioessays, 23,* 288–294.

Doty, R. W. (1968). Neural organization of deglutition. In C. F. Code (Ed.), *Handbook of physiology: Alimentary canal* (pp. 1861–1902). Washington, DC: American Physiological Society.

Dourish, C. T., Rycroft, W., & Iversen, S. D. (1989). Postponement of satiety by blockade of brain cholecystokinin (CCK-B) receptors. *Science, 245,* 1509–1511.

Dow, B. M. (2002). Orientation and color columns in monkey visual cortex. *Cerebral Cortex, 12,* 1005–1015.

Downey, J., Ehrhardt, A. A., Schiffman, M., Dyrenfurth, I., & Becker, J. (1987). Sex hormones in lesbian and heterosexual women. *Hormones and Behavior, 21,* 347–357.

Doyle, T. F., Bellugi, U., Korenberg, J. R., & Graham, J. (2004). "Everybody in the world is my friend" hypersociability in young children with Williams syndrome. *American Journal of Medical Genetics, 124,* 263–273.

Doyon, S. (2001). The many faces of ecstasy. *Current Opinion in Pediatrics, 13,* 170–176.

Drapeau, E., Mayo, W., Aurousseau, C., Le Moal, M., Piazza, P. V., & Abrous, D. N. (2003). Spatial memory performances of aged rats in the water maze predict levels of hippocampal neurogenesis. *Proceedings of the National Academy of Sciences of the United States of America, 100,* 14385–14390.

Drellishak, R. (1996). Genetic testing. Retrieved April 28, 2004, from http://www.lib.uchicago.edu/~rd13hd/testing.html

Drevets, W. C. (2001). Neuroimaging and neuropathological studies of depression: Implications for the cognitive-emotional features of mood disorders. *Current Opinion in Neurobiology, 11,* 240–249.

Drevets, W. C., Ongür, D., & Price, J. L. (1998). Neuroimaging abnormalities in the subgenual prefrontal cortex: Implications for the pathophysiology of familial mood disorders. *Molecular Psychiatry, 3,* 220–226.

Drewnowski, A., Henderson, S. A., & Barratt-Fornell, A. (1998). Genetic sensitivity to 6-n-propylthiouracil and sensory responses to sugar and fat mixtures. *Physiology & Behavior, 63,* 771–777.

Drewnowski, A., Henderson, S. A., & Barratt-Fornell, A. (2001). Genetic taste markers and food preferences. *Drug Metabolism and Disposition, 29,* 535–538.

Drewnowski, A., Henderson, S. A., Hann, C. S., Berg, W. A., & Ruffin, M. T. (2000). Genetic taste markers and preferences for vegetables and fruit of female breast care patients. *Journal of the American Dietetic Association, 100,* 191–197.

Driver, H. S., & Taylor, S. R. (2000). Exercise and sleep. *Sleep Medicine Reviews, 4,* 387–402.

Driver, J., & Vuilleumier, P. (2001). Perceptual awareness and its loss in unilateral neglect and extinction. *Cognition, 79,* 39–88.

Dronkers, N. F., Pinker, S., & Damasio, A. (2000). Language and the aphasias. In E. R. Kandel, J. H. Schwartz, & T. M. Jessell (Eds.), *Principles of neural science* (4th ed., pp. 1169–1187). New York: McGraw-Hill.

Dronkers, N. F., Wilkins, D. P., Van Valin, R. D., Jr., Redfern, B. B., & Jaeger, J. J. (2004). Lesion analysis of the brain areas involved in language comprehension. *Cognition, 92,* 145–177.

Drummond, S. P. A., Brown, G. G., Stricker, J. L., Buxton, R. B., Wong, E. C., & Gillin, J. C. (1999). Sleep deprivation-induced reduction in cortical functional response to serial subtraction. *NeuroReport, 10,* 3745–3748.

Dryden, J. (2004, February). *Magnetic treatment studied for depression.* Retrieved July 20, 2005, from http://mednewsarchive.wustl.edu/medadmin/PAnews.nsf/0/B6FAAED1EA50D54986256E46006C2C51

Dubb, A., Gur, R., Avants, B., & Gee, J. (2003). Characterization of sexual dimorphism in the human corpus callosum. *Neuroimage, 20,* 512–519.

Duchniewska, K., & Kokoszka, A. (2003). The protective mechanisms of the basic rest-activity cycle as an indirect manifestation of this rhythm in waking: Preliminary report. *International Journal of Neuroscience, 113,* 153–163.

Duffy, S. N., Craddock, K. J., Abel, T., & Nguyen, P. V. (2001). Environmental enrichment modifies the PKA-dependence of hippocampal LTP and improves hippocampus-dependent memory. *Learning & Memory, 8,* 26–34.

Duncan, C. P. (1949). The retroactive effect of electroshock on learning. *Journal of Comparative and Physiological Psychology, 42,* 32–44.

Dunnett, S. B., Lane, D. M., & Winn, P. (1985). Ibotenic acid lesions of the lateral hypothalamus: Comparison with 6-hydroxydopamine-induced sensorimotor deficits. *Neuroscience, 14,* 509–518.

Durany, N., Michel, T., Zochling, R., Boissl, K. W., Cruz-Sanchez, F. F., Riederer, P., et al. (2001). Brain-derived neurotrophic factor and neurotrophin 3 in schizophrenic psychoses. *Schizophrenia Research, 52,* 79–86.

Dutton, D. G., & Aron, A. P. (1974). Some evidence for heightened sexual attraction under conditions of high anxiety. *Journal of Personality and Social Psychology, 30,* 510–517.

Duzel, E., Picton, T. W., Cabeza, R., Yonelinas, A. P., Scheich, H., Heinze, H. J., et al. (2001). Comparative electrophysiological and hemodynamic measures of neural activation during memory-retrieval. *Human Brain Mapping, 13,* 104–123.

Dykens, E. M., Hodapp, R. M., & Leckman, J. F. (1994). *Behavior and development in fragile X syndrome.* Thousand Oaks, CA: Sage.

Dykes, R. W. (1983). Parallel processing of somatosensory information: A theory. *Brain Research, 287,* 47–115.

Eaker, E. D., Sullivan, L. M., Kelly-Hayes, M., D'Agostino, R. B., Sr., & Benjamin, E. J. (2004). Anger and hostility predict the development of atrial fibrillation in men in the Framingham Offspring Study. *Circulation, 109,* 1267–1271.

Ebadi, M., Govitrapong, P., Phansuwan-Pujito, P., Nelson, F., & Reiter, R. J. (1998). Pineal opioid receptors and analgesic action of melatonin. *Journal of Pineal Research, 24,* 193–200.

Edwards, J. S., & Palka, J. (1971). Neural regeneration: Delayed formation of central contacts by insect sensory cells. *Science, 172,* 591–594.

Eid, J., Johnsen, B. H., Saus, E. R., & Risberg, J. (2004). Stress and coping in a week-long disabled submarine exercise. *Aviation, Space, and Environmental Medicine, 75,* 616–621.

Eisenberger, N. I., Lieberman, M. D., & Williams, K. D. (2003). Does rejection hurt? An fMRI study of social exclusion. *Science, 302,* 290–292.

Electromagnetic Stimulation. (2000–2006). Electromagnetic stimulation shows promise for treatment-resistant depression. Retrieved March 10, 2006, from http://www.healthyplace.com/Communities/Depression/treatment/tms/index.asp

Eliot, R. S. (1979). *Stress and the major cardiovascular disorders.* Mount Kisco, NY: Futura.

Elliott, R. (2003). Executive functions and their disorders. *British Medical Bulletin, 65,* 49–59.

Ellison, G. (1995). The N-methyl-D-aspartate antagonists phencyclidine, ketamine and dizocilpine as both behavioral and anatomical models of the dementias. *Brain Research. Brain Research Reviews, 20,* 250–267.

Elsworth, J. D., Brittan, M. S., Taylor, J. R., Sladek, J. R., Jr., al-Tikriti, M. S., Zea-Ponce, Y., et al. (1996). Restoration of dopamine transporter density in the striatum of fetal ventral mesencephalon-grafted, but not sham-grafted, MPTP-treated parkinsonian monkeys. *Cell Transplantation, 5,* 315–325.

Emre, M. (2003). Dementia associated with Parkinson's disease. *Lancet. Neurology, 2,* 229–237.

Engel, J., Jr. (1992). Recent advances in surgical treatment of temporal lobe epilepsy. *Acta Neurologica Scandinavica. Supplementum, 140,* 71–80.

Engen, T. (1982). *The perception of odors.* New York: Academic Press.

Engleman, H. M., Kingshott, R. N., Martin, S. E., & Douglas, N. J. (2000). Cognitive function in the sleep apnea/hypopnea syndrome (SAHS). *Sleep, 23,* S102–S108.

Enz, R. (2001). GABA(C) receptors: A molecular view. *Biological Chemistry, 382,* 1111–1122.

Epstein, A. N., Fitzsimons, J. T., & Rolls, B. J. (1970). Drinking induced by injection of angiotensin into the brain of the rat. *Journal of Physiology, 210,* 457–474.

Ergenzinger, E. R., Glasier, M. M., Hahm, J. O., & Pons, T. P. (1998). Cortically induced thalamic plasticity in the primate somatosensory system. *Nature Neuroscience, 1,* 226–229.

Erhardt, S., Hajos, M., Lindberg, A., & Engberg, G. (2000). Nicotine-induced excitation of locus coeruleus neurons is blocked by elevated levels of endogenous kynurenic acid. *Synapse, 37,* 104–108.

Erlacher, D., & Schredl, M. (2004). Time required for motor activity in lucid dreams. *Perceptual and Motor Skills, 99,* 1239–1242.

Ernst, M., Moolchan, E. T., & Robinson, M. L. (2001). Behavioral and neural consequences of prenatal exposure to nicotine. *Journal of the American Academy of Child and Adolescent Psychiatry, 40,* 630—641.

Ervin, F. R., Mark, V. H., & Stevens, J. R. (1969). Behavioral and affective response to brain stimulation in man. In J. Zubin & C. Shagass (Eds.), *Neurobiological aspects of psychopathology* (pp. 54–65). New York: Grune & Stratton.

Eskandar, E. N., Shinobu, L. A., Penney, J. B., Jr., Cosgrove, G. R., & Counihan, T. J. (2000). Stereotactic pallidotomy performed without using microelectrode guidance in patients with Parkinson's disease: Surgical technique and 2-year results. *Journal of Neurosurgery, 92,* 375–383.

Estes, W. K. (1999). Models of human memory: A 30-year retrospective. In C. Izawa (Ed.), *On human memory: Evolution, progress, and reflections on the 30th anniversary of the Atkinson-Shiffrin model* (pp. 59–86). Mahwah, NJ: Erlbaum.

Estok, P. J., & Rudy, E. B. (1996). The relationship between eating disorders and running in women. *Research in Nursing & Health, 19,* 377–387.

Ethell, D. W., & Buhler, L. A. (2003). Fas ligand-mediated apoptosis in degenerative disorders of the brain. *Journal of Clinical Immunology, 23,* 439–446.

Ettenberg, A., Pettit, H. O., Bloom, F. E., & Koob, G. F. (1982). Heroin and cocaine intravenous self-administration in rats: Mediation by separate neural systems. *Psychopharmacology (Berlin), 78,* 204–209.

Eustace, L. W., Kang, D. H., & Coombs, D. (2003). Fetal alcohol syndrome: A growing concern for health care professionals. *Journal of Obstetric, Gynecologic, and Neonatal Nursing, 32,* 215–221.

Everitt, B. J., & Stacey, P. (1987). Studies of instrumental behavior with sexual reinforcement in male rats (*Rattus norvegicus*): II. Effects of preoptic area lesions, castration, and testosterone. *Journal of Comparative Psychology, 101,* 407–419.

Fabbro, F., Tavano, A., Corti, S., Bresolin, N., De Fabritiis, P., & Borgatti, R. (2004). Long-term neuropsychological deficits after cerebellar infarctions in two young adult twins. *Neuropsychologia, 42,* 536–545.

Factor, S. A., & Friedman, J. H. (1997). The emerging role of clozapine in the treatment of movement disorders. *Movement Disorders, 12,* 483–496.

Fadda, P., Scherma, M., Fresu, A., Collu, M., & Fratta, W. (2003). Baclofen antagonizes nicotine-, cocaine-, and morphine-induced dopamine release in the nucleus accumbens of rat. *Synapse, 50,* 1–6.

Fannon, D., Tennakoon, L., Sumich, A., O'Ceallaigh, S., Doku, V., Chitnis, X., et al. (2000). Third ventricle enlargement and developmental delay in first-episode psychosis: Preliminary findings. *British Journal of Psychiatry, 177,* 354–359.

Fantini, M. L., Ferini-Strambi, L., & Montplaisir, J. (2005). Idiopathic REM sleep behavior disorder: Toward a better nosologic definition. *Neurology, 64,* 780–786.

Faraday, A. (1974). *The dream game.* New York: Harper & Row.

Farah, M. J. (2000). *The cognitive neuroscience of vision.* Malden, MA: Blackwell.

Faraone, S. V., Skol, A. D., Tsuang, D. W., Bingham, S., Young, K. A., Prabhudesai, S., et al. (2002). Linkage of chromosome 13q32 to schizophrenia in a large veterans affairs cooperative study sample. *American Journal of Medical Genetics, 114,* 598–604.

Farbman, A. I. (1994). The cellular basis of olfaction. *Endeavour, 18,* 2–8.

Farbman, A. I. (1997). Injury-stimulated neurogenesis in sensory systems. *Advances in Neurology, 72,* 157–161.

Fatemi, S. H., Earle, J., Kanodia, R., Kist, D., Emamian, E. S., Patterson, P. H., et al. (2002). Prenatal viral infection leads to pyramidal cell atrophy and macrocephaly in adulthood: Implications for genesis of autism and schizophrenia. *Cellular and Molecular Neurobiology, 22,* 25–33.

Fava, M. (2003). The role of serotonergic and noradrenergic neurotransmitter systems in the treatment of psychological and physical symptoms of depression. *Journal of Clinical Psychiatry, 64,* 26–29.

Fawcett, J. W., Rosser, A. E., & Dunnett, S. B. (Eds.). (2002). *Brain damage, brain repair.* Oxford: Oxford University Press.

Federmeier, K. D., Kleim, J. A., & Greenough, W. T. (2002). Learning-induced multiple synapse formation in rat cerebellar cortex. *Neuroscience Letters, 332,* 180–184.

Federoff, I. C., Polivy, J., & Herman, C. P. (1997). The effect of pre-exposure to food cues on the eating behavior of restrained and unrestrained eaters. *Appetite, 28,* 33–47.

Federoff, I. C., Polivy, J., & Herman, C. P. (2003). The specificity of restrained versus unrestrained eaters' responses to food cues: General desire to eat, or craving for the cued food? *Appetite, 41,* 7–13.

Fendrich, R., Wessinger, C. M., & Gazzaniga, M. S. (2001). Speculations on the neural basis of islands of blindsight. *Progress in Brain Research, 134,* 353–366.

Ferguson, C. P., & Pigott, T. A. (2000). Anorexia and bulimia nervosa: Neurobiology and pharmacotherapy. *Behavior Therapy, 31,* 237–263.

Ferini-Strambi, L., & Zucconi, M. (2000). REM sleep behavior disorder. *Clinical Neurophysiology, 111,* S136–S140.

Fernandez, H. H., Friedman, J. H., Jacques, C., & Rosenfeld, M. (1999). Quetiapine for the treatment of drug-induced psychosis in Parkinson's disease. *Movement Disorders, 14,* 484–487.

Fernandez, J. R., & Allison, D. B. (2004). Rimonabant Sanofi-Synthelabo. *Current Opinion in Investigational Drugs, 5,* 430–435.

Fernandez-Espejo, E. (2004). Pathogenesis of Parkinson's disease: Prospects of neuroprotective and restorative therapies. *Molecular Neurobiology, 29,* 15–30.

Ferrari, P. F., Galleses, V., Rizzolatti, G., & Fogassi, L. (2003). Mirror neurons responding to the observation of ingestive and communicative mouth actions in the monkey ventral premotor cortex. *European Journal of Neuroscience, 17,* 1703–1714.

Ficca, G., & Salzarulo, P. (2004). What in sleep is for memory? *Sleep Medicine, 5,* 225–230.

Field, A. E., Austin, S. B., Taylor, C. B., Malspeis, S., Rosner, B., Rockett, H. R., et al. (2003). Relation between dieting and weight change among preadolescents and adolescents. *Pediatrics, 112,* 900–906.

Files, F. J., Denning, C. E., & Samson, H. H. (1998). Effects of the atypical antipsychotic remoxipride on alcohol self-administration. *Pharmacology, Biochemistry, and Behavior, 59,* 281–285.

Fin, C., Da Cunha, C., Bromberg, E., Schmitz, P. K., Bianchin, M., Medina, J. H., et al. (1995). Experiments suggesting a role for nitric oxide in the hippocampus in memory processes. *Neurobiology of Learning and Memory, 63,* 113–115.

Finger, S. (1994). *Origins of neuroscience: A history of explorations into brain function.* New York: Oxford University Press.

Finger, S. (2000). *Minds behind the brains: A history of the pioneers and their discoveries.* New York: Oxford University Press.

Fink, G. R., Halligan, P. W., Marshall, J. C., Frith, C. D., Frackowiak, R. S. J., & Dolan, R. J. (1996). Where in the brain does visual attention select the forest and the trees? *Nature, 382,* 626–628.

Fink, M. (2001). Convulsive therapy: A review of the first 55 years. *Journal of Affective Disorders, 63,* 1–15.

Fiorino, D. F., Coury, A., Fibiger, H. C., & Phillips, A. G. (1993). Electrical stimulation of reward sites in the ventral tegmental area increases dopamine transmission in the nucleus accumbens of the rat. *Behavioural Brain Research, 55,* 131–141.

Fisch, H., Hyun, G., Golden, R., Hensle, T. W., Olsson, C. A., & Liberson, G. L. (2003). The influence of paternal age on Down syndrome. *Journal of Urology, 169,* 2275–2278.

Fitzpatrick, D. C., Kuwada, S., & Batra, R. (2002). Transformations in processing interaural time differences between the superior olivary complex and inferior colliculus: Beyond the Jeffress model. *Hearing Research, 168,* 79–89.

Fitzsimons, T. L., & Le Magnen, J. (1969). Eating as a regulatory control of drinking in the rat. *Journal of Comparative and Physiological Psychology, 67,* 273–283.

Flanagan-Cato, L. M., Calizo, L. H., & Daniels, D. (2001). The synaptic organization of VMH neurons that mediate the effects of estrogen on sexual behavior. *Hormones and Behavior, 40,* 178–182.

Fletcher, P. J. (1998). A comparison of the effects of risperidone, raclopride, and ritanserin on intravenous self-administration of d-amphetamine. *Pharmacology, Biochemistry, and Behavior, 60,* 55–60.

Floter, A., Nathorst-Boos, J., Carlstrom, K., & von Schoultz, B. (2002). Addition of testosterone to estrogen replacement therapy in oophorectomized women: Effects on sexuality and well-being. *Climacteric, 5,* 357–365.

Flourens, P. J. M. (1965). Pierre Jean Marie Flourens on the functions of the brain (M. D. Boring, Trans.). In R. J. Herrnstein & E. G. Boring (Eds.), *A source book in the history of psychology.* Cambridge, MA: Harvard University Press. (Original work published 1824)

Flynn, J. P. (1972). Patterning mechanisms, patterned reflexes, and attack behavior in cats. In J. K. Cole & D. D. Jensen (Eds.), *Nebraska symposium on motivation* (pp. 125–153). Lincoln, NE: University of Nebraska Press.

Fogarty, F., Russell, J. M., Newman, S. C., & Bland, R. C. (1994). Epidemiology of psychiatric disorders in Edmonton. Mania. *Acta Psychiatrica Scandinavica. Supplementum, 376,* 16–23.

Fogoros, R. N. (2006). FDA disappoints on Rimonabant. Retrieved April 25, 2006, from http://heartdisease.about.com/b/a/245084.htm

Foley, A. G., Hedigan, K., Roullet, P., Moricard, Y., Murphy, K. J., Sara, S. J., et al. (2003). Consolidation of memory for odour-reward association requires transplant polysialylation of the neural cell adhesion molecule in the rat hippocampal dentate gyrus. *The Journal of Neuroscience Research, 74,* 570–576.

Folic Acid. (2001, July 26). Folic acid 'doubles twin chance'. *BBC News.* Retrieved April 23, 2004, from http://news.bbc.co.uk/1/hi/health/1456028.stm

Folic Acid Information. (2001). Folic acid information: Folic acid fortification begins. Retrieved July 23, 2001, from http://www.sbaa.org/html/sbaa_folic.html

Fonberg, E. (1988). Dominance and aggression. *International Journal of Neuroscience, 41,* 201–213.

Ford, C. S., & Beach, F. A. (1951). *Patterns of sexual behavior.* New York: Harper Colophon Books.

Formisano, E., Kim, D. S., Di Salle, F., van de Moortele, P. F., Ugurbil, K., & Goebel, R. (2003). Mirror-symmetric tonotopic maps in human primary auditory cortex. *Neuron, 40,* 859–869.

Foster, R. G., Argamaso, S., Cloeman, S., Colwell, C. S., Lederman, A., & Provencio, I. (1993). Photoreceptors regulating circadian behavior: A mouse model. *Journal of Biological Rhythms, 8,* S17–S23.

Fox, M. J. (2002). *Lucky man: A memoir.* New York: Hyperion.

Frank, M. E. (1985). On the neural code for sweet and salty taste. In D. W. Pfaff (Ed.), *Taste, olfaction, and the central nervous system* (pp. 107–128). New York: Rockefeller University Press.

Franken, I. H. (2003). Drug craving and addiction: Integrating psychological and neuropsychopharmacological approaches. *Progress in Neuro-Psychopharmacology & Biological Psychiatry, 27,* 563–579.

Franzek, E., & Beckmann, H. (1998). Different genetic background of schizophrenia spectrum psychoses: A twin study. *American Journal of Psychiatry, 155,* 76–83.

Franzen, E. A., & Myers, R. E. (1973). Neural control of social behavior: Prefrontal and anterior temporal cortex. *Neuropsychologia, 11,* 141–157.

Franzon, R. C., Montenegro, M. A., Guimaraes, C. A., Guerreiro, C. A., Cendes, F., & Guerreiro, M. M. (2004). Clinical, electroencephalographic, and behavioral features of temporal lobe epilepsy in childhood. *Journal of Child Neurology, 19,* 418–423.

Freed, C. R., Greene, P. E., Breeze, R. E., Tsai, W. Y., DuMouchel, W., Kao, R., et al. (2001). Transplantation of embryonic dopamine neurons for severe Parkinson's disease. *New England Journal of Medicine, 344,* 710–719.

Freeman, E. W. (2004). Luteal phase administration of agents for the treatment of premenstrual dysphoric disorder. *CNS Drugs, 18,* 453–468.

Freud, S. (1938). The interpretation of dreams. In A. A. Brill (Ed. and Trans.), *The basic writings of Sigmund Freud* (pp. 183–549). New York: The Modern Library.

Frey, W. H., & Langseth, M. (1985). *Crying: The mystery of tears.* New York: Winston Press.

Fried, P. A. (2002). Adolescents prenatally exposed to marijuana: Examination of facets of complex behaviors and comparisons with the influence of in utero cigarettes. *Journal of Clinical Pharmacology, 42,* 97S–102S.

Fried, P. A., Watkinson, B., & Gray, R. (2003). Differential effects on cognitive functioning in 13- to 16-year-olds prenatally exposed to cigarettes and marihuana. *Neurotoxicology and Teratology, 25,* 427–436.

Friedman, M. I., & Stricker, E. M. (1976). The physiological psychology of hunger: A physiological perspective. *Psychological Review, 83,* 409–431.

Friedman, M., & Rosenman, R. H. (1974). *Type A behavior and your heart.* New York: Knopf.

Friedman, M., Byers, S. O., Diamant, J., & Rosenman, R. H. (1975). Plasma catecholamine response of coronary-prone subjects (type A) to a specific challenge. *Metabolism, 24,* 205–210.

Friedman-Hill, S. R., Robertson, L. C., & Treisman, A. (1995). Parietal contributions to visual feature binding: Evidence from a patient with bilateral lesions. *Science, 269,* 853–855.

Fritsch, G., & Hitzig, E. (1960). On the electrical excitability of the cerebrum. In G. Von Bonin (Trans.), *Some papers on the cerebral cortex.* Springfield, IL: Charles C. Thomas. (Original work published 1870)

Fukuda, M., Ono, T., Nishino, H., & Nakamura, K. (1986). Neuronal responses in monkey lateral hypothalamus during operant feeding behavior. *Brain Research Bulletin, 17,* 879–883.

Fulton, J. F., & Jacobsen, C. F. (1935). The functions of the frontal lobes: A comparative study in monkeys, chimpanzees, and man. *Advances in Modern Biology, 4,* 113–123.

Fuster, J. M. (2004). Upper processing stages of the perception-action cycle. *Trends in Cognitive Sciences, 8,* 143–145.

Fuster, J. M., Bodner, M., & Kroger, J. K. (2000). Cross-modal and cross-temporal association in neurons of frontal cortex. *Nature, 405,* 347–351.

Gabrieli, J. D. (1998). Cognitive neuroscience of human memory. *Annual Review of Psychology, 49,* 87–115.

Gabrieli, J. D., Cohen, N. J., & Corkin, S. (1988). The impaired learning of semantic knowledge following bilateral medial temporal-lobe resection. *Brain & Cognition, 7,* 157–177.

Gackenbach, J., & LaBerge, S. (1988). *Conscious mind, sleeping brain: Perspectives on lucid dreaming.* New York: Plenum.

Galaburda, A. M., & Bellugi, U. (2000). V. Multi-level analysis of cortical neuroanatomy in Williams syndrome. *Journal of Cognitive Neuroscience, 12,* 74–88.

Galaburda, A. M., Wang, P. P., Bellugi, U., & Rossen, M. (1994). Cytoarchitectonic anomalies in a genetically based disorder: Williams syndrome. *Neuroreport, 5,* 753–757.

Gale, C., & Martyn, C. (1998). Larks and owls and health, wealth, and wisdom. *BMJ, 317,* 1675–1677.

Gale, S. M., Castracane, V. D., & Mantzoros, C. S. (2004). Energy homeostasis, obesity and eating disorders: Recent advances in endocrinology. *Journal of Nutrition, 134,* 295–298.

Galynker, I. I., Cai, J., Ongseng, F., Finestone, H., Dutta, E., & Serseni, D. (1998). Hypofrontality and negative symptoms in major depressive disorder. *Journal of Nuclear Medicine, 39,* 608–612.

Gammie, S. C., Huang, P. L., & Nelson, R. J. (2000). Maternal aggression in endothelial nitric oxide synthase-deficient mice. *Hormones and Behavior, 38,* 13–20.

Gandour, J., Larsen, J., Dechongkit, S., Ponglorpisit, S., & Khunadorn, F. (1995). Speech prosody in affective contexts in Thai patients with right hemisphere lesions. *Brain and Language, 51,* 422–443.

Gangitano, M., Mottaghy, F. M., Pascual-Leone, A. (2004). Modulation of premotor mirror neuron activity during observation of unpredictable grasping movements. *European Journal of Neuroscience, 20,* 2193–2202.

Gann, H., Feige, B., Hohagen, F., van Calker, D., Geiss, D., & Dieter, R. (2001). Sleep and the cholinergic rapid eye movement sleep induction test in patients with primary alcohol dependence. *Biological Psychiatry, 50,* 383–390.

Gao, J., Zhang, J. X., & Xu, T. L. (2002). Modulation of serotonergic projection from dorsal raphe nucleus to basolateral amygdala on sleep-waking cycle of rats. *Brain Research, 945,* 60–70.

Garb, J. L., & Stunkard, A. J. (1974). Taste aversions in man. *American Journal of Psychiatry, 131,* 1204–1207.

Garbarino, S., Beelke, M., Costa, G., Violani, C., Lucidi, F., Ferrillo, F., et al. (2002). Brain function and effects of shift work: Implications for clinical neuropharmacology. *Neuropsychobiology, 45,* 50–56.

Garbutt, J. C., Krantzler, H. R., O'Malley, S. S., Gastfriend, D. R., Pettinati, H. M., Silverman, B. L., et al. (2005). Efficacy and tolerability of long-acting injectable naltrexone for alcohol dependence: A randomized controlled trial. *JAMA, 293,* 1617–1625.

Garcia, J., Kimeldorf, D. J., & Hunt, E. L. (1961). The use of ionizing radiation as a motivating stimulus. *Psychological Review, 68,* 383–395.

Garcia, J., Kimeldorf, D. J., & Koelling, R. A. (1955). Conditioned aversion to saccharin resulting from exposure to gamma radiation. *Science, 122,* 157–158.

Gardiner, T. W., & Stricker, E. M. (1985). Impaired drinking responses of rats with lesions of nucleus medianus: Circadian dependence. *American Journal of Physiology, 248,* R224–R230.

Gardner, E. L. (2002). Addictive potential of cannabinoids: The underlying neurobiology. *Chemistry and Physics of Lipids, 121,* 267–290.

Gardner, H. (1983). *Frames of mind: The theory of multiple intelligences.* New York: Basic Books.

Gardner, H. (2003, April). *Multiple intelligences after twenty years.* Paper presented at the meeting of the American Educational Research Association, Chicago, IL.

Garfinkel, P. E., Kline, S. A., Stancer, H. C. (1973). Treatment of anorexia nervosa using operant conditioning techniques. *Journal of Nervous and Mental Disease, 157,* 428–433.

Gartrell, N. K., Louiaux, D. L., & Chase, T. N. (1977). Plasma testosterone in homosexual and heterosexual women. *American Journal of Psychiatry, 134,* 1117–1118.

Gass, P., Reichardt, H. M., Strekalova, T., Henn, F., & Tronche, F. (2001). Mice with targeted mutations of glucocorticoid and mineralocorticoid receptors: Models for depression and anxiety. *Physiology & Behavior, 73,* 811–825.

Gawande, A. (1998, September 21). The pain perplex. *New Yorker,* 86, 88, 90, 92–94.

Gazzaniga, M. S. (1967). The split brain in man. *Scientific American, 217,* 24–29.

Gazzaniga, M. S. (1977). Consistency and diversity in brain organization. *Annals of the New York Academy of Sciences, 299,* 415–423.

Gazzaniga, M. S. (1983). Right hemisphere language following brain bisection: A 20-year perspective. *American Psychologist, 38,* 525–537.

Gazzaniga, M. S. (1989). Organization of the human brain. *Science, 245,* 947–952.

Gazzaniga, M. S. (1995). Consciousness and the cerebral hemispheres. In M. S. Gazzaniga (Ed.), *The cognitive neurosciences* (pp. 1391–1400). Cambridge, MA: The MIT Press.

Gazzaniga, M. S. (1998). The split brain revisited. *Scientific American, 279,* 50–55.

Gazzaniga, M. S., & LeDoux, J. E. (1978). *The integrated mind.* New York: Plenum.

Gazzaniga, M. S., & Sperry, R. W. (1967). Language after section of the cerebral commissures. *Brain, 90,* 131–148.

Gazzaniga, M. S., Fendrich, R., & Wessinger, C. M. (1994). Blindsight reconsidered. *Current Directions in Psychological Science, 3,* 93–96.

Gazzaniga, M. S., LeDoux, J. E., & Wilson, D. H. (1977). Language, praxis, and the right hemisphere: Clues to some mechanisms of consciousness. *Neurology, 27,* 1144–1147.

Geddes, J. R., Burgess, S., Hawton, K., Jamison, K., & Goodwin, G. M. (2004). Long-term lithium therapy for bipolar disorder: Systematic review and meta-analysis of randomized controlled trials. *American Journal of Psychiatry, 161,* 217–222.

Gegenfurtner, K. R., & Kiper, D. C. (2003). Color vision. *Annual Review of Neuroscience, 26,* 181–206.

Georgopoulos, A. P., Taira, M., & Lukashin, A. (1993). Cognitive neurophysiology of the motor cortex. *Science, 260,* 47–52.

Geracioti, T. D., Jr., Kling, M. A., Joseph-Vanderpool, J. R., Kanayama, S., Rosenthal, N. E., Gold, P. W., et al. (1989). Meal-related cholecystokinin secretion in eating and affective disorders. *Psychopharmacology Bulletin, 25,* 444–449.

Geracioti, T. D., Jr., & Liddle, R. A. (1988). Impaired cholecystokinin secretion in bulimia nervosa. *New England Journal of Medicine, 319,* 683–688.

Geracioti, T. D., Jr., Liddle, R. A., Altemus, M., Demitrack, M. A., & Gold, P. W. (1992). Regulation of appetite and cholecystokinin secretion in anorexia nervosa. *American Journal of Psychiatry, 149,* 958–961.

Geracioti, T. D., Jr., Loosen, P. T., Ekhator, N. N., Schmidt, D., Chambliss, B., Baker, D. G., et al. (1997). Uncoupling of serotonergic and noradrenergic systems in depression: Preliminary evidence from continuous cerebrospinal fluid sampling. *Depression & Anxiety, 6,* 89–94.

Geraud, G., Arné-Bès, M. C., Güell, A, & Bes, A. (1987). Reversibility of hemodynamic hypofrontality in schizophrenia. *Journal of Cerebral Blood Flow and Metabolism, 7,* 9–12.

Gerra, G., Borella, F., Zaimovic, A., Moi, G., Bussandri, M., Bubici, C., et al. (2004). Buprenorphine versus methadone for opioid dependence: Predictor variables for treatment outcome. *Drug and Alcohol Dependence, 75,* 37–45.

Gerra, G., Marcato, A., Caccavari, R., Fontanesi, B., Delsignore, R., Fertonani, G., et al. (1995). Clonidine and opiate receptor antagonists in the treatment of heroin addiction. *Journal of Substance Abuse Treatment, 12,* 35–41.

Gerrits, M. A., & van Ree, J. M. (1996). Effects of nucleus accumbens dopamine depletion on motivational aspects involved in initiation of cocaine and heroin self-administration in rats. *Brain Research, 713,* 114–124.

Geschwind, N. (1991). Specializations of the human brain. In W. S.-Y. Wang (Ed.), *Emergence of language: Development and evolution: Readings from "Scientific American" magazine* (pp. 72–87). New York: W. H. Freeman.

Geschwind, N. (1992). The organization of language and the brain. In S. M. Kosslyn & R. A. Andersen (Eds.), *Frontiers in cognitive neuroscience* (pp. 634–640). Cambridge, MA: The MIT Press.

Geschwind, N., & Galaburda, N. (1987). *Cerebral lateralization: Biological mechanisms, associations and pathology.* Cambridge, MA: The MIT Press.

Ghez, C., Hening, W., & Gordon, J. (1991). Organization of voluntary movement. *Current Opinion in Neurobiology, 1,* 664–671.

Gianola, S., Savio, T., Schwab, M. E., & Rossi, F. (2003). Cell-autonomous mechanisms and myelin-associated factors contribute to the development of Purkinje axon intracortical plexus in the rat cerebellum. *The Journal of Neuroscience, 23,* 4613–4624.

Gianoulakis, C. (2001). Influence of the endogenous opioid system on high alcohol consumption and genetic predisposition to alcoholism. *Journal of Psychiatry & Neuroscience, 26,* 304–318.

Gianoulakis, C. (2004). Endogenous opioids and addiction to alcohol and other drugs of abuse. *Current Topics in Medicinal Chemistry, 4,* 39–50.

Gibson, E. L., & Booth, D. A. (2000). Food-conditioned odour rejection in the late stages of the meal, mediating learnt control of meal volume by aftereffects of food consumption. *Appetite, 34,* 295–303.

Giduck, S. A., Threatte, R. M., & Kare, M. R. (1987). Cephalic reflexes: Their role in digestion and possible roles in absorption and metabolism. *Journal of Nutrition, 117,* 1191–1196.

Giles, D. E., Biggs, M. M., Rush, A. J., & Roffwarg, H. P. (1988). Risk factors in families of unipolar depression. I. Psychiatric illness and reduced REM latency. *Journal of Affective Disorders, 14,* 51–59.

Giles, D. E., Kupfer, D. J., Rush, A. J., & Roffwarg, H. P. (1998). Controlled comparison of electrophysiological sleep in families of probands with unipolar depression. *American Journal of Psychiatry, 155,* 192–199.

Girard, B., Cuzin, V., Guillot, A., Gurney, K. N., & Prescott, T. J. (2003). A basal ganglia inspired model of action selection evaluated in a robotic survival task. *Journal of Integrative Neuroscience, 2,* 179–200.

Gizzi, M. S., Katz, E., Schumer, R. A., & Movshon, J. A. (1990). Selectivity for orientation and direction of motion of single neurons in cat striate and extrastriate visual cortex. *Journal of Neurophysiology, 63,* 1529–1543.

Gladfelter, W. E., & Brobeck, J. R. (1962). Decreased spontaneous locomotor activity in the rat induced by hypothalamic lesions. *American Journal of Physiology, 203,* 811–817.

Glass, D. C. (1977). *Behavior patterns, stress, and coronary disease.* Hillsdale, NJ: Erlbaum.

Glazener, C. M., Evans, J. H., & Peto, R. E. (2003). Alarm interventions for nocturnal enuresis in children. *Cochrane Database of Systematic Reviews,* CD002911.

Glowa, J. R., Rice, K. C., Matecka, D., & Rothman, R. B. (1997). Phentermine/fenfluramine decreases cocaine self-administration in rhesus monkeys. *Neuroreport, 8,* 1347–1351.

Goda, Y., & Davis, G. W. (2003). Mechanisms of synapse assembly and disassembly. *Neuron, 40,* 243–264.

Goda, Y., & Sudhof, T. C. (1997). Calcium regulation of neurotransmitter release: Reliably unreliable? *Current Opinion in Cell Biology, 9,* 513–518.

Goeders, N. E., Lane, J. D., & Smith, J. E. (1984). Self-administration of methionine enkephalin into the nucleus accumbens. *Pharmacology, Biochemistry, and Behavior, 20,* 451–455.

Goff, D. C., & Evins, A. E. (1998). Negative symptoms in schizophrenia: Neurobiological models and treatment response. *Harvard Review of Psychiatry, 6,* 59–77.

Gold, P. W., & Chrousos, G. P. (1999). The endocrinology of melancholic and atypical depression: Relation to neurocircuitry and somatic consequences. *Proceedings of the Association of American Physicians, 111,* 22–34.

Gold, P. W., Goodwin, F. K., & Chrousos, G. P. (1988). Clinical and biochemical manifestations of depression: Relation of the neurobiology of stress: II. *New England Journal of Medicine, 319,* 413–420.

Gold, R. M. (1973). Hypothalamic obesity: The myth of the ventromedial nucleus. *Science, 182,* 488–490.

Gold, R. M., Jones, A. P., & Sawchenko, P. E. (1977). Paraventricular area: Critical focus of a longitudinal neurocircuitry mediating food intake. *Physiology & Behavior, 18,* 1111–1119.

Goldberg, J. L., & Barres, B. A. (2000). The relationship between neuronal survival and regeneration. *Annual Review of Neuroscience, 23,* 579–612.

Goldenberg, G., & Spatt, J. (1994). Influence of size and site of cerebral lesions on spontaneous recovery of aphasia and on success of language therapy. *Brain & Language, 47,* 684–698.

Goldman, B. D. (1999). The circadian timing system and reproduction in mammals. *Steroids, 64,* 679–685.

Goldstein, A. (1976). Opioid peptide (endorphins) in pituitary and brain. *Science, 193,* 1081–1086.

Goldstein, B., Little, J. W., & Harris, R. M. (1997). Axonal sprouting following incomplete spinal cord injury: An experimental model. *Journal of Spinal Cord Medicine, 20,* 200–206.

Goldstein, I., Lue, T. F., Padma-Nathan, H., Rosen, R. C., Steers, W. D., & Wicker, P. A. (1998). Oral sildenafil in the treatment of erectile dysfunction. Sildenafil Study Group. *New England Journal of Medicine, 338,* 1397–1404.

Golla, H., Thier, P., & Haarmeier, T. (2005). Disturbed overt but normal covert shifts of attention in adult cerebellar patients. *Brain, 128,* 1525–1535.

Gonzalez, F., Perez, R., Justo, M. S., & Ulibarrena, C. (2001). Binocular interaction and sensitivity to horizontal disparity in visual cortex in the awake monkey. *International Journal of Neuroscience, 107,* 147–160.

Goodale, M. A., & Humphrey, G. K. (1998). The objects of action and perception. *Cognition, 67,* 181–207.

Goodale, M. A., & Milner, A. D. (1992). Separate visual pathways for perception and action. *Trends in Neuroscience, 15,* 20–25.

Goodale, M. A., Meenan, J. P., Bülthoff, H. H., Nicolle, D. A., Murphy, K. J., & Racicot, C. I. (1994). Separate neural pathways for the visual analysis of object shape in perception and prehension. *Current Biology, 4,* 604–610.

Goode, E. (1998). *Drugs in American society* (5th ed.). New York: McGraw-Hill.

Goodglass, H., Kaplan, E., & Barresi, B. (2001a). *The assessment of aphasia and related disorders* (3rd ed.). Philadelphia: Lippincott Williams & Wilkins.

Goodglass, H., Kaplan, E., & Barresi, B. (2001b). *Boston Diagnostic Aphasia Examination stimulus cards* (3rd ed.). Philadelphia: Lippincott Williams & Wilkins.

Goodwin, G. M., & Geddes, J. R. (2003). Latest maintenance data on lithium in bipolar disorder. *European Neuropsychopharmacology, 13,* S51–S55.

Goodwin, M., Gooding, K. M., & Regnier, F. (1979). Sex pheromone in the dog. *Science, 203,* 559–561.

Goodyear, B. G., Nicolle, D. A., & Menon, R. S. (2002). High resolution fMRI of ocular dominance columns within the visual cortex of human amblyopes. *Strabismus, 10,* 129–136.

Gordon, N. (1997). Nutrition and cognitive function. *Brain Development, 19,* 165–170.

Gorski, R. A. (1997). Gonadal hormones and the organization of brain structure and function. In D. Magnusson (Ed.), *The lifespan development of individuals: Behavioral, neurobiological, and psychosocial perspectives: A synthesis* (pp. 315–340). New York: Cambridge University Press.

Gorski, R. A. (2002). Hypothalamic imprinting by gonadal steroid hormones. *Advances in Experimental Medicine and Biology, 511,* 57–70.

Gorski, R. A., Harlan, R. E., Jacobson, C. D., Shryne, J. E., & Southam, A. M. (1980). Evidence for the existence of a sexually dimorphic nucleus in the preoptic area of the rat. *Journal of Comparative Neurology, 193,* 529–539.

Gorter, R. W. (1999). Cancer cachexia and cannabinoids. *Forschende Komplementarmedizin, 6*(Supplement 3), 21–22.

Goscinski, I., Kwiatkowski, S., Polak, J., Orlowiejska, M., & Partyk, A. (1997). The Klüver-Bucy syndrome. *Journal of Neurosurgical Sciences, 41,* 269–272.

Gottesman, I. I. (1991). *Schizophrenia genesis: The origins of madness.* New York: W. H. Freeman/Times Books/Henry Holt.

Gottesmann, C. (1988). What the cerveau isolé preparation tells us nowadays about sleep-wake mechanisms? *Neuroscience and Biobehavioral Reviews, 12,* 39–48.

Gottesmann, C. (1996). The transition from slow-wave sleep to paradoxical sleep: Evolving facts and concepts of the neurophysiological processes underlying the intermediate stage of sleep. *Neuroscience and Biobehavioral Reviews, 20,* 367–387.

Gottlieb, B., Beitel, L. K., & Trifiro, M. A. (2004, April 8). Androgen insensitivity syndrome. Retrieved June 30, 2005, from http://www.geneclinics.org/profiles/androgen/details.html

Gotz, J., Streffer, J. R., David, D., Schild, A., Hoerndli, F., Pennanen, L., et al. (2004). Transgenic animal models of Alzheimer's disease and related disorders: Histopathology, behavior and therapy. *Molecular Psychiatry, 9,* 664–683.

Gould, E., Beylin, A., Tanapat, P., Reeves, A., & Shors, T. J. (1999). Learning enhances adult neurogenesis in the hippocampal formation. *Nature Neuroscience, 2,* 260–265.

Gould, E., Reeves, A. J., Graziano, M. S., & Gross, C. G. (1999). Neurogenesis in the neocortex of adult primates. *Science, 286,* 548–552.

Gould, E., & Tanapat, R. (1999). Stress and hippocampal neurogenesis. *Biological Psychiatry, 46,* 1472–1479.

Gould, E., Tanapat, P., Hastings, N. B., & Shors, T. J. (1999). Neurogenesis in adulthood: A possible role in learning. *Trends in Cognitive Sciences, 3,* 186–192.

Goussakov, I. V., Fink, K., Elger, C. E., & Beck, H. (2000). Metaplasticity of mossy fiber synaptic transmission involves altered release probability. *The Journal of Neuroscience, 20,* 3434–3441.

Gowers, S. G., & Shore, A. (2001). Development of weight and shape concerns in the aetiology of eating disorders. *British Journal of Psychiatry, 179,* 236–242.

Grabowski, J. (2001). Complementary examination of medications for drug abuse: Preclinical, human laboratory, and clinical research. In M. E. Carroll & J. B. Overmier (Eds.), *Animal research and human health: Advancing human welfare through behavioral science* (pp. 155–175). Washington, DC: American Psychological Association.

Grady, K. L., Phoenix, C. H., & Young, W. C. (1965). Role of the developing rat testis in differentiation of the neural tissues mediating mating behavior. *Journal of Comparative and Physiological Psychology, 59,* 176–182.

Graham, C. A. (2002). Methods for obtaining menstrual-cycle data in menstrual-synchrony studies: Commentary on Schank (2001). *Journal of Comparative Psychology, 116,* 313–315.

GrandPre, T., Li, S., & Strittmatter, S. M. (2002). Nogo-66 receptor antagonist peptide promotes axonal regeneration. *Nature, 417,* 547–551.

Grant, J., Valian, V., & Karmiloff-Smith, A. (2002). A study of relative clauses in Williams syndrome. *Journal of Child Language, 29,* 403–416.

Grant, M. M., & Weiss, J. M. (2001). Effects of chronic antidepressant drug administration and electroconvulsive shock on locus coeruleus electrophysiologic activity. *Biological Psychiatry, 49,* 117–129.

Grant, S., London, E. D., Newline, D. B., Villemagne, V. L., Liu, X., Contoreggi, C., et al. (1996). Activation of memory circuits during cue-elicited cocaine craving. *Proceedings of the National Academy of Sciences of the United States of America, 93,* 12040–12045.

Grau, J. W., & Joynes, R. L. (2001). Spinal cord injury: From animal research to human therapy. In M. E. Carroll & J. B. Overmier

(Eds.), *Animal research and human health: Advancing human welfare through behavioral science* (pp. 209–226). Washington, DC: American Psychological Association.

Graves, J. A. (2001). From brain determination to testis determination: Evolution of the mammalian sex-determining gene. *Reproduction, Fertility, and Development, 13,* 665–672.

Graves, J. A. (2002a). Evolution of the testis-determining gene—The rise and fall of SRY. *Novartis Foundation Symposium, 244,* 86–97.

Graves, J. A. (2002b). The rise and fall of SRY. *Trends in Genetics, 18,* 259–264.

Gray, C. M., Engel, A. K., Konig, P., & Singer, W. (1992). Synchronization of oscillatory neuronal responses in cat striate cortex: Temporal properties. *Visual Neuroscience, 8,* 337–347.

Gray, J. A. (1972). The psychophysical nature of introversion-extroversion: A modification of Eysenck's theory. In V. D. Neblitsyn & J. A. Gray (Eds.), *Biological basis of individual behavior.* New York: Academic Press.

Gray, J. J., & Hoage, C. M. (1990). Bulimia nervosa: Group behavior therapy with exposure plus response prevention. *Psychological Reports, 66,* 667–674.

Gray, K. A., Day, N. L., Leech, S., & Richardson, G. A. (2005). Prenatal marijuana exposure: Effect on child depressive symptoms at ten years of age. *Neurotoxicology and Teratology, 27,* 439–448.

Greco, M. A., Magner, M., Overstreet, D., & Shiromani, P. J. (1998). Expression of cholinergic markers in the pons of Flinders rats. *Brain Research. Molecular Brain Research, 55,* 232–236.

Greek, R., & Greek, J. (2000). Animal research and human disease. *JAMA, 283,* 743.

Green, J. T. (2004). The effects of ethanol on the developing cerebellum and eyeblink classical conditioning. *Cerebellum, 3,* 178–187.

Greenlee, M. W., Lang, H. J., Mergner, T., & Seeger, W. (1995). Visual short-term memory of stimulus velocity in patients with unilateral posterior brain damage. *The Journal of Neuroscience, 15,* 2287–2300.

Greer, M. K., Lyons-Crews, M., Mauldin, L. B., & Brown, F. R., 3rd. (1989). A case study of the cognitive and behavioral deficits of temporal lobe damage in *herpes simplex encephalitis. Journal of Autism and Developmental Disorders, 19,* 317–326.

Greicius, M. (1996). Genetic testing for Huntington's Disease. Retrieved April 28, 2004, from http://www.lkwdpl.org/hdsa/hdgreic.htm

Griebel, G., Perrault, G., & Sanger, D. J. (1999). Orphanin FQ, a novel neuropeptide with anti-stress-like activity. *Brain Research, 836,* 221–224.

Grill-Spector, K., Knouf, N., & Kanwisher, N. (2004). The fusiform face area subserves face perception, not generic within-category identification. *Nature Neuroscience, 7,* 555–562.

Grilo, C. M., & Masheb, R. M. (2000). Onset of dieting vs. binge eating in outpatients with binge eating disorder. *International Journal of Obesity and Related Metabolic Disorders, 24,* 404–409.

Groenewegen, H. J. (2003). The basal ganglia and motor control. *Neural Plasticity, 10,* 107–120.

Groos, G., & Hendriks, J. (1982). Circadian rhythms in electrical discharge of rat suprachiasmatic neurones recorded in vitro. *Neuroscience Letters, 34,* 283–288.

Grossman, F., & Potter, W. Z. (1999). Catecholamines in depression: A cumulative study of urinary norepinephrine and its major metabolites in unipolar and bipolar depressed patients versus healthy volunteers at the NIMH. *Psychiatry Research, 87,* 21–27.

Grossman, S. P. (1972). The ventromedial hypothalamus and aggressive behaviors. *Physiology & Behavior, 9,* 721–725.

Grunhaus, L., Shipley, J. E., Eiser, A., Pande, A. C., Tandon, R., Krahn, D. D., et al. (1997). Sleep-onset rapid eye movement after electroconvulsive therapy is more frequent in patients who respond less well to electroconvulsive therapy. *Biological Psychiatry, 42,* 191–200.

Grunhaus, L., Shipley, J. E., Eiser, A., Pande, A. C., Tandon, R., Remen, A., et al. (1994). Shortened REM latency postECT is associated with rapid recurrence of depressive symptomatology. *Biological Psychiatry, 36,* 214–222.

Grunt, J. A., & Young, W. C. (1952). Differential reactivity of individuals and the response of the male guinea pig to testosterone propionate. *Endocrinology, 51,* 237–248.

Grutzendler, J., & Morris, J. C. (2001). Cholinesterase inhibitors for Alzheimer's disease. *Drugs, 61,* 41–52.

Guarraci, F. A., Megroz, A. B., & Clark, A. S. (2004). Paced mating behavior in the female rat following lesions of three regions responsive to vaginocervical stimulation. *Brain Research, 999,* 40–52.

Guay, A. T., Perez, J. B., Jacobson, J., & Newton, R. A. (2001). Efficacy and safety of sildenafil citrate for treatment of erectile dysfunction in a population with associated organic risk factors. *Journal of Andrology, 22,* 793–797.

Gubbay, J., Collignon, J., Koopman, P., Capel, B., Economou, A., Munsterberg, A., et al. (1990). A gene mapping to the sex-determining region of the mouse Y chromosome is a member of a novel family of embryonically expressed genes. *Nature, 346,* 245–250.

Gucciardi, E., Celasun, N., Ahmad, F., & Stewart, D. E. (2004). Eating disorders. *BMC Women's Health, 4,* S21.

Guimaraes, C. A., Franzon, R. C., Souza, E. A., Schmutzler, K. M., Montenegro, M. A., Queiroz, Lde S., et al. (2004). Abnormal behavior in children with temporal lobe epilepsy and ganglioglioma. *Epilepsy & Behavior, 5,* 788–791.

Gulbenkian, S., Uddman, R., & Edvinsson, L. (2001). Neuronal messengers in the human cerebral circulation. *Peptides, 22,* 995–1007.

Gulevich, G., Dement, W., & Johnson, L. (1966). Psychiatric and EEG observations on a case of prolonged (264 hours) wakefulness. *Archives of General Psychiatry, 15,* 29–35.

Gunston, G. D., Burkimsher, D., Malan, H., & Sive, A. A. (1992). Reversible cerebral shrinkage in kwashiorkor: An MRI study. *Archives of Disease in Childhood, 67,* 1030–1032.

Gupta, P., Banerjee, G., & Nandi, D. N. (1989). Modified Masters Johnson technique in the treatment of sexual inadequacy in males. *Indian Journal of Psychiatry, 31,* 63–69.

Gurney, K., Prescott, T. J., & Redgrave, P. (2001a). A computational model of action selection in the basal ganglia. I. A new functional anatomy. *Biological Cybernetics, 84,* 401–410.

Gurney, K., Prescott, T. J., & Redgrave, P. (2001b). A computational model of action selection in the basal ganglia. II. Analysis and simulation of behaviour. *Biological Cybernetics, 84,* 411–423.

Gurney, K., Prescott, T. J., Wickens, J. R., & Redgrave, P. (2004). Computational models of the basal ganglia: From robots to membranes. *Trends in Neurosciences, 27,* 453–459.

Guthrie, J. P., Ash, R. A., & Bendapudi, V. (1995). Additional validity evidence for a measure of morningness. *Journal of Applied Psychology, 80,* 186–190.

Gutierrez, G., & Domjan, M. (1997). Differences in the sexual conditioned behavior of male and female Japanese quail (*Coturnix japonica*). *Journal of Comparative Psychology, 111,* 135–142.

Gutierrez, J., Alvarez-Ordas, I., Rojo, M., Marin, B., & Menendez-Patterson, A. (1989). Reproductive function and sexual behaviour in female rats exposed to immobilization stress or ACTH injections during gestation. *Physiologia Bohemoslovaca, 38,* 13–20.

Gutierrez, R., De la Cruz, V., Rodriguez-Ortiz, C. J., & Bermudez-Rattoni, F. (2004). Perirhinal cortex muscarinic receptor blockage impairs taste recognition memory formation. *Learning & Memory, 11,* 95–101.

Gutman, M. B., Jones, D. L., & Ciriello, J. (1989). Contribution of nucleus medianus to the drinking and pressor responses to angiotenin II acting at subfornical organ. *Brain Research, 488,* 49–56.

Guzman-Marin, R., Alam, M. N., Szymusiak, R., Drucker-Colin, R., Gong, H., & McGinty, D. (2000). Discharge modulation of rat dorsal raphe neurons during sleep and waking: Effects of preoptic/basal forebrain warming. *Brain Research, 875,* 23–34.

Haber, S. N. (2003). The primate basal ganglia: Parallel and integrative networks. *Journal of Chemical Neuroanatomy, 26,* 317–330.

Habib, M., Gayraud, D., Oliva, A., Regis, J., Salamon, G., & Khalil, R. (1991). Effects of handedness and sex on the morphology of the corpus callosum: A study with brain magnetic resonance imaging. *Brain & Cognition, 16,* 41–61.

Hadland, K. A., Rushworth, M. F., Gaffan, D., & Passingham, R. E. (2003). The effect of cingulate lesions on social behaviour and emotion. *Neuropsychologia, 41,* 919–931.

Haft, J. I. (1974). Cardiovascular injury induced by sympathetic catecholamines. *Progress in Cardiovascular Diseases, 17,* 73–86.

Halac, I., & Zimmerman, D. (2004). Coordinating care for children with Turner syndrome. *Pediatric Annals, 33,* 189–196.

Halford, J. C. (2004). Clinical pharmacology for obesity: Current drugs and those in advanced development. *Current Drug Targets, 5,* 637–646.

Halford, J. C., Cooper, G. D., & Dovey, T. M. (2004). The pharmacology of human appetite suppression. *Current Drug Targets, 5,* 221–240.

Hall, E. J., & Sykes, N. P. (2004). Analgesia for patients with advanced disease: I. *Postgraduate Medical Journal, 80,* 148–154.

Hallett, M. (2001). Plasticity of the human motor cortex and recovery from stroke. *Brain Research: Brain Research Reviews, 36,* 169–174.

Halliday, G., Cullen, K., & Harding, A. (1994). Neuropathological correlates of memory dysfunction in the Wernicke-Korsakoff syndrome. *Alcohol and Alcoholism. Supplement, 2,* 245–251.

Halliday, G. M., McRitchie, D. A., Macdonald, V., Double, K. L., Trent, R. J., & McCusker, E. (1998). Regional specificity of brain atrophy in Huntington's disease. *Experimental Neurology, 154,* 663–672.

Halligan, P. W., & Marshall, J. C. (2001). Graphic neglect—More than the sum of the parts. *NeuroImage, 14,* S91–S97.

Hallschmid, M., Benedict, C., Born, J., Fehm, H. L., & Kern, W. (2004). Manipulating central nervous mechanisms of food intake and body weight regulation by intranasal administration of neuropeptides in man. *Physiology & Behavior, 83,* 55–64.

Halpern, B. P. (2000). Glutamate and the flavor of foods. *Journal of Nutrition, 130,* 910S–914S.

Halpern, J. H., & Pope, H. G., Jr. (2003). Hallucinogen persisting perception disorder: What do we know after 50 years? *Drug and Alcohol Dependence, 69,* 109–119.

Halpern, M., & Martinez-Marcos, A. (2003). Structure and function of the vomeronasal system: An update. *Progress in Neurobiology, 70,* 245–318.

Hamburg, D. A., Lunde, D. T., Moos, R. H., & Yalom, I. D. (1968). Studies of distress in the menstrual cycle and postpartum period. In R. P. Michael (Ed.), *Endocrinology and human behavior* (pp. 94–116). New York: Oxford University Press.

Hamer, D. H., Hu, S., Magnuson, V. L., Hu, N., & Pattatucci, A. M. (1993). A linkage between DNA markers on the X chromosome and male sexual orientation. *Science, 261,* 321–327.

Han, J. S. (2004). Acupuncture and endorphins. *Neuroscience Letters, 361,* 258–261.

Han, P. W., & Liu, A. C. (1966). Obesity and impaired growth of rats force fed 40 days after hypothalamic lesions. *American Journal of Physiology, 211,* 229–231.

Hansson, E., & Ronnback, L. (2003). Glial neuronal signaling in the central nervous system. *The FASEB Journal, 17,* 341–348.

Harding, A., Halliday, G., Caine, D., & Kril, J. (2000). Degeneration of anterior thalamic nuclei differentiates alcoholics with amnesia. *Brain, 123,* 141–154.

Hardy, J., Cowburn, R., Barton, A., Reynolds, G., Lofdahl, E., O'Carroll, A. M., et al. (1987). Region-specific loss of glutamate innervation in Alzheimer's disease. *Neuroscience Letters, 73,* 77–80.

Hardy, J., & Selkoe, D. J. (2002). The amyloid hypothesis of Alzheimer's disease: Progress and problems on the road to therapeutics. *Science, 297,* 353–356.

Harhangi, B. S., de Rijk, M. C., van Duijn, C. M., Van Broeckhoven, C., Hofman, A., & Breteler, M. M. (2000). APOE and the risk of PD with or without dementia in a population-based study. *Neurology, 54,* 1272–1276.

Hariri, A. R., Bookheimer, S. Y., & Mazziotta, J. C. (2000). Modulating emotional responses: Effects of a neocortical network on the limbic system. *Neuroreport, 11,* 43–48.

Hariri, A. R., Mattay, V. S., Tessitore, A., Kolachana, B., Fera, F., Goldman, D., et al. (2002). Serotonin transporter genetic variation and the response of the human amygdala. *Science, 297,* 400–403.

Harlow, J. M. (1868). Recovery from the passage of an iron bar through the head. *Massachusetts Medical Society Publication, 2,* 329–347.

Harris, D., & Batki, S. L. (2000). Stimulant psychosis: Symptom profile and acute clinical course. *American Journal on Addictions, 9,* 28–37.

Harris, G. J., Pearlson, G. D., Peyser, C. E., Aylward, E. H., Roberts J., Barta, P. E., Chase, G. A., et al. (1992). Putamen volume reduction on magnetic resonance imaging exceeds caudate changes in mild Huntington's disease. *Annals of Neurology, 31,* 69–75.

Harrison, P. J. (1999). The neuropathology of schizophrenia: A critical review of the data and their interpretation. *Brain, 122,* 593–624.

Harrison, P. J. (2004). The hippocampus in schizophrenia: A review of the neuropathological evidence and its pathophysiological implications. *Psychopharmacology, 174,* 151–162.

Hartje, W., Ringelstein, E. B., Kistinger, B., Fabianek, D., & Willmes, K. (1994). Transcranial Doppler ultrasonic assessment of middle cerebral artery blood flow velocity changes during verbal and visuospatial cognitive tasks. *Neuropsychologia, 32,* 1443–1452.

Hartline, H. K. (1938). The response of single optic nerve fibers of the vertebrate eye to illumination of the retina. *American Journal of Physiology, 121,* 400–415.

Hartline, H. K. (1949). Inhibition of activity of visual receptors by illuminating nearby retinal areas in the *Limulus* eye. *Federation Proceedings, 8,* 69.

Hartsfield, C. L. (2002). Cross talk between carbon monoxide and nitric oxide. *Antioxidants and Redox Signalling, 4,* 301–307.

Harvey, J. A. (2004). Cocaine effects on the developing brain: Current status. *Neuroscience and Biobehavioral Reviews, 27,* 751–764.

Harvey, J. A., Romano, A. G., Gabriel, M., Simansky, K. J., Du, W., Aloyo, V. J., et al. (2001). Effects of prenatal exposure to cocaine on the developing brain: Anatomical, chemical, physiological and behavioral consequences. *Neurotoxicity Research, 3,* 117–143.

Harvey, P. D., Lombardi, J., Leibman, M., Parrella, M., White, L., Powchik, P., et al. (1997). Age-related differences in formal thought disorder in chronically hospitalized schizophrenic patients: A cross-sectional study across nine decades. *American Journal of Psychiatry, 154,* 205–210.

Hashimoto, K., & Kano, M. (2003). Functional differentiation of multiple climbing fiber inputs during synapse elimination in the developing cerebellum. *Neuron, 38,* 785–796.

Hassanain, M., & Levin, B. E. (2002). Dysregulation of hypothalamic serotonin turnover in diet-induced obese rats. *Brain Research, 929,* 175–180.

Hatten, M. E. (1990). Riding the glial monorail: A common mechanism for glial-guided neuronal migration in different regions of the developing mammalian brain. *Trends in Neurosciences, 13,* 179–184.

Haugh, R. M., & Markesbery, W. R. (1983). Hypothalamic astrocytoma. Syndrome of hyperphagia, obesity, and disturbances of behavior and endocrine and autonomic function. *Archives of Neurology, 40,* 560–563.

Hauri, P., (1979). What can insomniacs teach us about the functions of sleep? In R. Drucker-Colin, M. Shkurovich, & M. B. Sterman (Eds.), *The functions of sleep* (pp. 251–271). New York: Academic Press.

Havens, M. D., & Rose, J. D. (1992). Investigation of familiar and novel chemosensory stimuli by golden hamsters: Effects of castration and testosterone replacement. *Hormones and Behavior, 26,* 505–511.

Hawke, C. C. (1950). Castration and sex crimes. *American Journal of Mental Deficiency, 55,* 220–226.

Hawkins, R. D., Carew, T. J., & Kandel, E. R. (1986). Effects of interstimulus interval and contingency on classical conditioning of the Aplysia siphon withdrawal reflex. *The Journal of Neuroscience, 6,* 1695–1701.

Hawkins, R. D., Greene, W., & Kandel, E. R. (1998). Classical conditioning, differential conditioning, and second-order conditioning of the Aplysia gill-withdrawal reflex in a simplified mantle organ preparation. *Behavioral Neuroscience, 112,* 636–645.

Hawkins, R. D., Kandel, E. R., & Siegelbaum, S. A. (1993). Learning to modulate transmitter release: Themes and variations in synaptic plasticity. *Annual Review of Neuroscience, 16,* 625–665.

Hawkins, R. D., Lalevic, N., Clark, G. A., & Kandel, E. R. (1989). Classical conditioning of the Aplysia siphon-withdrawal reflex exhibits response specificity. *Proceedings of the National Academy of Sciences of the United States of America, 86,* 7620–7624.

Hawkins, R. D., Son, H., & Arancio, O. (1998). Nitric oxide as a retrograde messenger during long-term potentiation in hippocampus. *Progress in Brain Research, 118,* 155–172.

Hawkins, R. D., Zhuo, M., & Arancio, O. (1994). Nitric oxide and carbon monoxide as possible retrograde messengers in hippocampal long-term potentiation. *Journal of Neurobiology, 25,* 652–665.

Haydon, P. G. (2001). GLIA: Listening and talking to the synapse. *Nature Reviews: Neuroscience, 2,* 185–193.

Haynes, A. C., Chapman, H., Taylor, C., Moore, G. B., Cawthorne, M. A., Tadayyon, M., et al. (2002). Anorectic, thermogenic and anti-obesity activity of a selective orexin-1 receptor antagonist in ob/ob mice. *Regulatory Peptides, 104,* 153–159.

Hazlett, E. A., & Buchsbaum, M. S. (2001). Sensorimotor gating deficits and hypofrontality in schizophrenia. *Frontiers in Bioscience, 6,* D1069–D1072.

Hazlett, E. A., Buchsbaum, M. S., Jeu, L. A., Nenadic, I., Fleischman, M. B., Shihabuddin, L., et al. (2000). Hypofrontality in unmedicated schizophrenia patients studied with PET during performance of a serial verbal learning task. *Schizophrenia Research, 43,* 33–46.

Hebb, D. O. (1949). *The organization of behavior: A neuropsychological theory.* Oxford, England: Wiley.

Hebb, D. O. (1959). Karl Spencer Lashley: 1890–1958. *American Journal of Psychology, 72,* 142–150.

Hebb, D. O. (1972). *Textbook of psychology* (3rd ed.). Philadelphia: Saunders.

Hebert, L. E., Scherr, P. A., Bienias, J. L., Bennett, D. A., & Evans, D. A. (2003). Alzheimer disease in the U. S. population: Prevalence estimates using the 2000 census. *Archives of Neurology, 61,* 802–803.

Hebert, L. E., Scherr, P. A., McCann, J. J., Beckett, L. A., & Evans, D. A. (2001). Is the risk of developing Alzheimer's disease greater for women than for men? *American Journal of Epidemiology, 153,* 132–136.

Heck, D., & Sultan, F. (2002). Cerebellar structure and function: Making sense of parallel fibers. *Human Movement Science, 21,* 411–421.

Heckers, S., & Konradi, C. (2002). Hippocampal neurons in schizophrenia. *Journal of Neural Transmission, 109,* 891–905.

Heckmann, J. M., LeePan, E. B., & Eastman, R. W. (2001). High-dose immunosuppressive therapy in generalized myasthenia gravis—A 2-year follow-up study. *South African Medical Journal, 91,* 765–770.

Hedges, D. W., Allen, S., Tate, D. F., Thatcher, G. W., Miller, M. J., Rice, S. A., et al. (2003). Reduced hippocampal volume in alcohol and substance naive Vietnam combat veterans with posttraumatic stress disorder. *Cognitive and Behavioral Neurology, 16,* 219–224.

Hegde, J., & Van Essen, D. C. (2000). Selectivity for complex shapes in primate visual area V2. *The Journal of Neuroscience, 20,* RC61.

Hegde, M. (2001). *Introduction to communicative disorders* (3rd ed.). Austin, TX: Pro-Ed.

Heidel, E., & Davidowa, H. (1998). Interactive effects of cholecystokinin-8S and serotonin on spontaneously active neurons in ventromedial hypothalamic slices. *Neuropeptides, 32,* 423–429.

Heiman, J. R. (1975). The psychology of erotica: Women's sexual arousal. *Psychology Today, 8,* 90–94.

Heimer, G., Bar-Gad, I., Goldberg, J. A., & Bergman, H. (2002). Dopamine replacement therapy reverses abnormal synchronization of pallidal neurons in the 1-methyl-4-phenyl-1,2,3,6-tetrahydropyridine primate model of parkinsonism. *The Journal of Neuroscience, 22,* 7850–7855.

Heimer, L., & Larsson, K. (1966/1967). Impairment of mating behavior in male rats following lesions in the preoptic-anterior hypothalamic continuum. *Brain Research, 3,* 248–263.

Heinrichs, R. W. (1993). Schizophrenia and the brain. Conditions for a neuropsychology of madness. *American Psychologist, 48,* 221–233.

Heinsbroek, R. P., van Haaren, F., Feenstra, M. G., Boon, P., & van de Poll, N. E. (1991). Controllable and uncontrollable footshock and monoaminergic activity in the frontal cortex of male and female rats. *Brain Research, 551,* 247–255.

Heinz, A., Romero, B., Gallinat, J., Juckel, G., & Weinberger, D. R. (2003). Molecular brain imaging and the neurobiology and genetics of schizophrenia. *Pharmacopsychiatry, 36,* S152–S157.

Heinz, A., Schafer, M., Higley, J. D., Krystal, J. H., & Goldman, D. (2003). Neurobiological correlates of the disposition and maintenance of alcoholism. *Pharmacopsychiatry, 36,* S255-S258.

Heiss, W. D., Kessler, J., Thiel, A., Ghaemi, M., & Karbe, H. (1999). Differential capacity of left and right hemispheric areas for compensation of poststroke aphasia. *Annals of Neurology, 45,* 430–438.

Heitkamp, H. C., Schmid, K., & Scheib, K. (1993). Beta-endorphin and adrenocorticotropic hormone production during marathon and incremental exercise. *European Journal of Applied Physiology and Occupational Physiology, 66,* 269–274.

Hellekant, G., Ninomiya, Y., & Danilova, V. (1998). Taste in chimpanzees: III. Labeled-line coding in sweet taste. *Physiology & Behavior, 65,* 191–200.

Hellekant, G., Ninomiya, Y., DuBois, G. E., Danilova, V., & Roberts, T. W. (1996). Taste in chimpanzee: I. The summated response to sweeteners and the effect of gymnemic acid. *Physiology & Behavior, 60,* 469–479.

Hellige, J. B. (1993). Unity of thought and action: Varieties of interaction between the left and right cerebral hemispheres. *Current Directions in Psychological Science, 2,* 21–25.

Hellige, J. B., Taylor, K. B., Lesmes, L., & Peterson, S. (1998). Relationships between brain morphology and behavioral measures of hemispheric asymmetry and interhemispheric interaction. *Brain & Cognition, 36,* 158–192.

Helm, K. A., Rada, P., & Hoebel, B. G. (2003). Cholecystokinin combined with serotonin in the hypothalamus limits accumbens dopamine release while increasing acetylcholine: A possible satiation mechanism. *Brain Research, 963,* 290–297.

Heneka, M. T., Galea, E., Gavriluyk, V., Dumitrescu-Ozimek, L., Daeschner, J., O'Banion, M. K., et al. (2002). Noradrenergic depletion potentiates beta-amyloid-induced cortical inflammation: Implications for Alzheimer's disease. *The Journal of Neuroscience, 22,* 2434–2442.

Hennig, J., Laschefski, U., & Opper, C. (1994). Biopsychological changes after bungee jumping: Beta-endorphin immunoreactivity as a mediator of euphoria? *Neuropsychobiology, 29,* 28–32.

Hennig, J., Speck, O., Koch, M. A., & Weiller, C. (2003). Functional magnetic resonance imaging: A review of methodological aspects and clinical applications. *Journal of Magnetic Resonance Imaging, 18,* 1–15.

Hensley, K., Carney, J. M., Mattson, M. P., Aksenova, M., Harris, M., Wu, J. F., et al. (1994). A model for beta-amyloid aggregation and neurotoxicity based on free radical generation by the peptide: Relevance to Alzheimer disease. *Proceedings of the National Academy of Sciences of the United States of America, 91,* 3270–3274.

Hernandez-Gonzalez, M., Guevara, M. A., Cervantes, M., Morali, G., & Corsi-Cabrera, M. (1998). Characteristic frequency bands of the cortico-frontal EEG during the sexual interaction of the male rat as a result of factorial analysis. *Journal of Physiology, Paris, 92,* 43–50.

Herrero, M. T., Barcia, C., & Navarro, J. M. (2002). Functional anatomy of thalamus and basal ganglia. *Child's Nervous System, 18,* 386–404.

Hershberger, S. L. (1997). A twin registry study of male and female sexual orientation. *Journal of Sex Research, 34,* 212–222.

Hertz-Pannier, L., Chiron, C., Jambaque, I., Renaux-Kieffer, V., Van de Moortele, P. F., Delalande, O., et al. (2002). Late plasticity for language in a child's non-dominant hemisphere: A pre- and post-surgery fMRI study. *Brain, 125,* 361–372.

Hetherington, A. W., & Ranson, S. W. (1942). Hypothalamic lesions and adiposity in the rat. *The Anatomical Record, 78,* 149–172.

Heyser, C. J., Roberts, A. J., Schulteis, G., & Koob, G. F. (1999). Central administration of an opiate antagonist decreases oral ethanol self-administration in rats. *Alcoholism, Clinical and Experimental Research, 23,* 1468–1476.

Hickey, M. A., & Chesselet, M. F. (2003). Apoptosis in Huntington's disease. *Progress in Neuro-psychopharmacology & Biological Psychiatry, 27,* 255–265.

Hicks, R. A., Kilcourse, J., & Sinnott, M. A. (1983). Type A-B behavior and caffeine use in college students. *Psychological Reports, 52,* 338.

Higley, J. D., Mehlman, P. T., Higley, S. B., Fernald, B., Vickers, J., Lindell, S. G., et al. (1996a). Excessive mortality in young free-ranging male nonhuman primates with low cerebrospinal fluid 5-hydroxyindoleacetic acid concentrations. *Archives of General Psychiatry, 53,* 537–543.

Higley, J. D., Mehlman, P. T., Poland, R. E., Taub, D. M., Vickers, J., Suomi, S. J., et al. (1996b). CSF testosterone and 5-HIAA correlate with different types of aggressive behaviors. *Biological Psychiatry, 40,* 1067–1082.

Hill, D. W., Hill, C. M., Fields, K. L., & Smith, J. C. (1993). Effects of jet lag on factors related to sport performance. *Canadian Journal of Applied Physiology, 18,* 91–103.

Himashree, G., Banerjee, P. K., & Selvamurthy, W. (2002). Sleep and performance: Recent trends. *Indian Journal of Physiological Pharmacology, 46,* 6–24.

Hindler, C. G. (1989). Epilepsy and violence. *British Journal of Psychiatry, 155,* 246–249.

Hines, M., Brook, C., & Conway, G. S. (2004). Androgen and psychosexual development: Core gender identity, sexual orientation and recalled childhood gender role behavior in women and men with congenital adrenal hyperplasia (CAH). *Journal of Sex Research, 41,* 75–81.

Hirota, H., Matsuoka, R., Kimura, M., Imamura, S., Joh-o, K., Ando, M., et al. (1996). Molecular cytogenetic diagnosis of Williams syndrome. *American Journal of Medical Genetics, 64,* 473–477.

Hirschenhauser, K., Frigerio, D., Grammar, K., & Magnusson, M. S. (2002). Monthly patterns of testosterone and behavior in prospective fathers. *Hormones and Behavior, 42,* 172–181.

Hlastala, S. A. (2003). Stress, social rhythms, and behavioral activation: Psychosocial factors and the bipolar illness course. *Current Psychiatry Reports, 5,* 477–483.

Ho, A. K., Sahakian, B. J., Brown, R. G., Barker, R. A., Hodges, J. R., Ane, M. N., et al. (2003). Profile of cognitive progression in early Huntington's disease. *Neurology, 61,* 1702–1706.

Ho, L. W., Carmichael, J., Swartz, J., Wyttenbach, A., Rankin, J., & Rubinsztein, D. C. (2001). The molecular biology of Huntington's disease. *Psychological Medicine, 31,* 3–14.

Hobson, J. A. (1988). *The dreaming brain.* New York: Basic Books.

Hobson, J. A. (1992). Sleep and dreaming: Induction and mediation of REM sleep by cholinergic mechanisms. *Current Opinion in Neurobiology, 2,* 759–763.

Hobson, J. A. (1995). *Sleep.* New York: Scientific American Library.

Hobson, J. A., & McCarley, R. W. (1977). The brain as a dream state generator: An activation-synthesis hypothesis of the dream process. *American Journal of Psychiatry, 134,* 1335–1348.

Hobson, J. A., Pace-Schott, E. F., & Stickgold, R. (2000). Dreaming and the brain: Toward a cognitive neuroscience of conscious states. *Behavioral and Brain Sciences, 23,* 793–1121.

Hobson, J. A., Pace-Schott, E. F., Stickgold, R., & Kahn, D. (1998). To dream or not to dream? Relevant data from new neuroimaging and electrophysiological studies. *Current Opinion in Neurobiology, 8,* 239–244.

Hoebel, B. G. (1969). Feeding and self-stimulation. *Annals of the New York Academy of Sciences, 157,* 758–778.

Hoebel, B. G., & Teitelbaum, P. (1966). Weight regulation in normal and hypothalamic hyperphagic rats. *Journal of Comparative and Physiological Psychology, 61,* 189–193.

Hoekema, A., Stegenga, B., & De Bont, L. G. (2004). Efficacy and co-morbidity of oral appliances in the treatment of obstructive sleep apnea-hypopnea: A systematic review. *Critical Reviews in Oral Biology and Medicine, 15,* 137–155.

Hoffman, M. A., & Swaab, D. F. (1994). The human hypothalamus: Comparative morphometry and photoperiodic influences. *Progress in Brain Research, 93,* 133–147.

Hoffmann, G., Linkowski, P., Kerkhofs, M., Desmedt, D., & Mendlewicz, J. (1985). Effects of ECT on sleep and CSF biogenic amines in affective illness. *Psychiatry Research, 16,* 199–206.

Hoffmann, H., Janssen, E., & Turner, S. L. (2004). Classical conditioning of sexual arousal in women and men: Effects of varying awareness and biological relevance of the conditioned stimulus. *Archives of Sexual Behavior, 33,* 43–53.

Hohman, G. W. (1966). Some effects of spinal cord lesions on experienced emotional feelings. *Psychophysiology, 3,* 143–156.

Hollerman, J. R., Tremblay, L., & Schultz, W. (2000). Involvement of basal ganglia and orbitofrontal cortex in goal-directed behavior. *Progress in Brain Research, 126,* 193–215.

Holloway, R. L., Anderson, P. J., Defendini, R., & Harper, C. (1993). Sexual dimorphism of the human corpus callosum from three independent samples: Relative size of the corpus callosum. *American Journal of Physical Anthropology, 92,* 481–498.

Holmes, A., Murphy, D. L., & Crawley, J. N. (2002). Reduced aggression in mice lacking the serotonin transporter. *Psychopharmacology, 161,* 160–167.

Holy, T. E., Dulac, C., & Meister, M. (2000). Responses of vomeronasal neurons to natural stimuli. *Science, 289,* 1569–1572.

Holzmann, C., Schmidt, T., Thiel, G., Epplen, J. T., & Riess, O. (2001). Functional characterization of the Huntington's disease gene promoter. *Brain Research: Molecular Brain Research, 92,* 85–97.

Hooks, M. S., Colvin, A. C., Juncos, J. L., & Justice, J. B., Jr. (1992). Individual differences in basal and cocaine-stimulated extracellular dopamine in the nucleus accumbens using quantitative microdialysis. *Brain Research, 587,* 306–312.

Hormuzdi, S. G., Filippov, M. A., Mitropoulou, G., Monyer, H., & Bruzzone, R. (2004). Electrical synapses: A dynamic signaling system that shapes the activity of neuronal networks. *Biochimica et Biophysica Acta, 1662,* 113–137.

Horne, J., & Reyner, L. (1999). Vehicle accidents related to sleep: A review. *Occupational and Environmental Medicine, 56,* 289–294.

Horne, J. A., & Wilkinson, S. (1985). Chronic sleep reduction: Daytime vigilance performance and EEG measures of sleepiness, with particular reference to "practice" effects. *Psychophysiology, 22,* 69–78.

Houston, B. K., & Snyder, C. R. (1988). *Type A behavior: Research, theory, and intervention.* New York: Wiley.

Howard, J. L., Reifler, C. B., & Liptzin, M. B. (1971). Effects of exposure to pornography. In *Technical report of the Commission on Obscenity and Pornography* (Vol. 8, pp. 97–132). Washington, DC: U.S. Government Printing Office.

Hrdy, S. B. (1979). Infanticide among animals: A review, classification, and examination of the implications for the reproductive strategies of females. *Ethology and Sociobiology, 1,* 13–40.

Hsu, L. K. (2004). Eating disorders: Practical interventions. *Journal of the American Medical Women's Association, 59,* 113–124.

Hu, S., Pattatucci, A. M., Patterson, C., Li, L., Fulker, D. W., Cherny, S. S., et al. (1995). Linkage between sexual orientation and the chromosome Xq28 in males but not in females. *Nature Genetics, 11,* 248–256.

Huang, C. C., Su, T. P., & Wei, I. H. (2005). Repetitive transcranial magnetic stimulation for treating medication-resistant depression in Taiwan: A preliminary study. *Journal of the Chinese Medical Association, 68,* 202–203.

Hubel, D. H. (1967). Effects of distortion of sensory input on the visual system of kittens. *The Physiologist, 10,* 17–45.

Hubel, D. H., & Wiesel, T. N. (1963). Receptive fields of cells in striate cortex of very young, visually inexperienced kittens. *Journal of Neurophysiology, 26,* 994–1002.

Hubel, D. H., & Wiesel, T. N. (1965). Binocular interaction in striate cortex of kittens reared with artificial squint. *Journal of Neurophysiology, 28,* 1041–1059.

Hubel, D. H., & Wiesel, T. N. (1977). Functional architecture of macaque monkey visual cortex. *Proceedings of the Royal Society of London, B, 198,* 1–59.

Hubel, D. H., & Wiesel, T. N. (1979). Brain mechanisms of vision. *Scientific American, 241,* 150–162.

Hudson, T. J., Owen, R. R., Thrush, C. R., Han, X., Pyne, J. M., Thapa, P., et al. (2004). A pilot study of barriers to medication adherence in schizophrenia. *Journal of Clinical Psychiatry, 65,* 211–216.

Hudspeth, A. J. (1997). How hearing happens. *Neuron, 19,* 947–950.

Hughes, A. J. (1997). Drug treatment of Parkinson's disease in the 1990s. Achievements and future possibilities. *Drugs, 53,* 195–205.

Hughes, C. W., Kent, T. A., Campbell, J., Oke, A., Croskell, H., & Preskorn, S. H. (1984). Cerebral blood flow and cerebrovascular permeability in an inescapable shock (learned helplessness) animal model of depression. *Pharmacology, Biochemistry, and Behavior, 21,* 891–894.

Hughes, J., Smith, T. W., Kosterlitz, H. W., Fothergill, L. A., Morgan, B. A., & Morris, H. R. (1975). Identification of two related pentapeptides from the brain with potent opiate agonist activity. *Nature, 258,* 577–580.

Hughes, J. R. (1996). A review of the usefulness of the standard EEG in psychiatry. *Clinical EEG (Electroencephalography), 27,* 35–39.

Huh, G. S., Boulanger, L. M., Du, H., Riquelme, P. A., Brotz, T. M., & Shatz, C. J. (2000). Functional requirement for class I MHC in CNS development and plasticity. *Science, 290,* 155–159.

Hull, E. M., Du, J., Lorrain, D. S., & Matuszewich, L. (1997). Testosterone, preoptic dopamine, and copulation in male rats. *Brain Research Bulletin, 44,* 327–333.

Hultman, C. M., Wieselgren, I-M., & Oehman, A. (1997). Relationships between social support, social coping and life events in the relapse of schizophrenic patients. *Scandinavian Journal of Psychology, 38,* 3–13.

Hurvich, L. M., & Jameson, D. (1974). Opponent processes as a model of neural organization. *American Psychologist, 29,* 88–102.

Hussain, I. F., Brady, C. M., Swinn, M. J., Mathias, C. J., & Fowler, C. J. (2001). Treatment of erectile dysfunction with sildenafil citrate (Viagra) in parkinsonism due to Parkinson's disease or multiple system atrophy with observations on orthostatic hypotension. *Journal of Neurology, Neurosurgery, and Psychiatry, 71,* 371–374.

Hutton, M., Perez-Tur, J., & Hardy, J. (1998). Genetics of Alzheimer's disease. *Essays in Biochemistry, 33,* 117–131.

Huwig-Poppe, C., Voderholzer, U., Backhaus, J., Riemann, D., Konig, A., & Hohagen, F. (1999). The tryptophan depletion test. Impact on sleep in healthy subjects and patients with obsessive-compulsive disorder. *Advances in Experimental Medicine and Biology, 467,* 35–42.

Hwang, S. J., Ji, E. K., Lee, E. K., Kim, Y. M., Shin, D. Y., Cheon, Y. H., et al. (2004). Gender differences in the corpus callosum of neonates. *Neuroreport, 15,* 1029–1032.

Hyde, J. S., & DeLamater, J. D. (2000). *Understanding human sexuality* (7th ed.). New York: McGraw-Hill.

Hyman, A. M., & Frank, M. E. (1980). Sensitivities of single nerve fibers in the hamster chorda tympani to mixtures of taste stimuli. *Journal of General Physiology, 76,* 143–173.

Hyman, B. T., Van Hoesen, G. W., & Damasio, A. R. (1987). Alzheimer's disease: Glutamate depletion in the hippocampal perforant pathway zone. *Annals of Neurology, 22,* 37–40.

Hynd, M. R., Scott, H. L., & Dodd, P. R. (2004). Glutamate-mediated excitotoxicity and neurodegeneration in Alzheimer's disease. *Neurochemistry International, 45,* 583–595.

Imaizumi, K., Priebe, N. J., Crum, P. A., Bedenbaugh, P. H., Cheung, S. W., & Schreiner, C. E. (2004). Modular functional organization of cat anterior auditory field. *Journal of Neurophysiology, 92,* 444–457.

Imperato-McGinley, J., & Zhu, Y. S. (2002). Androgens and male physiology: The syndrome of 5alpha-reductase-2 deficiency. *Molecular and Cell Endocrinology, 198,* 51–59.

Inagaki, T., Shimutzu, Y., Tsubouchi, K., Momose, I., Miyaoka, T., et al. (2003). Korsakoff syndrome following chronic subdural hematoma. *General Hospital Psychiatry, 25,* 364–366.

Ingraham, L. J., & Wender, P. H. (1992). Risk for affective disorder and alcohol and other drug abuse in the relatives of affectively ill adoptees. *Journal of Affective Disorders, 26,* 45–51.

Insel, T. R. (1992). Oxytocin—A neuropeptide for affiliation: Evidence from behavioral, receptor autoradiographic, and comparative studies. *Psychoneuroendocrinology, 17,* 3–35.

Intranuovo, L. R., & Powers, A. S. (1998). The perceived bitterness of beer and 6-n-propylthiouracil (PROP) taste sensitivity. *Annals of the New York Academy of Sciences, 855,* 813–815.

Ishii, Y., Blundell, J. E., Halford, J. C., Upton, N., Porter, R., Johns, A., et al. (2004). Differential effects of the selective orexin-1 receptor antagonist SB-334867 and lithium chloride on behavioural satiety sequence in rats. *Physiology & Behavior, 81,* 129–140.

Ito, M. (2000). Mechanisms of motor learning in the cerebellum. *Brain Research, 886,* 237–245.

Iversen, L. (2003). Cannabis and the brain. *Brain, 126,* 1252–1270.

Ivry, R. (1997). Cerebellar timing systems. *International Review of Neurobiology, 41,* 555–573.

Izawa, C. (Ed.). (1999). *On human memory: Evolution, progress, and reflections on the 30th anniversary of the Atkinson-Shiffrin model.* Mahwah, NJ: Erlbaum.

Izquierdo, I. (1995). Role of the hippocampus, amygdala, and entorhinal cortex in memory storage and expression. In J. L. McGaugh, F. Bermudez-Rattoni, & R. A. Prado-Alcalá (Eds.), *Plasticity in the central nervous system: Learning and memory* (pp. 41–56). Hillsdale, NJ: Erlbaum.

Izquierdo, I., & Medina, J. H. (1993). Role of the amygdala, hippocampus and entorhinal cortex in memory consolidation and expression. *Brazilian Journal of Medical and Biological Research, 26,* 573–589.

Izumoto, Y., Inoue, S., & Yasuda, N. (1999). Schizophrenia and the influenza epidemics of 1957 in Japan. *Biological Psychiatry, 46,* 119–124.

Jackson, C. E., & Bryan, W. W. (1998). Amyotrophic lateral sclerosis. *Seminars in Neurology, 18,* 27–39.

Jackson, T., & Ramaswami, M. (2003). Prospects of memory-modifying drugs that target the CREB pathway. *Current Opinion in Drug Discovery & Development, 6,* 712–719.

Jacobsen, L. K., Mencl, W. E., Pugh, K. R., Skudlarski, P., & Krystal, J. H. (2004). Preliminary evidence of hippocampal dysfunction in adolescent MDMA ("ecstasy") users: Possible relationship to neurotoxic effects. *Psychopharmacology (Berlin), 173,* 383–390.

Jacobsen, P. B., Bovbjerg, D. H., Schwartz, M. D., Andrykowski, M. A., Futterman, A. D., Gilewski, T., et al. (1993). Formation of food aversions in cancer patients receiving repeated infusions of chemotherapy. *Behaviour Research & Therapy, 31,* 739–748.

Jacobson, C. D., & Gorski, R. A. (1981). Neurogenesis of the sexually dimorphic nucleus of the preoptic area in the rat. *Journal of Comparative Neurology, 196,* 519–529.

Jacobson, M. (1991). *Developmental neurobiology.* New York: Plenum Press.

Jakicic, J. M. (2002). The role of physical activity in prevention and treatment of body weight gain in adults. *Journal of Nutrition, 132,* 3826S–3829S.

James, W. (1884). What is an emotion? *Mind, 9,* 188–205.

Jan, C., Francois, C., Tande, D., Yelnik, J., Tremblay, L., Agid, Y., et al. (2000). Dopaminergic innervation of the pallidum in the normal state, in MPTP-treated monkeys and in parkinsonian patients. *European Journal of Neuroscience, 12,* 4525–4535.

Jancke, L., Shah, N. J., & Peters, M. (2000). Cortical activations in primary and secondary motor areas for complex bimanual movements in professional pianists. *Brain Research: Cognitive Brain Research, 10,* 177–183.

Jancke, L., Shah, N. J., Posse, S., Grosse-Ryuken, M., Muller-Gartner, H. W. (1998). Intensity coding of auditory stimuli: An fMRI study. *Neuropsychologia, 36,* 875–883.

Janowitz, H. D., & Grossman, M. I. (1949). Some factors affecting the food intake of normal dogs and dogs with esophagostomy and gastric fistula. *American Journal of Physiology, 159,* 143–148.

Janowitz, H. D., & Hollander, F. (1953). Effect of prolonged intragastric feeding on oral ingestion. *Federation Proceedings, 12,* 72.

Janowsky, D. S., Overstreet, D. H., & Nurnberger, J. I., Jr. (1994). Is cholinergic sensitivity a genetic marker for the affective disorders? *American Journal of Medical Genetics, 54,* 335–344.

Jarvelainen, J., Schurmann, M., & Hari, R. (2004). Activation of the human primary motor cortex during observation of tool use. *Neuroimage, 23,* 187–192.

Jay, S. M., & Elliott, C. H. (1990). A stress inoculation program for parents whose children are undergoing painful medical procedures. *Journal of Consulting and Clinical Psychology, 58,* 799–804.

Jemmott, J. B., 3rd, Borysenko, J. Z., Borysenko, M., McClelland, D. C., Chapman, R., Meyer, D., et al. (1983). Academic stress, power motivation, and decrease in secretion rate of salivary secretory immunoglobulin A. *Lancet, 1*(8339), 1400–1402.

Jentsch, J. D., & Roth, R. H. (1999). The neuropsychopharmacology of phencyclidine: From NMDA receptor hypofunction to the dopamine hypothesis of schizophrenia. *Neuropsychopharmacology, 20,* 201–225.

Jesberger, J. A., & Richardson, J. S. (1985). Animal models of depression: Parallels and correlates to severe depression in humans. *Biological Psychiatry, 20,* 764–784.

Jessell, T. M., & Sanes, J. R. (2000). The induction and patterning of the nervous system. In E. R. Kandel, J. H. Schwartz, & T. M. Jessell (Eds.), *Principles of neural science* (4th ed., pp. 1019–1040). New York: McGraw-Hill.

JFK Jr.: The truth behind the crash. (2000). Salon.com. Retrieved from http://archive.salon.com/news/feature/2000/07/07/kennedy

Johansen, J., & Johansen, K. M. (1997). Molecular mechanisms mediating axon pathway formation. *Critical Reviews in Eukaryotic Gene Expression, 7,* 95–116.

Johnson, B. W., McKenzie, K. J., & Hamm, J. P. (2002). Cerebral asymmetry for mental rotation: Effects of response hand, handedness and gender. *Neuroreport, 13,* 1929–1932.

Johnson, D. F., Ackroff, K., Peters, J., & Collier, G. H. (1986). Changes in rats' meal patterns as a function of the caloric density of the diet. *Physiology & Behavior, 36,* 929–936.

Johnson, H., & Cowey, A. (2000). Transneuronal retrograde degeneration of retinal ganglion cells following restricted lesions of striate cortex in the monkey. *Experimental Brain Research, 132,* 269–275.

Johnson, J. S., & Newport, E. L. (1989). Critical period effects in second language learning: The influence of maturational state on the acquisition of English as a second language. *Cognitive Psychology, 21,* 60–99.

Johnson, R. F., Moore, R. Y., & Morin, L. P. (1988). Loss of entrainment and anatomical plasticity after lesions of the hamster retinohypothalamic tract. *Brain Research, 460,* 297–313.

Johnstone, E. C. (1998). Predictive symptomatology, course, and outcome in first-episode schizophrenia. *International Clinical Psychopharmacology, 13,* S97–S99.

Jones, B. E. (2003). Arousal systems. *Frontiers in Bioscience, 8,* 438–451.

Jones, B. E., Bobillier, P., & Jouvet, M. (1969). [Effect of destruction of neurons containing catecholamines of the mesencephalon on the wake-sleep cycle in cats]. *Comptes Rendus des Séances de la Société de Biologie et de ses Filiales, 163,* 176–180.

Jones, E. (1953). *The life and work of Sigmund Freud* (Vol. 1). New York: Basic Books.

Jones, E. G., & Pons, T. P. (1998). Thalamic and brainstem contributions to large-scale plasticity of primate somatosensory cortex. *Science, 282,* 1121–1125.

Jones, T. A., Chu, C. J., Grande, L. A., & Gregory, A. D. (1999). Motor skills training enhances lesion-induced structural plasticity in the motor cortex of adult rats. *The Journal of Neuroscience, 19,* 10153–10163.

Jope, R. S. (1999). Anti-bipolar therapy: Mechanism of action of lithium. *Molecular Psychiatry, 4,* 117–128.

Jordan, A. S., & McEvoy, R. D. (2003). Gender differences in sleep apnea: Epidemiology, clinical presentation and pathogenic mechanisms. *Sleep Medicine Reviews, 7,* 377–389.

Jordan, H. A. (1969). Voluntary intragastric feeding: Oral and gastric contributions to food intake and hunger in man. *Journal of Comparative and Physiological Psychology, 68,* 498–506.

Joseph, J. E. (2001). Functional neuroimaging studies of category specificity in object recognition: A critical review and meta-analysis. *Cognitive, Affective & Behavioral Neuroscience, 1,* 119–136.

Jouvet, M. (1967) Neurophysiology of the states of sleep. *Physiological Reviews, 47,* 117–177.

Jouvet, M. (1969). Biogenic amines and the states of sleep. *Science, 163,* 32–41.

Jouvet, M. (1972). The role of monoamines and acetylcholine-containing neurons in the regulation of the sleep-waking cycle. *Ergebnisse der Physiologie, Biologischen Chemie und Experimentellen Pharmakologie, 64,* 166–307.

Jouvet, M. (1974). Monoaminergic regulation of the sleep-waking cycle in the cat. In F. O. Schmitt & F. G. Worden (Eds.), *The neurosciences: Third study program* (pp. 499–508). Cambridge, MA: The MIT Press.

Jouvet, M., & Renault, J. (1966). [Persistence of insomnia after lesions of the nuclei of the raphe in the cat.] *Comptes Rendus des Séances de la Société de Biologie et de ses Filiales, 160,* 1461–1465.

Julien, E., & Over, R. (1988). Male sexual arousal across five modes of erotic stimulation. *Archives of Sexual Behavior, 17,* 131–143.

Julien, R. M. (2005). *A primer of drug action* (10th ed.). New York: Worth.

Kaas, J. H., Nelson, R. J., Sur, M., & Merzenich, M. M. (1981). Organization of somatosensory cortex in primates. In F. O. Schmitt, F. G. Worden, G. Adelman, & S. G. Dennis (Eds.), *The organization of the cerebral cortex* (pp. 237–261). Cambridge, MA: The MIT Press.

Kaelber, W. W., Mitchell, C. L., & Way, J. S. (1965). Some sensory influences on savage (affective) behavior in cats. *American Journal of Physiology, 209,* 866–870.

Kales, A., Soldatos, C. R., Bixler, E. O., & Kales, J. D. (1983). Early morning insomnia with rapidly eliminated benzodiazepines. *Science, 220,* 95–97.

Kalin, N. H., Shelton, S. E., & Davidson, R. J. (2004). The role of the central nucleus of the amygdala in mediating fear and anxiety in the primate. *The Journal of Neuroscience, 24,* 5506–5515.

Kallman, F. J. (1952). Comparative twin study on the genetic aspects of male homosexuality. *Journal of Nervous and Mental Disease, 115,* 283–298.

Kalra, S. P., Clark, J. T., Sahu, A., Dube, M. G., & Kalra, P. S. (1988). Control of feeding and sexual behaviors by neuropeptide Y: Physiological implications. *Synapse, 2,* 254–257.

Kalra, S. P., & Kalra, P. S. (2003). Neuropeptide Y: A physiological orexigen modulated by the feedback action of ghrelin and leptin. *Endocrine, 22,* 49–56.

Kalynchuk, L. E. (2000). Long-term amygdala kindling in rats as a model for the study of interictal emotionality in temporal lobe epilepsy. *Neuroscience and Biobehavioral Reviews, 24,* 691–704.

Kalynchuk, L. E., Pinel, J. P., & Treit, D. (1999). Characterization of the defensive nature of kindling-induced emotionality. *Behavioral Neuroscience, 113,* 766–775.

Kalynchuk, L. E., Pinel, J. P., Treit, D., Barnes, S. J., McEachern, J. C., & Kippin, T. E. (1998). Persistence of the interictal emotionality produced by long-term amygdala kindling in rats. *Neuroscience, 85,* 1311–1319.

Kaminski, L. C., Henderson, S. A., & Drewnowski, A. (2000). Young women's food preferences and taste responsiveness to 6-n-propylthiouracil (PROP). *Physiology & Behavior, 68,* 691–697.

Kanamori, N., Sakai, K., & Jouvet, M. (1980). Neuronal activity specific to paradoxical sleep in the ventromedial medullary reticular formation of unrestrained cats. *Brain Research, 189,* 251–255.

Kandel, E. R. (2000a). Cellular mechanisms of learning and the biological basis of individuality. In E. R. Kandel, J. H. Schwartz, & T. M. Jessell (Eds.), *Principles of neural science* (4th ed., pp. 1247–1279). New York: McGraw-Hill.

Kandel, E. R. (2000b). Disorders of mood: Depression, mania, and anxiety disorders. In E. R. Kandel, J. H. Schwartz, & T. M. Jessell (Eds.), *Principles of neural science* (4th ed., pp. 1209–1226). New York: McGraw-Hill.

Kandel, E. R., Kupfermann, I., & Iversen, S. (2000). Learning and memory. In E. R. Kandel, J. H. Schwartz, & T. M. Jessell (Eds.), *Principles of neural science* (4th ed., pp. 1227–1246). New York: McGraw-Hill.

Kang, H., Sun, L. D., Atkins, C. M., Soderling, T. R., Wilson, M. A., & Tonegawa, S. (2001). An important role of neural activity-dependent CaMKIV signaling in the consolidation of long-term memory. *Cell, 106,* 771–783.

Kanner, A. M. (2004). Is major depression a neurologic disorder with psychiatric symptoms? *Epilepsy & Behavior, 5,* 636–644.

Kanold, P. O., Kara, P., Reid, R. C., & Shatz, C. J. (2003). Role of subplate neurons in functional maturation of visual cortical columns. *Science, 301,* 521–525.

Kaplan, H. S. (1974). *The new sex therapy: Active treatment of sexual dysfunctions.* New York: Brunner/Mazel.

Kaplan, J. A., Brownell, H. H., Jacobs, J. R., & Gardner, H. (1990). The effects of right hemisphere damage on the pragmatic interpretation of conversational remarks. *Brain and Language, 38,* 315–333.

Kapsimalis, F., & Kryger, M. H. (2002). Gender and obstructive sleep apnea syndrome, Part 2: Mechanisms. *Sleep, 25,* 499–506.

Karagogeos, D. (2003). Neural GPI-anchored cell adhesion molecules. *Frontiers in Bioscience, 8,* s1304–s1320.

Karmiloff-Smith, A., Brown, J. H., Grice, S., & Paterson, S. (2003). Dethroning the myth: Cognitive dissociations and innate modularity in Williams syndrome. *Developmental Neuropsychology, 23,* 227–242.

Karmiloff-Smith, A., Grant, J., Berthoud, I., Davies, M., Howlin, P., & Udwin, O. (1997). Language and Williams syndrome: How intact is "intact"? *Child Development, 68,* 246–262.

Karmiloff-Smith, A., Tyler, L. K., Voice, K., Sims, K., Udwin, O., Howlin, P., et al. (1998). Linguistic dissociations in Williams syndrome: Evaluating receptive syntax in on-line and off-line tasks. *Neuropsychologia, 36,* 343–351.

Kasahara, J., Fukunaga, K., & Miyamoto, E. (2001). Activation of calcium/calmodulin-dependent protein kinase IV in long term potentiation in the rat hippocampal CA_1 region. *Journal of Biological Chemistry, 276,* 24044–24050.

Katz, L. C., & Shatz, C. J. (1996). Synaptic activity and the construction of cortical circuits. *Science, 274,* 1133–1138.

Kawamura, M., Midorikawa, A., & Kezuka, M. (2000). Cerebral localization of the center for reading and writing music. *Neuroreport, 11,* 3299–3303.

Keck, P. E., & McElroy, S. L. (2003). Bipolar disorder, obesity, and pharmacotherapy-associated weight gain. *Journal of Clinical Psychiatry, 64,* 1426–1435.

Keck, P. E., Jr., McElroy, S. L., & Arnold, L. M. (2001). Bipolar disorder. *The Medical Clinics of North America, 85,* 645–661.

Keesey, R. E., & Powley, T. L. (1986). The regulation of body weight. *Annual Review of Psychology, 37,* 109–133.

Keim, N. L., Stern, J. S., & Havel, P. J. (1998). Relation between circulating leptin concentrations and appetite during a prolonged, moderate energy deficit in women. *American Journal of Clinical Nutrition, 68,* 794–801.

Keller, K. L., Steinmann, L., Nurse, R. J., & Tepper, B. J. (2002). Genetic taste sensitivity to 6-n-propylthiouracil influences food preference and reported intake in preschool children. *Appetite, 38,* 3–12.

Keller, M. B., Klein, D. N., Hirschfeld, R. M., Kocsis, J. H., McCullough, J. P., Miller, I., et al. (1995). Results of the DSM-IV mood disorder field trial. *American Journal of Psychiatry, 152,* 843–849.

Kelly, D. D. (1991a). Sexual differentiation of the nervous system. In E. R. Kandel, J. H. Schwartz, & T. M. Jessel (Eds.), *Principles of neural science* (3rd ed., pp. 959–973). Norwalk, CT: Appleton & Lange.

Kelly, D. D. (1991b). Sleep and dreaming. In E. R. Kandel, J. H. Schwartz, & T. M. Jessell (Eds.), *Principles of neural science* (3rd ed., pp. 792–804). Norwalk, CT: Appleton & Lange.

Kelly, J. P. (1991). Hearing. In E. R. Kandel, J. H. Schwartz, & T. M. Jessell (Eds.), *Principles of neural science* (3rd ed., pp. 481–499). Norwalk: CT: Appleton & Lange.

Kelly, J. P., Wrynn, A. S., & Leonard, B. E. (1997). The olfactory bulbectomized rat as a model of depression: An update. *Pharmacology & Therapeutics, 74,* 299–316.

Kelso, S. R., & Brown, T. H. (1986). Differential conditioning of associative synaptic enhancement in hippocampal brain slices. *Science, 232,* 85–87.

Kemble, E. D., Blanchard, D. C., Blanchard, R. J. (1990). Effects of regional amygdaloid lesions on flight and defensive behaviors of wild black rats (*Rattus rattus*). *Physiology & Behavior, 48,* 1–5.

Kemble, E. D., Blanchard, D. C., Blanchard, R. J., & Takushi, R. (1984). Taming in wild rats following medial amygdaloid lesions. *Physiology & Behavior, 32,* 131–134.

Kendall, A. L., Hantraye, P., & Palfi, S. (2000). Striatal tissue transplantation in non-human primates. *Progress in Brain Research, 127,* 381–404.

Kendler, K. S., Myers, J. M., O'Neill, F. A., Martin, R., Murphy, B., MacLean, C. J., et al. (2000). Clinical features of schizophrenia and linkage to chromosomes 5q, 6p, 8p, and 10p in the Irish study of high-density schizophrenia families. *American Journal of Psychiatry, 157,* 402–408.

Kendler, K. S., Pedersen, N., Johnson, L., Neale, M. C., & Mathe, A. A. (1993). A pilot Swedish twin study of affective illness, including hospital- and population-ascertained subsamples. *Archives of General Psychiatry, 50,* 699–706.

Kendler, K. S., Thornton, L. M., Gilman, S. E., & Kessler, R. C. (2000). Sexual orientation in a U.S. national sample of twin and nontwin sibling pairs. *American Journal of Psychiatry, 157,* 1843–1846.

Kennedy, N., Boydell, J., Kalidindi, S., Fearon, P., Jones, P. B., van Os, J., et al. (2005). Gender differences in incidence and age at onset of mania and bipolar disorder over a 35-year period in Camberwell, England. *American Journal of Psychiatry, 162,* 257–262.

Kensinger, E. A., Ullman, M. T., & Corkin, S. (2001). Bilateral medial temporal lobe damage does not affect lexical or grammatical processing: Evidence from amnesic patient H.M. *Hippocampus, 11,* 347–360.

Kent, A. (2004). Huntington's disease. *Nursing Standard, 18,* 45–51.

Kentta, G., & Hassmen, P. (1998). Overtraining and recovery. A conceptual model. *Sports Medicine, 26,* 1–16.

Kerchner, M., & Ward, I. L. (1992). SDN-MPOA volume in male rats is decreased by prenatal stress, but is not related to ejaculatory behavior. *Brain Research, 581,* 244–251.

Kerkhof, G. A. (1998). The 24-hour variation of mood differs between morning- and evening-type individuals. *Perceptual and Motor Skills, 86,* 264–266.

Keverne, E. B. (1999). The vomeronasal organ. *Science, 286,* 716–720.

Keverne, E. B. (2004). Importance of olfactory and vomeronasal systems for male sexual function. *Physiology & Behavior, 83,* 177–187.

Keysers, C., Kohler, E., Umilta, M. A., Nanetti, L., Fogassi, L., & Gallese, V. (2003). Audiovisual mirror neurons and action recognition. *Experimental Brain Research, 153,* 628–636.

Killestein, J., Uitdehaag, B. M., & Polman, C. H. (2004). Cannabinoids in multiple sclerosis: Do they have a therapeutic role? *Drugs, 64,* 1–11.

Kilts, C. D., Schweitzer, J. B., Quinn, C. K., Gross, R. E., Faber, T. L., Muhammad, F., et al. (2001). Neural activity related to drug craving in cocaine addiction. *Archives of General Psychiatry, 58,* 334–341.

Kim, H. T., Kim, I. H., Lee, K. J., Lee, J. R., Park, S. K., Chun, Y. H., et al. (2002). Specific plasticity of parallel fiber/Purkinje cell spine synapses by motor skill learning. *Neuroreport, 13,* 1607–1610.

Kim, M-S., & Robertson, L. C. (2001). Implicit representations of space after bilateral parietal lobe damage. *Journal of Cognitive Neuroscience, 13,* 1080–1087.

Kim, S. S. (2003). Role of fluoxetine in anorexia nervosa. *The Annals of Pharmacotherapy, 37,* 890–892.

Kimura, A., Caria, M. A., Melis, F., & Asanuma, H. (1994). Long-term potentiation within the cat motor cortex. *Neuroreport, 5,* 2372–2376.

King, B. M. (1980). A re-examination of the ventromedial hypothalamic paradox. *Neuroscience and Biobehavioral Reviews, 4,* 151–160.

King, C., & Quigley, S. (1985). *Reading and deafness.* San Diego: College-Hill Press.

King, C. T., Garcea, M., & Spector, A. C. (2000). Glossopharyngeal nerve regeneration is essential for the complete recovery of quinine-stimulated oromotor rejection behaviors and central patterns of neuronal activity in the nucleus of the solitary tract in the rat. *The Journal of Neuroscience, 20,* 8426–8434.

King, D. P., & Takahashi, J. S. (2000). Molecular genetics of circadian rhythms in mammals. *Annual Review of Neuroscience, 23,* 713–742.

Kinnamon, S. C., Dionne, V. E., & Beam, K. G. (1988). Apical localization of K^+ channels in taste cells provides the basis for sour taste transduction. *Proceedings of the National Academy of Sciences of the United States of America, 85,* 7023–7027.

Kinomura, S., Larsson, J., Gulyás, B., & Roland, P. E. (1996). Activation by attention of the human reticular formation and thalamic intralaminar nuclei. *Science, 271,* 512–515.

Kipman, A., Gorwood, P., Mouren-Simeoni, M. C., & Ades, J. (1999). Genetic factors in anorexia nervosa. *European Psychiatry, 14,* 189–198.

Kirchgessner, A. L., & Sclafani, A. (1988). PVN-hindbrain pathway involved in the hypothalamic hyperphagia-obesity syndrome. *Physiology & Behavior, 42,* 517–528.

Kirik, D., Winkler, C., & Bjorklund, A. (2001). Growth and functional efficacy of intrastriatal nigral transplants depend on the extent of nigrostriatal degeneration. *The Journal of Neuroscience, 21,* 2889–2896.

Kirk, K. M., Bailey, J. M., Dunne, M. P., & Martin, N. G. (2000). Measurement models for sexual orientation in a community twin sample. *Behavior Genetics, 30,* 345–356.

Klebaur, J. E., Bevins, R. A., Segar, T. M., & Bardo, M. T. (2001). Individual differences in behavioral responses to novelty and amphetamine self-administration in male and female rats. *Behavioural Pharmacology, 12,* 267–275.

Kleim, J. A., Vij, K., Ballard, D. H., & Greenough, W. T. (1997). Learning-dependent synaptic modifications in the cerebellar cortex of the adult rat persist for at least four weeks. *The Journal of Neuroscience, 17,* 717–721.

Klein, D. N., & Santiago, N. J. (2003). Dysthymia and chronic depression: Introduction, classification, risk factors, and course. *Journal of Clinical Psychology/In Session, 59,* 807–816.

Klein, D. N., Schwartz, J. E., Rose, S., & Leader, J. B. (2000). Five-year course and outcome of dysthymic disorder: A prospective, naturalistic follow-up study. *American Journal of Psychiatry, 157,* 931–939.

Klein, S. B. (1982). *Motivation: Biosocial approaches.* New York: McGraw-Hill.

Klein, S. B. (2002). *Learning principles and applications* (4th ed.). New York: McGraw-Hill.

Kleinman, L., Lowin, A., Flood, E., Gandhi, G., Edgell, E., & Revicki, D. (2003). Costs of bipolar disorder. *Pharmacoeconomics, 21,* 601–622.

Klüver, H., & Bucy, P. C. (1939). Preliminary analysis of functions of the temporal lobes in monkeys. *Archives of Neurology and Psychiatry, 42,* 979–1000.

Knoll, J. (2000). (-)Deprenyl (Selegiline): Past, present and future. *Neurobiology (Budapest, Hungary), 8,* 179–199.

Knutson, J. F., Murray, K. T., Husarek, S., Westerhouse, K., Woodworth, G., Gantz, B. J., et al. (1998). Psychological change over 54 months of cochlear implant use. *Ear and Hearing, 19,* 191–201.

Ko, G. Y., & Kelly, P. T. (1999). Nitric oxide acts as a postsynaptic signaling molecule in calcium/calmodulin-induced synaptic potentiation in hippocampal CA_1 pyramidal neurons. *The Journal of Neuroscience, 19,* 6784–6794.

Kobasa, S. C. (1979). Stressful life events, personality, and health: An inquiry into hardiness. *Journal of Personality and Social Psychology, 37,* 1–11.

Kobasa, S. C., Maddi, S. R., & Zola, M. A. (1983). Type A and hardiness. *Journal of Behavioral Medicine, 6,* 41–51.

Kobatake, E., & Tanaka, K. (1994). Neuronal selectivities to complex object features in the ventral visual pathway of the macaque cerebral cortex. *Journal of Neurophysiology, 71,* 856–867.

Koch, R., Burton, B., Hoganson, G., Peterson, R., Rhead, W., Rouse, B., et al. (2002). Phenylketonuria in adulthood: A collaborative study. *Journal of Inherited Metabolic Disease, 25,* 333–346.

Kocsis, J. D., Akiyama, Y., Lankford, K. L., & Radtke, C. (2002). Cell transplantation of peripheral-myelin-forming cells to repair the injured spinal cord. *Journal of Rehabilitation Research and Development, 39,* 287–298.

Kodama, F., Ogawa, T., Sugihara, S., Kamba, M., Kohaya, N., Kondo, S., et al. (2003). Transneuronal degeneration in patients with temporal lobe epilepsy: Evaluation by MR imaging. *European Radiology, 13,* 2180–2185.

Koechlin, E., Ody, C., & Kouneiher, F. (2003). The architecture of cognitive control in the human prefrontal cortex. *Science, 302,* 1181–1185.

Koenig, J. I., Kirkpatrick, B., & Lee, P. (2002). Glucocorticoid hormones and early brain development in schizophrenia. *Neuropsychopharmacology, 27,* 309–318.

Koksal, F., Domjan, M., Kurt, A., Sertel, O., Orung, S., Bowers, R., et al. (2004). An animal model of fetishism. *Behaviour Research and Therapy, 42,* 1421–1434.

Kolarsky, A., Freund, K., Machek, J., & Polak, O. (1967). Male sexual deviation. Association with early temporal lobe damage. *Archives of General Psychiatry, 17,* 735–743.

Kolb, B. (1995). *Brain plasticity and behavior.* Mahwah, NJ: Erlbaum.

Kolb, B., & Whishaw, I. Q. (2003). *Fundamentals of human neuropsychology* (5th ed.). New York: Worth.

Komaki, G., Matsumoto, Y., Nishikata, H., Kawai, K., Nozaki, T., Takii, M., et al. (2001). Orexin-A and leptin change inversely in fasting non-obese subjects. *European Journal of Endocrinology, 144,* 645–651.

Komarova, N. L., Niyogi, P., & Nowak, M. A. (2001). The evolutionary dynamics of grammar acquisition. *Journal of Theoretical Biology, 209,* 43–59.

Komarova, N. L., & Nowak, M. A. (2001). Natural selection of the critical period for language acquisition. *Proceedings of the Royal Society of London. Series B, Biological Science, 268,* 1189–1196.

Komarova, N. L., & Nowak, M. A. (2003). Language dynamics in finite populations. *Journal of Theoretical Biology, 221,* 445–457.

Koob, G. F. (1992). Drugs of abuse: Anatomy, pharmacology and function of reward pathways. *Trends in Pharmacological Sciences, 13,* 177–184.

Koopman, P., Gubbay, J., Vivian, N., Goodfellow, P., & Lovell-Badge, R. (1991). Male development of chromosomally female mice transgenic for Sry. *Nature, 351,* 117–121.

Kopelman, M. D., Wilson, B. A., & Baddeley, A. D. (1989). The autobiographical memory interview: A new assessment of autobiographical and personal semantic memory in amnesic patients.

Journal of Clinical and Experimental Neuropsychology, 11, 724–744.

Kopka, S. L., Geran, L. C., & Spector, A. C. (2000). Functional status of the regenerated chorda tympani nerve as assessed in a salt taste discrimination task. *American Journal of Physiology. Regulatory, Integrative and Comparative Physiology, 278,* R720–R731.

Kordower, J. H., Rosenstein, J. M., Collier, T. J., Burke, M. A., Chen, E. Y., Li, J. M., et al. (1996). Functional fetal nigral grafts in a patient with Parkinson's disease: Chemoanatomic, ultrastructural, and metabolic studies. *Journal of Comparative Neurology, 370,* 203–230.

Kosaki, H., Hashikawa, T., He, J., & Jones, E. G. (1997). Tonotopic organization of auditory cortical fields delineated by parvalbumin immunoreactivity in macaque monkeys. *Journal of Comparative Neurology, 386,* 304–316.

Kosslyn, S. M. (1987). Seeing and imagining in the cerebral hemispheres: A computational approach. *Psychological Review, 94,* 148–175.

Kostowski, W., Giacalone, E., Garattini, S., & Valzelli, L. (1969). Electrical stimulation of midbrain raphe: Biochemical, behavioral and bioelectrical effects. *European Journal of Pharmacology, 7,* 170–175.

Kotrla, K. J., & Weinberger, D. R. (1995). Brain imaging in schizophrenia. *Annual Review of Medicine, 46,* 113–122.

Koukounas, E., & McCabe, M. (1997). Sexual and emotional variables influencing sexual response to erotica. *Behaviour Research and Therapy, 35,* 221–230.

Koukounas, E., & McCabe, M. P. (2001). Sexual and emotional variables influencing sexual response to erotica: A psychophysiological investigation. *Archives of Sexual Behavior, 30,* 393–408.

Kouri, E. M., & Halbreich, U. (1998). Hormonal treatments for premenstrual syndrome. *Drugs of Today (Barcelona, Spain),* 34, 603–610.

Kovelman, J. A., & Scheibel, A. B. (1984). A neurohistological correlate of schizophrenia. *Biological Psychiatry, 19,* 1601–1621.

Kow, L. M., Mobbs, C. V., & Pfaff, D. W. (1994). Roles of second-messenger systems and neuronal activity in the regulation of lordosis by neurotransmitters, neuropeptides, and estrogen: A review. *Neuroscience and Biobehavioral Reviews, 18,* 251–268.

Kozel, F. A., & George, M. S. (2002). Meta-analysis of left prefrontal repetitive transcranial magnetic stimulation (rTMS) to treat depression. *Journal of Psychiatric Practice, 8,* 270–275.

Kozlowski, S., & Drzewiecki, K. (1973). The role of osmoreception in portal circulation in control of water intake in dogs. *Acta Physiologica Polonica, 24,* 325–330.

Krack, P., Poepping, M., Weinert, D., Schrader, B., & Deuschl, G. (2002). Thalamic, pallidal, or subthalamic surgery for Parkinson's disease? *Journal of Neurology, 247,* II122–134.

Kraly, F. S. (2004). Eating provides important physiological signals for satiety and drinking. *Physiology & Behavior, 82,* 49–52.

Kraly, F. S., Tribuzio, R. A., Kim, Y. M., Keefe, M. E., Braun, C. J., & Newman, B. H. (1995). Angiotensin AT_1 and AT_2 receptors contribute to drinking elicited by eating in rats. *Physiology & Behavior, 58,* 1099–1109.

Kramer, T. H., Sclafani, A., Kindya, K., & Pezner, M. (1983). Conditioned taste aversion in lean and obese rats with ventromedial hypothalamic knife cuts. *Behavioral Neuroscience, 97,* 110–119.

Krantz, D. S., & Manuck, S. B. (1984). Acute psychophysiologic reactivity and risk of cardiovascular disease: A review and methodologic critique. *Psychological Bulletin, 96,* 435–464.

Krantz, M. J., & Mehler, P. S. (2004). Treating opioid dependence. Growing implications for primary care. *Archives of Internal Medicine, 164,* 277–288.

Kriegsfeld, L. J., Dawson, T. M., Dawson, V. L., Nelson, R. J., & Snyder, S. H. (1997). Aggressive behavior in male mice lacking the gene for neuronal nitric oxide synthase requires testosterone. *Brain Research, 769,* 66–70.

Kringelbach, M. L. (2004). Food for thought: Hedonic experience beyond homeostasis in the human brain. *Neuroscience, 126,* 807–819.

Krupa, D. J., Thompson, J. K., & Thompson, R. F. (1993). Localization of a memory trace in the mammalian brain. *Science, 260,* 989–991.

Kubin, L. (2001). Carbachol models of REM sleep: Recent developments and new directions. *Archives Italiennes de Biologie, 139,* 147–168.

Krupa, D. J., & Thompson, R. F. (1997). Reversible inactivation of the cerebellar interpositus nucleus completely prevents acquisition of the classically conditioned eye-blink response. *Learning & Memory, 3,* 545–556.

Kubitz, K. A., Landers, D. M., Petruzzello, S. J., & Han, M. (1996). The effects of acute and chronic exercise on sleep. A meta-analytic review. *Sports Medicine, 21,* 277–291.

Kuffler, S. W. (1953). Discharge patterns and functional organization of mammalian retina. *Journal of Neurophysiology, 16,* 37–68.

Kuhnle, U., & Bullinger, M. (1997). Outcome of congenital adrenal hyperplasia. *Pediatric Surgery International, 12,* 511–515.

Kulikowski, J. J., Walsh, V., McKeefry, D., Butler, S. R., & Carden, D. (1994). The electrophysiological basis of colour processing in macaques with V4 lesions. *Behavioural Brain Research, 60,* 73–78.

Kunkel-Bagden, E., Dai, H. N., & Bregman, B. S. (1993). Methods to assess the development and recovery of locomotor function after spinal cord injury in rats. *Experimental Neurology, 119,* 153–164.

Kurzthaler, I., Hummer, M., Miller, C., Sperner-Unterweger, B., Gunther, V., Wechdorn, H., et al. (1999). Effect of cannabis use on cognitive functions and driving ability. *Journal of Clinical Psychiatry, 60,* 395–399.

Kuzniecky, R. (1997). Magnetic resonance and functional magnetic resonance imaging: Tools for the study of human epilepsy. *Current Opinion in Neurology, 10,* 88–91.

Laan, E., Everaerd, W., & Evers, A. (1995). Assessment of female sexual arousal: Response specificity and construct validity. *Psychophysiology, 32,* 476–485.

LaBar, K. S., Gatenby, J. C., Gore, J. C., LeDoux, J. E., & Phelps, E. A. (1998). Human amygdala activation during conditioned fear acquisition and extinction: A mixed-trial fMRI study. *Neuron, 20,* 937–945.

LaBar, K. S., LeDoux, J. E., Spencer, D. D., & Phelps, E. A. (1995). Impaired fear conditioning following unilateral temporal lobectomy in humans. *The Journal of Neuroscience, 15,* 6846–6855.

Labbate, L. A., Croft, H. A., & Oleschansky, M. A. (2003). Antidepressant-related erectile dysfunction: Management via avoidance, switching antidepressants, antidotes, and adaptation. *Journal of Clinical Psychiatry, 64,* 11–19.

LaBerge, S. (1993). Lucid dreaming. In M.Carskadon (Ed.), *Encyclopedia of sleep and dreaming* (pp. 338–341). New York: Macmillan.

LaBerge, S., Greenleaf, W., & Kedzierski, B. (1983). Physiological responses to dreamed sexual activity during lucid REM sleep. *Psychophysiology, 20,* 454–455.

LaBerge, S., Levitan, L., & Dement, W. (1986). Lucid dreaming: Physiological correlates of consciousness during REM sleep. *Journal of Mind and Behavior, 7,* 251–258.

Lacerda, A. L., Keshavan, M. S., Hardan, A. Y., Yorbik, O., Brambilla, P., Sassi, R. B., et al. (2004). Anatomic evaluation of the orbitofrontal cortex in major depressive disorder. *Biological Psychiatry, 55,* 353–358.

Lacro, J. P., Dunn, L. B., Dolder, C. R., Leckband, S. G., & Jeste, D. V. (2002). Prevalence of and risk factors for medication nonadherence in patients with schizophrenia: A comprehensive review of recent literature. *Journal of Clinical Psychiatry, 63,* 892–909.

Laforce, R., Jr., & Doyon, J. (2001). Distinct contribution of the striatum and cerebellum to motor learning. *Brain and Cognition, 45,* 189–211.

Lai, Y. Y., & Siegel, J. M. (2003). Physiological and anatomical link between Parkinson-like disease and REM sleep behavior disorder. *Molecular Neurobiology, 27,* 137–152.

Lalonde, R., & Botez-Marquard, T. (1997). The neurobiological basis of movement initiation. *Reviews in the Neurosciences, 8,* 35–54.

Laman, J. D., 't Hart, B. A., Brok, H., Meurs, M., Schellekens, M. M., Kasran, A., et al. (2002). Protection of marmoset monkeys against EAE by treatment with a murine antibody blocking CD40 (mu5D12). *European Journal of Immunology, 32,* 2218–2228.

Landisman, C. E., & Ts'o, D. Y. (2002). Color processing in macaque striate cortex: Electrophysiological properties. *Journal of Neurophysiology, 87,* 3138–3151.

Lanfumey, L., & Hamon, M. (2004). 5-HT1 receptors. *Current Drug Targets. CNS and Neurological Disorders, 3,* 1–10.

Lang, A. E., Duff, J., Saint-Cyr, J. A., Trepanier, L., Gross, R. E., Lombardi, W., et al. (1999). Posteroventral medial pallidotomy in Parkinson's disease. *Journal of Neurology, 246,* II28–II41.

Langbehn, D. R., Brinkman, R. R., Falush, D., Paulsen, J. S., Hayden, M. R.; International Huntington's Disease Collaborative Group. (2004). A new model for prediction of the age of onset and penetrance for Huntington's disease based on CAG length. *Clinical Genetics, 65,* 267–277.

Lange, C. G. (1887). *Über gemutsbewegungen* (H. Kurella, Trans.). Leipzig: Thomas. (Original work published 1885)

Langston, J. W. (2005). The promise of stem cells in Parkinson disease. *Journal of Clinical Investigation, 115,* 23–25.

Langston, J. W., Ballard, P., Tetrud, J. W., & Irwin, I. (1983). Chronic Parkinsonism in humans due to a product of meperidine-analog synthesis. *Science, 219,* 979–980.

Lao, L., Bergman, S., Hamilton, G. R., Langenberg, P., & Berman, B. (1999). Evaluation of acupuncture for pain control after oral surgery: A placebo-controlled trial. *Archives of Otolaryngology—Head & Neck Surgery, 125,* 567–572.

Larsson, K. (1964). Mating behavior in male rats after cerebral cortex ablation: II. Effects of lesions in the frontal lobes compared to lesions in the posterior half of the hemispheres. *Journal of Experimental Zoology, 155,* 203–214.

Lasco, M. S., Jordan, T. J., Edgar, M. A., Petito, C. K., & Byne, W. (2002). A lack of dimorphism of sex or sexual orientation in the human anterior commissure. *Brain Research, 936,* 95–98.

Lashley, K. S. (1950). In search of the engram. In Society for Experimental Biology (Great Britain), *Physiological mechanisms in animal behaviour* (pp. 454–482). Cambridge, England: Cambridge University Press.

Lashley, K. S. (1963). *Brain mechanisms and intelligence.* New York: Dover. (Original work published 1929)

Lassonde, M., Sauerwein, H. C., & Lepore, F. (1995). Extent and limits of callosal plasticity: Presence of disconnection symptoms in callosal agenesis. *Neuropsychologia, 33,* 989–1007.

Latham, E. E., & Thorne, B. M. (1974). Septal damage and muricide: Effects of strain and handling. *Physiology & Behavior, 12,* 521–526.

Lauderback, C. M., Hackett, J. M., Huang, F. F., Keller, J. N., Szweda, L. I., Markesbery, W. R., et al. (2001). The glial glutamate transporter, GLT-1, is oxidatively modified by 4-hydroxy-2-nonenal in the Alzheimer's disease brain: The role of Abeta1-42. *Journal of Neurochemistry, 78,* 413–416.

Lauderback, C. M., Kanski, J., Hackett, J. M., Maeda, N., Kindy, M. S., & Butterfield, D. A. (2002). Apolipoprotein E modulates Alzheimer's Abeta(1-42)-induced oxidative damage to synaptosomes in an allele-specific manner. *Brain Research, 924,* 90–97.

Laumann, E., Gagnon, J. H., Michael, R. T., & Michaels, S. (1994). *The social organization of sexuality: Sexual practices in the United States.* Chicago: University of Chicago Press.

Lauterbach, E. C. (2004). The neuropsychiatry of Parkinson's disease and related disorders. *The Psychiatric Clinics of North America, 27,* 801–825.

Law, A., Logan, H., & Baron, R. S. (1994). Desire for control, felt control, and stress inoculation training during dental treatment. *Journal of Personality and Social Psychology, 67,* 926–936.

Lawrence, D. G., & Kuypers, H. G. (1968a). The functional organization of the motor system in the monkey: I. The effects of bilateral pyramidal lesions. *Brain, 91,* 1–14.

Lawrence, D. G., & Kuypers, H. G. (1968b). The functional organization of the motor system in the monkey: II. The effects of lesions of the descending brain-stem pathways. *Brain, 91,* 15–36.

Lazarus, R. S. (1993). From psychological stress to the emotions: A history of changing outlooks. *Annual Review of Psychology, 44,* 1–21.

Lazarus, R. S., & Lazarus, B. N. (1994). *Passion and reason: Making sense of our emotions.* New York: Oxford University Press.

Le Foll, B., & Goldberg, S. R. (2005). Cannabinoid CB_1 receptor antagonists as promising new medications for drug dependence. *The Journal of Pharmacology and Experimental Therapeutics, 312,* 875–883.

Leclerc, R. (1985). Sign-tracking behavior in aversive conditioning: Its acquisition via a Pavlovian mechanism and its suppression by operant contingencies. *Learning & Motivation, 16,* 63–82.

LeDoux, J. E. (1995). Emotions: Clues from the brain. *Annual Review of Psychology, 46,* 209–235.

LeDoux, J. E. (1996). *The emotional brain: The mysterious underpinnings of emotional life.* New York: Simon & Schuster.

LeDoux, J. E., Iwata, J., Cicchetti, P., & Reis, D. J. (1988). Different projections of the central amygdaloid nucleus mediate autonomic and behavioral correlates of conditioned fear. *The Journal of Neuroscience, 8,* 2517–2529.

Lee, A. K., & Wilson, M. A. (2002). Memory of sequential experience in the hippocampus during slow wave sleep. *Neuron, 36,* 1183–1194.

Lee, D., Port, N. L., Kruse, W., & Georgopoulos, A. P. (2001). Neuronal clusters in the primate motor cortex during interception of moving targets. *Journal of Cognitive Neuroscience, 13,* 319–331.

Lee, G. P., Bechara, A., Adolphs, R., Arena, J., Meador, K. J., Loring, D. W., et al. (1998). Clinical and physiological effects of stereotaxic bilateral amygdalotomy for intractable aggression. *Journal of Neuropsychiatry and Clinical Neurosciences, 10,* 413–420.

Lee, H. K., Takamiya, K., Han, J. S., Man, H., Kim, C. H., Rumbaugh, G., et al. (2003). Phosphorylation of the AMPA receptor GluR1 subunit is required for synaptic plasticity and retention of spatial memory. *Cell, 112,* 631–643.

Lehman, B. M. (2003). Affective language and humor appreciation after right hemisphere brain damage. *Seminars in Speech and Language, 24,* 107–119.

Lehrer, P. M., Carr, R., Sargunaraj, D., & Woolfolk, R. L. (1994). Stress management techniques: Are they all equivalent, or do they have specific effects? *Biofeedback and Self-Regulation, 19,* 353–401.

Lei, S., Pelkey, K. A., Topolnik, L., Congar, P., Lacaille, J. C., & McBain, C. J. (2003). Depolarization-induced long-term depression at hippocampal mossy fiber-CA_3 pyramidal neuron synapses. *The Journal of Neuroscience, 23,* 9786–9795.

Leibowitz, S. F., & Alexander, J. T. (1998). Hypothalamic serotonin in control of eating behavior, meal size, and body weight. *Biological Psychiatry, 44,* 851–864.

Leibowitz, S. F., Weiss, G. F., Yee, F., & Tretter, J. B. (1985). Noradrenergic innervation of the paraventricular nucleus: Specific role in control of carbohydrate ingestion. *Brain Research Bulletin, 14,* 561–567.

Lein, E. S., Hohn, A., & Shatz, C. J. (2000). Dynamic regulation of BDNF and NT-3 expression during visual system development. *Journal of Comparative Neurology, 420,* 1–18.

Leisman, G., & Koch, P. (2000). Continuum model of mnemonic and amnesic phenomena. *Journal of the International Neuropsychological Society, 6,* 593–607.

Lemieux, G., Davignon, A., & Genest, J. (1956). Depressive states during Rauwolfia therapy for arterial hypertension; a report of 30 cases. *Canadian Medical Association Journal, 74,* 522–526.

Lemmer, B., Kern, R. I., Nold, G., & Lohrer, H. (2002). Jet lag in athletes after eastward and westward time-zone transition. *Chronobiology International, 19,* 743–764.

Lenard, L., Jando, G., Karadi, Z., Hajnal, A., & Sandor, P. (1988). Lateral hypothalamic feeding mechanism: Iontophoretic effects of kainic acid, ibotenic acid and 6-hydroxydopamine. *Brain Research Bulletin, 20,* 847–856.

Lennartz, R. C., & Weinberger, N. M. (1992). Frequency selectivity is related to temporal processing in parallel thalamocortical auditory pathways. *Brain Research, 583,* 81–92.

Lenneberg, E. H. (1969). On explaining language. *Science, 164,* 635–643.

Lenneberg, E. H. (1993). Toward a biological theory of language development. In M. H. Johnson (Ed.), *Brain development and cognition: A reader* (pp. 39–46). Malden, MA: Blackwell Publishers.

Lenox, R. H., & Hahn, C. G. (2000). Overview of the mechanism of action of lithium in the brain: Fifty-year update. *Journal of Clinical Psychiatry, 61,* 5–15.

Leonard, B. E. (1997). Action mechanisms of antidepressants. In A. Honig & H. M. van Praag (Eds.), *Depression: Neurobiological, psychopathological and therapeutic advances* (pp. 459–470). New York: Wiley.

Leppamaki, S., Partonen, T., Vakkuri, O., Lonnqvist, J., Partinen, M., & Laudon, M. (2003). Effect of controlled-release melatonin on sleep quality, mood, and quality of life in subjects with seasonal or weather-associated changes in mood and behaviour. *European Neuropsychopharmacology, 13,* 137–145.

Lerner, A. G., Gelkopf, M., Oyffe, Il, Finkel, B., Katz, S., Sigal, M., et al. (2000). LSD-induced hallucinogen persisting perception disorder treatment with clonidine: An open pilot study. *International Clinical Psychopharmacology, 15,* 35–37.

Leroi, I., O'Hearn, E., Marsh, L., Lyketsos, C. G., Rosenblatt, A., Ross, C. A., et al. (2002). Psychopathology in patients with degenerative cerebellar diseases: A comparison to Huntington's disease. *American Journal of Psychiatry, 159,* 1306–1314.

Leuner, B., Mendolia-Loffredo, S., Kozorovitskiy, Y., Samburg, D., Gould, E., & Shors, T. J. (2004). Learning enhances the survival of new neurons beyond the time when the hippocampus is required for memory. *The Journal of Neuroscience, 24,* 7477–7481.

LeVay, S. (1991). A difference in hypothalamic structure between heterosexual and homosexual men. *Science, 253,* 1034–1037.

Levenson, R. W., & Ekman, P. (2002). Difficulty does not account for emotion-specific heart rate changes in the directed facial action task. *Psychophysiology, 29,* 397–405.

Levenson, R. W., Ekman, P., & Friesen, W. V. (1990). Voluntary facial action generates emotion-specific autonomic nervous system activity. *Psychophysiology, 27,* 363–384.

Levi-Montalcini, R., & Hamburger, V. (1951). Selective growth stimulating effects of mouse sarcoma on the sensory and sympathetic nervous system of the chick embryo. *Journal of Experimental Zoology, 116,* 321–361.

Levin, B. E. (2000). The obesity epidemic: Metabolic imprinting on genetically susceptible neural circuits. *Obesity Research, 8,* 342–347.

Levin, B. E., & Dunn-Meynell, A. A. (2000). Defense of body weight against chronic caloric restriction in obesity-prone and -resistant rats. *American Journal of Physiology. Regulatory, Integrative and Comparative Physiology, 278,* R231–R237.

Levin, B. E., & Dunn-Meynell, A. A. (2002). Defense of body weight depends on dietary composition and palatability in rats with diet-induced obesity. *American Journal of Physiology. Regulatory, Integrative and Comparative Physiology, 282,* R46–R54.

Levin, B. E., Dunn-Meynell, A. A., Balkan, B., & Keesey, R. E. (1997). Selective breeding for diet-induced obesity and resistance in Sprague-Dawley rats. *American Journal of Physiology, 273,* R725–R730.

Levin, B. E., Dunn-Meynell, A. A., & Banks, W. A. (2004). Obesity-prone rats have normal blood-brain barrier transport but defective central leptin signaling before obesity onset. *American Journal of Physiology. Regulatory, Integrative and Comparative Physiology, 286,* R143–R150.

Levin, B. E., & Keesey, R. E. (1998). Defense of differing body weight set points in diet-induced obese and resistant rats. *American Journal of Physiology, 274,* R412–R419.

Levin, E. D. (1988). Psychopharmacological effects in the radial-arm maze. *Neuroscience and Biobehavioral Reviews, 12,* 169–175.

Levin, R. J. (1998). Sex and the human female reproductive tract—What really happens during and after coitus. *International Journal of Impotence Research, 10,* S14–S21.

Levin, R. J. (2002). The physiology of sexual arousal in the human female: A recreational and procreational synthesis. *Archives of Sexual Behavior, 31,* 405–411.

Levine, J., Leventhal, U., Lerner, V., & Belmaker, R. H. (2001). Inositol treatment has no effect on the dexamethasone suppression test. *The World Journal of Biological Psychiatry, 2,* 190–192.

Levy, H. L. (1987). Maternal phenylketonuria. Review with emphasis on pathogenesis. *Enzyme, 38,* 312–320.

Levy, J. (1985, May). Right brain, left brain: Fact and fiction. *Psychology Today,* 38–44.

Levy, J., Trevarthen, C., & Sperry, R. W. (1972). Perception of bilateral chimeric figures following hemispheric deconnexion. *Brain, 95,* 61–78.

Levy, L. M., Henkin, R. I., Lin, C. S., & Finley, A. (1999). Rapid imaging of olfaction by functional MRI (fMRI): Identification of presence and type of hyposmia. *Journal of Computer Assisted Tomography, 23,* 767–775.

Levy-Lahad, E., Tsuang, D., & Bird, T. D. (1998). Recent advances in the genetics of Alzheimer's disease. *Journal of Geriatric Psychiatry and Neurology, 11,* 42–54.

Lewin, R. (1985). Parkinson's disease: An environmental cause? *Science, 229,* 257–258.

Lewis, D. J. (1979). Psychobiology of active and inactive memory. *Psychological Bulletin, 86,* 1054–1083.

Lewis, S. J., Dove, A., Robbins, T. W., Barker, R. A., & Owen, A. M. (2003). Cognitive impairments in early Parkinson's disease are accompanied by reductions in activity in frontostriatal neural circuitry. *The Journal of Neuroscience, 23,* 6351–6356.

Lewy, A. J., Bauer, V. K., Cutler, N. L., & Sack, R. L. (1998). Melatonin treatment of winter depression: A pilot study. *Psychiatry Research, 77,* 57–61.

Li, N., He, S., Parrish, C., Delich, J., & Grasing, K. (2003). Differences in morphine and cocaine reinforcement under fixed and progressive ratio schedules; effects of extinction, reacquisition and schedule design. *Behavioural Pharmacology, 14,* 619–630.

Li, X. B., Inoue, T., Nakagawa, S., & Koyama, T. (2004). Effect of mediodorsal thalamic nucleus lesion on contextual fear conditioning in rats. *Brain Research, 1008,* 261–272.

Liao, J., & Schultz, P. G. (2003). Three sweet receptor genes are clustered in human chromosome 1. *Mammalian Genome, 14,* 291–301.

Liechti, M. E., & Vollenweider, F. X. (2001). Which neuroreceptors mediate the subjective effects of MDMA in humans? A summary of mechanistic studies. *Human Psychopharmacology, 16,* 589–598.

Lien, H. C., Sun, W. M., Chen, Y. H., Kim, H., Hasler, W., & Owyang, C. (2003). Effects of ginger on motion sickness and gastric slow-wave dysrhythmias induced by circular vection. *American Journal of Physiology, 284,* G481–G489.

Liguori, A., Gatto, C. P., & Jarrett, D. B. (2002). Separate and combined effects of marijuana and alcohol on mood, equilibrium and simulated driving. *Psychopharmacology (Berlin), 163,* 399–405.

Lilenfeld, L. R., Kaye, W. H., Greeno, C. G., Merikangas, K. R., Plotnicov, K., Pollice, C., et al. (1998). A controlled family study of anorexia nervosa and bulimia nervosa: Psychiatric disorders in first-degree relatives and effects of proband comorbidity. *Archives of General Psychiatry, 55,* 603–610.

Limosin, F., Rouillon, F., Payan, C., Cohen, J. M., & Strub, N. (2003). Prenatal exposure to influenza as a risk factor for adult schizophrenia. *Acta Psychiatrica Scandinavica, 107,* 331–335.

Lin, L., Faraco, J., Li, R., Kadotani, H., Rogers, W., Lin, X., et al. (1999). The sleep disorder canine narcolepsy is caused by a mutation in the hypocretin (orexin) receptor 2 gene. *Cell, 98,* 365–376.

Lin, L., Hungs, M., & Mignot, E. (2001). Narcolepsy and the HLS region. *Journal of Neuroimmunology, 117,* 9–20.

Lin, W., & Kinnamon, S. C. (1999). Physiological evidence for ionotropic and metabotropic glutamate receptors in rat taste cells. *Journal of Neurophysiology, 82,* 2061–2069.

Lindsley, D. B. (1944). Electroencephalography. In J. M. Hunt (Ed.), *Personality and the behavioral disorders* (Vol. 2, pp. 1033–1103). New York: Ronald Press.

Lindstrom, J. M. (2000). Acetylcholine receptors and myasthenia. *Muscle & Nerve, 23,* 453–477.

Lindstrom, L. H. (1996). Clinical and biological markers for outcome in schizophrenia: A review of a longitudinal follow-up study in Uppsala schizophrenia research project. *Neuropsychopharmacology, 14,* 23S–26S.

Lindvall, O. (1998). Update on fetal transplantation: The Swedish experience. *Movement Disorders, 13,* 83–87.

Lindvall, O. (2000). Neural transplantation in Parkinson's disease. *Novartis Foundation Symposium, 231,* 110–123.

Lindvall, O. (2003). Stem cells for cell therapy in Parkinson's disease. *Pharmacological Research, 47,* 279–287.

Lindvall, O., & Hagell, P. (2001). Cell therapy and transplantation in Parkinson's disease. *Clinical Chemistry and Laboratory Medicine, 39,* 356–361.

Linnet, K. M., Dalsgaard, S., Obel, C., Wisborg, K., Henriksen, T. B., Rodriguez, A., et al. (2003). Maternal lifestyle factors in pregnancy risk of attention deficit hyperactivity disorder and associated behaviors: Review of the current evidence. *American Journal of Psychiatry, 160,* 1028–1040.

Lino, A., Silvy, S., Condorelli, L., & Rusconi, A. C. (1993). Melatonin and jet lag: Treatment schedule. *Biological Psychiatry, 34,* 587.

Lisanby, S. H., Maddox, J. H., Prudic, J., Devanand, D. P., & Sackeim, H. A. (2000). The effects of electroconvulsive therapy on memory of autobiographical and public events. *Archives of General Psychiatry, 57,* 581–590.

Liu, Y. C., Salamone, J. D., & Sachs, B. D. (1997). Lesions in medial preoptic area and bed nucleus of stria terminalis: Differential effects on copulatory behavior and noncontact erection in male rats. *The Journal of Neuroscience, 17,* 5245–5253.

Livingstone, M., & Hubel, D. (1988). Segregation of form, color, movement, and depth: Anatomy, physiology, and perception. *Science, 240,* 740–749.

Lockhart, R. S., & Craik, F. I. (1990). Levels of processing: A retrospective commentary on a framework for memory research. *Canadian Journal of Psychology, 44,* 87–112.

Loewi, O. (1960). An autobiographical sketch. *Perspectives in Biology and Medicine, 4,* 3–25.

Loftus, E. (2003). Our changeable memories: Legal and practical implications. *Nature Reviews. Neuroscience, 4,* 231–234.

Logan, C. G., & Grafton, S. T. (1995). Functional anatomy of human eyeblink conditioning determined with regional cerebral glucose metabolism and positron-emission tomography. *Proceedings of the National Academy of Sciences of the United States of America, 92,* 7500–7504.

Logue, A. W. (1991). *The psychology of eating & drinking: An introduction* (2nd ed.). New York: W. H. Freeman.

LoLordo, V. M. (2001). Learned helplessness and depression. In M. E. Carroll & J. B. Overmier (Eds.), *Animal research and human health: Advancing human welfare through behavioral science* (pp. 63–77). Washington, DC: American Psychological Association.

Long, J. W. (1984). *Clinical management of prescription drugs.* New York: Harper Collins.

Loosen, P. T., Purdon, S. E., & Pavlou, S. N. (1994). Effects on behavior of modulation of gonadal function in men with gonadotropin-releasing hormone antagonists. *American Journal of Psychiatry, 151,* 271–273.

Lopez-Larson, M. P., DelBello, M. P., Zimmerman, M. E., Schwiers, M. L., & Strakowski, S. M. (2002). Regional prefrontal gray and white matter abnormalities in bipolar disorder. *Biological Psychiatry, 52,* 93–100.

Lord, T., & Kasprzak, M. (1989). Identification of self through olfaction. *Perceptual and Motor Skills, 69,* 219–224.

Loring, D. W., Meador, K. J., Lee, G. P., Murro, A. M., Smith, J. R., Flanigin, H. F., et al. (1990). Cerebral language lateralization: Evidence from intracarotid amobarbital testing. *Neuropsychologia, 28,* 831–838.

Lott, I. T., & Head, E. (2005). Alzheimer disease and Down syndrome: Factors in pathogenesis. *Neurobiology of Aging, 26,* 383–389.

Louie, K., & Wilson, M. A. (2001). Temporally structured replay of awake hippocampal ensemble activity during rapid eye movement sleep. *Neuron, 29,* 145–156.

Louis-Sylvestre, J., Giachetti, I., & Le Magnen, J. (1984). Sensory versus dietary factors in cafeteria-induced overweight. *Physiology & Behavior, 32,* 901–905.

Louis-Sylvestre, J., Larue-Achagiotis, C., & Le Magnen, J. (1980). Oral induction of the insulin hyper-responsiveness in rats with ventromedial hypothalamic lesions. *Hormone and Metabolic Research, 12,* 671–676.

Louis-Sylvestre, J., & Le Magnen, J. (1980). Fall in blood glucose level precedes meal onset in free-feeding rats. *Neuroscience and Biobehavioral Reviews, 4,* 13–15.

Lowe, J., & Carroll, D. (1985). The effects of spinal injury on the intensity of emotional experience. *British Journal of Clinical Psychology, 24,* 135–136.

Luboshitzky, R., & Lavie, P. (1999). Melatonin and sex hormone interrelationships—A review. *Journal of Pediatric Endocrinology & Metabolism,* 12, 355–362.

Luders, E., Rex, D. E., Narr, K. L., Woods, R. P., Jancke, L., Thompson, P. M., et al. (2003). Relationships between sulcal asymmetries and corpus callosum size: Gender and handedness. *Cerebral Cortex, 13,* 1084–1093.

Luft, A. R., Smith, G. V., Forrester, L., Whitall, J., Macko, R. F., Hauser, T. K., et al. (2002). Comparing brain activation associated with isolated upper and lower limb movement across corresponding joints. *Human Brain Mapping, 17,* 131–140.

Lugaz, O., Pillias, A. M., & Faurion, A. (2002). A new specific ageusia: Some humans cannot taste L-glutamate. *Chemical Senses, 27,* 105–115.

Lynch, G. (1986). *Synapses, circuits, and the beginnings of memory.* Cambridge, MA: The MIT Press.

Lynch, G., & Baudry, M. (1984). The biochemistry of memory: A new and specific hypothesis. *Science, 224,* 1057–1063.

Lynch, M. A. (2004). Long-term potentiation and memory. *Physiological Reviews, 84,* 87–136.

Lyness, S. A. (1993). Predictors of differences between Type A and B individuals in heart rate and blood pressure reactivity. *Psychological Bulletin, 114,* 266–295.

Lyons, M. J., Eisen, S. A., Goldberg, J., True, W., Lin, N., Meyer, J. M., et al. (1998). A registry-based twin study of depression in men. *Archives of General Psychiatry, 55,* 468–472.

Maas, J. B. (1998). *Power sleep.* New York: Villard.

Maas, J. W., Dekirmenjian, H., & Fawcett, J. (1971). Catecholamine metabolism, depression and stress. *Nature, 230,* 330–331.

Maas, J. W., Dekirmenjian, H., & Fawcett, J. A. (1974). MHPG excretion by patients with affective disorders. *International Pharmacopsychiatry, 9,* 14–26.

MacDonald, A. W., III, Cohen, J. D., Stenger, V. A., & Carter, C. S. (2000). Dissociating the role of the dorsolateral prefrontal and anterior cingulate cortex in cognitive control. *Science, 288,* 1835–1838.

MacDonald, M. E., Gines, S., Gusella, J. F., & Wheeler, V. C. (2003). Huntington's disease. *Neuromolecular Medicine, 4,* 7–20.

MacIntosh, C. G., Morley, J. E., Wishart, J., Morris, H., Jansen, J. B., Horowitz, M., et al. (2001). Effect of exogenous cholecystokinin (CCK)-8 on food intake and plasma CCK, leptin, and insulin concentrations in older and young adults: Evidence for increased CCK activity as a cause of the anorexia of aging. *The Journal of Clinical Endocrinology and Metabolism, 86,* 5830–5837.

MacKay, E. M., Calloway, J. W., & Barnes, R. H. (1940). Hyperalimentation in normal animals produced by protamine-insulin. *Journal of Nutrition, 20,* 59–66.

MacLean, P. D. (1949). Psychosomatic disease and the "visceral brain": Recent developments bearing on the Papez theory of emotion. *Psychosomatic Medicine, 11,* 338–353.

MacLean, P. D. (1970). The limbic brain in relation to the psychoses. In P. Black (Ed.), *Physiological correlates of emotion.* New York: Academic Press.

Maddison, S., Wood, R. J., Rolls, E. T., Rolls, B. J., & Gibbs, J. (1980). Drinking in the rhesus monkey: Peripheral factors. *Journal of Comparative and Physiological Psychology, 94,* 365–374.

Madhav, T. R., Pei, Q., Grahame-Smith, D. G., & Zetterstrom, T. S. (2000). Repeated electroconvulsive shock promotes the sprouting of serotonergic axons in the lesioned rat hippocampus. *Neuroscience, 97,* 677–683.

Maffei, L., & Galli-Resta, L. (1990). Correlation in the discharges of neighboring rat retinal ganglion cells during prenatal life. *Proceedings of the National Academy of Sciences of the United States of America, 87,* 2861–2864.

Maguire, C., Casey, M., Kelly, A., Mullany, P. M., & Lynch, M. A. (1999). Activation of tyrosine receptor kinase plays a role in expression of long-term potentiation in the rat dentate gyrus. *Hippocampus, 9,* 519–526.

Mahant, N., McCusker, E. A., Byth, K., Graham, S.; Huntington Study Group. (2003). Huntington's disease: Clinical correlates of disability and progression. *Neurology, 61,* 1085–1092.

Mahl, G. F. (1950). Anxiety, HCl secretion, and peptic ulcer etiology. *Psychosomatic Medicine, 12,* 158–169.

Majewska, M. D., Harrison, N. L., Schwartz, R. D., Barker, J. L., & Paul, S. M. (1986). Steroid hormone metabolites are barbiturate-like modulators of the GABA receptor. *Science, 232,* 1004–1007.

Malamud, N. (1967). Psychiatric disorder with intracranial tumors of the limbic system. *Archives of Neurology, 17,* 113–123.

Maldonado, R., Robledo, P., Chover, A. J., Caine, S. B., & Koob, G. F. (1993). D_1 dopamine receptors in the nucleus accumbens modulate cocaine self-administration in the rat. *Pharmacology, Biochemistry, and Behavior, 45,* 239–242.

Malenka, R. C. (2003). Synaptic plasticity and AMPA receptor trafficking. *Annals of the New York Academy of Sciences, 1003,* 1–11.

Malhotra, A., Ayas, N. T., & Epstein, L. J. (2000). The art and science of continuous positive airway pressure therapy in obstructive sleep apnea. *Current Opinion in Pulmonary Medicine, 6,* 490–495.

Malinow, R., & Malenka, R. C. (2002). AMPA receptor trafficking and synaptic plasticity. *Annual Review of Neuroscience, 25,* 103–126.

Manahan-Vaughan, D., Herrero, I., Reymann, K. G., & Sanchez-Prieto, J. (1999). Presynaptic group 1 metabotropic glutamate receptors may contribute to the expression of long-term potentiation in the hippocampal CA_1 region. *Neuroscience, 94,* 71–82.

Mandal, M. K., Borod, J. C., Asthana, H. S., Mohanty, A., Mohanty, S., & Koff, E. (1999). Effects of lesion variables and emotion type on the perception of facial emotion. *The Journal of Nervous and Mental Disease, 187,* 603–609.

Mandzia, J., & Black, S. E. (2001). Neuroimaging and behavior: Probing brain behavior relationships in the 21st century. *Current Neurology and Neuroscience Reports, 1,* 553–561.

Mann, J. J., & Malone, K. M. (1997). Cerebrospinal fluid amines and higher-lethality suicide attempts in depressed inpatients. *Biological Psychiatry, 41,* 162–171.

Mann, J. J., McBride, P. A., Brown, R. P., Linnoila, M., Leon, A. C., DeMeo, M., et al. (1992). Relationship between central and peripheral serotonin indexes in depressed and suicidal psychiatric inpatients. *Archives of General Psychiatry, 49,* 442–446.

Mann, K. (2004). Pharmacology of alcohol dependence: A review of the clinical data. CNS *Drugs, 18,* 485–504.

Manns, J. R., Hopkins, R. O., Reed, J. M., Kitchener, E. G., & Squire, L. R. (2003). Recognition memory and the human hippocampus. *Neuron, 37,* 171–180.

Manrique, M., Cervera-Paz, F. J., Huarte, A., & Molina, M. (2004). Prospective long-term auditory results of cochlear implantation in prelinguistically deafened children: The importance of early implantation. *Acta Oto-laryngologica. Supplementum,* 55–63.

Maquet, P. (2001). The role of sleep in learning and memory. *Science, 294,* 1048–1052.

Maquet, P., Laureys, S., Peigneux, P., Fuchs, S., Petiau, C., Phillips, C., et al. (2000). Experience-dependent changes in cerebral activation during human REM sleep. *Nature Neuroscience, 3,* 831–836.

Maquet, P., Peigneux, P., Laureys, S., Boly, M., Dang-Vu, T., Desseilles, M., et al. (2003). Memory processing during human sleep as assessed by functional neuroimaging. *Revue Neurologique, 159,* 6S27–6S29.

Maquet, P., Péters, J.-M., Aerts, J., Delfiore, G., Degueldre, C., Luxen, A., et al. (1996). Functional neuroanatomy of human rapid-eye-movement sleep and dreaming. *Nature, 383,* 163–166.

Marder, S. R. (1999). Antipsychotic drugs and relapse prevention. *Schizophrenia Research, 35,* S87–S92.

Margules, D. L., & Stein, L. (1967). Neuroleptics versus tranquilizers: Evidence from animal behavior studies of mode and site of action. In H. Brill et al. (Eds.), *Neuropsychopharmacology* (pp. 108–120). Amsterdam: Elsevier.

Marino, S., Hoogervoorst, D., Brandner, S., & Berns, A. (2003). Rb and p107 are required for normal cerebellar development and granule cell survival but not for Purkinje cell persistence. *Development, 130,* 3359–3368.

Mark, V. H., & Ervin, F. R. (1970). *Violence and the brain.* New York: Harper & Row.

Markianos, M., Botsis, A., & Arvanitis, Y. (1992). Biogenic amine metabolites in plasma of drug-naive schizophrenic patients: Associations with symptomatology. *Biological Psychiatry, 32,* 288–292.

Marks, G. A., Shaffery, J. P., Oksenberg, A., Speciale, S. G., & Roffwarg, H. P. (1995). A functional role for REM sleep in brain maturation. *Behavioural Brain Research, 69,* 1–11.

Marrocco, R. T., Witte, E. A., & Davidson, M. C. (1994). Arousal systems. *Current Opinion in Neurobiology, 4,* 166–170.

Marsh, L., Suddath, R. L., Higgins, N., & Weinberger, D. R. (1994). Medial temporal lobe structures in schizophrenia: Relationship of size to duration of illness. *Schizophrenia Research, 11,* 225–238.

Martin, A. (1998). Pharmacology update: What's new in the treatment of depression. *Psychoanalysis & Psychotherapy, 15,* 131–134.

Martini, F. H. (1998). *Fundamentals of anatomy and physiology* (4th ed.). Upper Saddle River, NJ: Prentice-Hall.

Martini, F. H. (2003). *Fundamentals of anatomy and physiology* (6th ed.). San Francisco: Benjamin Cummings.

Martone, M., Butters, N., Payne, M., Becker, J. T., & Sax, D. S. (1984). Dissociations between skill learning and verbal recognition in amnesia and dementia. *Archives of Neurology, 41,* 965–970.

Marzella, P. L., Hill, C., Keks, N., Singh, B., & Copolov, D. (1997). The binding of both [3H]nemonapride and [3H]raclopride is increased in schizophrenia. *Biological Psychiatry, 42,* 648–654.

Masand, P., Popli, A. P., & Weilburg, J. B. (1995). Sleepwalking. *American Family Physician, 51,* 649–654.

Massi, M., De Caro, G., Mazzarella, L., & Epstein, A. N. (1986). The role of the subfornical organ in the drinking behavior of the pigeon. *Brain Research, 381,* 289–299.

Masters, W., & Johnson, V. (1966). *Human sexual response.* Boston: Little, Brown.

Masters, W., & Johnson, V. (1970). *Human sexual inadequacy.* Boston: Little, Brown.

Matos, F. F., Guss, V., & Korpinen, C. (1996). Effects of neuropeptide Y (NPY) and [D-Trp32]NPY on monoamine and metabolite levels in dialysates from rat hypothalamus during feeding behavior. *Neuropeptides, 30,* 391–398.

Matsumoto, R., Nair, D. R., LaPresto, E., Najm, I., Bingaman, W., Shibasaki, H., et al. (2004). Functional connectivity in the human language system: A cortico-cortical evoked potential. *Brain, 127,* 2316–2330.

Matsunami, H., Montmayeur, J. P., & Buck, L. B. (2000). A family of candidate taste receptors in human and mouse. *Nature, 404,* 601–604.

Matsuo, K., Nakai, T., Kato, C., Moriya, T., Isoda, H., Takehara, Y., et al. (2000). Dissociation of writing processes: functional magnetic resonance imaging during writing of Japanese ideographic characters. *Cognitive Brain Research, 9,* 281–286.

Matthews, K. A., & Haynes, S. G. (1986). Type A behavior pattern and coronary disease risk. Update and critical evaluation. *American Journal of Epidemiology, 123,* 923–960.

Mattick, R. P., Kimber, J., Breen, C., & Davoli, M. (2004). Buprenorphine maintenance versus placebo or methadone maintenance for opioid dependence. *Cochrane Database of Systematic Reviews, 3,* CD002207.

Mattson, M. P. (2003). Excitotoxic and excitoprotective mechanisms: Abundant targets for the prevention and treatment of neurodegenerative disorders. *Neuromolecular Medicine, 3,* 65–94.

Matuszewich, L., Lorrain, D. S., & Hull, E. M. (2000). Dopamine release in the medial preoptic area of female rats in response to hormonal manipulation and sexual activity. *Behavioral Neuroscience, 114,* 772–782.

Mavanji, V., & Datta, S. (2002). Sleep-wake effects of yohimbine and atropine in rats with a clomipramine-based model of depression. *Neuroreport, 13,* 1603–1606.

Mavri, A., Stegnar, M., & Sabovic, M. (2001). Do baseline serum leptin levels predict weight regain after dieting in obese women? *Diabetes, Obesity & Metabolism, 3,* 293–296.

Max, M., Shanker, Y. G., Huang, L., Rong, M., Liu, Z., Campagne, F., et al. (2001). Taslr3, encoding a new candidate taste receptor, is allelic to the sweet responsiveness locus Sac. *Nature Genetics, 28,* 58–63.

Mayer, J. (1953). Glucostatic mechanism of regulation of food intake. *New England Journal of Medicine, 249,* 13–16.

Mayer, J. (1955). Regulation of energy intake and the body weight: The glucostatic theory and the lipostatic hypothesis. *Annals of the New York Academy of Sciences, 63,* 15–43.

Mayer, J. (1978). *Overweight: Causes, cost and control.* Englewood Cliffs, NJ: Prentice-Hall.

McCall, W. V. (2001). Electroconvulsive therapy in the era of modern psychopharmacology. *International Journal of Neuropsychopharmacology, 4,* 315–324.

McCargar, L. J. (1996). Can diet and exercise really change metabolism? *Medscape Women's Health, 1,* 5.

McCarthy, M. E., & Waters, W. F. (1997). Decreased attentional responsivity during sleep deprivation: Orienting response latency, amplitude, and habituation. *Sleep, 20,* 115–123.

McClintock, M. K. (1971). Menstrual synchrony and suppression. *Nature, 229,* 244–245.

McClintock, M. K. (1998). Whither menstrual synchrony? *Annual Review of Sex Research, 9,* 77–95.

McCormick, D. A. (1989). Acetylcholine: Distribution, receptors, and actions. *Seminars in the Neurosciences, 1,* 91–101.

McDonald, E. R., Wiedenfeld, S. A., Hillel, A., Carpenter, C. L., & Walter, R. A. (1994). Survival in amyotrophic lateral sclerosis. The role of psychological factors. *Archives of Neurology, 51,* 17–23.

McDonald, W. I., Compston, A., Edan, G., Goodkin, D., Hartung, H. P., Lublin, F. D., et al. (2001). Recommended diagnostic criteria for multiple sclerosis: Guidelines from the International Panel on the diagnosis of multiple sclerosis. *Annals of Neurology, 50,* 121–127.

McDowell, I. (2001). Alzheimer's disease: Insights from epidemiology. *Aging (Milano), 13,* 143–162.

McElroy, S. L., Casuto, L. S., Nelson, E. B., Lake, K. A., Soutullo, C. A., Keck, P. E., Jr., et al. (2000). Placebo-controlled trial of sertraline in the treatment of binge eating disorder. *American Journal of Psychiatry, 157,* 1004–1006.

McElroy, S. L., Hudson, J. I., Malhotra, S., Welge, J. A., Nelson, E. B., & Keck, P. E., Jr. (2003). Citalopram in the treatment of binge-eating disorder: A placebo-controlled trial. *Journal of Clinical Psychiatry, 64,* 807–813.

McEwen, B. S. (1998). Stress, adaptation, and disease. Allostasis and allostatic load. *Annals of the New York Academy of Sciences, 840,* 33–44.

McEwen, B. S. (1999). Stress and hippocampal plasticity. *Annual Review of Neuroscience, 22,* 105–122.

McEwen, B. S. (2000a). Allostasis, allostatic load, and the aging nervous system: Role of excitatory amino acids and excitotoxicity. *Neurochemical Research, 25,* 1219–1231.

McEwen, B. S. (2000b). Effects of adverse experiences for brain structure and function. *Biological Psychiatry, 48,* 721–731.

McEwen, B. S. (2000c). The neurobiology of stress: From serendipity to clinical relevance. *Brain Research, 886,* 172–189.

McEwen, B. S., & Magarinos, A. M. (2001). Stress and hippocampal plasticity: Implications for the pathophysiology of affective disorders. *Human Psychopharmacology, 16,* S7–S19.

McEwen, B. S., & Wingfield, J. C. (2003). The concept of allostasis in biology and medicine. *Hormones and Behavior, 43,* 2–15.

McGaugh, J. L., Cahill, L., & Roozendaal, B. (1996). Involvement of the amygdala in memory storage: Interaction with other brain systems. *Proceedings of the National Academy of Sciences of the United States of America, 93,* 13508–13514.

McGinnis, M. Y., Montana, R. C., & Lumia, A. R. (2002). Effects of hydroxyflutamide in the medial preoptic area or lateral septum on reproductive behaviors in male rats. *Brain Research Bulletin, 59,* 227–234.

McGinty, D., & Szymusiak, R. (2003). Hypothalamic regulation of sleep and arousal. *Frontiers in Bioscience, 8,* 1074–1083.

McInnis, K. J. (2000). Exercise and obesity. *Coronary Artery Disease, 11,* 111–116.

McKinley, M. J., Allen, A. M., Burns, P., Colvill, L. M., & Oldfield, B. J. (1998). Interaction of circulating hormones with the brain: The roles of the subfornical organ and the organum vasculosum of the lamina terminalis. *Clinical and Experimental Pharmacology & Physiology. Supplement, 25,* S61–S67.

McLaughlin, T., Torborg, C. L., Feller, M. B., & O'Leary, D. D. (2003). Retinotopic map refinement requires spontaneous retinal waves during a brief critical period of development. *Neuron, 40,* 1147–1160.

McMahon, P. M., Araki, S. S., Neumann, P. J., Harris, G. J., & Gazelle, G. S. (2000). Cost-effectiveness of functional imaging tests in the diagnosis of Alzheimer disease. *Radiology, 217,* 58–68.

Mearow, K. M. (1998). The effects of NGF and sensory nerve stimulation on collateral sprouting and gene expression in adult sensory neurons. *Experimental Neurology, 151,* 14–25.

Mechoulam, R., & Parker, L. (2003). Cannabis and alcohol—A close friendship. *Trends in Pharmacological Sciences, 24,* 266–268.

Medina, L. S., Aguirre, E., Bernal, B., & Altman, N. R. (2004). Functional MR imaging versus Wada test for evaluation of language lateralization: Cost analysis. *Radiology, 230,* 49–54.

Medved, V., Petrovic, R., Isgum, V., Szirovicza, L., & Hotujac, L. (2001). Similarities in the pattern of regional brain dysfunction in negative schizophrenia and unipolar depression: A single photon emission-computed tomography and auditory evoked potentials. *Progress in Neuro-Psychopharmacology & Biological Psychiatry, 25,* 993–1009.

Meehan, H. L., Bull, S. J., Wood, D. M., & James, D. V. B (2004). The overtraining syndrome: A multicontextual assessment. *Sport Psychologist, 18,* 154–171.

Meeks, G. J., Grantham-McGregor, S. M., Chang, S. M., Himes, J. H., & Powell, C. A. (1995). Activity and behavioral development in stunted and nonstunted children and response to nutritional supplementation. *Child Development, 66,* 1785–1797.

Mehlman, P. T., Higley, J. D., Faucher, I., Lilly, A. A., Taub, D. M., Vickers, J., et al. (1995). Correlation of CSF 5-HIAA concentration with sociality and the timing of emigration in free-ranging primates. *American Journal of Psychiatry, 152,* 907–913.

Meichenbaum, D. (1996). Stress inoculation training for coping with stressors. *The Clinical Psychologist, 49,* 4–7.

Meijer, J. H., & Rietveld, W. J. (1989). Neurophysiology of the suprachiasmatic circadian pacemaker in rodents. *Physiological Reviews, 69,* 671–707.

Meijer, J. H., van der Zee, E. A., & Dietz, M. (1988). Glutamate phase shifts circadian activity rhythms in hamsters. *Neuroscience Letters, 86,* 177–183.

Meis, S., & Pape, H. C. (2001). Control of glutamate and GABA release by nociceptin/orphanin FQ in the rat lateral amygdala. *Journal of Physiology, 532,* 701–712.

Melendez, R. I., Rodd-Henricks, Z. A., Engleman, E. A., Li, T. K., McBride, W. J., & Murphy, J. M. (2002). Microdialysis of dopamine in the nucleus accumbens of alcohol-preferring (P) rats during anticipation and operant self-administration of ethanol. *Alcoholism, Clinical and Experimental Research, 26,* 318–325.

Melfi, R. S., & Garrison, S. J. (2004). Communication disorders. Retrieved September 10, 2004, from http://www.emedicine.com/pmr/topic153.htm

Meltzer, H. Y., Kennedy, J., Dai, J., Parsa, M., & Riley, D. (1995). Plasma clozapine levels and the treatment of L-DOPA-induced psychosis in Parkinson's disease. A high potency effect of clozapine. *Neuropsychopharmacology, 12,* 39–45.

Melzack, R. (1999). From the gate to the neuromatrix. *Pain, Supplement 6,* S121–S126.

Melzack, R. (2001). Pain and the neuromatrix in the brain. *Journal of Dental Education, 65,* 1378–1382.

Melzack, R., & Wall, P. D. (1965). Pain mechanisms: A new theory. *Science, 150,* 971–979.

Melzack, R., & Wall, P. D. (1982). *The challenge of pain.* Harmondsworth, England: Penguin.

Mendelson, J. (1967). Lateral hypothalamic stimulation in satiated rats: The rewarding effects of self-induced drinking. *Science, 157,* 1077–1079.

Mendelson, W. B. (1987). *Human sleep: Research and clinical care.* New York: Plenum Press.

Menendez, L., Lastra, A., Hidalgo, A., & Baamonde, A. (2004). The analgesic effect induced by capsaicin is enhanced in inflammatory states. *Life Sciences, 74,* 3235–3244.

Meredith, M. (1994). Chronic recording of vomeronasal pump activation in awake behaving hamsters. *Physiology & Behavior, 56,* 345–354.

Meredith, M. (2001). Human vomeronasal organ function: A critical review of best and worst cases. *Chemical Senses, 26,* 433–445.

Meredith, M., Marques, D. M., O'Connell, R. O., & Stern, F. L. (1980). Vomeronasal pump: Significance for male hamster sexual behavior. *Science, 207,* 1224–1226.

Mereu, G., Fa, M., Ferraro, L., Cagiano, R., Antonelli, T., Tattoli, et al. (2003). Prenatal exposure to a cannabinoid agonist produces memory deficits linked to dysfunction in hippocampal long-term potentiation and glutamate release. *Proceedings of the National Academy of Sciences of the United States of America, 100,* 4915–4920.

Merlotti, L., Roehrs, T., Zorick, F., & Roth, T. (1991). Rebound insomnia: Duration of use and individual differences. *Journal of Clinical Psychopharmacology, 11,* 368–373.

Merrick, J., Aspler, S., & Schwarz, G. (2003). Phenylalanine-restricted diet should be life long. A case report on long-term follow-up of an adolescent with untreated phenylketonuria. *International Journal of Adolescent Medicine and Health, 15,* 165–168.

Merry, D. E., & Korsmeyer, S. J. (1997). Bcl-2 gene family in the nervous system. *Annual Review of Neuroscience, 20,* 245–267.

Mervaala, E., Kononen, M., Fohr, J., Husso-Saastamoinen, M., Valkonen-Korhonen, M., Kuikka, J. T., et al. (2001). SPECT and neuropsychological performance in severe depression treated with ECT. *Journal of Affective Disorders, 66,* 47–58.

Mervis, C. B. (2003). Williams syndrome: 15 years of psychological research. *Developmental Neuropsychology, 23,* 1–12.

Mervis, C. B., & Klein-Tasman, B. P. (2000). Williams syndrome: Cognition, personality, and adaptive behavior. *Mental Retardation and Developmental Disabilities Research Reviews, 6,* 148–158.

Meschke, L. L., Holl, J. A., & Messelt, S. (2003). Assessing the risk of fetal alcohol syndrome: Understanding substance use among pregnant women. *Neurotoxicology and Teratology, 25,* 667–674.

Messerli, P., Pegna, A., & Sordet, N. (1995). Hemispheric dominance for melody recognition in musicians and non-musicians. *Neuropsychologia, 33,* 395–405.

Mesulam, M. M. (1998). Some cholinergic themes related to Alzheimer's disease: Synaptology of the nucleus basalis, location of m2 receptors, interactions with amyloid metabolism, and perturbations of cortical plasticity. *Journal of Physiology, Paris, 92,* 293–298.

Methippara, M. M., Alam, M. N., Szymusiak, R., & McGinty, D. (2003). Preoptic area warming inhibits wake-active neurons in the perifornical lateral hypothalamus. *Brain Research, 960,* 165–173.

Meyers, R. (1942). The modification of alternating tremor, rigidity, and festination by surgery of the basal ganglia. *Research Publications B: Association for Research in Nervous and Mental Disease, 21,* 692–665.

Michael, R. P. (1969). Effects of gonadal hormones on displaced and direct aggression in pairs of rhesus monkeys of opposite sex. In S. Garattini & E. B. Sigg (Eds.), *Aggressive behaviour* (pp. 172–178). New York: Wiley.

Michael, R. P. (1980). Hormones and sexual behavior in the female. In D. T. Krieger & J. C. Hughes (Eds.), *Neuroendocrinology* (pp. 223–231). Sunderland, MA: Sinauer Associates.

Miczek, K. A., Maxson, S. C., Fish, E. W., & Faccidomo, S. (2001). Aggressive behavioral phenotypes in mice. *Behavioural Brain Research, 125,* 167–181.

Mierzejewski, P., Koros, E., Goldberg, S. R., Kostowski, W., & Stefanski, R. (2003). Intravenous self-administration of morphine and cocaine: A comparative study. *Polish Journal of Pharmacology, 55,* 713–726.

Miller, E. K., & Cohen, J. D. (2001). An integrative theory of prefrontal cortex function. *Annual Review of Neuroscience, 24,* 167–202.

Miller, J. L. (2000). Alzheimer's disease FAQs. Retrieved March 8, 2005, from http://www.athealth.com/Consumer/disorders/Alzheimers.html

Miller, N. E., Bailey, C. J., & Stevenson, J. A. (1950). Decreased "hunger" but increased food intake resulting from hypothalamic lesions. *Science, 112,* 256–259.

Miller, R. R., & Springer, A. D. (1973). Amnesia, consolidation, and retrieval. *Psychological Review, 80,* 69–79.

Miller, T. Q., Smith, T. W., Turner, C. W., Guijarro, M. L., & Hallet, A. J. (1996). A meta-analytic review of research on hostility and physical health. *Psychological Bulletin, 119,* 322–348.

Mills, C. B. (1980). Effects of context on reaction time to phonemes. *Journal of Verbal Learning & Verbal Behavior, 19,* 75–83.

Mills, E. M., Rusyniak, D. E., & Sprague, J. E. (2004). The role of the sympathetic nervous system and uncoupling proteins in the thermogenesis induced by 3,4-methylenedioxymethamphetamine. *Journal of Molecular Medicine, 82,* 787–799.

Milner, B. (1965). Memory disturbance after bilateral hippocampal lesions. In P. M. Milner & S. E. Glickman (Eds.), *Cognitive processes and the brain* (pp. 97–111). Princeton, NJ: Van Nostrand.

Milner, B. (1970). Memory and the medial temporal regions of the brain. In K. H. Pribram & D. E. Broadbent (Eds.), *Biology of memory* (pp. 29–50). New York: Academic Press.

Milner, P. M. (1989). The discovery of self-stimulation and other stories. *Neuroscience and Biobehavioral Reviews, 13,* 61–67.

Milo, T. J., Kaufman, G. E., Barnes, W. E., Konopka, L. M., Crayton, J. W., Ringelstein, J. G., et al. (2001). Changes in regional cerebral blood flow after electroconvulsive therapy for depression. *The Journal of ECT, 17,* 15–21.

Minerbo, G., Albreck, D., Goldberg, E., Lindberg, T., Nakari, M., Martinez, C., et al. (1994). Activity of peptidergic neurons in the amygdala during sexual behavior in the male rat. *Experimental Brain Research, 97,* 444–450.

Mirsky, A. F., Bieliauskas, L. A., French, L. M., Van Kammen, D. P., Jonsson, E., & Sedvall, G. (2000). A 39-year follow-up of the Genain quadruplets. *Schizophrenia Bulletin, 26,* 699–708.

Mirsky, A. F., DeLisi, L. E., Buchsbaum, M. S., Quinn, O. W., Schwerdt, P., Siever, L. J., et al. (1984). The Genain Quadruplets: Psychological studies. *Psychiatry Research, 13,* 77–93.

Misanin, J. R., Miller, R. R., & Lewis, D. J. (1968). Retrograde amnesia produced by electroconvulsive shock after reactivation of a consolidated memory trace. *Science, 160,* 554–555.

Mishkin, M., Suzuki, W. A., Gadian, D. G., & Vargha-Khadem, F. (1999). Hierarchical organization of cognitive memory. In N. Burgess, K. J. Jeffery, & J. O'Keefe (Eds.), *The hippocampal and parietal foundations of spatial cognition* (pp. 290–302). London: Oxford University Press.

Misra, K., & Pandey, S. C. (2003). Differences in basal levels of CREB and NPY in nucleus accumbens regions between C57BL/6 and DBA/2 mice differing in inborn alcohol drinking behavior. *Journal of Neuroscience Research, 74,* 967–975.

Mitchell, R. L., Elliott, R., Barry, M., Cruttenden, A., & Woodruff, P. W. (2003). The neural response to emotional prosody, as revealed by functional magnetic resonance imaging. *Neuropsychologia, 41,* 1410–1421.

Mittelman, M. S. (2000). Effect of support and counseling on caregivers of patients with Alzheimer's disease. *International Psychogeriatrics, 12,* 341–346.

Mittwoch, U. (2004). The elusive action of sex-determining genes: Mitochondria to the rescue? *Journal of Theoretical Biology, 228,* 359–365.

Miwa, T., Moriizumi, T., Horikawa, I., Uramoto, N., Ishimaru, T., Nishimura, T., et al. (2002). Role of nerve growth factor in the olfactory system. *Microscopy Research and Technique, 58,* 197–203.

Mochida, G. H., & Walsh, C. A. (2001). Molecular genetics of human microcephaly. *Current Opinion in Neurology, 14,* 151–156.

Moeller, F. G., Hasan, K. M., Steinberg, J. L., Kramer, L. A., Dougherty, D. M., Santos, R. M., et al. (2005). Reduced anterior corpus callosum white matter integrity is related to increased impulsivity and reduced discriminability in cocaine-dependent subjects: Diffusion tensor imaging. *Neuropsychopharmacology, 30,* 610–617.

Mohr, J. P. (1980). Revision of Broca aphasia and the syndrome of Broca's area infarction and its implications in aphasia theory. In R. H. Brookshire (Ed.), *Clinical aphasiology conference proceedings* (pp. 1–16). Minneapolis, MN: BRK.

Molina, V., Sanz, J., Reig, S., Martinez, R., Sarramea, F., Luque, R., et al. (2005). Hypofrontality in men with first-episode psychosis. *The British Journal of Psychiatry, 186,* 203–208.

Moller, C., Wiklund, L., Sommer, W., Thorsell, A., & Heilig, M. (1997). Decreased experimental anxiety and voluntary ethanol consumption in rats following central but not basolateral amygdala lesions. *Brain Research, 760,* 94–101.

Mombaerts, P. (1999). Molecular biology of odorant receptors in vertebrates. *Annual Review of Neuroscience, 22,* 487–509.

Mombaerts, P. (2001). The human repertoire of odorant receptor genes and pseudogenes. *Annual Review of Genomics and Human Genetics, 2,* 493–510.

Money, J. (1961). Components of eroticism in man. I. The hormones in relation to sexual morphology and sexual desire. *Journal of Neurochemistry, 132,* 239–248.

Money, J. (1980). *Love and love sickness.* Baltimore: Johns Hopkins University Press.

Money, J., & Ehrhardt, A. (1972). *Man and woman, boy and girl: The differentiation and dimorphism of gender identity from conception to maturity.* Baltimore: Johns Hopkins University Press.

Money, J., Schwartz, M., & Lewis, V. G. (1984). Adult erotosexual status and fetal hormonal masculinization and demasculinization: 46,XX congenital virilizing adrenal hyperplasia and 46,XY androgen-insensitivity syndrome compared. *Psychoneuroendocrinology, 9,* 405–414.

Monnikes, H., Lauer, G., & Arnold, R. (1997). Peripheral administration of cholecystokinin activates c-Fos expression in the locus coeruleus/subcoeruleus nucleus, dorsal vagal complex and paraventricular nucleus via capsaicin-sensitive vagal afferents and CCK-A receptors in the rat. *Brain Research, 770,* 277–288.

Monroe, R. R. (1970). *Episodic behavioral disorders: A psychodynamic and neurophysiologic analysis.* Cambridge, MA: Harvard University Press.

Monterosso, J. R., Flannery, B. A., Pettinati, H. M., Oslin, D. W., Rukstalis, M., O'Brien, C. P., et al. (2001). Predicting treatment response to naltrexone: The influence of craving and family history. *American Journal on Addictions, 10,* 258–268.

Montmayeur, J. P., Liberles, S. D., Matsunami, H., & Buck, L. B. (2001). A candidate taste receptor gene near a sweet taste locus. *Nature Neuroscience, 4,* 492–498.

Montorsi, F., & Althof, S. E. (2004). Partner responses to sildenafil citrate (Viagra) treatment of erectile dysfunction. *Urology, 63,* 762–767.

Montplaisir, J. (2004). Abnormal motor behavior during sleep. *Sleep Medicine, 5,* S31–S34.

Montreys, C. R., & Borod, J. C. (1998). A preliminary evaluation of emotional experience and expression following unilateral brain damage. *International Journal of Neuroscience, 96,* 269–283.

Moorcroft, W. H. (1987). An overview of sleep. In J. Gackenback (Ed.), *Sleep and dreams* (pp. 3–29). New York: Garland.

Moore, B. O., & Deutsch, J. A. (1985). An antiemetic is antidotal to the satiety effects of cholecystokinin. *Nature, 315,* 321–322.

Moore, R. Y. (1982). The suprachiasmatic nucleus and the organization of a circadian system. *Trends in Neurosciences, 5,* 404–407.

Moore, R. Y. (1997). Circadian rhythms: Basic neurobiology and clinical applications. *Annual Review of Medicine, 48,* 253–266.

Moore, R. Y., Card, J. P., & Riley, J. N. (1980). The suprachiasmatic hypothalamic nucleus: Neuronal ultrastructure. *Neuroscience Abstract, 6,* 758.

Moore, R. Y., & Eichler, V. B. (1972). Loss of a circadian adrenal corticosterone rhythm following suprachiasmatic lesions in the rat. *Brain Research, 42,* 201–206.

Moore-Ede, M. C. (1993). *The twenty-four hour society.* Reading, MA: Addison-Wesley.

Moore-Ede, M. C., Sulzman, F. M., & Fuller, C. A. (1982). The clocks that time us. Cambridge, MA: Harvard University Press.

Morfit, N. S., & Weekes, N. Y. (2001). Handedness and immune function. *Brain and Cognition, 46,* 209–213.

Morgan, R. E., & Riccio, D. C. (1998). Memory retrieval processes. In W. T. O'Donohue (Ed.), *Learning and behavior therapy* (pp. 464–482). Needham Heights, MA: Allyn & Bacon

Mori, K. (2003). Grouping of odorant receptors: Odour maps in the mammalian olfactory bulb. *Biochemical Society Transactions, 31,* 134–136.

Morien, A., Garrard, L., & Rowland, N. E. (1999). Expression of Fos immunoreactivity in rat brain during dehydration: Effect of duration and timing of water deprivation. *Brain Research, 816,* 1–7.

Morley-Fletcher, S., Palanza, P., Parolaro, D., Vigano, D., & Laviola, G. (2003). Intrauterine position has long-term influence on brain mu-opioid receptor density and behaviour in mice. *Psychoneuroendocrinology, 28,* 386–400.

Morrow, B. A., Elsworth, J. D., & Roth, R. H. (2002). Prenatal cocaine exposure disrupts non-spatial, short-term memory in adolescent and adult male rats. *Behavioural Brain Research, 129,* 217–223.

Morrow, C. E., Vogel, A. L., Anthony, J. C., Ofir, A. Y., Dause, A. T., & Bandstra, E. S. (2004). Expressive and receptive language functioning in preschool children with prenatal cocaine exposure. *Journal of Pediatric Psychology, 29,* 543–554.

Mors, O., Mortensen, P. B., & Ewald, H. (2001). No evidence of increased risk for schizophrenia or bipolar affective disorder in persons with aneuploidies of the sex chromosomes. *Psychological Medicine, 31,* 425–430.

Morse, D., Sethi, J., & Choi, A. M. (2002). Carbon monoxide-dependent signaling. *Critical Care Medicine, 30,* S12–S17.

Mortensen, P. B., Pedersen, C. B., Melbye, M., Mors, O., & Ewald, H. (2003). Individual and familial risk factors for bipolar affective disorders in Denmark. *Archives of General Psychiatry, 60,* 1209–1215.

Moruzzi, G., & Magoun, H. W. (1949). Brain stem reticular formation and activation of the EEG. *Electroencephalography and Clinical Neurophysiology, 1,* 455–473.

Mosher, J. T., Birkemo, L. S., Johnson, M. F., & Ervin, G. N. (1998). Sulfated cholecystokinin (26–33) induces mild taste aversion conditioning in rats when administered by three different routes. *Peptides, 19,* 849–857.

Mosher, J. T., Johnson, M. F., Birkemo, L. S., & Ervin, G. N. (1996). Several roles of CCKA and CCKB receptor subtypes in CCK-8-induced and LiCl-induced taste aversion conditioning. *Peptides, 17,* 483–488.

Movshon, A. (1990). Visual processing of moving images. In H. Barlow, C. Blakemore, & M. Weston-Smith (Eds.), *Images and understanding: Thoughts about images; ideas about understanding* (pp. 122–137). New York: Cambridge University Press.

Moyer, C. A., Sonnad, S. S., Garetz, S. L., Helman, J. I., & Chervin, R. D. (2001). Quality of life in obstructive sleep apnea: A systematic review of the literature. *Sleep Medicine, 2,* 477–491.

Moyer, K. E. (1976). *The psychobiology of aggression.* New York: Harper & Row.

Mueller, T. I., Leon, A. C., Keller, M. B., Solomon, D. A., Endicott, J., Coryell, W., et al. (1999). Recurrence after recovery from major depressive disorder during 15 years of observational follow-up. *American Journal of Psychiatry, 156,* 1000–1006.

Muhlnickel, W., Elbert, T., Taub, E., & Flor, H. (1998). Reorganization of auditory cortex in tinnitus. *Proceedings of the National Academy of Sciences of the United States of America, 95,* 10340–10343.

Müller, J. (1838). *Handbuch der Physiologie des Menschen für Vorlesungen.* Coblenz: J. Hölscher.

Mundell, E. J. (2004, October 11). Caminiti's death puts spotlight on steroids. *HealthScout.* Retrieved from http://www.heartinfo.org/ms/news/521728/main.html

Munoz, M. T., & Argente, J. (2004). New concepts in anorexia nervosa. *Journal of Pediatric Endocrinology & Metabolism, 17,* 473–480.

Murdoch, B. E., Afford, R. J., Ling, A. R., & Ganguley, B. (1986). Acute computerized tomographic scans: Their value in the localization of lesions and as prognostic indicators in aphasia. *Journal of Communication Disorders, 19,* 311–345.

Murphy, C., Jernigan, T. L., & Fennema-Notestine, C. (2003). Left hippocampal volume loss in Alzheimer's disease is reflected in performance on odor identification: A structural MRI study. *Journal of the International Neuropsychological Society, 9,* 459–471.

Murphy, K. J., & Regan, C. M. (1998). Contributions of cell adhesion molecules to altered synaptic weightings during memory consolidation. *Neurobiology of Learning and Memory, 70,* 73–81.

Murray, A. M., Hyde, T. M., Knable, M. B., Herman, M. M., Bigelow, L. B., Carter, J. M., et al. (1995). Distribution of putative D_4 receptors in postmortem striatum from patients with schizophrenia. *The Journal of Neuroscience, 15,* 2186–2191.

Murray, J. B. (2002). Phencyclidine (PCP): A dangerous drug, but useful in schizophrenia research. *The Journal of Psychology, 136,* 319–327.

Mushlin, A. I., Mooney, C., Holloway, R. G., Detsky, A. S., Mattson, D. H., & Phelps, C. E. (1997). The cost-effectiveness of magnetic resonance imaging for patients with equivocal neurological symptoms. *International Journal of Technology Assessment in Health Care, 13,* 21–34.

Musso, M., Weiller, C., Kiebel, S., Muller, S. P., Bulau, P., & Rijntjes, M. (1999). Training-induced brain plasticity in aphasia. *Brain, 122,* 1781–1790.

Mustanski, B. S., Dupree, M. G., Nievergelt, C. M., Bocklandt, S., Schork, N. J., & Hamer, D. H. (2005). A genome-wide scan of male sexual orientation. *Human Genetics, 116,* 272–278.

Muthane, U., Jain, S., & Gururaj, G. (2001). Hunting genes in Parkinson's disease from the roots. *Medical Hypotheses, 57,* 51–55.

Muzzin, P., Cusin, I., Charnay, Y., & Rohner-Jeanrenaud, F. (2000). Single intracerebroventricular bolus injection of a recombinant adenovirus expressing leptin results in reduction of food intake and body weight in both lean and obese Zucker *fa/fa* rats. *Regulatory Peptides, 92,* 57–64.

Myers, R. E., & Sperry, R. W. (1953). Interocular transfer of a visual form discrimination habit in cats after section of the optic chiasma and corpus callosum. *Anatomical Record, 115,* 351–352.

Myers, R. E., & Sperry, R. W. (1958). Interhemispheric communication through the corpus callosum: Mnemonic carry-over between the hemispheres. *AMA Archives of Neurology and Psychiatry, 80,* 298–303.

Naber, D. (2000). Long-term phase of schizophrenia: Impact of atypical agents. *International Clinical Psychopharmacology, 15,* S11–S14.

Nadasdy, Z., Hirase, H., Czurko, A., Csicsvari, J., & Buzsaki, G. (1999). Replay and time compression of recurring spike sequences in the hippocampus. *The Journal of Neuroscience, 19,* 9497–9507.

Nader, K., Majidishad, P., Amorapanth, P., & LeDoux, J. E. (2001). Damage to the lateral and central, but not other, amygdaloid nuclei prevents the acquisition of auditory fear conditioning. *Learning & Memory (Cold Spring Harbor, NY), 8,* 156–163.

NADS. (2005). Down syndrome facts. Retrieved February 25, 2005, from http://www.nads.org/pages/facts.htm

Naegelé, B., Thouvard, V., Pépin, J. L., Lévy, P., Bonnet, C., Perret, J. E., et al. (1995). Deficits of cognitive executive functions in patients with sleep apnea syndrome. *Sleep, 18,* 43–52.

Nagao, H., Yamaguchi, M., Takahash, Y., & Mori, K. (2002). Grouping and representation of odorant receptors in domains of the olfactory bulb sensory map. *Microscopy Research and Technique, 58,* 168–175.

Nagao, T., Wada, K., Kuwagata, M., Nakagomi, M., Watanabe, C., Yoshimura, S., et al. (2004). Intrauterine position and postnatal growth in Sprague-Dawley rats and ICR mice. *Reproductive Toxicology, 18,* 109–120.

Nakaji, P., Meltzer, H. S., Singel, S. A., & Alksne, J. F. (2003). Improvement of aggressive and antisocial behavior after resection of temporal lobe tumors. *Pediatrics, 112,* e430.

Nakamura, K., Ono, T., Tamura, R., Indo, M., Takashima, Y., & Kawasaki, M. (1989). Characteristics of rat lateral hypothalamic neuron responses to smell and taste in emotional behavior. *Brain Research, 491,* 15–32.

Nakazato, M., Murakami, N., Date, Y., Kojima, M., Matsuo, H., Kangawa, K., et al. (2001). A role for ghrelin in the central regulation of feeding. *Nature, 409,* 194–198.

Naoi, M., Maruyama, W., Yagi, K., & Youdim, M. (2000). Anti-apoptotic function of L-(-)deprenyl (Segeline) and related compounds. *Neurobiology (Budapest, Hungary), 8,* 69–80.

Narabayashi, H. (1972). Stereotaxic amygdalotomy. In B. Eleftheriou (Ed.), *The neurobiology of the amygdala* (pp. 459–483). New York: Plenum.

Narr, K. L., van Erp, T. G., Cannon, T. D., Woods, R. P., Thompson, P. M., Jang, S., et al. (2002). A twin study of genetic contributions to hippocampal morphology in schizophrenia. *Neurobiology of Disease, 11,* 83–95.

National Center for Health Statistics. (2003). *National Vital Statistics Reports, 52*(9), 9. Retrieved February 9, 2005, from http://www.cdc.gov/nchs/Default.htm

National Multiple Sclerosis Society. (2003). Corticosteroids. *National MS Society Information Sourcebook.* Retrieved June 8, 2004, from http://www.nationalmssociety.org/sourcebook.asp

Navarro, J. F., Maldonado, E., Pedraza, C., & Cavas, M. (2001). Attitudes toward animal research among psychology students in Spain. *Psychological Reports, 89,* 227–236.

Negri-Cesi, P., Colciago, A., Celotti, F., & Motta, M. (2004). Sexual differentiation of the brain: Role of testosterone and its active metabolites. *Journal of Endocrinological Investigation, 27,* 120–127.

Nehlig, A. (1999). Are we dependent upon coffee and caffeine? A review on human and animal data. *Neuroscience and Biobehavioral Reviews, 23,* 563–576.

Nelson, J. A. (2000). Audiological rehabilitation. In R. Gilliam, T. Marquardt, & F. Martin (Eds.), *Communication sciences and disorders* (pp. 147–176). San Diego: Singular.

Nemechek, P. M., Polsky, B., & Gottlieb, M. S. (2000). Treatment guidelines for HIV-associated wasting. *Mayo Clinic Proceedings, 75,* 386–394.

Nemeroff, C. B. (1988). The role of corticotropin-releasing factor in the pathogenesis of major depression. *Pharmacopsychiatry, 21,* 76–82.

Nemeroff, C. B. (1998). The neurobiology of depression. *Scientific American, 278,* 42–49.

Neve, R. L., McPhie, D. L., & Chen, Y. (2001). Alzheimer's disease: Dysfunction of a signalling pathway mediated by the amyloid precursor protein? *Biochemical Society Symposium,* (67), 37–50.

Nguyen, P. V., Abel, T., Kandel, E. R., & Bourtchouladze, R. (2000). Strain-dependent differences in LTP and hippocampus-dependent memory in inbred mice. *Learning & Memory, 7,* 170–179.

Nichols, C. S., & Russell, R. M. (1990). Analysis of animals rights literature reveals the underlying motives of the movement: Ammunition for counter offense by scientists. *Endocrinology, 127,* 985–989.

Nicholson, P. J., & D'Auria, D. A. (1999). Shift work, health, the working time regulations and health assessments. *Occupational Medicine (Oxford, England), 49,* 127–137.

Nicolle, M. W. (2002). Myasthenia gravis. *Neurologist, 8,* 2–21.

Nierenberg, A. A., Dougherty, D., & Rosenbaum, J. F. (1998). Dopaminergic agents and stimulants as antidepressant augmentation strategies. *Journal of Clinical Psychiatry, 59,* 60–64.

Nightingale, S., Orgill, J. C., Ebrahim, I. O., de Lacy, S. F., Agrawal, S., & Williams, A. J. (2005). The association between narcolepsy and REM behavior disorder (RBD). *Sleep Medicine, 6,* 253–258.

Nilsson, M., Perfilieva, E., Johansson, U., Orwar, O., & Eriksson, P. S. (1999). Enriched environment increases neurogenesis in the adult rat dentate gyrus and improves spatial memory. *Journal of Neurobiology, 39,* 569–578.

Nishimura, H., Doi, K., Iwaki, T., Hashikawa, K., Oku, N., Teratani, T., et al. (2000). Neural plasticity detected in short- and long-term cochlear implant users using PET. *Neuroreport, 11,* 811–815.

Nishino, S., Okura, M., & Mignot, E. (2000). Narcolepsy: Genetic predisposition and neuropharmacological mechanisms. *Sleep Medicine Reviews, 4,* 57–99.

Nissenkorn, A., Michelson, M., Ben-Zeev, B., & Lerman-Sagie, T. (2001). Inborn errors of metabolism: A cause of abnormal brain development. *Neurology, 56,* 1265–1272.

Nixon, P. D. (2003). The role of the cerebellum in preparing responses to predictable sensory events. *Cerebellum, 2,* 114–122.

Noble, E. P. (2000). Addiction and its reward process through polymorphisms of the D_2 dopamine receptor gene: A review. *European Psychiatry, 15,* 79–89.

Noble, E. P. (2003). D_2 dopamine receptor gene in psychiatric and neurologic disorders and its phenotypes. *American Journal of Medical Genetics, 116B,* 103–125.

Nolan, B. C., Nicholson, D. A., & Freeman, J. H., Jr. (2002). Blockade of $GABA_A$ receptors in the interpositus nucleus modulates expression of conditioned excitation but not conditioned inhibition of the eyeblink response. *Integrative Physiological and Behavioral Science, 37,* 293–310.

Nordin, S., & Murphy, C. (1998). Odor memory in normal aging and Alzheimer's disease. *Annals of the New York Academy of Sciences, 855,* 686–693.

Norman, A. B., Norman, M. K., Hall, J. F., & Tsibulsky, V. L. (1999). Priming threshold: A novel quantitative measure of the reinstatement of cocaine self-administration. *Brain Research, 831,* 165–174.

Norrholm, S. D., & Ouimet, C. C. (2001). Altered dendritic spine density in animal models of depression and in response to antidepressant treatment. *Synapse, 42,* 151–163.

Novak, C. M., Smale, L., & Nunez, A. A. (2000). Rhythms in *Fos* expression in brain areas related to the sleep-wake cycle in the diurnal *Arvicanthis niloticus. American Journal of Physiology. Regulatory, Integrative and Comparative Physiology, 278,* 1267–1274.

Novak, M. A., & Petto, A. J. (Eds.). (1991). *Through the looking glass: Issues of psychological well-being in captive nonhuman primates.* Washington, DC: American Psychological Association.

Nowak, M. A., Plotkin, J. B., & Krakauer, D. C. (1999). The evolutionary language game. *Journal of Theoretical Biology, 2000,* 147–162.

Nudo, R. J. (2003). Functional and structural plasticity in motor cortex: Implications for stroke recovery. *Physical Medicine and Rehabilitation Clinics of North America, 14,* S57–76.

Nudo, R. J., Plautz, E. J., & Frost, S. B. (2001). Role of adaptive plasticity in recovery of function after damage to motor cortex. *Muscle & Nerve, 24,* 1000–1019.

Nutt, D. J. (2002). The neuropharmacology of serotonin and noradrenaline in depression. *International Clinical Psychopharmacology, 17,* S1–S12.

Nutt, D. J., & Malizia, A. L. (2001). New insights into the role of the GABA(A)-benzodiazepine receptor in psychiatric disorder. *British Journal of Psychiatry, 179,* 390–396.

Nyberg, J., Sandnabba, K., Schalkwyk, L., & Sluyter, F. (2004). Genetic and environmental (inter)actions in male mouse lines selected for aggressive and nonaggressive behavior. *Genes, Brain, and Behavior, 3,* 101–109.

Nyberg, L., Cabeza, R., & Tulving, E. (1996). PET studies of encoding and retrieval: The HERA model. *Psychonomic Bulletin & Review, 3,* 135–148.

O'Brien, C. P., Volpicelli, L. A., & Volpicelli, J. R. (1996). Naltrexone in the treatment of alcoholism: A clinical review. *Alcohol, 13,* 35–39.

O'Kane, G., Kensinger, E. A., & Corkin, S. (2004). Evidence for semantic learning in profound amnesia: An investigation with patient H.M. *Hippocampus, 14,* 417–425.

O'Leary, C. M. (2004). Fetal alcohol syndrome: Diagnosis, epidemiology, and developmental outcomes. *Journal of Paediatrics and Child Health, 40,* 2–7.

O'Malley, A., O'Connell, C., Murphy, K. J., & Regan, C. M. (2000). Transient spine density increases in the mid-molecular layer of hippocampal dentate gyrus accompany consolidation of a spatial learning task in the rodent. *Neuroscience, 99,* 229–232.

O'Neill, M. J., & O'Neill, R. J. (1999). Whatever happened to SRY? *Cellular and Molecular Life Sciences, 56,* 883–893.

Oades, R. D. (1981). Impairments of search behaviour in rats after haloperidol treatment, hippocampal or neocortical damage suggest a mesocorticolimbic role in cognition. *Biological Psychology, 12,* 77–85.

Oades, R. D., Klimke, A., Henning, U., & Rao, M. L. (2002). Relations of clinical features, subgroups and medication to serum monoamines in schizophrenia. *Human Psychopharmacology, 17,* 15–27.

Oatley, K., & Toates, F. M. (1969). The passage of food through the guts of rats and its uptake of fluid. *Psychonomic Science, 16,* 225–226.

Oda, K., Okubo, Y., Ishida, R., Murata, Y., Ohta, K., Matsuda, T., et al. (2003). Regional cerebral blood flow in depressed patients with white matter magnetic resonance hyperintensity. *Biological Psychiatry, 53,* 150–156.

Oesterheld, J. R., Armstrong, S. C., & Cozza, K. L. (2004). Ecstasy: Pharmacodynamic and pharmacokinetic interactions. *Psychosomatics, 45,* 84–87.

Ogawa, S., Robbins, A., Kumar, N., Pfaff, D. W., Sundaram, K., & Bardin, C. W. (1996). Effects of testosterone and 7 alpha-methyl-19-nortestosterone (MENT) on sexual and aggressive behaviors in two inbred strains of male mice. *Hormones and Behavior, 30,* 74–84.

Ohye, C., Shibazaki, T., Zhang, J., & Andou, Y. (2002). Thalamic lesions produced by gamma thalamotomy for movement disorders. *Journal of Neurosurgery, 97,* 600–606.

Okubo, Y., Suhara, T., Suzuki, K., Kobayashi, K., Inoue, O., Terasaki, O., et al. (1997). Decreased prefrontal dopamine D_1 receptors in schizophrenia revealed by PET. *Nature, 385,* 634–636.

Olds, J. (1962). Hypothalamic substrates of reward. *Psychological Review, 42,* 554–604.

Olds, J., & Milner, P. (1954). Positive reinforcement produced by electrical stimulation of septal area and other regions of rat brain. *Journal of Comparative and Physiological Psychology, 47,* 419–427.

Olfson, M., Mechanic, D., Hansell, S., Boyer, C. A., Walkup, J., & Weiden, P. J. (2000). Predicting medication noncompliance after hospital discharge among patients with schizophrenia. *Psychiatric Services, 51,* 216–222.

Oliveira, A. A., Jr., & Hodges, H. M. (2005). Alzheimer's disease and neural transplantation as prospective cell therapy. *Current Alzheimer Research, 2,* 79–95.

Olney, J. W. (2002). New insights and new issues in developmental neurotoxicology. *Neurotoxicology, 23,* 659–668.

Oostra, B. A., & Willemsen, R. (2002). The X chromosome and fragile X mental retardation. *Cytogenetic and Genome Research, 99,* 257–264.

Opitz, B., Mecklinger, A., & Friederici, A. D. (2000). Functional asymmetry of human prefrontal cortex: Encoding and retrieval of verbally and nonverbally coded information. *Learning & Memory, 7,* 85–96.

Oppenheim, R. W. (1991). Cell death during development of the nervous system. *Annual Review of Neuroscience, 14,* 453–501.

Ornstein, R. E. (1997). *The right mind: Making sense of the hemispheres.* Orlando, FL: Harcourt.

Oshima, A., Miyano, H., Yamashita, S., Owashi, T., Suzuki, S., Sakano, Y., et al. (2001). Psychological, autonomic and neuroendocrine responses to acute stressors in the combined dexamethasone/CRH test: A study in healthy subjects. *Journal of Psychiatric Research, 35,* 95–104.

Otani, S. (2002). Memory trace in prefrontal cortex: Theory for the cognitive switch. *Biological Reviews of the Cambridge Philosophical Society, 77,* 563–577.

Ott, G. E. (2001). Bupropion and sleep: Acute, chronic, and predictive effects in depressed patients. *Dissertation Abstracts International: Section B: The Sciences & Engineering, 61,* 4076.

Ouagazzal, A. M., Moreau, J. L., Pauly-Evers, M., & Jenck, F. (2003). Impact of environmental housing conditions on the emotional responses of mice deficient for nociceptin/orphanin FQ peptide precursor gene. *Behavioural Brain Research, 144,* 111–117.

Packard, M. G., & Cahill, L. (2001). Affective modulation of multiple memory systems. *Current Opinion in Neurobiology, 11,* 752–756.

Packard, M. G., & Teather, L. A. (1997). Double dissociation of hippocampal and dorsal-striatal memory systems by posttraining intracerebral injections of 2-amino-5-phosphonopentanoic acid. *Behavioral Neuroscience, 111,* 543–551.

Pahwa, R., Lyons, K. E., Wilkinson, S. B., Troster, A. I., Overman, J., Kieltyka, J., et al. (2001). Comparison of thalamotomy to deep brain stimulation of the thalamus in essential tremor. *Movement Disorders, 16,* 140–143.

Paige, N. M., Hays, R. D., Litwin, M. S., Rajfer, J., & Shapiro, M. F. (2001). Improvement in emotional well-being and relationships of users of sildenafil. *Journal of Urology, 166,* 1774–1778.

Palace, E. M. (1995). Modification of dysfunctional patterns of sexual response through autonomic arousal and false physiological feedback. *Journal of Consulting and Clinical Psychology, 63,* 604–615.

Palmiter, R. D., Erickson, J. C., Hollopeter, G., Baraban, S. C., & Schwartz, M. W. (1998). Life without neuropeptide Y. *Recent Progress in Hormone Research, 53,* 163–199.

Pang, S. F., Pang, C. S., Poon, A. M., Lee, P. P., Liu, Z. M., & Shiu, S. Y. (1998). Melatonin: A chemical photoperiodic signal with clinical significance in humans. *Chinese Medical Journal, 111,* 197–203.

Pani, L. (2002). Clinical implications of dopamine research in schizophrenia. *Current Medical Research and Opinion, 18,* S3–S7.

Pantelis, C., Brewer, W. J., & Maruff, P. (2001). Olfactory cortex. In W. E. Craighead & C. B. Nemeroff (Eds.), *The Corsini encyclopedia of psychology and behavioral science* (3rd ed., vol. 3, pp. 1090–1098). New York: Wiley.

Papez, J. W. (1937). A proposed mechanism of emotion. *Archives of Neurology and Psychiatry, 38,* 725–744.

Paredes, R. G. (2003). Medial preoptic area/anterior hypothalamus and sexual motivation. *Scandinavian Journal of Psychology, 44,* 203–212.

Paredes, R. G., Tzschentke, T., & Nakach, N. (1998). Lesions of the medial preoptic area/anterior hypothalamus (MPOA/AH) modify partner preference in male rats. *Brain Research, 813,* 1–8.

Parker, K. J., Schatzberg, A. F., & Lyons, D. M. (2003). Neuroendocrine aspects of hypercortisolism in major depression. *Hormones and Behavior, 43,* 60–66.

Parrott, A. C. (2001). Human psychopharmacology of Ecstasy (MDMA): A review of 15 years of empirical research. *Human Psychopharmacology, 16,* 557–577.

Parry, B. L. (2002). Jet lag: Minimizing its effects with critically timed bright light and melatonin administration. *Journal of Molecular Microbiology and Biotechnology, 4,* 463–466.

Parsian, A., Racette, B., Goldsmith, L. J., & Perlmutter, J. S. (2002). Parkinson's disease and apolipoprotein E: Possible association with dementia but not age at onset. *Genomics, 79,* 458–461.

Pasierb, S. J., & Harrison, M. F. (2002, February 20). A drug lesson worth remembering. *San Diego Union-Tribune.* Retrieved May 19, 2005, from http://www.cnoa.org/whats-new-article-10.htm

Patrick, L. (2002). Eating disorders: A review of the literature with emphasis on medical complications and clinical nutrition. *Alternative Medicine Review, 7,* 184–202.

Paukert, M., Osteroth, R., Geisler, H. S., Brandle, U., Glowatzki, E., Ruppersberg, J. P., et al. (2001). Inflammatory mediators potentiate ATP-gated channels through the P2X(3) subunit. *The Journal of Biological Chemistry, 276,* 21077–21082.

Paul, P. V. (1998). *Literacy and deafness: The development of reading, writing, and literate thought.* Boston: Allyn and Bacon.

Paul, P. V. (2001). *Language and deafness* (3rd ed.). San Diego: Singular Thomson Learning.

Paulin, M. G. (1997). Neural representations of moving systems. *International Review of Neurobiology, 41,* 515–533.

Pauls, D. L., Morton, L. A., & Egeland, J. A. (1992). Risks of affective illness among first-degree relatives of bipolar I old-order Amish probands. *Archives of General Psychiatry, 49,* 703–708.

Paulson, H. L., & Fischbeck, K. H. (1996). Trinucleotide repeats in neurogenetic disorders. *Annual Review of Neuroscience, 19,* 79–107.

Pause, B. M., Miranda, A., Goder, R., Aldenhoff, J. B., & Ferstl, R. (2001). Reduced olfactory performance in patients with major depression. *Journal of Psychiatric Research, 35,* 271–277.

Pause, B. M., Raack, N., Sojka, B., Goder, R., Aldenhoff, J. B., & Ferstl, R. (2003). Convergent and divergent effects of odors and emotions in depression. *Psychophysiology, 40,* 209–225.

Payne, J. L., Quiroz, J. A., Zarate, C. A., Jr., & Manji, H. K. (2002). Timing is everything: Does the robust upregulation of noradrenergically regulated plasticity genes underlie the rapid antidepressant effects of sleep deprivation? *Biological Psychiatry, 52,* 921–926.

Pearce, B. D., Valadi, N. M., Po, C. L., & Miller, A. H. (2000). Viral infection of developing GABAergic neurons in a model of hippocampal disinhibition. *Neuroreport, 11,* 2433–2438.

Pearl, P. L., Wallis, D. D., & Gibson, K. M. (2004). Pediatric neurotransmitter diseases. *Current Neurology and Neuroscience Reports, 4,* 147–152.

Pecina, S., & Berridge, K. C. (2000). Opioid site in nucleus accumbens shell mediates eating and hedonic 'liking' for food: Map based on microinjection Fos plumes. *Brain Research, 863,* 71–86.

Pecina, S., Cagniard, B., Berridge, K. C., Aldridge, J. W., & Zhuang, X. (2003). Hyperdopaminergic mutant mice have higher "wanting" but not "liking" for sweet rewards. *The Journal of Neuroscience, 23,* 9395–9402.

Peck, J. W., & Novin, D. (1971). Evidence that osmoreceptors mediating drinking in rabbits are in the lateral preoptic area. *Journal of Comparative and Physiological Psychology, 74,* 134–147.

Pedrosa-Sanchez, M., & Sola, R. G. (2003). [Modern day psychosurgery: A new approach to neurosurgery in psychiatric disease]. *Revista de Neurologia, 36,* 887–897.

Penfield, W., & Jasper, H. (1954). *Epilepsy and the functional anatomy of the brain.* Boston: Little, Brown.

Penicaud, L., Pajot, M. T., & Thompson, D. A. (1990). Evidence that receptors controlling growth hormone and hyperglycemic responses to glucoprivation are located in the hindbrain. *Endocrine Research, 16,* 461–475.

Pentney, A. R. (2001). An exploration of the history and controversies surrounding MDMA and MDA. *Journal of Psychoactive Drugs, 33,* 213–221.

Perecman, E., & Brown, J. W. (1981). Phonemic jargon: A case report. In J. W. Brown (Ed.), *Jargonaphasia* (pp. 177–255). New York: Academic Press.

Pereda, A. E., Bell, T. D., Chang, B. H., Czernik, A. J., Nairn, A. C., Soderling, T. R., et al. (1998). Ca^{2+}/calmodulin-dependent kinase II mediates simultaneous enhancement of gap-junctional conductance and glutamatergic transmission. *Proceedings of the National Academy of Sciences of the United States of America, 95,* 13272–13277.

Perkins, K. A., Levine, M. D., Marcus, M. D., & Shiffman, S. (1997). Addressing women's concerns about weight gain due to smoking cessation. *Journal of Substance Abuse Treatment, 14,* 173–182.

Perl, D. P. (2000). Neuropathology of Alzheimer's disease and related disorders. *Neurologic Clinics, 18,* 847–864.

Perlstein, W. M., Carter, C. S., Noll, D. C., & Cohen, J. D. (2001). Relation of prefrontal cortex dysfunction to working memory and symptoms in schizophrenia. *American Journal of Psychiatry, 158,* 1105–1113.

Perlstein, W. M., Dixit, N. K., Carter, C. S., Noll, D. C., & Cohen, J. D. (2003). Prefrontal cortex dysfunction mediates deficits in working memory and prepotent responding in schizophrenia. *Biological Psychiatry, 53,* 25–38.

Perrone-Capano, C., & Di Porzio, U. (2000). Genetic and epigenetic control of midbrain dopaminergic neuron development. *The International Journal of Developmental Biology, 44,* 679–687.

Pertwee, R. G. (2002). Cannabinoids and multiple sclerosis. *Pharmacology & Therapeutics, 95,* 165–174.

Petibois, C., Cazorla, G., Poortmans, J. R., & Deleris, G. (2003). Biochemical aspects of overtraining in endurance sports: The metabolism alteration process syndrome. *Sports Medicine, 33,* 83–94.

Petitto, L. A. (2000a). On the biological foundations of human language. In K. Emmorey & H. Lane (Eds.), *The signs of language revisited: An anthology to honor Ursula Bellugi and Edward Klima* (pp. 449–473). Mahwah, NJ: Erlbaum.

Petitto, L. A. (2000b). The acquisition of natural signed languages: Lessons in the nature of human language and its biological foundations. In C. Chamberlain, J. P. Morford, & R. I. Mayberry (Eds.), *Language acquisition by eye* (pp. 41–50). Mahwah, NJ: Erlbaum.

Petkov, N., & Kruizinga, P. (1997). Computational models of visual neurons specialised in the detection of periodic and aperiodic oriented visual stimuli: Bar and grating cells. *Biological Cybernetics, 76,* 83–96.

Pettinati, H. M., Volpicelli, J. R., Pierce, J. D., Jr., & O'Brien, C. P. (2000). Improving naltrexone response: An intervention for medical practitioners to enhance medication compliance in alcohol dependent patients. *Journal of Addictive Diseases, 19,* 71–83.

Petty, F. (1994). Plasma concentrations of gamma-aminobutyric acid (GABA) and mood disorders: A blood test for manic depressive disease? *Clinical Chemistry, 40,* 296–302.

Pevet, P. (2000). Melatonin and biological rhythms. *Biological Signals and Receptors, 9,* 203–212.

Pevet, P. (2003). Melatonin: From seasonal to circadian signal. *Journal of Neuroendocrinology, 15,* 422–426.

Pfaff, D. W. (1997). Hormones, genes, and behavior. *Proceedings of the National Academy of Sciences of the United States of America, 94,* 14213–14216.

Pfaff, D. W., & Sakuma, Y. (1979a). Facilitation of the lordosis reflex of female rats from the ventromedial nucleus of the hypothalamus. *Journal of Physiology, 288,* 189–202.

Pfaff, D. W., & Sakuma, Y. (1979b). Deficit in the lordosis reflex of female rats caused by lesions in the ventromedial nucleus of the hypothalamus. *Journal of Physiology, 288,* 203–210.

Pfaus, J. G., Dramsma, G., Wenkstern, D., & Fibiger, H. C. (1995). Sexual activity increases dopamine transmission in the nucleus accumbens and striatum of female rats. *Brain Research, 693,* 21–30.

Pfaus, J. G., Kippin, T. E., & Coria-Avila, G. (2003). What can animal models tell us about human sexual response? *Annual Review of Sex Research, 14,* 1–63.

Pfeiffer, C. A. (1936). Sexual differences of the hypophyses and their determination by the gonads. *American Journal of Anatomy, 58,* 195–225.

Phan, K. L., Wager, T. D., Taylor, S. F., & Liberzon, I. (2004). Functional neuroimaging studies of human emotions. *CNS Spectrums, 9,* 258–266.

Phelps, E. A., Delgado, M. R., Nearing, K. I., & LeDoux, J. E. (2004). Extinction learning in humans: Role of the amygdala and vmPFC. *Neuron, 43,* 897–905.

Phelps, E. A., O'Connor, K. J., Gatenby, J. C., Gore, J. C., Grillon, C., & Davis, M. (2001). Activation of the left amygdala to a cognitive representation of fear. *Nature Neuroscience, 4,* 437–441.

Phenylketonuria. (2000). Phenylketonuria (PKU): Screening and management. *NIH Consensus Statement, 17,* 1–33.

Phoenix, C. H., Goy, R. W., Gerall, A. A., & Young, W. C. (1959). Organizing action of prenatally administered testosterone propionate on the tissues mediating mating behavior in the female guinea pig. *Endocrinology, 65,* 369–382.

Phornphutkul, C., Fausto-Sterling, A., & Gruppuso, P. A. (2000). Gender self-reassignment in an XY adolescent female born with ambiguous genitalia. *Pediatrics, 106,* 135–137.

Pilcher, J. J., & Walters, A. S. (1997). How sleep deprivation affects psychological variables related to college students' cognitive performance. *Journal of American College Health, 46,* 121–126.

Pillard, R. C., & Bailey, J. M. (1998). Human sexual orientation has a heritable component. *Human Biology, 70,* 347–365.

Pillmann, F., Rohde, A., Ullrich, S., Draba, S., Sannemuller, U., & Marneros, A. (1999). Violence, criminal behavior, and the EEG: Significance of left hemispheric focal abnormalities. *The Journal of Neuropsychiatry and Clinical Neurosciences, 11,* 454–457.

Pilosky, L. S., Costa, D. C., Ell, P. J., Murray, R. M., Verhoeff, N. P., & Kerwin, R. W. (1992). Clozapine, single photon emission tomography, and the D_2 dopamine receptor blockade hypothesis of schizophrenia. *Lancet, 340,* 199–202.

Pisella, L., & Mattingley, J. B. (2004). The contribution of spatial remapping impairments to unilateral visual neglect. *Neuroscience and Biobehavioral Reviews, 28,* 181–200.

Pitcher, G. M., & Henry, J. L. (2004). Nociceptive response to innocuous mechanical stimulation is mediated via myelinated afferents and NK-1 receptor activation in a rat model of neuropathic pain. *Experimental Neurology, 186,* 173–197.

Pittenger, C., & Kandel, E. (1998). A genetic switch for long-term memory. *Comptes Rendus de l'Academie des Sciences. Serie III, Sciences de la Vie, 321,* 91–96.

Placidi, G. P., Oquendo, M. A., Malone, K. M., Huang, Y. Y., Ellis, S. P., & Mann, J. J. (2001). Aggressivity, suicide attempts, and depression: Relationship to cerebrospinal fluid monoamine metabolite levels. *Biological Psychiatry, 50,* 783–791.

Plaud, J. J., & Martini, J. R. (1999). The respondent conditioning of male sexual arousal. *Behavior Modification, 23,* 254–268.

Plenger, P. M., Breier, J. I., Wheless, J. W., Ridley, T. D., Papanicolaou, A. C., Brookshire, B., et al. (1996). Lateralization of memory for music: Evidence from the intracarotid amobarbital procedure. *Neuropsychologia, 34,* 1015–1018.

Plessinger, M. A. (1998). Prenatal exposure to amphetamines. Risks and adverse outcomes in pregnancy. *Obstetrics and Gynecology Clinics of North America, 25,* 119–138.

Ploj, K., Roman, E., Bergstrom, L., & Nylander, I. (2001). Effects of neonatal handling on nociceptin/orphanin FQ and opioid peptide levels in female rats. *Pharmacology, Biochemistry, and Behavior, 69,* 173–179.

Plomin, R., DeFries, J. C., McClearn, G. E., & Rutter, M. (1997). *Behavioral genetics* (3rd ed.). New York: W. H. Freeman.

Plous, S. (1996). Attitudes toward the use of animals in psychological research and education. *American Psychologist, 51,* 1167–1180.

Poe, G. R., Nitz, D. A., McNaughton, B. L., & Barnes, C. A. (2000). Experience-dependent phase-reversal of hippocampal neuron firing during REM sleep. *Brain Research, 855,* 176–180.

Poeck, K., Huber, W., & Willmes, K. (1989). Outcome of intensive language treatment in aphasia. *Journal of Speech & Hearing Disorder, 54,* 471–479.

Poggio, G. E. (1995). Mechanisms of stereopsis in monkey visual cortex. *Cerebral Cortex, 5,* 193–204.

Poldrack, R. A., & Gabrieli, J. D. (1997). Functional anatomy of long-term memory. *Journal of Clinical Neurophysiology, 14,* 294–310.

Polivy, J., & Herman, C. P. (1993). Etiology of binge eating: Psychological mechanisms. In C. G. Fairburn & G. T. Wilson (Eds.), *Binge eating: Nature, assessment, and treatment* (pp. 173–205). New York: The Guilford Press.

Polman, C. H., Wolinsky, J. S., & Reingold, S. C. (2005). Multiple sclerosis diagnostic criteria: Three years later. *Multiple Sclerosis, 11,* 5–12.

Pons, S., & Marti, E. (2000). Sonic hedgehog synergizes with the extracellular matrix protein vitronectin to induce spinal motor neuron differentiation. *Development, 127,* 333–342.

Pons, T. P., Garraghty, P. E., Friedman, D. P., & Mishkin, M. (1987). Physiological evidence for serial processing in somatosensory cortex. *Science, 237,* 417–420.

Ponton, C. W., Moore, J. K., & Eggermont, J. J. (1999). Prolonged deafness limits auditory system developmental plasticity: Evidence from an evoked potentials study in children with cochlear implants. *Scandinavian Audiology. Supplementum, 51,* 13–22.

Popova, N. K., Nikulina, E. M., & Kulikov, A. V. (1993). Genetic analysis of different kinds of aggressive behavior. *Behavior Genetics, 23,* 491–497.

Porter, R. H. (1998–1999). Olfaction and human kin recognition. *Genetica, 104,* 259–263.

Porter, R. J., Lunn, B. S., & O'Brien, J. T. (2003). Effects of acute tryptophan depletion on cognitive function in Alzheimer's disease and in the healthy elderly. *Psychological Medicine, 33,* 41–49.

Postle, B. R., & D'Esposito, M. (1999). Dissociation of human caudate nucleus activity in spatial and nonspatial working memory: An event-related fMRI study. *Brain Research. Cognitive Brain Research, 8,* 107–115.

Postle, B. R., & D'Esposito, M. (2003). Spatial working memory activity of the caudate nucleus is sensitive to frame of reference. *Cognitive, Affective & Behavioral Neuroscience, 3,* 133–144.

Poustie, V. J., & Rutherford, P. (2000). Dietary interventions for phenylketonuria. *Cochrane Database of Systematic Reviews,* (2), CD001304.

Powell, N. B., Schechtman, K. B., Riley, R. W., Li, K., Troell, R., & Guilleminault, C. (2001). The road to danger: The comparative risks of driving while sleepy. *Laryngoscope, 111,* 887–893.

Powley, T. L. (1977). The ventromedial hypothalamic syndrome, satiety, and a cephalic phase hypothesis. *Psychological Review, 84,* 89–126.

Powley, T. L. (2000). Vagal circuitry mediating cephalic-phase responses to food. *Appetite, 34,* 184–188.

Powley, T. L., & Keesey, R. E. (1970). Relationship of body weight to the lateral hypothalamic feeding syndrome. *Journal of Comparative and Physiological Psychology, 70,* 25–36.

Prang, P., Del Turco, D., & Kapfhammer, J. P. (2001). Regeneration of entorhinal fibers in mouse slice cultures is age dependent and can be stimulated by NT-4, GDNF, and modulators of G-proteins and protein kinase C. *Experimental Neurology, 169,* 135–147.

Preston, K. L., Umbricht, A., & Epstein, D. H. (2000). Methadone dose increase and abstinence reinforcement for treatment of continued heroin use during methadone maintenance. *Archives of General Psychiatry, 57,* 395–404.

Preti, G., Cutler, W. B., Garcia, C. R., Huggins, G. R., & Lawley, H. J. (1986). Human axillary secretions influence women's menstrual cycles: The role of donor extract of females. *Hormones and Behavior, 20,* 474–482.

Preti, G., Wysocki, C. J., Barnhart, K. T., Sondheimer, S. J., & Leyden, J. J. (2003). Male axillary extracts contain pheromones that affect pulsatile secretion of luteinizing hormone and mood in women recipients. *Biology of Reproduction, 68,* 2107–2113.

Prien, R. F., Caffey, E. M., Jr., & Klett, C. J. (1973). Prophylactic efficacy of lithium carbonate in manic-depressive illness. Report of the Veteran Administration and National Institute of Mental Health collaborative study group. *Archives of General Psychiatry, 28,* 337–341.

Proietto, J., & Thorburn, A. W. (2003). The therapeutic potential of leptin. *Expert Opinion on Investigational Drugs, 12,* 373–378.

Provencio, I., Wong, S., Lederman, A. B., Argamaso, S. M., & Foster, R. G. (1994). Visual and circadian responses to light in aged retinally degenerate mice. *Vision Research, 34,* 1799–1806.

Przewlocki, R., & Przewlocka, B. (2001). Opioids in chronic pain. *European Journal of Pharmacology, 429,* 79–91.

Puerta-Fonolla, A. J. (1998). Morphogenesis of the human genital tract. *Italian Journal of Anatomy and Embryology, 103,* 3–15.

Pugh, J. R., & Raman, I. M. (2005). $GABA_A$ receptor kinetics in the cerebellar nuclei: Evidence for detection of transmitter from distant release sites. *Biophysical Journal, 88,* 1740–1754.

Pulvermueller, F. (1996). Hebb's concept of cell assemblies and the psychophysiology of word processing. *Psychophysiology, 33,* 317–333.

Purdy, S. C., Kelly, A. S., & Thorne, P. R. (2001). Auditory evoked potentials as measures of plasticity in humans. *Audiology and Neuro-otology, 6,* 211–215.

Putnam, S. K., Du, J., Sato, S., & Hull, E. M. (2001). Testosterone restoration of copulatory behavior correlates with medial preoptic dopamine release in castrated male rats. *Hormones and Behavior, 39,* 216–224.

Putnam, S. K., Sato, S., & Hull, E. M. (2003). Effects of testosterone metabolites on copulation and medial preoptic dopamine release in castrated male rats. *Hormones and Behavior, 44,* 419–426.

Qu, T., Brannen, C. L., Kim, H. M., & Sugaya, K. (2001). Human neural stem cells improve cognitive function of aged brain. *Neuroreport, 12,* 1127–1132.

Quarta, D., Ferre, S., Solinas, M., You, Z. B., Hockemeyer, J., Popoli, P., et al. (2004). Opposite modulatory roles for adenosine A_1 and A_{2A} receptors on glutamate and dopamine release in the shell of the nucleus accumbens. Effects of chronic caffeine exposure. *Journal of Neurochemistry, 88,* 1151–1158.

Quinnell, T. G., & Smith, I. E. (2004). Obstructive sleep apnea in the elderly: Recognition and management considerations. *Drugs & Aging, 21,* 307–322.

Rachels, J. (1986). Darwin's moral lapse. *National Forum,* 66, 22–24.

Rachman, S. (1966). Sexual fetishism: An experimental analogue. *The Psychological Record, 16,* 293–296.

Raffaele, R., Vecchio, I., Giammusso, B., Morgia, G., Brunetto, M. B., & Rampello, L. (2002). Efficacy and safety of fixed-dose oral sildenafil in the treatment of sexual dysfunction in depressed patients with idiopathic Parkinson's disease. *European Urology, 41,* 382–386.

Rahkila, P., Hakala, E., Alen, M., Salminen, K., & Laatikainen, T. (1988). Beta-endorphin and corticotropin release is dependent on a threshold intensity of running exercise in male endurance athletes. *Life Sciences, 43,* 551–558.

Rahola, J. G. (2001). Antidepressants: Pharmacological profile and clinical consequences. *International Journal of Psychiatry in Clinical Practice, 5,* S19–S28.

Raineteau, O., Fouad, K., Bareyre, F. M., & Schwab, M. E. (2002). Reorganization of descending motor tracts in the rat spinal cord. *European Journal of Neuroscience, 16,* 1761–1771.

Raineteau, O., & Schwab, M. E. (2001). Plasticity of motor systems after incomplete spinal cord injury. *Nature Reviews. Neuroscience, 2,* 263–273.

Rainville, P. (2002). Brain mechanisms of pain affect and pain modulation. *Current Opinion in Neurobiology, 12,* 195–204.

Rajkowksi, J., Kubiak, P., & Aston-Jones, G. (1994). Locus coeruleus activity in monkey: Phasic and tonic changes are associated with altered vigilance. *Brain Research Bulletin, 35,* 607–616.

Rakic, P. (2003). Elusive radial glial cells: Historical and evolutionary perspective. *Glia, 43,* 19–32.

Rakic, P., & Caviness, V. S., Jr. (1995). Cortical development: View from neurological mutants two decades later. *Neuron, 14,* 1101–1104.

Rakic, S., & Zecevic, N. (2000). Programmed cell death in the developing human telencephalon. *European Journal of Neuroscience, 12,* 2721–2734.

Ralph, M. R., Foster, R. G., Davis, F. C., & Menaker, M. (1990). Transplanted suprachiasmatic nucleus determines circadian period. *Science, 247,* 975–978.

Ramachandran, V. S., Rogers-Ramachandran, D., & Cobb, S. (1995). Touching the phantom limb. *Nature, 377,* 489–490.

Ramamurthi, B. (1988). Stereotactic operation in behaviour disorders. Amygdalotomy and hypothalamotomy. *Acta Neurochirurgica. Supplement, 44,* 152–157.

Rami-Gonzalez, L., Bernardo, M., Boget, T., Salamero, M., Gil-Verona, J. A., & Junque, C. (2001). Subtypes of memory dysfunction associated with ECT: Characteristics and neurobiological bases. *The Journal of ECT, 17,* 129–135.

Raming, K., Krieger, J., Strotmann, J., Boekhoff, I., Kubick, S., Baumstark, C., et al. (1993). Cloning and expression of odorant receptors. *Nature, 361,* 353–356.

Ramirez, O. A., Nordholm, A. F., Gellerman, D., Thompson, J. K., & Thompson, R. F. (1997). Conditioned eyeblink response: A role for the $GABA_B$ receptor? *Pharmacology, Biochemistry, & Behavior, 58,* 127–132.

Rao, G. M. (1995). Oxytocin induces intimate behaviors. *Indian Journal of Medical Sciences, 49,* 261–266.

Rao, R., & Georgieff, M. K. (2000). Early nutrition and brain development. In C. A. Nelson (Ed.), *The Minnesota symposia on child psychology, Vol. 31: The effects of early adversity on neurobehavioral development* (pp. 1–30). Mahwah, NJ: Erlbaum.

Rapkin, A. J., Pollack, D. B., Raleigh, M. J., Stone, B., & McGuire, M. T. (1995). Menstrual cycle and social behavior in vervet monkeys. *Psychoneuroendocrinology, 20,* 289–297.

Rasmussen, T., & Milner, B. (1977). The role of early left-brain injury in determining lateralization of cerebral speech functions. *Annals of the New York Academy of Sciences, 299,* 355–369.

Rauchs, G., Bertran, F., Guillery-Girard, B., Desgranges, B., Kerrouche, N., Denise, P., et al. (2004). Consolidation of strictly episodic memories mainly requires rapid eye movement sleep. *Sleep, 27,* 395–401.

Rauschecker, J. P. (1998). Parallel processing in the auditory cortex of primates. *Audiology and Neuro-otology, 3,* 86–103.

Rauschecker, J. P., & Tian, B. (2000). Mechanisms and streams for processing of "what" and "where" in auditory cortex. *Proceedings* *of the National Academy of Sciences of the United States of America, 97,* 11800–11806.

Rauschecker, J. P., & Tian, B. (2004). Processing of band-passed noise in the lateral auditory belt cortex of the rhesus monkey. *Journal of Neurophysiology, 91,* 2578–2589.

Rauschecker, J. P., Tian, B., & Hauser, M. (1995). Processing of complex sounds in the macaque nonprimary auditory cortex. *Science, 268,* 111–114.

Ravinet Trillou, C., Arnone, M., Delgorge, C., Gonalons, N., Keane, P., Maffrand, J. P., et al. (2003). Anti-obesity effect of SR141716, a CB1 receptor antagonist, in diet-induced obese mice. *American Journal of Physiology. Regulatory, Integrative and Comparative Physiology, 284,* R345–R353.

Ray, O., & Ksir, C. (2006). *Drugs, society, and human behavior* (11th ed.). New York: McGraw-Hill.

Raz, A., Frechter-Mazar, V., Feingold, A., Abeles, M., Vaadia, E., & Bergman, H. (2001). Activity of pallidal and striatal tonically active neurons is correlated in mptp-treated monkeys but not in normal monkeys. *The Journal of Neuroscience, 21,* RC128.

Recanzone, G. H. (2000). Spatial processing in the auditory cortex of the macaque monkey. *Proceedings of the National Academy of Sciences of the United States of America, 97,* 11829–11835.

Recanzone, G. H., Guard, D. C., Phan, M. L., & Su, T. K. (2000). Correlation between the activity of single auditory cortical neurons and sound-localization behavior in the macaque monkey. *Journal of Neurophysiology, 83,* 2723–2739.

Recanzone, G. H., & Wurtz, R. H. (1999). Shift in smooth pursuit initiation and MT and MST neuronal activity under different stimulus conditions. *Journal of Neurophysiology, 82,* 1710–1727.

Redfern, P. A. (1970). Neuromuscular transmission in new-born rats. *The Journal of Physiology, 209,* 701–709.

Redmond, A. M., Kelly, J. P., & Leonard, B. E. (1997). Behavioural and neurochemical effects of dizocilpine in the olfactory bulbectomized rat model of depression. *Pharmacology, Biochemistry, and Behavior, 58,* 355–359.

Reed, J. M., & Squire, L. R. (1997). Impaired recognition memory in patients with lesions limited to the hippocampal formation. *Behavioral Neuroscience, 111,* 667–675.

Rees, T. M., & Brimijoin, S. (2003). The role of acetylcholinesterase in the pathogenesis of Alzheimer's disease. *Drugs of Today (Barcelona, Spain), 39,* 75–83.

Reeve, C. (2002). Christopher Reeve Q&A. Retrieved April 19, 2004, from http://www.christopherreeve.org/ChristopherReeve/ChristopherReeve.cfm?ID=331&c=57

Reeves, A. G., & Plum, F. (1969). Hyperphagia, rage, and dementia accompanying a ventromedial hypothalamic neoplasm. *Archives of Neurology, 20,* 616–624.

Reidelberger, R. D., Hernandez, J., Fritzsch, B., & Hulce, M. (2004). Abdominal vagal mediation of the satiety effects of CCK in rats. *American Journal of Physiology. Regulatory, Integrative and Comparative Physiology, 286,* R1005–R1012.

Reinscheid, R. K., Nothacker, H., & Civelli, O. (2000). The orphanin FQ/nociceptin gene: Structure, tissue distribution of expression and functional implications obtained from knockout mice. *Peptides, 21,* 901–906.

Reisenzein, R. (1983). The Schachter theory of emotion: Two decades later. *Psychological Bulletin, 94,* 239–264.

Reiter, R. J. (1993). The melatonin rhythm: Both a clock and a calendar. *Experientia, 49,* 654–664.

Reiter, R. J. (1998). Melatonin and human reproduction. *Annals of Medicine, 30,* 103–108.

Remes-Troche, J. M., Tellez-Zenteno, J. F., Estanol, B., Garduno-Espinoza, J., & Garcia-Ramos, G. (2002). Thymectomy in myasthenia gravis: Response, complications and associated conditions. *Archives of Medical Research, 33,* 545–551.

Rempel-Clower, N. L., Zola, S. M., Squire, L. R., & Amaral, D. G. (1996). Three cases of enduring memory impairment after bilateral damage limited to the hippocampal formation. *The Journal of Neuroscience, 16,* 5233–5255.

Renehan, W. E., Jin, Z., Zhang, X., & Schweitzer, L. (1996). Structure and function of gustatory neurons in the nucleus of the solitary tract: II. Relationships between neuronal morphology and physiology. *Journal of Comparative Neurology, 367,* 205–221.

Reneman, L. (2003). Designer drugs: How dangerous are they? *Journal of Neural Transmission. Supplementum,* (66), 61–83.

Resnick, S. M., Gottesman, I. I., & McGue, M. (1993). Sensation seeking in opposite-sex twins: An effect of prenatal hormones? *Behavior Genetics, 23,* 323–329.

Ressler, K. J., Sullivan, S. L., & Buck, L. B. (1994). Information coding in the olfactory system: Evidence for a stereotyped and highly organized epitope map in the olfactory bulb. *Cell, 79,* 1245–1255.

Reynolds, D. V. (1969). Surgery in the rat during electrical analgesia induced by focal brain stimulation. *Science, 164,* 444–445.

Reynolds, G. P., Abdul-Monim, Z., Neill, J. C., & Zhang, Z. J. (2004). Calcium binding protein markers of GABA deficits in schizophrenia—Postmortem studies and animal models. *Neurotoxicity Research, 6,* 57–61.

Reynolds, G. P., Zhang, Z. J., & Beasley, C. L. (2001). Neurochemical correlates of cortical GABAergic deficits in schizophrenia: Selective losses of calcium binding protein immunoreactivity. *Brain Research Bulletin, 55,* 579–584.

Rhees, R. W., Al-Saleh, H. N., Kinghorn, E. W., Fleming, D. E., & Lephart, E. D. (1999). Relationship between sexual behavior and sexually dimorphic structures in the anterior hypothalamus in control and prenatally stressed male rats. *Brain Research Bulletin, 50,* 193–199.

Rhees, R. W., Shryne, J. E., & Gorski, R. A. (1990). Termination of the hormone-sensitive period for differentiation of the sexually dimorphic nucleus of the preoptic area in male and female rats. *Brain Research. Developmental Brain Research, 52,* 17–23.

Rhodes, G., Byatt, G., Michie, P. T., & Puce, A. (2004). Is the fusiform face area specialized for faces, individuation, or expert individuation? *Journal of Cognitive Neuroscience, 16,* 189–203.

Ricci, L. C., & Wellman, M. M. (1990). Monoamines: Biochemical markers of suicide? *Journal of Clinical Psychology, 46,* 106–116.

Ricci, M. R., & Levin, B. E. (2003). Ontogeny of diet-induced obesity in selectively bred Sprague-Dawley rats. *American Journal of Physiology. Regulatory, Integrative and Comparative Physiology, 285,* R610–R618.

Rice, C. M., Halfpenny, C. A., & Scolding, N. J. (2003). Stem cells for the treatment of neurological disease. *Transfusion Medicine, 13,* 351–361.

Rice, G., Anderson, C., Risch, N., & Ebers, G. (1999). Male homosexuality: Absence of linkage to microsatellite markers at Xq28. *Science, 284,* 665–667.

Rice, J., Reich, T., Andreasen, N. C., Endicott, J., Van Eerdewegh, M., Fishman, R., et al. (1987). The familial transmission of bipolar illness. *Archives of General Psychiatry, 44,* 441–447.

Rice, J. R. (1989). Children's language acquisition. *American Psychologist, 44,* 149–156.

Richter, C. P. (1957). On the phenomenon of sudden death in animals and man. *Psychosomatic Medicine, 19,* 191–198.

Richter, C. P. (1967). Psychopathology of periodic behavior in animals and man. In J. Zubin & H. F. Hunt (Eds.), *Comparative psychopathology* (pp. 205–227). New York: Grune & Stratton.

Ridley, R. M., Warner, K. A., Maclean, C. J., Gaffan, D., & Baker, H. F. (2001). Visual agnosia and Klüver-Bucy syndrome in marmosets (*Callithrix jacchus*) following ablation of inferotemporal cortex, with additional mnemonic effects of immunotoxic lesions of cholinergic projections to medial temporal areas. *Brain Research, 898,* 136–151.

Riemann, D., Voderholzer, U., & Berger, M. (2002). Sleep and sleep-wake manipulations in bipolar depression. *Neuropsychobiology, 45,* 7–12.

Rilea, S. L., Roskos-Ewoldsen, B., & Boles, D. (2004). Sex differences in spatial ability: A lateralization of function approach. *Brain and Cognition, 56,* 332–343.

Ring, H. A., & Serra-Mestres, J. (2002). Neuropsychiatry of the basal ganglia. *Journal of Neurology, Neurosurgery, and Psychiatry. 72,* 12–21.

Risch, S. C., Kalin, N. H., & Janowsky, D. S. (1981). Cholinergic challenges in affective illness: Behavioral and neuroendocrine correlates. *Journal of Clinical Psychopharmacology, 1,* 186–192.

Ritter, A. J. (2002). Naltrexone in the treatment of heroin dependence: Relationship with depression and risk of overdose. *The Australian and New Zealand Journal of Psychiatry, 36,* 224–228.

Ritter, R. C., Slusser, P. G., & Stone, S. (1981). Glucoreceptors controlling feeding and blood glucose: Location in the hindbrain. *Science, 213,* 451–452.

Rivinus, T. M., Biederman, J., Herzog, D. B., Kemper, K., Harper, G. P., Harmatz, J. S., et al. (1984). Anorexia nervosa and affective disorders: A controlled family history study. *American Journal of Psychiatry, 141,* 1414–1418.

Rizzo, M., & Vecera, S. P. (2002). Psychoanatomical substrates of Balint's syndrome. *Journal of Neurology, Neurosurgery, and Psychiatry, 72,* 162–178.

Rizzolatti, G., & Craighero, L. (2004). The mirror-neuron system. *Annual Review of Neuroscience, 27,* 169–192.

Roberts, S. B., Savage, J., Coward, W. A., Chew, B., & Lucas, A. (1988). Energy expenditure and intake in infants born to lean and overweight mothers. *New England Journal of Medicine, 318,* 461–466.

Robertson, L., Treisman, A., Friedman-Hill, S., & Grabowsky, M. (1997). The interaction of spatial and object pathways: Evidence from Balint's syndrome. *Journal of Cognitive Neuroscience, 9,* 295–317.

Robinson, B. W., & Mishkin, M. (1968). Alimentary responses to forebrain stimulation in monkeys. *Experimental Brain Research, 4,* 330–366.

Robinson, D., Woerner, M. G., Alvir, J. M., Bilder, R., Goldman, R., Geisler, S., et al. (1999). Predictors of relapse following response from a first episode of schizophrenia or schizoaffective disorder. *Archives of General Psychiatry, 56,* 241–247.

Robison, B. L., & Sawyer, C. H. (1987). Hypothalamic control of ovulation and behavioral estrus in the cat. *Brain Research, 418,* 41–51.

Roca, C. A., Schmidt, P. J., Altemus, M., Deuster, P., Danaceau, M. A., Putnam, K., et al. (2003). Differential menstrual cycle regulation of hypothalamic-pituitary-adrenal axis in women with premenstrual syndrome and controls. *The Journal of Clinical Endocrinology and Metabolism, 88,* 3057–3063.

Rodin, J. (1985). Insulin levels, hunger, and food intake: An example of feedback loops in body weight regulation. *Health Psychology, 4,* 1–24.

Rodin, J. (1990). Comparative effects of fructose, aspartame, glucose, and water preloads on calorie and macronutrient intake. *American Journal of Clinical Nutrition, 51,* 428–435.

Rodin, J., Reed, D., & Jamner, L. (1988). Metabolic effects of fructose and glucose: Implications for food intake. *American Journal of Clinical Nutrition, 47,* 683–689.

Roehrs, T., Vogel, G., & Roth, T. (1990). Rebound insomnia: Its determinants and significance. *American Journal of Medicine, 88,* 39S–42S.

Roelink, H., Augsburger, A., Heemskerk, J., Korzh, V., Norlin, S., Ruiz i Altaba, A., et al. (1994). Floor plate and motor neuron induction by vhh-1, a vertebrate homolog of hedgehog expressed by the notochord. *Cell, 76,* 761–775.

Roenneberg, T., & Merrow, M. (2003). The network of time: Understanding the molecular circadian system. *Current Biology, 13,* R198–R207.

Roffwarg, H. P., Muzio, J. N., & Dement, W. C. (1966). Ontogenetic development of human sleep-dream cycle. *Science, 152,* 604–609.

Rogers, J. L., & Kesner, R. P. (2004). Cholinergic modulation of the hippocampus during encoding and retrieval of tone/shock-induced fear conditioning. *Learning & Memory, 11,* 102–107.

Rohner-Jeanrenaud, F. (2000). Hormonal regulation of energy partitioning. *International Journal of Obesity and Related Metabolic Disorders, 24,* S4–S7.

Rohsenow, D. J. (2004). What place does naltrexone have in the treatment of alcoholism? *CNS Drugs, 18,* 547–560.

Rojo, M., Marin, B., & Menendez-Patterson, A. (1986). Prenatal stress: Effects on sexual receptivity in female rats. *Revista Espanola de Fisiologia, 42,* 379–381.

Rolls, E. T. (2004a). The functions of the orbitofrontal cortex. *Brain and Cognition, 55,* 11–29.

Rolls, E. T. (2004b). Convergence of sensory systems in the orbitofrontal cortex in primates and brain design for emotion. *The Anatomical Record. Part A, Discoveries in Molecular, Cellular, and Evolutionary Biology, 281,* 1212–1225.

Rolls, E. T., Burton, M. J., & Mora, F. (1976). Hypothalamic neuronal responses associated with the sight of food. *Brain Research, 111,* 53–66.

Rolls, E. T., Burton, M. J., & Mora, F. (1980). Neurophysiological analysis of brain-stimulation reward in the monkey. *Brain Research, 194,* 339–357.

Romanski, L. M., Tian, B., Fritz, J., Mishkin, M., Goldman-Rakic, P. S., & Rauschecker, J. P. (1999). Dual streams of auditory afferents target multiple domains in the primate prefrontal cortex. *Nature Neuroscience, 2,* 1131–1136.

Rommelspacher, H., Smolka, M., Schmidt, L. G., Samochowiec, J., & Hoehe, M. R. (2001). Genetic analysis of the mu-opioid receptor in alcohol-dependent individuals. *Alcohol, 24,* 129–135.

Rosen, R. C. (2000). Prevalence and risk factors of sexual dysfunction in men and women. *Current Psychiatry Reports, 2,* 189–195.

Rosenblatt, A., Brinkman, R. R., Liang, K. Y., Almqvist, E. W., Margolis, R. L., Huang, C. Y., et al. (2001). Familial influence on age of onset among siblings with Huntington disease. *American Journal of Medical Genetics, 105,* 399–403.

Rosenthal, D. (Ed.). (1963). *The Genain quadruplets.* Oxford, England: Basic Books.

Rosenzweig, M. R., & Bennett, E. L. (1996). Psychobiology of plasticity: Effects of training and experience on brain and behavior. *Behavioural Brain Research, 78,* 57–65.

Ross, M. J., & Berger, R. S. (1996). Effects of stress inoculation training on athletes' postsurgical pain and rehabilitation after orthopedic injury. *Journal of Consulting and Clinical Psychology, 64,* 406–410.

Rosser, A. E., & Dunnett, S. B. (2003). Neural transplantation in patients with Huntington's disease. *CNS Drugs, 17,* 853–867.

Rossion, B., Caldara, R., Seghier, M., Schuller, A. M., Lazeyras, F., & Mayer, E. (2003). A network of occipito-temporal face-sensitive areas besides the right middle fusiform gyrus is necessary for normal face processing. *Brain, 126,* 2381–2395.

Rossion, B., Schiltz, C., Robaye, L., Pirenne, D., & Crommelinck, M. (2001). How does the brain discriminate familiar and unfamiliar faces? A PET study of face categorical perception. *Journal of Cognitive Neuroscience, 13,* 1019–1034.

Rosvold, H. E., Mirsky, A. F., & Pribram, K. H. (1954). Influence of amygdalectomy on social behavior in monkeys. *Journal of Comparative and Physiological Psychology, 47,* 173–178.

Rouquier, S., Blancher, A., & Giorgi, D. (2000). The olfactory receptor gene repertoire in primates and mouse: Evidence for reduction of the functional fraction in primates. *Proceedings of the National Academy of Sciences of the United States of America, 97,* 2870–2874.

Rousmans, S., Robin, O., Dittmar, A., & Vernet-Maury, E. (2000). Autonomic nervous system responses associated with primary tastes. *Chemical Senses, 25,* 709–718.

Routtenberg, A., & Lindy, J. (1965). Effects of the availability of rewarding septal and hypothalamic stimulation on bar pressing for food under conditions of deprivation. *Journal of Comparative and Physiological Psychology, 60,* 158–161.

Rozental, R., Giaume, C., & Spray, D. C. (2000). Gap junctions in the nervous system. *Brain Research. Brain Research Reviews, 32,* 11–15.

Rozin, P., Ebert, L., & Schull, J. (1982). Some like it hot: A temporal analysis of hedonic responses to chili pepper. *Appetite, 3,* 13–22.

Rubin, B. D., & Katz, L. C. (1999). Optical imaging of odorant representations in the mammalian olfactory bulb. *Neuron, 23,* 499–511.

Rusak, B., & Groos, G. (1982). Suprachiasmatic stimulation phase shifts rodent circadian rhythms. *Science, 215,* 1407–1409.

Rush, A. J., Giles, D. E., Schlesser, M. A., Orsulak, P. J., Parker, C. R., Jr., Weissenburger, J. E., et al. (1996). The dexamethasone suppression test in patients with mood disorders. *Journal of Clinical Psychiatry, 57,* 470–484.

Russek, M. (1971). Hepatic receptors and the neurophysiological mechanisms controlling feeding behavior. *Neurosciences Research, 4,* 213–282.

Ryan, B. C., & Vandenbergh, J. G. (2002). Intrauterine position effects. *Neuroscience and Biobehavioral Reviews, 26,* 665–678.

Sack, R. L., Brandes, R. W., Kendall, A. R., & Lewy, A. J. (2000). Entrainment of free-running circadian rhythms by melatonin in blind people. *New England Journal of Medicine, 343,* 1070–1077.

Sackeim, H. A., Prudic, J., Devanand, D. P., Nobler, M. S., Lisanby, S. H., Peyser, S., et al. (2000). A prospective, randomized, double-blind comparison of bilateral and right unilateral electroconvulsive therapy at different stimulus intensities. *Archives of General Psychiatry, 57,* 425–434.

Sacks, O. (1987). *The man who mistook his wife for a hat.* New York: HarperCollins.

Sacks, O. (1990). The man who mistook his wife for a hat and other clinical tales. New York: HarperPerennial.

Sadato, N., Okada, T., Kubota, K., & Yonekura, Y. (2004). Tactile discrimination activates the visual cortex of the recently blind naive to Braille: A functional magnetic resonance imaging study in humans. *Neuroscience Letters, 359,* 49–52.

Saeed, S. A., & Bruce, T. J. (1998). Seasonal affective disorders. *American Family Physician, 57,* 1340–1346, 1351–1352.

Sakai, K. (1980). Some anatomical and physiological properties of pontomesencephalic tegmental neurons with special reference to the PGO waves and postural atonia during paradoxical sleep in the cat. In J. A. Hobson & M. A. Brazier (Eds.), *The reticular formation revisited* (pp. 427–447). New York: Raven Press.

Sakai, R. R., & Epstein, A. N. (1990). Dependence of adrenalectomy-induced sodium appetite on the action of angiotensin II in the brain of the rat. *Behavioral Neuroscience, 104,* 167–176.

Salamone, J. D., & Correa, M. (2002). Motivational views of reinforcement: Implications for understanding the behavioral functions of nucleus accumbens dopamine. *Behavioural Brain Research, 137,* 3–25.

Salim, A., Kim, K. A., Kimbrell, B. J., Petrone, P., Roldan, G., & Asensio, J. A. (2002). Kluver-Bucy syndrome as a result of minor head trauma. *Southern Medical Journal, 95,* 929–931.

Salman, M. S. (2002). The cerebellum: It's about time! But timing is not everything—new insights into the role of the cerebellum in timing motor and cognitive tasks. *Journal of Child Neurology, 17,* 1–9.

Salorio, C. F., Hammond, P. B., Schwartz, G. J., McHugh, P. R., & Moran, T. H. (1994). Age-dependent effects of CCK and devazepide in male and female rats. *Physiology & Behavior, 56,* 645–648.

Sanchez Galan, L., Diez Sanchez, M. A., Llorca Ramon, G., & del Canizo Fernandez-Roldan, A. (2000). Personality study in profoundly deaf adults. *Revue de Laryngologie-Otologie-Rhinologie, 121,* 339–343.

Sanchez-Lastres, J., Eiris-Punal, J., Otero-Cepeda, J. L., Pavon-Belinchon, P., & Castro-Gago, M. (2003). Nutritional status of mentally retarded children in northwest Spain: II. Biochemical indicators. *Acta Paediatrica, 92,* 928–934.

Sanders, R. J. (1989). Sentence comprehension following agenesis of the corpus callosum. *Brain and Language, 37,* 59–72.

Sanes, J. N., & Donoghue, J. P. (2000). Plasticity and primary motor cortex. *Annual Review of Neuroscience, 23,* 393–415.

Sanes, J. N., Wang, J., & Donoghue, J. P. (1992). Immediate and delayed changes of rat motor cortical output representation with new forelimb configurations. *Cerebral Cortex, 2,* 141–152.

Sanes, J. R., & Jessell, T. M. (2000a). The formation and regeneration of synapses. In E. R. Kandel, J. H. Schwartz, & T. M. Jessell (Eds.), *Principles of neural science* (4th ed., pp. 1087–1114). New York: McGraw-Hill.

Sanes, J. R., & Jessell, T. M. (2000b). The guidance of axons to their targets. In E. R. Kandel, J. H. Schwartz, & T. M. Jessell (Eds.), *Principles of neural science* (4th ed., pp. 1063–1086). New York: McGraw-Hill.

Santonastaso, P., Friederici, S., & Favaro, A. (2001). Sertraline in the treatment of restricting anorexia nervosa: An open controlled trial. *Journal of Child and Adolescent Psychopharmacology, 11,* 143–150.

Sarason, I. G., & Sarason, B. R. (2004). *Abnormal psychology: The problem of maladaptive behavior* (11th ed.). Upper Saddle River, NJ: Prentice Hall.

Sarno, M. T. (1998). Recovery and rehabilitation in aphasia. In M. T. Sarno (Ed.), *Acquired aphasia* (3rd ed., pp. 595–631). San Diego: Academic Press.

Sasaki-Adams, D. M., & Kelley, A. E. (2001). Serotonin-dopamine interactions in the control of conditioned reinforcement and motor behavior. *Neuropsychopharmacology, 25,* 440–452.

Sato, Y., Wada, H., Horita, H., Suzuki, N., Shibuya, A., Adachi, H., et al. (1995). Dopamine release in the medial preoptic area during male copulatory behavior in rats. *Brain Research, 692,* 66–70.

Satz, P. (1979). A test of some models of hemispheric speech organization in the left- and right-handed. *Science, 203,* 1131–1133.

Sauerwein, H. C., Lassonde, M. C., Cardu, B., & Geoffroy, G. (1981). Interhemispheric integration of sensory and motor functions in agenesis of the corpus callosum. *Neuropsychologia, 19,* 445–454.

Saunders, T., Driskell, J. E., Johnston, J. H., & Salas, E. (1996). The effect of stress inoculation training on anxiety and performance. *Journal of Occupational Health Psychology, 1,* 170–186.

Sawa, A., Tomoda, T., & Bae, B. I. (2003). Mechanisms of neuronal cell death in Huntington's disease. *Cytogenetic and Genome Research, 100,* 287–295.

Sawaki, L., Boroojerdi, B., Kaelin-Lang, A., Burstein, A. H., Butefisch, C. M., Kopylev, L., et al. (2002). Cholinergic influences on use-dependent plasticity. *Journal of Neurophysiology, 87,* 166–171.

Sawrey, W. L., Conger, J. J., & Turrell, E. S. (1956). An experimental investigation of the role of psychological factors in the production of gastric ulcers in rats. *Journal of Comparative and Physiological Psychology, 49,* 457–461.

Sax, L. (2002). How common is intersex? A response to Anne Fausto-Sterling. *Journal of Sex Research, 39,* 174–178.

Schachter, S. (1964). The interaction of cognitive and physiological determinants of emotional state. In L. Berkowitz (Ed.), *Advances in experimental social psychology* (Vol. 1, pp. 49–79). New York: Academic Press.

Schachter, S. (1971). Some extraordinary facts about obese humans and rats. *American Psychologist, 26,* 129–144.

Schachter, S., & Singer, J. E. (1962). Cognitive, social, and physiological determinants of emotional state. *Psychological Review, 69,* 379–399.

Schafer, D., & Greulich, W. (2000). Effects of parkinsonian medication on sleep. *Journal of Neurology, 247,* 24–27.

Schank, J. C. (2000). Menstrual-cycle variability and measurement: Further cause for doubt. *Psychoneuroendocrinology, 25,* 519–526.

Schank, J. C. (2001a). Measurement and cycle variability: Reexamining the case for ovarian-cycle synchrony in primates. *Behavioural Processes, 56,* 131–146.

Schank, J. C. (2001b). Menstrual-cycle synchrony: Problems and new directions for research. *Journal of Comparative Psychology, 115,* 3–15.

Schank, J. C. (2002). A multitude of errors in menstrual-synchrony research: Replies to Weller and Weller (2002) and Graham (2002). *Journal of Comparative Psychology, 116,* 319–322.

Schank, J. C. (2004). Avoiding synchrony as a strategy of female mate choice. *Nonlinear Dynamics, Psychology, and Life Sciences, 8,* 147–176.

Schapira, A. H. (2001). Causes of neuronal death in Parkinson's disease. *Advances in Neurology, 86,* 155–162.

Scharrer, E. (1999). Control of food intake by fatty acid oxidation and ketogenesis. *Nutrition, 15,* 704–714.

Schatzman, M., Worsley, A., & Fenwick, P. (1988). Correspondence during lucid dreams between dreamed and actual events. In J. Gackenbach & S. LaBerge (Eds.), *Conscious mind, sleeping brain* (pp. 155–179). New York: Plenum.

Scheibel, A. B., & Conrad, A. S. (1993). Hippocampal dysgenesis in mutant mouse and schizophrenic man: Is there a relationship? *Schizophrenia Bulletin, 19,* 21–33.

Scheich, H., & Zuschratter, W. (1995). Mapping of stimulus features and meaning in gerbil auditory cortex with 2-deoxyglucose and c-Fos antibodies. *Behavioural Brain Research, 66,* 195–205.

Schenck, C. H., Bundlie, S. R., Ettinger, M. G., & Mahowald, M. W. (1986). Chronic behavioral disorders of human REM sleep: A new category of parasomnia. *Sleep, 9,* 293–308.

Schenkel, E., & Siegel, J. M. (1989). REM sleep without atonia after lesions of the medial medulla. *Neuroscience Letters, 98,* 159–165.

Schmid, R., Schick, T., Steffen, R., Tschopp, A., & Wilk, T. (1994). Comparison of seven commonly used agents for prophylaxis of seasickness. *Journal of Travel Medicine, 1,* 203–206.

Schmitt, M. (1973). Influences of hepatic portal receptors on hypothalamic feeding and satiety centers. *American Journal of Physiology, 225,* 1089–1095.

Schnapf, J. L., & Baylor, D. A. (1987). How photoreceptor cells respond to light. *Scientific American, 256,* 40–47.

Schneider, M. L., Moore, C. F., & Kraemer, G. W. (2001). Moderate alcohol during pregnancy: Learning and behavior in adolescent rhesus monkeys. *Alcoholism, Clinical and Experimental Research, 25,* 1383–1392.

Schneider, M. L., Moore, C. F., & Kraemer, G. W. (2004). Moderate level alcohol during pregnancy, prenatal stress, or both and limbic-hypothalamic-pituitary-adrenocortical axis response to stress in rhesus monkeys. *Child Development, 75,* 96–109.

Schnitzler, A., & Ploner, M. (2000). Neurophysiology and functional neuroanatomy of pain perception. *Journal of Clinical Neurophysiology, 17,* 592–603.

Schoenlein, R. W., Peteanu, L. A., Mathies, R. A., & Shank, C. V. (1991). The first step in vision: Femtosecond isomerization of rhodopsin. *Science, 254,* 412–415.

Schoorlemmer, G. H., Johnson, A. K., & Thunhorst, R. L. (2000). Effect of hyperosmotic solutions on salt excretion and thirst in rats. *American Journal of Physiology. Regulatory, Integrative and Comparative Physiology, 278,* R917–R923.

Schotzinger, R., Yin, X., & Landis, S. (1994). Target determination of neurotransmitter phenotype in sympathetic neurons. *Journal of Neurobiology, 25,* 620–639.

Schrag, A., Samuel, M., Caputo, E., Scaravilli, T., Troyer, M., Marsden, C. D., et al. (1999). Unilateral pallidotomy for Parkinson's disease: Results after more than 1 year. *Journal of Neurology, Neurosurgery, and Psychiatry, 67,* 511–517.

Schreiner, L., & Kling, A. (1953). Behavioral changes following rhinencephalic injury in cat. *Journal of Neurophysiology, 16,* 643–659.

Schubotz, R. I., & von Cramon, D. Y. (2001). Functional organization of the lateral premotor cortex: fMRI reveals different regions activated by anticipation of object properties, location and speed. *Brain Research: Cognitive Brain Research, 11,* 97–112.

Schuell, H., Jenkins, J. J., & Jimenez-Pabon, E. (1964). *Aphasia in adults: Diagnosis, prognosis, and treatment.* New York: Harper & Row.

Schultz, W. (2002). Getting formal with dopamine and reward. *Neuron, 36,* 241–263.

Schulze-Rauschenbach, S. C., Harms, U., Schlaepfer, T. E., Maier, W., Falkai, P., & Wagner, M. (2005). Distinctive neurocognitive effects of repetitive transcranial magnetic stimulation and electroconvulsive therapy in major depression. *British Journal of Psychiatry, 186,* 410–416.

Schwartz, M. D., Jacobsen, P. B., & Bovbjerg, D. H. (1996). Role of nausea in the development of aversions to a beverage paired with chemotherapy treatment in cancer patients. *Physiology & Behavior, 59,* 659–663.

Schwartz, T. H., Haglund, M. M., Lettich, E., & Ojemann, G. A. (2000). Asymmetry of neuronal activity during extracellular microelectrode recording from left and right human temporal lobe neocortex during rhyming and line-matching. *Journal of Cognitive Neuroscience, 12,* 803–812.

Schwartz, W. J., & Gainer, H. (1977). Suprachiasmatic nucleus: Use of 14C-labeled deoxyglucose uptake as a functional marker. *Science, 197,* 1089–1091.

Schwarz, D. W., Dezso, A., & Neufeld, P. R. (1993). Frequency selectivity of central auditory neurons without inner ear. *Acta Otolaryngologica, 113,* 266–270.

Schwarzschild, M. A., Xu, K., Oztas, E., Petszer, J. P., Castagnoli, K., Castagnoli, N., Jr., et al. (2003). Neuroprotection by caffeine and more specific A2A receptor antagonists in animal models of Parkinson's disease. *Neurology, 61,* S55–S61.

Sclafani, A. (1971). Neural pathways involved in the ventromedial hypothalamic lesion syndrome in the rat. *Journal of Comparative and Physiological Psychology, 77,* 70–96.

Sclafani, A., & Kluge, L. (1974). Food motivation and body weight levels in hypothalamic hyperphage rats: A dual lipostat model of hunger and appetite. *Journal of Comparative and Physiological Psychology, 86,* 28–46.

Scott, A. J. (2000). Shift work and health. *Primary Care, 27,* 1057–1079.

Scott, S. K., Young, A. W., Calder, A. J., Hellawell, D. J., Aggleton, J. P., & Johnson, M. (1997). Impaired auditory recognition of fear and anger following bilateral amygdala lesions. *Nature, 385,* 254–257.

Scoville, W. B., & Milner, B. (1957). Loss of recent memory after bilateral hippocampal lesions. *Journal of Neurology, Neurosurgery, and Psychiatry, 20,* 11–21.

Seed, J. A., Dixon, R. A., McCluskey, S. E., & Young, A. H. (2000). Basal activity of the hypothalamic-pituitary-adrenal axis and cognitive function in anorexia nervosa. *European Archives of Psychiatry and Clinical Neuroscience, 250,* 11–15.

Segraves, R. T., & Althof, S. (1998). Psychotherapy and pharmacotherapy of sexual dysfunctions. In P. E. Nathan & J. M. Gorman (Eds.), *A guide to treatments that work* (pp. 447–471). New York: Oxford University Press.

Seidl, R., Cairns, N., Singewald, N., Kaehler, S. T., & Lubec, G. (2001). Differences between GABA levels in Alzheimer's disease and Down syndrome with Alzheimer-like neuropathology. *Naunyn-Schmiedebergs Archiv fur Pharmakologie, 363,* 139–145.

Seifritz, E. (2001). Contribution of sleep physiology to depressive pathophysiology. *Neuropsychopharmacology, 25,* S85–S88.

Selemon, L. D., Rajkowska, G., & Goldman-Rakic, P. S. (1995). Abnormally high neuronal density in the schizophrenic cortex. A morphometric analysis of prefrontal area 9 and occipital area 17. *Archives of General Psychiatry, 52,* 805–818.

Seligman, M. E. P. (1975). *Helplessness: On depression, development, and death.* San Francisco: W.H. Freeman.

Selkoe, D. J. (1992). Aging brain, aging mind. *Scientific American, 267,* 134–142.

Selkoe, D. J. (2000). Toward a comprehensive theory for Alzheimer's disease. Hypothesis: Alzheimer's disease is caused by the cerebral accumulation and cytotoxicity of amyloid beta-protein. *Annals of the New York Academy of Sciences, 924,* 17–25.

Selye, H. (1956). *The stress of life.* New York: McGraw-Hill.

Sem-Jacobson, C. W. (1968). *Depth-electrographic stimulation of the human brain and behavior: From fourteen years of studies and treatment of Parkinson's disease and mental disorders with implanted electrodes.* Springfield, IL: Thomas.

Setlow, B., & McGaugh, J. L. (1999). Involvement of the posteroventral caudate-putamen in memory consolidation in the Morris water maze. *Neurobiology of Learning and Memory, 71,* 240–247.

Shaikh, M. B., Steinberg, A., & Siegel, A. (1993). Evidence that substance P is utilized in medial amygdaloid facilitation of defensive rage behavior in the cat. *Brain Research, 625,* 283–294.

Shaldubina, A., Agam, G., & Belmaker, R. H. (2001). The mechanism of lithium action: State of the art, ten years later. *Progress in Neuro-Psychopharmacology & Biological Psychiatry, 25,* 855–866.

Sham, P. C., Morton, N. E., & Rice, J. P. (1992). Segregation analysis of the NIMH Collaborative Study: Family data on bipolar disorder. *Psychiatric Genetics, 2,* 175–184.

Shapiro, M. (2001). Plasticity, hippocampal place cells, and cognitive maps. *Archives of Neurology, 58,* 874–881.

Sharma, K. N., Anand, B. K., Dua, S., & Singh, B. (1961). Role of stomach in regulation of activities of hypothalamic feeding centers. *American Journal of Physiology, 201,* 593–598.

Shastry, B. S. (2005). Bipolar disorder: An update. *Neurochemistry International, 46,* 273–279.

Shatz, C. J. (1992). The developing brain. *Scientific American, 267,* 60–67.

Shatz, C. J. (1996). Emergence of order in visual system development. *Proceedings of the National Academy of Sciences of the United States of America, 93,* 602–608.

Shaw, C. E., Al-Chalabi, A., & Leigh, N. (2001). Progress in the pathogenesis of amyotrophic lateral sclerosis. *Current Neurology and Neuroscience Reports, 1,* 69–76.

Shaw, S. H., Mroczkowski-Parker, Z., Shekhtman, T., Alexander, M., Remick, R. A., Sadovnick, A. D., et al. (2003). Linkage of a bipolar disorder susceptibility locus to human chromosome 13q32 in a new pedigree series. *Molecular Psychiatry, 8,* 558–564.

Shaywitz, B. A., Shaywitz, S. E., Pugh, K. R., Mencl, W. E., Fulbright, R. K., Skudlarski, P., et al. (2002). Disruption of posterior brain systems for reading in children with developmental dyslexia. *Biological Psychiatry, 52,* 101–110.

Shaywitz, S. E., Shaywitz, B. A., Pugh, K. R., Fulbright, R. K., Constable, R. T., Mencl, W. E., et al. (1998). Functional disruption in the organization of the brain for reading in dyslexia. *Proceedings of the National Academy of Sciences of the United States of America, 95,* 2636–2641.

Shear, P. K., Sullivan, E. V., Lane, B., & Pfefferbaum, A. (1996). Mammillary body and cerebellar shrinkage in chronic alcoholics with and without amnesia. *Alcoholism, Clinical and Experimental Research, 20,* 1489–1495.

Sheehy, R., & Horan, J. J. (2004). Effects of stress inoculation training for 1st-year law students. *International Journal of Stress Management, 11,* 41–55.

Sheline, Y., Bardgett, M. E., & Csernansky, J. G. (1997). Correlated reductions in cerebrospinal fluid 5-HIAA and MHPG concentrations after treatment with selective serotonin reuptake inhibitors. *Journal of Clinical Psychopharmacology, 17,* 11–14.

Shelton, R. C. (1999). Treatment options for refractory depression. *Journal of Clinical Psychiatry, 60,* 57–63.

Shen, J., & Ryan, M. (2003). Olfactory dysfunction and disorders. Retrieved from http://www.utmb.edu/otoref/Grnds/Olfactory-2003-1126/Olfactory-2003-1126.htm

Shepherd, R. K., & Clark, G. M. (1985). Progressive ototoxity of neomycin monitored using derived brainstem response audiometry. *Hearing Research, 18,* 105–110.

Sher, L. (2000). The role of brain thyroid hormones in the mechanisms of seasonal changes in mood and behavior. *Medical Hypotheses, 55,* 56–59.

Sher, L. (2004). Alcoholism and seasonal affective disorder. *Comprehensive Psychiatry, 45,* 51–56.

Sheremata, W. A., Minagar, A., Alexander, J. S., & Vollmer, T. (2005). The role of alpha-4 integrin in the aetiology of multiple sclerosis: Current knowledge and therapeutic implications. *CNS Drugs, 19,* 909–922.

Shi, C., & Davis, M. (2001). Visual pathways involved in fear conditioning measured with fear-potentiated startle: Behavioral and anatomic studies. *The Journal of Neuroscience, 21,* 9844–9855.

Shih, J. C., & Chen, K. (1999). MAO-A and -B knock-out mice exhibit distinctly different behavior. *Neurobiology (Budapest, Hungary), 7,* 235–246.

Shih, J. C., Chen, K., & Ridd, M. J. (1999a). Monoamine oxidase: From genes to behavior. *Annual Review of Neuroscience, 22,* 197–217.

Shih, J. C., Chen, K., & Ridd, M. J. (1999b). Role of MAO A and B in neurotransmitter metabolism and behavior. *Polish Journal of Pharmacology, 51,* 25–29.

Shimomura, K., Low-Zeddies, S. S., King, D. P., Steeves, T. D., Whiteley, A., Kushla, J., et al. (2001). Genome-wide epistatic interaction analysis reveals complex genetic determinants of circadian behavior in mice. *Genome Research, 11,* 959–980.

Shinotoh, H., Namba, H., Fukushi, K., Nagatsuka, S., Tanaka, N., Aotsuka, A., et al. (2000). Progressive loss of cortical acetylcholinesterase activity in association with cognitive decline in Alzheimer's disease: A positron emission tomography study. *Annals of Neurology, 48,* 194–200.

Shiota, M., Sudou, M., & Ohshima, M. (1996). Using outdoor exercise to decrease jet lag in airline crewmembers. *Aviation, Space, and Environmental Medicine, 67,* 1155–1160.

Ship, J. A., & Weiffenback, J. M. (1993). Age, gender, medical treatment, and medication effects on smell identification. *Journal of Gerontology, 48,* M26–M32.

Shono, M., Shono, H., Takasaki, M., Ito, Y., Muro, M., Iwasaka, T., et al. (2001). A new method to analyze basic rest-activity cycle. *Psychiatry and Clinical Neurosciences, 55,* 169–170.

Shors, T. J., Foy, M. R., Levine, S., & Thompson, R. F. (1990). Unpredictable and uncontrollable stress impairs neuronal plasticity in the rat hippocampus. *Brain Research Bulletin, 24,* 663–667.

Shors, T. J., Miesegaes, G., Beylin, A., Zhao, M., Rydel, T., & Gould, E. (2001). Neurogenesis in the adult is involved in the formation of trace memories. *Nature, 410,* 372–376.

Shors, T. J., Townsend, D. A., Zhao, M., Kozorovitskiy, Y., & Gould, E. (2002). Neurogenesis may relate to some but not all types of hippocampal-dependent learning. *Hippocampus, 12,* 578–584.

Shostak, Y., Ding, Y., Mavity-Hudson, J., & Casagrande, V. A. (2002). Cortical synaptic arrangements of the third visual pathway in three primate species: *Macaca mulatta, Saimiri sciureus,* and *Aotus trivirgatus. The Journal of Neuroscience, 22,* 2885–2893.

Shuren, J. E., Schefft, B. K., Yeh, H. S., Privitera, M. D., Cahill, W. T., & Houston, W. (1995). Repetition and the arcuate fasciculus. *Journal of Neurology, 242,* 596–598.

Shutts, D. (1982). *Lobotomy: Resort to the knife.* New York: Van Nostrand Reinhold.

Siderowf, A. (2001). Parkinson's disease: Clinical features, epidemiology and genetics. *Neurologic Clinics, 19,* 565–578.

Siderowf, A., & Stern, M. (2003). Update on Parkinson's disease. *Annals of Internal Medicine, 138,* 651–658.

Siegel, A., Schubert, K. L., & Shaikh, M. B. (1997). Neurotransmitters regulating defensive rage behavior in the cat. *Neuroscience and Biobehavioral Reviews, 21,* 733–742.

Sills, T. L., Onalaja, A. O., & Crawley, J. N. (1998). Mesolimbic dopaminergic mechanisms underlying individual differences in sugar consumption and amphetamine hyperlocomotion in Wistar rats. *European Journal of Neuroscience, 10,* 1895–1902.

Simon, H., Scatton, B., & le Moal, M. (1980). Dopaminergic A10 neurones are involved in cognitive functions. *Nature, 286,* 150–151.

Simpson, J. B., Epstein, A. N., & Camardo, J. S., Jr. (1978). Localization of receptors for the dipsogenic action of angiotensin II in the subfornical organ of rat. *Journal of Comparative and Physiological Psychology, 92,* 581–601.

Sinclair, D. (1981). *Mechanisms of cutaneous sensation.* Oxford: Oxford University Press.

Singer, W., & Gray, C. M. (1995). Visual feature integration and the temporal correlation hypothesis. *Annual Review of Neuroscience, 18,* 555–586.

Singh, A. N., Srivastava, S., & Jainar, A. K. (1999). Pharmacotherapy of chronic alcoholism: A review. *Drugs of Today (Barcelona, Spain), 35,* 27–33.

Singh, D., Vidaurri, M., Zambarano, R. J., & Dabbs, J. M., Jr. (1999). Lesbian erotic role identification: Behavioral, morphological, and hormonal correlates. *Journal of Personality and Social Psychology, 76,* 1035–1049.

Singh, S., & Mallick, B. N. (1996). Mild electrical stimulation of pontine tegmentum around locus coeruleus reduces rapid eye movement sleep in rats. *Neuroscience Research, 24,* 227–235.

Singh, V., & Malone, D. A., Jr. (2001). Should amphetamines be added to SSRI therapy to enhance the antidepressant effect? *Cleveland Clinic Journal of Medicine, 68,* 748–749.

Sinisi, A. A., Pasquali, D., Notaro, A., & Bellastella, A. (2003). Sexual differentiation. *Journal of Endocrinological Investigation, 26,* 23–28.

Sjostrom, L., Garellick, G., Krotkiewski, M., & Luyckx, A. (1980). Peripheral insulin in response to the sight and smell of food. *Metabolism, 29,* 901–909.

Skinner, B. F. (1938). *The behavior of organisms: An experimental analysis.* Englewood Cliffs, NJ: Prentice-Hall.

Skinner, B. F. (1980). The experimental analysis of operant behavior: A history. In R. W. Rieber & K. Salzinger (Eds.), *Psychology: Theoretical-historical perspectives* (pp. 191–202). New York: Academic Press.

Sklar, P., Pato, M. T., Kirby, A., Petryshen, T. L., Medeiros, H., Carvalho, C., et al. (2004). Genome-wide scan in Portuguese Island families identifies 5q31-5q35 as a susceptibility locus for schizophrenia and psychosis. *Molecular Psychiatry, 9,* 213–218.

Skuse, D., Morris, J., & Lawrence, K. (2003). The amygdala and development of the social brain. *Annals of the New York Academy of Sciences, 1008,* 91–101.

Sloan, D. M., & Kornstein, S. G. (2003). Gender differences in depression and response to antidepressant treatment. *The Psychiatric Clinics of North America, 26,* 581–594.

Slobin, D. I. (1966). Grammatical transformations and sentence comprehension in childhood and adulthood. *Journal of Verbal Learning & Verbal Behavior, 5,* 219–227.

Slotnick, B. M., & McMullen, M. F. (1972). Intraspecific fighting in albino mice with septal forebrain lesions. *Physiology & Behavior, 8,* 333–337.

Smith, A. M., Fried, P. A., Hogan, M. J., & Cameron, I. (2004). Effects of prenatal marijuana on response inhibition: An fMRI study of young adults. *Neurotoxicology and Teratology, 26,* 533–542.

Smith, A. W., & Baum, A. (2003). The influence of psychological factors on restorative function in health and illness. In J. Suls & K. A. Wallston (Eds.), *Social psychological foundations of health and illness* (pp. 432–457). Malden, MA: Blackwell Publishers.

Smith, C. A., Collins, C. T., Cyna, A. M., & Crowther, C. A. (2003). Complementary and alternative therapies for pain management in labour. *Cochrane Database of Systematic Reviews,* CD003521.

Smith, G. P., & Epstein, A. N. (1969). Increased feeding in response to decreased glucose utilization in the rat and monkey. *American Journal of Physiology, 217,* 1083–1087.

Smith, G. P., & Gibbs, J. (1975). Cholecystokinin: A putative satiety signal. *Pharmacology, Biochemistry & Behavior, 3,* 135–138.

Smith, K. M., Larive, L. L., & Romanelli, F. (2002). Club drugs: Methylenedioxymethamphetamine, flunitrazepam, ketamine hydrochloride, and gamma-hydroxybutyrate. *American Journal of Health-System Pharmacy, 59,* 1067–1076.

Smith, K. R. (1974). The problem of stimulation deafness. II. Histological changes in the cochlea as a function of tonal frequency. *Journal of Experimental Psychology, 37,* 304–317.

Smith, L. L. (2000). Cytokine hypothesis of overtraining: A physiological adaptation to excessive stress. *Medicine and Science in Sports and Exercise, 32,* 317–331.

Smith, L. L. (2003). Overtraining, excessive exercise, and altered immunity: Is this a T helper-1 versus T helper-2 lymphocyte response? *Sports Medicine, 33,* 347–364.

Smith, M., & Pereda, A. E. (2003). Chemical synaptic activity modulates nearby electrical synapses. *Proceedings of the National Academy of Sciences of the United States of America, 100,* 4849–4854.

Smith, P. F. (2002). Cannabinoids in the treatment of pain and spasticity in multiple sclerosis. *Current Opinion in Investigational Drugs, 3,* 859–864.

Snowdon, C. T. (1969). Motivation, regulation, and the control of meal parameters with oral and intragastric feeding. *Journal of Comparative and Physiological Psychology, 69,* 91–100.

Snyder, S. H., & D'Amato, R. J. (1986). MPTP: A neurotoxin relevant to the pathophysiology of Parkinson's disease. The 1985 George C. Cotzias lecture. *Neurology, 36,* 250–258.

Soares, J. C., & Mann, J. J. (1997). The functional neuroanatomy of mood disorders. *Journal of Psychiatric Research, 31,* 393–432.

Soares, S. R., Vidal, F., Bosch, M., Martinez-Pasarell, O., Nogues, C., Egozcue, J., et al. (2001). Acrocentric chromosome disomy is increased in spermatozoa from fathers of Turner syndrome patients. *Human Genetics, 108,* 499–503.

Soderpalm, B., Ericson, M., Olausson, P., Blomqvist, O., & Engel, J. A. (2000). Nicotinic mechanisms involved in the dopamine activating and reinforcing properties of ethanol. *Behavioural Brain Research, 113,* 85–96.

Solanto, M. V. (1998). Neuropsychopharmacological mechanisms of stimulant drug action in attention-deficit hyperactivity disorder: A review and integration. *Behavioural Brain Research, 94,* 127–152.

Soldatos, C. R., & Kales, A. (1986). Treatment of sleep disorders. In R. M. Berlin & C. R. Soldatos (Eds.), *Sleep disorders in psychiatric practice.* Longwood, FL: Rylandic.

Solms, M. (2000). Dreaming and REM sleep are controlled by different brain mechanisms. *The Behavioral and Brain Sciences, 23,* 843–850.

Solomon, D. A., Keller, M. B., Leon, A. C., Mueller, T. I., Lavoie, P. W., Shea, M. T., et al. (2000). Multiple recurrences of major depressive disorder. *American Journal of Psychiatry, 58,* 819–820.

Sonino, N., & Fava, G. A. (1998). Psychosomatic aspects of Cushing's disease. *Psychotherapy and Psychosomatics, 67,* 140–146.

Sonino, N., & Fava, G. A. (2001). Psychiatric disorders associated with Cushing's syndrome. Epidemiology, pathophysiology and treatment. *CNS Drugs, 15,* 361–373.

Sonino, N., & Fava, G. A. (2002). Residual symptoms in depression an emerging therapeutic concept. *Progress in Neuro-Psychopharmacology & Biological Psychiatry, 26,* 763–770.

Sood, B., Delaney-Black, V., Covington, C., Nordstrom-Klee, B., Ager, J., Templin, T., et al. (2001). Prenatal alcohol exposure and childhood behavior at age 6 to 7 years: I. Dose-response effect. *Pediatrics, 108,* E34.

Sorbi, S., Forleo, P., Tedde, A., Cellini, E., Ciantelli, M., Bagnoli, S., et al. (2001). Genetic risk factors in familial Alzheimer's disease. *Mechanisms of Ageing and Development, 122,* 1951–1960.

Sothern, M. S. (2001). Exercise as a modality in the treatment of childhood obesity. *Pediatric Clinics of North America, 48,* 995–1015.

Sotillo, M., Carretie, L., Hinojosa, J. A., Tapia, M., Mercado, F., Lopez-Martin, S., et al. (2005). Neural activity associated with metaphor comprehension: Spatial analysis. *Neuroscience Letters, 373,* 5–9.

Spanagel, R. (2003). Alcohol addiction research: From animal models to clinics. *Best Practice and Research: Clinical Gastroenterology, 17,* 507–518.

Spaner, D., Bland, R. C., & Newman, S. C. (1994). Epidemiology of psychiatric disorders in Edmonton: Phenomenology and comorbidity: Major depressive disorder. *Acta Psychiatrica Scandinavica, 89,* 7–15.

Speakman, M. T., & Kloner, R. A. (1999). Viagra and cardiovascular disease. *Journal of Cardiovascular Pharmacology and Therapeutics, 4,* 259–267.

Spear, N. E., & Riccio, D. C. (1994). *Memory: Phenomena and principles.* Needham Heights, MA: Allyn & Bacon.

Sperry, R. W. (1961). Cerebral organization and behavior. *Science, 133,* 1749–1757.

Sperry, R. W. (1974). Lateral specialization in the surgically separated hemispheres. In F. Schmitt & F. Worden (Eds.), *Neurosciences third study program* (Vol. 3, pp. 5–19). Cambridge, MA: The MIT Press.

Sperry, R. W. (1982). Some effects of disconnecting the cerebral hemispheres. *Science, 217,* 1223–1226.

Sperry, R. W., Stamm, J. S., & Miner, N. (1956). Relearning tests for interocular transfer following division of optic chiasma and corpus callosum in cats. *Journal of Comparative & Physiological Psychology, 49,* 529–533.

Spreux-Varoquaux, O., Alvarez, J. C., Berlin, I., Batista, G., Despierre, P. B., Gilton, A., et al. (2001). Differential abnormalities in plasma 5-HIAA and platelet serotonin concentrations in violent suicide attempters: Relationships with impulsivity and depression. *Life Sciences, 69,* 647–657.

Springer, S. P., & Deutsch, G. (1998). *Left brain, right brain* (5th ed.). New York: W. H. Freeman.

Squire, L. R. (1986). Mechanisms of memory. *Science, 232,* 1612–1619.

Squire, L. R. (1987). *Memory and brain.* London: Oxford University Press.

Squire, L. R. (1998). Memory systems. *Comptes Rendus de l'Academie des Sciences. Serie III, Sciences de la Vie, 321,* 153–156.

Squire, L. R., Amaral, D. G., & Press, G. A. (1990). Magnetic resonance imaging of the hippocampal formation and mammillary nuclei distinguish medial temporal lobe and diencephalic amnesia. *The Journal of Neuroscience, 10,* 3106–3117.

Squire, L. R., Stark, C. E. L., & Clark, R. E. (2004). The medial temporal lobe. *Annual Review of Neuroscience, 27,* 279–306.

Squire, L. R., & Zola, S. M. (1996). Structure and function of declarative and nondeclarative memory systems. *Proceedings of the*

National Academy of Sciences of the United States of America, 93, 13515–13522.

Squitieri, F., Gellera, C., Cannella, M., Mariotti, C., Cislaghi, G., Rubinsztein, D. C., et al. (2003). Homozygosity for Cag mutation in Huntington disease is associated with a more severe clinical course. *Brain, 126,* 946–955.

Srinivasan, V. (1997). Melatonin, biological rhythm disorders and phototherapy. *Indian Journal of Physiology and Pharmacology, 41,* 309–328.

St. George-Hyslop, P. H. (2000). Molecular genetics of Alzheimer's disease. *Biological Psychiatry, 47,* 183–199.

Staba, R. J., Wilson, C. L., Fried, I., & Engel, J., Jr. (2002). Single neuron burst firing in the human hippocampus during sleep. *Hippocampus, 12,* 724–734.

Staddon, J. E. R. (1998). The dynamics of memory in animal learning. In M. Sabourin, F. Craik, & M. Roberts (Eds.), *Advances in psychological science, Vol. 2. Biological and cognitive aspects* (pp. 259–274). Hove, England: Psychology Press/Erlbaum.

Stallone, D., & Nicolaidis, S. (1989). Increased food intake and carbohydrate preference in the rat following treatment with the serotonin antagonist metergoline. *Neuroscience Letters, 102,* 319–324.

Standaert, D. G., & Young, A. B. (1996). Treatment of central nervous system degenerative disorders. In J. G. Hardman, L. E. Limbird, P. B. Molinoff, R. W. Ruddon, & A. G. Gilman (Eds.), *Goodman & Gilman's the pharmacological basis of therapeutics* (9th ed., pp. 503–513). New York: McGraw-Hill.

Standridge, J. B. (2004). Pharmacotherapeutic approaches to the treatment of Alzheimer's disease. *Clinical Therapeutics, 26,* 615–630.

Stanford, L. R. (1987). Conduction velocity variations minimize conduction time differences among retinal ganglion cell axons. *Science, 238,* 358–360.

Stanley, B. G., Anderson, K. C., Grayson, M. H., & Leibowitz, S. F. (1989). Repeated hypothalamic stimulation with neuropeptide Y increases daily carbohydrate and fat intake and body weight gain in female rats. *Physiology & Behavior, 46,* 173–177.

Starbuck, E. M., & Fitts, D. A. (2001). Influence of the subfornical organ on meal-associated drinking in rats. *American Journal of Physiology. Regulatory, Integrative and Comparative Physiology, 280,* R669–R677.

Stark, C. P., Alpern, H. P., Fuhrer, J., Trowbridge, M. G., Wimbish, H., & Smock, T. (1998). The medial amygdaloid nucleus modifies social behavior in male rats. *Physiology & Behavior, 63,* 253–259.

Starr, P. A., Wichmann, T., van Horne, C., & Bakay, R. A. (1999). Intranigral transplantation of fetal substantia nigra allograft in the hemiparkinsonian rhesus monkey. *Cell Transplantation, 8,* 37–45.

Stasheff, S. F., & Barton, J. J. (2001). Deficits in cortical visual function. *Ophthalmology Clinics of North America, 14,* 217–242.

Steele, M. T., Ma, O. J., Watson, W. A., Thomas, H. A., Jr., & Muellerman, R. L. (1999). The occupational risk of motor vehicle collisions for emergency medicine residents. *Academic Emergency Medicine, 6,* 1050–1053.

Stein, L., & Wise, C. D. (1973). Amphetamine and noradrenergic reward pathways. In E. Usdin & S. H. Snyder (Eds.), *Frontiers in catecholamine research.* New York: Pergamon.

Steinbaum, S. R. (2004). The metabolic syndrome: An emerging health epidemic in women. *Progress in Cardiovascular Diseases, 46,* 321–336.

Steinhausen, H. C. (2002). The outcome of anorexia nervosa in the 20th century. *American Journal of Psychiatry, 159,* 1284–1293.

Stephan, F. K., & Zucker, I. (1972). Circadian rhythms in drinking behavior and locomotor activity of rats are eliminated by hypothalamic lesions. *Proceedings of the National Academy of Sciences of the United States of America, 69,* 1583–1586.

Sterbing, S. J., & Schrott-Fischer, A. (2003). Neuronal responses in the inferior colliculus of mutant mice (Bronx waltzer) with hereditary inner hair cell loss. *Hearing Research, 177,* 91–99.

Steriade, M. (1996). Arousal: Revisiting the reticular activating system. *Science, 272,* 225–226.

Sterling, P., & Eyer, J. (1988). Allostasis: A new paradigm to explain arousal pathology. In S. Fisher & J. Reason (Eds.), *Handbook of life stress, cognition and health* (pp. 629–649). New York: Wiley.

Sternberg, E. M. (2002). Walter B. Cannon and "'voodoo' death": A perspective from 60 years on. *American Journal of Public Health, 92,* 1564–1566.

Stewart, J. J., Wood, M. J., Wood, C. D., & Mims, M. E. (1991). Effects of ginger on motion sickness susceptibility and gastric function. *Pharmacology, 42,* 111–120.

Stickgold, R., Hobson, J. A., Fosse, R., & Fosse, M. (2001). Sleep, learning, and dreams: Off-line memory reprocessing. *Science, 294,* 1052–1057.

Stickgold, R., & Walker, M. (2004). To sleep, perchance to gain creative insight? *Trends in Cognitive Sciences, 8,* 191–192.

Stober, G., Pfuhlmann, B., Nurnberg, G., Schmidtke, A., Reis, A., Franzek, E., et al. (2001). Towards the genetic basis of periodic catatonia: Pedigree sample for genome scan I and II. *European Archives of Psychiatry and Clinical Neuroscience, 251,* I25–I30.

Stober, G., Seelow, D., Ruschendorf, F., Ekici, A., Beckmann, H., & Reis, A. (2002). Periodic catatonia: Confirmation of linkage to chromosome 15 and further evidence for genetic heterogeneity. *Human Genetics, 111,* 323–330.

Stockhorst, U., Klosterhalfen, S., & Steingrueber, H.-J. (1998). Conditioned nausea and further side-effects in cancer chemotherapy: A review. *Journal of Psychophysiology, 12,* 14–33.

Stockhorst, U., Wiener, J. A., Klosterhalfen, S., Klosterhalfen, W., Aul, C., & Steingrueber, H.-J. (1998). Effects of overshadowing on conditioned nausea in cancer patients: An experimental study. *Physiology & Behavior, 64,* 743–753.

Stoddard-Apter, S. L., & MacDonnell, M. F. (1980). Septal and amygdalar efferents to the hypothalamus which facilitate hypothalamically elicited intraspecific aggression and associated hissing in the cat. An autoradiographic study. *Brain Research, 193,* 19–32.

Stoerig, P., & Cowey, A. (1997). Blindsight in man and monkey. *Brain, 120,* 535–559.

Stork, O., Welzl, H., Cremer, H., & Schachner, M. (1997). Increased intermale aggression and neuroendocrine response in mice deficient for the neural cell adhesion molecule (NCAM). *European Journal of Neuroscience, 9,* 1117–1125.

Stricker, E. M. (1983). Thirst and sodium appetite after colloid treatment in rats: Role of the renin-angiotensin-aldosterone system. *Behavioral Neuroscience, 97,* 725–737.

Stricker, E. M., Rowland, N., Saller, C. F., & Friedman, M. I. (1977). Homeostasis during hypoglycemia: Central control of adrenal secretion and peripheral control of feeding. *Science, 196,* 79–81.

Stricker, E. M., & Verbalis, J. G. (1991). Caloric and noncaloric controls of food intake. *Brain Research Bulletin, 27,* 299–303.

Stricker, E. M., & Zigmond, M. J. (1984). Brain catecholamines and the central control of food intake. *International Journal of Obesity, 8,* 39–50.

Stricker-Krongrad, A., Richy, S., & Beck, B. (2002). Orexins/hypocretins in the ob/ob mouse: Hypothalamic gene expression, peptide content and metabolic effects. *Regulatory Peptides, 104,* 11–20.

Strober, M., Freeman, R., Lampert, C., Diamond, J., & Kaye, W. (2000). Controlled family study of anorexia nervosa and bulimia nervosa: Evidence of shared liability and transmission of partial syndromes. *American Journal of Psychiatry, 157,* 393–401.

Stromberg, I., Tornqvist, N., Johansson, S., Bygdeman, M., & Alqvist, P. M. (2001). Evidence for target-specific outgrowth from subpopulations of grafted human dopamine neurons. *Microscopy Research and Technique, 54,* 287–297.

Struder, H. K., & Weicker, H. (2001). Physiology and pathophysiology of the serotonergic system and its implications on mental and physical performance. Part I. *International Journal of Sports Medicine, 22,* 467–481.

Stunkard, A., Berkowitz, R., Tanrikut, C., Reiss, E., & Young, L. (1996). d-fenfluramine treatment of binge eating disorder. *American Journal of Psychiatry, 153,* 1455–1459.

Stunkard, A. J., Van Itallie, T. B., & Reis, B. B. (1955). The mechanism of satiety: Effect of glucagon on gastric hunger contractions in man. *Proceedings of the Society for Experimental Biology and Medicine, 89,* 258–261.

Sturm, R. (2002). The effects of obesity, smoking, and drinking on medical problems and costs. Obesity outranks both smoking and drinking in its deleterious effects on health and health costs. *Health Affairs (Project Hope), 21,* 245–253.

Stutts, J. C., Wilkins, J. W., Scott, O. J., & Vaughn, B. V. (2003). Driver risk factors for sleep-related crashes. *Accident: Analysis and Prevention, 35,* 321–331.

Su, T. P., Huang, C. C., & Wei, I. H. (2005). Add-on rTMS for medication-resistant depression: A randomized, double-blind, sham-controlled trial in Chinese patients. *Journal of Clinical Psychiatry, 55,* 930–937.

Suddath, R. L., Christison, G. W., Torrey, E. F., Casanova, M. F., & Weinberger, D. R. (1990). Anatomical abnormalities in the brains of monozygotic twins discordant for schizophrenia. *New England Journal of Medicine, 322,* 789–794.

Sudzak, P. D., Glowa, J. R., Crawley, J. N., Schwartz, R. D., Skolnick, P., & Paul, S. M. (1986). A selective imidazobenzodiazepine antagonist of ethanol in the rat. *Science, 234,* 1243–1247.

Sugaya, K. (2005). Possible use of autologous stem cell therapies for Alzheimer's disease. *Current Alzheimer Research, 2,* 367–376.

Sugaya, K., & Brannen, C. L. (2001). Stem cell strategies for neuroreplacement therapy in Alzheimer's disease. *Medical Hypotheses, 57,* 697–700.

Sullivan, E. V., Rosenbloom, M. J., Desmond, J. E., & Pfefferbaum, A. (2001). Sex differences in corpus callosum size: Relationship to age and intracranial size. *Neurobiology of Aging, 22,* 603–611.

Sultan, C., Lumbroso, S., Paris, F., Jeandel, C., Terouanne, B., Belon, C., et al. (2002). Disorders of androgen action. *Seminars in Reproductive Medicine, 20,* 217–228.

Sultan, C., Paris, F., Terouanne, B., Balaguer, P., Georget, V., Poujol, N., et al. (2001). Disorders linked to insufficient androgen action in male children. *Human Reproduction Update, 7,* 314–322.

Suri, R. E., Bargas, J., & Arbib, M. A. (2001). Modeling functions of striatal dopamine modulation in learning and planning. *Neuroscience, 103,* 65–85.

Susswein, A. J., Katzoff, A., Miller, N., & Hurwitz, I. (2004). Nitric oxide and memory. *Neuroscientist, 10,* 153–162.

Sutter, M. L., & Schreiner, C. E. (1991). Physiology and topography of neurons with multipeaked tuning curves in cat primary auditory cortex. *Journal of Neurophysiology, 65,* 1207–1226.

Suzuki, E., Kanba, S., Nibuya, M., Adachi, S., Sekiya, U., Shintani, F., et al. (1994). Longitudinal changes in symptoms and plasma homovanillic acid levels in chronically medicated schizophrenic patients. *Biological Psychiatry, 36,* 654–661.

Swaab, D. F., Gooren, L. J., & Hofman, M. A. (1995). Brain research, gender and sexual orientation. *Journal of Homosexuality, 28,* 283–301.

Swain, R. A., & Thompson, R. F. (1993). In search of engrams. In F. M Crinella & J. Yu (Eds.), *Brain mechanisms: Papers in memory of Robert Thompson* (pp. 27–39). New York: The New York Academy of Sciences.

Swann, A. C. (2005). Long-term treatment in bipolar disorder. *The Journal of Clinical Psychiatry, 66,* 7–12.

Swann, A. C., Koslow, S. H., Katz, M. M., Maas, J. W., Jevaid, J., Secunda, S. K., et al. (1987). Lithium carbonate treatment of mania. Cerebrospinal fluid and urinary monoamine metabolites and treatment outcome. *Archives of General Psychiatry, 44,* 345–354.

Sweet, W. H., Ervin, F., & Mark, V. H. (1969). The relationship of violent behavior to focal cerebral disease. In S. Garattini & E. B. Sigg (Eds.), *Aggressive behavior* (pp. 336–352). New York: Wiley.

Swithers, S. E., & McCurley, M. (2002). Effects of 2-mercaptoacetate on ingestive behavior in 18- and 21-day-old rats. *Behavioural Brain Research, 136,* 511–520.

Szabo, S. (1998). Hans Selye and the development of the stress concept. Special reference to gastroduodenal ulcerogenesis. *Annals of the New York Academy of Sciences, 851,* 19–27.

Szabo, S. T., & Blier, P. (2001). Effect of the selective noradrenergic reuptake inhibitor reboxetine on the firing activity of noradrenaline and serotonin neurons. *European Journal of Neuroscience, 13,* 2077–2087.

Szeto, C. Y., Tang, N. L., Lee, D. T., & Stadlin, A. (2001). Association between mu opioid receptor gene polymorphisms and Chinese heroin addicts. *Neuroreport, 12,* 1103–1106.

Taheri, S., & Mignot, E. (2002). The genetics of sleep disorders. *The Lancet Neurology, 1,* 242–250.

Taheri, S., Zeitzer, J. M., & Mignot, E. (2002). The role of hypocretins (orexins) in sleep regulation and narcolepsy. *Annual Review of Neuroscience, 25,* 283–313.

Taira, M., Boline, J., Smyrnis, N., Georgopoulos, A. P., & Ashe, J. (1996). On the relations between single cell activity in the motor cortex and the direction and magnitude of three-dimensional static isometric force. *Experimental Brain Research, 109,* 367–376.

Takagi, S. F. (1984). The olfactory nervous system of the old world monkey. *Japanese Journal of Physiology, 34,* 561–573.

Takahashi, T., Sasaki, M., Itoh, H., Ozone, M., Yamadera, W., Hayshida, K., et al. (2000). Effect of 3 mg melatonin on jet lag syndrome in an 8-h eastward flight. *Psychiatry and Clinical Neurosciences, 54,* 377–378.

Takakusaki, K., Oohinata-Sugimoto, J., Saitoh, K., & Habaguchi, T. (2004). Role of basal ganglia-brainstem systems in the control of postural muscle tone and locomotion. *Progress in Brain Research, 143,* 231–237.

Takeda, M., Tachibana, H., Shibuya, N., Nakajima, Y., Okuda, B., Sugita, M., et al. (1999). Pure anomic aphasia caused by a subcortical hemorrhage in the left temporo-parieto-occipital lobe. *Internal Medicine, 38,* 293–295.

Talesa, V. N. (2001). Acetylcholinesterase in Alzheimer's disease. *Mechanisms of Ageing and Development, 122,* 1961–1969.

Tanaka, K. (2000). Mechanisms of visual object recognition studied in monkeys. *Spatial Vision, 13,* 147–163.

Tannenbaum, G. A., Paxinos, G., & Bindra, D. (1974). Metabolic and endocrine aspects of the ventromedial hypothalamic syndrome in the rat. *Journal of Comparative and Physiological Psychology, 86,* 404–413.

Tanner, B. A. (2004). Multimodal behavioral treatment of non-repetitive, treatment-resistant nightmares: A case report. *Perceptual and Motor Skills, 99,* 1139–1146.

Taylor, J. S., & Bampton, E. T. (2004). Factors secreted by Schwann cells stimulate the regeneration of neonatal retinal gangion cells. *Journal of Anatomy, 204,* 25–31.

Taylor, L., Faraone, S. V., & Tsuang, M. T. (2002). Family, twin, and adoption studies of bipolar disease. *Current Psychiatry Reports, 4,* 130–133.

Taylor, S. E. (2003). *Health psychology* (5th ed.). Boston: McGraw-Hill.

Teitelbaum, P. (1955). Sensory control of hypothalamic hyperphagia. *Journal of Comparative and Physiological Psychology, 48,* 156–163.

Teitelbaum, P., Cheng, M. F., & Rozin, P. (1969). Stages of recovery and development of lateral hypothalamic control of food and water intake. *Annals of the New York Academy of Sciences, 157,* 849–860.

Teitelbaum, P., & Epstein, A. N. (1962). The lateral hypothalamic syndrome: Recovery of feeding and drinking after lateral hypothalamic lesions. *Psychological Review, 69,* 74–90.

Teitelbaum, P., & Stellar, E. (1954). Recovery from the failure to eat produced by hypothalamic lesions. *Science, 120,* 894–895.

Temple, C. M., Jeeves, M. A., Vilarroya, O. O. (1990). Reading in callosal agenesis. *Brain and Language, 39,* 235–253.

Teng, E., Stefanacci, L., Squire, L. R., & Zola, S. M. (2000). Contrasting effects on discrimination learning after hippocampal lesions and conjoint hippocampal-caudate lesions in monkeys. *The Journal of Neuroscience, 20,* 3853–3863.

Tepass, U., Truong, K., Godt, D., Ikura, M., & Peifer, M. (2000). Cadherins in embryonic and neural morphogenesis. *Nature Reviews: Molecular Cell Biology, 1,* 91–100.

Tervaniemi, M., Medvedev, S. V., Alho, K., Pakhomov, S. V., Roudas, M. S., Van Zuijen, T. L., et al. (2000). Lateralized automatic auditory processing of phonetic versus musical information: A PET study. *Human Brain Mapping, 10,* 74–79.

Terzian, H., & Ore, G. D. (1955). Syndrome of Klüver and Bucy reproduced in man by bilateral removal of the temporal lobes. *Neurology, 5,* 373–380.

Teter, C. J., & Guthrie, S. K. (2001). A comprehensive review of MDMA and GHB: Two common club drugs. *Pharmacotherapy, 21,* 1486–1513.

Thal, D. J., Marchman, V., Stiles, J., Aram, D., Trauner, D., Nass, R., et al. (1991). Early lexical development in children with focal brain injury. *Brain and Language, 40,* 491–527.

Thase, M. E., Trivedi, M. H., & Rush, A. J. (1995). MAOIs in the contemporary treatment of depression. *Neuropsychopharmacology, 12,* 185–219.

Thayer, R., Collins, J., Noble, E. G., & Taylor, A. W. (2000). A decade of aerobic endurance training: Histological evidence for fibre type transformation. *Journal of Sports Medicine and Physical Fitness, 40,* 284–289.

Thomas, M., Sing, H., Belenky, G., Holcomb, H., Mayberg, H., Dannals, R., et al. (2000). Neural basis of alertness and cognitive performance impairments during sleepiness. I. Effects of 24 h of sleep deprivation on waking human regional brain activity. *Journal of Sleep Research, 9,* 335–352.

Thompson, C. K. (2000). Neuroplasticity: Evidence from aphasia. *Journal of Communication Disorders, 33,* 357–366.

Thompson, J. C., Snowden, J. S., Craufurd, D., & Neary, D. (2002). Behavior in Huntington's disease: Dissociating cognition-based and mood-based changes. *The Journal of Neuropsychiatry and Clinical Neurosciences, 14,* 37–43.

Thompson, J. L., Manore, M. M., & Thomas, J. R. (1996). Effects of diet and diet-plus-exercise programs on resting metabolic rate: A meta-analysis. *International Journal of Sport Nutrition, 6,* 41–61.

Thompson, R. (1993). Centrencephalic theory, the General Learning System, and subcortical dementia. In F. M Crinella & J. Yu (Eds.), *Brain mechanisms: Papers in memory of Robert Thompson* (pp. 197–223). New York: The New York Academy of Sciences.

Thompson, R., & Dean, W. (1955). A further study of the retroactive effects of ECS. *Journal of Comparative and Physiological Psychology, 48,* 488–491.

Thompson, R. F., & Krupa, D. J. (1994). Organization of memory traces in the mammalian brain. *Annual Review of Neuroscience, 17,* 519–549.

Thorne, B. M. (1993). "By the way, rats with olfactory bulb lesions are vicious." *Annals of the New York Academy of Sciences, 702,* 131–147.

Thorne, B. M., & Henley, T. B. (1997). *Connections in the history and systems of psychology.* Boston: Houghton Mifflin.

Thorne, B. M., & Henley, T. B. (2005). *Connections in the history and systems of psychology* (3rd ed.). Boston: Houghton Mifflin.

Tian, B., Reser, D., Durham, A., Kustov, A., & Rauschecker, J. P. (2001). Functional specialization in rhesus monkey auditory cortex. *Science, 292,* 290–293.

Timmann, D., Watts, S., & Hore, J. (1999). Failure of cerebellar patients to time finger opening precisely causes ball high-low inaccuracy in overarm throws. *Journal of Neurophysiology, 82,* 103–114.

Tollin, D. J. (2003). The lateral superior olive: A functional role in sound source localization. *Neuroscientist, 9,* 127–143.

Tomida, I., Pertwee, R. G., & Azuara-Blanco, A. (2004). Cannabinoids and glaucoma. *British Journal of Ophthalmology, 88,* 708–713.

Tominaga, S., Satoh, S., Nagase, H., Tanaka, K., & Inoue, S. (1993). Hypergastric acid secretion in rats with ventromedial hypothalamic lesions. *Physiology & Behavior, 53,* 1177–1182.

Tonkonogy, J. M., & Geller, J. L. (1992). Hypothalamic lesions and intermittent explosive behavior. *The Journal of Neuropsychiatry and Clinical Neurosciences, 4,* 45–50.

Tootell, R. B., Reppas, J. B., Kwong, K. K., Malach, R., Born, R. T., Brady, T. J., et al. (1995). Functional analysis of human MT and related visual cortical areas using magnetic resonance imaging. *The Journal of Neuroscience, 15,* 3215–3230.

Tordoff, M. G., Rawson, N., & Friedman, M. I. (1991). 2,5-anhydro-D-mannitol acts in liver to initiate feeding. *American Journal of Physiology, 261,* R283–R288.

Tordoff, M. G., Schulkin, J., & Friedman, M. I. (1987). Further evidence for hepatic control of salt intake in rats. *American Journal of Physiology, 253,* R444–R449.

Torrey, E. F., Miller, J., Rawlings, R., & Yolken, R. H. (1997). Seasonality of births in schizophrenia and bipolar disorder: A review of the literature. *Schizophrenia Research, 28,* 1–38.

Torrey, E. F., Rawlings, R. R., Ennis, J. M., Merrill, D. D., & Flores, D. S. (1996). Birth seasonality in bipolar disorder, schizophrenia, schizoaffective disorder and stillbirths. *Schizophrenia Research, 21,* 141–149.

Toru, M., Watanabe, S., Shibuya, H., Nishikawa, T., Noda, K., Mitsushio, H., et al. (1988). Neurotransmitters, receptors and neuropeptides in post-mortem brains of chronic schizophrenic patients. *Acta Psychiatrica Scandinavica, 78,* 121–137.

Touhara, K. (2002). Odor discrimination by G protein-coupled olfactory receptors. *Microscopy Research and Technique, 58,* 135–141.

Tracy, J. A., Thompson, J. K., Krupa, D. J., & Thompson, R. F. (1998). Evidence of plasticity in the pontocerebellar conditioned stimulus pathway during classical conditioning of the eyeblink response in the rabbit. *Behavioral Neuroscience, 112,* 267–285.

Tranel, D., & Damasio, A. R. (1988). Non-conscious face recognition in patients with face agnosia. *Behavioural Brain Research, 30,* 235–249.

Trojano, L., Grossi, D., Linden, D. E., Formisano, E., Goebel, R., Cirillo, S., et al. (2002). Coordinate and categorical judgements in spatial imagery. An fMRI study. *Neuropsychologia, 40,* 1666–1674.

Tronnier, V. M., Fogel, W., Kronenbuerger, M., & Steinvorth, S. (1997). Pallidal stimulation: An alternative to pallidotomy? *Neurosurgical Focus, 2,* e10.

Trujillo, K. A., Belluzzi, J. D., & Stein, L. (1989). Effects of opiate antagonists and their quaternary analogues on nucleus accumbens self-stimulation. *Behavioural Brain Research, 33,* 181–188.

Tsai, G., & Coyle, J. T. (1998). The role of glutamatergic neurotransmission in the pathophysiology of alcoholism. *Annual Review of Medicine, 49,* 173–184.

Tsai, G. E., Ragan, P., Chang, R., Chen, S., Linnoila, V. M., & Coyle, J. T. (1998). Increased glutamatergic neurotransmission and oxidative stress after alcohol withdrawal. *American Journal of Psychiatry, 155,* 726–732.

Tsang, Y. C. (1938). Hunger motivation in gastrectomized rats. *Journal of Comparative and Physiological Psychology, 26,* 1–17.

Tsuang, M. T. (1998). Genetic epidemiology of schizophrenia: Review and reassessment. *The Kaohsiung Journal of Medical Sciences, 14,* 405–412.

Tsuang, M. T. (2000). Schizophrenia: Genes and environment. *Biological Psychiatry, 47,* 210–220.

Tsuang, M. T., & Faraone, S. V. (1990). *The genetics of mood disorders.* Baltimore: Johns Hopkins University Press.

Tsuda, A., & Hirai, H. (1976). Psychological stress and development of gastric lesions in animals. *Japanese Psychological Review, 19,* 116–139.

Tsuda, A., & Tanaka, M. (1985). Differential changes in noradrenaline turnover in specific regions of rat brain produced by controllable and uncontrollable shocks. *Behavioral Neuroscience, 99,* 802–817.

Tsuda, A., Tanaka, M., Hirai, H., & Pare, W. P. (1983). Effects of coping behavior on gastric lesions in rats as a function of predictability of shock. *Japanese Psychological Research, 25,* 9–15.

Tucker, D. M. (1981). Lateral brain function, emotion, and conceptualization. *Psychological Bulletin, 89,* 19–46.

Tucker, V. A. (2000). The deep fovea, sideways vision and spiral flight paths in raptors. *Journal of Experimental Biology, 203,* 3745–3754.

Tulving, E. (1972). Episodic and semantic memory. In E. Tulving & W. Donaldson (Eds.), *Organisation of memory* (pp. 381–403). New York: Academic Press.

Tulving, E. (1983). *Elements of episodic memory.* New York: Oxford University Press.

Tulving, E. (1998). Brain/mind correlates of human memory. In M. Sabourin, F. Craik, & M. Roberts (Eds.), *Advances in psychological science, Vol. 2. Biological and cognitive aspects* (pp. 441–460). Hove, England: Psychology Press.

Tulving, E. (2002). Episodic memory: From mind to brain. *Annual Review of Psychology, 53,* 1–25.

Tulving, E., & Markowitsch, H. J. (1997). Memory beyond the hippocampus. *Current Opinion in Neurobiology, 7,* 209–216.

Tuszynski, M. H., & Blesch, A. (2004). Nerve growth factor: From animal models of cholinergic neuronal degeneration to gene therapy in Alzheimer's disease. *Progress in Brain Research, 146,* 441–449.

Tuszynski, M. H., Roberts, J., Senut, M. C., U, H. S., & Gage, F. H. (1996). Gene therapy in the adult primate brain: Intraparenchymal grafts of cells genetically modified to produce nerve growth factor prevent cholinergic neuronal degeneration. *Gene Therapy, 3,* 305–314.

Tuszynski, M. H., Thal, L., Pay, M., Salmon, D. P., U, H. S., Bakay, R., et al. (2005). A phase 1 clinical trial of nerve growth factor gene therapy for Alzheimer disease. *Nature Medicine, 11,* 551–555.

Tuszynski, M. H., U, H. S., Alksne, J., Bakay, R. A., Pay, M. M., Merrill, D., et al. (2002). Growth factor gene therapy for Alzheimer disease. *Neurosurgical Focus (Electronic Resource), 13,* e5.

Uccelli, A., Giunti, D., Capello, E., Roccatagliata, L., & Mancardi, G. L. (2003). EAE in the common marmoset *Callithrix jacchus. International MS Journal, 10,* 6–12.

Udry, J. R., & Morris, N. M. (1968). Distribution of coitus in the menstrual cycle. *Nature, 220,* 593–596.

Ulett, G. A., Han, S., & Han, J. S. (1998). Electroacupuncture: Mechanisms and clinical application. *Biological Psychiatry, 44,* 129–138.

Ulloa-Montoya, F., Verfaillie, C. M., & Hu, W. S. (2005). Culture systems for pluripotent stem cells. *Journal of Bioscience and Bioengineering, 100,* 12–27.

Ulm, R. R., Volpicelli, J. R., & Volpicelli, L. A. (1995). Opiates and alcohol self-administration in animals. *Journal of Clinical Psychiatry, 56,* 5–14.

Ungerleider, L. G., Doyon, J., & Karni, A. (2002). Imaging brain plasticity during motor skill learning. *Neurobiology of Learning and Memory, 78,* 553–564.

Ungerleider, L. G., & Mishkin, M. (1982). Two cortical visual systems. In D. J. Ingle, M. A. Goodale, & R. J. W. Mansfield (Eds.), *Analysis of visual behavior* (pp. 549–586). Cambridge, MA: The MIT Press.

Unterwald, E. M. (2001). Regulation of opioid receptors by cocaine. *Annals of the New York Academy of Sciences, 937,* 74–92.

Urani, A., & Gass, P. (2003). Corticosteroid receptor transgenic mice: Models for depression? *Annals of the New York Academy of Sciences, 1007,* 379–393.

Uys, J. D., Stein, D. J., Daniels, W. M., & Harvey, B. H. (2003). Animal models of anxiety disorders. *Current Psychiatry Reports, 5,* 274–281.

Vaccarino, F. J., Schiff, B. B., & Glickman, S. E. (1989). Biological view of reinforcement. In S. B. Klein & R. R. Mowrer (Eds.), *Contemporary learning theories: Instrumental conditioning and the impact of biological constraints on learning* (pp. 111–142). Hillsdale, NJ: Erlbaum.

Valensi, P., Doare, L., Perret, G., Germack, R., Paries, J., & Mesangeau, D. (2003). Cardiovascular vagosympathetic activity in rats with ventromedial hypothalamic obesity. *Obesity Research, 11,* 54–64.

Valenstein, E. S. (Ed.). (1980). *The psychosurgery debate: Scientific, legal, and ethical perspectives.* San Francisco: W. H. Freeman.

Valenstein, E. S., Cox, V. C., & Kakolewski, J. W. (1969). The hypothalamus and motivated behavior. In J. Tapp (Ed.), *Reinforcement* (pp. 242–285). New York: Academic Press.

Vallada, H. P., Vasques, L., Curtis, D., Zatz, M., Kirov, G., Lauriano, V., et al. (1998). Linkage analysis between bipolar affective disorder and markers on chromosome X. *Psychiatric Genetics, 8,* 183–186.

Vallbo, A. B., & Johansson, R. S. (1984). Properties of cutaneous mechanoreceptors in the human hand related to touch sensation. *Human Neurobiology, 3,* 3–14.

Van Bockstaele, E. J. (1998). Morphological substrates underlying opioid, epinephrine and gamma-aminobutyric acid inhibitory actions in the rat locus coeruleus. *Brain Research Bulletin, 47,* 1–15.

Van Bockstaele, E. J., Cestari, D. M., & Pickel, V. M. (1994). Synaptic structure and connectivity of serotonin terminals in the ventral tegmental area: Potential sites for modulation of mesolimbic dopamine neurons. *Brain Research, 647,* 307–322.

Van Boven, R. W., Hamilton, R. H., Kauffman, T., Keenan, J. P., & Pascual-Leone, A. (2000). Tactile spatial resolution in blind braille readers. *Neurology, 54,* 2230–2236.

van den Berg, P., Wertheim, E. H., Thompson, J. K., & Paxton, S. J. (2002). Development of body image, eating disturbance, and general psychological functioning in adolescent females: A replication using covariance structure modeling in an Australian sample. *The International Journal of Eating Disorders, 32,* 46–51.

van der Lee, S., & Boot, L. M. (1955). Spontaneous pseudopregnancy in mice. *Acta Physiologica et Pharmacologica Néerlandica, 4,* 442–444.

Van Der Leeden, M., Van Dongen, K., Kleinhout, M., Pfaff, J., De Groot, C. J., De Groot, L., et al. (2001). Infants exposed to alcohol prenatally: Outcome at 3 and 7 months of age. *Annals of Tropical Paediatrics, 21,* 127–134.

van der Veght, B. J., de Boer, S. F., Buwalda, B., de Ruiter, A. J., de Jong, J. G., & Koolhaas, J. M. (2001). Enhanced sensitivity of postsynaptic serotonin-1A receptors in rats and mice with high trait aggression. *Physiology & Behavior, 74,* 205–211.

Van der Werf, Y. D., Jolles, J., Witter, M. P., & Uylings, H. B. (2003). Contributions of thalamic nuclei to declarative memory functioning. *Cortex, 39,* 1047–1062.

Van Dongen, H. P., Maislin, G., Mullington, J. M., & Dinges, D. F. (2003). The cumulative cost of additional wakefulness: Dose-response effects on neurobehavioral functions and sleep physiology from chronic sleep restriction and total sleep deprivation. *Sleep, 26,* 117–126.

van Elst, L. T., Woermann, F. G., Lemieux, L., Thompson, P. J., & Trimble, M. R. (2000). Affective aggression in patients with temporal lobe epilepsy: A quantitative MRI study of the amygdala. *Brain, 123,* 234–243.

Van Gaal, L. F., Rissanen, A. M., Scheen, A. J., Ziegler, O., Rossner, S., & RIO-Europe Study Group. (2005). Effects of the cannabinoid-1 receptor blocker rimonabant on weight reduction and cardiovascular risk factors in overweight patients: 1-year experience from the RIO-Europe study. *Lancet, 365,* 1389–1397.

Van Goozen, S. H., Frijda, N. H., Wiegant, V. M., Endert, E., & Van de Poll, N. E. (1996). The premenstrual phase and reactions to aversive events: A study of hormonal influences on emotionality. *Psychoneuroendocrinology, 21,* 479–497.

Vanduffel, W., Fize, D., Mandeville, J. B., Nelissen, K., Van Hecke, P., Rosen, B. R., et al. (2001). Visual motion processing investigated using contrast agent-enhanced fMRI in awake behaving monkeys. *Neuron, 32,* 565–577.

Vargha-Khadem, F., Gadian, D. G., Watkins, K. E., Connelly, A., Van Paesschen, W., & Mishkin, M. (1997). Differential effects of early hippocampal pathology on episodic and semantic memory. *Science, 277,* 376–380.

Varney, N. R., Pinkston, J. B., & Wu, J. C. (2001). Quantitative PET findings in patients with posttraumatic anosmia. *The Journal of Head Trauma Rehabilitation, 16,* 253–259.

Varon, D., Pritchard, P. B., 3rd, Wagner, M. T., & Topping, K. (2003). Transient Klüver-Bucy syndrome following complex partial status epilepticus. *Epilepsy & Behavior, 4,* 348–351.

Vasquez, E., & Vanegas, H. (2000). The antinociceptive effect of PAG-microinjected dipyrone in rats mediated by endogenous opioids of the rostral ventromedial medulla. *Brain Research, 854,* 249–252.

Velazquez-Moctezuma, J., Dominguez, S. E., & Cruz Rueda, M. L. (1993). The effect of prenatal stress on adult sexual behavior in rats depends on the nature of the stressor. *Physiology & Behavior, 53,* 443–448.

Velkoska, E., Morris, M. J., Burns, P., & Weisinger, R. S. (2003). Leptin reduces food intake but does not alter weight regain following food deprivation in the rat. *International Journal of Obesity and Related Metabolic Disorders, 27,* 48–54.

Vermetten, E., Vythilingam, M., Southwick, S. M., Charney, D. S., & Bremner, J. D. (2003). Long-term treatment with paroxetine increases verbal declarative memory and hippocampal volume in posttraumatic stress disorder. *Biological Psychiatry, 54,* 693–702.

Verney, E. G. (1947). The antidiuretic hormone and the factors which determine its release. *Proceedings of the Royal Society, Series B, 135,* 25–106.

Verster, J. C., Veldhuijzen, D. S., & Volkerts, E. R. (2004). Residual effects of sleep medication on driving ability. *Sleep Medicine Reviews, 8,* 309–325.

Verster, J. C., Volkerts, E. R., Schreuder, A. H., Eijken, E. J., van Heuckelum, J. H., Veldhuijzen, D. S., et al. (2002). Residual effects of middle-of-the-night administration of zaleplon and zolpidem on driving ability, memory functions, and psychomotor performance. *Journal of Clinical Psychopharmacology, 22,* 576–583.

Vertes, R. P., & Eastman, K. E. (2000). The case against memory consolidation in REM sleep. *The Behavioral and Brain Sciences, 23,* 867–876.

Verzeano, M., & Negishi, K. (1960). Neuronal activity in cortical and thalamic networks. *The Journal of General Physiology, 43,* 177–195.

Vgontzas, A. N., & Kales, A. (1999). Sleep and its disorders. *Annual Review of Medicine, 50,* 387–400.

Vicari, S., Albertoni, A., Chilosi, A. M., Cipriani, P., Cioni, G., & Bates, E. (2000). Plasticity and reorganization during language development in children with early brain injury. *Cortex, 36,* 31–46.

Vickery, R. M., Morris, S. H., & Bindman, L. J. (1997). Metabotropic glutamate receptors are involved in long-term potentiation in isolated slices of rat medial frontal cortex. *Journal of Neurophysiology, 78,* 3039–3046.

Vigh, B., Manzano, M. J., Zadori, A., Frank, C. L., Lukats, A., Rohlich, P., et al. (2002). Nonvisual photoreceptors of the deep brain, pineal organs and retina. *Histology and Histopathology, 17,* 555–590.

Viljoen, D., Croxford, J., Gossage, J. P., Kodituwakku, P. W., & May, P. A. (2002). Characteristics of mothers of children with fetal alcohol syndrome in the Western Cape Province of South Africa: A case control study. *Journal of Studies on Alcohol, 63,* 6–17.

Vingerhoets, G., & Stroobant, N. (1999). Lateralization of cerebral blood flow velocity changes during cognitive tasks. A simultaneous bilateral transcranial Doppler study. *Stroke, 30,* 2152–2158.

Virkkunen, M., Eggert, M., Rawlings, R., & Linnoila, M. (1996). A prospective follow-up study of alcoholic violent offenders and fire setters. *Archives of General Psychiatry, 53,* 523–529.

Viskontas, I. V., McAndrews, M. P., & Moscovitch, M. (2000). Remote episodic memory deficits in patients with unilateral temporal lobe epilepsy and excisions. *The Journal of Neuroscience, 20,* 5853–5857.

Visser, P. J., Krabbendam, L., Verhey, F. R., Hofman, P. A., Verhoeven, W. M., Tuinier, S., et al. (1999). Brain correlates of memory dysfunction in alcoholic Korsakoff's syndrome. *Journal of Neurology, Neurosurgery, and Psychiatry, 67,* 774–778.

Viswanathan, N., & Davis, F. C. (1995). Suprachiasmatic nucleus grafts restore circadian function in aged hamsters. *Brain Research, 686,* 10–16.

Vitaterna, M. H., King, D. P., Chang, A. M., Kornhauser, J. M., Lowrey, P. L., McDonald, J. D., et al. (1994). Mutagenesis and mapping of a mouse gene, Clock, essential for circadian behavior. *Science, 264,* 719–725.

Vochteloo, J. D., & Koolhaas, J. M. (1987). Medial amygdala lesions in male rats reduce aggressive behavior: Interference with experience. *Physiology & Behavior, 41,* 99–102.

Voderholzer, U., Hornyak, M., Thiel, B., Huwig-Poppe, C., Kliemen, A., Konig, A., et al. (1998). Impact of experimentally induced serotonin deficiency for tryptophan depletion on sleep EEG in healthy subjects. *Neuropsychopharmacology, 18,* 112–124.

Vogel, G. W., Buffenstein, A., Minter, K., & Hennessey, A. (1990). Drug effects on REM sleep and on endogenous depression. *Neuroscience & Biobehavioral Reviews, 14,* 49–63.

Voldsgaard, P., Schiffman, J., Mednick, S., Rodgers, B., Christensen, H., Bredkjaer, S., et al. (2002). Accuracy of retrospective reports of infections during pregnancy. *International Journal of Methods in Psychiatric Research, 11,* 184–186.

Volkow, N. D., Chang, L., Wang, G. J., Fowler, J. S., Ding, Y. S., Sedler, M., et al. (2001a). Low level of brain dopamine D_2 receptors in methamphetamine abusers: Association with metabolism in the orbitofrontal cortex. *American Journal of Psychiatry, 158,* 2015–2021.

Volkow, N. D., Chang, L., Wang, G. J., Fowler, J. S., Franceschi, D., Sedler, M., et al. (2001b). Loss of dopamine transporters in methamphetamine abusers recovers with protracted abstinence. *The Journal of Neuroscience, 21,* 9414–9418.

Volkow, N. D., Chang, L., Wang, G. J., Fowler, J. S., Leonido-Yee, M., Franceschi, D., et al. (2001c). Association of dopamine transporter reduction with psychomotor impairment in methamphetamine abusers. *American Journal of Psychiatry, 158,* 377–382.

Volkow, N. D., & Fowler, J. S. (2000). Addiction, a disease of compulsion and drive: Involvement of the orbitofrontal cortex. *Cerebral Cortex, 10,* 318–325.

Vollenweider, F. X., Vollenweider-Scherpenhuyzen, M. F., Babler, A., Vogel, H., & Hell, D. (1998). Psilocybin induces schizophrenia-like psychosis in humans via a serotonin-2 agonist action. *Neuroreport, 9,* 3897–3902.

Vollenweider, F. X., Vontobel, P., Hell, D., & Leenders, K. L. (1999). 5-HT modulation of dopamine release in basal ganglia in psilocybin-induced psychosis in man—A PET study with [11C] raclopride. *Neuropsychopharmacology, 20,* 424–433.

Volpicelli, J. R., Alterman, A. I., Hayashida, M., & O'Brien, C. P. (1992). Naltrexone in the treatment of alcohol dependence. *Archives of General Psychiatry, 49,* 876–880.

vom Saal, F. S., & Bronson, F. H. (1980). Sexual characteristics of adult female mice are correlated with their blood testosterone levels during prenatal development. *Science, 208,* 597–599.

vom Saal, F. S., Grant, W. M., McMullen, C. W., & Laves, K. S. (1983). High fetal estrogen concentrations: Correlation with increased adult sexual activity and decreased aggression in male mice. *Science, 220,* 1306–1309.

Vonk, R. (1997). Attitudes toward animal research. *American Psychologist, 52,* 1248–1249.

Votruba, S. B., Horvitz, M. A., & Schoeller, D. A. (2000). The role of exercise in the treatment of obesity. *Nutrition, 16,* 179–188.

Wada, Y., & Yamamoto, T. (2001). Selective impairment of facial recognition due to a haematoma restricted to the right fusiform and lateral occipital region. *Journal of Neurology, Neurosurgery, and Psychiatry, 71,* 254–257.

Wager-Smith, K., & Kay, S. A. (2000). Circadian rhythm genetics: From flies to mice to humans. *Nature Genetics, 26,* 23–27.

Wagner, G. C., Beuving, L. J., & Hutchinson, R. R. (1980). The effects of gonadal hormone manipulations on aggressive target-biting in mice. *Aggressive Behavior, 6,* 1–7.

Wagner, U., Gais, S., & Born, J. (2001). Emotional memory formation is enhanced across sleep intervals with high amounts of rapid eye movement sleep. *Learning & Memory, 8,* 112–119.

Wagner, U., Gais, S., Haider, H., Verleger, R., & Born, J. (2004). Sleep inspires insight. *Nature, 427,* 352–355.

Walker, A., Rosenberg, M., & Balaban-Gil, K. (1999). Neurodevelopmental and neurobehavioral sequelae of selected substances of abuse and psychiatric medications in utero. *Child and Adolescent Psychiatric Clinics of North America, 8,* 845–867.

Walker, J. R., Ahmed, S. H., Gracy, K. N., & Koob, G. F. (2000). Microinjections of an opiate receptor antagonist into the bed nucleus of the stria terminalis suppress heroin self-administration in dependent rats. *Brain Research, 854,* 85–92.

Walker, M. P., Liston, C., Hobson, J. A., & Stickgold, R. (2002). Cognitive flexibility across the sleep-wake cycle: REM-sleep enhancement of anagram problem solving. *Brain Research. Cognitive Brain Research, 14,* 317–324.

Wallace, A. F. C. (1956). *Tornado in Worcester: An exploratory study of individual and community behavior in an extreme situation.* Disaster Study Number 3, Washington, DC: National Academy of Sciences–National Research Council.

Wallace, T., & Thorne, B. M. (1978). The effect of lesions in the septal region on muricide, irritability, and activity in the Long-Evans rat. *Physiological Psychology, 6,* 36–42.

Wallen, K., & Zehr, J. L. (2004). Hormones and history: The evolution and development of primate female sexuality. *Journal of Sex Research, 41,* 101–112.

Walsh, B. T., Agras, W. S., Devlin, M. J., Fairburn, C. G., Wilson, G. T., Kahn, C., et al. (2000). Fluoxetine for bulimia nervosa following poor response to psychotherapy. *American Journal of Psychiatry, 157,* 1332–1334.

Walsh, B. T., Fairburn, C. G., Mickley, D., Sysko, R., & Parides, M. K. (2004). Treatment of bulimia nervosa in a primary care setting. *American Journal of Psychiatry, 161,* 556–561.

Walsh, D., Nelson, K. A., & Mahmoud, F. A. (2003). Established and potential therapeutic applications of cannabinoids in oncology. *Support Care Cancer, 11,* 137–143.

Walsh, J. K. (2004). Clinical and socioeconomic correlates of insomnia. *Journal of Clinical Psychiatry, 65,* 13–19.

Walsh, V., Carden, D., Butler, S. R., & Kulikowski, J. J. (1993). The effects of V4 lesions on the visual abilities of macaques: Hue discrimination and colour constancy. *Behavioural Brain Research, 53,* 51–62.

Walters, A. S., McHale, D., Sage, J. I., Hening, W. A., & Bergen, M. (1990). A blinded study of the suppressibility of involuntary movements in Huntington's chorea, tardive, dyskinesia, and L-dopa-induced chorea. *Clinical Neuropharmacology, 13,* 236–240.

Wand, G., Levine, M., Zweifel, L., Schwindinger, W., & Abel, T. (2001). The cAMP-protein kinase A signal transduction pathway modulates ethanol consumption and sedative effects of ethanol. *The Journal of Neuroscience, 21,* 5297–5303.

Wang, G. J., Volkow, N. D., Chang, L., Miller, E., Sedler, M., Hitzemann, R., et al. (2004). Partial recovery of brain metabolism in methamphetamine abusers after protracted abstinence. *American Journal of Psychiatry, 161,* 242–248.

Wang, J., Yeckel, M. F., Johnston, D., & Zucker, R. S. (2004). Photolysis of postsynaptic caged Ca^{2+} can potentiate and depress mossy fiber synaptic responses in rat hippocampal CA_3 pyramidal neurons. *Journal of Neurophysiology, 91,* 1596–1607.

Wang, K., Hoosain, R., Yang, R. M., Meng, Y., & Wang, C. Q. (2003). Impairment of recognition of disgust in Chinese with Huntington's or Wilson's disease. *Neuropsychologia, 41,* 527–537.

Wang, W., Cain, B. M., & Beinfeld, M. C. (1998). Adult carboxypeptidase E-deficient fat/fat mice have a near-total depletion of brain CCK 8 accompanied by a massive accumulation of glycine and arginine extended CCK: Identification of CCK 8 Gly as the immediate precursor of CCK 8 in rodent brain. *Endocrine, 9,* 329–332.

Wang, X., Dow-Edwards, D., Anderson, V., Minkoff, H., & Hurd, Y. L. (2004). In utero marijuana exposure associated with abnormal amygdala dopamine D_2 gene expression in the human fetus. *Biological Psychiatry, 56,* 909–915.

Wangsness, M. (2000). Pharmacological treatment of obesity. Past, present, and future. *Minnesota Medicine, 83,* 21–26.

Wardlaw, J. M., Keir, S. L., Seymour, J., Lewis, S., Sandercock, P. A., Dennis, M. S., et al. (2004). What is the best imaging strategy for acute stroke? *Health Technology Assessment, 8,* iii, ix–x, 1–180.

Warner, J. (2005). Dopamine may play new role in depression. Retrieved March 10, 2006, from http://www.webmd.com/content/Article/109/109242.htm

Warwick-Evans, L. A., Masters, I. J., & Redstone, S. B. (1991). A double-blind placebo controlled evaluation of acupressure in the treatment of motion sickness. *Aviation, Space, and Environmental Medicine, 62,* 776–778.

Wass, T. S., Persutte, W. H., & Hobbins, J. C. (2001). The impact of prenatal alcohol exposure on frontal cortex development in utero. *American Journal of Obstetrics and Gynecology, 185,* 737–742.

Watanabe, T. (2003). Lucid dreaming: Its experimental proof and psychological conditions. *Journal of International Society of Life Information Science, 21,* 159–162.

Waterhouse, B. D., Sessler, F. M., Cheng, J. T., Woodward, D. J., Azizi, S. A., & Moises, H. C. (1988). New evidence for a gating action of norepinephrine in central neuronal circuits of mammalian brain. *Brain Research Bulletin, 21,* 425–432.

Watkins, L. H., Rogers, R. D., Lawrence, A. D., Sahakian, B. J., Rosser, A. E., & Robbins, T. W. (2003). Impaired planning but intact decision making in early Huntington's disease: Implications for specific fronto-striatal pathology. *Neuropsychologia, 38,* 1112–1125.

Watson, C. P. (1994). Topical capsaicin as an adjuvant analgesic. *Journal of Pain & Symptom Management, 8,* 425–433.

Watson, J. B., Mednick, S. A., Huttunen, M., & Wang, X. (1999). Prenatal teratogens and the development of adult mental illness. *Development and Psychopathology, 11,* 457–466.

Wauquier, A., & Sadowski, B. (1978). Behavioral measurements of excitability changes in reward sites in the dog: A frequency dependent effect. *Physiology & Behavior, 21,* 165–168.

Webb, W. (1988). An objective behavioral model of sleep. *Sleep, 11,* 488–496.

Webb, W. (1992). *Sleep: The gentle tyrant* (2nd ed.). Boston: Anker.

Webb, W. B., & Agnew, H. W., Jr. (1970). Sleep stage characteristics of long and short sleepers. *Science, 168,* 146–147.

Wehr, T. A., Wirz-Justice, A., Goodwin, F. K., Duncan, W., & Gillin, J. C. (1979). Phase advance of the circadian sleep-wake cycle as an antidepressant. *Science, 206,* 710–713.

Weiller, C., Isensee, C., Rijntjes, M., Huber, W., Muller, S., Bier, D., et al. (1995). Recovery from Wernicke's aphasia: A positron emission tomographic study. *Annals of Neurology, 37,* 723–732.

Weinberger, D. R., Berman, K. F., & Illowsky, B. P. (1988). Physiological dysfunction of dorsolateral prefrontal cortex in schizophrenia. III. A new cohort and evidence for a monoaminergic mechanism. *Archives of General Psychiatry, 45,* 609–615.

Weingarten, H. P., & Powley, T. L. (1981). Pavlovian conditioning of the cephalic phase of gastric acid secretion in the rat. *Physiology & Behavior, 27,* 217–221.

Weisenberg, M. (1998). Cognitive aspects of pain and pain control. *The International Journal of Clinical and Experimental Hypnosis, 46,* 44–61.

Weisfeld, G. E., Czilli, T., Phillips, K. A., Gall, J. A., & Lichtman, C. M. (2003). Possible olfaction-based mechanisms in human kin recognition and inbreeding avoidance. *Journal of Experimental Child Psychology, 85,* 279–295.

Weiskrantz, L. (2004). Roots of blindsight. *Progress in Brain Research, 144,* 229–241.

Weiskrantz, L., Warrington, E. K., Sanders, M. D., & Marshall, J. (1974). Visual capacity in the hemianopic field following a restricted occipital ablation. *Brain, 97,* 709–728.

Weiss, F., Ciccocioppo, R., Parsons, L. H., Katner, S., Liu, X., Zorrilla, E. P., et al. (2001). Compulsive drug-seeking behavior and relapse. Neuroadaptation, stress, and conditioning factors. *Annals of the New York Academy of Sciences, 937,* 1–26.

Weiss, J. M. (1968). Effects of coping responses on stress. *Journal of Comparative and Physiological Psychology, 65,* 251–260.

Weiss, J. M., & Simson, P. G. (1986). Depression in an animal model: Focus on the locus ceruleus. *Ciba Foundation Symposium, 123,* 191–215.

Weiss, J. M., Simson, P. G., Ambrose, M. J., Webster, A., & Hoffman, L. J. (1985). Neurochemical basis of behavioral depression. In E. Katkin & S. Manuck (Eds.), *Advances in behavioral medicine* (Vol. 1, pp. 232–275). Greenwich: JAI.

Weiss, J. M., Stone, E. A., & Harrell, N. (1970). Coping behavior and brain norepinephrine level in rats. *Journal of Comparative and Physiological Psychology, 72,* 153–160.

Weiss, M. J. (2002). Hardiness and social support as predictors of stress in mothers of typical children, children with autism, and children with mental retardation. *Autism, 6,* 115–130.

Weisz, N., Wienbruch, C., Hoffmeister, S., & Elbert, T. (2004). Tonotopic organization of the human auditory cortex probed with frequency-modulated tones. *Hearing Research, 191,* 49–58.

Weitzman, E. D. (1981). Sleep and its disorders. *Annual Review of Neuroscience, 4,* 381–417.

Weitzman, E. D., Kripke, D. F., Goldmacher, D., McGregor, P., & Nogeire, C. (1970). Acute reversal of the sleep-waking cycle in man. Effect on sleep stage patterns. *Archives of Neurology, 22,* 483–489.

Weitzman, M., Byrd, R. S., Aligne, C. A., & Moss, M. (2002). The effects of tobacco exposure on children's behavioral and cognitive functioning: Implications for clinical and public health policy and future research. *Neurotoxicology and Teratology, 24,* 397–406.

Weller, A., & Weller, L. (1997). Menstrual synchrony under optimal conditions: Bedouin families. *Journal of Comparative Psychology, 111,* 143–151.

Weller, A., & Weller, L. (2002a). Menstrual synchrony can be assessed, inherent cycle variability notwithstanding: Commentary on Schank (2001). *Journal of Comparative Psychology, 116,* 316–318.

Weller, L., & Weller, A. (2002b). Menstrual synchrony and cycle variability: A reply to Schank (2000). *Psychoneuroendocrinology, 27,* 519–526.

Weller, L., Weller, A., Koresh-Kamin, H., & Ben-Shoshan, R. (1999a). Menstrual synchrony in a sample of working women. *Psychoneuroendocrinology, 24,* 449–459.

Weller, L., Weller, A., & Roizman, S. (1999b). Human menstrual synchrony in families and among close friends: Examining the importance of mutual exposure. *Journal of Comparative Psychology, 113,* 261–268.

Wellman, P. J. (2000). Norepinephrine and the control of food intake. *Nutrition, 16,* 837–842.

Wellman, P. J., Davies, B. T., Morien, A., & McMahon, L. (1993). Modulation of feeding by hypothalamic paraventricular nucleus alpha 1- and alpha 2-adrenergic receptors. *Life Sciences, 53,* 669–679.

Wernicke, C. (1874). *Der aphasische Symptomenkomplex: Eine psychologische Studie auf anatomischer Basis.* Breslau, Poland: Cohn and Weigert.

Wesensten, N. J., Balkin, T. J., & Belenky, G. (1999). Does sleep fragmentation impact recuperation? A review and reanalysis. *Journal of Sleep Research, 8,* 237–245.

Westbrook, G. L. (2000). Seizures and epilepsy. In E. R. Kandel, J. H. Schwartz, & T. M. Jessell (Eds.), *Principles of neural science* (4th ed., pp. 910–935). New York: McGraw-Hill.

Westergaard, G. C., Cleveland, A., Trenkle, M. K., Lussier, I. D., & Higley, J. D. (2003). CSF 5-HIAA concentration as an early screening tool for predicting significant life history outcomes in female specific-pathogen-free (SPF) rhesus macaques (Macaca mulatta) maintained in captive breeding groups. *Journal of Medical Primatology, 32,* 95–104.

Westheimer, G. (1999). Gestalt theory reconfigured: Max Wertheimer's anticipation of recent developments in visual neuroscience. *Perception, 28,* 5–15.

Westrin, A., & Nimeus, A. (2003). The dexamethasone suppression test and CSF-5-HIAA in relation to suicidality and depression in suicide attempters. *European Psychiatry, 18,* 166–171.

Wever, E. G. (1949). *A theory of hearing.* New York: Wiley.

Wever, E. G., & Bray, C. W. (1930). The nature of acoustic responses: The relation between sound frequency and frequency of impulses in the auditory nerve. *Journal of Experimental Psychology, 13,* 373–387.

Wexler, N. S., Lorimer, J., Porter, J., Gomez, F., Moskowitz, C., Shackell, E., et al. (2004). Venezuelan kindreds reveal that genetic and environmental factors modulate Huntington's disease age of onset. *Proceedings of the National Academy of Sciences of the United States of America, 101,* 3498–3503.

Wheatley, M. D. (1944). The hypothalamus and affective behavior in cats. A study of the effects of experimental lesions with anatomic correlations. *Archives of Neurology & Psychiatry (Chicago), 52,* 296–316.

Whytt, R. (1768). *The works of Robert Whytt, M.D.* (3rd ed., published by his son). Edinburgh: Balfour, Auld, and Smellie.

Wible, C. G., Anderson, J., Shenton, M. E., Kricun, A., Hirayasu, Y., Tanaka, S., et al. (2001). Prefrontal cortex, negative symptoms, and schizophrenia: An MRI study. *Psychiatry Research, 108,* 65–78.

Widner, H., Tetrud, J., Rehncrona, S., Snow, B., Brundin, P., Gustavii, B., et al. (1992). Bilateral fetal mesencephalic grafting in two patients with parkinsonism induced by 1-methyl-4-phenyl-1,2,3,6-tetrahydropyridine (MPTP). *New England Journal of Medicine, 327,* 1556–1563.

Wiesel, T. N., & Hubel, D. H. (1963). Single cell responses in striate cortex of kittens deprived of vision in one eye. *Journal of Neurophysiology, 26,* 1003–1017.

Wilford, B. B. (1981). *Drug abuse: A guide for the primary care physician.* Chicago: American Medical Association.

Williams, B. M., Luo, Y., Ward, C., Redd, K., Gibson, R., Kuczaj, S. A., et al. (2001). Environmental enrichment: Effects on spatial memory and hippocampal CREB immunoreactivity. *Physiology & Behavior, 73,* 649–658.

Williams, G., Bing, C., Cai, X. J., Harrold, J. A., King, P. J., & Liu, X. H. (2001). The hypothalamus and the control of energy homeostasis: Different circuits, different purposes. *Physiology & Behavior, 74,* 683–701.

Williams, G., Cai, X. J., Elliott, J. C., & Harrold, J. A. (2004). Anabolic neuropeptides. *Physiology & Behavior, 81,* 211–222.

Williams, G., Harrold, J. A., & Cutler, D. J. (2000). The hypothalamus and the regulation of energy homeostasis: Lifting the lid on a black box. *The Proceedings of the Nutrition Society, 59,* 385–396.

Williams, J. E., Nieto, F. J., Sanford, C. P., & Tyroler, H. A. (2001). Effects of an angry temperament on coronary heart disease risk: The Atherosclerosis Risk in Communities Study. *American Journal of Epidemiology, 154,* 230–235.

Williams, J. E., Paton, C. C., Siegler, I. C., Eigenbrodt, M. L., Nieto, F. J., & Tyroler, H. A. (2000). Anger proneness predicts coronary heart disease risk: Prospective analysis from the atherosclerosis risk in communities (ARIC) study. *Circulation, 101,* 2034–2039.

Willner, P. (1997). The dopamine hypothesis of schizophrenia: Current status, future prospects. *International Clinical Psychopharmacology, 12,* 297–308.

Wilson, B. E. (2004, May 26). 5-alpha-reductase deficiency. *eMedicine.* Retrieved June 3, 2005, from http://www.emedicine.com/ped/topic1980.htm

Wilson, J. D. (2001). Androgens, androgen receptors, and male gender role behavior. *Hormones and Behavior, 40,* 358–366.

Wilson, R., Raynal, D., Guilleminault, C., Zarcone, V., & Dement, W. B. (1973). REM sleep latencies in daytime sleep recordings of narcoleptics. *Sleep Research, 2,* 166.

Wilson, R. I., Godecke, A., Brown, R. E., Schrader, J., & Haas, H. L. (1999). Mice deficient in endothelial nitric oxide synthase exhibit a selective deficit in hippocampal long-term potentiation. *Neuroscience, 90,* 1157–1165.

Winokur, G., Clayton, P. J., & Reich, T. (1969). *Manic-depressive illness.* St. Louis: Mosby.

Winokur, G., Coryell, W., Endicott, J., Akiskal, H., Keller, M., Maser, J. D., et al. (1995a). Familial depression versus depression identified in a control group: Are they the same? *Psychological Medicine, 25,* 797–806.

Winokur, G., Coryell, W., Keller, M., Endicott, J., & Leon, A. (1995b). A family study of manic-depressive (bipolar I) disease. Is it a distinct illness separable from primary unipolar depression? *Archives of General Psychiatry, 52,* 367–373.

Winters, L., Cornblatt, B. A., & Erlenmeyer-Kimling, L. (1991). The prediction of psychiatric disorders in late adolescence. In E. F. Walker (Ed.), *Schizophrenia: A life-course developmental perspective. Personality, psychopathology, and psychotherapy series* (Vol. 18, pp. 123–127). San Diego: Academic Press.

Wise, R. A. (2002). Brain reward circuitry: Insights from unsensed incentives. *Neuron, 36,* 229–240.

Wisniewski, A. B., Migeon, C. J., Meyer-Bahlburg, H. F. L., Gearhart, J. P., Berkovitz, G. D., Brown, T. R., et al. (2000). Complete androgen insensitivity syndrome: Long-term medical, surgical, and psychosexual outcome. *The Journal of Clinical Endocrinology & Metabolism, 85,* 2664–2669.

Wolfson, A. R., & Carskadon, M. A. (1998). Sleep schedules and daytime functioning in adolescents. *Child Development, 69,* 875–887.

Wolfson, C., Oremus, M., Shukla, V., Momoli, F., Demers, L., Perrault, A., et al. (2002). Donepezil and rivastigmine in the treatment of Alzheimer's disease: A best-evidence synthesis of the published data on their efficacy and cost-effectiveness. *Clinical Therapeutics, 24,* 862–886.

Wong, C. G., Bottiglieri, T., & Snead, O. C., 3rd. (2003). GABA, gamma-hydroxybutyric acid, and neurological disease. *Annals of Neurology, 54,* S3–12.

Wong, M. T., Lumsden, J., Fenton, G. W., & Fenwick, P. B. (1994). Electroencephalography, computed tomography and violence ratings of male patients in a maximum-security mental hospital. *Acta Psychiatrica Scandinavica, 90,* 97–101.

Wong-Riley, M. (1979). Changes in the visual system of monocularly sutured or enucleated cats demonstrable with cytochrome oxidase histochemistry. *Brain Research, 171,* 11–28.

Wood, R. I. (1998). Integration of chemosensory and hormonal input in the male Syrian hamster brain. *Annals of the New York Academy of Sciences, 855,* 362–372.

Woodruff-Pak, D. S. (2001). Insights about learning in Alzheimer's disease from the animal model. In M. E. Carroll & J. B. Overmier (Eds.), *Animal research and human health: Advancing human welfare through behavioral science* (pp. 323–336). Washington, DC: American Psychological Association.

Woodruff-Pak, D. S., Papka, M., & Ivry, R. B. (1996). Cerebellar involvement in eyeblink classical conditioning in humans. *Neuropsychology, 10,* 443–458.

Woods, J. R. (1998). Maternal and transplacental effects of cocaine. *Annals of the New York Academy of Sciences, 846,* 1–11.

Woods, S. C., Schwartz, M. W., Baskin, D. G., & Seeley, R. J. (2000). Food intake and the regulation of body weight. *Annual Review of Psychology, 51,* 255–277.

Woods, S. C., Seeley, R. J., Porte, D., Jr., & Schwartz, M. W. (1998). Signals that regulate food intake and energy homeostasis. *Science, 280,* 1378–1383.

Woods, T. M., Cusick, C. G., Pons, T. P., Taub, E., & Jones, E. G. (2000). Progressive transneuronal changes in the brainstem and thalamus after long-term dorsal rhizotomies in adult macaque monkeys. *The Journal of Neuroscience, 20,* 3884–3899.

Worthington, J. J., 3rd, & Peters, P. M. (2003). Treatment of antidepressant-induced sexual dysfunction. *Drugs of Today, 39,* 887–896.

Wu, L.-G., & Saggau, P. (1997). Presynaptic inhibition of elicited neurotransmitter release. *Trends in Neuroscience, 20,* 204–212.

Wysocki, C. J., & Preti, G. (2004). Facts, fallacies, fears, and frustrations with human pheromones. *Anatomical Record, 281A,* 1201–1211.

Xi, Z. X., & Stein, E. A. (1998). Nucleus accumbens dopamine release modulation by mesolimbic $GABA_A$ receptors—an in vivo electrochemical study. *Brain Research, 798,* 156–165.

Yamanaka, A., Beuckmann, C. T., Willie, J. T., Hara, J., Tsujino, N., Mieda, M., et al. (2003). Hypothalamic orexin neurons regulate arousal according to energy balance in mice. *Neuron, 38,* 701–713.

Yamasaki, H., LaBar, K. S., & McCarthy, G. (2002). Dissociable prefrontal brain systems for attention and emotion. *Proceedings of the National Academy of Sciences of the United States of America, 99,* 11447–11451.

Yamashita, H., Akabane, T., & Kurihara, Y. (1995). Activity and stability of a new sweet protein with taste-modifying action, curculin. *Chemical Senses, 20,* 239–243.

Yan, Q. S., & Yan, S. E. (2001). Activation of 5-HT (1B/1D) receptors in the mesolimbic dopamine system increases dopamine release from the nucleus accumbens: A microdialysis study. *European Journal of Pharmacology, 418,* 55–64.

Yang, E. H., Hla, K. M., McHorney, C. A., Havighurst, T., Badr, M. S., & Weber, S. (2000). Sleep apnea and quality of life. *Sleep, 23,* 535–541.

Yaniv, D., Desmedt, A., Jaffard, R., & Richter-Levin, G. (2004). The amygdala and appraisal processes: Stimulus and response complexity as an organizing factor. *Brain Research Reviews, 44,* 179–186.

Yates, A., Leehey, K., & Shisslak, C. M. (1983). Running—An analogue of anorexia? *New England Journal of Medicine, 308,* 251–255.

Yau, K. W. (1991). Calcium and light adaptation in retinal photoreceptors. *Current Opinion in Neurobiology, 1,* 252–257.

Yee, F., MacLow, C., Chan, I. N., & Leibowitz, S. F. (1987). Effects of chronic paraventricular nucleus infusion of clonidine and alpha-methyl-paratyrosine on macronutrient intake. *Appetite, 9,* 127–138.

Yoburn, B. C., Glusman, M., Potegal, M., & Skaredoff, L. (1981). Facilitation of muricide in rats by cholinergic stimulation of the lateral hypothalamus. *Pharmacology, Biochemistry, and Behavior, 15,* 747–753.

You, Z. B., Chen, Y. Q., & Wise, R. A. (2001). Dopamine and glutamate release in the nucleus accumbens and ventral tegmental area of rat following lateral hypothalamic self-stimulation. *Neuroscience, 107,* 629–639.

Young, K. A., Manaye, K. F., Liang, C., Hicks, P. B., & German, D. C. (2000). Reduced number of mediodorsal and anterior thalamic neurons in schizophrenia. *Biological Psychiatry, 47,* 944–953.

Young, L. J. (1999). Oxytocin and vasopressin receptors and species-typical social behaviors. *Hormones and Behavior, 36,* 212–221.

Young, L. J., Lim, M. M., Gingrich, B., & Insel, T. R. (2001). Cellular mechanisms of social attachment. *Hormones and Behavior, 40,* 133–138.

Yousem, D. M., Maldjian, J. A., Siddiqi, F., Hummel, T., Alsop, D. C., Geckle, R. J., et al. (1999). Gender effects on odor-stimulated functional magnetic resonance imaging. *Brain Research, 818,* 480–487.

Yui, K., Goto, K., & Ikemoto, S. (2004). The role of noradrenergic and dopaminergic hyperactivity in the development of spontaneous recurrence of methamphetamine psychosis and susceptibility to episode recurrence. *Annals of the New York Academy of Sciences, 1025,* 296–306.

Zadra, A. L., & Pihl, R. O. (1997). Lucid dreaming as a treatment for recurrent nightmares. *Psychotherapy and Psychosomatics, 66,* 50–55.

Zamble, E., Mitchell, J. B., & Findlay, H. (1986). Pavlovian conditioning of sexual arousal: Parametric and background manipulations. *Journal of Experimental Psychology. Animal Behavior Processes, 12,* 403–411.

Zareparsi, S., Camicioli, R., Sexton, G., Bird, T., Swanson, P., Kaye, J., et al. (2002). Age at onset of Parkinson disease and apolipoprotein E genotypes. *American Journal of Medical Genetics, 107,* 156–161.

Zarrindast, M. R., Bakhsha, A., Rostami, P., & Shafaghi, B. (2002). Effects of intrahippocampal injection of GABAergic drugs on memory retention of passive avoidance learning in rats. *Journal of Psychopharmacology, 16,* 313–319.

Zehr, J. L., Maestripieri, D., & Wallen, K. (1998). Estradiol increases female sexual initiation independent of male responsiveness in rhesus monkeys. *Hormones and Behavior, 33,* 95–103.

Zekanowski, C., Religa, D., Graff, C., Filipek, S., & Kuznicki, J. (2004). Genetic aspects of Alzheimer's disease. *Acta Neurobiologiae Experimentalis, 64,* 19–31.

Zeng, H., Chattarji, S., Barbarosie, M., Rondi-Reig, L., Philpot, B. D., Miyakawa, T., et al. (2001). Forebrain-specific calcineurin knockout selectively impairs bidirectional synaptic plasticity and working/episodic-like memory. *Cell, 107,* 617–629.

Zesiewicz, T. A., & Hauser, R. A. (2001). Neurosurgery for Parkinson's disease. *Seminars in Neurology, 21,* 91–101.

Zgaljardic, D. J., Borod, J. C., Foldi, N. S., & Mattis, P. (2003). A review of the cognitive and behavioral sequelae of Parkinson's disease: Relationship to frontostriatal circuitry. *Cognitive and Behavioral Neurology, 16,* 193–210.

Zhang, L., Zhou, F. M., & Dani, J. A. (2004). Cholinergic drugs for Alzheimer's disease enhance in vitro dopamine release. *Molecular Pharmacology, 66,* 538–544.

Zhang, Y., Loonam, T. M., Noailles, P. A., & Angulo, J. A. (2001). Comparison of cocaine- and methamphetamine-evoked dopamine and glutamate overflow in somatodendritic and terminal field regions of the rat brain during acute, chronic, and early withdrawal conditions. *Annals of the New York Academy of Sciences, 937,* 93–120.

Zhdanova, I. V. (2004). Advances in the management of insomnia. *Expert Opinion on Pharmacotherapy, 5,* 1573–1579.

Zhdanova, I. V., & Tucci, V. (2003). Melatonin, circadian rhythms, and sleep. *Current Treatment Options in Neurology, 5,* 225–229.

Zhdanova, I. V., Cantor, M. L., Leclair, O. U., Kartashov, A. I., & Wurtman, R. J. (1998). Behavioral effects of melatonin treatment in non-human primates. *Sleep Research Online, 1,* 114–118.

Zhdanova, I. V., Geiger, D. A., Schwagerl, A. L., Leclair, O. U., Killiany, R., Taylor, J. A., et al. (2002). Melatonin promotes sleep in three species of diurnal nonhuman primates. *Physiology and Behavior, 75,* 523–529.

Zhdanova, I. V., Lynch, H. J., & Wurtman, R. J. (1997). Melatonin: A sleep-promoting hormone. *Sleep, 20,* 899–907.

Zhdanova, I. V., & Wurtman, R. J. (1997). Efficacy of melatonin as a sleep-promoting agent. *Journal of Biological Rhythms, 12,* 644–650.

Zhdanova, I. V., Wurtman, R. J., Morabito, C., Piotrovska, V. R., & Lynch, H. J. (1996). Effects of low oral doses of melatonin, given 2–4 hours before habitual bedtime, on sleep in normal young humans. *Sleep, 19,* 423–431.

Zhdanova, I. V., Wurtman, R. J., Regan, M. M., Taylor, J. A., Shi, J. P., & Leclair, O. U. (2001). Melatonin treatment for age-related insomnia. *The Journal of Clinical Endocrinology and Metabolism, 86,* 4727–4730.

Zhdanova, I. V., Wurtman, R. J., & Wagstaff, J. (1999). Effects of a low dose of melatonin on sleep in children with Angelman syndrome. *Journal of Pediatric Endocrinology & Metabolism, 12,* 57–67.

Zhou, J. N., & Swaab, D. F. (1999). Activation and degeneration during aging: A morphometric study of the human hypothalamus. *Microscopy Research and Technique, 44,* 36–48.

Zimbardo, P. G., Andersen, S. M., & Kabat, L. G. (1981). Induced hearing deficit generates experimental paranoia. *Science, 212,* 1529–1531.

Zinbarg, R. E., & Mineka, S. (2001). Understanding, treating, and preventing anxiety, phobias, and anxiety disorders. In M. E. Carroll & J. B. Overmier (Eds.), *Animal research and human health: Advancing human welfare through behavioral science* (pp. 19–28). Washington, DC: American Psychological Association.

Zisapel, N. (2001). Circadian rhythm sleep disorders: Pathophysiology and potential approaches to management. *CNS Drugs, 15,* 311–328.

Zola-Morgan, S., & Squire, L. R. (1985). Amnesia in monkeys after lesions of the mediodorsal nucleus of the thalamus. *Annals of Neurology, 17,* 558–564.

Zola-Morgan, S., & Squire, L. R. (1993). Neuroanatomy of memory. *Annual Review of Neuroscience, 16,* 547–563.

Zola-Morgan, S., Squire, L. R., & Amaral, D. G. (1986). Human amnesia and the medial temporal region: Enduring memory impairment following a bilateral lesion limited to field CA_1 of the hippocampus. *The Journal of Neuroscience, 6,* 2950–2967.

Zola-Morgan, S., Squire, L. R., & Ramus, S. J. (1994). Severity of memory impairment in monkeys as a function of locus and extent of damage within the medial temporal lobe memory system. *Hippocampus, 4,* 483–495.

Zoppelt, D., Koch, B., Schwarz, M., & Daum, I. (2003). Involvement of the mediodorsal thalamic nucleus in mediating recollection and familiarity. *Neuropsychologia, 41,* 1160–1170.

Zuckerman, L., & Weiner, I. (2003). Post-pubertal emergence of disrupted latent inhibition following prenatal immune activation. *Psychopharmacology, 169,* 308–313.

Name Index

Subject Index

Interpreting Cell Activity Figures

Neurons are unique among cells in that they are highly specialized for receiving and sending information through the cell membrane. They accomplish this in two ways: by ion flow and by neurotransmitter activity. In interpreting figures that show this cell activity, you will find it helpful to be familiar with certain visual conventions of the diagrams.

Ion Flow

For neurons to receive and send information they need to effectively interact with their external environment. The neuron's interaction with the external environment is achieved in part through the controlled exchange of positively and negatively charged particles called ions. Ions change the electrical state of a cell as they flow through its membrane. Ion flow is typically represented in figures that show a cell membrane in cross section.

High-magnification representations show in detail the components of the cell membrane, which is made up of two rows of lipid molecules, the inner and outer surfaces of the membrane. Because the lipid bilayer is typically impenetrable, proteins embedded in the membrane serve as either channels or pumps for the flow of ions.

Filled circles represent ions, and arrows indicate movement of those ions during cell activity. Ions are usually labeled with the element abbreviation and the charge (for example, Na^+ for sodium, K^+ for potassium, Cl^- for chloride). Ions move through the cell membrane by two methods. The first is by a passive flow through membrane channels, which may occur when ions near an open channel are attracted to oppositely charged ions across the membrane (an electrical gradient flow), or when ions move across the membrane from an area where they are highly concentrated to an area of low concentration (a concentration gradient flow). The second is active transport of ions through the membrane via the pumping action of embedded proteins.

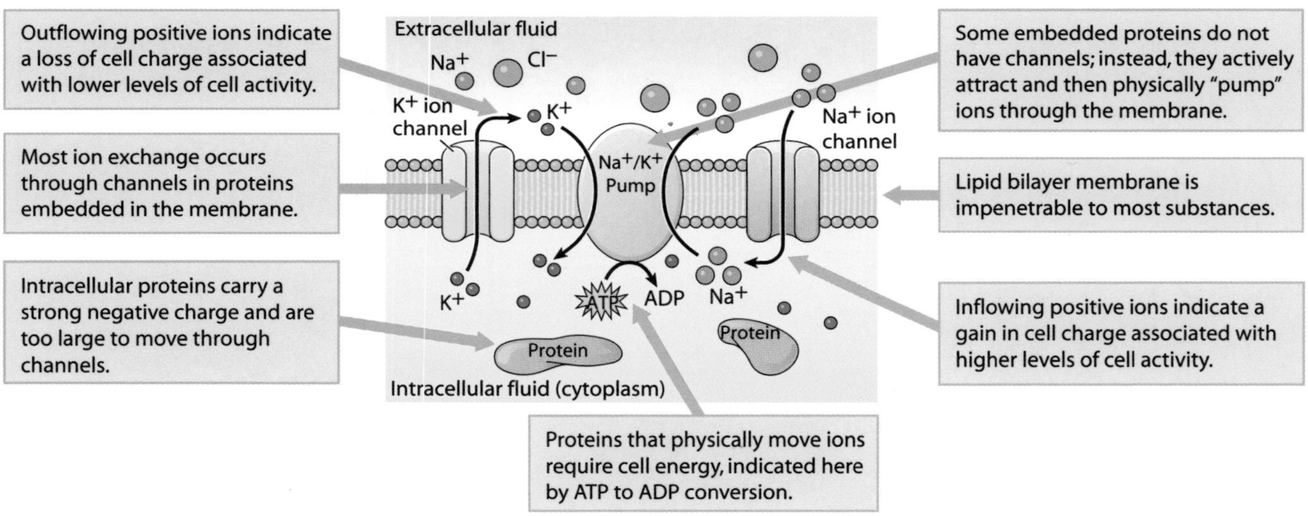
Outflowing positive ions indicate a loss of cell charge associated with lower levels of cell activity.
Most ion exchange occurs through channels in proteins embedded in the membrane.
Intracellular proteins carry a strong negative charge and are too large to move through channels.
Extracellular fluid
Na+
Cl−
K+ ion channel
K+
Na+/K+ Pump
Na+ ion channel
K+
ATP
ADP
Na+
Protein
Protein
Intracellular fluid (cytoplasm)
Some embedded proteins do not have channels; instead, they actively attract and then physically "pump" ions through the membrane.
Lipid bilayer membrane is impenetrable to most substances.
Inflowing positive ions indicate a gain in cell charge associated with higher levels of cell activity.
Proteins that physically move ions require cell energy, indicated here by ATP to ADP conversion.

Low-magnification representations (opposite page, top) show less detail, on the assumption that you are familiar with the membrane components represented in high-magnification figures. For example, an arrow may depict ion movement through the membrane without indicating flow through a protein channel. Low-magnification representations are generally used to show a larger area of ion activity, such as movement of a signal along a length of axon.